Steiner & Woods
EU Law

THIRTEENTH EDITION

Lorna Woods

Philippa Watson

Marios Costa

OXFORD
UNIVERSITY PRESS

UNIVERSITY PRESS

Great Clarendon Street, Oxford, OX2 6DP,
United Kingdom

Oxford University Press is a department of the University of Oxford.
It furthers the University's objective of excellence in research, scholarship,
and education by publishing worldwide. Oxford is a registered trade mark of
Oxford University Press in the UK and in certain other countries

Tenth edition 2009
Eleventh edition 2012
Twelfth edition 2014

Impression: 1

Published in the United States of America by Oxford University Press
198 Madison Avenue, New York, NY 10016, United States of America

British Library Cataloguing in Publication Data
Data available

Library of Congress Control Number: 2017933152

ISBN 978-0-19-879561-2

Printed in Great Britain by
Bell & Bain Ltd., Glasgow

In memory of Jo Steiner

Preface

The European Union has changed significantly since this book was first published in 1988. In terms of achievements, membership of the Union, originally called the European Economic Community, has risen to the current number of 28. The goal of the internal market, set down in the 1986 Single European Act, has been largely achieved. The year 1992 saw the signing at Maastricht of the Treaty on European Union, committing members to new goals, not least to economic and monetary union, and increasing governmental cooperation in the fields of foreign and security policy and justice and home affairs. Additionally, the concept of citizenship of the Union was born. More problematically, resistance to what is perceived as continued transfer of power to the Union is increasing. Since Maastricht, the Union seems to have been in a process of almost constant treaty revision, with the Treaties of Amsterdam, Nice and Lisbon, as well as the failed Constitutional Treaty. New challenges have arisen with the sovereign debt crisis and its impact on the Eurozone. In 2016, a referendum in the United Kingdom came out in favour of leaving the EU, the first Member State to be on the verge of leaving.

The purpose of this thirteenth edition is not to chart the political developments in the Union and its relationship with Member States and would-be Member States, except in outline. Instead, it aims to continue the approach adopted in previous editions of providing an accurate and succinct account of the present state of European Union law. There is still a need for a single textbook of manageable size, concise but not simplistic, covering the major areas of EU law—constitutional, institutional and administrative as well as substantive—to cater for the growing body of students (and not only lawyers) from around the world who wish to study EU law, and for practitioners who realise that they can no longer afford to ignore it. The advent of the internal market and the continuing expansion substantively and geographically of the Union has simply reinforced that need.

A book of this type cannot of necessity provide an in-depth account of the EU institutions, nor can it cover all areas of substantive law. Much EU law, for example in the field of company, commercial or environmental law, or the law relating to employment or consumer protection, is increasingly, and more appropriately, treated in specialised works on these subjects. Some topics, such as agriculture or common foreign and security policy are too large or too specialised for inclusion. Others, such as competition law, are the subject of detailed monographs and dedicated periodicals. The aim of the book therefore is to provide as comprehensive an oversight as possible of the topic, the detail being readily accessible elsewhere. The book continues to concentrate on the more highly developed areas of EU law, what one might describe as fundamental Union law—the law relating to the free movement of goods, persons and services; competition law; and discrimination—and on the remedies available for breaches of Union law.

There are a number of changes to this edition. All chapters have been revised in the light of jurisprudential developments in the field. More detail on Article 50 TEU has been included in the light of forthcoming Brexit and the chapters on judicial review and discrimination have been thoroughly revised. This edition again includes a chapter on the Area of Freedom and Security, although detailed consideration of asylum lies outside the scope of the textbook. In the light of this, and the fact that the separate pillar structure has been abandoned, as with the previous edition, more detail on the second and third pillars has been included in a number of constitutional and administrative chapters. The changes to structure with regard to the free movement of persons have been continued. Given that state aid has become a specialist subject in its own right, regretfully the decision was made for the twelfth edition not to cover the area in this book, and this remains the case for this edition. Given the continuing Eurozone crisis, a brief overview of the institutional framework for economic and monetary union has been included with the discussion of free movement of capital, although a detailed analysis lies outside the scope of this book.

As before, the book aims to provide sufficient insight into the principles of EU law, including its current difficulties, and the processes of the European institutions, to enable the reader to pursue studies, resolve problems, and enforce rights in areas of law whether or not covered by the book, as and when the need arises. The principal sources of EU law and a selection of textbooks are listed at the end of the book. Each chapter provides a list of further reading.

The textbook was originally written in 1988 by Jo Steiner, who was joined by Lorna Woods in 1996 for the fifth and subsequent editions, with Jo Steiner retiring from the writing of the book after the seventh edition. For the eighth and ninth editions Lorna Woods was joined in the writing by Christian Twigg-Flesner; since the eleventh edition, the book has been written by Lorna Woods and Philippa Watson. Marios Costa, who contributed three chapters to the twelfth edition, now joins as author for the thirteenth edition.

It is with great sadness that we report that Jo, who had such a clear-sighted view of EU law and a distinctive voice in explaining it, died in 2015. She will be missed.

Our thanks go to all of those who helped in the preparation of this book: to colleagues in respective institutions for their helpful comments and suggestions and to our families and friends for their unflinching support and encouragement, and for providing a welcome distraction from the demands of academic research.

Lorna Woods, Philippa Watson and Marios Costa
March 2017

Guide to the Online Resource Centre

Steiner & Woods EU Law is accompanied by a free Online Resource Centre which contains a range of resources designed to support you throughout your EU law module:

www.oxfordtextbooks.co.uk/orc/steiner_woods13e/

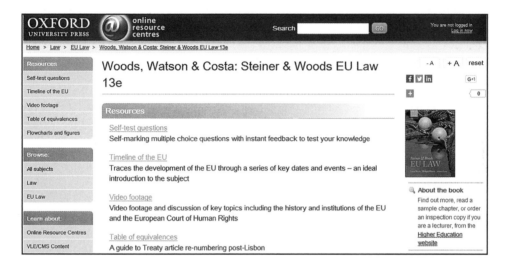

Get started…

If you're studying EU law for the first time the Online Resource Centre provides a range of resources to help build your understanding and prepare for your first lectures including:

- an interactive timeline of the development of the EU
- video clips of key moments in the EU's development
- a quick-reference and searchable guide to EU Article renumbering.

Prepare for exams…

The Online Resource Centre includes a range of tools designed to help with your revision including:

- self-test questions with instant feedback
- downloadable flowcharts and figures from the book
- a guide to further web resources to help you pursue areas of interest.

Stay up to date…

The Online Resource Centre provides updates on key developments in EU law, including the impact of Brexit, as well as links to the latest EU law blogs and the European Commission's YouTube channel.

Outline contents

Detailed contents

PART II

PART III

Abbreviations

ACTA	Anti-Counterfeiting Trade Agreement
AFSJ	Area of Freedom, Security and Justice
BEPG	broad economic policy guidelines
BT Rev	British Tax Review
Bull EC	Bulletin of the European Communities
CAP	Common Agricultural Policy
CCT	common customs tariff
CDE	*Cahiers de Droit Européen*
CEAS	Common European Asylum System
CET	common external tariff
CFI	Court of First Instance (prior to Lisbon)
CFLQ	Child and Family Law Quarterly
CFSP	common foreign and security policy
CJ	Court of Justice
CJEL	Columbia Journal of European Law
CJEU	Courts of Justice of the European Union (post Lisbon)
CJQ	Civil Justice Quarterly
CLJ	Cambridge Law Journal
CMLR	Common Market Law Reports
CML Rev	Common Market Law Review
COREPER	Committee of Permanent Representatives
COSAC	Conference of Parliamentary Committees for Union Affairs of Parliaments of the European Union
CSP	Contingency Social Plan
CYELS	Cambridge Yearbook of European Legal Studies
DBA	Dutch Bar Association
D/G	Directorate-General
EAGGF	European Agriculture Guidance and Guarantee Fund
EBA	European Banking Authority
EBL Rev	European Business Law Review
EC	European Community/Communities, Treaty Establishing the European Community
ECB	European Central Bank
ECFL Rev	European Company and Financial Law Review

ECHR	European Convention for the Protection of Human Rights and Fundamental Freedoms 1950
ECJ	European Court of Justice (prior to Lisbon)
ECLR	European Competition Law Review
ECL Rev	European Constitutional Law Review
ECN	European Competition Network
ECOFIN	Council of Economic and Finance Ministers
ECOSOC	Economic and Social Council
ECR	European Court Reports (official reports of the judgments of the European Court, English version)
ECSC	European Coal and Steel Community
ECtHR	European Court of Human Rights
EDRF	European Regional Development Fund
EEA	European Economic Area
EEC	European Economic Community
EFSF	European Financial Stability Facility
EFSM	European Financial Stabilisation Mechanism
EFTA	European Free Trade Association
EHRLR	European Human Rights Law Review
EIOPA	European Insurance and Occupational Pensions Authority
EIPR	European Intellectual Property Review
EJIL	European Journal of International Law
EJSS	European Journal of Sport Science
ELJ	European Law Journal
EL Rev	European Law Review
EMU	Economic and Monetary Union
ENP	European Neighbourhood Policy
ENISA	European Network and Information Security Authority
EPL	*European Public Law*
ERCL	European Review of Contract Law
ERM	exchange rate mechanism
ESCB	European System of Central Banks
ESM	European Stability Mechanism
ESMA	European Securities and Markets Authority
ESRB	European Systemic Risk Board
EUCFR	European Charter of Fundamental Rights
EU Const	European Constitutional Law Review
EUPM	European Union Police Mission
Euratom	European Atomic Energy Community
Eur J Crime Cr L Cr J	European Journal of Crime, Criminal Law and Criminal Justice

FCC	German Federal Constitutional Court
FSP	foreign and security policy
FYR	Former Yugoslav Republic
GATT	General Agreement on Tariffs and Trade
GBER	General Block Exemption
GC	General Court
GG	Grundgesetz (Basic Law of the Federal Republic of Germany)
GLJ	German Law Journal
Harv Int'l LJ	*Harvard International Law Journal*
IBLJ	International Business Law Journal
ICJ	International Court of Justice
ICLQ	*International and Comparative Law Quarterly*
ICN	International Competition Network
ICT	intra-corporate transferee
ICTY	International Criminal Tribunal for the former Yugoslavia
IGC	intergovernmental conference
IIA	interinstitutional agreements
IIC	International Review of Industrial Property and Copyright Law
ILJ	Industrial Law Journal
ILO	International Labour Organisation
IML	Internal Market Integration System
Int J Const L	International Journal of Constitutional Law
Int'l J Refugee L	International Journal of Refugee Law
ISO	International Standards Organisation
JBL	Journal of Business Law
JCMS	Journal of Common Market Studies
J Env L	Journal of Environmental Law
JEPP	Journal of European Public Policy
JHA	justice and home affairs
JIEL	Journal of International Economic Law
JO	Journal Officiel (French version of OJ)
JR	Judicial Review
LIEI	Legal Issues of European Integration
LQR	Law Quarterly Review
MAD	Market Abuse Directive
MCA	Monetary Compensatory Amount
MEQR	measure having equivalent effect to quantitative restrictions
MFF	multiannual financial framework
MJ	Municipal Journal
MJECL	Maastricht Journal of European and Comparative Law

MLR	Modern Law Review
OECD	Organisation for Economic Co-operation and Development
OJ	Official Journal (of the European Union)
OMC	Open Method of Coordination
OMT	Outright Monetary Transaction
PL	Public Law
PNR	passenger name records
PQD	Professional Qualification Directive
QMV	qualified majority voting
RGM	relevant geographical market
RPM	relevant product market
RQMV	reverse qualified majority voting
SEA	Single European Act
SEPA	Single Euro Payments Area
SGEI	services of general economic interest
SGP	stability and growth pact
SLR	Statute Law Review
SME	small and medium-sized enterprises
SSM	Single Supervisory Mechanism
SSNIP	small but significant and non-transitory increase in prices
TCN	third country national
TEU	Treaty on European Union
TFEU	Treaty on the Functioning of the European Union
ToA	Treaty of Amsterdam
TSCG	Treaty on Stability, Coordination and Governance
UNHCR	United Nations High Commissioner for Refugees
UNICE	Union des industries de la communauté européenne (federation of European employers' groups)
WashLRev	Washington Law Review
WTO	World Trade Organization
Yale LJ	Yale Law Journal
YEL	Yearbook of European Law

Unless otherwise stated, cases cited were decided by the CJ.

Table of cases

Page numbers in **bold** indicate that an extract is reproduced in the text

Court of Justice: numerical

General Court: alphabetical

General Court: numerical

European Court of Human Rights (ECtHR)

Table of legislation

Page numbers in **bold** indicate that an extract is reproduced in the text

EU secondary legislation

Regulations

National Legislation

Estonia

Finland

France

Germany

Ireland

Netherlands

United Kingdom

Part I

From EEC to EU: a brief history of the development of the Union

1.1 Introduction

The European Union (EU) is no ordinary international law organisation. It is unique but its extra-ordinary success has led it to be a model for regional trading organisations across the globe. The purpose of this chapter is to provide a brief overview of how the European Economic Community (EEC) developed into the European Union, identifying key points. The development of the organisation will be traced chronologically, by reference to the main treaties amending the original Treaty of Rome (1957): the Single European Act (1987); the Maastricht Treaty (1993); the Amsterdam Treaty (1999); the Nice Treaty (2003); and, most recently, the Lisbon Treaty (2009). Certain underlying themes and tensions will be identified, as well as the theories that have been used to explain the development of the EU. There are three vectors of development:

- enlargement;
- substantive scope of the EU's activities;
- the nature of the EU and the way it works.

It is these perennial issues, or the way the Union institutions and the Member States choose to deal with them, that have shaped the way the EU works and, indeed, will shape the future of the EU.

1.2 Development prior to the Single European Act

The EEC came into existence following the signing of the Treaty of Rome in 1957 by the six original Member States: France, Germany, Italy, Belgium, The Netherlands and Luxembourg. A second Rome Treaty signed by the same six states created the European Atomic Energy Community (Euratom) on the same day. These treaties, but particularly the EEC Treaty, represented the culmination of a movement towards international cooperation, which had been growing throughout the twentieth century, and which was given particular impetus in Europe following the devastation inflicted by the Second World War.

The institutional model for the EEC had already been provided by the European Coal and Steel Community (ECSC) set up in 1951 with the Treaty of Paris by the same six states. However, the substantive scope of the EEC was altogether wider. The ECSC was concerned only with creating a single market in coal and steel; the EEC was designed to create an economic community. Although its aims were primarily economic, to create a single 'common' market in Europe, they were not exclusively so. The founder members of the EEC were fired by ideals as well as economic practicalities. As stated in the preamble to the EEC Treaty, its signatories were 'Determined to lay the foundations of an ever closer union among the peoples of Europe', and 'Resolved by thus pooling their resources to preserve and strengthen peace and liberty'.

Although the institutional framework of the EEC, as of Euratom, was modelled on that of the ECSC, the three communities at the outset held only two institutions in common: the Assembly (subsequently renamed the Parliament) and the European Court of Justice (ECJ). It was not until the Merger Treaty 1965 that the other two main institutions merged. The High Authority, the executive body of the ECSC, merged with the EEC and Euratom Commission to form what is now the Commission and the Council of Ministers of the ECSC, with that of the EEC and Euratom to become a single Council. Thereafter the three communities continued to function as separate entities, but with shared institutions. The roles and powers of the institutions are discussed in Chapter 2.

In addition to the EU Treaties, there is another agreement, the European Economic Area (EEA) Agreement. It is an agreement providing for a single market between the EU Member States and Iceland, Liechtenstein and Norway. While some EU law applies as a result of the EEA Agreement, its substantive scope is narrower than that of the EU Treaties.

1.3 Enlargement

1.3.1 Current membership

The UK, Denmark and the Republic of Ireland were the first additional states to join the Communities in 1973. (Norway joined at the same time but subsequently withdrew following a referendum which came out against membership.) This accession was the first of many, which has led the size of the EU to more than quadruple: from 6 to 28, with more states seeking to join.

In 1979 Greece, and in 1986 Spain and Portugal, signed acts of accession bringing the then total membership to 12. Membership increased again with the accession of Austria, Finland and Sweden on 1 January 1995. Norway held a second referendum, which again resulted in a vote against membership. Expansion continued with the largest number of countries joining what had become the EU in one go, ten, acceding in 2004. These new Member States, sometimes referred to as the EU10, are, in alphabetical order: Cyprus, Czech Republic, Estonia, Hungary, Latvia, Lithuania, Malta, Poland, Slovakia and Slovenia, resulting in an EU of 25. Two more Member States joined on 1 January 2007, Bulgaria and Romania, despite some concerns about compliance with the Union *acquis* (see COM(2006) 549 final). Most recently, Croatia became a Member State on 1 July 2013. While further countries seek to join the EU, there are questions about existing Member States. Notably, the UK held a referendum in which approximately 52 per cent of those voting were in favour of the UK leaving the EU (see 1.10).

1.3.2 Process for joining the EU

The process of joining the EU involves several stages. Typically, before a country even applies for accession to the EU, it will sign an association agreement, as for some countries being ready to apply for membership itself requires preparation. The aim of the association agreement is to help the would-be candidate country adapt to meet the conditions of EU membership (see 1.3.3). Given the recent history in the Western Balkans, a special process, the Stabilisation and Association Process, has been introduced to deal with the circumstances there. When a country finally formally applies for membership, the Commission prepares an opinion on the country's readiness to begin negotiations, which is then presented to the Council. This process of assessing a would-be Member State's progress continues: during the accession period, the Commission will review progress of the country and publish its views on that progress. Assuming a positive decision is made in Council on the country's readiness to join the EU, the applicant country will then be recognised as a candidate country, at which point formal negotiations are opened between the candidate country and the EU. The negotiations have the aim of concluding an accession treaty. After the signing of the accession treaty, there is usually a period before the treaty comes into force to allow, inter alia, the acceding state time to complete any internal steps (eg, holding a referendum) necessary for it to accede to the EU.

1.3.3 Conditions for membership

Before a country can accede to the EU, it must satisfy the terms of Article 49 of the Treaty on European Union (TEU), Article 6 TEU and the Copenhagen Criteria. Article 49 requires that a state be European; Article 6 requires respect for democracy, the rule of law, and respect for human rights. The Copenhagen criteria are the:

- political criterion (respect for democracy and human rights);
- economic criterion (the need for viable market economies and the capacity to cope with competitive pressure and market forces within the EU);
- ability to adopt the Union *acquis* (ie the current body of EU law).

In 1995, the Madrid European Council added a further practical requirement: that the candidate country must adjust its administrative structures and practices so as to ensure the effective implementation of the EU *acquis* in practice. More recently, there has been recognition that the EU itself must be able to cope with continued enlargement.

1.3.4 Beyond enlargement: EU Neighbourhood Policy

In addition to the interventions and negotiations as part of the EU enlargement, the EU also engages in what is called the European Neighbourhood Policy (ENP). This development is part of the increasing geographic influence of the EU, which extends more broadly than the territories of the Member States. The ENP was originally developed following the European Commission communication, 'Wider Europe' (COM(2003) 104 final) and a subsequent communication 'European Neighbourhood Policy: strategy paper' (COM(2004) 373 final) in 2004. It had the aim of preventing divisions occurring between new Member States and their neighbour countries by building upon common values: democracy and human rights; rule of law; good governance; market economy principles; and sustainable development. There seems to be a double objective. Firstly, it aims to assist the spread of EU values beyond the EU in the interests of creating a wider area of stability and security. The attainment of this area of stability and security is the second objective. The ENP builds on existing agreements and operates through action plans agreed between the EU and individual neighbouring countries. The system works on the basis that the relevant neighbour country agrees to undertake reforms in areas relevant to the 'common values' in return for incentives, including funding and increased access to markets. Progress is monitored.

Finally, it should be noted that the Lisbon Treaty provides a new legal and institutional framework for EU foreign policy (see 1.9.2) and, in particular, provides in Article 8 TEU for the development of a 'special relationship' with neighbouring countries. Whether the objectives of the spread of EU values pulls in the same direction as the EU's security objectives or, rather, is in tension with it, remains to be seen.

1.4 Kick-starting the internal market: the Single European Act

An important step in the development of both the EU's institutional processes and its substantive scope took place in 1986 with the signing by the then 12 Member States of the Single European Act (SEA). A White Paper issued by the Commission in 1985 had revealed that many barriers still existed to the achievement of the single internal market. The result was a new treaty, the SEA. The principal purpose of the SEA was to eliminate the remaining barriers to the single internal market within the deadline of 31 December 1992, to be achieved by a massive programme of harmonisation of legislation (see Chapter 16). In addition, the SEA extended the sphere of what was at that stage Community competence and introduced a number of procedural changes designed to accelerate the Community decision-making process (see Chapter 3). The SEA undoubtedly injected a new dynamism. By February 1992, 218 of the 282 proposals, forming the entire programme for the completion of the internal market, had been adopted. Although the 1992 programme reached its termination date, it is important to remember that the provisions the SEA introduced remain and are still used as a basis for legislation (see Chapter 16), as barriers to the internal remain even now (see, eg, the Services Directive, discussed in Chapter 22).

1.5 Wider or deeper? Treaty on European Union

The late 1980s saw a growing movement within the Community towards closer European union. In December 1989, two intergovernmental conferences were convened pursuant to cooperation procedures introduced by the SEA to consider the questions of (1) economic and monetary union and (2) political union. The conferences, which lasted for a year, resulted in the signing of the Treaty of Maastricht on 7 February 1992. The Maastricht Treaty is significant in terms of two out of the three vectors identified in 1.1: (1) the increase in the substantive scope of EU competence; and (2) the nature of the EU.

The Maastricht Treaty had the effect of amending the treaty that had established the EEC (Treaty of Rome—the EEC Treaty). It comprised two distinct parts. One part (at that time, Article G), consisting of 86 paragraphs, introduced substantial amendments to the former EEC Treaty, and renamed it the European Community (EC) Treaty. This change of name reflected the Treaty's wider purposes. It was subsequently renamed again by the Treaty of Lisbon (see 1.9).

The second part of the Maastricht Treaty stood as a separate treaty establishing the European Union (Article 1 TEU). It set out a number of general principles and provided specifically for

(1) cooperation, with a view to adopting joint action, in the field of foreign and security policy (FSP), and eventually defence and (2) cooperation and the framing of common policies in justice and home affairs (JHA). These two areas of cooperation came to be referred to as the second and third pillars, respectively, of the European Union (see 1.5.3). The remaining pillar was made up of the EC, together with Euratom and, prior to its expiry in 2002, ECSC. The communities comprising this pillar, referred to as the first pillar of the Union, were together called the European Communities. The Union structure was often represented pictorially, as a temple. The three pillars we have just described support a 'roof' containing the Union's objectives. The whole structure stood on a pediment of the common, concluding provisions. Note that, following Lisbon, this pillar structure no longer exists (see 1.9.2), but it is important to be aware of as it had important constitutional and institutional consequences.

Maastricht was due to come into effect on 1 January 1993, following ratification as required by all Member States. As a result of difficulties, political and legal, causing delay in ratification in some Member States (notably the UK, Denmark and Germany), the Treaty did not enter into force until 1 November 1993. From that date until the entry into force of the Lisbon Treaty, the EEC Treaty became the EC Treaty. Given the removal of the distinction between the EC and the EU by the Treaty of Lisbon (see 1.9), the terms EC and Community have been replaced throughout this book to avoid confusion, except where context requires a distinction to be made between EC and EU.

1.5.1 Monetary union

Like the SEA, Maastricht extended the scope of Union competence and strengthened its institutional machinery; in particular, the powers of the European Parliament (see Chapter 2). Perhaps one of the most politically sensitive issues was the introduction of provisions designed to lead to full economic and monetary union by 1999. The fact that, of the then Member States, both Britain and Denmark negotiated provisions allowing them to opt out of this process, indicates the importance of this issue. Even Germany, one of the driving forces behind monetary union, experienced difficulties: the validity of Germany's entry into the single currency was challenged, albeit unsuccessfully, before the German constitutional court. In the recent economic crisis it seems that, in retrospect, some concerns about the euro were valid. Shortly after the entry into force of the Lisbon Treaty, the institutional provisions for the euro were revised in March 2011 in order to allow the establishment of the European Stability Mechanism (see Chapter 20). It remains to be seen what impact the Euro crisis has, not only on the structure of the euro provisions but also on the EU itself.

The Treaty also contains provisions detailing the institutions necessary to run the single currency (Articles 134–5 and 282–4 TFEU). Crucially, there is no exit mechanism should Member States think it desirable to leave the euro. More details on monetary union can be found in Chapter 20.

Eleven states were initially identified as having satisfied the convergence criteria: Belgium, Germany, Spain, France, Ireland, Italy, Luxembourg, The Netherlands, Austria, Portugal and Finland (the UK, Denmark and Sweden having, for the time being, opted out of monetary union). Greece became the 12th Member State to join the Eurozone, on 1 January 2002. All the new Member States should join the euro if they meet the convergence criteria. Estonia, Latvia and Lithuania have joined the ERM as a preliminary step. Slovenia joined the Eurozone in January 2007; Malta and Cyprus joined in January 2008, as did Slovakia on 1 January 2009. Subsequently Estonia joined and then Latvia. Enthusiasm for early adoption of the euro has faded somewhat due to the current economic situation, but, despite the sovereign debt crisis, at the time of writing no Eurozone state has left the euro.

1.5.2 **Union citizenship**

The TEU also introduced the notion of citizenship of the Union (Article 20 TFEU). On the face of it, citizenship seems a relatively straightforward notion. It entitles EU nationals to certain rights such as freedom of movement throughout the Union (see Chapters 21–25) and the right to vote and to stand in municipal elections or elections to the European Parliament in any Member State in which they are resident.

There has been much debate about the significance of European citizenship. Some saw it as the beginning of the development of a common European identity or as a means to ameliorate the democratic deficit within the Union (see Chapter 3). Others have criticised it for being no more than a label for the rights of free movement already incorporated in the Treaties. The Treaty allows the Member States to increase the rights attaching to the notion of citizenship, but two decades on they have not done so. Development has mainly been through case law (see Chapters 20–23). While the links of nationality to individual Member States remain strong, according to some commentators, judicial extension of rights—particularly social rights—upsets the balance between the powers of Member States and those of the EU.

1.5.3 **The other two pillars of the Union**

Although the second and third pillars could have been seen as extending the powers transferred to the European level, they could also have been seen as maintaining the autonomy of the nation state. Decision-making within these pillars was, under the TEU, predominantly in the hands of the Council representing the Member States, and, although these two pillars shared the institutions of the former EC, the other institutions were limited in the role they played in both policymaking and enforcement. Decision-making in these two pillars could thus be characterised as being primarily intergovernmental in nature, in contrast with the supranational approach found in the first pillar. In addition, all decisions were required to be made unanimously. Consequently progress towards making effective policies within these areas was slow. The TEU contained provisions whereby some of the policies in JHA could be transferred to what at that stage was the EC (under what was originally Article K.9 TEU). These provisions are often referred to as 'passarelle provisions'. In the context of the original JHA, the assumption was that such a transfer must surely increase the speed of common policy-making in those areas. These provisions have to a large extent been superseded by events, given the 'de-pillarisation' of the EU with Lisbon, though some passarelle provisions remain with regard to the possibility of changing the decision-making procedures in respect of sensitive policy areas (see 1.9).

1.6 Impact of the Treaty of Amsterdam

Original Article N(2) TEU provided that an intergovernmental conference (IGC) should be held in 1996. The purpose of the review was to revise the policies and institutional structure of the Union to ensure its effectiveness (Article 2 TEU) and constitutes a stage in the development of the EU's working processes. This was an issue gaining evermore relevance with the increase of Union competence under the TEU and the further expansion of Union membership. As the IGC discussions progressed, it became clear that the issues to be decided coalesced round three broad, interlinked themes: democracy, transparency and efficiency (discussed further in Chapters 2 and 3). The review process continued into June 1997, when a draft treaty was agreed at Amsterdam. This treaty, the Treaty of Amsterdam (ToA), was signed on 2 October 1997 and came into force on 1 May 1999. The ToA renumbered all Treaty articles, but since the Treaty of Lisbon again renumbered the Treaty articles, we will use post-Lisbon Treaty numbering.

1.6.1 **Strengthening the EC pillar**

The ToA, when compared with the ambitious TEU, may seem to have achieved little; indeed, when one considers the stresses to which the EU will increasingly find its decision-making subject in an EU of 28 or more, the ToA could be criticised for failing to deal adequately with the difficult institutional questions involved. Nonetheless, the ToA can still be seen as constituting a cautious but significant expansion of the Union's scope. The (then) EC pillar was strengthened by streamlining its decision-making powers and by the allocation of new competences (see Chapter 3). Certain provisions, for example those relating to the admission of third-country nationals, were moved from the then third pillar (JHA) to what was at that time the EC pillar. In addition, the Schengen Agreement, which dealt with controls at internal borders (an agreement outside the EC/EU framework between a number of the EU Member States), and its associated decisions were, in effect, incorporated into the then EC Treaty. Some completely new provisions were also introduced, such as those relating to unemployment. The Protocol on Social Policy, originally annexed to the EC Treaty by the TEU, was incorporated into the main body of the Treaty, replacing the previous social-policy provisions.

1.6.2 **Equality and fundamental rights**

These changes reflect a shift of emphasis away from the mainly economic conception of the EU to a more political idea, founded on fundamental rights and principles. In particular, the provision prohibiting discrimination on grounds of nationality (Article 18 TFEU) was developed by the insertion of a new clause (Article 19 TFEU) authorising the Council to 'take appropriate action to combat discrimination based on sex, racial or ethnic origin, religion or belief, disability, age or sexual orientation'.

Although not phrased in the absolute terms of Article 18 TFEU, it reinforces the idea of non-discrimination as a fundamental principle, which the European courts have invoked and used to significant effect in their case law. Indeed, some of the case law on age discrimination is potentially far-reaching in its effects (see Chapters 5, 6 and 27). Further, the promotion of the equality of men and women is now identified in Article 8 TFEU as a task of the Union. Post-Lisbon, this requirement has been strengthened, as Article 10 TFEU requires the Union, in defining all its policies, to combat discrimination whether based on sex, racial or ethnic origin, religion or belief, disability, age or sexual orientation.

The concern with fundamental principles is also evidenced by amended Article 7 TEU. This provides that any Member State found to have committed a persistent and serious breach of the fundamental principles listed in Article 2 TEU may be suspended from voting in the Council of Ministers, although it will remain subject to obligations arising out of the Union membership, such as compliance with Union legislation. The principles listed in Article 2 TEU are: human dignity, freedom, democracy, equality, the rule of law and respect for human rights, including the rights of persons belonging to minorities. Article 7 TEU has been amended to strengthen procedural safeguards, specifically to allow the Union to act to prevent violations occurring (Article 7(1) TEU) in addition to the power to act when 'serious and persistent breach' has occurred (Article 7(2) TEU). The amended Article 7 conferred new powers on the Commission regarding monitoring of fundamental rights in the Union and in the identification of potential risks. As a response, the Commission issued a communication outlining its views on when the conditions of Article 7 TEU would be satisfied (COM(2003) 606 final). There have been a number of occasions on which the possibility of using Article 7 TEU has been discussed. For example, the European Parliament proposed activating the process in relation to constitutional changes introduced in Hungary (See Resolution of 3 July 2013 on the Situation of Fundamental Rights: standards and practices in Hungary (A7-0229/2013), para 87). Nonetheless, there seems to be reluctance amongst the Member States to use this process, suggesting it is more political than justiciable in nature. Respect for the rule of law, however, was evidenced by the expansion of the Court's jurisdiction in relation to the area of freedom, security and justice (discussed further in Chapters 10 and 26).

1.6.3 Closer cooperation

The last main change introduced by the ToA was the introduction of provisions allowing for 'closer cooperation' by Member States. This is often referred to as an example of the principle of 'flexibility', described as the leitmotif of the ToA. It allows differing conceptions of the European ideal and different degrees of commitment to coexist within the Union framework. As such, it is a variant of the concepts variously described as 'multi-speed Europe', 'Europe of variable geometry' and 'Europe of concentric circles' prior to the 1996 IGC. The ToA allowed Member States wishing to cooperate more closely in specific areas within the general scope of the Treaties, but which are not yet subject to Union legislation, to do so. Although the Union had, in effect, accepted this approach in specific policy areas, such as the UK and Danish opt-out of monetary union under the TEU and the UK opt-out of the Protocol on Social Policy in the TEU, this was the first time that a *general* provision (now, as amended, Articles 20 TEU and 326–34 TFEU) allowing for such separate development within the Union framework, was incorporated.

Note that these provisions were amended by Nice (see 1.7.1), would have been amended by the Constitution had it come into force (see 1.8), and have again been affected by Lisbon (see further 1.9 and 3.8.6).

This provision for closer cooperation may bring some advantages, notably by preventing the frustration of the integrationist aims of the majority of Member States by the minority, thus relieving the tensions between the Member States which disagree about the depth of European integration and allowing compromise within the Union. It also carries disadvantages. In particular, the boundary between matters falling only within the sphere of EU law proper and areas permitting closer cooperation may be unclear. In any event, the very fact that the Union contemplates an approach where some Member States go ahead regardless of the wishes of others will undermine the ideas of community and solidarity which are fundamental to the creation of both the internal market and an ever closer union. It seems, however, that 'flexibility' is now an unavoidable part of ensuring agreement within the Union and allowing it to develop.

1.7 Preparations for enlargement: Treaty of Nice

It has been suggested that the ToA failed to deal with one of the main issues identified by the 1996 IGC—that of preparing the EU for enlargement. As noted in 1.1, such expansion is one of the vectors of the EU's development. On that basis, the swift progression from treaty negotiation (in respect of the ToA) to treaty negotiation (regarding the Treaty of Nice) is not that surprising. Just two months after the ToA was signed, the European Council at the Cologne Summit in 1999 called for an IGC with a mandate to address certain unresolved issues: size and composition of the Commission; the weighting of votes in Council; and the extension of qualified majority voting (QMV). At the same time, wider discussions were taking place about the legitimacy of the Union and the scope of its powers. There was consequently a debate as to whether the issues to be dealt with by the Nice Treaty should be broadened. In the event, the Treaty remained relatively narrowly focused, although following the 2000 Feira European Council, it also dealt with 'enhanced cooperation'. Difficult constitutional questions, including the status of the Charter of Fundamental Rights, the form of which had been agreed prior to Nice, were deferred until the

2004 IGC. The Treaty of Nice then might well be described as dealing with the leftovers of the ToA but going no further.

1.7.1 Changes to the TEU: enhanced cooperation

The main changes to the former common foreign and security policy (CFSP) and JHA pillars related to the provisions on closer cooperation, renamed 'enhanced cooperation', and revised to relax the conditions for use of the procedure. The number of Member States needed to cooperate has been reduced. The provision accepts a greater degree of potential impact of any consequent legislation on non-participating Member States and on the *acquis*. Whereas the original version used the phrase 'does not affect', the amended version refers to these interests being respected. Nonetheless, the provisions were not used. Lisbon introduced yet more changes (see 1.9.2).

1.7.2 Changes to the EC pillar

As already noted, certain institutional changes were included in Nice: these are discussed further in Chapter 2. Changes were also made to the court structure, significantly strengthening the role of what is now called the General Court, which gained the right to hear some preliminary rulings procedures (see Part II). The closer cooperation provisions were amended as noted in 1.7.1 (but see also 1.9.2). Further, co-decision and QMV were extended to a wider range of substantive provisions.

1.7.3 Ratification of the Treaty of Nice

Although it may not have had the great ambitions of TEU, Nice ran into difficulties when the Member States sought the approval of the Treaty within their own legal orders. Surprisingly, perhaps, the Irish voted 'no' to the Nice Treaty in June 2001. This was an embarrassing result, as the institutional rebalancing contained in Nice was viewed as the necessary precursor to further enlargement, which was already being negotiated. It was only in October 2002 that a second Irish referendum accepted the Treaty of Nice. Ireland finally lodged its instrument of ratification on 18 December 2002. As provided in the Nice Treaty, it came into force on 1 February 2003.

1.8 Doomed: Treaty establishing a Constitution for Europe

Although the Declaration on the Future of Europe attached to the Treaty of Nice identified specific issues that would need to be addressed: the delimitation of powers between the EU and the Member States; the simplification of the Treaties; and the role of the national parliaments within the EU, it also called for 'a wider and deeper debate about the future of the European Union'. The Laeken Declaration confirmed the issues to be addressed by the next round of treaty negotiations. It confirmed the points identified in the Nice Declaration and emphasised the importance of bringing Europe closer to its citizens. In doing so, however, it raised the possibility of reorganising the Treaties so as to introduce a constitutional text for the EU. Such a text would be important for setting down the future characteristics of the Union; indeed the fact that the word 'constitutional' was introduced was seen by some as significant. Unusually by comparison with the intergovernmental nature of previous treaty revisions, the Laeken Declaration provided for the establishment of a Convention on the Future of Europe. Its function was to identify and discuss the relevant issues before drawing up a final document containing the possible options for the Union's future development to form a starting point for the IGC's discussions.

The resulting treaty, the Treaty establishing a Constitution for Europe (the Constitution), was signed on 29 October 2004. Significantly, referenda held in France and the Netherlands produced a 'no' vote, and the governments of both countries accepted this outcome. Nonetheless, 13 Member States ratified it. As a result, the Union entered a period of reflection to consider how to proceed. The outcome was the Treaty of Lisbon (see 1.9). Before we consider Lisbon, a few points about the Constitution should be noted.

Despite the grand title, the Constitution can be seen as reordering, clarifying and simplifying rather than adding much that was totally new. It certainly did not change the nature of the EU. Nonetheless it would have introduced changes, some of which, though small, were significant. Crucially, it would have repealed all existing Treaties and the current pillar structure, thus removing the distinction between Community and Union. It also identified the powers, or competence, of the Union and the Member States expressly (Chapters 3 and 16), and would have formally incorporated the doctrine of primacy of Union law (Chapter 4). Some changes were proposed to the operation of the institutions, mainly to improve efficiency of decision-making (see Chapter 2) and to contain the size of the institutions with the increased size of the Union. Particular controversy surrounded the proposed introduction of a formal president of the Council, as well as the post of a foreign minister.

Some limited areas of Union competence were to be added and the scope of some areas amended. Thus we saw references to space, energy, humanitarian aid and territorial cohesion. Although not hitherto mentioned in the Treaties, the introduction of these areas would have reflected existing Union practice. Similarly, areas such as sport have been the subject of declarations attached to Treaties, if not part of the formal Union competence. Article I–44 Constitutional Treaty dealt with enhanced cooperation. A minimum of one-third of the Member States were required to participate, a lower percentage than under Nice, but enhanced cooperation was expressed to be used only as a last resort and within the framework of Union non-exclusive competence. Finally, there were changes to the types of Union legislation and their terminology, discussed further in Chapter 3.

How do we assess the impact of the Constitution? On the one hand it sought formally to introduce the notion of constitution, with all its implications of statehood. On the other, the word constitution had been used in the context of the Community and the Union for some considerable time: the Court of Justice (CJ) in its judgment in *Parti Ecologiste 'Les Verts' v European Parliament* (case 294/83) referred to the EC Treaty as a constitutional document and the debates about statehood of the Union arose in the context of European citizenship, introduced by TEU. In terms of the text itself, the Constitution did not constitute a huge turning point. As with many of the previous Treaties, it was a reaction to the concerns afflicting the EU at that time. In this case, the triggers seem to have been the need to 'tidy up' the Union's procedures in the face of the expansion in membership and, importantly, to try to deal with the increased public disaffection with the EU. Thus we see an increased emphasis on democracy, participation, the rights of individuals, and the values of the Union. Vaclav Havel, President of the Czech Republic, sought a:

concise, clearly formulated and universally understandable constitution [which] would simply make it easier for the citizens of an integrating Europe to recognise what the European Union stands for; to understand it better; and, consequently, to identify with it.

With the abandonment of the Constitution, this task fell to Lisbon. Whether this aim has been achieved is another matter.

1.9 Democracy and effectiveness? Treaty of Lisbon

The 50th anniversary of the EU took place in 2007. To mark the occasion, its representatives signed the Berlin Declaration, which identified the themes, values and aspirations of the EU. It also sought to re-start the process of treaty negotiation:

> With European Unification, a dream of earlier generations has become a reality. Our history reminds us that we must protect this for the good of future generations. For that reason we must always renew the political shape of Europe in keeping with the times. That is why today, 50 years after the signing of the Treaties of Rome, we are united in our aim of placing the European Union on a renewed common basis before the European Parliament elections in 2009.

Thus, in June 2007, the EU summit agreed a new IGC mandate for institutional reform. A new Reform Treaty was agreed and signed at a special summit in Lisbon on 13 December 2007. This is the Treaty of Lisbon. It came into force on 1 January 2009, despite problems in the ratification process.

There has been intense debate, both academic and political, about the impact of the Treaty of Lisbon. It is clear that it comprises much of what was contained in the Constitution; indeed the starting point for discussions on the Lisbon Treaty was the Constitution. For the leaders of a number of Member States—such as the 'no' voting states of France and the Netherlands—it was important that the new Treaty be distinguished from the Constitutional Treaty. At the same time, sufficient proposed reforms from the Constitutional Treaty needed to be retained to attract the support of the Member States which had ratified the Constitutional Treaty, as well as to make the EU workable for the future. In the UK particularly, there was political debate as to whether the Treaty should attract a referendum; however the government pressed ahead without, and the UK officially ratified the Treaty of Lisbon on 16 July 2008. An attempt to challenge the decision, on the basis of legitimate expectations, was unsuccessful (*R, on the application of Wheeler v Office of the Prime Minister, Secretary of State for Foreign and Commonwealth Affairs and Speaker of the House of Commons* [2008] EWHC 1409 (Admin)). Ratification was fairly smooth in almost all of the Member States; however in a case of history repeating itself, the Irish—after a poorly orchestrated 'yes' campaign—voted no, apparently due to concerns about the right to mandate a commissioner, taxation, military neutrality and abortion. Concessions—or clarifications—were given on these points. Notably, all Member States will be able to nominate a Commissioner. The Czechs had to wait until a decision of their constitutional court on the constitutionality of ratification. Whilst that court approved ratification, the Czech implementing legislation now contains a provision that no further transfer of power to the EU may take place without the express permission of the Czech parliament. Although the German parliament approved Lisbon, ratification was delayed pending legal challenges filed by a number of appellants. The Federal Constitutional Court (FCC) gave a conditional approval to the Lisbon Treaty. While the Treaty itself is compatible with the German constitution, ratification could not proceed until an accompanying law dealing with 'bridging clauses' (which allow for an extension of Union competence), usually referred to as passarelles, had been amended, so as to ensure democratic control of the process but potentially limiting further integration. The FCC also held that Union law deemed to violate requirements of the judgment could be declared inapplicable in Germany. In a return to *Brunner* language (see Chapters 3 and 4) the FCC emphasised its place in the legal hierarchy as final arbiter of any disputes between German and EU legal orders (see Chapter 4 for further details). A brief overview of Lisbon follows.

1.9.1 **Themes of the Lisbon Treaty**

We have seen that much of the post-TEU impetus for treaty making was a desire to make the EU function efficiently, especially in an EU of 28 Member States. Lisbon has other themes, however. It is notable that it has a much greater emphasis on values, specifically those which value the human as a political and social animal rather than as an economic actor. Article 2 TEU specifies:

> The Union is founded on the values of respect for human dignity, freedom, democracy, equality, the rule of law and respect for human rights, including the rights of persons belonging to minorities. These values are common to the Member States in a society in which pluralism, non-discrimination, tolerance, justice, solidarity and equality between men and women prevail.

Perhaps the key example of this is the change in status of the Charter of Fundamental Rights: it is now binding (see 6.4). The Lisbon Treaty is also focused on freedom and security, as the changes to the provisions on criminal law illustrate. Another central concern relates to democracy: a number of the changes reflect a concern about the role of the national legislature through the involvement of the national parliaments in EU processes (see 1.9.3 and 3.5.3), through emphasis on the principle of conferral (see 1.9.2 and 3.2) and in the attempt to delimit EU competence more carefully. Some of these provisions on democracy operate by emphasising the Member States as the original source of EU power. Seen this way, the inclusion of provisions to deal with the possibility of a Member State choosing to leave the EU also fits here. One final theme, arising from some of the institutional innovations, such as the new High Representative and the EU's legal personality, but also some of the substantive provisions (see 3.3.2), is the endeavour to give the EU an external profile on the world stage.

1.9.2 **Constitutional issues**

Like the Constitution, Lisbon disposed of the pillar structure, though there remains a distinction between the former first and third pillars on the one hand and CFSP on the other. The first and third pillars of the EU have in effect been merged into a single system: what was the EC Treaty and what is now the Treaty on the Functioning of the European Union (TFEU). CFSP remains in the TEU, with a different institutional structure. So whilst JHA became subject to the greater involvement of the Union institutions as part of the Area of Freedom, Security and Justice, with presumably greater scrutiny of actions at Union level, the CFSP remains essentially intergovernmental in form. Whilst the court's jurisdiction has been extended as regards the former JHA, subject to some limitations, it remained largely excluded as regards CFSP. Nonetheless, the role of determining the boundaries falls to the Court, as discussed in Chapters 2 and 3.

As part of the Lisbon changes, the EC Treaty was renamed the TFEU, another classic in the Union tendency to pick 'un-user friendly' terminology. References to the 'Community' became references to the 'Union'. Further, the EU was given a single legal personality; previously the Union had no legal personality, although the former Community did. The inclusion of the old JHA within what was the EC pillar meant that some case law, emphasising the culturally specific nature of criminal sanctions, for example, *Commission v Council (environmental crimes)* (case C-176/03), has been consigned to history by Lisbon.

The Charter did not have legal status prior to Lisbon, though the European courts referred to it in some judgments (see, eg, *Parliament v Council (family reunification)* (case C-540/03)). The Constitution envisaged including the Charter of Fundamental Rights in the constitutional treaties themselves. Lisbon abandoned this format, but gave the Charter the same status as the Treaties. This achieved effectively the same end by a different route. The precise impact of this change is hard to assess, though some have suggested that if the scope of application of the Charter is understood in the light of European citizenship, it will be very broad indeed. The British negotiated an 'opt-out', as they have in relation to some of the provisions formerly in the JHA, and the Poles have also 'opted out' of the Charter provision; the scope of this 'opt-out' is discussed in Chapter 6. Like the Constitution, Lisbon requires the accession of the EU to the European Convention for the Protection of Human Rights and Fundamental Freedoms (ECHR) (see 6.5.2).

Finally, and with great symbolic significance, an exit clause has been introduced; hitherto the possibility of a Member State leaving the EU was not envisaged in the Treaties. Now, a mechanism has been introduced for that to happen. This is discussed further at 1.10.

Lisbon emphasised the division of competence between the EU and the Member States, re-emphasising that competence is granted to the EU on a limited basis and residual power remains with the Member States. The previous Article 5 EC, which set out the principle of subsidiarity was reformulated in the EU Treaty. A new Title (Title I) in the TFEU on *Categories and areas of Union competence* reflects the ambition to provide a more transparent and better organised catalogue than the previous Treaties (see Chapter 3). In this, there are similarities to the approach adopted in the Constitution. Another point of similarity to the Constitution is the approach taken to enhanced cooperation. Lisbon removed the amendments inserted by Nice. The criteria for permission to use enhanced cooperation include a minimum number of nine Member States (currently just under one-third of Member States) to participate and a requirement that this is a 'last resort'. While the enhanced cooperation provisions have now been used, in some instances this has already given rise to dispute (see 3.8.6).

1.9.3 **Institutional matters**

The main impetus for reform was a desire to make the EU function more effectively. Although there are differences between Lisbon and the Constitution, there are also marked similarities in approach. Lisbon introduced a permanent Council president and a High Representative of the EU for foreign affairs (see Chapter 2). The number of Commissioners and MEPs was in principle reduced, though note the concession to Ireland, so that one Commissioner per Member State was retained. A 'double majority' rule for Council decisions made by QMV will be introduced (see Chapter 3), but, due to Polish opposition, did not come in to force immediately. In terms of seeking to prevent further 'mission creep' on the part of the EU institutions, the role of national parliaments has been strengthened (Article 12 TEU, as amended by Lisbon). The so-called 'orange-card' system will allow national parliaments to review legislative proposals for compliance with the subsidiarity principle, thus introducing a political solution to an essentially political question about the appropriate boundaries of EU competence. This is linked to the approach which is a theme of the Lisbon Treaty, that is, that competence granted to the EU is limited, as we can see in Articles 4 and 5 TEU.

1.9.4 **Policy matters**

We have noted the change consequent to the proposed abolition of the pillar structure. Linked to this development, and reflecting a changing approach to these policy areas, is the extension of QMV to approximately 40 policy areas, including asylum, immigration, police cooperation and judicial cooperation in criminal matters. A significant change arises from the inclusion of matters formerly dealt with under the third pillar by the 'Community method'. New areas, such as climate change and energy solidarity, have also been introduced into Lisbon and, at the request of the French, a reference to 'free and undistorted competition', found in the Constitution, was removed as an objective of the Union. This change is unlikely to undermine competition policy which has been central to the common market project for the last half-century. Its downgrading perhaps reflects the wider aims of the Union.

1.9.5 **Key differences from the Constitution**

Whilst the issues that were addressed in the Constitution still needed addressing, it was equally obvious that a treaty that was exactly the same as the one that had been rejected by the voters of two Member States could not be put forward with any degree of legitimacy. Lisbon therefore needed to fulfil some symbolic, as well as practical, functions. Crucially, it was needed to put an end to the process of reform started by the Laeken Declaration; essentially saying the EU has now been reformed and thus bring an end to discussions about the nature of the EU and how to improve it. Bringing these debates to an end would allow the institutions of the EU freedom to concentrate on their mission, rather than justifying their very existence. With the impact of economic downturn, refocusing the Union on problem solving becomes increasingly important.

The key differences between the Constitutional Treaty and the Treaty of Lisbon are as follows:

(1) Arguably the most notable difference is the change in format of implementation. The Constitution was to re-establish the EU in a new treaty which would have replaced all of the old Treaties; the Treaty of Lisbon on the other hand amended the existing EU Treaties, even though the EC Treaty was renamed as part of this process. The Lisbon proposals are less radical, and they leave the existing Treaties as a rather untidy bundle of provisions. Certainly in approach, then, Lisbon is significantly less far-reaching than the grand recasting of the Treaties envisaged by the Constitution. Like the previous Treaties, with the exception of the Constitution, Lisbon is an amending Treaty and, read on its own, makes little sense, as it cross refers to the original Treaty of Rome as variously amended; Lisbon contains only changes to that text. Whilst an attempt is made to impose a certain order through renumbering, this is of dubious helpfulness as the net result is that anyone reading materials has to be familiar with the numbering which will be introduced by Lisbon, the post-ToA numbers and the original numbers;

(2) Under the Constitution, primacy of the EU Treaties and EU law was to be given explicit recognition; under the Lisbon Treaty, primacy is recognised in an annexed declaration. This is another example of the softening in approach between the Constitutional Treaty and Lisbon, and may reflect a pragmatic desire not to destabilise the relationship between the Union legal order and those of Member States, by removing the principle of supremacy from its case law basis in to the form of a treaty provision. Note that one consequence of the structural changes (and 'horizontal' amendments) is that it would appear to be EU law rather than EC law, which is supreme (see further Chapter 4);

(3) The various symbols and terminology, which were criticised for carrying overtones of statehood, such as the European flag, anthem and motto, have been abandoned. The restatement of the position as to competence and the emphasis on subsidiarity (see Chapter 3)—although both principles were included in the Constitutional Treaty—reflect a similar reframing of the EU as an international organisation rather than the EU as nascent state;

(4) Under the Constitution the office of the 'minister for foreign affairs' was to be created, again a term with state-like overtones. As already noted at 1.9.3, Lisbon created a 'High Representative of the Union for Foreign Affairs and Security Policy', a much less contentious name for what might be the same job;

(5) The change in approach to fundamental rights: whilst the Constitution highlighted the significance of the Charter of Fundamental Rights, in Lisbon it is dealt with by a

cross-reference and is not incorporated into the Treaty structure itself. This distinction may have a symbolic significance, though the Charter will, post-Lisbon, have a similar effect.

This leaves us with the question of whether Lisbon is merely the Constitution repackaged. There are many areas in which the Lisbon Treaty takes the same approach as the Constitution would have done, using the same provisions almost word-for-word. Like the Constitution, Lisbon makes little change to the substantive policies at the heart of the internal market. There are significant differences, however, in the way Lisbon achieves its aims and, crucially, many of the controversial elements relating to the statist overtones in the Constitution have been removed. It is not the same treaty; it is, however, very similar.

1.10 Withdrawal under Article 50 TEU and Brexit

The Treaty of Lisbon famously introduced the right for a Member State to leave, or withdraw from, the EU. On one level, this is nothing new: the decision of a Member State to leave the EU was always possible under usual rules of international law. With the Lisbon Treaty, these rules are now displaced and Article 50 TEU provides the route by which a Member State may leave the EU. Before considering the text of Article 50 and the questions it raises, we should recognise that the inclusion of an exit route in the Treaty framework was a significant symbolic step. It opens the possibility of a destination for the Member States of the EU other than the 'ever-closer' union to which the Treaties have hitherto pointed. Nonetheless, a negotiated exit may have the benefit of allowing better future relations between the EU and the exiting Member State and so may lead to a better outcome than a Member State seeking to leave just under the principles of international law.

No Member State has—at the time of writing—yet left the EU. On 23 June 2016 a majority of the UK population who voted, voted to leave the EU. Shortly after, it became apparent that the process by which a Member State leaves raises a number of difficult questions; indeed the provisions in Article 50 TEU have been described as incomplete and unclear (see, eg, Hillion). The text of Article 50 follows.

Article 50 TEU

(1) Any Member State may decide to withdraw from the Union in accordance with its own constitutional requirements.

(2) A Member State which decides to withdraw shall notify the European Council of its intention. In the light of the guidelines provided by the European Council, the Union shall negotiate and conclude an agreement with that State, setting out the arrangements for its withdrawal, taking account of the framework for its future relationship with the Union. That agreement shall be negotiated in accordance with Article 218(3) of the Treaty on the Functioning of the European Union. It shall be concluded on behalf of the Union by the Council, acting by a qualified majority, after obtaining the consent of the European Parliament.

(3) The Treaties shall cease to apply to the State in question from the date of entry into force of the withdrawal agreement or, failing that, two years after the notification referred to in paragraph 2, unless the European Council, in agreement with the Member State concerned, unanimously decides to extend this period.

(4) For the purposes of paragraphs 2 and 3, the member of the European Council or of the Council representing the withdrawing Member State shall not participate in the discussions of the European Council or Council or in decisions concerning it. A qualified majority shall be defined in accordance with Article 238(3)(b) of the Treaty on the Functioning of the European Union.

(5) If a State which has withdrawn from the Union asks to rejoin, its request shall be subject to the procedure referred to in Article 49.

The procedure comprises four elements:

- notification by existing Member State;
- adoption of negotiating guidelines by the European Council;
- negotiation of exit agreement;
- cessation of applicability of Treaties to exiting Member State.

Although Article 50(1) TEU seems straightforward, the internal 'constitutional requirements' of the withdrawing Member State may be complex and contentious in themselves, as can be seen in the response to the British referendum. As a matter of British constitutional law, it was not clear who should make the decision to leave, and there were sharply differing views as to whether parliamentary approval was required. This lack of clarity led to litigation: *R (Miller and Another) v Secretary of State for Exiting the European Union and Others* ([2017] UKSC 5). The Supreme Court ruled that an Act of Parliament was required, though the Court was not unanimous in its opinion. A more detailed discussion of British national constitutional law lies outside the scope of this book. There are, however, further uncertainties which relate to the interpretation of Article 50 TEU as a matter of EU law. These uncertainties concern the who, what and when of the process. While it may be that the process of Brexit answers some of the questions, it may well be that some remain.

1.10.1 'Who'?

It is accepted that the decision to notify lies in the hands of the Member State seeking to leave the EU. A matter of internal activity (such as the holding of a referendum) does not automatically trigger Article 50; a notification must be made, though there are no conditions in the TEU as to what any such notification should look like. The choice whether to make such a notification and the timing of that notification are decisions for the leaving Member State. It cannot be required to give an Article 50 notification and the notification itself is not subject to the approval of the EU institutions or other Member States. The 'Three Knights Opinion' suggests that Article 50 permits a Member State to notify its intention to leave the EU subject to the fulfilment of its constitutional requirements (such as Parliamentary approval of the deal as actually negotiated) and that if the constitutional requirements were not met, the notice would lapse, or could be unilaterally revoked. Whether this view accords with the meaning of Article 50 TEU cannot be known unless the CJ rules on the point.

Questions arise as to which institution within the EU should lead the negotiations and what is being negotiated. Usually external agreements are negotiated under Article 218(2) TFEU, which specifies the Commission as the negotiator. Article 50 TEU, however, refers to Article 218(3) TFEU, rather than Article 218(2) TFEU. This means that the Council must nominate the body which will carry out the negotiations, rather than it being the role of the Commission by operation of the TFEU. As regards the UK referendum result, the European Commission has set up a 'task force' to deal with negotiations, with Commissioner Michel Barnier as chief negotiator.

The negotiated agreement must be approved. Article 50(2) TEU refers to a qualified majority of remaining Member States. It also requires the consent of the European Parliament, but it is not clear whether MEPs from the exiting Member State may vote. Furthermore, the TEU is silent as to what sort of majority is required.

1.10.2 'What'?

Some politicians suggested that the negotiations would involve negotiations as to the future relationship between the leaving State and the EU. This would have the advantage of ensuring that there was no gap in arrangements between exit and new trade agreements coming into force. It would also mean that the simplified approval arrangements for the exit agreement would apply to any treaties setting up the future arrangements, rather than those treaties having to go through the normal EU approval process. Unfortunately, it is not clear that this view is supported by the text of Article 50(2) which merely requires the negotiations to 'take account of', not negotiate, the future relationship between the EU and the exiting State.

A question of considerable importance is whether, once notification has been given, it is possible to rescind the notification. Once again, Article 50 TEU is silent on this point and there have been arguments put forward to support either the possibility that a change of mind is possible, or—to the contrary—not possible. The argument then turns on how Article 50 is interpreted. Apart from the argument in the 'Three Knights Opinion' where the conditions of Article 50 have not been met, possible constructions are:

- an implied right to withdraw notification, which would be supported by the fact that the provision envisages the possibility of a Member State changing its mind as Article 50(5) allows a Member State to apply to rejoin the EU;

- that the extent to which a Member State may change its mind is dealt with by Article 50(5) TEU and that there are policy reasons not to allow a Member State to start the leaving process just as a bargaining strategy; or

- that the matter has not been dealt with at all in Article 50 TEU, which brings us to the Vienna Convention on the Law of Treaties. Article 68 Vienna Convention specifies that a notification of an intention to withdraw from a treaty 'may be revoked at any time before it comes into effect'. This general provision is subject to any specific arrangements in the relevant treaty, which, on this construction of Article 50 TEU, are absent.

Litigation has been commenced before the Irish courts with the intention of seeking a reference to the CJ, on whether Article 50 TEU, once triggered, is revocable by the British government without the consent of the other Member States. At the time of writing the success or otherwise of this action is not known.

A further question is whether triggering Article 50 automatically means triggering the exit procedure for the EEA Agreement, which has its own provision, s 127, setting out the mechanism for withdrawal. Permission to bring judicial review action against the Secretary of State for Exiting the EU on this point was refused by the English High Court on the basis that the application was premature (3 February 2017).

1.10.3 'When'?

On the face of the text, given that the choice to notify lies in the hands of the exiting Member State, the timing of the start of the process is also under the control of that Member State—though there may be political pressures to take into account. Once the notification has been given, a two-year period starts within which the negotiations should conclude. While it might be thought possible to start negotiations before notification has been given (perhaps informal discussions), the institutions only have authority to start negotiating formally after any such notification.

The TEU envisages the possibility of an extension of time, but significantly this requires the agreement of all Member States. A single Member State could block any such extension. We then see a shift in balance of power which rests with the exiting Member State up to the point of notification but thereafter shifts to the EU. This point together with the uncertainty about the ability to revoke a notification, suggests a Member State should be wary of notifying before it is ready to go through the negotiation process.

1.11 Theories of integration

Although the development of the Union is usually described as a linear progression towards a specified goal, it has also been argued that the integration process has actually fallen into different phases
with key characteristics. These phases may even suggest that, despite the rhetoric of an 'ever-closer
Union', the end goal of the Union is not well defined or even necessarily agreed upon. Different
theories have been put forward to describe and explain these different phases, though the degree
to which it is possible to describe each such phase only by reference to an individual theory is debatable. The main schools of thought follow.

1.11.1 Functionalism

Functionalism was a theory which was popular during the Union's early years. As its name implies,
it is based on identifying specific, discrete economic areas, usually those perceived as 'non-
contentious', in which Member States are encouraged to cooperate. Technocrats (technical experts
in the relevant field) would manage these fields in the interests of the Union as a whole. Unlike
politicians, they would not be influenced by the need to retain power. Instead, technocrats were
perceived as making rational choices. Functionalism can be used to describe the ECSC prior to its
demise.

1.11.2 Neofunctionalism

What was the European Community was much broader than the ECSC. Neofunctionalism developed as a way of describing this endeavour. It has similarities to functionalism in that it, too, is
based on cooperation in specific areas. Neofunctionalism argues, however, that those involved in
the process became key players to whom allegiance may be transferred; thus it accepts that the state
is not a single unified actor and, indeed, that states are not the only players on the international
stage. In this, it was an appropriate theory of European integration and some have described it as
the dominant ideology of the early years. Central to neofunctionalism is 'spill-over' which has both
a functional and political aspect. The functional aspect was based on the idea that elements of the
economy do not exist in isolation and that integration in one area would lead to pressure in other
areas. Integration in non-contentious areas spills over into other, more sensitive areas. As regards
the political aspect, the theory was that in areas which had been integrated, interest groups would
be expected to focus their attention on the Union level, as that was where the regulatory power lay
and would also add to pressure for further integration.

   The process results in a diminution of national governmental power and a matching increase
in the power of the technocratic level to deal with sensitive issues. Whilst attractive at a superficial
level, the theory was criticised, as it did not describe the reality of later Union development.

1.11.3 Intergovernmentalism

Both of the above theories can be described as forms of supranationalism. Supranationalism argues
that power is located above the nation state. This view is challenged by intergovernmentalism
which means literally between governments. It assumes that the central actors are the states themselves, which essentially act to protect their own interests and power base. On this view, integration
occurs because such behaviour is in the rational best interests of the states, as they seek to acquire
and maintain the support of domestic interest groups by promising to attain the preferences which
those interest groups have articulated. Underlying this is the assumption that groups in society

recognise that increasing the flow of goods, services, etc gives rise to benefits, which leads to the policy coordination in the sphere of economic policy.

The Union can be seen as containing elements that illustrate a supranational aspect, but also intergovernmental elements. Intergovernmentalism can be seen in the Luxembourg Accords, in which the then Member States agreed that one Member State could effectively veto a measure in its national interest. The sections of the Union Treaty which deal with CFSP vest most power in the Council, made up of representatives of the Member States' governments. Agreement in these spheres was by agreement of all Member States. In contrast, the powers of the institutions are unusual in their scope and their independence from the Member States (see further Chapter 2). The use of QMV in Council (see Chapter 3) introduces the possibility of Member States being outvoted with the consequence that a Member State may be obliged to implement policies with which it might not agree. This is not easily compatible with a view of Member States each acting in their own interest unless membership of the Union itself is taken into account.

1.11.4 **Multi-level governance**

To some extent the discussion in academic writing about the tension between supranationalism and intergovernmentalism has been replaced during the 1990s with writings on the subject of multi-level governance. Certainly intergovernmentalism has been criticised as being very state-centric. Multi-level governance seeks to explain how the Union is governed rather than focusing on the nature of the integration process. Theories in this school of thought allow a broader range of actors to appear in the discussion of EU governance, important with the introduction of new methods of governance such as open method coordination (see Chapter 3). Thus states do not have a monopoly of control, and in particular do not monopolise the links between sub-state actors and the Union level. This results in a picture which is not just based on a conception of the EU as driven by the Member States or by the actions of the EU institutions and may be more relevant given the dual sources of legitimacy of the EU (the states and their peoples); the tendency to technocratic solutions (involving 'experts' of various sources); the move towards different regulatory solutions, which involve other actors in setting and enforcing standards; and de-centralised enforcement through national courts and regulatory authorities.

1.12 **Conflicting attitudes towards the Union**

It should be noted that the frequency of treaty revision has increased dramatically during the 1990s. While the EEC Treaty survived from 1957 to the SEA of 1986 relatively unchanged, since then there have been four treaty revisions that have been brought into force: TEU, ToA, Nice and Lisbon, as well as the proposed revisions contained in the Constitution. The significance of this development is unclear. One might suggest that it reflects the political changes occurring during the 1990s, particularly in Europe. Alternatively, the change could reflect the dissatisfaction of the Member States (and their population) with the current EU. The difference between the European Communities and the other two pillars created by the TEU was illustrative of the conflicting attitudes held by Member States and individuals towards the Union since its inception, as exemplified by the divergent views expressed by politicians. Although academic literature may now focus on the way the EU operates, within political debate, tensions remain as to the nature of the EU and its future. These tensions seemed particularly apparent during the negotiation and ratification of the TEU and subsequent Treaties, with the 'fiscal compact' to amend the provisions on economic and monetary union (EMU) (see Chapter 20) as well as with Brexit. This issue is not new, nor has it gone away.

One ongoing problem is that there are two main competing visions of Europe: the intergovern-mental and the federal. In *Brunner v European Union Treaty* ([1994] 1 CMLR 57) Germany's power to ratify the TEU was challenged as being contrary to the German constitution. It was argued that in transferring further powers and competence to the EU institutions, the TEU was seeking to cre-ate a Euro-state. The German constitutional court found, it is submitted correctly, that the EU was a federation of states not a Euro-state. Nevertheless, the loss of autonomy of action of the Member States consequent on membership of the EU has certainly been considerable. This has increased during the life of the EU as more and more powers have been transferred to the Union by successive Treaties. This process has been emphasised by the increased use of both qualified majority voting and co-decision. Some integrationists approve of this as part of the process of achieving an 'ever-closer union'. Others fear the loss of sovereignty and see the EU as having grown beyond the loose association of states within a free trade area that the EU was 'intended' to be. The concern about controlling EU competence permeates the approach to the treaty revision at Lisbon. The response in a number of Member States, where challenges were brought before the various national con-stitutional courts, suggests that the proposals are not enough. According to a press release from one challenger in Germany, EU integration has been characterised by 'continuous breaches of the stability pact, a presumptuous over-stepping of power by the European Commission, unaccount-able leadership and dissolution of the separation of powers' (*Frankfurter Allgemeine Zeitung*, 26 January 2009).

Sometimes these differing views of the EU result in Member States being characterised as either Euro-sceptic or pro-Europe, but a degree of caution must be exercised about such generalisations. There is a difference between political rhetoric and legal reality. Out of the group of 28 Member States, it is perhaps surprising that Italy and France, both original Member States, had a much less impressive record of compliance than Denmark, which is often perceived as more Euro-sceptic. According to the 2004 Commission *Review on Implementation of Community Law* (COM(2005) 570), all the EU-15 States had a much less impressive implementation record than the new Member States, though this may be due to the pressures of proving compliance with the Copenhagen criteria and acceding to the EU, than evidence of a long-term political intention to ensure prompt imple-mentation of all Union legislation. Furthermore, there is a tendency for Member States' representa-tives to put national interest—or national political pressures—over the Union interest. This is not just the case with France (see its ban on British beef in defiance of the Union position) or the UK (veto on introduction of Union tax on interest income, thought to threaten the UK bond market), but with all Member States (see the impact of the Greek position on the accession of Turkey, or Portugal on the diversion of Union funding to new Member States).

With the introduction of monetary union, and its current problems, the transfer of further com-petence to the EU and the proposed expansion in membership, the question 'where next?' assumes a new significance as Member States try to fight for their own view on the future of Europe. The ToA, re-emphasised by Nice and Lisbon, sought to solve the problem by the principle of 'flexibility'; opt-outs have become common in the treaty-revision process. The danger is that a flexible Europe could become a fragmented Europe. Arguably, any risk of fragmentation could increase with further expansion, as the Union will have not just more voices, but a greater variety of interests to satisfy.

1.13 **Conclusions: the future**

The EU has changed considerably over its half century or more of existence. Its membership has increased and the Union seems set to continue its eastward expansion. The EU is now a significant trading bloc: the American CIA gave the GDP of the EU as $14,820,000,000,000 in 2010, the largest

GDP in the world. This is, however, the combined GDP of all Member States and there is considerable variance between the Member States. The scope of the Union's substantive activities has also developed, developing not just internal policies with its own Member States, but also an external profile. While the EU has always had a concern to ensure community and peace in Europe, the emphasis has changed. Originally, the central element of the EU was the trade aspect; now 'The Union's aim is to promote peace, its values and the well-being of its peoples' (Article 3(1) TEU). At the same time, the working methods of its institutions have been amended, with a focus on efficiency, transparency and democracy.

While some may be tempted to portray this development as a move along a pre-determined path to federal statehood, such a portrayal would be inaccurate. Instead, the EU's development seems more like a continuing process in which both aims are shifted and the mechanisms for achieving them are changed in response to the environment in which the EU, from time to time, finds itself. While the original Treaty was set up to rebuild Europe after the Second World War, the current Union has different challenges: a global recession, the threat of terrorism and the environmental problems of pollution, dwindling natural resources and global warming. As a global player, the EU has a chance to redefine its role and the world in which we live. We can see the EU as a success story looking at its expansion and (overall) its wealth, as well as the fact that the EU Member States have enjoyed a significant period free from conflict between themselves. The EU story has not been without its difficulties, however, as the almost constant revision of the Treaties and the difficulties encountered in the ratification of those Treaties from Maastricht onwards, as well as Brexit, illustrate. The differences between the Member States in terms of size, wealth and attitudes towards debt and taxation, as well as towards the EU itself, may mean that going forward these difficulties will remain. These internal tensions and differences may threaten the ability of the EU to respond to external circumstances, despite its long history of change. For the first time, the EU envisages, in its post-Lisbon incarnation, the express possibility for a Member State to withdraw. How the EU will develop, if at all, therefore is a question that history alone will answer.

Further reading

Avbelj, M, 'Theory of European Union' (2011) 36 EL Rev 818.

Bradley, K, 'Institutional design in the Treaty of Nice' (2001) 38 CML Rev 1095.

Church, CH and Phinnemore, D, *Understanding the European Constitution: An introduction to the EU Constitutional Treaty* (Routledge, 2006).

Craig, P, 'The Lisbon Treaty: Process, architecture and substance' (2008) 33 EL Rev 137.

Curtin, D, 'The constitutional structure of the Union: A Europe of bits and pieces' (1993) 30 CML Rev 17.

Dawson, M, 'Three Waves of New Governance in the European Union' (2011) 36 EL Rev 208.

Delacourt, C, 'The *Acquis Communautaire*: Has the concept had its day?' (2001) 38 CML Rev 829.

Dougan, M, 'The Treaty of Lisbon 2007: Winning minds, not hearts' (2008) 45 CML Rev 609.

Edwards, D, 'The impact of the single market' (1987) 24 CML Rev 19.

Edwards, D, et al, In the Matter of Article 50 of the Treaty on European Union: Opinion, 10 February 2017 ('Three Knights Opinion'), available at: **www.bindmans.com/uploads/files/documents/Final_Article_50_Opinion_10.2.17.pdf**.

Ehlermann, CD, 'Differentiation, flexibility, closer cooperation: The new provisions of the Amsterdam Treaty' (1998) 4 ELJ 246.

Hillion, C, 'Accession and withdrawal in the law of the European Union' in A Arnull and D Chalmers (eds), *The Oxford Handbook of European Union Law* (Oxford University Press, 2015), 126.

House of Lords Select Committee on the Constitution, *The Invoking of Article 50*, 4th Report of Session 2016–17 (HL Paper 44), 13 September 2016.

Lazowski, A, 'Withdrawal from the European Union and alternatives to membership' (2012) 37 EL Rev 523.

Martinico, G, 'Dating Cinderella: On Subsidiarity as a Political Safeguard of Federalism in the European Union' (2011) EPL 649.

Meyring, B, 'Intergovernmentalism and supranationality: Two stereotypes of a complex reality' (1997) 22 EL Rev 221.

Pinelli, C, 'The discourses on post-national governance and the democratic deficit absent on EU Government' (2013) 9 ECL Rev 177.

Schütze, R, *From Dual to Cooperative Federalism: The Changing Structure of European Law* (Oxford University Press, 2009).

Somek, A, 'Postconstitutional treaty' [2007] German LJ 1121.

Usher, J, 'Variable geometry or concentric circles: Patterns for the European Union' (1997) 46 ICLQ 243.

2 Institutions of the Union: composition and powers

2.1 Introduction

One of the defining features of the Union is the scope and level of power given to its institutions. Its objectives and the way the institutions fulfil those objectives affect the nature of the EU itself and the scope and content of EU law. Chapter 2 outlines the composition and powers of the institutions and the relationship between them.

In considering the institutions and the way they work, there are a number of underlying points. First, it is the different powers ascribed to the institutions and the way they have to work together that provide the 'checks and balances' within the Union legal order, the so-called 'institutional balance'. This point is implied in the wording of Article 13(2) TEU, which states:

> Each institution shall act within the limits of the powers conferred upon it in the Treaties, and in conformity with the procedures, conditions and objectives set out in them.

It is important to note that we should not approach a review of the institutions from the perspective of traditional notions of governmental functions: legislative, executive, administrative and judicial. It is the institutional balance that prevents one institutional actor from becoming too powerful, rather than the more traditional notion of 'separation of the powers'. Another key point in this area is that the powers of the respective institutions have evolved over time. The institutional balance is not a static notion. It reflects the development of the Union—and our expectations of it in terms of effectiveness, responsibility and accountability. The institutional balance is not just about limiting the power of the institutions, but has a positive side in that the political institutions at least must cooperate to achieve anything at all, though the nature of the relationship between the individual institutions has varied. It is possible to see some of the institutions representing various interests: the Commission as supranational and integrationist, the Council as intergovernmental and incorporating the individual state interests, though to categorise any one institution as *entirely* intergovernmental or supranational is to overstate the position. The institutional balance has also been affected by the emergence of other actors of various sorts which do not fall within the definition of 'institution' for the purposes of the Treaty, yet these bodies also have a role in policymaking and its implementation and enforcement. Finally, we should note that the powers of the institutions vary depending on the different areas of competence, although with the changes introduced by Lisbon many of these differences have been reduced or eradicated. Nonetheless, the ways in which these different fields of competence interrelate also affect the institutional balance. This latter issue is discussed further in Chapter 3.

2.2 The institutions

A preliminary question is 'What are the institutions?' While the term can be used generically to refer to bodies involved generally in the governance of the EU, it has a specific meaning within the Treaties.

The original list of institutions has expanded over the successive Treaty amendments. Article 13 TEU currently provides that the institutions are:

- the European Parliament;
- the Council;
- the European Council;
- the Commission;
- the Court of Justice;
- the European Central Bank;
- the Court of Auditors.

Note that it is in the post-Lisbon TEU that we find the first explicit reference to the European Council as an institution, although it has existed for rather longer. Article 13(4) TEU identifies two more bodies, which are not technically institutions: the Economic and Social Committee, and the Committee of the Regions. Lisbon also formalised the role of national parliaments in the EU legislative process, specifically as regards the scrutiny of proposals to ensure respect for the principles of subsidiarity and proportionality (see 3.5.3).

The original institutions operated only within the EEC. When Maastricht introduced the pillar structure (see Chapter 1), the institutions were given roles and responsibilities in the other pillars too. This was the idea of institutional unity within the Union. In the former second and third pillars, however, the roles of some of the institutions (eg, the European Parliament) were more limited than in the former Community pillar. With the Lisbon Treaty, the three-pillar structure was abandoned. The consequence of this 'depillarisation' was that most of these limitations and differences in the roles of the institutions died away. The main responsibilities of the various institutions are set out in Articles 14–19 TEU.

2.3 European Parliament (Article 14 TEU; Articles 223–34 TFEU)

2.3.1 Appointment

As created by the Treaty of Rome in 1957, the European Parliament was not a democratic body. It consisted of representatives of Member States who were required to be members of a national parliament. The introduction of direct elections, which occurred in 1979, resulted in increased democracy and increased concentration and expertise, since members are responsible to their electorate, and, as anyone is now eligible to stand, many are no longer subject to the rigorous demands of the 'dual mandate' at home and in Europe. MEPs are elected for five years (Article 14(3) TEU).

The significance of the European Parliament, and particularly its manner of appointment, is that it creates a direct link between the national electorates and the Union political institutions. There are limits to seeing the Parliament as creating a pan-European democracy. Constituencies are still organised on a national basis. A perennial complaint is that, despite the introduction of direct elections, a uniform system of election has not been introduced. It should also be noted that recent elections have revealed a low voter turnout, which may cast doubt on the claims of the European Parliament to legitimacy on the basis of the direct election of its members. Finally, some have suggested that there is no EU 'demos', or EU polity, on which pan-EU democracy could be based. Instead, there are a group of nationally based polities.

2.3.2 Composition

To date, each Member State has been allocated a number of MEPs roughly dependent on the size of the Member State in population terms. Currently the members are allocated as shown in Table 2.1.

Table 2.1 Allocation of MEPs to Member States

Member State	Number of MEPs
Belgium	21
Denmark	13
Germany	96
Ireland	11
France	74
Italy	73
Luxembourg	6
Netherlands	26
UK	73
Greece	21
Spain	54
Portugal	21
Sweden	20

(Continued)

Table 2.1 *(Continued)*

Member State	Number of MEPs
Austria	18
Finland	13
Czech Republic	21
Estonia	6
Cyprus	6
Lithuania	11
Latvia	8
Hungary	21
Malta	6
Poland	51
Slovenia	8
Slovakia	13
Bulgaria	17
Romania	32
Croatia	11

The division of MEPs among the Member States has always been subject to criticism: Germany has fewest representatives per head of population, whilst Luxembourg has a disproportionately high number of representatives given its size. Moreover, the Czech Republic and Hungary are, arguably, underrepresented. Again, this may cast doubt on the representative nature of democracy in the European Parliament. Article 14(2) TEU specifies that the maximum number of MEPs shall be 750 plus the President and that representation shall be degressively proportional, with a minimum number of 6 MEPs and a maximum of 96. With future enlargement envisaged, these rules mean that reallocation of MEPs will eventually have to take place, with revision envisaged prior to the 2019 elections, though Brexit may relieve this pressure somewhat. Each time a change happens, shifts in the power relationships within the European Parliament will occur.

Members meet in plenary sessions of approximately one week per month in Strasbourg, although the majority of Parliament's committee meetings, where much important preparatory work is done, are held in Brussels. The rest take place in Strasbourg or, occasionally, Luxembourg. Members, who are drawn from 75 political parties, sit in broad, multinational political groupings; they are required to vote 'on an individual and personal basis' and 'they shall not be bound by any instructions and shall not receive a binding mandate' (Act Concerning Direct Elections, Article 4(1)). Both the Statute for Members of the European Parliament and the Code of Conduct for Members of the European Parliament reiterate that MEPs are free and independent. These also regulate practical matters, such as pay.

MEPs are elected within national systems along national-party lines. Although MEPs sit in broad political groupings, not in national blocks, the European Parliament does not have what might be termed a 'European political consciousness'. Article 10(4) TEU, however, contains an expression of the importance of political parties at the European level for the formation of 'a European political awareness' and the expression of 'the will of the citizens of the Union'. Article 224 TFEU specifies that the European Council is to enact regulations governing political parties and, in particular, their funding.

The Parliament has a president, elected by the Parliament for a two-and-a-half-year term (see Article 14(4) TEU). There are also 14 vice-presidents. Together the president and vice-presidents constitute the Bureau of the Parliament, which is the body responsible for the Parliament's administrative, organisational and staff matters, as well as for budgetary matters. The agenda of the Parliament is set by the 'Conference of Presidents', a group made up of the president and the leaders of the various political groups in the Parliament; it also establishes the terms of reference for the various Parliamentary committees, of which the Parliament has 20 standing committees. Subcommittees and temporary committees can also be established. These committees fulfil a vital role in the functioning of the Parliament, as they comment on the legislative proposals put forward by the Commission in their respective areas of expertise and can also produce own initiative reports. For example, the Committee on Foreign Affairs put forward a report with a proposal for a European Parliament recommendation to the Council on the mandate of the International Criminal Tribunal for the former Yugoslavia (A6-0112/2009).

2.3.3 **Functions**

As befitted a non-elected body, the original Parliament had few powers. Its functions were advisory and supervisory. It was not intended as a legislative body. Following the introduction of direct elections, Parliament has played an increasingly important role in the legislative process and has been given the final say over certain aspects of the budget. Budgetary procedure will be discussed further at 2.9. The TEU, ToA, Nice and Lisbon have further and (together) substantially increased its powers, so that it is no longer limited to the merely consultative but is a co-legislator. This development is linked to the wider role of the Union and the need to ensure its democratic legitimacy. The Parliament's functions are set out in Article 14 TEU as follows:

> The European Parliament shall, jointly with the Council, exercise legislative and budgetary functions. It shall exercise functions of political control and consultation as laid down in the Treaties. It shall elect the President of the Commission.

2.3.3.1 **Consultative and advisory role**

There are still areas in which the Parliament's role is limited to being consulted on a proposal by the Council. In these areas the Council must seek, and is obliged to consider, Parliament's opinion, although there is no obligation on the Council to follow it. This is an essential procedural requirement. Legislation has been successfully challenged when, although the Parliament had been consulted on an initial draft of the legislation, it was not consulted following substantial amendment to the draft (*Parliament v Council (road taxes)* (case C-21/94)). In *Roquette Frères SA v Council* (case 138/79) and *Maizena GmbH v Council* (case 139/79) a regulation of the Council was annulled because, although Parliament's opinion had been sought, the regulation had been passed by the Council before that opinion had been obtained. Nonetheless, in *Parliament v Council (obligation to consult the Parliament)* (case C-65/93), where the Parliament's opinion was required as a matter of some urgency, the Council made all efforts to obtain that opinion in time. In failing to meet the deadline, the Parliament, according to the Court, had failed in its duty of cooperation. The Court, as a consequence, refused to annul the contested regulation. How far the Parliament's duty of cooperation extends is not clear. The Advocate-General in this case was clearly unhappy about the effect such a decision would have on the institutional balance and thought that any changes to it would be more appropriately dealt with by Treaty amendment.

A requirement to consult Parliament or merely to keep it informed of developments in a particular field can be seen in the CFSP, where the usual assumption about the equality of Parliament with the Council in decision-making terms is not applicable. In general, CFSP tends towards a more intergovernmental approach. Nonetheless, as with the earlier case law, the involvement of the Parliament must be taken seriously, as can be seen by the jurisprudence on Article 218 TFEU.

Article 218 TFEU deals with the procedure for negotiating and concluding agreements with third countries or with international organisations. Different procedures apply depending on the substantive matter of the agreement. Matters pertaining exclusively to the CFSP are treated separately from other agreements (Article 218(6) TFEU) and do not require the consent of the Parliament. In relation to the procedure for negotiating such agreements, Article 218(10) TFEU provides:

> The European Parliament shall be immediately and fully informed at all stages of the procedure.

This provision applies to agreements within the field of CFSP as to others.

It seems that post-Lisbon the Parliament is still prepared to litigate to protect its powers. In *Parliament v Council (Somali pirates II)* (case C-263/14) (see further 3.7.9), the Court acknowledged that the Parliament's role was limited in the field of CFSP. Nonetheless, the Parliament is accorded some form of oversight role. The Court held (at para 71):

> while the purpose of the requirement to inform the Parliament fully and immediately is not to enable the Parliament to participate in the negotiation and conclusion of agreements concerning the CFSP, that requirement allows it, in addition to undertaking a check of the appropriate legal basis for measures adopted as part of the CFSP, to exercise its own powers with full knowledge of the European Union's external action as a whole.

Moreover, in its reasoning the Court at para 70 referred back to its early jurisprudence on the Parliament's powers in cases such as *Roquette Frères* to make the point that:

> participation by the Parliament in the legislative process is the reflection, at Union level, of a fundamental democratic principle that the people should participate in the exercise of power through the intermediary of a representative assembly. As regards the procedure for negotiating and concluding international agreements, the information requirement laid down in Article 218(10) TFEU is the expression of that democratic principle, on which the European Union is founded. [citations omitted]

In sum, with the increasing use of what is now the ordinary legislative procedure, the use of consultation procedures is much rarer, although still envisaged by the Treaties (see Article 289 TFEU). In practice, it seems that it is within CFSP that this procedure will most commonly still be used.

2.3.3.2 Legislative role

The power of the European Parliament has increased over time, reflecting the dual source of the Union's legitimacy—not only the Member States, but also the citizens of those states. As well as a right to be *consulted*, and to participate in *conciliation* and *cooperation* procedures, the TEU introduced for Parliament a right of *co-decision* with the Council in certain defined areas. This procedure, following Lisbon, is called the 'ordinary legislative procedure' (Article 289 TFEU). Thus, under this procedure, the European Parliament has a significant power of veto in matters subject to the procedure; effectively the Parliament is an equal partner in the legislative process using this procedure. While originally this procedure was to apply in a number of areas previously governed by the less onerous cooperation procedures and in some new spheres of activity introduced by Maastricht (eg, health, consumer protection), subsequent Treaties extended the areas in which the procedure is used, with the result that the cooperation procedures in future will largely disappear. Following Lisbon, yet more fields (eg, agriculture and energy) use the ordinary legislative procedure. Significantly, this procedure forms, as its name now implies, the default legislative procedure in the EU, reaffirming the strength of the Parliament's involvement. These procedures will be examined further in Chapter 3.

Parliament was also given a new power of initiative by Maastricht. Under Article 225 TFEU it may, acting by a majority of its members, request the Commission to submit any appropriate proposals on matters on which it considers that a Union act is required for the purpose of implementing the Treaty. It has been suggested that, provided Parliament stays within the guidelines set out in its rules of procedure, these requests are likely to be considered sympathetically by the Commission. To date, Parliament has exercised these rights sparingly.

Although the European Parliament's powers have been increased, there are weaknesses in the ways it fulfils its responsibilities. The European Parliament does not have great expertise in highly technical areas. Further, under Article 225 TFEU it may *request* policy initiatives; it does not have the *right* of policy initiative, although the Commission would, if it chose not to respond, give reasons why.

Although not strictly legislative in nature, it is convenient to return to the European Parliament's role in Treaty negotiations here. Since Lisbon its powers have increased, though, as noted at 2.3.3.1, its role varies on the policy field. According to Article 218 TFEU, the consent of the European Parliament is required in relation to agreements listed at Article 218(6)(a) TFEU. The list includes 'agreements covering fields to which either the ordinary legislative procedure applies, or the special legislative procedure where consent by the European Parliament is required' (Article 218(6)(a)(v)). Thus, Parliament can veto international agreements. Again, the obligation in Article 218(10) TFEU, to keep the Parliament informed, applies here. The exercise of Parliament's right of veto can be seen in the European Parliament's response to the proposed Anti-Counterfeiting Trade Agreement (ACTA). The initial proposal put forward by the Commission was voted down on 4 July 2012 by a significant margin (478 votes to 39, with 165 abstentions), on the basis of concerns about the impact on individuals' fundamental rights (data protection and privacy) in relation to the enforcement procedures for intellectual property rights. This was the first time that the European Parliament asserted its new power.

The EU has entered into a number of agreements with the USA. One such agreement concerns the provision of financial data to US authorities of details of banking transactions carried out by individuals in the interests of the fight against terrorism. When this agreement was reached, the European Parliament expressed concerns about the protection of individuals' privacy (indeed it voted a first proposal of this agreement down too), but were given reassurances by the European Commission on this point. Subsequently, leaked documents indicated that the US authorities were carrying out extensive surveillance, including of EU nationals, in breach of the terms of the agreement. In addition to calling for a full investigation of the matter, the European Parliament agreed a resolution (23 October 2013 (2013/2831(RSP))) stating, inter alia, that the European Parliament:

> 11. Considers that, although Parliament has no formal powers under Article 218 TFEU to initiate the suspension or termination of an international agreement, the Commission will have to act if Parliament withdraws its support for a particular agreement; points out that, when considering whether or not to give its consent to future international agreements, Parliament will take account of the responses of the Commission and the Council in relation to this Agreement;
>
> 12. Asks the Commission, in the light of the above, to suspend the Agreement.

While the Commission asserted that there was no wrong-doing under the agreement, this seems more broadly to be an attempt by the European Parliament to use existing legal powers to exert more wide-reaching political influence.

2.3.3.3 Supervisory role

In its supervisory role, Parliament exercises direct political control over the Commission. Commissioners must reply orally or in writing to its questions. The Commission must publish a general report which is discussed in Parliament in open session. Parliament meets members of the Commission in committees, and in practice, though this is not required by law, members of Parliament are consulted by the Commission at the pre-legislative stage. Parliament also has the power to dismiss the Commission, by passing a vote of censure (Article 234 TFEU). Such a motion must be carried by a two-thirds majority of the votes cast, which must represent a majority of the members of Parliament. A particular weakness of this sanction is the fact that the existing Commissioners will remain in office until their replacements are appointed. There is nothing to prevent the Member States from suggesting the same Commissioners be reappointed. Nonetheless, it was the Parliament's dissatisfaction with the conduct of the Commission that resulted in the Commissioners resigning in 1999. Some, but not all, of the Commissioners were reappointed. Prior to Maastricht, Parliament had no say in the appointment of new Commissioners. This was remedied; under Article 17(7) TEU, Parliament must be consulted on the nomination of the president and the appointment of Commissioners and the Commission as a whole has to be approved by Parliament. Parliament approves the appointment of the president individually and then the president and the other Commissioners together as a group.

The Council is not subject to the control of Parliament, but is subject to extensive supervision. Parliament reports on the activities of the Council three times a year, and the president of the Council must present an address to Parliament at the beginning of every year. This is followed by a general debate. The incoming president also presents a survey of the previous six months' presidency, and the chairman of the conference of foreign ministers reports to Parliament once a year on the progress of European political cooperation. Since Lisbon, there is a new role of 'European Council President' (see 2.12.1), who is required to report to Parliament after each meeting of the European Council. Unlike proceedings in the Council and the Commission, proceedings in Parliament are published in the *Official Journal* (see the discussion on transparency in Chapter 3).

Parliament also has standing to challenge the legality of acts adopted by the other institutions in accordance with Article 263 TFEU (see Chapter 12). It is through such challenges that Parliament enforces its rights and seeks to ensure that the correct treaty base is used for legislative measures. This is important because the treaty base still affects the degree of parliamentary involvement in the legislative process (eg, scope of CFSP, see 2.3.3.1). Judicial review under Article 263 TFEU has been used vigorously for these purposes. In passing, it should be noted that the Parliament's power in this regard was extended under the Treaty of Nice and it now also has the power to request advisory opinions under Article 218 TFEU from the Court of Justice.

Role of the European Ombudsman

To broaden Parliament's role it was given power under the TEU to set up a temporary committee of inquiry to investigate alleged contraventions or maladministration in the implementation of Union law (except where the alleged facts are being examined before a court or subject to legal proceedings), and has been required to appoint an Ombudsman to receive and enquire into complaints of maladministration in the activities of the EU institutions or bodies (with the exception of the CJ and the General Court acting in their judicial capacity). At the end of an investigation, the Ombudsman is under an obligation to produce a report to the Parliament and to the institution under investigation. The original complainant is also notified of the result. The Ombudsman has also to produce an annual report to Parliament. In addition, any natural or legal person residing or having its registered office in a Member State is to be given the right to address a petition to the European Parliament on a matter which comes within the Union's fields of activity, and which affects him, her or it directly. These provisions can be found in Articles 226–8 TFEU. Criticism of the system relates to the Ombudsman's lack of binding powers, though compliance with the Ombudsman's rulings is high.

Protection of Human Rights

One area of the Parliament's activities which is sometimes overlooked is the work that it does in promoting human rights. We will see when looking at the role of general principles of Union law (Chapter 6) that the Parliament was instrumental in persuading the other institutions to recognise the importance of human rights and, in particular, the European Convention on the Protection of Human Rights. The Parliament is not concerned only with human-rights protection within the Union. The European Parliament also established a subcommittee to identify urgent cases of human-rights abuse throughout the world, and the facts surrounding each case. In appropriate circumstances it will put forward resolutions on specific cases to the whole Parliament. The passing of such resolutions can raise the profile of certain issues and can therefore play a useful role in generating pressure to remedy the problem. The subcommittee also produces an annual report and the degree of reaction that it provokes in countries criticised by it is indicative of its influence.

2.4 European Council (Article 15 TEU; Articles 235–6 TFEU)

Although the European Council had been in existence since 1974, it was not recognised in the EC Treaty until the Single European Act (SEA). Article 2 SEA provided:

> The European Council shall bring together Heads of State or of government of the Member States and the President of the Commission of the European Communities. They shall be assisted by a Minister for Foreign Affairs and by a member of the Commission. They shall meet at least twice a year.

Since Lisbon, the European Council has been recognised as an institution of the EU (Article 13(1) TEU). The European Council comprises the Heads of State or government for the Member States, together with the president of the European Council and the president of the Commission. The High Representative of the Union for Foreign Affairs (a post introduced by Lisbon) will also participate (see further 2.11.2). The function of the European Council is defined at Article 15(1) TEU as:

> provid[ing] the Union with the necessary impetus for its development and . . . defin[ing] the general political directions and priorities thereof. It shall not exercise legislative functions.

The European Council, however, will generally be required to act by consensus (Article 15(4) TEU).

The changing level of recognition awarded to the European Council is an example of the changing relationships between the institutions and also an example of the way that the institutional set-up can respond and accept political reality. Despite the relatively few references in the Treaties to the European Council and the fact it does not have a legislative function, it does not do to underestimate its importance; its membership comprises the leaders of the Member States and it serves to set the general direction of the EU itself.

2.5 Council (Article 16 TEU; Articles 237–43 TFEU)

The Council was formerly known as the Council of Ministers. Despite the similarity in name, the Council is a different institution from the European Council.

2.5.1 Appointment

The Council consists of representatives of the Member States, one from each Member State, who must be 'at ministerial level, authorised to commit the government of that Member State' (Article 16(2) TEU). Ministerial representatives tend not to be appointed specifically for their role within the Council; appointment is a consequence of their appointment within the domestic system; they are national politicians. A common concern about the Council is that it represents the views of the Member States and the individual members of the Council look to the national interest, rather than the Union common interest, when making their decisions. Although ministerial representatives may be accountable as part of an individual Member State's government through that Member State's parliamentary system, there is no body, at European or national level, to hold the Council itself accountable (see further 3.9.1).

2.5.2 Composition

The Council is not a fixed body. Although it is limited to one voting delegate from each state, membership may fluctuate depending on the topic under discussion. For example, where matters of agriculture are at stake, the ministers of agriculture will normally participate; if the matters relate to general economic policy, the finance ministers may be present.

Specific configurations of the Council based on subject matter have been identified. This varying membership has led to criticism that the Council lacks coherence: there is no one who is responsible for coordinating policies. This approach means that the role of bodies assisting the Council, notably COREPER (discussed further in 2.5.5) is crucial in the legislative process.

The fact that different 'configurations' exist is recognised in the Treaties (Article 16(6) and (9) TEU, Article 236 TFEU). The Lisbon Treaty did not impose a restriction on the number of different configurations, but two improvements were made. First, there is a 'General Affairs Council' responsible for ensuring consistency in the work of the different Council configurations (Article 16(6) TEU). Secondly, the European Council has been given the power to specify, by qualified majority, the various configurations of the Council of Ministers (Article 236 TFEU). Note that two configurations identified in the Treaty are: the 'General Affairs Council' (as already noted) and a 'Foreign Affairs Council' (Article 16 TEU).

2.5.3 Functions

The role of the Council is now found in Article 16(1) TEU.

> The Council shall, jointly with the European Parliament, exercise legislative and budgetary
> functions. It shall carry out policy-making and coordinating functions as laid down in the Treaties.

It remains to be seen whether there is any change in approach given the reformulation of the Union's mission to take into account and to protect non-economic values, including respect for human rights (Article 2 TEU).

There is arguably a tension between the demands of a minister's role as a national politician and his or her obligations as a member of Council under the Treaties. When the Council meets in its legislative capacity it will meet in public (Article 16(8) TEU). While this is desirable from the perspective of ensuring transparency of decision-making (see 3.9), it may make it more difficult for the Council to reach agreement. Making concessions, especially against stated national policy, may be harder in the public eye.

Since the Council has the final power of decision on most secondary legislation some control by the Member States is thus assured. However, in most cases it can only act on the basis of a proposal from the Commission. Furthermore, other institutions are involved in the decision-making process to an increasing degree. Nonetheless, since legislation (even under the co-decision procedure) cannot be enacted without the consent of the Council, its methods of voting are crucial.

2.5.4 The emergence of qualified majority voting

It is generally the case today that most decisions by the Council are taken by qualified majority voting (QMV) (Article 16(3) TEU). However, this has not always been the case. The existence of QMV is one of the more unusual, and perhaps controversial, aspects of EU law—whenever a new area is opened up to QMV, objections are raised against 'giving up the veto' in respect of that area. Yet, there are good reasons for having this form of majority.

Historically, some more sensitive areas of the Treaty were required to be implemented only by unanimous vote (eg, the original Article 100 EEC on the approximation of laws). It was, however, intended that once the period of adjustment to membership, known as the transitional period, provided by the Treaty of Rome in its original form had expired, Member States would be required to move towards QMV. This did not happen. A crisis in the Council in 1962 resulted, at the insistence of the French, in the Luxembourg Accords (1966). Under the Accords, where vital national interests are at stake, Member States may insist on a unanimous vote. The Accords noted 'a divergence of views on what should be done in the event of a failure to reach agreement'. It has been suggested that this approach is partly a reaction against the judicial activism of the time.

The Luxembourg Accords did not have the force of law, but they were followed in practice, with the result that in many cases the Council sought unanimity where the Treaty would not have required it. In only one case, in 1982, was a measure passed by the Council by QMV against the wishes of the UK government, in a situation in which it was suggested that the UK was abusing its veto by attempting to force the Council's hand in a matter unrelated to the measure under discussion.

QMV is a system of weighted voting. Clearly, from the Union standpoint it makes for more rapid and effective decision-making than unanimity as the consent of all parties is not required. It is, however, controversial because, as noted in Chapter 1, it runs contrary to the idea that a nation state is a sovereign entity and the government (or ruler) of that entity has freedom to choose which policies to implement within that state. With QMV (and also with simple majority voting) a Member State could be put in the position of being under a Treaty obligation to put in place a policy for which it had not voted. Though this is true, there is a positive side to the loss of veto, in that Member States 'in the minority' on a given issue now have an incentive to negotiate positively to try to arrive at an outcome which is more acceptable to them than perhaps the original proposal had been. This perhaps introduces a more supranational—or Union focused—element to the Council than might at first appear.

Perhaps the most significant innovation of the SEA was to increase the number of areas in which voting was to be by qualified majority. The majority of legislation required to complete the internal market was enacted by qualified majority. The TEU, ToA and Nice all further increased the scope for QMV, introducing QMV into what are now Article 192 (environment), Article 157 (equal pay) and Article 122 TFEU (difficulties in economic situation), respectively. Lisbon broadened the use of QMV further still. According to Article 16(3) TEU, QMV is now the default position in Council decision-making. It provides that:

> The Council shall act by a qualified majority except where the Treaties provide otherwise.

There are still some sensitive areas where unanimity may be required. There are also areas, such as social security, where QMV may be used, but where there is also an 'emergency brake procedure'. Article 48 TFEU envisages that the Council and the European Parliament will adopt legislative measures in the field of social security using the ordinary legislative procedure. Although the default position is the use of QMV, the provision further specifies that:

> Where a member of the Council declares that a draft legislative act referred to in the first subparagraph would affect important aspects of its social security system...it may request that the matter be referred to the European Council. In that case, the ordinary legislative procedure shall be suspended.

The possibility remains that the measure may still be passed. An emergency brake mechanism can also be seen in Article 82(3) TFEU, regarding judicial cooperation in criminal matters.

Member States have so far been prepared to accede to QMV in the areas in which it has been required. It should be noted that, in practice, the approach is still very much to seek consensus, even though the reaching of such consensus does take place against a backdrop where, ultimately, it is not required. In some cases, however, they have challenged the appropriateness of the legal basis of a measure demanding such a vote (see further Chapters 3 and 16). While the increased use of QMV may have reduced the likelihood of generally popular measures being blocked, such a possibility still exists. In this circumstance, another route forward exists: the use of the enhanced cooperation mechanism. Although the provisions were first introduced by the Amsterdam Treaty (see Chapter 1), they were first used only in 2010 and have already proved contentious (see 3.8.6).

A difficulty with QMV was the determination of the respective strength of each Member State's vote, an issue which gained in complexity whenever new countries joined the existing Member States. Prior to the succession of Finland, Sweden and Austria, which joined in 1995, concern was expressed that the number of votes required to block a proposal would increase. Eventually, the Ioannina Compromise (1994) was agreed with the result that the blocking minority increased to 71 per cent of the new total, but if states carrying together 23 to 25 votes intended to vote against the proposal then negotiations would continue in an attempt to satisfy their concerns.

The Ioannina Compromise raised concerns that the attitudes of Member States had not changed since the Luxembourg Accords, the 1966 agreement between Member States that a decision of the Council may be vetoed by a member whose national interests are at stake and which limited the use of QMV. A contrary view has also been suggested. Although clearly there are difficulties, the Ioannina Compromise does represent some progress because under its terms the Member States are committed to trying to come to some form of compromise acceptable to all. Contrast this with the Luxembourg Accords, where Member States merely agreed to disagree.

Further attempts were made to improve the system over successive Treaty amendments. Now, in recognition of the dual source of legitimacy in the EU, the Treaties provide a system of majority which reflects those two sources. Article 16(4) TEU provides that a qualified majority comprises two elements:

> (a) at least 55 per cent of the Members of Council comprising at least 15 of them (thus representing the interests of the states)
> (b) states representing at least 65 per cent of the population of the Union.

The new system will not have to be adjusted to maintain (or change) relative power on the accession of any new Member States, or the departure of any Member State. The description using percentages will accommodate this automatically. Moreover, a blocking minority would have to comprise at least four Council members, or the qualified majority would be deemed to have been attained. Further, from 1 November 2014, where the Council is not acting on a proposal from the Commission, the qualified majority will be at least 72 per cent of the members of the Council, representing at least 65 per cent of the Union's population. There are also special provisions relating to areas of policy where some Member States have negotiated an opt-out (Article 238 TFEU). Following strong Polish lobbying, a long transitional period was included in the Treaties, with two transitional periods (one until 31 October 2014, and the second from 1 November 2014 until 31 March 2017) being laid out in the Protocol on Transitional Provisions. Essentially, the effect of these transitional periods was the temporary maintenance of the old system. The intention of the Lisbon changes was clearly to simplify the concept of a 'qualified majority', but only practical experience will demonstrate if that will be the effect of this provision. The complexity attendant on the transitional period is not an auspicious start.

2.5.5 **COREPER**

Since the Council is not a permanent body, meeting only a few days a month, and its members have full-time responsibilities at home, much of its preparatory work has been taken over by the Committee of Permanent Representatives (COREPER) (see Article 240(1) TFEU). Article 16(7) TEU recognises this fact, expressly giving COREPER the responsibility for preparing the work of the Council (see also Article 240(1) TFEU). It is for the Council to decide the composition of COREPER but it is a permanent and full-time body, consisting of representatives of Member States. Its main task is to scrutinise and sift proposals coming from the Commission prior to a final decision being made by the Council. COREPER is assisted in turn by a number of working groups, operating at different levels and in specialised areas. This sifting process, from working group to COREPER to Council, enables the more straightforward issues to be decided at the appropriate level, leaving the Council to focus on the more difficult or controversial decisions. Since the ToA, the Treaties expressly recognise the power of COREPER to make procedural decisions where provided for by the Council's Rules of Procedure (see now Article 240(1) TFEU). COREPER operates by dividing matters into category A and category B. Category A matters tend to be adopted by the Council without further discussion. Thus, COREPER has an agenda-setting role for discussions in Council as well as effectively being the decision-maker for matters COREPER deems non-problematic.

Although COREPER and the working groups might be crucial in ensuring the Council can operate as a decision-making body, their use is problematic in terms of transparency and accountability.

This is because the committee structures underpinning COREPER are complex and, generally, members of COREPER are not elected but are national appointments (see also Chapter 3).

2.6 Commission (Article 17 TEU; Articles 244–50 TFEU)

2.6.1 Appointment

Note that the term 'Commission' is used in two ways: first to describe the high-level political appointments constituting the 'College of Commissioners'; and, secondly, to describe the permanent bureaucracy in Brussels. Whilst the staff members of the bureaucracy apply for jobs (after having passed an entrance examination), the Commissioners themselves are nominated by individual Member States, and agreed amongst the Member States. They are political appointments. They are appointed for a period of five years (Article 17(3) TEU), and may be reappointed. Voting on this point is by QMV. Since the TEU, the Parliament has been given an increasing role in the appointment process (see 2.3.3), lending the Commissioners and especially the president of the Commission, a greater degree of legitimacy. The process in Article 17(7) TEU envisages the election of a president for the Commission on the proposal of the European Council. The European Parliament votes as to whether to approve the nomination. If not, another candidate is put forward following the same procedure. The new president is then involved in the selection of the rest of the Commissioners with the European Council. The Commission as a body is then subject to the approval of the European Parliament. On appointment, the Commissioners each take an oath before the Court of Justice in which he or she undertakes to respect the Treaties and to carry out his or her duties independently and in the interests of the Union. Given that the Lisbon Treaty gave the Charter of Fundamental Rights legal force, when the members of the second Barroso Commission gave their undertakings (2010), they specifically included respect for the Charter in their oath.

2.6.2 Composition

The present Commission consists of 28 members (one from each Member State), chosen on the grounds of their general competence and 'whose independence is beyond doubt' (Article 245 TFEU). Continuing on a 'one commissioner per member State' basis would make the Commission unwieldy and would also make it difficult for it to continue to function as it currently does. The Treaty of Nice accepted that change was necessary. According to a protocol adopted at Nice, once there were 27 Commissioners the Council would determine both the number of Commissioners and the mechanism by which they are to be selected. Some form of rotation was envisaged based on the principle of 'equality' and reflecting 'satisfactorily the demographic and geographical range of all the Member States'. This principle found its way into the Lisbon Treaty, which provided that, after the expiry of a transitional period on 31 October 2014, the number of Commissioners would be limited to a number equal to two-thirds the number of Member States, Commissioner posts rotating on a system (to be determined by Council) 'reflecting the demographic and geographical range of all the Member States' (Article 17(5) TEU). Following the Irish 'no' vote (see Chapter 1) this proposal has not come into being. Instead, the Council of Ministers used its powers under Article 17(5) TEU to return to the pre-Lisbon position. It seems that the system of one Commissioner per Member State will continue.

Although appointees of the Member States, they must, in the performance of their duties, remain independent of their respective appointing Member States, and Member States are under an obligation to respect the Commissioners' independence (Article 245 TFEU). Whilst Article 245 TFEU requires Commissioners to 'refrain from any action incompatible with their duties', the probity of some Commissioners has been the subject of adverse comment (see 2.6.3).

The Commission is headed by a president appointed from among the Commissioners (2.6.1). In addition, the Commission comprises the 'double-hatted' High Representative, who is also a vice-president of the Commission, the other vice-presidents (for the Commission 2010–14, there are eight vice-presidents) and the remainder of the 'ordinary' Commissioners.

The Commission is divided into directorates-general, each one responsible for certain aspects of Community policy (eg, D-G Competition), and headed by a director-general. Commissioners are given responsibility for particular directorates (a 'portfolio'). Portfolios vary considerably in size and prestige. Although Commissioners are supposed to be generally competent, whether they have any particular expertise in the portfolio allocated to them is a matter of luck rather than judgement, as individual Member States seek to ensure that its commissioner has the most prestigious portfolio possible. One might argue that, as a result, the interests (or prestige) of individual Member States take priority over the interests of the Union. This approach received much criticism and changes to allow the president greater control were introduced by the Prodi Commission, which have now found their way into the Treaty (Article 248 TFEU; see 2.6.4).

2.6.3 **Probity**

As noted in 2.6.2, Commissioners are expected to carry out their functions with a high degree of probity; it is a term of their appointment that they be independent. Article 245 TFEU allows a Commissioner who fails in his or her duties to be retired compulsorily or deprived of his right to a pension or other benefits.

It was concerns about fraud and mismanagement that led to the setting-up of a Committee of Independent Experts, which delivered a damning report in 1999. This led to the resignation of all Commissioners en bloc; the principal problem was not necessarily the Commissioners themselves, but the persons to whom responsibility had been contracted out. This led to a process of review and reform under the leadership of Prodi, the new Commission president, which led to a greater system of accountability, including over contracted-out functions, and to the changes in management powers noted in 2.6.4.

In this context we should note *Commission v Edith Cresson* (case C-432/04), a case which concerns a member of the Commission who was part of the Commission that had resigned en bloc.

Cresson

In this case, Mrs Cresson had wanted to appoint an acquaintance as a personal adviser despite being told that the rules did not allow for this appointment. Nonetheless, the adviser worked for Mrs Cresson for two years. It was discovered that he had been paid for numerous tasks which were fictitious. The Commission sought a declaration that Mrs Cresson had breached the obligations arising from her status as a Commissioner and that she be deprived of her right to a pension or other benefits. Whilst Mrs Cresson had no knowledge of the fictitious tasks, the appointment was in clear breach of Commission rules. The Court determined that the finding of breach was sufficient and therefore did not deprive her of her pension.

Similar issues can also be seen in the later case of *Dalli v Commission* (case C-394/15P). Further concerns have arisen in the context of the relationship between Commissioners, lobbyists, special advisers and industry and the risk of conflicts of interest. Most recently, the ad hoc ethical committee (established by Decision C(2003)3750 final), which has responsibility for considering among other issues the compatibility with the Treaties of former Commissioners' envisaged post-office activities, considered whether the decision of former Commission President José Manuel Barroso to take up a senior position with Goldman Sachs bank was consistent with Article 245 TFEU in the light of the Commission's Code of Conduct. The Ad Hoc Ethical Committee found that there had been no violation of the rules (Opinion, 26 October 2016), leading the European Ombudsman to note that she may open an official inquiry into the matter (Press Release, No 13/2016, 31 October 2016). This would not be the first such inquiry.

2.6.4 Management powers of the Commission president

The Nice Treaty gave more power to the president regarding the management of the Commissioners (Article 248 TFEU), although these changes substantially reflect changes introduced by the working rules of the Prodi Commission ([2000] OJ L308/26). In particular, Prodi suggested that the portfolios of the Commissioners should be allocated on a more rational basis rather than as a matter of horse trading between the various Member States. The changes introduced by Lisbon reflect the need to give management power to the Commission president. Article 248 TFEU provides:

> the responsibilities incumbent upon the Commission shall be structured and allocated among its members by its President, in accordance with Article 17(6) [TEU]. The President may reshuffle the allocation of those responsibilities during the Commission's term of office.

Articles 246–7 TFEU deal with the retirement or resignation of Commissioners. Since the Treaty of Nice, it has been possible for an individual Commissioner to be 'compulsorily retired'. Article 247 TFEU provides that either the Council or the Commission may make an application to the Court of Justice to this effect where the Commissioner no longer fulfils the conditions required for the performance of his duties or if he has been guilty of serious misconduct. (For an example of these provisions in action, see *Dalli*.)

2.6.5 Functions

The role of the Commission is set out in Article 17 TEU:

> 1. The Commission shall promote the general interest of the Union and take appropriate initiatives to that end. It shall ensure the application of the Treaties, and of measures adopted by the institutions pursuant to them. It shall oversee the application of Union law under the control of the Court of Justice of the European Union. It shall execute the budget and manage programmes. It shall exercise coordinating, executive and management functions, as laid down in the Treaties. With the exception of the common foreign and security policy, and other cases provided for in the Treaties, it shall ensure the Union's external representation. It shall initiate the Union's annual and multiannual programming with a view to achieving interinstitutional agreements;
> 2. Union legislative acts may only be adopted on the basis of a Commission proposal, except where the Treaties provide otherwise. Other acts shall be adopted on the basis of a Commission proposal where the Treaties so provide.

While Article 17 TEU identifies a number of specific tasks, they can be grouped together in four main categories:

- initiator;

- watchdog;
- executive;
- external representation.

2.6.5.1 Initiator

First, the Commission acts as initiator or 'motor' of Union action. It has described itself as 'the driving force behind European integration' ((2000)COM 34), although some commentators have criticised this view of the Commission as having a unitary goal, since its policies are fragmented and sometimes conflict with each other. Nonetheless, all important decisions made by the Council must be made on the basis of proposals from the Commission (subject to the Council's power to 'request the Commission to undertake any studies which the Council considers desirable for the attainment of the common objectives, and to submit to it any appropriate proposals' (see Article 241 TFEU) and the Parliament's powers to request the Commission to submit proposals) (Article 225 TFEU).

A new procedure introduced by the Treaty of Lisbon is the provision that allows a group of citizens to invite the European Commission to submit a proposal (Article 11(4) TEU). To take advantage of this opportunity there must be more than one million citizens who make the request and they must be nationals of 'a significant number of Member States'. Given that it will be logistically difficult to coordinate such a request, it seems unlikely that this procedure would be much used. The procedural requirements are set out in Article 21 TFEU.

The Commission may formulate proposals on any matter provided for under the TFEU, either where the power is specifically granted or under the more general power provided by Article 352 TFEU. Clearly, given the need for agreement by the political bodies (the Council and the Parliament), the Commission's power of initiative was limited to what was politically acceptable; measures must, of necessity, be diluted for common consumption. Further, proposals must take into account the rights protected by the EU Charter on Fundamental Rights (see Commission Strategy for Effective Implementation) (COM(2010) 573/4). Nevertheless, the importance of this power should not be underestimated. The power of initiative allows the Commission to frame the terms of the debate in Council and Parliament through the way it drafts and amends the proposals.

A corollary of the right to initiate legislation is the right to withdraw a legislative proposal. A recent case, *Council v Commission* (*Macro-Financial Assistance*) (case C-409/13) addressed the question of whether the power of the Commission in this regard was unlimited.

Macro-Financial Assistance

The case concerned a proposal made by the Commission for a regulation laying down the basic framework for macro-financial assistance to third countries. The Commission proposal envisaged limited oversight for its choice of recipient countries. The Parliament and the Council objected to this approach, as there would be insufficient political and democratic scrutiny of the decision-making process. They agreed that the matter be dealt with on the basis of the ordinary legislative procedure—as envisaged in Article 212 TFEU, the Treaty provisions dealing with the grant of macro-financial assistance. The Commission considered this to be unacceptable and decided to withdraw the proposal.

The Council (but not the Parliament) initiated proceedings against the Commission seeking annulment of the Commission's decision to withdraw the proposal.

The questions before the Court were whether there were any limits on the Commission's power and, if so, what were they?

As regards the first question, the Court—referring to Article 17(2) TEU in conjunction with Articles 289 TFEU and 293 TFEU—held:

> Just as it is, as a rule, for the Commission to decide whether or not to submit a legislative proposal and, as the case may be, to determine its subject-matter, objective and content, the Commission has the power, as long as the Council has not acted, to alter its proposal or even, if need be, withdraw it [para 74].

Nonetheless, accepting that the Commission had an unfettered choice as to when to do so would give the Commission a very strong position in the formulation of legislation. The other institutions would be under the threat that they had to agree to the Commission's ideas or lose the chance to legislate—effectively this is a power of veto. Accepting this approach, in the view of the Court, would change the institutional balance (para 75).

The Court then considered the conditions on which the Commission could withdraw a proposal. It stated that the Commission 'must state to the Parliament and the Council the grounds for the withdrawal, which, in the event of challenge, have to be supported by cogent evidence or arguments' (para 76). It seems that the Commission cannot withdraw a proposal merely because it does not like the proposed changes. The power to withdraw seems limited to instances where the proposed change 'distorts the proposal for a legislative act in a manner which prevents achievement of the objectives pursued by the proposal and which, therefore, deprives it of its raison d'être' (para 83). Whether or not this standard is easy for the Commission to meet, the significance in the ruling lies in the fact that the Court has claimed the power to review the Commission's actions in this regard and that the principles set down will affect the Commission's power of initiative generally.

The Commission has other responsibilities which also give it control: it sets the legislative timetable for the year; and it formulates more general policy guidance through its white papers.

2.6.5.2 Watchdog

Secondly, the Commission acts as the Union watchdog: it has been described as the guardian of the Treaties. Member States are obliged under Article 4(3) TEU to:

> …take any appropriate measure, general or particular, to ensure fulfilment of the obligations arising out of the Treaties or resulting from the acts of the institutions of the Union.
>
> The Member States shall facilitate the achievement of the Union's tasks and refrain from any measure which could jeopardise the attainment of the Union's objectives.

It is the Commission's task to seek out and bring to an end any infringements of EU law by Member States, if necessary by proceedings under Article 258 TFEU (see Chapter 11) before the Court of Justice. The Commission has complete discretion in this matter (see *Alfons Lütticke GmbH v Commission* (case 48/65) noted in Chapter 11).

Since the entry into force of the Lisbon Treaty, the Charter has binding force. The Commission therefore may now take actions against a Member State for failure to comply with the Charter when a Member State is acting within the scope of EU law. More broadly, the Commission may trigger—as may the other institutions—the Article 7 TEU procedure (Article 7(1) TEU); that is, to take action against a Member State where there is a clear risk of a serious breach by a Member State of the values referred to Article 2 TEU, which include respect for human rights (see further Chapter 6).

As the Commission noted in its 'Communication on Article 7 of the Treaty on European Union' (COM(2003) 606 final):

> ... amended Article 7 confers new powers on the Commission in its monitoring of fundamental rights in the Union and in the identification of potential risks. The Commission intends to exercise its new right in full and with a clear awareness of its responsibility. (p. 3)

By contrast with the enforcement role relating to the Charter as part of EU law, the enforcement role here—as it concerns the conditions for being a Member State—is in principle not limited to the scope of EU law. It is different too in the fact that any proposed solutions are principally political rather than judicial in nature (see Article 7(2) and (3) TEU).

2.6.5.3 Executive

Thirdly, the Commission functions as the executive of the Union. Once a policy decision has been taken by the Council, the detailed implementation of that policy, often requiring further legislation, falls to the Commission, acting under powers delegated by the Council and the European Parliament (Articles 290 and 291 TFEU). Prior to Lisbon, in exercising its powers of implementation the Commission was subject to the supervision of a range of advisory, management and regulatory committees, comprising national civil servants and appointed by the Council for that purpose. This process was referred to as 'comitology'. It was suggested that this system undermined the Commission's authority. Comitology has also been criticised for adding to the lack of transparency over democratic accountability in the decision-making process. Lisbon brought a complete change to the system, limiting the circumstances in which comitology-style procedures will operate in relation to 'implementing acts' under Article 291 TFEU (see Chapter 3).

2.6.5.4 External representation

Finally, in pursuit of the Union's external trade policies, the Commission is required to act as negotiator, leaving agreements to be concluded by the Council (Articles 218 and 207(3) TFEU). Where agreements are to be concluded, the Commission makes recommendations to the Council, which in turn authorises the Commission to open the necessary negotiations. The Council and the Commission are responsible for ensuring that the agreements negotiated are compatible with internal Union policies and rules, including respect for human rights. Certain agreements can only be concluded after the assent of the European Parliament has been obtained (Article 218(6)(a) TFEU). The roles of the institutions are different in relation to the common foreign and security policy, where the High Representative for Foreign Affairs takes over the Commission's role (Article 218(3) TFEU; see further 2.12.2).

2.7 Economic and Social Committee (Articles 301–4 TFEU)

The Economic and Social Committee plays a consultative role in the Union decision-making process. Its members are appointed by the Council in their personal capacity, and represent a variety of sectional interests such as farmers, workers, trade unionists, or merely members of the general public. Where consultation is provided for by the Treaty this is an essential procedural requirement: such consultation must also be referred to in any resulting legislation. The Committee may also be consulted by the Council and the Commission and, following Lisbon, by the European

Parliament whenever they consider it appropriate. In addition, it is entitled to advise the institutions on its own initiative on all questions affecting Union law (see Article 13(4) TEU and Articles 300–4 TFEU). Lisbon extended the term of appointment to five years from the previous four.

2.8 Committee of the Regions

This committee was established by the TEU to represent regional interests, and to act (like the Economic and Social Committee) in an advisory capacity in specified circumstances, as provided by the Treaties (eg, Articles 165—education; 167—culture; 177 and 178—regional development). Although the committee is supposed to represent the regions, Member States take a different approach to whether representatives should be determined regionally or centrally. Following Lisbon, the composition of the Committee of the Regions is decided by the Council, acting unanimously on a proposal from the Commission. The committee does not represent one particular set of interests and so its members may be pursuing divergent if not conflicting goals. In any event its powers are weak: the Treaty only requires that it be consulted and, unlike the Parliament, it cannot rely on the judicial review mechanism in Article 263 TFEU to ensure its powers are respected.

2.9 Budgetary procedures (Articles 313–16 TFEU)

These are laid down by Article 314 TFEU. As might be expected, the Commission is responsible for drawing up a preliminary draft budget for approval by both the Council and the European Parliament. Since Lisbon, the European Parliament has power of approval over the entire budget; prior to Lisbon its powers were limited to certain specified areas. In this regard, it is now on an equal footing with the Council. If there is a disagreement between them, it is taken to a conciliation committee in the same way as for legislative proposals (3.8.1). While both institutions must cooperate to agree the budget, according to Article 314(9) TFEU, the confirmation that the budget has been agreed is signed by the President of the European Parliament alone. This point was confirmed in *Council v European Parliament* (case C-77/11), when the Council challenged the confirmation of the 2011 budget by the president of the European Parliament without the document being co-signed by the President of the Council.

Note, however, that the resources provided to the EU are in the control of the Member States (via the Council) and the annual budget must be drawn up within the framework of a multiannual financial framework (MFF) (Article 312 TFEU). The MFF sets the maximum amount of commitment appropriations in the EU budget each year for broad policy areas. It is laid down by the Council, using a special legislative procedure, but the Council must obtain the consent of the European Parliament; the previous agreement will continue to operate until the MFF is agreed.

2.10 Court of Auditors (Articles 285–7 TFEU)

The Court of Auditors was established in 1975 under the Budgetary Powers Treaty ([1977] OJ L359/ 1). Article 285 TFEU provides that the Court of Auditors comprises one member from each of the Member States. Article 286 TFEU specifies that its members shall be completely independent in the performance of their duties. Appointment is by the Council of Ministers after consultation with Parliament (Article 286(2) TFEU). Following Nice, the term of office is six years. Its function is to exercise control and supervision over the implementation of the budget by carrying out an audit. Its creation represents an important step forward in the accountability of the institutions, particularly the Commission. Its annual report is published in the *Official Journal*. It must provide both the Parliament and the Council with a statement of assurance as to the reliability of the Union accounts and the legality of the underlying transactions (Article 287(1) TFEU) which, since Amsterdam, has been published in the *Official Journal*. Article 287 TFEU also requires the Court of Auditors to report any cases of irregularity. It is, however, limited in its effectiveness because there seems to be no one conception amongst the Member States of what it is intended to do. Secondly, there is no one body to respond to the Court of Auditors' reports to ensure that the Union is getting value for the money it spends. This is worrying in a time where there is increased public concern about the amounts of public spending and potential fraud within the Union. Indeed, the Court of Auditors has refused to sign off the budget for the past 11 years, although 'significant improvements' in budgetary controls compared to previous years were noticed.

2.11 Court of Justice of the European Union (Article 19 TEU; Articles 251–81 TFEU)

Article 19(1) TEU describes the courts that together make up the Court of Justice of the European Union (CJEU):

> The Court of Justice of the European Union shall include the Court of Justice, the General Court and specialised courts.

Each of the courts making up the CJEU has its own jurisdiction and judicial personnel.

All cases before the CJEU are allocated a number, the last two digits of which refer to the year in which the action was started. Since the setting up of the General Court (GC) (formerly Court of First Instance) in 1988, all Court of Justice (CJ) (formerly European Court of Justice) cases start with the letter 'C'; all cases before the General Court have the prefix 'T-'. Cases with the suffix 'P' are appeals from the GC, and those followed by 'R' are applications for interim relief. 'PPU' indicates the urgent preliminary reference procedures.

2.11.1 Appointment

There is currently one judge from each Member State (Article 19(2) TEU), chosen 'by common accord of the governments of the Member States' (Article 253 TFEU). The inclusion of judges from all the Member States allows the various national legal traditions to be reflected. The judges have a variety of backgrounds within the legal sphere, but are not appointed to represent the political interests of their 'home' Member State. All must be 'persons whose independence is beyond doubt' (Article 253 TFEU).

As the appointment of judges proposed by Member States occurred without the possibility of challenge, the Lisbon Treaty introduced a novelty in the appointment of judges and advocates-general aimed at securing the quality of the CJEU and its judgments. Article 255 TFEU establishes a panel to give an opinion on the suitability of candidates proposed by the Member States, which itself is made up of senior lawyers, mainly judges. This also reflects moves to greater transparency in the appointment process, although the system may still be criticised. The Member States nominate only one candidate at a time and so there is no choice between candidates who may have different strengths (particularly as to the substantive areas of their expertise); the panel may say merely 'yes' or 'no'. The panel can only react to Member States' choices and so cannot choose new appointments on the basis of what the CJEU might need in terms of different areas of expertise. Finally, there is no possibility of reviewing the decision by a Member State not to re-nominate a judge who has come to the end of his or her tenure. The threat of not being reselected has the potential to undermine judicial independence, especially where politically sensitive cases are in issue.

Judges are appointed for a six-year term, as are the judges of the General Court. They are eligible for reappointment, but there is no express guarantee that they could not be removed during their term. Appointments are staggered so that not all judges are replaced at the same time, thus building some continuity into decision-making from one rotation of judges to the next. In practice, some of the judges and advocates-general have had a long term of office: Jacobs, a former British advocate-general, was at the Court from 1988 to 2006.

The judges of the CJ are assisted by the advocates-general. Advocates-general are appointed on the same basis as the judges, and have the same term of office: six years.

2.11.2 **Composition**

There are currently 28 judges. Although it could sit with all 28 members, given its increasing workload, the court may sit in chambers of three or five judges, or a Grand Chamber of 15 judges (Article 16 Statute of the Court of Justice). The CJ will now only sit with all members in the small instances specified in Article 16 of its Statute (including proceedings to dismiss the European Ombudsman or a Member of the European Commission who has failed to fulfil his or her obligations) and where the Court considers that a case is of exceptional importance. The case of *Thomas Pringle v Government of Ireland* (case C-370/12) is an example of a case on which the CJ sat as a full court. Whereas a Member State could previously request a hearing before a full court, it will now only be possible to insist on a hearing before the Grand Chamber. Grand Chamber hearings are also held when an institution is a party to the proceedings or when the matter is important or complex. The CJ is currently assisted by eight advocates-general. Five of the eight advocates-general are nominated as of right by the five 'big' Member States: Germany, France, the United Kingdom, Italy and Spain, with the remaining three slots being allocated to the remaining Member States on an alphabetical basis. The boundary between the 'big' Member States and the others may hark back to a smaller EU. It certainly looks odd where Poland, which is only slightly smaller than Spain, has no permanent advocate-general. The number of advocates-general may be increased to 11 at the request of the CJEU, six of which would be held permanently, allowing Poland a permanent advocate-general, the remaining five being rotated between the other Member States. At the time of writing, no such request has been made.

The CJEU may face further reform due to the pressures of enlargement. More Member States mean more judges, more different languages and a wider range of legal traditions. It remains to be seen how the Court will cope with these pressures in terms of working method. The CJEU has commented that increasing the number of judges would mean the CJEU 'would cross the invisible boundary between a collegiate court and a deliberative assembly'. The use of chambers or a devolved system of justice, however, may cause problems in ensuring uniformity between the different chambers, especially given the different legal traditions in which each judge will be grounded.

2.11.3 **Functions**

The task of the CJEU is to 'ensure that in the interpretation and application of this Treaty the law is observed' (Article 19(1) TEU). It is the supreme authority on all matters of Union law, and in this capacity may be required to decide matters of constitutional law (see, eg, Chapters 4 and 6), administrative law (see Chapters 12 and 13), social law (Chapter 27) and economic law (Chapter 29) in matters brought directly before it or on application from national courts. Its jurisdiction is principally over the acts of the institutions and Member States within the Union's sphere of activity. Prior to Lisbon, there were consequently limitations on the CJEU's jurisdiction: the European Council lay outside its powers of review (*Roujansky v Council* (case T-584/93)); the majority of the TEU (including CFSP) provisions were likewise excluded from its jurisdiction (former Article 46 TEU), although the CJEU did have the power to police the boundaries between what lay within its jurisdiction and what lay outside.

The position changed radically with the Lisbon Treaty. With the incorporation of what were JHA provisions in TFEU, limitations on the CJEU's jurisdiction regarding these provisions have been removed. Post-Lisbon, the CJEU still has no jurisdiction with regard to the CFSP provisions, however (Article 275 TFEU), although it may rule on the boundary between Union law and the CFSP provisions, (Article 40 TEU) to ensure that there is no encroachment upon the *acquis communautaire*. The relevant provisions defining the scope of the Court's jurisdiction with regard to CFSP are now Articles 24(1) and 40 TFEU, as well as the first paragraph of Article 275 TFEU. Article 24(1) TEU excludes the Court's jurisdiction with the exception of the circumstances identified in Article 40 TEU and Article 275 TFEU.

Article 40

The implementation of the common foreign and security policy shall not affect the application of the procedures and the extent of the powers of the institutions laid down by the Treaties for the exercise of the Union competences referred to in Articles 3 to 6 of the Treaty on the Functioning of the European Union.

Similarly, the implementation of the policies listed in those Articles shall not affect the application of the procedures and the extent of the powers of the institutions laid down by the Treaties for the exercise of the Union competences under this Chapter.

While the scope of the CJEU's powers with regard to CFSP have not been exhaustively delineated, it is clear at least some aspects of the CFSP must lie outside its jurisdiction, as otherwise there would be no need for the boundary process envisaged in Article 40 TEU (a point recognised by the Full Court in Opinion 2/13 at paras 249–52). The scope of Article 40 TEU was considered in *H v Council* (case C-455/14P).

H v Council

This case concerned the appeal of a person seconded to the European Union Police Mission (EUPM) in Bosnia and Herzegovina. H brought an action for annulment of a EUPM decision and a claim for compensation before the General Court, but that Court held that it did not have jurisdiction because of Article 24(1) TEU. The matter was appealed to the Court of Justice.

The Court confirmed that the effect of Article 24(1) TEU was that it did not have jurisdiction with respect to the provisions relating to the CFSP or with respect to acts adopted on the basis of those provisions. Referring to earlier judgments on this point (*Parliament v Council* (case C-658/11) and *Elitaliana v Eulex Kosovo* (case C-439/13P)), it stated that:

> the aforementioned provisions introduce a derogation from the rule of general jurisdiction which Article 19 TEU confers on the Court to ensure that in the interpretation and application of the Treaties the law is observed, and they must, therefore, be interpreted narrowly [para 40].

The Court continued, not by reference to the need to ensure the effectiveness of Union law, but to the fact that the Union:

> is founded, in particular, on the values of equality and the rule of law. The very existence of effective judicial review designed to ensure compliance with provisions of EU law is inherent in the existence of the rule of law [para 41, citations omitted].

So, while the end point—a reasonably wide interpretation of the jurisdiction of the European courts—may seem similar to the pre-Lisbon wording of the Treaties, the reasoning now emphasises the EU as being based on the rule of law.

The Lisbon Treaty also gave the Charter of Fundamental Rights legal force, a charter which lies within the CJEU's jurisdiction, potentially adding to the CJEU's powers of review (see Chapter 6).

An advocate-general's function is to assist the Court by presenting his 'submissions'—a detailed analysis of all the relevant issues of fact and law together with his recommendations to the Court. Under the current Statute of the Court, Article 20 permits the Court to decide not to have a submission from the advocate-general if the case raises no new point of law. This possibility has already been used extensively.

Although the advocate-general's recommendations are not always followed, where they are they are useful as a means of ascertaining the reasoning behind the Court's decision. The judgment itself, which is a single collegiate decision, is, to common law eyes, sometimes terse, cryptic, with little indication of the reasoning on which it is based. Even where the advocate-general's recommendations are not followed they may still be invoked as persuasive authority in a subsequent case.

In its practices and procedures the CJEU draws on continental models; in developing the substantive law it draws on principles and traditions from all the Member States. The judgments from both the CJ and GC are given in the name of the entire chamber; there is no room for dissenting opinions, which may adversely affect the reasoning in the judgment as finally agreed. Although the CJEU seeks to achieve consistency in its judgments, its precedents are not binding in the English sense; it always remains free to depart from previous decisions in the light of new facts. An example of the CJ expressly, and somewhat abruptly, departing from previous jurisprudence on the scope of Article 34 TFEU can be found in the infamous cases of *Bernard Keck and Daniel Mithouard* (cases C-267 and 268/91), in which the CJ stated 'contrary to what has previously been decided'. This judgment has been the subject of some criticism, as the CJ never precisely identified which previous case law it overturned (see further Chapter 18). Similarly, the judgment of the ECJ in *Mettock and Others v Ireland* (case C-127/08) suggested that *Secretary of State for the Home Department v Akrich* (case C-109/01) should be 'reconsidered'.

As the TFEU is a framework treaty the CJEU has been extremely influential in 'filling the gaps', and in doing so has created law in bold, and, to those accustomed to English methods of interpretation, often surprising ways. As Lord Diplock pointed out in *R v Henn and Darby* [1981] AC 850:

> The European Court, in contrast to English courts, applies teleological rather than historical methods to the interpretation of the Treaties and other [Union] legislation. It seeks to give effect to what it conceives to be the spirit rather than the letter of the Treaties; sometimes, indeed, to an English judge, it may seem to the exclusion of the letter. It views the [Union] as a living and expanding [organism] and the interpretation of the provisions of the Treaties as changing to match [its] growth.

The CJEU (particularly the CJ) has, on occasion, been criticised for its activism in its constitutional development of the Union legal order and more recently in the context of European citizenship. It has been this dynamism, or the consequences thereof, which led to the suggestion that the jurisdiction of the CJEU be limited by the 1996 IGC. This suggestion was not taken up. Indeed, the reverse seems the case: the Court's jurisdiction was extended, as we have noted with the changes introduced by Lisbon. Thus the CJEU remains a powerful, nearly omnipresent, actor in the EU.

2.11.4 **General Court**

In 1986 the SEA provided for the setting up of a new tribunal, then called the 'Court of First Instance' (CFI) which forms part of the CJEU (Article 19(1) TEU). It is now the General Court (GC). Approval for this court was obtained in October 1988 ([1989] OJ C215/1). Originally, there was one judge per Member State. Following the 2015 revision to the Statute of the CJEU, there will be two judges per Member State (Regulation 2015/2422 on Statute of CJEU ([2015] OJ L341/14)). They, as in the CJ, may sit in chambers. There are no advocates-general. Its jurisdiction includes applications for judicial review and damages by 'natural and legal persons', under Articles 263 and 265 TFEU, respectively. A number of specialised tribunals and offices, such as the European Union Civil Service Tribunal, the Community Plant Variety Office or the European Chemicals Agency, have been introduced and the GC may hear actions against their decisions. There is a right of appeal on matters of law from this court to the CJ. An applicant cannot appeal against a decision of the GC unless new facts come to light (*ISAE/VP v Commission* (case C-130/91); see further Chapters 7 and 11).

The GC's jurisdiction can be extended under provisions introduced by the Treaty of Nice and now found in Article 256 TFEU. Crucially, it will have jurisdiction to hear preliminary references 'in specific areas laid down by the Statute [of the Court]', although to date no areas have been allocated to the GC. Article 257 TFEU provides for the possibility for some areas, such as staff cases, to be dealt with by judicial panel.

2.12 **Lisbon Treaty**

In the preceding sections, we noted the impact of the Lisbon Treaty on existing institutions and bodies. In addition, there are two further significant developments:

- the creation of the separate office of 'European Council President';
- the establishment of a 'High Representative of the Union for Foreign Affairs and Security Policy'.

Both developments have parallels with similar proposals found in the Constitution which sparked considerable controversy, because the existence of a political figurehead and of a foreign minister might be seen as a further step towards a European state. However, on closer examination, these fears were overstated, and both positions are a development of existing roles.

2.12.1 **Council President**

Article 15(5) TEU established a European Council President, elected by the European Council, for a period of two-and-a-half years, renewable once. The Council President is not a current head of state or government, or entitled to hold any other national office (Article 15(6) TEU). He or she is responsible for chairing the European Council and managing its work, endeavouring to facilitate cohesion and consensus within the European Council and representing the Union externally on matters falling within the CFSP, although this must be without prejudice to the powers of the High Representative.

2.12.2 High Representative for Foreign Affairs and Security Policy

The High Representative for Foreign Affairs and Security is a member of the Commission and constitutes one of its vice-presidents; as such he or she is subject to the approval of the European Parliament on appointment. The High Representative is appointed by the European Council, acting by a qualified majority (Article 18 TEU). The European Council may terminate the appointment using the same procedure. The High Representative is responsible for conducting the Union's CFSP and the common security and defence policy. As such, she presides over the Foreign Affairs Council (Article 18(3) TEU). Within the Commission, the High Representative is responsible for coordinating external actions within the Commission to ensure its consistency. Some commentators have expressed concern about the hybrid nature of this role; somewhere between Commission and Council. In particular, some feel that the post may disturb the institutional balance between institutions, as this role seems almost to be part of two of them.

A new, autonomous body was set up, the European External Action Service under Council Decision 2010/427/EU ([2010] OJ L201/30), which describes itself as the Union's 'diplomatic service'. It is headed by the High Representative for Foreign Affairs and Security Policy.

2.13 EU Institutions outside the EU Framework

Following the financial crisis, there have been a number of treaties negotiated between some, but not all, Member States of the EU. These treaties may affect the EU Treaties, specifically by allocating tasks to the institutions of the EU, or changing the way those institutions operate in specific policy fields. Examples are the Treaties establishing the European Financial Stability Facility (EFSF) and the European Stabilisation Mechanism (ESM) (the 'Fiscal Compact', see Chapter 20). Remember, the EU Treaties provide that the institutions may only act within the competence conferred on them by the Treaties (see Article 13(2) TEU).

This raises the questions of whether these sorts of changes should have been incorporated in the EU Treaties (because of their link with and effect on those Treaties), and whether the use of such mechanisms have the effect of circumventing the legal requirements for Treaty amendments. To what extent is the use of the EU institutions in this way legitimate? Further, are there constraints on this use, especially given the possibility of using the enhanced cooperation procedure to allow some, but not all, Member States to agree further integration? While these decisions affect non-participating Member States, the European Parliament may also find that its role is limited by recourse to such procedures. It may mean activities carried out outside the EU framework are not under the supervision of the European Parliament as a result. The use of this sort of approach may not only affect the institutional balance, but also the level of protection granted to private parties by the Charter of Fundamental Rights since it seems that such additional treaties do not fall within the scope of EU law (see Chapter 6).

This granting of additional powers to EU institutions is not new. The European Parliament—in the context of seeking to protect its prerogatives—has previously sought to challenge powers conferred upon the European Commission by agreement of all the Member States. *Parliament v Council and Commission* (the *Bangladesh* case) (cases C-181 and 248/91) concerned the validity of a decision by (all of) the Member States, meeting within the Council, to grant financial aid to Bangladesh and to confer power upon the Commission to manage that aid. *Parliament v Council (European development fund)* (the *Lomé Convention* case) (case C-316/91) dealt with the decision by the *Council* to establish a special system, distinct from the EU's usual budgetary procedure, to administer Member States' assistance to African, Caribbean and Pacific countries within the framework of the Lomé Convention. In each case, the Court upheld the decision. Further obligations could be imposed on the institutions provided that they were compatible with the relevant institution's Treaty obligations. The principle elaborated in these cases was potentially broad, although its application in these cases related to a specific, narrow set of facts. Essentially, the institutions were acting as agents of the Member States to coordinate financial schemes.

With the Fiscal Pact, the issue of using EU institutions outside the EU framework was raised again, in the case of *Pringle*.

Pringle

The case concerned a challenge to the amendment to Article 136 TFEU, to allow the introduction of a permanent stability mechanism, and to the establishment of a separate treaty outside the EU Treaties to deal with Eurozone problems. The case was brought by a member of the Irish parliament against the Irish government in the Irish courts, and the competent national court referred a number of questions to the CJ. As part of the arguments, the legitimacy of the use of Union institutions in this way was raised. The ESM is based on the Commission and the European Central Bank in terms of assessing need and agreeing loans (including the conditions of the loan) and monitoring compliance with the terms of the loan.

Building on its previous case law, the CJ upheld the use of the institutions. It held that Member States:

> are entitled, in areas which do not fall under the exclusive competence of the Union, to entrust tasks to the institutions, outside the framework of the Union, such as the task of coordinating a collective action undertaken by the Member States or managing financial assistance....[provided] those tasks do not alter the essential character of the powers conferred on those institutions by the EU and FEU treaties [para 158].

The *Pringle* judgment raises many issues. The following paragraphs describe three main points from the many.

The CJ's judgment leaves the question about what a change to an institution's 'essential nature' would look like. The starting point must be that the role is not incompatible with the institution's role under the EU Treaties, or undermines the attainment of EU objectives. At para 163 of its judgment in *Pringle*, the CJ noted that the Commission is obliged by Article 17(1) TEU to 'promote the general interest of the Union' and to 'oversee the application of Union law.' Given that the objective of the ESM was ensuring the stability of the euro 'by its involvement in the ESM Treaty, the Commission promotes the general interest of the Union' (para 164). The Court took a similar approach as regards the role of the ECB. On this basis, the constraints imposed by the 'essential nature' test operate at a very general level and would consequently seem to be easy to satisfy. It would be hard to think of circumstances in which it could not be argued that the Commission was acting 'to promote the general interest of the Union'.

Additionally, the Court confirmed that the existence of the enhanced cooperation provisions does not prevent the use of the non-judicial institutions in Treaties between Member States, at least where the Treaties concerned do not relate to an issue within the EU's 'specific competences' (ie areas of exclusive competence, or areas where the EU has exercised its shared competence to the extent that it has pre-empted Member States' action within the meaning of Article 3(2) TEU).

Article 20 TEU, which contains provisions relating to enhanced cooperation (see Chapter 3), does not contain an obligation on Member States to use it. It provides a mechanism which they may use. This leaves us with the question of why Member States, given the duty of cooperation and good faith which applies to all Member States, should choose not to use the enhanced cooperation mechanism.

While a mechanism to support struggling economies may well have suited EU objectives as well as those of some, if not all, Member States, there are questions about process here. Is it appropriate that such far-reaching mechanisms are established without consulting other institutions, notably the European Parliament? Note, the European Parliament has co-decision powers in internal legislation as well as a role in agreeing external agreements. In the *Bangladesh* and *Lomé Convention* cases, the advocate-general suggested that all that was needed was the agreement of the institution concerned implying that the possible impact on the institutional balance need not be considered. Those tasks were, however, much more narrowly confined than the responsibilities of the Fiscal Pact. Participation by an EU institution in such a venture will affect all institutions, and those institutions may have views as to the desirability of such participation from its perspective of the good of the EU. This may affect the institutional balance of the institutions, undermining the ability of some institutions to participate in the determination of Union policy.

Similar questions arose in *Peter Gauweiler and Others v Deutscher Bundestag* (case C-62/14) in relation to the legality of the Outright Monetary Transaction (OMT) programme which was part of a series of measures taken by the ECB in response to the Euro crisis (see Chapter 20). The CJ in *Gauweiler* took a similar view to that which it adopted in *Pringle*, confirming this approach.

A final issue with the Fiscal Compact should be noted. By contrast with the earlier examples, which envisaged extra tasks for the Commission, the Fiscal Compact also envisages a role for the CJ. The Court will have a role in adjudicating, where appropriate, on the enforcement mechanism contained in the Fiscal Compact in a procedure which bears similarities to the enforcement procedure in Article 258 TFEU, including the possibility of financial penalty in accordance with Article 260 TFEU (see Chapter 11). The legal basis for the Court's role is Article 273 TFEU, which provides:

> The Court of Justice shall have jurisdiction in any dispute between Member States which relates to the subject matter of the Treaties if the dispute is submitted to it under a special agreement between the parties.

2.14 Conclusions

When looking at the institutions, it is important to remember that they operate as a system, and individual institutions should not be seen in isolation; what is crucial is the relationship between them, and the other actors that increasingly play a role in Union policymaking. It is tempting to see different institutions as representatives for different ideas—supranationalism versus intergovernmentalism, and democracy versus a technocratic or interstate method. The shifting relationships and relative strengths of the institutions on this basis reflect the approach of the Union. In many respects, this is an oversimplification; even the Council can be seen to have some integrationist tendencies and the Parliament cannot be considered an ideal of democracy. In practice, then, the institutions have had to learn to cooperate and to negotiate the hard points to permit any actions to be taken. This complicity of all institutions in the process is the basis of policymaking and the way in which over-ambitious or over-mighty institutions are, on the whole, controlled.

Nonetheless, difficulties remain. The current institutional structure of the Union was established for a system with a more limited membership and substantive scope. Since then there has been enlargement so that membership of the Union has more than quadrupled. It became accepted that what was in essence the original institutional structure was unable to function effectively in the modern Union and that institutional problems would only be exacerbated by further enlargement. Not only is it more difficult to reach agreement between a greater number of representatives, but with eastward expansion the Member States reflect a greater diversity of interests, traditions and languages. In addition to the sheer weight of numbers, there will be a risk of fragmentation as the Union becomes less cohesive. The current Member States were aware of this problem even before the ToA, resulting in a protocol being annexed to the ToA regarding proposed institutional reform. Subsequent Treaties brought incremental change but the issues relating to the operations of the institutions remained on the agenda through the Nice revisions to Lisbon. In formal terms, Lisbon has dealt with many of the issues—though it should be noted that some changes will not come into force for a considerable period and others have already been undone. In this new settlement, one of the 'winners' was the European Parliament; the CJEU also benefited from an extension of its jurisdiction. From previous experience, it is clear that institutional arrangements are dynamic and the whole story is not told in the words of the Treaties alone. We must wait to see, therefore, how this settlement works in practice.

Further reading

Bradley, K, 'The European Parliament and treaty reform: Building blocks and stumbling blocks' in D O'Keeffe and P Twomey (eds), *Legal Issues of the Amsterdam Treaty* (Hart Publishing, 1999).

Chamon, M, 'The institutional balance, an ill-fated principle of EU law?' (2015) 21 EPL 371.

Craig, P, 'The Treaty of Lisbon: Process, architecture and substance' (2008) 33 EL Rev 137.

Craig, P, 'Pringle and the use of EU institutions outside the EU legal framework: foundations, procedure and substance' (2013) 9 ECL Rev 263.

Dawson, M and de Witte, F, 'Constitutional balance in the EU after the euro-crisis' (2013) 76 MLR 817.

De Baere, G and Van den Sanden, T, 'Interinstitutional gravity and pirates of the parliament on stranger tides: The continued constitutional significance of the choice of legal basis in post-Lisbon external action' (2016) 12 ECL Rev 85.

Dehousse, R, 'European institutional architecture after Amsterdam: Parliamentary system or regulatory structure?' (1998) 35 CML Rev 595.

Hartley, T, 'Constitutional and institutional aspects of the Maastricht Treaty' (1993) 42 ICLQ 213.

Laffan, B, 'Becoming a "living institution": The evolution of the European Court of Auditors' (1999) 37 JCMS 252.

Lang, JT, 'Checks and balances in the European Union: The institutional structure and the "community method"' (2006) 12 EPL 127.

Peers, S, 'Towards a new form of EU law? The use of EU institutions outside the EU legal framework' (2013) 9 ECL Rev 37.

Rasmussen, H, 'Between self-restraint and activism: A judicial policy for the European Court' (1988) 13 EL Rev 28.

Sharpston, E and De Baere, G, 'The Court of Justice as a constitutional adjudicator' in A Arnull et al (eds), *A Constitutional Order of States? Essays in EU Law in Honour of Alan Dashwood* (Hart Publishing, 2011).

Smulders, B and Eisele, K, 'Reflections on the institutional balance, the Community method and the interplay between jurisdictions after Lisbon' (2012) 31 YEL 112.

Tridimas, T, 'The Court of Justice and judicial activism' (1996) 21 EL Rev 199.

Usher, J, 'Institutional aspects of the Constitutional Treaty: Which way does it go?' (2005) 37 Bracton LJ 30.

Vajda, C, 'Democracy in the European Union: What has the Court of Justice to say?' (2015) Cambridge Journal of International and Comparative Law 226.

Van Elsuwege, P, 'EU external action after the collapse of the pillar structure: In search of new balance between delimitation and consistency' (2010) 47 CML Rev 987.

Woods, L, 'Consistency in the Chambers of the European Court of Justice: A case study on the free movement of goods' (2012) 31 CJQ 338.

Xhaferri, Z, 'Delegated acts, implementing acts and institutional balance implications post-Lisbon' (2013) 20 Maastricht Journal 557.

3 Scope of the EU Treaty: laws and lawmaking

3.1 Introduction

The EU would be nothing if it had no powers to enact legislation to take forward the obligations contained in the Treaties. Given the supremacy of the resulting EU law, we must question the scope, the nature and source of those powers, and how the EU and its institutions exercise them. This chapter therefore considers, first, the scope of the Treaties and the type of competence that the EU may exercise in relation to the different policy areas (3.2–3.4, 3.10). It secondly investigates the question of when the EU should exercise those powers, and how, through the doctrines of subsidiarity and proportionality (3.5–3.6). Thirdly, and developing from issues flagged in Chapter 2, it looks at legislative procedures and whether there is sufficient transparency in and democratic control over EU lawmaking (3.7–3.8). In this analysis, transparency may be adversely affected by the complexity, as well as by the degree of openness, of lawmaking procedures. Democracy has links to the EU institutional balance in that the institutions' respective democratic credentials vary. So, we must also consider the changes that the various Treaties have effected and the consequences those changes have had on the institutions' respective policy and lawmaking roles (3.9).

3.2 Conferred competence

It is an underlying principle that the EU may only act in the policy fields which the Member States have conferred upon it; this is the 'principle of conferral' and what we mean by 'attributed competence'. This point is made in Article 5 TEU and is re-affirmed by the statement in Article 13(1) TEU, that the institutions may only act within their powers. While these principles have been long established in the Treaties, there are two aspects which had not been explicitly stated before Lisbon. First, it is the Member States that confer the powers on the EU (through the Treaties); the Member States remain 'masters of the Treaties'. This point can be seen in the text of Article 1 TEU which reads:

> By this Treaty, the high contracting parties establish among themselves a *European Union*, hereinafter called 'the Union', on which the Member States confer competences to attain objectives they have in common.

Secondly, those powers which are not conferred on the EU remain with the Member States (Article 4(1) TEU and Article 5(2) TEU; Declaration in relation to the delimitation of competences). The use of the word 'conferral' implies that the relationship between the Member States and the Union is one of delegation.

These changes may have been introduced in response to a concern that the EU was exhibiting 'mission creep', that is, accumulating more and more powers at the expense of the Member States, and that it was therefore necessary to reaffirm the nature and source of the EU's powers. We noted in Chapter 1 that successive Treaty amendments saw the cumulative expansion of EU competence resulting in a Union with a broad sphere of action. This, together with the fact that the Member States are under an obligation to 'take any appropriate measure, general or particular, to ensure fulfilment of the obligations arising out of the Treaties or resulting from the acts of the institutions of the Union' (Article 4(3) TEU), meant the impact of the EU on national legislative choices was huge. It is not surprising that Lord Denning MR was moved to say, even in the relatively early years, in *HP Bulmer Ltd v J Bollinger SA* ([1974] Ch 401), 'the Treaty is like an incoming tide. It flows into the estuaries and up the rivers. It cannot be held back'.

The concerns about the impact of expanded EU competence on Member States can also be seen in the landmark decision of the German Federal Constitutional Court (FCC) in *Brunner*. The case concerned a challenge to the German ratification of the Maastricht Treaty. Although the FCC upheld the powers of the German Parliament to ratify the Maastricht Treaty, it sounded a number of warnings about the powers of the Union and its institutions. Effectively, any further transfer of powers to Union level would need express democratic approval to be binding. The FCC argued (at para 33):

> Because the principle of limited powers is adhered to, no power to extend its powers is conferred on the European Union . . . and the claiming of further functions and powers by the European Union . . . is made dependent on supplementation and amendment of the Treaty and is therefore subject to the affirmative decision of the national parliaments.

Despite this affirmation, the introduction of the principle of subsidiarity by the Maastricht Treaty (see 3.5) and the changes introduced by Lisbon, it seems that national constitutional courts remain concerned about 'mission creep'. When the question of the acceptability of the Lisbon Treaty was referred to the Czech constitutional court, it approved the Lisbon Treaty, but the enabling Czech legislation was subject to a requirement that no further competence could be transferred without the express consent of the Czech Parliament. In its decision on the Lisbon Treaty, the FCC made a similar point. It emphasised the principle of 'conferral' and the obligation in EU law 'to respect the constituent power of the Member States as masters of the Treaties'. This issue of respect is one the FCC has the power to review. The question of the boundary between national and Union competence is an ongoing issue, as can be seen from the continuing stream of cases concerning EU competence, which continue to appear before the national constitutional courts. (See Chapter 4 for more detail.)

3.3 The scope of EU competence

The Treaties have always contained provisions identifying the general objectives of the Union and then introducing more specific tasks to achieve those objectives; the list has been amended, elaborated and lengthened over successive Treaty amendments. These provisions describe the areas in which the EU may act and for which purpose. The objectives are currently found in Article 3 TEU (with the more specific tasks found in Article 3(3) and (4) TEU). Article 3 TEU states:

1. The Union's aim is to promote peace, its values and the well-being of its peoples;

2. The Union shall offer its citizens an area of freedom, security and justice without internal frontiers, in which the free movement of persons is ensured in conjunction with appropriate measures with respect to external border controls, asylum, immigration and the prevention and combating of crime;

3. The Union shall establish an internal market. It shall work for the sustainable development of Europe based on balanced economic growth and price stability, a highly competitive social market economy, aiming at full employment and social progress, and a high level of protection and improvement of the quality of the environment. It shall promote scientific and technological advance.

   It shall combat social exclusion and discrimination, and shall promote social justice and protection, equality between women and men, solidarity between generations and protection of the rights of the child.
   It shall promote economic, social and territorial cohesion, and solidarity among Member States.
   It shall respect its rich cultural and linguistic diversity, and shall ensure that Europe's cultural heritage is safeguarded and enhanced;

4. The Union shall establish an economic and monetary union whose currency is the euro;

5. In its relations with the wider world, the Union shall uphold and promote its values and interests and contribute to the protection of its citizens. It shall contribute to peace, security, the sustainable development of the Earth, solidarity and mutual respect among peoples, free and fair trade, eradication of poverty and the protection of human rights, in particular the rights of the child, as well as to the strict observance and the development of international law, including respect for the principles of the United Nations Charter.

While the current version of these objectives is similar to its predecessor provisions, the Lisbon Treaty made some changes of note to these general provisions. The Union always had a range of socio-economic objectives as its goals, but these were based on the creation of a common market and—latterly—an economic and monetary union. While the internal market and the economic and monetary union remain, Lisbon changed the emphasis: the starting point is peace and the well-being of the Union's peoples, as well as respect for the Union's values.

The Union's values are described in Article 2 TEU and, again, are not focused on the economic. Article 2 TEU provides:

The Union is founded on the values of respect for human dignity, freedom, democracy, equality, the rule of law and respect for human rights, including the rights of persons belonging to minorities. These values are common to the Member States in a society in which pluralism, non-discrimination, tolerance, justice, solidarity and equality between women and men prevail.

It is only when we get to para 3 of Article 3 TEU that we see the first reference to the creation of the internal market, but even here there are changes post-Lisbon. Notably, Article 3(3) TEU now refers to 'a highly competitive social market economy, aiming at full employment and social pro-gress'. Previously there had been a reference to 'a harmonious, balanced and sustainable develop-ment of economic activities, a high level of employment and social protection' (former Article 2 TEC), and former Article 4 TEC had referred to an 'open market economy'. Additionally, there are some new objectives, such as 'solidarity between generations and protection of the rights of the child'. Interestingly, there is now no reference to free competition being an objective of the Union, though the more detailed provisions on competition law in TFEU have not been amended (Chapters 1, 28 and 29). The French government requested the change to the text to make the point that free compe-tition is a means to an end, not the objective itself. There is, in general, a greater emphasis on human values and the well-being of people than previously. Article 2 TEU does not provide legally binding rights. Nonetheless, it is a significant provision. It describes the underlying spirit of the Union in that it states the common values on which the Union is founded. There have been suggestions from both the European Parliament and the European Commission concerning the possibility of monitoring—and possibly enforcing—Member States' compliance with these values (see, eg: strong resolutions on Hungary and European complicity in the CIA rendition/secret detention; Council Conclusions, June 2013; Commissioner Reding, SPEECH/13/677). (On human rights see further Chapter 6.)

Article 3 TEU describes the main objectives of the Union but does not itself impose specific legal obligations on the Member States. The detailed obligations are found, in the main, in TFEU (the ex-ception is CFSP). Article 1(1) TFEU states:

> This Treaty organises the functioning of the Union and determines the areas of, delimitation of, and arrangements for exercising its competences.

The provisions of the TFEU delineate the scope of the various Union policies, as well as the steps that may or must be taken for their implementation. Some examples of Union policy areas are found in Box 3.1. Although Article 3 TEU does not have direct legal impact, it has interpretative value; it may be used to clarify the scope of the more precise Treaty obligations.

Box 3.1   Examples of Union policies

agriculture

economic and monetary affairs

employment and social affairs

environment

foreign and security policy

internal market

justice, freedom and security

public health

sport

transport

3.3.1 General principles

In addition to the goals and tasks enunciated in Articles 2–3 TEU, the Treaties contain other provi-sions laying down principles underlying the Union. This list of principles has been expanded by the successive Treaty amendments and covers a range of issues. Article 4(3) TEU provides for the duty of sincere cooperation, a principle which has been in the Treaties since the beginning and which the CJ has used to great effect in developing the law (see, eg, indirect effect at 5.3). A central principle is that of subsidiarity, as well as proportionality (see 3.5 and Chapter 6). Respect for human rights is found in Article 6 TEU, as well as Article 2 TEU. By contrast to the position under the doomed Constitutional Treaty, primacy of the EU is not encapsulated as a principle in either the TEU or TFEU; instead there is a Declaration (Declaration 17) attached to the Lisbon Treaty restating the existing legal position (see Chapter 4). Most of the other principles can be found grouped together in Part I of the TFEU and they reiterate some of the objectives found in Articles 2 and 3 TEU. Thus we see an emphasis on the promotion of equality, particularly sex equality and the fight against social exclusion, as well as the prohibition on discrimination (Article 10 TFEU, as well as in Articles 18 and 19 TFEU), whether on the basis of sex, race, religion and belief, disability, age or sexual orientation. An addition introduced by the Lisbon Treaty is the statement about the 'equality of Member States before the Treaties' (Article 4(2) TEU). This was felt to re-state the position found in the case law of the CJ; a proposal to establish a principle of equality between the Member States was not accepted, because the position of the Member States varies in a number of respects, for example their rights to appoint judges and the number of MEPs. Since the ToA, the EU has emphasised environmental protection, and this is now found as a principle in Article 11 TFEU. Other principles described in the TFEU are a mixed bag of ideas: consumer protection; respect for animal welfare; the role of public services; open government; the right of data protection; and respect for religious bodies under national law (Article 17 TFEU).

While these provisions may not confer rights on which individuals could rely directly, they identify principles which should inform the Union and its institutions when carrying out their tasks. Article 7 TFEU specifies that the Union must ensure consistency between its policies and activities, taking all of its objectives into account. Some principles seem to impose stronger obligations on the Union. Article 10 TFEU specifies that 'in defining and implementing its policies and activities, the Union shall aim to combat discrimination . . .', whereas Article 9 TFEU dealing with social protection merely requires the Union to take the specified requirements 'into account'. Environmental protection must be integrated into Union policies (Article 11 TFEU); consumer protection, as with Article 9 TFEU, must merely be 'taken into account' (Article 12 TFEU).

3.3.2 External competence

While the European Union always has had some external competence, we can divide this competence into two main aspects:

- that focused on economic aspects connected with the Union's trade activities;
- more general foreign policy.

3.3.2.1 Trade

The external competence connected with the Union's trade activities has existed since the original Treaty of Rome, although Treaty amendments have expanded its range of activities (see Article 207 TFEU). Thus the original Treaty of Rome provided that the then Community had legal personality (former Article 281 EC) to allow it to conclude agreements on the common commercial policy. Since Lisbon, the EU has had legal personality. As noted in 2.3.3.2 the procedure for concluding such agreements is found in what is now Article 218 TFEU. Successive Treaty amendments have extended the policy areas in respect of which the Union could act, adding areas such as: environment and research; development cooperation; external representation of the single currency; and economic, financial and technical cooperation with third countries. These provisions are now found in Title V of TFEU on International Agreements. As well as these Treaty developments, the CJ interpreted the scope of the EU's external competence broadly, using the doctrine of implied powers (3.6.2). Given that the EU has exclusive competence in this area (see 3.4), the scope of the common commercial policy is significant.

The line between Union competence under Article 207 TFEU and that of the Member States in this area is not clear-cut and has changed, as *Opinion 1/94, Opinion 1/08* and *Daiichi Sankyo Co Ltd Sanofi–Aventis Deutschland GmbH v DEMO Anonimos Viomikhaniki kai Emporiki Etairia Farmakon* (case C-414/11) show.

Opinion 1/94

This case concerned the competence of the Union to enter into the World Trade Organization (WTO) agreements as part of the Union's common commercial policy competence (Article 207 TFEU). The WTO Agreements are broad in scope, including trade in services (GATS) and harmonizing trade-related aspects of intellectual property rights (TRIPS). The Member States contested the Union's competence, arguing that ascribing the power to the Union to conclude the agreement (exclusively) would allow the avoidance of procedural rules for and limitations on lawmaking with regards to internal Union matters, particularly with regard to the proper legal base for harmonization of Member States' laws. The difficulty is that there are close links between what is agreed externally and what is permitted internally, so a measure intended to harmonise trade between the EU and its trading partners can have substantial impacts on the regulation of internal trade as well. The CJ accepted these arguments on the basis that the TRIPS agreement did not relate specifically to international trade. The result was that competence was split between the EU and the Member States.

As well as the practical implications of requiring duplicate membership of the WTO for the Member States and the EU, the case left difficult questions about when an agreement would specifically relate to trade so as to trigger exclusive Union competence, especially as TRIPS stands for trade-related aspects of intellectual property.

The Commission has sought to argue that changes to the Treaties would result in changes to the scope of the Union's competence under Article 207 TFEU. In *Opinion 1/08* it unsuccessfully argued, in the context of negotiations to amend commitments under GATS consequent on the accession of new Member States, that the Nice amendments would be deprived of full effectiveness unless Union exclusive competence were to be extended. Significantly, Article 207 TFEU has since been revised to include explicit reference to 'commercial aspects of intellectual property', raising the question of whether this change would affect the CJ's reasoning about mixed competence and intellectual property in *Opinion 1/94*. The CJ returned to the question, and in another Grand Chamber judgment—*Daiichi Sankyo*—reversed its conclusions about competence found in *Opinion 1/94*. Indeed, the CJ held that *Opinion 1/94* was no longer relevant; the allocation of competence of the European Union and the Member States must be determined on the basis of the Treaty now in force (para 48).

Daiichi Sankyo

The case arose in the context of a dispute in Greece concerning the marketing by DEMO of a generic medicinal product whose active ingredient is a substance allegedly protected by patent rights of Daiichi

Sankyo. The outcome of the dispute would be affected by the interpretation accorded to certain provisions of the TRIPS agreement. The Greek court essentially wanted to know whether this was a matter primarily for Greek law and the national court.

The CJ determined the scope of Article 207 TFEU to be where:

A European Union act falls within the common commercial policy if it relates specifically to international trade in that it is essentially intended to promote, facilitate or govern trade and has direct and immediate effects on trade. [para 50]

It then went on to argue:

It follows that, of the rules adopted by the European Union in the field of intellectual property, only those with a specific link to international trade are capable of falling within the concept of 'commercial aspects of intellectual property' in Article 207(1) TFEU and hence the field of the common commercial policy. That is the case of the rules in the TRIPS Agreement [paras 52–3].

We can suggest that this change is related to the textual amendments underpinning the CJ's argument in para 48, but the fact is that the definition of the CCP in para 50 is not that far away from the definition used by the CJ in *Opinion 1/94*. What has changed is the CJ's factual assessment that TRIPS has a specific link to international trade: in *Opinion 1/94* the CJ thought there was no such link; in *Daiichi Sankyo* the CJ is of the opposite view.

The CJ has had to address external competence in other areas. Notably, the provisions establishing the Area of Freedom, Security and Justice allow for Union action to facilitate cross border service of documents in court cases. The question arose as to whether the negotiation of the Lugano Convention, dealing with conflicts of national jurisdiction and enforcement of judgments in civil and commercial matters, was within the exclusive competence of the Union (*Opinion 1/03*). The CJ emphasised that the Lugano Convention would affect the uniform and consistent application of Union rules and that the conclusion of the Lugano Convention fell entirely within the exclusive competence of the Union.

3.3.2.2 Foreign and Security Policy

The Treaty of Maastricht gave the Union the power to define a Common Foreign and Security Policy (CFSP, formerly the second pillar, see Chapter 1), which is very broad in its terms, defined as 'all areas of foreign policy and all questions relating to the Union's security' (Article 24 TEU). This area falls within the remit of the High Representative for Foreign Affairs and Security Policy (see 2.12.2).

While the Member States had agreed on the desirability of 'enhancing cohesion of [EU] external policies', concern about the potential impact of this policy area on Member States' sovereignty resulted in the provisions relating to CFSP remaining in the TEU post-Lisbon. Despite the separation between the commercial and more general aspects of the EU's external policy, the policy comprises a single framework, as evidenced by the fact that Article 21(1) TEU (dealing with CFSP) refers to the provisions in the TFEU detailing the EU's external competence and Article 205 TFEU (relating to external commercial policy) refers to the relevant provisions in the TEU on CFSP.

3.3.2.3 Impact of Lisbon

While the scope of the EU's external powers seems not to have been materially affected by Lisbon, two points should be noted. First, Article 3(5) TEU specifically refers to the Union's external competence, stating that 'in its relations with the wider world, the Union shall uphold and promote its values and interests', specifically contributing to 'peace, security and sustainable development of the earth, solidarity and mutual respect among peoples, free and fair trade, eradication of poverty and protection of human rights'. Whether these aims would limit or otherwise change the Union's external competence is far from clear. Given that the Union's activities should already take at least some of these concerns into account, arguably there should not be much difference in substantive approach. Secondly, while the existence of Union powers might constitute nothing new, there are questions about who—Union or Member States—gets to exercise that competence (see further 3.4).

3.4 Types of competence

We have noted the concerns about 'mission creep' in 3.2. This in part was based on the fact that the circumstances in which the Union should act were not clear, despite the introduction of the principle of subsidiarity (see 3.5) by the Maastricht Treaty. To support the principle of subsidiarity, post-Lisbon the TFEU identifies three types of EU competence in Article 2 TFEU:

- exclusive competence;
- shared competence;
- supporting, coordinating or supplementing competence (Article 24 TEU).

Exclusive competence means that only the EU may act; in such circumstances, Member States may act only where specifically empowered so to do by the EU. Save for some limited cases identified in Article 4 TFEU, shared competence means that both the EU and the Member States may act, but when the EU has acted, Member States may act only to the extent that the EU has not done so, to the extent that Member States are permitted to act by the EU, or to the extent that the EU has ceased to act. Protocol 25 on the Exercise of Shared Competence clarifies that:

> when the Union has taken action in a certain area, the scope of this exercise of competence only covers those elements governed by the Union acting question and therefore does not cover the whole area.

For the third category of competence, 'supporting' the EU may act to support, coordinate and supplement actions of the Member States but may not enact harmonising legislation. Even where 'supporting competence' is in issue, the Union may introduce harmonising measures where those measures also tackle an issue having an adverse impact on the internal market. The precise degree of impact required to justify such harmonising measures has given rise to unclear case law (discussed in Chapter 16).

Articles 2–6 TFEU ascribe the various EU policy areas to one or other of the three categories of EU competence (see Table 3.1). There is no category of exclusive Member State competence, although the TEU specifies that competences not conferred upon the Union remain with the Member States (Article 4(1) TEU). Even in such circumstances, Member States may not act in a way incompatible with Union law. This point, and the linked question of the scope of Union law, have become increasingly important in the context of protection of human rights (see Chapter 6).

Table 3.1 Division of competence

Exclusive	Shared	Supporting
Customs union Competition rules	All policy areas not mentioned in Articles 3 and 6 TFEU, specifically:	Human health Industry
Monetary policy (for euro Member States)	Internal market	Culture
	Social policy aspects found in TFEU	Tourism
Conservation of marine biological resources under the common fisheries policy	Economic, social and territorial cohesion	Education, vocational training, youth and sport
Common commercial policy	Agriculture and fisheries (except marine conservation)	Civil protection
NB rules on conclusion of international agreements/ external policy	Environment	Administrative cooperation
	Consumer protection	
	Transport	
	Trans-European energy networks	
	Area of freedom, security and justice	
	Common safety concerns in public health matters, for the aspects defined in TFEU	

The list of policies falling within the shared competence is not exhaustive. Article 4(1) TFEU states:

> The Union shall share competence with the Member States where the Treaties confer on it a competence which does not relate to the areas referred to in Articles 3 and 6.

There were also some difficult areas to ascribe to one category or another. Article 4(3) and (4) TFEU identify some policies where, although the policy seems to be ascribed to the shared competence category, this does not precisely fit with the description of the legal bases found in TFEU. Rather than shared competence, it seems that in areas such as research, technological development and space, and of development cooperation and humanitarian aid, the EU's competence is in addition to Member States' competence rather than displacing it. Further, Article 5 TFEU describes a number of policies (economic policies, employment policies) which are complementary to EU action. Due to the operation of Article 4(1) TFEU which defines shared competence as everything that is not in Articles 3 and 6 TFEU, it seems that these policies have been categorised as being shared competence.

Interestingly, the Union has not been granted exclusive competence in areas relating to the creation of the internal market, for example, in free movement of goods, persons and services, although the Commission had argued for this position. The denial of exclusive competence was presumably because of the potential breadth of internal market measures.

Article 3(2) TFEU has also given rise to some interpretive concerns. It specifies that:

> The Union shall also have exclusive competence of the conclusion of an international agreement when its conclusion is provided for in a legislative act of the Union or is necessary to enable the Union to exercise its internal competence, or in so far as its conclusion may affect common rules or alter their scope.

Some commentators have suggested that this phraseology broadens the scope of Union exclusive competence beyond the boundaries defined by the CJ in its jurisprudence on implied powers and external policy, though the wording of the provision has clear similarities to that jurisprudential position (see 3.3.2 and 3.6.2). Note also that the CFSP provisions, which are found in the TEU not the TFEU, are not included in the three-group categorisation found in Article 2 TFEU.

Although these provisions have the advantage of relative brevity and simplicity, the real test would be likely to arise in the application of the provisions and the determination in individual cases of where the boundaries lie between the different types of competence. Note also that the scope of the Union's respective competences is to be determined by the provisions specific to each area (Article 2(6) TFEU), that is the provisions which, inter alia, reflect the substantive provisions of the TFEU.

3.5 **Subsidiarity**

3.5.1 **General**

At 3.2 we noted the concerns about mission creep. One mechanism to address this concern introduced into the Treaties by the Maastricht Treaty was the principle of subsidiarity. As Article 5(1) TEU states, subsidiarity, together with the principle of proportionality, operates to constrain the principle of conferral. Subsidiarity decides, where there are multiple layers of government, at which level policy decisions will be made. There is thus a distinction between the question of whether EU competence exists, and the question of whether the EU should exercise that competence. The preamble to the TEU suggests that subsidiarity requires that decisions should be taken as closely as possible to the citizen, a point now re-affirmed by Article 10(3) TEU. This requirement suggests that action at the Union level would be the exception rather than the rule. The principle of subsidiarity itself, found in Article 5(3) TEU, may, however, point in a different direction.

Article 5(3) TEU, second paragraph states:

> Under the principle of subsidiarity, in areas which do not fall within its exclusive competence, the Union shall act only if and in so far as the objectives of the proposed action cannot be sufficiently achieved by the Member States, either at central level or at regional better achieved at Union level.

Clearly, the principle of subsidiarity does not apply if the Union is exercising exclusive competence (as defined in Article 4 TFEU).

3.5.2 **Test for the exercise of concurrent powers**

Looking now at the principle of subsidiarity itself, it can be seen that the idea in the second paragraph of Article 5(3) TEU can be broken down into two further blocks:

(1) that no Union action should be taken unless the action cannot be sufficiently achieved by the Member States

(2) that because of the proposed scale or effects of the measure, the Union can better achieve the end result desired.

This test raises several issues: it is a test of comparative efficiency ('Commission Communication to the Council and the European Parliament', Bull EC 10-1992, 116) which might, in the context of achieving goals such as common trading rules throughout the Union, be seen to favour action at Union level. How this fits in with the definition of subsidiarity, which states that the principle of subsidiarity requires that decision-making should be made as close to the citizen as possible (Preamble; Article 10(3) TEU), is not clear. Further, when will 'sufficiently' be satisfied? Do these questions relate to the scale or the effect of the proposed action?

Some writers suggested that, in any event, these issues are not appropriately decided by the CJEU because of their political nature. In view of the fact that a number of cases have already raised this issue (eg, *UK v Council* (case C-84/94) and *Germany v Parliament* (case C-233/94)), it seems that the CJEU has not, so far, refused jurisdiction and is now unlikely to do so. It has been reluctant to exercise a high level of review, however.

Annexed to the Lisbon Treaty is a protocol on subsidiarity and proportionality; while this seems more focused on ensuring the implementation of the principles than in clarifying the meaning of either subsidiarity or proportionality, it does contain the requirement that, '[t]he reasons for concluding that a Union objective can be better achieved at Union level shall be substantiated by qualitative and, wherever possible, quantitative indicators'. It remains to be seen whether this requirement has any impact on the legislative proposals put forward.

3.5.3 **Role of the national parliaments**

Article 5(3) TEU provides that the principle of subsidiarity is to be applied in accordance with the Protocol on the application of the principles of subsidiarity and proportionality. To support application of the subsidiarity principle, this protocol sets out a procedure whereby national parliaments may ensure compliance with the principle of subsidiarity as envisaged in Article 12(b) TEU.

The protocol provides that any national parliament, or any chamber of such a parliament, may within eight weeks from the date of transmission of the draft legislative act, send a reasoned opinion stating why it considers that the draft piece of legislation does not comply with the principle of subsidiarity. If a given percentage of the national parliaments agree, the draft must be reviewed. The relevant institutions may decide to maintain, amend or withdraw the draft, but reasons must be given for the decision and, in the context of the ordinary legislative procedure, where a simple majority (decided by using an allocation of votes among the national parliaments) support the non-compliance of the proposed legislative act with the principle of subsidiarity and the Commission decides to maintain the proposal, the Commission must justify the proposal's compliance with subsidiarity in a reasoned opinion, which is then considered in the legislative process by the European Parliament and the Council. In addition, the Commission is under an obligation prior to proposing legislative acts to consult widely.

To date, the system has been used three times. The first instance concerned a Commission proposal concerning the right to strike. In response to the 'yellow card', the Commission decided to drop the proposal. The second instance related to the Commission's proposal to establish a European Prosecutor's office to ensure EU-wide criminal law enforcement of fraud which specifically affects the financial interests of the Union. Despite the yellow card, the Commission decided to maintain the proposal. In its justification ('Communication on the review of the proposal for a Council Regulation on the establishment of the European Public Prosecutor's Office with regard to the principle of subsidiarity, in accordance with Protocol No 2' (COM(2013) 851 final)), the Commission pointed to a lack of continuity, equivalence and efficacy in enforcement action taken among Member States and to the absence of a common EU prosecution policy. On this basis, EU-level action adds significantly to the fight against financial crime. The third yellow card arose in 2016 in relation to the Commission's proposal to revise the 1996 Posted Workers Directive. So far, the 'orange card' (which arises when votes against the proposal reach the threshold of 28) has not been triggered.

The national parliaments participate in the Conference of Parliamentary Committees for Union Affairs of Parliaments of the European Union (COSAC). The most recent bi-annual report of COSAC (Twenty Fourth Bi-annual Report: Developments in the European Union Procedures and Practices Relevant to Parliamentary Scrutiny, 4 November 2015) discussed how to make the 'yellow card' procedure more effective. Notably, national parliaments requested an extension of the time period from eight weeks to twelve weeks and improvements to the Commission's responses to any reasoned opinions issued. Whether improvements can be effected without requiring Treaty amendment is the subject of debate.

The report also discussed the possibility of introducing a 'green card' (enhanced political dialogue) procedure. This was based on proposals by Danish Folketing at COSAC, and by the UK's House of Lords EU Committee's *Report on The Role of National Parliaments in the EU* (House of Lords European Union Committee, The Role of National Parliaments in the European Union, 9th Report of Session 2013–14, HL Paper 151, 24 March 2014). The Dutch Tweede Kamer also produced a report on the role of national parliaments. Although the reports differed in detail, there is a common theme: that the national parliaments should be permitted to make legislative suggestions to the Commission, thereby influencing the development of EU policy. The first such initiative concerned food waste and took the form of a letter dated 25 July 2015 from the House of Lords European Union Committee to the President of the Commission and signed by the chairpersons of 16 COSAC members. In the letter the signatories emphasised that this was not a challenge to the Commission's right of initiative nor a challenge to the role of the European Parliament as co-legislator (which itself only has a limited right of initiative under Article 225 TFEU), but an attempt to participate in the formulation of policy. The 24th COSAC Report supports the initiative though it is as yet unclear whether this mechanism will be formalised.

Prior to the UK's referendum on EU membership, the British government proposed the introduction of a 'red card' system to further strengthen the role of national parliaments by giving 'national parliaments the right to block legislation that need not be agreed at the European level' (Speech of William Hague, 31 May 2013). It proposed that a 55 per cent majority of national parliaments should be required for blocking legislation, and it could be used only in cases where an argument could be made that Member States would be better able to regulate individually (the 'subsidiarity principle'). Importantly, the proposal also made it clear that this 'red card' system would not apply to existing EU legislation. Implementing this proposal does not require Treaty amendment; the obligation is on the 'representatives of the Member States acting in their capacity as members of the Council' to 'discontinue the consideration of the draft legislative act in question unless the draft is amended to accommodate the concerns expressed in the reasoned opinions' (Decision of the Heads of State or

Government, meeting within the European Council, Concerning a New Settlement for the United Kingdom within the European Union, attached to the Conclusions of the European Council, 18 and 19 February 2016 at Annex A, para 3). Whether or not these changes would be in any way useful given the limited recourse to the yellow and orange cards, the changes will only take effect once the UK notifies the EU that the UK intends to remain a member of the EU. In the light of the referendum result, this is currently unlikely.

3.5.4 Principle of proportionality

The final element of subsidiarity is that contained in the third paragraph of Article 5. It states:

> Under the principle of proportionality, the content and form of Union action shall not exceed what is necessary to achieve the objectives of the Treaties.

This requirement, an expression of the proportionality principle which permeates EU law (see Chapter 6), may have an impact on the type of action proposed by the Union. As with subsidiarity itself, the Commission must justify the proportionality of any proposed measure. Rather than adopting an approach which prescribes the obligations of the Member States in minute detail, this would require the Union simply to provide the outline, leaving the Member States to fill in the detail.

3.6 Basis for Union action

As noted in Chapter 2, the three main institutions of the Union—the Commission, the Council and the European Parliament—are empowered to legislate (subject to review by the CJEU) on any of the matters within the framework. Many of the Treaty provisions, for example, the articles relating to free movement of goods and workers (Articles 30, 34 and 45 TFEU respectively) contain obligations that are sufficiently precise to be applicable as they stand (see further Chapter 5). Others provide for, and often require, further measures of implementation before they can take full legal effect. To enact legislation, the institutions must identify a provision in the Treaties which gives them power to act and which forms the legal basis for the legislation. Some of the provisions provide a very specific legal base. For example, Article 53 TFEU specifies that the institutions may issue directives for 'the mutual recognition of diplomas, certificates and other evidence of formal qualifications . . .' Other provisions, however, may provide for a much broader field of activity, such as Article 114 TFEU (see 3.6.1 and Chapter 16). Given that different Treaty bases may provide for different procedures for enacting legislation, the issue of appropriate Treaty base can give rise to dispute. Equally, there may be challenges as to whether the proposed action falls within the scope of the claimed Treaty base.

3.6.1 Broad provisions for action

3.6.1.1 Internal market clauses

Article 115 TFEU provides for the 'approximation' (ie harmonisation) of such laws as directly affect the establishment or functioning of the internal market by unanimous vote. Article 114 TFEU makes similar provision for measures which have as their object the establishing or functioning of the internal market, in most cases, by qualified majority vote (QMV) (see Chapter 16). Both these provisions are broad, and their precise extent and relationship to each other and to other Treaty provisions is sometimes open to discussion (see discussion of the *Tobacco Advertising Directive case* (*Germany v Parliament and Council* (case C-376/98)) at 16.4.1). Although these seem to have similar scope, in practice the Treaty base of choice is Article 114 TFEU, leaving the exceptional circumstances not covered by Article 114 TFEU to the more procedurally restrictive Article 115 TFEU.

3.6.1.2 Flexibility clause

Even where the institutions are not specifically empowered to act, Article 352 TFEU provides:

> If action by the Union should prove necessary, within the framework of the policies defined in the Treaties, to attain one of the objectives set out in the Treaties, and the Treaties have not provided the necessary powers, the Council, acting unanimously on a proposal from the Commission and after obtaining the consent of the European Parliament, shall adopt the appropriate measures. Where the measures in question are adopted by the Council in accordance with a special legislative procedure, it shall also act unanimously on a proposal from the Commission and after obtaining the consent of the European Parliament.

This blanket power, sometimes known as the 'flexibility clause', has been used as a basis for legislation on matters of regional or social policy (eg, equal treatment for men and women) which fell within the broad aims of the Union, as expressed in the preamble, but which were not spelt out specifically in the Treaty. Many of these matters have now been incorporated expressly into the TFEU by subsequent Treaty amendments. Although Article 352 TFEU is potentially wide, concerns about its use to extend Treaty competence by the back door are limited by the fact that the consent of all Member States to any proposed measure is required. This point does not, however, recognise that Article 352 TFEU permits the European Parliament a very limited role by comparison with the position it would have were its powers of competence to be expanded by formal Treaty amendment. Given the breadth of Articles 114–15 TFEU, recourse to the flexibility clause seems to have become less frequent. The expansion of express Union competence by various Treaties and the related political tensions (discussed at 3.2) render it less likely that Article 352 TFEU will be used as extensively as in the early years of the EU.

Lisbon amended the text of Article 352 TFEU to require that the European Commission must draw the attention of national parliaments to draft legislation based on this provision. Further, Lisbon amended the provision to extend the power of using the flexibility clause to objectives defined in either of the Treaties (rather than by reference to 'attaining, in the course of the operation of the common market, one of the objectives set out in the Treaties'), but it cannot be used either for circumventing any prohibition on harmonisation found in the Treaty or as a basis for attaining objectives pertaining to the CFSP.

3.6.2 Implied powers

The CJ has also determined that the Union has implied powers, so that when powers which are not specifically enumerated in the Treaty are required to achieve a Union goal, the Union is deemed to have the necessary powers. There are two possible formulations of this doctrine. The first is a narrow approach. It states that the existence of a power implies the existence of any other power that is reasonably necessary for the exercise of the original power. This was the approach taken by the CJ in *Fédération Charbonnière de Belgique v High Authority* (case 8/55). The second approach is wider. It was taken in *Germany v Commission* (cases 281, 283–5 and 287/85) where the powers of the Commission arising out of original Article 118 (which has been amended significantly and is now Article 153 TFEU) were the subject of dispute. The article, as then formulated, provided the Commission with a task—that of promoting close cooperation between Member States in the social field—but did not give the Commission any specific legislative powers. Germany therefore argued that the proposed legislative act of the Commission was outside the Treaty. The CJ commented that, to avoid rendering provisions such as the then Article 118 EEC totally ineffective, the powers necessary for carrying out the task must be inferred. This is a significant decision because there are many instances where the Commission has been allocated a task but not been given legislative power.

It is not just internally that the Court has deduced Union competence. Following *Commission v Council (European Road Transport Agreement)* (the *ERTA* case) (case 22/70) and *Opinion 1/76* it was thought that the Union would have implied powers to act in the international sphere in relation to matters with respect to which the Union has power to act within the Union under the TFEU. In addition, the *ERTA* case appeared to suggest that the competence of the Union, in this regard, was exclusive: Member States were precluded from acting. *ERTA* is now an old case, though Article 3(2) TEU (discussed at 3.4) was understood by some to be an attempt to codify this line of jurisprudence. Confirmation that the *ERTA* approach remains good law even after the changes introduced by Lisbon came in *Opinion 1/13 on the Hague Convention on Child Abduction* as regards the procedures to be adopted in relation to new accessions to the Convention. As such, it was the first decision on the meaning of Article 3(2) TEU.

Opinion on Hague Convention on Child Abduction

The Hague Convention dates back to 1980. At that time the scope of EU law did not extend to family matters and thus only EU Member States were signatories to it. Over the years, EU competence changed with the EU starting to adopt regulations in this field, notably Regulation 2201/2003 (the Brussels IIa Regulation) on recognition of judgments in matrimonial matters. Moreover, non-EU states wished to sign the Convention and it was this aspect that triggered the case. Member States had—as individual acts and not jointly through EU procedures—accepted accession of these additional states to the Convention. The Commission took the view that the matter fell within the exclusive competence of the Union under Article 3(2) TEU and that accession should be dealt with by a Council decision following a Commission proposal. The Commission requested an opinion from the CJ under Article 218(11) TFEU. The Court confirmed that—following an *ERTA*-style analysis—there was a risk that Regulation 2201/2003 would be affected by individual action. The Court concluded that:

> the exclusive competence of the EU encompasses the acceptance of the accession of a third State to the 1980 Hague Convention. [para 90]

3.7 Union acts

The legislative powers of the Union institutions are laid down in Article 288 TFEU:

> To exercise the Union's competences, the institutions shall adopt regulations, directives, decisions, recommendations and opinions.

Note that prior to Lisbon, the other two pillars of the Union used different legal instruments to give effect to policy decisions. For example, under CFSP there were references to common positions and joint actions; under the former JHA we saw not only common positions but also framework decisions and conventions. Lisbon abolished the pillar system so in principle the types of legal act in use will be common to all areas of policy.

The measures in Article 288 TFEU, described as 'acts', are defined as follows:

> A regulation shall have general application. It shall be binding in its entirety and directly applicable in all Member States.
>   A directive shall be binding, as to the result to be achieved, upon each Member State to which it is addressed, but shall leave to the national authorities the choice of form and methods.
>   A decision shall be binding in its entirety upon those to whom it is addressed.
>   Recommendations and opinions shall have no binding force.

There is a division between binding and non-binding acts. Only the first three are binding. Non-binding acts are a form of soft law. Article 288 TFEU is open to criticism because, beyond this basic division, it does not provide a clear definition of each of the types of act. Nor does it distinguish between legislation and administrative acts, which most Member States' legal systems do. To a certain extent, it has fallen to the CJEU to fill in some of the detail.

3.7.1 Regulations

The principal feature of a regulation is its general application: it is a normative rather than an individual act, designed to apply to situations in the abstract. The Court has held that 'the Regulation, being of an essentially normative character, is applicable not to a limited identifiable number of persons but rather to categories of persons envisaged both in the abstract and as a whole' (*Conféderation Nationale des Producteurs de Fruits et Légumes v Council* (cases 16 and 17/62)). Since it is 'binding in its entirety and directly applicable in all Member States' it does not require further implementation to take effect. It may give rise to rights and obligations for states and individuals as it stands. Indeed, it has been held (*Leonesio v Ministero dell' Agricoltura e delle Foreste* (case 93/71)) that the rights bestowed by a regulation cannot be subjected, at the national level, to implementing provisions diverging from those laid down by the regulation itself (see further 5.2.4).

3.7.2 Directives

A directive is binding 'as to the result to be achieved, upon each Member State to which it is addressed', but allows Member States a discretion as to the form and method of implementation. Thus it is a measure intended to be addressed to, and binding on states, either individually or collectively.

3.7.3 Decisions

A decision is an individual act designed to be addressed to a specified person or persons. As a 'binding' act it has the force of law and does not therefore require implementation in order to take effect. Decisions may be addressed to states or individuals.

3.7.4 Recommendations and opinions

Since they have no binding force, they are ineffective in law, although clearly of persuasive authority (see *Grimaldi v Fonds des Maladies Professionnelles* (case C-322/88) noted in Chapter 5).

3.7.5 Acts *sui generis*

Article 288 TFEU does not provide an exhaustive list of legal acts and the Court has recognised acts not identified by Article 288 TFEU. These are usually described as *sui generis* acts and include rules relating to the internal management of the Union, such as rules of procedure. Article 295 TFEU provides for the existence of interinstitutional agreements (IIA), which may be of a binding nature.

3.7.6 **Boundary between different types of act**

The line between these acts is not as clear-cut as Article 288 TFEU would suggest. It was held in *Confédération Nationale des Producteurs de Fruits et Légumes* that the true nature of an act is determined not by its form but by its content and object. The label attached to the measure is not decisive, and in the case of *International Fruit Co NV v Commission (No 1)* (cases 41–4/70) what was termed a regulation was found to comprise a 'bundle of decisions'. Measures have been found to be hybrid—to contain some parts in the nature of a regulation, and other parts in the nature of decisions (see Advocate-General Warner's submissions in *NTN Toyo Bearing Co Ltd v Council* (case 113/77)). In ascertaining the true nature of the act, the essential distinction seems to be between a regulation, which is normative, applicable not to a limited identifiable number of designees but rather to categories of persons envisaged both in the abstract and as a whole, and a decision, which concerns designated persons individually (*Confédération Nationale des Producteurs de Fruits et Légumes*). The nature of a directive has not been called into question, but considerable controversy has arisen over its effects. These will be discussed in Chapter 5.

3.7.7 **Publication**

With regard to publication, Article 297 TFEU provides:

1. Legislative acts adopted under the ordinary legislative procedure shall be signed by the President of the European Parliament and by the President of the Council.
   Legislative acts adopted under a special legislative procedure shall be signed by the President of the institution which adopted them.
   Legislative acts shall be published in the Official Journal of the European Union. They shall enter into force on the date specified in them or, in the absence thereof, on the twentieth day following that of their publication;

2. Non-legislative acts adopted in the form of regulations, directives or decisions, when the latter do not specify to whom they are addressed, shall be signed by the President of the institution which adopted them.
   Regulations and directives which are addressed to all Member States, as well as decisions which do not specify to whom they are addressed, shall be published in the Official Journal of the European Union. They shall enter into force on the date specified in them or, in the absence thereof, on the twentieth day following that of their publication.
   Other directives, and decisions which specify to whom they are addressed, shall be notified to those to whom they are addressed and shall take effect upon such notification.

3.7.8 **Soft law**

In addition to the above types of law specified in Article 288 TFEU, the Commission has used new ways of developing policy, for example, by issuing guidelines (eg, in the field of competition—see Chapter 29). In the area of competition law, the Commission has issued notices. A notice provides guidance on the Commission's policy in particular fields but is non-binding. Therein lies the difficulty: while these documents are often of great importance and are relied on by individuals, as non-binding instruments they may not be open to challenge before the GC (see Chapter 12). Their creation is informal, ad hoc and not subject to the rules laid down in the Treaty for the enactment of other forms of Union legislation. It is difficult to hold the policymakers to account and this has further implications for democracy.

Despite possible problems with informal approaches to lawmaking, a further move towards the use of soft-law methods can be seen following the conclusions of the Lisbon Council Summit (European Council 2002). There the European Council formally established its Open Method of Coordination (OMC). This is a method of rule-making which allows for the agreement of policy guidelines through exchanges of information on best practice, benchmarking, monitoring, target-setting and peer review. This approach potentially allows discretion on best practice to be exercised by national regulatory bodies. It has the disadvantage of other soft-law methods: OMC allows the democratic structures of the European Parliament to be bypassed, increasing concerns about any democratic deficit in policymaking.

Another change in the approach to regulation, perhaps in line with concerns about proportionality, is the move towards co-regulation and self-regulation found in the institutions' documents on better governance. In its White Paper on European Governance, (COM(2001) 428), the Commission suggested that '[t]he Union must renew the Community method by following a less top-down approach and complementing its policy tools more effectively with non-legislative instruments'. The IIA on Better Law-Making (16 December 2003) set out, for the first time, the general framework for the use of co-regulation and self-regulation within the EU. Co-regulation and self-regulation both involve private actors in (informal) rule-setting, and in this they can be distinguished from OMC which involves public actors. The difference between co- and self-regulation is that co-regulation envisages some form of legislative framework. This can be seen in the definition of co-regulation given in the IIA on Better Law-Making (para 18):

> . . . the mechanism whereby a *[Union] legislative act* entrusts the attainment of the objectives defined by *the legislative authority* to parties which are recognised in the field (such as economic operators, the social partners, non-governmental organisations, or associations).

It implies that the European legislature first sets the essential legal framework, that the stakeholders or parties concerned then fill in the details and that public authorities, often the Commission, monitor the outcome. Co-regulation may also envisage that these rules may be validated in some way by public authorities. By contrast, self-regulation does not pre-suppose such legislative activity. It is defined in the same document (para 22) as:

> . . . the possibility for economic operators, the social partners, non-governmental organisations or associations to adopt *amongst themselves* and for themselves common guidelines at European level (particularly codes of practice or sectoral agreements).

The IIA on Better Law-Making was updated in 2016. While these forms of rule-making may fit well with a system of multi-level governance and some perspectives on subsidiarity, this approach also raises concerns about who is making decisions about standards, on what basis and in whose interests.

3.7.9 **Acts under the CFSP**

As noted in Chapter 1, the approach under the CFSP is much more intergovernmental than in other policy areas.

The European Council and the Council are the key players in CFSP. The role of the European Council is to identify the principles and general guidelines for the approach to be adopted in regard to relevant policies. The Council takes the decisions for defining and implementing the policy based on those guidelines (Article 26 TEU). The role of the other institutions is limited, although the 'double-hatted Commissioner' (the High Representative of the Union for Foreign Affairs and Security Policy) has a role in ensuring the unity and effectiveness of Union policy in this area. Article 36 TEU provides that the High Representative shall consult the European Parliament, and, indeed, take its views into consideration (see Chapter 2). The European Parliament may also ask questions or make recommendations. It has no legal power to change the outcome of Council choices, though. Decisions, according to Article 31 TEU, are to be taken by the European Council and the Council, acting unanimously.

The mechanisms for pursuing the objectives of the CFSP are found in Article 25 which, in addition to noting the guidelines, provides that the Union shall 'adopt decisions'; this change in text introduced by Lisbon replaces a list of other forms of action (eg, common positions), the status of which was never clear. Note, however, that a decision by Council under CFSP is not a 'legislative act' for the purposes of Article 289 TFEU, though it is—obviously—a Union legal act.

The boundary between the pillars has never been clear-cut. Given the different powers of the various institutions under the CFSP and the other policy areas in the TFEU, there has sometimes been dispute as to the appropriate basis for Union action. While the CJ's jurisdiction is limited with regard to CFSP, it does have the power to determine the boundary between CFSP and the TFEU. In determining the boundaries between the pillars under the old structure, the CJ gave a broad interpretation to the needs of the TFEU (*Commission v Council (moratorium on small arms)* (case C-91/05)). Article 40 TEU (which replaces the former provision, Article 47 TEU) specifies that:

> The implementation of the common foreign and security policy shall not affect the application of the procedures and the extent of the powers of the institutions laid down by the Treaties for the exercise of the Union competences referred to in Articles 3 to 6 of the Treaty on the Functioning of the European Union.
>
> Similarly, the implementation of the policies listed in those Articles shall not affect the application of the procedures and the extent of the powers of the institutions laid down by the Treaties for the exercise of the Union competences under this Chapter.

The CJ has had occasion to review the scope of CFSP on a number of occasions, for example in *Somali pirates II*.

Somali Pirates II

The EU established a mission, known as Operation Atalanta, to secure sea lanes from piracy. It was launched in 2008 (Joint Action 2008/851/CFSP on a European Union military operation to contribute to the deterrence, prevention and repression of acts of piracy and armed robbery off the Somali coast [2008] OJ L301/33 as amended by Council Decision 2012/174/CFSP ([2012] OJ L89/69)) and based on the following provisions: Article 14 TEU; the third paragraph of Article 25 TEU; and Article 28(3) TEU. The mission's main activity was capturing pirates, but an ancillary question related to where the pirates who were caught should be tried and what their rights should be. There was a concern about standards in the Somali courts, although the Member States did not want to bring the pirates before their own courts. The solution, as permitted under the United Nations Convention on the Law of the Sea, was to ensure that trials took place in a number of states in the region but subject to human rights guarantees. That solution necessitated the negotiation of an agreement with the relevant third states (known as Transfer Agreements). The Council wrote to the European Parliament, informing it that the High Representative had been authorised, pursuant to Article 37 TEU, to open negotiations regarding Transfer Agreements with the Republics of Mauritius, Mozambique, South Africa, Tanzania and Uganda. Council decisions were subsequently adopted in relation to each Transfer Agreement and the Parliament notified.

The Parliament brought an action to annul the decision underpinning the signing of the Transfer Agreement, challenging the legal base used because the Transfer Agreement did not relate 'exclusively' to the CFSP in the meaning of Article 218(6). The legal base—according to the Parliament—should have been Article 37 TEU but also Articles 82 and 87 TFEU. This would have resulted in the Parliament having a greater role in the process. The Parliament's action was unsuccessful.

The approach in *Somali pirates II* illustrates a number of points. First, that Article 40 TEU places the CFSP and other areas of EU external action on an equal footing. Secondly, that the Court will use a 'centre of gravity approach' as it has done in the context of other boundary disputes (see, eg, *Commission v Council* (*titanium dioxide*) (case C-300/89)). So, the choice of the legal basis, including one adopted in order to conclude an international agreement, rests on objective factors amenable to judicial review, including the aim and content of the measure. In assessing the situation here, the Court emphasised the ancillary purpose of the Council decision concluding the Transfer Agreement to the overarching objective of strengthening the fight against piracy (paras 45–55). Thus the underpinning framework and rationale for the Decision was that of the CFSP.

3.8 Lawmaking process

As we have seen in Chapter 2, the legislative process involves three out of the five institutions: the Commission as initiator, the Council and the European Parliament. The relative importance of the Parliament's role varies according to the nature of the legislation and procedure used. The two main variables relate to the voting in Council (whether unanimity or QMV is used—see 2.5.4) and the degree to which the Parliament is involved (see 2.3.3). The role of the Parliament has increased in significance through the successive changes in rules. This point is reflected by the fact that Article 289 TFEU now identifies two types of legislative procedure: the ordinary legislative procedure, in which the Parliament is effectively a co-legislator, and special legislative procedures, where the rules may vary. In the majority of cases, as its name suggests, the procedure that will be used is the ordinary legislative procedure.

In addition to the legislative acts, which are defined in Article 289(3) TFEU as those acts made by these two legislative procedures, the Treaties provide for the possibility of other acts being adopted by different procedures. The resulting act is a 'legal act', not a 'legislative act' within Article 289(3) TFEU. The significance of the distinction between a legal act and a legislative act is that some provisions of the Treaties apply only to legislative acts. For example, the rule that the Council will meet in public applies only to the discussions relating to legislative acts. Article 290 TFEU allows the incorporation of a power of delegation in relation to legislative acts only (see 3.8.4).

As noted in 3.2, the institutions can only act within the scope of the powers conferred on them. Union acts must make their legal basis within the Treaty clear. They must 'state the reasons on which they are based and shall refer to any proposals or opinions which were required to be obtained pursuant to this Treaty' (Article 296 TFEU). This is done in the preamble to the legislation. It is an essential procedural requirement. Any act that does not comply will be subject to annulment (see Chapter 12, Article 263 TFEU and Chapter 10, Article 267 TFEU). Further, the freedom of the institutions to legislate is now counterbalanced by the notion of subsidiarity (Article 5 TEU, see 3.5).

According to the protocol on subsidiarity annexed to the Lisbon Treaty, draft legislative acts should contain a detailed statement making it possible to appraise compliance with the principles of subsidiarity and proportionality. Acts will further be reviewed by national parliaments.

3.8.1 Ordinary legislative procedure

This procedure was originally called the co-decision procedure. Introduced by the Maastricht Treaty and amended by the ToA, and it improved the bargaining power of Parliament. Here, Parliament, as with the cooperation procedure, has two opportunities to review the proposal. The procedure is now set out in Article 294 TFEU. At its simplest, both institutions can adopt the Commission's proposal unamended (see Figure 3.1). If Parliament approves the common position, the act is adopted (usually by QMV in the Council, see 2.5.4). The TFEU does not expressly deal with the possibility of the Parliament rejecting a proposal at this stage, though the Parliament's internal rules envisage that possibility. In such a case, the Parliament would ask the Commission to withdraw its proposal, though the Commission may refuse to do so.

The Parliament may suggest amendments to a proposal. The document would then be re-examined by the Commission, which may choose to include or reject any or all of the Parliament's amendments in a new draft. The Council finalises its position at first reading on the basis of the Commission's proposal. It may accept the new form of document acting by qualified majority (see Figure 3.2); if it does not act with the support of the Commission, unanimity is required. It is thus easier for the Council to adopt the suggestions of the Parliament than to agree its own proposals. If it does not accept the proposal it will adopt a position, which is then sent to the Parliament for consideration (Article 294(5) TFEU). At its second reading, the Parliament may accept, reject or propose amendments. In the case of amendments, these plus a Commission opinion come before the Council for its second reading.

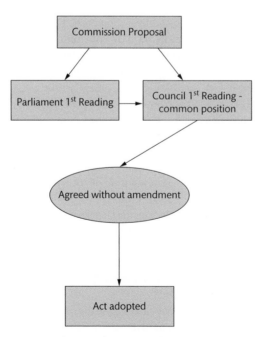

Figure 3.1 Adoption of Commission's proposal unamended

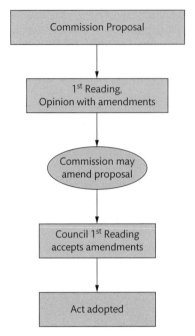

Figure 3.2 Adoption following Parliamentary amendment

If the Council does not adopt the new form of the proposal then the Conciliation Committee, made up of the members of the Council or their representatives and an equal number of representatives of the Parliament, meets to try to reach a compromise (see Figure 3.3) (Article 294(8)(b) TFEU). If the Conciliation Committee approves a joint text, it is then sent to the Council and the Parliament for a third reading (Article 294(13) TFEU). Both institutions must approve the text for it to be adopted; either (or both) may reject it. This is more problematic for the European Parliament than the Council, as the representatives in the Conciliation Committee may not be representative of the Parliament as a whole.

Although the Council's common position may be affirmed, ultimately Parliament may veto a piece of legislation. It is also more difficult to ignore the Commission's views on the form of the amended proposal; if it wishes so to do, the Council must act unanimously.

Co-decision as originally introduced by Maastricht was a long-winded and complex procedure. The amendments introduced by the ToA went some way to improving this situation. The procedure was streamlined by the ToA and in such a way as to tilt the balance of power a little more in the direction of the Parliament. Prior to the ToA, in the event of the Parliament rejecting the Council's common position entirely at its second reading, the Conciliation Committee was convened at that stage to try to reach a solution. Now, in such an event, the act shall be deemed not to be adopted. The power of the Council to reaffirm its common position in the absence of agreement in the Conciliation Committee (albeit subject to rejection by Parliament), originally granted under TEU, was removed by the ToA. If the institutions fail to reach an agreement through the Conciliation Committee, the proposed legislation will fall.

Following Lisbon, there are no longer any cases where the ordinary legislative procedure is combined with unanimity in Council: QMV is used (see 2.5.4). There are a few areas—criminal law and social security for migrants—where an individual Member State can utilise the 'emergency brake' procedures, which will result in an attempt to resolve the issue in the European Council. Lisbon extends the use of the ordinary legislative procedure to some areas which were originally in the JHA pillar (including the majority of the criminal law and policing measures) but also to key policies such as agriculture, fisheries and external trade.

The ordinary legislative procedure now seems to have given the Parliament real power within the legislative process, and in this it is not necessarily the impact of the use of the veto that is important,

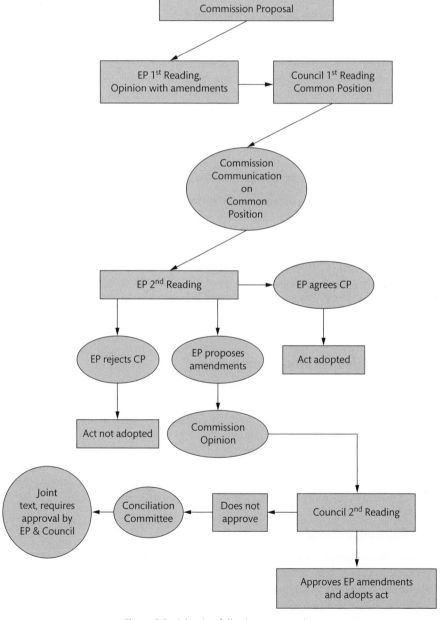

Figure 3.3 Adoption following compromise

but the threat of the use of the veto. In being able to introduce amendments to the draft legislation, the Parliament has to some degree an agenda-setting role too; these amendments can also form part of the basis of discussions in the Conciliation Committee.

To improve effectiveness of the legislative process, the institutions participate in 'trilogues'. These are meetings which occur outside the formal Treaty provisions in which the three institutions try to negotiate an acceptable compromise on the text of a legislative proposal before the Commission proposes a redraft. This occurred, for example, in the process of amending the Television without Frontiers Directive for the second time (now, the Audiovisual Media Services Directive (Directive 2010/13 ([2010] OJ L95/1)) (codified version)). Nonetheless, the procedure is not without its critics. Even after amendment, the procedure remains complex. The procedure, especially when the Conciliation Committee system is activated, adds to the length and complexity of the legislative process. The proceedings of neither the trilogue meetings nor the Conciliation Committee are open to the public, which leads to questions as to how transparent and democratic the process actually is.

The European Ombudsman adopted a decision requesting changes to the trilogues following a strategic inquiry into their transparency (OI/8/2015/JAS), in particular suggesting that more documentation should be made public. The 2016 IIA on Better Law-Making, includes a strong commitment to legislative transparency but does not cover all the suggestions made by the Ombudsman; it remains to be seen how the institutions will respond.

3.8.2 Special legislative procedures: consultation procedure

This procedure was the original procedure found in the Treaty of Rome. It now arises as part of the special legislative procedure mentioned in Article 289(2) TFEU. Until the SEA, consultation was the usual form of legislative process. It is still used in some areas. An example of these areas is Article 89 TFEU, which deals with cross-border police operations, and economic and monetary policy (Articles 126(13), 129(4) TFEU). Consultation now seems to be the exception, rather than the rule.

The consultation procedures require the Council to consult the European Parliament before it adopts an act. Parliament's views must be considered but have no binding effect on the Council (see *Roquette Frères* discussed in Chapter 2). Indeed, the Council do not need to give any reasons for its disregard of the Parliament's views.

3.8.3 Special legislative procedures: assent

The assent procedure was also introduced by the SEA. As the name suggests, a measure to be adopted by the assent procedure may only be so adopted if the European Parliament gives its consent. While the Parliament cannot amend the proposal, this procedure gives the Parliament considerable power. It is used only in limited circumstances such as external relations (Article 218(6)(a) TFEU), the establishment of the European Public Prosecutor's Office (Article 68(1) TFEU), and action against discrimination under Article 19(1) TFEU. The disadvantage with the assent procedure is that there is no mechanism by which the Council and Parliament might resolve their differences: the only option for Parliament is to agree or block the proposal entirely.

3.8.4 Delegated and implementing acts

The Treaties always have provided for the possibility of the Commission making acts to implement Union policy. The pre-Lisbon comitology regime referred to the process whereby the Commission's freedom to implement Union policies was supervised by expert committees, whose members were appointed by the Council (formerly based on Article 202 EC). These committees often had the power to block the proposed Commission measure and to refer the matter to the Council.

While giving rise to some difficulties, the CJ confirmed at an early stage that such delegation to a committee is permissible, provided the matter dealt with by the committee was one of implementation rather than determining general policy (*Einfuhr-und Vorratsstelle für Getreide und Futtermittel v Köster* (case 25/70)), a boundary that is sometimes a little hard to determine. Many legal systems allow the delegation of powers to prevent the entire legislative process from being clogged up with matters of detail; such delegation also permits issues to be dealt with by experts. It is important to note that members of the committees of national experts see themselves as experts and not as national representatives. This can bring its own problems, as science and its interpretation is not neutral, notwithstanding claims of scientific objectivity. Within the Union another benefit in the system can be identified: Member States have an interest in overseeing rule-making for the purposes of implementing policy, as they are responsible for applying the resulting rules within their respective jurisdictions.

There were concerns about comitology committees; in particular, that Union practice is not transparent and was problematic from a democratic perspective. The House of Lords noted:

> The fact that these committees exist is fairly well-known. But who sits on them, when they meet, how they work and what they decide is something of a mystery, except to insiders, assiduous Brussels watchers and a few academics and students [House of Lords Select Committee, 1999].

One problem was that there was no complete list of the committees and their members, and the procedures for appointing the committees were complex, incoherent and opaque. Further, the rights of the European Parliament as co-legislator could be undermined if key decision-making is shifted from primary legislation to a delegated system. Furthermore, there was no process of scrutiny either at EU or national level for appointment to the committees.

Some of the difficulties about transparency and access were alleviated by reforms in 1999 which, inter alia, listed the committees allowed for greater involvement by the European Parliament and provided that comitology committees were subject to the right of access to documents. The 1999 Comitology Decision (Council Decision 1999/468), which was revised in 2006, provided for four types of comitology procedure. In particular, it introduced the 'regulatory procedure with scrutiny' procedure, which gave the Parliament better oversight and a right of veto over the Commission implementing measures based on acts enacted jointly by the Parliament and the Council. Post-Lisbon, comitology has effectively been divided into two. Article 290 TFEU, which introduces a procedure for 'delegated acts', deals with the old 'regulatory procedure with scrutiny matters'. Article 291 TFEU introduces the implementing powers procedure, which effectively deals with the rest.

As a result of this change, the Comitology Decision has been replaced by a new regulation (Regulation 182/2011 ([2011] OJ L 55/13)) to implement Article 291 TFEU. It provides that committees supervising the Commission's use of *implementing powers* operate on one of two types of procedure: an advisory procedure (Article 4 Regulation 182/2011) or an examination procedure (Article 5 Regulation 182/2011). The examination procedure gives more power to the committee to block a Commission measure, though the Commission may appeal against an adverse ruling. It will apply in fields such as agriculture, fisheries, environment, health, trade and taxation. As regards the advisory procedure (which is the same as under the 2006 version of the Comitology Decision), the Commission has the obligation to take utmost account of the committee's views without being bound by them. The new Regulation confers on both the Council and the Parliament a right of scrutiny, so that either institution may inform the Commission that it has exceeded its powers.

As noted, Article 290 TFEU introduces a new power for 'delegated acts'. It provides:

> A legislative act may delegate to the Commission the power to adopt non-legislative acts of general application to supplement or amend certain non-essential elements of the legislative act.

Article 290 TFEU does not require implementing rules. There is no general framework providing the terms on which a legislative act may delegate power to the Commission so legislators will be free to set the objectives, scope, duration and the conditions to which the delegation is subject each time a legislative act delegates power to the Commission. To allow some control over the use of this provision Article 290(2) TFEU provides that the delegation may be subject to its revocation by either the Parliament or the Council, or the delegated act may be subject to a 'negative assent', that is, only where the Parliament does not object. Note that in the context of delegated acts, and by contrast to the former comitology procedure, there is no requirement that the Commission consult the Member States' representatives; there is no power for those representatives to block a proposed Commission delegated act. Nonetheless, it seems that the Commission intends to consult on draft delegated acts (see, eg, Delegated Act on the Detailed Rules for A Unique Identifier for Medicinal Products for Human Use, and Its Verification, based on Directive 2011/62 ([2011] OJ L174/ 74)). Given that the delegating act and implementing act are subject to different levels of oversight, and constitute two mutually exclusive groups of act, it may well be that the boundary between them will become the subject of litigation. To date the CJ has not developed the definitions of the two types of act nor the distinctions between them. It has however suggested that the level of review as to whether the right sort of act has been selected is that of 'manifest errors of assessment' (*Commission v Parliament and Council* (*biocides*) (case C-427/12)).

3.8.5 Enhanced cooperation

As noted in Chapter 1, the ToA introduced provisions allowing for 'closer cooperation' between some but not all Member States in areas covered by the Treaties, with the exception of areas of exclusive Union competence (Article 20 TEU). There are also specific rules for CFSP (Article 329 TFEU). Essentially, this allows the agreement of secondary legislation but which has a limited ambit in terms of the Member States bound (Article 20(4) TEU); any measures agreed under this procedure do not form part of the *acquis* and therefore do not have to be accepted as such by candidate countries. The first example of the enhanced cooperation procedure being used was in the Council Decision of 12 July 2010 authorising enhanced cooperation in the area of the law applicable to divorce and legal separation (see Council Regulation (EU) No 1259/2010 implementing enhanced cooperation in the area of the law applicable to divorce and legal separation ([2010] OJ L189/12)).

The enhanced cooperation procedure involves a request by one (or more) Member States to the Commission to take action. The Commission will assess the request and it may submit a proposal to the Council. If the Commission decides not to present a proposal, it will explain its reasons to the Member States concerned (Article 329(1) TFEU). The second paragraph of Article 329(1) TFEU specifies that, following the presentation of a proposal by the Commission, the decision whether to authorise the enhanced cooperation is that of the Council after obtaining the consent of the European Parliament. Once a proposal has been put forward, all Member States may participate in the Council's deliberations, but those participating in enhanced cooperation take part in the vote (Article 20(3) TEU; Article 330 TFEU).

There are conditions pertaining to the use of the enhanced cooperation procedure. At least nine Member States must participate in the cooperation, and the procedure can only be used as a last resort, when 'the objectives of such cooperation cannot be attained within a reasonable period by the Union as a whole' (Article 20(2) TEU). Even then, cooperation must be open at any time to all Member States (Article 328 TFEU). Further, Article 20(1) TEU requires that enhanced cooperation must 'aim to further the objectives of the Union, protect its interests and reinforce its integration process'. To similar effect, not only must cooperation comply with Union law, but Article 326 TFEU specifies that:

> cooperation shall not undermine the internal market or economic, social and territorial cohesion. It shall not constitute a barrier to or discrimination in trade between Member States, nor shall it distort competition between them.

The competences, rights and obligations of those Member States which do not participate in the enhanced cooperation must also be respected (Article 327 TFEU). Bearing in mind that the effect of the enhanced cooperation procedure is to allow a two-speed EU on a particular topic, these conditions would always raise difficult questions. They were examined in *Italy v Council* (case C-295/11) and *Spain v Council* (case C-274/11) regarding the unitary patent.

Unitary Patents Cases

Attempts to create a common patent system within the normal EU system (Article 118 TFEU) had failed. Twelve Member States then requested the use of the enhanced cooperation procedure to create a unitary patent system in the EU, and the European Parliament and the Council both agreed. The proposal was that patents would be examined and granted in one of the official languages of the European Patent Office—English, French or German—and the patent would be enforceable within all participating countries. All the Member States agreed to participate, apart from Spain and Italy, which were unhappy that their respective languages would not be official languages in the proposed system. Both of these countries filed actions for annulment of the Council decision which authorised the use of enhanced cooperation, arguing in slightly different terms that the conditions set down in the Treaty for the use of enhanced cooperation were not met.

The Italian and Spanish governments put forward a number of arguments, some of which referred to the specificities of the patent system. The remaining arguments dealt with conditions set down in the Treaty and an argument that this case involved a misuse of powers, as the enhanced cooperation procedure was being used to avoid limitations in the TFEU on rules relating to language (which required unanimity). In this there are parallels to concerns raised in the cases on the appropriate Treaty base to be used for certain legislation.

The CJ started by rejecting the argument based on misuse of power. This doctrine requires an evidenced intent to evade Treaty procedures (para 33). On this basis, the use of the enhanced cooperation procedure when negotiations have been unsuccessful:

> does not amount to misuse of powers, but rather, having regard to its being impossible to reach common arrangements for the whole Union within a reasonable period, contributes to the process of integration (para 37).

The CJ held that the 'last resort' criterion must be understood in the light of the objectives of enhanced cooperation in Article 20(1) TEU, including the reinforcement of its integration process. So, 'only those situations in which it is impossible to adopt such legislation in the foreseeable future' justify the use of the procedure (para 50). In the Court's view, its duty is to review whether the Council 'carefully and impartially assessed the relevant factors leading to its decision and gave adequate reasons for its conclusions' (para 54).

The challenge based on the measure's impact on the internal market was dismissed, as any impact could only be determined once the measure authorised by the enhanced cooperation procedure had itself been agreed. This puts non-participating Member States in the position of having to mount two legal challenges if they disagree with the use of enhanced cooperation: one relating to the decision to use enhanced cooperation (as here); and one relating to the measure adopted as a result of the use of the enhanced cooperation procedure. The CJ's approach leaves questions relating to the 'internal market' criterion unresolved.

The final question in the *Unitary Patents Cases* concerned the rights of non-participating Member States. This is a difficult issue as the nature of enhanced cooperation itself is to mean non-participating states will not participate in the discussions on the relevant topic and therefore might find the outcome less to their liking than if they had participated. It means that later participation results in acquiescing to those decisions. Unsurprisingly, the CJ rejected the Spanish and Italian claims:

> While it is, admittedly, essential for enhanced cooperation not to lead to the adoption of measures that might prevent the non-participating Member States from exercising their competences and rights or shouldering their obligations, it is, in contrast, permissible for those taking part in this cooperation to prescribe rules with which those non-participating States would not agree if they did take part in it (para 82).

The CJ has reached a balanced conclusion in this judgment; a narrow interpretation of the provisions would have left the enhanced cooperation procedure unusable in real terms. Nonetheless, its reasoning in para 82 did not adequately address the question of whether it would really be possible for a such a state subsequently to agree to measures. Spain initiated such a second set of proceedings: *Spain v European Parliament and Council* (case C-146/13). They were unsuccessful.

3.8.6 'Passerelle' provisions and Treaty amendment

3.8.6.1 Passerelle clauses

A passerelle provision is one which allows the legislative process to be changed without recourse to formal Treaty amendment. Usually, the passerelle will operate to change the relevant legislative process from special legislative processes and unanimity to ordinary legislative process using QMV. There are two types of passerelle clause:

- specific clauses relating to a particular provision in the Treaties;
- a general clause applying to all European policies.

There are six specific passerelle clauses, comprising:

- judicial cooperation concerning family law with cross-border implications (Article 81(3) TFEU);
- social affairs, with regard to areas currently governed by a special legislative procedure (Article 153(2)(b) TFEU);
- environmental issues (measures with a fiscal aspect, those affecting town planning and energy policy) (Article 192(2) TFEU);

- the multiannual financial framework (Article 312(2) TFEU); provides for a move to QMV but not for the use of ordinary legislative procedure;

- reinforced cooperation in areas governed by unanimity or by a special legislative procedure;

- common foreign and security policy (Article 31(3) TEU).

Where the change involves a move from the use of a special legislative procedure to the ordinary legislative procedure, the European Parliament will be consulted; where there is a change to the voting procedures in Council from unanimity to QMV, the Council will make this decision unanimously, without consulting Parliament.

The general passerelle clause was introduced by Lisbon and is found at Article 48(7) TEU. It allows for the change from unanimity to QMV in relation to the TFEU and Title V TEU and for the change from use of special legislative procedure to the use of ordinary legislative procedure within the TFEU. The decision will be taken by the European Council acting unanimously, after obtaining the consent of the European Parliament. Any such decision must be notified to the national parliaments, which may oppose such a decision. This involvement of the national parliaments may be a response to concerns about the 'competence creep' of the EU.

3.8.6.2 Revision of the Treaties

The general passerelle clause is effectively a procedure for revising the Treaties and is one of two such simplified revision procedures. Article 48(6) TEU contains the other procedure. It allows for revisions to provisions in Part Three of the TFEU relating to the internal policies and action of the EU. Again, the decision to rely on the revision procedure will be made unanimously by the European Council, after consulting the European Parliament and the Commission (and the European Central Bank (ECB) as regards monetary policy). Any such decision must be approved by each of the Member States in accordance with their respective constitutional requirements. Significantly, the provision specifies in its third paragraph that any such decision 'shall not increase the competences conferred on the Union', reflecting concerns about balance of competence between the EU and the Member States seen in Chapter 1 and 3.4 and 3.5.

The remainder of Article 48 TEU deals with the 'ordinary revision procedure', which, prior to Lisbon, was the only procedure for revising the Treaties generally. The process is designed to provide for more significant Treaty amendment than the simplified procedures already discussed, such as changes to increase the competences conferred on the Union. The Lisbon Treaty changed the process aiming to make the system more democratic by normally requiring the convening of a Convention to discuss amendments to the Treaties (Article 48(3) TEU). Another change is the awarding of a right of initiative in this regard to the European Parliament (Article 48(2) TEU).

3.8.6.3 Brake and accelerator clauses

In some sensitive policy areas, in order to get agreement that the ordinary legislative procedure might be used, the Member States agreed the insertion of 'brake clauses'. The areas in which the brake clause may operate are:

- the coordination of social security systems for migrant workers (Article 48 TFEU, para 2);

- judicial cooperation in criminal matters (Article 82(3) TFEU);

- establishment of common rules for certain criminal offences (Article 83(3) TFEU).

The brake clause provides that where a proposed piece of legislation, in the opinion of a Member State, threatens either its social security system or its criminal justice system (depending on the legislation proposed), the concerned Member State may bring the matter to the European Council. As a result, the legislative procedure is suspended and the European Council may:

- either send the draft back to the Council, in which case the legislative process using the ordinary legislative procedure continues, but taking into account the observations made; or

- stop the procedure permanently and request a new proposal from the Commission, if appropriate.

The use of the brake procedure may mean that other Member States are prevented from proceeding with a measure. As regards Articles 82 and 83 TFEU, in such a situation, the enhanced co-operation procedure (discussed in 3.8.5) is simplified by the accelerator procedure, provided the requisite number of states agrees to the proposal.

Additionally, the accelerator procedure is applicable to police cooperation (Article 87(3) TFEU) and to the creation of a European Public Prosecutor's Office (Article 86(1) TFEU).

3.9 Problems in the lawmaking process—democracy, transparency and efficiency

Prior to the 1996 IGC leading to the ToA, a reflection group was established to consider the issues that needed to be addressed. Its reports revealed that the central issues which the 1996 IGC had to tackle were democracy, transparency and, as already discussed in Chapter 2, efficiency. We will look mainly at the first two of these issues, identifying the problem as presented at the 1996 IGC, and then assessing what not only the ToA but also subsequent amending Treaties have done to improve the position.

3.9.1 Democracy

The EU decision-making process has often been criticised for its lack of democratic legitimacy. This is frequently referred to as the 'democratic deficit'. Before we go on to look at some specific issues, some have suggested that this criticism is misplaced. Critics of the 'democratic deficit argument' propose that the European constitutional settlement is focused on the limited nature of the EU powers both in terms of the type of power exercised and the salience of those powers.

The first aspect concerns the argument that the EU policies are focused on regulatory aspects of policy, which are efficiency-enhancing and therefore wealth-creating, rather than redistributive. Greater legitimacy is required for the redistributive policies because in redistribution one group loses out to the benefit of another; with efficiency-enhancing policies, in theory, everyone benefits. This gives efficiency-enhancing policies 'output legitimacy', that is, justification focuses on the consequences of the policy.

The second argument is based on salience. Salience concerns the importance or relevance of something. The salience argument in this context states that the policies dealt with by the EU are of low interest to voters and therefore it makes sense to leave such issues to the technocratic approach. Unfortunately, this argument assumes limited competence, which does not reflect the growth of Union powers. Criminal law, for example, a matter of great concern to the general populace, falls within Union competence; public services are likewise affected by internal market and competition provisions. This suggestion that the democratic deficit argument is not appropriate may, given the nature of the EU, itself not be the most convincing.

The problem of democratic legitimacy has bedevilled the Union for some time. One of the reasons for the introduction of European citizenship, it seems, was a desire to create a greater connection between individuals and the Union. Nonetheless, concerns—and the attempts to address them—remained, and the democratic legitimacy of the Union was one of the central themes of the Constitution and then Lisbon. Not only was one of the Union's values expressed to be a respect for democracy (Article 2 TEU), which was not new, but a separate title, Title II of the TEU, was entitled 'Provisions on Democratic Principles', emphasising the significance of democracy within the Union order. In particular, Article 19(1) TEU states that 'the functioning of the Union shall be founded on representative democracy', though the obligation on the institutions is stated to be to involve citizens by 'appropriate means' (Article 11(1) TEU), without specifying those means. The question is whether Lisbon adds anything new.

One of the main concerns is the lack of democratic accountability of the institutions. The Commission is not elected at all, the Commissioners being political appointments by individual Member States. As we have seen in Chapter 2, however, changes have been made to increase the European Parliament's control over the appointment process. Although the Council usually constitutes members of the national parliaments, those members tend not to have been elected for the purpose of serving as a member of the Council of Ministers and any control is therefore indirect and applies only to the individual members rather than the Council as a body. The Belgian people will only have control over the Belgian ministers but not, for example, the Danish ministers. Ministers can avoid taking responsibility for a decision by passing it on to ministers of the other Member States. The quality of democratic control will rest with each of the national parliaments, so its standard may well vary throughout the Union. Two changes introduced by Lisbon may be of relevance here:

- the rule that legislative decision-making in Council should take place in public;
- the provisions to increase the role of national parliaments in the legislative process (Article 12 TEU; protocol on the role of national parliaments in the European Union).

As noted in the discussion of subsidiarity, the Treaty of Lisbon envisages a greater role for the involvement of national parliaments prior to the enactment of European legislation, with the introduction of the 'yellow' and 'orange card' system. Although we might still comment that there could be variation in the level of oversight, with national parliaments perhaps having neither the time nor the inclination to review Union legislation thoroughly, at least now national parliaments have the possibility of having a voice in the legislative process.

Another concern is the use of non-elected bodies in the decision-making process. There are many of these, for example the Economic and Social Council (ECOSOC) and the Committee of the Regions. These fulfil an advisory role only. We have also noted the role of the comitology committees (see 3.8.4 and 'soft law'). Of more concern here is COREPER (see 2.5.5), which plays an important role in filtering out perceived non-contentious issues from high level political discussions. It has been argued that in so doing, although technically the final decision is the Council's, in effect COREPER is functioning as a decision-making body. In deciding whether issues are contentious or not, COREPER frames the terms of the debate in Council, potentially having the effect of discouraging debate on certain issues. The role of COREPER is likely to remain strong.

The only directly elected body, the European Parliament, has historically been the weakest of the institutions involved in the decision-making process, although the introduction of the ordinary legislative procedure and the extension of its use to the majority of policy areas have meant that the European Parliament is now effectively a co-legislator.

One problem with relying on the European Parliament to assuage democratic concerns is the 'no demos' theory. This posits that, for democracy to work, there needs to be a 'demos', or a group of people. The common membership of the group is such that members of that group allow their own interests sometimes to be outweighed by the interests of others. It is suggested that what we have within the EU is actually a multitude of groups of people—so we see the crucial plural in the phrase 'peoples of the Union'—and on this basis there is no common demos across the EU which the institutions, particularly, the European Parliament might represent. This is a theoretical criticism which no amount of tinkering with the powers of the European Parliament can solve.

3.9.2 **Transparency**

The complexity of the legislative procedures means that decision-making is not transparent. Consequently, it is difficult for individuals to become involved in the process and to hold the decision-makers accountable. The suggestion was to simplify these procedures, without altering the institutional balance. Similarly, improvements could be made in the way documents are drafted and made available. The IIA on Better Law-Making between the European Parliament, the Council and the Commission (2003, revised 2016) aims to improve lawmaking; it focuses not just on the text of the document, but addressing questions about the necessity for law through the use of impact assessments and the possibility of the use of alternative mechanisms, such as co-regulation. There are three other IIAs:

- the IIA on common guidelines for the quality of drafting legislation;
- the IIA on an accelerated working method for the codification of Union texts;
- the IIA on a structured use of the re-casting technique for legal acts.

The Commission produces an annual report on 'Better Lawmaking' which includes a section on how these IIAs have been implemented.

While, undoubtedly, the institutions are making attempts to improve the accessibility of documents, both in terms of their availability (through on-line databases) and improving the comprehensibility of the documents (especially by consolidating texts, where an act is amended), the fact remains that finding, understanding and using EU texts is still pretty much the preserve of the EU cognoscente.

The availability of documents is another part of the overall problem revolving around the way the decision-making process, particularly at Council level, operates. The calls for more openness and better access to documents date back to 1992 and a Protocol annexed to the Maastricht Treaty. Since then, there have been repeated documents that emphasise the need for public access, particularly to Council and Commission documents. While change came, initially it seemed that it would be hard to move away from an institutional assumption of confidentiality, as can be seen in the case of *Carvel v Council* (case T-194/94). This case relied on the 1993 Code of Practice to seek the annulment of a Council decision refusing to reveal Council meeting minutes to the applicant. The GC held that although the Code might permit the withholding of documents when certain specified interests would be threatened by their disclosure, such witholding cannot be automatic. The rights of citizens to see documents must be balanced against the other interests. In this case the Council had *automatically* refused to reveal the minutes on the basis that all minutes are confidential. Since there was no attempt to take the claims of the applicant into account, the Council was therefore held to be in breach of the Code. Although this did not mean that citizens have an automatic right to see all documents, it was a step forward in that the Council has to consider whether it is proper to refuse access, arguably changing the attitude of ministers towards the release of non-controversial information. Subsequent case law made it clear that exceptions to rights of access are to be construed narrowly, a point made expressly in *WWF (UK) v Commission* (case T-105/95). In *Rothmans International BV v Commission* (case T-188/97), the GC held that comitology committees were covered by the right of access to documents. Further, institutions should consider whether partial access to documents is possible where full disclosure is not (*Mattila v Council* (case C-353/01P)). There seems then to have been at least some degree of change in attitude and that access is now (more) the norm. Certainly, Lisbon provided a general principle on access to documents in Article 15(3) TFEU (replacing Article 255(2) EC). While its terms are broadly the same as its predecessor provision (though it covers a broader range of bodies), its placement in the Title containing Provisions having General Application suggests the principle is viewed as important. The right of access has been implemented by Regulation 1049/2001 on Access to Information ([2001] OJ L145/43, as reviewed in 2007).

Although there has, in general, been an acceptance of the need for transparency, a note of caution must be sounded. The right to access documents is subject to limitation in the public or private interest (Article 15(3), para 2 TFEU). Article 4 of the Regulations contains a list of exceptions, comprising nine different categories divided into three groups.

The first group consists of: public security; defence and military matters; international relations; financial, economic or monetary policy; and privacy and integrity of an individual (especially regarding personal data). Article 4(1) specifies that the appropriate test for determining whether access should be allowed to documents in any of these categories is whether public access would undermine the protection of the public interest. Article 9 provides for extra protection of the public interest in relation to 'sensitive documents' dealing with issues falling under Article 4(1)(a). A wide discretion exists in this context, with the CJEU concluding its powers in this regard are limited to verifying whether the procedural rules and the duty to state reasons have been complied with, the facts have been accurately stated and whether there has been a manifest error of assessment of the facts or a misuse of powers (see, eg, *Sison v Council* (cases T-110, 150 and 405/03, on appeal C-266/05P)). In *Sophie in't Veld v Council* (case T-529/09), while it upheld her claim in part, the GC accepted that a refusal to allow access in the context of international negotiations was acceptable to allow a 'certain level of discretion to allow mutual trust between negotiators and the development of a free and effective discussion'. Nonetheless, as the CJ agreed on appeal (case C-350/12P), the mere fact that a document concerns an interest protected by an exception is not itself sufficient to justify the refusal but rather the institution must specify how the interest would be undermined by the release of the document. The CJ continued that the wide discretion does not remove the obligation to explain by the institution concerned, as discussed later.

The second group of concerns (Article 4(2)) comprises the commercial interests of private persons; court proceedings and legal advice; and inspections, investigations and audits. The test here is whether public access would undermine the protection of one of these interests themselves. Finally, Article 4(3) provides that documents relating to a matter on which a decision has not yet been taken 'shall be refused if the disclosure of the document would seriously undermine the institution's decision-making process, unless there is an overriding public interest in disclosure'. The CJ has noted that in the context of legislative decision-making, there is a specific interest in allowing access in that openness contributes to strengthening democracy by enabling citizens to scrutinise all the information which has formed the basis for a legislative act (see, eg, *Sweden and Turco v Council* (cases C-39 and 52/05P), para 46).

The CJ has regularly reiterated its approach from the early cases on access to documents that exceptions to the right of access must be interpreted strictly, and the assessment must be made on the facts of each individual case. So, an institution refusing access to a document must explain how disclosure of that document could specifically and actually undermine the interest protected by the Article 4 exception upon which it is relying. Moreover, the risk of the interest being undermined must be reasonably foreseeable and must not be purely hypothetical (see, eg, *Sweden v MyTravel and Commission* (case C-506/08P)). Further, the fact that a document falls into a particular category of document cannot of itself trigger the application of the claimed exception (*Sweden v Commission* (case C-65/05P)). Thus the fact that a document is entitled 'legal advice' does not automatically bring it within the exception in Article 4(2) (*Turco*). The CJ emphasised that access of documents was necessary for the conferring of legitimacy on the institutions and their workings in the eyes of European citizens, a point it reiterates in many cases; it is a lack of information and of debate which is contributing to the perceived lack of legitimacy of the decision-making process overall. Even though Article 4(2) of the Regulation accepted that the institutions needed to be able to access frank legal advice, the institutions may not rely on the exception by making broad assertions without more evidence. In coming to its decision, the CJ re-emphasised the three-stage approach for assessing disclosure: (1) identify which documents are covered by the exception; (2) identify the relevant Union interest; and (3) balance the right of access against the Union interest. Crucially, a reasoned decision must be given. As well as emphasising the links between transparency and democracy, this case illustrates the differences in approaches between the institutions and some of the Member States.

It is questionable whether transparency is a general principle of Union law (see Chapter 6). The Advocate-General suggested it should be viewed as such in *Hautala v Council* (case C-353/99P), but the CJ expressly rejected this idea. While Member States' approaches may vary, the right of access is found in the European Charter on Fundamental Rights, which now has legal force. The significance of transparency has been highlighted again more recently (see, eg, *Sweden v Council* (case C-65/05)). The long stream of challenges to institutional decisions not to release information on the basis of these interests suggests that we still have some way to go until we have truly open government at EU level.

3.9.3 Efficiency

The institutions have also been criticised for being inefficient, especially with regard to the time-consuming need to reach unanimity. This problem can only get worse with enlargement of the Union. QMV was extended to new policy areas by both ToA and Nice, and Lisbon continues this trend. Notwithstanding this development, difficulties remain. Notably, the Union lawmaking processes remain extremely complex, inevitably taking considerable time to reach agreement. This is compounded by the need to work in all official languages. The number of languages has risen with enlargement and, although it is likely that not all documents will be translated into all languages, all legally binding documents of general application, as the situation currently stands, will be. In addition to problems relating to efficiency, the need to translate into all official languages increases the risk of small differences in the meaning of key terms between the different language versions. (See also Chapter 10.)

3.10 Sources of EU law

The sources of EU law comprise the following:

(1) The TEU, TFEU and protocols.

(2) EU secondary legislation. This group comprises directives and decisions. Recommendations and opinions are of persuasive force only.

(3) International agreements as are entered into by Union institutions on behalf of the Union pursuant to their powers under the Treaties. These agreements may result from accession by the Union to existing agreements, such as GATT, or from new agreements such as the Lomé Convention. Conventions entered into by Member States, on the other hand, cannot be considered as forming part of Union law. Despite the apparent clarity of the provision, there has been some erosion of this principle. Note that some international human rights treaties have been found to inspire principles of Union law (see further Chapter 6). Further, the Commission has suggested that the UN Convention on the International Sale of Goods, to which some but not all Member States are parties, should be viewed as Union law.

(4) Judicial decisions. This comprises the entire jurisprudence of the CJEU irrespective of whether the ruling comes from a preliminary reference, judicial review action or an opinion. The importance and the extent of the contribution of the CJEU in particular to the corpus of EU law will become apparent in the course of this book.

As a matter of international law, the law arising from all these sources is binding on Member States who are obliged, under Article 4(3) TEU, to 'take all appropriate measures, whether general or particular, to ensure fulfilment' of all these obligations.

3.11 Conclusions

The Union has the competence to make law in a broad range of areas, albeit constrained by a procedural framework. It is perhaps this breadth of scope that has led to concern about the lawmaking procedures. As a result of this, successive Treaty revisions have amended the lawmaking procedures, which have affected the institutional balance. Over the years, the role of the European Parliament has increased, arguably increasing the Union's democratic credentials as a result. Whether the increase in power of the European Parliament is sufficient to assuage concerns about mission creep is debatable; following Lisbon there is a clear endeavour to ensure that the Union is understood to be a creature of conferred powers. Nonetheless, problems with the efficiency, democratic accountability and transparency of the procedures remain, as a glance at the issues dealt with by the Convention on the Future of Europe, the resulting Constitution and its successor, the Lisbon Treaty, illustrate. There are, however, other concerns: in particular, the vexed question of the proper scope of Union competence. There are two main aspects to this issue. The first is the identification of the scope of Union activities; the second the determination of exclusive and concurrent competence, particularly important in the context of subsidiarity. Although Lisbon attempts to deal with these, it is unlikely to solve all these difficulties that have dogged the Union for some period, especially given the fact that the Union legal order has changed and continues to change over time. It is to be hoped, however, that some of these problems will be ameliorated.

Further reading

Ankersmit, L, 'The scope of the Common Commercial policy after Lisbon: The Daiichi Sankyo and Conditional Access Services Grand Chamber judgments' (2014) 41 LIEI 193.

Armstrong, KA, 'The new governance of fiscal discipline' (2013) 38 EL Rev 601.

Barrett, G, '"The king is dead, long live the king": The recasting by the Treaty of Lisbon of the provisions of the constitutional treaty concerning national parliaments' (2008) 33 EL Rev 66.

Bellamy, R, 'Democracy without democracy? Can the EU's democratic "outputs" be separated from the democratic "inputs" provided by competitive parties and majority rule?' (2010) 17 JEPP 2.

Chamon, M, 'Clarifying the divide between delegated and implementing acts?' (2015) 42 LIEI 175.

Cooper, I, 'A yellow card for the striker: National parliaments and the defeat of EU legislation on the right to strike' (2015) 22 JEPP 1406.

Craig, P, 'Delegated acts, implementing acts and the new comitology regulation' (2011) 36 EL Rev 671.

Crum, B, 'Saving the Euro at the Cost of Democracy?' (2013) 51 JCMS 614.

Cygan, A, 'The parliamentarisation of EU decision-making? The impact of the Treaty of Lisbon on national parliaments' (2011) 36 EL Rev 478.

Dashwood, A, 'States in the European Union' (1998) 23 EL Rev 201.

Davies, G, 'Subsidiarity: The wrong idea, in the wrong place, at the wrong time' (2006) 43 CML Rev 63.

De Baere, G, 'EU external action' in C Barnard and S Peers (eds), European Union Law (Oxford University Press, 2014).

de Búrca, G, 'The quest for legitimacy in the European Union' (1996) 59 MLR 349.

Emilou, N, 'Subsidiarity: An effective barrier against enterprises of ambition' (1992) 29 CML Rev 383.

Fabbrini, F, 'Enhanced cooperation under scrutiny: revisiting the law and practice of multi-speed integration in light of the first involvement of the EU judiciary' (2013) 40 LIEI 197.

Føllesdal, A and Hix, S, 'Why there is a democratic deficit in the EU: A response to Majone and Moravcsik' (2006) 44 JCMS 533.

Habermas, J, 'The crisis of the European Union in the light of the constitutionalization of international law' (2012) 23 EJIL 335.

Joerges, C, 'Integration through de-legislation?' (2008) 33 EL Rev 291.

Kiiver, P, 'The early-warning system for the principle of subsidiarity: The national parliament as a Conseil d'Etat for Europe' (2011) 36 EL Rev 98.

Konstadinides, T, 'EU foreign policy under the doctrine of implied powers: Codification drawbacks and constitutional limitations' (2014) 39 EL Rev 511.

Koopmans, T, 'The role of law in the next stage of European integration' (1986) 35 ICLQ 925.

Kuijper, PJ, 'The case law of the Court of Justice of the EU and the allocation of external relations powers. Whither the traditional role of the executive in EU foreign relations?' in M Cremona and A Thies (eds), The European Court of Justice and external relations law (Hart Publishing, 2014).

Lamping, M, 'Enhanced cooperation—a proper approach to market integration in the field of unitary patent' (2011) 42 IIC 879.

Majone, G, 'Unity in diversity: European integration and the enlargement process' (2008) 33 EL Rev 457.

O'Keefe, D and Twomey, P (eds), Legal Issues of the Maastricht Treaty (Wiley Chancery Law, 1994).

Ott, A, 'The legal bases for international agreements post-Lisbon: Of pirates and The Philippines' (2014) 21 Maastricht Journal 739.

Peers, S, EU Justice and Home Affairs, 3rd edn (Oxford University Press, 2011), Ch 2.

Peers, S and Costa, M, 'Accountability for Delegated and Implementing Acts After the Treaty of Lisbon' (2012) 18 ELJ 427.

Rasmussen, H, *On Law and Policy-making in the European Communities* (Martinus Nijhoff, 1986).

Scott, J and Trubeck, D, 'Mind the gap: Law and new approaches to governance in the European Union' (2002) 8 ELJ 1.

Swaine, ET, 'Subsidiarity and self interest: Federalism at the European Court of Justice' (2000) 41 Harv Int'l LJ 1.

Verbruggen, P, 'Does co-regulation strengthen EU legitimacy?' (2009) 15 ELJ 425.

Verellen, T, 'The ERTA doctrine in the post-Lisbon era: Note under judgment in *Commission v Council* (C-114/12) and Opinion 1/13' (2015) 21 CJEL 383.

4 Principle of supremacy of EU law

4.1 Introduction

The wide scope of the Treaties, covering a number of areas normally reserved for national law alone, coupled with the extended application by the CJ of the principle of direct effects (Chapter 5), led inevitably to a situation of conflict between national and EU law. In such a case, which law was to prevail? The way in which that conflict was resolved was of crucial importance to the Union legal order; it was a constitutional problem of some magnitude for Member States. It affects our understanding not only of the relationship between Member States and what is now the Union, but also their respective autonomy and sovereignty. In one sense, this is a tale of a power struggle, or the story of the birth of a new form of legal order. It is also the story of the development of multi-level cooperation, where each judgment constitutes part of a judicial dialogue. After considering the problem of priorities in traditional international law, this chapter will review the development of the CJ's case law on supremacy of Union law and the significance of the Lisbon Treaty. We will then look at the other side of the coin and identify the problems and solutions from the perspective of the national courts.

4.2 The problem of priorities

The original Treaty of Rome (and subsequently the TFEU and the TEU) is silent on the issue of which law should in the case of conflict take priority, and always has been. Perhaps in the early days this was a diplomatic omission; perhaps it was not thought necessary to make the matter explicit, since the extent to which Union law might be directly effective was not envisaged at the time of signing the Treaty of Rome. In the absence of guidance, the matter was left to be decided by the courts of Member States, assisted by the CJ in its jurisdiction under Article 267 TFEU (see Chapter 10). As with the concept of direct effects (see Chapter 5), the CJ has proved extremely influential in developing the law.

The question of priorities between directly effective international law and domestic law is normally seen as a matter of national law, to be determined according to the constitutional rules of the state concerned. It will depend on a number of factors. Primarily it will depend on the terms on which international law has been incorporated into domestic law, which in turn will depend on whether the state is monist or dualist in its approach to international law. If monist, it will be received automatically into national law from the moment of its ratification, without the need for further measures of incorporation. If dualist, international law will not become binding internally, as part of domestic law, until it is incorporated by a domestic statute. But whether received automatically, by process of 'adoption', or incorporated by statute, by way of 'transformation', the incorporation of international law does not itself settle the question of priorities. The status accorded to international law will depend, in the case of each state, on the extent to which that state has provided for this, either in its constitution, where it has a written constitution, or, where it has no written constitution, in its statute of incorporation.

As we will see in 4.4, there is wide variation in the way in which, and the extent to which, Member States of the Union have provided for this question of priorities. Where states have a written constitution, there may be express provision for this issue. A state which does not have a written constitution, and which is dualist, such as the UK, must provide for priorities in the statute of incorporation itself. This statute will have the same status as any other statute. As such it will be vulnerable to the doctrine of implied repeal, or *lex posterior derogat priori*, whereby any inconsistency between an earlier and a later statute is resolved in favour of the latter. The later statute is deemed to have impliedly repealed the earlier one (see *Ellen Street Estates Ltd v Minister of Health* [1934] 1 KB 590, but see 4.4.3 as to how the British courts have approached this issue).

Given the differences from state to state it is clear that if national courts were to apply their own constitutional rules to the question of priorities between domestic law and EU law, there would be no uniformity of application, and the primacy of EU law could not be guaranteed throughout the Union. This was the principal reason advanced by Advocate-General Roemer in *Algemene Transport-en Expeditie Onderneming Van Gend en Loos NV v Nederlandse Administratie der Belastingen* (case 26/62) for denying the direct effects of what was then Article 12 EEC (now Article 30 TFEU). Not only would this weaken the effect of Union law, it would undermine solidarity among the Member States, and in the end threaten the Union itself. Thus, for the EU supremacy was central its effectiveness, if not its existence. It is no doubt reasons such as these which led the CJ to develop its own constitutional rules to deal with the problem, in particular the principle of supremacy, or primacy, of EU law.

4.3 The Court of Justice's contribution

4.3.1 Development of the principle of supremacy

The first cautious statement of the principle of supremacy of EU law came in the case of *Van Gend en Loos*.

Van Gend en Loos

The principal question in the case was the question of the direct effects of what was at that time Article 12 EEC (now Article 30 TFEU). The conflict, assuming that article was found to be directly effective, was between Article 30 TFEU and an *earlier* Dutch law. Under Dutch law, if Article 30 TFEU were directly effective it would, under the Dutch Constitution, take precedence over domestic law. So the questions referred to the CJ under Article 267 TFEU did not raise the issue of sovereignty directly. Nevertheless, in addition to declaring that what is now Article 30 TFEU was directly effective, the Court went on to say that:

the Community [now Union] constitutes a new legal order in international law, for whose benefit the States have limited their sovereign rights, albeit within limited fields.

Although the main emphasis of the judgment relates to the doctrine of direct effect, it is also significant because, by referring to the 'new legal order', the CJ indicated that the Union was not just a 'normal' international law organisation. In particular, the Union had an independent status as well as, arguably, greater impact on the national legal systems of the Member States. It is difficult to overstate the importance of this step from treaty organisation to independent legal order.

The conflict in *Costa v ENEL* (case 6/64) posed a more difficult problem for the Italian courts, raising the issue of implied repeal.

Costa

This case involved an alleged conflict between a number of Treaty provisions and an Italian statute nationalising the electricity company of which the defendant, Signor Costa, was a shareholder, but here the Italian law was later in time than the Treaty provision. On being brought before the Milan tribunale for refusing to pay his bill (the princely sum of L1,925, or approximately £1.10), Signor Costa argued that the company was in breach of EU law. The defendants argued *lex posterior*; the Italian Act nationalising the electricity company was later in time than the Italian Ratification Act, the act incorporating EU law, and therefore took priority.

The Italian court referred this question of priorities to the CJ. It also referred the matter to its own constitutional court. This time the principle of supremacy was clearly affirmed by the CJ. It cited *Van Gend en Loos*; the Member States had 'limited their sovereign rights'. It went further. It looked to the Treaty and noted that Article 288 TFEU indicated that there had been a transfer of powers to the Union institutions; what is now Article 4(3) TEU underlined Member States' commitment to observe Union law. The Court concluded:

> The reception, within the laws of each Member State, of provisions having a Community [now Union] source, and more particularly of the terms and of the spirit of the Treaty, has as a corollary the impossibility, for the Member State, to give preference to a unilateral and subsequent measure against a legal order accepted by them on a basis of reciprocity . . .
>
> Such a measure cannot be inconsistent with that legal system. The executive force of Community [now Union] law cannot vary from one State to another in deference to subsequent domestic laws, without jeopardizing the attainment of the objectives of the Treaty . . .
>
> The obligations undertaken under the Treaty establishing the Community [now Union] would not be unconditional, but merely contingent, if they could be called into question by subsequent legislative acts of the signatories . . .
>
> It follows from all these observations that the law stemming from the Treaty, an independent source of law, could not, because of its special and original nature, be overridden by domestic legal provisions, however framed, without being deprived of its character as Community [now Union] law and without the legal basis of the Community [now Union] itself being called into question.
>
> The transfer, by Member States, from their national orders in favour of the Community [now Union] order of the rights and obligations arising from the Treaty, carries with it a clear limitation of their sovereign right upon which a subsequent unilateral law, incompatible with the aims of the Community [now Union], cannot prevail.

The reasoning used by the CJ is worthy of note as, in developing its argument, the CJ uses a teleological—or purposive—approach that is not tied in particularly closely to the actual wording of the Treaty. The CJ's substantive arguments can be divided into two main groups:

(1) those relating to the *nature* of the Union;

(2) those relating to the *purposes* of the Union.

The first category comprises the CJ's assertion about the independent nature of the new Union legal order and the mechanism by which this legal order was created: the permanent limitation of Member States' sovereign rights. There is no express basis in the Treaty for either of these points. The other arguments, referring to the aims of the Treaty, are more practical. They look to the purpose of the Union and the need to ensure that those goals are not undermined. These arguments are based on the need to make Union law effective. Effectiveness itself becomes a leitmotif of the CJ's judgments in many areas and while it might sound merely pragmatic, it has had a huge influence on the development of Union law (see 6.9 and Chapter 8).

In the case of *Internationale Handelsgesellschaft mbH* the CJ went even further.

Internationale Handelsgesellschaft

Here, the conflict was between not a Treaty provision and a domestic statute, but between an EU regulation and provisions of the German Constitution. The claimant argued that the regulation infringed, inter alia, the principle of proportionality enshrined in the German Constitution and sought to nullify the regulation on those grounds. Normally, any ordinary law in breach of the constitution is invalid, since the constitution is superior in the hierarchy of legal rules to statute law. EU law had been incorporated into German law by statute, the Act of Ratification. There was no provision in the constitution that the constitution could be overridden by EU law. Article 24 GG (at that stage the relevant provision) merely provided for 'the transfer of sovereign powers to intergovernmental institutions'.

So the question before the German Administrative Court was: if there were a conflict between the regulation and the German Constitution, which law should prevail? As in *Costa*, the German judge referred the question to the CJ and his own federal constitutional court (FCC).

The ruling from the CJ was in the strongest terms. The legality of a Union act cannot be judged in the light of national law:

> the law born from the Treaty [cannot] have the courts opposing to it rules of national law *of any nature whatever* . . . the validity of a Community [now Union] instrument or its effect within a Member State cannot be affected by allegations that it strikes at either the fundamental rights as formulated in that State's constitution or the principles of a national constitutional structure [emphasis added].

Underlying this judgment one can see concerns similar to those expressed in *Costa*: the need to ensure the effectiveness of Union law, whatever the cost to the national legal order. If the CJ's ruling seems harsh in the light of the importance of the rights protected in a state's constitution, many of which are regarded as fundamental human rights, it is worth adding that the Court went on to say that respect for such rights was one of the principal aims of the Union and as such it was part of its own (albeit unwritten) law (see Chapter 6). In any event, following *Internationale Handelsgesellschaft*, it is clear that—from the CJ's perspective—the (high) status of national law will not protect that national law from being overridden by EU law. In *Amministrazione delle Finanze dello Stato v Simmenthal SpA* (case 106/77), the CJ went still further: EU laws take priority over subsequent national laws (see 4.3.2). Implied repeal does not apply; Union law is effectively entrenched.

The principle of supremacy of Union law applies not only to internal domestic laws, but also to obligations entered into with third countries, that is, countries outside the EU. In the *ERTA* case the CJ held, in the context of a challenge to an international road transport agreement to which the

Union was a party, that once the Union, in implementing a common policy, lays down common rules, Member States no longer have the right, individually or collectively, to contract obligations towards non-Member States affecting these common rules. And where the Union concludes a treaty in pursuance of a common policy, this excludes the possibility of a concurrent authority on the part of the Member States. This means that where a state attempts to exercise concurrent authority it will be overridden to the extent that it conflicts with Union law. This principle does not, however, appear to apply to Member States' pre-accession agreements with third countries. Where such agreements are 'not compatible' with the Treaties, Member States are required to 'take all appropriate steps to eliminate the incompatibilities established' (Article 351 TFEU). In *R v Secretary of State for the Home Department, ex parte Evans Medical Ltd* (case C-324/93), the CJ conceded that provisions of such an agreement contrary to Union law may continue to be applied where the performance of that agreement may still be required by non-Member States which are parties to it.

Evans Medical

Evans Medical concerned a prohibition on importing heroin into the UK, which resulted from the Single Convention on Narcotic Drugs concluded in New York on 30 March 1961 (a time when the UK had not joined the EU). While in principle the prohibition on imports would be contrary to the Treaty provision on the free movement of goods (now Article 34 TFEU), Member States need not give that provision full effect when it would be contrary to the obligations the states had already contracted under international law. Here, the CJ noted that there was no equally effective means of ensuring the objectives of the Convention.

The Court has, however, urged national courts to give effect to such provisions only to the extent that it is necessary to meet the demands of that agreement (*Office national del'emploi v Minne* (case C-13/93) concerning the relationship of Directive 76/207 on equal treatment with an ILO Convention).

The case of *Yassin Abdullah Kadi and Al Barakaat International Foundation v Council* (cases C-402 and 415/05P) shows a further development in this area.

Kadi

The background to this case is the fight against terrorism, according to which the UN Security Council adopted a number of resolutions for the freezing of assets of people thought to be involved in terrorism. All Member States are members of the UN, and as a prior agreement, must be respected by the Union. The Council adopted two common positions under the CFSP, which were then implemented by regulations to which a list was attached, updated in accordance with decisions made at UN level, as to whose assets should be frozen. Kadi was one such and he sought to challenge the legality of the EU action on the basis, inter alia, of human-rights concerns.

The CJ (overruling a decision of the General Court) emphasised the autonomy of the EU and its constitutional status as a legal order based on the rule of law. On this reasoning, the obligations imposed on the Member States and the relationship between them and the EU were unaffected by any international agreement whatever its nature. In reaching this conclusion, the CJ distinguished between the international obligations of the EU and the effect of Union norms, regardless of their source. On this basis, the CJ was able to review the Union measures implementing the UN Resolutions. The impact of this judgment was to reassert the coherence and autonomy of the *Union* legal order, and to re-emphasise its constitutional basis. As regards the relationship of the EU and other international organisations, it suggests that the EU constitutes an impermeable layer protecting its own inner organisational structure; it also reminds us that to the extent that the EU is still an international law body, it sees itself in a different light from other such bodies. This concern to ensure the autonomy of the EU legal order also underpinned the CJ's reasoning in its *Opinion on the creation of a European Patents Court* (EPC) (*Opinion 1/09*).

Opinion on Patents Court

The Member States proposed to establish a specialised court to deal with disputes relating to the proposed European patent; this court was to follow EU law and would have been able to make references to the CJ. The CJ, having reiterated its duty to ensure the autonomy of the EU legal system (para 67) reasoned, 'The judicial system of the European Union is moreover a complete system of legal remedies and procedures designed to ensure review of the legality of acts of the institutions' which was made up of the CJEU and the courts of the Member States (para 66). On this basis, the Member States were not permitted to establish the EPC.

Thus, subject to the narrow exception in *Evans Medical*, as far as the CJ is concerned *all* EU law, whatever its nature, must take priority over *all* conflicting domestic law and international law, whether it be prior or subsequent to Union law.

All these cases show a common theme in the CJ's approach: the need to ensure the effectiveness of Union law. The position can be summarised as follows. The Court's reasoning is pragmatic, based on the purpose, the general aims and spirit of the Treaties. States freely signed the Treaties; they agreed to take all appropriate measures to comply with EU law (Article 4(3) TEU); the Treaties created their own institutions, and gave those institutions power to make laws binding on Member States (Article 288 TFEU). They agreed to set up an institutionalised form of control by the Commission (under Article 258 TFEU—see Chapter 11) and the Court. The Union would not survive if states were free to act unilaterally in breach of their obligations. If the aims of the Union are to be achieved, there must be uniformity of application.

4.3.2 **National procedural rules: problems for the national courts**

National courts were understandably reluctant to disregard their own constitutional rules and the Italian and German constitutional courts in *Costa* and *Internationale Handelsgesellschaft mbH v Einfuhr- und Vorratsstelle fur Getreide und Futtermittel (Solange I)* ([1974] 2 CMLR 540), adhering to their own traditional view, refused to acknowledge the absolute supremacy of EU law.

There were other problems too for national courts—problems of application. Even if the principle of primacy of EU law were accepted in theory, what was a national judge to do in practice when faced with a conflict? No English judge can declare a statute void or unlawful (subject to limited powers in respect of the Human Rights Act); in most countries with a written constitution only the constitutional court has power to declare a domestic law invalid for breach of the constitution, if it has such a power at all. Must the national judge wait for the offending national law to be repealed or legally annulled before he can give precedence to EU law?

The CJ suggested a solution to this problem in *Simmenthal*.

Simmenthal

This case involved a conflict between a Treaty provision, the then Article 30 EEC (now 34 TFEU) on the free movement of goods, and an Italian law passed *subsequent* to the Italian Act incorporating EU law, a similar clash to the one in *Costa*. Following *Costa*, the Italian Constitutional Court had revised its view and declared that it would be prepared to declare any national law conflicting with EU law invalid. When the problem arose in *Simmenthal* the Italian judge, the Pretore di Susa, was perplexed. Should he apply EU law at once to the case before him, or should he wait until his own constitutional court had declared the national law invalid? He referred this question to the CJ.

The Court's reply was predictable:

> any recognition that national legislative measures which encroach upon the field within which the Community [now Union] exercises its legislative power or which are otherwise incompatible with the provisions of Community [now Union] law had any legal effect would amount to a corresponding denial of the effectiveness of obligations undertaken unconditionally and irrevocably by Member States pursuant to the Treaty and would thus imperil the very foundations of the Community [now Union] [para 18].
> . . . a national court which is called upon . . . to apply provisions of Community [now Union] law is under a duty to give full effect to those provisions, if necessary refusing . . . to apply any conflicting provision of national legislation, even if adopted subsequently, and it is not necessary for the court to request or await the prior setting aside of such provision by legislative or other constitutional means [para 24].

The reasoning behind the judgment is clear. Unless Union law is given priority over conflicting national law at once, from the moment of its entry into force, there can be no uniformity of application throughout the Union. Union law would be rendered ineffective. According to the CJ, national judges faced with a conflict between national law, whatever its nature, and Union law, must ignore, must shut their eyes to national law; they need not, indeed must not, wait for the law to be changed. Any incompatible national law is automatically inapplicable.

The principles expressed in *Simmenthal* were applied by the Court in *R v Secretary of State for Transport, ex parte Factortame Ltd (Factortame I)* (case C-213/89).

Factortame I

The case concerned a claim before the English courts by a group of Spanish fishermen for an interim injunction to prevent the application of certain sections of the Merchant Shipping Act 1988, which denied them the right to register their boats in the UK, and which the claimants alleged were in breach of EU law. The question of the 'legality' of the British provisions under Union law had yet to be decided, following a separate reference to the CJ. The British courts were being asked to give primacy to a *putative* Union right over an allegedly conflicting national law, and to grant an interim injunction against the Crown, something which they considered they were not permitted to do under national law.

Following a reference by the then House of Lords asking whether it was obliged to grant the relief in question as a matter of Union law, the CJ pointed out that national courts were obliged to ensure the legal protection which persons derive from the direct effect of provisions of Union law. Moreover:

> The full effectiveness of Community [now Union] law would be . . . impaired if a rule of national law could prevent a court seised of a dispute governed by Community [now Union] law from granting

interim relief in order to ensure the full effectiveness of the judgment to be given on the existence of the rights claimed under Community [now Union] law. It follows that a court which in those circumstances would grant interim relief, if it were not for a rule of national law, is obliged to set aside that rule [para 21].

Supremacy and the effectiveness of EU law have thus had a broad range of consequences within the Member States' respective legal systems. As we saw in *Simmenthal*, the effectiveness of EU law means that any national provisions which limit decisions about the validity of national law to certain bodies (eg, a rule which stated that only the national constitutional court may strike down or disapply national rules) would themselves be contrary to the requirements of EU law. This principle has been repeated on many occasions since (eg, *Melki and Abdeli* (case C-188-9/10)—identity checks within 20 km of nations border and free movement of persons) even if the consequence of the application of supremacy means that there is a legal vacuum while the Member State in question re-legislates so as to comply with Union law (*Winner Wetten GmbH v Bürgermeisterin der Stadt Bergheim* (case C-409/06) German rules creating a gambling monopoly—incompatible with free movement rules).

The obligation on Member States to ensure the full effectiveness of Union law requires national courts not only to 'disapply' the offending national law but also to supply a remedy which is not available under national law (eg, *Factortame*; see also *Unibet (London) Ltd and Unibet (International) Ltd v Justitiekanslern* (case C-432/05)—availability of interim relief decision on EU law issue must be possible). The obligation to disapply inconsistent national law extends beyond the courts to administrative agencies. In *Gervais Larsy v Institut national d'assurances sociales pour travailleurs indépendants (Inasti)* (case C-118/00), reasoning from its judgments in *Simmenthal* and *Factortame*, the CJ held that the national social security institution, INASTI, should disapply national laws that precluded effective protection of Larsy's Union law rights (para 53). (See also *Consorzio Industrie Fiammeferi (CIF) v Autorita Grante della Concorrenza e del Mercato* (case C-198/01)—disapplication of national legislation incompatible with the competition provisions.) The potential impact on the national legal systems is huge; the issue of procedural rules and remedies and the doctrine of effectiveness is discussed further in Chapter 8.

A finding that a provision of national law is 'inapplicable' because of its incompatibility with Union law does not, however, result in its annulment, or even prevent its application in situations falling outside the scope of Union law.

IN.CO.GE.'90

Ministero delle Finanze v IN.CO.GE. '90 (cases C-10 and 22/97) concerned a series of disputes between the Ministry of Finance and IN.CO.GE.'90 relating to the detailed rules governing repayment of the *tassa di concessione governativa* (registration charge) for entering companies on the register of companies. In a previous case (*Ponente Carni and Cispadana Costruzioni v Amministrazione delle Finanze dello Stato* (cases C-71 and 178/91)), the CJ had held that the way the administration charge was calculated was incompatible with Union law. IN.CO.GE.'90 sought repayment as a civil matter, but the Ministry of Finance argued that a specific regime dealing with tax matters was applicable (together with specific time bar rules). So the question referred was whether the setting aside of the national decree establishing the registration charge meant that claims for repayment should be dealt with as a normal debt recovery or under the special fiscal rules. The legislation that gave the debt its fiscal character was not applicable, but was it appropriate to deal with the situation as though the rules had not existed?

The Court held that 'it does not follow from *Simmenthal* that a domestic rule which is incompatible with EC [now EU] law is non-existent'.

ICI v Colmer (case C-264/96) deals with matters outside the scope of EU law.

ICI

Here, the CJ found a system of tax relief for holding companies with a seat in the EU discriminatory, and therefore contrary to EU law, when applied to subsidiary companies in other Member States, but lawful in a situation where holding companies control subsidiaries in non-Member States. Despite its inapplicability in the former context, the national court was under no obligation to disapply national law in the latter situation, since that lay outside the scope of EU law.

However:

Where the same legislation must be disapplied as contrary to EC [now EU] law in a situation covered by Community [now Union] law it is for the competent body of the Member State concerned to remove that legal uncertainty insofar as it might affect rights deriving from Community [now Union] rules.

The case of *Kapferer v Schlank and Schick* (case C-234/04) concerned the principle of *res judicata*, whereby judicial decisions which have become final can no longer be called into question. Referring to *res judicata*, the CJ held that, subject to the rules of equivalence and effectiveness (see Chapter 8), a national court did not have to disapply procedural rules which enshrined this principle, even if disapplying those rules would allow it to end an infringement of Union law caused by a ruling inconsistent with Union law. The CJ, however, came to the opposite conclusion in *Ministero dell'Industria, del Commercio e dell'Artigianato v Lucchini SpA, formerly Lucchini Siderurgica SpA* (case C-119/05), where it held that the national law upholding the principle of *res judicata* should be disapplied. This case, which goes against the run of authorities, should perhaps be regarded as exceptional rather than implying a new disregard for *res judicata*, which the CJ has recognised as being a general principle of law (see Chapter 6). The CJ had the opportunity to consider the matter again in *Fallimento Olimpiclub Srl v Amministrazione dell'Economia e delle Finanze and Agenzia delle Entrate* (case C-2/08), which concerned the application of the VAT rules. The CJ re-emphasised its approach in *Kapferer*, and distinguished *Lucchini* as applying to a 'highly specific situation' where the Commission had exclusive competence to determine whether the state aid granted was compatible with the common market. Note, however, that the CJ held that the effectiveness of Union law would be impaired if the application of the *res judicata* doctrine meant that it prevents the same issue being investigated in other cases dealing with the same issue.

4.3.3 **EU rules which do not have direct effect**

It may be noted that all the earlier landmark rulings of the Court, up to and including *Simmenthal*, were expressed in terms of directly effective Union law, that is, rules that gave rise to rights that could be relied on within the national legal system. Until the CJ introduced the principle of indirect effects in *von Colson v Land Nordrhein-Westfalen* (case 14/83) (see Chapter 5) and the principle of state liability in *Francovich* (cases C-6 and 9/90) (see Chapter 9), it was thought that national courts would only be required to apply, and give priority to, EU law which was directly effective. This proved not to be the case; indeed supremacy has to a large extent driven the developments in enforcement in EU law which seek to limit the circumstances where an individual may not access EU law. The obligation on national courts to interpret domestic law to comply with EU directives which are not directly effective (because invoked horizontally), as extended in *Marleasing SA v La Comercial Internacional de Alimentación SA* (case C-106/89), impliedly requires those courts to give priority to EU law. The reasoning in cases such as *CIA Security International SA v Signalson SA* (case C-194/94) (see 5.2.13) and in *Mangold v Helm* (case C-144/04) (see 5.2.14) is based on supremacy. Similarly, although the granting of a remedy in damages against the state under *Francovich* ('state liability') does not require the *application* of Union law, the remedy, based on Member States' obligation to guarantee full and effective protection for individuals' rights under Union law, is premised on the supremacy of EU law. This obligation was held in *Francovich* (at para 42) to apply to all rights 'which parties enjoy under [Union] law'. That protection cannot be achieved unless those rights prevail over conflicting provisions of national law. As *Brasserie du Pêcheur SA v Germany* and *R v Secretary of State for Transport, ex parte Factortame* (cases C-46 and 48/93)—two more cases establishing the conditions for the doctrine of state liability—subsequently made clear, individuals' Union rights, including the right to damages, must prevail over *all* acts of Member States, legislative, executive or judicial, which are contrary to Union law.

4.3.4 **Supremacy after Lisbon**

The CJ's early case law referred to the Community. After Maastricht the question arose, would supremacy apply to the second and third pillars too; to EU law in general? The Treaties were silent on this point. Arguments could be put forward to support either position. The limitations on the institutions' powers in the second and third pillars, which rendered them more intergovernmental in nature, might suggest that the 'new legal order' arguments found in *Costa* regarding the Community might not be applicable. Conversely, the effectiveness arguments would apply just as much to those provisions as to the provisions in the then Community pillar. In the case of *Pupino (Maria)* (case C-105/03), which concerned third pillar provisions, the CJ held that the Member States' duty of loyalty applied in that context just as much as in the context of the first pillar provisions of the Community.

Pupino

The case concerned the interpretation of Council Framework Decision 2001/220/JHA on the standing of victims in criminal proceedings ([2001] OJ L82/1) in the context of criminal proceedings against Mrs Pupino, a nursery school teacher charged with inflicting injuries on pupils. The prosecutors wished to adopt special measures in view of the children's age, but national rules did not allow for this. The question arose as to whether those rules were compatible with the Framework Decision and, if so, what the national court could do. The Italian government argued that framework decisions (made under the then JHA pillar) and directives (under the Communities pillar) were different and separate sources of law and consequently that the obligation on a national court in respect of a directive to interpret national law in conformity with the directive could not be transposed to framework decisions.

The CJ rejected that argument because the legal effects of a framework decision were described in similar terms to that of a directive, and that their binding character thus 'place[d] on national authorities, and particularly national courts, an obligation to interpret national law in conformity' (para 34). The CJ returned to the effectiveness argument seen in the early supremacy cases and argued—referring to different legal provisions but to similar effect—that:

> It would be difficult for the Union to carry out its task effectively if the principle of loyal cooperation, requiring in particular that Member States take all appropriate measures, whether general or particular, to ensure fulfilment of their obligations under European Union law, were not also binding in the area of police and judicial cooperation in criminal matters, which is moreover entirely based on cooperation between the Member States and the institutions, as the Advocate General has rightly pointed out in paragraph 26 of her Opinion (para 42).

Pupino therefore supports a more extensive view of supremacy.

In the post-Lisbon world, the distinctions between the pillars have to a large extent been eradicated (though some provisions relating to FSP remain separate). To what extent can we say that we have supremacy of Union law in its entirety?

While the Constitutional Treaty would have included a re-statement of the principle of supremacy (in Article I-6), which stated that all Union law would have primacy, political reaction was such that no comparable provision is found in the Lisbon Treaty. Instead, it contains a Declaration (Declaration 17 Concerning Primacy).

The Declaration, which does not have binding legal effect, states that:

> [t]he conference recalls that, in accordance with well settled case law of the EU Court of Justice, the Treaties and the law adopted by the Union on the basis of the Treaties have primacy over the law of Member States, under the conditions laid down by the said case law.

Interestingly, the Declaration also contains a reference to a legal Opinion of the Council Legal Service, which states that:

> [t]he fact that the principle of primacy will not be included in the future treaty shall not in any way change the existence of the principle and the existing case-law of the Court of Justice.

It is not quite clear on what basis the legal Opinion draws this conclusion, especially as the wording between the Opinion and the Declaration differs. It is perhaps an attempt to pretend that the Constitution, and particularly Article I-6, never happened. Nonetheless, the abolition of the pillar structure may change the position in that the formal distinctions between the different aspects of EU law have been removed. There is no such thing as EC law, so how can we limit supremacy thereto? The integration of JHA matters into the TFEU certainly makes it difficult to argue that there is a difference between those provisions and former Community law. The CFSP provisions, however, even after Lisbon, remain separate in the TEU, especially given the reasoning in *Pupino*. It is here that the difference in approach between the Declaration and the Opinion of the Council's Legal Service might seem significant. The Opinion harks back to the old structure, referring to the 'Community' and perhaps allows houseroom to arguments based on a pillar-based structure, so that we might argue the provisions of CFSP do not have supremacy. The terms of the Declaration are different. They refer to the fact that 'the Treaties and the law adopted by the Union on the basis of the Treaties have primacy'—that is, both the TEU and TFEU. This would suggest that EU law in its entirety and not just aspects deriving from TFEU have primacy. Despite the claim that Lisbon makes no difference to the legal position, the de-pillarisation could have the consequence of extending the scope of supremacy from what was Community law to all EU law.

4.4 The Member States' response

Given the expanded membership of the Union, for reasons of space alone it is not possible to discuss the response of each of the Member States; a full comparative survey of the position in other Member States must fall outside this book. Further, for the newest Member States, it may well still be too soon for all possible problems to work their way through the judicial system, although there are already a number of constitutional court rulings from the newer Member States in this area. It would be naive to suggest that the newer Member States would have no difficulties absorbing the doctrine of primacy, as they should have been aware of it on entry. As illustrated by the UK, whose politicians knew of the doctrine at the time of accession, legal reality is often different from political aspirations.

4.4.1 Shades of supremacy

The existence of supremacy of EU law seems clear from the perspective of the CJ. It is important to remember that there is another perspective: that from the Member States' judiciary. So, although the CJ might rule that Union law is supreme, this principle requires acceptance by the courts of the Member States if it is to have any real effect. We should also note that the views of each of the Member State's courts may be different from one another, as each will be based in the constitutional structures of the respective Member State. In considering the question of supremacy from the Member States' perspective, then, we should bear in mind that each Member State may accept supremacy to a different degree for different reasons.

This scale of intensity may be described by looking at the answers to a range of questions. The first is the question of whether each of the Member States and their courts recognise the principle of supremacy of EU law. In general, the answer to this question is 'yes' (see 4.4.2). Even if the Member States have accepted supremacy, this does not mean that they accept the basis on which the CJ has justified supremacy, as set out in *Costa*. A Member State may choose to accept supremacy on the basis of its own constitution (see 4.4.3). Furthermore, we might question the degree of acceptance of supremacy. According to the CJ, EU law takes priority over any element of national law, whatever its status. National courts may choose to view supremacy in a somewhat more limited fashion, perhaps by regarding constitutions or fundamental rights protection as being in some way excluded from the principle of supremacy (see 4.4.4). The scope of EU law itself and consequently the substantive scope of supremacy may also be contentions, as can be seen in discussions about the circumstances in which the EU Charter of Fundamental Rights applies (see Chapter 6). Underlying all this is the fundamental question: who gets to decide this question (see 4.4.5)? This issue is sometimes referred to as '*Kompetenz-Kompetenz*', as this issue has loomed large in German literature. Essentially it is addressing the question of whether the EU or the Member States have the authority to determine the boundary of competence between the EU and the Member States.

4.4.2 Acceptance of supremacy

Those states which were early members of the EU have accepted the principle of supremacy. Given the points in time at which the CJ established the principle, perhaps this is not surprising, though it should be noted that it has taken some courts longer than others to accept supremacy. For example, the Italian Constitutional Court seemed to accept supremacy in the 1974 case of *Frontini v Ministero delle Finanze* ([1974] 2 CMLR 372), while the French courts were still undecided until the case of *Nicolo* in 1989 ([1990] 1 CMLR 173). The British courts accepted in the UK in *Factortame II* ([1991] 1 AC 603) (see 4.4.3). With the exception of the sensitivities relating to abortion, which arose in *Society for the Protection of the Unborn Child Ltd v Grogan* (case C-159/90) and which resulted in a protocol to the Maastricht Treaty on the subject, the Irish courts likewise seem to have accepted the principle of supremacy. A similar pattern of recognition of supremacy can be seen in the newer Member States.

4.4.3 Basis of acceptance

The position in France (Décision No 2004-505 DC–19.11.2004, Traité établissant une Constitution pour l'Europe) and Italy (*Granital*, Decision No 170, 1984), as it was also in Germany (see 4.4.4), was that supremacy was based principally on provisions in the national constitution. Indeed, some of these provisions were specifically enacted so as to deal with the position of the European Union (eg, article 88–1 of the French Constitution and article 23 of the German Constitution; see also article 29 of the Irish Constitution), a process that can also be found in relation to the newer Member States (eg, Poland and Estonia). The British position was less clear-cut.

The status of Union law in the UK derives from the European Communities Act 1972. While s 2(1) provides for the direct applicability of EU law, s 2(4) is the section relevant to the question of primacy. It does not expressly say EU law is supreme. Section 2(4) provides (emphasis added):

> The provision that may be made under subsection (2) above includes, subject to schedule 2 to this Act, any such provision (of any such extent) as might be made by Act of Parliament, and *any enactment passed or to be passed*, other than one contained in this part of this Act [ie an enactment of a non-Union nature], *shall be construed and have effect subject to the foregoing provisions of this section* [ie obligations of a Union nature].

There was considerable wavering in the early years on the question of primacy, but in 1979 the Court of Appeal in *Macarthys Ltd v Smith* ([1979] ICR 785) took the 'European' view, invoking the CJ in *Costa* and *Simmenthal*. The current British position is found in the ruling of what is now the Supreme Court in *Factortame Ltd v Secretary of State for Transport* ([1990] 2 AC 85). Lord Bridge suggested that the combined effect of sub-ss (1) and (4) of the European Communities Act 1972, s 2, was:

> as if a section were incorporated in Part II [the impugned part] of the Merchant Shipping Act 1988 which in terms enacted that the provisions with respect to registration of British fishing vessels were to be without prejudice to the directly enforceable Community [now Union] rights of nationals of any Member State of the EEC [now EU].

He suggested that if it were to be found that the British Act was in breach of the claimants' directly effective Union rights, the latter rights would 'prevail' over the contrary provisions of the 1988 Act.

Subsequently, in applying the CJ's ruling (in case C-213/89) that national courts must grant interim relief against the Crown where this was necessary to protect individuals' Union rights, the House of Lords, unanimously, granted that relief (*R v Secretary of State for Transport, ex parte Factortame Ltd* [1991] 1 AC 603 at 645). Here, clearly, no question of 'interpretation' of national law was possible; the House simply gave 'priority' to Union law. In justification, Lord Bridge pointed out that the principle of supremacy of Union law, if it was not always inherent in the Treaty, was:

> well established in the jurisprudence of the Court long before the United Kingdom joined the [Union]. Whatever limitation of its sovereignty Parliament accepted when it enacted the European Communities Act was entirely voluntary.

As a corollary, it seems that the doctrine of implied repeal has changed. In the context of 'constitutional' Acts of Parliament, such as the European Communities Act (and the Human Rights Act), express intention to repeal the act is required. Such acts will not be repealed through inconsistency with a later act. (See *Thoburn v Sunderland CC* (*metric martyrs* case) [2003] QB 151, QBD concerning criminal charges brought against individuals who sold products in imperial units rather than metric as required by EU law.)

Thus the British courts have been willing to accord supremacy to directly effective Union law, either by a (fictional) 'construction' of domestic law, or, where necessary, by applying EU law directly, in priority over national law. As suggested by Lord Bridge in *Factortame*, this appears to rest on the implied intentions of Parliament. However, should Parliament expressly attempt to repudiate its EU obligations, the courts would be obliged to give effect to its wishes:

> If the time should come when our Parliament deliberately passes an Act—with the intention of repudiating the Treaty or any provision in it—or intentionally of acting inconsistently with it—and says so in express terms—then . . . it would be the duty of our courts to follow the statute of our Parliament [*per* Lord Denning in *Macarthys Ltd v Smith* [1979] ICR 785 at 789].

As Laws LJ noted in the *metric martyrs* case, any changes have been introduced as a matter of English law, not as a direct requirement of Union law. The fact that EU law takes effect in the UK only by virtue of the domestic legal order was reiterated in s 18 of the European Union Act 2011. While the principle of supremacy is accepted in the UK courts, the scope of that acceptance may deserve further consideration as can be seen in the Supreme Court's ruling in *HS2* (*R (Buckinghamshire County Council) v Secretary of State for Transport* [2014] UKSC 3).

> ### HS2
>
> The case concerned the challenge to the governmental decision to proceed with plans for a high speed rail link between London through the Midlands to the north of England. The challenge was based on EU law and concerned the decision-making process, specifically the extent to which the legislative form chosen (a hybrid bill) complied with the requirement for an environmental impact assessment (required by Directive 2011/92 ([2012] OJ L26/3)). The problem lay in the combined impact of the party whip system and the limited review in the select committee on the possibility of review as required by an environmental impact assessment. This raised questions about the extent to which the domestic courts can review decision-making in Parliament (rather than the substance of the resulting decision) and came into conflict with a constitutional principle recognised in Article 9 Bill of Rights (1689).

The underlying issue was whether the 1972 Act was limited in its scope, so that there is a need for express Parliamentary authority for violations of fundamental rights or of fundamental constitutional principles. While the Supreme Court avoided the conflict on the facts (and did not make a reference), the issue was considered. Importantly, their Lordships agreed that this was a question of domestic law, not a question for the CJ. The Supreme Court also held, at para 207:

> It is, putting the point at its lowest, certainly arguable (and it is for the United Kingdom law and courts to decide) that there may be fundamental principles, whether contained in other constitutional instruments or recognised at common law, of which Parliament when it enacted the European Communities Act 1972 did not either contemplate or authorise the abrogation.

In sum, if the British courts have changed in their approach to statutory interpretation in the context of Union law, the principle of parliamentary sovereignty remains intact.

Given their post-war history, there were some questions about how new Member States would adapt to a system within which the CJ claimed priority. Their respective constitutions each claim supremacy in respect of the relevant Member State and each emphasise the principles of sovereignty and independence. Nonetheless, within most of the new Member States, similar approaches to EU supremacy can be seen to that taken in the older Member States. Relationships between national law and EU law are to be dealt with through the prism of national law. Given the differences in the various legal systems, the precise reasoning has varied and, in some instances, the judgments seemed very strongly worded. Notably, the Polish Constitutional Tribunal handed down two decisions, both of which emphasised the supremacy of the Polish Constitution, even as it accepted the supremacy of EU law over national (non-constitutional) law (*European Arrest Warrant* case (case P 1/05), judgment 27 April 2005; *Accession Treaty* case (case K 18/04), judgment 11 May 2005).

The Estonian position stands as a stark and rare contrast. The legislation introduced to allow Estonia to join the euro was challenged as being contrary to the constitution which reserved the power to issue Estonian currency to the Bank of Estonia. As part of its judgment (*Opinion on the Interpretation of the Constitution* CRCSC 3-4-1-3-06, decision of 11 May 2006), the Constitutional Review Chamber of the Supreme Court expressly accepted the supremacy of EU law over even the Estonian Constitution, arguing:

> As a result of the adoption of the Constitution of the Republic of Estonia Amendment Act the European Union law became one of the grounds for the interpretation and application of the Constitution.
>
> In the substantive sense this amounted to a material amendment of the entirety of the Constitution to the extent that it is not compatible with the European Union law. To find out which part of the Constitution is applicable, it has to be interpreted in conjunction with the European Union law which became binding for Estonia through the Accession Treaty. At that, only that part of the Constitution is applicable, which is in conformity with the European Union law or which regulates the relationships that are not regulated by the European Union law. The effect of those provisions of the Constitution that are not compatible with the European Union law and thus inapplicable, is suspended. This means that within the spheres, which are within the exclusive competence of the European Union or where there is a shared competence with the European Union, the European Union law shall apply in the case of a conflict between Estonian legislation, including the Constitution, with the European Union law.

4.4.4 Scope of supremacy

The case of Germany, which made the original reference in *Internationale Handelsgesellschaft*, has given rise to a significant body of case law. In the case applying the CJ's ruling, *Internationale Handelsgesellschaft* (*Solange I*), the FCC sought to exclude the protection of human rights from the scope of supremacy. The FCC held that even though the German Constitution permitted the transfer of sovereign rights to inter-state institutions through Treaty ratification, it did not permit its amendment by any means other than the formal process set down in the Constitution. In this case, the FCC was concerned to ensure that the guarantees relating to fundamental rights were not undermined. To some extent, in *Application of Wünsche Handelsgesellschaft* (*Solange II*) ([1987] 3 CMLR 225), its position in *Internationale Handelsgesellschaft* was reversed. Following *Solange II*, as long as EU law itself ensured the effective protection of fundamental rights, a ruling from the CJ under Article 267 TFEU would not, the FCC held, be subject to review.

Germany is not the only Member State which reserves the right to review EU law for compatibility with human rights. The Italian Constitutional Court has made similar claims, albeit limited to fundamental constitutional principles (*Fragd* Corte costituzionale, Sentenza No 232/1989, 21 April 1989); similarly, the French *Conseil Constitutional* limits its review to features constituting the 'constitutional identity' of France (CC Décision no 2006-540 DC, 27 July 2006). Likewise, the UK

Supreme Court in *HS2* affirmed the FCC's approach and significance of the state's constitutional identity (discussed further later).

Human rights are not the only issue which concerns the German FCC: as we see in *Brunner*. In addition to ensuring the protection of fundamental human rights guaranteed under the German Constitution, it will decide whether the Union institutions have acted within their powers under the Treaties.

Brunner

Brunner involved a challenge to the German Federal Parliament's power to ratify the TEU. It was argued that the transfer via the proposed Act of Ratification of further powers and competences to the European Union would threaten human rights and democratic principles protected under the German Constitution. The FCC found these allegations unfounded. The TEU did not establish a European state but a federation of states. It equipped the Union only with specific competences and powers in accordance with the principle of limited individual competences and established a principle of subsidiarity for the Union. It would permit no further extension of Union competence under Article 352 TFEU (Chapter 3). If the Union institutions or organisations were to develop the Treaty in a way not covered by the Treaty in the form that was the basis for the Act of Accession the resultant legislative instruments would not be binding within the sphere of German sovereignty. If parts of the Union legal order were to breach fundamental rights protected under the German Constitution it would declare those provisions inapplicable. Accordingly, the FCC would review legal instruments of European institutions and agencies to see whether they remained within the sovereign rights conferred on them or transgressed them. Germany was one of the masters of the Treaty with the intention of long-term membership: but it could ultimately revoke its adherence by a contrary act.

Germany is not alone in its concerns regarding national democracy. The British government, for example, had similar concerns about the need to protect national democracy by limiting the further transfer of powers to the EU. The European Union Act 2011 provided that an Act of Parliament will be required for all types of EU Treaty change and before the government can agree to the use of a passerelle (see Chapter 1). Where the use of a passerelle would constitute a transfer of competence to the EU, a referendum would be required. The ratification of the Lisbon Treaty raised similar concerns with regard to passarelle clauses in the Czech Republic (*Treaty of Lisbon II* (Pl. ÚS 29/09)).

A third possible limitation on the scope of supremacy from the German perspective was introduced with the *Lisbon* judgment (2 BvE, 2/08, judgment 30 June 2009). This limitation concerned the constitutional identity of Germany and defined a number of areas in particular in which it should be reserved to the state to act. The *Lisbon* judgment has been criticised, in particular in relation to the rationale for the selection of these areas of state sovereignty.

The FCC had the opportunity to consider the identity criterion again in the subsequent *Data Retention* case (BVerfG, 1 BvR 256/08, 2 March 2010).

Data Retention

The case concerned the implementation of the Data Retention Directive (Directive 2006/24 ([2006] OJ L105/64)). This Directive, as an exception to the e-Privacy Directive (Directive 2002/58 ([2002] OJ L201/37)) required *all* communications traffic data to be captured and stored by communications services providers for a period of up to two years. It permitted some Member State discretion and, seemingly, the German legislators took advantage of this when implementing the Directive into German law. This was problematic from a German constitutional point of view, as in the *Population Census* case (BVerfGe

65, 1) the FCC held that the right to informational self-determination broadly guarantees the ability of individuals to decide for themselves about the disclosure and use of their personal data. Here, the FCC held that the problem lay not with the Directive, but with the way it had been implemented and thus avoided direct conflict, once again, with the CJ. It did, however, describe informational self-determination to be part of the constitutional identity of Germany, which must be protected.

The *Brunner* judgment seemed designed to send a very clear message to the Union about the strength of review which the FCC was prepared to undertake. Whether it will in practice undertake such a review is, however, questionable. While the FCC post-*Brunner* received a number of applications challenging EU action, particularly on the basis of respect for human rights in the 'Banana litigation', it has managed to avoid open conflict with the CJ. The banana regime, which was set up in 1993 by Regulation 404/93 ([1993] OJ L47/1), and which operated to the serious disadvantage of German importers, was challenged by Germany on the grounds that it breached the Union's international obligations (inter alia, GATT) and violated vested property rights protected under the German Constitution. Despite strong arguments, acknowledged by Advocate-General Gulmann, that there were 'circumstances which might provide a basis for a finding that the Regulation was invalid' the CJ found that there was no illegality in the Union's market organisation of bananas (*Germany v Council* (*banana regime*) (case C-280/93); see further Chapter 12).

This case, which was extremely thin in its reasoning, for which it was roundly criticised, even by a former judge of the CJ (see the article by Everling noted in the further reading section at the end of this chapter), did little to stem the flood of actions before the German (and not only German) courts seeking to suspend the application of the contested regulation and/or to obtain compensation for damage suffered as a result of its application. The matter did not end until the Administrative Court, which had made a reference in *Atlanta Fruchthandelsgesellschaft mbH v Bundesamt für Ernährung und Forstwirtschaft* (case C-465/93) on further questions even after the CJ's decision in case C-280/93 and was still not satisfied by the CJ's response, referred the question back to the FCC. It was only in 2000, four years later, that the FCC delivered its ruling, declaring in a much-criticised judgment that the Administrative Court's application was inadmissible. The FCC argued that in *Solange II* and *Brunner* it had found the level of human-rights protection in Germany and within the EU legal order to be comparable. To succeed in a challenge against Union law, it would be necessary to show that the level of protection guaranteed by the CJ fell below the German level of protection. In the case in issue, the referring Administrative Court had not pointed to any decline in human rights standards since *Solange II*. Some commentators have suggested that this ruling constituted evidence of renewed cooperation between the FCC and the CJ. Indeed, some suggested that in the light of this judgment and another broadly contemporaneous case, *Alcan* (BVerfG, judgment 17 February 2000) the threat to supremacy suggested by *Brunner* had been dispersed and even that *Brunner* had partially been repealed. The reiteration of the *Brunner* approach in *Lisbon* and the *Data Protection* case rebuts this possibility (see also *Honeywell* below), but, as some critics have suggested, the FCC sets such high hurdles before it will find the Union in violation of human rights that it will never act on these issues.

This point can be made in relation to the conditions the FCC has imposed on the transfer of further competence to the EU, too. The political unease regarding the Treaty of Lisbon reawakened old concerns about competence creep resulting in references to the FCC, including the question of whether the '*Brunner* test' is satisfied by the guarantees in Lisbon (*Lisbon* judgment). While the FCC approved the Lisbon Treaty, it broadly reiterated its approach in *Brunner* and emphasised that the EU has 'autonomy to rule which is independent but derived' and ultimately subject to review by the

Member States to ensure their constitutional identities are respected. Shortly after the *Lisbon* decision, the question as to whether the EU exceeded its powers on this basis came before the FCC in *Honeywell* (2 BvR 2661/06).

Honeywell

Honeywell argued that the CJ's ruling in *Mangold* concerning age discrimination should not be applied in Germany as it was an *ultra vires* judgment. The FCC acknowledged that its *Lisbon* judgment ascribed it the power to review the *vires* of the European institutions, but then emphasised that any such review must be carried out in a manner that is open towards EU law.

The test for review seems high. According to the FCC, the complained of acts must be manifestly in breach of competence; and the impugned act must lead to a *significant* shift to the detriment of the Member States in the structure of competence between Member States and the European Union. Applying this principle to the case in issue, the outcome in the *Mangold* case was not a *sufficiently manifest* example of a breach. The FCC argued that:

> even a putative further development of the law on the part of the European Court of Justice that would no longer be justifiable in terms of legal method would only constitute a sufficiently quantified infringement of its competences if it also had the effect of establishing competences in practice.

This was not in the case with regard to the *Mangold* ruling, as the Union had already legislated on age discrimination.

The *Honeywell* judgment was not unanimous. One dissenting judge, Landau, argued that the decision in this case 'transgressed the consensus' on which the FCC's *Lisbon* judgment was based, by introducing the double test of a manifest breach and a shift in competence. (See also *Aid Measures for Greece and the Euro Rescue Package*, 2 BvR 987/10, 2 BvR 1485/10, 2 BvR 1099/10, judgment 7 September 2011.)

Another expression of German concern about the scope of EU law—specifically the Charter—arose in the *Anti-Terror Database* case (1 BvR 1215/07, judgment 24 April 2013).

Anti-Terror Database

The complainant challenged the constitutionality of the German Act on Setting up a Standardised Central Counter-Terrorism Database of Police Authorities and Intelligence Services of the Federal Government and the *Länder*, which regulates the exchange of information between the police and intelligence agencies. It poses a threat to the right to privacy of those people whose personal information is collected and exchanged. The FCC determined that the challenged provisions pursue nationally determined objectives which 'are not determined by EU law,' and can regard it 'only in part' (paras 88–9).

This determination meant that, in the eyes of the FCC, according to Article 51 EUCFR, the Charter did not apply. The FCC concluded that there was no need to refer the case to the CJ.

This case can be seen as the FCC signalling a limit to the applicability of the EU Charter in circumstances which are not closely connected with EU law and reasserting the competence of national constitutional courts to deal with constitutional issues (including human rights protection) in their respective territories. This is the more noticeable as the FCC's judgment was handed down shortly after a decision of the CJ, *Åklagaren v Åkerberg Fransson* (case C-617/10), which was seen by some—seemingly including the judges in the FCC—as an example of 'competence creep' through an expansive interpretation of the scope of EU law. The FCC argued that the ruling in *Fransson* should not be read in such a way as to render it an 'obvious' *ultra vires* act under German law or so as to endanger the protection and enforcement of the fundamental rights in Member States in such a way that would question the identity of the Basic Law's constitutional order—that is, repeating the concerns of the *Lisbon* and *Honeywell* judgments. To ensure the 'cooperative relationship' between the FCC and the CJ, the FCC therefore opted for the narrower interpretation. The fact that it did not make a reference to the CJ on the question, although EU rules affecting the substance of the case exist (eg, data protection), is significant, and indicates an assertion of its right to make a decision about the boundaries of the CJ's involvement.

The terms of *Honeywell* came to the fore in the *Gauweiler* litigation concerning the programme for Outright Monetary Transactions (OMT) in which both the scope of EU law and the nature of German constitutional identity were in question. The litigation argued that the OMT concerned economic policy and was therefore outside the remit of the European System of Central Banks. The FCC in a majority decision thought the matter lay outside EU competence—in fact was a 'manifest transgression' in *Honeywell* terms —but in so doing made its first ever reference to the CJ on the basis that a narrow interpretation of the programme could mean that it was, after all, legal. In so doing the FCC reiterated its claim to Kompetenz-Kompetenz, reaffirming German constitutional identity (as distinct from national identity as understood in the scope of Article 4(2) TEU). In its judgment, the FCC suggested that it was not alone in its understanding of constitutional identity—that other constitutional courts took the same view: Denmark, Estonia, France, Ireland, Italy, Latvia, Poland, Sweden, Spain and the Czech Republic.

The matter was heard before the CJ as *Gauweiler*. The CJ found the OMT to be lawful. In so doing, however, it did not reiterate its case law on autonomy and the primacy of EU law, and its exclusive jurisdiction to rule on the validity of EU law (see Chapter 12), but rather focused on the substance of the powers awarded to the EU, perhaps seeking to avoid direct collision with the FCC. The matter returned to the FCC, where that court found that the OMT passed scrutiny in terms of the scheme itself but held that, given that there is a difference between policy and its implementation, any such implementation must be kept under review to ensure that the conditions specified in the CJ's reasoning justifying the legality of the measure would in fact be met.

It could be said that this is just another example of the CJ and the FCC avoiding collisions: the CJ by sticking to a substantive analysis in its ruling; and the FCC by retreating to its long standing 'so long as . . .' approach in which the measure in issue is approved by conditions for any future approval are reiterated. While to some extent this is true, it is not the whole story. Note first that, in its statement on the policy, the FCC does not say that OMT is not *ultra vires*, just not 'manifestly so', as required by the *Honeywell* judgment. The FCC's judgment also re-emphasises that EU law is based on the delegation of power to the EU, so that the EU's (and the CJ's powers) are limited by the constitutions of the several Member States. If this is accepted more broadly, then the uniformity of EU law and its supremacy could be under threat.

The FCC is not the only court to challenge the vires of CJEU rulings. Perhaps one of the most controversial judgments in the relationship between the EU national constitutional courts was the ruling of the Czech Constitutional Court (CCC) in 2012 (case Pl. US 5/12).

Case Pl. US 5/12: Czech Constitutional Court

The background to the case concerned an internal dispute between the CCC and the Czech Supreme Administration Court over the CCC case law on Slovak pensions, which allowed more favourable treatment of Slovak nationals in certain circumstances relating to the dissolution of the Czech and Slovak Federal Republic on 31 December 1992. The Administrative Court referred questions on the compatibility of the case law with EU law (specifically Regulation 1408/71 on social security) to the CJ. The CJ in *Landtová v Česká správa socialního zabezpečení* (case C-399/09) had ruled that there was incontrovertible evidence of discrimination on the grounds of nationality contrary to EU law. The national law was then amended but in a subsequent but similar case, the CCC held expressly that the ruling of the CJ was *ultra vires*. The CCC argued that an EU regulation which governed coordination of pension systems among Member States generally should not be applied to the entirely specific situation of dissolution of the Czechoslovak federation and its consequences. It therefore held that the amendment to national law was incompatible with the Constitution. In its judgment, the CCC reiterated its own previous case law on the relationship between national courts and the EU and the circumstances in which constitutional courts maintain their role of supreme guardians of constitutionality, but also linked its reasoning with that of the German FCC.

Are these cases the beginning of a new trend of challenges to the CJEU, or one-off decisions arising from specific facts?

4.4.5 **'Kompetenz-kompetenz'**

While some courts have not made the point in express terms, it seems that all the constitutional courts of the Member States regard themselves as having the power to review the boundary of EU competence. According to the FCC in *Brunner*, German sovereignty remains intact, and that court will itself decide whether the institutions of the Union have acted within their powers under the Treaties. Consequently, the potential for conflict remains, though it should be noted that while the relations between the national courts can be portrayed as a power struggle, they can also be seen as a form of judicial dialogue, in which both levels of judiciary participate so as to avoid open disagreement.

4.5 Conclusions

The CJ, in introducing the notion of supremacy, was instrumental in providing a view of the Union as a body that went beyond what was normal for an international law organisation. In a number of key judgments it identified the Union as an independent legal order, supreme over the national legal systems. One of the mechanisms used to justify this was the effectiveness of Union law, a doctrine that the CJ has used again and again in different contexts to justify the development of Union law in a particular direction. As has been noted, however, the success of this project cannot be ascribed entirely to the CJ. To a large part, it has been dependent on the cooperation of the Member States, particularly their courts. In a relatively short space of time the courts of Member States, despite their different constitutional rules and traditions, have adapted to the principle of supremacy of EU law. They have done so in a variety of ways: by bending and adapting their own constitutional rules; and by devising new constitutional rules to meet the new situation. Different Member States have shown different degrees of deference. While they have argued for the supremacy of Union law, it has been on the basis of national legal provisions, not the provisions of Union law itself. Their acceptance of supremacy is thus conditional. There remains the potential for conflict on specific issues, as the human rights cases illustrate (see Chapter 6). Credit for national courts' acceptance of the principle of supremacy of EU law must go to the CJ, which has supplied persuasive reasons for doing so. Nonetheless, equal credit must go to the courts of Member States, which have contrived to embrace the principle of primacy of Union law while at the same time insisting that ultimate political and judicial control remains within the Member States. As the cases relating to the ratification of the Lisbon Treaty indicate, the courts of Member States, particularly their supreme courts, will be vigilant, and use all the means at their disposal, to ensure that the EU institutions do not exceed their powers or transgress fundamental constitutional rights, particularly in the post-Lisbon political climate. As Kumm suggests, 'they need to keep a handle on the emergency brake'; but they would disapply a Union act or a ruling from the CJ only where that act or that ruling was manifestly and gravely erroneous. While we might see this as true judicial dialogue, note that the CJ has not shied away from the ultimate step: a claim for damages against the state in respect of judicial breaches of Union law (see *Köbler v Austria* (case C-224/01) and *Traghetti del Mediterraneo SpA v Italy* (case C-173/03) discussed in Chapter 9).

Further reading

See also the reading list at the end of Chapter 5.

Alonso Garcia, R, 'The Spanish Constitution and the European Constitution: The script for a virtual collision and other observations on the principle of primacy' (2005) 6 German LJ 1010.

Alter, KJ, *Establishing the Supremacy of EC Law* (Oxford University Press, 2001).

Avbelj, M, 'Supremacy or primacy of EU law–(Why) Does it Matter?' (2011) 17 ELJ 744.

Craig, P, 'Constitutionalising constitutional law' [2014] Public Law 373.

Craig, P and Markakis, M, '*Gauweiler* and the Legality of Outright Monetary Transactions' (2016) 41 EL Rev 1.

Danielsen, JH, 'One of many national constraints on European integration: Section 20 of the Danish Constitution' (2010) 16 EPL 181.

Everling, U, 'Will Europe slip on bananas? The *bananas* judgment of the European Court and national courts' (1996) 33 CML Rev 401.

Fahey, E, 'A constitutional crisis in a teacup: The supremacy of EC law in Ireland' (2009) 15 EPL 515.

Herdegen, M, 'Maastricht and the German Constitutional Court: Constitutional restraints for an ever closer union' (1994) 31 CML Rev 235.

Keleman, R, Daniel, 'On the Unsustainability of Constitutional Pluralism: European Supremacy and the Survival of the Eurozone' (2016) 23 Maastricht Journal of European and Comparative Law 136.

Komarek, J, 'The place of constitutional courts in the EU' (2013) 9 ECL Rev 420.

Kowalik-Bańczyk, K, 'Polish constitutional tribunal and the idea of supremacy of EU law' (2005) 6 German LJ 1355.

Kumm, M, 'Who is the arbiter of constitutionality in Europe?' (1999) 36 CML Rev 351.

Lenaerts, K and Corthaut, T, 'Of birds and hedges: The role of primacy in invoking norms of EU law' (2006) 31 EL Rev 287.

Oliver, P, 'The French Constitution and the Treaty of Maastricht' (1994) 43 ICLQ 1.

Peers, S, 'Taking supremacy seriously' (1998) 23 EL Rev 146.

Steiner, J, 'Coming to terms with EEC directives' (1990) 106 LQR 144.

Wende, M, 'Lisbon before the courts: Comparative perspectives' (2011) 7 ECL Rev 96.

Zuleeg, M, 'The European Constitution under European constraints: The German scenario' (1997) 22 EL Rev 19.

5 Principles of direct applicability and direct effects

5.1 Introduction

It has already been seen that EU law takes priority over national law in its sphere of application and that domestic courts are under an obligation to give full effect to EU law (Chapter 4). With this in mind, the question then arises to what extent individuals can rely on EU law before the national courts, particularly where a Member State has failed to implement a particular measure, or where the implementation is in some way defective and does not provide the full extent of the rights an individual should enjoy by virtue of the relevant EU measure. To deal with this question, and very much in accordance with the principle of supremacy, the CJ has developed three interrelated doctrines:

- direct effect;
- indirect effect;
- state liability.

Taken together, these seek to ensure that individuals are given the greatest possible level of protection before their national courts. This chapter considers the scope of the doctrines of direct and indirect effect, as well as identifying difficulties in the jurisprudence. While the CJ has emphasised that directives cannot have direct effect as against individuals, its case law shows a range of developments that operate to undermine the simplicity of this position. This can be seen in the Court's approach to the definition of a public body and in the introduction of the doctrine of indirect effect. More recently, questions have arisen concerning the idea of incidental direct effect, triangular situations and the consequences of the judgments in *Mangold* and *Kücükdeveci v Swedex (Grand Chamber)* (case C-555/07).

The third mechanism developed by the CJ to encourage the full implementation of EU law is the doctrine of state liability. It is different from direct effects and indirect effects as it does not affect the meaning of national law (which is the consequence of direct effects and indirect effects). Rather, state liability seeks to compensate an individual for losses caused by a Member State's failure to implement EU law. State liability will therefore be dealt with separately, in Chapter 9.

5.2 Doctrine of direct effects

5.2.1 Direct applicability

Provisions of international law which are found to be capable of application by national courts *at the suit of individuals* are also termed 'directly applicable'. This ambiguity (the same ambiguity is found in the alternative expression 'self-executing') has given rise to much uncertainty in the context of EU law. For this reason it was suggested by Winter (see the further reading section at the end of this chapter) that the term 'directly effective' be used to convey this secondary meaning. Although this term has generally found favour amongst British academic writers, the CJ as well as the British courts tend to use the two concepts of 'direct applicability' and 'direct effects' interchangeably. However, for purposes of clarity it is proposed to use the term 'directly effective' or 'capable of direct effects' in this secondary meaning, to denote those provisions of EU law which give rise to rights or obligations which individuals may enforce before their national courts.

Not all provisions of directly applicable international law are capable of direct effects. Some provisions are regarded as binding on, and enforceable by, states alone; others are too vague to form the basis of rights or obligations for individuals; others are too incomplete and require further measures of implementation before they can be fully effective in law. Whether a particular provision is directly effective is a matter of construction, depending on its language and purpose as well as the terms on which the Treaty has been incorporated into domestic law. Although most states apply similar criteria of clarity and completeness, specific rules and attitudes inevitably differ, and since the application of the criteria often conceals an underlying policy decision, the results are by no means uniform from state to state.

5.2.2 Relevance of direct effect in EU law

The question of the direct effects of Union law is of paramount concern to EU lawyers. If a provision of EU law is directly effective, domestic courts must not only apply it but, following the principle of primacy of EU law (Chapter 4), must do so in priority over any conflicting provisions of national law. Since the scope of the Treaties is wide, the more generous the approach to the question of direct effects, the greater the potential for conflict.

Which provisions will then be capable of direct effect? The TFEU merely provides in Article 288 that regulations (but only regulations) are 'directly applicable'. Since, as has been suggested, direct applicability is a necessary precondition for direct effects, this would seem to imply that only regulations are capable of direct effects.

This has not proved to be the case. In a series of landmark decisions, the CJ has extended the principle of direct effects to Treaty articles, directives, decisions, and even to provisions of international agreements to which the EU is a party.

5.2.3 Treaty articles

The question of the direct effect of a treaty article was first raised in *Van Gend en Loos*.

> ### *Van Gend en Loos*
>
> Van Gend en Loos challenged the amount of import duty charged by the Dutch authorities in relation to a shipment of ureaformaldehyde. The company argued that the Dutch government was not permitted

under the then Treaty of Rome to increase, after the entry into force of that Treaty, the amount of duty payable in respect of trade between Member States.

Article 30 prohibits states from 'introducing between themselves any new customs duties on imports or exports or any charges having equivalent effect'.

The Dutch administrative tribunal asked the CJ:

Whether [Article 30 TFEU] has an internal effect . . . in other words, whether the nationals of Member States may, on the basis of the Article in question, enforce rights which the judge should protect?

It was argued on behalf of the defendant customs authorities that the obligation in Article 30 TFEU was addressed to states and was intended to govern rights and obligations between states. Such obligations were not normally enforceable at the suit of individuals. Moreover the Treaty had expressly provided enforcement procedures under what are now Articles 258–9 TFEU (see Chapter 11) at the suit of the Commission or Member States, respectively. Advocate-General Roemer suggested that Article 30 TFEU was too complex to be enforced by national courts; if such courts were to enforce Article 30 TFEU directly there would be no uniformity of application.

Nonetheless, the CJ held that Article 30 TFEU was directly effective. The Court stated that:

this Treaty is more than an agreement creating only mutual obligations between the contracting parties . . . [Union] law . . . not only imposes obligations on individuals but also confers on them legal rights.

These rights would arise:

not only when an explicit grant is made by the Treaty, but also through obligations imposed, in a clearly defined manner, by the Treaty on individuals as well as on Member States and the Community institutions.

. . . The text of Article [30 TFEU] sets out a clear and unconditional prohibition, which is not a duty to act but a duty not to act. This duty is imposed without any power in the States to subordinate its application to a positive act of internal law. The prohibition is perfectly suited by its nature to produce direct effects in the legal relations between the Member States and their citizens.

And further:

The vigilance of individuals interested in protecting their rights creates an effective control additional to that entrusted by Articles [258–9] to the diligence of the Commission and the Member States.

Apart from its desire to enable individuals to invoke the protection of EU law the Court clearly saw the principle of direct effects as a valuable means of ensuring that EU law was enforced uniformly in all Member States, even when Member States had not themselves complied with their obligations.

It was originally thought that, as the Court suggested in *Van Gend*, only prohibitions such as (the then) Article 25 EEC ('standstill' provisions) would qualify for direct effects; this was found in *Alfons Lütticke GmbH v Hauptzollamt Saarlouis* (case 57/65) not to be so. The article under consideration was at that time Article 95(1) and (3) EEC (now Article 110 TFEU). It contains a prohibition on states introducing discriminatory taxation; the then Article 95(3) EEC contained a positive obligation that

'Member States shall, not later than at the beginning of the second stage, repeal or amend any provisions existing when this Treaty enters into force which conflict with the preceding rules'. Lütticke, which imported powdered milk, was subject to a discriminatory taxation regime and sought to challenge it.

The CJ found that the then Article 95(1) EEC was directly effective and what was Article 95(3) EEC, which was subject to compliance within a specified time limit, would, the Court implied, become directly effective once that time limit had expired.

The Court has subsequently found a large number of Treaty provisions to be directly effective. All the basic principles relating to free movement of goods and persons, competition law and discrimination on the grounds of sex and nationality may now be invoked by individuals before their national courts.

In deciding whether a particular provision is directly effective certain criteria are applied:

- the provision must be sufficiently clear and precise;
- the provision must be unconditional;
- the provision must leave no room for the exercise of discretion in implementation by Member States or Union institutions.

The criteria are, however, applied generously, with the result that many provisions which are not particularly clear or precise, especially with regard to their scope and application, have been found to produce direct effects. Even where they are conditional and subject to further implementation they have been held to be directly effective once the date for implementation is past. The Court reasons that while there may be discretion as to the means of implementation, there is no discretion as to ends.

In *Van Gend* the principle of direct effects operated to confer rights on Van Gend exercisable against the Dutch customs authorities. Thus the obligation fell on an organ of the state, to whom Article 30 TFEU was addressed. But Treaty obligations, even when addressed to states, may fall on individuals too. May they be invoked by individuals against individuals?

Van Gend implies so, and this was confirmed in *Defrenne v Sabena (Defrenne II)* (case 43/75).

Defrenne II

Ms Defrenne was an air hostess employed by Sabena, a Belgian airline company. She brought an action against Sabena based on what was then Article 119 EEC Treaty (now, after amendment, Article 157 TFEU). It provided that:

> Each Member State shall during the first stage ensure and subsequently maintain the application of the principle that men and women should receive equal pay for equal work.

Ms Defrenne claimed, inter alia, that by paying their male stewards more than their air hostesses, when they performed identical tasks, Sabena was in breach of the then Article 119 EEC. The gist of the questions referred to the CJ was whether, and in what context, that provision was directly effective. Sabena argued that the Treaty articles so far found directly effective, such as former Article 12 EEC, concerned the relationship between the state and its subjects, whereas former Article 119 EEC was primarily concerned with relationships between individuals. It was thus not suited to produce direct effects. The Court, following Advocate-General Trabucci, disagreed, holding that:

> the prohibition on discrimination between men and women applies not only to the action of public authorities, but also extends to all agreements which are intended to regulate paid labour collectively, as well as to contracts between individuals.

This same principle was applied in *Walrave v Association Union Cycliste Internationale* (case 36/74) to Article 18 TFEU (originally Article 7 EEC) which provides that:

> Within the scope of application of this Treaty, and without prejudice to any special provisions contained therein, any discrimination on grounds of nationality shall be prohibited.

Walrave and Koch

The claimants, Walrave and Koch, were pacemakers on motorcycles in medium-distance bicycle races with so-called 'stayers', that is, competitors in the race who cycle in the lee of the motorcycle. New rules were introduced which required pacemakers and stayers to be of the same nationality. Walrave and Koch sought to invoke Article 18 TFEU in order to challenge the rules of the defendant association which they claimed were discriminatory.

The CJ held that the prohibition of any discrimination on grounds of nationality:

> does not only apply to the action of public authorities but extends likewise to rules of any other nature aimed at regulating in a collective manner gainful employment and the provision of services.

To limit the prohibition in question to acts of a public authority would risk creating inequality in their application. Even now, the precise scope of the horizontal nature of the provisions relating to free movement of individuals (Articles 45, 49 and 56 TFEU respectively) is not clear. Whilst the judgment in *Walrave* can be read as a form of effectiveness, which could then extend the scope of the provisions to all non-state actors, it can equally be read as relating to collective agreements, or to situations where there is a violation of the principle of non-discrimination. Subsequent cases have not cleared up this ambiguity (see Chapter 21). It was generally accepted that the provisions on the free movement of goods (Articles 34–5 TFEU) did not have horizontal direct effect, although the CJ's jurisprudence operated to compensate for this limitation (see Chapter 19).

The case of *Fra.bo SpA v Deutsche Vereinigung des Gas- und Wasserfaches eV (DVGW)–Technisch-Wissenschaftlicher Verein* (case C-171/11) seems to change the position.

Fra.bo SpA

The German Regulation on General Conditions for Water Supply specified that only materials and devices that carried a compliance mark could be used by contractors. One such mark was awarded by DVGW, a non-profit, private law body. It refused to renew its certification for Fra.bo's products and Fra.bo challenged this decision. The matter was referred to the CJ regarding the compatibility of DVGW's relationship with the industry under the Regulations and the impact of its decisions on the free movement of goods (and competition law). The CJ recognised that the DVGW was a body independent of government, over whose activities the relevant Member State had no decisive influence. So, could Article 34 TFEU apply? The applicants argued that private-law bodies are, in certain circumstances, bound to observe the free movement of goods, a point with which the CJ seemed to agree. It suggested that the key point was whether:

> in the light of inter alia the legislative and regulatory context in which it operates, the activities of a private-law body such as the DVGW has the effect of giving rise to restrictions on the free movement of goods in the same manner as do measures imposed by the State [para 26].

The CJ concluded that as DVGW 'had the power to regulate the entry into the German market of products' in question, Article 34 TFEU applies (para 31). Many Treaty provisions have now been successfully invoked vertically and horizontally. The fact of their being addressed to, and imposing obligations on, states has been no bar to their horizontal effect.

Note that while the Charter has, since Lisbon, been given legal effect, the extent to which Charter provisions can be regarded as directly effective—especially in disputes between private parties—is uncertain (see 5.2.14 with regard to their impact on directives and, generally, Chapter 6).

5.2.4 **Regulations**

A regulation is described in Article 288 TFEU as of 'general application . . . binding in its entirety and directly applicable in all Member States'. It is clearly intended to take immediate effect without the need for further implementation.

Regulations are thus by their very nature apt to produce direct effects. However, even for regulations, direct effects are not automatic. There may be cases where a provision in a regulation is conditional, or insufficiently precise, or requires further implementation before it can take full legal effect. Conversely, if a regulation requires implementation it may fail the test for direct effects, as happened in *Azienda Agricola Monte Arcosu v Regione Autonoma della Sardegna* (case C-403/98). There the EU regulation left it to the Member State to define the word 'farmer', which gave the Member States too much discretion for the provision to have direct effects. Further, where a regulation provides that it shall not come into force for a given period or where there is a special derogation for a Member State, the regulation will not be capable of having direct effects until any such limit has expired (*Enosi Efoploiston Aktoploias and Others v Ipourgos Emporikis Naftilias and Ipourgos Aigaiou* (case C-122/09) temporary exemption from free movement of services for Greek island cabotage).

Since a regulation is of 'general application', where the criteria for direct effects are satisfied, it may be invoked vertically or horizontally. In *Antonio Muñoz Cia SA v Frumar Ltd* (case C-253/00), the CJ confirmed that regulations by their very nature operate to confer rights on individuals which must be protected by the national courts.

Muñoz

Regulation 2200/96 ([1996] OJ L297/1) laid down the standards by which grapes are classified. Muñoz brought civil proceedings against Frumar who had sold grapes under particular labels which did not comply with the corresponding standard. The relevant provision in the Regulation did not confer rights specifically on Muñoz, but applied to all operators in the market. A failure by one operator to comply with the provision could have adverse consequences for other operators. The CJ held that, since the purpose of the Regulation was to keep products of unsatisfactory quality off the market, and to ensure the full effectiveness of the Regulation, it must be possible for a trader to bring civil proceedings against a competitor to enforce the Regulation.

This decision is noteworthy for three reasons. First, as with the early case law on the Treaty articles, the CJ reasons from the need to ensure the effectiveness of Union law. Secondly, it also confirms that, as directly applicable measures, regulations can apply horizontally between private parties as well as vertically against public bodies. Thirdly, in terms of enforcement, it also seems to suggest that it is not necessary that rights be conferred expressly on the claimant before that individual may rely on the sufficiently clear and unconditional provisions of a regulation (contrast the position for directives at 5.2.8).

5.2.5 **Directives: accepting the principle of direct effects**

The position of directives is more complex. A directive is (Article 288 TFEU) 'binding, as to the result to be achieved, upon each Member State to which it is addressed, but shall leave to the national authorities the choice of form and methods'.

Because directives are not described as 'directly applicable', it was originally thought that they could not produce direct effects. Moreover the obligation in a directive is addressed to states, and gives the state some discretion as to the form and method of implementation; its effect thus appeared to be conditional on the implementation by the state. Given that unconditionality is part of the test for direct effects, this fact militates against directives having the potential to have direct effects.

This was not the conclusion reached by the CJ, however, which found, in *Grad v Finanzamt Traunstein* (case 9/70) that a directive could be directly effective.

Grad

The claimant was a haulage company seeking to challenge a tax levied by the German authorities that the claimant claimed was in breach of a directive and decision. The Directive required states to amend their VAT systems to comply with a common European system and to apply this new VAT system to, inter alia, freight transport from the date of the Directive's entry into force. The German government argued that only regulations were directly applicable. Directives and decisions took effect internally only via national implementing measures. As evidence they pointed out that only regulations were required to be published in the *Official Journal*. The CJ disagreed. The fact that only regulations were described as directly applicable did not mean that other binding acts were incapable of such effects:

> It would be incompatible with the binding effect attributed to Decisions by Article [288 TFEU] to exclude in principle the possibility that persons affected may invoke the obligation imposed by a Decision . . . the effectiveness of such a measure would be weakened if the nationals of that State could not invoke it in the courts and the national courts could not take it into consideration as part of [Union] law.

Although expressed in terms of a decision, it was implied in the judgment that the same principle applied in the case of directives.

The direct effect of directives was established beyond doubt in a claim based on a free-standing directive in *Van Duyn v Home Office* (case 41/74).

Van Duyn

The claimant sought to invoke Article 3 Directive 64/221 to challenge the Home Office's refusal to allow her to enter to take up work with the Church of Scientology. Under EU law Member States are allowed to deny EU nationals rights of entry and residence only on the grounds of public policy, public security and public health (see Chapter 25). Article 3 Directive 64/221 provided that measures taken on the grounds of public policy must be based exclusively on the personal conduct of the person concerned. Despite the lack of clarity as to the scope of the concept of 'personal conduct' the CJ held that Mrs Van Duyn was entitled to invoke the Directive directly before her national court. It suggested that even if the provision in question was not clear the matter could be referred to the CJ for interpretation under Article 267 TFEU.

So, both directives and decisions may be directly effective. Whether they will in fact be so will depend on whether they satisfy the criteria for direct effects—they must be sufficiently clear, precise and unconditional, leaving no room for discretion in implementation. These conditions were satisfied in *Grad*. Although the Directive was not unconditional in that it required action to be taken by the state, and gave a time limit for implementation, once the time limit expired the obligation became absolute. At that stage there was no discretion left. *Van Duyn* demonstrates that it is not necessary for a provision to be particularly precise for it to be deemed 'sufficiently' clear. *Riksskatterverket v Soghra Gharehveran* (case C-441/99) concerned a directive which sought to protect employees in the event of their employer's insolvency. The Court had held (eg, in *Francovich*) that the relevant Directive was not sufficiently clear and precise in terms of how that protection was to be put into practice to be directly effective. Swedish law, however, designated that the state would be liable to fulfil the obligation to meet claims for pay guaranteed under the Directive (as permitted but not required by the Directive). The Court thus held that a provision in a directive could be directly effective even where it contained a discretionary element if the Member State had already exercised that discretion. The reason for this was that it could then no longer be argued that the Member State still had to take measures to implement the provision.

The reasoning in *Grad*, which was followed in *Van Duyn*, has been repeated on many occasions to justify the direct effect of directives. The more recent formulation of the test for direct effects, that the provision in question should be 'sufficiently clear and precise and unconditional', is the one that is generally used.

Although the CJ has taken, and continues to take, a very broad approach to the test for direct effects, it is not unlimited in scope as can be seen in *Comitato di Coordinamento per la Difesa della Cava v Regione Lombardia* (case C-236/92).

Comitato di Coordinamento per la Difesa della Cava

The Court found that Article 4 Directive 75/442 on the Disposal of Waste, which required states to 'take the necessary measures to ensure that waste is disposed of without endangering human health and without harming the environment', was not unconditional or sufficiently precise to be relied on by individuals before their national courts. It 'merely indicated a programme to be followed and provided a framework for action' by the Member States. The Court suggested that in order to be directly effective the obligation imposed by the Directive must be 'set out in unequivocal terms'.

In *El Corte Inglés SA v Rivero* (case C-192/94) the CJ found Article 169 TFEU, which requires the Union to take action to achieve a high level of consumer protection, insufficiently clear, precise and unconditional to be relied on as between individuals. This may be contrasted with its earlier approach to Article 166 TFEU, which required the Union institutions to lay down general principles for the implementation of a vocational training policy, which was found, albeit together with the non-discrimination principle of Article 18 TFEU, to be directly effective (see *Gravier v City of Liège* (case 293/83)).

5.2.6 Direct effect of directives: when does the obligation arise?

A directive cannot be directly effective before the time limit for implementation has expired. A claim to the contrary was tried unsuccessfully in the case of *Pubblico Ministero v Ratti* (case 148/78).

> ### Ratti
>
> Mr Ratti, a solvent manufacturer, sought to invoke two harmonisation directives on the labelling of dangerous preparations to defend a criminal charge based on his own labelling practices. These practices, he claimed, were not illegal according to the Directive. The CJ held that since the time limit for the implementation of one of the Directives had not expired it was not directly effective. He could, however, rely on the other Directive for which the implementation date had passed.

In *Inter-Environnement Wallonie ASBL v Region Wallonie* (case C-129/96), the CJ held that even within the implementation period Member States are not entitled to take any measures which could seriously compromise the result required by the Directive. This obligation applies irrespective of whether the domestic measure which conflicts with a directive was adopted to implement that Directive or not (*ATRAL SA v Belgium* (case C-14/02)). In *Mangold* (see further 5.2.14), the CJ strengthened this view. According to its ruling, the obligation on a national court to set aside domestic law in conflict with a directive before its period for implementation has expired appears to be even stronger where the directive in question merely aims to provide a framework for ensuring compliance with a general principle of Union law, such as non-discrimination on the grounds of age (see further Chapter 6).

5.2.7 Directives: faulty implementation

Even when a state has implemented a directive the directive may still be directly effective. The CJ held this to be the case in *Verbond van Nederlandse Ondernemingen (VNO) v Inspecteur der Invoerrechten en Accijnzen* (case 51/76), thereby allowing the Federation of Dutch Manufacturers to invoke the Second VAT Directive despite faulty implementation of the provision by the Dutch authorities. The grounds for the decision were that the useful effect of the Directive would be weakened if individuals could not invoke it before national courts. By allowing individuals to invoke the Directive the Union can ensure that national authorities have kept within the limits of their discretion. Indeed, it seems possible to rely on even a properly implemented directive if it is not properly applied in practice (*Marks and Spencer plc v Commissioners of Customs and Excise* (case C-62/00)).

> ### Marks and Spencer
>
> *Marks and Spencer* concerned a VAT directive, which both sides agreed had not been properly implemented. Companies as a result had overpaid tax. When it was realised (following a decision of the CJ on the relevant provision) that the UK's understanding of the EU law requirements was incorrect, the government sought to limit its exposure to claims for repayment by limiting the time period in which such claims could be brought. The CJ held that the fact that the UK had now correctly implemented the Directive could not take away the right of Marks and Spencer under EU law to claim back the overpaid tax. The Court held:
>
> > the adoption of national measures correctly implementing a directive does not exhaust the effects of the directive. Member States remain bound actually to ensure full application of the directive even after the adoption of those measures. Individuals are therefore entitled to rely before national courts, against the State, on the provisions of a directive which appear, so far as their subject-matter is concerned, to be unconditional and sufficiently precise whenever the full application of the directive is not in fact secured, that is to say, not only where the directive has not been implemented or has been implemented incorrectly, but also where the national

> measures correctly implementing the directive are not being applied in such a way as to achieve
> the result sought by it [para 27].

Arguably, the principle could apply to enable an individual to invoke a 'parent' directive even before the expiry of the time limit, where domestic measures have been introduced for the purpose of complying with the directive (see *Officier van Justitie v Kolpinghuis Nijmegen* (case 80/86) discussed in 5.3.2).

5.2.8 **Must rights be conferred by the directive?**

The CJ's test for direct effects (the provision must be sufficiently clear, precise and unconditional) has never expressly included a requirement that the directive should be intended to give rise to rights for the individual seeking to invoke its provisions. However, the justification for giving direct effect to EU law has always been the need to ensure effective protection for individuals' Union rights. Furthermore, the CJ has, in a number of cases, suggested that an individual's right to invoke a directive may be confined to situations in which he can show a particular interest in that directive. In *Becker v Finanzamt Munster-Innenstadt* (case 8/81), in confirming and clarifying the principle of direct effect as applied to directives, the Court held that 'provisions of Directives can be invoked by individuals *insofar as they define rights which individuals are able to assert against the state*' (emphasis added).

Drawing on this statement in *Verholen v Sociale Verzekeringsbank, Amsterdam* (cases C-87 to 89/90), the Court suggested that only a person with a direct interest in the application of the directive could invoke its provisions: this was held in *Verholen* to include a third party who was directly affected by the directive.

> ### *Verholen*
>
> The husband of a woman suffering sex discrimination as regards the granting of a social security benefit, contrary to Directive 79/7, was able to bring a claim based on the Directive in respect of disadvantage to himself consequential on the discriminatory treatment of his wife.

In most recent cases in which an individual seeks to invoke a directive directly, the existence of a direct interest is clear. The question of his or her standing has not therefore been in issue. Normally the rights he or she seeks to invoke, be it, for example, a right to equal treatment or to employment protection, are contained in the directive. Its provisions are clearly, if not explicitly, designed to benefit persons such as the individual. There are circumstances, however, where the interest is not so clear. In many cases where the nature of the right is far from clear—such as in the context of an environmental directive (see, eg, *Wells v Secretary of State for Transport, Local Government and the Regions* (case C-201/02) discussed in 5.2.12) or in the cases concerning the procedural requirements of the Technical Regulation Directive (Directive 98/34 now codified as Directive 2015/1535 ([2015] OJ L241/1)) (eg, *Unilever Italia SpA v Central Food SpA* (case C-443/98) discussed in 5.2.13)—the CJ has still found the directive in issue capable of having direct effects. So, while *Verholen* seems to suggest a more limited view of the circumstances in which an individual may claim direct effects, the issue of whether rights are granted by the provision in issue does not seem to have been developed as a requirement for a finding of direct effects, or at least not one that is regularly applied by the CJ.

5.2.9 **Member States' initial response**

Initially national courts were reluctant to concede that directives could be directly effective. The Conseil d'État, the supreme French administrative court, in *Minister of the Interior v Cohn-Bendit* ([1980] 1 CMLR 543), refused to follow *Van Duyn* and allow the claimant to invoke Directive 64/221. The English Court of Appeal in *O'Brien v Sim-Chem Ltd* ([1980] ICR 429) found the Equal Pay Directive (Directive 75/117) not to be directly effective on the grounds that it had purportedly been implemented in the Equal Pay Act 1970 (as amended in 1975). *VNO* (discussed in 5.2.7) was apparently not cited before the Court. The German Federal Tax Court, the Bundesfinanzhof, in *VAT Directives* ([1982] 1 CMLR 527) took the same view on the direct effects of the Sixth VAT Directive, despite the fact that the time limit for implementation had expired and existing German law appeared to run counter to the Directive. The courts' reasoning in all these cases ran on similar lines: Article 288 TFEU expressly distinguishes regulations and directives; only regulations are described as 'directly applicable'; directives are intended to take effect within the national order via national implementing measures.

On a strict interpretation of Article 288 TFEU this is no doubt correct. On the other hand the reasoning advanced by the CJ is compelling. The obligation in a directive is 'binding "on Member States" as to the result to be achieved'; the useful effects of directives would be weakened if states were free to ignore their obligations and enforcement of EU law were left to direct action by the Commission or Member States under Articles 258 or 259 TFEU. Moreover states are obliged under Article 4(3) TEU) to:

> take all appropriate measures . . . to ensure fulfilment of the obligations arising out of this Treaty or resulting from action taken by the institutions of the Union.

If they have failed in these obligations, why should individual litigants not have a chance to enforce their rights?

5.2.10 **Vertical and horizontal direct effects: a necessary distinction**

The reasoning of the CJ is persuasive where an individual seeks to invoke a directive against the state on which the obligation to achieve the desired results has been imposed. In cases such as *VNO*, *Van Duyn* and *Ratti*, the claimant sought to invoke a directive against a public body, an arm of the state. This is known as *vertical* direct effect, reflecting the relationship between the individual and the state. Yet as with Treaty articles, there are a number of directives, impinging on labour, company or consumer law, for example, which a claimant may wish to invoke against a private person. Is the Court's reasoning in favour of direct effects adequate as a basis for the enforcement of directives against individuals? This is known as *horizontal* direct effect, reflecting the relationship between individuals.

The arguments for and against horizontal effects are finely balanced. Against horizontal effects is the fact of uncertainty. Prior to the entry into force of the TEU, directives were not required to be published, though in practice they usually were. More compelling, the obligation in a directive is addressed to the state. The CJ argued in *Becker* that the state should not benefit from its failure to implement.

Becker

The Court, following dicta in *Ratti*, had justified the direct application of the Sixth VAT Directive against the German tax authorities on the grounds that the obligation to implement the Directive had been placed on the state. It followed that:

> a Member State which has not adopted, within the specified time limit, the implementing measures prescribed in the Directive, cannot raise the objection, as against individuals, that it has not fulfilled the obligations arising from the Directive.

This reasoning is clearly inapplicable in the case of an action against a private person.

In favour of horizontal effects is the fact that directives have always in fact been published; that Treaty provisions addressed to, and imposing obligations on, Member States have been held to be horizontally effective; that it would be anomalous, and offend against the principles of equality, if an individual's rights to invoke a directive were to depend on the status, public or private, of the party against whom he wished to invoke it; and that the useful effect of Union law would be weakened if individuals were not free to invoke the protection of Union law against *all* parties.

Although a number of references were made in which the issue of the horizontal effects of directives was raised, the CJ for many years avoided the question, either by declaring that the claimant's action lay outside the scope of the directive, as in *Burton v British Railways Board* (case 19/81) (Equal Treatment Directive (Directive 76/207)) or by falling back on a directly effective Treaty provision, as in *Worringham and Humphreys v Lloyds Bank Ltd* (case 69/80) in which the then Article 119 EEC (now Article 157 TFEU) was applied instead of Directive 75/117, the Equal Pay Directive.

The nettle was finally grasped in *Marshall v Southampton & South West Hampshire Area Health Authority (Teaching)* (case 152/84).

Marshall

Mrs Marshall was seeking to challenge the health authority's compulsory retirement age of 65 for men and 60 for women as discriminatory, in breach of the Equal Treatment Directive (Directive 76/207). The difference in age was permissible under the Sex Discrimination Act 1975, which expressly excluded 'provisions relating to death or retirement' from its ambit. The Court of Appeal referred two questions to the CJ:

(1) Was a different retirement age for men and women in breach of Directive 76/207?

(2) If so, was Directive 76/207 to be relied on by Mrs Marshall in the circumstances of the case?

The relevant circumstances were that the area health authority, though a 'public' body, was acting in its capacity as employer.

The question of vertical and horizontal effects was fully argued. The Court, following a strong submission from Advocate-General Slynn, held that the compulsory different retirement age was in breach of Directive 76/207 and could be invoked against a public body such as the health authority. Moreover:

> where a person involved in legal proceedings is able to rely on a Directive as against the State he may do so regardless of the capacity in which the latter is acting, whether employer or public authority.

On the other hand, following the reasoning of *Becker*, since a directive is, according to Article 288 TFEU, binding only on 'each Member State to which it is addressed':

> It follows that a Directive may not of itself impose obligations on an individual and that a provision of a Directive may not be relied upon as such against such a person.

If this distinction was arbitrary and unfair:

> Such a distinction may easily be avoided if the Member State concerned has correctly implemented the Directive in national law.

So, with *Marshall* the issue of the horizontal effect of directives was, it seemed, finally laid to rest (albeit in an *obiter* statement, since the health authority was arguably a public body at the time). By denying their horizontal effect on the basis of Article 288 TFEU the Court strengthened the case for their vertical effect. The decision undoubtedly served to gain acceptance for the principle of vertical direct effects by national courts (see, eg, *R v London Boroughs Transport Committee, ex parte Freight Transport Association* [1990] 3 CMLR 495—judicial review of goods vehicle licensing conditions).

Nonetheless, the question of whether a directive might have horizontal effects continues to be asked. In 1993, in the case of *Dori v Recreb Srl* (case C-91/92), the Court was invited to change its mind on the issue of horizontal direct effects in a claim based on Directive 85/577 on Door-step Selling, which had not at the time been implemented by the Italian authorities, against a private party. Advocate-General Lenz urged the Court to reconsider its position in *Marshall* and extend the principle of direct effects to allow for the enforcement of directives against *all* parties, public and private, in the interest of the uniform and effective application of Union law. This departure from its previous case law was, he suggested, justified in the light of the completion of the internal market and the entry into force of the Maastricht Treaty, in order to meet the legitimate expectations of citizens of the Union seeking to rely on Union law.

The Court, no doubt mindful of national courts' past resistance to the principle of direct effects, and the reasons for that resistance, declined to follow the Advocate-General's advice and affirmed its position in *Marshall*: Article 288 TFEU distinguished between regulations and directives; the case law establishing vertical direct effects was based on the need to prevent states from taking advantage of their own wrong; to extend this case law and allow directives to be enforced against individuals:

> would be to recognise a power to enact obligations for individuals with immediate effect, whereas the [Union] has competence to do so only where it is empowered to adopt Regulations.

This decision has repeatedly been confirmed in subsequent cases, such as *El Corte*, *Arcaro* (case C-168/95) and in *Carp v Ecorad* (case C-80/06).

However, in denying horizontal effects to directives in *Dori*, the Court was at pains to point out that alternative remedies might be available based on principles introduced by the Court prior to *Dori*, namely the principle of indirect effects and the principle of state liability introduced in *Francovich*—see Chapter 9). The CJ has repeated this approach in other cases in which it rejected the horizontal effect of directives. So, *Francovich* was suggested as providing an alternative remedy in *El Corte* where it was again confirmed that directives could not have horizontal direct effect. The case concerned a dispute concerning a consumer (Rivero) and a finance company in respect of a loan she had taken out to pay for a holiday and which she ceased to repay due to shortcomings in the relevant travel agency's service. She sought to argue that she could rely on terms of EU consumer protection legislation as against the companies as the EU Treaties seek to ensure a high level of consumer protection (a provision also introduced by Maastricht, now 169 TFEU). The CJ confirmed that such changes in the Treaty could not affect the existing case law even in relation to consumer protection legislation. A similar reiteration can be found in *Pfeiffer and Others v Rotes Kreuz, Kreisverband Waldshut eV* (cases C-397 and 403/01) (discussed further at 5.3.2) which concerned the application of the Working Time Directive (Directive 93/104 ([1993] OJ L307/18)) to workers in an emergency service run by the German Red Cross. Here it emphasised, in the strongest possible terms, that a court was obliged to interpret domestic law in so far as possible in accordance with a directive (see paras 110–13 and 5.3). This is one mechanism by which the CJ has sought to mitigate the adverse consequences of the prohibition of horizontal effects on some claimants. There are other mechanisms, including:

- broad interpretation of the concept of 'public body';
- its approach to three party situations;
- incidental directive effect.

We must also consider the implications of *Mangold* and subsequent decisions.

5.2.11 Vertical direct effects: reliance against public body

The concept of a 'public' body, or an 'agency of the State', against whom a directive may be invoked, is unclear. In *Fratelli Costanzo SPA v Comune di Milano* (case 103/88), in a claim against the Comune di Milano based on the Comune's alleged breach of the Public Procurement Directive (Directive 71/305), the Court held that since the reason for which an individual may rely on the provisions of a directive in proceedings before the national courts is that the obligation is binding on all the authorities of the Member States, where the conditions for direct effect were met:

> all organs of the administration, including decentralised authorities such as municipalities, are obliged to apply these provisions.

The area health authority in *Marshall* was deemed a 'public' body, as was the Royal Ulster Constabulary in *Johnston v Chief Constable of the Royal Ulster Constabulary* (case 222/84). But what of the status of publicly owned or publicly run enterprises such as the former British Rail or British Coal? Or semi-public bodies? Are universities 'public' bodies and what is the position of privatised utility companies, or banks such as RBS, which are in the main owned by the taxpayer?

These issues arose for consideration in *Foster v British Gas* (case C-188/89).

Foster

In a claim against the British Gas Corporation in respect of different retirement ages for men and women, based on Equal Treatment Directive 76/207, the English Court of Appeal had held that British Gas, a statutory corporation carrying out statutory duties under the Gas Act 1972 at the relevant time, was not a public body against which the Directive could be enforced. On appeal the Supreme Court sought clarification on this issue from the CJ.

The CJ refused to accept British Gas's argument that there was a distinction between a nationalised undertaking and a state agency and ruled (at para 18) that a Directive might be relied on against organisations or bodies which were subject to the authority or control of the State or had special powers beyond those which result from the normal relations between individuals. Applying this principle to the specific facts of *Foster* it ruled (at para 20) that a directive might be invoked against:

> a body, whatever its legal form, which has been made responsible, pursuant to a measure adopted by the State, for providing a public service under the control of the State and has for that purpose special powers beyond those which result from the normal rules applicable in relations between individuals.

On this interpretation a nationalised undertaking such as the then British Gas would be a 'public' body against which a directive might be enforced, as the then House of Lords subsequently decided in *Foster*.

The CJ's ruling in *Foster* gave rise to difficulties, however. The CJ described a 'public body' twice: once in para 18, and again in para 20, using slightly different language each time. The principle expressed in para 18 is wider than that of para 20, the criteria of 'control' and 'powers' being expressed as alternative, not cumulative. As such it is wide enough to embrace any nationalised undertaking, and even bodies such as universities with a more tenuous public element, but which are subject to *some* state authority or control.

This possibility was acknowledged by the English Court of Appeal in *National Union of Teachers v Governing Body of St Mary's Church of England (Aided) Junior School* ([1997] 3 CMLR 630) when, contrary to the reasoning in the earlier case of *Rolls-Royce v Doughty* ([1992] ICR 538), it suggested that the concept of an emanation of the state should be a 'broad one'.

Nonetheless, the CJ's approach to the test for whether a particular body is an 'emanation of the state' for the purpose of enforcement of directives is unpredictable. It has adopted the para 18 test in one case and the para 20 test in another. For example, in *Vassallo v Azienda Ospedaliera Ospedale San Martino die Genova e Cliniche Universitarie Convenzionate* (case C-180/04), the Court adopted the para 18 formulation. The case addressed the effect in national law of Directive 1999/70 concerning the framework agreement on fixed-term work ([1999] OJ L175/43), that obliged Member States to impose on state institutions (including, see para 26, the respondent in that case) mandatory rules as to the stability of long-term employment. Conversely, it took the para 20, cumulative approach in *Rieser Internationale Transporte GmbH v Autobahnen-und Schnellstrassen-Finanzierrungs-AG (Asfinag)* (case C-157/02) concerning Directive 93/89 ([1993] OJ L220/1) and discriminatory tolls on the Brenner motorway. The body was a joint-stock company but its shares were held by the Austrian government. It was held to be a public body. This is no doubt confusing for national courts, but even if they were to adopt a generous approach, no matter how generously the concept of a 'public' body is defined, as long as the public/private distinction exists there can be no uniformity in the application of directives as between one state and another. Neither will it remove the anomaly as between individuals. Where a state has failed to fulfil its obligations in regard to directives, whether by non-implementation or inadequate implementation, an individual would, it appears, following *Marshall*, be powerless to invoke a directive in the context of a 'private' claim.

5.2.12 Three-party situations

It must be borne in mind that one of the principal justifications for rejecting 'horizontal direct effect' has been that directives cannot, of themselves, impose obligations on individuals. In two-party situations, this reasoning is straightforward. It is less so in a three-party situation where an individual is seeking to enforce a right under a directive against the Member State where this would have an impact on a third party. This is sometimes called a 'triangular situation' or 'triangular direct effects'. The issue arose in *Wells*.

Wells

Mrs Wells challenged the government's failure to carry out an environmental impact assessment (as required under Directive 85/337 ([1985] OJ L175/40)) when authorising the recommencement of quarrying works. The UK government argued that to accept that the relevant provisions of the Directive had direct effect would result in 'inverse direct effect' in that the UK government would be obliged to deprive another individual (the quarry owners) of their rights.

The CJ dismissed this argument. While the CJ accepted that:

> an individual may not rely on a directive against a Member State where it is a matter of a State obligation directly linked to the performance of another obligation falling, pursuant to that directive, on a third party

nonetheless,

> mere adverse repercussions on the rights of third parties, even if the repercussions are certain, do not justify preventing an individual from invoking the provisions of a directive against the Member State concerned.

This is a fine boundary and it would be for the national courts to consider whether to require compliance with the directive in the particular case, or whether to compensate the individual for any harm suffered.

A similar approach can be seen in *Arcor AG & Co KG and Others v Bundesrepublik Deutschland, Deutsche Telekom AG intervening* (case C-152–4/07).

Arcor

The case concerned a decision by the German telecommunications authority, approving a connection charge for calls from Deutsche Telekom's national network to a connection partner to cover the costs of maintaining the local telecommunications infrastructure. Third-party telecommunications operators sought to challenge that decision and it was this challenge that formed the basis of the reference.

The CJ held that the decision was incompatible with the directives regulating the area, relying on its decision in *Wells*, although the referring court had not raised the question in these terms. *Arcor* illustrates that, while triangular situations are common in environmental cases, they may be found more broadly than in just that area of law.

In coming to its conclusion in *Wells*, the CJ relied, in part, on case law developed in the context of Directive 83/189 (OJ [1983] L109/8) on the enforceability of technical standards which have not been notified in accordance with the requirements of that Directive (see 5.2.13), sometimes called incidental direct effect. Despite this common history, it is arguable that there are differences between the triangular situation and the case of incidental direct effect. Both, however, operate to blur the boundaries of the horizontal situation.

5.2.13 'Incidental' horizontal effect

There have been cases in which individuals have sought to exploit the principle of direct effects not for the purposes of claiming Union rights denied them under national law, but simply in order to establish the illegality of a national law and thereby prevent its application to them. In this case, the effect of the directive would be felt horizontally. The starting point for this line of case law is *CIA Security*. It involves Directive 83/189 (Directive 83/189 has been replaced and extended, by Directive 98/34 ([1998] OJ L204/ 37) (now codified as Directive 2015/1535 ([2015] OJ L241/1)), amended by Directive 98/44 ([1998] OJ L217/18), see 16.3.6). The Directive, which is designed to facilitate the operation of the single market, lays down procedures for the provision of information by Member States to the Commission in the field of technical standards and regulations. Article 8 prescribes detailed procedures requiring Member States to notify, and obtain clearance from, the Commission for any proposed national regulatory measures in the areas covered by the Directive.

CIA Security

The case concerned a Belgian rule according to which security alarms had to meet Belgian standards. These standards were 'technical regulations' and, according to Directive 83/189 ([1983] OJ L109/8), should have been notified to the Commission before the standards came into force. The parties to the case were competitors, and in this action Signalson alleged that CIA Security used alarms which did not comply with the Belgian standards and should not therefore be allowed.

Clearly, this is an action between private parties and equally clearly, if the Belgian regulation on standards for alarms stood, CIA would lose its case. It is at this point that the Directive becomes relevant. CIA Security argued that the Belgian regulations were inapplicable to the case before the national court because they had not been notified to the Commission—contrary to the requirements in Article 8 of the Directive.

Contrary to its finding in the earlier case of *Enichem Base v Comune di Cinsello Balsamo* (case C-380/87), involving very similar facts and the same Directive, the CJ accepted this argument, distinguishing *Enichem* on the slenderest of grounds. The Court confirmed that the relevant provisions of Directive 83/189 were directly effective. While a number of Member States argued that the Directive provided for no consequences were there to be non-compliance with the obligation to notify, the Court saw things differently. It reasoned that, given the Directive's general aim of eliminating or restricting obstacles to trade:

> The effectiveness of [Union] control will be that much greater if the directive is interpreted as meaning that breach of the obligation to notify constitutes a substantial procedural defect such as to render the technical regulations in question inapplicable to individuals.

Thus the effects of the Directive fell horizontally on the claimant, whose actions, based on national law, failed.

The *CIA Security* principle was confirmed and extended to a contractual relationship between two companies in *Unilever*.

Unilever Italia

Italy planned to introduce legislation on the geographical origins of various kinds of olive oil and notified this in accordance with Article 8 of the Directive after the Commission requested that this be done. The Commission subsequently decided to adopt a Union-wide measure and invoked the 'stand-still' procedure in Article 9 of the Directive, which requires a Member State to delay adoption of a technical regulation for 12 months if the Commission intends to legislate in the relevant field. Italy nevertheless adopted its measure before the 12-month period had expired. The dispute leading to the Article 267 TFEU reference arose when Unilever supplied Central Foods with olive oil which had not been labelled in accordance with Italian law. Unilever argued that Italian legislation should not be applied because it had been adopted in breach of Article 9 of the Directive.

A number of Member States argued that to apply the reasoning in *CIA Security* more generally would be tantamount to allowing horizontal direct effects of directives, contrary to the Court's position in *Faccini Dori*. Advocate-General Jacobs argued that the *CIA* principle could not affect contractual relations between individuals, primarily because to hold otherwise would infringe the principle of legal certainty. The Court disagreed and held that the national court should refuse to apply the Italian legislation. It noted that there was no reason to treat the dispute relating to unfair competition in *CIA Security* differently from the contractual dispute in *Unilever*. The Court acknowledged the established position that directives cannot have horizontal direct effect, but went on to say that this did not apply in relation to Articles 8–9 of Directive 83/189. The Court argued:

> In such circumstances, and unlike the case of non-transposition of directives with which the case-law cited by those two Governments is concerned, Directive 83/189 does not in any way define the substantive scope of the legal rule on the basis of which the national court must decide the case before it. It creates neither rights nor obligations for individuals.

It seems therefore, that the Court has sought to distinguish this situation from the horizontal situation in cases such as *Marshall* and *Faccini Dori*. The key is in the nature of the obligation: as can be seen from the quotation from *Unilever*, in this case the European obligation is procedural. It does not grant rights which are enforced; the consequence of European law is to remove national law, but not to substitute substantive European law in its place.

Article 8 Directive 83/189 was again invoked in *Lemmens* (case C-226/97), this time as a defence.

Lemmens

Lemmens was charged in Belgium with driving above the alcohol limit. Evidence as to his alcohol level at the relevant time had been provided by a breath analysis machine. Invoking *CIA Security*, he argued that the Belgian regulations with which breath analysis machines in Belgium were required to conform had not been notified to the Commission, as required by Article 8 Directive 83/189. He argued that the consequent inapplicability of the Belgian regulations regarding breath analysis machines impinged on the evidence obtained by using those machines; it could not be used in a case against him.

The CJ refused to accept this argument. It looked to the purpose of the Directive, which was designed to protect the interest of free movement of goods. The Court concluded:

> Although breach of an obligation (contained in the Directive) rendered (domestic) regulations inapplicable inasmuch as they hindered the marketing of a product which did not conform with its provisions, it did not have the effect of rendering unlawful any use of the product which conformed with the unnotified regulations. Thus the breach (of Article 8) did not make it impossible for

evidence obtained by means of such regulations, authorized in accordance with the regulations, to be relied on against an individual.

This distinction, between a breach affecting the marketing of a product, as in *CIA Security*, and one affecting its use, as in *Lemmens*, is fine, and hardly satisfactory, but remains good law. While *Lemmens* did not involve a third-party situation, the invocation by the defendant of Article 8 Directive 83/189 did smack of abuse. The refinement introduced in *Lemmens* may thus be seen as an attempt by the CJ to impose some limits on the principle of incidental direct effects as affected by *CIA Security* and as applied to directives.

The initial reaction to *CIA Security* was that the Court appeared to accept that directives could have horizontal direct effect. After *Unilever*, it is clear that this has not been its intention. However, this area remains one of some uncertainty. The position now seems to be that private parties to a contract for the sale or supply of goods need to investigate whether there are any relevant technical regulations and, if so, whether they have been notified in accordance with the Directive. There may then be a question of whether the limitation introduced by *Lemmens* comes into play. The end result appears to be the imposition on private parties of rights and obligations of which they could not have been aware–this was the main reason *against* the acceptance of horizontal direct effect in the case of directives. Although the Court in *Unilever* was at pains to restrict this line of cases to Directive 83/189 (and its replacement, Directive 98/34 ([1998] OJ L204/37), now codified as Directive 2015/1535 ([2015] OJ L241/1)), this is not convincing, especially since the CJ has on occasion (eg, *Panagis Parfitis* (case C-441/93) concerning a minority shareholder's rights in company reorganisation) accepted that individuals could invoke other directives to challenge national law, despite its adverse impact on third parties. Nevertheless, the CJ has maintained its approach under this Directive (see, eg, *Lidl Italia Srl v Comune di Stradella* (case C-303/04) –Italian law precluding sale of non-biodegradable cotton buds could not be relied on as it was a technical regulation which had not been notified), and it would appear to be best to regard the case law under Directive 98/34 (now codified as Directive 2015/1535 ([2015]OJ L241/1)) (and its predecessor) as being confined to the context of that and similar directives (see also, eg, *R v Medicines Control Agency ex parte Smith & Nephew* (case C-201/94) in the context of the authorisation of medicinal products under Directive 65/65 (superseded by 1993 measures), permitting the holder of a marketing authorisation to rely on Article 5 of that Directive in challenging the grant of an authorisation to a competitor). It should also be noted that the CJ has not adopted this approach in analogous situations involving decisions (*Ecorad* see 5.2.17).

5.2.14 **Directives and general principles of EU law**

The final set of circumstances in which a directive may have consequences in the horizontal situation is when the directive gives expression to a general principle of Union law. This rather contentious point derives from *Mangold*.

> ### *Mangold*
>
> The case arose from an employment dispute where the employer (Mr Helm), as well as the employee (Mr Mangold), was a private individual. The employee sought to argue that the terms of his contract, permitted under German law, were contrary to Article 6(1) Directive 2000/78 establishing a general framework for equal treatment in employment and occupation ([2000] OJ L303/16). The CJ held that the German rule was incompatible with Article 6(1). It seemed that the mere principle that directives should not have horizontal effect would not be a bar to this ruling. The CJ continued:

> . . . Observance of the general principle of equal treatment, in particular in respect of age, cannot as such be conditional upon the expiry of the period allowed the Member States for the transposition of a directive intended to lay down a general framework for combating discrimination on the grounds of age.

Mangold gave rise to much criticism because it implicitly runs contrary to the long line of case law limiting direct effects in the interest of legal certainty. Indeed, some commentators thought the case was an aberration. The CJ, however, reaffirmed its approach in another age discrimination case, *Kücükdeveci*.

Kücükdeveci

The national rules in this case concerned the amount of notice which should be given to an employee in the case of termination of the contract of employment. The general rule was that the longer the employment relationship had lasted, the longer the period of notice due. Periods of employment accrued before the employee reached a certain age were, however, discounted and it was this that Kücükdeveci claimed constituted age discrimination contrary to the same directive as in *Mangold*: Directive 2000/78.

The CJ reaffirmed the point it had made in *Mangold*, that age discrimination constituted a general principle of EU law, and continued that a national court must do all that lay within its jurisdiction to ensure the effectiveness of EU law, including the disapplication of any national law which is inconsistent with EU law.

The issue arose again, in *Association de Médiation Sociale* (AMS) (case C-176/12).

Association de Médiation Sociale (AMS)

The case is based on Directive 2002/14 containing certain rights of consultation for employees and Article 27 EUCFR. That provision states:

> Workers or their representatives must, at the appropriate levels, be guaranteed information and consultation in good time in the cases and under the conditions provided for by Union law and national laws and practices.

The Directive specified a minimum number of employees (50) before an employer would be bound by the consultation and representation obligations contained in the Directive. The French implementing legislation excluded certain categories of employee from being included in this calculation. The case concerns Laboubi who worked for AMS and was appointed a union representative. AMS argued that it had fewer than 11 staff and that it was consequently not required under the relevant national legislation to take measures for the representation of employees, such as the election of a staff representative. The trade union wanted to argue that the French implementing legislation was not in compliance with the Directive, but AMS was not a public body. The union sought to argue that Article 27 EUCFR meant the Directive should be given some form of horizontal effect.

While the CJ accepted that French law was incompatible with the Directive and that Article 27 EUCFR is guaranteed in the legal order of the European Union, the CJ nevertheless held that neither Article 27 EUCFR on its own, nor in conjunction with the terms of the Directive, could not be invoked in a private dispute. Article 27 EUCFR must be given more specific expression by provisions of EU law or national law to be fully effective.

Crucially, and by distinction from *Kücükdeveci*, Article 27 EUCFR did not confer a right, whereas, at least according to the CJ:

> the principle of non-discrimination on grounds of age at issue in [*Kücükdeveci*], laid down in Article 21(1) of the Charter, is sufficient in itself to confer on individuals an individual right which they make invoke as such (para. 47).

A further twist in this story was introduced in *Dansk Industri (DI) v Estate of Karsten Eigil Rasmussen* (case C-441/14), which again concerned the implications of the prohibition on discrimination in disputes between private parties.

DI

Rasmussen left his employment at Ajos and went to work elsewhere. Under national law, an employee who had worked as long for his employer as Rasmussen had for Ajos would normally be entitled to severance pay. Rasmussen, however, had reached retirement age, though in fact he continued to work. National law excluded retired persons from receiving the severance payment. Rasmussen sought to claim the payment given that the national law did not comply with the terms of the Discrimination Directive. Ajos argued that the application of a rule as clear and unambiguous as that laid down in Paragraph 2a(3) of the domestic law could not be precluded on the basis of the general principle of EU law prohibiting discrimination on grounds of age without jeopardising the principles of the protection of legitimate expectations and legal certainty.

The concern that the national court had was that, while it was clear that it could not apply the Directive in the context of a dispute between two private parties, was there an underlying EU general principle prohibiting age discrimination that could be applied and how should that principle be balanced against principles of legal certainty and legitimate expectations?

The CJ reiterated its case law about horizontal direct effect and then held—following *Kücükdeveci*—that if a national court could not apply the directive, nor interpret its law in a manner consistent with the directive, 'it is nonetheless under an obligation to provide, within the limits of its jurisdiction, the legal protection which individuals derive from EU law and to ensure the full effectiveness of that law, disapplying if need be any provision of national legislation contrary to that principle' (para 35), so 'if it considers that it is impossible for it to interpret the national provision at issue in a manner that is consistent with EU law, the national court must disapply that provision' (para 37). So while the directive is not relied on directly, the underlying principle results in the striking down of national law so as to allow the remaining national law to be interpreted consistently with EU law.

The full consequences of these rulings are still uncertain especially as a number of other directives may be viewed as giving rise to general principles of EU law or fundamental rights. Clearly, not all directives will benefit from the *Mangold/Kücükdeveci* reasoning. This reasoning, however, begs the question as to which general principles or which provisions in the Charter are going to be such as grant a 'sufficient' right. It could be argued that the *Mangold* argument may be used in relation to those directives too, especially in relation to rights recognized by the Charter which—since Lisbon—has had legal force. The Data Protection Directive (Directive 95/46 ([1995] OJ L281/31)) is a clear example: there is even a right to data protection in the EU Charter of Fundamental Rights. By distinguishing *Kücükdeveci* in *AMS*, the CJ has not done away entirely with that line of case law but has hardly clarified the question about when it would apply.

5.2.15 No direct effect to impose criminal liability

One important limitation to the direct effect principle was confirmed in *Berlusconi and Others* (cases C-387, 391 and 403/02).

Berlusconi

Here, Italian company legislation had been amended after proceedings against Mr Berlusconi and others had been commenced to make the submission of incorrect accounting information a summary offence, rather than an indictable offence. The Italian criminal code provides that a more lenient penalty introduced after proceedings have been commenced but prior to judgment should be imposed, and in the instant cases, proceedings would therefore have to be terminated as the limitation period for summary offences had expired. The CJ was asked if Article 6 of the First Company Law Directive (Directive 68/151) could be relied upon directly against the defendants.

Having observed that the Directive required an appropriate penalty and that it was for the national court to consider whether the revised provisions of Italian law were appropriate, the Court confirmed that it is not permissible to rely on the direct effect of a directive to determine the criminal liability of an individual (paras 73–8). In so holding, the CJ followed the principles developed in the context of indirect effect (5.3.2) and which reflect general principles of law (see Chapter 6).

5.2.16 Direct effect of directives: conclusions

As a general rule, directives cannot take direct effect in the context of a two-party situation where both parties are individuals. Directives can only be relied upon against a Member State (in a broad sense) by an individual. Although there is some uncertainty as to the precise test to be used, it seems the scope of 'public body' is broad, thus limiting the scope of the prohibition on the horizontal direct effect of directives. It is also apparent that the clear-cut distinction between vertical and horizontal direct effect in two-party situations becomes blurred when transposed into a tripartite context. The enforcement by an individual of an obligation on the Member State may affect the rights of other individuals, which, according to *Wells*, is a consequence of applying direct effect, but does not appear to change its vertical nature. The rather specific context of notification and authorisation directives, which may also have an effect on relationships not involving Member States, adds to the uncertainty, as do the cases following *Mangold*. But whilst the framework may seem settled, the debate as to whether directives *should* have horizontal direct effect is one that is unlikely to go away soon. Although this seems to be a complex and problematic area, we can tackle the issues relating to the direct effect by reference to a number of questions set out in Figure 5.1.

5.2.17 Decisions

A decision is 'binding in its entirety upon those to whom it is addressed' (Article 288 TFEU).

Decisions may be addressed to Member States, singly or collectively, or to individuals. Although, like directives, they are not described as 'directly applicable', they may, as was established in *Grad*, be directly effective provided the criteria for direct effects are satisfied. The direct application of decisions does not pose the same theoretical problems as directives, since they will only be invoked

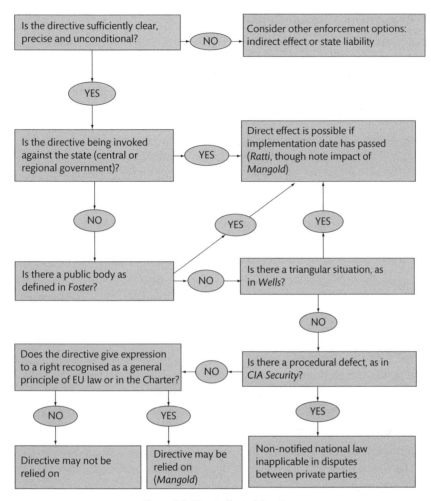

Figure 5.1 Direct effect of directives

against the addressee of the decision. If the obligation has been addressed to him and is 'binding in its entirety', there seems no reason why it should not be invoked against him, providing, of course, that it satisfies the test of being sufficiently clear, precise and unconditional. In the case of *Foselev Sud-Ouest-Sarl v Administration des douanes et droits indirects* (case C-18/08), which concerned a decision permitting the state to exempt certain vehicles from motor tax, the CJ held that due to the element of choice left to the Member State, the individual could not rely on the decision to obtain such an exemption. An individual may seek to rely on a decision addressed to a Member State against that Member State (eg, *Foselev Sud-Ouest-Sarl*). In *Ecorad*, Ecorad sought to rely on the contents of a decision, adopted according to the terms of a directive, addressed to a Member State in the context of a contractual dispute with Carp. Carp claimed it was not bound by the decision. The CJ reviewed the cases on the horizontal application of directives and concluded that:

the considerations underpinning the case-law referred to in the preceding paragraph with regard to directives apply mutatis mutandis to the question whether Decision 1999/93 may be relied upon as against an individual [para 21].

5.2.18 **Recommendations and opinions**

Since recommendations and opinions have no binding force it would appear that they cannot be invoked by individuals, directly or indirectly, before national courts. However, in *Grimaldi*, in the context of a claim by a migrant worker for benefit in respect of occupational diseases, in which he sought to invoke a Commission recommendation concerning the conditions for granting such benefit, the CJ held that national courts were:

> bound to take [Union] recommendations into consideration in deciding disputes submitted to them, in particular where they clarify the interpretation of national provisions adopted in order to implement them or where they are designed to supplement binding [EU] measures.

Such a view is open to question. It may be argued that recommendations, as non-binding measures, can at the most only be taken into account in order to resolve ambiguities in domestic law.

5.2.19 **International agreements to which the EU is a party**

There are three types of international agreements capable of being invoked in the context of EU law arising from the Union's powers under Articles 243, 260, 294 and 272 TFEU—see Chapter 3. These comprise:

- agreements concluded by the Union institutions falling within the treaty-making jurisdiction of the EU;
- 'hybrid' agreements, such as the WTO agreements, in which the subject matter lies partly within the jurisdiction of Member States and partly within that of the EU;
- agreements concluded prior to the Treaty of Rome, such as GATT, which the EU has assumed as being within its jurisdiction, by way of succession.

There is no indication in the Treaties that such agreements may be directly effective.

The CJ has effectively devised a three-stage test (confirmed in *Ioannis Katsirardas OE v Ipourgos Ikonomikon* (case C-160/09)):

(1) It is in the first instance for the parties to the international law agreement to determine its effects within their national legal orders;

(2) If the agreement is silent, it falls to the CJ to determine the question;

(3) It will take account of the spirit, general scheme and terms of the agreement in so doing.

Nonetheless, the CJ's case law on the direct effect of these agreements has not been wholly consistent. It purports to apply similar principles to those which it applies in matters of 'internal' law. A provision of an association agreement will be directly effective when 'having regard to its wording and the purpose and nature of the agreement itself, the provision contains a clear and precise obligation which is not subject, in its implementation or effects, to the adoption of any subsequent measure'. Applying these principles in some cases, such as *International Fruit Co NV v Produktschap voor Groenten en Fruit (No 3)* (cases 21 and 22/72), the Court, in response to an enquiry as to the direct effects of Article XI GATT, held, following an examination of the agreement as a whole, that the article was not directly effective. In others, such as *Conceria Daniele Bresciani v Amministrazione delle Finanze* (case 87/75) and *Hauptzollamt Mainz v* CA *Kupferberg & Cie KG* (case 104/81), Article 2(1) of the Yaoundé Convention and Article 21 of the EC–Portugal trade agreement were examined respectively on their individual merits and found to be directly effective. The reasons for these differences are at not at first sight obvious, particularly since the provisions in all three cases were almost identical in wording to, what was at that time, the EC Treaty articles already found directly effective. The suggested reason (see Hartley in the further reading section at the end of this chapter) for this inconsistency is the conflict between the CJ's desire to provide an effective means of enforcement of international agreements against Member States and the lack of a solid legal basis on which to do so. The Court justifies divergences in interpretation by reference to the scope and purpose of the agreement in question, which are clearly different from, and less ambitious than, those of the Treaties (*Opinion 1/91* (on the draft EEA Treaty)). As a result, the criteria for direct effects tend to be applied more strictly in the context of international agreements entered into by the EU.

Since the *International Fruit Co* cases the Court has maintained consistently that GATT rules cannot be relied upon to challenge the lawfulness of a Union act except in the special case where the Union provisions have been adopted to implement obligations entered into within the framework of GATT. Because GATT rules are not unconditional, and are characterised by 'great flexibility', direct effects cannot be inferred from the 'spirit, general scheme and wording of the Treaty'. This principle was held in *Germany v Council* (case C-280/93) to apply not only to claims by individuals but also to actions brought by Member States. As a result the opportunity to challenge Union law for infringement of GATT rules is seriously curtailed. Despite strong arguments in favour of the direct applicability of WTO provisions from Advocate-General Tesauro in *T Hermes International v FH Marketing Choice BV* (case C-53/96), the Court has not been willing to change its mind. It appears that there is near-unanimous political opposition to the direct application of WTO. (See also *Merck Genéricos–Produtos Farmacêuticos Lda v Merck & Co Inc, and Merck Sharp & Dohme Lda* (case C-431/05)). However, where the agreement or legislation issued under the agreement confers clear rights on *individuals* the CJ has not hesitated to find direct effects (eg, *Sevince v Staatssecretaris van Justitie* (case C-192/89); *Office national de l'emploi v Bahia Kziber* (case C-18/90)).

5.2.20 **Temporal limitations to the principle of direct effects**

A situation in which an individual was not able to rely on Union law arose in the case of *Rechberger and Greindle v Austria* (case C-140/97). The case, a claim based on *Francovich*, concerned Austria's alleged breaches of Directive 90/134 on package travel ([1990] OJ L158/59) both before Austria's accession, under the EEA Agreement, and, following accession, under the then EC Treaty. The CJ held that where the obligation to implement the Directive arose under the EEA Agreement, it had no jurisdiction to rule on whether a Member State was liable under that agreement prior to its accession to the European Union (see also *Ulla-Brith Andersson v Swedish State* (case C-321/97)).

5.3 **Principle of indirect effects**

Although the CJ has not shown willing to allow horizontal direct effect of directives, it has developed an alternative tool by which individuals may rely on directives against another individual. This tool is known as the principle of 'indirect effect', which is an interpretative tool to be applied by domestic courts interpreting national legislation which conflicts with a directive in the same area. It is sometimes also called the principle of consistent interpretation.

The principle of indirect effects was introduced in a pair of cases decided shortly before *Marshall*, namely: *von Colson* and *Harz v Deutsche Tradax GmbH* (case 79/83).

> ### *Von Colson*
>
> Both cases were based on Article 6 Equal Treatment Directive (Directive 76/207). Article 6 provides that:
>
> > Member States shall introduce into their national legal systems such measures as are necessary to enable all persons who consider themselves wronged by failure to apply to them the principle of equal treatment . . . to pursue their claims by judicial process after possible recourse to other competent authorities.
>
> The claimants had applied for jobs with their respective defendants. Both had been rejected. It was found by the German court that the rejection had been based on their sex, but it was justifiable. Under German law they were entitled to compensation only in the form of travelling expenses. This they claimed did not meet the requirements of Article 6. Ms von Colson was claiming against the prison service; Ms Harz against Deutsche Tradax GmbH, a private company. So the vertical/horizontal, public/private anomaly was openly raised and argued in preliminary ruling proceedings before the CJ.

The Court's solution was ingenious. Instead of focusing on the vertical or horizontal effects of the Directive it turned to what is now Article 4(3) TEU. Article 4(3) TEU requires states to 'take appropriate measures' to ensure fulfilment of their Union obligations.

This obligation, the Court said, applies to *all* the authorities of Member States, including the courts. It thus falls on the courts of the Member States to interpret national law in such a way as to ensure that the objectives of the Directive are achieved. It was for the German courts to interpret German law in such a way as to ensure an effective remedy as required by Article 6 of the Directive. The result of this approach is that although Union law is not applied directly—it is not 'directly effective'—it may still be applied indirectly as domestic law by means of interpretation.

The success of the *von Colson* principle of indirect effect depended on the extent to which national courts perceived themselves as having discretion, under their own constitutional rules, to interpret domestic law to comply with Union law. We will consider first how the CJ has developed the scope of the doctrine before identifying some limitations on when it may be used.

5.3.1 **The scope of the doctrine: *Marleasing***

The CJ considered the scope of the 'indirect effect' doctrine in some depth in *Marleasing*.

> ### *Marleasing*
>
> In this case, which was referred to the CJ by the Court of First Instance, Oviedo, the claimant company was seeking a declaration that the contracts setting up the defendant companies were void on the grounds of 'lack of cause', the contracts being a sham transaction carried out in order to defraud their creditors. This was a valid basis for nullity under Spanish law. The defendants argued that this question was now governed by Directive 68/151 ([1968] OJ L65/8). The purpose of Directive 68/151 was to protect the members of a company and third parties from, inter alia, the adverse effects of the doctrine of nullity. Article 11 of the Directive provides an exhaustive list of situations in which nullity may be invoked. It does not include 'lack of cause'. The Directive should have been in force in Spain from the date of accession in 1986, but it had not been implemented. The Spanish judge sought a ruling from the CJ on whether, in these circumstances, Article 11 of the Directive was directly effective.

The CJ reiterated the view it expressed in *Marshall* that a directive cannot of itself 'impose obligations on private parties'. It reaffirmed its position in *von Colson* that national courts must *as far as possible* interpret national law in the light of the wording and purpose of the directive in order to achieve the result pursued by the directive (para 8). And it added that this obligation applied *whether the national provisions in question were adopted before or after the directive*. It concluded by ruling specifically, and without qualification, that national courts were 'required' to interpret domestic law in such a way as to ensure that the objectives of the directive were achieved (para 13).

Given that in *Marleasing* no legislation had been passed, either before or after the issuing of the Directive, to comply with the Directive, and given the CJ's suggestion that the Spanish court must nonetheless strive to interpret domestic law to comply with the directive, it seems that, according to the CJ, it is not necessary to the application of the *von Colson* principle that the relevant national measure should have been introduced for the purpose of complying with the Directive, nor even that a national measure should have been specifically introduced at all.

5.3.2 **The limits of *Marleasing***

There are three main constraints on the use of the doctrine of indirect effects as far as it affects national law, which are:

- the limits of natural language (or the *contra legum* principle);
- non-imposition of criminal sanctions;
- non-retroactivity.

While these constraints can be seen separately, they reflect a common concern: that the EU respects principles relating to the rule of law and the protection of fundamental rights. Respect for these values may also affect the meaning ascribed to Union law by national authorities, which in turn will affect the interpretation of national law, as can be seen in *NS v Secretary of State for the Home Department and Secretary of State for the Home Department v ME* (cases C–411 and 493/10).

NS

NS concerned decisions by the UK authorities to return people seeking asylum in the UK to other Member States through which those individuals had travelled en route to the UK. In principle, this is permitted by the relevant regulations provided those other countries satisfy certain criteria. While the applicants claimed that their return would lead to a risk of their human rights being breached because the conditions for asylum seekers in the destination Member State were low, the UK government argued that it could presume—on the basis of the system set up by a number of pieces of EU legislation—that conditions in other Member States were adequate and the UK could apply its national rules accordingly.

The CJ held:

> Member States must not only interpret their national law in a manner consistent with European Union law but also make sure that they do not rely on an interpretation of an instrument of secondary legislation which would be in conflict with the fundamental rights protected by the European Union legal order or with the other general principles of European Union law [para 77].

Looking at the *contra legum* principle, the strict line taken in *Marleasing* (5.3.1) was modified in *Wagner Miret v Fondo de Garantíra Salaria* (case C-334/92), in a claim against a private party based on Directive 80/987 ([1980] OJ L283/23). This Directive is an employee protection measure designed, inter alia, to guarantee employees arrears of pay in the event of their employer's insolvency. Citing its ruling in *Marleasing* the Court suggested that, in interpreting national law to conform with the objectives of a directive, national courts must *presume* that the state intended to comply with Union law. They must strive 'as far as possible' to interpret domestic law to achieve the result pursued by the directive. But if the provisions of domestic law cannot be interpreted in such a way (as was found to be the case in *Wagner Miret*) the state may be obliged to make good the claimant's loss on the principles of state liability laid down in *Francovich*.

Wagner Miret thus represents a tacit acknowledgement on the part of the Court that national courts will not always feel able to 'construe' domestic law to comply with an EU directive, particularly when the provisions of domestic law are clearly at odds with that directive, and there is no evidence that the national legislature intended national law to comply with its provisions, or with a ruling on its provisions by the CJ. This limitation proved useful for courts which were unwilling to follow *Marleasing*. Thus, in *R v British Coal Corporation, ex parte Vardy* ([1993] ICR 720), a case decided after, but without reference to, *Marleasing*, the English High Court found that it was 'not possible' to interpret a particular provision of the Trade Union and Labour Relations Act 1992 to produce the same meaning as was required by the relevant directive (see also *Re Hartlebury Printers* [1993] 1 All ER 470 at 478b, ChD). More recently, the High Court has had difficulty interpreting the Copyright Designs and Patents Act 1988 in accordance with the Copyright Directive (Directive 2001/29 ([2001] OJ L167/10)) (*Football Association Premier League Ltd and Others v QC Leisure and Others* ([2008] EWHC 2897)), paras 73–5).

Thus the indirect application of EU directives by national courts cannot be guaranteed. Some reluctance on the part of national courts to comply with the *von Colson* principle, particularly as applied in *Marleasing*, is hardly surprising. It may be argued that in extending the principle of indirect effect in this way the CJ is attempting to give horizontal effect to directives by the back door, and impose obligations, addressed to Member States, on private parties, contrary to their understanding of domestic law. Where such is the case, as the then House of Lords remarked in *Duke v GEC Reliance Ltd* ([1988] AC 618) (see also *Finnegan v Clowney Youth Training Programme Ltd* ([1996] 1 AC 546)), this could be 'most unfair'. Indeed, the dividing line between giving 'horizontal direct effect' to a directive and merely relying on the interpretative obligation under the doctrine of 'indirect effect' can be a very fine and technical one in the circumstances of a particular case, as evidenced by *Pfeiffer*.

Pfeiffer

This case involved an interpretation of the notion of 'working time' in the context of the Working Time Directive. German case law had developed a distinction between duty time, on-call time and stand-by time, with only the first being regarded as 'working time'. Emergency workers employed by the German Red Cross had challenged a provision in their collective labour agreement which, they argued, extended their working time beyond the prescribed 48-hour limit. The Court suggested that this agreement may be in breach of the Directive, but that the claimants could not rely on the Directive itself as against their employer. Having restated the basic principle that national law must be interpreted in accordance with the Treaty, in particular where this has been enacted to implement a directive, the Court went on to say that this obligation was not restricted to the provisions themselves, but extended to:

national law as a whole in order to assess to what extent it may be applied so as not to produce a result contrary to that sought by the directive [para 115].

A national court must do 'whatever lies within its jurisdiction' to ensure compliance with EU law. The CJ did not go so far as to state expressly that existing case law might have to be reviewed to ensure such compliance, but the force of its reasoning appears to point in that direction. On the facts of the case, the outcome would be very close to allowing the individuals to invoke the direct effect of the Directive against their employer.

In *DI* which concerned the impact of the prohibition of age discrimination on a provision of Danish law which it was not possible to interpret in accordance with the Discrimination Directive (see further 5.2.14), the CJ went further. It expressly stated that a 'national court cannot validly claim in the main proceedings that it is impossible for it to interpret the national provision at issue in a manner that is consistent with EU law by mere reason of the fact that it has consistently interpreted that provision in a manner that is incompatible with EU law' (para 34). In brief, inconsistent case law must change direction to comply with EU law. This pronouncement does not seem dependent on the facts of the case—specifically the involvement of general principles here.

The CJ in *Adeneler v ELOG* (case C-212/04) referred to another limitation on indirect effect: legal certainty and non-retroactivity. This line of reasoning finds its basis in the case of *Kolpinghuis Nijmegen*, where in the context of criminal proceedings against Kolpinghuis for breach of Directive 80/777 on Water Purity ([1980] OJ L299/1), which at the relevant time had not been implemented by the Dutch authorities, the Court held that national courts' obligation to interpret domestic law to comply with EU law was:

> limited by the general principles of law which form part of [Union] law [see Chapter 6] and in particular the principles of legal certainty and non-retroactivity.

Although expressed in the context of criminal liability, to which these principles were 'especially applicable', it was not suggested that the limitation should be confined to such situations. Where an interpretation of domestic law would run counter to the legitimate expectations of individuals *a fortiori* where the state is seeking to invoke a directive against an individual to determine or aggravate his criminal liability, as was the case in *Arcaro* (discussed later), the doctrine will not apply. Where domestic legislation has been introduced to comply with a Union directive, it is legitimate to expect that domestic law will be interpreted in conformity with Union law, provided that it is capable of such an interpretation (cf *Pfeiffer* discussed earlier). Where legislation has not been introduced with a view to compliance domestic law may still be interpreted in the light of the aims of the directive as long as the domestic provision is reasonably capable of the meaning contended for. But in either case an interpretation which conflicts with the clear words and intentions of domestic law is unlikely to be acceptable to national courts. This has repeatedly been acknowledged by the Court (*Wagner Miret* and *Arcaro*: discussed in more detail later).

Pfeiffer could, however, be seen as a more unsympathetic approach to the limits of interpretation. A similarly unsympathetic approach to the difficulties of the national court can be seen in *Quelle AG v Bundesverband der Verbraucherzentralen und Verbraucherverbände* (case C-404/06). There the national court had ruled that there was only one possible interpretation of national law. The court was prohibited under its national law from making a ruling *contra legem*. Quelle therefore argued that the reference should be declared inadmissible as the referring court would not be able to take account of any interpretation of the relevant directive from the CJ, which contradicted national law. The CJ rejected the argument, on the basis of the separation of functions between the CJ and the national court (see Chapter 10). It continued:

> The uncertainty as to whether the national court—following an answer given by the Court of Justice to a question referred for a preliminary ruling relating to interpretation of a directive—may, in

compliance with the principles laid down by the Court . . . interpret national law in the light of that answer cannot affect the Court's obligation to rule on that question [para 22].

In effect, the CJ held here that the problems of dealing with the doctrine of indirect effect are for the national court. It should not be thought that *Quelle* signals an end to the *contra legem* principle. It was a ruling of one of the chambers. The Grand Chamber shortly before *Quelle* in *Impact v Minister for Agriculture and Food and Others* (case C-268/06) reaffirmed the *contra legem* principle, holding that the national court's duty under indirect effect is 'limited by general principles of law, particularly those of legal certainty and non-retroactivity' and therefore indirect effect 'cannot serve as the basis for an interpretation of national law *contra legem*' (para 100). *Quelle* and *Pfeiffer* seem then to be exceptions, but the uncertainty they introduced is not helpful. A strong obligation to interpret in conformity with EU law, such as in *Quelle* and *Pfeiffer*, could be seen again. *DI*, discussed earlier, could be seen in this light. There, faced with the outright incompatibility of a national provision with EU law, the CJ said that the national court should disapply that provision—presumably thereby allowing an interpretation that was consistent with EU law. It should be noted that *DI* concerned the application of a general principle (age discrimination) which may limit the circumstances in which national courts are obliged to go to such lengths.

Arcaro could also be seen as introducing further limitations on the scope of indirect effect. There, the CJ held that the:

obligation of the national court to refer to the content of the directive when interpreting the relevant rules of its own national law *reaches a limit where such an interpretation leads to the imposition on an individual of an obligation laid down by a directive which has not been transposed* or, more especially, where it has the effect of determining or aggravating, on the basis of the directive and in the absence of a law enacted for its implementation, the liability in criminal law of persons who act in contravention of that directive's provisions.

The Court has subsequently affirmed that the obligation to interpret domestic law in accordance with EU law cannot result in criminal liability independent of a national law adopted to implement an EU measure, particularly in light of the principle of non-retroactivity of criminal penalties in Article 7 ECHR (*Criminal Proceedings against X ('Rolex')* (case C-60/02)). This reasoning has also been applied in the context of direct effect (see *Berlusconi* discussed in 5.2.15).

The phrase 'imposition on an individual of an obligation' in *Arcaro* could be interpreted to mean that indirect effect could never require national law to be interpreted so as to impose obligations on individuals not apparent on the face of the relevant national provisions. It is submitted, however, that the CJ's view in *Arcaro* is limited to the context of criminal proceedings, and that the application of the doctrine of indirect effect can result in the imposition of civil liability not found in domestic law (see also Advocate-General Jacobs in *Centrosteel Srl v Adipol GmbH* (case C-456/98), paras 31–5).

This seems to be the result of *Oceano Grupo Editorial v Rocio Murciano Quintero* (case C-240/98).

Oceano Grupo

Oceano had brought a claim in a Barcelona court for payment under a contract of sale for encyclopaedias. The contract contained a term which gave jurisdiction to the Barcelona court rather than a court located near the consumer's home. That court had doubts regarding the fairness of the jurisdiction clause. The Unfair Contract Terms Directive (Directive 93/13 ([1993] OJ L95/29)) required that public bodies be able to take steps to prevent the continued use of unfair terms. It also contains a list of unfair terms, including a jurisdiction clause, but this only became effective in Spanish law *after* Oceano's claim arose. Spanish law did contain a general prohibition on unfair terms which could have encompassed the jurisdiction clause, but the scope of the relevant Spanish law was unclear. The question arose whether the Barcelona court should interpret Spanish legislation in accordance with the Unfair Contract Terms Directive. The CJ reaffirmed the established position that a:

> national court is obliged, when it applies national law provisions predating or postdating [a directive], to interpret those provisions, so far as possible, in the light of the wording of the directive [para 32].

The Court went on to say that in light of the emphasis on public enforcement in the Unfair Contract Terms Directive, the national court may be required to decline of its own motion the jurisdiction conferred on it by an unfair term. As a consequence, Oceano would be deprived of a right which it might otherwise have enjoyed under existing Spanish law. This latter consideration should not prevent the national court from interpreting domestic law in light of the Directive. In terms of the scope of the doctrine of indirect effect, it would be nonsensical to distinguish between cases which involve the imposition of obligations and those which concern restrictions on rights. Often, in a relationship between individuals, one individual's right is an obligation placed on another individual. The reasoning in *Arcaro* is best confined to the narrow context of criminal penalties.

5.3.3 Indirect effect: when does the obligation arise?

Some questions have arisen as to the point in time at which the obligation to use a consistent interpretation arises and, in particular, should it be the date the directive is enacted, or the date by which it must be implemented. This question came before the CJ in *Adeneler*. The CJ distinguished a positive and a negative duty for the courts of Member States. The positive aspect is the obligation to interpret all national law in line with the directive; that arises from the date by which the directive must be transposed. The negative aspect is based on the CJ's reasoning in *Inter-Environnement Wallonie* (see 5.2.6). According to this line of reasoning, the national courts must, once the directive is in force (but before it is due to be transposed), refrain from interpreting national law in a way liable seriously to compromise the attainment of the result prescribed by the directive. *Mangold* (discussed in 5.2.14) puts a gloss on this principle; here the interpretative obligation came into play before the date the Directive was due to be implemented in Germany. Is this, then, another change consequent on the value to be ascribed to general principles? The Directive in question allowed Member States an additional period in which to put appropriate measures in place to implement the Directive under the obligation to report progress to the Commission. This objective would be 'rendered redundant if the Member State were to be permitted, during the period allowed for implementation of the directive, to adopt measures incompatible with the objectives pursued by that act'. This reasoning then relates to quite a specific set of circumstances. If we return to the CJ's general ruling about the effect of general principles (5.2.14)—that their effectiveness is not conditional on the expiry of implementation periods—this suggests that, at least where general principles are in issue, the principle in *Inter-Environnement Wallonie* has been broadened. That *Mangold* does not have a broader effect as regards the interpretation of the directives generally is supported by the fact that the post-*Mangold* case of *Adeneler* re-affirms the position in *Inter-Environnement Wallonie*.

It may therefore be stated that the doctrine of indirect effect continues to be significant. However, there will be circumstances when it will not be possible to apply it. In such a situation, as the Court suggested in *Wagner Miret*, it will be necessary to pursue the alternative remedy of a claim in damages against the state under the principles laid down in *Francovich* (see Chapter 9). It may be significant that in *El Corte* the Court, in following the *Dori* ruling that a directive could not be invoked directly against private parties, did not suggest a remedy based on indirect effect, as it had in *Dori*, but focused only on the possibility of a claim against the state under *Francovich*.

5.3.4 Indirect effect in other contexts

The discussion has, so far, concentrated on the application of this principle in the context of directives. However, in *Maria Pupino* (case C-105/03), the CJ held that the obligation to interpret national law in accordance with European rules could extend to framework decisions adopted under pre-Lisbon Article 34(2) TEU, and that a national court is required to interpret domestic law, in so far as possible, in accordance with the wording and purpose of a corresponding framework decision. The decision was controversial, because it extended the notion of indirect effect into a domain in which the approach to lawmaking was strongly intergovernmental. Of course, post-Lisbon many of the distinctions based on the pillar system have disappeared (see Chapters 1 and 4), although the key area of CFSP remains, subject to its own rules, in the TEU. The key point now regarding *Pupino* is whether the same reasoning the CJ used in that case in relation to the old third pillar (JHA), could be used in relation to the current actions under CFSP.

5.4 Conclusions

The principle of direct effects, together with its twin principle of supremacy of EU law, discussed in Chapter 4, has played a crucial part in securing the application and integration of Union law within national legal systems. By giving individuals and national courts a role in the enforcement of Union law it has ensured that EU law is applied, and Union rights enforced, even though Member States have failed, deliberately or inadvertently, to bring national law and practice into line with Union law. Thus, as the Court suggested in *Van Gend*, the principle of direct effects has provided a means of control over Member States additional to that entrusted to the Commission under Article 258 TFEU and Member States under Article 259 TFEU (see further Chapter 11). While undoubtedly successful to the point where the central frameworks of both direct and indirect effects are generally accepted in the national courts, there are still points of difficulty. With regard to direct effects, the fundamental difficulty remains the horizontal direct effect of directives. Although *Marshall* should have put an end to this discussion, the question re-occurs—perhaps because of the anomalies the prohibition on the horizontal direct effect of directives creates. The CJ's response has been to develop lines of case law which seems to aim to limit the impact of the *Marshall* ruling and to ensure effectiveness of Union law. We can see this in the Court's broad approach to public bodies, in its development of the doctrine of indirect effect and 'incidental direct effect' as well as, more recently, in the *Mangold* line of cases. The consequence has, however, been some uncertainty in the application of the direct effects doctrine as well as a concern that the CJ is overstepping the boundaries (see *Honeywell* decision, Chapter 4). Indirect effect has always been a doctrine of uncertain effect. While in practice the doctrine national courts turn to first, it is to some extent unreliable as it depends on the scope the national court has in interpretation. Given that there are shortfalls in both these mechanisms of enforcement, the doctrine of state liability (discussed in Chapter 9) remains a potentially useful alternative cause of action.

Further reading

Amstutz, M, 'In-between worlds: *Marleasing* and the emergence of interlegality in legal reasoning' (2005) 11 ELJ 766.

Bronckers, M, 'From "direct effect" to "muted dialogue": Recent developments in the European courts' case law on the WTO and beyond' (2008) 11 JIEL 885.

Craig, P, "The legal effect of directives: Policy, rules and exceptions' (2009) 34 EL Rev 349.

de Mol, M, 'The novel approach of the CJEU on the horizontal direct effect of the EU principle of non-discrimination: (Unbridled) expansionism of EU law?' (2011) 18 MJ 109.

Dougan, M, 'Community directives: Explaining CIA Security?' (2001) 60 CLJ 231.

Hartkamp, AS, 'The effect of the EC Treaty in private law: On direct and indirect horizontal effect of primary Community law' (2010) 18 European Review of Private Law 527.

Hartley, T, 'International agreements and the Community legal system: Some recent developments' (1983) 8 EL Rev 383.

Lackoff, K and Nyssens, H, 'Direct effect of directives in triangular situations' (1998) 23 EL Rev 397.

Lenz, M, 'Horizontal what? Back to basics' (2000) 25 EL Rev 502.

Prechal, S and De Vries, S, 'Seamless web of judicial protection in the internal market?' (2009) 34 EL Rev 5.

Steiner, J, 'Coming to terms with EEC directives' (1990) 106 LQR 144.

Winter, TA, 'Direct applicability and direct effects' (1972) 9 CML Rev 425.

General principles of law

6.1 Introduction

This chapter will focus upon the development of general principles of law and will be structured into four topics. First, it will consider the development of general principles by the jurisprudence of the CJEU. Secondly, it will look at the EU Charter of Fundamental Rights (EUCFR). Thirdly, it will outline the EU's relationship with the ECHR and the progress that has been made towards the EU's accession to the ECHR. The final topic will be an introduction to key rights recognised by the EU. This chapter does not provide a full survey of the substantive rights which are now recognised in Union law. Such a discussion is beyond the scope of this book and readers should refer to the specialist texts which are now available.

6.2 Overview of the Treaty framework and development of general principles

Article 2 TEU identifies the values on which the EU is based and it reads as follows:

> The Union is founded on the values of respect for human dignity, freedom, democracy, equality, the rule of law and respect for human rights, including the rights of persons belonging to minorities.

Article 6 TEU recognises the special role of the ECHR and identifies the sources of EU fundamental rights and their legal status. It provides that:

> 1. The Union recognises the rights, freedoms and principles set out in the Charter of Fundamental Rights of the European Union of 7 December 2000, as adapted at Strasbourg, on 12 December 2007, which shall have the same legal value as the Treaties.
>   The provisions of the Charter shall not extend in any way the competences of the Union as defined in the Treaties.

> The rights, freedoms and principles in the Charter shall be interpreted in accordance with the general provisions in Title VII of the Charter governing its interpretation and application and with due regard to the explanations referred to in the Charter, that set out the sources of those provisions.
>
> 2. The Union shall accede to the European Convention for the Protection of Human Rights and Fundamental Freedoms. Such accession shall not affect the Union's competences as defined in the Treaties.
>
> 3. Fundamental rights, as guaranteed by the European Convention for the Protection of Human Rights and Fundamental Freedoms and as they result from the constitutional traditions common to the Member States, shall constitute general principles of the Union's law.

Given the emphasis on the protection of human rights and general principles in the Treaties, it may seem surprising that such protection was excluded from the scope of the original Community's range of activities and it was initially left to the courts to develop this area of law. Yet, after the concept of direct effect and the principle of supremacy of EU law, the third major contribution of the CJEU, and the CJ in particular, has been the introduction of general principles of law into the corpus of EU law.

The development of the Union's human rights role was incremental, in response at least in part to concerns raised by the constitutional courts of various Member States about the doctrine of supremacy of EU law (see Chapter 4), but now seems well entrenched in the Union's architecture. While a desire to protect fundamental human rights is laudable, there are potential problems in this area. Three main issues can be identified. The first relates to the level of protection that the CJ and the GC have awarded to general principles, especially when the actions of the institutions themselves are under review. The second is about the relationship between the EU protection of human rights and that provided by other bodies, particularly the European Court of Human Rights (ECtHR). Finally, what is the scope of the EU's human rights jurisdiction and its impact on the legal systems of the Member States?

Beyond the CJEU's contribution, the strengthening of respect for human rights can also be seen in the introduction of an enforcement mechanism in Article 7 TEU by the ToA. Article 7 TEU provides that where there has been a determination of a serious and persistent breach of the values mentioned in Article 2 TEU, the Council may—following a reasoned proposal by one-third of the Member States, by the European Parliament or by the European Commission—suspend certain of the rights of the offending Member State, including its voting rights. Were this provision used, it could have serious consequences for the Member State in question; such a Member State would lose its opportunity to influence the content of Union legislation by which it would be bound, even in sensitive areas where otherwise it could have vetoed legislation. Thus, one might suggest that the need to comply with fundamental principles is being taken very seriously indeed. It is likely that this provision will be used only rarely given the severity of the breach needed to trigger the procedure, which itself is long-winded, requiring unanimity (excluding the offending Member State) in the first instance. While the Commission put forward a Communication proposing a framework within which to analyse the conditions for applying Article 7 TEU (COM (2003)606 final) the procedure has not been used. Given the potential consequences for Member States, however, the complexity of the procedure is perhaps appropriate. Finally, Article 269 TFEU gives the CJ the jurisdiction to decide on the legality of a decision under Article 7 TEU on procedural grounds only.

6.2.1 **Initial phase**

Article 263 TFEU gives the CJEU power to review the legality of Union acts on the basis of, inter alia, 'infringement of this Treaty', or 'any rule of law relating to its application'. Article 340(2) TFEU, which governs Union liability in tort, provides that liability is to be determined 'in accordance with the general principles common to the laws of the Member States'. Article 19 TEU, governing the role of the CJEU, provides that the Court 'shall ensure that in the interpretation and application of the treaties the law is observed'. The Court's first tentative recognition of fundamental human rights on the basis of this unwritten law was in the case of *Stauder v City of Ulm* (case 29/69).

Stauder

The applicant was claiming entitlement to butter at a reduced price provided under a Union scheme to persons in receipt of welfare benefits. He was required under German law to divulge his name and address on the coupon which he had to present to obtain the butter. He challenged this law as representing a violation of his fundamental human rights (namely, equality of treatment). The CJ, on reference from the German court on the validity of the relevant Union decision, held that, on a proper interpretation, the Union measure did not require the recipient's name to appear on the coupon.

This interpretation, the Court held, contained nothing capable of prejudicing the fundamental human rights enshrined in the general principles of law and protected by the Court. Thus, the CJ recognised the existence of those principles.

One of the reasons for what has been described as the Court's 'naked lawmaking' in this area is best illustrated by the case of *Internationale Handelsgesellschaft*. The German courts were faced with a conflict between a regulation requiring the forfeiture of deposits by exporters if export was not completed within an agreed time, and a number of principles of the German constitution, in particular, the principle of proportionality. It is in the nature of constitutional law that it embodies a state's most fundamental principles. Although these principles were of particular importance, for obvious reasons, in post-war Germany, other Member States had also written constitutions embodying similar principles and rights. Clearly it would not have done for EU law to conflict with such principles. Indeed, as the German Federal Constitutional Court (FCC) made clear ([1974] 2 CMLR 540), were such a conflict to exist, national constitutional law would take precedence over EU law. This would have jeopardised not only the principle of primacy of EU law, but also the uniformity of application so necessary to the success of the new legal order. So while the CJ asserted the principle of primacy of EU law in *Internationale Handelsgesellschaft*, it was quick to point out that respect for fundamental rights was in any case part of EU law. By recognising the concern and providing an EU-level response, the CJ minimised the threat to the acceptance of the new EU legal order.

6.2.2 **Sources of rights: traditions common to the Member States**

Having identified that the Union legal order respects general principles, we are faced with the task of identifying them. In the absence of any indication as to the scope or content of these general principles or the unidentified 'law' referred to in Article 263 TFEU and Article 19 TEU, it has been left to the CJEU to put flesh on the bones provided by the Treaty.

As explained earlier, the CJ in *Internationale Handelsgesellschaft* identified national constitutional traditions as one source of such principles. It argued that, while Union law cannot be reviewed by reference to national rules and standards, those standards might be *analogous* to those found in the Union system. Thus, '[t]he protection of such rights, whilst inspired by the constitutional traditions common to the Member States, must be ensured within the framework of the structure and object-ives of the [Union]'. Member States' legal traditions can constitute the source of a right to be pro-tected, but ultimately the existence and scope of such a right are issues of EU law. The role of national constitutions in informing the meaning of general principles is now recognised in Article 6(3) TEU.

While this was a neat piece of legal reasoning, seemingly reconciling the concerns of both national constitutional courts and the CJ, it gave rise to questions about which rights should be recognised and to what degree. It may be argued that if the problem of conflict between Union law and national law is to be avoided in *all* Member States it is necessary for *any* human right upheld in the constitution of *any* Member State to be protected under EU law (a 'maximalist' approach). The alternative is to suggest that only those traditions common to *all* Member States should be recognised. Either position gives rise to difficulties, either imposing rights on some Member States with the maximalist position or downgrading the rights of some Member States with the minimalist position. The CJ has sought to find a middle way which can be seen in the context of *Hoechst v Commission* (cases 46/87 and 227/88). The case arose in the context of a claim based on the right to the inviolability of the home. The Court, following a comprehensive review by Advocate-General Mischo of the laws of all the then Member States on this question, distinguished between this right as applied to the 'private dwelling of physical persons', which was common to all Member States (and which would by implication be protected as part of Union law), and the protection offered to commercial premises against intervention by public author-ities, which was subject to 'significant differences' in different Member States. In the latter case the only common protection, provided under various forms, was protection against arbitrary or disproportionate intervention on the part of public authorities.

Similarly, in *Australian Mining & Smelting Europe Ltd v Commission* (case 155/79), in considering the principle of professional privilege, the Court found that the scope of protection for confidenti-ality for written communications between lawyers and their clients varied from state to state; only privilege as between independent (as opposed to in-house) lawyers and their clients was generally accepted, and would be upheld as a general principle of Union law.

While the CJ undertook a comparative review to come to its conclusion, the judgment in *AM & S* did give rise to criticism that the CJ focused too heavily on the common law tradition and foisted on the other Member States something that was mainly a UK principle. (Cf privilege for in-house lawyers: *Akzo Nobel Chemicals and Akcros Chemicals v Commission* (case C-550/07P).) If *AM & S* constituted an example of the CJ inventing a common principle (or taking a max-imalist approach, perhaps), other examples can be found too. The CJ's assertion that age dis-crimination constitutes a general principle of EU law has been repeatedly challenged, not least by a number of advocates-general (see Opinions in *Palacios de la Villa v Cortefi el Servicios SA* (case C-411/05), *Maruko v Versorgungsanstalt der deutschen Bühnen* (case C-267/06), *Lindorfer v Council* (case C-277/04P) and *Bartsch v Bosch und Siemens Hausgeräte (BSH) Altersfürsorge GmbH* (case C-427/06)). The latest judicial approach with regards the application of the gen-eral principle of age discrimination can be seen in *DI* examined in Chapter 5 and in 6.7. The CJ ruled that the national court should disapply the inconsistent national provision and proceed with an interpretation that is consistent with the general principle of EU law that prohibits age discrimination.

While there is some uncertainty in the CJ's approach, it seems that, where certain rights are pro-tected to differing degrees and in different ways in Member States, the Court will look for some *common* underlying principle to uphold as part of Union law. Even if a particular right protected in a Member State is not universally protected; where there is an apparent conflict between that right and EU law, the Court will strive to interpret Union law so as to ensure that the substance of that right is not infringed.

One particular problem area is where an individual seeks to extend the nature of the fundamental principles recognised in his or her home state by reference to rights protected in other Member States and recognised as such by the CJ. This can be illustrated by contrasting two cases which arose out of similar circumstances: *Wachauf v Germany* (case 5/88) and *R v Ministry of Agriculture, Fisheries and Food, ex parte Bostock* (case C-2/93).

Wachauf

Wachauf was a tenant farmer who, upon the expiry of his tenancy, requested compensation arising out of the loss of 'reference quantities' on the discontinuance of milk production. When this was refused, he claimed that this was an infringement of his right to private property, protected under the German constitution. The German authorities claimed that the rules they applied were required by the Union Regulation, but the CJ held that on its proper interpretation the Regulation required no such thing: although the Regulation did not itself provide the right to compensation, equally it did not preclude it. The discretion thereby given to the Member States by the Regulation should be exercised in accordance with fundamental rights, thus in practice meaning that the applicant should receive the compensation.

Bostock

Bostock, similarly, had been a tenant farmer. Following *Wachauf* he argued that he, too, should be entitled to compensation for the value of the reference quantities on the expiry of his lease. Unlike the situation in Germany, though, this right was not protected by British law at the time when Bostock's lease ended. Bostock therefore sought to challenge that British law on the basis that the provisions breached general principles of non-discrimination and unjust enrichment. Despite its approach in *Wachauf*, the CJ ruled that the right to property protected by the Union legal order did not include the right to dispose of the 'reference quantities' for profit. The CJ held that the question of unjust enrichment, as part of the legal relations between lessor and lessee, was a matter for national law and therefore fell outside the scope of Union law.

The CJ implicitly accepted the level of protection awarded by Germany not to be excessive, though it clearly differed from that provided by the UK. It is difficult to reconcile these two cases if one accepts that general principles accepted by the CJ should apply across the EU. It might, however, be argued that the CJ is sensitive to the cultural particularities of certain rights for individual Member States. In *Omega Spielhallen- und Automatenaufstellungs-GmbH v Oberbürgerme isterin der Bundesstadt Bonn* (case C-36/02), the German authorities sought to prevent a laser-dome game operating on the grounds that a game based on shooting people infringed respect for human dignity which is specifically protected by German constitution: no such problem arose in the UK where the game originated. The CJ ruled that:

> Since both the [Union] and its Member States are required to respect fundamental rights, the protection of those rights is a legitimate interest which, in principle, justifies a restriction of the obligations imposed by [Union] law, even under a fundamental freedom guaranteed by the Treaty such as the freedom to provide services [para 35].

Omega Spielhallen might be seen as showing deference to the German sensitivity to the need to protect human dignity.

6.2.3 Sources of rights: ECHR and other international human rights Treaties

Following *Internationale Handelsgesellschaft* the scope for human-rights protection was further extended in the case of *J Nold KG v Commission* (case 4/73).

Nold

J Nold KG, a coal wholesaler, was seeking to challenge a decision taken under the ECSC as being in breach of the company's fundamental right to the free pursuit of business activity guaranteed by the German basic law. While the Court did not find for the company on the merits of the case, it asserted its commitment to fundamental rights in the strongest terms. As well as stating that fundamental rights form an integral part of the general principles of law, the observance of which it ensures, it went on to say:

> In safeguarding these rights, the Court is bound to draw inspiration from constitutional traditions common to the Member States, and it cannot therefore uphold measures which are incompatible with fundamental rights recognised and protected by the constitutions of those States. Similarly, international treaties for the protection of human rights on which the Member States have collaborated or of which they are signatories, can supply guidelines which should be followed within the framework of [Union] law.

The reasons for this inclusion of principles of certain international Treaties as part of EU law are clearly the same as those upholding fundamental constitutional rights; it is a way to minimise the risk of conflict.

In this context, the most important international treaty concerned with the protection of human rights is the ECHR, to which all Member States are now signatories. The Court has on a number of occasions confirmed its adherence to the rights protected therein. This can be seen in *R v Kirk* (case 63/83).

R v Kirk

The case arose in the context of criminal proceedings against Kirk, the captain of a Danish fishing vessel, for fishing in British waters (a matter subsequently covered by EU regulations). The principle of non-retroactivity of penal measures, enshrined in Article 7 ECHR, was invoked by the CJ and applied in Captain Kirk's favour. The EU Regulation, which would have legitimated the British rules under which Captain Kirk was charged, could not be applied to penalise him retrospectively.

Note that neither the ECHR, nor the rulings of the Strasbourg Court, are seen as part of EU law. In *Mannesmannröhren-Werke AG v Commission* (case T-112/98), the GC emphasised that although the ECHR has special significance in defining the scope of fundamental rights recognised by the Union, the Court has no jurisdiction to apply the ECHR itself. The GC therefore rejected arguments based directly on Article 6 ECHR in relation to an application to annul a Commission decision, but allowed the application on other grounds (see 6.6.7). The view of the GC with regard to invoking ECHR articles may be technically correct, but it sits somewhat uneasily with its other judgments and with those of the CJ in which both courts appeared more willing to refer directly to ECHR provisions, and even to the jurisprudence of the ECtHR itself (see, eg, *Roquette Frères* (case C-94/00); *Orfanopoulos v Land Baden-Wurttemberg* (case C-482/01), citing *Boultif v Switzerland* concerning right to family life; *Connolly v Commission* (case C-274/99P): civil servants' freedom of expression under Article 10 ECHR). The boundary between using the ECHR as an 'inspiration' and drawing directly on it as a source of law may have been hard to discern in practice, but the distinction allows space for the CJEU to come to its own conclusions on the scope of the rights. Other international treaties concerned with human rights referred to by the Court as constituting a possible source of general principles are the European Social Charter (1971) and ILO Convention 111, 1958 (*Defrenne v Sabena (Defrenne III)* (case 149/77)). In *Ministère Public v Levy* (case C-158/91) the Court suggested that a Member State might even be obliged to apply a national law which conflicted with a ruling of its own on the interpretation of Directive 76/207 ([1976] OJ L39/40) where this was necessary to ensure compliance with an international convention (in this case ILO Convention 89, 1948) concluded prior to that state's entry into the EU. The list has grown over the years, with the CJ adding, for example, Convention on the Protection and Promotion of the Diversity of Cultural Expressions (*UTECA v Administración General del Estado* (case C-222/07)—rules to provide funding for European cinematographic works) and the UN Convention on the Rights of the Child (*Dynamic Medien Vertriebs GmbH v Avides Media AG* (case C-244/06)—rules providing for age labelling of videos). It is possible that this list may increase. Note also that in its dealings with the outside world, the EU and its institutions post-Lisbon are required to have 'respect for the principles of the United Nations Charter' (Article 3(5) TEU).

The relationship between EU and international law more generally has been the subject of consideration in *Kadi*.

Kadi

The case relates to the freezing of funds of persons allegedly connected to, inter alia, the Taliban and Bin Laden. In particular, the factual backdrop concerned Union measures implementing UN resolutions on economic sanctions. Effectively, these measures allowed for the freezing of individuals' assets, without prior warning. The matter came before the GC, as an action for annulment. It held that the courts are not empowered to review decisions of the UN, including the Security Council, even in the light of the fundamental rights recognised by Union law. The GC based this decision on the fact that, according to its interpretation of the requirements of international law, the obligations of the Member States of the United Nations prevail over any other obligation. The Union, although not itself a member of the UN, must, in the GC's view, be bound by the obligations flowing from the Charter of the United Nations. Nonetheless, the GC reserved the rights of the Union courts to check the lawfulness of the Council Regulation (which implemented the UN Security Council Resolution and was under challenge in this case), and therefore implicitly the underlying resolution, by reference to the higher rules of international law (*jus cogens*), from which neither the Member States nor the bodies of the Union should, under international law, be able to derogate. This includes provisions intended to secure universal protection of fundamental human rights. On the facts, the GC found the application unfounded.

The CJ heard the appeal in *Kadi* and approached the matter in a completely different way, overturning the GC's internationalist approach. Advocate-General Maduro in his Opinion emphasised that

> . . . there is a real possibility that the sanctions taken against the appellant within the [Union] may be disproportionate or even misdirected, and might nevertheless remain in place indefinitely. The Court has no way of knowing whether that is the case in reality, but the mere existence of that possibility is anathema in a society that respects the rule of law [para 53].

While the CJ accepted that the EU (and its Member States) were subject to international obligations, such as those contained in the UN, this does not change the allocation of powers within the

EU. Furthermore, the EU was characterised by the CJ, drawing on its previous jurisprudence (see Chapter 4), as an autonomous legal order built on the rule of law and respect for fundamental human rights. Thus there is a distinction between international obligations and the effect of Union norms, and the fact that Union measures might arise from those international obligations does not affect the fact that Union law must comply with human rights, as recognised by the EU. On this basis, the CJ in *Kadi* reviewed whether the EU implementing measures (not the UN resolutions) complied with a number of procedural rights and the right to respect for property and highlighted that judicial review was a constitutional guarantee of the EU. In this, it is arguable that the CJ was taking a stronger line than the ECtHR had when faced with the same issue. This is a significant judgment, which re-emphasises the centrality of the rule of law and the protection of human rights within the EU.

6.2.4 Scope of general principles

General principles of law are not to be confused with the fundamental principles of Union law, as expressed in the EU Treaty, for example, the principles of free movement of goods and persons, although there may be some overlap or commonality between the two. General principles of law constitute the 'unwritten' law of the Union and they have been developed—or discovered—over time by the CJ. The CJ has not provided an exhaustive list of general principles so in theory the range of general principles to which EU law is subject may increase as the Union develops. We have seen at 6.2.2 that there may be some variance between the Member States as to what constitutes a general principle, though there seems to be consensus about the main civil and political rights (such as the right to a private life and freedom of expression) even if there may be disagreement as to what this means in a given case. The CJ has identified characteristics of general principles in *Audiolux v Groupe Bruxelles Lambert SA (GBL) and Others and Bertelsmann AG and Others* (case C-101/08).

Audiolux

The case concerned a shareholder dispute in which the minority shareholders in a company argued that certain references to 'the equality of shareholders' and, more specifically, the protection of minority shareholders in various EU directives dealing with company law were a manifestation of a general principle of Union law. In particular, it was argued that dominant shareholders should be under an obligation to offer to buy shares from minority shareholders on the same terms as it acquired its dominant shareholding. The CJ rejected this argument.

In coming to this conclusion, the CJ stated that the general principles of Union law have constitutional status. It contrasted that status with the principle proposed by Audiolux which was sufficiently detailed as to require secondary Union legislation to put it into effect. On that basis, the principle proposed by Audiolux was not an independent general principle of Union law. While many of the general principles are fundamental human rights, not all general principles fall in this category. Some principles of good governance, such as proportionality or subsidiarity, are also general principles. We consider some of the general principles at 6.6.

6.2.5 Circumstances in which general principles may be used: scope of EU law

While issues pertaining to general principles arise in a wide range of circumstances, they can only arise within the scope of EU law. In *Kaur v Lord Advocate* ([1980] 3 CMLR 79), an attempt was made to invoke Article 8 ECHR—('respect for family life') by an Indian immigrant seeking to challenge a deportation order made under the Immigration Act 1971. She failed on the grounds that the Convention had not been incorporated into UK law. Its alleged incorporation via the European Communities Act 1972 did not enable a party to invoke the Convention before a Scottish court in a matter wholly unrelated to EU law. The CJ has no power to examine the compatibility with the ECHR of national rules which do not fall therein (*Cinéthèque SA v Fédération Nationale des Cinémas Françaises* (cases 60 and 61/84), noting the different approach of Advocate-General and Court, and contrast *Karner Industrie-Auktionen GmbH v Troostwijk GmbH* (case C-71/02)—prohibition of references in auction details to the fact that the goods came from an insolvent estate).

Another example can be seen in *Gueye and Salmerón Sánchez* (cases C-489/09 and 1/10) which concerned Spanish rules that provided that those who have been convicted of an act of domestic violence should be subject to an additional restraining order preventing cohabitation between victim and abuser. The victims thought that this constituted a violation of their right to family life. The CJ avoided ruling on this delicate issue (although the Advocate-General noted the need for balancing of interests), pointing out that EU law covered procedural criminal law rather than substantive criminal law and that therefore the issue lay outside its jurisdiction.

While EU law is clearly in issue when general principles are used to interpret the scope of a piece of secondary legislation (eg, *Tietosuojavaltuutettu v Satakunnan Markkinaporssi Oy and Satamedia Oy* (case C-73/07), concerning the Data Protection Directive (Directive 95/46), to challenge the validity of such an act (see, eg, *Digital Rights Ireland ltd and Seitlinger and Others* (cases C-293 and 594/12)), or to challenge an administrative act of the institutions (see, eg, cases at 6.6.4), the situation is a little more complex when considering national measures. In *Bartsch*, Advocate-General Sharpston, summarising the case law, identified three categories of circumstance when national measures would fall within the scope of EU law (see Box 6.1).

Box 6.1   General principles in national law

- Implementation of EU law, irrespective of the degree of the discretion the Member State enjoys and whether the national measure goes beyond what is strictly necessary for implementation (*SpA Eridania-Zuccherifi and SpA Società Italiana per l'Industria degli Zuccheri v Minister of Agriculture and Forestry, Minister for Industry, Trade and Craft Trades, and SpA Zuccherifi ci MeridionaliEridania* (case 230/78)—Italian measures implementing Regulation 3331/74 ([1974] OJ L359/18)); (eg, *Klensch v Secrétaire d'État à l'Agriculture et à la Viticulture* (cases 201 and 202/85));

- National rules seeking to rely on a derogating provision under EU law (*Elliniki Radiophonia Tileorassi AE v Dimotiki Etairia Pliroforissis* (case C-260/89));

- It falls within the scope of Union law because some specific substantive rule of EU law is applicable to the situation. (*Commission v UK (fisheries conservation)* (case 804/79)—Member States acting as trustees of the Union in an area of exclusive Union competence: fisheries.)

When Member States implement Union rules, either by legislative act or as administrators for the Union, they must not infringe fundamental rights. National rules may be challenged on this basis. This can be seen in the case of *Commission v Germany (housing conditions)* (case 249/86).

Housing Conditions

The Commission challenged Germany's rules enforcing Regulation 1612/86 ([1986] OJ L142/20) which permitted the family of a migrant worker to install themselves with the worker in a host country provided that the worker has housing available for the family of a standard comparable with that of similarly employed national workers. Germany enforced this in such a way as to make the residence permit of the family conditional on the existence of appropriate housing for the duration of the stay. The CJ interpreted the Regulation as requiring this only in respect of the beginning of their period of residence. Since the Regulation had to be interpreted in the light of Article 8 ECHR concerning respect for family life, a fundamental principle recognised by Union law, German law was incompatible with Union law.

When Member States are implementing obligations contained in Union law, they must do so without offending against any fundamental rights recognised by the Union. In *Wachauf* the CJ held that:

> Since those requirements are also binding on the Member States when they implement [Union] rules, the Member States must, as far as possible, apply those rules in accordance with those requirements [para 19].

The problem lies in defining the boundary between Union law and purely domestic law, as can be seen in, for example, *Karner*.

Karner

The case related to advertising on the internet. The CJ held that the national rules complained of were not selling arrangements and therefore they would not fall within Article 34 TFEU (see Chapter 18). In this aspect, the case is different from the preceding cases, as those cases concerned situations where the national legislation fell within the relevant Treaty provision. Despite the fact that the situation seemed to lie outside the prohibition in Article 34 TFEU (thus rendering a consideration of a derogation unnecessary), the CJ then went on to give the national court 'guidance as to interpretation necessary to enable it to assess the compatibility of that legislation with the fundamental rights whose observance the Court ensures' (para 49).

According to the CJ, in this case the national legislation fell within the scope of application of EU law (an issue to which we return in relation to the Charter).

The scope of Union law could be construed very widely, as evidenced by the approach of the Advocate-General in *Konstantinidis v Stadt Altensteig-Standesamt* (case C-168/91).

Konstantinidis

The case related to a Greek national working in Germany. He complained that the German authorities had mistransliterated his name in official registers. He argued that the error exposed him to a risk of confusion of identity on the part of potential clients, resulting in an interference with his right of establishment under TFEU. The Advocate-General suggested that, as the applicant had exercised his right of free movement under Article 49 TFEU, the national provisions affecting him fell within the scope of Union law and continued to do so; therefore he was entitled to the protection of his human rights by the CJ.

The Court did not go this far in *Konstantinidis*, although some of the citizenship cases can be seen in this light (see *Garcia Avello v Etat Belge* (case C-148/02), *Carpenter (Mary) v Secretary of State for the Home Department* (case C-60/00), *Kunqian Catherine Zhu and man Lavette Chen (Chen) v Secretary of State for the Home Department* (case C-200/02), Chapter 21).

Most Treaty rules provide for some derogation in order to protect important public interests (eg, Articles 36 and 45(3) TFEU). The CJ has insisted that any derogation from the fundamental principles of Union law must be narrowly construed. When Member States do derogate, their rules may be reviewed in the light of general principles, as the question of whether the derogation is within permitted limits is one of Union law. Most, if not all, derogations are subject to the principle of proportionality.

The *ERT* case (see Box 6.1) concerned the establishment by the Greek government of a monopoly broadcaster. The CJ held that this would be contrary to Article 56 TFEU regarding the freedom to provide services. Although the Treaty provides for derogation from Article 56 TFEU in Articles 52 and 62 TFEU, any justification provided for by Union law must be interpreted in the light of fundamental rights, in this case the principle of freedom of expression embodied in Article 10 ECHR. In *Schmidberger v Austria* (case C-112/00), Advocate-General Jacobs argued that the right to freedom of expression and assembly permits a derogation from the free movement of goods (Article 34 TFEU) in a context where the main transit route across the Alps was blocked by a demonstration for a period of 28 hours on a single occasion and steps were taken by the Austrian authorities to ensure that the disruption to the free movement of goods was not excessive. The CJ came to the same end conclusion, noting the wide margin of discretion given to the national authorities in striking a balance between fundamental rights and Treaty obligations.

One issue in this context is whether fundamental human rights should properly be seen as derogating from Treaty freedoms, perhaps falling within the scope of the public policy objection, or whether they should be seen as operating to limit Treaty freedoms at an earlier point in the legal analysis. In *Omega Spielhallen* (see 6.2.2), human dignity was seen as forming part of the public policy grounds of derogation. In her Opinion in this case, Advocate-General Stix-Hackl emphasised the importance of the protection of human dignity, and suggested that public policy should be interpreted in the light of the Union law requirement that human dignity should be protected. Recognition that human rights protection forms part of the public policy exception can also be seen in *Dynamic Medien* (see 6.2.3). Nonetheless, this still leaves human rights protection with the status of an exception to Treaty freedoms rather than constraining the scope of those rights in the first place. The potential problem is that exceptions to the Treaty freedoms are normally narrowly construed and subject to the proportionality test, which hardly puts them on the same footing as the economic Treaty freedom. In *Schmidberger*, the Advocate-General suggested that rather than the usual proportionality test, in such cases the different interests should be balanced; whether this approach is consistently adopted in cases concerning fundamental rights, remains to be seen; it was not adopted by the CJ in *Omega Spielhallen*.

6.3 Assessment

There has been a change in approach towards general principles, specifically but not exclusively with regards to human rights, over the course of the Union's existence. The CJ introduced the idea of general principles on a very thin legal basis which questions whether the development by the CJ of those principles is actually legitimate. The political institutions also recognise the importance of general principles. While a good thing in and of itself, respect for general principles is also important in helping to protect the individual against the acts of increasingly powerful Union institutions, bodies, offices and agencies. There is another side to the coin, though. There is a risk that the EU courts and the courts of other international human rights bodies (specifically the ECHR) might come to different conclusions as to the appropriate level of protection to be awarded.

In this context, it should be noted that some commentators have raised questions about whether the EU courts are really seeking to protect human rights or are rather seeking to protect their own jurisdiction (notably Coppell and O'Neill). The background to this is the CJ's motivation for introducing general principles, which can be seen as political (ie to stave off a rebellion by the German and Italian constitutional courts) rather than out of a genuine concern for human rights. Certainly, the fact that a particular principle is upheld by the CJ and appears to be breached does not automatically lead to a decision in favour of the claimant. Fundamental rights are not absolute rights. As the Court pointed out in *Nold*, rights of this nature are always subject to limitations laid down in the public interest, and, in the Union context, limits justified by the overall objectives of the Union (eg, *O'Dwyer v Council* (cases T-466, 469, 473–4 and 477/93)). The pursuit of these objectives can result in some hard decisions (eg, *Dowling v Ireland* (case C-85/90)), although the Court has held that it may not constitute a 'disproportionate and intolerable interference, impairing the very substance of those rights' (*Wachauf* at para 18).

It has been argued that the CJ is more likely to support human rights when they support internal market objectives or limit Member State freedom rather than the actions of the institutions (eg, *ERT*). This viewpoint has been challenged and it is certainly possible to find examples of cases where the EU courts have protected general principles (such as *Kadi*). Whether this is enough to allay all qualms about the EU courts as protectors of human rights is another question. The CJ may also be more confident in upholding rights claims now that the EUCFR has the same legal status as the EU Treaties themselves.

6.4 The EU Charter of Fundamental Rights

6.4.1 Background

In 1999, the Cologne European Council set up a Convention to produce a draft Union charter as an alternative mechanism to ensure the protection of fundamental rights. This was completed in time for the 2000 European Council meeting at Nice, where the European institutions solemnly proclaimed the Charter (EUCFR). Initially, the EUCFR did not have legal effect, but this position changed with Lisbon. Thus, Article 6(1) TEU states:

> the Union recognises the rights, freedoms and principles set out in the Charter of Fundamental Rights . . . which shall have the same legal value as the Treaties.

6.4.2 Structure and content

The EUCFR is divided into six substantive chapters: dignity, freedoms, equality, solidarity rights, citizenship rights (see also Chapter 24) and justice.

The EUCFR is to be interpreted in accordance with a number of horizontal provisions (see 6.4.3 and 6.4.4). The EUCFR consists of a mixture of human rights found in the ECHR, rights derived from other international conventions and provisions of the TFEU. The Council of the European Union has published a booklet which explains the origin of each of the rights contained in the EUCFR, known as the Explanations (see the further reading section in Chapter 6). The provisions cover a broad range of rights and principles, some of which are familiar (freedom of expression, the right to private life, right to a fair trial), while some are less usual features of a catalogue of fundamental rights (access to services of general economic interest, consumer protection), and some are very specific to the EU (right to petition the European Parliament). To the extent that individual provisions are based on provisions in the TFEU (see, eg, healthcare: Article 35 EUCFR; Article 168 TFEU), it is not clear whether the right in the EUCFR constitutes an independent right, with its own scope.

It should also be noted that there is a difference between 'rights' and 'principles' in that principles will, according to Article 52(5) EUCFR, be enforceable only via implementing legislation, although they may still influence the interpretation of EU law. Problematically, the EUCFR does not identify which provisions are rights and which principles. The Explanations give some examples, but there is no complete list, thereby giving rise to some uncertainty in this regard. According to the Explanations, principles include Article 25 EUCFR on the rights of the elderly, Article 26 EUCFR on the integration of persons with disabilities and Article 37 EUCFR on environmental protection. The Explanations also suggest that some provisions, such as Article 33 EUCFR on family and professional life, contain elements of both rights and principles. The House of Lords Select Committee noted that, if the Explanations are reflected in practice, then some social and economic rights—which are usually viewed as aspirational rather than enforceable—may in this context give rise to justiciable rights.

6.4.3 Horizontal provisions: scope

The question of defining the scope of the Charter is important because it determines the conditions under which national law is subject to judicial review. By virtue of Article 51(1) EUCFR, the provisions of the EUCFR are addressed to the institutions and bodies of the Union and to the Member States only when they are implementing Union law. As far as the institutions and bodies of the Union are concerned, due regard is to be had to the principle of subsidiarity. It is when we consider the impact of the Charter on the Member States and their legal systems that the position becomes unclear and contentious. There had been a suggestion that, because Article 51(1) EUCFR refers just to the Member States, the Charter did not affect horizontal relationships. This seems to be refuted by *AMS* (discussed at 5.2.14). Although the CJ rejected the possibility of Article 27 EUCFR applying to a dispute between private parties, this ruling seemed to be based very much on its facts. The fact that the CJ dealt with the issue by reference to the nature of the obligation found in Article 27 EUCFR suggests that some other provisions could have a horizontal effect. The law here is not yet clear.

We have also just seen that Article 51(1) EUCFR provides that fundamental rights are binding on Member States 'only when they are implementing Union law'. This phrase suggests that the Charter applies to a narrower range of circumstances than general principles (see Box 6.1 above, identifying three different categories, including implementation). The Explanations to the Charter, which are authoritative, then state that 'it follows unambiguously from the case-law of the Court of Justice' that Member States are bound by fundamental rights 'when they act within the scope of EU law', and cite the case of *ERT*. Significantly, *ERT* concerned Member States' *derogation* from EU law, not their implementation of it. Arguably, the Explanations give a broader reach to the scope of application of the EUCFR than Article 51(1) EUCFR does on its own. Some light has been thrown on the meaning of the scope of EU law within Article 51(1) EUCFR in the problematic case of *Fransson*.

Fransson

The case concerned a Swedish fisherman. The Swedish tax authorities accused him of incorrectly reporting his income, which affected the assessment of Value Added Tax (VAT) due. He was given a fine for tax offences, part of which related to a VAT offence. The VAT system is based on Directive 2006/112 ([2006] OJ L347/1), but the Swedish penalties were not based on the Directive. Subsequently, the Public Prosecutor commenced criminal proceedings against him for tax evasion in relation to the same year that the penalties were levied. When the prosecution came before the national court, it wanted to know whether the duplication in administrative and criminal proceedings was problematic in the light of Article 50 EUCFR (*ne bis in idem*; otherwise known as 'double jeopardy'). On the facts of the case, however, it was far from clear that the situation fell within the scope of EU law, a concern which the Advocate-General shared. The CJ, however, disagreed with the Advocate-General and determined that the circumstances did fall within the scope of EU law and therefore applicability of EU law entailed applicability of the fundamental rights guaranteed by the Charter.

In coming to its conclusion, the CJ addressed the possible different approaches to Article 51(1). It held that:

> ... the Charter's field of application so far as concerns action of the Member States is defined in Article 51(1) thereof, according to which the provisions of the Charter are addressed to the Member States only when they are implementing European Union law.
>
> That article of the Charter thus confirms the Court's case-law relating to the extent to which actions of the Member States must comply with the requirements flowing from the fundamental rights guaranteed in the legal order of the European Union.
>
> The Court's settled case-law indeed states, in essence, that the fundamental rights guaranteed in the legal order of the European Union are applicable in all situations governed by European Union law, but not outside such situations. In this respect the Court has already observed that it has no power to examine the compatibility with the Charter of national legislation lying outside the scope of European Union law. On the other hand, if such legislation falls within the scope of European Union law, the Court, when requested to give a preliminary ruling, must provide all the guidance as to interpretation needed in order for the national court to determine whether that legislation is compatible with the fundamental rights the observance of which the Court ensures [case law omitted] [paras 17–19].

The CJ's reasoning is interesting to note, especially as regards the phrases it uses to describe the field of application of the Charter. It began by referring to 'implementing EU law' (para 17) and then to 'situations governed by EU law', and 'the scope of EU law' (para 19) the final phrase being familiar from its pre-Charter case law on general principles. It seems to use these three phrases interchangeably, thereby equating 'implementation' with 'scope' and eradicating any possible difference between them. In sum, it seems that 'implementing' in Article 51(1) EUCFR covers all three sets of circumstances identified with regard to general principles (Box 6.1) as the scope of EU law. Insofar as the CJ feels the need to justify this reasoning, it does so by referring to the text of the Explanations.

Part of the contentious nature of this case is, however, the nature of its connection with EU law, which could be described as tenuous. The Court determined that the Swedish tax penalties and criminal proceedings for tax evasion, constituted implementation of Directive 2006/112 and of Article 325 TFEU (provisions on combatting fraud), even though the legislation had not been designed to transpose the Directive. The CJ itself says the measures are only 'in part' within the EU body of law. We can read *Fransson* widely, to say that the ruling in *Fransson* is generally applicable and therefore any Member State action or inaction falls within the scope of Union law. This reading could be wide indeed, given that national measures need only be related 'in part' to the content of any directive. Furthermore, any such national measures need not even explicitly implement or transpose Union legislation, provided its purpose corresponds to those formulated in primary or secondary Union law. A narrower reading of the impact of *Fransson* is also possible; this takes the specific facts into account. Here we could say that the Swedish authorities were acting as agent of the EU in ensuring that the EU's resources (derived from VAT payments) were protected. This seems to be the approach that the FCC took in a ruling it handed down quite shortly after *Fransson*. In its *Counter-Terrorism Database judgment* (1 BvR 1215/07, discussed in Chapter 4), the FCC specifically confined *Fransson* to its facts and ruled that the Counter-Terrorism Database Act pursues nationally determined objectives and any effect on the functioning of the legal relationships under EU law would be merely indirect.

By contrast, where EU law rights are clearly not in issue, the CJ will decline jurisdiction as can be seen, for example, in *Sociedade Agrícola e Imobiliária da Quinta de S. Paio Lda v Instituto da Segurança Social IP* (case C-258/13). Here, the applicant was seeking legal aid to bring an action under national law. When its application was refused, the Sociedade Agrícola argued that it had a right to legal aid under Article 47 of the Charter, which provides for a right for effective legal protection. The CJ in the earlier case of *DEB Deutsche Energiehandels-und Beratungsgesellschaft* (case C-279/09), which concerned a state liability action under EU law, had held that a right to legal aid existed. Here, however, the reliance on the Charter would have been independent of any EU law right, potentially giving the Charter a broad field of application, which was not constrained by the scope of substantive EU law. The CJ rejected the claim, distinguishing *DEB* on the basis that Sociedade Agrícola had not submitted the request for legal aid in order to protect the rights conferred on it by Union law. In sum, and referring back to the distinction made in *Fransson* (para 19), where a legal situation does not fall within the scope of Union law, the Charter provisions relied upon cannot, of themselves, form the basis for such jurisdiction.

In this context, note Article 51(2) EUCFR provides:

> The Charter does not extend the field of application of Union law beyond the powers of the Union or establish any new power or task for the Union, or modify powers and tasks as defined in the Treaties.

While this restatement of the law might not seem contentious, it was felt sufficiently important to justify a declaration and a protocol. The Declaration concerning the Charter of Fundamental Rights of the European Union attached to the Treaty of Lisbon simply restates, word for word, the text of Article 51(2) EUCFR. It is hard to see what this adds. The protocol, Protocol (No 30) on the Application of the Charter of Fundamental Rights of the European Union to Poland and to the United Kingdom is the so-called 'opt-out'. This is a misnomer; it is not an opt-out, it is an interpretive protocol. Article 1 Protocol 30 deals with the impact of the EUCFR in the domestic legal systems of Poland and the UK. It provides:

> The Charter does not extend the ability of the Court of Justice of the European Union, or any court or tribunal of Poland or of the United Kingdom, to find that the laws, regulations or administrative provisions, practices or action of Poland or of the United Kingdom are inconsistent with the fundamental rights, freedoms and principles that it reaffirms.

The scope of the protocol, amongst other issues, was considered in *NS*.

NS

The case concerned an asylum seeker in the UK who first entered the EU through Greece. The Dublin Regulation, which governs this aspect of EU asylum law, provides that in this case the competent Member State to consider the asylum claim should have been Greece. NS challenged his transfer to Greece, claiming that his human rights would be infringed by such a transfer as Greece would be unable to process his application. The English courts referred a number of questions, including one about the impact of the protocol questioning whether the EUCFR was relevant where a Member State was exercising a permitted discretion under the Regulation.

This was given short shrift by the CJ. It confirmed that the protocol was not an opt-out, but a document which clarified the interpretation of the EUCFR. In sum, the matter concerned the Dublin Regulation which was a matter of EU law to which fundamental rights protection applied and the CJ's answers to the substantive issues:

> do not require to be qualified in any respect so as to take account of Protocol (No 30) on the application of the Charter of Fundamental Rights of the European Union to Poland and the United Kingdom.

In a subsequent case concerning a judicial review of a rejection of asylum, which came before the High Court in England, *AB, R (on the application of) v Secretary of State for the Home Department*, the judge hearing the case had to deal with claims under Article 7 EUCFR (respect for private life) and Article 8 EUCFR (protection of personal data). In the course of that judgment he noted that the British view 'that the effect of the seventh protocol is to prevent any new justiciable rights from being created is not one shared by the Court of Justice of the European Union' (para 13, citing *NS*). This is a fact of constitutional significance because of the wider breadth of the Charter by comparison with the ECHR and because the political decision to try to exclude certain rights from being justiciable in the UK has been unsuccessful. As Mostyn J in *AB* noted, the result is that as regards the right to protection of personal data, which is separately protected under the Charter but which is not expressly part of the ECHR and has therefore not been incorporated into UK domestic law by the Human Rights Act, 'by virtue of the decision of the court in Luxembourg, and notwithstanding the terms of the opt-out, the claimant is entitled,…surprising though it may seem, to assert a violation of it in these domestic proceedings before me' (para 16). This position has given rise to consternation in UK political circles.

Article 52(1) EUCFR provides that limitations on the exercise of the rights and freedoms guaranteed by the EUCFR must be provided by law. Any such limitations must be proportionate and are only permitted if they are necessary and genuinely meet objectives recognised by the EU. In this, there are similarities to the approach taken with regard to the derogation provisions in the ECHR. Article 52(2) EUCFR further confirms that those rights which derive from the Treaties are subject to the conditions and limitations that apply to the corresponding Treaty provisions.

6.4.4 Horizontal provisions: compatibility with national constitution and with the ECHR

Article 53 EUCFR provides that the Charter will not restrict or adversely affect fundamental rights as recognised in their respective fields of application, by Union law and international law and by international agreements to which the EU or all the Member States are party, including the ECHR, and by the Member States' constitutions. According to the Explanations,

> [t]his provision is intended to maintain the level of protection currently afforded within their respective scope by Union law, national law and international law. Owing to its importance, mention is made of the ECHR.

Article 53 EUCFR was introduced to ensure that the Charter would not result in a reduction of the level of protection of fundamental rights in the Member States' respective legal orders and perhaps to allow space for national peculiarities (such as those noted in *Omega Spielhallen*) to be taken into account. The CJ had the opportunity to consider the scope of this provision in *Stefano Melloni v Ministerio Fiscal* (case C-399/11).

Melloni

The Italian courts sentenced Mr Melloni *in absentia* to 10 years' imprisonment for bankruptcy fraud and the Italian authorities sought to rely on the European arrest warrant to secure his return and imprisonment. Melloni would have no right to appeal against his sentence should he be returned to Italy. He challenged the Spanish order agreeing to his return. When the case came before the Tribunal Constitucional (Spanish constitutional court), that court asked the CJ whether, in the light of Article 53 EUCFR, the Framework Decision establishing the arrest warrant would allow the Spanish courts to make the surrender of Mr Melloni subject to the possibility of judicial review of his conviction, as would be the position in Spain as required by the case law of the Tribunal Constitucional. The CJ rejected an interpretation of Article 53 of the Charter which would permit a Member State to apply its standard of protection for fundamental rights so as to give priority to national constitutional norms over the application of EU law (see paras 55–7). It based its reasoning on the need to protect the supremacy of EU law. It continued that:

> by virtue of the principle of primacy of EU law, which is an essential feature of the EU legal order…rules of national law, even of a constitutional order, cannot be allowed to undermine the effectiveness of EU law on the territory of that State [para 61].

This judgment returns the CJ clearly to its early and long-standing approach in cases such as *Internationale Handelsgesellschaft* (see 6.2.1 and Chapter 4). Member States' own standards may only be relied upon where EU law is implemented in the national legal order provided that the level of protection provided by the EUCFR—as interpreted by the Court—and primacy, unity and effectiveness of EU law are not compromised. While this ruling is hardly surprising in terms of the CJ's approach to supremacy, it may not be popular with some of the constitutional courts in the Member States.

Article 52(3) EUCFR deals with the complex problem of overlap between the ECHR and the EUCFR. It specifies that those rights in the EUCFR which correspond with ECHR rights must be given the same meaning and scope as the ECHR rights. EU law may provide more generous protection, but not a lower level of protection than guaranteed under the ECHR and other international instruments (Article 53).

The consequences of Article 52(3) EUCFR are not yet known. If, however, certain EUCFR rights (such as those based on the ECHR) are regarded as free-standing rights, then the CJ may be in danger of 'competing' with the ECtHR. The CJ would be obliged to interpret EUCFR rights in accordance with the ECHR, but a difficulty may arise if the CJ interprets an ECHR-based right in one way and the Court of Human Rights subsequently takes a different view. Member States may then still face a conflict between complying with their obligations under European law, in particular the doctrine of supremacy (see Chapter 4) and under the ECHR, respectively. It is submitted that in such a case, the ECHR should prevail. This seems to be the current position under the CJ's case law. In *Roquette*, the question arose whether business premises could be protected under Article 8 ECHR against 'dawn raids' by the Commission under Regulation 17 (now replaced by Regulation 1/2003). In its earlier decision in *Hoechst*, the CJ had held that Article 8 required no such protection. However, subsequent ECHR case law has extended the scope of Article 8 to cover business premises. In *Roquette*, the CJ held that the case law under the ECHR must be taken into account in applying the *Hoechst* decision. The CJ therefore appears to recognise that ECHR case law can have an impact on the scope of fundamental rights guaranteed by Union law. A similar judicial dialogue can be seen taking place in *NS*. A number of cases have come before the ECtHR on similar facts to those in *NS*. In *KRS v UK* (Application No 32733/08), the ECtHR held that returning an asylum seeker to Greece would not constitute a violation of fundamental rights. Subsequently, in *MSS v Belgium and Greece* (Application No 30696/09), that court reviewed its position in the light of new evidence and held that such a transfer would constitute a violation. The CJ in *NS* specifically referred to the changing position of the ECtHR in coming to its own conclusion: that such a transfer would constitute an infringement of Article 4 EUCFR. Interestingly, it has been noted that the ECtHR has likewise taken account of relevant case law of the CJ. It seems that in their respective jurisdictions the two courts are endeavouring to minimise conflict. The existence of this judicial dialogue has been recognised in a declaration attached to the Lisbon Treaty on Article 6(2) TEU (see also 6.5). Whilst this is good practice, the risk of inconsistency remains.

6.4.5 **CJ's reaction**

Even before the EUCFR became binding, the CJ had already mentioned the EUCFR in a number of judgments by way of reference in confirming that the European legal order recognises particular fundamental rights. For example, in *R v Secretary of State for Health, ex parte British American Tobacco (BAT)* (case C-491/01), the Court observed that:

> the right to property . . . is recognised to be a fundamental human right in the [Union] legal order, protected by the first subparagraph of Article 1 of the First Protocol to the European Convention on Human Rights ('ECHR') and *enshrined in Article 17 of the Charter of Fundamental Rights of the European Union* [para 144, emphasis added].

These references cover a wide range of rights.

In *Günter Fuß v Stadt Halle* (case C-243/09), the Court referred to the right to effective judicial protection contained in Article 47 EUCFR: it did not refer either to general principles of EU law or to Article 6 or 13 ECHR (see similarly *Gascogne Sack Deutschland* (case C-40/12P) discussed in 6.6.4). In some cases, however, the CJ has considered the scope of Charter rights in the light of ECHR jurisprudence. *J McB v LE* (case C-400/10) concerned the interpretation of Regulation 2201/2003 ([2003] OJ L338/1) on jurisdiction and the recognition and enforcement of judgments in matrimonial matters. The questions referred concerned the procedural matters covered by the Regulation, rather than with substantive national law. The CJ noted the similarity between Article 7 EUCFR and Article 8 ECHR and concluded 'Article 7 of the Charter must therefore be given the same meaning and the same scope as Article 8(1) of the ECHR, as interpreted by the case-law of the European Court of Human Rights'. The CJ then proceeded to deal with the question by reference to specific

ECHR case law on this subject. The focus is, however, on the meaning of the EUCFR on which the judgment is based.

6.5 Relationship with ECHR

6.5.1 Historical development

All Member States of the EU have signed the ECHR, and in most Member States the Convention has been incorporated into domestic law. (In the UK, the ECHR was incorporated by the Human Rights Act 1998, which came into force in October 2000.) When incorporated, the Convention's provisions may be invoked before the domestic courts in order to challenge *national* rules or procedures which infringe the rights protected by the Convention. Even without the Convention being incorporated into domestic law, the Member States are bound by its terms, and individuals, after they have exhausted national remedies, have a right to bring a claim under the Convention to the ECtHR.

The CJ has done a great deal to ensure the protection of human rights within the context of the application of Union law, whether by Union institutions or by Member States. But, as the ECHR has not so far been incorporated into *Union* law, its scope has been limited in some key respects (eg, actions of the institutions) and the relationship between the ECHR and the Union legal system is somewhat unclear. The difficulties are illustrated by the decision of the ECtHR in *Matthews v UK* (ECtHR judgment, 18 February 1999).

Matthews

The case concerned the rights of UK nationals resident in Gibraltar to vote in European Parliamentary elections. They were excluded from participating in the elections as a result of the 1979 agreement between the Member States which established direct elections in respect of the European Parliament. The applicants argued that this was contrary to Protocol 1 Article 3 ECHR, which provides that signatory states to the Convention are under an obligation 'to hold free elections at reasonable intervals by secret ballot, under conditions which will ensure the free expression of the opinion of the people in the choice of the legislature'. The British government argued that not only was Union law not within the jurisdiction of the ECHR (as the Union had not acceded to the Convention), but also that the UK government could not be held responsible for joint acts of the Member States. The ECtHR found, however, that there had been a violation of the Convention.

The Court held that states which are party to the ECHR retain residual obligations in respect of the rights protected by the Convention, even as regards areas of lawmaking which had been transferred to the Union. Such a transfer of power is permissible, provided Convention rights continue to be secured within the Union framework. In this context the ECtHR noted the CJ's jurisprudence in which the CJ recognised and protected Convention rights. In this case, however, the existence of the direct elections was based on a *sui generis* international instrument entered into by the UK and the other Member States which could not be challenged before the CJ, as it was not a normal Union act. Furthermore, the TEU, which extended the European Parliament's powers to include the right to the ordinary legislative procedure, thereby increasing the Parliament's claim to be considered a legislature and taking it within the terms of Protocol 1 Article 3 ECHR, was equally an act which could not be challenged before the CJ. There could, therefore, be no protection of Convention rights in this regard by the CJ. Arguing that the ECHR is intended to guarantee rights that are not theoretical or illusory, the ECtHR held that:

> The United Kingdom, together with all other parties to the Maastricht Treaty, is responsible *ratione materiae* under Article 1 of the Convention and, in particular, under Article 3 of Protocol 1, for the consequences of that Treaty [para 33].

It may be noted that it is implicit in the reasoning in this judgment that the EU is regarded by the ECtHR as being the creature of the Member States, which remains fundamentally responsible for the Union's actions—and for those of the Union. This corresponds with the conception of the EU expressed by some of the Member States' constitutional courts (eg, see the FCC's reasoning in *Brunner* (discussed in Chapter 4).

Arguably, this judgment opens the way for the Member States to be held jointly responsible for those Union acts that currently fall outside the jurisdiction of the CJEU, sealing lacunae in the protection offered to individual human rights within the Union legal order. The difficulty is, of course, that in this case only the UK was the defendant. The British government is dependent on the co-operation of the other Member States to enable it to fulfil its own obligations under the ECHR. It is possible that a case could be brought under the ECHR against all Member States jointly. (See, eg, *Société Guerin Automobiles* (Application No 51717/99), inadmissible on other grounds; *DSR Senator Lines* (Application No 56672/00) (Grand Chamber), dismissed as the applicant could not claim on the facts to be a victim, though note third-party representations, including that of the ICJ.) Although this would not obviate the need for cooperation to remedy any violation found, it would avoid the situation where one Member State alone was carrying the responsibility for Union measures that were the choice of all (or most) Member States.

The implication that the ECtHR will step in only where there is no effective means of securing human rights protection within an existing international body (ie, that the CJ has primary responsibility for these issues in the EU) is underlined by its approach in another case involving another European supranational organisation, Euratom (*Waite and Kennedy v Germany*, ECtHR judgment, 18 February 1999). There the Court emphasised the necessity for an independent review board which is capable of protecting fundamental rights that exist within the organisational structure. We can also see this approach in *Bosphorus Airways v Ireland* (ECtHR judgment, 30 June 2005 (GC)), which concerned alleged human rights violations resulting from Union secondary legislation which the CJ had upheld. There the ECtHR held that it would not interfere provided the rights protection awarded by the CJ was equal to that under the ECHR, noting that in this context, 'equal' means equivalent or comparable rather than identical (para 155). It should be noted that in a concurring judgment, one of the ECtHR judges did make the point that, although there have been reviews of CJ jurisprudence, they have looked at the level of protection in a general or formal way, rather than looking at the substance of a right in an individual case (Concurring Opinion of Judge Ress, para 2), highlighting a potential weakness in the system of protection awarded to individuals.

Despite the concerns expressed by some about the approach in *Bosphorus*, it seemed that the position that EU acts gave adequate protection to human rights was accepted in *KRS v UK* (Application No 32733/08) concerning reliance on the Dublin Regulation (Regulation 343/2003 ([2003] OJ L50/1)) concerning asylum seekers. The ECtHR discussed its ruling in *Bosphorus* in *MSS v Belgium and Greece* (Application No 30696/09). The case concerned the European asylum system set up under the Dublin Regulation. Essentially, Belgium sought to return MSS to Greece, the Member State which, under the Dublin Regulation, had responsibility for assessing the asylum claim, despite the fact that conditions in Greece were poor. In assessing whether Belgium could so rely, the scope and impact of *Bosphorus* arose. The ECtHR noted that its judgment in *Bosphorus* was restricted to the former EC pillar of the EU, not the third pillar, an interesting point though, following Lisbon, seemingly of historical significance. The court also considered that Belgium could not rely on the presumption of equivalence found in *Bosphorus* because the Regulation provides Member States with a choice whether or not to intervene, notwithstanding the normal rules in the Dublin Convention, and Belgium chose not to do so. While in the absence of any rebutting evidence a Member State may assume its fellow Member States meet the conditions set down in the Dublin system, in this case the shortfalls in the Greek system were apparent and therefore Belgium was in breach of its obligations. While this case does not expressly change *Bosphorus*, it does make it clear that Member States do not have an automatic 'get out of jail free' card from liability in areas controlled by EU law. In the subsequent CJ decision, *NS*, the CJ took into account the ECtHR reasoning in *MSS* when interpreting the obligations flowing from the Dublin system.

The Strasbourg court has been willing to consider the adequacy of EU level protection in more detail again, in *Michaud v France* (Application No 12323/11). The case concerned the obligation under the Money Laundering Directive (Directive 2005/60 ([2005] OJ L309/15)) for lawyers to report reasonable suspicions of money laundering or terrorist financing and its compatibility with Article 8 ECHR. The Court declined to apply the *Bosphorus* presumption of equivalent protection for two reasons:

(1) The Directive grants some space to Member States to make choices about implementation, effectively following the reasoning in *MSS*; and

(2) The *Conseil d'Etat* had not made preliminary ruling to the CJ, nor had the CJ any other opportunity to examine the question.

While the first reason may be unsurprising in the light of *MSS*, the second reason is new and suggests that where issues are not referred to the CJ, the ECtHR will review EU law—or at least its implementation in Member States. The ECtHR affirmed the *Bosphorus* presumption and its approach in *Michaud* in *Avotiņš v Latvia* (Application No 17502/07). Some had expressed concern that the ECtHR might be less willing to deploy the *Bosphorus* presumption after the CJ's ruling in *Opinion 2/13* (discussed at 6.5.2). It is therefore significant that *Avotiņš* was handed down after *Opinion 2/13*.

6.5.2 Lisbon and accession

Despite the efforts of both sets of courts, there remain concerns about the completeness and coherence of protection of human rights within the EU. Deferring to the CJ concentrates a significant degree of power in that Court, against whose rulings there is no appeal. One suggested safeguard for fundamental rights would be for the Union to accede to the ECHR. Questions of human rights and, in particular, interpretation of the ECHR, could then be taken to the ECtHR, a court which specialises in human rights. This would minimise the risk of the CJEU misinterpreting the ECHR and avoid the possibility of two conflicting lines of case law developing (eg, *Orkem v Commission* (case 374/87) and *Funke v France* (case SA 256A) ([1993] 1 CMLR 897)). It has also been suggested that accession to the ECHR will provide the EU with external review, thus increasing its credibility as an organisation which subjects itself to the same standards with which it expects others to comply.

When this question arose in the 1990s, the CJ ruled that accession to the ECHR was not within the then powers of the Union: Treaty amendment would be required before the Union could take this step (*Opinion 2/94 on the Accession by the Community to the European Convention on Human Rights*). This was one of the issues discussed by the Convention on the Future of Europe preparing for the 2004 IGC. Against this background, the TEU post-Lisbon finally provides the EU with the power to accede to the ECHR; indeed, Article 6(2) TEU provides:

The Union shall accede to the European Convention for the Protection of Human Rights and Fundamental Freedoms. Such accession shall not affect the Union's competences as defined in the Treaties.

As a result, negotiations were ongoing since Lisbon came into force to achieve this end. Although the ECHR was amended to allow the accession of a non-state party (Protocol 14, amending Article 59(2) ECHR came into force 1 June 2010), and talks on the EU's accession to the ECHR started on 7 July 2010, matters were not entirely straightforward. The second sentence in Article 6(2) TEU (cited earlier) imposes limits on accession or its consequences for the EU, though it is not entirely clear what this sentence means. Further, Protocol 8 relating to Article 6(2) TEU contains conditions which must be met for accession to take place, specifically reiterating the point that accession shall not affect the competences of the EU, nor affect, 'the power of its institutions'. Practical questions also arose: what status should the EU have in the institutions of the ECHR—for example, should there be a judge for the EU? Non-EU Member States might be concerned that the EU Member States would thereby have double representation on the Committee of Ministers, were the EU to have a representative in that body. Other questions related to how actions against Member States and the EU should be organised (the co-respondent mechanism) and, crucially, the relationship between the Strasbourg and Luxembourg courts. There was also the substantive issue of the elements of the ECHR to which the EU will commit itself, in particular whether it will accept any optional protocols. Despite these difficult issues, a text agreement (see Box 6.2) was finalised.

Box 6.2 Key points in the Draft Accession Agreement

- The EU will accede to the ECHR itself and to protocols which all current member States have ratified:
  - Protocol 1 (on property and education amongst others);
  - Protocol 6 (abolition of the death penalty in times of peace) (but not Protocol 13 concerning the death penalty in all circumstances);
- The EU has obligations only with regard to acts, measures or omissions of its institutions, bodies, offices or agencies, or of persons acting on their behalf and within the EU's competence;
- An act, measure or omission of organs of a member State of the European Union or of persons acting on its behalf shall be attributed to that State, even if such act, measure or omission occurs when the State implements the law of the European Union (but note possibility of 'co-respondent mechanism');
- Co-respondent mechanism establishes joint responsibility for violations of the ECHR where it was caused by complying with EU law, but participation depends on the consent of EU and the relevant Member State;
- Where the EU is a co-respondent, the CJ will, in situations in which it has not yet assessed 'the compatibility with the Convention rights at issue of the provision of European Union law' at stake, be given the opportunity to make such an assessment;
- Participation of the EU in the Parliamentary Assembly of the Council of Europe (when electing judges) and in the Committee of Ministers of the Council of Europe (amongst others when supervising judgments) is also covered.

Nevertheless, as required by Article 218(11) TFEU, the CJ on 18 December 2014 gave a ruling (*Opinion 2/13*) on the compatibility of the proposed agreement with the EU legal order. This is a complex judgment that raises significant legal questions. A detailed analysis of the judgment is beyond the scope of this book. For the time being it can be said that, post the delivery of the *Opinion 2/13*, the EU is unable to proceed with the accession to the ECHR on the basis of the draft agreement. The CJ referred to Article 1(2) TEU which reads as follows:

> [t]his Treaty marks a new stage in the process of creating an ever closer union among the peoples of Europe, in which decisions are taken as openly as possible and as closely as possible to the citizen.

and concluded that the draft accession agreement is incompatible with the unique characteristics of EU law. Of particular importance are the principles of supremacy and direct effect of EU law. Similarly, the CJ highlighted the principle of autonomy of EU law. In the words of the judiciary:

> For the purposes of that review, it must be noted that . . . the conditions to which accession is subject under the Treaties are intended, particularly, to ensure that accession does not affect the specific characteristics of the EU and EU law [para 164].

Additionally the CJ highlighted that:

> The autonomy enjoyed by EU law in relation to the laws of the Member States and in relation to international law requires that the interpretation of those fundamental rights be ensured within the framework of the structure and objectives of the EU (see, to that effect, judgments in *Internationale Handelsgesellschaft*, EU:C:1970:114, paragraph 4, and *Kadi and Al Barakaat International Foundation v Council and Commission*, EU:C:2008:461, paragraphs 281 to 285) [para 170].

Additionally, the CJ noted that the draft agreement did not exclude the possibility of Member States having higher human rights standards than those provided by fully harmonised EU law (para 189). Also, the CJ ruled that the draft agreement left open the possibility of Member States' courts being able to send EU law related questions to the ECtHR before they make a reference to the CJ. In the eyes of the CJ, that failure undermines the preliminary reference procedure provided by Article 267 TFEU (para 196).

The CJ also concluded that the draft agreement is in violation of Article 344 TFEU which gives exclusive jurisdiction to the CJ to decide on EU law disputes between Member States (paras 201–14). In relation to the co-respondent system which sought to establish that both the EU and the relevant Member State could be parties to a case before the ECtHR, the CJ again found that to be in violation of EU law since the ECtHR would be deciding on the interpretation of EU law (paras 215–35). Finally, according to the CJ, the ECtHR cannot have jurisdiction to decide on the validity of Common Foreign and Security Policy issues.

Consequently, the draft accession agreement would need to be amended in order to comply with the requirements of *Opinion 2/13*. It seems, therefore, that the accession is unlikely to happen in the foreseeable future.

6.6 Rules of administrative justice

This section and 6.7–6.9 outline the substance of some of the general principles. The general principles of Union law have been expanded through the case law of the CJ to cover a wide variety of rights and principles developed from many sources. We will now look at some specific examples of those rights. The following is not, however, an exhaustive list, and there may be degrees of overlap between the categories mentioned.

6.6.1 **Proportionality**

This was the principle invoked in *Internationale Handelsgesellschaft*. Proportionality is formally recognised in Article 5(4) TEU which provides that '[u]nder the principle of proportionality, the content and form of Union action shall not exceed what is necessary to achieve the objectives of the Treaty' (see 6.8). Similarly, Article 5 of the Protocol on the Application of the Principles of Subsidiarity and Proportionality requires that draft EU legislation 'be justified with regard to the principles of subsidiarity and proportionality. Any draft legislation should contain a detailed statement making it possible to appraise compliance with the principles of subsidiarity and proportionality. . .'. The principle, applied in the context of administrative law, requires that the means used to achieve a given end must be no more than that which is appropriate and necessary to achieve legitimately that end. The test thus puts the burden on an administrative authority to justify its actions and requires some consideration of possible alternatives. In this respect it is a more rigorous test than one based on reasonableness.

The principle has been invoked on many occasions as a basis of challenge to EU secondary legislation, often successfully. For example, it was applied in *R v Intervention Board for Agricultural Produce, ex parte ED & F Man (Sugar) Ltd* (case 181/84) in the context of a claim by ED & F Man (Sugar) Ltd before the English Divisional Court, on facts very similar to *Internationale Handelsgesellschaft*.

ED & F Man (Sugar)

Here the claimant, ED & F Man (Sugar) Ltd, was seeking repayment of a security of £1,670,370 forfeited when it failed to comply with an obligation to submit licence applications to the Board within a specified time limit. Due to an oversight they were a few hours late. The claimant's claim rested on the alleged illegality of the EU regulations governing the common organisation of the sugar market. The Regulations appeared to require the full forfeiture of the deposit (lodged by the exporter at the time of the initial offer to export) in the event of a breach of both a *primary* obligation to export goods as agreed with the Commission and a *secondary* obligation to submit a licence application following the initial offer within a specified time limit. The CJ held, on a reference from the Divisional Court on the validity of the Regulations, that to require the same forfeiture for breach of the secondary obligation as for the primary obligation was disproportionate, and to the extent that the Regulation required such forfeiture, it was invalid. As a result of this ruling, the claimant was held entitled in the Divisional Court to a declaration that the forfeiture of its security was unlawful: a significant victory for the claimant.

The proportionality principle has also been applied in the context of the TFEU, for example, in the application of the provisions relating to freedom of movement for goods and persons. Under these provisions, Member States are allowed some scope for derogation from the principle of free movement, but derogations must be 'justified' on one of the grounds provided (Articles 36 and 45(3) TFEU). This has been interpreted by the CJ as meaning that the measure must be *no more than is necessary* to achieve the desired objective (see Chapters 19 (goods), and 25 (persons)).

Proportionality can also be used in the context of Member States' actions as can be seen in *Watson and Belmann* (case 118/75).

Watson

The proportionality principle was invoked in the sphere of the free movement of persons to challenge the legality of certain action by the Italian authorities. One of the defendants, Ms Watson, was claiming rights of residence in Italy. The right of free movement of workers expressed in Article 45 TFEU is regarded as a fundamental Union right, subject only to 'limitations' which are 'justified' on the grounds of public policy, public security or public health (Article 45(3) TFEU). The Italian authorities sought to invoke this derogation to expel Ms Watson from Italy. The reason for the defendants' expulsion was that they had failed to comply with certain administrative procedures, required under Italian law, to record and monitor their movements in Italy. The CJ, on reference from the Italian court, held that, while states were entitled to impose penalties for non-compliance with their administrative formalities, these must not be disproportionate; and they must never provide a ground for deportation. Expulsion was regarded by the CJ as disproportionate and not necessary in order to attain the objectives pursued by the legislation in question.

Likewise, in *Wijsenbeek* (case C-378/97) the CJ held that, although Member States were still entitled to check the documentation of EU nationals moving from one Member State to another, any penalties imposed on those whose documentation was unsatisfactory must be proportionate: in this case, imprisonment for failure to carry a passport was seen as disproportionate. (See further Chapter 25.)

Similarly, in the context of goods, in a case brought against Germany in respect of its beer purity laws (*Commission v Germany (German beer purity laws)* (case 178/84)), a German law imposing an absolute ban on additives was found in breach of Article 34 TFEU and not 'justified' on public-health grounds under Article 36 TFEU. Since the same (public health) objective could have been achieved by other less restrictive means, the ban was not 'necessary' and it was therefore disproportionate.

Watson, *Wijsenbeek* and *German beer purity laws* all concerned Member States' actions in derogation from the Treaty freedoms. Proportionality may also come into play in the context of Member States' actions to implement EU law. An example of this can be seen in *Danske Svineproducenter v Justitsministeriet* (case C-316/10).

Danske Svineproducenter

The case concerned Regulation 1/2005, ([2005] OJ L3/1) on the protection of animals during transport. The applicant argued that the standards contained in national law, which provided detailed requirements concerning the transport by road of pigs in respect of internal transport height, inspection height and loading density, were contrary to Regulation 1/2005. After confirming that the mere fact that the EU rules were in a regulation did not preclude more detailed national rules to implement the Regulation, the CJ identified limitations on Member States' freedom of action which included proportionality. The CJ held that the principle, which applies to, inter alia, the legislative and regulatory authorities of the Member States when they apply EU law, requires that measures implemented by means of a provision must be appropriate for attaining the objective pursued and must not go beyond what is necessary to achieve it.

There has been a refinement of the principle of proportionality. In the case of *Südzucker Mannheim/Ochsenfurt AG v Hauptzollamt Mannheim* (case C-161/96) the CJ confirmed the distinction between primary and secondary (or administrative) obligations made in *ED & F Man (Sugar)*. The breach of a secondary obligation should not be punished as severely as a breach of a primary obligation. (See also *ED & F Man (Sugar)* discussed earlier.) On the facts of the case in *ED & F Man (Sugar)*, the CJ held that a failure to comply with customs formalities by not producing an export licence was a breach of a primary and not a secondary obligation. The CJ stated that the production of the export licence was necessary to ensure compliance with export requirements and thus the production of the export licence was part of the primary obligation. On this reasoning, it may be difficult to distinguish between primary and secondary obligations.

Further, the CJ has held that, where an institution has significant discretion in the implementation of policies, such as in CAP, the CJ may only interfere if the 'measure is manifestly inappropriate having regard to the objectives which the competent institution is seeking to pursue' (*banana regime*) (para 90). The same is also true of actions of Member States where they have a broad discretion in the implementation of Union policy (see *R v Minister of Agriculture, Fisheries and Food, ex parte National Federation of Fishermen's Organisations* (case C-44/94)).

6.6.2 Legal certainty

The principle of legal certainty was invoked by the CJ in *Defrenne II*. The principle, which is one of the widest generality, has been applied in more specific terms as:

- the principle of legitimate expectations;
- the principle of non-retroactivity;
- the principle of *res judicata*.

The principle of legitimate expectations, derived from German law, means that, in the absence of an overriding matter of public interest, Union measures must not violate the legitimate expectations of the parties concerned. A legitimate expectation is one which might be held by a reasonable person as to matters likely to occur in the normal course of his affairs. It does not extend to anticipated windfalls or speculative profits. In *Efisol SA v Commission* (case T-336/94) the GC commented that an individual would have no legitimate expectations of a particular state of affairs existing where a 'prudent and discriminating' trader would have foreseen the development in question. Furthermore, in *Re Banana Regime*, the CJ held that no trader may have a legitimate expectation that an existing Union regime will be maintained. In that the principle requires the encouragement of a reasonable expectation, a reliance on that expectation, and some loss resulting from the breach of that expectation, it is similar to the principle of estoppel in English law.

The principle was applied in *August Töpfer & Co GmbH v Commission* (case 112/77) (see Chapter 12).

August Töpfer

August Töpfer & Co GmbH was an exporter which had applied for, and been granted, a number of export licences for sugar. Under Union law, as part of the common organisation of the sugar market, certain refunds were to be payable on export, the amount of the refunds being fixed in advance. If the value of the refund fell, due to currency fluctuations, the licence holder could apply to have his licence cancelled. This scheme was suddenly altered by a regulation, and the right to cancellation withdrawn, being substituted by provision for compensation. This operated to Töpfer's disadvantage, and it sought to have the Regulation annulled, for breach, inter alia, of the principle of legitimate expectations. Although it did not succeed on the merits, the principle of legitimate expectations was upheld by the Court.

(See also *CNTA SA v Commission* (case 74/74), monetary compensation scheme ended suddenly and without warning: Chapter 14.) In *Opel Austria GmbH v Council* (case T-115/94) the Court held that the principle of legitimate expectations was the corollary of the principle of good faith in public international law. Thus, where the Union had entered into an obligation and the date of entry into force of that obligation is known to traders, such traders may use the principle of legitimate expectations to challenge measures contrary to any provision of the international agreement having direct effect.

The principle of non-retroactivity, applied to Union secondary legislation, precludes a measure from taking effect before its publication. Retrospective application will only be permitted in exceptional circumstances, where it is necessary to achieve particular objectives and will not breach individuals' legitimate expectations. Such measures must also contain a statement of the reasons justifying the retroactive effect (*Diversinte SA v Administración Principal de Aduanos e Impuestos Especiales de la Junqueros* (case C-260/91)).

In *Kirk* the principle of non-retroactivity of penal provisions (activated in this case by a Union regulation) was invoked successfully. However, retroactivity may be acceptable where the retroactive operation of the rule in question improves an individual's position (see, eg, *Road Air BV v Inspecteur der Invoerrechten en Accijnzen* (case C-310/95)).

This principle also has relevance in the context of national courts' obligation to interpret domestic law to comply with Union law when it is not directly effective (the *von Colson* principle, see Chapter 5). In *Pretore di Salò v Persons Unknown* (case 14/86) in a reference from the Salò magistrates' court on the compatibility of certain Italian laws with the Water Purity Directive (Directive 78/659), which had been invoked against the defendants in criminal proceedings, the Court held that:

> A Directive cannot of itself have the effect of determining or aggravating the liability in criminal law of persons who act in contravention of the provisions of the Directive.

The Court went further in *Kolpinghuis Nijmegen*. Here, in response to a question concerning the scope of national courts' obligation of consistent interpretation under the *von Colson* principle, the Court held that that obligation was 'limited by the general principles of law which form part of [Union] law and in particular the principles of legal certainty and non-retroactivity'. Thus national courts are not required to interpret domestic law to comply with EU law in violation of these principles. This would appear to apply even where the EU law in question has direct effects, at least where criminal proceedings are in issue (see *Berlusconi*, discussed in Chapter 5). Note that Article 49(3) EUCFR specifies that penalties should not be disproportionate to the criminal offence.

Problems also arise over the temporal effects of CJ rulings under Article 267 TFEU. In *Defrenne* (see Chapter 5) the Court held that, given the exceptional circumstances, 'important considerations of legal certainty' required that its ruling on the direct effects of the then Article 119 EEC (now Article 157 TFEU) should apply prospectively only. It could not be relied on to support claims concerning pay periods prior to the date of judgment, except as regards workers who had already brought legal proceedings or made an equivalent claim. However, in *Amministrazione delle Finanze dello Stato v Ariete SpA* (case 811/79) and *Amministrazione delle Finanze dello Stato v Meridionale Industria Salumi Srl* (cases 66, 127 and 128/79) the Court affirmed that *Defrenne* was an exceptional case. In a 'normal' case a ruling from the CJ was retroactive; the Court merely declared the law as it always was. This view was approved in *Barra v Belgium* (case 309/85) concerning access to educational and vocational training. However, in *Blaizot v University of Liège* (case 24/86), a case decided the same day as *Barra*, 'important considerations of legal certainty' again led the Court to limit the effects of its judgment on the lines of *Defrenne*. It came to the same conclusion in *Barber v Guardian Royal Exchange Assurance Group* (case 262/88), which affected UK rules setting different retirement ages for men and women. These cases indicate that in exceptional cases, where the Court introduces a new principle, or where the judgment may have serious effects as regards the past, the Court will be prepared to limit the effects of its rulings. *Kolpinghuis Nijmegen* may now be invoked to support such a view. Nevertheless, the Court did not limit the effect of its judgment in *Francovich* contrary to Advocate-General Mischo's advice, despite the unexpectedness of the ruling and its 'extremely serious financial consequences' for Member States. Nor did it do so in *Marshall v Southampton & South West Hampshire Health Authority (Teaching) (Marshall II)* (case C-271/91) when it declared that national courts were obliged, by Article 5 Directive 76/207 ([1976] OJ L39/40) and their general obligation under Article 5(3) TEU to ensure that the objectives of the directives might be achieved, to provide full compensation to persons suffering loss as a result of infringements of the Directive, a matter which could not have been deduced either from the CJ's case law or from the actual wording of the Directive (see further Chapter 8).

The question of the temporal effect of a ruling from the CJ under Article 267 TFEU was considered by the Italian constitutional court in *SpA Fragd v Amministrazione delle Finanze dello Stato*, Decision No 232 of 21 April 1989 in the light of another general principle. Although the point did not arise out of the reference in question, the Italian court considered the effect that a ruling under Article 267 TFEU holding a Union measure void should have on the referring court if the CJ had held that the ruling would apply for future cases only, excluding the judgment in which it was given. The Italian constitutional court suggested that in the light of the right to judicial protection given under the Italian constitution, such a holding should have effect in the case in which the reference was made. A finding of invalidity with purely prospective effect would offend against this principle and would therefore be unacceptable.

Res judicata is a principle accepted in both the civil- and common-law traditions; its significance has been recognised also by the ECtHR (see, eg, *Brumarescu v Romania* (Application No 28342/05)). Essentially it operates to respect the binding force of a final judgment in a matter; once any relevant time limits for appeal have expired, the judgment cannot be challenged. The CJ has recognised this principle in many cases. In *Köbler*, the CJ held that:

> attention should be drawn to the importance, both for the [Union] legal order and national legal systems, of the principle of *res judicata*. In order to ensure both stability of the law and legal relations and the sound administration of justice, it is important that judicial decisions which have become definitive after all rights of appeal have been exhausted or after expiry of the time-limits provided for in that connection can no longer be called into question [para 38].

Applying this in *Kapferer* the CJ ruled that in the light of *res judicata*, a national court does not have to disapply domestic rules of procedure conferring finality on a decision, even though doing so would enable it to remedy an infringement of Union law by the decision at issue. Surprisingly, in *Lucchini*, the CJ came to the opposite conclusion. An undertaking was seeking to claim state aid, which had been granted by the Italian government in breach of the state aid rules. The undertaking had a decision of an Italian court to this effect, whose judgment was protected by the principle of *res judicata*. In proceedings to challenge this decision, the CJ addressed the question of whether Union law precluded the application of *res judicata*. The CJ concluded that it did. The Advocate-General in *Lucchini* pointed out that the principle is not absolute; the systems of the various Member States allow exceptions under certain strict conditions and the ECtHR has accepted this. *Lucchini* is best regarded as an isolated case on exceptional facts.

6.6.3 **Procedural rights**

Where a person's rights are likely to be affected by EU law, EU secondary legislation normally provides for procedural safeguards (eg, Regulation 1/2003, ([2003] OJ L1/1), competition law; and Citizens' Rights Directive (Directive 2004/38 ([2004] OJ L158/77)), free movement of workers, Chapter 25). However, where such provision does not exist, or where there are lacunae, general principles of law may be invoked to fill those gaps.

6.6.4 **Natural justice: the right to a hearing**

The right to natural justice, and in particular the right to a fair hearing, was invoked, this time from English law, in *Transocean Marine Paint Association v Commission* (case 17/74) by Advocate-General Warner. The case, which arose in the context of competition law, was an action for annulment of the Commission's decision, addressed to the claimant association, that their agreements were in breach of EU law. The court, following Advocate-General Warner's submissions, asserted a general rule that a person whose interests are perceptibly affected by a decision taken by a public authority must be given the opportunity to make his views known. Since the Commission had failed to comply with this obligation its decision was annulled. The principle was affirmed in the well-known case of *Hoffman-La Roche & Co AG v Commission* (case 85/76), in which the court held that observance of the right to be heard is, in all proceedings in which sanctions, in particular fines and periodic payments, may be imposed, a fundamental principle of law which must be respected even if the proceedings in question are administrative proceedings.

Another aspect of the right to a fair hearing is the notion of 'equality of arms'. This is exemplified in a series of cases against the Commission following a Commission investigation into alleged anti-competitive behaviour on the part of ICI and another company, Solvay. In *Solvay SA v Commission* (case T-30/91) the GC stated that the principle of equality of arms presupposed that both the Commission and the defendant company had equal knowledge of the files used in the proceeding. That was not the case here, as the Commission had not informed Solvay of the existence of certain documents. The Commission argued that this did not affect the proceedings because the documents would not be used in the company's defence. The Court took the view that this point was not for the Commission to decide, as this would give the Commission more power vis-à-vis the defendant company because it had full knowledge of the file whereas the defendant did not. Equally, in the *ICI plc v Commission (soda ash)* (cases T-36 and 37/91) the Commission's refusal to grant ICI access to the file was deemed to infringe the rights of the defence.

There are, however, limits to the rights of the defence: in *Descom Scales Manufacturing v Council* (case T-171/94), the CJ held that the rights of the defence do not require the Commission to provide a written record of every stage of the investigation detailing information which needed still to be verified. In this case, the Commission had notified the defendant company of the position although it had not provided a written record and the CJ held that this was sufficient.

The right to a hearing within Article 6 ECHR also includes the right to a hearing within a reasonable period of time. The CJ, basing its reasoning on Article 6 ECHR, thus held that, in respect of a case that had been pending before the GC for 5 years and 6 months, the GC had been in violation of its obligation to dispose of cases within a reasonable time (*Baustahlgewerbe v Commission* (case C-185/95P)).

The CJ handed down a judgment on the reasonable time requirement contained in Article 47 EUCFR in relation to a challenge to competition proceedings before the GC in *Gascogne Sack*. As regards the assessment of the length of time, the CJ reiterated that such an assessment should take place in the light of the circumstances specific to each case, such as 'the complexity of the case and the conduct of the parties' (para 96), although this is not an exhaustive list. In this case, the length of the proceedings before the GC could not be justified by any such particular circumstances. This constituted, according to the CJEU, 'a sufficiently serious breach of a rule of law that is intended to confer rights on individuals' (para 106), referring back to the case law on actions for non-contractual liability against EU institutions.

This approach then raises a second question: what is an appropriate remedy where justice has already taken so long, bearing in mind that Article 47 EUCFR also specifies that Member States must provide an effective remedy. The CJ had a choice. It could take the approach it did in *Baustahlgewerbe* and reduce the fine imposed on the undertakings, or it could take the approach it had taken in *Der Grüne Punkt–Duales System Deutschland v Commission* (case C-385/07P). *Der Grüne Punkt* concerned the level of fee payable under a trade-mark agreement relating to the system for the collection and recovery of used packaging in Germany that raised questions about abuse of a dominant position. Again, the claim was that proceedings had taken too long. In that case, the Grand Chamber suggested that the appropriate remedy was through an action for non-contractual liability pursuant to Articles 268 and 340(2) TFEU. In *Gascogne Sack* the CJ followed its reasoning in *Der Grüne Punkt*. This is not entirely satisfactory as it leaves the applicant with another court case, potentially to be heard by the same court, the GC, the behaviour of which gave rise to the claim in the first place.

The right to a hearing has arisen in more difficult circumstances, that of the freezing of assets of persons thought to be involved in, or supporting, terrorism. Even in these circumstances, the European courts have reiterated the principle of the right to be heard (*OMPI v Council* (*OMPI I*) (case T-228/02)). Nonetheless, the GC recognised that this right is subject to broad limitations in the interests of the overriding requirement of public security, which relate to all aspects of procedural justice rights, including the hearing of certain types of evidence. It seems in these circumstances the right to a hearing is limited to a right to be notified as soon as possible as to the adoption of an economic sanction; given this finding, the duty to state reasons has a still greater significance than it usually would have. The rule of law is protected by the right to seek a review of the decision-making process subsequently. In *OMPI II* (case T-256/07) the GC clarified that the right to a hearing does not necessitate a formal hearing if the relevant legislation does not provide for it; nor is there a right to continuous conversation. Rather, it suffices if the persons involved have the right to make their views known to the competent authorities (see *OMPI II*, para 93; see also *Common Market Fertilisers v Commission* (cases T-134–5/03), para 108).

The Charter likewise contains a right to a fair trial in Article 47 EUCFR, as well as the right to an effective remedy. This article has already been relied on in a significant number of cases, though successful claims are much rarer.

6.6.5 The duty to give reasons

The duty was affirmed in *Union Nationale des Entraîneurs et Cadres Techniques Professionels du Football (UNECTEF) v Heylens* (case 222/86).

Heylens

In this case, M Heylens, a Belgian and a professional football trainer, was the defendant in a criminal action brought by the French football trainers' union, UNECTEF, as a result of his practising in Lille as a professional trainer without the necessary French diploma, or any qualifications recognised by the French government as equivalent. M Heylens held a Belgian football trainers' diploma, but his application for recognition of this diploma by the French authorities had been rejected on the basis of an adverse opinion from a special committee, which gave no reasons for its decision. The CJ, on a reference from the Tribunal de Grande Instance, Lille, held that the right of free movement of workers, granted by Article 45 TFEU, required that a decision refusing to recognise the equivalence of a qualification issued in another Member State should be subject to legal redress which would enable the legality of that decision to be established with regard to Union law, and that the person concerned should be informed of the reasons upon which the decision was based.

Similarly in *Al-Jubail Fertiliser Company (SAMAD) v Council* (case C-49/88) in the context of a challenge to a Council regulation imposing antidumping duties on the import of products manufactured by the applicants, the Court held that since the applicants had a right to a fair hearing the institutions were under a duty to supply them with all the information which would enable them effectively to defend their interests. Moreover if the information is supplied orally, as it may be, the Commission must be able to prove that it was in fact supplied.

The duty to give reasons was considered in the *OMPI* cases noted in 6.6.4. These have a greater significance due to the potential for a limited right to a hearing. In *OMPI II*, the GC emphasised that the Council was under an obligation to provide actual and specific reasons justifying the inclusion of a person on a sanctions list. This requires the Council not only to identify the legal conditions found in the underlying regulation, but why the Council considered that they applied to the particular person, justifying their inclusion on the sanctions list. The duty to give reasons does not, however, include the obligation to respond to all points made by the applicant.

6.6.6 **The right to due process**

As a corollary to the right to be informed of the reasons for a decision is the right, alluded to in *Heylens*, to legal redress to enable such decisions and reasons to be challenged. This right was established in *Johnston*.

Johnston

The case arose from a refusal by the RUC (now the Police Service of Northern Ireland) to renew its contracts with women members of the RUC Reserve. Although the measure was admittedly discriminatory, since it was taken solely on the grounds of sex, the Chief Constable claimed that it was justified, arguing from the 'public policy and public security' derogation of Articles 34 TFEU (goods) and 45 TFEU (workers), and from Article 347 TFEU, which provides for the taking of measures in the event of, inter alia, 'serious internal disturbances affecting the maintenance of law and order'. The Secretary of State had issued a certificate under relevant national legislation stating that the refusal of renewal was done in the interests of national security. The Court considered the requirement of judicial control, provided by Article 6 Directive 76/207, which requires states to enable persons who 'consider themselves wronged' to 'pursue their claims by judicial process after possible recourse to the competent authorities'. This provision, the Court said, reflected:

> a general principle of law which underlies the constitutional traditions common to the Member States. That principle is also laid down in Articles 6 and 13 of the European Convention for the Protection of Human Rights and Fundamental Freedoms . . . It is for the Member States to ensure effective judicial control as regards compliance with the applicable provisions of [Union] law and of national legislation intended to give effect to the rights for which the Directive provides.

The CJ went on to say that Article 53(2) of the Sex Discrimination (Northern Ireland) Order 1976, in requiring the Secretary of State's certificate to be treated as conclusive evidence that the conditions for derogation are fulfilled, allowed the competent authority to deprive an individual of the possibility of asserting by judicial process the rights conferred by the Directive. Such a provision was contrary to the principle of effective judicial control laid down in Article 6 of the Directive.

In the *OMPI* cases, the GC made clear that reasons of public security could not remove the decisions and the decision-making processes at issue from the scope of judicial review (see also *Kadi*, para 344 and comments of the Advocate-General at para 45), although that review may necessarily be limited. In *OMPI II*, the GC clarified (at paras 138–41) the scope and standard of review, at least as regards decisions concerning economic sanctions. While the Council has broad discretion as to whether to impose sanctions, the GC must ensure that a threefold test is satisfied: whether the requirements of the applicable law are fulfilled; whether the evidence contains all information necessary to assess the situation and whether it is capable of supporting the inferences drawn from it; and whether essential procedural guarantees have been satisfied. The GC seems to have taken a surprisingly tough stance in favour of the protection of procedural rights here.

Thus general principles of law act as a curb not only on the institutions of the Union but also on Member States, which are required, in the context of EU law, to accommodate these principles alongside existing remedies and procedures within their own domestic systems of administrative law and may result eventually in some modification in national law itself. There are, in any event, problems in determining the boundaries between matters of purely national law and matters of Union law (see 6.2.5).

6.6.7 Right to protection against self-incrimination

The right to a fair trial and the presumption of innocence of 'persons charged with a criminal offence' contained in Article 6 ECHR are undoubtedly rights which will be protected as general principles of law under Union law (see also Articles 47 and 48 EUCFR). However, in *Orkem* and *Solvay* the CJ held that the right under Article 6 not to give evidence against oneself applied only to persons charged with an offence in criminal proceedings; it was not a principle which could be relied on in relation to infringements in the economic sphere, in order to resist a demand for information such as may be made by the Commission to establish a breach of EU competition law. This view was placed in doubt following a ruling from the ECtHR in the case of *Funke v France*.

Funke

Funke involved a claim, for breach of Article 6 ECHR, in respect of a demand by the French customs' authorities for information designed to obtain evidence of currency and capital transfer offences. Following the applicant's refusal to hand over such information fines and penalties were imposed. The ECtHR held that such action, undertaken as a 'fishing expedition' in order to obtain documents which, if found, might produce evidence for a prosecution, infringed the right, protected by Article 6(1) ECHR, of anyone charged with a criminal offence (within the autonomous meaning of that phrase in Article 6 ECHR), to remain silent and not incriminate himself.

It appears that Article 6 ECHR, according to its 'autonomous meaning', is wide enough to apply to investigations conducted under the Commission's search-and-seizure powers under competition law, and that *Orkem* and *Solvay* may no longer be regarded as good law. This view, assimilating administrative penalties to criminal penalties, appears to have been taken by the CJ in *Otto BV v Postbank NV* (case C-60/92). Moreover, in *Mannesmannröhren-Werke*, also a case involving a request for information about an investigation into anti-competitive agreements, the GC held that although Article 6 ECHR could not be invoked directly before the Court, Union law offered 'protection equivalent to that guaranteed by Article 6 of the Convention' (para 77). A party subject to a Commission investigation could not be required to answer questions that might involve an admission of involvement in an anti-competitive agreement, although it would have to respond to requests for general information.

Note that the rights granted by the EUCFR additionally include the principle that no one can be convicted of a criminal offence that has not been enshrined in law (Article 49 EUCFR), a right which has been recognised by the CJ as a general principle (see, eg, *Kirk* and *Pretore di Salò*, both discussed in 6.6.2). Furthermore, Article 50 provides that no-one can be tried or punished twice in criminal proceedings for the same criminal offence. This was the right in issue in *Fransson* (see 6.4.3).

6.7 Equality

The principle of equality means, in its broadest sense, that persons in similar situations are not to be treated differently unless the difference in treatment is objectively justified. This, of course, gives rise to the question of what are similar situations. Discrimination can only exist within a framework in which it is possible to draw comparisons, for example, the framework of race, sex, nationality, colour, religion. The equality principle will not apply in situations which are deemed to be 'objectively different' (see *Les Assurances du Crédit SA v Council* (case C-63/89), public export credit insurance operations different from other export credit insurance operations). What situations are regarded as comparable, subject to the equality principle, is clearly a matter of political judgement. The TFEU expressly prohibits discrimination on the grounds of nationality (Article 18 TFEU) and, to a limited extent, sex (Article 157 TFEU provides for equal *pay* for men and women for equal work; and note Article 10 TFEU). The ToA introduced further provisions, giving the EU powers to regulate against discrimination on grounds of race, religion, sexual orientation or disability (Article 19 TFEU). Directive 2000/43 ([2000] OJ L180/22) has been adopted to combat discrimination, both direct and indirect, on grounds of racial or ethnic origin, in relation to employment matters, social protection, education and access to public goods and services (see, eg, *Centrum voor gelijkheid van kansen en voor racismebestrijding v Feryn* (case C-54/07)). Directive 2000/78 ([2000] OJ L303/16) was adopted to combat discrimination on the grounds of religion or belief, disability, age or sexual orientation with regard to employment and occupation. The practical implications of Directive 2000/78 can be seen in the context of *Samira Achbita v G4S Secure Solutions NV* (case C-157/15) and *Asma Bougnaoui Association de défense des droits de l'homme (ADDH) v Micropole* (case C-188/15). Both cases relate to the compatibility of rules restricting the wearing of religious symbols at work (in both cases Islamic headscarves) with the prohibition of direct and indirect discrimination in employment provided by Directive 2000/78. Advocate-General Kokott in her Opinion in *Achbita* and Advocate-General Sharpston in her Opinion in *Bougnaoui* seem to have different understandings on whether a ban on Islamic headscarves at work can be found as directly discriminatory. For Kokott, a prohibition of wearing religious symbols at work should not in any case be considered as directly discriminatory since it does not relate to:

> individuals' immutable physical features or personal characteristics—such as gender, age or sexual orientation—rather than with modes of conduct based on a subjective decision or conviction, such as the wearing or not of a head covering at issue here [para 45].

On the other hand Sharpston considers religion as part of one's identity. She argues that:

> [i]t would be entirely wrong to suppose that, whereas one's sex and skin colour accompany one everywhere, somehow one's religion does not [para 118].

The differences in these Opinions are not surprising because of the fairly contentious issues that they examine. The CJ gave a joined judgment which permits, under certain conditions, rules banning the wearing of visible religious symbols. These cases are discussed further in Chapter 27.

There has been some discussion as to whether the above-mentioned aspects of discrimination constitute separate general principles of law, as seemed to be suggested by the CJ in *Mangold* (see also 6.2.6). Although a number of advocates-general have discussed the issue, it is indicative of the matter's sensitive nature that in each of the cases, the CJ handed down rulings without addressing the *Mangold* point. (See, eg, *Sonia Chacón Navas v Eurest Colectividades SA* (case C-13/05) concerning disability discrimination; and see Opinion of Advocate-General at paras 46–56; *Lindorfer* and the Opinion of the Advocate-General at paras 87–97 and 132–8; *Palacios de la Villa* and *Maruko* on discrimination based on sexual orientation—see Opinion of Advocate-General at para 78; *The Queen, on the application of The Incorporated Trustees of the National Council on Ageing (Age Concern England) v Secretary of State for BERR* (case C-388/07) and *Bartsch*.) The CJ reaffirmed its approach in *Kücükdeveci* without, however, clarifying this question.

The latest judicial approach with regards to the application of the general principle of age discrimination can be seen in *DI*. While normally an employee would not be able to rely on a directive directly against a private employer, where the directive in question gives expression to a general principle the limitation on horizontal effect of the directive does not seem to apply. In *DI*, the national court was unsure as to whether the inconsistent national provision should be disapplied at the expense of the principle of legal certainty and legitimate expectations. The CJ ruled that the national court should proceed with an interpretation that is consistent with EU law on the basis of the general principle of EU law which prohibits discrimination on grounds of age. The CJ found that the national court:

> is nonetheless under an obligation to provide, within the limits of its jurisdiction, the legal protection which individuals derive from EU law and to ensure the full effectiveness of that law, disapplying if need be any provision of national legislation contrary to that principle [para 35].

Overall, the CJ found that the underlying principle of the Directive is a general principle of EU law that prohibits discrimination and as such it can be relied upon in disputes between individuals. Of particular importance is the obligation of the national judge to strike down the conflicting national law. The consequences of the *DI* ruling are further examined in detail in Chapter 5.

A general principle of equality is clearly wider in scope. This approach can be seen in the context of the first isoglucose case, *Royal Scholten-Honig (Holdings) Ltd v Intervention Board for Agricultural Produce* (cases 103 and 145/77).

Isoglucose

Here, the claimants, who were glucose producers, together with other glucose producers, sought to challenge the legality of a system of production subsidies whereby sugar producers were receiving subsidies financed in part by levies on the production of glucose. Since glucose and sugar producers were in competition with each other the claimants argued that the Regulations implementing the

> system were discriminatory, that is, in breach of the general principle of equality, and therefore invalid. The CJ, on a reference on the validity of the Regulations from the English court, agreed. The Regulations were held invalid.

(See also *Firma Albert Ruckdeschel & Co v Hauptzollamt Hamburg–St Annen* (case 117/76); *Moulins et Huileries de Pont-à-Mousson SA v Office National Interprofessionel des Céréales* (cases 124/76 and 20/77).)

6.8 Subsidiarity

The principle of subsidiarity in its original philosophical meaning, as expressed by Pope Pius XI (Encyclical letter, 1931), is that:

> It is an injustice, a grave evil and disturbance of right order for a larger and higher association to arrogate to itself functions which can be performed efficiently by smaller and lower societies.

It was invoked in the Union context during the 1980s when the Union's competence was extended under the Single European Act. It was incorporated into that Act, in respect of environmental measures, in the then Article 130r EC, and introduced into the former EC Treaty by the Maastricht Treaty. The Protocol on the application of the principles of subsidiarity and proportionality, was annexed to the then EC Treaty by the ToA. Currently, Article 5 TEU requires the Union to act 'only if and so far as the objectives of the proposed action cannot be sufficiently achieved by the Member States, and can therefore, by reason of the scale or the effects of the proposed action, be better achieved at Union level'.

As expressed in Article 5 TEU, subsidiarity appears to be a test of comparative efficiency; as such it lacks its original philosophical meaning, concerned with fostering social responsibility. As we saw in Chapter 3, the TEU now provides that decisions of the European Union 'be taken as closely as possible to the people'.

The principle of subsidiarity in its narrow form in Article 5 TEU has, on occasion, been referred to as a ground for challenge of EU legislation (eg, *British American Tabacco*; *UK v Council (Working Time Directive)* (case C-84/94); *R v Secretary of State for Health, ex parte Swedish Match* (case C-210/03)), but this has not to date succeeded.

6.9 Effectiveness

The doctrine of effectiveness is not usually recognised as a general principle of Union law, save—perhaps—when it is equated with the idea of effective judicial protection. Nonetheless, the principle is ubiquitous and has had a significant effect on the development of Union law. Notably, it was an effectiveness argument that was used to develop the doctrine of supremacy, direct effect (*Van Gend en Loos* and *Costa*, as well as state liability (*Francovich*), and was used to extend the loyalty principle now found in Article 4(3) TEU to the former third pillar (*Pupino*).

As we shall see in Chapter 8, it has been used to ensure effective protection for EU law, and for individuals' rights; indeed sometimes the CJ seems to blur the boundaries between the two (eg, *Courage Ltd v Bernard Creehan* (case C-453/99)). Following Lisbon, Article 19 TEU expressly requires

Member States to provide remedies so as to ensure effective legal protection of Union law rights. Further, Article 47 EUCFR guarantees the right to an effective remedy (including the right to legal aid—see *DEB* discussed earlier). Despite the potential overlap between effectiveness of EU law and the right to effective remedies, it is probably best to differentiate between the two principles.

6.10 Conclusions

The EU constitutes of a legal order founded on respect for human rights and other similar principles. This orientation has been given great visibility by the terms of Article 2 TEU, as well as the more specific provisions in Articles 6 and 7 TEU. Given the range of sources that provide protection for human rights that are now expressed (or referred to) in the Treaties, it is surprising to remember that there was no scope for human rights protection in the original Treaty of Rome. The shift is in no small part due to the activities of the CJ and its jurisprudence on general principles, supported of course by the reaction of the Member States and the institutions of the EU in the successive Treaty amendments, as well as through the judicial dialogue with the ECtHR. While this change is no doubt a good thing, there are still issues to note. The very multiplicity of sources means the system for human rights protection is complex, and the overlapping regimes lead frequently to questions about their interrelationship—especially when it comes to recognition of rights and the scope and level of protection awarded them. We have seen that there have been questions about the motivation of the CJ in this regard. While *Bosphorus* suggested that the EU level of protection through general principles is adequate, there has been some narrowing in the field to which it applies. With the changes introduced by Lisbon we have seen a greater emphasis on the EUCFR, though it will take some time, particularly post *Opinion 2/13*, for the consequences of accession of the EU to the ECHR—if it happens—to be understood. Underlying this is the question of the scope of EU law and the power of the courts to review national acts for compliance with EU standards. This issue existed even under the general principles approach, though it did not have the high profile the issue attracted when viewed through the lens of the EUCFR. In sum, the protection of human rights is more visible after Lisbon, there are more avenues to such protection, but whether the scope and level of protection has increased is debatable.

Further reading

Ashiagbor, D, 'Economic and social rights in the European Charter of Fundamental Rights' (2004) 1 EHRLR 62.

Coppel, J and O'Neill, A, 'The European Court of Justice: Taking rights seriously?' (1992) 29 CMLR 669.

Council of the EU, *Charter of Fundamental Rights of the European Union: Explanations relating to the complete text of the Charter* (Office for Official Publications of the European Communities, 2001).

De Búrca, G, 'After the EU Charter of Fundamental Rights: The Court of Justice as a human rights adjudicator?' (2013) 20 MJ 168.

Eeckhout, P, 'Opinion 2/13 on EU Accession to the ECHR and Judicial Dialogue—Autonomy or Autarky?' (2015) Jean Monnet Working Paper 01/2015.

Knook, A, 'The Court, the Charter, and the vertical division of powers in the European Union' (2005) 42 CML Rev 367.

Leczykiewicz, D, 'Horizontal application of the Charter of Fundamental Rights' (2013) 38 EL Rev 479.

Mancini, GF, 'The making of a constitution for Europe' (1989) 26 CML Rev 594.

Micheau, C, 'The *Werner Mangold* case: An example of legal militancy' (2007) 13 EPL 587.

Papadopoulos, T, 'Criticising the horizontal direct effect of the EU general principle of equality' (2011) EHRLR 437.

Peers, S, 'The EU's Accession to the ECHR: The Dream Becomes a Nightmare' (2015) 16 GLJ 213.

Peers, S, 'Supremacy, equality and human rights' (2010) 35 EL Rev 849.

Peers, S, Hervey, T, Kenner, J and Ward, A (eds), *The EU Charter of Fundamental Rights: A Commentary* (Hart Publishing, 2014).

Polakiewicz, J, 'EU law and the ECHR: Will the European Union's accession square the circle?' (2016) 6 EHRLR 592.

Sarmiento, D, 'Who's afraid of the Charter? The Court of Justice, national courts and the new framework of fundamental rights protection in Europe' (2013) 50 CML Rev 1267.

Spaventa, E, 'A Very Fearful Court? The Protection of Fundamental Rights in the European Union after Opinion 2/13' (2015) 22 MJECL 35.

Van Bockel, B and Wattel, P, 'New wine into old wineskins: The scope of the Charter of Fundamental Rights of the EU after *Akerberg Fransson*' (2013) 38 EL Rev 866.

Weiler, JHH and Lockhart, NJS, '"Taking rights seriously" seriously?: The European Court and its fundamental rights jurisprudence' (1995) 32 CML Rev 51 (Part I) and 579 (Part II).

Weiss, W, 'Human rights in the EU: Rethinking the role of the European Convention on Human Rights after Lisbon' (2011) 7 ECLR 64 and 71.

Woods, L, 'Freedom of expression in the EU' (2006) 12 EPL 371.

Part II

Framework for enforcement

7.1 Introduction

The discussion in Part II which by no means covers the whole range of Union law, illustrates the extent to which EU law permeates our lives. In addition to the law stemming from the Treaties, a wealth of secondary legislation has been, and is in the constant process of being, enacted, covering a wide and ever-increasing range of activities. Much of this law is directly effective (see Chapter 5), and will, under the principle of primacy of EU law (see Chapter 4), take precedence over any conflicting rules of national law. It thus forms an important source of *rights* and *obligations* for both states and individuals.

An effective system of enforcement requires that the rights arising under EU law may be enforced against three groups of people:

- *the institutions of the Union*, who, in their lawmaking or administrative capacity, may have acted or failed to act in breach of EU law;

- *Member States*, which, in carrying out or failing to carry out their obligations under the Treaties or secondary legislation, may have acted in breach of EU law;

- *individuals*, who in failing to comply with their obligations under the Treaties or secondary legislation may have acted in breach of EU law.

The TFEU Treaty itself provides an extensive range of remedies. It provides, by way of *direct* action before the CJEU, which comprises the CJ and the GC, for actions against the Council, the Commission, the European Central Bank, the European Parliament and of the European Council. It also enables actions to be taken against Union bodies, offices or agencies, and against Member States. Union secondary legislation may be challenged *indirectly* before the courts of Member States, and questions of validity referred to the CJ under Article 267 TFEU (see Chapter 10). Chapters 12–14 are concerned primarily with the means whereby states, and sometimes individuals, may challenge the acts or failure to act of the European Parliament, the European Council, the Council, the Commission or the European Central Bank *directly* before the European Courts. The Treaty of Lisbon enlarges the functions of the CJ. Articles 35 and 46 of the TEU and Article 68 of the EC Treaty have been repealed, with the result that the 'third pillar' is brought into the mainstream of EU law. Article 19(3) TEU gives the CJ jurisdiction over the law of the EU, which now includes the Charter of Fundamental Rights and the Area of Freedom, Security and Justice unless the Treaties provide otherwise. The CFSP largely remains outside the jurisdiction of the CJ (see also 3.7.9 and 16.4.3), but the CJ has jurisdiction to review the legality of Council decisions providing for restrictive measures against natural or legal persons (Article 24(1) TEU; Article 275 TFEU).

7.2 Action before the European Courts

7.2.1 Actions against the institutions of the Union

These comprise actions:

(a) for judicial review, in the form of actions to 'review the legality of acts of the Council and the Commission other than recommendations or opinions' (Article 263 TFEU), the 'annulment action', and, Article 277 TFEU, the 'plea of illegality', and an action for 'failure to act' (Articles 232, 265 TFEU);

(b) for damages (Article 246 TFEU);

(c) in respect of disputes between the Union and its servants ('staff cases') (Article 270 TFEU).

7.2.1.1 Significance of judicial review

There are two ways in which control over the institutions needs to be exercised. First, it is necessary to ensure that the legislation issued by the institutions is valid; that is, that the institution is empowered to adopt the measure in question, that it has been adopted according to the correct procedures, and for the purposes for which it was enacted. This constitutes a check on the institutions' *activities* and is provided under Article 263 TFEU and, as an adjunct to that article, Article 277 TFEU. Article 267 TFEU also provides for the possibility of a similar review via the national courts and preliminary ruling mechanism, discussed further at 7.3.4. Secondly, there is a need to check on the institutions' *inactivity*—to ensure that the institutions do not fail to act when they are under a legal duty to do so. This is provided by Article 265.

Judicial review under Articles 263 and 265 requires an examination of three separate questions. First there is the question of *locus standi*: does this applicant have the right, personally, to bring proceedings? Secondly, has he brought his action in time? These two questions relate to admissibility. And thirdly, if the first questions are answered in the affirmative, is he entitled to succeed on the merits? Whilst in much of this book we can see the profound influence that the actions of private actors have had on the development of the EU law, in the case of actions brought pursuant to Articles 263 and 265 TFEU, private bodies have been restrained from playing such an extensive role by the limited *locus standi* rules. Indeed, much of the argument in any given case is often about *locus standi*, and many cases never proceed to a decision on substance.

7.2.1.2 Jurisdiction of the GC

All claims by natural and legal persons under (a) and (b), including the areas such as the competition rules of the EU, decisions taken pursuant to Regulation 40/94 (Union trade mark, as amended) and Regulation 2100/94 (Union plant-variety rights), are now dealt with by the GC, with a right of appeal on a point of law to the CJ (Article 299 TFEU). Claims under (c) were until 31 August 2016 within the jurisdiction of the Civil Service Tribunal but jurisdiction over such claims was transferred to the GC with effect from 1 September 2016 (Regulation 2016/92 ([2016] OJ L200/137)).

Following the Treaty of Nice, the jurisdiction of the GC was changed. It retained the right to hear direct actions, but the amended Article 225 EC introduced the possibility of some specialist areas being referred to judicial panels, with the GC hearing appeals from the decisions of those panels. As noted in 2.11.4, the first such panel was the Civil Service Tribunal whose jurisdiction was subsumed into that of the GC as from 1 September 2016. Article 257 TFEU further amended Article 225a EC to provide that specialised courts are to be established by regulation adopted by the Council and the European Parliament following the ordinary legislative procedure. The regulation establishing the specialised courts will lay down the rules on the organisation of the court and the extent of the jurisdiction conferred upon it. Decisions given by a specialist court may be subject to the right of appeal on a point of law only or if the regulation establishing the specialist court so provides, on matters of fact also. The specialist courts will establish their rules of procedure in agreement with the CJ. The rules must be approved by the Council. There are currently no specialist courts.

7.2.1.3 Appeals to the CJ in judicial review cases

Appeal is limited to points of law and must be based on the grounds of lack of competence of the GC, breach of procedure before it which adversely affects the interests of the appellant or infringement of Union law by the GC (Article 58 of the Statutes of the Court of Justice of the European Union). An appeal must contain the pleas in law and legal arguments relied on. It must indicate precisely the contested elements of the judgment that the appellant seeks to have set aside, as well as the legal arguments specifically advanced in support of the appeal. That requirement is not satisfied by an appeal confined to repeating the pleas and arguments previously submitted to the GC. Such an approach would constitute no more than a re-examination by the CJ of the application submitted to the GC. The CJ has no jurisdiction to do this. Likewise, an attempt to raise new issues falls outside the CJ's jurisdiction as an appeal court.

Furthermore, Article 169 of the Rules of Procedure of the Court of Justice provides that an appeal must contain the pleas in law and the legal arguments relied on in the appeal; this means that an appeal must indicate *precisely* the contested elements of the judgment which the appellant seeks to have set aside, and the legal arguments *specifically* advanced in support of the appeal. The CJ has commented that this requirement 'is not satisfied by an appeal confined to repeating or reproducing word for word pleas in law and arguments previously submitted to the Court of First Instance [now General Court], including those based on facts expressly rejected by that court' (*John Deere Ltd v Commission* (case C-7/95P)).

The CJ also has no jurisdiction to establish facts or examine evidence. The appraisal by the GC of the evidence does not constitute a point of law which is subject to review by the CJ unless the evidence has been fundamentally misconstrued (see *John Deere* and also *Hilti v Commission* (case C-53/92P), para 42). After a period when the CJ seemed to dispose of appeals from the GC on matters of intellectual property law on the facts, as can be seen in *Proctor & Gamble v OHIM (Baby Dry)* (case C-383/99P), the CJ has reverted to this approach. In *DKV Deutsche Krankenversicherung AG v OHIM* (case C-104/00P), the CJ held that the GC has exclusive jurisdiction to find the facts and to appraise them. That assessment of the facts cannot be reviewed unless 'the clear sense of the evidence before it has been distorted' (para 22). Coming to the same conclusion, the Advocate-General in this case suggested that the role of the CJ as 'highest interpreter of the law' was to 'lay down principles of general application' (Opinion, para 59).

7.2.2 Actions against Member States

These comprise:

(a) action by the Commission against a Member State for failure 'to fulfil an obligation under this Treaty' (Article 258 TFEU);

(b) action by a Member State against another Member State for failure 'to fulfil an obligation under this Treaty' (Article 259 TFEU);

(c) action by the Commission or an interested Member State against a Member State—for breach of its obligation to comply with a decision of the Commission under Article 88(2) (Article 108(2) TFEU (state aids) and Article 114 (9) TFEU (unilateral restrictions imposed by a Member State on free movement of goods));

(d) proceedings brought by the Commission under Article 298 (Article 348 TFEU) where emergency measures have been taken by a Member State which prevent the functioning of the internal market.

The proceedings specified in (b), (c) and (d) may be brought directly before the CJ. Note that indirect challenges to Member States' actions or inaction can be brought using the preliminary reference procedure. Although the CJ is involved in such procedures the action is commenced in the national courts and discussed in 7.3.

7.2.2.1 **Right to intervene**

Member States and Union institutions have a right to intervene in cases before the Court. This right is also open to any other person establishing an interest in the result of any case submitted to the Court, except in cases between institutions of the Union or between Member States and institutions of the Union. In *British Coal Corporation v Commission* (case T-367/94), a case based on the parallel provisions of the statutes of the ECSC, the Court held that an applicant must establish a 'direct, existing interest in the grant by the Court of the order as sought and not purely an interest in relation to the plea in law advanced'. The fact that representative associations have a right to intervene in order to protect their members in cases raising questions of principle liable to affect those members cannot be relied on in support of an individual application to intervene (see also *Dorsch Consult Ingenieurgesellschaft mbH v Council and Commission* (case T-184/95)).

7.2.2.2 **Interim relief**

Although actions before the courts do not have suspensory effect, the courts may, 'if [they] consider that the circumstances so require it, order that the application of the contested act be suspended' (Article 278 TFEU). They may also order 'any necessary interim measures in any of the above proceedings' (Article 279 TFEU). However, action under Article 278 TFEU is admissible only if the applicant is challenging that measure 'in proceedings before the Court'. Similarly an action under Article 279 TFEU will be admitted only if it is made 'by a party to the case before the Court and relates to that case'. Interim measures may not be ordered 'unless there are circumstances giving rise to urgency and factual and legal grounds establishing a prima facie case for the measures applied for'. The urgency of the application will be assessed according to the necessity for such an order in order to prevent serious and irreparable damage. Parties wishing to establish the existence of 'serious and irreparable damage' for the purpose of obtaining the suspension of a Union act must provide documentary evidence both as regards the specific damage suffered or likely to be suffered and the causative link between that damage and the contested act (*Descom Scales Manufacturing Co Ltd v Council* (case C-6/94R), application for suspension of anti-dumping regulation rejected for lack of evidence). Purely financial damage cannot in principle be regarded as irreparable (*Cargill v Commission* (case 229/88R)). The interim measures requested must be of such a nature as to prevent the alleged damage (*Commission v United Kingdom (merchant shipping rules)* (case 246/89R)).

In such proceedings relief can be very speedy. In *Commission v Ireland (Dundalk water scheme)* (case 45/87R) an interim injunction was granted *ex parte* within three days of application.

Antonissen

Antonissen v Council (case C-393/96P/R) concerned a claim for an interim award of damages. The case came on appeal to the President of the CJ from the President of the GC, who had rejected the applicant's request. The applicant sought provisional damages, pending a final ruling in a claim for compensation against the Union. The applicant, a dairy farmer, had been refused a milk quota on the basis of an allegedly invalid EU regulation. As a result he had received a request for payment of a substantial supplementary levy, threatening to cause him severe financial distress. The President of the CJ allowed his appeal. He held that if an interim order is justified, prima facie—in law and in fact—and it is urgent, in order to avoid serious and irreparable damage, it must be made before a decision is reached in the main proceedings.

An absolute prohibition on obtaining, in interim proceedings, part of the compensation claimed in the main proceedings, and seeking to protect the applicant's interest, would not be compatible with the individual's right to effective judicial protection. Such payment may be necessary to ensure the practical effect of the judgment in the main application. However, before ordering such payment the Court must examine the applicant's assets to assess whether it would be possible to recover any payment by way of advance when the final judgment is delivered. Recourse to such a remedy must be restricted to situations in which the prima facie case is strong and the urgency is undeniable.

7.2.3 **Action against individuals**

There is no provision in the TFEU for direct action before the CJ *against individuals*. Individuals may, however, be vulnerable to fines and penalties under Union secondary legislation (eg, Regulation 1/2003). Decisions imposing such fines may be challenged before the GC. The CJ has unlimited jurisdiction in regard to the penalties provided in such regulations.

7.3 **Action before national courts**

7.3.1 **Basic principles**

In addition to these direct remedies before the European Courts, questions of infringement of Union law by Union institutions and Member States may also be raised before national courts. In describing regulations as 'directly applicable' (Article 288 TFEU) and in providing a means whereby national courts might refer questions of interpretation and validity of EU law to the CJ (Article 267 TFEU), the Treaty clearly envisaged a role for national courts in the enforcement of EU law. This role has been greatly enlarged by the development by the CJ of the principle of direct effect and, more recently, the principles of indirect effect and state liability under *Francovich* (see Chapters 5 and 9). A ruling on the interpretation of Union law may reveal that a national law or practice is inconsistent with Union law; a ruling that a provision of an EU regulation, directive or decision is invalid renders it unenforceable against the individual concerned. In both cases it may provide the basis for a claim in damages before the national courts. With the decentralisation of enforcement under the competition and rules, national courts assume a far greater role in the enforcement of such rules than has hitherto been the case.

7.3.2 Significance of actions before national courts

This possibility of obtaining remedies via their national courts is of particular importance for individuals, since they have no *locus standi* to bring a direct action before the CJ in respect of infringements of Union law by Member States, nor any power to compel the Commission to bring such an action (see *Alfons Lütticke GmbH v Commission* (case 48/65)—Chapters 12 and 13). Further, their *locus standi* in direct actions against the Union institutions for judicial review is limited. Moreover, national courts remain the only forum in which actions can be brought *by* individuals in respect of infringements of Union law *against* individuals. Union law may be invoked as a defence to a criminal charge (eg, *Ratti*), to resist payment of a charge exacted, or support a claim for the return of money withheld, in breach of EU law (eg, *Van Gend en Loos*). It may provide a basis for an injunction, to prevent or put an end to action in breach of Union law (eg, *Garden Cottage Foods Ltd v Milk Marketing Board* [1982] QB 1114, CA; [1984] AC 130, House of Lords) or a declaration, for example, that a particular national measure is illegal, being based on an invalid EU regulation (eg, *Royal Scholten-Honig*). It may also provide the basis for a claim in damages, either on the principles of direct or indirect effect, against parties acting in breach of substantive provisions of EU law, or, under *Francovich*, against the state itself for its failure to comply with its obligation under Article 4(3) TEU to 'take any appropriate measures general or particular to ensure fulfilment of the obligations arising out of the Treaties or resulting from the acts taken of the institutions of the Union'. Thus acts of Member States or of Union institutions which are illegal under Union law may be challenged, and remedies provided. While the illegal acts are not set aside as a result of the action, they cannot be enforced.

It has long been recognised that some of the key developments in the Union legal order have arisen as the result of an Article 267 TFEU reference from a national court, and that private actors consequently have a role in facilitating the enforcement of Union law as they seek the means to enforce their rights.

7.3.3 Remedies in national courts

Where individuals seek to assert their Union rights before national courts or tribunals, they may do so in the context of any proceedings of national law, public or private, in which Union rights are relevant, in pursuit of any remedy, interim or final, available under national law. The issue of remedies is discussed in Chapter 8. Here it is worthwhile noting that while the Union does not have the competence to harmonise national legal systems' rules and remedies, they are subject to certain principles laid down by the CJ, for example, the principle of effectiveness.

7.3.4 Jurisdiction of the European courts to give preliminary rulings

To assist national courts in their task of enforcing Union law, Article 267 TFEU gives the CJ jurisdiction to give preliminary rulings concerning the interpretation of Union law and the validity of acts of the institutions at the request of national courts. The discussion in Chapter 10 will show the significance of this procedure in terms of the institutional architecture and the role of the national courts in enforcing Union law. Originally, only the CJ had the power to give preliminary rulings but, following the Treaty of Nice, some part of this jurisdiction may fall to the GC, though this has not yet been made operational. According to Article 256(3) TFEU, the GC may be granted jurisdiction to hear and determine questions referred for a preliminary ruling 'in specific areas laid down by statute'. These decisions could be reviewed by the CJ should there be a 'serious risk of the unity or consistency of Union law being affected'; even within these limits, there will be the possibility of review of the GC's decisions by the CJ. According to Article 62 of the Statute of the Court of Justice, the decision as to whether review is necessary is to be made by the First Advocate-General of the Court of Justice, not the parties to the case.

Although the CJ has no power to *decide* the issue before the national court, an interpretation on the matter of Union law involved, or on the validity of the act in question, will normally be sufficient to establish whether an infringement of EU law has occurred. On this basis the national court may then supply the appropriate remedy.

7.4 Conclusions

The role played by the CJ in securing the enforcement of Union law against both EU institutions and Member States cannot be overstated. Recognising and respecting the limitations of the remedies provided under the TFEU, it has provided, via the principles of direct effect, indirect effect, and state liability in damages, an extremely effective alternative means of enforcement of Union law by individuals, within the courts of Member States. It has insisted on the effective protection of individuals' Union rights by these courts, even when the rights have not been expressly, or even impliedly, granted to individuals. This principle of effective judicial protection has sometimes revealed the deficiencies in national legal systems and extended the scope of legal protection of individuals in matters of Union law. This has spilt, and will continue to spill, over into domestic law, raising the standard of judicial protection in matters of purely national law.

In contrast, the approach of the CJ and GC regarding challenges to the actions of the institutions, especially where the challenge comes from a non-privileged applicant, fails to protect the interests of the individual adequately. As discussed in Chapter 12, the narrow view taken of *locus standi* for non-privileged applicants by the European courts has given rise to some adverse criticism. It has made the possibility of challenging the validity of Union measures via national courts and the preliminary ruling mechanism particularly important. The jurisdiction of the courts in the context of judicial review remains important, as it is one mechanism by which the institutional balance of the Union is maintained.

Further reading

Broberg, M and Fenger, N, *Preliminary References to the European Court of Justice*, 2nd edn (Oxford University Press, 2014).

Craig, P, *The Lisbon Treaty: Law, Politics and Treaty Reform* (Oxford University Press, 2010) Ch 4.

Gutman, K, 'The evolution of the action for damages against the European Union and its place in the system of judicial protection' (2011) 48 CML Rev 695.

Lenaerts, K, Marelis, I and Gutman, K, *EU Procedural Law* (Oxford University Press, 2014).

Piris, J-C, *The Lisbon Treaty: A Legal and Political Analysis* (Cambridge University Press, 2010) Ch 28.

8 Remedies in national courts

8.1 Introduction

The preceding chapters have identified that the CJ, relying to a significant extent on the need to make EU law effective, extended the possible mechanisms by which individuals could seek access to rights derived from EU law in their national courts. This chapter takes a step forward and focuses on how the CJ has developed the principles of 'equivalence' and 'effectiveness'—key concepts underlying the CJ's approach to procedure and remedies—to limit what is termed 'national procedural autonomy'. In this area we see the use of the principle of 'effectiveness' in different contexts: referring either more generally to effective judicial protection; or meaning effective protection (and enforcement) of EU rights. Intertwined in this debate are the differing elements of the right to a fair trial: access to a court is certainly central, but there are other concerns which may affect the outcome, notably legal certainty and the principle of *res judicata*. Against this background, one particular issue should be addressed: to what extent does EU law require the creation of new remedies in national legal systems for EU law rights?

8.2 General principles regarding national procedural rules

8.2.1 Overview of principles

Extending access to substantive rights means nothing unless it is possible, in procedural terms, to access the national court system to obtain a remedy for any violation of those substantive rights. In *Heylens*, the Court stated:

> since free access to employment is a fundamental right which the Treaty confers individually on each worker in the [Union], the existence of a remedy of a judicial nature against any decision of a national authority refusing the benefit of that right is essential in order to secure for the individual effective protection for his right [para 14].

Rules relating to *locus standi*, periods of limitation and quantum of damages can all have an effect on whether it would be possible to bring an action and if any such action would, in practice, be worth bringing before the national courts. The Treaties contain a number of general provisions from which the CJ has developed a number of principles relating to remedies and access to justice.

Article 4(3) TEU provides:

> Pursuant to the principle of sincere cooperation, the Union and the Member States shall, in full mutual respect, assist each other in carrying out the tasks which flow from the Treaties.
>
> The Member States shall take any appropriate measure, general or particular, to ensure fulfilment of the obligations arising out of the Treaties or resulting from the acts of the institutions of the Union.
>
> The Member States shall facilitate the achievement of the Union's tasks and refrain from any measures which could jeopardise the attainment of the Union's objectives.

Article 19 TEU specifies:

> Member States shall provide remedies sufficient to ensure effective legal protection in the fields covered by Union law.

Article 47 of the Charter of Fundamental Rights, which it will be recalled was elevated to Treaty status by virtue of Article 6 TEU, provides:

> Everyone whose rights and freedoms guaranteed by the law of the Union are violated has the right to an effective remedy before a tribunal in compliance with the conditions laid down in this article.
>
> Everyone is entitled to a fair and public hearing within a reasonable time by an independent and impartial tribunal previously established by law. Everyone shall have the possibility of being advised, defended and represented.
>
> Legal aid shall be made available to those who lack sufficient resources in so far as such aid is necessary to ensure effective access to justice.

In addition to these provisions, in a number of specific areas directives prescribe remedies that Member States must make available to those whose rights have been denied. Examples include public procurement remedies directives (Directive 89/665 ([1989] OJ L395/33)) and Directive 92/13 ([1992] OJ L76/14) as amended extensively by Directive 2007/66 ([2007] OJ L335/31)) and the equality of treatment directives discussed in Chapter 27.

The CJ has laid down a number of principles which must be observed by national courts in claims involving EU law. It has held that:

> In the absence of [Union] rules it is for the domestic systems of each Member State to designate the courts having jurisdiction and the procedural conditions governing actions at law intended to ensure the protection of the rights which subjects derive from the direct effects of [Union law], it being understood that such conditions cannot be less favourable than those relating to similar actions of a domestic nature nor render virtually impossible or excessively difficult the exercise of rights conferred by [Union law]. [See *Rewe Zentralfinanz v Landwirtschaftskammer Saarland* (case 33/76), *Peterbroeck van Campenhout & Cie SCS v Belgium* (case C-312/93), *Van Schijndel v Stichting Pensioenfonds voor Fysiotherapeuten* (cases C-430 and 431/93) and *Wells*.]

The CJ referred in a number of cases to the principle that national rules should not 'render impossible or excessively difficult the exercise of the rights conferred'. The CJ has not always used this formulation of the effectiveness principle. Another version, enunciated in *Harz* requires that the remedies and sanctions provided for breach of Union law must have a real deterrent effect and must be 'such as to guarantee full and effective protection' for individuals' Union rights. It is arguable that the two different formulations give the principle of effectiveness a different scope, the 'impossible or excessively difficult test' being narrower than the requirement for 'full and effective protection' of EU law rights. The differences between the two approaches to effectiveness are discussed further in 8.3.2.

An approach which starts from the presumption that national rules will, in principle, be accepted by the CJ as sufficient to guarantee EU law rights also respects the integrity of national legal systems. However, the general principles of non-discrimination and effectiveness limit the principle of national procedural autonomy in cases where national legal systems do not meet these standards. Article 4(3) TEU has been relied upon by the CJ as a legal basis for its approach to national procedures and remedies, although this provision does not specifically address the question of procedures or remedies.

8.2.2 Equivalence and effectiveness

The CJEU's approach may be seen to embody three separate principles:

(1) The principle of national procedural autonomy ('it is for the domestic systems of each Member State to designate . . . effects of [Union] law');

(2) The principle of non-discrimination ('conditions cannot be less favourable than those . . . of a domestic nature');

(3) The principle of effectiveness ('nor render impossible or excessively difficult the exercise of rights conferred' or 'full and effective protection').

Since the national remedy provided for a claim based on domestic law may not be exactly comparable to a claim based on EU law, or, although seemingly comparable, may operate to the detriment of the party relying on EU law, commentators and even the Court, have tended to merge the first and second principles (ie the principles of national treatment and non-discrimination) into a single principle of *equivalence* discussed in 8.4.

There are a number of difficulties with the approach that the CJ has adopted. One relates to the fact that procedures and remedies will not be uniform across the Member States, meaning that an individual in one Member State might be able to bring an action or be awarded a certain amount of damages that an individual in another Member State, relying on the same substantive right and factual situation, would not. The second set of problems relate to the scope of equivalence and effectiveness and their impact on the principle of national procedural autonomy.

8.2.3 Difficulties in application of national procedural autonomy with the principles of equivalence and effectiveness

A number of difficulties can be identified in the application of national procedural autonomy when considering the principles of equivalence and autonomy. First, it may not be easy to assess what is an 'equivalent' national remedy. EU law is *sui generis*. It cuts across the boundaries and classifications of national law. Even where domestic law provides a remedy in the context of a similar claim, for example in restitution, or in the field of employment law, such claims may be dealt with in different courts, subject to different procedures and different limitations as to time or the award of damages. Some potential remedies may be more 'effective' than others. How, then, is equivalence to be assessed? What is the minimum acceptable level? Does the principle of effectiveness require that the most generous treatment be accorded to claims based on EU law? Secondly, there are circumstances in which an equivalent domestic remedy may not exist. EU law is supreme over all national law. Where individuals seek to invoke their Union rights in order to challenge national law, they may do so against any law, whatever its nature. In most Member States, concepts of sovereignty may prohibit challenge to the legality of statute or, *a fortiori*, constitutional law. Furthermore, in most Member States there are lacunae, gaps in the legal protection of individuals, arising from traditional privileges and immunities. Sometimes these limitations are justified, sometimes they are not. What remedy or procedure is to be provided by national courts in these circumstances?

The CJ, in its jurisdiction under Article 267 TFEU, has provided guidance on these matters. Its approach to the principles of equivalence and effectiveness has developed over the years, from an absolutist, interventionist approach in cases such as *Marshall II, Emmott v Minister for Social Welfare* (case C-208/90) and *Factortame I* and *II*, towards a more 'hands-off' approach, described by Tridimas as a policy of 'selective deference to national rules of procedure'. As we shall see, despite these general trends the CJ will still have moments of activism, particularly where areas of exclusive Union competence are concerned, and the case law is therefore somewhat uncertain. There are two main concerns. The first relates to whether, by focusing on effectiveness over equivalence, the CJ has created a requirement for super remedies, which may then spill over into national law generally. The alternative position is that there is a distinction between rights derived from EU law and those which are not. The second issue relates to the competence of the Member States to maintain their own legal systems. Due to the shifting meaning of the terminology used, it is not always clear whether the CJ is protecting enforcement or individuals' rights; or protecting the coherence of the EU legal system as a whole.

8.3 Meaning of 'effectiveness'

In some circumstances it will be clear that an effective remedy has not been provided. For example, rules that deny access to the courts altogether, such as a rule restricting payment of a duty held by the CJ to be contrary to EU law to claimants who have brought an action for repayment before the delivery of that judgment, as was the situation in *Barra*, will clearly be ineffective in protecting the Union law rights of persons bringing their claim, based on that judgment, after the date of judgment (see also *Deville v Administration des Impôts* (case 240/87)). But there are many situations in which the position is not so clear. Many of the important cases in this area have arisen in the field of sex-discrimination legislation. Some of those cases were based on specific requirements in directives which required remedies to be provided. We might ask, therefore, to what extent is that jurisprudence representative of the approach taken by the CJ in other policy fields? We will consequently consider the jurisprudence relating to procedural rules in two segments: that relating to sex-discrimination legislation and then the more general case law.

8.3.1 Jurisprudence in the field of sex-discrimination legislation

A significant number of cases in this area have arisen in the context of sex-discrimination legislation, notably—though not exclusively— The Equal Treatment Directive (Directive 76/207 ([1976] OJ L39/40)), now repealed and replaced by Directive 2006/54 ([2006] OJ L204/23), the 'Recast Directive'. Crucially, Article 6 of the Recast Directive, like the Equal Treatment Directive, requires Member States to provide judicial remedies for those with a substantive claim under the Directive. The starting point for this line of jurisprudence was *von Colson*, discussed also in Chapter 5. *Von Colson* concerned two women who applied for jobs but who were not appointed. They claimed successfully that they had been discriminated against on the grounds of their gender. The damages in the case were assessed on the basis of the claimants' actual loss, in this case, travelling expenses. The question referred to the CJ was whether this was sufficient, or, in the words of the CJ's jurisprudence, 'effective'. The CJ remarked that:

> if a Member State chooses to penalize breaches of [the prohibition on sex discrimination] by the award of compensation, then in order to ensure that it is effective and that it has a deterrent effect, that compensation must in any event be adequate in relation to the damage sustained and must therefore amount to more than purely nominal compensation such as, for example, the reimbursement only of the expenses incurred in connection with the application [para 26].

This judgment can be seen to be making a number of points. First, it reaffirmed that remedies must be effective. This point is linked, as we have seen, to the idea that without adequate recompense from the perspective of the victim, a right has little value. Secondly, the CJ also looked to the impact of the remedy on the body responsible for the violation of EU law: any compensation must be such as to make the violation of EU law-derived rights much less attractive.

The CJ developed the effectiveness principle in this field significantly during the early 1990s. This can be seen in the context of *Dekker v VJV-Centrum Plus* (case C-177/88).

Dekker

This case concerned a claim that the applicant had been discriminated against on the basis that she had not been employed because she was pregnant. Under national law, claims for redress could be subject to a requirement of fault on the part of the defendant, or a claim could be subjected to arguments based on justification; the right to compensation was not absolute even once discrimination had been shown. The CJ, basing its judgment on *von Colson*, held that, to be effective, 'any infringement of the prohibition suffices in itself to make the person guilty fully liable' [para 26].

This ruling would seem to have pushed the boundaries of the effectiveness requirement wider than in *von Colson*. In contrast to *von Colson*, the damages that would have been awarded under national law in this case were not necessarily only nominal. In the words of the early judgments, it could not be said that the national rules operated to make the exercise of substantive rights 'impossible in practice'.

In *Marshall II*, two national rules were in issue: a statutory ceiling on the amount of damages that could be awarded for sex-discrimination claims; and the jurisdictional limitation on the relevant tribunal which meant that it could not award interest on damages. Again, reasoning from *von Colson*, the CJ, based on the Equal Treatment Directive, now repealed and replaced by the 'Recast Directive', held that where damages were awarded for breaches of individuals' rights under the Directive, national courts must provide 'full' compensation, including interest on the award from the date of judgment. A system in which compensation was subject to statutory limits, as provided under the UK Sex Discrimination Act 1975, would not be 'sufficiently effective to achieve the objectives of the Directive'. A principle of full compensation required that 'reparation be commensurate with the loss or damage sustained'. This case was a step forward from *von Colson*, as the Court describes in more detail the requirements of an effective remedy. Rather than describing the lower end of what would be required—that is, more than nominal—the Court imposed a higher test: that the remedy be *full* compensation. This ruling, generally applied, could have had potentially far-reaching consequences.

However, the Court has been prepared to accept some limits to the principle of full compensation. In *R v Secretary of State for Social Security, ex parte Sutton* (case C-66/95), in a claim based on Directive 79/7 ([1979] OJ L6/24) on equal treatment for men and women in social security, it accepted a statutory bar on the payment of interest on backdated social security entitlements, even though the wording of the Directive on which the applicants sought to rely, requiring Member States to ensure that persons alleging discrimination are able to 'pursue their claims by judicial process', was virtually identical to that on which the applicants based their claim in *Marshall II*. *Marshall* was distinguished on the basis that there the award of interest was an 'essential component of compensation for the purpose of ensuring real equality of treatment'. In contrast, *Sutton* 'concerned the "right to receive interests on amounts payable by way of social security benefits". Those social security benefits paid by the competent bodies which must . . . examine whether the conditions laid down in the relevant legislation were fulfilled'.

The benefits paid to Ms Sutton in no way constituted reparation for loss or damage sustained and thus the reasoning in *Marshall II* need not be applied: ' . . . amounts paid by way of social security are not compensatory in nature with the result that the payment of interest cannot be required'. The Court in *Sutton* was similarly reserved in its comments on the possibility of recovery of interest on arrears of payment in an alternative claim based on *Francovich* (discussed in Chapter 9). It enunciated the principles governing state liability in damages but insisted that it was for the national court to assess, in the light of those principles, whether the claimant was entitled to reparation for the loss she had suffered, and to determine the amount of such reparation.

However, *Marshall II* was followed in *Draehmpaehl v Urania Immobilienservice OHG* (case C-180/95), a case decided on the same day as *Sutton*. In a claim by a man, the Court held that a limit of three months' wages as compensation for sex discrimination as regards access to employment (the job advertisement requested female applicants), and a six-month aggregate limit where several applicants were involved, would not guarantee effective judicial protection for individuals' Union rights. A three-month limit would only be acceptable as reasonable if the employer could prove that the applicants would not have been given the job in the absence of discrimination. Clearly, if the applicant would have been given the job in the absence of discrimination, the limits on compensation in this case would not have been sufficient to compensate for the damage sustained. Although *Marshall II* may have been limited, it is not extinct.

A separate line of cases deals with the issue of time limits. In general, the CJ had rules that a limitation of a 'reasonable' period would not make it 'impossible in practice' to exercise Union law rights. We have seen that this phrase was extended in the context of amount of damages for sex-discrimination cases. How would the CJ approach the question of time limits for sex discrimination? This was addressed by the CJ in *Emmott*, a case which arose in respect of Directive 79/7.

Emmott

The case concerned a challenge to the Irish authorities' refusal to grant Ms Emmott disability benefit. She claimed that this was discriminatory, in breach of Directive 79/7 on equal treatment for men and women in matters of social security. At the time when her cause of action arose she was unaware that it was directly effective. When she became aware that it was, following a ruling from the Court in *McDermott v Minister for Social Welfare* (case 286/85), she applied to the minister for her case to be reviewed. Her application was deferred pending a ruling from the CJ in *Cotter v Minister for Social Welfare* (case C-377/89). When she was finally granted leave to institute proceedings, she was found to be out of time.

The High Court of Ireland referred to the CJ a question for a preliminary ruling, to ascertain whether it was contrary to Union law for the authorities of a Member State to rely on national procedural rules, in particular relating to time limits, in defending claims based on EU directives. The minister argued that, even though a directive had not been implemented, or properly implemented, the principle of direct effect enabled the individual effectively to assert his Union law rights, at least against a 'public' body.

The Court held that the principle of direct effect provided only a minimum guarantee: as long as a directive has not been properly implemented the individual is in a state of uncertainty; the individual is unaware of the full extent of his or her rights. Therefore the competent authorities of Member States cannot rely, in an action against them based on the directive, on national procedural rules relating to time limits for bringing proceedings as long as that Member State has not properly implemented that directive into national law.

One important point to note about *Emmott* is that (like *Cotter* and *McDermott*), the CJ's reasoning is significantly different from that used in the damages cases. Although both lines of case law are aimed at ensuring the full effectiveness of Union law rights, *Emmott* is based on the principle of estoppel, that is, the state cannot benefit from its own wrongdoing. It has been suggested, notably by Advocate-General Jacobs, that it was because the state was in the wrong and indeed created the problem in *Emmott*, that the CJ took such an uncompromising stance in that case.

This decision, expressed in the broadest terms, gave rise to some alarm in Member States. It might be acceptable in a case in which the Member State's failure to implement a Union directive is clear, or when, as in *Emmott*'s case, it was 'excessively difficult', as a result of action by the national authorities, for the claimant to enforce her rights. But it was likely to cause injustice and be contrary to the principle of legal certainty, when applied in cases of inadvertent failure on the part of the state and when it exposed public bodies, acting bona fide according to their legitimate understanding of the law, to a flood of retrospective claims. It might be years before a directive was found not to have been 'properly' implemented into national law. Nor was it clear whether *Emmott* applied solely to the non- or faulty implementation of directives. The reasoning on which the decision was based might be applied to any breach of Union law, including claims under *Francovich*.

Perhaps recognising that it had gone too far, the Court distinguished *Emmott* in *Steenhorst-Neerings v Bestuur van de Bedrijfsvereniging voor Detailhandel* (case C-338/91).

Steenhorst-Neerings

In this case the Court held that a statutory limit on the retrospective payment of invalidity benefit (not in itself a limitation period, although similar in its effect) was not contrary to EU law, being justified by the need to preserve the financial equilibrium of social security funds. There was a difference between national rules fixing time limits for bringing an action, as in *Emmott*, and rules which merely limited the retroactive effect of claims. In the case of *Emmott* the time limit for bringing proceedings was an absolute bar on bringing claims, whereas *Steenhorst-Neerings* imposed a limit on the period of time for which benefits should not be paid retroactively. The aim of such a rule is quite different from that of a rule imposing mandatory time limits for bringing a claim. The restriction on the retroactive effect of the claim in *Steenhorst-Neerings* reflected the need 'to preserve the financial balance in a welfare scheme in which claims submitted by insured persons in the course of a year must be covered by the contributions collected in the same year'.

Steenhorst-Neerings was followed, on similar facts, in *Johnson v Chief Adjudication Officer* (case C-410/92), in which the benefit in question was non-contributory, therefore posing no threat to the financial balance of social security funds (see also *Alonso-Pérez v Bundesanstat für Arbeit* (case C-394/93), three-month ceiling on the retrospective payment of family benefits did not render the exercise of Union rights impossible). It seems that time limits will be set aside only when they render the exercise of Union rights absolutely impossible and that *Emmott* is limited to its facts.

Similar thinking, albeit to different effect, lay behind the Court's ruling in *Magorrian v Eastern Health and Social Services Board* (case C-246/96).

Magorrian

This case concerned a claim for the retrospective payment of certain pension benefits to which the applicant, a female part-time worker, found she was entitled under Article 157 TFEU following a ruling from the CJ (see *Fisscher v Voorhuis Hengelo BV* (case C-128/93), Chapter 27). Her claim, which related to the period from 1976 to 1990, was subject to a two-year limitation period running from the date of commencement of her action. The defendant Board opposed her claim, relying on *Steenhorst-Neerings* and *Johnson*. The Court distinguished these cases. The claim in this case was not, it held, for the retrospective award of certain additional benefits but for the recognition of entitlement to full membership of an occupational scheme through acquisition of Mental Health Officer status, which confers entitlement to the additional benefits. The two-year limitation rule prevented the entire record of service from 1976 to 1990 being taken into account for the purposes of calculating the additional benefits which would be payable even after the date of the claim. It 'struck at the very essence' of the applicant's rights and would not be permissible under Union law.

The CJ took the same view of the same rule in *Preston v Wolverhampton NHS Healthcare Trust* (case C-78/98). Although the CJ accepts the need for limitation periods, even those imposing a short period of time in which would-be applicants must act, where the rule affects the underlying principle of non-discrimination, the substantive right in issue in these cases, the Court still seems prepared to strike down national time limits.

Other cases have raised issues relating to national rules concerning the evidence that may be relied upon in order to establish discrimination. Often this evidence is in the hands of the person or entity against whom the allegation of discriminatory conduct is made. To what extent does that evidence have to be made available to a claimant seeking to prove 'facts from which it may be presumed that there has been direct or indirect discrimination'? This point was addressed in the case of *Kelly v National University of Ireland* (case C-104/10).

Kelly

In this case an unsuccessful applicant for a vocational training course wished to have access to information held by the course provider on the qualifications of other applicants for the course to establish whether he had been a victim of discrimination. The CJ held that he was not entitled to that information under Article 4(1) Directive 97/80 ([1998] OJ L14/6), now Article 19(1), Directive 2006/54 ([2006] OJ L204/23), but the Court refined its ruling somewhat by stating that if a refusal to disclose information could compromise the achievement of the objective of the Directive and hence its effectiveness then the position might be otherwise: a national court could not apply such rules of evidence. In the case of Mr Kelly the course provider had offered to provide him with part of the information he requested. It was up to the national court to ascertain in these circumstances whether the provision of more information was necessary in order to enable Mr Kelly to make his claim and therefore render Article 4(1) effective.

Meister v Design Carrier Systems GmbH (case C-415/10) raised similar issues to *Kelly* but the CJ noted that unlike *Kelly*, Ms Meister had not been provided with any information she sought to have disclosed. It was for the national court to assess in such circumstances whether the refusal of disclosure was such as to compromise the achievement of the directives Ms Meister relied upon in her claim. The CJ noted that discrimination can be established by 'any means including on the basis of statistical evidence'. From these cases it can be concluded that disclosure of evidence may be required if there is no other means by which a claimant can establish or is in a position to reasonably establish his case.

8.3.2 **The creation of new remedies?**

We have seen the starting point of the CJ's jurisprudence being the concept of national procedural autonomy. As the CJ confirmed in *Rewe-Handelsgesellschaft Nord mbH v Hauptzollamt Kiel* (case 158/80), a Member State is not required to create new remedies for Union law rights, subject always to the principles of equivalence and effectiveness. It is the consequences of the application of effectiveness that gives rise to problems here, in a number of ways.

The first point to note is that in some instances the Court has seen the remedy as forming part of the substantive right. In cases involving repayment of charges levied in breach of Union law, the Court has held that repayment of the sums is a consequence of, and an adjunct to, the right not to pay customs duties. If there was no right to repayment, the substantive right itself would be undermined. This in practice requires a specific form of remedy to be available as a matter of EU law, although the procedural elements of such a claim will fall to be determined by national law, subject always to the principles of equivalence and effectiveness. Although the Court has not phrased this idea in terms of effectiveness itself, in other circumstances it has recognised that judicial remedies are, in principle, necessary to secure effective protection for the individual's rights.

We have also seen that in developing the notion of effectiveness, the CJ has required that national rules which impede the effectiveness of Union law should be disapplied. In this context, there is a fine line between the disapplication of rules and the creation of new remedies. *Factortame I* is a good example. In that case, national rules precluded the granting of interim relief by injunction against the Crown. The CJ held that the national courts should set aside this rule. The consequence was that the English courts were required to apply a remedy which existed in its national legal systems but which had hitherto not been available in the circumstances of *Factortame I*. The immediate result of the application of the ruling was that EU-derived rights could possibly be treated more favourably than those based in domestic law. The English courts recognised that it is difficult to justify a difference in available remedies in similar situations based on whether the applicant's claim was based on EU law or not. One might have argued that the *Factortame I* ruling was an isolated case, and, in the light of the CJ's more cautious approach to the principle of effectiveness, it was not to be seen as suggesting that the 'no new remedies' principle had been eliminated entirely. *Francovich*, however, suggested that it had again been eroded. The Court in *Francovich* introduced the notion of the liability of the state in damages to its citizens for breach of its EU law obligations. It can be seen as another enforcement mechanism for EU law rights, and is discussed in Chapter 9. As will be seen there, *Francovich* created substantive rights for individuals in certain circumstances, with national legal systems again to provide the procedural framework within which individuals can exercise those rights. Although the CJ has provided some guidance as to the requirements to be satisfied regarding a successful claim under state liability, the remainder of the cause of action will also be determined within the national legal system. All elements determined by the national legal system are subject to the requirements of effectiveness and equivalence. The end result is that a cause of action and remedy is to be provided as a matter of EU law, requiring Member States to provide remedies should their national legal system not already provide them in those circumstances. This approach can be seen in the context of *Palmisani v INPS* (case C-261/95).

Palmisani

This case concerned a claim for damages for losses suffered as a result of the belated transposition of Directive 80/987 ([1980] OJ L283/23) on the protection of employees in the event of their employers' insolvency. INPS was the agency responsible for managing the fund set up to guarantee employees' arrears of wages as required by the Directive. Following the CJ's ruling in *Francovich*, the Directive had finally been implemented in Italy by legislative decree. Under the decree, claims for compensation from INPS were limited to not more than one year from the date of entry into force of the decree. The claimant's claim, having been brought outside this period, had been rejected by the Italian court. He argued before the CJ that the one-year limitation period was unlawful, being contrary to the requirement of equivalence and effectiveness.

The CJ ruled that:

[EU] law does not preclude a Member State from requiring any action for reparation of the loss or damage sustained as a result of the belated transposition of the Directive to be brought within a limitation period of one year from the date of its transposition into national law [para 39].

Metallgesellschaft & Hoechst

Metallgesellschaft & Hoechst v Inland Revenue (case C-410/98) concerned a ruling of the British tax authorities which imposed advance corporation tax on subsidiary companies whose parents were not UK resident. It was thus discriminatory. The applicants challenged the imposition of the tax, claiming the interest they would have earned had they not been subject to the advance taxation. It was far from clear under English law that restitution would be available in these circumstances.

The Court ruled that it was the premature levying of the tax that created the lack of equality contrary to Article 49 TFEU. To protect the rights to equality guaranteed by the freedom of establishment, the Court characterised the claim as one for damages for loss of interest due to a breach of Article 49 TFEU. The Court went further and, reasoning from *Marshall II* (paras 24–32), held that interest on the sum claimed was also due.

The Court has also looked to the substance of the EU law rights in other circumstances, not concerned with claims for repayment. In *Courage*, the CJ held that a right of action in damages against another private party for breach of Article 101 TFEU must, in principle, be available. In reaching this conclusion, the Court argued that:

[t]he full effectiveness of Article 85 [now 101] of the Treaty and, in particular, that practical effect of the prohibition laid down in Article 85(1) [now 101(1)] would be put at risk if it were not open to any individual to claim damages for loss caused to him by a contract or by conduct liable to restrict or distort competition [para 26].

Similar trends to those identified in *Metallgesellschaft & Hoechst* can be seen here. Again there is an emphasis on the effectiveness of the substantive right which requires a cause of action to be provided, irrespective of the provisions of the national legal system. Nonetheless, in the light of *Courage*, discussed earlier, it is difficult to maintain that EU law does not in some circumstances require that new remedies be provided. This was confirmed further by the decision in *Muñoz*, involving Regulation 2200/96 ([1996] OJ L297/1) on the standards for the classification of grapes.

Muñoz

Muñoz brought civil proceedings against Frumar who had sold grapes under particular labels which did not comply with the relevant standard. Although the Regulation did not confer rights on individuals such as Muñoz, but applied to all operators in the market, it was accepted that failing to comply with the Regulation could have adverse consequences for other operators. Referring to the principle of effectiveness, the Court held that a trader must be able to bring civil proceedings against a competitor to ensure that the Regulation is enforced effectively (assuming that the provisions in issue are directly applicable).

This seems to cement the position in *Courage*, and it is now the case that, insofar as a provision of EU law is directly applicable (as opposed to directly effective—see Chapter 5), it is open to be invoked in civil proceedings even though the provision itself does not confer rights on an individual (see also Betlem in the further reading section at the end of this chapter). In *Unibet*, the CJ seemed to require Member States to create new remedies where the enforcement of EU law rights so requires, suggesting that this is an application of the effectiveness principle. In one sense, this may well be true, as the CJ has already used the principle to require national courts to use national remedies in novel circumstances and against branches of government that would normally enjoy immunity from suit (eg, *Factortame*). Crucially, the CJ here investigated the possibility that a national legal system may have to develop a self-standing cause of action to challenge the compatibility of national law with Union law. On the other hand, it can be seen also that the CJ emphasised the national autonomy principle. Its starting point was to assess the adequacy of existing domestic arrangements and, in particular, the CJ was prepared to accept that a self-standing remedy need not be provided where the same matter could be examined indirectly in the course of alternative judicial proceedings. Whilst the outcome on the facts in *Unibet* might not be startling, the implications of some of the CJ's statements may revitalise the question of whether 'euro' remedies will be required.

8.4 Principle of 'equivalence'

Whilst much of the earlier case law considered in some detail the requirements of effectiveness, less attention was paid to the notion of 'equivalence'. The principle of equivalence requires that claims based on EU law must be treated in the same way as claims under national law. For example, a national court must exercise its powers in the same way in proceedings governing domestic law and EU law. Where a national appellate court may raise of its own motion the validity of national legal measure in the light of national rules of public policy (even where no issue of invalidity had been raised at first instance) it must also exercise such a power with respect to EU law measures (*Erika Jőrös v Aegon Magyarország Hitel Zrt* (case C-397/11)).

Clearly, a rule that discriminates, directly or indirectly, against claimants relying on EU law will be contrary to Union law. Such was the case in *Bickel and Franz* (case C-274/96). The case concerned the rules of the Trento-Alto region of Italy, which provided that the German language was to have the same status as Italian in relations between *citizens of that area* and the judicial and administrative authorities, but which did not extend to persons of Austrian and German nationality and residence, were held to be discriminatory in their effect, contrary to Article 18 TFEU. Since then, the CJ has had to consider more directly the question of equivalence.

On the question of equivalence in *Palmisani*, the applicant pointed to other, more generous, limitation rules governing claims for damages and to the 'manifest difference' between, for example, the five-year limitation period for reparation in general claims for non-contractual liability and the one-year period allowed for claims based on *Francovich*. The Court held that to ascertain comparability, 'the essential characteristics of the domestic system of reference must be examined'. Prior to the passing of the legislative decree there was no remedy in Italy for such a claim: 'If the domestic system [was] incapable of serving as a basis for a claim under *Francovich* no other relevant comparisons [could] be made'. The Member State must therefore make reparation for the consequences of the loss or damage caused to the claimant on the basis of national rules of liability, provided that they satisfy the requirement of effectiveness.

In *Edis v Ministero delle Finanze* (case C-231/96), national time limits were again the subject of challenge.

> ### Edis
>
> This case concerned a shorter time limit imposed for claims for the recovery of payments made regarding charges which had not actually been due, when compared with the time limits for payments made for other sums paid but not due. The applicant had made payments for charges that had not been due; it claimed that the principle of equivalence meant that the longer of the two periods should be applied, as the charges had their basis in EU law. The matter was referred to the CJ.

The CJ began by reiterating the principle that procedural rules must apply without distinction to actions originating in Union law and those based on national law. The Court continued, however, to make the point that this principle of equivalence did not mean that national legal systems could not distinguish between different types of action, such as making a distinction, as in this case, between rules regarding challenges to charges and levies and those relating to the recovery of sums paid in other circumstances, unless the less favourable rules applied only for actions based on Union law. The CJ concluded that the principle of equivalence could not 'be interpreted as obliging a Member State to extend its most favourable rules governing recovery under national law to all actions for repayment of charges or dues levied in breach of Union law' (para 36).

The Court continued:

> [Union law] does not in principle preclude the legislation of a Member State from laying down, alongside a limitation period applicable under the ordinary law to actions between individuals for the recovery of sums paid but not due, special detailed rules governing claims and legal proceedings to challenge the imposition of charges and other levies. The position would only be different if those detailed rules applied solely to actions based on [Union law] for the repayment of such charges and levies [para 37].

National rules are thus permitted to distinguish between different circumstances such as whether public bodies are parties to the action.

This passage in *Edis* was cited verbatim in a similar claim for repayment of the Italian registration charge in *IN.CO.GE '90*. Here the Court held that 'any reclassification of the legal relationship between the tax authorities and certain companies in that state . . . in such circumstances . . . is a matter for national law'.

Similarly, in *Nunes* (case C-186/98) the Court upheld the right of a Member State to impose criminal penalties for the improper use of the European Social Fund, even though the Regulation governing misuse of such funds provided only for civil remedies. The Court held that where a Union regulation failed to provide specifically for any penalty for an infringement of Union law, Article 4(3) TEU required Member States to take all measures necessary to ensure the application and effectiveness of that law. The choice of penalties remained at Member States' discretion, provided that the penalty chosen complied with the principle of equivalence, and was 'effective, proportionate and dissuasive'.

The Court has had further opportunity to consider equivalence in a number of cases subsequently. In *Levez v TH Jennings (Harlow Pools) Ltd* (case C-326/96), in a claim for damages in respect of sex discrimination brought under Article 157 TFEU and Directive 75/117, the Court was asked to consider a two-year time limit on arrears of payment of damages under the UK Equal Pay Act in the light of the principles of equivalence and effectiveness. It was argued that the claim, brought before an industrial tribunal, could have been brought before a county court, by analogy with claims for unlawful deductions from wages or unlawful discrimination in terms of employment on grounds of race or disability, which were subject to more generous limitation rules. The Court held that it was 'for national courts to ascertain whether the procedural rules intended to safeguard rights derived from [Union law] were safeguarded under national law and complied with the principle of equivalence'. A rule of national law would be deemed equivalent 'where the purpose and cause of action are similar'. However, citing *Edis*, it held that 'that principle is not to be interpreted as requiring Member States to extend their most favourable rules to all actions brought . . . in the field of employment law'. In assessing equivalence, the national court must consider 'the purpose and essential characteristics of allegedly similar domestic actions'. It must review the different procedures as a whole and weigh the relative advantages and disadvantages of each. On the facts it was found that the two-year period could not be enforced against the applicant, since, having been misled by her employer, she had no way of determining whether she was being discriminated against, or to what extent: 'To allow her employer to rely on the two-year rule would be to deprive his employee of the means provided by the Directive of enforcing the principle of equal pay before the court'. Thus, *in these particular circumstances* the remedy provided was ineffective. In applying the CJ's ruling in *Levez*, the Employment Appeal Tribunal ([1999] 3 CMLR 715) found that the two-year limitation period provided under the Equal Pay Act did not satisfy the requirement of equivalence, since it had been introduced in order to give effect to Britain's EU obligations and it applied only to equal-pay claims based on sex discrimination. This is, it is submitted, a somewhat stricter line than that taken by the CJ in *Palmisani*.

The Supreme Court referred further questions to the CJ on how to identify a 'similar' cause of action in *Preston*. The CJ re-emphasised the general balancing approach which it had taken in the effectiveness cases of *Peterbroeck* and *Van Schijndel*; see 8.3.2. It commented that the relevant national rules must be considered in their general context and concluded, in terms very similar to those used in *Van Schijndel*, that:

> the national court must verify objectively, in the abstract, whether the rules at issue are similar taking into account the role played by those rules in the procedure as whole, as well as the operation of that procedure and special feature of those rules . . . [para 63].

8.5 Impact of EU law on national remedies

Although EU law does not in principle prescribe specific remedies and procedures to be adopted by national courts in actions based on EU law, the obligation to ensure that national remedies are effective, or sufficiently effective, to protect individuals' Union rights has on occasions required the modification of national law, even the provision of new remedies. These will now be considered, bearing in mind that some of the earlier cases might be decided differently today.

8.5.1 **Interim relief**

In *Factortame I* the Court held that English courts were obliged to provide interim injunctions against the Crown where there was no other means of protecting individuals' Union rights, even though, as the Supreme Court had found in that case ([1990] 2 AC 85), no such remedy was available as a matter of national law. Following the CJ's ruling, the Supreme Court granted the requested relief ([1991] 1 AC 603 at 645).

In *Zuckerfabrik Süderdithmarschen AG v Hauptzollamt Itzehoe* (cases C-143/88 and 92/89) the CJ laid down Union criteria for the granting of interim relief pending a ruling from the CJ under Article 267 TFEU on the validity of a Union act, based on the principles applicable to the exercise of its own jurisdiction to grant such relief under Articles 278–9 TFEU. Relief should be granted only if the facts and legal circumstances are such as to persuade the court:

- that serious doubts exist about the validity of the Union measures on which the contested administrative decision is based;
- in cases of urgency;
- to avoid serious and irreparable damage to the party seeking the relief.

Given that the granting of interim relief pending a ruling on the *validity* of Union law involved a new situation for national courts, and that the suspension of a Union act would have serious implications for the Union legal order, it is not surprising that the Court provided a common Union solution here. However, although it might have been desirable, in the interests of the coherence of legal remedies, to require national courts to apply the same criteria in a claim for interim relief pending a ruling on the *interpretation* of Union law, the Court is not now likely to do so.

Zuckerfabrik Süderdithmarschen AG concerned the granting of *suspensory* measures pending a ruling on the validity of a Union measure under Article 267 TFEU. In *Atlanta Fruchthandelsgesellschaft mbH* the Court held, in the context of a claim for interim relief in the form of a grant of licences to import bananas from third countries pending a ruling on the validity of a Council regulation setting up a common banana regime, that the principles laid down in *Zuckerfabrik Süderdithmarschen AG* also applied to the grant of *positive* measures. It was not possible to make a distinction between an order designed to preserve an existing position and an order intended to create a new legal position. In deciding whether to grant such relief, national courts must respect existing decisions from the CJ on the matter in question whether under Article 267 TFEU or Article 263 TFEU; they must take into account the Union interest, particularly the damage which the non-application of a Union regulation may cause to an established Union regime. National courts may also consider the repercussions which an interim order may entail on important individual interests and even on national interests, economic and social. If the grant of interim relief represents a financial risk for the Union the national court must be in a position to require the applicant to provide adequate guarantees, such as the deposit of money or other security. The decision whether or not to grant interim relief is a difficult one, not to be taken lightly, particularly when it involves the suspension of a normative act, a Union regulation, as was the case in *Atlanta Fruchthandelsgesellschaft mbH*.

Zuckerfabrik Süderdithmarschen AG and *Atlanta Fruchthandelsgesellschaft mbH* concerned the national courts' powers to grant interim relief pending a ruling from the CJ on the validity of a Union act, a regulation. In the subsequent case of *T Port GmbH & Co KG v Bundesanstalt für Landwirtschaft und Ernährung* (case C-68/95), the GC refused to take the next logical step when it held that national courts had no power to order interim measures pending a decision on the EU institutions' *failure to act*. Indeed the national courts had no jurisdiction to refer questions concerning such alleged failures to the CJ. Judicial review of alleged failures on the part of the institutions could only be carried out by the Union courts. Given the limited access of individuals to the Union courts under Article 265 TFEU this decision appears to have left a gap in the judicial protection of individuals (see further Chapter 13).

8.5.2 Challenge to statutory provisions

Claims based on Union law will often involve a challenge to legislative acts or omissions. In many cases the challenge is indirect, ancillary to the principal action based on Union law. If the national court finds the provisions of a national statute incompatible with Union law, it may grant the remedy requested and simply 'disapply' them, on the principles established in *Simmenthal II* (see Chapter 4). This can also be seen in the context of *R v Secretary of State for Employment, ex parte Equal Opportunities Commission* ([1993] 1 WLR 872).

Equal Opportunities Commission

This case concerned a direct challenge to a domestic statute, something which was clearly not permitted in English law. The Equal Opportunities Commission (EOC) applied for a declaration that certain provisions of the Employment Protection (Consolidation) Act 1978 were contrary to EU sex-discrimination law and an order of mandamus requiring the Secretary of State to rectify the breach. A majority of the Court of Appeal thought that it would be 'wrong and unconstitutional for the Courts to grant a declaration or mandamus in an attempt to enforce obligations of Union law which, if they existed, did so only in international law'.

The Supreme Court disagreed, and granted a declaration that the provisions in question were *incompatible* with EU law (the claim for mandamus was not pursued) ([1995] 1 AC 1). There was no need to declare that the UK or the Secretary of State were in *breach* of their obligations under Union law. A declaration of incompatibility would suffice for the purposes sought by the EOC and was capable of being granted consistently with the precedent afforded by *Factortame II*.

The question of whether free-standing remedy to challenge the compatibility of national law with Union law was raised by the Swedish courts in *Unibet*. The CJ held that when it was possible to reach this route incidentally, through another legal action, there was no need for a free-standing remedy. The CJ did seem to suggest that there might be some circumstances where this would be insufficient—for example, where criminal charges were involved.

8.5.3 Damages

As the case law discussed above illustrates, national rules limiting the amount of damages that may be awarded will not always be successful. The approach taken in *Marshall II* requiring 'full' compensation can be seen in other areas, such as the state liability cases, such as *Danila Bonifaci and Others and Wanda Berto and Others v Istituto Nazionale della Previdenza Sociale (INPS)* (cases C-94 and 95/95). Applying this principle in *Brasserie du Pêcheur* the CJ held that a 'total exclusion' of loss of profit as a head of damage would not be permissible. Even an award of exemplary damages 'could not be ruled out' if such damages could be awarded pursuant to a similar claim or action founded on domestic law (para 89).

The case law is not entirely clear, however, as the Court has sought to distinguish the approach to whether interest should be awarded by reference to the nature of the right at stake, as the sex-discrimination cases illustrate. Article 6 Equal Treatment Directive (Directive 76/207) was amended by Directive 2002/73, and now limits the cases in which an upper limit on the amount of damages could be imposed in advance. This is, of course, of no help in other areas and the problem remains regarding the principles to be applied in determining whether limitations on damages and interest on damages are 'effective' for the purposes of EU law. In *Evans v Secretary of State for the Environment, Transport and the Regions and the Motor Insurers' Bureau* (case 63/01), a case under the Second Insurance Directive, the CJ held that compensation awarded under the rules implementing Article 1(4) Directive 84/5 'must take account of the effluxion of time until actual payment of the sums awarded in order to guarantee adequate compensation for the victims', which suggests that the obligation to award interest may extend to other areas of EU law.

8.5.4 **Restitution**

There have been many claims before national courts for the return of money paid in breach of Union law. The TFEU prohibits the imposition of customs duties or charges having equivalent effect, and discriminatory taxation (see Chapter 17). These charges are normally levied by national authorities. As early as 1960 the CJ held, in the context of a claim for sums levied in breach of the ECSC Treaty, that once a Member State had been found to have breached Union law it must take the necessary measures to make good the lawful effects of the breach, making restitution for sums wrongfully levied as a result of that breach (*Humblet v Belgium* (case 6/60)). There is now a consistent line of authority to this effect (see, eg, *Express Dairy Foods Ltd v Intervention Board for Agricultural Produce* (case 130/79)).

8.5.5 **Time limits**

In *Express Dairy Foods*, the Court suggested that a 'reasonable' period of limitation would not make it 'impossible in practice' for national courts effectively to protect individuals' Union rights. This principle, consistently invoked, was put in doubt by the Court's decision in *Emmott*, decided in 1991. Subsequent case law retreated from the approach in *Emmott*. In *Palmisani*, on the question of the effectiveness of the remedy provided, with its one-year limitation rule, the Court held that although in principle reparation must be commensurate with the loss or damage sustained (see *Marshall II* and *Brasserie du Pêcheur*), 'reparation cannot always be ensured by the retroactive and proper application in full of the measures implementing the Directive'. The setting of 'reasonable' limitation periods was permitted under EU law. A one-year limitation period such as the one in question 'cannot be regarded as making it excessively difficult or *a fortiori* impossible to lodge a claim for compensation'. Thus the one-year limitation period would not be incompatible with EU law.

In *Preston*, the CJ found a six-month bar on proceedings (following termination of employment) acceptable under EU law. In *Fantask A/S v Industriministeriet* (case C-188/95) the CJ accepted a Danish statutory five-year limitation period for the recovery of debts, running from the date on which the debt became payable, in the context of a challenge to the Ministry's refusal to reimburse company registration charges levied from the applicant in breach of Directive 69/335. The Court held that it had:

> acknowledged, in the interests of legal certainty, which protects the taxpayer and the authorities concerned, that the setting of reasonable limitation periods for bringing proceedings [was] compatible with [Union] law. Such periods cannot be regarded as rendering impossible or

> excessively difficult the exercise of rights conferred by [Union] law, even if the expiry of those periods necessarily entails the dismissal, in whole or in part, of the action brought [para 48].

This paragraph was cited by the Court in *Levez* and *Edis*.

The five-year limitation period was re-examined in *Fantask* and found to be neither discriminatory nor unreasonable. Distinguishing *Emmott*, the Court held that *Emmott* was 'justified on the particular facts of the case, in which the time bar had the result of *depriving the applicant of any opportunity whatsoever* to rely on her right to equal treatment under the Union Directive'. It seems that reasonable limitation rules will be acceptable, since they do not render the exercise of Union rights impossible or excessively difficult; but where they 'deprive the applicant of any opportunity whatsoever' to rely on her rights, or 'strike at the very essence of those rights', or where the applicant has been misled as to her Union rights, as in *Levez*, they will not be permitted. These principles have been reaffirmed by the CJ. In *Grundig Italiana SpA v Ministero delle Finanze* (case C-255/00), the CJ had to deal with the national rules which shortened the period within which claims for sums paid but not due could be recovered. Crucially, the CJ confirmed that such changes could be made, referring again to the 'practically impossible' test, but then went on to hold that such a change requires transitional arrangements to deal with the situation where such a change of time limits would have the effect of retroactively depriving individuals of rights to repayment, or of allowing such claimants too short a period in which to assert their rights. Rather than leaving this matter for the national court to assess, the CJ determined that the 90-day transitional period allowed by the national legislation was too short to allow 'normally diligent tax payers [to] familiarise themselves with the new regime and commence proceedings in circumstances which do not compromise their chances of success' (para 40). This is a slightly more stringent approach to assessing national rules than that taken about other aspects of time limits since *Emmott*, as the CJ did not require that there be a total bar to the exercise of the rights before the national rule is set aside. This aspect of the ruling, however, concerned only one aspect of the issue of time limits, that of the transitional arrangements. In contrast, in *Recheio-Cash & Carry SA v Fazenda PublicaRe-gisto Nacional de Pessoas Colectivas, and Ministério Público* (case C-30/02), a 90-day limitation period for launching a claim for the repayment of charges levied in breach of Union law was held to be compatible with the principle of effectiveness. This case concerned the limitation period itself, rather than transitional arrangements, so issues about allowing time for acclimatisation to a new system do not arise. Nonetheless, it is noteworthy that the Court did not refer to *Grundig Italiana* in its judgment.

The trend of case law since *Emmott* indicates that the Court will be slow to regard Member States' limitation rules as unreasonable except of course where, as was the case in *Emmott*, the time limit acts as a bar to the enforcement of an EU law right. Nevertheless, the acceptance of reasonable limitation rules will inevitably operate to modify the principle of full compensation, as occurred in *Fantask*, in which the applicant sought, unsuccessfully, to recover company registration charges levied in breach of Union law over a nine-year period, from 1983 to 1992. The precise limits of what will be regarded as reasonable remain unclear.

8.6 Conclusions

The law in this area divides the responsibility for procedural rules and remedies between European and national law. The underlying principle is that in the absence of harmonising measures the national legal system should apply, subject to the EU law rules of equivalence and effectiveness. There seems to be little difference in the CJ's approach to cases where EU law has specifically required that a remedy be provided and those areas where there is no such express requirement. The case law identified in this chapter shows clear parallels in the approach taken by the CJ, both in its expansive phase and when it has become more cautious. The division between national rules and those of EU law reflects the division between the CJ and the national courts shown in Article 267 TFEU. There the national courts have the responsibility for hearing the case, determining the facts and making a ruling in the light of EU law requirements as interpreted by the CJ.

The balance between the two court systems has not been static, reflecting different approaches by the CJ. The cases of the early years show deference to the autonomy of the national legal systems. Nevertheless, more emphasis on effectiveness can be seen immediately prior to the Treaty of Maastricht. The problem with this approach is that EU rights could end up being treated more favourably than rights deriving from national law. It seems that the CJ recognised this difficulty and has subsequently adopted an approach which seeks to balance the two extremes and recognised the importance of the national legal systems in providing the legal framework within which EU law operates and which fall to the national courts to assess. The principles of EU law do not mean that national rules will automatically fail. Nor does the new approach, however, mean that the national courts will not be required to disapply national rules or create new remedies. In each case, it will be a matter for the facts: the precise scope of the rules in question and their interplay with the substantive EU law rights.

Further reading

Accetto, M and Zleptnig, S, 'The principle of effectiveness: Rethinking its role in Community law' (2005) 11 EPL 375.

Anagnostaras, G, 'The quest for an effective remedy and the measure of protection afforded to putative Community law rights' (2007) 32 EL Rev 727.

Betlem, G, 'Torts, A European Ius Commune and the Private Enforcement of Community law' (2004) 64 CLJ 126.

Coppell, J, 'Domestic limitations on recovery for breach of EU law' (1998) ILJ 259.

Dougan, M, 'Cutting your Losses in the enforcement deficit: A Community right to the recovery of unlawfully levied charges?' (1998) 1 CYELS 233.

Drake, S, 'Scope of courage and the principle of 'individual liability' for damages: Further development of the principle of effective judicial protection by the Court of Justice' (2006) 31 EL Rev 841.

Kilpatrick, C, Novitz, T and Skidmore, P (eds), *The Future of Remedies in Europe* (Hart Publishing, 2000).

Lang, JT, 'The duties of national authorities under Community law' (1998) 23 EL Rev 109.

Nebbia, P, 'Damages actions for the infringement of EC competition law: Compensation or deterrence?' (2008) 33 EL Rev 23.

Prechal, S, 'Community law in national courts: The lessons from *Van Schijndel*' (1998) 35 CML Rev 681.

Prechal, S, 'Member State liability and direct effect: What's the difference after all?' (2006) 17 EBL Rev 299.

Ross, M, 'Refining effective enjoyment' (1990) 15 EL Rev 476.

Ross, M, 'Effectiveness in the European legal order(s): Beyond supremacy to constitutional proportionality?' (2006) 31 EL Rev 476.

Snyder, F, 'The effectiveness of European Community law' (1993) 56 MLR 19.

Steiner, J, 'How to make the action fit the case: Domestic remedies for breach of EEU law' (1987) 12 EL Rev 102.

Steiner, J, 'From direct effects to *Francovich*: Shifting means of enforcement of Community law' (1993) 18 EL Rev 3.

Steiner, J, 'The limits of state liability for breach of European Community law' [1998] EPL 69.

Tridimas, T, *The General Principles of EU Law*, 2nd edn (Oxford University Press, 2007).

Van Cleijneubreugel, P, 'Judge-made standards of national procedure in the post-Lisbon constitutional framework' (2012) 37 EL Rev 90.

Woods, L and Smith, F, 'Causation in *Francovich*: The neglected problem' (1997) 46 ICLQ 925.

State liability

9.1 Introduction

The preceding chapters have identified how the CJ extended the possible mechanisms by which individuals could enforce their EU law rights before their national courts. Perhaps the most significant development in this area over the past three decades has been the creation and development of the principle of state liability in *Francovich* and subsequent cases. This case law enables individuals, on a national level, to seek a remedy for losses suffered as a result of the failure by a Member State to implement, or apply correctly, provisions of Union law. While the national courts have largely accepted this development, the potential impact on the autonomy of the national legal systems remains a sensitive matter. This chapter will outline the development of the state liability doctrine and examine its scope and the conditions for such liability, as well identifying its relationship with other provisions.

9.2 Principle of state liability under *Francovich*

9.2.1 The *Francovich* ruling

The shortcomings, for the aggrieved EU citizen, of the principles of direct and indirect effect, particularly in the context of enforcement of directives, as already explained in Chapter 5, led the CJ to develop a third and separate principle in *Francovich*, the principle of state liability.

> ### *Francovich*
>
> In this case, the claimants, a group of ex-employees, were seeking arrears of wages following their employers' insolvency. Their claim (like that in the subsequent case of *Wagner Miret* (see Chapter 5)) was based on Directive 80/987, which required Member States, inter alia, to provide for a guarantee fund to ensure the payment of employees' arrears of wages in the event of their employers' insolvency. Since a claim against their former employers would have been fruitless (they being insolvent and 'private' parties), they brought their claim for compensation against the state.
>
> There were two aspects to their claim. The first was based on the state's breach of the claimants' (alleged) substantive rights contained in the Directive, which they claimed were directly effective. The second was based on the state's primary failure to implement the Directive, as required under Articles 288 TFEU and Article 4 TEU. The Court had already held, in Article 258 TFEU proceedings, that Italy was in breach of its Union obligations in failing to implement the Directive (*Commission v Italy* (case 22/87)).

With regard to the first claim, the Court found that the provisions in question were not directly effective since they were not sufficiently clear, precise and unconditional. Although the content of the right, and the class of intended beneficiaries, was clear, the state had discretion as to the appointment of the guarantee institution; it would not necessarily itself be liable under the Directive. The claimants were, however, entitled in principle to succeed in their second claim. The Court held that where, as here, a state had failed to implement an EU directive it would be obliged to compensate individuals for damage suffered as a result of its failure to implement the directive if certain conditions were satisfied—that is, where:

(a) the directive involved rights conferred upon individuals;

(b) the content of those rights could be identified on the basis of the provisions of the directive;

(c) there was a causal link between the state's failure and the damage suffered by the persons affected.

The Court's reasoning was based on: (1) the Member States' obligation to implement directives under Article 288 TFEU and their general obligation under what was then Article 10 EC, now Article 4(3) TEU, to 'take all appropriate measures . . . to ensure fulfilment of' their obligations under Union law; (2) its jurisprudence in *Van Gend en Loos* and *Costa* that certain provisions of Union law are intended to give rise to rights for individuals; and (3) that national courts are obliged to provide effective protection for those rights, as established in *Simmenthal* and *Factortame I*—see further Chapter 4. It concluded that 'a principle of state liability for damage to individuals caused by a breach of Union law for which it is responsible is inherent in the scheme of the Treaty'.

Thus, where the three conditions of *Francovich* are fulfilled, individuals seeking compensation as a result of activities and practices which are inconsistent with EU directives may proceed directly against the state. It provides for the right of compensation for a Member State's failure to comply with its EU law obligations to do so and, as well as providing protection for individuals' rights, consequently creates a mechanism for enforcement of Union law.

9.2.2 Scope of the principle

The reasoning in *Francovich* is compelling; its implications for Member States, however, remained unclear. Although what was in issue in the main proceedings was a state's liability for the non-implementation of a directive, *Francovich* appeared to lay down a wider principle of liability for all breaches of Union law 'for which the state is responsible'. Apart from the three conditions for liability, which are themselves open to interpretation, what other conditions would have to be fulfilled? Would liability be strict or dependent on culpability, even serious culpability, as was the case with actions for damages against Union institutions under Article 340 TFEU (see Chapter 14)? In the case of non-implementation of directives, as in *Francovich* itself, the state's failure is clear; *a fortiori* when established by the Court under Article 258 TFEU. But in cases of faulty or inadequate implementation it is not. The state's 'failure' may only become apparent following an interpretation of the directive by the Court (see, eg, the sex-discrimination cases such as *Marshall* and *Barber*—see Chapter 27). In such an instance, the case for imposing liability in damages on the state is less convincing, since non-implementation or incorrect implementation may be due to legal uncertainty (a lack of clarity as to what precisely the Member States are required to do to fulfil their obligations).

9.2.2.1 Type of action

Many of these issues were referred to the CJ for interpretation in the joined cases of *Brasserie du Pêcheur* (which related to a claim for damages brought by a French Brewery against Germany in relation to the beer purity legislation that prohibited the sales of beer with additives) and *Factortame* (which concerned a claim brought by Spanish fishermen against the UK in relation to the Merchant Shipping Act 1998 which prohibited them from fishing in UK waters). The Court clarified that the principle of state liability is not confined to a failure to implement directives; rather, *all* domestic acts and omissions, legislative, executive and judicial, in breach of Union law, can give rise to liability. Provided the conditions for liability are fulfilled it applies to breaches of *all* Union law, whether or not directly effective. However, arguing from the principles applicable to the Union's non-contractual liability under Article 340(2) TFEU, the Court held that where a Member State is faced with situations involving choices comparable to those made by Union institutions when they adopt measures pursuant to a Union policy it will be liable only where three conditions are met (see paras 50 and 51 of the judgment):

(a) the rule of law infringed must be intended to confer rights on individuals;

(b) the breach must be sufficiently serious;

(c) there must be a direct causal link between the breach of the obligation resting on the state and the damage sustained by the injured parties.

The 'decisive test' for whether a breach is sufficiently serious is whether the institution concerned has 'manifestly and gravely exceeded the limits of its discretion' (para 55). The factors to be taken into account in assessing this question included:

> the clarity and precision of the rule breached, the measure of discretion left by that rule to the national or [Union] authorities, whether the infringement and the damage caused was intentional or voluntary, whether any error of law was excusable or inexcusable, the fact that the position taken by a [Union] institution may have contributed towards the omission, and the adoption or retention of national measures or practices contrary to [Union] law [para 56].

9.2.2.2 For whose actions is the state liable?

One question left open by *Brasserie de Pêcheur* is the extent of a Member State's liability. There can be little doubt as to the state's liability for actions taken by the government itself in the context of the obligation to implement Union law measures. But what about other organs of the state? In *Commission v Belgium* (case 77/69), the CJ found that the principle of the supremacy of Union law would bind all agencies and organs of a Member State including those of a constitutionally independent character. As a result, the state is liable for their non-compliance with EU law. In *Haim v Kassenzahnartzliche Vereinigung Nordrhein* (case C-424/97) it was established that a legally independent body may be liable under *Francovich*, as well as the Member State itself.

In *AGM-COS MET Srl v Suomen Valtio and Tarmo Lehtinen* (case C-470/03), the Court held, that an individual official may be liable in addition to a Member State for any damage caused by that individual's actions which are in breach of Union law.

Lehtinen

Article 4(1) Directive 98/37 on machinery (now Directive 2006/42) requires that Member States do not restrict the marketing and use of machinery which complies with the Directive. Lehtinen was an official who had been involved in safety inspections of vehicle lifts in respect of which he had doubts as to their safety. His actions included making various public statements about his concerns, although Finland did nothing to arrange for the machinery to be withdrawn from the market. The manufacturer's sales plummeted in the wake of this, and an action was brought for state liability.

The Court held that statements such as the ones made by Lehtinen, if attributable to the state as giving the impression of reflecting official rather than personal opinions (which was for the national court to determine), could give rise to liability. It went on to say that Lehtinen's statements could be a breach of Article 4(1) of the Directive and could not be justified on the basis of public health or freedom of expression. As the provision conferred rights on individuals and left no discretion to the Member States, the conditions for liability were satisfied. Crucially, as well as the Member State itself, the individual official could also be held liable under national law. The Court appears to treat this as the corollary of its ruling in *Haim* that a public body may also be liable under the state liability principle. In the words of the Court:

> [Union] law does not preclude an individual other than a Member State from being held liable, in addition to the Member State itself, for damage caused to individuals by measures which that individual has taken in breach of [Union] law (see, to that effect, *Haim*, paragraph 32) [para 98].

A similar argument could be made about the actions of regional and local government.

Brasserie de Pêcheur also suggested that there may be liability for judicial failures, which was controversial. In *Köbler*, the CJ confirmed that such liability may arise in particular circumstances.

Köbler

The case concerned the refusal by the Austrian Administrative Supreme Court (Verwaltungsgerichtshof) to grant Mr Köbler a 'length of service' increment on the basis that the payment would be a loyalty bonus, for which time spent in similar positions in other Member States could not be taken into account. This was an inaccurate interpretation of Union law and in direct conflict with an earlier ruling by the CJ (*Schöning-Kougebetopoulou v Freie und Hansestadt Hamburg* (case C-15/96)), and Mr Köbler therefore brought a new claim under *Francovich* for the failure of the Verwaltungsgerichtshof to apply Union law correctly.

The CJ stated that, in international law, state liability can arise on the basis of acts by the legislature, executive and judiciary, and that the same must be true of Union law (para 32). In addition, the principle of effectiveness (see 8.3) requires that there must be instances when a state will incur liability for actions by its courts which are in breach of Union law (para 33). However, the CJ limited this to instances where courts are adjudicating at the last instance (para 33) and emphasised the mandatory jurisdiction of such a court under Article 267 TFEU to request a preliminary ruling on the interpretation of Union law (see Chapter 10). The Court ruled that:

> in the light of the essential role played by the judiciary in the protection of the rights derived by individuals from [EU] rules, the full effectiveness of those rules would be called in question and the protection of those rights would be weakened if individuals were precluded from being able, under certain conditions, to obtain reparation when their rights are affected by an infringement of [EU] law attributable to a decision of a court of a Member State adjudicating at last instance [para 33].

In order to ensure the effective protection of individuals' rights under Union law, there has to be a possibility of claiming compensation for damage caused by an infringement of these rights by a court adjudicating at last instance (para 36). Such an infringement must be manifest, and it is for the national legal system to designate the courts that would hear such claims. This ruling, it is submitted, follows logically from the principle of state liability, and its restrictions to courts of last instance is entirely appropriate because at that point there would be no possibility of an appeal against a ruling which infringes an individual's Union rights. In order to avoid opening the floodgates to claims of state liability or Article 267 references in such circumstances, the CJ was at pains to emphasise that 'state liability for an infringement of Union law by a decision of a national court adjudicating at last instance can be incurred only in the exceptional case where the court has manifestly infringed the applicable law' (para 53), although this is not limited to intentional fault or serious misconduct by the national court (*Traghetti*). Whether this will serve as an appropriate brake to such actions remains to be seen.

In coming to its conclusion, the Court in *Köbler* had to deal with several fundamental objections. The first was that the principle of *res judicata* (finality of judgments) might be undermined by imposing liability on the state for a serious infringement of Union law (see generally 6.6.2). The Court, replied to this by stating that state liability in such circumstances would not affect the finality of the judgment at issue. At a technical level, that may be correct, although it cannot be denied that the authority of the ruling in the original case would be undermined. Secondly, there was concern that the independence of the judiciary may be affected, and the authority of the court undermined, by the possibility of a state liability claim. This, too, was given short shrift by the Court, simply denying that there would be 'any particular risk to the independence' of the court concerned (para 42), and that the possibility of a state liability action might be 'regarded as enhancing the quality of a legal system and . . . the authority of the judiciary' (para 43). However, the Court did not expand on this in any detail, and its assertion remains somewhat unconvincing. Finally, there was concern as to whether there would be an appropriate domestic court which might hear a claim for state liability. In this regard, the CJ referred back to established principles according to which it is for national legal systems to determine the appropriate court to hear such claims. That, however, does not solve the difficulties that may arise in practice. Presumably, a Member State found liable before a domestic court has a right of appeal. In the UK, this might produce the rather strange situation whereby the Supreme Court might eventually be called upon to hear a case in state liability based on one of its own judgments. Whilst the basic outcome in *Köbler* therefore can be defended at a purely logical level, there are many practical difficulties which remain unresolved by this decision. As a final point, it may be noted that in *Köbler* itself, the CJ thought that the breach by the Austrian Verwaltungsgerichtshof was not sufficiently serious for a claim in state liability to succeed.

9.2.2.3 Liability only where measure confers rights

One of the key requirements of liability under *Francovich/Brasserie de Pêcheur* is that the rule of law infringed must be intended to confer rights on individuals. Consequently, where a directive in issue does not confer rights on individuals, then there can be no claim under *Francovich*. Thus, in *Peter Paul v Germany* (case C-222/02), the failure of the German banking supervisory authority correctly to supervise a bank, which subsequently failed, in accordance with the relevant directive (Directive 94/19, now Directive 2014/49 ([2014] OJ L173/149)) did not permit depositors to maintain an action for compensation for lost deposits beyond the maximum threshold of £20,000 provided for in the Directive. This was because the obligation to ensure supervision was not combined with an independent right to compensation for the consequences of any failure in that regard, and the individual rights under this Directive were limited to a specified amount of compensation (which had been paid already).

9.2.3 Conditions of liability

For liability to arise it is not necessary for the infringement of Union law to have been established by the CJ under Article 258 TFEU; nor is it necessary to prove fault on the part of the national institution concerned *going beyond that of a sufficiently serious breach of Union law*. In *Brasserie du Pêcheur* the Court rephrased the three conditions laid down in *Francovich* and incorporated a requirement that the breach be sufficiently serious. Condition (b) of *Francovich* (the content of the right infringed must be sufficiently clear) may now be regarded as contained within the definition of 'sufficiently serious'.

The Court based its decision on its past case law, particularly its reasoning in *Francovich*: states are obliged under Article 4(3) TEU to provide effective protection for individuals' Union rights and ensure the full effect of Union law. As regards its own jurisdiction to rule on the matter of states' liability in damages, it reasoned that, since the Treaty had failed to provide expressly for the consequences of breaches of Union law, it fell to the Court, pursuant to its duty under Article 19 TEU, to ensure that 'in the interpretation and application of this Treaty the law is observed'.

Despite the hostility with which this decision was greeted in some quarters, it is submitted that the Court's ruling on the question of, and conditions for, liability is prima facie consistent with existing principles and, provided that the multiple test in para 56 of *Brasserie de Pêcheur* (see 9.2.2.1) of what will constitute a 'sufficiently serious' breach is rigorously applied, strikes a fair balance between the interests of the Union in enforcing Union law and the interests of Member States in restricting liability to culpable breaches of Union law.

9.2.3.1 Meaning of 'sufficiently serious'

For liability to arise, the institution concerned must have 'manifestly and gravely exceeded the limits of its discretion': the breach must be 'inexcusable'. If there is to be equality of *responsibility* as between the liability of the Union under Article 340(2) TFEU and Member States under *Francovich*, the criterion of a 'sufficiently serious' breach laid down in *Brasserie du Pêcheur* should be interpreted strictly. The question remaining was whether the Court would apply the 'sufficiently serious' test to *all* claims based on *Francovich*, including claims for damage resulting from breaches of Union law which do *not* involve legislative 'choices' analogous to those made by Union institutions when implementing policy. Alternatively it might continue to 'interpret' Member States' actions as involving such choices, as it did, surprisingly, in *Brasserie du Pêcheur*. To limit the application of the sufficiently serious test to situations in which Member States are involved in 'legislative choices', by analogy with the position of Union institutions under Article 340(2) TFEU (see Chapter 14), as was suggested in *Brasserie du Pêcheur*, would be to ignore the essential difference between the position of Member States, when *implementing* Union law, and that of Union institutions when *making* Union law. Since liability depends on the breach by a Member State of a Union obligation, liability should in all cases depend on whether the breach is sufficiently serious. This is reflected in the multiple test laid down in para 56.

Given the lack of clarity at times of Union law, and that Member States are obliged to respect it, it is submitted that the crucial element in para 56 will often be the clarity and precision of the rule breached, as suggested by Advocate-General Tesauro in *Brasserie du Pêcheur*.

This view obtained some support in *R v Her Majesty's Treasury, ex parte British Telecommunications plc* (case C-392/93), a case decided shortly after *Brasserie du Pêcheur*.

> ### BT
>
> This case, brought by BT, concerned the alleged improper implementation of Council Directive 90/351 on public procurement in the water, energy, transport and telecommunication sectors ([1990] OJ L297/1). BT, which claimed to have been financially disadvantaged as a result of this wrongful implementation, was claiming damages based on *Francovich*. The Court, appearing to presume that

the other conditions for liability were met, focused on the question whether the alleged breach was sufficiently serious. It applied the test of para 56 of *Brasserie du Pêcheur*. Although it found that the UK implementing regulations were contrary to the requirements of the Directive, it suggested that the relevant provisions of the Directive were sufficiently unclear as to render the UK's error excusable. At para 43 of its judgment the Court said that the article in question (Article 8(1)) was:

> imprecisely worded and was reasonably capable of bearing, as well as the construction applied to it [by the CJ] the interpretation given to it by the United Kingdom in good faith and on the basis of arguments which are not entirely void of substance. The interpretation, which was also shared by other Member States, was not manifestly contrary to the wording of the Directive or to the objective pursued by it.

This interpretation was, it is submitted, generous to the UK. The Court held that in the context of the transposition of directives, 'a restrictive approach to state liability is justified' for the same reasons as apply to Union liability in respect of legislative measures, namely:

> to ensure that the exercise of legislative functions is not hindered by the prospect of actions for damages whenever the general interest requires the institutions or Member States to adopt measures which may adversely affect individual interests [para 40].

The Court adopted a rather different approach in *R v Ministry of Agriculture, Fisheries and Food, ex parte Hedley Lomas (Ireland) Ltd* (case C-5/94).

Hedley Lomas

This case concerned a claim for damages by an exporter, Hedley Lomas, for losses suffered as a result of a UK ban on the export of live sheep to Spain. The ban was imposed following complaints from animal welfare groups that Spanish slaughterhouses did not comply with the requirements of Council Directive 74/577 on the stunning of animals before slaughter ([1974] OJ L316/10). The Spanish authorities had implemented the Directive, but had made no provision for monitoring compliance or providing sanctions for non-compliance. The UK raised the matter with the Commission, which, following discussion with the Spanish authorities, decided not to take action against Spain under Article 258 TFEU. Although the UK ban was clearly in breach of Article 35 TFEU, the UK argued that it was justified on the grounds of the protection of health of animals under Article 36 TFEU (for further discussion of the substantive issues see Chapter 19). However, the UK provided no evidence that the Directive had in fact been breached, either by particular slaughterhouses or generally.

The Court found that the ban was in breach of Article 35 TFEU, and was not justified under Article 36 TFEU. The fact that the Spanish authorities had not provided procedures for monitoring compliance with the Directive or penalties for non-compliance was irrelevant. 'Member States must rely on trust in each other to carry out inspections in their respective territories' [para 19]. Furthermore, the breach was 'sufficiently serious' to give rise to liability under *Francovich*. The Court suggested [para 28] that:

> where, at the time when it committed the infringement, the Member State in question was not called upon to make any legislative choices and had only considerably reduced, or even no, discretion, the mere infringement of [Union law] may be sufficient to establish the existence of a sufficiently serious breach.

The ruling in *Hedley Lomas*, delivered two months after *BT*, was surprising. While a finding that the UK would in principle be liable in damages was justified on the facts, the UK having produced no evidence of breach of the Directive constituting a threat to animal health to justify the ban under Article 36 TFEU, the suggestion that a 'mere infringement' of Union law might be sufficient to create liability where the state is not 'called upon to make any legislative choices' or has 'considerably reduced, or no, discretion' is questionable. While a state may have a choice as to the 'form and method of implementation' of directives, and some discretion under the Treaty to derogate from basic Treaty rules, its discretion is strictly circumscribed, and it has no discretion to act in breach of Union law. The UK had no more 'legislative' discretion in implementing Directive 90/531 in *BT*, indeed possibly less, than it had under Article 36 TFEU in *Hedley Lomas*. Indeed, prior to the Court's decision in *Hedley Lomas*, it was thought that a Member State *would* have discretion to derogate from the prohibition of Article 35, where this was necessary to protect a genuine public interest (see Chapter 19). To pursue the analogy between the Union's liability for 'legislative choices involving choices of economic policy' and Member States' liability under *Francovich*, as the Court has done in all these cases, is to disguise the fact that *the two situations are not similar*. The principal reason for limiting liability under *Francovich* is not because Member States' 'discretion' in implementing Union law must not be fettered, but because the rules of Union law are often not clear. To hold them liable in damages for 'mere infringements' of such rules, thereby introducing a principle akin to strict liability, would not only be politically dangerous, it would be contrary to the principle of legal certainty, itself a respected principle of Union law (for further analysis see Chapter 14).

Nevertheless the principle of liability for a 'mere infringement' of Union law in situations in which Member States are not required to make legislative choices was invoked by the CJ in *Dillenkofer v Germany* (cases C-178, 179, 188, 189 and 190/94). In that case Germany's failure fully to implement Directive 90/314, designed to protect consumers in the event of travel organisers' insolvency, was on a par with that of the Italian government in *Francovich*, was clearly 'inexcusable', and therefore, as the Court acknowledged, 'sufficiently serious' to warrant liability. Similarly, in *Rechberger and Greindle v Austria*, concerning the same Directive, the CJ found that the implementing measures set the period for the commencement of claims at a date some months later than the time limit for implementation of the Directive, which was 'manifestly' incompatible with the Directive, and sufficiently serious to attract liability. In neither *Hedley Lomas* nor *Dillenkofer* did the Court attempt to apply the multiple test laid down in para 56 of *Brasserie du Pêcheur*.

However, in *Denkavit International BV v Bundesamt für Finanzen* (cases C-283, 291 and 292/94), which were cases involving claims for damages resulting from the faulty implementation of a Directive decided shortly after *Dillenkofer*, the Court followed its approach in *BT*. On the basis of a strong submission from Advocate-General Jacobs, it applied the criteria of para 56 of *Brasserie du Pêcheur* and concluded that, as a result of the lack of clarity and precision of the relevant provisions of the Directive, and the lack of clear guidance from the Court's previous case law, Germany's breach of Union law could not be regarded as sufficiently serious to justify liability. Significantly, the Court did not draw a distinction, for the purposes of liability, between acts of Member States involving 'choices of economic policy' and 'mere infringements' of Union law.

In an attempt to rationalise this aspect of state liability, Advocate-General Jacobs in *Sweden v Stockholm Lindöpark AB* (case C-150/99) commented on the origins of the phrase 'sufficiently serious breach'. At para 59 of his Opinion, he noted that:

> In French, the Court has always used—originally with regard to liability incurred by the [Union]—the term 'violation suffisamment caractérisée'. This is now normally translated into English as 'sufficiently serious breach'. However, the underlying meaning of 'caractérisé', which gives rise to its inherent implication of seriousness, includes the notion that the breach (or other conduct) has been clearly established in accordance with its legal definition, in other words, that it is a definite,

clear-cut breach. This may help to explain why the term was previously translated as 'sufficiently flagrant violation' and may throw additional light on the choice of factors which the Court has indicated should be taken into consideration when deciding whether a breach is 'sufficiently serious'.

On this reasoning, in order to be sufficiently serious, the breach of Union law would have to be definite and clear-cut. Nevertheless, establishing whether a breach is of that nature can be a difficult issue, and the approach by the CJ to the assessment of the matter of a 'sufficiently serious' breach has not been fully consistent. In *Lindöpark*, the Court effectively followed *Hedley Lomas*.

Lindöpark

Lindöpark had not been entitled to deduct VAT on goods and services used for the purposes of its business activities under Swedish law and Sweden was thus in breach of the sixth VAT Directive (Directive 91/680 ([1991] OJ L376/1)). Sweden amended its VAT legislation with effect from 1 January 1997, to bring it into line with the sixth VAT Directive, following which Lindöpark was entitled to deduct VAT. It claimed for a return of VAT payments made between Sweden's accession to the Union on 1 January 1995 and 1 January 1997. The CJ observed that the right to deduct VAT was capable of being directly effective. Although the question of Member State liability did not strictly speaking arise, the CJ was nevertheless prepared to indicate whether Sweden had committed a sufficiently serious breach. It noted that 'given the clear wording of [the directive], the Member State concerned was not in a position to make any legislative choices and had only a considerably reduced, or even no, discretion'. The mere infringement of the Directive was therefore enough to create liability.

Although the CJ has, in some cases, concluded whether a breach was sufficiently serious to give rise to liability, that assessment is properly left to the national courts, with the CJ only able to provide general guidance (which is correct, in principle, given the nature of the CJ's jurisdiction under Article 267). Thus, in *Norbrook Laboratories Ltd v Minister of Agriculture, Fisheries and Food* (case C-127/95), a case involving a claim for damages for wrongful implementation of Union directives on the authorisation of veterinary products, the CJ, following an extensive examination of the provisions of the Directive allegedly breached, which revealed a number of clear breaches, invoked the *Hedley Lomas/Dillenkofer* dictum:

> Where . . . the Member State was not called upon to make legislative choices, and had considerably reduced, if no discretion, the mere infringement of [Union law] may be sufficient to establish the existence of a sufficiently serious breach [para 109].

The CJ then left it to the national court to assess whether the conditions for the award of damages were fulfilled. Similarly, in *Klaus Konle v Austria* (case C-302/97), in a claim for damages for losses suffered as a result of laws of the Tyrol governing land transactions, allegedly contrary to Article 52 TFEU and Article 70 of the Act of Accession, the Court examined these provisions for their compatibility with Union law, and finding some (but not all) of the laws to be 'precluded' by Union law, left it to the national court 'to apply the criteria to establish the liability of Member States for damage caused to individuals by breaches of Union law in accordance with the guidelines laid down by the Court of Justice'.

If national courts are to assess this crucial question of the seriousness of the breach, it is essential that these guidelines are clear. The multiple criteria laid down in para 56 of *Brasserie du Pêcheur* are clear and comprehensive. The *Hedley Lomas* requirement, that in some circumstances a 'mere infringement' of Union law will suffice to establish liability, clouds the issue. It is submitted that if it is to be invoked, it will be applicable only *following* an examination of the Union law allegedly breached under the multiple test in para 56; for only then will the issue of whether the state has any 'discretion' in the exercise of its legislative powers be resolved. If the aim, and the substance, of the Union obligation allegedly infringed is 'manifest', the state will have no discretion to act in its breach. If it is not, the breach will not be sufficiently serious. Nevertheless, it was invoked in *Haim* alongside the multiple test of para 56 and has been referred to since, though in cases in which the CJ seems to suggest that the clarity and precision of the rule are key (*R, on the application of Synthon BV v Licensing Authority of the Department of Health* (case C-452/06), para 39).

One factor which may assist the national court is the rulings by the CJ on the interpretation of the measure in issue. Indeed, it seems that even if there is some ambiguity in the text of the relevant measure, the *BT* approach will not be followed where the CJ has interpreted a particular provision of Union law and a Member State has subsequently failed to apply that provision in accordance with the CJ's interpretation in *Gervais Larsy*. In that case, it can no longer be said that the Member State has a legislative choice. However, where the exact position only emerges gradually through several rulings by the Court, the national court can take this into account when considering the clarity of the rule in question and whether any errors of law were excusable or inexcusable (*Test Claimants in the FTI Group Litigation v Commissioners of Inland Revenue* (case C-446/04)). This approach can be contrasted with the outcome of the CJ in *Robins v Secretary of State for Work and Pensions* (case C-278/05).

Robins

In this case, the CJ held that the UK had incorrectly implemented Article 8 Directive 80/987 on protecting employees in the event of insolvency of their employer by not ensuring that a sufficient proportion of expected pension benefits were protected. The UK's liability turned on the interpretation of 'protect' in Article 8, and as its meaning had been unclear prior to the interpretation given in this case, it seemed unlikely that the UK's breach would be sufficiently serious, although it was for the national court to come to a final decision.

9.2.3.2 The claimant must prove that damage has been suffered

It is also important that the claimant is able to establish that he has suffered loss or damage. This can be seen in *Schmidberger v Austria*.

Schmidberger

In this case, Austria had allowed a public protest to take place on the main motorway across the Alps which closed the motorway for 28 hours. Schmidberger claimed damages for delay to his business of transporting goods from Germany to Italy on the basis that this amounted to a breach of Articles 34–6 TFEU (see Chapter 19).

Advocate-General Jacobs noted that it was necessary for the claimant to establish loss or damage which is attributable, by a direct causal link, to a sufficiently serious breach of Union law. Importantly, this included a right to claim for lost profit. However, if the claimant is unable to establish the existence of any loss or damage, then there cannot be a claim for state liability. The Advocate-General was willing to accept that it may not be possible to quantify exactly the loss suffered, in which case this may be calculated on an appropriate flat-rate basis. On the facts, the Advocate-General thought that the breach of Articles 34–6 TFEU in that case was not sufficiently serious. Austria had authorised a 28-hour demonstration which blocked the main transit route across the Alps, which was technically a breach of Articles 34–6, but this had to be balanced against the freedom of expression of the demonstrators (see further Chapter 6). This and the short duration of the disruption would not be a sufficiently serious breach of Union law. The CJ, having decided that there was no breach of Articles 34–6, did not address the question of state liability in its judgment. As far as the requirement that damage be proven is concerned, it is submitted that the reasoning of this Advocate-General is sound.

9.2.3.3 The damage must have been caused by the breach

It is also necessary that the claimant can demonstrate that any damage suffered was caused by the Member State's breach of EU law. In *Brinkmann Tabakfabriken GmbH v Skatteministeriet* (case C-319/96), a case along the more moderate line in *BT*, the Court found that the Danish authorities' failure properly to implement Directive 79/32 ([1979] OJ L10/8) on taxes other than turnover taxes affecting the consumption of manufactured tobacco was not sufficiently serious to incur liability. The classification adopted by the authorities, which resulted in the applicant having to pay the higher rates of taxes, was not 'manifestly contrary' to the wording and aim of the Directive. It was not clear from the Directive whether the tobacco rolls imported by the applicant, which had to be wrapped in paper to be smoked, constituted 'cigarette tobacco' or 'cigarettes'. Significantly, both the Commission and the Finnish government supported the classification adopted by the Danish authorities. The question of liability turned on the question of causation. The Directive in question had not been implemented in Denmark by legislative decree, although the authorities had given immediate (albeit imperfect) effect to its provisions. There was no direct causal link between that former (legislative) failure and the damage suffered by the applicant. It is implicit in the decisions that, contrary to the view of some commentators, provided that the requirements of a directive are complied with in practice, a failure to implement a directive by legislative means will not necessarily constitute a sufficiently serious breach to warrant liability.

9.2.4 *Brasserie du Pêcheur* in the English courts

In 1997 the CJ's ruling in *Brasserie du Pêcheur* and *Factortame* was applied in the English High Court with a view to ascertaining whether the UK's action in introducing the Merchant Shipping Act 1988 in fact constituted a sufficiently serious breach of Union law (*R v Secretary of State for Transport, ex parte Factortame Ltd (Factortame V)* [1998] 1 CMLR 1353). Hobhouse LJ considered the CJ's case law on state liability and concluded that whether or not a Member State's action involved the exercise of discretion (ie, 'legislative choices') the same test, requiring proof of a sufficiently serious breach of Union law, applied. That test, requiring a 'manifest and grave disregard of whatever discretion the Member State might possess', was based on the same principles as applied to Union liability under Article 288(2), and was a relatively difficult one to meet. He concluded that the UK's breach as regards the Merchant Shipping Act 1988 was sufficiently serious to warrant liability and referred the case back to the Divisional Court to decide the question of causation. Two factors in particular were cited by Hobhouse LJ as rendering the breach of Union law (Article 49 TFEU) sufficiently serious:

(1) The UK had introduced the measures in question in primary legislation in order to ensure that the implementation would not be delayed by legal challenge (at the time it was thought that primary legislation could not be challenged, but see now *Factortame I*, noted in Chapter 4);

(2) The Commission had from the start been opposed to the legislation on the grounds that it was (in its opinion) contrary to Union law.

Both the Court of Appeal and the Supreme Court agreed with Hobhouse LJ that the UK's breach of Union law was sufficiently serious to warrant liability. Both courts applied the multiple test laid down in para 56 of *Brasserie du Pêcheur* (although they suggested that the list was 'not exhaustive') and found that the balance tipped in favour of the respondents. In pressing ahead with its legislation, against the advice of the Commission, despite its clear adverse impact on the respondents, and in a form (statute) which it was thought could not be challenged, the UK government was clearly taking a 'calculated risk'. Lord Slynn did, however, express the opinion, contrary to the view of Hobhouse LJ and the Court of Appeal, that the considered views of the Commission, although of importance, could not be regarded as conclusive proof as to:

● whether there had been a breach of Union law;

● whether the breach (if any) was sufficiently serious to justify an award of damages.

Lords Hoffmann and Clyde expressed a similar view; the position taken by the Commission was 'a relevant factor to be taken into account' in deciding whether a breach was sufficiently serious, but it was not conclusive.

Following the House of Lords' decision in *Factortame*, Sullivan J in the English High Court, in assessing the seriousness of the Department of Social Security's breach of Article 7(1) of the Sex Discrimination Directive (Directive 79/7) in *R v Department of Social Security, ex parte Scullion* ([1999] 3 CMLR 798), also applied the multiple test of para 56 of *Brasserie du Pêcheur*, which he described as the 'global' or 'basket' approach, and decided that, since there the scope of Article 7(1) was not clear at the relevant time, and there was no evidence that the Department had sought legal advice on the matter either from the Commission or from its own legal advisers, the breach was sufficiently serious.

9.2.5 Relationship of the principle of state liability with direct effect

The principle of state liability is an important complement to the principles of direct and indirect effect in the effective enforcement of EU law, particularly in the context of enforcement of directives. A good example is *Francovich* itself, following the CJ's denial of the direct effects of the relevant provisions of Directive 80/987 ([1980] OJ L283/23).

One question that arises is whether state liability can be used in preference to direct effect and indirect effect, or whether it can only be used if neither of these two mechanisms are available. In this regard, the CJ has pointed out a gap in protection—in particular due to the fact that directives do not have horizontal effect—can be remedied through the use of state liability. The doctrine on this view has a subsidiary role in enforcing EU law rights. In *Brasserie du Pêcheur* the CJ viewed state liability in a slightly different light, seeing it as a corollary of direct effect (para 22). Nonetheless, the preferred approach seems to see state liability as the approach of last resort. It was suggested in *Lindöpark* that a damages claim is unnecessary where the applicant can obtain relief by instituting an alternative course of action set down in national law. Some commentators have suggested that

Bonifaci implies it is possible to make admissibility of such proceedings dependent on the exhaustion of other domestic remedies which offer full reinstatement of rights. None of this however requires such an approach before an action in state liability may be brought.

9.2.6 Classifying state liability in national law

The principle of state liability remains a hybrid concept, part national, part Union law, with national courts ultimately responsible for applying the conditions to a particular case. This has created problems for national courts. Prior to *Brasserie du Pêcheur* it was assumed, following *Francovich*, that a claim for damages against the state must be brought on the same basis, and according to the same rules, as the 'equivalent' claim based on national law.

However, regrettably, as noted earlier, the rules governing state liability laid down in *Brasserie du Pêcheur* were not comprehensive. It is left to national courts to decide, according to the principles applicable to equivalent claims based on national law, whether the Union law breached was intended to benefit persons such as the applicant (condition (a)); whether there existed the appropriate direct causal link between the state's breach and the applicant's damage (condition (c)), which was raised, but not decided, in *Schmidberger* and whether the damage suffered was of a kind in respect of which damages might be awarded.

Although a principle of state liability for executive acts, and judicial remedies in respect of such acts, already exists in all Member States, these claims will now also be subject to the rules laid down in *Brasserie du Pêcheur*. As with legislative acts, existing national remedies may need to be modified to ensure that they are effective in protecting individuals' rights; alternatively (and preferably) claims may be brought under a new *Francovich* tort.

A principle of liability for judicial acts in breach of Union law, as laid down in *Brasserie du Pêcheur*, clearly breaks new constitutional ground in most if not all Member States. If available in theory, it is unlikely to be applied freely in practice. There is a degree of freedom for the Member States to specify the circumstances in which Member State liability may arise, provided that these are not stricter than those laid down in Union law. Thus, in *Traghetti*, Italian legislation excluded state liability for judicial functions involving the interpretation of legal provisions or the assessment of facts and evidence by limiting liability exclusively to cases of intentional fault and serious misconduct of national courts.

And as to limiting liability, following on from its ruling in *Köbler*, the Court observed that whilst the interpretation of the law is part of the essence of judicial activity, it is possible that a manifest breach of Union law might occur during the process of interpretation (para 35).

In *Lehtinen*, the Court held that national law may lay down specific conditions, provided that they do not make it impossible or excessively difficult in practice to obtain compensation caused by a Member State's breach of Union law. The Finnish limitation to damage caused by a criminal offence, the exercise of public authority, or on the basis that there are other especially serious reasons for awarding compensation were too restrictive because there may be conduct otherwise giving rise to liability not covered by these factors. This issue has been discussed in more detail in Chapter 8.

9.3 Conclusions

The principle of state liability provides individuals with a strong tool before their national courts to secure the enforcement of their rights under Union law. However, as the *Francovich* case law on state liability has shown, there may be many hurdles to overcome in establishing a successful claim. To succeed in a claim for damages the applicant must establish that the law infringed was intended to confer rights on individuals and that the breach is sufficiently serious (as well as the requisite damage and causation). In cases of non-implementation of directives, as in *Francovich* or *Dillenkofer*, where there is no doubt about the nature of the Union obligation, the breach is likely to be sufficiently serious. However, where the Union obligation allegedly breached is less clear, the breach may well be found to be excusable. This, then, is a limitation on the ability of the doctrine to provide an effective remedy—or an effective enforcement mechanism—in every circumstance. Nonetheless, the introduction of state liability was a significant moment in the jurisprudence of the CJ as it undermined the principle found in the legal systems of many Member States: that the state would not be liable for legislative (in)action. At a systemic level, the introduction of the doctrine emphasises that in the field of Union (if not Union) law, Member States play a subordinate role.

Further reading

Anagnostaras, G, 'The principle of state liability for judicial breaches: The impact of European Union law' (2001) 7 EPL 281.

Anagnostaras, G, 'Erroneous Judgments and the prospect of damages: The scope of the principle of governmental liability for Judicial Breaches' (2006) 31 EL Rev 735.

Beutler, B, 'State liability for breaches of community law by national courts: Is the requirement of a manifest infringement of the applicable law an insurmountable obstacle?' (2009) 46 CML Rev 773.

Biondi, A, 'In Praise of *Francovich*' in P Maduro and L Azoulai (eds), *The Past and Future of EU Law* (Hart Publishing, 2010).

Cabral, P and Chaves, MC, 'Member State liability for decisions of national courts adjudicating at last instance' (2006) 13 MJECL 109.

Cruz, J, '*Francovich* and imperfect law' in P Maduro and L Azoulai (eds), *The Past and Future of EU Law* (Hart Publishing, 2010) p 418.

Davies, A, 'State Liability for Judicial Decisions in European Union and International Law' (2012) 61 ICLQ 585.

Dougan, M, 'The vicissitudes of life at the coalface: Remedies and procedures for enforcing union law before national courts' in P Craig and G de Búrca (eds), *The Evolution of EU Law*, 2nd edn (Oxford University Press, 2011).

Gutman, K, 'The evolution of the action for damages against the European Union and its place in the system of judicial protection' (2011) 48 CML Rev 695.

Lock, T, 'Is private enforcement of EU law through State liability a myth? An assessment 20 years after *Francovich*' (2012) 49 CML Rev 1675.

Prechal, S, 'Member State liability and direct effect: What's the difference after all?' (2006) 17 EBL Rev 299.

Vajda, C, 'Liability for breach of Union law: A survey of the CJEU cases post *Factortame*' (2006) 17 EBL Rev 257.

Van den Berg, R and Schafer, HB, 'State liability for infringements of the EC Treaty' (1998) 23 EL Rev 552.

Van Cleijneubreugel, P, 'Judge-made standards of national procedure in the post-Lisbon constitutional framework' (2012) 37 EL Rev 90.

Van Gerven, W, 'Bridging the gap between Union and national law: Towards a principle of homogeneity of legal remedies' (1995) 32 CML Rev 679.

Wattel, PJ, '*Köbler, CILFIT and Welthgrove*, We can't go on meeting like this' (2004) 41 CML Rev 177.

10

The preliminary rulings procedure

10.1 Introduction

The EU legal system is enforced through many routes and the role of individuals in the enforcement and development of Union law has been vital. This has been possible through private actions begun in the national courts where private litigants seek to assert their directly effective rights derived from Union law. In practice this private enforcement of EU law before national courts has been critical to the success of the European legal order; at the same time it has been important to ensure that this action before such a multiplicity of courts and tribunals does not prejudice uniform interpretation and application of EU law. The system devised to achieve this objective is created by Article 267 TFEU. National courts and tribunals, faced with a question of EU law, the determination of which is essential for the resolution of the dispute before it, but the meaning of which provision is not clear, may (and sometimes must) ask the CJ for its view on the interpretation of that provision. The national court may suspend proceedings before it and make a 'reference' to the CJ to obtain a 'preliminary ruling' on any point of EU law relevant to the proceedings. After the CJ has given its view on the point of Union law, the case is remitted to the national court for a final ruling in light of the legal opinion received. The CJ does not have the power to make final orders or enforce its judgments in the Member States' national legal systems.

This chapter seeks to consider the relationship between the national courts and the CJ in the context of preliminary rulings. In particular we consider the following key issues:

(1) The relative importance of the Article 267 TFEU preliminary reference procedure to the development of Union law and European integration, and the role of individuals in that process;

(2) The extent to which the national courts are willing and able to gain access to the CJ in order to resolve questions of Union law before them;

(3) How far the Article 267 system has ensured that Union law is interpreted uniformly throughout the Member States;

(4) The nature of the relationship between the national courts and the CJ, and whether that remains one of cooperation between equal partners or whether it has evolved into something more hierarchical, with the CJ effectively acting as a supreme court for the Union;

(5) The extent to which the Article 267 TFEU procedures adequately protect fundamental rights and give effective remedies to private litigants.

10.2 The text of Article 267 TFEU and an overview of the procedure

Article 267 TFEU provides that:

(1) The Court of Justice of the European Union shall have jurisdiction to give preliminary rulings concerning:

(a) the interpretation of the Treaties;

(b) the validity and interpretation of acts of the institutions, bodies, offices or agencies of the Union;

(2) Where such a question is raised before any court or tribunal of a Member State, that court or tribunal may, if it considers that a decision on the question is necessary to enable it to give judgment, request the Court to give a ruling thereon;

(3) Where any such question is raised in a case pending before a court or tribunal of a Member State against whose decisions there is no judicial remedy under national law, that court or tribunal shall bring the matter before the Court;

(4) If such a question is raised in a case pending before a court or tribunal of a Member State with regard to a person in custody, the Court of Justice of the European Union shall act with the minimum of delay.

References for preliminary rulings may also be made on the interpretation of provisions of international agreements concluded by the EU with third states or international organisations (*Haegeman v Belgium* (case 181/ 73)). In the case of Freedom, Security and Justice, there are limitations to the CJ's jurisdiction under Article 267. Article 276 TFEU provides that the CJ 'shall have no jurisdiction to review the validity or proportionality of operations carried out by the police or other law enforcement services of a Member State or the exercise of the responsibilities incumbent upon Member States with regard to the maintenance of law and order and the safeguarding of internal security'. The CFSP, which remains in the TEU, continues by Article 275 TFEU to fall outside the preliminary rulings procedure. Article 267 TFEU also applies to questions relating to the Euratom Treaty and the Unified Patents Convention.

Article 256(3) TFEU envisages that the GC could be given jurisdiction to hear and determine preliminary rulings in specific areas laid down by the Statute of the Court of Justice. Should the GC be endowed with such jurisdiction, provision could be made for review of those rulings by the CJ 'should there be a serious risk of the unity or consistency of Union law being affected' (Article 256(3) TFEU). Should the GC itself consider that any case requires a decision of principle likely to affect the Union or consistency of Union law, it could refer the case to the CJ for a ruling.

10.2.1 The historical importance of the Article 267 procedure

The reference procedure has been very valuable to the individual, since it has provided him or her with a means of access to the CJ, albeit via the national courts, to challenge Member State actions alleged to breach Union law and to challenge the compatibility of acts of the Union institutions with the Union legal order. It will be recalled that there is no possibility for individuals themselves to begin enforcement action against a Member State under Article 258 TFEU. This is reserved to the Commission. Similarly, individuals have found it difficult to begin direct actions before the GC under Article 263 against the acts and legislation of Union institutions, bodies, offices or agencies because of the restrictive rules on standing (see Chapter 12). By virtue of Article 267, the individual has been able indirectly to challenge the validity of actions by Member States (eg, *Van Gend en Loos*). By instituting proceedings before national courts challenging domestic measures implementing Union law a reference can be obtained for a ruling to the CJ, on the validity of Union legislation. Article 267 thus enables an individual to obtain an appropriate remedy from his national court where the CJ finds a Union measure to be unlawful. (See Chapter 6 and, eg, *Royal Scholten-Honig*—regulation invalid for breach of principle of equality.)

10.2.1.1 Impact on development of Union law

The importance of the Article 267 procedure has been greatly increased by the development by the CJ of the concept of direct effect. Where originally only 'directly applicable' regulations might have been expected to be invoked before national courts, these courts may now be required to apply Treaty articles, decisions and even directives. Even where Union law is not directly effective it may be invoked before national courts on the principles of indirect effect or state liability under *Francovich*. As a result, national courts now play a major role in the enforcement of Union law. As we will see, the cooperative relationship between the CJ and the national courts has been a key factor in the success of the preliminary rulings procedure.

The CJ has also used the preliminary ruling procedure to develop many principles vital for the substantive development of Union law. A glance through the other chapters of this book will reveal that the majority of cases cited, and almost all the major principles of EU Law established by the CJ, were decided in the context of references to that court for preliminary rulings under Article 267. Cases such as *Van Gend en Loos*, *Costa* and *Defrenne II*, concerned with questions of interpretation of Union law, enabled the CJ to develop the crucial concepts of direct effect and the supremacy of Union law. *Internationale Handelsgesellschaft; Stauder* and *Royal Scholten-Honig* (see Chapter 6), which raised questions of the validity of Union law, led the way to the incorporation of general principles of law into the Union legal order. The principle of state liability in damages was laid down in *Francovich* in preliminary ruling proceedings. In all areas of EU law, the Article 267 procedure has played a major role in developing the substantive law. Preliminary rulings are the most common type of proceedings dealt with by the CJ.

10.2.2 Nature of the preliminary rulings procedure

The preliminary ruling procedure is not an appeals procedure. It merely provides a means whereby national courts, may apply to the CJ for a ruling on the interpretation or validity of points of EU law necessary to resolve disputes before them. It is a matter for the national courts to decide whether or not to make a reference. The Court cannot compel a reference; neither can the parties to the proceedings. It is an example of shared jurisdiction, depending for its success on mutual cooperation.

As Advocate-General Lagrange said in *De Geus en Uitdenbogerd v Robert Bosch GmbH* (case 13/61), the first case to reach the CJ on an application under the preliminary rulings procedure:

> Applied judiciously—one is tempted to say loyally—the provisions of [Article 267] must lead to a real and fruitful collaboration between the municipal courts and the Court of Justice of the Communities with mutual regard for their respective jurisdiction.

10.3 The broad approach of the Court to Article 267 references

The CJ has adopted a purposive approach in its rulings on the meaning of Union law aiming to strengthen the effectiveness of Union law and build the single market. It actively encourages cooperation with national courts to ensure the uniform and effective application of EU law. Rarely does it rule references to be inadmissible. It has accepted references from a wide range of bodies (see 10.3.1 and 10.3.2) and it has shown flexibility in its handling of references from national courts, for example by rephrasing questions or indeed raising points *ex officio* which it sees are necessary to ensure a satisfactory resolution to the national proceedings (see 10.3.6).

10.3.1 What is a 'court or tribunal'?

Jurisdiction to refer to the CJ under Article 267 is conferred on 'any court or tribunal'. The proceedings that give rise to the reference for a preliminary ruling must lead to a legally binding decision of a judicial nature (*El Yassini v Secretary of State for the Home Department* (case C-416/96); *Cartesio Okató és Szolgáltató bt* (case C-210/06); *Valeri Hariev Belov v ChEZ Elektro Balgaria AD and ChEZ Raspredelenie Balgaria AD* (case C-394/11)) with rare exceptions (eg, *Nordsee Deutsche Hochseefischerei GmbH* (case 102/81) discussed at 10.3.2; *Corbiau v Administration des Contributions* (case C-24/92) (a fiscal authority is not a court or tribunal); *Victoria Film A/S v Riksskattenverkert* (case C-134/97) (a court exercising its administrative duties is not a court or tribunal)).

The concept of a 'court or tribunal' has been interpreted in the widest sense. Whether a particular body qualifies as a court or tribunal within Article 267 is a matter of *Union law*. National-law classifications are not determinative. The court or tribunal making the reference must be situated in one of the Member States. (*Department of Health and Social Security v Christopher Stewart Barr and Montrose Holdings* (case C-355/89) reference from the Deputy High Bailiffs' Court, Isle of Man refused.) The court or tribunal must be 'of a Member State'.

Miles

In *Paul Miles v European Schools* (case C-196/09) the CJ held that it had no jurisdiction to rule on a reference for a preliminary ruling from the Complaints Board of the European Schools. Although the Complaints Board had been created by all the Member States and by the Union, 'the fact remains that it is a body of an international organisation, which despite its functional links which it has with the Union remains formally distinct from it and from the Member States' [para 42].

The CJ has set down a number of criteria by which a 'court or tribunal' might be identified, comprising:

- statutory origin;
- permanence;

- *inter partes* procedure;
- compulsory jurisdiction;
- the application of rules of law;
- independence of the body making the reference.

(See *Dorsch Consult v Bundesbaugesellschaft Berlin* (case C-54/96), para 23; *Pretore di Salò*; *Abrahamsson and Anderson v Fogelqvist* (case C-407/98); *Cartesio; Synetairismos Farmakopoion Aitolias & Akarnanias v GlaxoSmithKline plc* (case C-53/03); *Miles.*)

Broekmeulen

In *Broekmeulen v Huisarts Registratie Commissie* (Case 246/80) the Court was faced with a reference from the appeal committee of the Dutch professional medical body. One of the questions referred was whether the appeal committee was a 'court or tribunal' within what is now Article 267 TFEU. The Court held that it was:

> in the practical absence of an effective means of redress before the ordinary courts, in a matter concerning the application of Union law, the appeal committee, which performs its duties with the approval of the public authorities and operates with their assistance, and whose decisions are accepted following contentious proceedings and are in fact recognised as final, must be deemed to be a court of a Member State for the purpose of [Article 267].

It was held that it was imperative, to ensure the proper functioning of Union law, that the CJ should have the opportunity of ruling on issues of interpretation and validity raised before such a body.

More recently, the CJ has held that a person appointed to hear appeals against home affairs ministry decisions in immigration cases, an immigration adjudicator, could make a reference (*El-Yassini*). In this case, the office of Immigration Adjudicator was a permanent office, established by statute which gives the officer in question the power to hear and determine disputes in accordance with rules set down by statute. The CJ further agreed with the Advocate-General, who had emphasised the *inter partes* nature of the procedure (para 20) and the fact that the adjudicators are required to give reasons for their decisions.

The CJ was subsequently criticised by the Advocate-General in *François de Coster v Collège des bourgmestre et échevins de Watermael-Boitsfort* (case C-17/00) for an approach to the interpretation of a 'court or tribunal' that is confused, especially as regards the criteria of whether the body is established by law, the independent nature of the body and the need for *inter partes* procedure, as well as the requirement that the body's decision be of a judicial nature. Although in cases such as *Criminal Proceedings against X* (cases C-74 and 129/95), in which the CJ declared it did not have jurisdiction because the prosecutor making the reference was not independent, and *Dorsch Consult*, in which the Court emphasised the need for the referring body to carry out its responsibilities 'independently' (para 35), in other instances, such as *El-Yassini*, the CJ has not stringently assessed the requirement of independence. Another such example is *Gabalfrisa v AEAT* (cases C-110–47/98). There the CJ held that the Spanish Economic-Administrative Courts, which do not form part of the judiciary but are part of the Ministry of Economic Affairs and Finance, fell within Article 267. The CJ accepted that the separation of functions between the departments of the Ministry responsible for tax collection and the Economic–Administrative Courts, which ruled on complaints lodged against the collection departments, was sufficient to ensure independence, despite the Opinion of Advocate-General Saggio in that case to the contrary.

In *de Coster*, the Court, contrary to the view of the Advocate-General, accepted the reference. It noted that the body in question was 'a permanent body, established by law, that it gives legal rulings and that the jurisdiction thereby invested in it concerning local tax proceedings is compulsory' (para 12). In the subsequent *Schmid* case (case C-516/99), however, the CJ went to great lengths to distinguish the Fifth Appeal Chamber for the Regional Finance Authority, the referring body in *Schmid*, from the bodies found to fall within the definition of a 'court or tribunal' in *Dorsch Consult* and *Gabalfrisa*, which the Advocate-General in *de Coster* had criticised. Like the bodies in those cases, the appeal chamber was linked in organisational terms to the body whose decisions it reviewed.

10.3.2 Can arbitrators be a 'court or tribunal'?

The position of arbitrators has given rise to problems in this context. The Court took a narrow view of a 'court or tribunal' in the early case of *Nordsee*.

Nordsee

This case arose from a joint shipbuilding project which involved the pooling of aid. The parties agreed that in the event of a dispute they would refer their differences to an independent arbitrator. Their agreement excluded the possibility of recourse to the ordinary courts. They fell into disagreement and a number of questions involving the interpretation of certain Union regulations were raised before the arbitrator. He sought a ruling from the CJ as to, inter alia, whether he was a 'court or tribunal' within the meaning of Article 267. The Court held that he was not.

According to the Court, the key issue was the nature of the arbitration. *In Nordsee* the public authorities of Member States were not involved in the decision to opt for arbitration, nor were they called upon to intervene automatically before the arbitrator. If questions of Union law were raised before such a body, the ordinary courts might be called upon to give them assistance, or to review the decision; it would be for those courts to refer questions of interpretation or validity of Union law to the CJ.

The Court's decision in *Nordsee* ignored the fact that in this case recourse to the courts was excluded, and the arbitrator was thus required to interpret a difficult point of Union law, of central importance in the proceedings, unaided. Since in *Nordsee* there was no effective means of redress before the ordinary courts, the decisions of the arbitrator were recognised as final. It seems that the only factor distinguishing it from *Broekmeulen* was the element of *public* participation or control. This, it seems, will be essential. Certainly, in subsequent cases, such as *Handels–og Kontorfunktionaerernes Forbund i Danmark v Dansk Arbejdsgiveforening for Danfoss* (case 109/88), the CJ has focused on the compulsory nature of an arbitrator's jurisdiction, by contrast to the position in *Nordsee*, when the parties agreed to refer their dispute to arbitration.

The position was confirmed in *Denuit v Transorient* (case C-125/04) involving a dispute under the Package Travel Directive (Directive 90/314) before the arbitration panel of the Belgian Travel Dispute Committee. Having confirmed its case law, the CJ rejected the reference on the basis that the panel was not a 'court or tribunal', because the parties were 'under no obligation, in law or in fact, to refer their disputes to arbitration' (at para 16). No regard was had to the fact that, in a consumer situation, arbitration may be the only formal procedure which may practically be available to a consumer because of the comparatively high cost of court action; a matter which surprises in view of the increasing emphasis on out-of-court procedures in consumer cases.

10.3.3 The question must be a matter of Union law

The Court is only empowered to give rulings on matters of Union law. It has no jurisdiction to interpret domestic law, nor to pass judgment on the compatibility of domestic law with Union law. The

Court has frequently been asked such questions (eg, *Van Gend en Loos; Costa; Netherlands v Ten Kate Holding BV* (case C-511/03)), since it is often the central problem before the national court. But as the Court said in *Costa*:

> a decision should be given by the Court not upon the validity of an Italian law in relation to the Treaty, but only upon the interpretation of the above-mentioned [Treaty] Articles in the context of the points of law stated by the Giudice Conciliatore.

Where the Court is asked to rule on such a matter it will merely reformulate the question and return an abstract interpretation on the point of Union law involved. This respects the division of competences laid down in the Treaty and avoids the CJ becoming involved in national law issues over which it has no jurisdiction.

The Court can give preliminary rulings where national law refers to a provision of EU law (*Dzodzi v Belgium* (cases C-297/88 and 197/89)) but its jurisdiction is confined to provisions of EU law; it cannot deal with purely national law (*Punch Graphic Prepress Belgium* (case C-371/11)).

10.3.4 The Court's role is one of interpretation of Union law not application to the facts

The Court maintains a dividing line in principle between interpretation and application. It has no jurisdiction to rule on the application of Union law by national courts. However, since the application of Union law often raises problems for national courts, the Court, in its concern to provide national courts with 'practical' or 'worthwhile' rulings, will sometimes, when interpreting Union law, also offer unequivocal guidance as to its application (see, eg, *Stoke-on-Trent City Council v B&Q* (case C-169/91); *BT; Arsenal Football Club v Reed* (case C-206/01); *Feryn*).

10.3.5 The Court must not interfere with the matters within national court discretion

The Court maintains a strict policy of non-interference over matters of what to refer, when to refer and how to refer. Such matters are left entirely to the discretion of the national judge. As the Court said in *De Geus en Uitdenbogerd*, its jurisdiction depends 'solely on the existence of a request from the national court'. However, it has no jurisdiction to give a ruling when, at the time when it is made, the procedure before the court making it has already been terminated (*Fratelli Pardini SpA v Ministero del Commercio con l'estero* (case 338/85); *Grogan*). In contrast, the Court does have jurisdiction where a court is involved in preparatory inquiries in criminal proceedings which may or may not lead to a formal prosecution, where the question of Union law may determine whether the inquiries will continue (*Criminal proceedings against X ('Rolex')* (case C-60/02)).

No formal requirements are imposed on the framing of the questions. Where the questions are inappropriately phrased the Court will merely reformulate the questions, answering what it sees as the relevant issues (*Haribo Lak Ritzen Han Riegal v Finanzamt Linz* (cases C-436 and 437/08)). It may interpret what it regards as the relevant issues even if they are not raised by the referring court (eg, *OTO SpA v Ministero delle Finanze* (case C-130/92); *Land Oberösterreich v ČEZ* (case C-115/08)). Nor will it question the timing of a reference. However, since 'it is necessary for the national court to define the legal context in which the interpretation requested should be placed', the Court has suggested that it might be convenient for the facts of the case to be established and for questions of purely national law to be settled at the time when the reference is made, in order to enable the

Court to take cognisance of all the features of fact and law which may be relevant to the interpretation of Union law which it is called upon to give (*Irish Creamery Milk Suppliers Association v Ireland* (cases 36 and 71/80); approved in *Pretore di Salò*). In *Telemarsicabruzzo SpA v Circostel* (cases C-320, 321 and 322/90) it rejected an application for a ruling from an Italian magistrates' court on the grounds that the reference had provided no background factual information and only fragmentary observations on the case. The CJ has since reaffirmed this approach in several cases (eg, *Pretore di Genova v Banchero* (case C-157/92); *Monin Automobiles v France* (case C-386/92)). The CJ has held, however, that the need for detailed factual background to a case is less pressing when the questions referred by the national court relate to technical points (*Vaneetveld v Le Foyer SA* (case C-316/93)) or where the facts are clear, for example, because of a previous reference (*Crispoltoni v Fattoria Autonoma Tabacchi* (cases C-133, 300 and 362/92)). The concern seems to be that not only must the CJ know enough to give a useful ruling in the context, but that there is also enough information for affected parties to be able to make representations. This, according to the CJ, is especially relevant in competition cases (*Deliége v Ligue Francophone de Judo et Disciplines Associées ASBL, Ligue Belge de Judo ASBL and Others* (case C-191/97), paras 30 and 36) (see further Chapter 29). The Court has issued an 'Information Note on references from national courts for a preliminary ruling' ([2011] OJ C160/1, replacing guidance issued in 2009), consolidating its rulings in these cases. In November 2016 a recommendation was issued to national courts and tribunals on the initiation of preliminary ruling proceedings ([2016] OJ C439/1).

The circumstances in which the CJ will decline jurisdiction are discussed at 10.4.

10.3.6 National courts may refer cases on the validity of Union measures

As confirmed in Article 267 TFEU itself, the validity of Union measures may be called into question within national proceedings. Thus, for example, a regulation or directive passed by the Council and Parliament may be argued to be *ultra vires* the TFEU. If an individual is adversely affected by the measure, he may begin proceedings in the national courts to challenge it. The national courts have often made references to the CJ in such cases. The CJ has been receptive to such cases (subject to the limits discussed at 10.4.4) and is willing to rule that EU measures are invalid in responding to Article 267 references (see eg, *Digital Rights Ireland Ltd v Minister for Communications, Marine and Natural Resources and Others* (case C-293/12)). The only limit placed upon national courts is that they themselves do not have the power to declare EU measures invalid (see *Foto-Frost v Hauptzollamt Lübeck-Ost* (case 314/85)). The CJ has been keen to maintain exclusive jurisdiction because of the risk that national courts may undermine the effectiveness and uniformity of Union law if they were competent unilaterally to declare Union measures invalid. The CJ has however confirmed that national courts can grant interim relief suspending the implementation of EU measures that they believe to be invalid in *Zuckerfabrik Süderdithmarschen AG*. The national courts must use this power with great care and make an urgent reference to the CJ. This is a good example of the cooperative nature of the relationship between the CJ and the national courts. The CJ sought to balance the concerns of national courts about invalid EU legislation affecting individuals with its own concerns about the effectiveness and uniform application of Union law.

10.3.7 The practical reality of the CJ's jurisdiction

Some of the previously discussed limitations of the Court's jurisdiction are more apparent than real. The line between matters of Union law and matters of national law, between interpretation and application are more easily drawn in theory than in practice. An interpretation of Union law may leave little room for doubt as to the legality of a national law and little choice to the national judge in matters of application if he is to comply with his duty to give priority to Union law. The Court has on occasions suggested that a particular national law is incompatible with Union law (eg, *R v Secretary of State for Transport, ex parte Factortame Ltd* (case C-221/89); *Johnston*). The Court may even offer specific guidance as to the application of its ruling. In the *BT* case, for example, the CJ commented:

> Whilst it is in principle for the national courts to verify whether or not the conditions of State liability for a breach of [Union law] are fulfilled, in the present case the Court has all the necessary information to assess whether the facts amount to a sufficiently serious breach of [Union law].

The Court then went on to hold that there had been no breach. Further, in rephrasing and regrouping the questions the Court is able to select the issues which it regards as significant, without apparently interfering with the discretion of the national judge.

It may be argued that some encroachment by the CJ on to the territory of national courts' jurisdiction is necessary to ensure the correct and uniform application of Union law. However, the CJ has at times been accused of blurring the boundaries between its jurisdiction and that of the national courts.

The potential difficulties arising from the CJ overstepping the boundary between its role of interpreting Union law and the national courts' role of applying that ruling to the facts can be seen in the case of *Arsenal Football Club v Reed* ([2002] All ER (D) 180 (Dec)).

Arsenal Football Club

The case before the national court concerned the action commenced by Arsenal to prevent Reed from continuing to sell souvenirs which carried its name and logos. The national court referred a number of questions to the CJ on the interpretation of the Trade Mark Directive (see case C-206/01). The main issue was whether trade-mark protection extended only to the circumstances in which the sign was used as a trade-mark or whether an infringement would occur irrespective of how the marks were used. The CJ held:

> In a situation which is not covered by Article 6(1) of the First Council Directive 89/104/EEC of 21 December 1988 to approximate the laws of the Member States relating to trade marks, where a third party uses in the course of trade a sign which is identical to a validly registered trade mark on goods which are identical to those for which it is registered, the trade mark proprietor of the mark is entitled, in circumstances such as those in the present case, to rely on Article 5(1)(a) of that directive to prevent that use. It is immaterial that, in the context of that use, the sign is perceived as a badge of support for or loyalty or affiliation to the trade mark proprietor.

The phrase 'in circumstances such as those in the present case' would seem to give the national court little freedom in its determination of the case for which the preliminary ruling was originally made. In the *Arsenal* case, however, the referring court accepted the argument of the defendant's counsel to the effect that in the course of its judgment and in particular by tying the operative part of its judgment to the facts of the case, the CJ had made a determination of fact which in some aspects was inconsistent with the finding of fact made by the national court. On this basis, the national court commented: 'If this is so, the CJ has exceeded its jurisdiction and I am not bound by its final conclusion. I must apply its guidance on the law to the facts as found at the trial' (para 27).

It further remarked:

> The courts of this country cannot challenge rulings of the [CJ] within its areas of competence. There is no advantage to be gained by appearing to do so. Furthermore national courts do not make references to the [CJ] with the intention of ignoring the result. On the other hand, no matter how tempting it may be to find an easy way out, the High Court has no power to cede to the [CJ] a jurisdiction it does not have [para 28].

Although the national court in this case—the High Court—pointed to the limits of the CJ's jurisdiction as the basis for its decision it did point out that there was the possibility of an appeal to the Court of Appeal, which might make a different application of the law to the facts. This is what happened subsequently (see [2003] 2 CMLR 25), when the Court of Appeal held that the CJ's reference to the facts was *not* at variance with those of the trial judge, but that there was a difference in legal reasoning. The trial judge had therefore been wrong to disagree with the CJ in this case, although the Court of Appeal did confirm the principle on which the first-instance decision was based. We can see in *Reed* a good example of a case where the CJ was perceived to have exceeded its proper jurisdiction as a court of reference by taking the final decision on the case away from the national court. The nature of cooperation requires that both national courts and the CJ respect each other's jurisdictions.

10.4 The Court's refusal to give rulings in some cases

There are limitations on the CJ's willingness to accept references for preliminary rulings. One practical, thus justifiable, limitation that we have already seen is that the CJ will refuse jurisdiction when the referring court has not included enough information to enable the CJ to give a ruling on the question referred (see eg, *Telemarsicabruzzo SpA*). This situation can be remedied by a further reference from the national court providing further information to assist the CJ. In other cases the CJ has found that there is no genuine dispute before the national court which requires a ruling from it.

10.4.1 The CJ can decline to hear cases brought in artificial proceedings

The most important limitation was first laid down by the CJ in the cases of *Foglia v Novello (No 1)* (case 104/79) and *Foglia v Novello (No 2)* (case 244/80). Here for the first time the Court refused its jurisdiction to give a ruling on a question of Union law.

> ### *Foglia v Novello I* and *Foglia v Novello II*
>
> The questions, which were referred by an Italian judge, concerned the legality under Union law of an import duty imposed by the French on the import of wine from Italy. It arose in the context of litigation between two Italian parties. Foglia, a wine producer, had agreed to sell wine to Mrs Novello, an exporter. In making their contract the parties agreed that Foglia should not bear the cost of any duties levied by the French in breach of Union law. When duties were charged and eventually paid by Foglia, he sought to recover the money from Mrs Novello. In his action before the Italian court for recovery of the money that court sought a preliminary ruling on the legality under Union law of the duties imposed by the French. The CJ refused its jurisdiction. The proceedings, it claimed, had been artificially created in order to question the legality of the French law; they were not 'genuine'. The parties were no more successful the second time when the judge referred the case back to the CJ having not received a

satisfactory answer to his previous reference. In a somewhat peremptory judgment the Court declared that the function of Article 267 was to contribute to the administration of justice in the Member States; not to give advisory opinions on general or hypothetical questions.

The CJ's decision has been criticised. Although the parties had contrived their contractual arrangements so as to bring a claim in their own national court, rather than challenging the French duty in the French courts, they did genuinely think the duty was in breach of Union law and the Italian judge called upon to decide the case was faced with a real problem, central to which was the issue of Union law. If, in his discretion, he sought guidance from the CJ in this matter, surely it was not for that Court to deny it. The principles expressed in *Foglia* were, however, applied in *Meilicke v ADV/ ORGA AG* (case C-83/91). Here the Court refused to answer a lengthy and complex series of questions relating, inter alia, to the interpretation of the second Company Law Directive. The dispute between the parties centred on a disagreement as to the interpretation of certain provisions of German company law. It appeared that the EU Directive was being invoked in order to prove the theories of one of the parties (a legal scholar). The Court held that it had no jurisdiction to give advisory opinions on hypothetical questions submitted by national courts. The reasons are partly those of effective case management but also to prevent the courts becoming a forum for political rather than legal disputes.

In the *Foglia* decision the Court held it 'must display special vigilance when . . . a question is referred to it with a view to permitting the national court to decide whether the legislation of another Member State is in accordance with Union law': *Foglia (No 2)*. This assessment is supported by the case of *Bacardi-Martini SAS v Newcastle United Football Company Ltd* (case C-318/00).

Bacardi-Martini

Bacardi entered into a contract for advertising time on an electronic revolving display system during a match between Newcastle and Metz, a French football club. The match was to be televised live in the United Kingdom and France. Although the advertising deal was in compliance with English law, it contravened French law and Newcastle therefore pulled out of the advertising agreement. Bacardi brought an action against Newcastle, claiming that it could not rely on the French law to justify its actions, as the French law was incompatible with Article 56 TFEU on the freedom to provide services. The High Court made a reference on this point. When discussing the question of admissibility, the CJ referred to *Foglia* and the special need for vigilance when the law of another Member State was in issue; it then reviewed whether the national court had made it clear why an answer was necessary. The CJ concluded:

> In those circumstances, the conclusion must be that the Court does not have the material before it to show that it is necessary to rule on the compatibility with the Treaty of legislation of a Member State other than that of the court making the reference [para 53].

From this case it seems that, although a national court is not precluded from referring questions relating to the national laws of other Member States, the CJ will review the justification for the reference more stringently than it would otherwise do.

10.4.2 The case must relate to a cross-border issue and not a purely internal situation

Another area in which the CJ has sometimes limited references has been when the subject matter of the case is 'internal' and does not involve Union law directly. Internal law issues are governed by national not Union law. The CJ has generally been careful not to rule on cases which appear to concern internal situations because to do so would be to assume a power not conferred upon it by the TFEU. This issue came before the Court in *Dzodzi*. Here the Court was prepared to provide a ruling on the interpretation of EU social security law in a purely 'internal' matter, for the purpose of clarifying provisions of Belgian law invoked by a Togolese national. The Court held that it was 'exclusively for national courts which were dealing with a case to assess, with regard to the specific features of each case, both the need for a preliminary ruling in order to enable it to give judgment, and the relevance of the question'. Following *Dzodzi*, in *Leur Bloem v Inspecteur der Belastingdienst/ Ondernemingen Amsterdam 2* (case C-28/95), the CJ held that it has jurisdiction to interpret provisions of Union law where the facts of the case lie outside these provisions but are applicable to the case because the national law governing the main dispute has transposed the Union rule to a non-Union context ('spontaneous harmonisation'). This is subject to the proviso that national law does not expressly prohibit it (*Kleinwort Benson Ltd v City of Glasgow District Council* (case C-346/93)). Similarly, the CJ has accepted references for preliminary rulings in circumstances where a national provision is tied into a Union rule in order to avoid non-discrimination even in purely internal situations (*Doris Salzmann* (case C-300/01)—an internal situation affected by rules on free movement of capital in Article 63 TFEU).

10.4.3 A preliminary ruling must be 'objectively required'

Another potential limitation on the CJ's willingness to accept references can be seen in *Monin Automobiles—Maison du Deux-Roues* (case C-428/93). There the CJ suggested that the questions referred must be 'objectively required' by the national court as 'necessary to enable that court to give judgment' in the proceedings before it as required under Article 267(2).

> ### Monin Automobiles
>
> This case concerned a company which was in the process of being wound up. The company argued that it should not be finally wound up until certain questions relating to Union law had been answered. Conversely, the company's creditors thought that the company had been artificially kept in existence for too long already and should be wound up immediately. The national court referred the EU-law questions to determine the strength of the company's argument. The CJ held that, although there was a connection between the questions and the dispute, answers to the question would not be *applied* in the case. The CJ therefore declined jurisdiction.

10.4.4 The parties must challenge Union measures directly under Article 263 TFEU if they have standing

Another limitation on the CJ's willingness to give preliminary rulings relates to cases where a party is seeking to challenge an EU measure indirectly using proceedings in the national courts. Whilst we saw that often the CJ will rule on such issues where national courts refer questions to the CJ under Article 267 (see 10.3.7), there are some limits to this open-door policy. The Court has been concerned to prevent parties using Article 267 to get round the rules on direct challenges under Article 263. This was the situation in *TWD Textilwerke GmbH v Germany* (case C-188/92) where the Court refused to give a ruling on the validity of a Commission decision, addressed to the German government, demanding the recovery from the applicants of state aid granted by the government in breach of Union law. Its refusal was based on the fact that the applicants, having been informed by the government of the Commission's decision, and advised of their right to challenge it under Article 263, had failed to do so within the two-month limitation period. Having allowed this period to expire the Court held that the applicants could not, in the interests of legal certainty, be permitted to attack the decision under national proceedings. This would defeat the restrictions on challenging Union acts imposed by Article 263 because a party could wait many months or years before attempting to invalidate long-standing EU decisions or legislation.

This decision, as it might be taken to be, has caused concern, calculated to drive parties, perhaps prematurely, into action under Article 263, for fear of being denied a later opportunity to challenge Union legislation under Article 267 (see further, Chapter 12). However, the CJ has since mitigated some of the effects of its judgment in *TWD*. In *R v Intervention Board for Agriculture, ex parte Accrington Beef Co Ltd* (case C-241/95), the parties had not sought to bring an action for annulment within the time limits set out in Article 263 TFEU. Nonetheless, the CJ was prepared to hear the preliminary ruling reference because it was not clear, as the parties were seeking to challenge a regulation, that they would have had standing to bring an action under Article 263 (see also *Atzeni and Others v Regione autonoma della Sardegna* (cases C-346 and 529/03), discussed at 12.3.3.4). It seems therefore that Article 267 can be used in such cases as long as it is not obvious that the party would have had standing to challenge the Union measure directly under Article 263.

10.5 National courts and the reference procedure

It is up to the national-court judge whether to decide to refer matters to the CJ. The discretion is entirely his—it is he who has to decide whether a reference is necessary to decide the case before him. The parties to the case cannot compel a reference. As will be seen, in some cases Article 267 imposes a duty to refer cases but there is no means of compelling this if a national court declines to do so. The CJ has thus relied very much upon judges cooperating with it in order to develop Union law and to ensure uniform application throughout the Member States. In this sense, national courts are also part of the Union legal order.

10.5.1 When must a national court refer and when does it have choice?

Although any court or tribunal may refer questions to the CJ under Article 267, a distinction must be drawn between those courts or tribunals which have a discretion to refer ('permissive' jurisdiction) and those for which referral is mandatory ('mandatory' jurisdiction). Under Article 267(3), where a question concerning interpretation is raised 'in a case pending before a court or tribunal of a Member State, *against whose decisions there is no judicial remedy under national law*, that court or tribunal *shall* bring the matter before the Court' (emphasis added). For all courts other than those within Article 267(3) referral is discretionary. The Treaty therefore created a system whereby most of the time the national courts would have a choice about when to refer questions to the Court. Decisions of national courts which are disputed (including on points of Union law) could be appealed internally (subject to the national law regarding appeals of the particular Member State). Only when a case could go no further within the domestic legal system does the Treaty require a reference.

10.5.2 Article 267(3): The mandatory obligation to refer for courts against whom no appeal lies

The purpose of Article 267(3) must be seen in the light of the function of Article 267 as a whole, which is to prevent a body of national case law not in accordance with the rules of Union law from coming into existence in any Member State (*Hoffmann-La Roche AG v Centrafarm Vertiebsgesellschaft Pharmazeutischer Erzeugnisse mbH* (case 107/76); *Skatterverket v Gourmet Classic Ltd* (case C-458/06). To this end Article 267(3) seeks to ensure that, when matters of Union law arise, there is an obligation to refer to the CJ if the proceedings can go no further in the domestic court system. This purpose should be kept in mind when questions of interpretation of Article 267(3) arise.

The scope of Article 267(3) is not entirely clear. While it obviously applies to courts or tribunals at the apex of the legal system whose decisions are *never* subject to appeal (the 'abstract theory'), such as the Supreme Court in England, or the Conseil d'État in France, it is less clear whether it applies also to courts whose decisions *in the case in question* are not subject to appeal (the 'concrete theory'), such as the Italian magistrates' court (*giudice conciliatore*) in *Costa* (no right of appeal because the sum of money involved was too small). Furthermore, if leave to appeal is required to go to a higher court and this is refused, does this mean the lower court becomes a court 'against whose decisions there is no judicial remedy under national law'? In the UK we see this in appeals from the Court of Appeal where leave to the Supreme Court is refused, or when the High Court refuses leave for judicial review from a tribunal decision. These cases all involve courts not at the apex of the system but whose decision has effectively concluded the domestic proceedings. If a point of Union law remained in dispute, the parties would not have had the benefit of a ruling from the CJ and so their fundamental rights might have been impaired. Furthermore, the interpretation and application of Union law in that Member State might be wrong, thus threatening the uniformity of the Union law system across the Member States.

The judgment of the CJ in *Costa* was seen, albeit *obiter*, to support the wider, 'concrete' theory. In that case, in the context of a reference from the Italian magistrates' court, from which there was no appeal due to the small amount of money involved, the Court said, with reference to the then Article 177(3) EEC (now 267(3) TFEU): 'By the terms of this Article . . . national courts against whose decisions, *as in the present case*, there is no judicial remedy, *must* refer the matter to the Court of Justice' (emphasis added). Taking into account the function of Article 267(3) and particularly its importance for the individual, this would have seemed to be the better view.

The issue was finally resolved by the CJ in favour of the concrete theory in *Lyckeshog* (case C-99/00). The CJ ruled that where there was a right for a party to seek to appeal against the decision under challenge, that was not a final court. It followed that if there was no right to appeal against the decision then that court was a 'final court' regardless of its status in the judicial hierarchy.

In *Lyckeshog* the CJ was also asked whether national courts are 'final' courts for the purposes of Article 267(3) if an appeal against their decision is possible but only with leave to appeal having been granted by a higher court (or the lower court itself). The CJ noted that the function of the obligation on courts against whose decisions there was no judicial remedy to refer questions to the CJ was to prevent a body of national case law coming into being that was inconsistent with the requirements of Union law. The CJ argued that 'the fact that examination of the merits of such appeals is subject to a prior declaration of admissibility by the supreme court does not have the effect of depriving the parties of a judicial remedy' (para 16). In coming to this conclusion, the CJ noted that 'uncertainty as to the interpretation of the law applicable, including [Union] law, may give rise to review, at last instance, by the supreme court' (para 17). In this light, the CJ concluded that, where leave depends on permission from a superior 'final' court, that latter court is obliged to grant the requested leave and make a reference to the CJ when a question of Union law arises. Any other course would frustrate the purpose of Article 267 and amount to a denial of the individual's Union law rights. This approach was confirmed in *Cartesio*. In *Köbler* the CJ held that a failure on the part of a court of last resort to comply with the obligation to refer a question under Article 267(3) might render the Member State of whose judicial system it forms part, liable in damages to an individual who had as a result of a refusal to refer, been deprived of his or her lawful rights under Union law.

10.5.3 Article 267(2): courts that have a discretion whether to refer or not

Courts or tribunals which do not fall within Article 267(3) enjoy, according to the CJ, an unfettered discretion in the matter of referrals. This reflects the importance of the cooperative nature of the relationship between the CJ and national courts. The CJ has sought to respect the unfettered jurisdiction of national courts, where a case falls under Article 267(2), by refraining from being prescriptive about when cases should be referred to it. A court or tribunal at any level is free, 'if it considers that a decision on the question is necessary to enable it to give judgment', to refer to the CJ in any kind of proceedings, including interim proceedings (*Hoffmann-La Roche*), at any stage in the proceedings. In *De Geus en Uitdenbogerd*, the Court held that national courts have jurisdiction to refer whether or not an appeal is pending; the CJ is not even concerned to discover whether the decision of the national judge has acquired the force of *res judicata* (see also Chapter 6). However, following *Pardini* and *Grogan*, if proceedings have been terminated and the Court is aware of this fact, it may refuse jurisdiction on the grounds that its ruling is not necessary to enable the national court to give judgment.

10.5.4 When does a 'question' of Union law arise?

Whether a national court is a final court or merely one that has a discretion to refer cases to the CJ, the national judge must consider if a case raises a 'question' of Union law such that a ruling from the CJ is '*necessary* to enable it to give judgment'. If the case does raise such a question then, if the court is a final court, the judge must, in principle, refer the case to the CJ. The question must raise issues of doubt as to the meaning of the Union law.

Guidelines on these matters have been supplied by the CJ to national courts. It is submitted that as the ultimate arbiter on matters of Union law the CJ must decide whether a 'question' of Union law arises. We can see a tension in relation to this issue. On the one hand the CJ has been keen to encourage references to be made to ensure uniformity of application of Union law. On the other hand, there has been the concern that overloading the CJ with references diminishes the effectiveness of judicial protection for parties because of the delay this produces. The CJ has therefore sought to encourage national courts to deal with Union law points the meaning of which is either clear or can be deduced from previous CJEU judgments.

In *CILFIT Srl v Ministero della Sanità* (case 283/81) the CJ tried to balance the responsibilities of national courts and itself.

CILFIT

This case was a reference from the Italian Supreme Court, the Cassazione, and concerned national courts' mandatory jurisdiction under Article 267(3). On a literal reading of Article 267(2) and (3) it would appear that the question of whether 'a decision on a matter of [Union] law is necessary' only applies to the national courts' discretionary jurisdiction under Article 267(2). Thus in principle the highest national court would have to refer all questions of Union law to the CJ even if not strictly necessary to resolve the case before it. This would have been an absurd result whereby the lower courts had more discretion than the supreme court. However, in *CILFIT* the CJ held that:

> it followed from the relationship between [Article 267 TFEU (2) and (3)] that the courts or tribunals referred to in [Article 267 TFEU (3)] have the same discretion as any other national court or tribunal to ascertain whether a decision on a question of [Union] law is necessary to enable them to give judgment.

Thus both final courts and other courts have the power to consider if the 'question' of Union law that requires resolution through a ruling from the CJ is actually material to deciding the case before them. While it is clearly not necessary for 'final' courts to refer questions of Union law in every case, a lax approach by such courts towards their need to refer, resulting in non-referral, may lead to an incorrect application of Union law and, for the individual concerned, a denial of justice. Since *Köbler*, 'final' courts choosing not to make a reference run the risk of imposing liability on the Member State of whose judicial system they form part, under *Francovich*, should they get the point of Union law significantly wrong (see 9.2.2.2).

10.5.4.1 **Previous rulings**

Where there has been a previous ruling on a point of Union law there will be no need for a national court to refer the same point again to the CJ. *Da Costa en Schaake NV v Nederlandse-Belastingadministratie* (cases 28–30/62) concerned a question of interpretation almost identical to a matter already decided by the Court in *Van Gend en Loos*. Like *CILFIT*, it arose in a case concerning the court's mandatory jurisdiction under Article 267(3). While asserting that Article 267(3) 'unqualifiedly' required national courts to submit to the CJ 'every question of interpretation raised before the court', the Court added that this would not be necessary if the question was materially identical to a question which had already been the subject of a preliminary ruling in a similar case.

Where the matter involves the legality of a *Union measure*, the national court must refer a question to the CJ as it is only that court which can pronounce on the validity of Union measures. This was made clear in *Gaston Schul v Minister van Landbouw* (case C-461/03), a case which questions the validity of Article 4(1)–(2) of Commission Regulation 1423/95 on import rules for products in the sugar sector ([1995] OJ L141/16). The provisions corresponded with those in another regulation (1484/95) which had been declared invalid by the CJ in an earlier decision (*Kloosterbooer Rotterdam BV v Minister van Landbouw Natuurbeheer en Visserij* (case C-317/99)). The Dutch court in *Gaston* therefore asked whether it was still subject to the mandatory obligation to refer the question of validity to the CJ under Article 267(3). The CJ held that questions of *validity* of Union law differed from questions of *interpretation*, and a reference should always be made, even where there is an earlier ruling dealing with corresponding provisions in another measure (para 25). The possible time delay was not a justification for changing the position that questions of invalidity are only for the CJ to decide upon (para 23).

10.5.4.2 *Acte clair*

For some time, it seemed that once a relevant 'question' of Union law had arisen before a final court, so long as the point had not been previously ruled upon by the CJ, the national court must make a reference. This was so even if the point of law was very simple and incapable of more than one interpretation. The CJ was under some pressure from the highest courts within the Member States to allow them some latitude in deciding whether in such circumstances to refer in such cases. The CJ eventually accepted a very limited version of *acte clair* in *CILFIT*. *Acte clair* is a doctrine originating in French administrative law whereby, if the meaning of a provision is clear, no 'question' of interpretation arises. *CILFIT* concerned a question from the Italian Supreme Court concerning its obligation under Article 267(3). The national court asked if Article 267 created an absolute obligation to refer, or was referral conditional on a prior finding of a reasonable interpretative doubt in relation to the question of Union law? The CJ held that there was no need to refer if the matter was: (a) irrelevant; (b) materially identical to a question already the subject of a preliminary ruling; or (c) so obvious as to leave 'no scope for reasonable doubt'. This third criteria may be taken as endorsing a version, albeit a narrow one, of *acte clair*. Of particular importance to its third criterion is the Court's *dictum* that, in deciding whether a matter was free from doubt, account must be taken of the specific characteristics of Union law, its particular difficulties and the risk of divergence in judicial interpretation. The CJ also required the national court to consider each of the different language versions of the Union law measure under consideration. Thus, if *acte clair* is to be invoked by a final court so as not to refer a case to the CJ, the issue of Union law must meet the *CILFIT* criteria which may be difficult to do.

The CJ's caution is probably justified as there is some danger that national courts acting in accordance with their own views without seeking a reference may make errors of interpretation even in relation to matters they consider to be 'obvious'. This was revealed in the Court of Appeal in the case of *R v Henn and Darby* ([1978] 1 WLR 1031). There, Lord Widgery suggested that it was clear from the case law of the CJ that a ban on the import of pornographic books was not a quantitative restriction within Article 34 TFEU. A subsequent referral on this matter by the Supreme Court revealed that it undoubtedly was. Lord Diplock, giving judgment in the Supreme Court ([1981] AC 850), warned English judges not to be too ready to hold that, because the meaning of an English text seemed plain to them, no question of interpretation was involved: the CJ and the English courts have very different styles of interpretation and may ascribe different meanings to the same provision. He did, however, approve a version of *acte clair* consistent with that of the CJ in *Da Costa en Schaake NV* and *CILFIT* in *Garland v British Rail Engineering Ltd* ([1983] 2 AC 751) when he suggested that where there was a 'considerable and consistent line of case law' from the CJ the answer would be 'too obvious and inevitable' to be capable of giving rise to what could properly be called a question within the meaning of Article 267.

In two recent cases the CJ has held that it is the sole responsibility of national courts at last instance to determine 'alone' and 'independently' whether the meaning of any legal provisions is obvious beyond reasonable doubt (*Ferreira da Silva e Brito v Portugal* (case C-160/14); *X v Inspecteur van Rijksbelastingdienst and T. A. and van Dijk v Stattssecretaris van Fianciën* (cases C-72 and 197/14)). In *Ferreira da Silva e Brito,* a case involving the interpretation of the concept of a 'transfer of a business' within the meaning of Directive 2001/23 ([2001] OJ L82/16), the fact that lower courts had given contradictory judgments on the point of EU law in issue did not prevent a court of last instance from refraining from making a reference for a preliminary ruling to the CJ if the interpretation it proposed to give to that provision was so obvious that there was no reasonable doubt as to its correctness. However, in the circumstances of that particular case, the CJ found that the Portuguese Supreme Court was obliged to make a reference given both the conflicting lines of case law in the Portuguese lower courts and the fact that the concept of a 'transfer of a business' 'frequently gives rise to difficulties of interpretation in the various Member States' (para 44). In *X and Van Dijk*, the CJ held that a national court or tribunal of last instance was not obliged to make a reference on the sole ground that a lower national court, in a similar case and involving the same legal issue, had referred a question to the CJ for a preliminary ruling, nor was it obliged to await that ruling before giving judgment.

The doctrine of *acte claire*, depending as it does on a subjective assessment as to what is clear, can all too easily be used as a means of avoiding referral. This appears to have occurred in *Minister of the Interior v Cohn-Bendit* ([1980] 1 CMLR 543).

Cohn-Bendit

In this case, heard by the French Conseil d'État, the supreme administrative court, Cohn-Bendit sought to invoke a directive to challenge a deportation order made by the French authorities. Certain provisions of the Directive had already been declared by the CJ to be directly effective (*Van Duyn*; see Chapter 5). Despite urgings from the Commissaire du Gouvernement, M Genevois, that in such a situation the Conseil d'État must either follow *Van Duyn* and apply the Directive or seek a ruling from the Court under Article 267(3), the Conseil d'État declined to do either. In its opinion, the law was clear. The Directive was not directly effective.

10.5.4.3 The question may not be relevant to the case

The CJ had confirmed in *CILFIT* that there was no obligation to refer questions relating to Union law that were not relevant to the case before the national court. This is in one sense obvious, but there is potential for final national courts to misuse this discretion so as to decline to refer cases that should be referred. A court may avoid its obligations under Article 267(3) by deciding the case before it without considering the possibility of referral (see, eg, *Mees v Belgium* [1988] 3 CMLR 137, Belgian Conseil d'État). In *Wellcome Foundation Ltd v Secretary of State for Social Services* ([1988] 1 WLR 635) the Supreme Court, in considering the factors to be taken into account by a licensing author-ity in issuing a licence to parallel import a trade-mark medicine, thought it 'highly undesirable to embark on considerations of [Union] law which might have necessitated a referral to the Court of Justice under Article [267]'. This suggests the national court did not consider closely enough the rele-vance of Union law to the case in question.

In contrast, the German FCC has emphasised national courts' duty to refer under Article 267(3), according to the *CILFIT* criteria, in the strongest terms. In quashing the German Bundesfinanzhof's decision on the direct effects of directives in *VAT Directives* ([1982] 1 CMLR 527), and in *Kloppenburg v Finanzamt Leer* ([1989] 1 CMLR 873), the FCC held that a court subject to Article 267(3) which deliberately departs from the case law of the CJ and fails to make a reference under that article is acting in breach of Article 101 of the German constitution. The principle of *acte clair* could not operate where there existed a ruling from the CJ to the contrary (*VAT exemption* [1989] 1 CMLR 113). In *Patented Feedingstuffs* ([1989] 2 CMLR 902), the same court declared that it would review an 'arbitrary' refusal by a court subject to Article 267(3) to refer to the CJ. A refusal would be arbitrary:

- where the national court gave no consideration at all to a reference in spite of the accepted relevance of Union law to the judgment and the court's doubt as to the correct answer;
- where the law consciously departs in its judgment from the case law of the CJ on the relevant questions, and nevertheless does not make a reference or a fresh reference;
- where there is not yet a decisive judgment of the CJ on point, or such judgments may not have provided an exhaustive answer to the relevant questions or there is a more than remote possibility of the CJ developing its case law further, and the national court exceeds to an indefensible extent the scope of its necessary judicial discretion, as where there may be contrary views of the relevant question of Union law which should obviously be given preference over the view of the national court.

It is suggested that these principles, applied in good faith, would ensure that a reference to the CJ will be made in the appropriate case. Although a decision of a domestic court rather than of the CJ, these principles should prove useful to the courts from all the Member States.

Even if the CJ has already ruled on a similar question, national courts are not precluded from requesting a further ruling. This point was made in *Da Costa en Schaake NV*. There the Court held, in the context of a reference for interpretation of a question substantially the same as that referred in *Van Gend en Loos*, that the Court should retain a legal right to depart from its previous judg-ments. It may recognise its errors in the light of new facts. In *International Chemical Corporation SpA v Amministrazione delle Finanze dello Stato* (case 66/80), it held that while national courts could assume from a prior declaration of invalidity that a regulation was invalid, they should not be deprived of an opportunity to refer the same issue if they have a 'real interest' in making a further reference.

10.5.4.4 National courts can ignore national rules of precedent in order to refer cases

This discretion to refer is in no way affected by national rules of precedent within the Member State. This important principle was established in the case of *Rheinmühlen-Düsseldorf v Einfuhr- und Vorratsstelle für Getreide und Futtermittel* (case 146/73).

Rheinmühlen-Düsseldorf

In this case, which concerned an attempt by a German cereal exporter to obtain an export rebate under Union law, the German federal tax court (the Bundesfinanzhof), hearing the case on appeal from the Hessian tax court (Hessische Finanzgericht), had quashed the Hessian court's judgment and remitted the case to that court for a decision on certain issues of fact. The Hessian court was not satisfied with the Bundesfinanzhof's ruling since questions of Union law were involved. It sought a ruling from the CJ on the interpretation of the Union law, and also on the question of whether it was permissible for a lower court to refer in this way when its own superior court had already set aside its earlier judgment on appeal. On an appeal by Rheinmühlen-Düsseldorf to the Bundesfinanzhof challenging the Hessian court's right to refer to the CJ, the Bundesfinanzhof itself referred certain questions to the CJ. The principal question, raised in both cases, was whether Article 267 gave national courts an unfettered right to refer or whether that right is subject to national provisions whereby lower courts are bound by the judgments of superior courts.

The Court's reply was in the strongest terms. The object of the preliminary rulings procedure, the Court held, was to ensure that in all circumstances the law was the same in all Member States. No provision of domestic law can take away the power provided by Article 267. The lower court must be free to make a reference if it considers that the superior court's ruling could lead it to give judgment contrary to Union law. It would only be otherwise if the question put by the lower court were substantially the same.

The CJ's view may be compared with that of Wood J in the Employment Appeal Tribunal in *Enderby v Frenchay Health Authority* ([1991] ICR 382). Here he suggested that lower English Courts were bound even in matters of Union law by decisions of their superior courts; thus they should not make references to the CJ but should leave it to the Supreme Court, *a fortiori* when the Supreme Court has decided on a particular issue that British law does not conflict with Union law. Wood J's observations are clearly at odds with Union law. It appears that *Rheinmühlen-Düsseldorf* was not cited before the tribunal. A reference to the CJ was subsequently made in this case by the Court of Appeal ([1992] IRLR 15) resulting in a ruling (case C-127/92) and a decision on an important issue of equal pay for work of equal value contrary to that of Wood J and in the claimant's favour.

10.5.4.5 How should non-final courts exercise their discretion to refer?

When the national court hears a case in which there arises a question of Union law a number of factors will obviously have to be taken into account in deciding whether or not to refer. These are largely questions for domestic courts according to the particular features of the domestic legal system. They have not been subject to detailed scrutiny by the CJ because they are largely outside its jurisdiction.

There has been some interesting discussion in the lower courts of the UK on this question. In an early opinion, Lord Denning in *HP Bulmer* sitting in the Court of Appeal adopted a broad approach which required the national judge to consider a wide range of factors before making a reference. He suggested that a decision would only be 'necessary' if it was 'conclusive' to the judgment. Even then it would not be necessary if:

- the CJ had already given judgment on the question; or
- the matter was reasonably clear and free from doubt.

Although the criteria in both cases are similar, the first and third *CILFIT* criteria are clearly stricter; it would be easier under Lord Denning's guidelines to decide that a decision was not 'necessary'.

If courts within the area of discretionary jurisdiction consider, applying the *CILFIT* criteria, that a decision from the CJ is necessary, how should they exercise their discretion? With regard to other factors, Lord Denning suggested in *HP Bulmer* that time, cost, workload of the CJ and the wishes of the parties should be taken into account by national courts in the exercise of their discretion. In a contrasting view, however, Bingham J in *Commissioners of Customs and Excise v Samex ApS* ([1983] 3 CMLR 194) said that factors such as time and cost need to be treated with care, weighing in the fact that deferring a referral may in the end increase the time and cost to the parties: there may be cases where it is appropriate to refer at an early stage. He also stressed the CJ's 'panoramic' view of the Union law system that a national judge would find it impossible to match. The more difficult and uncertain the issue of Union law, the greater the likelihood of appeal, requiring, in the end, a referral to the CJ under Article 267(3). The workload of the CJ is an increasing problem and no doubt a reason for some modification in recent years of its open-door policy. However, whereas it may justify non-referral in a straightforward case, it should not prevent referral where the point of Union law is difficult or novel. The *CILFIT* criteria should operate to prevent unnecessary referrals.

On the question of timing, the CJ has suggested that the facts of the case should be established and questions of purely national law settled before a reference is made (*Irish Creamery*). This would avoid referrals being made too early, and enable the Court to take cognisance of all the features of fact and law which may be relevant to the issue of Union law on which it is asked to rule. A similar point was made by Lord Denning MR in *HP Bulmer* ('decide the facts first') and approved by the Supreme Court in *Henn and Darby*. However, Lord Diplock did concede in *Henn and Darby* that in an urgent, for example, interim, matter, where important financial interests are concerned, it might be necessary to refer *before* all the facts were found. It is of course also possible that an issue of Union law may so clearly need to be resolved that it would be good case management to refer a question before a full finding of facts since the facts to be proved may depend upon the response to the preliminary ruling. In other cases a clear ruling on a point of law will encourage the parties to settle out of court.

The wishes of the parties also need to be treated with caution. If the point of Union law is relevant (which under *CILFIT* it must be) and difficult or uncertain, clearly *one* of the parties' interests will be better served by a referral. The CJ has held that the question of referral is one for the national court and that a party to the proceedings in the context of which the reference is made cannot challenge a decision to refer, even if that party thinks that the national court's findings of fact are inaccurate (*SAT Fluggesellschaft mbH v European Organization for the Safety of Air Navigation* (case C-364/92)).

10.6 What is the temporal effect of a ruling from the CJ?

There are a number of issues concerning the effect of a preliminary ruling by the CJ. A preliminary ruling is in effect an interpretation of a particular provision or provisions of Union law. Its ramifications can therefore often go well beyond the particular proceedings that led to the reference. Rulings from the CJ can affect legal relations across all the Member States and have wide economic and social consequences. There have therefore been some cases in which the CJ has limited the temporal effects of its rulings so that they are only 'prospective' and do not affect prior legal relations. These cases are exceptional. More narrowly, clearly a ruling from the CJ under Article 267 is binding in the individual case and will govern the legal effects between the parties. Given Member States' obligation under Article 4(3) TEU to 'take all appropriate measures . . . to ensure fulfilment of the obligations arising out of the Treaties or resulting from acts of the institutions of the Union' the ruling should also be generally applied. This does not preclude national courts from seeking a further ruling on the same issue should they have a 'real interest' in making a reference (*Da Costa en Schaake* NV–interpretation; *International Chemical Corporation*–validity).

10.6.1 Rulings involving interpretation are generally retrospective in effect

Preliminary rulings, since they interpret Union law, take effect retroactively (*ex tunc*, ie from the moment of entry into force of the provision subject to the ruling). Exceptionally, the Court itself may decide that the ruling take such effect only from the date of judgment (*ex nunc*) or other point in time (*Association Belge des Consommateurs Test Achats ASBL and Others v Conseil des ministers* (case C-236/09)). In *Defrenne II* the Court was prepared to limit the effect of the then Article 119 (now 157 TFEU) to claims lodged prior to the date of judgment. 'Important considerations of legal certainty', the Court held, 'affecting all the interests involved, both public and private, make it impossible to reopen the question as regards the past'. The Court was clearly swayed by the arguments of the British and Irish governments that a retrospective application of the equal pay principle would have serious economic repercussions on parties (ie employers) who had been led to believe they were acting within the law.

However, in *Ariete SpA* and *Salumi Srl* the Court made it clear that *Defrenne* was to be an exceptional case. As a general rule an interpretation under Article 267 of a rule of Union law 'clarifies and defines where necessary the meaning and scope of that rule as it must be or ought to be understood and applied *from the time of its coming into force*' (emphasis added). A ruling under that article must therefore be applied to legal relationships arising prior to the date of the judgment provided that the conditions for its application by the national court are satisfied.

It is for the CJ *alone* to decide on the temporal restrictions as regards the effects of the interpretation which it gives.

These principles were applied in *Blaizot* and *Barra*.

Blaizot and *Barra*

Both cases involved a claim for reimbursement of the Belgian *minerval*, based on *Gravier* (see Chapter 23). In both cases the claims were in respect of periods prior to the CJ's ruling in *Gravier*. In *Barra* it was not disputed that the course for which the *minerval* had been charged was vocational; but Blaizot's university course in veterinary medicine was, the defendant university argued, not vocational, not being within the scope of the *Gravier* ruling.

Since Barra's case fell squarely within *Gravier* and the Court had imposed no temporal limits on the effect of its judgment in *Gravier* itself, that ruling was held to apply retrospectively in Barra's favour. *Blaizot*, on the other hand, raised new issues. In deciding that university education could, and a course in veterinary science did, constitute vocational training the Court, clearly conscious of the impact of such a ruling on Belgian universities if applied retroactively, decided that 'important considerations of legal certainty' required that the effects of its ruling should be limited on the same lines as *Defrenne*— that is, to future cases and those lodged prior to judgment.

In *Barber* the Court was again persuaded by 'overriding considerations of legal certainty' to limit the effects of its ruling that employers' contracted-out pension schemes fell within the then Article 119 EEC (now 157 TFEU). Unfortunately the precise scope of the non-retroactivity principle that 'Article 119 [now 157] may not be relied upon in order to *claim entitlement* to a pension with effect prior to that of this judgment (except in the case of workers . . . who have initiated proceedings before this date or raised an equivalent claim under the applicable national law)' was disputed as being unclear. A protocol to the Maastricht Treaty and further cases to spell out the precise temporal scope of the *Barber* ruling (see Chapter 27) were necessary. Despite its commitment to the principle of legal certainty, the Court has chosen not to limit the effect of its rulings in a number of cases in which it has introduced new and unexpected principles with significant consequences for Member States and even (in the case of Treaty articles) for individuals. It did not limit the effects of its judgment in *Francovich* despite Advocate-General Mischo's warnings as to the 'extremely serious' financial consequences for Member States if the judgment were not so limited: nor did it do so when it laid down a principle of full compensation for breach of a directly effective directive in *Marshall II*. Where a ruling is likely to result in serious consequences, whether for states or 'public' or private bodies, for example employers, Member States would be advised to take advantage of their opportunity to intervene in Article 267 proceedings as they are entitled to do, to argue against retroactivity, as they did successfully in *Defrenne* and *Barber*.

The effects of the CJ's strict approach to retroactivity may be mitigated by its more recent approach to Member States' procedural rules. In a number of cases (*IN.CO.GE* '90 and *Edis*), it has held that the principle of retroactivity should not prevent the application of detailed procedural rules (in these cases relating to limitation of actions) governing legal proceedings under national law, provided that these national rules do not make it 'impossible or excessively difficult' for individuals to exercise their Union rights (see further Chapter 8).

The impact of an interpretation on previous rulings by domestic administrative authorities which conflict with the CJ's ruling was considered in *Kühne & Heitz NV v Productschap voor Pluimvee en Eieren* (case C-453/00).

Kühne & Heitz

The case involved a claim for reimbursement of export refunds made by a Dutch administrative authority against Kühne. The latter's objection had been rejected by a court and the claim had therefore become a final decision by the administrative authority. The CJ then delivered a ruling (*Voogd Vleesimport en-export* (case C-151/93)) which rendered the previous Dutch decision incorrect. Kühne therefore requested a reopening of the administrative procedure.

The CJ held that there was an obligation on administrative authorities to comply with an interpretation given by the Court in respect of all legal relationships, because the effect of a ruling is to clarify and define the meaning of a European rule 'as it ought to have been understood and applied from the time of its coming into force' (para 21). This was subject to the principle of legal certainty, requiring finality of administrative decisions once a reasonable time limit for legal remedies had expired or those remedies had been exhausted (para 24); in such circumstances, there was no obligation to reopen previous decisions which had become final. However, on the facts of the case, the Dutch authority could reopen its decision, and the CJ held that in such a situation, where a decision had become final and was based on a misinterpretation of Union law adopted without a preliminary ruling, and the matter had been raised without delay after the CJ's interpretation, the administrative authority should review its decision.

10.6.2 Rulings as to the validity of Union measures: more flexible temporal effects

The cases considered above relate to rulings on interpretation. Where matters of validity of Union measures are concerned, the Court's approach is more flexible. This is logical because where a prima facie valid Union measure has been in place for some time, the finding that it is invalid may entail serious consequences for those who relied upon it. On grounds of legal certainty there are good arguments to decide in each case what effect the finding of invalidity should have. The CJ has adopted the same approach to the effects of a ruling of invalidity to those of a successful annulment action, as a result of which the illegal act is declared void. However, arguing from Article 264, which enables the Court, in a successful annulment action, to limit the effects of a regulation which it has declared void (see Chapter 12), the Court has limited the effects of a finding of invalidity in a number of cases, sometimes holding the ruling to be purely prospective (ie, for the future only, *excluding* the present case, eg, *Roquette Frères v France* (case 145/79); policy doubted in *Roquette Frères SA v Hauptzollamt Geldern* (case C-228/92), see Chapter 12). The Court has not so far insisted that the effect of a ruling of invalidity can only be limited in the case in which the ruling itself is given. The Court is more likely to be prepared to limit the effects of a ruling on validity than one on interpretation. Where matters of validity are concerned parties will have relied legitimately on the provision in question. A retrospective application of a ruling of invalidity may produce serious economic repercussions: thus it may not be desirable to reopen matters as regards the past. On the other hand too free a use of prospective rulings in matters of interpretation would seriously threaten the objectivity of the law, its application to all persons and all situations. Moreover, as the Court no doubt appreciates, a knowledge on the part of Member States and individuals that the law as interpreted may not be applied retrospectively could foster a dangerous spirit of non-compliance.

10.7 The increasing workload of the CJ: the need for reform

The current system governing preliminary rulings is under stress as, despite the *acte clair* doctrine, the number of references made to the CJ remains high.

There are many proposals to reform the current system to ensure that the CJ can better provide effective judicial protection by removing the delays in the reference system. The difficulty remains one of how to reduce the number of references without damaging the uniform interpretation of EU law. The easy access of national courts to the CJ has been the key to the relationship between domestic and EU legal systems.

The CJ itself has introduced new rules into its Rules of Procedures and Statute that allow for expedited procedures to be used in some cases which are simple or raise no new issues. Thus the CJ has taken steps to devote fewer resources to cases that do not merit them because they are legally straightforward. This change emphasises the importance of the CJ in the Union's court system, suggesting a more hierarchical structure to the system than that found in the early days. Article 104(3) allows the CJ to dispense with oral hearings and proceed simply by issuing a 'reasoned order' where the case referred raises identical issues upon which the CJ has already ruled or is free from reasonable doubt. Thus if a national court refers a case that meets the *CILFIT* criteria, the CJ can deal swiftly with the matter. The Statute was also amended by the Nice Treaty so that where no new point of law arises, the CJ can dispense with the requirement for an advocate-general's opinion. These procedural steps have helped to focus the CJ's resources upon cases that really need them because they raise new issues of EU law but they have preserved the crucial right of access that national courts have to refer any question that they wish to.

At the same time the CJ is aware that the volume of references for preliminary rulings, and the resultant delay in dispensing with cases before it, may prejudice effective judicial protection. Thus Article 104a of the Rules of Procedure provides for an accelerated procedure where the case involves a matter of 'exceptional urgency'. This provision is particularly important in cases involving persons in detention, those facing deportation or children. The Court can fix a hearing date within weeks in these cases.

10.8 Conclusions

The success of the preliminary rulings procedure depends on a fruitful collaboration between the CJ and the courts of Member States. Generally speaking this collaboration has been successful. The CJ has rarely refused its jurisdiction or attempted to interfere with national courts' discretion in matters of referral and application of Union law. National courts have generally been ready to refer; cases in which they have unreasonably refused to do so are rare. Equally rare are the cases in which the CJ has exceeded the bounds of its jurisdiction without justification. However, this very separation of powers, the principal strength of Article 267, is responsible for some of its weaknesses. The decision whether to refer and what to refer rests entirely with the national judge. No matter how important referral may be to the individual concerned, he cannot compel referral; he can only seek to persuade. And although the CJ will extract the essential matters of Union law from the questions referred, it can only give judgment in the context of the questions referred (see *Hessische Knappschaft v Maison Singer et Fils* (case 44/65)). Thus, it is essential for national courts to ask the right questions. As the relevance of the questions can only be assessed in the light of the factual and legal circumstances of the case in hand, these details must also be supplied.

As the body of case law from the CJ has developed and national courts have acquired greater confidence and expertise in applying Union law and ascertaining its relevance to the case before them, there should be less need to resort to Article 267. The initial issue, of whether a decision on a 'question' of Union law arises during the proceedings, has become crucial. As we have seen, *CILFIT* has supplied guidelines to enable national courts to answer this question. Where a lower court is in doubt as to whether a referral is necessary the matter may be left to be decided on appeal. On the other hand, where a final court has the slightest doubt as to whether a decision is necessary, it should always refer—bearing in mind the purpose of Article 267(3) and its particular importance for the individual litigant. The danger that final courts will fail to refer seems to have been one of the factors that influenced the CJ in its ruling in *Köbler* which allows individuals to sue for damages where a reference was not made when it should have been. This case, along with others like *CILFIT* and *Foglia* is illustrative of the trend that we have noted whereby the CJ has been positioning itself not as an equal partner in a horizontally structured relationship, but as a superior court. Some might even say it sees itself as the supreme court for the Union. In so doing, it has sought to put itself firmly in control of the development of European law and not simply to act as the servant of the national courts.

Further reading

Alexander, W, 'The temporal effects of preliminary rulings' (1988) 8 YEL 11.

Anagnostaras, G, 'Preliminary problems and jurisdiction uncertainties: The admissibility of questions referred by bodies performing quasi-judicial functions' (2005) 30 EL Rev 878.

Barnard, C and Sharpston, E, 'The changing face of Article 177 references' (1997) 34 CML Rev 1113.

Bebr, G, 'Arbitration tribunals and Article 177' (1985) 22 CML Rev 498.

Bebr, G, 'The reinforcement of the constitutional review of Community acts under Article 177 EEC' (1988) 25 CML Rev 684.

Broberg, M and Fenger, N, *Preliminary References to the European Court of Justice*, 2nd edn (Oxford University Press, 2014).

Broberg, M, 'National Courts of Last Instance Failing to make a Preliminary Reference The (Possible) Consequences flowing Therefrom' (2016) 22 EPL 243.

de la Mare, T and Donnelly, C, 'Preliminary Rulings and EU Legal Integration: Evolution and Stasis' in P Craig and G de Búrca (eds), *The Evolution of EU Law*, 2nd edn (Oxford University Press, 2011).

Editorial, '*Quis custodiet* the European Court of Justice?' (1993) 30 CML Rev 905.

Fenger, N and Broberg, M, 'Finding light in the darkness: On the actual application of the *acte claire* doctrine' (2011) 30 YEL 180.

Komarek, J, 'In the courts we trust? On the need for hierarchy and differentiation in the preliminary ruling procedure' (2007) 32 EL Rev 467.

Kornezov, A, 'The new format of the acte claire doctrine and its consequences' (2016) 53 CML Rev 1317.

Lenaerts, K, 'The Rule of Law and the Coherence of the Judicial System of the European Union' (2007) 44 CML Rev 1625.

O'Keeffe, D, 'Appeals against an order to refer under Article 177 of the EEC Treaty' (1984) 9 EL Rev 87.

Rasmussen, H, 'The European Court's *acte clair* strategy in *CILFIT*' (1984) 9 CML Rev 242.

Rasmussen, H, 'Between self-restraint and activism: A judicial policy for the European Court' (1988) 13 EL Rev 28.

Tridimas, T, 'Knocking on heaven's door: "Fragmentation, efficiency and defiance in the Preliminary Ruling Procedure"' (2002) 40 CML Rev 9.

Tridimas, T, 'Constitutional review of Member State action: The virtues and vices of an incomplete jurisdiction' (2011) 9 Int J Const L 737.

Enforcement actions

11.1 Introduction

We have already seen that it is vital for the success of the Union that Member States comply with their obligations under the Treaties. Member States are subject to the 'principle of sincere co-operation' whereby the Union and the Member States 'shall in full mutual respect assist each other in carrying out the tasks which flow from the Treaties' (Article 4(3) TEU). Member States should ensure that they implement Union legislation by the due date, notify the Commission, where required, of the implementation of such legislation in their national legal orders and comply with decisions made by the Commission (eg, in the field of state aid) and judgments of the CJEU made under Article 267 TFEU. There is a danger that this obligation would be ineffective were there no mechanism by which Member States that infringe Union law could be pursued. Indeed, the Commission would find it much more difficult to fulfil one of its main objectives, which is to ensure compliance with Treaty obligations (Article 17(1) TEU), if it did not have strong tools to support it in this task. The key provision in this context is Article 258 TFEU. Originally infringement proceedings resulted in a declaration by the CJ of a failure on the part of a Member State to fulfil its obligations under Union law. Article 260 TFEU now provides for the imposition of financial penalties in two sets of circumstances:

(1) Where a Member State has not complied with judgment of the CJEU following infringement proceedings (Article 260(2) TFEU);

(2) Where a Member State has failed to notify the Commission of measures transposing a directive into national law (Article 260(3) TFEU).

The Commission has issued a communication on the implementation of Article 260(3) (SEC 2010 1371 Final).

This is not to say that Union law cannot be enforced by individuals. They have the right, albeit limited, to bring proceedings under Articles 263 and 265 TFEU (see Chapters 7 and 13) for annulment of acts of the Union institutions, bodies, offices, agencies and the European Central Bank, and to bring proceedings against such entities for failure to act when required to do so under the Treaties. Moreover, and importantly, individuals can bring proceedings before national courts and tribunals to enforce their Union law rights. Such proceedings may result in a reference for a preliminary ruling to the CJ under Article 267 TFEU (see Chapter 10).

11.2 Outline of enforcement mechanism

The principal mechanism provided by the Treaties to pursue infringements of Union law by Member States is the direct action before the CJ under Article 258 TFEU, which provides:

> If the Commission considers that a Member State has failed to fulfil an obligation under the Treaties, it shall deliver a reasoned opinion on the matter after giving the State concerned the opportunity to submit its observations.
>
> If the state concerned does not comply with the opinion within the period laid down by the Commission the latter may bring the matter before the Court of Justice of the European Union.

A second procedure, in similar terms, provides for action by a Member State under Article 259 TFEU against another Member State for failure to fulfil its obligations under the Treaties.

Also, the Commission is empowered to bring a Member State directly before the CJ under Article 108 TFEU (infringement of Union rules on state-aid provision (see Chapter 30), Article 114 TFEU (improper use of derogation powers provided by Article 114) and Article 248 TFEU (measures taken by Member States to protect essential security interests or to prevent serious internal disturbances, see Chapter 20).

11.2.1 Substantive areas covered by Article 258

The Commission's power under Article 258 applies to the 'Treaties'. This may include breaches of the Union's international agreements (*Commission v Germany* (case C-61/94)). A transitional period was created, by Protocol (No 36) to the Treaty of Lisbon, in respect of acts adopted under the old third pillar arrangements. For a period of five years after the entry into force of the Treaty of Lisbon, the Commission could not bring proceedings under Article 258 in respect of acts the field of police and judicial cooperation adopted under the third pillar arrangements, except where those acts were amended after the entry into force of the Treaty of Lisbon.

11.2.2 Development of enforcement procedure

Article 258 was not designed as a punitive measure. Until the passing of the Maastricht Treaty (1992) no sanction was provided against Member States found by the CJ to be in breach of their obligations; they were merely required 'to take the necessary measures to comply with the judgment of the Court' (Article 260 TFEU). Although no time limit was prescribed for a Member State's compliance with judgments issued against it, the Court had held (*Commission v Italy* (case 69/86)) that implementation of a judgment must be undertaken immediately and must be completed within the shortest possible time. Where a state failed to comply with these obligations the Commission could only seek to enforce the judgment by further proceedings before the CJEU. While few such actions were taken in the early days of the Union, their number increased alarmingly in the course of the 1980s. As a result, Article 228 EC (the then relevant provision) was amended by the Maastricht Treaty to allow the Commission to propose to the Court the imposition of fines and penalties on Member States which had failed to comply with a judgment against them in what is now Article 258 TFEU proceedings.

11.3 Purpose of enforcement actions

The purpose of Article 258 TFEU is threefold. First, and primarily, it seeks to *ensure compliance* by Member States with their Union obligations. Secondly, it provides a valuable non-contentious *procedure for the resolution of disputes* between the Commission and Member States over matters of Union law: at least one-third of all Article 258 TFEU proceedings are settled at the preliminary informal stage. Finally, where cases do reach the CJ they serve not only to bring particular breaches of Union law to light, but also to *clarify* the law for the benefit of all Member States.

It is no doubt on account of the latter function that the Court has held that even if a state has complied with its obligations prior to the hearing before the Court, the Commission is entitled to judgment; it is not necessary for the Commission to show the existence of a 'legal interest' (*Commission v Italy (ban on pork imports)* (case 7/61)). It is in the general interest of the Union to obtain a declaration of any failure to fulfil obligations under the Treaties in order to clarify the law and thereby the extent of the obligations of the Member States, because this may assist other Member States in ensuring that they comply with Union law (*Commission v France (conservation and management of fisheries)* (case C-333/99) para 23).

11.4 Liability of Member States

11.4.1 **Member States as defendants**

Member States are responsible for compliance with the Treaties by any agency of that state, executive, legislative or judicial. The responsibility of the state is engaged 'whatever the organ of the state whose action or inaction constitutes a failure, even if it concerns an institution which is constitutionally independent' (*Commission v Belgium* (case 77/69)). A Member State is responsible for violations of the Treaties by its autonomous regions (*Commission v Germany* (case C-383/00)).

The Commission, on the basis of the *Lyckeskog* case regarding the obligation on the courts of final resort of Member States to refer questions for preliminary rulings to the CJ (discussed in Chapter 10) and the fact that the Swedish Supreme Court referred very few questions, sent a reasoned Opinion to Sweden (see Bernitz in the further reading section at the end of this chapter). In *Köbler* (see Chapter 9) the CJ found that the state was liable for failure on the part of the judiciary to ensure compliance with Union law.

11.4.2 **Meaning of 'failure'**

A state's 'failure' may be in respect of any binding obligation arising from Union law. This would cover obligations arising from the Treaties and the general principles of Union law from international agreements entered into by the Union and third countries where the obligation lies within the sphere of Union competence; from Union regulations, directives and decisions 'failure' can include any wrongful act or omission, ranging from a failure to notify an implementation measure, to partial implementation, to faulty implementation, to non-implementation of Union law, or simple maintaining in force national laws or practices incompatible with EU law. The Commission has brought actions in the case of relatively minor breaches of obligations when this seems to be part of a consistent practice and will also bring actions where the breach is caused by a general administrative practice. In *Commission v Ireland (waste management)* (case C-494/01), the CJ accepted that separate individual breaches could together constitute a general and persistent breach, though the Commission will each time have to prove its case on the facts (cf *Commission v Germany (expulsion on criminal conviction)* (case C-441/02)).

As the case of *Commission v France (angry farmers)* (case C-265/95) also makes clear, the failure to fulfil an obligation may also arise in circumstances where the state has failed to take action to prevent other bodies from breaching EU law. In this case, the French authorities' failure to take action in the face of blockades of imported products was found, following an Article 258 action by the Commission, to be a breach of Article 34 TFEU in conjunction with Article 4(3) TEU (see further Chapter 18, and discussion at 11.6.2). Thus failure can include the Member States' positive obligations too.

11.5 Procedure

The Commission becomes aware of Member States' failures to comply with its obligations under Union law in a variety of ways: from its own enquiries; from (increasingly) complaints from the public; from complaints from interested groups (consumer groups, non-governmental organisations (NGOs)); or from other institutions or bodies such as the European Parliament or the Ombudsman.

The sensitive nature of an action under Article 258 TFEU is reflected in its procedure. It follows a number of stages. The initial stages, both formal and informal, between the Commission and the Member State, are designed to achieve an amicable solution. If this fails it may become necessary for the Commission to commence judicial proceedings before the CJ. The procedure excludes the involvement of third parties, even if they are affected by Member States' non-compliance or have brought the matter to the attention of the Commission. To maintain the involvement of third parties in the infringement process, the Commission issued a Communication on Relations with Complainants (COM(2002) 141) setting out how it will conduct its relationship with complainants. That said, it is important to remember that a complainant does not have a right to require that the Commission should bring an action against a Member State; this decision lies within the Commission's broad discretion. The Commission has developed a number of IT tools to assist in the management of infringement proceedings. After registration and assessment the Commission decides how to handle a complaint. It can either start infringement proceedings or proceed more informally through the EU Pilot scheme, which is designed to resolve compliance issues without resort to infringement proceedings. EU Pilot is an online database which shares information on the details of a particular case with the relevant parties. The Commission sends a query to the government of the Member State which allegedly has not complied with its EU law obligations. A response is required within 10 weeks. The Commission then has a further 10 weeks to consider the Member State's position. If it considers that the response of the Member State is unsatisfactory, it may start infringement proceedings. The average time taken by each Member State in 2015 to respond to a query was 70 days. In 2015, 75 per cent of complaints were resolved by the EU Pilot scheme (EU Single Market Scoreboard Edition 07/2016).

The settlement of complaints on a national level has been assisted by SOLVIT, a service provided by national administrations. Each Member State has a SOLVIT centre which helps citizens who encounter difficulties in other Member States where public authorities do not correctly apply EU legislation. The SOLVIT centre in the Member State of residence of the citizen (the 'home Member State') sends the citizen's complaint to the SOLVIT centre in the Member State whose authorities are allegedly at fault in their application of EU law (the 'host Member State') which will follow up with the relevant public authority. On average the home Member State responds to the complainant within seven days. SOLVIT acts as a filter enabling the speedy resolution of complaints at the most appropriate level thus leaving more complex issues to be resolved by the European Commission.

11.5.1 **Informal proceedings**

The Commission begins proceedings informally with a notification to the state concerned of its alleged failure, to which the Member State is required to respond. Many cases are resolved at this stage. Infringements sometimes occur inadvertently, often because it is not clear just what is required of a Member State. In other cases the Commission may have misunderstood the position of the Member State or the state of its national law. The Commission has a broad discretion in terms of the cases it chooses to bring, and even when to conclude them. The CJ will not concern itself with the Commission's motives in bringing proceedings nor what its objectives might be in doing do (*Commission v United Kingdom* (case 416/85)). Where cases are not resolved at this stage the Commission starts formal proceedings.

11.5.2 **Formal proceedings: first stage**

11.5.2.1 **Formal notice**

The Commission opens proceedings by letters of formal notice, setting out why it believes that the Member State in question has not fulfilled its obligations and inviting the Member State to submit its observations. So that the Member State has a full opportunity to put its case, the Commission must first inform the state of its grounds of complaint. The complaint need not at this stage be fully reasoned, but the state must be informed of *all* the charges which may be raised in an action before the Court.

> ### *Payment of Export Rebates*
>
> In *Commission v Italy (payment of export rebates)* (case 31/69) the Commission alleged that Italy was in breach of its Union law obligations in failing to pay certain export rebates to its farmers, required under EU regulations; in opening the proceedings the Commission charged Italy with breaches up to 1967, but failed to mention a number of breaches committed after that date. When the matter came before the Court, the Court refused to consider the later breaches. The Court said that the Member States must be given an adequate and realistic opportunity to make observations on the alleged breach of Treaty obligations.

In deciding whether a state has had such an opportunity the Court may take into account communications made by the Commission during the informal stage.

The Commission must send a letter of formal notice which is identified as relating to Article 258 proceedings. It seems that a formal letter sent under a different provision of EU law will not suffice.

> ### *Rubber Materials*
>
> In *Commission v France (rubber materials)* (case C-230/99), France had notified the Commission under Directive 83/189 (see 16.3.5) of a draft order concerning rubber materials. The Commission felt that, if implemented, the order would affect the free movement of goods, and delivered a detailed opinion under the Directive, setting out its objections to the proposed French order. France rejected the Commission's opinion and adopted the order. The Commission subsequently sent a reasoned opinion pursuant to Article 258 (see 11.5.2.2). The Court ruled that the enforcement action was inadmissible because the Commission had failed to follow the correct procedure by not sending a formal notice under Article 258 before submitting its reasoned opinion. Moreover, a formal notice must allege a prior failure by the Member State to whom it is addressed to comply with Union law, which could not be the case here

as the opinion sent under Directive 83/189 related to a draft measure. The CJ took the view that it would violate the principle of legal certainty should the function of the opinion change, that is, from notification under Directive 83/189 to a letter of formal notice under Article 258, depending on whether the Member State amended its proposed legislation in accordance with the opinion.

11.5.2.2 Reasoned opinion

Following the submission of the state's observations to the Commission, assuming that the case is not settled at this stage, the Commission issues a 'reasoned opinion'. The reasoned opinion will record the infringement and require the state to take action to end it, normally within a specified time limit. Although it cannot introduce issues not mentioned in the formal notice, this does not mean that the reasoned opinion and the formal notice have to be exactly the same. In particular, the Commission may limit the scope of the enquiry (*Commission v Italy* (case C-279/94)). Further, although the opinion must be 'reasoned' it need not set out the Commission's case in full. In the *ban on pork imports* case the Court held, in response to the Italian government's claim that the Commission's reasoned opinion was inadequate, that the reasoned opinion need only contain a coherent statement of the reasons which had convinced the Commission that the Italian government had failed to fulfil its obligations. The only purpose of the reasoned opinion was to specify the point of view of the Commission in order to inform the government concerned.

11.5.2.3 Challenging a reasoned opinion

In *Commission v Germany* (case C-191/95) Germany challenged the admissibility of Article 258 proceedings on a number of grounds. The first of these related to the Commission's decision to issue the reasoned opinion in breach of the principle of collegiality. Germany argued that the Commissioners themselves at the time did not have all the facts to enable them to make such a decision; furthermore they had not seen the draft reasoned opinion. The CJ held that the decision to issue a reasoned opinion could not be described as a measure of administration or management and could not be delegated by the Commissioners themselves to their officers. Nonetheless, this does not mean that the Commissioners have to agree the wording of the reasoned opinion; it is sufficient if they have the information on which the decision to send a reasoned opinion is based.

The CJ has held (*Lütticke* (case 48/65)) that the reasoned opinion is merely a step in the proceedings; it is not a binding act capable of annulment under Article 263 TFEU (see Chapter 12). While the defendant state may choose to impugn the Commission's opinion in proceedings under Article 258 before the Court, where the Member State complies with the opinion, a third party, possibly adversely affected by the Commission's opinion, has no equivalent right. However, in *Amministrazione della Finanze dello Stato v Essevi SpA* (cases 142 and 143/80) the Court held that the Commission has no power in Article 258 TFEU proceedings to determine conclusively the rights and duties of a Member State. These may only be determined, and their conduct appraised, by a judgment of the Court. The Commission may not, in the opinion which it is obliged to deliver under Article 258, exempt a Member State from compliance with its obligations under the Treaty or prevent individuals from relying, in legal proceedings, on the rights conferred on them by the Treaty to contest any legislative or administrative measure of a Member State which may be incompatible with Union law. Thus, a third party, dissatisfied with the Commission's opinion, could raise the issue of the legality of the Member State's action indirectly before his national court and seek a referral on the relevant questions of interpretation to the CJ under Article 267 TFEU. This was done in *Essevi SpA* in a domestic action for the recovery of taxes levied allegedly in breach of Article 110 TFEU.

The same principle would apply where the Commission has decided in its discretion not to institute or pursue Article 258 TFEU proceedings.

Lütticke (case 48/65)

Alfons Lütticke GmbH had complained to the Commission that its own (German) government was acting in breach of EU law by introducing a levy on imported powdered milk. As an importer of powdered milk, the levy affected it adversely. It asked the Commission to take action under Article 258 against Germany. The Commission refused. Germany had since withdrawn the levy and the Commission decided in its discretion not to take action. It was a political compromise. Lütticke, on the other hand, wished to establish the infringement in order to recover for losses suffered while the German law was in force. Since Article 258 gave the Commission discretion in the matter, there was no way in which its refusal to bring proceedings could be challenged either under Article 263 TFEU (annulment action) or Article 265 TFEU (failure to act) (see Chapters 12 and 13). However, in a parallel action before its national courts in *Alfons Lütticke GmbH v Hauptzollamt Saarlouis* (case 57/65), it succeeded in obtaining a ruling under Article 267 from the CJ on the direct effects of Article 110 TFEU, the article which it alleged the German government had breached. Since the article was found directly effective, it could be applied in the company's favour.

11.5.2.4 **Time limits**

While there are no time limits in respect of the stages leading up to the reasoned opinion, thereby giving both parties time for negotiation, the Commission will normally impose in its reasoned opinion a time limit for compliance. A Member State will not be deemed in breach of its obligations until that time limit has expired. Where the Commission does not impose a time limit the Court has held that a reasonable time must be allowed. A Member State cannot be relieved of its obligations merely because no time limit has been imposed (*Commission v Italy (premiums for reducing dairy production)* (case 39/72)). The Commission has complete discretion in the matter of time limits, subject to the possibility of review by the Court. The Court may dismiss an action under Article 258 on the grounds of inadequate time limit. An action by the Commission against Belgium for its failure adequately to implement *Gravier* was dismissed on the grounds that the compliance period of 15 days prescribed by the Commission in its reasoned opinion did not give Belgium sufficient time to respond to its complaints, either before or after the issuing of its reasoned opinion (*Commission v Belgium (university fees)* (case 293/85)). On the other hand, in *Commission v Belgium* (case 85/85) a compliance period of 15 days was held to be reasonable in the light of the extensive information provided by the Commission at the informal stage.

11.5.3 **Formal proceedings: second stage**

If a Member State fails to comply with the Commission's reasoned opinion within the specified time limit, proceedings move to the final, judicial stage before the Court. The Court will examine the situation as it prevailed when the time limit set in the reasoned opinion expired, and will not take account of any subsequent changes (*Commission v France* (case C-147/00)). However, the action taken before the Court must be based on the same grounds as stated in the reasoned opinion and may not introduce new grounds (*Commission v Italy (customs agents)* (case C-35/96) and *Commission v Italy (trade fairs, markets and exhibitions)* (case C-439/99)). It is possible to limit the subject matter of the proceedings (*Commission v Austria (law prohibiting employment of women in specific posts)* (case C-203/03)), or to rephrase the grounds for complaint as long as this does not change its substance (*Commission v UK (sixth VAT Directive)* (case C-305/03)). Moreover, if the Member State concerned amends its legislation in order to comply with EU law, but does so incompletely, the Commission may withdraw its action in part but continue it with regard to the domestic provisions that are not in compliance (*Commission v France (product liability)* (case C-177/04)).

Again, the initiative rests with the Commission, which '*may* bring the matter before the Court of Justice' (Article 258 TFEU). No time limits are imposed on the Commission in commencing the second stage; however, this position seems to be qualified by a requirement that the length of the pre-litigation procedure must not have adversely affected the rights of defence of the Member State concerned (*conservation and management of fisheries* case), para 25; *Commission v Netherlands (reduced rate of levy on manioc)* (case 96/89)).

In the reasoned opinion, the Commission is obliged to set out the subject matter of the dispute, the submissions and a brief statement of the grounds on which the application is based. With regard to the latter, it is not enough simply to refer to all the reasons set out in the letter of formal notice and the reasoned opinion (*Commission v Germany (labelling of dangerous substances)* (case C-43/90)).

Reasoned opinions and indeed other communications relating to proceedings under Article 258, such as letters of formal notice, are confidential (*WWF*; *Petrie v Commission* (case T-191/99)).

Proceedings before the CJ are by way of a full hearing of all the facts and issues. Interested Member States (but not individuals: *Commission v Italy (import of foreign motor vehicles)* (case 154/85R)) are entitled to intervene in the proceedings. The Commission is entitled to request, and the Court to order, interim measures (eg, *merchant shipping rules*; *Dundalk water scheme*). Applications for interim relief may, however, only be made 'by a party to the case before the Court' and where it 'relates to' that case.

11.6 **Burden of proof**

The Commission bears the burden of proof in Article 258 proceedings (*Commission v United Kingdom* (case C-434/01)). It must set out the legal basis of its case against the defendant Member State, and details of the facts and circumstances which it believes are indicative of that Member States' alleged failure to comply with its obligations under the Treaties.

11.7 **Common defences**

11.7.1 **Reciprocity**

The defence of *reciprocity*, an accepted principle of international law, even entrenched in some Member States' constitutions (eg, France, Article 55), whereby in the event of a breach of his obligations by one party the other party is likewise relieved of his, was rejected by the Court in *Commission v Luxembourg and Belgium (import of powdered milk products)* (cases 90 and 91/63). Here the governments argued that their alleged breach of Article 30 TFEU would have been legal but for the Commission's failure to introduce certain measures which they were authorised to enact. This argument, based on reciprocity, the Court held, was not applicable in the context of Union law. The Union was a new legal order; it was not limited to creating reciprocal obligations. Union law governed not only the powers, rights and obligations of Member States, but also the *procedures* necessary for finding and sanctioning all violations that might occur.

The defence of reciprocity was also rejected in the context of a failure by another Member State to comply with a similar obligation; it made no difference that Article 258 TFEU proceedings had not been instituted against that state in respect of a similar breach (*Commission v France (restrictions on imports of lamb)* (case 232/78); *Steinike und Weinlig v Bundesamt für Ernährung und Forstwirtschaf* (case 78/76)).

11.7.2 **Necessity and *force majeure***

Similar reasoning to that advanced in the *import of powdered milk products* case led to the rejection of a defence of *necessity* in the *ban on pork imports* case. The Treaty provided for procedures to be followed in cases of emergency. Their existence precluded unilateral action on the part of Member States.

A defence based on *force majeure* was rejected in *Commission v Italy (transport statistics)* (case 101/84). Here Italy was charged with non-implementation of a Union directive; the reason for its non-implementation was that the data-processing centre involved in the implementation of the directive had been bombed. The Court held that while this might amount to *force majeure*, which could provide an excuse for non-implementation, a delay of four-and-a-half years, as in this case, was inexcusable. As the Court said, 'time will erode the validity of the excuse'.

The concept of *force majeure* was considered in the case of *McNicholl v Ministry of Agriculture* (case 296/86), not in Article 258 TFEU proceedings, but in order to challenge via the preliminary rulings procedure the forfeiture of a deposit for failing to comply with an export undertaking as required by Union law. The Court held that:

> whilst the concept of *force majeure* does not presuppose an absolute impossibility of performance, it nevertheless requires that non-performance of the act in question be due to circumstances beyond the control of persons pleading *force majeure*, that the circumstances be abnormal and unforeseeable and that the consequences could not have been avoided through the exercise of all due care.

This principle should be equally applicable in Article 258 proceedings. Where it is clear that the fulfilment of a Union obligation will be impossible, a Member State should alert the Commission at the earliest opportunity in order to ascertain whether a compromise arrangement can be made (*Commission v Italy (non-implementation of state aid decision)* (case C-349/93)).

The CJ faced a situation of civil disorder, by French farmers blocking imports of agricultural produce, contrary to Article 34 TFEU, in the *angry farmers* case. Here, despite complaints by the Commission, the French authorities had failed to take any significant action to prevent the demonstrations, arguing that more determined action might lead to more serious breaches of public order or even to social conflict. The CJ refused to accept these arguments:

> Apprehension of internal difficulties could not justify a failure by a Member State to apply [Union] law correctly . . . It was for a Member State to guarantee the full scope and effect of that law, to ensure its proper implementation, unless the state could show that action by it could have consequences for public order with which it could not cope.

The government had failed to adduce any evidence of the latter. Although a serious threat to public order might justify non-intervention by the police, that argument could only be adduced with regard to a specific incident, and not, as in the case in question, in a general way, covering all the incidents cited.

11.7.3 **Constitutional difficulties**

Another defence, frequently raised and consistently rejected by the Court, is based on *constitutional, institutional or administrative difficulties* within a Member State. As the Court held in *Commission v Italy (admission to the occupation of road haulage)* (case 28/81), a Member State cannot plead the provisions, practices or circumstances existing in its own legal system in order to justify a failure to comply with obligations resulting from Union directives. The same reasoning would apply to a failure to comply with any other Union law obligations (eg, the *premiums for reducing dairy production* case—regulation).

Similarly in *Commission v United Kingdom (tachographs)* (case 128/78) the Court refused to accept an argument based on *political* (ie trade union) difficulties, submitted as justification for a failure to implement a Union regulation on the installation of tachographs.

11.7.4 *De facto* **compliance**

Another popular but equally unsuccessful defence rests on the argument that although Union law may not be applied *de jure*, administrative practices ensure that Union law is in fact applied, and so the Member State in question is in compliance with its Union law obligations. This argument was advanced in *Commission v France (French merchant seamen)* (case 167/73), in an action based on the French Code Maritime. The code was clearly discriminatory, since it required a ratio of three French nationals to one non-national in certain jobs. The French government's argument that the code was not enforced in practice was unsuccessful. Enforcement by administrative practices, the Court held, is not enough. The maintenance of national laws contrary to Union law gives rise to an ambiguous state of affairs, and leaves citizens of a Member State in a state of uncertainty (see also *Commission v Ireland (Directive on meat products)* (case C-381/92)).

Similar reasons led to the rejection of another argument in the same case based on the *direct effect* of Union law. If the Union law in question, in this case what was then Article 7 of the EEC Treaty (now Article 18 TFEU), were directly effective, argued the French, this would be enough to ensure that the state fulfilled its obligations. The Court did not agree (see also *Commission v Belgium (type approval Directives)* (case 102/79)).

The Court took a (seemingly) more moderate line in *Commission v Germany (nursing directives)* (case 29/84). Here it conceded that a defence based on direct effect might succeed if the state's administrative practices guaranteed that the relevant directives would be applied fully and ensured that the legal position was clear and that all persons concerned were fully aware of their rights. These requirements were not, however, found to be satisfied in this case. It is submitted that they will rarely be satisfied. This seems to be borne out in the case of *Commission v Italy (freedom of establishment)* (case 168/85), in which the Court held that the right of citizens to plead directly applicable provisions of the Treaty before national courts is only a minimum guarantee and insufficient in itself to ensure full and complete application of the Treaty.

11.7.5 **Domestic law is in compliance**

A variation on the defence of '*de facto* compliance' is either that existing domestic law already adequately implements the corresponding Union law rule, or that the legislation that has been adopted to give effect to such a rule will be interpreted by the courts in accordance with it (in line with the principle of 'indirect effect'; see Chapter 5). The CJ has accepted that existing domestic law can be sufficient to give effect to an EU directive, even where the words of the domestic measure depart from the text of the directive itself. Provided that the general legal context ensures the full application of a directive in a sufficiently clear and precise manner, a Member State will be deemed to have fulfilled its obligations (see, eg, the *nursing directives* case, para 23; and *Commission v Spain (conditional access services)* (case C-58/02), para 26). In *conditional access services*, Spain sought to rely on its existing criminal code provisions on the violation of intellectual property rights as being equivalent to the requirements of the Directive on conditional access services (Directive 98/84 ([1998] OJ L320/54)), but this was rejected by the court (see also *Commission v Italy (unfair contract terms)* (case C-372/99) and *Commission v Netherlands (unfair contract terms)* (case C-144/99)).

Where legislation has been adopted to give effect to an EU obligation, but the wording of that legislation differs from the European text, there is an obvious risk that domestic law may not comply with EU law. However, the mere fact that a different wording has been chosen may not be conclusive evidence of a failure to comply with EU law if there is no corroborating evidence such as court judgments (see, in particular, *Commission v United Kingdom (liability for defective products)* (case C-300/95)).

11.7.6 **Treaty derogation**

Where there is a derogation from a Treaty obligation in the Treaty itself, provided the terms of that derogation are satisfied then it goes without saying that an Article 258 TFEU action would be unsuccessful for non-compliance with the obligation for which a derogation has been permitted.

11.7.7 **Public order**

In *R v Chief Constable of Sussex, ex parte International Trader's Ferry Ltd* ([1999] 1 CMLR 1320) the Supreme Court was asked to consider whether a failure by the Sussex constabulary to adequately police animal-rights protestors seeking to obstruct the export of live cattle from local ports was in breach of Union law. Faced with mounting and unsustainable costs, the chief constable had decided to reduce policing from five to three days per week. Although that failure might constitute a barrier to exports, in breach of Article 35 TFEU, it was argued that the breach was justified under Article 36 TFEU on public-policy grounds. Given that there was no likelihood of obtaining funds from the government, and that the police had a continuing obligation to protect the general public against crime and disorder, the restrictions on policing were neither unreasonable nor disproportionate. This argument was accepted by the Supreme Court. The question is, would it have been accepted by the CJ?

In the *angry farmers* case, the Court conceded in principle, it is submitted correctly, that the need to preserve public order is, in an appropriate situation, a valid defence. Given the competing demands of public order in *R v Chief Constable of Sussex* and the necessity, in the face of finite public funds, to strike a balance between them, it may be argued that the Supreme Court was right in concluding that the chief constable's decision, taken conscientiously, to reduce policing at the ports, was justified, albeit on public-policy or public-order grounds rather than simply on the grounds of cost, and was not disproportionate.

More recently, in *Commission v Italy (motorbike trailers)* (case C-110/05), the CJ accepted that the Italian rules regarding the use of trailers might constitute a measure having equivalent effect contrary to Article 34 TFEU, but that the measure was justified by reasons relating to the protection of road safety. This case makes the point that a Member State may rely on 'imperative requirements' to justify such measures under Article 258 as much as Article 34 TFEU (see Chapter 19).

11.8 Consequences of a ruling and of a failure to comply

11.8.1 **Obligations following a ruling under Article 258 TFEU**

If the Court finds that the Member State has failed to fulfil its obligations under the Treaties, the Member State is 'required to take the necessary measures to comply with the judgment of the Court of Justice' (Article 260 TFEU). Until the Maastricht Treaty the only sanction against a state which had failed to comply with a ruling from the Court under Article 258 TFEU was a second action under that Article for failure to comply with its obligation. The number of such repeat actions had been steadily increasing. This was serious and could have led to prolonged non-compliance in the face of which little could be done. Although the CJ had provided individuals with a means of enforcement of their Union rights via the principles of direct and indirect effect and state liability under *Francovich*, these remedies were uncertain and unequal in their applica-tion, and provided a remedy only in the individual case. Following its clarification in *Brasserie du Pêcheur*, a remedy under *Francovich* will only be available in circumstances where the state has 'manifestly and gravely' acted or failed to act in breach of Union law. A state will not be liable in damages for 'excusable' failures. Thus infringement proceedings remain crucial to ensuring that Member States comply with their obligations under the Treaties; other methods of redress may not be as effective.

11.8.2 Penalty payments for continuing failure to comply

The Maastricht Treaty added a further weapon to the Court's armoury. Providing for the imposition of financial penalties in two sets of circumstances: (1) failure of a Member State to comply with a judgment of the CJ; and (2) failure of a Member State to notify measures transposing a directive into national law, Article 260(2) TFEU provides:

> If the Commission considers that the Member State concerned has not taken such measures [to comply with the Court's judgment under Article 258] it may bring the case before the Court, after giving the State an opportunity to submit its observations. It shall specify the amount of the lump sum or penalty payment to be paid by the Member State concerned which it considers appropriate in the circumstances.
>
> If the Court of Justice finds that the Member State concerned has not complied with its judgment it may impose a lump sum or penalty payment on it.

Article 260(3) provides that where a Member State has failed to fulfil its obligation 'to notify meas-ures transposing a directive adopted under a legislative procedure' the Commission may bring pro-ceedings before the CJ requesting that it find an infringement and imposing a financial penalty. The obligation to make the payment takes effect on the date set by the Court in its judgment.

Article 260 TFEU is significant: it marks a shift in the enforcement powers of the Union towards Member States. For the first few years after Maastricht, there were no actions involving the impos-ition of fines. In 1996 and 1997, the first fines were proposed, and the first case in which a penalty was imposed was *Commission v Greece* (case C-387/97). In this case, Greece was found to have failed to comply with an earlier judgment in Article 258 proceedings (case C-45/91). The Court therefore exercised its powers under Article 260(2) TFEU and imposed a penalty of EUR 20,000 for each day of delay in ensuring compliance with the earlier judgment. Ultimately, Greece paid EUR 5.4 million in penalties before it finally complied with the judgment in March 2001 (19th Annual Report on Monitoring the Application of Union Law (COM(2002) 324 final, p 14).

There is no limit to the level of fines that may be imposed by the Court, although the Commission is required to propose a fine when it commences proceedings. Initially it was not clear how the Commission was going to calculate the fines, and it was only in November 1997 (four years after the relevant provision came into effect) that the Commission published guidance on calculating the penalty payments (COM(97) 299). A new notice was issued in December 2005 (SEC(2005) 1658), which applies to all Article 260 TFEU cases started after 1 January 2006 and which consolidates Commission practice and CJ rulings to date. This notice was updated in 2010 (SEC(2010) 923/3).

Initially the Commission requested periodic penalty payments rather than a lump sum. This may have been the result of an ambiguity in Article 260(2) authorising the CJ to impose 'a lump sum *or* penalty payment' (emphasis added). In *Commission v France (control measures for fishing activities)* (case C-304/02), the CJ held that the word 'or' should be understood in a cumulative rather than an alternative sense, and that it would be possible to impose both a lump sum and penalty payment. The lump sum would reflect the failure of the Member State to comply with the earlier judgment (particularly where there has been a long delay), whereas the penalty payment would act as an incentive to the Member State to bring the infringement to an end as soon as possible (para 81). Consequently, the Commission has changed its practice and will now request a lump-sum penalty as well as a periodic payment (SEC(2005) 1658). The lump sum is intended to penalise the continuation of the infringement between the dates of the judgment in the Article 258 TFEU proceedings and of the Article 260 proceedings, whereas the penalty payment is to cover each day of delay after a judgment under Article 260 TFEU. In *Commission v Luxembourg* (case C-576/11) a judgment of 28 November 2013, the CJ ordered Luxembourg to pay a lump sum of EUR 2 million and a penalty payment of EUR 2,800 for each day of delay in taking the measures necessary to comply with a judgment delivered some seven years earlier (23 November 2006). On 17 October 2013 in *Commission v Belgium* (case C-533/11), Belgium was ordered to pay a lump sum of EUR 10 million and a penalty payment of EUR 859,404 for each six-month period of delay in taking measures necessary to comply with a judgment of 8 July 2004.

In considering what sort of financial penalty to request the Commission will take into account the seriousness of the infringement, its duration and the need for deterrence to prevent future infringements (para 6). The notice then spells out the approach the Commission adopts in calculating the penalty payment. It starts from a standard flat rate amount currently set at EUR 600 per day. This amount is multiplied by a 'seriousness coefficient' ranging from 1 to 20. This is followed by a 'duration coefficient' which increases that sum by a multiplier of between 1 and 3 (at a rate of 0.10 per month from the date of the Article 258 judgment). That sum is then multiplied by a further factor specific to each Member State based on its GDP and number of votes in Council.

As far as the lump sum is concerned, a minimum sum for each Member State is specified in the notice. This will be requested unless a sum calculated by multiplying a daily amount by the number of days the infringement persists exceeds that amount. The 'daily amount' is calculated in the same way as the daily penalty payment. The number of days will be the period between the first judgment (under Article 258 TFEU) and the judgment under Article 260 TFEU. In this regard, it should be noted that the Commission does have a degree of discretion as to the timing of launching Article 260 proceedings, which may affect the duration of the period on the basis of which the lump sum is calculated. It remains to be seen whether this fact could form the basis for a claim of discriminatory treatment by the Commission against a particular Member State, or whether the time it takes the Commission to take action under Article 260 reflects the nature and seriousness of the infringement.

The combination of lump sum and penalty payments could therefore result in the imposition of considerable financial penalties, which may act as a strong deterrent. The CJ has made it clear that it is not bound by the Commission guidance, although it regards it as 'a useful point of reference' (*Commission v Greece* (case C-387/97), paras 89–90; *Commission v Spain (bathing water)* (case C-278/01), para 41; the *control measures for fishing activities* case, para 103), and it has, so far, calculated the penalty on the basis of the criteria specified by the Commission (although not always applying the same factors). It has made it clear that the Commission can propose a penalty, but that the ultimate decision is for the Court, and that the Court may depart from the criteria stated in the notice, for example, by adopting a duration coefficient that exceeds the maximum of 3 (the *product liability* case, para 71).

> ### Bathing Water
>
> In this case Spain had failed to comply with the Bathing Water Directive (Directive 76/160 ([1976] OJ L31/1)) even after an adverse judgment under Article 258 TFEU (see *Commission v Spain* (case C-92/96)). Having found that Spain continued to be in breach, the CJ addressed the question of penalty payments. A difficulty with imposing a daily payment was that the nature the obligation imposed by the Directive (improvements to the quality of bathing waters) meant that compliance could only be established on an annual basis once the water had been analysed and a report submitted. The CJ accepted that it would be unfair to impose a daily fine at the same level up to the point when a report confirming compliance was received, because Spain may in fact have complied sooner. The Court therefore imposed a penalty payment which would only be payable annually, and be calculated on the basis of the percentage of Spanish bathing waters not in compliance with the Directive.

This decision is important in that it creates a balance between ensuring that the fine achieves its objective of securing compliance and the need to avoid penalising a Member State which has already complied.

11.9 Action by Member States (Article 259 TFEU)

In addition to enforcement actions brought by the Commission, there may be situations in which one Member State has reason to complain about an infringement of Union law by another Member State. In such circumstances, if the Commission fails to act, then a Member State may wish to bring infringement proceedings itself. This possibility is provided for in Article 259 TFEU, which states:

> A Member State which considers that another Member State has failed to fulfil an obligation under the Treaties may bring the matter before the Court of Justice of the European Union.
>
> Before a Member State brings an action against another Member State for an alleged infringement of an obligation under the Treaties, it shall bring the matter before the Commission.
>
> The Commission shall deliver a reasoned opinion after each of the States concerned has been given the opportunity to submit its own case and its observations on the other party's case both orally and in writing.
>
> If the Commission has not delivered an opinion within three months of the date on which the matter was brought before it, the absence of such opinion shall not prevent the matter from being brought before the Court.

The procedure is thus similar to that of Article 258 TFEU, save that it is initiated by a Member State which, if the Commission fails to deliver a reasoned opinion within three months, is entitled to bring the matter before the CJ. In addition, both parties are entitled to state their case and comment on the other's case, both orally and in writing.

The issuing of a reasoned opinion by the Commission cannot preclude the complainant state from bringing proceedings before the Court if it is dissatisfied with the opinion or if it wishes to obtain a final judgment from the Court. This latter occurred in *France v United Kingdom (fishing net mesh sizes)* (case 141/78).

The procedure provided under Article 259 TFEU has rarely been used; Member States seem cautious about bringing an action under this provision because, since no Member State has a perfect record for the implementation of Union law, there is a danger that a defendant state might bring a retaliatory action against a complainant state. It is likely to be deemed more politic to bring the alleged infringement to the attention of the Commission, leaving the Commission to act under Article 258 TFEU. Nonetheless, the Article 259 TFEU procedure was used in *Belgium v Spain* (case C-388/95), concerning the rules regarding the application of the wine denomination, Rioja. It is interesting to note that the dispute brought in other Member States, which intervened in favour of one side or the other, revealed a split in opinion between the main wine-growing states and others. The CJ found in favour of Spain. More recently, Spain used the procedure against the UK in respect of voting rights for commonwealth citizens in Gibraltar and lost (*Spain v UK* (case C-145/04)). In contrast to *Belgium v Spain*, no other Member States intervened, perhaps reflecting the politically sensitive, bilateral nature of the dispute.

In case of dispute between Member States, the Treaty also provides a further, voluntary procedure. Under Article 273 TFEU, Member States may agree to submit to the CJ any dispute relating to the subject matter of the Treaty. It is on the basis of this provision that the Eurozone States will award jurisdiction to the Court in relation to the Fiscal Pact being agreed outside the Treaty framework (see Article 3(2) and all of the Treaty, and further Chapter 20).

11.10 Special enforcement procedures: state aid, breach of Article 114(4) TFEU procedures and measures to prevent serious internal disturbances

These procedures, which apply only within the areas specified, operate 'in derogation from the provisions of Articles 258 and 259'. There are certain essential differences between these procedures and Articles 258-9. In the case of Article 108(2) TFEU the Commission, after giving the parties concerned an opportunity to submit their comments, issues a *decision* requiring the Member State concerned to alter or abolish the disputed aid within a specified time limit. If the state concerned does not comply with the decision within the prescribed time, the Commission or any other interested state may bring the matter to the CJ. Since a *decision*, unlike a reasoned opinion, is a binding act it may be subject to challenge under Article 263 TFEU (*Commission v Belgium* (case 156/77), see Chapter 12).

Article 348 TFEU provides an accelerated procedure whereby the Commission can, without preliminaries, bring a Member State directly before the CJ if it considers that that state is making improper use of its powers provided under Articles 346-7 TFEU. Under these provisions Member States are empowered to take emergency measures to protect essential security interests (Article 296 TFEU), or in the event of serious internal disturbances, war or threat of war, or for the purposes of maintaining peace and international security (Article 347 TFEU). A ruling of the Court under Article 348 is given in camera.

Article 114(9) TFEU also provides for an accelerated procedure whereby the Commission and any Member State may bring a state before the Court if it considers that a Member State has made improper use of the powers of derogation provided for in Article 114(4) in deciding 'to maintain national provisions on grounds of major needs referred to in Article 36, or relating to the protection of the environment or the working environment', or in Article 114(5) (see also Chapter 16).

11.11 Conclusions

The compliance of the Member States with their Union obligations is vital in ensuring the success of the Union. Without the enforcement procedure provided in Article 258 TFEU, and crucially that in Article 260 TFEU, it seems that there would be a much lower level of compliance. The procedure itself seems to work tolerably well, although the Commission has, on occasion, been slow to proceed to the second stage of the formal procedure, and the exclusion of parties affected by Member States' non-compliance has given rise to adverse comment. The possibility of imposing penalty payments appears to have encouraged Member States to put a stop to continuous infringements more quickly than would otherwise have been the case. Yet, there is still a general problem with most Member States as far as complying with Union law is concerned, and there is a steady stream of cases under Article 258.

The case law which is developing under Article 260 TFEU seems to be marking a new period of activism by the CJ, at least with regard to persistent failures to comply with TFEU law. The Court appears to have lost its patience with countries that disregard judgments under Article 258 TFEU and has given a very strong indication that penalties under Article 260 should be punitive, as well as remedial. The Commission has responded by changing its practice, as confirmed in the 2005 Guidelines (as amended in 2010 SEC(2010) 923/3).

The recent enlargement of the Union may increase the Commission's workload in this area significantly if it is to fulfil its role as 'guardian of the Treaties' adequately. Early indications are that the countries which joined in 2004 generally managed to ensure that their national legal systems had implemented the *acquis communautaire*, although there have already been some instances of inconsistent application, and failures to comply outright.

Further reading

Commission's Annual Reports on the Monitoring and Application of Union Law (published at <**http://ec.europa.eu/dgs/secretariat_general/publications/laws_procedures/index_en.htm**>).

Hilson, C, 'Legality review of Member State discretion and directives' in T Tridimas and P Nebbia (eds), *European Law for the 21st Century* (Hart Publishing, 2004).

Prete, L and Smulders, B, 'The coming of age of infringement proceedings' (2010) 47 CML Rev 9.

Timmermans, C, 'Use of the infringement procedure in cases of judicial errors' in JW de Zwaan, JH Jans and FA Nelissen (eds), *The European Union: An ongoing process of integration* (TMC Asser Press, 2004).

Wenneras, P, 'A new dawn for Commission enforcement under Articles 258 and 260 EC: General and persistent (GAP) infringements, lump sums and penalty payments' (2006) 43 CML Rev 31.

Wenneras, P, 'Sanctions against Member States under Article 260 TFEU: Alive but not kicking?' (2012) 49 CML Rev 145.

12 Direct action for annulment

12.1 Introduction

One of the fundamental means by which the actions of the executive and the legislature can be controlled is through the process of judicial review. The possibility of challenging the legality of administrative and legislative acts characterises every democratic society. Judicial review enables an independent court to consider whether a legally binding measure violates procedural or substantive rules of law and should therefore be rendered inapplicable. Binding acts of the Union institutions are subject to review through a number of routes (see Chapter 7). The most direct way of review is to challenge the legality of a particular measure.

This chapter examines the operation of the Article 263 TFEU procedure in detail. There are four main elements:

- the types of act that are subject to review;
- the bodies that may bring an action for review;
- the time within which an action may be brought;
- the grounds on which such an action may be based.

We will consider each of these aspects in turn but first will provide an overview of the provision.

12.2 Judicial review: overview

There are a number of ways in which the CJEU can decide on the legality of measures adopted by EU institutions, offices, bodies and agencies. Article 263 TFEU provides a mechanism for a direct challenge to the legality of Union acts. The further provision is Article 267 TFEU concerning the indirect review which can be exercised by the CJ via the preliminary referencing procedure. A third possibility to challenge is provided by Article 277 TFEU, which permits a claim incidental to a main action that an act of general application adopted by an institution, body, office or agency of the Union should not be applicable.

If proceedings under Article 263 TFEU are successful, Article 264(1) TFEU provides that the act in question shall be declared void. This does not necessarily mean that the entire act should be declared void—if the provision annulled can be severed from the act as a whole, that provision alone can be considered void, the remainder of the act remaining intact.

Article 263 TFEU provides:

> The Court of Justice of the European Union shall review the legality of legislative acts of the Council, of the Commission and of the European Central Bank, other than recommendations and opinions, and of acts of the European Parliament and of the European Council intended to produce legal effects vis-à-vis third parties. It shall also review the legality of acts of bodies, offices or agencies of the Union intended to produce legal effects vis-à-vis third parties.
>
> It shall for this purpose have jurisdiction in actions brought by a Member State, the European Parliament, the Council or the Commission on grounds of lack of competence, infringement of an essential procedural requirement, infringement of the Treaties or of any rule of law relating to their application, or misuse of powers.
>
> The Court shall have jurisdiction under the same conditions in actions brought by the Court of Auditors, by the European Central Bank and by the Committee of the Regions for the purpose of protecting their prerogatives.
>
> Any natural or legal person may, under the conditions laid down in the first and second paragraphs, institute proceedings against an act addressed to that person or which is of direct and individual concern to them and against a regulatory act which is of direct concern to them and does not entail implementing measures.
>
> Acts setting up bodies, offices and agencies of the Union may lay down specific conditions and arrangements concerning actions brought by natural or legal persons against acts of these bodies, offices or agencies intended to produce legal effects in relation to them.
>
> The proceedings provided for in this Article shall be instituted within two months of the publication of the measure, or of its notification to the plaintiff, or, in the absence thereof, of the day on which it came to the knowledge of the latter, as the case may be.

The Treaty of Lisbon amended substantially the wording of what was Article 230 EC Treaty. This is now reflected in Article 263 TFEU which states that whatever the type of the act (directive, decision, regulation), it can be challenged directly. This is a welcome development since it incorporates the pre-Lisbon case law on Article 230 EC and also clarifies that private parties can challenge any type of act, legislative or non-legislative, that affects them directly and individually as well as any regulatory act that affects them directly and does not entail implementing measures.

12.2.1 **Acts that may be challenged**

The *ERTA* case states:

> 42. An action for annulment must . . . be available in the case of all measures adopted by the institutions, whatever their nature or form, which are intended to have legal effects.

Three main categories of acts are reviewable under Article 263 TFEU: legislative acts, regulatory acts and acts. The concept of 'regulatory act' appeared for the first time in Article 263 TFEU. It is not defined in that treaty. The question of what was a regulatory act within the meaning of Article 263 TFEU arose in *Inuit Tapiriit Kanatami and Others v European Parliament and Council* (case T-18/10).

Inuit

A group of entities consisting of seal hunters, trappers and other organisations representing the interests of Inuit, sought for the annulment of Regulation 1007/2009, under Article 263(4) TFEU, which prohibits the marketing of seal products. The GC dismissed the action as inadmissible and defined the term regulatory act as follows:

> . . . it must be held that the meaning of 'regulatory act' for the purposes of the fourth paragraph of Article 263 TFEU must be understood as covering all acts of general application apart from legislative acts.

As can be seen in the *Inuit* case a regulatory act is a non-legislative act. It thus encompasses recommendations and opinions and any other acts of general application such as, for example, resolutions.

On appeal, (*Inuit Tapiriit Kanatami and Others* (C-583/11P)), the CJ confirmed the approach taken by the GC about the definition of the term regulatory act and dismissed the appeal. In *Inuit* 'acts' were held to encompass any act addressed to a natural or legal person and any act whether legislative or regulatory, which is of direct and individual concern to them (including legislative and regulatory acts which require implementing measures).

Microban v Commission (case T-262/10) shows the development in the Court's thinking and constitutes the latest judicial position in the area.

Microban

The dispute concerned the challenge of a Commission's decision implementing EU legislation in relation to plastic materials intended to come into contact with foodstuffs. The Commission's decision to withdraw from the list of permitted additives a material called 'triclosan', had the effect of banning the marketing of triclosan in the EU. The applicants were engaged in the marketing of that material and they sought the annulment of the Commission's decision. The GC ruled that the decision of the Commission to withdraw triclosan from the list of the permitted additives was a 'regulatory act' since it was a non-legislative act of general application which produced legal effects to categories of persons in a general and abstract way. The GC found that the decision was adopted by the Commission in the exercise of implementing powers and not in the exercise of legislative powers.

Moreover, the GC found that a regulatory act is a non-legislative act of general application.

In this regard, reviewable acts must produce legal effects vis-á-vis third parties (Article 263(1) TFEU). In the *ERTA* case, the measure was a Council resolution setting out the position to be taken by the Council in the preparation of the road-transport agreement. The Commission sought to challenge this resolution, since it considered that the matter lay outside the Council's sphere of competence. The action was declared admissible.

Similarly in *Cimenteries CBR Cementsbedrijven NV v Commission (Noordwijk's Cement Accord)* (cases 8–11/66), the act challenged was a registered letter sent by the Commission to the applicant in the context of EU competition proceedings to the effect that the companies' immunity from fines was at an end. The letter was not called a 'decision'. Since it produced legal effects for the companies concerned and brought about a change in their legal position it was an act capable of annulment under Article 263 TFEU. A similar approach can be seen with regard to a decision not to investigate an alleged case of state aid (*Athinaiki Techniki AE v Commission* (case C-521/06 P)). In *France v Commission (pension funds communication)* (case C-57/95) the CJ held that a communication, which was phrased in imperative language, was intended to have legal effects and could be challenged. A further example is the status of letters from the Commission, as can be seen in the contrasting cases of *Infront WM AG v Commission* (case T-33/01) and *max.mobil v Commission* case (case T-54/99, on appeal case C-141/02P).

Infront

The applicant sought to challenge a Commission letter to the UK government, indicating that the Commission had no objection to measures taken, in accordance with Article 3a Television without Frontiers Directive (Directive 89/552, as amended), by the UK to ensure the broadcast of football World Cup finals on free-to-air television. In defence, it was argued that the letter was not a decision, but was analogous to a definition of position of an intention not to take action under Article 258 TFEU, which is not susceptible of review. Further, the legal effects stemmed from the underlying national law, not the Commission letter, which did not change the legal position. The GC disagreed and held the letter was susceptible of review as it concluded the verification procedure which the Commission is obliged to carry out under the Television without Frontiers Directive. It therefore triggers the mutual recognition system in the Directive, according to which other Member States are obliged to prevent broadcasters established under their respective jurisdictions from avoiding national regulation about access to television content. The matter was appealed (case C-125/06P) where the CJ agreed that the action was admissible.

Not all letters issued by the Commission will necessarily be capable of challenge.

---

max.mobil

The underlying complaint concerned pricing in the telecommunications market in Austria. max.mobil complained to the Commission, asking it to take action under Article 106 TFEU. The Commission, referring to its existing policy in this area, declined to do so and wrote to max.mobil to this effect. max.mobil sought to challenge this letter; the Commission argued that it was of an informative nature only. The GC agreed with max.mobil, suggesting that on the basis of previous case law (notably *Bundesverband der Bilanzbuchhalter eV v Commission* (case C-107/95P), discussed in Chapter 13), an individual had the right to have a diligent and impartial treatment of the complaint; thus the Commission must consider the matter before coming to its decision. The letter, in the view of the GC, was therefore a decision on this basis which was subject to review. The CJ, on appeal, disagreed. It argued that 'the fact that max.mobil has a direct and individual interest in the annulment of the Commission's decision to refuse to act on its complaint is not such as to confer on it the right to challenge that decision' (para 70). The CJ concluded that the letter to max.mobil was of an informative nature only.

It is difficult to reconcile the approach in *max.mobil* with that taken by the GC in *Air France v Commission* (case T-3/93). Here, a mere statement by a Commission spokesman, not published but reported by the press agencies, that a proposed acquisition of Dan-Air by British Airways lay outside the scope of the Commission's competence under Regulation 4064/89, was held to be capable of annulment, since it confirmed the Commission's position 'beyond all doubt'. The fact that the statement was not addressed to a particular person and was given orally was not relevant: it was the content and legal effect of the measure which were crucial. It may be that one way of reconciling these cases is to note that the broader approach to the notion of a decision is taken by the GC, the CJ seemingly taking a narrower approach.

Both courts have held, in contrast to the case law discussed above, that preliminary measures, designed simply to pave the way for a final decision, are not reviewable (see *Nashua Corporation v Commission* (cases C-133 and 150/87)). In *Dysan Magnetics Ltd v Commission* (case T-134/95), the opening by the Commission of a dumping investigation, a purely preparatory measure which preceded the adoption of definitive anti-dumping duties, and which did not have an immediate and irreversible effect on the legal situation of concerned undertakings, was held not to be open to challenge under Article 263 TFEU. In *Philip Morris International and Others v Commission* (cases T-377, 379 and 380/00; T-260 and 272/01), the Commission's decision to commence proceedings against various tobacco manufacturers in an American court was challenged by the defendants to that action, but the GC held that the action was inadmissible because the decision to commence proceedings had no binding legal effects on the applicants. The legal effects, if any, would derive from the decision of the American court.

12.2.2 Acts of Parliament

Although only acts of the Council and the Commission were expressed to be capable of challenge under the original Article 173 EEC, the Court had, prior to the passing of the TEU, admitted challenges to acts of the European Parliament having binding legal effect on third parties (see *Luxembourg v Parliament* (case 230/81); *Parti Ecologiste ('Les Verts') v Parliament* (case 294/83)). In *Luxembourg v Parliament* (case 230/81), Luxembourg was seeking to challenge Parliament's resolution to move its seat from Luxembourg to Strasbourg and Brussels. In *'Les Verts' v Parliament*, the Green Party sought to challenge a decision of the Bureau of Parliament on the allocation of campaign funds for the 1984 European elections. Clearly Parliament's acts in these cases produced significant legal effects for both applicants (cf *Les Verts v Parliament* (case 190/84)).

Contrast these cases with *Le Pen v Parliament (France, intervening)* (case T-353/00 and case C-208/03P) which concerned the question of a declaration of the President of the Parliament, and turned on the issue of whether the declaration had legal effects. In earlier cases (*Council v Parliament* (case 34/86) and *Council v Parliament* (case C-284/90)), the CJ had held that a declaration could have legal effects. The *Le Pen* case was different. The declaration here consisted of recognition of the legal position in France, rather than creating legal effects of its own. Thus, when looking at acts giving rise to legal effects, it is not sufficient that the act be of the type that could give rise to legal effects, but it must itself give rise to such effects.

The principles established in cases such as *'Les Verts'* have now been incorporated into Article 263 TFEU. In general terms, the CJEU has accepted that internal rules of organisation for the Parliament do not have legal effects on third parties (ie externally) and are therefore not capable of being reviewed (*Weber v Parliament* (case C-314/91)). A declaration of the European Parliament waiving the rights and immunities of one of its members went beyond the 'internal' and therefore was capable of being subject to review (*Mote v Parliament* (case T-345/05)).

12.2.3 Acts of other bodies

The Court may only review 'the legality of acts of bodies, offices or agencies of the Union intended to produce legal effects vis-à-vis third parties'. Acts adopted within the institutional framework of such entities are not reviewable. Thus in *Commission v Council* (case C-25/94), a decision by the Committee of Permanent Representatives (COREPER), and in *Parliament v Council* (case C-181/91), a decision of the Member States meeting in Council (but not of the *Council* as such), could not be challenged.

12.2.4 **Review under TEU**

The CJ's jurisdiction under Article 263 TFEU is, of course, currently limited to Union acts. The CFSP provisions, post Lisbon, remain in the TEU and, in principle, Article 275 TFEU excludes the CJ's jurisdiction with respect to them and to acts adopted on the basis of those provisions. However. Article 275(2) specifies that the CJ may review the legality of restrictive measures against natural or legal persons under Chapter 2, Title V TEU, and the CJ will continue to have the power to review the boundary between the different areas of jurisdiction (see Chapters 2 and 3).

12.3 *Locus standi*: who may bring an action?

The question of *locus standi* (or standing)—that is, of who should be entitled to challenge the legality of a particular measure—is controversial. On the one hand, it may be desirable to provide for broad *locus standi* to ensure that the legislature is subject to adequate control. On the other hand, it is equally desirable to ensure that somebody who is wholly unconnected with the adoption or effects of a legally binding act is not in a position to challenge its validity, as this would otherwise possibly lead to excessive challenges with adverse consequences both on legal certainty and on the Court's workload. There are strict *locus standi* requirements in Article 263 TFEU. Applicants are divided into privileged, semi-privileged and non-privileged applicants. The main controversy in recent years has been over the restricted interpretation given by the Court to the *locus standi* rules on non-privileged applicants. Strict *locus standi* requirements for private litigants constitute one of the very few areas of EU law where the legal literature is almost unanimous in finding fundamental gaps in judicial protection.

12.3.1 **Privileged applicants**

Member States, the European Parliament, the Council and the Commission are entitled to challenge *any* binding act under Article 263 TFEU. As such, they are referred to as privileged applicants. A 'Member State' for the purposes of Article 263 TFEU does not include governments of regions or of autonomous communities (*Région Wallonne v Commission* (case C-95/97)). However, regional authorities may intervene, if they have legal personality under their domestic law, as a non-privileged applicant. As such, they must satisfy the requirements of direct and individual concern (*Comunidad Autonoma de Cantabria v Council* (case T-238/97)). It is arguable that regional authorities should have semi-privileged status to protect their prerogatives, but this has not been given serious consideration by the Member States or the Union.

12.3.1.1 Semi-privileged applicants

Article 263(3) TFEU grants semi-privileged position to the Court of Auditors, the ECB and the Committee of the Regions. The CJ's jurisdiction is confined to reviewing such acts of those institutions that are necessary for the protection of their prerogatives.

12.3.2 **Non-privileged applicants**

The *locus standi* of individuals under Article 263 TFEU is much more limited than that of privileged or semi-privileged applicants. A 'natural or legal person' is entitled only to challenge:

- an act addressed to that person, or which is of direct and individual concern to them;
- a regulatory act which is of direct concern to them and does not entail implementing measures.

A 'natural or legal person' includes a state which is not a Member State of the EU (*Gibraltar v Council* (case C-298/89)) as well as autonomous regions of a Member State.

All claims by natural or legal persons are brought before the GC with a right of appeal to the CJ on points of law only (see Chapter 7).

No problem with standing exists where the decision is addressed to the applicant, with one minor exception (to be discussed in Chapter 13). Provided the applicants bring the action within the two-month time limit, their claim will be admissible. Many such decisions have been successfully challenged (eg, in competition law).

Where the decision is not addressed to the applicant it is more difficult to establish *locus standi* and many actions have been held inadmissible.

12.3.2.1 Representative bodies

The Court has traditionally been unwilling to exercise jurisdiction to entertain actions by trade or other associations under Article 263 TFEU, maintaining that 'defence of a common interest is not enough to establish admissibility'. However, the GC held in *Associazione Italiana Tecnico Economica del Cemento (AITEC) v Commission* (cases T-447–9/93) that a trade association would be permitted to bring an action against a decision addressed to 'another person' where it represented the individual interests of some of its members whilst at the same time protecting the interests of the section as a whole. The GC noted that 'in these circumstances collective action brings procedural advantages'. As a result, Italian and British associations of cement producers were able to challenge a Commission decision addressed to the Greek government approving the grant of state aid to a Greek producer, Heracles, and succeeded in obtaining its annulment. Likewise a trade union and a works council, as 'recognised representatives' of employees affected by a proposed merger under Merger Regulation 4064/89, were held entitled to challenge a Commission decision approving Nestlé's takeover of Perrier SA (see *Comité Central d'Entreprise de la Société Générale des Grandes Sources v Commission* (case T-96/92) and *Aktionsgemeinschaft Recht und Eigentum eV v Commission* (case T-114/00)—an association formed to protect the collective interests of its members—had *locus standi* to challenge a Commission decision not to instigate the formal procedure under Article 108(2) TFEU, on behalf of those members who would have been parties concerned within the meaning of Article 108(2) TFEU). In *Federolio v Commission* (case T-122/96), the GC identified three situations when an association would be granted *locus standi*:

- the trade association has been expressly granted procedural rights;
- it represents the individuals or undertakings which themselves have standing;
- the trade association itself is affected—for example if its right to negotiate is affected.

This will still leave many associations or pressure groups without *locus standi* (see, eg, *Stichtling Greenpeace Council v Commission* (case T-585/93), the subject of an unsuccessful appeal (case C-321/95P)). Perhaps this is not surprising, given the stringency of the test applied to individuals.

12.3.3 Challenging acts addressed to another person

An act addressed to a person other than the plaintiff may be challenged provided it is of direct and individual concern to him and against a regulatory act which is of direct concern to him and does not entail implementing measures. In order for the action of annulment to be considered admissible all the criteria need to be satisfied.

Further, it now seems that the GC requires an individual seeking to challenge a decision to show a legal interest in bringing the proceedings *Schmitz-GothaFahrzeugwerke v Commission* (case T-167/

01). In the absence of such a legal interest being proved, the Court will not proceed to examine the question of the standing of an application (*Olivieri v Commission* (case T-326/99)). The CJ has apparently accepted this extra requirement (*Rendo and Others v Commission* (case C-19/93 P), para 13)). It seems in this regard that the burden of proof lies with the applicant (*Sniace SA v Commission* (case T-141/03), paras 31–2). In *Flaherty* (T-218/03), the applicant had a legal interest in bringing proceedings to challenge a decision but was found not to have standing, although the applicant was identified in the Annex to the contested decision.

Flaherty

The GC held that individuals who were intending to build a boat, the name of which was listed in the Annex to the contested decision, did not have an interest as the boat was 'fictional', that is, it did not, at the time of the decision, exist. It further held the applicants were not individually concerned.

The CJ reversed the decision as regards the applicants' interest, arguing that they were listed in the relevant annex because they had applied for support under a particular scheme and the contested decision denied them that support. The fact that they had not yet built the boat (for which they needed the support) did not change this assessment.

The CJ in *Flaherty and Others v Commission* (cases C-373, 379, and 382/06P) overturned the GC on the question of whether the applicants were individually concerned.

12.3.3.1 The measure must be, as far as the applicant is concerned, an act which is of direct and individual concern or a regulatory act which is of direct concern and requires no implementing measures

The CJ has consistently held that in assessing admissibility, the form of any particular act is irrelevant: what is critical is the essential nature of the act if it is to be of direct and individual concern to the individual. The objective of this rule is to prevent the Union institutions from being in a position, merely by choosing the form of the act, to determine whether the act can be challenged. The applicant, because of his characteristics or circumstances, or those of the limited group of which he is a member, must be more particularly affected by the act than others which are also affected. Thus a regulation, although of general application, might have more of a specific impact on one or more individuals than on the rest of the class of person to which it applies. In *Salamander AG and Others v Parliament and Council* (cases T-172 and 175–7/98) the Court ruled that '. . . in certain circumstances, however, even a legislative measure which applies to economic operators generally may be of direct and individual concern to some of them. . .'. Therefore, the form of the measure is not of crucial importance as long as the measure is of a direct and individual concern to the litigant. But as a general rule, individual challenges to regulations are difficult. Few such challenges have succeeded. In *Koninklijke Scholten-Honig NV v Council and Commission* (case 101/76) the applicant glucose producers' attempt to challenge certain regulations requiring glucose producers to pay levies on the production of glucose, for the benefit of sugar producers, was held, despite the merits of the case, to be inadmissible. (See also *Calpak SpA v Commission* (cases 789 and 790/79)—attempt (failed) by Italian pear processors to challenge a regulation fixing production aids for pear processors.)

Whether a regulation is of direct and individual concern to an individual is a subjective matter involving an assessment of its impact upon the applicant. In *ex parte Accrington Beef Co Ltd*, the CJ acknowledged that an individual seeking to challenge a regulation could not be sure whether or not he would have *locus standi* under Article 263 TFEU—it all depended on his individual circumstances.

In *Confédération Nationale des Producteurs de Fruits et Légumes* the Court held that to determine the legal nature of an act it is necessary to consider the nature and content of an act rather than its form. It is the substance, not the label, which is crucial. A true regulation is a measure of general application, that is, normative; it applies to objectively determined situations and produces legal effects on categories of persons viewed abstractly and in their entirety. On the other hand the essential feature of a decision, which is defined as 'binding upon those to whom it is addressed' (Article 288 TFEU) arises from the limitation of the persons to whom it is addressed; a decision concerns designated persons individually. This can be seen in the context of *International Fruit Co NV*.

International Fruit Co NV

Here, the applicants, a group of fruit importers, were held entitled to challenge a Union regulation laying down the quantity of import licences to be issued for a certain period. The quantity of licences was calculated on the basis of applications from, inter alia, the applicants, received during the preceding week; thus it applied to a finite number of people and was issued in response to their applications. Although it appeared to be a general measure it was found in fact to be a disguised bundle of decisions addressed to each applicant.

The CJ has also suggested that a measure may be 'hybrid' in nature, that is, it may be a measure of general application which is, nonetheless, in the nature of a decision for certain 'designated individuals'. In the *Japanese ball-bearings* cases (cases 113 and 118–21/77) four major Japanese producers of ball bearings were held entitled to challenge an EU anti-dumping regulation. Although the measure was of general application, some of its articles specifically referred to the applicants. For them, it was in the nature of a decision. In *Allied Corporation v Commission* (cases 239 and 275/82) some of the applicant companies seeking to annul an anti-dumping regulation were charged with illegal dumping in the regulation itself. The CJ held that although measures involving anti-dumping duties were:

> as regards their nature and scope, of a legislative character, inasmuch as they apply to all traders concerned taken as a whole, the provision may nonetheless be of direct and individual concern to those producers and exporters who are charged with practising dumping.

On this basis the applicant producers' and exporters' claims were held to be admissible.

It may be noted that in *Allied*, the measures challenged were regulations but the CJ did not consider the question whether they were in the nature of a decision to the applicants. It appeared to be sufficient that the applicants had established direct and individual concern. This approach was adopted in a number of cases, principally, but not exclusively, in the context of challenge to regulations imposing anti-dumping duties. Under EU anti-dumping rules such duties, which are normally levied on importation of the product concerned, can only be imposed by regulation. Such regulations may adversely affect undertakings such as producers and exporters situated outside the Union who have no opportunity to challenge the measures in an action before the courts of Member States. The Court has admitted a number of challenges to regulations by producers or exporters who were able to establish that they were identified in the measures adopted by the Commission or the Council or were concerned in the Commission's preliminary investigations (see *Nashua Corporation* (12.2.1)), *Neotype v Commission* (case C-305/86)): also by importers whose retail prices for the goods in question or whose business dealings with the manufacturer of those goods played a part in establishing the existence of dumping (*Enital v Commission* (case C-304/86); *Gestetner Holdings plc v Commission* (case C-156/87)). Such claims were admissible because (as well as the applicants being directly concerned) the factors cited above were deemed to constitute individual concern. In *Extramet Industrie SA v Council* (case C-358/89), the CJ went further and admitted a challenge to a 'true' regulation by an *independent* importer whose retail prices and business dealings in the goods in question were *not* taken into account in establishing the existence of dumping, simply because he was able to establish individual (as well as direct) concern.

Also, outside the area of anti-dumping, in *Sofrimport SARL v Commission* (case C-152/88), the CJ allowed an applicant importer to challenge a regulation suspending imports into the EU of apples from certain third countries solely on the basis that it was of direct and individual concern to the applicant. *Codorniu SA v Council* (case C-309/89) is another example of a successful challenge by an individual to a regulation.

Codorniu

In this case the principal producer of quality sparkling wine in Spain, and holder of graphic trade-mark rights in the title 'Gran Cremant di Codorniu' was allowed to challenge Union regulations on the description of sparkling wines in which the word 'cremant' was to be reserved for certain quality sparkling wines produced in France and Luxembourg. Although the measures in question were legislative measures applicable to traders in general they were of individual concern to the applicant because of trade-mark rights, considered by the CJ as a significant element which distinguished the applicants from all the other traders in the field.

These cases show that in the context of a challenge to an act where the applicant can prove direct and (particularly) individual concern his action will be admissible. This approach is, as Advocate-General Jacobs pointed out in *Extramet*, consistent with the general scheme and purpose of Article 263 and necessary to ensure effective judicial protection for those (such as manufacturers and exporters in countries outside the EU) who may have no other means to challenge regulations by which they may be seriously affected.

There have been few examples of challenge by natural or legal persons to directives. In *Gibraltar* (noted earlier) the Court refused to admit a challenge to an EU directive by the government of Gibraltar (found to be a natural or legal person) on the grounds that directives, being 'normally a form of indirect regulatory or legislative measure' were not open to challenge by such persons. Since the directive in question, although affecting the applicants by excluding them from its territorial scope, applied to 'objectively determined situations' the applicants' claim was inadmissible. Here, however, unlike the applicants mentioned earlier who succeeded in establishing *locus standi* to challenge regulations, the applicants were unable to prove individual concern. In *Salamander* (see 12.3.2), concerning a challenge to the Tobacco Advertising Directive (Directive 98/43 ([1998] OJ L213/9)), the GC seemed to suggest that a directive could in principle be capable of challenge by individuals provided they could show direct and individual concern. In this case, however, the applicants were unable to show direct concern.

12.3.3.2 The act must be of individual concern to the applicant

The concept of individual concern has been construed very restrictively by the CJ (and GC). Because it operates to exclude so many cases it is often the first criterion to be examined, as it was in *Plaumann & Co v Commission* (case 25/62).

Plaumann

Plaumann & Co were importers of clementines who sought to annul a Commission decision, addressed to the German government, refusing the government permission to reduce its customs duties on clementines imported from outside the EU. Plaumann claimed that, as a large-scale importer of such clementines, they were 'individually concerned'. The Court disagreed. The importing of clementines, the Court held, was an activity which could be carried out by anyone at any time. There was nothing in the decision to distinguish Plaumann from any other importer of clementines.

In order to establish individual concern, the applicant must prove that the decision affects him or her because of:

certain characteristics which are peculiarly relevant to him, or by reason of circumstances in which he is differentiated from all other persons, and not by the mere fact that he belongs to a class of persons who are affected.

The so-called '*Plaumann*' test became the classic test for individual concern. It was crucially confirmed in *Unión de Pequeños Agricultores (UPA) v Council* (case C-50/00; see 12.3.3.5). It is, however, more easily stated than applied, since it does not specify *what* characteristics 'peculiarly relevant to him' the applicant must prove to establish individual concern or what circumstances will differentiate him from all other persons.

It will *not* be sufficient to prove that his business interests have been adversely affected, as was clearly the case in *Plaumann*. *Nor* is it sufficient that they were affected in a different way, or more seriously, than other similar traders. These arguments were rejected in *Calpak* in which the applicant claimed that the Commission's mode of calculation of aid for the pear-processing industry operated particularly unfairly on itself as a private company as compared with other pear producers such as public companies and cooperatives.

Equally it is not sufficient that the applicant's identity is known to, or ascertainable by, the Commission when the measure is passed as can be seen in *UNICME v Council* (case 123/77).

UNICME

In this case an association of Italian motorcycle importers was seeking to annul a Commission regulation, authorising the Italian government to impose temporary quotas on motorcycles imported from Japan. The measure was in retaliation for the imposition by the Japanese of a quota on the import of Italian ski boots. Members of the association were the only persons concerned and they were all concerned. Their identity was ascertainable and many had already applied for import licences. Their application was held inadmissible.

The Court found it unnecessary to consider whether the contested measure was a true regulation, as it was not of direct or individual concern to the applicants. It 'would only affect the interests of the applicants when their request for a licence was refused'. 'The possibility of determining more or less precisely the number or even the identity of the persons to whom the measure applies by no means implies that it must be regarded as being of individual concern to them'. While the former statement may be open to question as a ground for denying direct and individual concern, since it could be applied to *any* act addressed to a third party, the latter recurs consistently in the Court's case law on individual concern.

Will a measure be deemed of individual concern if a causal connection can be proved between a particular act and the applicant's own case? This was not found to be the case in *Spijker Kwasten BV v Commission* (case 231/82).

Spijker Kwasten

Here the Commission issued a decision, at the request of the Dutch government, enabling the government to ban the import of Chinese brushes for a six-month period, from July to 31 December 1982. Prior to the above request being made the applicant had applied for a licence to import such brushes. There was no doubt a causal link between its application and the Dutch government's request. The request and the Commission's decision were prompted by its application. Moreover the company was the only importer of these brushes in Holland, and the only one likely to want to import them during the six-month period in question. Yet it was held not to be individually concerned. The measure, the Court held, was of general application. There was nothing to stop others applying for licences during that same period.

This case also confirmed a point established earlier in *Glucoseries Réunies v Commission* (case 1/64), that the fact that the applicant (in this case the sole producer of glucose in Belgium and the principal exporter of glucose in France) is the *only* person likely to be affected by the measure is not a characteristic peculiarly relevant to him such as to give rise to individual concern, as long as there is a theoretical possibility that others can enter the field and be affected by the same measure.

What characteristic peculiarly relevant to him must the applicant then prove in order to establish individual concern?

12.3.3.2.1 Acts referable specifically to applicant's situation and affecting a closed class

Although there is no single satisfactory test, a common thread runs through most of the cases in which individual concern has been held to exist. In almost every case the act which the applicant seeks to challenge, although addressed to another person, is referable specifically to his situation. Moreover, not only does it affect him as though he were the person addressed, but it affects him either *alone* or as a member of a fixed and *closed* class; no one else is capable of entering the field and being affected by the same measure.

For example, the measure may have been issued in response to a licence or tender application as can be seen in *Alfred Toepfer KG v Commission* (cases 106 and 107/63).

Alfred Toepfer

Toepfer had, amongst others, requested a licence from the German government to import cereals from France. The Commission's decision, made at the request of the German government, was a confirmation of the government's measure refusing to grant the import certificate. The only persons affected by the decision were those who had already applied for licences. They were individually concerned.

A similar situation arose in *Werner A Bock KG v Commission* (case 62/70).

Werner A Bock

The firm of Bock had applied for a permit to import a consignment of Chinese mushrooms, for which it already had a firm offer. As Chinese mushrooms, at the time, were in free circulation in the EU, the German government, if it wished to prohibit their import into Germany, needed authorisation from the Commission to do so. Following Bock's application, the German government, on 11 September, applied to the Commission for that authorisation, which the Commission granted by a decision on 15 September. The Court held that Bock was individually concerned; the decision was passed in response to its application.

A similar connection existed in *Philip Morris Holland BV v Commission* (case 730/79). Here the decision in question, which was addressed to the Dutch government, requested the government to refrain from granting state aid to the applicant tobacco company, Philip Morris. The Court assumed without argument that the company was individually concerned. In *Consorzio Gruppo di Azione Locale 'Murgia Messapica' v Commission* (case T-465/93) the applicant consortium had applied for grants from the Union Leader programme: they were found to be individually concerned by the Commission's decision addressed to the Italian authorities rejecting their application for aid. In *International Fruit Co NV*, discussed earlier, measure was found not to be a true regulation at all, but a bundle of decisions.

International Fruit Co NV

This case concerned a Commission 'regulation' controlling the issue of import licences for apples from non-Member States. The regulation was issued by the Commission on the basis of applications received during the preceding week, following an assessment of the overall situation. It applied *only* to those who had applied for licences during that week. It was held to be of individual concern to the applicants.

The courts have noted that a person will be individually concerned should their existing rights be affected by the decision. This can be seen clearly in the *Infront* case (see 12.2.1), which concerned the exclusive rights to broadcast certain football matches, which were acquired by Infront before the UK (acting under the then Television without Frontiers Directive) determined that those matches should be broadcast free to air. Being the holder of an intellectual property right may give a strong claim to be individually concerned by a measure affecting those rights (see also *Codorniu* below).

However, even a 'true' regulation can be of individual concern to *some* individuals, as it can be in the nature of a decision to some individuals, if it is referable expressly or impliedly to their particular situation, either alone or as a member of a known and *closed* class (*Japanese ball-bearing case; Allied*); CAM SA v Commission (case 100/74), overruling *Compagnie Française Commerciale et Financière SA v Commission* (case 64/69)). Likewise in *Codorniu* the applicant producers of sparkling wine were differentiated from all other producers of sparkling wine because they were prevented by the regulation from exercising their registered trade-mark right in 'Gran Cremant di Codorniu'. *Sofrimport* also concerned a successful challenge of this nature.

> ### Sofrimport
>
> The applicants, who were fruit importers, were seeking to annul a number of Commission regulations suspending the issue of import licences for apples from Chile and fixing quantities of such imports from third countries. Under one of the regulations (Regulation 2702/72) the Commission was required under Article 3 to take into account, when exercising its powers under the regulations, the 'special position of products in transit' when the regulations come into force. The applicants had goods in transit when the contested regulations came into force. The CJ held that they were individually concerned. 'Such persons constituted a restricted group *which could not be extended* after the contested measure took effect.'

12.3.3.2.2 Acts issued as a result of proceedings initiated by applicant or in which the applicant has played a legitimate part

A rather different situation arises when the act is not 'directed at' an applicant but issued as a result of proceedings in which the applicant exercised his procedural rights. An example can be seen in *Metro-SB-Grossmärkte GmbH & Co KG v Commission* (case 26/76).

> ### Metro-SB-Grossmärkte GmbH
>
> In this case the applicant was seeking to challenge a decision issued to another firm, SABA, in the context of EU competition proceedings. The decision was issued following a complaint by Metro under Article 3 of Regulation 17/62 (now repealed) that SABA was acting in breach of Article 101 TFEU. The Court held, on the question of admissibility, that since persons with a legitimate interest were entitled, under Article 3 of Regulation 17/62, to request the Commission to investigate the infringement, they should be allowed to institute Article 263 TFEU proceedings in order to protect that interest. Thus Metro was individually concerned.

Participation in proceedings before the Union institutions will only confer the quality of 'individual concern' on an applicant if he or she enjoys specific guarantees pertaining to the challenged act (*Boehringer v Commission and Council and Boehringer Ingelheim Vetmedica v Council and Commission* (cases T-125 and 156/96)). If the position were otherwise the mere sending of a comment on a proposed legislative initiative could be capable of conferring the quality of 'individual concern' upon an applicant—an absurd outcome (*CSR Pampryl v Commission* (case T-114/99)).

12.3.3.2.3 Anti-dumping and competition cases

Overall, the Court has treated standing requirements in areas such as anti-dumping, competition law and state aids more generously. In this regard, where the applicant is a complainant or has been concerned in the preliminary investigations he will be individually concerned on the principles outlined earlier. But he will also be deemed to be individually concerned where his retail prices or business dealings have been used as a basis for establishing the existence of dumping (see *Enital*). However, in the absence of these factors, the CJ was not in its earlier case law prepared to find individual concern. In *Allied* (12.3.3.1), independent importers (as opposed to manufacturers and exporters) who had not been involved in the preliminary proceedings and who were affected simply as members of a class, failed to establish individual concern.

12.3.3.3 A regulatory act not entailing any implementing measures

The question of whether a particular regulatory act entails implementing measures is problematic. Some acts may require some minor form of implementing measure such as, for example, the designating of a body responsible for gathering statistical information. That type of implementing measure will not affect the substantive rights of an applicant and therefore may need to be distinguished from implementing measures which may alter his position and which may therefore render a challenge to legality premature before their adoption. A number of cases in which the applicant has succeeded in establishing *locus standi*, such as *Alfred Toepfer* and *Werner A Bock* have involved decisions of confirmation (*Toepfer*) or authorisation (*Bock*). In these cases it seems to have been presumed that the measures were of direct concern to the applicants. In the more recent cases the CJ and GC seem to have returned to the language of 'no discretion' and 'automatic'. Thus, in *Infront* the CJ held the test:

> requires the contested [Union] measure to affect directly the legal situation of the individual and leave no discretion to its addressees, who are entrusted with the task of implementing it, such implementation being purely automatic and resulting from [Union] rules without the application of other intermediate rules [para 47].

Nonetheless, here the CJ was referring to the term of the Television without Frontiers Directive which required Member States to recognise other Member States' systems for ensuring certain content was available on free-to-air television, once the Commission had approved the content to be so provided, and it found the test to be satisfied. In *Commission v Ente per Le Ville vesuviane* and *Ente per le Ville vesuviance v Commission* (cases C-444 and 455/07P), the CJ took a less favourable stance, although it relied on exactly the same test.

Ente per Le Ville

The case concerned the closure of financial assistance from the European Regional Development Fund (EDRF) for some projects in Ente. Although Ente was named as the beneficiary, the application was made by the Italian state. Requests to the Commission by the Italian state for the payments to be made to Ente had not been made by the due deadline. Representatives of Ente sought to challenge the Commission's decision. The CJ held that because the grants were applied for through the Italian state and it was still possible that the Italian government could have changed its mind, Ente was not directly concerned.

Acts need not, of course, be addressed to Member States. In the past where decisions have been addressed to natural or legal persons, the GC has often taken a narrow view of when these decisions could be said to affect other persons directly. The Commission's decision to approve Nestlé's takeover of Perrier in *Comité* (see 12.3.2.1) was found not to be of direct concern to the applicant employee representative bodies. Any disadvantage suffered by employees following the merger would result from action by the merged undertaking itself, subject to the protection provided for employees in these circumstances under national and Union law. It did not result directly from the Commission's decision. The applicants were only directly concerned by the decision to the extent that their procedural rights, granted to 'recognised representatives' under the Merger Regulation, might have been infringed. More recently, a supplier under a contract with the Ukraine, which received financial aid from the Union, was held not to be directly affected by a Commission decision that its contracts did not satisfy the Union's criteria for release of payments to the Ukraine

(*Richco Commodities Ltd v Commission* (case T-509/93)). The GC pointed out that there was no legal relationship between the supplier and the Commission. The fact that the contract was expressed to be conditional on payment of the aid was irrelevant; standing under Article 263 TFEU cannot be dependent on decisions made in commercial negotiations. This ruling may now be open to question. In a series of cases on appeal from the GC regarding the same point, the CJ has held the individual to be directly concerned (see, eg, *Glencore Grain Ltd v Commission* (cases C-403 and 404/96)). These difficulties can also be seen in *Telefónica v Commission* (case C-274/12 P).

Telefónica

The case concerned a decision from the Commission addressed to Spain in relation to a state aid scheme, which was found by the Commission to be incompatible with the internal market law. *Telefónica*, a Spanish telephone company, benefited from the aid scheme and faced the danger of paying back the aid it had received from the Spanish state, therefore the company sought for the annulment of the Commission's decision. The CJ, on appeal, ruled that the GC rightly dismissed *Telefónica's* action. The CJ held that the Commission's decision confirmed that the state aid scheme in issue was incompatible with the internal market law. Further action was required by the Spanish government to recover that aid. Accordingly, further implementing measures within the meaning of Article 263(4) TFEU were necessary.

The approach taken by the CJ in *Telefónica* is problematic since a simple finding that the state aid was unlawful was seen as requiring an implementing measure. It is therefore difficult to identify a significant number of legal measures that will not require some form of minor implementation at the national level. More recently, in *T and L* (case C-456/13P), the CJ focused on the notion of implementing measures.

T and L

The applicants in this case attempted to challenge the validity of EU regulations that set out excessive tariffs on sugar imported from third countries. Based on the Regulations, the national authorities needed to ensure that the requirements set out in the Regulations were met and to notify the Commission about the relevant quantity allowed to be imported. The Regulations in question left no discretionary powers to the national authorities which they only needed to confirm that the requirements provided by the Regulations were met. Yet, the CJ held that doing so required some form of implementing measures even though the national authorities carried out only a mechanical application in order to see whether the import licence should be granted.

Overall, the latest jurisprudence of the CJEU requires that the measures in question are capable of producing legal effects by themselves and as such do not require any further action at the national level. (See *Canon Europa v Commission* case (C-552/14P).)

12.3.3.4 Can the restrictive interpretation of *locus standi* for individuals be justified?

There is no doubt that it is the fear of opening floodgates to litigation, together with a desire not unduly to hamper the institutions in their task of implementing Union policies, problems common to all administrative law systems, that has led the courts to a strict interpretation of this provision, particularly concerning the *locus standi* of individuals. The CJ responded to the criticism of its case law on *locus standi* under Article 263 in *UPA* stating that it is for the Member States to reform the system currently in force. In justifying its narrow approach to *locus standi* under this provision, the courts have often referred to the possibility of alternative means of challenge to the validity of Union law under Article 267 TFEU in proceedings before national courts (eg, *Spijker Kwasten; UNICME*). According to the CJ, the Treaty guarantees judicial review of the Union acts by establishing a complete system of judicial remedies that consist of direct actions for annulment and of indirect review under the preliminary referencing procedure. Any binding Union act can be challenged in preliminary rulings proceedings (see Chapter 10). It has been suggested that this roundabout approach to matters of validity (which can only be decided authoritatively by the CJ) is prompted by a desire to filter out unnecessary claims and ensure that only the claims of genuine merit reach the CJ. One such claim was *Royal Scholten-Honig*, in which the claimant finally succeeded in obtaining a declaration of invalidity on a reference under Article 267 TFEU having failed to establish *locus standi* in an action under Article 263 TFEU (*Koninklijke Scholten-Honig NV v Council and Commission* (case 101/76)) on the grounds that the disputed measure was a true regulation and therefore had no direct or individual effect on the applicant.

But a challenge to the legality of a Union measure in the context of a preliminary ruling may be problematic.

TWD Textilwerke Deggendorf GmbH

In this case, the CJ refused to exercise its jurisdiction under Article 267 TFEU to pronounce on the validity of a Commission decision, addressed to the German government, requiring the government to recover state aids paid to the applicant in breach of what are now Articles 107–8 TFEU. The German government had informed the applicants of the existence of the decision and of their right to challenge it under Article 263 TFEU, but the applicants took no action under this article. Instead they sought to challenge the decision later, in the context of domestic proceedings for recovery of the aid wrongfully paid. When the German judge referred to the CJ for a ruling on the validity of the Commission's decision, the CJ refused its jurisdiction on the grounds that the applicants could and should have challenged the decision directly under Article 263 TFEU. Since they had been informed of the decision and of their right to challenge it they could not circumvent the two-month limitation period of that article by resorting to action under Article 267 TFEU.

The implications of this decision are disturbing. Although the applicants were aware of the decision as soon as it was received and clearly would have had *locus standi* to challenge it under Article 263 TFEU, as being directly and individually concerned, it was not addressed to them. Nor had they been informed of its existence officially by the Commission. Can and should a notification and advice to act by a national government be deemed sufficient notice of a party's rights and obligations, when he is not the addressee of the decision, such as to require that he move immediately to action under Article 263 TFEU, or forfeit his right of challenge? Can this be deemed effective judicial protection for individuals' Union rights? Although the *TWD* ruling has been applied subsequently (eg, *Wiljo NV v Belgium* (case C-178/95)), the CJ has also recognised the difficulties for an applicant unsure of his *locus standi*. In *ex parte Accrington Beef Co Ltd* the CJ held that a reference for a preliminary ruling challenging the validity of a regulation was admissible despite the applicant's failure to bring a claim under Article 263 TFEU within the time limit, since it was not clear that the applicants would have had standing for a judicial review application. An Article 267 TFEU reference which came before the CJ in a case based on the same facts as those in which a judicial review action had been summarily dismissed by the GC was held to be admissible (*Atzeni*). The GC had dismissed the judicial review action for being out of time without considering the *locus standi* of *Atzeni*. When the matter came before the CJ via Article 267 TFEU, the CJ had to consider whether *TWD* applied. It emphasised that the *locus standi* of the applicants was not clear: they had not been mentioned in the decision addressed, in this case, to the Italian government; nor had the government informed them of the decision and of the possibility of reviewing it.

12.3.3.5 A false dawn: *Jégo-Quére* and *Unión de Pequeños Agricultores (UPA)*

Despite the frequent criticism of the restrictive interpretation given to direct and individual concern, the CJ has adhered to the view originally taken in *Plaumann*. However, a strong Advocate-General's opinion in *UPA* and the judgment by the GC in *Jégo-Quére et Cie v Commission* (case T-177/01) appeared to herald a more liberal attitude to the interpretation of individual concern.

UPA

In *UPA*, a trade association challenged a Commission regulation (Regulation 1638/98), but this application had been dismissed by the GC because UPA could not demonstrate individual concern. Moreover, the GC pointed out that UPA could have brought an action under national law and then asked for a reference to be made under Article 267 TFEU to question the legality of the regulation in question. UPA's argument that the restrictive interpretation of individual concern meant that there was no effective legal protection for individuals was rejected. On appeal, Advocate-General Jacobs was unconvinced by the GC's reasons for dismissing the application and reviewed extensively the arguments put forward for the restrictive interpretation of individual concern. He observed that a direct challenge under Article 263 TFEU would be more appropriate than the procedure under Article 267 TFEU, and that the restrictive approach taken to individual applicants was 'anomalous' in the light of the Court's case law on other aspects of judicial review (para 37).

The difficulty with the Article 267 TFEU route is that it requires an action before a national court which is not itself entitled to annul the contested measure. Instead, the national court must consider whether there is sufficient doubt as to its legality for a reference for a preliminary ruling to be made under Article 267 TFEU. Moreover, not all Union measures could give rise to an action before a national court; consequently, such measures could not be challenged through the Article 267 TFEU at all.

In relation to the test for individual concern itself, Advocate-General Jacobs argued that there was no reason why this should entail a requirement that an individual applicant was differentiated in some way for all others affected by the measure. If a measure adversely affects a large number of individuals and causes widespread harm, then this is a strong reason for accepting challenges by one or more of those individuals (para 59). Accordingly, the test of individual concern should be satisfied if a Union measure, by reason of an individual's particular circumstances, has, or is liable to have, a substantial adverse effect on his interests (para 60, and see paras 61–99 for a detailed justification).

The Advocate-General's Opinion in *UPA* found favour with the GC in *Jégo-Quére*, which was decided between the delivery of the Advocate-General's Opinion and the judgment in *UPA*. In *Jégo-Quére*, the applicant was found not to have individual concern within the meaning of the established *Plaumann* line of reasoning. The only possibility for the claimant to challenge the contested regulation was by violating the rules it laid down and then claiming their illegality by way of defence in national proceedings. Nonetheless, the GC held that individuals cannot be required to breach the law to gain access to justice (para 45). Accordingly, and largely in line with Advocate-General Jacob's Opinion in *UPA*, the GC proposed a revised test for individual concern. According to this:

> [a] person is to be regarded as individually concerned by a [Union] measure of general application that concerns him directly if the measure in question affects his legal position in a manner which is both definite and immediate, by restricting his rights or imposing obligations on him [para 51].

Although this judgment was welcomed by commentators throughout the Union, it appears to have been rather short-lived. When the CJ handed down its judgment in *UPA*, it reaffirmed the *Plaumann* jurisprudence on individual concern, and emphasised that there was a complete system of judicial protection in place at the Union level. It was for the Member States to ensure that they provide a system which ensures respect for the right to effective judicial protection and which would allow individuals to use the Article 267 TFEU route to challenge the validity of Union measures. The Court barely mentioned the Advocate-General's Opinion, and completely ignored the decision in *Jégo-Quére*. When it heard the appeal from the GC's decision in *Jégo-Quére* (case C-263/02), the CJ reiterated this reasoning. Despite the continued concerns of Advocate-General Jacobs, the CJ overturned the decision of the GC. The CJ has since reiterated this approach (see, eg, *PKK and KNK* (case C-299/05P)) and has, for example in *Ente per le Ville vesuviane* (case C-445/07), rejected claims that such an approach infringed the claimant's right to a fair trial.

12.4 Time limits

An applicant, whether an individual, a Member State or a Union institution, must bring a claim for annulment within two months of:

- the publication of the measure; or
- its notification to the claimant, or, in the absence thereof;
- the day on which it came to the knowledge of the latter, as the case may be (Article 263(3) TFEU).

The Rules of Procedure of the Court of Justice, as amended, provide that time runs from receipt by the person concerned of notification of the measure or, where the measure is published, from the end of the fourteenth day after its publication in the *Official Journal*.

Since regulations, directives and decisions adopted under the co-decision procedure and directives of the Council and the Commission addressed to all Member States are required to be published, time will run for them from the date of their entry into force, which will be either the date specified in the provisions or on the twentieth day following that of their publication (Article 297 TFEU). Other directives and decisions 'shall be notified to those to whom they are addressed and shall take effect upon such notification' (Article 297 TFEU). In the case of a measure addressed to a person other than the applicant, time will run from the date of the applicant's knowledge. This has been held to require 'precise knowledge' of both the contents of the measure in question and the grounds on which it is based. This is necessary to ensure that the applicant is able to exercise his right to initiate proceedings. Thus a summary of the measure will not suffice (*Commission v Socurte* (case C-143/95 P)). Once he is aware of the existence of the measure he must, however, ask for a full text within a reasonable period ('*Murgia Messapica*').

The 'date of knowledge' is the date on which the applicant became aware of the precise content of the measure. It is not the date on which he realised it could be challenged. Hence the importance of recognising an act as a measure capable of annulment.

The limitation period may be extended to take into account the distance between the CJ at Luxembourg and the applicant's place of residence. In the UK ten days are allowed. It may also be extended if the party concerned proves the existence of unforeseeable circumstances or *force majeure*. In *Bayer AG v Commission* (case C-195/91P) the CJ held that in order to establish such grounds the applicant must show 'abnormal difficulties, independent of the will of the person concerned, and apparently inevitable, even if all due care is taken'. Likewise, the concept of 'excusable error', justifying derogation from time limits, can concern only 'exceptional circumstances' in which the conduct of the EU institution has given rise to a pardonable confusion on the part of the party concerned. The applicant cannot rely on his or her own organisation's internal malfunctioning as an excuse for an error.

12.4.1 **Expiry of time limit**

Once the two-month time limit has expired a claimant cannot seek to challenge a measure by the back door, either by invoking Article 277 TFEU (*exception d'illégalité*, see *Commission v Belgium* (case 156/77)) or by alleging a failure to act when the institution concerned refuses by decision to amend or withdraw the disputed measure (see *Eridania v Commission* (cases 10 and 18/68)) or take the requested action (*Irish Cement Ltd v Commission* (cases 166 and 220/86), see Chapter 13). Time limits will not be allowed to run afresh when the addressee objects to the EU institution's initial reasoning and that institution (normally the Commission) merely confirms its original decision (*Control Union Gesellschaft für Warenkontrolle mbH v Commission* (case C-250/90)).

An indirect challenge using the preliminary rulings procedure before the applicant's national court will not be subject to the two-month limit. In actions before national courts national rules of limitation apply, provided they are adequate to ensure the effective protection of individuals' Union rights (see Chapter 8). However, following *TWD* it is possible that an individual who has *locus standi* under Article 263 TFEU will not be allowed to circumvent the time limit imposed by that Article by challenging legislation outside those limits under Article 267 TFEU. If this is the case, access to the Court under Article 267 TFEU should only be denied when the applicant's *locus standi* under Article 263 TFEU is unequivocally clear. As suggested earlier, this seems to have been the approach adopted and, for example, in *Eurotunnel and Others v SeaFrance* (case C-408/95), the challenge via Article 267 was allowed as it was not clear that the claim under Article 263 TFEU would have been admissible.

12.5 **The merits**

Once the Court has decided that the claim is admissible, the case will be decided on the merits. Article 263 TFEU provides four grounds for annulment, drawn directly from French administrative law. These are:

- lack of competence;
- infringement of an essential procedural requirement;
- infringement of the Treaty or any rule of law relating to its application;
- misuse of powers.

These categories are not mutually exclusive, and often more than one ground is cited in a given case. Nonetheless, in making an application, the applicant must identify clearly the facts and basic legal arguments of the case. In particular, the applicant should not rely on 'catch-all' references to documents annexed to the application. The GC has held that it is not for the Court to seek out and identify the grounds in which the application is based (see, eg, *Cipeke-Comércio e Indústria de Papel Lda v Commission* (case T-84/96), paras 29–4). However, it is not clear how this statement relates to the idea that the Court can consider an infringement of an essential procedural requirement of its own motion (see *Socurte-Sociedade de Curtumes a Sul do Tejo Lda v Commission* (case T-432–4/93), para 63). It seems, however, that the principle has gained acceptance. In *Laboratoires Servier v Commission* (case T-147/00, on appeal case C-156/03P), the GC annulled a Commission decision withdrawing marketing authorisation for certain medicinal products. It did so on its own motion, observing that the lack of competence of an institution that has adopted an act constitutes a ground of annulment for reasons of public policy, which must be raised by the Court. The CJ confirmed this approach in the appeal against the GC's decision.

12.5.1 Lack of competence

This is the equivalent of the English doctrine of substantive *ultra vires*. The institution responsible for adopting the measure in question must have the legal authority to do so. This may derive from the TFEU or from secondary legislation. In the *ERTA* case the Commission challenged the Council's power to participate in the shaping of the road transport agreement, since under the Treaty (Article 218 TFEU) it is the Commission which is empowered to negotiate international agreements and the Council whose duty it is to conclude them. On the facts the Court found that the Council had not exceeded its powers.

On a number of occasions Union law has been challenged as having been enacted under the wrong legal basis (see *Parliament v Council* (case C-295/90)). Clearly the choice of legal basis will be important, as it will determine the appropriate procedure to be followed and the vote required for the adoption of legislation (see Chapters 2 and 3).

The Court allows the institutions some latitude in their choice of legal base and their scope for action under that base. In *Germany v Commission* (case C-359/92) it held that Article 114 TFEU, which provides for the approximation of the provisions laid down by law, regulation or administrative action in Member States which have as their object the establishing and functioning of the internal market (see Chapter 16) was to be interpreted as 'encompassing the Council's power to lay down measures relating to a specific class of products and, if necessary, individual measures concerning those products'. Germany's challenge to Article 9 of Council Directive 92/59 on product safety, based on former Article 100a EEC (now Article 114 TFEU), which empowered the Commission to adopt decisions requiring Member States to take temporary measures in the event of a serious and immediate risk to the health and safety of consumers, failed. The choice of the wrong legal basis was also addressed in *Portugal v Council* (case C-268/94).

***

Portugal v Council

In this case the Portuguese government sought the annulment of a decision arguing that it had been based upon an incorrect Treaty provision. The decision referred to what are now Articles 144 and 211 TFEU respectively, dealing with commercial policy, which only required that the decision be adopted by qualified majority vote. The Portuguese government claimed that the agreement to which the decision related contained provisions aimed at protecting democracy and human rights in India, and should have been made under Article 352 TFEU, which would have required unanimity. The CJ held that on the facts of the case the provisions of the then Article 130y (now 211 TFEU) were broad enough to encompass the complained-of clauses, and that to rule otherwise would be to deprive the specific clauses of their substance.

We have seen that similar issues arise in relation to determining the allocation of powers between the pillars of the Union, and that the CJ has tended to favour an approach which gives the *acquis communautaire* the maximum protection (see, eg, *Kadi*, discussed in Chapter 4).

The Court is stricter in its approach to questions concerning the allocation of competence between the Union institutions (see, eg, *France, Netherlands and Spain v Commission* (case C-327/91)), and, as noted earlier, the CJ's decisions have protected the procedural rights of the European Parliament (see, eg, the *Lomé Convention* case).

12.5.2 Infringement of an essential procedural requirement

This is equivalent to procedural *ultra vires* in English law. Institutions, when enacting binding measures, must follow the correct procedures. These procedures may be laid down in the Treaties or secondary legislation. For example, Article 296 TFEU requires that all secondary legislation must state the reasons on which it is based, and must refer to proposals and opinions which were required to be obtained. The Court has held that reasons must not be too vague or inconsistent; they must be coherent; they must mention figures and essential facts on which they rely. They must be adequate to indicate the conscientiousness of the decision, and detailed enough to be scrutinised by the Court (*Germany v Commission (tariff quotas on wine)* (case 24/62)—Commission decision annulled; too vague, no facts and figures). The purpose of the requirement to give reasons is to enable those concerned to defend their rights and to enable the Court to exercise its supervisory jurisdiction. However, the Court will not annul an act for an insignificant defect. Nor will it annul an act on this ground unless the claimant can prove that, but for this defect, the result would have been different (*Distillers Co Ltd v Commission* (case 30/78)).

In *Roquette Frères SA v Council* (case 138/79) and *Maizena* a Council regulation was annulled on the grounds of the Council's failure to consult Parliament, as it was required to do under Article 43 TFEU. Although the Council had consulted Parliament, it was held not to have given Parliament sufficient time to express an opinion on the measure in question. Where no time limit is imposed it is presumed that Parliament must be given a reasonable time in which to express its opinion. In *Infront*, the letter to the UK government was signed by a director-general of the Commission who had not consulted the College of Commissioners. The letter was therefore annulled for failure to follow proper procedures.

12.5.3 Infringement of the Treaties or any rule of law relating to their application

Clearly, when an act is invalid for lack of competence or for an infringement of an essential procedural requirement, this may involve an infringement of the Treaties, but this ground of annulment is wider since it extends to *any* Treaty provision. In *Adams v Commission (No 1)* (case 145/83), an action for non-contractual liability (see Chapter 14), the Commission was found to have acted in breach of its duty of confidentiality under Article 339 TFEU.

Infringement of any rule of law relating to the Treaties' application is wider again, and certainly wider than any comparable rule of English law. This is where general principles of law, discussed at length in Chapter 6, are relevant. In *Royal Scholten-Honig* a Union regulation was held invalid for breach of the principle of equality. In *Transocean Marine Paint Association* (see Chapter 6) part of a decision was annulled for breach of the principle of natural justice. In *August Töpfer* a decision was annulled for breach of the principle of legal certainty, for infringement of the applicant's legitimate expectations. Although the Court will not lightly set aside legislation for breach of this principle and will expect businessmen to anticipate and guard against foreseeable developments, within the bounds of 'normal' economic risks, this is a ground of some potential (see *Amylum v Council* (case 108/81); *Mulder v Council* (case C-104/89)). Note, however, that a trader is unlikely to have legitimate expectations that do not accord with existing Union rules (see, eg, *Efisol SA*). Thus, it is difficult to argue that a requirement to pay back illegally granted state aid would be in breach of legitimate expectations. In *Opel Austria*, the GC held that the principle of legitimate expectations within the EU was the corollary of the principle of good faith in public international law. Where Union institutions have deposited their instruments of approval of an international agreement and the date of the entry into force of that agreement is known, any measures contrary to provisions of such agreements having direct effect will be in breach of legitimate expectations. In *A Racke Gmbh & Co v Hauptzollamt Mainz* (case C-162/96), the CJ held that the CJ's jurisdiction to review the validity of a Union act could not be limited as regards the grounds on which it could find a measure invalid. In this case, it held that a Union measure, a regulation, could be held to be invalid were it contrary to international law (cf *Kadi*).

Although it has not yet been done successfully, legislation could in principle be challenged for breach of the principle of subsidiarity, either as a general principle or as now expressed in Article 5 TEU (see Chapters 3 and 6). The German government raised the question of subsidiarity, albeit in a different context, in *Germany v Parliament* (case C-233/94). It sought to challenge Directive 94/19 ([1994] L135/5), arguing that there had been a breach of the duty to state reasons for the legislation as required by the then Article 190, in that the Directive did not explain how it complied with the principle of subsidiarity set out in Article 5 TEU. The CJ rejected this argument, stating that the necessary information could be inferred from the recitals to the Directive.

Because of the breadth of the concept of 'any rule of law relating to the [Treaty's] application', the acts of the EU institutions are vulnerable to attack on this ground. Thus the CJ has held that where the Union legislature has discretion to act in a complex economic situation, such as the implementation of the Union's agricultural policy, both as regards the nature and scope of the measures to be taken and the finding of basic facts, the Court, in reviewing the exercise of such a power:

> must confine itself to examining whether it contains a manifest error or constitutes a misuse of power or whether the authority in question did not clearly exceed the bounds of its discretion [*Commission v Council* (case C-122/94)].

The CJ's approach to the Union's liability in damages for legislative measures involving choices of economic policy, which the GC adopts also, reflects a similar concern not to fetter the discretion of the EU institutions when they are implementing Union policy. In this context the Court may be accused of occasionally going too far to protect the Union institutions (see *Germany v Council* (case C-280/93), see Chapter 6).

12.5.4 **Misuse of power**

This concept stems from the French *détournement de pouvoir*. It means, broadly, the use of a power for purposes other than those for which it was granted—for example, where powers granted to help one group (eg, producers) are used to benefit another (eg, distributors) (see *Simmenthal SpA v Commission* (case 92/78)). It has been defined by the CJ as:

> the adoption by a Union institution of a measure with the exclusive or main purpose of achieving an end other than that stated or evading a procedure specifically prescribed by the Treaty for dealing with the circumstances of the case [*Parliament v Commission* (case C-156/93)].

The concept is not confined to abuses of power, nor is an ulterior or improper motive essential; an improper or illegitimate use of power is all that is required. However, this provision has been narrowly interpreted. In *Fédération Charbonnière de Belgique*, in interpreting the comparable provision (Article 33) of the ECSC Treaty, the Court held that a measure will not be annulled for misuse of power if the improper use had no effect on its substance; nor will it be annulled if the authority had acted from mixed motives, proper and improper, as long as the proper purpose was dominant. It is thus a difficult ground to establish.

The case of *Werner A Bock* was considered, but not decided, on this ground. Although there was no clear collusion between the German government and the Commission over the issuing of the decision, there were definite signs of collaboration. The case was eventually decided, and the decision annulled, for breach of the principle of proportionality. The Commission's action was more than was necessary in the circumstances, since the quantities of mushrooms at stake were so small as to be insignificant.

There is much overlap between the above grounds. The Court rarely examines each one precisely and is often vague as to which ground forms the basis of its decision. This can be seen in the context of *BEUC v Commission* (case T-37/92).

BEUC

This case concerned the Commission's decision not to investigate the agreement between the British Society of Motor Manufacturers and the Japanese government limiting imports of Japanese cars to 11 per cent of total UK sales. This decision was prima facie contrary to Article 101, but was justified by the Commission, inter alia, because the agreement was permitted as a matter of UK policy. The GC annulled the decision simply on the ground that it constituted an 'error of law'. Despite the Court's lack of precision in these matters it is wise to plead as many grounds as seem applicable.

The grounds apply equally to an examination of the validity of a measure on reference from national courts under Article 267 TFEU. They also apply to an enquiry into the validity of regulations under Article 277 TFEU (12.8) and to an application for damages under Article 340 TFEU (Chapter 14) where the action is based on an illegal act of the institutions.

12.6 Consequences of a successful action

If an annulment action under Article 263 TFEU is successful the act will be declared void under Article 264 TFEU. A measure may be declared void in part only, provided that the offending part can be effectively severed. Under Article 264(2) TFEU, however, the Court may, following a successful action for annulment, 'state which of the effects of the Regulation which it has declared void shall be considered as definitive'. This has been done in the interests of legal certainty, to avoid upsetting past transactions based on a regulation, a normative act. It should be noted that in *Ecroyd v Commission* (case T-220/97), the GC held that should a court find a measure invalid, it is not enough to repeal that measure; the position of the complainants must also be addressed so that they do not continue to suffer loss. A successful action for damages under Article 340(2) TFEU could arise in these circumstances, as indeed it did in this case.

A slightly different point arose in *Commission v AssiDoman Kraft Products AB* (case C-310/97P).

> ### AssiDoman Kraft Products AB
>
> The case concerned certain fines imposed on a number of undertakings for breach of the competition rules. Some of the undertakings appealed against the Commission's decisions, resulting in the partial annulment of the Commission's decision and the reduction of the fines imposed on the appellant undertakings. Several other companies, which had also been fined but which had not been party to the appeal, then requested that the Commission reconsider their position in the light of the annulment ruling. The Commission refused, as it argued that the companies involved in the competition proceedings had each been addressed individually and therefore a finding of invalidity as regards a decision addressed to one company did not affect a similar decision addressed to another. The applicant companies sought to challenge before the European courts on the basis that the Commission was obliged to reconsider its decision by virtue of Article 266 TFEU. The matter finally came before the CJ, the GC having found in the companies' favour. The CJ overturned the GC's ruling, holding that the scope of Article 266 was limited in two ways. First, a ruling for annulment could not go further than the applicant requested, and thus the matter tried by the Union courts could relate only to aspects of the decision which affected the applicants. The CJ then held that although the operative part of the judgment and its reasoning were binding *erga omnes*, '[this] cannot entail annulment of an act not challenged before the Union judicature but alleged to be vitiated by the same illegality' (para 54).

12.7 Indirect review under Article 277 TFEU

12.7.1 Scope

Although Article 277 TFEU entitles 'any party' to attack a regulation 'notwithstanding the expiry' of the time limit laid down in Article 263 TFEU, it is not designed to provide a means of escaping the restrictions either of time or *locus standi* laid down in Article 263 TFEU. No action can be brought *directly* against a regulation under Article 277 TFEU. As the Court held in *Milchwerke Heinz Wöhrmann & Sohn KG v Commission* (cases 31 and 33/62), in the context of an action brought under Article 277 TFEU to annul three Commission decisions, a plea under Article 277 TFEU can be raised as an *incidental* matter *only* in the course of legal proceedings based on other provisions of the Treaty. In *Wöhrmann* the action was brought *solely* under Article 277 TFEU, since the time limit within which the decisions should have been challenged under Article 263 TFEU had elapsed. Thus, the application was rejected. (See also *Commission v Belgium* (case 156/77) and, more recently, *Comité des Salines de France v Commission* (case T-154/94).)

The purpose of Article 277 TFEU is to allow a party to question the legality of a general act on which a subsequent act (eg, a decision), or failure to act, is based. A decision is often, indeed normally, based on some general authorising act. Although a decision, in principle subject to challenge under Article 263 TFEU, may in itself be unimpeachable, it may be based on a general act that is not. A non-privileged applicant has no *locus standi* to challenge a general act under Article 263 TFEU. Even a privileged applicant under Article 263 TFEU may not be aware of the illegality of the general act until affected by some subsequent act issuing from that 'tainted' source. By this time the two months within which the original act should have been challenged may have elapsed. Article 277 TFEU provides a means whereby this underlying act may be challenged *indirectly*, free of time limit, before the CJ in proceedings in which it is 'in issue', in much the same way as questions concerning the validity of EU law may be raised indirectly in the context of domestic proceedings before national courts.

12.7.2 Proceedings in which Article 277 TFEU may be invoked

In theory Article 277 TFEU may be invoked in the context of any proceedings brought directly before the CJ in which it is relevant. This interpretation should be treated with caution. In *Hessische Knappschaft* the Court was not prepared to consider a claim under Article 277 TFEU in the context of a reference from a national court under Article 267 TFEU. However, in that case the parties had attempted to raise the plea of illegality as a new issue; it had not been raised in the reference by the national court. Their attempt to raise it before the CJ was thus seen by the Court as an interference with the national court's discretion, and, as such, unacceptable. Nevertheless, it would not be necessary to invoke Article 277 TFEU before a national court since these courts are free to refer to the CJ under Article 267 TFEU questions of validity of *any* Union act, and are not constrained by the time limit applicable to a direct challenge under Article 263 TFEU, subject, of course to the impact of *TWD*. This point seems to have been made in *Nachi Europe GmbH v Hauptzollamt Krefeld* (case C-239/99). The Court held that Article 277 TFEU could not be invoked in the context of a preliminary reference under Article 267 TFEU, because this is not regarded as a main action before the CJ (para 34). To hold otherwise would be to provide a duplicate means of challenge as Article 267 TFEU already provides for a challenge to the validity of the measure on which a domestic court has requested a ruling.

The main context in which Article 277 TFEU is likely to be invoked is to support a challenge under Article 263 TFEU to the validity of a measure based on the original, allegedly invalid, act. If the underlying act, challenged under Article 277 TFEU, is found invalid, it will be declared 'inapplicable' and the subsequent act, affecting the claimant, will be void. Thus the principal object of the exercise will be achieved.

12.7.3 Reviewable acts

Although Article 277 TFEU was expressed to apply only to acts of general application, the Court, in keeping with its approach in Article 263 TFEU, has held that Article 277 TFEU applies to any general act having binding force. This can be seen in *Simmenthal*.

Simmenthal

In this case the claimant, a meat processing company, was seeking to annul, under what is now Article 263(4) TFEU, a decision addressed to the Italian government, in which the company was directly and individually concerned. The basis of its claim for annulment was that the 'parent' measure, a general notice of invitation to tender, on which the decision was based, was invalid. The Court held that since the notice was a general act, which, although not in the form of a regulation, produced similar effects, it could be challenged under Article 277 TFEU. The challenge was successful and resulted in the annulment of the decision affecting the claimant.

Article 277 TFEU refers to acts of general application.

12.7.3.1 Is the scope for challenge under Article 277 TFEU limited to general measures?

The principal reason for making an 'exception' for regulations would appear to be to enable individuals, who are unable to challenge general acts under Article 263 TFEU, to do so when they seek, legitimately, to rely on their invalidity in the context of other proceedings before the Court.

A secondary reason would be that, since a regulation is 'of general application' and is not addressed to anyone, its invalidity may not be apparent to the claimant until a subsequent individual measure, based on the general measure, brings it to his attention. Both reasons, that is, lack of opportunity to challenge and absence of notification, would justify extending the scope of Article 277 TFEU to enable an individual to challenge, indirectly, any 'parent' act which was not addressed to him or in which he was not directly and individually concerned. The second reason would provide grounds for allowing a privileged applicant to challenge indirectly any 'parent' act which was not addressed to the applicant. This matter has yet to be decided by the Court.

12.7.4 *Locus standi*

Although *locus standi* under Article 277 TFEU appears to apply to 'any party', doubts have been expressed as to whether it extends to privileged applicants. It is argued that since Member States and institutions are entitled to seek annulment of *any* act under Article 263 TFEU, to allow them to invoke Article 277 TFEU would be to enable them to challenge acts which they should have challenged within the time limit laid down by Article 263 TFEU. However, Advocate-General Roemer in *Italy v Council* (case 32/65) took the view that a Member State *should* have *locus standi* under Article 277 TFEU, since the wording of the provision was in no way restrictive, and the illegality of the general provision might not become apparent until it was applied subsequently in a particular case. The Court did not comment on the matter, since it found that the regulations in issue were not relevant to the case, but its silence could be read as consent. Advocate-General Roemer's reasoning is persuasive. Moreover, Article 277 TFEU can never be used *merely* to circumvent a time limit; it can only be invoked as an incidental issue, when the claimant is affected by some subsequent act (or failure) arising from the original general act. This provides ample safeguard against abuse.

This point is illustrated by *Commission v Belgium* (case 156/77).

Commission v Belgium

Here Article 277 TFEU was raised as a defence to an enforcement action against Belgium for infringement of Union law relating to state aids. Belgium had failed to comply with a Commission decision of May 1976, requiring it to abolish certain state aids within a three-month period. No attempt had been made to challenge that decision. In proceedings brought by the Commission in December 1977 for non-compliance with the decision the Belgian government argued, invoking Article 277 TFEU, that the decision was invalid. The claim was held inadmissible. The Court found that Belgium's claim was, in essence, a claim for the annulment of the decision of May 1976. It had been free to contest this decision under Article 263 TFEU, but had failed to do so within the time limit. It could not allow this limit to elapse and then challenge the decision's legality under Article 277 TFEU.

This case, it is submitted, does not decide that Article 277 TFEU can never be raised in enforcement proceedings against Member States. Belgium's claim under the then Article 184 EEC was rejected on different and wholly legitimate grounds. They were not invoking the article as a collateral issue; their defence was based *solely* on the legality of a decision addressed to them which they had failed to challenge in time.

12.7.5 **Consequences of a successful challenge**

Where an action under Article 277 TFEU is successful, the regulation is declared 'inapplicable'. Since there is no time limit within which acts may be challenged under the article, it is not, for reasons of legal certainty, void, but voidable. However, a declaration of inapplicability will render a subsequent act, based on that act, void. Thus, although action under Article 277 TFEU is an 'incidental matter', it will be conclusive of the principal action before the Court. A declaration of inapplicability under this article may also be invoked to prevent the application of the invalid act in a subsequent case.

12.8 Conclusions

The procedure in Article 263 TFEU is an important cog in the judicial-review machinery, but it is not without shortcomings. The time limits can impose significant constraints and we have seen that other possible routes to challenge Union acts have been interpreted so as not to undermine this limitation. The greatest criticism has been of the restrictive test for the admissibility of actions by individuals and the attitude to the *locus standi* of trade associations and pressure groups is also rather restrictive. We saw earlier that the CJ in the *Inuit* appeal decided to reaffirm the rather unsatisfactory GC's order and therefore even post Lisbon private litigants still have to meet the requirements of direct and individual concern in relation to legislative acts since they cannot be considered as 'regulatory acts'. This approach imposes significant questions about the contribution of the Treaty of Lisbon as well as the contribution of the CJEU in relation to the strict *locus standi* requirements for private litigants.

Further reading

Albors-Llorens, A, 'Judicial Protection before the Court of Justice of the European Union' in C Barnard and S Peers (eds), *European Union Law* (Oxford University Press, 2014).

Albors-Llorens, A, 'The standing of private parties to challenge community measures: Has the European Court missed the boat?' (2003) 62 CLJ 72.

Arnull, A, 'Private applicants and the action for annulment under Article 173 of the EC Treaty' (1995) 32 CMLR 7.

Arnull, A, 'Private applicants and the action for annulment since *Cordoniu*' (2001) 38 CML Rev 7.

Balthasar, S, 'Locus Standi for challenges to regulatory acts by private applicants: The new Article 263(4) TFEU' (2010) 35 EL Rev 542.

Costa, M, *The Accountability Gap in EU law* (Routledge, 2016).

Enchelmeier, S, 'No-one slips through the net? Latest developments, and non-developments, in the European Court of Justice's jurisprudence on Art 263(4) EC' (2005) 24 YEL 173.

Harlow, C, 'Towards a theory of access for the European Court of Justice' (1992) 12 YEL 213.

Malleghem, P-A and Baeten, N, 'Before the law stands a gatekeeper—Or, what is a "regulatory act" in Article 263(4) TFEU? *Inuit Tapiriit Kanatami*' (2014) 51 CML Rev 1187.

Mancini, F and Keeling, D, 'Democracy and the European Court of Justice' (1994) 57 ML Rev 175.

Peers, S and Costa, M, 'Judicial Review of EU Acts after the Treaty of Lisbon; Order of 6 September 2011, Case T-18/10 *Inuit Tapiriit Kanatami and Others v Commission* & Judgment of 25 October 2011, Case T-262/10 *Microban v Commission*' (2012) 8 EU Const 82.

Tridimas, T and Poli, S, 'Locus Standi of individuals under Article 230(4): The return of Euridice?' in A Arnull, P Eeckhout and T Tridimas (eds), *Continuity and Change in EU Law: Essays in Honour of Sir Francis Jacobs* (Oxford University Press, 2008).

Vogt, M, 'Indirect judicial protection in EC law: The case of the plea of illegality' (2006) 31 EL Rev 364.

Ward, A, *Judicial Review and the Rights of Private Parties in EU Law*, 2nd edn (Oxford University Press, 2007).

Action for failure to act

13.1 Introduction

If the institutions of the European Union are to operate according to the rule of law, as they are obliged to do under Article 13 TEU, they must be answerable not only for their actions but for their failure to act in breach of Union law. Article 265 TFEU is a mirror of Article 263 which provides for judicial review of actions of the Union institutions. A complete system of judicial review requires not only that Union institutions, bodies and agencies act lawfully, but also that they act when they have a duty to do so. As with that provision, concern focuses on the extent to which non-privileged applicants are adequately protected by the Union legal order, in particular as regards the rules relating to *locus standi* and—consequently—the right of access to a court. Whilst much has been written about the scope of Article 263 TFEU, there has been much less attention paid to this provision, as relatively few cases brought under it have succeeded. Here the concept of an institution, body or agency 'defining its position' is key. This chapter, after outlining the scope of Article 265 TFEU, will consider who can bring an action, and what sorts of omissions are capable of being the subject of review. Finally, this chapter will consider the relationship of this provision with Article 263 TFEU, and consider the effects of a successful claim.

13.2 Overview of the provisions

The relevant provision is Article 265 TFEU, which provides as follows:

> Should the European Parliament, the European Council, the Council, the Commission or the European Central Bank in infringement of the Treaties, fail to act, the Member States and the other institutions of the Union may bring an action before the Court of Justice of the European Union to have the infringement established. This article shall apply, under the same conditions, to bodies, offices and agencies of the union which fail to act.
>
> The action shall be admissible only if the institution, body, office or agency concerned has first been called upon to act. If, within two months of being so called upon, the institution, body, office or agency concerned has not defined its position, the action may be brought within a further period of two months.
>
> Any natural or legal person may, under the conditions laid down in the preceding paragraphs, complain to the Court that an institution, body, office or agency of the Union has failed to address to that person any act other than a recommendation or an opinion.

Actions brought by a natural or legal person under Article 265 TFEU now fall within the jurisdiction of the GC, although appeal on points of law may be made to the CJ (see Chapter 7).

Articles 265 and 263 TFEU are essentially complementary remedies. As CJ held in *Chevalley v Commission* (case 15/70) when confronted with the applicant's uncertainty as to whether Articles 265 or 263 was the appropriate form of action, it is not necessary to characterise the proceedings as being under one or the other article, since both prescribe one and the same method of recourse. They represent two aspects of the same legal remedy. For this reason, any inconsistency between the two provisions should be resolved by applying the same principles to both. This is known as the 'unity principle', and it, or the coherence between the two provisions, remains a relevant factor referred to by the GC (see, eg, *Gestevision Telecinco v Commission* (case T-95/96)).

13.3 Reviewable omissions

The institution's failure to act must, first and foremost, be 'in infringement of the Treaties'. Since this would include legislation enacted under the Treaty it would apply to any failure on the part of the institution to act when it was under a legal duty to do so. In *Parliament v Council (common transport policy)* (case 13/83), in an action by Parliament under Article 265 alleging the Council's failure to implement a Union transport policy, the Court held that 'failure' can cover a failure to take a number of decisions; the nature of the acts which may be requested need not be clearly circumscribed as long as they are sufficiently identified. The failures alleged by Parliament in this case were:

- failure to introduce a common transport policy, as required by the then Article 74 EEC;
- failure to introduce measures to secure freedom to provide transport services, as required by the then Articles 75, 59, 60 and 61 EEC.

The Court held that Parliament was entitled to succeed on the second allegation but not on the first. While the second obligation was complete and legally perfect, and should have been implemented by the Council within the transitional period, the former obligation was insufficiently precise to constitute an enforceable obligation. Prior to the TEU, action under the then Article 175 EEC (now 265 TFEU) could be brought only against the Council or the Commission, but now action may also be brought against the European Parliament. Omissions of the Union are also subject to review under Article 265 TFEU. Although the Court of Auditors was awarded the power to bring actions under Article 263 by the ToA, its inaction is not subject to review under Article 265 TFEU.

Only non-binding acts in the form of recommendations and opinions are expressly excluded in the context of individual action under Article 265, third paragraph; a failure to act under Article 265 would only cover a failure to issue a binding act.

13.4 *Locus standi*

13.4.1 Privileged applicants

The Member States the European Parliament, the European Council, the Council and the European Central Bank are privileged applicants under Article 265. Privileged applicants enjoy a right to challenge *any* failure on the part of the Council and the Commission, ie an omission to adopt *any* binding act which these institutions have a duty to adopt.

It should be noted that there is no obligation on a Member State to bring an action under Article 265. This was confirmed by the CJ in *Ten Kate Holding BV*.

> ### Ten Kate Holding BV
>
> In this case, a Dutch manufacturer sought to bring an action against the Dutch government for failing to take action under Articles 263 and 265 TFEU. The Court held that neither provision imposed an obligation on a Member State to bring an action, and a Member State's decision not to bring an action would not constitute an infringement of that state's obligations under Union law (and therefore could not give rise to a claim in state liability under *Francovich*). However, the CJ emphasised that Union law did not preclude a domestic rule that would impose liability on the government of a Member State which could have brought an action under Articles 263 or 265 TFEU, but did not do so. This would be a matter entirely for domestic law and outside the jurisdiction of the CJ.

13.4.2 Individuals

13.4.2.1 Measures subject to challenge by individuals

In comparison with Member States and Union institutions, individuals, as under Article 263, have a limited *locus standi* under Article 265(3). Natural or legal persons may bring proceedings only where the institutions, bodies, offices or agencies of the Union have failed to address to that person any act other than a recommendation or an opinion. Since an act which is addressed to a designated person is in substance a decision, this seems to mean that an individual's *locus standi* is limited to a failure on the part of the Council or Commission to adopt what is in essence a *decision* addressed to *himself or herself*. The individual has no express *locus standi* to challenge an omission to address to *another person* a decision of direct and individual concern to himself or herself.

This apparent deficiency has been remedied by the Court. In *Nordgetreide GmbH & Co KG v Commission* (case 42/71), Advocate-General Roemer, invoking the unity principle, suggested that since Articles 263 and 265 TFEU constituted part of a coherent system, an individual should have a right to demand a decision vis-à-vis a third party in which the individual was directly and individually concerned as much as that third party. In *Bethell v Commission* (case 246/81) this right was implied when the Court, in rejecting Lord Bethell's claim as inadmissible, held that he had failed to show that the Commission had failed to adopt, in relation to him, a measure *which he was legally entitled to claim*. In the context of Article 265 TFEU, the equivalent to a decision of direct and individual concern under Article 263, it was a decision which the applicant was *legally entitled to claim*.

This test was relaxed in *T Port*. Reasoning from the unity principle and the test of direct and individual concern used for Article 263 TFEU actions, the CJ stated that Article 265(3) TFEU could be invoked where an institution has failed to act in respect of a measure which would have concerned the applicant in the same way (para 59). The GC has subsequently followed the *T Port* case in the more recent cases involving challenges to the funding of public service broadcasters (eg, *Gestevision Telecinco*), thus suggesting that this approach has now been consolidated into the courts' case law.

Many of the claims under Article 265 TFEU prior to *T Port* failed because the applicant was seeking the adoption of an act which he was not entitled to claim. For example, in *Ladbroke Racing Ltd v Commission* (case T-32/93), an individual complainant was held not to have a right to demand action by the Commission under the state aid provisions of Article 108 TFEU. This may be compared with the more recent case of *Bundesverband* (discussed in Chapter 12) in which the CJ accepted that in limited circumstances, details of which it did not elaborate, an applicant could demand action under Article 107 TFEU, although in *Commission v T-Mobile Austria* (case C-141/02P), the CJ appeared to move away from that view (see paras 68–9). In *Gestevision Telecinco*, the GC held that an individual could demand that the Commission make a decision at the end of the initial investigatory phase of state aid proceedings under Article 108 TFEU. Further, where the Commission has difficulty in determining whether the funding in issue constitutes state aid or whether it is compatible with the internal market 'the institution has a duty to gather all necessary views and to that end initiate the procedure under [Article 106(2) TFEU]'.

In both of these circumstances, Article 265 TFEU proceedings could be brought against a failure on the Commission's part to act. It may be that the easing of the test here and in *T Port* will result in an increase in the number of successful actions brought by individual applicants. Arguably, a more generous approach to individuals' *locus standi* under Article 265 TFEU is justified if individuals are to be denied access to the CJ to challenge an institution's failure to act under Article 257 TFEU.

On rather different reasoning in another failed claim in the earlier case of *Eridania*, the Court held that the applicants could not invoke Article 265 TFEU to obtain a revocation by the Commission of a decision addressed to third parties, as other methods of recourse, namely, Article 263, were provided by the Treaty; to allow parallel recourse via Article 265 would enable applicants to avoid the strict conditions (eg, time limits) laid down by Article 263 TFEU.

13.4.2.2 Challengeable acts

An applicant cannot bring proceedings to force a Union institution or any other entity specified in Article 265 TFEU to open an inquiry with respect to a third party or to address to them a decision (*Prodifarmia v Commission* (case T-3/90); *ENU v Commission* (case C-107/91)). It is clear that the act demanded must be in substance a decision.

Nordgetreide

In this case the applicant company was seeking the amendment by the Commission of a regulation. When the Commission rejected its request the company instituted two actions, one for failure to act, under Article 265 TFEU, and one under Article 263 TFEU for annulment of the Commission's decision refusing to act. The action under Article 265 TFEU would in any case have failed because, as Advocate-General Roemer pointed out, the company was seeking from the Commission what would have amounted to a normative act; in fact the Court found its claim inadmissible on different grounds (to be discussed below). The claim under Article 263 TFEU was also held inadmissible. Although the contested decision was addressed to the applicant, the Court held that a decision refusing to act (a 'negative' decision) would only be open to attack under Article 263 if the *positive* measure being sought were open to attack.

This same reasoning would apply to a refusal by the Commission to issue a decision to another person which the applicant was not entitled to claim. Thus, even though a decision may have been addressed to the applicant, Article 263 TFEU cannot be invoked as an adjunct to Article 265 TFEU to annul a decision not to act, in order to compel an institution to act *when it has no duty to do so at the behest of the applicant*. Although this has been attempted on a number of occasions, it has always failed (eg, *Lütticke* (case 48/65); *Star Fruit Company SA v Commission* (case 247/87); *J v Commission* (case T-5/94)—applicants demanding action by the Commission under Article 258 TFEU against a Member State; *Bethell*—applicant seeking to force Commission to take action under Article 109 TFEU against Member States' airlines).

13.4.2.3 **Procedural rights**

A case in which the applicant was entitled to demand action from the Commission, but in which its claim was surprisingly held inadmissible, was *Deutscher Komponistenverband v Commission* (case 8/71). Here the applicant alleged that the Commission had failed in its obligation under Union competition law (Regulation 17/62, now repealed) to grant it, as a complainant under Article 3 of that Regulation, a hearing. Advocate-General Roemer suggested that acts susceptible of action under Article 265 TFEU should cover any measures which give rise to legal effects for the applicant; they should then include measures of a procedural nature. The Court disagreed, holding that Article 265(3) TFEU only applied to a failure to adopt a decision; it did not cover the promulgation of a formal act. Nevertheless the Court did examine the merits and concluded that since the applicant had had an opportunity to make its submissions in writing there had been no failure to act on the part of the Commission.

It is submitted that Advocate-General Roemer's view is to be preferred to that of the Court. Since there was no doubt that the applicant was entitled to a hearing any failure to grant it that hearing should have been actionable under Article 265 TFEU. And if it was refused such a hearing, as it was, it should have been entitled to challenge that refusal under Article 263 TFEU, as the decision it requested (ie, a hearing) was one which it was entitled to demand.

This view seems to have been taken by the Court in *FEDIOL v Commission* (case 191/82).

FEDIOL

In this case, a Union federation of seed crushers and oil processors was seeking to compel the Commission to take action against alleged dumping practices on the part of Brazil. As undertakings which considered themselves injured or threatened by subsidised imports, the applicants were entitled under Regulation 3017/79 (the principal anti-dumping regulation) to lodge a complaint (Article 5), to be consulted (Article 6), and to receive information (Article 9). In April 1980 they lodged a complaint with the Commission. Following enquiries and negotiations with the Brazilian government the Commission decided to take no further action. In September 1981 FEDIOL instituted Article 265 TFEU proceedings. Following further correspondence between FEDIOL and the Commission, the Commission informed FEDIOL by letter in May 1982 that it intended to take no further action against Brazil. FEDIOL then brought Article 263 TFEU proceedings to annul the decision contained in that letter. The Court held that since the Regulation under which they complained recognised specific rights on the applicants' part, they were entitled to a review by the Court of any exercise of power by the Union institutions which might affect these rights. Thus the action was held admissible. Although the applicants could not compel the Commission to take action against Brazil, that being a matter within the Commission's discretion, they were entitled to a review by the Court of the Commission's decision in the letter of May 1982 to ensure that their procedural rights were respected.

This case may be contrasted with the earlier case of *GEMA v Commission* (case 125/78).

GEMA

Here GEMA initiated a complaint to the Commission under Article 3 of Regulation 17/62, alleging a breach by Radio Luxembourg of what is now Articles 101–2 TFEU. In March 1978 the Commission wrote to GEMA saying that it had decided not to pursue the matter. In May 1978 GEMA instituted Article 265 TFEU proceedings against this refusal to act. Subsequently, in March 1979, GEMA brought proceedings under Article 263 TFEU to annul the letter of March 1978. The action under Article 265 failed because the Commission was held to have defined its position in the letter of March 1978. The

> action under Article 263 failed on the grounds that, assuming that the letter could be contested, this did not entitle the applicants to a *final decision* on the existence of an infringement under Article 102 TFEU. In any case the letter had not been challenged in time and the parties' attempts to extend the limit on the grounds of fresh issues based on matters of fact and law failed.

On appeal in *Guérin Automobiles v Commission* (case C-282/95P), the CJ confirmed that a letter to a complainant was a definition of a position for the purposes of Article 265 TFEU, but that it could not be challenged because the letter was a preparatory stage in proceedings. The applicants were entitled under competition procedural rules to make representations, after which the Commission must make a decision which would have legally binding effects. It would be at this stage that an applicant could challenge a failure to act although it still could not force the Commission to take a decision that was favourable to the applicants.

Thus, in all of these cases the parties were only entitled in law to protection by way of review under Articles 265 and 263 TFEU to protect their procedural rights. They had no right to compel the Commission to institute proceedings against third parties; that was a matter within the Commission's discretion (see also *Ladbroke Racing Ltd v Commission* (case T-32/93)). Even in *Gestevision*, where the Commission seemed to be under an obligation to investigate the funding to state broadcasters further, this obligation arose out of the need to protect the procedural rights of all involved and did not entitle Gestevision to any particular finding on the question of state aid.

Where an individual does have a right to complain and to request action, as in *FEDIOL*, *GEMA* and *Guérin*, should the Commission take action and issue a decision to a third party, the complainant will be deemed to be directly and individually concerned and will be entitled to claim a full review of the decision under Article 263 TFEU (*Metro-SB-Grossmärkte GmbH*, see Chapter 12; *Timex Corporation v Council* (case 264/82); *COFAZ v Commission* (case 169/84); *British American Tobacco (BAT) Co Ltd & Reynolds v Commission* (cases 142 and 156/84)).

13.5 Procedure

Where the applicant has a right to require an institution to act, and the institution is under a corresponding duty to act, the applicant must first call upon the institution to act. No time limit is imposed within which proceedings must be commenced for the alleged failure to act, but the Court has held that proceedings must be brought within a reasonable time of the institution's having demonstrated its intention not to act (*Netherlands v Commission* (case 59/70)—case brought under Article 35 of the ECSC Treaty).

The institution, body office or agency then has two months within which it may either act in accordance with the request, or 'define its position'.

If the institution, body, office or agency fails to act or to define its position within that two-month period the claimant has a further two months within which to bring his case before the court, running from the date on which the institution should have defined its position. These limits are strictly enforced. In *Guérin* the Commission, responding to a complaint by Guérin concerning an alleged breach by Nissan of Article 101(1) TFEU, merely sent them a copy of Nissan's response to the complaint. When Guérin subsequently submitted their observations to the Commission in February 1995, the Commission failed to respond. In October 1995 they brought an action before the GC under Article 265 TFEU. The Court found the action inadmissible. Even supposing that the letter sent by the applicants in February 1995 could be regarded as an invitation to act in the sense of Article 265 TFEU, to which the Commission had failed to respond, the application to the GC should have been introduced within four months of the date on which the letter was sent, as required by that article.

It may sometimes be difficult to establish the point at which the institution can be said to have defined its position. In *CEVA and Pharmacia v Commission* (cases T-344 and 345/00), a letter which merely stated that the questions submitted by the applicants were still under consideration by the Commission was not a definition of position, whereas the subsequent adoption of a draft regulation was. The action under Article 265 TFEU could not proceed. However, a delay by a Union institution in defining its position which results in loss to an applicant may give rise to liability under Article 340 TFEU (see Chapter 14).

13.5.1 **Effect of definition of position**

Article 265 TFEU is silent as to what happens if the institution, body, office or agency concerned defines its position, but the Court held in *Lütticke* (case 48/65) that a definition of position brought proceedings under Article 265 TFEU to an end. The claimant in this case, it will be remembered, was attempting to persuade the Commission to bring an action under Article 258 TFEU against the German government for its alleged infringement of Article 110 TFEU. When the Commission refused to act Alfons Lütticke GmbH brought proceedings under Article 265 TFEU for failure to act. The Commission defined its position in a letter to Lütticke, again refusing to act, and Lütticke brought proceedings under Article 263 TFEU to annul that refusal. The Court, in the briefest of judgments, held that the Commission's refusal was a 'definition of position' which ended its failure to act. The action under Article 265 was therefore inadmissible.

With regard to the action under Article 263 TFEU, Advocate-General Gand's submissions were again convincing. The applicant would only be entitled to challenge the Commission's refusal to act (the 'negative decision'), he suggested, if it had been entitled to challenge the positive act which it alleged the Commission had failed to adopt. This it would not, since it had no right to demand action from the Commission vis-à-vis the German government. The Court, on the other hand, chose to treat the Commission's refusal not as a definition of position but as a 'reasoned opinion' under Article 258 TFEU, which, as a purely preliminary act, was not, the Court held, capable of annulment.

The Court did adopt reasoning similar to that of Advocate-General Gand in *Lütticke* (case 48/65) in *Star Fruit Company SA*.

Star Fruit Company SA

Here, as in *Lütticke* (case 48/65), the applicants, a firm of banana importers, were seeking to compel the Commission to institute Article 258 TFEU proceedings, this time against France in respect of the French regime regulating banana imports, which they considered was in breach of Article 34 TFEU. They had complained to the Commission and the Commission had acknowledged their request. The applicants subsequently brought Article 265 TFEU proceedings against the Commission for their failure to take action against France, and Article 263 TFEU proceedings for the annulment of the Commission's letter of acknowledgement.

On the claim for failure to act, the Court held that since the Commission was not required to instigate proceedings under Article 258 TFEU, but on the contrary had a discretionary power, 'individuals were not entitled to require that the institution adopt a particular position'.

On the claim under Article 263, the Court pointed out that by requesting the Commission to set in motion a procedure under Article 258 TFEU, the applicant was 'in reality requesting the adoption of acts which were not of direct and individual concern to it within the meaning of Article [263 TFEU], and which in any event it could not challenge by means of an action for annulment'.

13.5.2 **Definition of position and Article 263 TFEU**

The Court has, however, consistently followed its position in *Lütticke* (case 48/65) and held that, in Article 265 TFEU proceedings, a definition of position by the defendant entity ends its failure to act. In a situation *where he is entitled to demand action* from the institution concerned, he may challenge the taking of a position, as a decision addressed to himself, under Article 263 TFEU, and provided that he does so in time, his application should be admissible. It is submitted that *Lütticke* (case 48/65), with its special facts (applicant not entitled to demand action), and its judgment cast in terms of Article 258 TFEU, cannot be invoked to prevent such a challenge. *FEDIOL* supports this view. Although not described as such, the Commission's letter of May 1982, in which the Commission informed FEDIOL of its decision not to act, and which FEDIOL were held entitled to challenge under Article 263, was undoubtedly a 'definition of position' within Article 265 (see *GEMA*).

Where an institution defines its position and refuses to act, an applicant who is not entitled to demand that action cannot challenge that refusal under Article 263 TFEU; and even a legitimate claim under Article 265 TFEU is likely to result in an action to review that refusal under Article 263. In the latter case it is therefore essential that a definition of position be recognised as a decision capable of challenge under Article 263, and that it be challenged in time (cf *GEMA; Irish Cement Ltd*). The extent of the review conducted by the Court under Article 263 will depend on the extent of the applicant's rights. Since the institutions have wide discretionary powers in the pursuit of Union economic policy objectives, individuals' rights, at least where action vis-à-vis third parties are concerned, are likely to be limited and mainly of a procedural nature. However, as has been demonstrated in the *common transport policy* case, Article 265 offers considerable scope for privileged applicants.

In the *common transport policy* case, Parliament's case was heard under Article 265 TFEU, as the Council's 'definition of position' was found to be inadequate. As it neither confirmed nor denied the alleged failure (implementation of transport policy), and failed to reveal the Council's position with regard to the measure which the Council intended to adopt, it was held not to amount to a definition of position at all.

13.6 **Consequences of a successful action**

Whether the action is admitted before the Court under Article 265 TFEU, as a failure to act, or under Article 263 TFEU, as a claim for annulment of a decision not to act, the consequences of a successful action are the same. Under Article 266 TFEU: 'The institution whose act has been declared void or whose failure to act has been declared contrary to the Treaties shall be required to take the necessary measures to comply with the judgment of the Court of Justice'.

The institution will be required by the Court to take action to remedy its failure. It will not necessarily be the action required by the applicant. Should he wish to challenge the institution's implementation of the judgment he could do so under Article 263 TFEU.

No sanctions beyond the possibility of further action under Article 265 TFEU are provided for non-compliance with the Court's judgment. Unlike Article 260 TFEU, which was amended by Maastricht to provide for the imposition of fines and penalties on Member States which fail to comply with a judgment of the Court under Article 258 TFEU (see Chapter 11), Article 266 TFEU was not amended to provide for similar penalties against Union institutions in respect of their failures established under Article 265. Also, although Article 266(2) TFEU provides that the obligation imposed by Article 266(1) 'shall not affect any obligations which may result from the application of the second paragraph of Article 340' (governing the Union's non-contractual liability) the opportunity for individuals to obtain damages from the Union is, as will be seen, extremely limited (see Chapter 14).

13.7 Conclusions

It has been seen that the procedure under Article 265 TFEU complements the Article 263 TFEU procedure for directly challenging the validity of acts adopted by the institutions because it seeks to ensure that the institutions act on their powers whenever required. It is just as important to challenge legislation adopted by the institutions where this exceeds their powers as it is to challenge inaction when a positive step was required. Once Article 265 TFEU is invoked, the institution concerned must at least define its position. This, in turn, can then be reviewed under Article 263 TFEU, subject to the requirements on *locus standi* (see Chapter 12). Although a successful Article 265 claim may persuade the institution concerned to take action, this does not mean that the claimant will receive the decision he might prefer. Nevertheless, action by the Union institution would remove the uncertainty that could otherwise prevail if no action were taken at all.

14 Union liability in tort: action for damages

14.1 Introduction

We have already seen that there are various mechanisms in the Treaty by which the acts of the Union institutions can be reviewed (see Chapter 12). In addition to challenging acts directly and, if the challenge is successful, having these declared inapplicable, it may also be necessary to make good any loss that has been caused as a result of the adoption of a measure which is unlawful.

This chapter focuses upon the non-contractual liability of the Union provided for under Articles 268 and 340 TFEU. Although Article 340 TFEU is potentially of great utility, in practice its application has been limited by the CJEU. Whilst the approach to *locus standi* has been less stringent than that taken in relation to judicial review, the courts have taken a restrictive approach to the question of the test to show a violation of the Union's obligations. This chapter also examines the parallels between the action for damages and the action for state liability against the Member States. As we shall see, the CJ has attempted to develop the case law in both fields in the light of the jurisprudence of the other and in this the case of *Laboratoires Pharmaceutiques Bergaderm SA and Goupil v Commission* (case C-352/98) seems to have marked a significant shift in the courts' approach.

14.2 Scope of non-contractual liability

14.2.1 The Treaty provisions

According to Article 268 TFEU, 'The Court of Justice of the European Union shall have jurisdiction in disputes relating to the compensation for damage provided for in the second and third paragraph of Article 340'.

Article 340(2) and (3) TFEU provide that:

> In the case of non-contractual liability, the Union shall, in accordance with the general principles common to the laws of the Member States, make good any damage caused by its institutions or by its servants in the performance of their duties.
>   . . . the European Central Bank shall, in accordance with the general principles common to the laws of the Member States, make good any damage caused by its institutions or by its servants in the performance of their duties.

Thus, the Union may be liable for both *fautes de service*, that is, wrongful acts on the part of one of its institutions, and *fautes personelles*, wrongful acts on the part of its servants. Provided in both cases that the wrongful acts are committed in the performance of the perpetrator's official functions, the responsible institution may be sued. Where more than one institution is concerned, or where there is doubt as to which institution is responsible, both (or all) may be sued. In the case of *faute personelle*, the Union is liable on the principle of vicarious liability, albeit interpreted in a slightly narrower sense than that in which it is understood under English law (see *Sayag v Leduc* (case 9/69), proceedings under Article 188(2) of the Euratom Treaty, in which it was held that the Union is only liable for those acts of its servants which, by virtue of an internal relationship, are the *necessary* extension of the tasks entrusted to the institutions).

In applying Article 340(2) and (3) TFEU the CJEU is required to determine liability 'in accordance with the general principles common to the laws of Member States'. Where the principles of non-contractual liability, which embrace principles concerning the basis of liability (ie fault or non-fault), causation and damages are not 'common' to all Member States, the Court has drawn on the principles governing tortious liability in the Member States in order to develop its own specific principles of Union law. The process is thus different from its approach to the incorporation of general principles of law for the purposes of judicial review of Union law (see Chapter 6).

14.3 *Locus standi*

14.3.1 **Personal limitations**

Unlike the position in the area of judicial review, there are no personal limitations on the right to bring an action under Article 340(2) TFEU. There is no distinction between privileged and non-privileged applicants.

14.3.2 **Time limits**

A specific generous limitation period of five years is provided (Article 46 Statute of the Court of Justice), running from the occurrence of the event giving rise to liability. The Court has held that the limitation period cannot begin until all the requirements for liability, particularly damage, have materialised (*Birra Würhrer SpA v Council* (cases 256, 257, 265 and 267/80, and 5/81)). Where the damage results from a legislative measure, time runs not necessarily from the date of enactment but from the date on which the damaging effects of the measure arose, or, in the case of damages arising from an administrative act or omission, when the applicant becomes aware of that fact (see, eg, *Buhring v Council* (case T-246/93)). In disputes arising from individual measures the limitation period does not begin to run until damage has actually materialised *(Holcim (Deutschland) v Commission* (case C-282/05)).

14.3.3 **Relationship with Articles 263 and 265 TFEU**

The relative generosity of these *locus standi* provisions is important, since it may be possible to obtain a declaration of invalidity in the context of a claim for damages, thereby circumventing the *locus standi* limitations of Article 263 TFEU (see *Aktien-Zuckerfabrik Schöppenstedt v Council* (case 5/71)). The action for damages is a separate action from the judicial review action as can be inferred from the wording of the Treaty. Article 266 TFEU provides that the obligation to remedy a failure to act 'shall not affect any obligation which may result from the application of the second paragraph of Article 340'. This was the view taken in *Lütticke* (case 4/69). In this case, Lütticke, having failed to establish the Commission's failure to act under Article 265 TFEU (see Chapter 13), sought damages from the Commission in a separate action under Article 340(2) TFEU. The action was held admissible. The Court said that the action for damages provided for under Articles 268 and 340(2) TFEU was established as *an independent form of action with a particular purpose to fulfil*. It would be contrary to the independent nature of this action, as well as to the efficacy of the general system of forms of action created by the Treaty, to regard as a ground of inadmissibility the fact that, in certain circumstances, an action for damages might lead to a result similar to that of an action for failure to act under Article 265 TFEU. Although *Lütticke* failed on the merits (there being no wrongful failure), an important principle was established.

Similarly, in *Schöppenstedt* the Court held that the claimant company could sue the Council for damages on the basis of an allegedly illegal regulation even though as a 'natural or legal person' they would have no *locus standi* to seek its annulment under Article 263 TFEU. This point has been reiterated in *Holcim* where the CJ held that standing under Article 263 TFEU was not a relevant criterion for the application of Article 340 TFEU. In *Krohn & Co Import-Export GmbH & Co KG v Commission* (case 175/84), the Court held that since an action for non-contractual liability was an autonomous form of action, the expiry of the time limit for challenge under Article 263 TFEU did not render an action for damages inadmissible.

The Court did, however, make the point in *Krohn* that a claim might not be admissible if the purpose of the Article 340(2) TFEU action was purely to attain by another route the remedy provided by Article 263 TFEU, an approach reaffirmed by the GC in declaring an action inadmissible in *Cobrecaf SA v Commission* (case T-514/93) and reflecting that taken by the CJ regarding time limits on Article 267 TFEU references on the validity of Union acts (*TWD*) (see Chapters 10 and 12).

14.4 Elements of non-contractual liability

The basic elements of non-contractual liability are familiar. They embrace:

- wrongful conduct on the part of the institutions;
- damage to the claimant;
- causative link between the two.

For liability to arise, all three elements must be proved. The GC has noted that it is not necessary to deal with these elements in any particular order. If it seems likely that one of them will not be satisfied, the Court can deal with it first and, if appropriate, dismiss the application without discussing the remaining elements (*Elliniki Viomichania Oplon AE (EVO) v Council and Commission* (case T-220/96)).

14.5 Wrongful acts or omissions

Although, following continental traditions, non-contractual liability is not divided up into specific 'torts', wrongful acts and omissions may be grouped under three broad categories:

(1) Failures of administration. Union institutions, bodies, offices and agencies are under a duty of good administration. Failures of administration would include, for example, a failure to adopt satisfactory procedures, a failure to obtain the relevant facts before making the decision, the giving of misleading information, a failure to give the necessary information (eg, *Odigitria AAE v Council* (case T-572/93)—but no liability because of lack of causal link), or a significant delay in acting (*CEVA*—failure to act for a period of 19 months constituted a clear and serious breach of the principle of sound administration). In *Groupe Gascoigne v Commission* (case C-58/12P) the CJ found that a failure on the part of the GC to adjudicate within a reasonable time (proceedings lasted five years and nine months) gave rise to an action under Article 340 TFEU for compensation for financial losses linked to that failure.

As with negligence, the decision taken or advice offered need not be right as long as it is adopted according to the correct procedures and the conclusions reached are reasonable in the light of the information to hand;

(2) Negligent acts by servants in the performance of their duties. This category would also include a single negligent act. For example, in *Grifoni v Euratom* (case C-308/87), a case concerning the Euratom Treaty, Euratom contracted with Mr Grifoni to have the roof of a building repaired. While inspecting the roof, Grifoni fell off. The CJ held that Euratom was at fault in not providing the necessary guard rails;

(3) The adoption of wrongful (ie, illegal or invalid) acts having legal effect, or the wrongful failure to adopt a binding act when under a duty to do so.

14.5.1 Action taken under the TFEU

It is perhaps self-evident that liability cannot arise from action taken under primary legislation, that is, pursuant to the Treaties themselves. An example of this can be seen in *Édouard Dubois et Fils SA v Council* (case T-113/96).

> ### *Édouard Dubois*
>
> In this case, the applicant, a customs agent, was seeking damages for losses arising from the completion of the internal market. Following its completion on 1 January 1993 his business suffered 'an almost total and definitive cessation of its activities as a customs agent', resulting in material damage. The applicant claimed compensation. The GC held that the agreement to complete the single internal market contained in SEA, as an agreement between Member States, could not give rise to non-contractual liability on the part of the Union. Articles 268 and 340(2) TFEU, being also primary Union law, cannot be brought to bear on instruments of an equivalent level where this is not expressly provided for.

14.6 Establishing an unlawful act

The problem with an action for non-contractual liability lies not in establishing admissibility but in succeeding on the merits of the case. Originally, the CJ adopted a very restrictive approach

towards Union liability in tort, particularly towards liability resulting from the adoption of wrongful acts (or the wrongful failure to adopt an act). Indeed, there are strong policy reasons for limiting the non-contractual liability of public authorities. These bodies are charged by law to take
decisions in the general interest over a wide range of activities. These decisions often involve the
exercise of wide discretionary powers that affect a substantial section of the public. Sometimes
the decisions are unlawful. Whilst it is right that such decisions be subject to judicial review, it may
be argued that to expose public bodies to liability in damages for unlawful acts in the absence of
bad faith or an improper motive or (*quaere*) 'gross' negligence would unduly hamper the administrative process and impose an excessive burden on the public purse, *a fortiori* in a Union as large
as the EU.

For some time, the test to establish whether there was an unlawful act was the so-called
Schöppenstedt formula (from the *Schöppenstedt* case): where the action concerns a legislative measure which involves choices of economic policy, the Union incurs no liability unless a sufficiently
serious breach of a superior rule of law for the protection of the individual has occurred. A significant body of case law has built up under this formula. However, there had been concern that
the approach to Union liability under Article 340 TFEU and the development of state liability (see
Chapter 9) ought to be following the same principles. This nettle was grasped in *Brasserie du Pêcheur
and Factortame*, where the Court, in the context of a state-liability case, stated that the basis of liability under Article 340 TFEU and under the state-liability principle should be the same, because the
protection of individuals' rights cannot vary depending on whether a national authority or a Union
authority is responsible for the act or omission which is the subject of complaint. This was firmly
established in *Bergaderm*, a case decided under Article 340 TFEU.

14.6.1 Development of the *Schöppenstedt* formula: a brief overview

Before we set out the current position, it will be helpful to examine the approach adopted in this
area prior to *Bergaderm* under *Schöppenstedt*. It contains three essential elements:

- a legislative measure involving choices of economic policy;
- a breach of a superior rule of law for the protection of individuals;
- that the breach is 'sufficiently serious'.

These three requirements will now be examined in turn.

14.6.1.1 A legislative measure involving choices of economic policy

Although the term 'legislative act' relates primarily to regulations, it will apply to any binding act
which purports to lay down general rules. In *Gibraltar* (discussed in Chapter 12) the Court suggested,
albeit in the context of proceedings under Article 263 TFEU, that directives 'normally' constitute 'a
form of indirect regulatory or legislative measure'. It was accepted in *Odigitria* that an international
agreement dealing with fishing rights would be a legislative act involving economic policy because
of its impact on the Union's fisheries policy. The majority of legislative measures will involve choices
of economic policy, since the institutions enjoy wide discretionary powers in all areas of activity,
and it is possible to construe many measures even of a social nature as economic in the context of
the TFEU.

Following the CJ judgment in *Bergaderm* (see 14.6.2), in the case of wrongful acts it is no longer
crucial whether the measure is legislative or individual act. Now, the important consideration for
determining whether there was a wrongful act giving rise to liability is whether the institution concerned was involved in the exercise of any form of discretion.

14.6.1.2 A breach of a superior rule of law for the protection of individuals

Any general principle, such as equality or proportionality, accepted as part of Union law (see Chapter 6) would constitute a superior rule of law for the protection of individuals. Thus, a breach of the principle of legitimate expectations was argued successfully in a claim for damages in *Sofrimport* (see Chapter 12). Most fundamental principles of *Union* law (eg, freedom of movement for workers; non-discrimination between producers and consumers agriculture), whether expressed in the TFEU or in secondary legislation, could likewise form the basis of a claim for damages. In *Firma E Kampffmeyer v Commission* (cases 5, 7 and 13–24/66) a provision in a regulation directed at ensuring 'appropriate support for agricultural markets' was construed as intending to benefit, inter alia, the interests of individual undertakings such as importers. The claimants, as importers, were thus entitled to claim damages as a result of the Commission's action in breach of these provisions. It seems therefore that, as long as the rule of law can be construed as designed in part to benefit a particular class of people, it may be deemed to be 'for the protection of individuals'.

The original formulation of the test in *Schöppenstedt* refers to a 'superior rule of law', but the word 'superior' was dropped in later cases, referring to general principles such as proportionality simply as a 'rule of law' (see, eg, *Etablissements Biret v Council* (case T-210/00), para 53). Following *Bergaderm*, the focus is now on a rule intended to confer rights on individuals, in parallel with the rules on state liability, and the GC has expressly stated that there is no distinction to be made between a 'superior rule of law' and a rule of law (*Sison v Council* (case T-47/03), para 234).

14.6.1.3 The breach must be 'sufficiently serious'

Even under the old formula, a breach of a superior rule of law, including a fundamental rule such as the principle of equality, was not in itself sufficient to give rise to a claim in damages. The claimant must prove that the breach is 'sufficiently serious'. This principle has been very narrowly construed. In *Bayerische HNL Vermehrungsbetriebe GmbH & Co KG v Council* (cases 83 and 94/76, and 4, 15 and 40/77), the Court suggested that in a legislative field in which one of the chief features is the exercise of a wide discretion, the Union does not incur liability unless the institution concerned has '*manifestly and gravely disregarded the limits on the exercise of its power*'.

When interpreting this requirement, the Court adopted two broad approaches:

- the *effect* of the measure on the applicant, at the nature and extent of the harm to his interests;
- the nature of the breach.

An example of the first approach can be seen in *Bayerische HNL Vermehrungsbetriebe GmbH & Co KG v Council* (cases 83 and 94/76 and 4, 15 and 40/77).

> ### HNL
>
> An action was brought by a number of animal-feed producers for damages for loss suffered as a result of a regulation requiring animal-feed producers to purchase skimmed-milk powder, instead of the cheaper and equally effective soya, as a means of disposing of surplus stocks of milk. This regulation had been found by the Court in a prior preliminary ruling proceeding (*Bela-Mühle Josef Bergmann KG v Grows-Farm GmbH & Co KG* (case 114/76); *Granaria BV v Hoofdproduktschap voor Akkerbouwprodukten (No 1)* (case 116/76)) to be in breach of the principles of non-discrimination and proportionality. In deciding whether the breach was sufficiently serious, that is, whether the Commission had manifestly and gravely disregarded the limits on the exercise of its powers, the Court looked at the effect of the breach. It had affected a wide group of persons (all buyers of protein for the production of animal feed); the difference in price between the skimmed milk and soya had only a limited effect on production costs, insignificant

> beside other factors such as world prices; and the effect of the regulation on their profits did not exceed the normal level of risk inherent in such activities. The breach was not sufficiently serious.

Contrast the outcome in *HNL* with *P Dumortier Frères SA v Council* (cases 64 and 113/76; 167 and 239/78; 27, 28 and 45/79), where the claimants were a small, clearly defined group, and their loss went beyond the risks normally inherent in their business. In *Schneider v Commission* (case C-440/07P) the CJ, upholding the judgment of the GC, found that a breach of the rights of defence in competition proceedings would be a sufficiently serious breach of a rule intended for the protection of the individual.

In looking at the nature of a breach, the CJEU is effectively asking in what way, and to what extent, is the institution *culpable*?

It seems from the case law that both enquiries are relevant. The breach must be both serious as regards its effect on the applicant *and* inexcusable. This point is demonstrated in *Koninklijke Scholten-Honig NV v Council* (case 143/77) and *GR Amylum NV v Council* (cases 116 and 124/77), known as the 'Isoglucose' cases.

The 'Isoglucose' cases

The claimant glucose producers were seeking damages for losses suffered as a result of a Union regulation which imposed levies on the production of glucose in order to increase consumption of Union sugar. Clearly glucose and sugar were to some extent in competition with one another. The regulation had been found invalid, in breach of the principle of equality, in a prior preliminary ruling reference in *Royal Scholten-Honig*. The claimants were a small and closed group, and the damage which they suffered as a result of the regulation was described as 'catastrophic'. One firm, the Dutch firm Koninklijke Scholten-Honig NV, had been forced into liquidation. Yet they failed to obtain damages. Although the treatment of the glucose producers as compared with that of the sugar producers was 'manifestly unequal', the Court held that the defendants' errors were not of such gravity that their conduct could be regarded as 'verging on the arbitrary'.

In *Groupe Gascoigne* the CJ found that procedural delays before the GC breached Article 47 of the Charter of Fundamental Rights of the EU (which guarantees a hearing within a reasonable period of time) and that constituted sufficiently serious breach of a rule which is intended to confer rights on individuals.

14.6.2 The modern approach: *Bergaderm* and beyond

In view of the stringent nature of the *Schöppenstedt* formula it is not surprising that very few claims succeed. The Court had justified its strict approach on the basis of its:

> concern to ensure that the legislative function is not hindered by the prospect of actions for damages whenever the general interest requires the institutions . . . to adopt measures which may adversely affect individual interests [*R v HM Treasury*, ex parte *BT* (case C-392/93), para 40].

In its anxiety to protect the Union institutions, it applied the restrictive *Schöppenstedt* test in a seemingly indiscriminate manner to claims arising from actions which did not involve legislative choices. For this it has been rightly criticised. As Advocate-General Tesauro pointed out in *Brasserie du Pêcheur* on the date on which the opinion was handed down (26 November 1995), only eight awards of damages against Union institutions had been made. Although there have been a number of successful cases since then, these have tended to arise in the context of administrative failures rather than in circumstances involving economic policy (eg, *New Europe Consulting and Brown v Commission* (case T-231/97) and *Embassy Limousines v European Parliament* (case T-203/96)).

The emergence of the principle of state liability served to highlight the limitations of Article 340(2) TFEU and pointed to the need for a broader and more flexible test for liability capable of taking into account the different types of breach and the different situations of EU institutions and Member States.

The approach to state liability was elaborated in *Brasserie du Pêcheur*. Here the Court confirmed the concept of the 'sufficiently serious' breach as the basis for liability, but introduced, in para 56, a wide range of criteria by which the question of whether the breach was sufficiently serious might be judged (see further Chapter 9). These included:

> the clarity and precision of the [EU] rule breached, the measure of discretion left by that rule to the national or Union authorities, whether the infringement and the damage caused was intentional or voluntary, whether [the] error of law was excusable or inexcusable.

Subsequently, this test has been applied to all breaches of Union law, whether by EU institutions or by Member States. It enabled the court to decide, in a whole variety of circumstances, whether a breach of Union law, whether committed by an EU institution or by a Member State, was sufficiently serious to attract liability. The CJ clearly intended this approach to be used in all these circumstances, although it was not until *Bergaderm* that the application to Union liability was confirmed.

Bergaderm

The action in this case arose out of an amendment to Directive 76/768 ([1976] OJ L262/169) to limit the level of psolaren molecules in sun oils. Bergaderm was no longer able to sell its sun oil and the company was put into liquidation. It brought an action under Article 340(2) TFEU, claiming that the Commission had committed various wrongful acts (procedural errors, breach of the principle of proportionality and misuse of powers) during the adoption of the Adaptation Directive (which amended Directive 76/768), which had caused significant financial damages to Bergaderm. The claim was rejected by the GC (*Laboratoires Pharmaceutiques Bergaderm SA and Goupil v Commission* (case T-199/96)).

On appeal, the CJ brought Article 340 TFEU and state liability full circle. Having considered the test for state liability in *Brasserie du Pêcheur* (see Chapter 9), the Court held that there would be liability under Article 340 TFEU where a rule of law intended to confer rights on individuals had been infringed; the breach had to be sufficiently serious, and there had to be a direct causal link between the breach and the damage caused.

With regard to establishing whether a breach was 'sufficiently serious', the Court said that:

> as regards both Union liability under [Article 340] of the Treaty and Member State liability for breaches of Union law, the decisive test for finding that a breach of Union law is sufficiently serious is whether the Member State or the Union institution concerned manifestly and gravely disregarded the limits on its discretion [para 43].

This meant that the crucial factor in establishing whether there had been an unlawful act was the degree of discretion available to the institution concerned. The Court also noted that where there is no exercise of discretion, the *Hedley Lomas* principle developed in the context of Member State breaches of Union law (see Chapter 9) applies, according to which, if there is considerably reduced, or no, discretion, the mere infringement of Union law may be a sufficiently serious breach.

The new approach, in the wake of *Bergaderm*, therefore marks a departure from *Schöppenstedt* in three main aspects. First, it is no longer necessary to consider whether the rule infringed was a 'superior rule of law'; instead, the rule infringed has to be one intended to confer rights on individuals. Secondly, in establishing whether a breach is sufficiently serious, the criteria listed in para 56 of *Brasserie de Pêcheur* are now applied, rather than the cases on the effects of the breach and harm to the claimant. In *MyTravel Group plc v Commission* (case T-212/03), in the case of a third party affected by a Commission decision finding a merger to be incompatible with the internal market, which decision was subsequently annulled, the GC elaborated that:

> the right to compensation for damage resulting from the conduct of the institution becomes available where such conduct takes the form of action manifestly contrary to the rule of law and seriously detrimental to the interests of persons outside the institution and cannot be justified or accounted for by the particular constraints to which the staff of the institution, operating normally, are objectively subject [para 43].

The GC pointed to the complexity of the assessment required to be made by the Commission in vetting mergers and the degree of discretion it had to determine whether a merger was compatible with the internal market or not.

Finally, the focus has also shifted away from the question of whether the act complained about was administrative or legislative; instead, what matters now is the degree of discretion for the Union institution. In *Holcim* the CJ also reaffirmed that in determining discretion, this issue was not determined by whether the measure was general or individualised.

It seems therefore that the test for the application of Article 340(2) TFEU can still be reduced to a list of three elements, but these vary from those previously used. They can be summarised as follows:

- unlawful action;
- damage;
- causal link between the action and the damage.

Although the vast majority of cases involving Article 340 TFEU decided after *Bergaderm* have followed this new approach (eg, *Beamglow Ltd v Parliament, Council and Commission* (case T-383/00); *Medici Grimm KG v Council* (case T-364/03); *Holcim*), there are some decisions which have still been decided squarely on the basis of *Schöppenstedt*. Thus, in *CEVA*, an instance of Commission inaction under Regulation 1308/99 on Veterinary Medicinal Products ([1999] OJ L156/1), the GC regarded this as a breach of the principle of sound administration (a higher-ranking rule of law), and imposed liability on that basis.

14.6.3 **Individual acts**

It was assumed that the *Bergaderm* approach, as with the *Schöppenstedt* formula, would not apply to individual acts which do not involve the exercise of discretion. Since such acts affect only their addressees they do not raise the same floodgate problems, thus it is not necessary to subject them to such stringent criteria. The CJ has now expressly stated in *Holcim* that:

> the applicant is not justified in submitting that the criterion of a sufficiently serious breach of a rule of law applies only where a legislative act of the Union is at issue and is excluded when, as in the present case, an individual act is at issue. Contrary to what is argued, the [General Court] could not limit itself to making a finding of unlawfulness, but had to apply, as it correctly did, the criterion of the existence of a sufficiently serious breach [para 49].

(Contrast Advocate-General Tesauro's criticism of the Court's application of Article 340(2) TFEU in *Brasserie du Pêcheur*.)

Where an individual act is prima facie unlawful and threatens to cause damage to its addressee, it may be challenged under Article 263 TFEU. Where he fails to challenge the measure in time he may still bring an independent action under Article 340(2) TFEU where damage has occurred as a result of its application (*Krohn*). To succeed, however, it may not be enough to establish the illegality of the measure. Although there is little authority on this point it is thought that fault must be proved, although what may be deemed to constitute fault in this context remains unclear. In *Grifoni*, for example, a failure to provide a guard rail despite clear guidelines requiring their provision provided the basis for Union liability.

14.7 Liability for lawful acts

The CJEU has been somewhat shy of endorsing a principle of liability without fault in EU law. The GC had the opportunity to rule specifically on this matter in *Atlanta AG, Atlanta Handelsgesellschaft Harder & Co GmbH and Others v Council of the European Union and Commission of the European Communities* (case T-521/93) and *Édouard Dubois* but did not. The CJ had not, however, ruled out that possibility (see *Compagnie d'Approvisionnement v Commission* (cases 9 and 11/71); *Biovilac v Commission* (case 59/83)). In *Dorsch Consult* the GC commented, without specifically ruling on the point of whether liability could arise for a lawful act, that a precondition for such liability would in any event be the existence of 'unusual' and 'special' damage, which in this case was not satisfied. The matter has been discussed again, in the case of *FIAMM and FIAMM Technologies v Council and Commission* (case C-120/06P).

> ### *FIAMM Technologies*
>
> This case concerned compensation claimed for the damage suffered by the applicants after the United States was authorised under the World Trade Organization (WTO) rules to implement retaliatory measures following the EU failure to change its banana regime. The retaliatory measures were felt by other sectors. The GC had ruled against the applicants, although it suggested that liability could in principle arise even though there was no wrongful act.
>
> On appeal the CJ agreed with the GC that there was no wrongful act and further remarked that whilst the conditions for liability for wrongful acts were clear, the position was not so clear for liability for lawful acts.

In so doing, it seems to suggest that liability could arise for such acts. It then noted the suggestion, referring to *Dorsch Consult* (para 18) and *Biovilac* that in addition to the underlying action, there were at least three conditions of liability:

- damage;
- causal link;
- unusual and special nature of the damage.

The CJ then went on to re-emphasise that liability for legislative activity arose only in limited circumstances, as set down in *Bergaderm*. It concluded:

> that, as Union law currently stands, no liability regime exists under which the Union can incur liability for conduct falling within the sphere of its legislative competence in a situation where any failure of such conduct to comply with the WTO agreements cannot be relied upon before the Union courts [para 176].

The outcome of this judgment—beyond the facts in the case—is not clear, as the reasoning can be read three ways. First, as affirming the principle of liability for lawful acts but not in this case; secondly, as affirming the principle, but not for legislative acts or, finally, as overturning the GC's view that liability could arise for lawful acts. Presumably if the CJ had intended the latter interpretation, it would have said so and not discussed the particular difficulties of legislative acts.

14.8 Damage

Once it has been established that there was an unlawful act, it is necessary to consider if damage has been caused. This requirement will be considered in this section.

14.8.1 Only specific losses are recoverable

The CJEU is as restrictive in its approach to damages as it is to fault. Clearly, compensation will be awarded for damage to person or property provided the damage is sufficiently direct. The injured party bears the burden of proving the damage allegedly caused. Although it will in principle award damages for economic loss, such losses must be specific, not speculative. Only actual, certain and concrete damages are recoverable (*Société Roquette Frères v Commission* (case 26/74)). This can be seen in the context of *Firma E Kampffmeyer*.

> ### *Firma E Kampffmeyer*
>
> In this case the Court was prepared to award damages for lost profits on contracts which had already been concluded, which applicants had had to cancel as a result of the illegal decision, although these damages were reduced to only 10 per cent of the profits they might have expected to make, on account of the risks involved in the transactions in question. Applicants who had not concluded contracts prior to applying for import permits were awarded no damages at all.

The Court confirmed the same reasoning in *CNTA*.

> ### *CNTA*
>
> In this case the Court found that the Commission had breached the principle of legitimate expectation when it introduced a regulation, suddenly and without warning, which deprived the claimant of

export refunds at a particular rate, fixed in advance. Although the regulation was not in itself invalid, the Commission's mode of introduction of the measure was wrongful. Thus the Commission was liable in principle. However, although CNTA had entered into export contracts on the basis of its legitimate expectations, the Court held that it was only entitled to recover for losses actually suffered, not anticipated profits, and, since currency fluctuations at the time of import had resulted in its suffering no loss on the refunds themselves, it recovered no damages.

The CJ has held that the applicant must specify the amount of damages (*Camar and Tico v Commission* (cases T-79/96, 260/97 and 117/98)), save in limited circumstances (*Sinara Handel v Council and Commission* (case T-91/05), para 110) and those circumstances must be indicated (*Goldstein v Commission* (case T-262/97), para 25). In *CEVA*, the GC decided to rule that the Union was liable in damages even though it was not, at the time of judgment, possible to quantify the loss suffered by the applicant. In *Coldiretti and Others v Council and Commission* (case T-149/96) the applicants specified the different types of damage suffered and provided detailed estimates of the loss of profits suffered. In *Mulder* the CJ accepted that loss of profits could be claimed but held that a claimant had a duty to mitigate his loss and so any claim for damages resulting from an inability, due to the wrongful act of a Union institution, to carry out one type of economic activity, would have to take into account profits which could have been made for the carrying out of another type of economic activity.

14.8.2 Loss and third parties

Where the loss has been passed on to third parties, or could have been passed on in higher prices, no damages will be recoverable (*Interquell Stärke-Chemie GmbH & Co KG v Council* (cases 261 and 262/78), 'quellmehl' case). In *Dumortier* the claimants satisfied the Court that the losses could not have been passed on without risk of losing valuable markets. An injured party is expected to show reasonable diligence in limiting the extent of his loss; otherwise he must bear the damage himself (*Mulder*). In *Antillean Rice Mills NV v Commission* (cases T-480 and 483/93), the GC suggested that since the damage to the applicants was foreseeable they could have taken precautions against it. Since they did not, 'neither the fault nor the damage alleged by the applicants are such as to cause the Union to incur non-contractual liability'. This approach was also applied by the GC in *Dorsch Consult* where the GC held that the applicant had not shown actual and certain damage.

Dorsch Consult

The case concerned a contract for the provision of services in Iraq. The applicants had not been paid for the work done when the UN Security Council imposed a trade embargo on Iraq, which the European Union implemented within the Union. As a response to this, the Iraqi government froze all property, assets and income from them, held at the material time by the governments, undertakings, companies and banks of those states which had adopted 'arbitrary decisions' against Iraq. The applicants claimed that the Union was liable for the damage it had suffered from not being able to obtain payment from Iraq. The GC pointed out that the applicants had not tried to press for payment, even when the relevant Iraqi law was repealed.

14.8.3 Loss of a chance

In *Farrugia v Commission* (case T-230/94) the GC considered a claim for compensation for the loss of a chance.

> ### Farrugia
>
> The applicant claimed that an error on the part of the Commission concerning his nationality had deprived him of the opportunity of a fellowship in the field of research and technological development in the UK. The GC found that although the Commission had made a mistake the applicant had failed to prove that, in the absence of that mistake, he would have had a 'strong chance' of being awarded the fellowship he sought. This implies that the Court would consider a claim for loss of a chance of success provided that the chance was proved to be sufficiently strong. The Court did not indicate what standard of proof would be necessary to establish a 'strong chance' of success.

14.8.4 Payment of damages in national currency

Damages are payable in the applicant's national currency at the exchange rate applicable on the date of the judgment under Article 340(2) TFEU. Interest on that sum is payable from the date of judgment (*Dumortier*).

14.9 Causation

The Court is similarly restrictive in its approach to matters of causation. In *Dumortier* it said that the principles common to the laws of Member States cannot be relied on to deduce an obligation to make good every harmful consequence, even a remote one, of unlawful legislation. The damage must be a *sufficiently direct* consequence of the unlawful conduct of the institution concerned.

Thus in *Dumortier*, the parties were entitled to recover the refunds which had been unlawfully withheld as a result of the invalid regulation, but not for further alleged losses in the form of reduced sales or for general financial difficulties resulting in the closing of some factories. Even though these difficulties might have been exacerbated by the illegal regulation they were not a sufficiently direct consequence of the unlawful act to render the Union liable (see also *Blackspur DIY Ltd v Council* (case T-168/94)). Other factors such as obsolescence and financial stringency were responsible. Similarly, where a party engages in activities designed to replace activities denied or restricted as a result of Union law any operating losses incurred as a result of these activities will be deemed too remote, and not attributed to the Union (*Mulder*). A further example of this can be seen in *Elliniki Viomichania Oplon*. (See 14.8.2 and 14.9.2 for a further claim based on the Iraq embargo in *Dorsch Consult*.)

> ### Elliniki Viomichania Oplon
>
> This case concerned the trade embargo imposed on Iraq following its invasion of Kuwait. The Union had adopted Regulation 2340/90 ([1990] OJ L213/1) to implement the embargo. EVO had supplied ammunition to Iraq, but Iraq failed to pay sums due. It claimed that it could not pay because of two United Nations resolutions which also imposed an embargo on the country. EVO brought an action under Article 340 TFEU to recover the payment due from Iraq by way of a damages claim against the Union. The GC rejected the claim both because Iraq had not refused payment because of Regulation 2340/90 but because of the UN resolutions and because the Regulation itself did not apply to the particular contracts for which EVO was still owed payment. There was no causal link between the loss suffered and the Union act complained about.

14.9.1 **Break in the chain of causation**

The CJ (and now the GC) has taken the view that the acts of the applicants, and sometimes even their failure to act, will break the chain of causation. Traders are expected to act as prudent business people. For example, in a claim based on misleading information the required causal link will be established only if the information would have caused an error in the mind of a reasonable person (*Compagnie Continentale France v Council* (case 169/73); see also *SA Oleifici Mediterranei v EEC* (case 26/81) and *Antillean Rice Mills*). In *Efisol SA* the GC suggested that a legitimate expectation (as to a certain state of affairs) could not arise from conduct on the part of the (Union) administration which was inconsistent with Union rules. Thus it seems that the prudent trader is expected to know if a Union institution misapplies Union rules! An example of this can be seen in *International Procurement Services SA v Commission* (case T-175/94).

International Procurement Services SA

The applicant tenderer suffered loss in a contract with the Mozambique government. Following advice from the Commission the government reduced the payment originally agreed for the supply of steel billets by the applicant. Although the Commission was found to have indirectly influenced the Mozambique government's decision to pay the lower price, the applicant's damage was held by the GC to derive from two factors: the Mozambique government's refusal to pay the originally agreed price, and the applicant's failure to challenge that refusal in arbitration proceedings, as it was entitled to do. The fact that Internal Procurement Services had taken that course of action because it was 'in urgent need of liquid funds' would not have the effect of attaching responsibility for the damage to the defendants.

14.9.2 **Loss must be foreseeable**

Where other factors can be seen as contributing to the claimant's loss the damage is normally seen as too remote. The GC considered the nature of the causal link in *Dorsch Consult*. There, it commented that the applicant had not succeeded in showing that the adoption by the Iraqi government of a law freezing the applicants' assets in retaliation for the trade embargo imposed on Iraq was 'an objectively foreseeable consequence, in the normal course of events, of the adoption' of that Union's Regulation implementing the embargo. A requirement of foreseeability seems to have been introduced as a precondition to the finding of a causal link.

14.9.3 **Contributory negligence**

The Court does not as a general rule attempt to apportion blame on the basis of contributory negligence. It appears that apportionment is reserved for claims of particular merit. In *Adams* Adams' damages for the Commission's breach of confidence, which had caused him irreparable financial and emotional damage, were reduced by 50 per cent to take into account Adams' contribution in failing to protect his own interests. Similarly, in *Grifoni*, although Euratom was clearly at fault in not providing guard rails, equally Grifoni, an experienced contractor, should have known that he had to take some precautions himself. His damages were reduced, also by 50 per cent.

14.10 **Impact of other possible causes of action**

Where the Court rejects a claim for damages, as in the isoglucose cases (see 14.6.1.3), it often points out that applicants are not without a remedy. The action must be assessed having regard to the whole system of legal protection of individuals set up by the Treaty. Where a person suffers, or is likely to suffer, damage as a result of an unlawful act he may challenge that measure before his national courts and seek a ruling under Article 267 TFEU on its validity. The Court has said that the existence of such an action is by itself of such a nature as to ensure the effective protection of the individuals concerned. Not all would agree with this view. There may be no issue of national law in which to raise questions of EU law. As is borne out in *Koninklijke Scholten-Honig NV*, heavy, even irreparable, losses may be incurred while proceedings before the national courts are pending. An action before a national court may be successful in obtaining interim relief (see, eg, *Zuckerfabrik Süderdithmarschen AG*; *Antonissen*, noted in Chapter 7), or, in time, a declaration of invalidity, but where damage has occurred a national court cannot award compensation for wrongs attributable to the Union (see *Krohn*, discussed at 14.12).

Surely the most appropriate forum in which to challenge Union action (or inaction) would be before the European Courts under Article 263 TFEU (or Article 265 TFEU), alongside, or prior to, a claim for damages under Article 340(2) TFEU. Yet, as has been seen in Chapter 12, the individual has no *locus standi* to challenge or demand genuine legislative measures under these articles. Since the CJEU is understandably reluctant to expose the Union to unlimited claims, and, where the exercise of discretion by a Union institution is concerned, to fetter that discretion by the prospect of such exposure, arguably the most effective protection for applicants would be speedy interim relief from the CJEU to forestall the application of unlawful measures and prevent damage occurring. Although this may be obtained in an action under Article 340(2) TFEU (see *Kampffmeyer*, considered at 14.11), it would seem more logical, in the absence of damage, to proceed under Article 263 TFEU. Where damage is suffered as a result of lawful action on the part of the Union, perhaps the CJEU could be persuaded, in exceptional cases, to accept some form of strict liability on the principle of *égalité devant les charges publiques*. It cannot be right that a few should bear a disproportionate burden as a result of measures enacted in the interest of the many.

14.11 Relationship between Article 340(2) TFEU and other remedies

If a claim for damages for non-contractual liability, particularly a claim based on an unlawful legislative act, is unlikely to succeed for the many reasons outlined above, its value in the overall scheme of remedies available against the Union should not be underrated. Since an action under Article 340(2) TFEU is an independent form of action (*Lütticke*; *Schöppenstedt*; *Krohn*), an action for damages based on invalidity or wrongful failure may be effective in obtaining a declaration of invalidity or failure to act notwithstanding that the applicant has no *locus standi*, either personal or temporal, to challenge that same act (or inaction) in proceedings under Article 263 or Article 265 TFEU. Moreover, the Court has held (*Kurt Kampffmeyer Mühlenvereinigung KG v Council* (cases 56–60/74)) that where the damage to the claimant is imminent, or likely with a high degree of certainty to occur, the claimant may bring proceedings under Article 340(2)) *before* the damage has occurred. Although he may not be found entitled in principle to damages, he may obtain a declaration of invalidity or unlawful failure to act, including interim relief, in time to prevent the damage occurring.

It is submitted that the CJEU will admit such actions under Article 340(2) TFEU only where a claim for damages is genuine; it will not allow this provision to be used solely as a means of evading the *locus standi* limitations of Articles 263 and 265 TFEU (see *Krohn* and *Cobrecaf SA*).

14.12 Concurrent liability

As Union law is, to a large extent, implemented by national authorities, there may be cases in which it is unclear whether the cause of action—for example, for the return of money paid under an invalid regulation, or for a wrongful failure on the part of a national body to pay a sub-sidy to which the applicant feels he is entitled—lies against the national authority, in national courts, according to national law; or against a Union institution, before the GC; or against both. Motivated no doubt by a desire to reduce its workload and/or its potential liability, the Court, as illustrated by *Koninklijke Scholten-Honig NV* (and countless other cases), prefers to direct appli-cants to seek a remedy before their national courts, leaving questions of validity to be referred to the CJ, if necessary, under Article 267 TFEU. It is submitted that, largely as a result of this pref-erence, the case law on what might loosely be termed concurrent liability is both confusing and contradictory.

Initially, in cases such as *Firma E Kampffmeyer* and *R & V Haegeman Sprl v Commission* (case 96/71), the CJ espoused a doctrine of 'exhaustion of national law remedies'. In *Firma E Kampffmeyer* the applicant grain dealers were seeking, before the CJ, as a result of an invalid regulation:

- the return of levies paid to the German authorities;
- compensation for contracts cancelled.

They had already begun parallel proceedings before the German courts, but those proceedings had been stayed pending the outcome of the Union proceedings. The CJ held that the German court should first be given the opportunity to decide whether the German authorities were liable. The proceedings were stayed accordingly.

In *Haegeman* the applicant was seeking the annulment of a Commission decision refusing to return levies paid to the German authorities by the applicant as a result of an allegedly invalid regulation. This time, unlike *Firma E Kampffmeyer*, the levies had been paid into Union funds, and Haegeman had not instituted parallel proceedings before its national courts. Again the Court refused to admit the action. Haegeman's claim should have been made against the national author-ities to whom the refunds were originally paid.

There followed a series of cases in which claims before the CJ were made:

- for the return of sums unlawfully levied (eg, *Société Roquette Frères*);
- seeking payment of sums unlawfully withheld (*IBC v Commission* (case 46/75); *Lesieur Costelle et Associés SA v Commission* (cases 67–85/75)).

These were held to be inadmissible on the grounds that the applicants should have brought their actions before their national courts.

On the other hand in *Compagnie d'Approvisionnement; Merkur-Aussenhandels GmbH v Commission* (case 43/72); *Holtz & Willemsen GmbH v Council* (case 153/73); and *CNTA* the CJ was prepared to admit claims seeking payment of *sums unlawfully withheld* without requiring claimants to proceed first before their national courts.

In *Firma Gebrüder Dietz v Commission* (case 126/76) and *CNTA* the applicants were seeking dam-ages for losses suffered as a result of the sudden introduction by the Commission of monetary com-pensatory amounts in agriculture; they had not brought actions before their national courts. Their claims under Article 340(2) TFEU were held admissible.

In the second 'grits' and 'quellmehl' cases, and the 'isoglucose' cases, admitted under Article 340(2) TFEU, proceedings had already been brought and the invalidity of the measures in question decided, before the applicants' national courts.

From the above cases the following tentative conclusions may be drawn:

(1) A claim for the return of sums unlawfully paid to the relevant national authorities should always be brought before a national court, even though those sums may have been paid into Union funds (*Kampffmeyer, Haegeman; Roquette*; see also more recently *Industrie-en Handelsonderneming Vreugdenhil BV v Commission* (case C-282/90));

(2) A claim for sums unlawfully withheld, even when withheld by a national authority, may be brought *either* before national courts or the GC. The weight of authority (*Compagnie d'Approvisionnement; Merkur; Holtz & Willemsen; CNTA*) leans towards this view. However, the existence of *IBC* and *Costelle* render it advisable to bring such a claim before a national court, *provided* that no further damages are required from the Union *and* payment of the sums involved was required to be channelled through the national authority;

(3) A claim for unliquidated damages for losses suffered as a result of illegal Union action (eg, financial losses in *Dietz; CNTA; Dumortier*) can *only* be brought before the European courts under Article 340(2) TFEU. In this respect it is submitted that *Kampffmeyer* was wrong. Therefore, if these losses result from sums unlawfully withheld, the appropriate forum for recovery of *both* sums would be at the European level.

Further support for principles (2) and (3) above may also be derived from *Krohn*.

Krohn

Krohn & Co was seeking compensation for financial losses suffered as a result of its national (German) authority's refusal to grant it licences to import manioc from Thailand. In rejecting its application the authorities were acting on mandatory instructions from the Commission. Krohn brought an action before the German courts seeking an annulment of the national authority's decision and an injunction requiring it to issue the licences, and a parallel action before the CJ for compensation for losses suffered as a result of its action in denying him the licences. The Commission argued that the action under Article 340(2) TFEU was inadmissible, since:

(1) the refusal of the licence came from the national authority;

(2) the applicant should have exhausted its remedies before its national court;

(3) to admit liability would be equivalent to nullifying the Commission's decision, which the applicant had failed to challenge in time.

All three arguments were rejected by the Court. With regard to (1) the Court found that although the refusal emanated from the national authority, the unlawful conduct was to be attributed not to the German authorities but to the Union itself. The Commission was the 'true author' of the decision.

With regard to (2) the Court held that while admissibility may be dependent on national rights available to obtain the annulment of a national authority's decision, that would only be the case where national rights of action provide an effective means of protection for the individual concerned and are capable of resulting in compensation for the damage alleged.

Clearly, since the alleged 'tort' had been committed by the Union, only the Union would be liable to pay compensation.

The Court's response to (3) has already been noted. An action under Article 340(2) TFEU was an autonomous form of action with a particular purpose to fulfil (*Lütticke* (case 4/69)).

Thus, in deciding whether action should be brought before a national court or before the CJEU, the appropriate question is whether action before a national court can provide an *effective means of protection* for the claimant's interests. Where he merely seeks the return of money paid, or payment of money unlawfully withheld, or a declaration of invalidity or an injunction to prevent the application of the unlawful act, *a fortiori* when the wrongful act can be laid at the door of the national authorities (see *Société des Grands Moulins des Antilles v Commission* (case 99/74), and *Krohn*, in which it was held that national courts retain sole jurisdiction to order compensation for damage caused by national institutions), he should proceed before his national courts. Where he seeks damage from the Union for injury suffered as a result of wrongful acts attributable to the Union, his action must be before the GC (or CJ). This is a right which cannot be 'exhausted' before a national court. Where remedies are required of both national authorities and the Union, it will be necessary to proceed against both. Clearly he cannot recover twice for the same loss.

14.13 Conclusions

In dealing with claims under Article 340 TFEU, the European courts have to balance the conflicting interests of permitting flexibility in decision-making and protecting individuals who may suffer as a result of such action. For a long time, a very restrictive approach to claims brought under Article 340 TFEU was taken, but it is questionable whether this approach was entirely justified. The alignment of Union liability and state liability through *Brasserie de Pêcheur* and *Bergaderm* has improved this position to an extent, but it remains difficult for individuals seeking damages against the Union to succeed with their claim. Following *Brasserie du Pêcheur*, claims for damages under Article 340(2) TFEU should now be approached in the same way as claims under the state-liability principle. In situations where the defendant institution is acting pursuant to a wide discretion (which will often be the case in action taken under Article 340 TFEU), the list of factors to be taken into account in establishing whether a breach is sufficiently serious set out in para 56 of *Brasserie du Pêcheur* is now relevant. Moreover, it also appears that, following *Bergaderm*, it seems less relevant whether the measure complained of is of general or individual application. But although the applicant may succeed in establishing the existence of a sufficiently serious breach, he may still fail to establish that damage and causation. Although restrictive rules in relation to damage and causation may be justified to protect the Union against extensive liability to commercial undertakings for pure economic loss, it is questionable whether the rules as they currently are offer effective judicial protection for individuals. This has not changed to any significant extent in the wake of recent developments. Further, the position of the courts regarding liability for lawful acts still remains to be clarified fully. Despite these somewhat tentative extensions of the scope of Article 340 TFEU, it remains of limited use.

Further reading

Heukels, T and McDonnell, A (eds), *The Action for Damages in Community Law* (Kluwer, 1997).

Hilson, C, 'The role of discretion in EC law on non-contractual liability' (2005) 42 CML Rev 677.

Kuijper, PJ and Bronckers, M, 'WTO law in the European Court of Justice' (2005) 42 CML Rev 1313.

Schermers, H, Heukels, T and Mead, P (eds), *Non-contractual Liability of the European Communities* (Nijhoff Publications, 1988).

Steiner, J, 'The limits of state liability for breach of European Union Law' (1998) 4 EPL 69.

Wils, W, 'Concurrent liability of the Union and a Member State' (1992) 17 EL Rev 191.

Part III

15 Introduction to the internal market

15.1 Introduction

The creation of the internal market is one of the central purposes of the European Union (Article 3(3) TEU). So while the TEU refers to sustainable development and a social market economy, this is within the context of the creation of 'an area without internal frontiers in which the free movement of goods, persons, services and capital is ensured in accordance with the provisions of the Treaty' (Article 26(2) TFEU).

Prior to Lisbon, the Treaties also contained references to the 'common market', which includes, in addition to the four freedoms, common commercial policy—commercial relations with third countries—and competition policy. On this basis, it could be argued that the term 'common market' was slightly wider than 'internal market'. The CJ tended not to distinguish between the terms. Following Lisbon, all references to the 'common market' were replaced with the words 'internal market', removing the concept of the common market from the Union. However we refer to the objectives of the EU, the creation of the internal market is an essential and distinctive part of EU law. This chapter identifies certain common themes affecting those four freedoms which constitute the internal market: subsequent chapters look at the detail of these provisions.

15.2 Overview of the four freedoms

15.2.1 Free movement of goods

The principle of freedom of movement of goods has been described as a fundamental freedom, the 'cornerstone' of the internal market. For many Member States the opportunity of access for their goods to a single, European-wide market was, and remains, a primary reason for membership. The free play of market forces within that larger market would increase economic efficiency, widen consumer choice and enhance the Union's competitiveness in world markets. However, since the principle of freedom of movement was intended to apply to all goods, including goods imported from outside the Union, it was necessary to eliminate distortions of competition resulting from different national rules regulating trade with third countries by presenting a common commercial front to the outside world. To achieve these goals:

(1) the TFEU establishes a customs union which involves (Article 28 TFEU) (see Chapter 17):

   (a) 'the prohibition between Member States of customs duties on imports and exports and of all charges having equivalent effect' (Article 30 TFEU), and

   (b) 'the adoption of a common customs tariff in their relations with third countries'.

   This aspect of the free movement of goods falls within exclusive Union competence (Article 3 TFEU);

(2) the TFEU also seeks the elimination of quantitative restrictions on imports and exports and all measures having equivalent effect (Articles 34–5 TFEU);

(3) in addition states were required to adjust any state monopolies of a commercial character so as 'to ensure that . . . no discrimination regarding the conditions under which goods are procured and marketed exists between nationals of Member States' (Article 37 TFEU).

The provisions relating to the free movement of goods apply to both industrial and agricultural products—save, where agriculture is concerned, as otherwise provided in Articles 39–44 TFEU (Article 38 TFEU)—whether originating in Member States or coming from third countries which are in free circulation in Member States.

15.2.2 Free movement of people

The basic principles relating to the free movement of persons are contained in Articles 45–8 TFEU (workers), and Articles 49–54 TFEU (freedom of establishment). The freedom to provide services is often seen as providing for the free movement of people although it is identified separately within the four freedoms (see 15.2.3). These freedoms have been further substantiated by secondary legislation. The rules apply throughout the territories of the Member States of the Union.

The basic rights enshrined in these provisions, granted to EU nationals (defined according to the law of each Member State) and companies and firms formed in accordance with the law of one of the Member States (Article 54 TFEU), comprise the right freely to leave, or enter and reside in a Member State for the purposes of work or establishment (or the provision of services) and the right to be treated in the host Member State free from discrimination on the grounds of nationality. As we shall see later, the CJ has—at least as regards individuals—interpreted these provisions to a large extent in parallel, a process which has been reinforced by the introduction of European citizenship. The fact that there is such a large degree of similarity led to the restructuring of the chapters on free movement of people. Whereas early editions dealt with this topic by looking at the Treaty articles on workers, establishment, services and citizenship individually, this edition (as has its immediate predecessors) takes a horizontal approach, looking at each of the rights accorded to migrant EU nationals (access to the territory, economic rights and social rights), so commonalities and differences can be more easily seen, and duplication avoided.

These rights are not absolute; not even citizenship rights are absolute. Rights of entry and residence are subject to derogation on the grounds of public policy, public security and public health (Articles 45 and 52 TFEU; Directive 2004/38). Exceptions from the non-discrimination principle are provided for 'employment in the public service' (Article 45) and 'activities connected with the exercise of official authority' (Article 51 TFEU).

One of the key questions to be asked, in relation to free movement of people, is whether individuals claiming the rights fall within the scope of the Treaty. In this, we can see a broadening of protection in two ways: judicial and legislative. As regards the judicial activity, although the rights contained in the Treaty were originally expressed to be limited to those who are economically active—that is, workers or persons, natural or legal, exercising rights of establishment or providing services in the host state—broad definitions of the relevant terms, in particular the definition of worker, and generous interpretation on the part of the Court, have extended the scope of their protection in terms of people within the ambit of EU law. Furthermore, secondary legislation extended these rights to the families of economically active EU migrants, irrespective of their nationality (see Chapter 21). Legislative action also extended similar rights to a wider category of persons who were not economically active. This trend was then given Treaty recognition by the introduction of citizenship rights under Articles 21–5 TFEU, introduced by Maastricht. These rights have been consolidated and updated by the introduction of another directive, sometimes called the 'Citizenship Rights Directive' (Directive 2004/38). A separate regime applies to third-country nationals (see Chapter 26).

A second central question relates to the scope of the rights granted. While more detail on the scope of rights was expressly set out in secondary legislation, such as Regulation 492/2011 (former Regulation 1612/68) regarding workers, these rights have been supported by an extensive interpretation by the CJ. The CJ developed in many cases a discrimination-based argument so that with the expanded interpretation as to when free movement rights had been affected, and a broader scope to the Treaties themselves, the scope of rights available are broad, covering rights to education, the rights to war compensation and even the right to name your child in a certain way (see Chapter 23).

With this expansive interpretation, the focus shifts to questions of infringement and justification. In many cases involving social and ancillary rights in particular, infringement is clear to see on the basis of indirect discrimination (eg, residency clauses, and see further 15.3.3). Where measures do not directly discriminate, they may be justified. An increasingly common argument being used by the Member States is that the migrant claiming the right does not have sufficient connection with the host Member State; that there is no 'real link'. In principle it seems this argument can be used in relation to cases brought under an economic free movement right (eg, Article 45 TFEU) or under the citizenship provisions (*R, on the application of Dany Bidar v London borough of Ealing and Secretary of State for Education and Skills* (case C-209/03)), although whether it means the same thing in all circumstances is still not yet clear.

Citizenship rights, set out in Articles 21–5 TFEU, comprise the right 'to move and reside freely within the territory of the Member States', the right to stand and vote in municipal and European Parliament elections, and the right to petition the ombudsman and the European Parliament. We have noted that as regards the right of free movement, the CJ has interpreted the rights of citizens in line with the other free movement rights. Significantly, however, recent case law on citizenship has indicated that individuals who are EU citizens may claim rights in a very broad range of circumstances (see Chapter 21). The introduction of the concept of citizenship also raised questions as to what rights citizens should expect, and has fuelled the debate on whether the Union should do more to protect the individual citizen. Despite the opportunity to amend the citizenship provisions that successive Treaty revision provided, nothing was done expressly to expand the rights attaching to citizenship. Lisbon again rejected the possibility of adding to the citizenship provisions in the TFEU, though the existing provisions are more explicitly linked to the principle of non-discrimination and the provisions on the area of freedom, security and justice were strengthened (Chapter 26).

15.2.3 **Freedom to provide services**

The freedom to provide services is found in Articles 56–62 TFEU. In this book the freedom to provide services is treated as part of the free movement of people. When someone provides a service, it may also involve that person moving, even if temporarily, to the Member State where the service is received. However, it should be noted that services themselves can move, without necessarily requiring that a person also moves to provide the service. Examples of this principle can be seen in sectors such as broadcasting or insurance. Nonetheless, the same provisions of Article 56 TFEU *et seq* apply in this context as apply in relation to the provision of services where a person moves, although it may be that a difference in the way the provisions are interpreted can be seen in the two types of circumstance. The fundamental right comprises the freedom to access both the territory and market of other Member States and to be treated on the same basis as the nationals of the host Member State. A further significant development can be seen in relation to the right to receive services, especially as regards public service provided by the individual Member States. Jurisprudence of the CJ is eroding Member States' ability to control individuals' access to public services in other Member States. It has given rise to debate as to whether this case law allows for the most efficient use of such services across Europe or merely constitutes an unjustified erosion of national solidarity. This area is discussed in Chapter 24.

15.2.4 Free movement of capital

The provisions on capital and payments, substantially amended by Maastricht, are found in Articles 63–6 TFEU. In its post-Maastricht form, the central provision bears a resemblance to the approach taken in relation to the free movement of goods. Recent case law suggests that the CJ's approach has paralleled that taken in respect of the other three freedoms.

There are nonetheless, distinctive features relating to the provisions on capital. It should be noted that the TFEU distinguishes between payments and capital movements between Member States themselves and between Member States and third countries. In the latter situation the Council may, in limited circumstances, take measures limiting the movement of capital and payments from third countries (Article 75 TFEU).

Article 65 TFEU deals with tax, and permitted distinctions based on place of residence, as well as public-policy exceptions to the free movement of capital. Despite these provisions, it will be seen in the chapter on economic rights (Chapter 22) that Member States' freedom in the field of taxation has been curtailed. Article 65(2) TFEU provides that the provisions relating to capital are to operate without prejudice to the operation of restrictions on the freedom of establishment that are compatible with the TFEU. Effectively, this means that a person cannot seek to evade a legitimate restriction on establishment via the capital provisions. It seems, however, that the reverse might be true. The relationship between capital and the other provisions is discussed at 15.4 (see also Chapter 20).

Finally, Article 65(3) TFEU provides that any national measures taken on the basis of Article 65(1) are 'not to constitute a means of arbitrary discrimination or a disguised restriction on the free movement of capital'. This wording parallels that used in relation to the derogation from the free movement of goods found in Article 36 TFEU (see further Chapter 20).

15.3 Common themes in the free movement provisions

Although the terms of the freedoms are each worded slightly differently, certain common elements must be shown before a case for the application of one of the freedoms can be made. In all cases it seems that there must be both an economic element and an interstate factor to bring the situation within the scope of any of the freedoms. Note also that, although citizenship does not require an economic element, it does require some connection with another Member State to be shown. It has also been argued that a convergence can be seen in the approach taken to identifying the trigger for a finding of breach of the freedoms.

15.3.1 Economic activity

In the earlier years of the Union, to invoke the non-discrimination principle it was necessary for the migrant claimant to be or have been engaged in some form of economic activity in the host state. In *Walrave* (see also Chapter 5), in the context of a challenge to the cycling association's rules relating to 'pacemaker' cyclists, which were clearly discriminatory, it was held that the prohibition of discrimination on the grounds of nationality contained in former Article 7 EEC (currently Article 18 TFEU) does not apply to sports teams that have nothing to do with economic activity. The practice of sport is subject to Union law *only insofar as it constitutes an economic activity* (see further, eg, *Deliège*, discussed in Chapter 21). Just as the rights of free movement are only granted to workers and the self-employed and their families (albeit, as will be seen, very liberally interpreted), to invoke the principle of non-discrimination of Article 18 TFEU in this context, there had to be some economic nexus.

This principle has been considerably eroded over the past four decades, as the European Economic Community was transformed into the European Union. In *Gravier* and *Cowan v French Treasury* (case 186/87) the Court held that students (*Gravier*) and tourists (*Cowan*), temporarily resident in a Member State as recipients of services, were entitled to invoke the then Article 7 EEC (now Article 18 TFEU) to claim equality of treatment for certain financial benefits available under national law only to nationals of the host State (see also *Commission v Spain (museum admission)* (case C-45/93)—an entrance fee to museums charged to non-nationals was discriminatory and contrary to Article 18 TFEU).

Similarly the Directives extending free movement rights to persons of independent means, retired persons and students, now consolidated into the Citizenship Directive, also appeared to dilute the need for an economic link. Persons claiming under these Directives needed to be covered by medical insurance and need to have sufficient financial resources to avoid becoming a burden on the Member State though the extent of this limitation has been the subject of much litigation. Nonetheless, important questions regarding the scope of application of the non-discrimination principle in relation to those who are not economically self-supporting remain to be resolved, either by secondary legislation or by the Court. In general terms, the CJ has taken a generous approach.

Although goods are not usually considered in this light, economic aspects can be seen in the definition attributed to them by the CJ's jurisprudence. Though the terms are used interchangeably, 'goods' and 'products' are not defined in the TFEU. They were interpreted by the CJ in *Commission v Italy (export tax on art treasures)* (case 7/68) as anything capable of money valuation and of being the object of commercial transactions. It does not matter whether the individuals are moving goods as part of their business or in their private capacity, provided the items satisfy the definition of goods.

15.3.2 Internal situations and migration

An individual who has never sought to exercise his or her right to freedom of movement will not be able to rely on free movement rights. The matter will be regarded as 'wholly internal' (see, eg, *R v Saunders* (case 175/78); *Ministère Public v Gauchard* (case 20/87)). This principle, that EU law has no application to purely internal matters, can operate harshly as illustrated in *Morson v Netherlands* (cases 35 and 36/82).

Morson

Two mothers from Surinam wished to join their children in the Netherlands. Since they were not entitled to do so under Dutch law they sought to rely on EU law, which permits family members to join EU migrants. In this case the applicants were unsuccessful: since their children had never exercised their right to freedom of movement in the Union there was no factor connecting them with Union law.

Equally in *Firma Sloman Neptun Schiffahrts AG (Firma) v Seebetriebsrat Bodo Ziesemer of Sloman Neptun Schiffahrts AG* (cases C-72 and 73/91) the CJ held that it was not contrary to Union law to discriminate against migrant workers from third countries (ie countries outside the EU) in the absence of factors connecting them with Union law. Even in the context of citizenship, some transnational element must be identified (*Uecker Hecker and Jacquet* (cases C-64 and 65/96)).

The impact of this rule has been limited. Once a connecting factor has been established migrants will be able to rely on EU rights on returning to their own Member State (*R v Immigration Appeal Tribunal, ex parte Secretary of State for the Home Department* (the *Singh* case) (case C-370/90); see further Chapter 20). Further, in more recent cases involving citizenship, no cross-border movement was involved yet Union law applied (eg, *Garcia Avello*; *Chen*; see further Chapter 21).

A similar approach is taken in relation to goods. The Court has limited the circumstances in which an internal situation will be found through the width of the test used to determine when there is an impact on trade. The famous test in *Procureur du Roi v Dassonville* (case 8/74) refers to a measure 'directly or indirectly, actually or potentially' hindering trade being sufficient to trigger Article 34 TFEU, suggesting that an actual interstate element is not necessary in a particular case provided the possibility of such an effect can be shown. From the case law it seems possible that cases where a national trader selling or distributing national goods seeking to challenge a rule of the same Member State could fall within Article 34 TFEU, as happened in *Pistre* (cases C-321–4/94, discussed in Chapter 18). Similar approaches can be seen in relation to capital, services and establishment.

15.3.3 Discrimination or access to the market?

Because of the fundamental importance of the principle of free movement of goods the Treaty rules in this area have been strictly enforced, and exceptions, where provided, have been given the narrowest scope. In interpreting the rules the CJ looks not to the name of a particular national measure, nor to the motive for its introduction, but to its *effect* in the light of the aims of the Treaty; does it create an obstacle to the free movement of goods within the single internal market? Article 34 TFEU is not limited to circumstances in which a Member State has discriminated against imported goods. The provision, as seen by the CJ, is far wider than that. Interpreted in this way, many national measures, not overtly or intentionally protectionist, designed to achieve the most worthy objectives, have been found to be capable of hindering trade between Member States, prima facie in breach of Union law. Such measures, as will be seen, have nevertheless been permitted by the Court on an ad hoc basis where they could be proved to be 'objectively justified' as necessary to safeguard vital interests ('mandatory requirements'), such as the protection of health, the environment or the consumer.

A move away from an interpretation based on the need to show discrimination, whether direct or indirect, to one that focuses on the removal of obstacles to free movement can be seen in the context of persons too. The basic right contained in each of Articles 45, 49 and 56 TFEU is that migrant workers should not be discriminated against on grounds of nationality. This is reinforced by Article 18 TFEU which provides that:

> Within the scope of application of this Treaty, and without prejudice to any special provisions contained therein, any discrimination on grounds of nationality shall be prohibited.

This provision has been important in ensuring that the migrant individual and his family, once legally resident in the host Member State, receives parity of treatment with nationals of the host Member State in respect not only of employment rights but of social rights in general (see also 15.5 and Chapter 6).

The prohibition of discrimination on the grounds of nationality applies to all forms of discrimination, both overt and covert. It will often take the form of a residence or length-of-residence requirement as illustrated by *Sotgiu v Deutsche Bundespost* (case 152/73).

> ### Sotgiu
>
> Here, the claimant was an Italian national employed by the German post office in Germany. His family lived in Italy. Following the issue of a circular, post office workers separated from their families in Germany were to be paid an increased 'separation' allowance while workers who were living abroad at the time of recruitment would continue to be paid at the same rate. The rule was not overtly discriminatory, since it applied to all workers, regardless of nationality. But clearly its effects could fall more heavily on foreigners. The Court, on a reference from the Bundesarbeitsgericht held that the prohibition of discrimination (expressed here in Article 7(1) of Regulation 1612/68, but equally applicable to Article 18 TFEU) prohibited all covert forms of discrimination which, by the application of criteria other than nationality nevertheless led to the same result.

A residence criterion *could* have a discriminatory effect, prohibited by the Treaty and the Regulation. In *O'Flynn v Adjudication Officer* (case C-237/94), the CJ characterised four groups of conditions as potentially discriminatory, even if phrased in nationality-neutral terms. The conditions are:

- those which affect essentially migrant workers;
- those where the great majority of those affected are migrant workers;
- those which can be more easily satisfied by national workers than by migrant workers;
- those where there is a risk that they might operate to the particular detriment of migrant workers.

Thus, certain professional rules and codes of practices or even professional qualifications have been found to be indirectly discriminatory. By imposing conditions additional to those required in the worker's home state, and which may be more difficult or burdensome for the migrant worker to satisfy, they create obstacles to the free movement of persons in the same way as indistinctly applicable rules applied to goods (see Chapter 22).

Case law, such as *Union Royale Belge des Sociétés de Football Association (ASBL) v Bosman* (case C-415/93) in respect of workers; *Säger v Dennemeyer & Co Ltd* (case C-76/90) in respect of services; and *Gebhard v Consiglio dell'Ordine degli Avvocati e Procuratori di Milano* (case C-55/94) in respect of establishment, has developed this category of indirectly discriminatory measures. Indeed, these cases suggest that the Court phrases its arguments in terms of obstacles to trade and movement rather than as species of discrimination. In this again, we see parallels to the approach taken in relation to goods, and which can now also be found in the context of capital.

As in the case of goods, such measures may be permitted if they are objectively justified—that is, if they are not disproportionate and pursue legitimate ends. The extent to which these principles applicable to goods can be applied in the context of workers, establishment and services has been raised in a number of cases. (See, eg, the comments of the Advocates-General in *Bosman* and *Volker Graf v Filzmoser Maschinenbau* (case C-190/98); see Chapter 22.)

15.3.4 **Direct effect**

Although the free movement provisions are addressed to Member States, all the main articles have been found to be directly effective (see Chapter 5) and thus may be invoked by individuals.

15.3.5 **Need for harmonisation**

The Treaty derogations and the grounds for justification accepted by the Court, described as mandatory requirements or reasons of overriding public interest, clearly jeopardised the functioning of the single market. Nor was the problem confined to goods; it also applied to the other elements of the internal market. It became clear that if important public interests were to be protected without impairing the functioning of the internal market, action would have to be taken at Union level. Following the publication by the Commission in 1985 of a White Paper on the Completion of the Internal Market, Member States agreed to embark on a massive harmonisation programme, designed to provide common standards of protection, to be completed by 31 December 1992. This was enshrined in the SEA 1996 (Article 26 TFEU). To speed up the legislative process, a new article, Article 114 TFEU, was introduced into the TFEU, providing for the 'approximation' (ie harmonisation) of the 'provisions laid down by law, regulation or administrative action in Member States which have as their object the establishing and functioning of the internal market' (subject to some exceptions) by measures to be enacted by qualified majority vote, instead of, under Article 115 TFEU, by unanimity (see Chapter 16). This programme, an example of 'positive integration' (as opposed to the 'negative integration' achieved by decisions of the CJ rendering 'inapplicable' domestic measures contrary to EU law), has been largely successful.

In 2011, the Commission issued a Communication, 'Single Market Act—Twelve levers to boost growth and strengthen confidence "Working together to create new growth"' (COM(2011) 206 final). It recalled the central place of the internal market to prosperity but noted that the internal market still had shortcomings: areas where there are still barriers to trade and market fragmentation. Against this background, the Commission has (again) come up with an ambitious legislative programme to meet the 'Europe 2020' goals for 'smart, sustainable and inclusive growth' (COM(2010) 2020). It identified 12 areas in which it will seek to take action, which include action on intellectual property rights; consumer empowerment; services; networks (energy and transport infrastructure); and the digital single market. The digital single market alone led to significant legislative activity in the fields of copyright, e-commerce, broadcasting and telecommunications.

Another comparatively recent emphasis in the internal-market programme is that of simplifying legislation (SLIM), with the aim of increasing transparency and making cross-border transactions easier. The so-called open method of coordination (OMC) (discussed in Chapters 3 and 16) can also be seen as part of the attempt to lessen the regulatory burden on businesses. Chapter 16 also details new approaches to the eradication of differences in Member States' legal systems, such as reliance on agencies and EU-wide networks of regulators.

15.4 **Relationship between the freedoms**

The Court has held that the freedoms are mutually exclusive. This approach is supported by the terms of the TFEU itself. As noted at 15.2.4, the provisions on capital are expressed to apply without prejudice to the operation of the principles on establishment, and the service provisions are expressed to apply to situations 'insofar as they are not governed by the provisions relating to freedom of movement for goods, capital and persons'. Despite the similarity in approach between the freedoms identified earlier, it remains necessary to identify the scope of particular freedoms. It seems easy to identify where the boundary between goods and persons might arise, but other circumstances are less clear-cut. The boundary between services and establishment seems in some instances to be one of degree, rather than there being any qualitative difference between the subject matter of the two freedoms, though the introduction of the Services Directive (Directive 2006/123 ([2006] OJ L376/36)) may make it more important to make a distinction. (See further

Chapter 22.) It is also important, as we have noted (see 15.2.4), to distinguish between capital and establishment. Given that the provisions relating to capital may be relied upon by those in third countries, the classification of a measure as affecting establishment or capital has consequences for the group of persons who may rely on free movement rights in a given set of circumstances. More difficulties arise in relation to the boundary between goods and capital, on the one hand, and goods and services on the other.

In *R v Thompson* (case 7/78) goods were held to include collectors' coins in gold and silver, provided they were not coins in circulation as legal tender. The latter are covered by the provisions of the Treaty relating to capital (Article 63 TFEU, see *Bordessa* (cases C-358 and 416/93)).

In *Dundalk water supply* the concept of goods was held to apply not only to the sale of goods per se but to goods and materials supplied in the context of the provision of services. However, where goods are supplied in the context of the provision of services, to fall within the goods provisions of the Treaty, the importation or exportation of the goods in question must be an end in itself. Materials such as advertisements or tickets, supplied simply as an adjunct to a service—for example, a lottery—will fall within the provisions governing services, namely, Articles 56 and 57 TFEU (*Her Majesty's Customs and Excise v Schindler* (case C-275/92); see Chapter 22). The cases involving advertising of goods, especially those concerning broadcast advertising, illustrate the narrow boundary between goods and services (see, eg, *Konsummentombudsmannen v De Agostini (Svenska) Förlag AB and Komsummentombudsmannen v TV Shop i Sverge AB* (cases C-34-6/95), discussed further in Chapter 18). With the advent of digital content, which can be disseminated in many forms and across a range of platforms, the boundary between goods and services becomes problematic. For example, is there a reason why the CJ has treated one form of digital content (football matches on TV carried on encrypted satellite signals) as the provision of services in *Karen Murphy v Media Protection Services Ltd* (case C-429/08), yet treated software as a matter of goods in *UsedSoft GmbH v Oracle International Corp* (C-128/11)?

UsedSoft

This case concerned the extent to which Usedsoft could 'sell' secondhand software. While the reason that the software was treated as goods in *UsedSoft* might have been obvious had the software been handed over in physical form (eg, on a DVD), here the dataset of the program had been made available for online download—that is, not in physical form.

This question regarding the characterisation of digital goods and content is likely to occur again. The main value to such digital content is through copyright protection, and there are different rules relating to the extent that copyright protection will justify a barrier to free movement depending on whether goods or services are in issue.

In some instances, it seems that similar rules may be challenged by reference to different freedoms. In *Commission v Spain (shopping centres)* (case C-400/08), Catalonian planning laws which restricted the location of shopping centres were challenged (successfully) as a matter of freedom of establishment. Other planning cases, such as *Quietlynn v Louthend Borough Council* (case C-23/89) (see Chapter 18) have been viewed as a matter of the provision of goods. Further, in *Blanco Pérez* (cases C-570 and 571/07), restrictions on the territorial distribution of pharmacies was dealt with as a question of establishment. In *Commission v Germany (external pharmacies)*, those rules which dealt with the proximity of external pharmacies to hospitals were seen as a question of the free movement of goods. While it may be possible to distinguish between these cases on the facts (eg, the key point in the German case was the underlying contract to supply drugs to the hospital), it seems in some instances this distinction may be fine.

15.5 **The social dimension**

In addition to the rights conferred on those seeking to exercise their right to free movement, the Treaty seeks to increase social protection in areas such as employment and education. Where not already included, these goals were explicitly incorporated into the TEU by Maastricht. This social dimension has been re-emphasised by the changes introduced by Lisbon (Article 3(3) TEU; Article 9 TFEU). The purpose of EU *employment* legislation is to harmonise national laws, normally by direct- ive, to provide common standards of protection throughout the Union in the interest both of the worker and the more effective functioning of the single market. Harmonised standards are intended to create a level playing field, and avoid social dumping. It is thought that disparity between the laws of Member States as regards standards of employment protection will give a competitive advantage to states with lower standards. EU action in the field of *social rights* aims to promote and encourage the well-being of Union citizens, by action in the fields of public health or education, or to benefit the disabled, the deprived ('victims of social exclusion'), the elderly or victims of disaster. Measures here are designed to stimulate and complement rather than replace national provision, according to the principle of subsidiarity. Although there might not have been much direct action under the social policy provisions, workers' protection is also ensured by the general non-discrimination pro- visions (discussed in Chapter 23).

15.6 **Completion of the internal market: an Area of Freedom, Security and Justice**

The possibility of a frontier-free Europe has always been envisaged. This was re-emphasised by the insertion by the SEA of Article 26 TFEU, which provides for 'an area without internal frontiers in which the free movement of goods, persons, services and capital is ensured'. Progress on achieving an internal market in persons, by abolishing the barriers existing at the frontiers of Member States, was slow, partly because of the sensitivity of the area and partly because Member States were not agreed on whether the internal market in persons should include third-country nationals (TCNs) or be limited to EU nationals. The result was that certain Member States concluded an agreement outside the framework of the EU to achieve such an area. Under an agreement signed at Schengen in 1990, five Member States (Germany, France and the Benelux countries, later joined by Italy, Spain, Portugal and Greece) agreed to remove all checks on the movement of people across their borders (see further Chapter 26).

With the changes introduced by Maastricht, the Union began to develop, under the prior JHA pillar of the TEU, the foundations for a policy on TCNs. Although some decisions were made under JHA, progress in this area was slow. The need to reform the JHA was an important issue considered at Amsterdam.

Prior to the ToA, the majority of Member States had signed, if not ratified, the Schengen Agreement. The majority thus agreed at the 1996 IGC in effect to incorporate the terms of the Schengen Agreement into what is now the TFEU (the UK and Ireland opting out, and the Danish being undecided). Individuals lawfully resident within the EU are able to travel between Member States which have agreed to these provisions without being stopped at internal borders. Member States also agreed to develop common immigration and visa policies under these provisions. The provisions have been further strengthened by Lisbon. With 'de-pillarisation' the provisions in the old third pillar (the JHA) have been reintegrated into Title V of TFEU to create the provi- sions on an Area of Freedom, Security and Justice (AFSJ). Crucially, subject to some small limita- tions, decision-making in this area will be by the ordinary legislative procedure. This should give impetus to the Union's aim to complete the internal area (see Chapter 26 for further detail). These changes, especially the ability to move freely between Member States, benefit TCNs as well as EU citizens.

With the advent of the concept of European citizenship and the development of common immigration and asylum policies, there will be further pressure to extend the rights currently granted to EU workers and their families to all persons legitimately resident in the European Union. Although the concept of citizenship under Article 20 TFEU comprises only limited political rights, it provides for the granting of rights 'to move and reside freely within the territory of the Member States'. These provisions are already leading to social rights which apply to a more extensive group of EU citizens (see Chapter 28). It remains to be seen how far TCNs (who are not members of the family of EU nationals) legitimately resident in the Union will be able to claim equality of treatment with EU nationals. While some legislative proposals have been introduced, it is hard to avoid the suggestion that so far the emphasis as regards TCNs seems to have been directed more at keeping them out of the EU, rather than integrating them into the Union. As Weiler comments:

> It would be ironic that an ethos which rejected the nationalism of the Member States gave birth to a new European nation and European nationalism . . . We have made little progress if the Us becomes European (instead of German or French or British) and the Them becomes those outside the Community or those inside who do not enjoy the privileges of citizenship.

15.7 Conclusions

In sum, the internal market is central to much of the Union's activities, and the four freedoms in particular have operated to limit Member States' regulatory freedom in wide ranging policy fields, some at a first glance, unconnected with inter-state trade. The CJ has been a key driver in this, defining the scope of the four freedoms broadly and the exceptions narrowly. Although the consequences of many rulings have been deregulatory in effect, the CJ has at the same time played a part in extending social protection to migrants and their families. While it is possible to spot parallels in the CJ's reasoning between the freedoms, it is important to remember that there are key differences and that it remains important to identify which freedom is in issue. While many of the developments were as a result of judicial activity, the role of EU legislation, specifically harmonising legislation, must not be forgotten, as in increasing areas it, too, operates to displace or amend national laws.

The following chapters deal first with harmonisation then with the four freedoms. This part of the book also considers certain provisions relating to citizenship and the free movement of TCNs as part of the free movement of persons before we look at discrimination, one of the Treaty's key objectives and which was central to the early development of Union law. Finally we consider competition policy. The subject of state aids was formerly dealt with. Since the area is complex and of specialist nature, the topic has now been excluded from this work.

Further reading

Barnard, C, 'Fitting the remaining pieces into the goods and persons jigsaw?' (2001) 26 EL Rev 35.

Closa, C, 'The concept of citizenship in the Treaty on European Union' (1992) 29 CML Rev 1137.

Commission's Annual Report on the Internal Market: from 1993.

Curtin, D and Meijers, H, 'The principle of open government in Schengen and the European Union: Democratic retrogression?' (1995) 32 CML Rev 391.

Dougan, M, 'The constitutional dimension to the case law on Union citizenship' (2006) 31 EL Rev 613.

d'Oliveira, H, 'Nationality and the European Union after Amsterdam' in D O'Keeffe and P Twomey (eds), *Legal Issues of the Amsterdam Treaty* (Hart Publishing, 1999).

Hinarejos, A, 'Free movement, federalism and institutional choice: a Canada-EU comparison' (2012) 71 Cambridge Law Journal 537.

Mortelmans, K, 'The Common Market, the internal market and the single market: What's in a market?' (1998) 35 CML Rev 101.

O'Brien, C, 'Real links, abstract rights and false alarms: The relationship between the ECJ's "real link" case law and national solidarity' (2008) 33 EL Rev 643.

Snell, J, 'And then there were two: Products and citizens in Community law' in T Tridimas and P Nebbia (eds), *European Union Law for the Twenty-First Century: Rethinking the new legal order* (Hart Publishing, 2004).

Trstenjak, V and Beysen, E, 'The growing overlap of fundamental freedoms and fundamental rights in the case-law of the CJEU' (2013) 38 EL Rev 293.

Watson, P, 'Social policy after Maastricht' (1993) 30 CML Rev 481.

Weiler, JHH, 'The transformation of Europe' (1991) 100 Yale LJ 2403.

16 Harmonisation

16.1 Introduction

The objective of creating as well as completing the internal market requires the removal of barriers to the four freedoms.

Barriers to trade remain, as significant differences in the laws of the various Member States still exist, in particular where national laws are aimed at protecting various interests that are recognised by the Union. Although the removal of barriers would undoubtedly improve the workings of the internal market, it would not be enough simply to remove those national rules which affect the free movement of goods, services, persons and capital.

This chapter therefore considers the nature of harmonisation as well as discussing the different approaches taken by the Union to harmonisation itself. In this discussion, key issues concern the relationship between harmonising measures and underlying Treaty provisions, indirectly concerning the freedom of Member States to take individual action in harmonised fields. This discussion links into questions about the degree to which we require uniformity at Union level and the extent to which the Union can tolerate diversity. Given the impact of harmonising legislation, the legitimacy and effectiveness of the techniques adopted must also be considered (though see also Chapter 3). This chapter also reviews the scope of the Union's power to enact harmonising measures in the context of the internal market and the extent to which the Union effectively has a general power to regulate. Rather than being just a technical question of appropriate Treaty base, the scope of Article 114 TFEU has a constitutional aspect relating to the balance of powers within the Union and between the Union and the Member States. In this chapter, much of the discussion will relate to measures dealing with trade in goods; similar principles, however, also apply to the other freedoms.

16.2 The nature of harmonisation

16.2.1 Positive and negative harmonisation

The creation of similar standards throughout the Union would reduce the potential threat of a 'downward spiral' in standards arising from producers and service providers seeking to move their base to the Member State with the lowest regulatory burden. This process, by which the Union sets down a standard in a particular field that all the domestic legal systems must meet, is known as harmonisation. The form of harmonisation by which a common standard is introduced throughout the Union is sometimes referred to as 'positive' harmonisation, because new standards are introduced. The removal of existing barriers by the striking down of national laws (eg, under Articles 34, 45, 49 and 56 TFEU) is known as 'negative' harmonisation. This chapter focuses on positive harmonisation.

The original Treaty of Rome provided for the creation of common Union rules, not only in the areas marked out for common organisation, such as agriculture, but in all the areas of activity outlined in the Treaty, or falling within the broader objectives of the Union (see Article 352 TFEU and Chapter 3). A huge body of rules is now in place. Many of these rules, particularly, but not exclusively, those enacted under Articles 114–15 TFEU, seek to harmonise national laws, normally by means of directives. Although directives require implementation at national level, and leave national authorities some choice as to 'the form and method of implementation' (Article 288 TFEU; see Chapter 3), once the period allowed for implementation has expired, Member States are not free to enact or maintain domestic measures inconsistent with their obligations under the directive or with the general purposes of the directive. Where there is a conflict between provisions of national and Union law, Union law must prevail (see Chapter 4). A question that arises once harmonisation has taken place is the extent to which the Member States are free to derogate from their obligations under the Treaty, or to enact more stringent rules. These issues will be considered at 16.3.

Positive harmonisation may be seen to have a number of advantages over negative harmonisation. It seems possible at least in principle, to attain two objectives through the use of harmonising measures:

- the protection of the public interest;
- the creation of the internal market.

By contrast, where negative harmonisation is used, there seems to be a trade-off between the need to protect the public interest (letting the national rule stand) and the creation of the internal market (striking down the national rule). As will be seen, although mutual recognition facilitates free movement, disparities in national systems remain where 'mandatory requirements' and Treaty derogations operate to save national rules that prima facie constitute a barrier to trade, thus the barriers to trade remain with adverse consequences for the creation of the single market. Subsequent chapters indicate a similar process in relation to the other freedoms.

There are other possible advantages to positive harmonisation too. Inconsistent national measures will no longer be good law and they will also be replaced by the Union standards, reducing the risk of creating a regulatory gap, and in the case of an action against a public body, potentially may be relied on in national courts (see Chapter 5). Positive harmonisation might also be said to respect the division of powers within the Union. Laws and standards are properly made through the democratic process—that is, by the involvement of political institutions, rather than by the judicial process. Finally, in theory, the use of directives allows the various Member States to take account of legal principles already in existence within their individual legal systems and to ensure that the requirements of Union law blend in with that system, though the reality may leave Member States with little choice.

The difficulty with harmonisation is that, even using QMV (see Chapter 2), it can be difficult for Member States to come to an agreement. Thus, not only is legislative action difficult in the first place, but it can be problematic to amend a directive, with the result that standards become outdated. The difficulties of achieving consensus can be illustrated by reference to the rules harmonising the marketing of chocolate.

Labelling of chocolate

A directive on the marketing of chocolate was agreed in 1973 ([1973] OJ L228/23). The area was contentious because some Member States allowed the addition of vegetable fats to the cocoa butter used in chocolate, but other Member States, such as Italy, did not. The compromise position found in the Directive was not clear. The CJ clarified that the effect of the Directive was that the inclusion of vegetable fats could be permitted by individual Member States, but that 'chocolate' produced in this way could not claim the benefit of the free movement under the Directive. Some Member States retained stringent rules, effectively protecting their domestic market from chocolate with vegetable fat in it. It was not until 2000, approximately quarter of a century later, with the enactment of Directive 2000/36 ([2000] OJ L197/19) that the matter was resolved: chocolate made with vegetable fats became generally permissible but must be labelled as containing vegetable fats. Italy continued to have chocolate problems. Italian rules specified that products which do not contain vegetable fat other than cocoa butter could additionally carry the word 'pure' to describe the chocolate.

The CJ in *Commission v Italy (pure chocolate)* (case C-47/09) confirmed that in so doing, Italy had failed in its obligations to implement Directives 2000/36 related to cocoa products and chocolate intended for human consumption and 2000/13 on the labelling, presentation and advertising of foodstuffs. This example illustrates that even when harmonisation has occurred, national practices die hard.

16.2.2 **Harmonisation and unification**

Harmonisation may be contrasted with 'unification'. A process of unification would result in the complete replacement of particular aspects of the legal orders of the Member State with a new order adopted at the European level. For example, although it did not pursue this idea, in its Communication on European Contract Law (COM(2001) 398 final), the Commission considered among other things whether the entire system of contract law of the Member States might be replaced with a new European contract code. Unification would mean that existing legal principles would be replaced with new principles applicable throughout all the Member States. In contrast, although harmonisation may result in the creation of a common set of rules which have the same substantive scope, the implementation of these rules utilises the legal principles and concepts familiar to each particular Member State.

16.2.3 **Other forms of Union action**

It needs to be remembered that the Union does not focus exclusively on harmonisation. In some fields, such as public health, harmonisation is expressly precluded (see further 16.4.1). There are other means by which Union objectives can be supported, for example through the coordination of national measures—this is the approach taken in relation to social security arrangements. There, Regulation 883/2004 ([2004] OJ L166/1) provides for the coordination of Member States' social security schemes. It does not harmonise those systems: Member States remain responsible for the substance of their own social security systems. This type of approach is reflected now in the division of competence: Article 2(3) TFEU recognises that Union competence may support, coordinate or supplement national action rather than supplant it (as would be the case with harmonisation—Article 2(2) TFEU).

16.3 **Types of harmonisation**

There are several forms of harmonisation. These may be classed according to the degree of freedom left to the Member States to adopt measures that differ from the harmonised rules, either by setting a higher standard, or by maintaining existing lower standards. Some measures contain a mix of techniques. There is a certain lack of consensus about the number and types of categories of harmonisation; the types discussed in this section are the main forms of harmonisation usually found in EU law.

16.3.1 **Total harmonisation**

Total harmonisation leaves the Member States with no scope for further independent action in the field covered by the harmonising measure. In other words, Member States' competence to act has been pre-empted by Union action. As far as the area covered by a total harmonisation directive is concerned, Member States must ensure that their domestic system provides exactly what is required by that directive. It is not possible to introduce a stricter standard, as can be seen in *Commission v United Kingdom* (*dim-dip lights*) (case 60/86). In this case, the compatibility of a requirement introduced by the UK that all new cars should be equipped with dim-dip lights with the relevant directive, Directive 76/759 ([1976] OJ L262/71), was decided against the UK because the Directive specified exhaustively the types of lights which could be fitted to cars.

In its earlier decision in *Prantl* (case 16/83), the CJ stated that:

> once rules on the common organisation of the market may be regarded as forming a complete system, the Member States no longer have competence in that field unless [Union law] expressly provides otherwise [para 6].

Thus if a measure is a total harmonisation measure, Member States will not be free to adopt additional provisions covering the same sector even in relation to purely internal situations. These principles are not limited to technical rules relating to goods, but apply to all aspects of EU law. Thus, in *Chamber of Commerce Amsterdam v Inspire Art Ltd* (case C-167/01), Dutch legislation imposing disclosure obligations on branches of foreign companies exceeded the requirements of the Eleventh Company Law Directive (Directive 89/666 ([1989] OJ L395/36)), and was therefore not permitted. That Directive was exhaustive and a branch could not be required to disclose information beyond that required by the Directive.

The exclusion of higher domestic standards applies even where this might be of benefit to individuals, such as consumers, as can be seen in *Commission v France (Product Liability Directive)* (case C-52/00).

> ### *French Product Liability* Case
>
> The CJ held that France had incorrectly implemented several provisions of Directive 85/374 (Product Liability Directive [1985] OJ L210/29). Article 9 specifies that liability for property damage would only arise if the damage caused were to exceed 500 ECU. France chose not to implement this threshold and put forward two arguments to justify its position. It claimed first that the Directive should be interpreted in the light of Article 169 TFEU which permits a higher national level of protection than specified in relevant consumer protection directives. Moreover, the Product Liability Directive allowed the Member States to depart from several of the rules it laid down and permission to do likewise in relation to other areas covered by the Directive could be inferred. The CJ rejected France's contention and held that:
>
> > The margin of discretion available to the Member States . . . is *entirely determined by the directive itself* and must be inferred from its wording, purpose and structure [para 16].

Additionally, Member States may only derogate from the provisions of a total harmonisation directive in so far as the directive expressly permits. The fact that a directive permits derogation for particular aspects falling within the scope of the directive or leaves certain matters for domestic law does not change its character as a total harmonisation measure (*French product liability* case, para 19). This position was also adopted in *Sanchez v Medicina Asturiana SA* (case C-183/00), again involving Directive 85/374.

Sanchez

The Product Liability Directive establishes a system of strict liability for injury or property damage caused by defective products. Article 13 of the Directive preserves the application of other systems of contractual or non-contractual liability *based on other grounds*. Prior to the introduction of the Directive, Spain had adopted a system of strict liability which it did not repeal when it implemented the Directive. The earlier system was more favourable to the claimant. The CJ held that, although Article 13 did not prevent the maintenance of a fault-based system of product liability, it precluded the retention of a more extensive system of liability which uses the same basis as that in the Directive (ie strict liability).

Both cases described above illustrate the impact of a total harmonisation measure. Such a directive precludes Member States from adopting or retaining rules which cover the same ground as the directive and which are based on the same legal principles. This led to fears about the impact on the Member States' diversity from the threat of homogenised 'Euro-products'. To some extent, this fear is overstated as total harmonisation directives have typically contained a range of provisions variously allowing specific derogations, opt-out clauses and phased introduction of the obligations. While the resulting directives may be complex, these approaches allow some account to be taken of national differences. Thus, a total harmonisation measure may permit specific derogations by giving Member States the option whether to implement particular provisions in the directive.

In all cases, it will be necessary to identify exactly what the directive provides, and the scope of any opt-outs, and which aspects of the relevant field it regulates—that is, it is necessary to identify the 'occupied field', as areas which lie outside the field of a total harmonisation directive can still be regulated by the Member States, reflecting the fact that the internal market is an area of shared competence (Article 4(2)(a) TFEU). Member States' competence will always be subject to the requirement to comply with the Treaty, which, in practice, means the provisions on the four freedoms. This can be seen in *Inspire Art*.

Inspire Art

Here, the Dutch legislation on branches of foreign companies introduced several obligations on such branches that went beyond disclosure obligations, including the requirement to have a minimum share capital. The Directive on Branches (Directive 89/666) only dealt with disclosure obligations, and any additional requirements which had to be met by branches of foreign companies were within the domain of the Member States. The minimum capital requirement could therefore be imposed unless it conflicted with the freedom of establishment (Article 49 TFEU).

The CJ first considered whether this requirement was caught by Article 49 TFEU, and having found that it was, considered whether it could be justified on objective grounds, applying the *Säger* test (Chapter 22). On the facts, the minimum capital requirement was not justified and was therefore incompatible with the Treaty.

16.3.2 **The Union's power to re-legislate**

Although it is clear that Member States have no power of action once a total harmonisation measure has been adopted, the Union itself is able to amend existing harmonisation measures and thereby to re-legislate in an area in which it has previously adopted harmonising measures. This can be seen in *British American Tobacco*.

> #### *British American Tobacco*
>
> In this case, it was argued that Directive 2001/37 ([2001] OJ L194/26) on the manufacture, presentation and sale of tobacco products was void because, inter alia, it amended Directive 90/239 ([1990] OJ L137/36) on the maximum yield of tar of cigarettes. Both Directives had been adopted on the basis of Article 114 TFEU. The applicants' contention was that Directive 90/239 had already established a fully harmonised regime on the yield of tar of cigarettes and that the Union could therefore not legislate afresh, at least not in the absence of new scientific evidence.

The CJ held (at para 77) that although the *Member States* were no longer able to introduce a rule in this area, the *Union* was nevertheless able to amend earlier legislation to safeguard the general interests recognised by the Treaty.

The Court went on to hold that:

> It follows that, even where a provision of [Union] law guarantees the removal of all obstacles to trade in the area it harmonises, that fact cannot make it impossible for the [Union] legislature to adapt that provision in step with other considerations [para 78].

Such adaptation may be the result of new developments based on scientific facts (para 79), but may also follow from 'other considerations, such as the increased importance given to the social and political aspects of the anti-smoking campaign' (para 80). The Union has a general power to re-legislate, but can only exercise this power if there are scientific or other reasons for doing so.

16.3.3 **Minimum harmonisation**

There was a trend, commencing with the SEA, and particularly following Maastricht, towards minimum harmonisation and some provisions of the Treaty, post-SEA, specifically refer to minimum harmonisation. It has the advantage of allowing flexibility and diversity in the regulatory system. The main harmonising provisions (such as Articles 114–15 TFEU) make no express reference to minimum harmonisation and in more recent times, the focus seems to be turning away from this form of harmonisation in favour of maximum harmonisation (see, eg, Directive 2005/29 ([2005] OJ L149/22) on unfair commercial practices).

In a minimum harmonisation measure, the EU will set down a minimum standard with which all the Member States must comply. Beyond this minimum level, Member States are free to set their own standards, subject to the requirements of the TFEU. The main objective of minimum harmonisation is not to specify an absolute standard which must be met by all the Member States, but rather to reduce the differences that exist by narrowing the freedom given to the Member States to regulate particular aspects within their territory. Importantly, minimum harmonisation:

> does not limit [Union] action to the lowest common denominator, or even to the lowest level of protection established by the various Member States [UK v Council (Working Time Directive) (case C-84/94), para 56].

It simply indicates that there is a degree of freedom left to the Member States to exceed the standard set by such a measure.

Minimum harmonisation can only be of limited assistance in creating a level playing field. It may be useful to the extent that it sets a minimum standard below which none of the Member States may fall, but it still leaves room for divergence in standards between Member States. Minimum harmonisation does no more than to shift the boundaries of what is permissible, in that Member States are no longer free to maintain standards lower than those in a minimum harmonisation directive, but standards higher than those in such a directive can be maintained. Sometimes, the level of protection contained in a minimum harmonisation directive is high, in which case there would be only very limited scope for the Member States to adopt additional rules. In many instances, however, there will still be a considerable degree of variation between the Member States in respect of the area subject to minimum harmonisation because, with lower standards identifying the base level of protection, Member States will enjoy relative freedom to impose stricter standards. An added dimension to this problem is introduced when directives include optional provisions which Member States are permitted, but not obliged to, implement.

Arguably, minimum harmonisation and optional provisions undermine the purpose of harmonisation, because the continuing freedom to set standards above the baseline identified by the harmonising measure still subjects individuals and businesses to the possibility of divergent rules throughout the Union. These differences may impose extra burdens on producers, if applied to imported as well as domestic products, and are likely to create barriers to the internal market. If they do so, actually or potentially, will they be permitted to apply only to domestically produced goods, or may they be applied to all goods? If applicable only to domestic production, domestic producers will be disadvantaged. If applicable to all goods, when, and in what circumstances, will they be permitted?

16.3.4 **Minimum harmonisation and reverse discrimination**

In the case of a minimum harmonisation measure, it may be easier for the Member States to deviate from the harmonised standard than it is in the case of total harmonisation. Indeed, it is inherent in the concept of minimum harmonisation that Member States *will* introduce or retain rules which go beyond what is required of such a directive. However, it is clear that Member States cannot fall below the minimum standard introduced by a directive, and even where national legislation sets a higher standard than the relevant directive, the national measure has to comply with the Treaty. Thus, the final boundary is of course set by the four freedoms.

Confusingly, harmonisation measures, therefore, do not follow a single pattern. Some minimum harmonisation directives contain a 'market access' clause, whereas others do not. A market-access clause specifies that Member States may not prevent the import of products which comply with the minimum standard, but do not meet the higher standard imposed by the particular Member State. Such a provision was at issue in *R v Secretary of State for Health, ex parte Gallaher Ltd* (case C-11/92). The question was whether domestic producers could invoke a market access clause to challenge national rules which applied only to domestic production (reverse discrimination).

Gallaher

The case concerned a challenge by three leading UK cigarette producers to UK regulations implementing the Tobacco Directive (Directive 89/622 ([1989] OJ L395/36)). This Directive required Member States to provide, inter alia, for health warnings on cigarettes to cover 'at least' 4 per cent of the packet (Article 4(4)). It also contained a market-access clause. Member States were not to prohibit or restrict the sale of products which complied with the Directive (Article 8(1)). Nevertheless, the UK regulations provided for more extensive health warnings than required by the terms of the Directive, to cover 6 per cent of the packet, but these requirements were applicable only to domestic production. The CJ held that the stringent national measures were permitted.

Depending on the wording of the directive, where there is minimum harmonisation and a market access clause EU law will permit reverse discrimination, as it has done in other areas. Such a proposition was confirmed in *R v Minister of Agriculture, Fisheries and Food, ex parte Compassion in World Farming Ltd* (case C-1/96).

Compassion in World Farming

Here a British animal-welfare group was seeking to prevent the export of live calves to other Member States which permitted the rearing of calves in crates, a practice prohibited by the UK (and a Council of Europe Convention). Directive 91/629 ([1991] OJ L340/48), a harmonisation measure relating to the health of animals, laid down minimum common standards for the protection of live calves, but specifically allowed Member States to apply, within their own territory, stricter rules. In this way, as the CJ pointed out, the Directive aimed to strike a balance between the interests of animal protection and the smooth functioning of the organisation of the market in calves and derived products.

The CJ reasoned that:

a Member State cannot rely on Article 36 of the Treaty in order to restrict the export of calves to other Member States for reasons relating to the protection of the health of animals, which constitutes the specific objective of the harmonisation undertaken by the directive [para 64].

In reaching this conclusion, paras 18 and 19 of *Hedley Lomas*, which referred to a total harmonisation directive, were invoked. Although there might be questions in a given case as to the specific objective of the harmonisation, it can be seen that the CJ has unequivocally held that where a directive providing for minimum standards of harmonisation allows Member States to maintain stricter standards these can only be applied in their own territory to the state's own products. A similar approach is now being taken in the fields of services and establishment (see Chapter 22).

Gallaher has been criticised as tending to undermine competition in the internal market and discourage experiment and diversity. It is argued that Member States are unlikely to enact legislation in the interest of higher standards where this will result in a competitive disadvantage for domestic products.

However, in the light of the principle of subsidiarity, a system permitting reverse discrimination may be a more practical way of regulating Member States' freedom to supplement Union provision than ad hoc assessment by the Court under Article 36 TFEU or the rule of reason. Higher standards may even prove more attractive to consumers.

As noted, some directives contain no market access clause. In such a case, domestic measures over and above those required by the directive which restrict inter-state trade will be permissible provided they are justified under the rule of reason or Article 36 TFEU. Where the directive provides procedures for derogation, or, in the case of measures enacted under Article 114 TFEU, under Article 114(4) TFEU, those procedures must be followed (see 16.4.4).

16.3.5 **Technical harmonisation and the 'new approach'**

Originally, Member States had the power to lay down the performance objectives and design specifications, or 'technical standards', for goods manufactured and sold in their territory. Goods which did not comply with such technical standards could not be sold in that Member State. As seen in other chapters dealing with the four freedoms, some of these rules could be struck down as barriers to trade (see also mutual recognition), but others would be accepted as necessary by the CJ. Such a divergence in technical standards can lead to competitive distortions in much the same way as differences between national measures in other fields. That is why the Union has had a specific programme for the harmonisation of such technical standards, often referred to as 'technical harmonisation'.

In the field of technical harmonisation, the Union initially adopted a sector-by-sector approach to adopt very detailed technical specifications. In 1985, when it had become apparent that the slow progress would make it very difficult to complete the internal market, the Council adopted a resolution on the 'New Approach to Technical Harmonisation' ([1985] OJ C136). This approach meant that institutions would lay down so-called 'essential safety requirements' for a particular sector, but leave it to the European standardisation bodies to work out the detailed technical rules by which compliance with the requirements can be demonstrated. Compliance with a European standard is voluntary and producers can choose to meet the safety requirements another way. Compliance with the standard has the advantage that it creates a presumption that products comply with the essential safety requirements and should therefore be allowed to be marketed in all Member States. Compliance with European standards is indicated by the CE marking on the product. Producers can opt to comply with other standards (such as those created the International Standards Organisation (ISO)) or not to comply with a technical standard at all, but they must nevertheless satisfy the procedures for assessing conformity which will be set out in the relevant directive which specifies the essential safety requirements for a particular sector.

In addition to sector-specific measures, the institutions also adopted the Directive on General Product Safety (Directive 2001/95 ([2002] OJ L11/4)) which imposes a general requirement that all goods put on the internal market must be safe. Compliance with this general safety requirement can be demonstrated in the same manner as with sector-specific measures by complying with relevant European or national standards.

Directive 98/34 ([1998] OJ L204/37) (now codified as Directive 2015/1535 ([2015]OJ L241/1)) (which replaced Directive 83/189) (as amended) lays down a procedure for the provision of information in the field of technical standards and regulations which applies when a Member States adopts a new technical regulation. Such a measure must be notified to the Commission before it is adopted to ensure that its impact on the free movement of goods is minimised and that both the Commission and the other Member States are aware of the measure and given an opportunity to propose amendments to it. Given the fact that non-notified national measures may not be relied on (see the discussion in Chapter 5), the scope of the Directive—particularly the meaning of 'technical standards'—has gained in significance (see, eg, *Intercommunale Intermosane SCRL and Fédération de l'industrie et du gaz v Belgian State* (case C-361/10)—minimum requirements relating to certain electrical work to ensure the safety of those installations to protect the workers using them, rather than specifications relating to the product itself).

The advantage of the 'new approach' is seen to be threefold. First, there is the flexibility the new approach allows for manufacturers in that they identify the hazards to be dealt with, but do not predict the technological solutions for doing so. Secondly, this in theory leaves room for innovation, especially as standards can be updated more quickly than legislative responses. Finally, this provides advantages for the legislator, as new approach frameworks are easier to maintain. Of course, no system is perfect and the 'new approach' sometimes does not leave manufacturers much freedom of choice as to how they meet essential requirements. Given its significance, the standard agreeing process can be long and unwieldy, and commentators have noted that the membership of relevant committees is not representative. Nor is a technology-driven approach necessarily politically neutral; it limits regulatory choices, which has consequences for the social and cultural sphere.

At the same time as the Commission has sought to reinforce the 'new' approach to technical harmonisation, it also recognises, as part of the drive to 'better regulation', that measures in addition to binding legal measures may be used, such as guidelines, interpretative communications and other 'soft-law' measures, as well as using co-regulation and self-regulation (see, eg, COM(2007) 724 and 725 final). While these measures may be flexible, they do give rise to questions about the legitimacy and democratic credentials of the resulting standards (see further 16.4.3 on the development of EU agencies and Chapter 3).

16.3.6 **Other types of harmonisation**

Some harmonisation measures are limited to the cross-border context. If goods are sold across borders, the goods must comply with the harmonised standards used. For those who operate exclusively within the territory of one Member State, there is no need to comply with the Union standard. Sometimes, producers who do not operate across borders may be given the option of whether to comply with the Union or domestic standards. This may be of benefit to a producer who may intend to trade across borders in the future. Slot (see the further reading section at the end of this chapter) describes these two related forms as 'optional' and 'partial' harmonisation, respectively. Optional harmonisation allows a producer to select whether to follow the harmonised or the national rules. Partial harmonisation requires a producer to adopt the Union standard if he wishes to engage in cross-border trade. These forms of harmonisation may be less intrusive than other types but seem to be less frequently used.

16.3.7 **The 'country of origin' principle and mutual recognition**

First espoused by the Court of Justice in *Rewe-Zentral AG v Bundesmonopolverwaltung für Branntwein (Cassis de Dijon)* (case 120/78) in the context of 'negative harmonisation', the 'mutual recognition' principle has become a stalwart of EU law. In essence, the principle requires any Member State to admit onto its territory goods or services which are marketed lawfully in the originating Member State. It will thus rarely be possible to prevent the free circulation of goods within the internal market once these are sold lawfully in one Member State, although derogation remains possible (see further Chapter 19). To facilitate the operation of the principle of mutual recognition in practice, a regulation (Regulation 764/2008 ([2008] OJ L218/21)) on the application of certain national technical rules to products lawfully marketed in another Member State has been adopted. It sets down procedures that must be followed by a national authority which: seeks to prohibit the placing on the market of a product or type of product; requires the modification or additional testing of that product or type of product; or results in the withdrawal of that product or type of product from the market. The aim of the Regulation is to minimise the possibility of such technical rules creating unlawful obstacles to the free movement of goods between Member States (recital 4). The Regulation also requires the establishment of 'Product Contact Points' (Article 9(2)), the purpose of which is to provide the necessary information to enterprises so as to facilitate their ability to bring their products on to the market.

A variation of the 'country of origin' principle is occasionally used in legislation which also harmonises some parts of the relevant laws of the Member States (see, eg, Article 3 of the Audiovisual Media

Services Directive (Directive 2010/13 ([2010] OJ L95/1) (AVMSD))); also Article 3(1) of the Electronic Commerce Directive (Directive 2000/31 ([2000] OJ L178/1)). Under this principle, an operator in the internal market is only subject to regulation in his home Member State, and another Member State may not restrict that operator's activities in the host territory. Crucially, no derogations seem permissible, except where expressly provided for (see Article 3(2) AVMSD). For a trader seeking to sell goods or services in another Member State, this approach can be attractive, because it is only necessary to comply with the specific requirements imposed in the home country. However, it also gives rise to concerns about a 'race to the bottom', particularly where there is a significant variation in the level of regulation between the Member States (see further discussion in Chapter 22). Such concerns could be met by combining this principle with a maximum harmonisation measure, as all Member States' standards would then be the same. Even then the principle may be rejected (see, eg, the Directive on Unfair Commercial Practices (Directive 2005/29 ([2005] OJ L149/22)), the first proposal of which included a country of origin clause which was removed during the legislative process; see also the debate about a directive on services (see Chapter 22), especially where there are concerns about the level of protection conferred by the directive in question).

It is clear, however, that the country of origin principle has a role to play in the harmonisation landscape in that it can complement measures harmonising some aspects of domestic law. It may also be a bargaining tool in the legislative process to secure agreement on a harmonising measure, although, as more recent examples show, it can also have the opposite effect.

16.4 Article 114 TFEU and harmonisation

Much of the EU's harmonising legislation centres on the internal market, and it is therefore appropriate to consider the key provision in this regard, Article 114 TFEU, in some detail.

Before the adoption of the SEA, harmonisation measures were often adopted on the basis of Article 115 TFEU. This provision enables the adoption of harmonising directives which directly affect the establishment or functioning of the common market. It requires unanimity within the Council, and requires only that the Parliament be consulted. The unanimity requirement was blamed for the slow progress in completing the common market.

The SEA introduced what has become the most significant provision for the EU's harmonisation programme: Article 114 TFEU. Article 114(1) TFEU states that:

> Save where otherwise provided in the Treaties, the following provisions shall apply for the achievement of the objectives set out in Article 26. The European Parliament and the Council shall, acting in accordance with the ordinary legislative procedure and after consulting the Economic and Social Committee, adopt the measures for the approximation of the provisions laid down by law, regulation or administrative action in Member States which have as their object the establishment and functioning of the internal market.

In contrast to Article 115 TFEU, there is no requirement for unanimity. Moreover, since Maastricht, Parliament has been actively involved in the legislative process through the use of the ordinary legislative procedure. While most harmonising measures have been in the form of a directive, the text of the Treaty does not require the use of a directive. A regulation could also be used.

Article 114 TFEU can form the basis for two types of measures: those which have the object of *establishing* the internal market, and those which relate to the *functioning* of the internal market. The objective of Article 114 TFEU is to reduce or remove altogether competitive disadvantages caused by the higher cost of having to comply with rules which are stricter in some Member States than in others. In addition, it may extend to cover harmonising measures which affect goods irrespective of their ultimate destination, including goods manufactured exclusively for export, if there is a risk that their re-import could undermine the harmonising measure (see *British American Tobacco* at para 82, and see para 166 of Advocate-General Geelhoed's Opinion in the same case).

It must be noted that not all measures which may be significant for the internal market will be based on this provision. For example, the directives in the company-law field are generally adopted on the basis of Article 50 TFEU, especially Article 50(2)(g), although they are clearly of relevance to the internal market (eg, Directive 2005/56 on cross-border mergers of limited-liability companies ([2005] OJ L310/1)). However, such measures pursue a different objective and are not necessarily concerned with the establishment or functioning of the internal market as such, although sometimes the dividing line can be a fine one (cf Directive 68/151, adopted before Article 114 TFEU was introduced, and concerned, inter alia, with the protection of third parties dealing with companies, which seeks to introduce equivalent safeguards throughout the EU).

16.4.1 The extent of the Union's power to legislate under Article 114 TFEU

Article 114 TFEU has formed the basis of numerous directives. The Union has used its powers under this provision extensively. It seemed that the scope of legislation on the basis of this article was very broad; some commentators have suggested that it had been interpreted as a general power to regulate (see, eg, Wyatt). The extent of the Union's powers under this article was clarified in *Germany v Parliament and Council* (*Tobacco Advertising I*) (case C-376/98), but it is questionable the extent to which this case provided a new line of authority which limits Union competence, or was an anomaly in the otherwise broad interpretation of Article 114 TFEU.

> ### Tobacco Advertising I
>
> Here the case concerned the Tobacco Advertising Directive (Directive 98/43 ([2003] OJ L152/16)) which prohibited the advertising and sponsorship of tobacco products. In a challenge to the legality of the measures which were essentially based on health concerns, the CJ annulled the Directive. The Court emphasised that Article 114 TFEU could form the basis only for measures which are intended to improve the conditions for the establishment and functioning of the internal market, but that it did not give a general power to the Union legislature to regulate the internal market (para 83). Such a general power would conflict with Article 5(2) TEU, which provides that the Union must act within its powers (see further Chapter 3).

The Court went on to say that:

> a measure adopted on the basis of Article [114] of the Treaty must genuinely have as its object the improvement of the conditions for the establishment and functioning of the internal market [para 84].
>
> It is true . . . that recourse to Article [114 TFEU] as a legal basis is possible if the aim is to prevent the emergence of future obstacles to trade resulting from multifarious development of national laws. However, the emergence of such obstacles must be likely and the measure in question must be designed to prevent them [para 86].

It has therefore often been the case that Article 114 TFEU was used not only to harmonise existing divergences to facilitate the functioning of the internal market, but also to prevent the emergence of *future* obstacles to trade which could be caused by the diffuse development of the national legal systems. (See *R v Secretary of State for Health, ex parte Swedish Match* (case C-210/03), para 31.) However, a 'mere finding of disparities between national rules and of the abstract risk of obstacles to the exercise of fundamental freedoms or of distortions of competition' (para 84) would be insufficient to justify Union action. If a particular measure is aimed at eliminating distortions of competition, the Court has to be satisfied that this distortion is 'appreciable', because the powers of the Union legislature would otherwise be 'practically unlimited' (para 107, and see also the *titanium dioxide* case and *R v Secretary of State for Health, ex parte Alliance for Natural Health* (cases C-154 and 155/04)). The holding in *Tobacco Advertising* confirms the views of Advocate-General Fennelly, who observed that:

> the pursuit of equal conditions of competition does not give carte blanche to the [Union] legislator to harmonise any national rules that meet the eye . . . it would risk transferring general Member State regulatory competence to the [Union] if recourse to Article [114 TFEU] . . . were not subject to some test of the reality of the link between such measures and internal market objectives [Opinion, case C-376/98, para 89].

A measure could not be justified on the basis of Article 114 TFEU if its effect on the harmonisation of competitive conditions was 'merely incidental' (para 91). In *Tobacco Advertising I*, Directive 98/43 ([2003] OJ L152/16) prohibited outright advertising of, and sponsorship by, tobacco products. The CJ held that Article 114 TFEU was an inappropriate legal basis for the Directive because it not only failed to improve competition but sought to eliminate it altogether.

There is therefore a burden on the Union legislator to identify obstacles to the functioning of the internal market before adopting harmonising legislation on the basis of Article 114 TFEU. It is necessary to establish first of all that disparate national laws actually constitute a barrier to free movement or distort competition, and then that Union action contributes to the establishment and functioning of the internal market and goes no further. It seemed that this could have required a detailed analysis of the competitive conditions prevailing in a particular sector to establish whether an identified obstacle to free movement or competition is appreciable such as to justify Union action. It is debatable, however, whether the Court has consistently carried out such an assessment in subsequent case law: in some cases—and contrary to its reasoning in *Tobacco Advertising I*—it assumes that the existence of different regulatory approaches justify Union action (see, eg, *Alliance for Natural Health*). In the second *Tobacco Advertising Directive* case (*Germany v Parliament and Council* (case C-380/03)), the CJ argued that:

> where there are obstacles to trade, or it is likely that such obstacles will emerge in the future, because the member States have taken, or are about to take, divergent measures with respect to a product or a class of products, which bring about different levels of protection and thereby prevent the product or products concerned moving freely within the [Union], Article [114 TFEU] authorises the [Union] legislature to intervene by adopting appropriate measures . . . [para 41].

16.4.2 Article 114 TFEU and 'flanking policies'

A further question is to what extent Article 114 TFEU can be used as a legal basis to harmonise areas in which the Union does not have a direct competence to harmonise, or where there is more than one potential legal basis for a particular measure. In *Tobacco Advertising I*, it was argued that the Directive sought to harmonise public health legislation. Under Article

168 TFEU, the Union is expressly precluded from harmonising legislation in this area. The CJ emphasised that other Treaty articles may not be used to circumvent an express exclusion of harmonisation such as the one laid down in Article 168(4), but this did not rule out the possibility that harmonising measures adopted on the basis of other Treaty provisions could have an impact on the protection of human health (para 78). In *British American Tobacco*, Advocate-General Geelhoed emphasised that it must be possible to adopt harmonising measures under Article 114 TFEU to the extent that national measures within the field of public health create barriers to trade, but it is also clear that there is no independent power to harmonise public health legislation (see paras 112–14). The CJ confirmed that as long as a directive 'genuinely has as its object the improvement of the conditions for the functioning of the internal market', it would be possible to adopt it on the basis of Article 114 TFEU 'and it is no bar that the protection of public health was a decisive factor in the choices involved in the harmonising measures' (para 76).

On this basis, the Union has a degree of competence to harmonise all areas in which divergent national laws may adversely affect the operation of the internal market, but cannot adopt measures that have the effect of harmonising excluded areas beyond what is necessary to eliminate distortions of competition. This seems to be a very fine distinction to make and should require the Union legislator to be even more careful in adopting legislation on the basis of Article 114 TFEU.

An additional problem with 'flanking policies' may arise where a measure could be adopted on the basis of two or more Treaty provisions. For example, in *British American Tobacco*, the Directive in question had been adopted on the basis of both Article 114 and Article 207 TFEU. It was argued that this combined legal basis was inappropriate. The CJ observed that if a measure simultaneously pursues a number of objectives without one or more being secondary to a main objective, multiple legal bases may be acceptable. However, the Court regarded this as 'exceptional' and the general position is:

> If examination of a [Union] act shows that it has a twofold purpose ... and if one of these is identifiable as main or predominant, whereas the other is merely incidental, the act must be founded on a sole legal basis, that is, the one required by the main or predominant purpose [para 94].

In this case, all the relevant provisions could have been adopted on the basis of Article 114 TFEU, and the additional use of Article 207 TFEU was not permissible. This in itself did not mean that the Directive was invalid, however, because it only formed a 'purely formal defect' (see also *Swedish Match*, para 44).

However, if the use of multiple legal bases gives rise to an irregularity in the procedure used for the adoption of the directive concerned, the position would be different (see also *titanium dioxide*, paras 17–21). In *British American Tobacco*, the relevant legal bases were Articles 114 and 207 TFEU. In contrast to Article 114, which requires use of the ordinary legislative procedure, Article 207 TFEU at that stage simply required a decision by qualified majority in the Council, without any involvement by Parliament. The CJ did not regard this as a procedural irregularity, because both articles required a decision by qualified majority and the relevant procedure had, in fact, been followed. That case differed from *titanium dioxide*, where one of the conflicting legal bases required a unanimous decision. Although this view appears attractive, the CJ sidestepped the argument that use of the co-decision procedure under Article 207 TFEU was contrary to the separation of powers in the Treaty by holding that Article 207 was not required for the adoption of the directive.

16.4.3 Article 114 TFEU as the basis for establishing EU agencies

There has been a trend for Article 114 TFEU to be used as the Treaty legal basis for the establishment of a significant number of EU agencies. This can be seen in *United Kingdom v Parliament (ENISA)* (case C-217/04).

ENISA

Here, the case concerned the establishment of the European Network and Information Security Agency (ENISA), under Regulation 460/2004 [2004] OJ L77/1. The main aim of ENISA is to contribute to securing the EU's information society. In doing so, the agency helps the Commission and the Member States to meet the requirements of network and information security and to ensure the smooth functioning of the internal market in that field.

The UK government argued that only Article 352 TFEU (as it now is) can be the appropriate legal basis for the creation of the agency. The Court, however, ruled that Article 114 TFEU was the correct legal foundation.

Pursuant to the reasoning of the Court, the main objective of that agency was the completion of the internal market as an area without any internal frontiers in the field of information technology. The use of Article 114 TFEU was found to be acceptable not just because of the need for the advice, but also that the establishment of ENISA 'was an appropriate means for preventing the emergence of disparities likely to create obstacles to the smooth functioning of the internal market in the area', thus tying the reasoning back to the purpose of Article 114 TFEU and the case law on the use of that provision as the basis for harmonising legislation (see 16.4.1). The Court recognised that while Article 114 TFEU could only be used where the apparent objective of the measure was the establishment and functioning of the internal market, equally the legislature had a discretion as to the most appropriate means of harmonisation or approximation, especially in technical areas (para 43). This included:

> the establishment of a [Union] body responsible for contributing to the implementation of a process of harmonisation in situations where, in order to facilitate the uniform implementation and application of acts based on that provision, the adoption of non-binding supporting and framework measures seems appropriate.

The matter has arisen again more recently with the establishment of the three European Supervisory Authorities: the European Banking Authority (EBA); the European Insurance and Occupational Pensions Authority (EIOPA); and the European Securities and Markets Authority (ESMA). They were set up by the Union as a response to the continuing, unprecedented financial crisis. More specifically, the legal action concerned the annulment of Article 28 of Regulation 236/2012 ([2012] OJ L274/1) in *United Kingdom v Parliament and Council (ESMA)* (case C-270/12). The case concerned short selling and credit default swaps in relation to ESMA's power to ban 'short selling'.

ESMA

Short selling is a practice that allows for the sale of assets, usually securities, that are not owned by the seller at the moment of sale but have been 'borrowed' for the purpose of the sale, with the intention of profiting from a decline in the price of the assets before having to buy the assets back so that they

> can be 'returned' to their original owner. Article 28 of Regulation 236/2012 gives ESMA the power to intervene in the financial markets of the Member States in the event of a 'threat to the orderly functioning and integrity of financial markets or to the stability of the whole or part of the financial system in the Union'. Significantly, ESMA may take legally binding measures as against third parties; it is a regulatory agency. The UK challenged the validity of the Regulation, specifically its legal base of Article 114 TFEU.

In the view of the Advocate-General, there was no difficulty following the reasoning in the *ENISA* case in using Article 114 TFEU to establish ESMA. The responses of the Member States to the financial crisis in relation to short selling differed and there is a risk that, absent Union action, Member States would be likely to continue to take such different measures. The Advocate-General did not think that Article 114 TFEU could, however, be used as the basis of some of the powers which were granted to ESMA. In the view of the Advocate-General, ESMA's powers went beyond internal market powers: the effect of ESMA's powers is:

> to lift implementation powers … from the national level to the EU level when there is disagreement between ESMA and the competent national authority or between national authorities … Hence, the outcome of the activation of ESMA's powers under Article 28 … is not harmonisation, or the adoption of uniform practice at the level of the Member States, but the replacement of national decision making … with EU level decision making [Opinion, paras 50–2].

The Advocate-General seems to be reflecting the concerns found in the *Tobacco Advertising* case, discussed in 16.4.1. Nonetheless, the CJ rejected the argument that Article 114 TFEU should not have been used. It emphasised that ESMA's activities would involve reacting to market behaviour with cross-border implications (which national authorities alone could not resolve) and which would threaten the integrity of financial markets or the stability of the financial system (para 115).

16.4.4 Derogation under Article 114 TFEU

Where derogation may legitimately be sought from harmonisation measures enacted under Article 114(1), this will now be governed by Article 114(4)–(5) TFEU. Article 114(4), first introduced by the SEA in 1986, provides that where harmonising legislation has been passed by qualified majority, Member States who deem it necessary to *maintain* national provisions on grounds of major needs referred to in Article 36 TFEU, or relating to the protection of the environment or the working environment must notify the Commission and state the grounds for maintaining these rules. Similarly, Article 114(5) requires notification to the Commission if a Member State deems it necessary, after the adoption of a harmonising measure, to *introduce* national measures based on new scientific evidence relating to the protection of the environment or the working environment on grounds of a problem specific to that Member State (note that Article 114(5) does not refer to Article 36 TFEU as a ground for introducing new measures). These conditions are cumulative. It is implicit in the system that the Member State accepts that the national rule in issue is incompatible with the relevant directive.

Whether the Member State relies on Article 114(4) or (5), the Commission may then approve or reject the national provisions after having verified that they do not constitute a means of 'arbitrary discrimination or disguised restriction on trade between Member States', nor an obstacle to the functioning of the internal market (Article 114(6)). In making this assessment, the CJ has held that the Commission has a wide discretion (*Commission v Netherlands (diesel emissions)* (case

C-405/07P)), though this does not mean it is not amenable to review. There is no obligation on the Commission to give the Member State who made the notification, nor any other Member State, the right to make representations (*Denmark v Commission* (*use of sulphites, nitrites and nitrates in food*) (case C-3/00)). In the light of this, and given the width of its discretion, the procedural guarantees, such as the duty to give reasons, are particularly important.

The Commission must decide within six months, although this period may be extended by a further six months if the matter is complex and there is no danger to human health. If the Commission fails to act within that time, the national measure is deemed to have been approved. The Commission or any other Member State may bring the matter before the CJ if it considers that a state is making improper use of these powers.

Although expressed to apply only where harmonisation measures have been enacted by qualified majority, it has been suggested that the same procedure should be available where legislation has been passed unanimously; the Article 114(4) or (5) procedure is not in terms limited to Member States that have not agreed to the measure in question, and some scope for derogation should be available to meet emergencies not foreseen at the time when the legislation was passed. Moreover, in an emergency, arguably, it should not be necessary for a state to obtain *prior* approval for its actions from the Commission, provided that the need for action is genuine and urgent and the Commission is notified at the earliest possible time.

16.5 Conclusions

It has been seen that harmonisation is a fundamental, and perhaps the most significant, aspect of EU law. It is not without problems, however. One of the central difficulties relates to the fact that there is no one type of harmonisation: different approaches leave Member States varying degrees of legislative freedom. Although total harmonisation is necessary in some areas, there has been a minimum-harmonisation approach in some areas (such as consumer protection) to create at least a 'lowest common denominator' in the Member States. National measures which set a standard that exceeds a minimum-harmonisation measure are always potentially liable to challenge under provisions guaranteeing free movement. A second problem concerns the scope of the EU's power to enact harmonising measures, especially in relation to Article 114 TFEU. Despite the fact that harmonisation might seem to solve a number of problems with the operation of the internal market, the EU does not have a general power to regulate trade. The questions of the precise scope of Member States' power to legislate and the impact of the four freedoms on that competence will continue to be relevant.

Further reading

Andenas, M and Andersen, CB (eds), *Theory and Practice of Harmonisation* (Edward Elgar, 2012).

Braun, A, 'Trusts in the draft Common Frame of Reference: the "best solution" for Europe?' (2011) 70 CLJ 327.

Davies, G, 'Can selling arrangements be harmonised?' (2005) 30 EL Rev 370.

de Sadeleer, N, 'Procedures for derogations from the principle of approximation of laws under Article 95 EC' (2003) 40 CMLR 889.

Dougan, M, 'Minimum harmonisation and the internal market' (2000) 37 CMLR 853.

Fahey, E, 'Does the emperor have financial crisis clothes? Reflections on the legal basis of the European banking authority' (2011) 74 MLR 581.

Peers, S and Costa, M, 'Reassessing the accountability of EU decentralized agencies: Mind the Independence Gap' (2016) 22 EPL 645.

Picat, M and Soccio, S, 'Harmonisation of European contract law: Fiction or reality?' (2011) 4 IBLJ 371.

Poli, S, 'The legal basis of the internal market measures with a security dimension' (2010) 6 ECL Rev 13.

Ramsey, LE, 'The copy out technique: More of a "cop out" than a solution?' [1996] 17 SLR 3.

Schutze, R, 'Co-operative federalism constitutionalised: The emergence of complementary competences in the EC legal order' (2006) 31 EL Rev 167.

Slot, PJ, 'Harmonisation' (1996) 21 EL Rev 378.

Weber, F, 'European Integration assessed in the light of the "rules v standards" debate' (2013) 35 European Journal of Law and Economics 187.

Woods, L, *Free Movement of Goods and Services within the European Community* (Ashgate, 2004), Ch 13.

Customs union

17.1 Introduction

As we have seen in Chapters 3 and 15, the main mechanism for attaining the Union's goals is through the creation of the internal market. Central to the internal market is the free movement of goods, which aims to ensure that imported goods are not disadvantaged by extra costs of whatever nature. The most obvious way in which extra costs can be imposed on imports is by subjecting them to additional duties, such as customs duties, or by imposing a separate (and disadvantageous) taxation system on them. There are a number of relevant provisions in the Treaty to deal with this problem: Articles 28, 30 and 110 TFEU.

The articles in the TFEU go further than prohibiting such charges; they aim to create a customs union, which requires all Member States take a common approach to the import of goods from third countries. The TFEU, therefore, contains provisions for a common customs tariff (CCT) (Articles 31–2 TFEU). Allied to these provisions are Articles 3 and 206–7 TFEU, which provide for the establishment of a common commercial policy towards third countries.

This chapter briefly discusses the provisions establishing the CCT, before considering the prohibition on customs duties and on discriminatory taxation. In doing so, several key points should be noted. First, the prohibition on customs duties is one of the central features of the customs union. It has been interpreted broadly as a result, and any exceptions to the prohibition are strictly limited. The provisions on customs duties are linked to those on discriminatory taxation—the prohibition on discriminatory taxation serves to prevent Member States from circumventing the prohibition on customs duties by discriminating against imports via their internal taxation system. It is because of this link that the discriminatory taxation provisions are dealt with here, as part of the free movement of goods, despite the fact that within the Treaty they are located in a separate section dealing with taxation. Despite their common function, in some ways the taxation provisions are more problematic than those relating to customs duties. Taxation in general still remains part of the Member States' competence; further, in determining the scope of 'similar' products, the CJ has a certain degree of interpretive freedom. Although Article 110 TFEU does not require Member States to adopt any particular system of taxation, the rulings of the CJ under Article 110 TFEU have had an impact on Member States' policy choices. Article 110 TFEU jurisprudence is, to some degree, therefore contentious.

17.2 Common customs tariff

As part of its common commercial policy, and to ensure equal treatment in all Member States for goods imported into the EU from third countries, thereby enabling *all* goods in circulation within the Union to benefit equally from the free movement provisions, the Treaty provided for the introduction of the CCT, sometimes known as the common external tariff (CET). The CCT applies to all products imported into the Union from outside the EU, erecting a single tariff wall which no individual state is free to breach. Lisbon describes this area as falling within exclusive Union competence (Article 3(1)(e) TFEU).

The operation of the CCT is governed by Articles 31 and 32 TFEU and is enacted by directly applicable regulations. Under the CCT, goods are classified according to a common nomenclature, and are subject to common Union rules as to value and origin. Products are divided into lists, the classifications being derived from the Brussels Convention on Nomenclature for the Classification of Goods. The CCT is published by the Commission and is regularly updated. Once goods are imported into the Union—that is, when they have complied with import formalities and paid the relevant customs duties, the free movement provisions of the TFEU apply (Article 29 TFEU).

The Commission, subject to the Council's approval, has a central role in establishing and administering the CCT. In carrying out its task it is required to balance a number of (often conflicting) economic needs set out in Article 32 TFEU, in the light of the general aims of the Union. Although the Commission has an important role in the administration of the CCT, there is no such body as a Union customs service. The Union is dependent on the customs officers of the various Member States to implement the CCT. Duties raised under the CCT are payable to the Union and form part of its 'own resources'. Under Article 33 TFEU, the institutions may enact measures to strengthen the cooperation between Member States in this regard and between the Member States and the Commission.

17.3 Prohibition between Member States of customs duties on imports and exports and of all charges of equivalent effect

This area is governed by Articles 28 and 30 TFEU. Article 28 TFEU establishes the customs union and Article 30 TFEU is the mechanism whereby this is achieved, as it prohibits between Member States any customs duties.

Article 28 TFEU states:

> 1. The Union shall comprise a customs union which shall cover all trade in goods and which shall involve the prohibition between Member States of customs duties on imports and exports and of all charges having equivalent effect, and the adoption of a common customs tariff in the relations with third countries.
> 2. The provisions of Article 30 and of Chapter 2 of this Title shall apply to products originating in Member States and to products coming from third countries which are in free circulation in Member States.

Article 30 TFEU specifies:

> Customs duties on imports and exports and charges having equivalent effect shall be prohibited between Member States. This prohibition shall also apply to customs duties of a fiscal nature.

17.3.1 **Scope of the prohibition**

There are two types of prohibition in Article 30 TFEU:

- customs duties;
- charges equivalent to customs duties.

17.3.1.1 **Customs duties**

There is no definition of 'customs duties' in the TFEU, but they are generally understood as charges levied on goods—whether imports or exports—on the crossing of a border. Duties usually relate to the value of a product and often have a protectionist motive.

The prohibition applies to all duties, whether applied directly or indirectly. In *Van Gend en Loos* (discussed also in Chapter 4) the product in question had been reclassified under Dutch law, with the result that it became subject to a higher rate of duty. The CJ held that this would constitute a breach of what is now Article 30 TFEU.

The prohibition has also been held to apply to a charge on imports and exports into a *region* of a Member State, not only insofar as it is levied on goods entering that region from other Member States, but also when it is levied on goods entering that region from another part of the same state (*Simitzi v Kos* (cases C-485 and 486/93), *ad valorem* municipality tax imposed on imports into and exports from the Dodecanese (Greece)). This obligation was held to derive from the 'absolute nature' of the prohibition of all customs duties applicable to goods moving between Member States and emphasises the single nature of the European market. This approach also applies to additional charges levied on goods imported into a region which originated from a third country (*Société Cadi Surgélés v Ministre des Finances* (case C-126/94)), and to charges levied on goods *exported* from a region, irrespective of whether their final destination is within the same Member State, or abroad (*Carbonati Apuani Srol v Comune di Carrara* (case C-72/03)).

17.3.1.2 **Charges having equivalent effect**

If the meaning of 'custom duties' is clear, what are 'charges having equivalent effect' to a customs duty? It was held by the CJ in the case of *Sociaal Fonds voor de Diamantarbeiders* (cases 2 and 3/69), in the context of a challenge to a 'tax' imposed on imported diamonds, that it included any pecuniary charge, however slight, imposed on goods by reason of the fact that they cross frontiers. The charge need not be levied at the frontier; it can be imposed at any stage of production or marketing; but provided it is levied *by reason of importation* it will breach Article 30 TFEU (*Steinike und Weinlig*). This question of whether the charge is triggered by the crossing of a frontier is a key element to determine a charge falling within Article 30 TFEU.

17.3.2 **Distinction between customs duties and taxes**

A charge of equivalent effect to a customs duty may come in many guises, and is often disguised as a 'tax'. Since genuine taxes fall to be considered under Article 110 TFEU, it is necessary at the outset to distinguish between a charge falling within Article 30 TFEU and a genuine tax. A genuine tax was defined in *Commission v France (levy on reprographic machines)* (case 90/79) as one relating:

> to a general system of internal dues applied systematically to categories of products in accordance with objective criteria irrespective of the origin of the products.

To ascertain whether a 'tax' is genuine it must be examined to see whether it fits into an overall system of taxation or whether it has been superimposed on the system with a particular purpose in mind. Provided the tax is genuine, it may be imposed on imports even where the importing state produces no identical or similar product (*levy on reprographic machines*). In such a case it will not breach Article 30 TFEU but may be examined for its compatibility with Article 110 TFEU (see further 17.4).

17.3.3 **An effects-based test**

To breach Article 30 TFEU, a charge need not be introduced for protectionist reasons. It was pointed out in the *Sociaal Fonds* case that no diamond-mining industry existed in Belgium, and the proceeds of the charge were used for a most worthy purpose, to provide a social fund for workers in the diamond industry. These factors were held by the CJ to be irrelevant. Such duties are forbidden independently of the purpose for which they are levied and the destination of the charge. In reaching its decision the Court looked at the effect of the measure: any pecuniary charge imposed on goods by reason of the fact that they cross frontiers is an obstacle to the free movement of goods.

A similar conclusion was reached by the CJ in *Commission v Luxembourg (import on gingerbread)* (cases 2 and 3/62) in the context of a compensatory 'tax' on imported gingerbread.

> ### *Gingerbread* case
>
> The government claimed the 'tax' was introduced merely to compensate for the competitive disadvantage resulting from a high rate of domestic tax on rye, an ingredient of gingerbread. The purpose of the prohibition on measures of equivalent effect to customs duties, the Court held, was to prohibit not only measures ostensibly clothed with the classic nature of a customs duty but also those which, presented under other names or introduced by the indirect means of other procedures, would lead to the same discriminatory or protective *results* as customs duties. If compensatory 'taxes' of this type were allowed, states would be able to make up for all sorts of taxes at home by imposing a so-called balancing charge on imports. This would ensure that imported goods would lose any competitive advantage they might have as against the equivalent domestic product and thereby frustrate the objectives of the single market.

17.3.4 **Limitations on the prohibition**

Even when the charge is levied to benefit the importer, it may still breach Article 30 TFEU. In *Commission v Italy (statistical levy)* (case 24/68) a levy, applied to all imports and exports, regardless of source, the proceeds of which were used to finance an export statistical service for the benefit of importers and exporters, was found to be in breach of Articles 28–30 TFEU. The CJ held that the advantage to importers was so general and uncertain that it could not be considered a payment for service rendered (see also *W Cadsky SpA v Istituto Nazionale per il Commercio Estero* (case 63/74), in relation to charges on the *export* of goods).

This implies that a charge levied for a service rendered to the importer and which is *not* too general and uncertain would be permissible. This principle has, however, been given the narrowest possible interpretation. The CJ has held that where an inspection service is imposed in the general interest, for example for health or safety purposes or quality control, this cannot be regarded as a service rendered to the importer or exporter to justify the imposition of a charge

(*Rewe-Zentralfinanz eGmbH v Landwirtschaftskammer Westfalen-Lippe* (case 39/73)). This principle applies regardless of the nature of the agency, public or private, providing the service, and whether or not the charge is borne by virtue of a unilateral measure adopted by the authorities or as a result of a series of private contracts (*Édouard Dubois et Fils SA v Garonor Exploitation SA* (case C-16/94)). Even when such inspections are expressly *permitted* under EU law, as in *Commission v Belgium (health inspection service)* (case 314/82), the Court held that a charge for such a service cannot be regarded as a service rendered for the benefit of the importer. It is only when such services are mandatory, as part of a common Union regime, or arising from an international agreement into which the EU has entered (*Netherlands v P Bakker Hillegom BV* (case C-111/89)), that Member States are entitled to recover the cost, and no more than the cost, of the service (*Bauhuis v Netherlands* (case 46/76)).

Unless a service is required under Union law, it appears that only a service which gives a tangible benefit to the importer, or the imported goods, for example a finishing or packaging service, will be regarded as sufficient to justify a charge, and even then it will not be permissible if the 'service' is one imposed on the importer in the general interest. Where a genuine service is provided for the benefit of the importer the CJ has held that the charge must not exceed the value or the cost of the service (*Rewe-Zentralfinanz eGmbH*), or a sum proportionate to the service provided (*Commission v Denmark* (case 158/82)). A charge based on the value of the goods is not permissible (*Ford España SA v Spain* (case 170/88)). In *Donner v Netherlands* (case 39/82) the Court suggested that a charge by the Dutch Post Office for dealing with the payment of VAT on imported books on behalf of the claimant might be regarded as a payment for services rendered but left the national court to decide whether on the facts it was and, if so, whether it was proportionate.

Where a charge is imposed only upon domestically produced goods, the CJ appears to take a more lenient view as can be seen in *Apple and Pear Development Council v KJ Lewis Ltd* (case 222/82).

Apple and Pear Development

A number of growers challenged a compulsory levy imposed on growers of apples and pears in the UK. The proceeds of the levy went to finance the Apple and Pear Development Council, a semi-public body whose functions included research, the compilation of statistics, provision of information, publicity and promotion.

The CJ held that since the levy did not apply to imported products there was no breach of Articles 28–30 TFEU. The charge would only be illegal if it served to finance activities which were incompatible with EU law.

17.3.5 **Non-discriminatory charges**

All the cases considered so far have concerned unilateral charges, charges imposed only upon imported or exported products and not on the comparable domestic product (or vice versa). Clearly such charges undermine the principle of free trade and free competition within the common market and discriminate against imported products. What about a non-discriminatory charge, applied to a particular product regardless of source? Will this be capable of infringing Article 30 TFEU? This calls for a more subtle enquiry into:

- the nature of the charge and its mode of calculation;
- the destination of the charge, ie who receives the benefit.

Three situations may be considered:

(1) If the charge is identical in every respect and levied as part of a general system of taxation it will not fall within Article 30 TFEU and will be treated as a fiscal measure, and examined for its compatibility with Article 110 TFEU (prohibition on discriminatory taxation);

(2) If the same charge is levied on a particular product, regardless of source, it will nonetheless breach Article 30 TFEU if the charge on the imported or exported product is not imposed in the same way and determined according to the same criteria as apply to the domestic product. This point was made by the CJ in *Marimex SpA v Italian Minister of Finance (No 2)* (case 29/72) in the context of a challenge to a 'veterinary inspection tax' imposed on imported meat, live and dead, to ensure that it conformed to Italian health standards. Similar domestic products were subject to corresponding inspections which were also 'taxed', but they were conducted by different bodies according to different criteria. The CJ held that such a tax on imports would be in breach of the then Article 9 EEC (now 28 TFEU); even if the charge is levied at the same rate and according to identical criteria it may still breach Articles 28 and 30 TFEU if the proceeds of the charge are applied to benefit the domestic product *exclusively*.

This point was first made in *Capolongo v Azienda Agricola Maya* (case 77/72).

Capolongo

In this case, the Italians had introduced a charge on imported egg boxes, as part of an overall charge on cellulose products, the aim being to finance the production of paper and cardboard in Italy. Although the charge was imposed on all egg boxes, domestic and imported, the Court held it was in breach of the then Article 13 EEC (deleted by the ToA). Although applied to domestic and imported goods alike, it was discriminatory if it was intended exclusively to support activities which specifically benefited the domestic product.

The scope of *Capolongo* was restricted in the subsequent case of *Fratelli Cucchi v Avez SpA* (case 77/76).

Fratelli Cucchi

Here a dispute arose concerning the legality of a levy on imported sugar. Domestically produced sugar was subject to the same levy. The proceeds of the levy went to finance the sugar industry, to benefit two groups: the beet producers and the sugar-processing industry.

The CJ held that such a charge would be of equivalent effect to a customs duty if three conditions were fulfilled:

- if it has the *sole* purpose of financing activities for the specific advantage of the domestic product;
- if the taxed domestic product and the domestic product to benefit are the same;
- if the charges imposed on the domestic product are made up *in full*.

If these conditions are not fulfilled the charge will not breach Article 30 TFEU. However, where the same tax, levied on domestic and imported products alike, gives only *partial* benefit to the domestic product, it may be deemed a discriminatory tax, in breach of Article 110 TFEU (*Commission v Italy (reimbursement of sugar storage costs)* (case 73/79); *Cooperative Co-Frutta SRL v Amminstrazzione delle Finanze dello Stato* (case 193/85)). A grant to a particular industry may be adjudged a state aid in breach of Article 107 TFEU.

17.3.6 **Derogation from prohibition on customs duties**

The rules concerning charges of equivalent effect to a customs duty are strictly applied by the CJ. Indeed, in its anxiety to ensure that no pecuniary restriction, however small, shall create obstacles to trade, particularly to imports, the Court is even prepared to countenance a degree of reverse discrimination, since Member States are required themselves to finance measures such as health inspections which may be fully justified in the public interest (see *Rewe-Zentralfinanz eGmbH*). Nor does the Treaty or the Court provide for any derogation in this field. In the *export tax on art treasures* case the Italians argued that the tax was justified to protect their artistic heritage. Under Article 36 TFEU states are entitled to derogate from the prohibition on imposing quantitative restrictions on imports (Article 34 TFEU) or exports (Article 35 TFEU), or measures of equivalent effect, on the grounds of, inter alia, 'the protection of national treasures possessing artistic, historic or archaeological value'. The Court held that the then Article 36 EEC (now 36 TFEU) could never be invoked to justify a charge (see also *Marimex SpA*).

The only way for a Member State to defend a charge is to argue that:

- it does not fall within the definition of customs duty by virtue of it being part of an internal system of taxation, in which case it will be assessed by reference to Article 110 TFEU;
- it is required by Union law in accordance with the principles in *Bauhuis* (see 17.3.4);
- it is actually a payment for service rendered (see the *statistical levy* case and 17.3.4).

17.3.7 **Enforcing Article 30 TFEU**

Since Article 30 TFEU is directly effective, any sums paid under an illegal charge are recoverable. This might, in certain circumstances, require the relevant domestic bodies to reconsider a previous decision once it has become clear that charges should not have been made (*Kühne & Heitz*). Although repayment must be sought within the framework, and according to the rules, of national law, conditions must not be so framed as to render it excessively difficult or impossible in practice to exercise the rights conferred by Union law (*Amministrazione delle Finanze dello Stato v San Giorgio* (case 199/82), see further Chapter 8). The principle of unjust enrichment may be invoked to deny a claim for repayment where the charge has been incorporated into the price of goods and passed on to purchasers (*SpA San Giorgio; Weber's Wine World v Abgaberufungskommision Wien* (case C-147/01)). However, national authorities may not impose the burden of proving that a charge has *not* been passed on to those persons seeking reimbursement, nor may restrictive or onerous evidential requirements (such as documentary evidence alone) be imposed. Member States are not entitled to presume that illegal taxes have been passed on (*Commission v Italy (repayment of illegal taxes)* (case 104/86)). In *Just v Danish Ministry for Fiscal Affairs* (case 68/79), in a claim based on Article 110 TFEU, the Court held that national courts may take into account damage suffered by the person liable to pay the charge by reason of the restrictive effect of the charge on imports from other Member States.

This principle should also apply to damage suffered as a result of a charge in breach of Article 30 TFEU.

17.3.8 Approaching Article 30 TFEU

A structure for assessing whether or not a national measure infringes Article 30 TFEU is set out in Figure 17.1.

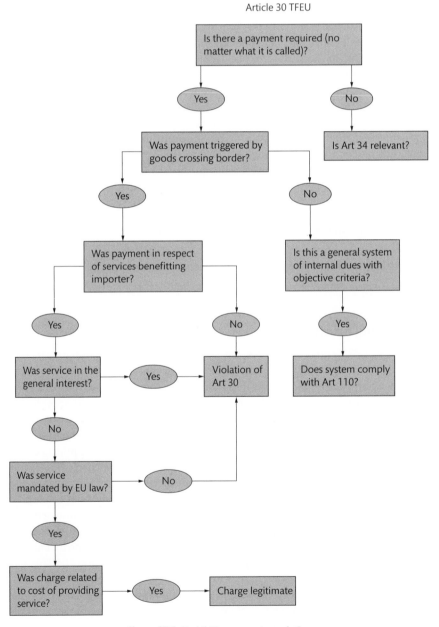

Figure 17.1 Prohibition on customs duties

17.4 Prohibition of discriminatory taxation

17.4.1 Meaning of taxation

As noted in 17.3.2, the Court draws a distinction between a charge having equivalent effect to a customs duty and a genuine tax. A genuine tax is a measure relating to a system of internal dues applied systematically to categories of products in accordance with objective criteria irrespective of the origin of the products in the *levy on reprographic machines* case. Even what may appear a genuine tax may be treated as a charge if it is earmarked to benefit only the domestic product subject to the tax (see *Fratelli Cucchi*, 17.3.5). The fact that it is levied by a body other than the state, or is collected for its own benefit and is a charge which is special or appropriate for a specific purpose, cannot prevent it from falling within the field of application of Article 110 TFEU (*Ianelli & Volpi SpA v Ditta Paola Meroni* (case 74/76)).

The line between a charge and a genuine tax may be hard to draw and may turn on slight differences in the facts. The Court held (*Fratelli Cucchi*, see 17.3.5) that the prohibition of customs duties and charges having equivalent effect and of discriminatory internal taxation are mutually exclusive. Therefore it is safer in case of doubt to invoke both Article 30 and Article 110 TFEU and leave the Court to define the boundaries.

Note also that Article 110 TFEU and Article 34 TFEU cover different ground and are mutually exclusive. If a measure falls under Article 110, it cannot be dealt with under Article 34 TFEU.

17.4.2 Scope of Article 110 TFEU

A 'genuine' tax must comply with Article 110 TFEU. It provides that:

> No Member State shall impose, directly or indirectly, on the products of other Member States any internal taxation of any kind in excess of that imposed directly or indirectly on similar domestic products.
>
> Furthermore, no Member State shall impose on the products of other Member States any internal taxation of such a nature as to afford indirect protection to other products.

While states are free to decide on the rate of taxation to be applied to a particular product and discriminate between different types of product (eg, *Outokumpu Oy* (case C-213/96), different sources of fuel), subject to certain overriding provisions of EU law (see further 17.4.6), they are not free to apply rates which discriminate, directly or indirectly, as between domestic and imported products which are similar or which afford indirect protection to the former. To do so would give a competitive advantage to the less highly taxed product and thereby distort competition within the single market. As the Court has held in a number of cases, a Member State's internal taxation system will be compatible with the requirements of Article 110 TFEU only if it is shown to be structured so as to exclude any possibility of having a discriminatory effect (see, eg, *Haahr Petroleum Ltd v Åbenrå Havn* (case C-90/94), concerning a duty on goods going through a port, irrespective of point of origin, where duty is calculated by reference to when the goods were loaded/weight/type of goods, which are objective criteria, see para 34).

There are a number of aspects to Article 110 TFEU. First, the issue of discriminatory taxation is clearly central to any discussion (see 17.4.3). Secondly, the meaning of 'products from other Member States' must be understood (see 17.4.4). Finally, note also that Article 110 TFEU contains two prohibitions:

- Article 110(1) TFEU which deals with 'similar' products;
- Article 110(2) TFEU which concerns goods which, although not exactly similar, are still in competition with each other.

The difference between the two provisions may be slight and therefore difficult to identify with precision. Indeed, in early case law the CJ did not always distinguish between the two subsections of Article 110, holding that the provision could be applied as a whole (see, eg, *Commission v France (spirits)* (case 168/78), para 13). The problem of adopting a 'global' approach to Article 110 TFEU is that it blurs the distinction between paragraphs (1) and (2) in terms of the consequences of a finding of a violation for Member States. A Member State is obliged to *equalise* the taxes on domestic and imported products when the Court has found a violation of Article 110(1) TFEU. In contrast, when there has been a violation of Article 110(2) TFEU, the Member State is required to remove the protective effect of the offending national rules. Such a requirement does not necessarily entail equalisation of the tax burdens on the goods in question; that is, the tax on imported products need not be identical to that on domestic products. It seems that in later cases the CJ has made greater efforts to distinguish between Article 110(1) and (2). For example, in *John Walker & Sons Ltd v Ministeriet for Skatter of Afgifter* (case 243/84), concerning whether liqueur fruit wine was comparable to whisky, the CJ found that the two products were not 'similar' for the purposes of Article 110(1), therefore the national rules would be assessed by reference to Article 110(2). The notion of similarity is discussed further at 17.4.5.

17.4.3 Discriminatory measures

17.4.3.1 Direct discrimination

Direct discrimination is discrimination based on 'nationality' or place of origin of the goods. Direct discrimination is rare but an early example can be seen in *Lütticke* (case 57/65).

> ### Lütticke
>
> Lütticke imported whole-milk powder from Luxembourg. The German authorities levied a duty and turnover tax on the import. Neither domestic natural milk nor domestic milk power were subject to such a tax and Lütticke challenged the legality of the tax. The CJ held that the tax was discriminatory contrary to the Treaty.

It is not necessary that all imported products are adversely affected; it is sufficient if just some imports are.

17.4.3.2 Indirect discrimination

A measure will be indirectly discriminatory if, although applicable to all goods, regardless of origin, it falls more heavily on the imported product. For example, in *Humblot v Directeur des Services Fiscaux* (case 112/84) a French car tax, calculated according to the power rating of the car, which imposed a disproportionately heavy burden on the more powerful cars, *all of which were imported*, was found to breach Article 110 TFEU. There was no apparent justification for the excessive difference between the rates charged on the different categories of car. It should be noted that a taxation system should not be discriminatory:

> *solely* because *only* imported products, in particular those from other Member States, come within the most highly taxed category [*Commission v Greece (taxation of cars)* (case 132/88), para 18, emphasis added].

Differentiating between products on objective grounds, which is permissible, can lead to imports and domestic products being treated differently because of the specific characteristics of the two categories of goods. Objective grounds for differentiation in treatment are considered in 17.4.6.

17.4.3.3 **No domestic competing products**

The Court has held that internal tax may be imposed on imported products even if there is no domestic production of a similar or competing product as long as it applies to the product as a class, irrespective of origin (*Fink-Frucht GmbH v Hauptzollamt München-Landsbergerstrasse* (case 27/67), concerning the imports of sweet peppers from Italy applied in *Commission v France* (case 90/79)).

The Court reasoned:

> Article [110 TFEU] is intended to remove certain restrictions on the free movement of goods. But to conclude that it prohibits the imposition of any internal taxation on imported goods which do not compete with domestic products would be to give it a scope exceeding its purpose. Internal taxes, and turnover tax in particular, are essentially fiscal in purpose. There is therefore no reason why certain imported products should be given privileged treatment because they do not compete with any domestic products capable of being protected [p 231].

In *Fink-Frucht*, the CJ also rejected the idea that internal taxes could be seen as contravening Article 34 TFEU, which prohibits quantitative restrictions (quotas) and measures having equivalent effect. It argued:

> Nor does internal taxation imposed under the conditions set out above come within the prohibition on quantitative restrictions and measures having equivalent effect, within the meaning of Article [34 TFEU]. Such restrictions, which are intended to limit the quantities imported, are in fact different both in their purpose and the way in which they operate from measures of a fiscal nature [p 231].

17.4.3.4 **High rates of taxation**

Subsequently, the Court has suggested that where there is no domestic production of a product and the 'tax' is set at such a level as to compromise the free circulation of trade within the Union, it cannot be deemed part of a general system of taxation (*Commission v Denmark (registration duty—absence of domestic production)* (case 47/88)). It may, however, fall within other provisions of the Treaty.

The Danish *registration duty* case concerned the registration duty for cars in Denmark. There, the CJ suggested that where Member States impose on products charges of such an amount, that the free movement of goods within the internal market would be impeded as far as those goods were concerned in circumstances where, because there is no comparable domestic production, it should be impermissible that the national rules would escape the application of the prohibitions contained in Article 110 TFEU. In this situation the CJ suggested the only alternative would be Article 34 TFEU (see paras 12–13 of the judgment). As the rules in this case constituted discriminatory taxation (depreciation of the cars' value was not taken into account in the same way for imports as for cars already on the market), the applicability of Article 34 TFEU was not dealt with.

The issue of 'excessive tax' arose again in *De Danske Bilimportører v Skatteministeriet, Told- og Skattestyrelsen* (case C-383/01). While the Danish government had removed the discriminatory element of the tax, which had been the main issue in the Danish *registration duty* case, the level of registration duty for cars in Denmark remained high. Article 110 TFEU could not address the situation, as there was no domestic production which the national measures protected (and therefore no discriminatory or protective taxation). The question was whether fiscal matters could only be dealt with by Article 110 TFEU (as seemed to be the implication of the reasoning in *Fink-Frucht* and subsequent cases) or whether it could be argued that such a tax—essentially because of the ineffectiveness of Article 110 TFEU in this particular sort of circumstance—could be a measure having an effect equivalent to a quantitative restriction on imports prohibited under Article 34 TFEU? The CJ dodged the question, referring to the principle in para 12 of the Danish *registration duty* case but arguing:

> It is however sufficient in that regard to state that, in any event, the figures communicated by the national court as to the number of new vehicles registered in Denmark, and thus imported into that Member State, do not in any way show that the free movement of that type of goods between Denmark and the other Member States is impeded.
>
> In those circumstances, it cannot be considered that a charge such as the Danish registration duty has ceased to be internal taxation, within the meaning of Article [110 TFEU], and should be classified as a measure having equivalent effect to a quantitative restriction, for the purposes of Article [34 TFEU], nor is it appropriate to examine the scope of the proviso adopted by the Court in paragraphs 12 and 13 of *Commission* v *Denmark* [paras 41–2].

In theory, the question remains open but the standard position, that fiscal matters should be dealt with by Article 110 TFEU, has frequently been repeated, for example in *Brzeziński v Dyrektor Izby Celnej w Warszawie* (case C-313/05), which concerned the compliance with EU law of the Polish regulations on excise duty on passenger cars imported from other EU Member States (para 50). Indeed, in *Brzeziński*, the requirement to submit a simplified declaration, which the CJ accepted was not 'a true obstacle of a fiscal nature' still did not fall within Article 34 as it was 'inextricably linked to the actual payment of the excise duty' (para 51). It seems the Danish *registration duty* case argument will be re-opened only in an extreme case, if at all.

17.4.3.5 Identification of discrimination

In assessing the question of discrimination, it is necessary to take into account not only the rate of direct and indirect internal taxation on domestic and imported products, but also the basis of assessment and the detailed rules for its collection. Where differences result in the imported product being taxed, *at the same stage of production or marketing*, more heavily than the similar domestic product, Article 110 TFEU is infringed (*Ianelli & Volpi SpA*). It may also be necessary to have regard to taxation levied at earlier stages of manufacture and marketing, particularly to ensure that goods are not taxed twice (*FOR v VKS* (case 54/72)). The Court insists on strict equality, rather than broad equivalence, to ensure 'transparency'. It has even applied Article 110 TFEU to penalties. In *Commission v France (infringement of VAT legislation)* (case 276/91) a provision of the French customs code, which provided for more severe penalties for VAT offences in relation to imported goods than for similar offences related to domestic transactions, was found to breach Article 110 TFEU. Although some difference in treatment might be justified for administrative reasons, in that VAT offences committed in other Member States were not as easily discoverable as those committed in the home Member State, this could not justify a manifest disproportion in the severity of the two categories of offences. It has been suggested that this decision, no doubt correct as to its result, would have been better based on Article 34 TFEU, or Article 16 TFEU, the general prohibition of discrimination on the grounds of nationality.

17.4.4 **Products from other Member States**

Although Article 110 TFEU is expressed as applying to the 'products of other Member States', the Court has held (*Co-Frutta*), arguing from *Criel, nee Donckerwolcke v Procureur de la République* (case 41/76)), that the prohibition of discriminatory taxation must apply, by analogy with the free movement of goods provisions, to goods from third countries in free circulation within the Member States. Similarly, although the reference to 'products of other Member States' would seem to imply that Article 110 TFEU only applies to taxes which discriminate against imports, the Court has held that in order to guarantee the neutrality of national systems of taxation, Article 110 TFEU will also apply to exports (*Statenskontrol v Larsen* (case 142/77)).

In *Stadtgemeinde Frohnleiten, Gemeindebetriebe Frohnleiten GmbH v Bundesminister für Land und Forstwirtschaft, Umwelt und Wasserwirtschaft* (case C-221/06), the Austrian government tried to argue that the charge on the tipping of waste products did not fall within Article 110 TFEU because the charge imposed pertained to a service. The CJ rejected this argument: Article 110 TFEU applies to internal taxation which is imposed on the use of imported products where those products are essentially intended for such use and have been imported solely for that purpose. Further, if the levy is imposed on the only use to which the items can be put, then charges on that activity fall within Article 110 TFEU.

17.4.5 **'Similar' products**

It is clear that products need not be identical to fall within Article 110 TFEU. What, then, is a 'similar' product? In the course of a number of judgments, mostly infringement proceedings against Member States under Article 263 TFEU (see Chapter 11), in respect of allegedly discriminatory taxation of alcoholic drinks (eg, the French *spirits* case), the Court has held that 'similar' must be interpreted widely. In assessing the question of similarity, classification of the product under the same heading in the CCT will weigh heavily, but it is not conclusive. The important factor is whether the products:

> have similar characteristics and meet the same needs from the point of view of consumers . . . not according to whether they are strictly identical but whether their use is similar or comparable [*Commission v Denmark (taxation of spirits)* (case 106/84)].

The concept of similarity is thus analogous to that of the relevant product market in EU competition law (see Chapter 29). Indeed, in *X* (case C-437/12) concerning the passenger-car and motorcycle tax payable when registering in the Netherlands a motor vehicle originating from another Member State, the CJ, in determining what was a similar product, remarked that domestic vehicles should 'be considered "similar products" to imported used vehicles if their characteristics and the needs which they serve place them in a competitive relationship' (para 23). This approach means that the territory covered by Article 110(1) and Article 110(2) TFEU (discussed at 17.4.7) remains very similar. To assess the question in the context of cars, the CJ in *X* gave a non-exhaustive list of characteristics to be taken into account: price, size, comfort, performance, fuel consumption, durability and reliability. A comparison must be made with a vehicle whose characteristics are closest to those of the imported vehicle—so model, type and other characteristics such as drive and equipment, age and mileage, general condition and brand are relevant factors. In *Commission v Italy (bananas)* (case 184/85), the CJ had to determine whether bananas were 'similar' fruit for the purposes of Article 110(1) TFEU. In making its assessment, the Court took into account the objective characteristics of bananas and other fruit, including the extent to which they could satisfy the same consumer need.

In this case, the CJ held that bananas were not similar to other fruit (although the national rules in the issue might fall within Article 110(2) TFEU).

To decide if the products meet the same consumer needs the Court has held (*Commission v UK (excise duties on wine)* (case 170/78)) that it is necessary to look not only at the present state of the market but also at possible developments—that is, the possibility of substituting one product for another. Taxation policy must not be allowed to crystallise consumer habits, for example, taxing wine much more heavily than beer (but see 17.4.6 on justification).

17.4.6 Objective grounds for differentiation

Different rates of taxation may, however, be applied to what appear to be 'similar' products provided they are based on objective criteria, designed to achieve economic policy objectives which are compatible with EU law, and are applied in such a way as to avoid discrimination against imports or afford indirect protection to domestic products. This reasoning was applied in *Commission v France (liqueur wines)* (case 196/85).

> ### Liqueur Wines
>
> The case concerned infringement proceedings for a system of differential taxation in which certain wines known as natural sweet wines or liqueur wines, production of which is 'traditional or customary', attracted more favourable tax rates than ordinary wine. The purpose of the special rate was to bolster the economy in areas largely dependent on the production of these wines, to compensate for the relatively rigorous conditions under which they are produced.
>
> The Court found the economic policy objectives pursued by the French to be justified. Such rules, it said, may not be regarded as contrary to Union law merely because they may be applied in a discriminatory manner if it is not proved that they have in fact been applied in such a manner.

Clearly in this case it felt that neither discrimination nor protectionist motives had been proved (see also *Chemial Farmaceutici SpA v DAF SpA* (case 140/79)). Where a system involving different rates of taxation, although prima facie objectively justified, in effect discriminates against the imported product or affords indirect protection to domestic products, it will not be permissible (*Bobie Getränkvertrieb GmbH v Hauptzollamt Aachen Nord* (case 127/75)). This principle can be seen in operation in *Commission v Greece (taxation of motor vehicles)* (case C-375/95), which concerned a Greek rule which provided that a reduced rate of tax would apply to cars using 'anti-pollution' technology. According to the Greek government, this reduced rate was not available to imports because the testing of each import to verify that it satisfied the relevant criteria was not practicable. The CJ responded that such consideration could not justify discriminatory taxation (see also *Outokumpu Oy* (17.4.2) and *Stadtgemeinde Frohnleiten* (17.4.4)). Reverse discrimination on the other hand will be permitted (*Peureux v Directeur des Services Fiscaux* (case 86/78)).

17.4.7 Taxation affording indirect protection to competing domestic products

Internal taxation will be contrary to Article 110 TFEU if it affords indirect protection to domestic products. Article 110(2) TFEU is intended to cover 'all forms of indirect tax protection in the case of products which, without being similar within the meaning of Article 110(1) TFEU, are nevertheless in competition, even partial, indirect or potential competition, with each other' (*Co-Frutta*). It is wider than Article 110(1) TFEU, because the competitive similarity does not have to be complete, and wider than the concept of the relevant product market in EU competition law. This point may be demonstrated by comparing *Co-Frutta* with the case of *United Brands v Commission* (case 27/76) (see Chapter 29). In *Co-Frutta* a consumer tax, imposed on both domestic and imported bananas but which in practice applied almost exclusively to imported products (domestic production being extremely small), and which was not applied to other fresh (principally home-produced) fruit was found to afford indirect protection to domestic production, in breach of Article 110(2) TFEU. In *United Brands*, on the other hand, bananas were found to constitute a separate product market; the relevant product market did not include other fresh fruit. Clearly a more generous approach to the question of competition is justified in the context of Article 110(2) TFEU, to safeguard the Union against fiscal protectionism on the part of Member States.

Since Article 110(2) TFEU does not depend on 'similarity' between the domestic and imported products, it will be necessary, in a claim based on this article, to demonstrate that the domestic and imported products, while not being similar, are in fact in competition with each other, and that the effect of the impugned tax regime is to afford indirect protection to the domestic product (*excise duties on wine*).

Excise Duties on Wine

This case concerned British rules, which subjected some wines to a rate of taxation approximately five times that applied to beer. In determining whether wine and beer were in fact in competition with each other, the Court held that 'to a certain extent at least, the two beverages were capable of meeting identical needs' (para 8).

It would seem that product substitutability is the basis on which the CJ will determine whether products are in competition. Further, as seems to be the case for determining similarity, consumer preferences will not be determinative because they are 'essentially variable in time and space' (*excise duties on wine*, para 8).

Once it has been determined that certain products are in competition, the next question is whether there is a 'protective effect'. In *Commission v Belgium (taxation of wine and beer)* (case 356/85), national rules detailing the level of tax on alcoholic drinks were in issue. Wine, an imported product, was taxed at 25 per cent, whereas beer, a domestic product, was taxed at 19 per cent. The CJ rejected the argument that the legislation provided a protective effect in favour of beer. The Court based its reasoning on the insignificant impact of the difference in tax rates on price.

The Court's approach in this case did not require complex market analysis but seems, rather, to have depended on a commonsense assessment of the impact of the tax differential. On the other side of the coin, the Court has taken an equally commonsense view of whether there is likely to be an impact, rather than requiring a detailed statistical analysis of the point. Statistics have, however, been used to show that apparently neutral rules do in fact discriminate.

17.5 Harmonisation of taxation

Although the Union has the power to harmonise laws relating to indirect taxation to the extent that it is necessary to ensure the establishment and functioning of the internal market (Articles 113 and 115 TFEU) and has made considerable progress in this area in the case of VAT, excise duties and corporation tax, Member States have understandably been reluctant to cede competence to the Union outside these areas. Proposals to approximate rates of indirect taxation within broad tax bands, introduced under the internal market programme, have not so far met with success. Since different tax regimes clearly have an adverse impact on the functioning of the internal market by distorting the 'normal' flow of trade and competition within the Union the Commission has expressed its intention to continue to seek progress in this area. However, since fiscal measures remain subject to a requirement of unanimity, as an exception to the principle of qualified majority voting introduced by Article 114 TFEU, which remains even after Lisbon, progress is likely to remain slow. More contentious issues arise where direct taxation has an impact on other policies, as has been seen in cases involving the free movement of persons and the freedom to provide services. Taxation also has an impact in the context of other areas, such as employment, the environment, public health, not to mention monetary union, for all of which the Union has competence. Nonetheless, legislative progress may well be slow, given the sensitivity of the issues involved and the fact that the need for unanimity remains.

17.6 Conclusions

In summary, we have two broad categories of charges: those that form part of a general system of taxation and those that apply when goods cross a border. This latter group is very hard to justify, even if the system is not intended to discriminate. The narrow grounds on which such charges might be justified concern (proportional) payment for services rendered, or the argument that the charge is not related to the crossing of the border but actually forms part of a system of general taxation. Even in this second main category of charges, direct discrimination cannot be justified. The Court's approach has been uncompromising. Since the creation of the customs union is one of the fundamental elements of the Union project the Court's broad interpretation of the relevant prohibitions is not surprising. Given the international-law trade context, in which overt protectionism is frowned on, the CJ's approach to customs duties and measures having equivalence caused, in general, little comment.

The provisions relating to taxation are the subject of greater discussion, touching as they do on an area of competence central to Member States' sovereignty. The breadth of some of the judgments has impinged on Member States' freedom to pursue other policy objectives, such as protection of the environment. It is somewhat ironic that increasingly, these other objectives are recognised as worthy of a high level of protection by the Treaty. A further irony for the Member States lies in the fact that, in failing to agree to harmonising legislation in all but limited fields of indirect taxation, they have effectively put the development of taxation policy in the hands of the CJ. This may result in decisions that have a greater impact on national taxation policies than any harmonised legislation.

Further reading

Barents, R, 'Recent case law on the prohibition of fiscal discrimination under Article 95' (1986) 23 CML Rev 641.

Danusso, M and Denton, R, 'Does the European Court of Justice look for a protectionist motive under Article 95?' (1991) 1 LIEI 67.

Easson, A, 'Fiscal discrimination: New perspectives on Article 95 of the EC Treaty' (1981) 18 CML Rev 521.

Grabitz, E and Zacher, C, 'Scope for action by Member States for the improvement of environmental protection under EEC law: The example of environmental taxes and subsidies' (1989) 26 CML Rev 423.

Schwartze, J, 'The Member States' discretionary powers under the tax provisions of the EEC Treaty' in J Schwartze (ed), *Discretionary Powers of the Member States in the Field of Economic Policies and their Limits under the EEC Treaty* (Nomos, 1988).

Thygesen, J, 'National tax law: Under the influence of EU rules for free movement of goods' (2013) 41 Intertax 351.

Tryfonidou, A, '*Carbonati Apuani Srl v Comune di Carrara*: Should we reverse "reverse discrimination"?' (2005) 16 King's College LJ 373.

Free movement of goods

18.1 Introduction

The rules relating to the abolition of measures having equivalent effect to quantitative restrictions have been central to the development of the single market. The abolition of customs duties and charges of equivalent effect and prohibition on discriminatory taxation would not have been sufficient to guarantee the free movement of goods within the internal market. In addition to pecuniary restrictions, there are other barriers to trade of a non-pecuniary nature, usually in the form of administrative rules and practices, protectionist and otherwise, equally capable of hindering the free flow of goods from state to state. Articles 34 and 35 TFEU are designed to eliminate these barriers.

The significance of these rules is based on the breadth of the circumstances in which they can come into play. The prohibition on measures having equivalent effect do not apply just to rules that apply at the border, or which intend to discriminate against imports (or exports). They apply in a much wider range of circumstances, catching national rules that may have been enacted for legitimate, non-trade-related reasons, such as worker protection, consumer protection or protection of the environment, and which apply to domestic goods as well as to imports or exports. Given the interplay between trade objectives and other policy aims, the central question is, 'Where does the proper scope of these articles end?' As we shall see, this question has given rise to a considerable amount of case law and academic criticism. The issue is important as the scope of Articles 34 and 35 TFEU may limit the powers of each of the Member States to regulate many matters that are not primarily trade-related. As a result, there is a tension between integration, driven by the Union institutions, and national regulatory competence.

Running parallel to this issue is another concern: that of the de-regulatory effect of the Treaty freedoms, which we also noted in Chapter 16. The effect of using Articles 34 and 35 TFEU is to strike down national legislation, thereby removing the rules regulating trade. This is sometimes called negative harmonisation. The difficulty is that a national rule may have been enacted for good reason. The CJ is therefore left with the task of balancing trade concerns with other concerns, as permitted by the Treaty derogation (Article 36 TFEU, discussed in Chapter 19) and through the rule of reason. Given that the CJ may not be the best body to assess such questions, it is sometimes suggested that the use of positive harmonisation, which involves the political institutions in the determination of agreed standards (see Chapters 3 and 16) is a better approach.

A further obstacle to the free movement of goods may be caused by the existence of what is referred to in the TFEU as a 'State monopoly of a commercial character'. Such monopolies exist where a Member State has restricted the right to sell particular goods to one body. State monopolies are clearly capable of obstructing the free movement of goods as their position in a particular market enables such monopolies to control the flow of goods in and out of the Member State, as well as the conditions under which trade in such goods takes place. Although a separate provision, Article 37 TFEU, deals with state monopolies, it is dealt with here because of the broad similarity of the potential effect on trade. When considering Article 37 TFEU and state monopolies, the relationship between this provision and competition provisions, notably state aid as well as Article 106 TFEU, should also be borne in mind. All these provisions seek to deal with state behaviour which has the effect of distorting, or reinforcing the distortion of, competition.

This chapter starts by looking at the elements common to the articles. Then, after considering the meaning of quantitative restriction, the chapter focuses on the development of the jurisprudence relating to measures having equivalent effect to quantitative restrictions. As we shall see, the case law has not been entirely consistent and the state of the law is *still* not completely clear, though the main principles are well established. We will look at the jurisprudence as falling broadly into three phases: the early years; the expansion of Article 34 TFEU following the case of *Cassis de Dijon* and the consequent problems; and finally *Keck* and the question of whether the CJ is now following a consistent policy. The chapter concludes with a consideration of Articles 35 (exports) and 37 TFEU.

18.2 Outline of provisions

18.2.1 Quantitative restrictions

As will be apparent, Articles 34 and 35 TFEU cover a much wider range of measures than Articles 28 and 30 TFEU, but unlike these latter articles, provision is made for derogation under Article 36 TFEU.

The principal provisions are:

- Article 34 TFEU, which prohibits quantitative restrictions, and all measures having equivalent effect, on *imports*;
- Article 35 TFEU, which contains a similar prohibition on *exports*.

The prohibition is twofold, embracing:

- quantitative restrictions;
- measures of equivalent effect to quantitative restrictions (MEQR).

Original Articles 31–3 EEC, which provided for the gradual abolition of import restrictions during the transitional period, were deleted by the ToA.

Article 36 TFEU provides that the prohibitions in Articles 34 and 35 TFEU will not apply to restrictions on imports and exports which are *justified* on a number of specified grounds (see Chapter 19).

Even where a particular activity falls within other provisions of the Treaty, such as the 'services' provisions, it may still fall foul of the Article 34 TFEU (*Dundalk water supply*) requirement that pipes required under a contract for the supply of services must comply with Irish specifications held in breach of Article 34 TFEU. The relationship between the four freedoms, together with the definition of 'goods', is discussed further in Chapter 15.

Note, however, that where a fiscal matter is in issue, and it can be dealt with under the discriminatory taxation provisions (Article 110 TFEU), it should be dealt with there. Similarly, a matter that concerns a customs duty should not be assessed under Article 34 TFEU but instead should be assessed by reference to Article 30 TFEU (see Chapter 17). The possibilities for derogation in relation to these provisions are different from that in relation to Article 34 TFEU (and, indeed, the other free movement provisions).

18.2.2 **State monopolies**

Article 37 TFEU states that:

> Member States shall adjust any State monopolies of a commercial character so as to ensure that no discrimination regarding the conditions under which goods are procured and marketed exists between nationals of Member States.

Member States must also refrain from introducing any new measure which is contrary to Article 37(1) TFEU or which restricts the scope of Articles 30, 34 or 35 TFEU (Article 37(2) TFEU). This does not mean that no new monopolies may be created, but rather that if such monopolies are formed, they must be compatible with the provisions on the free movement of goods.

There is no specific provision derogating from Article 37 TFEU; Article 36 TFEU cannot be used in this context.

18.3 Whose actions are caught?

To engage the articles, the actions challenged must be capable of being traced back by the categories of persons covered by the relevant article. These articles are addressed to, and relate to, measures taken by Member States. There are three ways in which the meaning of 'Member States' has been interpreted broadly.

18.3.1 **Application to the institutions**

First, the institutions are bound by the terms of the Treaty generally, including these provisions. Union institutions may derogate from the provisions of Articles 34 and 35 TFEU where they are expressly authorised to do so by other provisions of the Treaty, for example in implementing the common agricultural policy (Articles 39–44 TFEU) (*Rewe Zentrale AG v Direktor der Landwirtschaftskammer Rheinland* (case 37/83)).

18.3.2 **Public bodies**

Secondly, the term 'measures taken by Member States' has been interpreted in the widest sense. 'Measures' include the actions of all forms of government, whether central, regional or local, and extend to the activities of any public body, legislative, executive or judicial, or even semi-public body, such as a quango, exercising powers derived from public law (eg, *Apple and Pear Development*—establishment by government of development council for fruit production, with members appointed by minister).

Royal Pharmaceutical Society

In *R v Royal Pharmaceutical Society of Great Britain* (cases 266 and 267/87), pharmacists had to be a member of the society to practise as a pharmacist. The society, which was established by Royal Charter, set down rules with which its members had to comply. UK legislation empowered the society to impose disciplinary sanctions on members for professional misconduct.

The society specified that pharmacists should not substitute generic drugs for branded drugs when dispensing prescriptions. The importers of generic drugs sought to challenge this rule, but the question was whether it constituted a 'measure'.

In *Royal Pharmaceutical Society* the CJ held that measures adopted by professional bodies, such as the Royal Pharmaceutical Society, on which national legislation has conferred regulatory or disciplinary powers, were 'measures taken by Member States' subject to what is now Article 34 TFEU. In determining whether the actions of a body fall within the scope of Article 34 TFEU, the CJ will consider the body's functions, statutory basis, management and funding; its legal form will not be determinative as can be seen in *Commission v Germany (quality labels)* (case C-325/00).

Quality Labels case

Here, the fact that a body which awarded quality labels to German products was established as a private limited company did not take its actions outside Article 34 TFEU, despite the fact that the German government could not directly influence its actions. The CJ noted that the company was financed by a public body itself financed by compulsory contributions, its functions were determined, albeit broadly, by statute and it was subject to the supervision of the public body from which it derived its funding.

More recently, the CJ has held that, in principle, the opinions of a public official (expressed via interviews with the media) were sufficient to implicate the state, provided the persons to whom the statements were addressed could reasonably suppose that the statements were given by the official with the authority of his office (*Lehtinen*). This issue would be one for the national court to assess on the facts in a given case.

18.3.3 Horizontal direct effect

One question is whether Articles 34–7 TFEU have horizontal direct effect. Given the nature of Article 37 TFEU, it is unlikely that it is a question that has much relevance for this provision. Although there had been some debate on whether Articles 34 and 35 TFEU had horizontal effect, it seemed that these provisions did not and that they were limited to the actions of public bodies, however broadly those bodies were seen.

The position with regards Article 34 seems to have changed, however, as a result of *Fra.bo SpA* (discussed in Chapter 5). The case concerned a private standards setting body, the rules of which could have an effect on inter-state trade (cf *quality labels* discussed in 18.3.2). Rather than looking to the form of the body, the CJ instead considered the effect of its rules on trade, holding that the key question to answer was:

> whether, in the light of inter alia the legislative and regulatory context in which it operates, the activities of a private-law body such as the DVGW has the effect of giving rise to restrictions on the free movement of goods in the same manner as do measures imposed by the State [para 26].

It answered this question in the affirmative, holding that Article 34 TFEU applied. In this approach the Court now seems to be using a similar approach to that which it adopts in relation to the other freedoms—that is, looking at the effect of the rules. Note, the reasoning here is not limited to directly discriminatory measures.

Even before *Fra.bo*, the actions of individuals were not completely beyond the reach of these articles. The actions of individuals could be challenged indirectly by imposing positive obligations upon Member States. The starting point is the *angry farmers* case.

Angry Farmers

From 1993 certain groups of French farmers launched a systematic campaign to restrict the supply of agricultural products from other Member States, including threatening wholesalers and retailers to induce them to stock exclusively French products, imposing minimum selling prices for the products concerned, and the organisation of checks to verify whether those traders were complying with the instructions given. Other actions included vandalism as well as destruction of goods and means of transport. In some instances, French police were present but took no action. The Commission communicated its concerns about these activities to the French government, but instances continued to occur. The Commission brought an enforcement action before the CJ which was heard in 1997.

The problem here did not concern actions by the French state but rather its failure to take action to prevent private individuals from impeding the cross-border flow of goods. According to the Commission, the French government should have taken action to stop the farmers blockading imported agricultural produce and damaging property. The CJ agreed, stressing the fundamental nature of Article 34 TFEU and then referring to Article 4(3) TEU, which puts Member States under an obligation 'to take all necessary and appropriate measures' to ensure that Union fundamental freedoms are respected in their territory. This ruling makes it clear that Member States' obligations extend to positive measures as well as refraining from taking action incompatible with the TFEU.

The precise extent of this obligation remains uncertain, although *Schmidberger* (discussed later, as well as in Chapter 6) provides further guidance. In the *angry farmers* case, the CJ emphasised the duration and severity of the incidents in France and the passivity of the French authorities in this case. Note also that a Member State is only obliged to take 'necessary and proportionate' measures. Member States thus still retain some discretion in determining, for example, their policing policy, and would certainly not be obliged to quell every public demonstration. The question then is when does the Member State's obligation arise?

After the *angry farmers* case, a regulation, the so-called 'rapid intervention mechanism', was enacted to deal with obstacles to trade which originate in the action or inaction of the Member States (Regulation 2679/98 ([1998] OJ L337/8)). In defining 'inaction', the Regulation tracks the wording of the *angry farmers* case. The Regulation gives the Commission the power to intervene in such circumstances, providing the Commission with the possibility of taking a Member State before the CJ should obstacles covered by the Regulation continue in existence. The Regulation defines in Article 1 the notion of an 'obstacle' requiring action. It lists three cumulative requirements:

- the serious disruption of the free movement of goods;
- serious loss to individuals affected;
- the necessity of immediate state action.

This definition would seem to take one-off actions outside the scope of the Regulation. Such an approach would seem in line with the *angry farmers* case, which emphasised the severity and duration of the French farmers' action. In the *Schmidberger* case, however, the Advocate-General suggested that a one-day motorway blockade held in accordance with the relevant Member State's laws should trigger the application of Articles 34 and 35 TFEU where relevant, a view the Court followed. In the CJ's reasoning, the severity of the disruption would be relevant for justification for failure to act rather than the application of Articles 34 and 35 TFEU in the first place. Seemingly, there is now a divergence between the Treaty jurisprudence and specific secondary legislation.

18.4 Types of act caught by Articles 34 and 35 TFEU

We need also to consider whether the types of act challenged fall within the terms of the relevant articles. Articles 34 and 35 TFEU refer to 'measures', a term which clearly includes national legislative acts. The CJ will assess national legislation as it has been interpreted by national practice. According to the CJ's case law, 'measure' for the purpose of Article 34 TFEU is wider than legislation. It includes administrative acts, as *Commission v France (postal franking machine)* (case 21/84) shows. There, although a discriminatory law had been repealed, the administrative practice had not changed, the authorities showing a 'systematically unfavourable' attitude towards the approval of imported products. A measure does not need to be a binding act to fall within the prohibition as can be seen in the preamble to the Commission's Directive 70/50, and confirmed by the CJ in *Commission v Ireland ('buy Irish' campaign)* (case 249/81).

> ### *Buy Irish*
>
> In this case certain activities of the Irish Goods Council, a government-sponsored body charged with promoting Irish goods by, inter alia, advertising, principally on the basis of their Irish origin, were held to be in breach of the then Article 30 EEC (now Article 34 TFEU). Even though no binding measures were involved, the Board's actions were capable of influencing the behaviour of traders and thereby frustrating the aims of the Union.

This approach was reasserted in *Lehtinen*, where the views of an official were held to fall within Article 34 TFEU, provided that they appear to be the official position taken by the state and not the personal opinions of the individual.

As we have already seen from the *Angry Farmers* case, omissions can also constitute 'measures'.

18.5 Prohibition on quantitative restrictions (Article 34 TFEU)

Quantitative restrictions were interpreted in *Riseria Luigi Geddo v Ente Nazionale Risi* (case 2/73) as any measures which amount to a total or partial restraint on imports, exports or goods in transit. They would clearly include a ban, as was found to be the case in *ban on pork imports* and *R v Henn* (case 34/79)—ban on import of pornographic materials. They would also include a quota system, as in *Salgoil SpA v Italian Ministry for Foreign Trade* (case 13/68). The *Ditlev Bluhme* case (case C-67/97) confirms that a ban on imports operates as a quantitative restriction even if the prohibition extends to part only of a Member State's territory. This case concerned the Danish prohibition on the import onto the island of Læsø of live domestic bees or reproductive material for them, the aim of which was to protect the Læsø brown bee. This, the CJ held, was a quantitative restriction although it applied only to a small part of Denmark.

A covert quota system might operate by means of an import (or export) licence requirement. A licensing system might in itself amount to a quantitative restriction, or, alternatively, a measure of equivalent effect to a quantitative restriction. It was held in *International Fruit Co NV v Produktschap voor Groenten en Fruit* (cases 51–4/71) that even if the granting of a licence were a pure formality, the requirement of such a licence to import would amount to a breach of Article 34 TFEU. In that case it was deemed to be a measure of equivalent effect to a quantitative restriction.

Although Articles 34 and 35 TFEU identify two types of prohibited behaviour, quantitative restrictions and MEQR, it seems as though the case law no longer maintains a firm and consistent distinction between the two categories. Many cases which could be viewed as a quantitative measure have been considered as MEQR.

18.6 Prohibition on measures having equivalent effect to quantitative restrictions (Article 34 TFEU)

The concept of MEQR is altogether wider in scope than that of quantitative restrictions. Perhaps to the surprise of Member States, it has been interpreted very generously by both the Commission and the CJ to include not merely overtly protective measures or measures applicable only to imports or exports ('distinctly applicable' measures), but measures applicable to imports (or exports) and domestic goods alike ('indistinctly applicable' measures), often introduced (seemingly) for the most worthy purpose. The precise scope of Article 34 TFEU has therefore been the subject of much discussion, and central to the debate is the question of whether Article 34 TFEU is about discrimination, whether direct (distinctly applicable measures) or indirect (indistinctly applicable measures), or instead about ensuring that individual national markets are opened up to goods from other Member States (market access). It is questionable the degree to which the CJ has developed a consistent policy. There are three key cases: *Dassonville, Cassis de Dijon* and *Keck* (cases C-267–8/91), which may serve as landmarks as we navigate the development of the Article 34 TFEU jurisprudence. While the main elements of the jurisprudence are clear, there are grey areas near the boundaries.

18.6.1 *Dassonville* and the early years

It was generally accepted in the early years of the Union, that Article 34 TFEU caught measures that discriminated against imports, that is, were directly discriminatory by treating imports differently. The question was whether Article 34 TFEU could also catch indirectly discriminatory measures, which appeared on the face to treat imports and domestic products alike, but which in effect discriminated against imports. The Commission, in Directive 70/50 (which is no longer of legal effect), suggested that both direct and indirect discrimination should be caught. It was not until 1974 that the CJ, in the case of *Dassonville*, introduced its own definition of MEQR.

Dassonville

Dassonville concerned Belgian rules which required imported goods bearing certain designations of origin to have a certificate of authenticity from the authorities in the country of origin. Criminal proceedings were instituted against traders who acquired a consignment of Scotch whisky in free circulation in France and imported it into Belgium without being in possession of a certificate of origin from the British customs authorities.

The CJ determined that such a measure, which focused on imported goods, would fall within Article 34 TFEU, arguing:

> All trading rules enacted by Member States which are capable of hindering, directly or indirectly, actually or potentially, intra-[Union] trade are to be considered as measures having an effect equivalent to quantitative restrictions.

This definition, now known as the '*Dassonville* formula', has since been applied consistently, almost verbatim, by the CJ in subsequent cases. It is a broad, effects-based test. As became apparent, it is not necessary to show an actual hindrance to trade between Member States as long as the measure is capable of such effects. Unlike the competition provisions of Articles 101 and 102 TFEU, which require an 'appreciable effect' on trade and competition between Member States, the CJ has in the past held that Article 34 TFEU is not subject to a *de minimis* rule (*Officier Van de Justitie v Van de Haar and Kaveka de Meern BV* (case 177/82)—restrictions on sale of tobacco products).

Although *Dassonville*, as we shall see, is a broad test, there are some limitations. A measure which is not capable of hindering trade between Member States, which merely affects the flow of trade *within* a Member State, will not breach Article 34 TFEU. In *Sergius Oebel* (case 155/80) a German law banning the production and delivery to consumers and retail outlets of bakery products during the night hours, designed to protect workers in small and medium-sized bakeries, was held not to breach Article 34 TFEU because, although delivery of imported products through some outlets was precluded, 'trade within the [Union] remained possible at all times' (see also *Blesgen v Belgium* (case 75/81)). In *Quietlynn* (discussed also in Chapter 15) a licensing requirement for the sale of sex appliances by sex shops was held not to breach Article 34 TFEU, since the goods in question, which included imported goods, 'could be marketed through other channels'.

The case law of the Court has not been consistent on this point. In *Torfaen Borough Council v B&Q Plc* (case 145/88) the Court found that a ban on Sunday trading in England and Wales under the Shops Act 1950, the effect of which was to restrict the volume of imports to the shops trading in breach of the rules, was prima facie contrary to Article 34 TFEU, even though alternative outlets for the sale of these goods existed during the working week (see also *Union Départementale des Syndicats CGT de l'Aisne v Sidef Conforama* (case C-312/89) and *André Marchandise* and Others (case C-332/89)). Following a change in the Court's approach, these latter cases involving Sunday trading would be decided on a different basis today (see *Keck* and subsequent cases to be discussed at 18.6.4).

The CJ discussed the question of whether a national measure had an effect on inter-state trade in *Pistre* (see Chapter 15) which concerned a French rule limiting the marketing of products with the designation of 'montagne' to those originating in certain areas in France. The CJ held that this rule had a Union dimension. In the CJ's view, it did not matter that all the relevant facts arose in France; it was sufficient that the rule could affect inter-state trade. It would seem clear from this case, and other similar cases, that the question of internal situation is very closely linked to the question of whether there is hindrance to inter-state trade (see also 18.6.5). This connection can be seen from the CJ's more recent restatement of the position in *Karner*—rules on advertising:

> That principle has been upheld by the Court not only in cases where the national rule in question gave rise to direct discrimination against goods imported from other Member States (*Pistre and ors*, paragraph 44), but also in situations where the national rule applied without distinction to national and imported products and was thus likely to constitute a potential impediment to intra-[Union] trade covered by Article [34 TFEU] (see, to that effect, case C-448/98, *Guimont*, paras 21 and 22) [para 20].

18.6.1.1 **Reverse discrimination**

A measure falling within the *Dassonville* formula but which operates solely to the disadvantage of domestic production will not fall foul of Union law. The ban in *Oebel* on the production of bakery products during the night, which prevented Belgian bakers from benefiting from the early morning trade in adjacent Member States, was found not to breach what are currently Articles 18, 34 and 35 TFEU. The Court held that it was not contrary to the principle of non-discrimination on grounds of nationality for states to apply national rules where other states apply less strict rules to similar products. The CJ took the same view of a Dutch regulation concerning the permitted ingredients of cheese, which was only applicable to cheese produced in Holland (*Jongeneel Kaas BV v Netherlands* (case 237/82), see also approach to interpretation of Article 35 TFEU) and of a French law requiring French retailers to adhere to a minimum selling price for books, provided it was not applied to books which, having been exported, were reimported into France (*Association des Centres Distributeurs Edouard Leclerc v 'Au Blé Vert' Sàrl* (case 229/83)).

In this respect, as in other areas (eg, free movement of workers), the Court is prepared to accept a measure of reverse discrimination. While Member States must be compelled, in the interests of the single market, not to discriminate against, or in any way prejudice, imports, it seems that they may be safely left to act themselves in order to protect their own interests. There is now a consistent line of authority from the CJ to this effect.

18.6.1.2 **Pricing rules**

In the cases of *Tasca* (case 65/75) and *Openbaar Ministerie v van Tiggele* (case 82/77) the *Dassonville* test was applied in the context of a domestic law imposing maximum and minimum selling prices, respectively. The laws were indistinctly applicable, that is they applied to both domestic and imported goods. In both cases the issue of Article 34 TFEU arose in criminal proceedings against the defendants for breach of these laws. Tasca was accused in Italy of selling sugar above the permitted national maximum price; van Tiggele in Holland of selling gin below the national minimum price. Both pleaded that the measures were in breach of EU law. Applying the *Dassonville* test the CJ found that both measures were capable of breaching Article 34 TFEU. Regarding the maximum price, the Court held a maximum price does not in itself constitute a measure equivalent in effect to a quantitative restriction. It becomes so when fixed at a level such that the sale of imported products becomes, if not impossible, more difficult. The maximum price in *Tasca* could have that effect, in that importers of more highly priced goods might have to cut their profit margins or even be forced to sell at a loss. In *van Tiggele* the minimum price also acted as a hindrance to imports, since it would prevent the (possibly) lower price of imported goods from being reflected in the retail selling price. The Court suggested, however, that a prohibition on selling below cost price, or a minimum profit margin, would be acceptable, since it would have no adverse effect on trade between Member States (principle applied in *Commission v Italy (fixing of trading margins)* (case 78/82)).

In general, the CJ has continued this approach. In *Scotch Whisky Association and Others v The Lord Advocate and the Lord Advocate General for Scotland* (case C-333/14) which concerned the imposition of minimum prices for the sale of alcohol in an attempt to curb alcohol abuse, the Court held:

> the legislation at issue in the main proceedings prevents the lower cost price of imported products being reflected in the selling price to the consumer means, by itself, that that legislation is capable of hindering the access to the United Kingdom market of alcoholic drinks that are lawfully marketed in Member States other than the United Kingdom of Great Britain and Northern Ireland, and constitutes therefore a measure having an effect equivalent to a quantitative restriction within the meaning of Article 34 TFEU [para 32].

In *Deutsche Parkinson Vereinigung eV v Zentrale zur Bekämpfung unlauteren Wettbewerbs eV* (case C-148/15), a system of fixed prices for pharmaceutical drugs sold by pharmacies was held to affect imports more than domestic sales, thus falling within the terms of the prohibition in Article 34 TFEU. Note the boundary between these cases and those cases in which rules limiting traders' freedom to determine price (but not specifying the price) have been seen as selling arrangements. Examples of cases involving selling arrangements include *Keck* (discussed in 18.6.4), which concerned a prohibition on sale at a loss, and *Openbaar Ministerie v Etablissements Fr. Colruyt NV* (case C-221/15) concerning national regulation prohibiting the sale of tobacco products by retailers at prices lower than those indicated on the revenue stamp.

18.6.2 Indistinctly applicable measures: *Cassis de Dijon*

In applying the *Dassonville* formula in these early cases, the Court did not distinguish between distinctly (or directly discriminatory) and indistinctly applicable (or indirectly discriminatory) measures. The breadth of the formula, especially when applied 'mechanically', looking to the *effect* of the measure on inter-state trade rather than to the question of *hindrance*, despite the fact that a hindrance seems to be required by the terms of the *Dassonville* formula, bore harshly on Member States, particularly where the measure was indistinctly applicable and might be justified as in the public interest.

Perhaps taking heed of criticisms arising from its application of the *Dassonville* formula, the Court took a decisive step in the case of *Cassis de Dijon* and paved the way for a distinction in the treatment of distinctly and indistinctly applicable measures.

> ### *Cassis de Dijon*
>
> The question before the CJ in *Cassis de Dijon* concerned the legality under EU law of a German law laying down a minimum alcohol level of 25 per cent for certain spirits, which included cassis, a blackcurrant-flavoured liqueur. German cassis complied with this minimum, but French cassis, with an alcohol content of 15–20 per cent, did not. Thus although the German Regulation was indistinctly applicable, the result of the measure was effectively to ban French cassis from the German market. A number of German importers contested the measure, and the German court referred a number of questions to the CJ.

The CJ applied the *Dassonville* formula, thus confirming, should there have been any doubt, that Article 34 TFEU could apply to measures which, on their face, appeared to apply both to domestic products and imports.

18.6.2.1 Rule of reason

Crucially, the CJ developed a suggestion in its earlier *Dassonville* judgment that state measures falling within the formula might be acceptable where the restrictions on inter-state trade were 'reasonable', stating that:

> Obstacles to movement within the [Union] resulting from disparities between the national laws relating to the marketing of the products in question must be accepted insofar as those provisions may be recognised as being necessary in order to satisfy mandatory requirements relating in particular to the effectiveness of fiscal supervision, the protection of public health, the fairness of commercial transactions and the defence of the consumer.

This principle ('the first *Cassis de Dijon* principle'), that certain measures, though within the *Dassonville* formula, will not breach Article 34 TFEU if they are necessary to satisfy 'mandatory requirements' (now often referred to as matters of overriding public interest), has come to be known as the 'rule of reason', a concept borrowed from American anti-trust law, which also occasionally appears in the context of EU competition law (see Chapter 29).

Prior to *Cassis de Dijon*, it was assumed that any measure falling within the *Dassonville* formula would breach Article 34 TFEU and could be justified only on the grounds provided by Article 36 TFEU. Since *Cassis de Dijon*, at least where 'indistinctly applicable measures' are concerned, courts may apply a rule of reason to Article 34 TFEU. This means that if the measure is necessary in order to protect 'mandatory requirements', it will not breach Article 34 TFEU at all. 'Distinctly applicable measures', on the other hand, will normally breach Article 34 TFEU, but may be justified under Article 36 TFEU. This distinction is significant, since the mandatory requirements permitted under *Cassis de Dijon* are wider than the grounds provided under Article 36 TFEU, and, unlike that provision, are non-exhaustive (see Box 19.1 for examples), although the CJ refuses to contemplate a justification based on purely economic grounds (see, eg, *Duphar BV v Netherlands* (case 238/82) and, more recently, *Decker v Caisse Maladie des Employés Privés* (case C-120/95)). Any measure must be proportionate (see 19.3).

18.6.2.2 Mutual recognition

The Court established a second important principle in *Cassis de Dijon*. It suggested that there was no valid reason why:

> provided that [goods] have been lawfully produced and marketed in one of the Member States, [they] should not be introduced into any other Member State [para 14].

This is the principle of mutual recognition based on home country regulation.

Thus, national provisions making a product which was lawfully manufactured and marketed in another Member State subject to additional controls, save in the case of exceptions provided for or allowed by Union law, will constitute a MEQR. Is this principle, known as the principle of 'mutual recognition', not in conflict with the rule of reason? It is submitted that it is not. It merely gives rise to a presumption that goods which have been lawfully marketed in another state will comply with the 'mandatory requirements' of the importing state. This can be rebutted by evidence that further importing state measures are *necessary* to protect the interest concerned. Given the requirement of proportionality, that presumption will be hard to rebut; the burden of proving that a measure is necessary is a heavy one, particularly when, although justifiable in principle, it clearly operates as a hindrance to intra-Union trade.

18.6.2.3 Post-*Cassis de Dijon* application

The extent to which Member States are now limited, in the interests of the single market, in their ability to introduce indistinctly applicable and seemingly justifiable measures is illustrated by the case of *Commission v UK (Origin Marking of Retail Goods)* (case 207/83).

Origin Marking

Here the Commission claimed that a British regulation requiring certain goods (eg, clothing, textiles) sold retail to indicate their country of origin was in breach of Article 34 TFEU. The British government argued that the measure was justified on *Cassis de Dijon* principles in the interest of consumers, who regarded the origin of goods as an indication of their quality. The Court refused to accept this argument. It held that the Regulation merely enabled consumers to assert their prejudices, thereby slowing down the economic interpenetration of the Union. The quality of goods could also be indicated on the goods themselves or their packaging, and the protection of consumers sufficiently guaranteed by rules which enabled the use of false indications of origin to be prohibited. Whilst manufacturers remained free to indicate their own national origin it was not necessary to compel them to do so. The Regulation was in breach of Article 34 TFEU.

This judgment, initially surprising, demonstrates the Commission's and the Court's overriding concern to promote market integration by striking down national rules which tend to compartmentalise the market, particularly along national lines. In a single market, based on free competition, products must be allowed to compete on their merits, not on the basis of national origin. (See also *Apple and Pear Development*; the 'buy Irish' campaign case; and Chapter 29 on competition law.) The rules in respect of local or regional designations of origin of goods are now dealt with by secondary legislation (see Regulation 510/2006 on protection of geographical indications and designations of origin for agricultural products and foodstuffs ([2006] OJ L93/12), as amended; a separate system exists for wines and spirits).

18.6.3 'Over-extension' of Article 34 TFEU

Although the rule of reason has allowed Member States some latitude to enact or maintain indistinctly applicable measures that are capable of hindering trade between Member States to protect important national interests, while ensuring that such measures are subject to judicial control as to their proportionality, the rule has not been without its problems. These arose from a tendency to a lax, 'mechanical' application of the *Dassonville* formula, requiring measures which might affect the volume of imports overall, but with little potential to *hinder* imports, to be justified under the rule of reason. Certainly the idea of discrimination, or even indirect discrimination, seems to disappear in this body of cases where rules which equally affect domestic products were held to fall within Article 34 TFEU and following which Article 34 TFEU began to look like a 'right to trade' without any connection with the creation of the single market. (For a similar trend with regard to the right to regulate at Union level, see the scope of Article 114 TFEU discussed in Chapter 16.)

Defence lawyers in Member States were quick to exploit the 'Eurodefence' of Article 34 TFEU to charges involving a wide range of regulatory offences. Examples of such defences include challenges to Dutch laws restricting the use of free gifts for promotional purposes (*Openbaar Ministerie v Oosthoek's Uitgeversmaatschappij BV* (case 286/81)); to French laws prohibiting the door-to-door selling of educational materials (*Buet v Ministère Public* (case 382/87)); to English laws requiring the licensing of sex shops for the sale of sexual appliances (*Quietlynn*); to laws prohibiting 'eye-catching' price comparisons, as in *Schutzverband gegen Unwesen in der Wirtschaft v Yves Rocher GmbH* (case C-126/91); and a number of cases such as *Torfaen* pleading the illegality under Article 34 TFEU of national rules limiting Sunday trading. In all of these cases the legality of these measures under EU law was ultimately upheld, sometimes (eg, *Quietlynn*), on the grounds that Article 34 TFEU was not applicable at all, more often following the application of the rule of reason.

Given the result, these cases might be thought unproblematic, but there are difficulties relating to the approach of the CJ in determining the connection with Article 34 TFEU. The inclusion of a rule within the scope of Article 34 TFEU means that, in principle, the rule is unlawful and the burden of justification falls upon the state, not an easy task given the CJ's approach to proportionality. Further, not only was the scope of Article 34 TFEU very widely drawn, but the case law has not been consistent here as to whether it applied in the first place or whether the national rule would be justified by a rule of reason. Moreover, national courts face great difficulties in applying a rule of reason, particularly when there exists a number of possible justifications for the measure challenged and its harmful effect on trade between *Member States* (as opposed to between particular undertakings) is minimal. In these circumstances a national judge may be reluctant to entertain a challenge to domestic legislation, duly enacted by the national legislature, based on its lack of proportionality (see, eg, Hoffmann J in *Stoke-on-Trent City Council v B&Q plc* [1991] Ch 48).

These problems surfaced in the 'Sunday trading' cases. In *Torfaen*, the CJ had held that the rules in question, which prohibited large multiple shops such as the defendant's from opening on Sunday, might be justified to ensure that working hours be arranged to accord with 'national or regional socio-cultural characteristics', and directed the referring magistrates' court to examine the rules in the light of their proportionality. Unfortunately the precise grounds of justification permitted to protect such socio-cultural characteristics were not spelt out; nor was any guidance offered on the question of proportionality. Different British courts in different cases dealing with Sunday trading rules came to different conclusions. Courts which concluded that the socio-cultural purpose of the rules was to protect workers who did not want to work on Sunday not surprisingly concluded that the rules were disproportionate (eg, *B&Q Ltd v Shrewsbury & Atcham Borough Council* [1990] 3 CMLR 535); those which saw the rules as designed to 'preserve the traditional character of the British Sunday' legitimately concluded otherwise: the rules were not more than was necessary to achieve that end (eg, *Wellingborough Borough Council v Payless DIY Ltd* [1990] 1 CMLR 773). Despite a clear ruling from the Court in two cases subsequent to *Torfaen* and *Marchandise* that similar rules would be permissible under the rule of reason, the question of the legality of the English Sunday trading rules was only decided conclusively when the CJ, following a reference from the Supreme Court in *Stoke-on-Trent City Council v B&Q plc* (case C-169/91), applying the rule of reason in *Cassis de Dijon*, found that the rules were justified and not disproportionate.

18.6.4 *Keck and Mithouard*

Whether as a result of these problems and the uncertainty surrounding the scope of Article 34 TFEU in the case of non-discriminatory national rules with a minimal impact (in terms of hindrance) on intra-Union trade, resulting in some exploitation of Union rules, or of a new post-Maastricht commitment to the principle of subsidiarity, the Court, in *Keck and Mithouard*, signalled an important change of direction.

The approach to Article 34 TFEU had drawn a significant amount of academic comment, most of it critical. A range of suggestions were put forward to correct the perceived defects. One suggestion was that the CJ should return to the wording of *Dassonville* and look for a hindrance to inter-state trade to trigger the application of Article 34 TFEU (a *de minimis* approach). This is similar to the approach taken with regard to competition rules (see Chapter 29). Another was to draw a distinction between dual-burden and equal-burden rules. The former category places an additional burden on imports, and can therefore be seen as being akin to indirectly discriminatory rules. The rules in *Cassis de Dijon* could be seen as falling in this category. Equal-burden rules are rules which do not have a greater impact on imports though they may have an impact on trade. The Sunday trading rules could be an example of an equal-burden rule. The suggestion is that the boundary of Article 34 TFEU properly falls between the two categories, catching dual-burden rules but not equal-burden rules. Another suggestion focuses on the distinction between rules which relate to the characteristics of the goods, as in *Cassis de Dijon*, and rules which relate to the conditions of sale, such as the *Sunday Trading* cases. A further distinction may be made as regards this latter category between conditions of sale which apply generally, such as opening hours (sometimes called static conditions of sale) and those which relate to the marketing of the product itself, for example a ban on advertising a particular product (sometimes called dynamic conditions of sale).

The case of *Keck and Mithouard* concerned the legality under EU law of a French law prohibiting the resale of goods in an unaltered state at prices lower than their actual purchase price, in the interests of fair trading, to prevent 'predatory pricing' (see Chapter 29). Keck and Mithouard, who had been prosecuted for breach of this law, claimed that it was incompatible with EU law. Although Article 34 TFEU was not expressly invoked, the Court, to provide the French court with a 'useful' reply, focused on Article 34 TFEU, which was clearly the relevant article. It cited the *Dassonville* test. It pointed out that legislation such as the French law in question:

> may restrict the volume of sales, and hence the volume of sales of products from other Member States, insofar as it deprives traders of a method of sales promotion. But the question remains whether such a possibility is sufficient to characterise the legislation in question as a measure having equivalent effect to a quantitative restriction on imports.

It went on to suggest:

> in view of the increasing tendency of traders to invoke Article [34 TFEU] of the Treaty as a means of challenging any rules whose effect is to limit their commercial freedom even where such rules are not aimed at products of other Member States, the Court considers it necessary to re-examine and clarify its case law on this matter.

Citing the rule of reason from *Cassis de Dijon*, it drew a distinction between rules which lay down 'requirements to be met' by goods, such as those relating to designation, size, weight, composition, presentation, labelling and packaging, and rules relating to 'selling arrangements'. Rules governing 'requirements to be met' falling within the *Dassonville* formula remained subject to the rule of reason in *Cassis de Dijon*. However, 'contrary to what [had] previously been decided':

> the application to products from other Member States of national provisions restricting or prohibiting certain selling arrangements is not such as to hinder, directly or indirectly, actually or potentially, trade between Member States within the meaning of the *Dassonville* judgment, provided that those provisions apply to all affected traders operating within the national territory and provided that they affect in the same manner, in law and in fact, the marketing of domestic products and of those from other Member States.
>
> Where these conditions are fulfilled, the application of such rules to the sale of products from another Member State meeting the requirements laid down by that State is not by nature such as to prevent their access to the market or to impede access any more than it impedes the access of domestic products. Such rules therefore fall outside the scope of Article [34] of the Treaty.

Keck thus seemed to suggest that where a selling arrangement was in issue, the *Dassonville* test would not be satisfied and Article 34 TFEU would consequently not apply. The impact of such rules was likely to be too indirect or insignificant to constitute a MEQR; such rules do not in the view of the CJ impede access to the market. In this, traces of similarity with the approach of the Commission towards indistinctly applicable measures in Directive 70/50 can be seen. There the Commission accepted indistinctly applicable measures might have some impact on trade provided 'the restrictive effect of such measures on the free movement of goods exceeds the effects intrinsic to trade rules' (Article 3). We can also see similarities with the distinction between characteristics of the goods and their conditions of sale. *Keck* did not, however, seem to distinguish between static and dynamic rules. The CJ emphasised that the selling arrangement must apply equally in law and in fact, however, and it may be that static rules would be more likely to satisfy this test. Certainly, it is this proviso that was to prove to be significant in determining the direction of post-*Keck* case law. Initially, the new approach to Article 34 TFEU was affirmed in a number of cases (see Box 18.1).

Box 18.1 Examples of the application of *Keck*: Selling arrangements

Hünermund v Landesapothekerkammer Baden-Württemberg (case C-292/92)—prohibition on pharmacists advertising, outside pharmacy premises, pharmaceutical products which they are authorised to sell.

Commission v Greece (infant milk) (case C-391/92)—requirement for processed milk for infants to be sold only in pharmacies.

Groupement National des Négociants en Pommes de Terre de Belgique (Belgapom) v ITM Belgium SA (case C-63/94)—rules prohibiting sales yielding very low profit margins.

Banchero (case C-387/93)—rules reserving the retail sale of tobacco to authorised distributors.

By contrast with these cases involving 'selling arrangements', measures constituting 'requirements to be met', such as a Dutch law prohibiting dealings in gold and silver products not bearing a Dutch, Belgian or Luxembourg hallmark (*Houtwipper* (case C-293/93)) and German rules requiring the labelling of the contents of certain foods additional to that which was required under Union law (*Commission v Germany* (case C-51/94)) were examined, as *Keck* suggested, under the rule of reason and found not to be justified. Thus the approach to determining whether there is an MEQR can be rendered in diagrammatic form as seen in Figure 18.1.

While *Keck* has been controversial and the CJ has rarely found a selling arrangement to be outside Article 34, the CJ has not been prepared to abandon it completely as can be seen in *Ker-Optika bt v ANTSZ Déldunantuli Regionalis Intézete* (case C-108/09) and more recently, in *Etablissements Fr. Colruyt NV*. *Ker-Optika* which concerned Hungarian legislation banning the sale of contact lenses via the Internet. On the facts, the Hungarian government lost, but in reaching its conclusion classified the rules as selling arrangements under *Keck*, thus indicating that the *Keck* approach remained valid.

Etablissements Fr. Colruyt

The case concerned national rules prohibiting the sale of tobacco products by retailers at prices lower than those indicated on the revenue stamp. The rules were held not to concern the characteristics of those goods, but solely the arrangements under which they may be sold, and were therefore rules relating to selling arrangements. Not only did the rule apply to all traders but, since importers were free to set the price (on which duty was then assessed), the rules neither impeded nor hindered imports.

18.6.5 Weaknesses of the *Keck* approach

The move towards a more 'formalistic' approach towards Article 34 TFEU initiated in *Keck* has been both criticised as 'lacking in principle' and acclaimed for its 'tendency to cut back on unnecessary intrusions into the laws of the Member States in cases where access to the relevant national market is not at stake' (see the articles by Reich and Roth respectively, in the further reading section at the end of this chapter). Roth argues that the focus of Article 34 TFEU should be on access to the

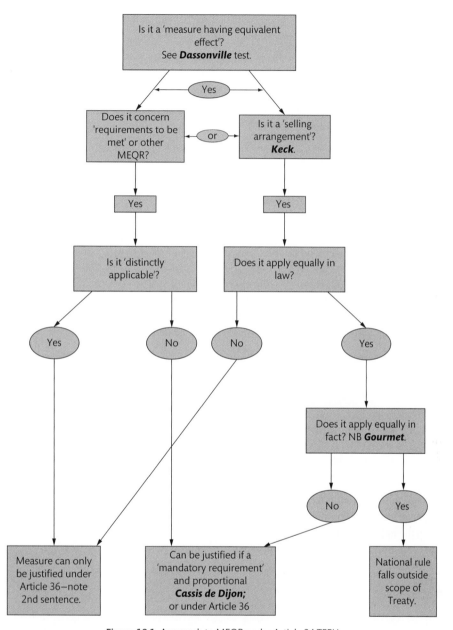

Figure 18.1 Approach to MEQR under Article 34 TFEU

(national) market, its purpose to promote inter-state trade in goods, not to ensure commercial free-dom as such. It is arguable that the more recent post-*Keck* cases see the CJ responding to some of these criticisms and, at least, considering questions such as the impact of a measure on access to the market. Perhaps a more appropriate way to view *Keck* is to consider, as the Advocate-General in *Volker Graf* suggested, the view that selling arrangements are harmless in internal market terms as a rebuttable presumption rather than as a rule. Even now, more than two decades after the decision, the jury seems still to be out on *Keck*.

There are two main areas of difficulty, (a) and (b), together with a third issue, (c), which has not—at least until recently—received much attention:

(a)   where the boundary between a selling arrangement and a requirement to be met lies, with the ancillary questions of whether the CJ has taken a consistent approach and whether the boundary lies in the right place (see 18.6.6);

(b)   the scope of the 'discrimination proviso' and whether a broad interpretation undermines the value of the *Keck* 'exception' (see 18.6.7);

(c)   whether there are only two categories of trading rule: selling arrangements and product requirements (see 18.6.8).

18.6.6 Meaning of 'selling arrangement'

There is no doubt that the 'formalistic' approach introduced in *Keck* creates uncertainty. The ambit of the phrase 'certain selling arrangements' is unclear and ultimately remains a Union concept the scope of which is controlled by the CJ. Some aspects of marketing (eg, advertising claims on packaging: *Verein gegen Unwesen In Handel und Gewerbe Köln eV v Mars GmbH* (case C-470/93); and *Verband Sozialer Wettbewerb eV v Clinique Laboratoires SNC et Estee Lauder Cosmetics GmbH* (case C-315/92)) can fall within the notion of a product requirement, as can the incorporation in a product of material for the purpose of increasing sales. One example of this occurred in *Vereinigte Familiapress Zeitungsverlags- und Vertriebs GmbH v Heinrich Bauer Verlag* (case C-368/95).

> #### *Familiapress*
>
> The case concerned the Austrian prohibition on prize draws or competitions in periodicals. Although the CJ accepted that publishers would include such games in publications with the hope of increasing circulation, this was not enough to bring the rule within *Keck*: the prohibition concerned the content of a magazine and therefore was a requirement to be met. Since it was an indistinctly applicable measure, it could, however, be justified under the *Cassis de Dijon* rule of reason.

The common theme in these cases is that the rules in question impose a dual burden on the manufacturer or importer; product requirements seem implicitly to involve *de facto* discrimination through the imposition of extra costs.

The CJ summed the position up in *Morellato v Comune de Padova* (case C-416/00).

> #### *Morellato*
>
> This case concerned the requirement to package bread made from partially baked dough, but finished off on-site, before sale, such packaging to contain certain information. Here the CJ held that the prior-packaging requirement did not mean it was necessary to alter the product. The rules therefore concerned selling arrangements and would be acceptable provided they applied equally in law and in fact.

The CJ specified:

> the need to alter packaging or the labelling of imported products prevents such requirements from constituting selling arrangements [para 29].

The approach in this case hints at difficulties with the boundary between a product requirement and a rule relating to selling arrangements. What would the classification of a rule be, for example, if certain information was required but not included on the label, but national law would be satisfied by additional packaging?

The question of a packaging requirement arose in *Georg Schwarz v Bürgermeister der Landeshauptstadt Salzburg* (case C-366/04).

Schwarz

Austrian law required chewing gum to be packaged if it was to be dispensed via certain types of vending machine, whereas other Member States, specifically Germany, did not impose this requirement. Those manufacturers of gum established in a state where there was no such requirement would therefore have to go to the extra expense of packaging the gum to distribute in Austria. Without considering the question of a selling arrangement, the CJ assumed that Article 34 TFEU was triggered and went on to assess and accept the question of justification under Article 36 TFEU.

The decision suggests that the CJ thought that the rule could not benefit from the selling arrangement 'exception'. There is clearly a fine line to be drawn here. One distinction between *Morellato* and *Schwarz* is that the obligation in *Schwarz* could fall on the producer rather than the retailer. Whereas retailers can be seen as supplying goods from multiple origins in one place, manufacturers deal with one product, but subject to potentially many regimes.

One particular problem area is that of advertising. One might argue that it falls within the ambit of 'selling arrangement' rather than 'requirements to be met'; indeed in *Leclerc-Siplec v TF1 Publicité SA* (case C-412/93) the CJ held that legislation which prohibits television advertising in a particular sector concerns selling arrangements for the products in that particular sector. Therefore, as the CJ suggested in *De Agostini*, even an outright ban on the advertising of certain products—here toys—will not fall within what is now Article 34 TFEU provided always that such measures apply to domestically produced and imported products equally in law and in fact. Sales promotions forming part of the packaging, as the *Mars* case (discussed earlier) illustrates, will conversely constitute a product requirement. The boundary between the two situations—sales promotion/advertising constituting a 'selling arrangement' on the one hand and product characteristics (including packaging) on the other—will not always be easy to identify.

More recently, the CJ in *A-Punkt Schmuckhandels GmbH v Claudia Schmidt* (case C-441/04) held that a prohibition on the doorstep sale of silver jewellery was a selling arrangement and compatible with Article 34 TFEU. In *Commission v Germany (hospital pharmaceutical supply)* (case C-141/07) rules imposed on pharmacists supplying products to hospitals were selling arrangements, albeit rules which might not operate equally.

From this list, it seems rules relating to place of sale of particular products, as well as limitations as to who can sell them, should be seen as selling arrangements. Contrast *Banchero* (noted in Box 18.1), concerning limitation on who could sell tobacco, with *Klas Rosengren and Others v Riksåklagaren* (case C-170/04, decision of the Grand Chamber). *Rosengren* concerned the Swedish alcohol monopoly and the consequent restriction on private individuals importing alcohol directly from overseas suppliers. Whilst the alcohol monopoly might seem to be a restriction on who can sell the product, the CJ categorised it as an MEQR rather than a selling arrangement.

A difficult case is *Alfa Vita Vassilopoulos and Carrefour-Marinopoulos* (cases C-158-9/04 and C-82/05) which concerned town planning rules imposing construction restrictions with regard to bakeries and the machinery that they must have and which affected shops baking partially pre-baked bread supplied to those shops in frozen form. The CJ considered this requirement to be a product requirement, although the rules related to the place where such bread was sold and not the bread itself. The reason given for the decision is that the rules affect the process of production of the product. Perhaps this approach is in line with *Morellato* and *Schwarz* because of the point in the production process at which the impact of the rule is felt: the earlier in the production process, the more likely it is to affect the nature of the product. Whether this is convincing or not, is another question. Here, it is arguable that the rules should not have been considered to be a product requirement as they had no direct link with the content of the product itself; and the dual burden justification normally found with regard to product requirements—for example in *Mars*—is not easily found here. In this context, *Alfa Vita* could be seen as evidence of a contraction of the scope of application of the selling arrangement 'exception' found in *Keck*.

18.6.7 **Non-discrimination in Keck**

It is not clear the extent to which the *Keck* assumption that selling arrangements should fall outside Article 34 TFEU is undercut by the requirement that any such selling arrangements should apply equally in law and, crucially, in fact. It is rare that a rule does not apply equally in law. One example can be seen in *Valev Visnapuu v Kihlakunnansyyttäjä (Helsinki)* (case C-198/14).

Visnapuu

The Finnish Law on Alcohol required retailers of alcohol to have a licence; this rule constitutes an exception to the general principle in the Law on Alcohol that the state-owned enterprise for the sale of alcohol has a monopoly on the retail sale of alcoholic beverages. Considering the requirement to obtain a licence, the CJ noted that since the state monopoly did not require a licence, the requirement to obtain a licence did not apply to all traders (para 104).

More often, the rule applies to all traders, but does not affect them all in the same manner. This point was raised in *De Agostini*. There, the prohibition applied to all adverts, whether they related to imported products or not. It therefore operated equally in law. The difficult question of whether it operated equally in fact was left by the CJ to the national court, although the CJ did note that in some circumstances the only practicable way to break into a new market will be through such advertising. Implicitly, this suggests that it would be difficult for a rule limiting advertising to apply equally in practice.

The CJ has generally left the question of assessment of whether there is equal application in fact to the national courts (see, eg, *Burmanjer and Others* (case C-20/03)). The CJ itself undertook the assessment of the equal operation of the selling arrangement in law and in fact in *Schutzverband gegen unlauteren Wettbewerb v TK-Heimdienst Sass GmbH* (case C-254/98), however.

TK-Heimdienst

Under Austrian legislation bakers, butchers and grocers may offer goods for sale on rounds from door to door, provided such sales are made by traders who have a permanent establishment in that district or in a municipality adjacent to it and the sales relate to the type of goods sold at that establishment. This rule became the subject of proceedings and the question as to whether the rule was compatible with Article 34 TFEU was referred. The CJ found that the rules constituted a selling arrangement; it then went on to consider whether the rules applied equally in law and in fact. The fact that traders established in one part of Austria would also be affected in respect of home delivery services in other areas of Austria does not change this assessment.

For the CJ, what was important was that:

> the national legislation impedes access to the market of the Member State of importation for products from other Member States more than it impedes access for domestic products.

This approach to 'equality in fact' seems to bring us back to questions about access to the market, characteristic of pre-*Keck* jurisprudence.

The problem of the equal application of selling arrangements arose again in the context of Swedish rules limiting the advertising of alcoholic beverages to publications directed to point of sale and the trade press. In *Konsumentombudsmannen (KO) Gourmet International Products AB (GIP)* (case C-405/98), a publisher challenged these rules on the basis that they were contrary to Articles 34 and 56 TFEU. In its judgment, the CJ restated the test in *Keck* and, following *TK-Heimdienst* closely, reiterated an approach based on access to the market (para 18). It then noted that *De Agostini* accepted the possibility that a prohibition might have a greater impact on imports than on domestic products. The Court concluded:

> Even without its being necessary to carry out a precise analysis of the facts characteristic of the Swedish situation, which it is for the national court to do, the Court is able to conclude that, in the case of products like alcoholic beverages, the consumption of which is linked to traditional social practices and to local habits and customs, a prohibition of all advertising directed at consumers in the form of advertisements in the press, on the radio and on television, the direct mailing of unsolicited material or the placing of posters on the public highway is liable to impede access to the market by products from other Member States more than it impedes access by domestic products, with which consumers are instantly more familiar [para 21].

The CJ in this case seems to give the national court very little scope but to follow the CJ's view that the national rules here do not apply equally in fact. It should be noted that the CJ did not state that all advertising will necessarily fall within Article 34 TFEU; it clearly seeks to limit the impact of its judgment by linking the type of product to 'traditional social practices'. Nonetheless, both *Gourmet International Products* and *TK-Heimdienst* suggest that the selling-arrangement/product-requirement distinction proposed in *Keck* will not always answer the question of whether a measure falls outside the scope of Article 34 TFEU or not. The problem, as the CJ seems to be recognising, is that even selling arrangements may have an impact on trade.

It is not clear the degree of impact, actual or potential, that is required before a selling arrangement does not operate equally in fact. In *Deutscher Apothekerverband eV v 0800 DocMorris* (case C-322/01) the CJ noted in respect of a prohibition on the mail order sale of medicinal products that, despite the fact that it limited the ability of German pharmacies to gain access to the entire German market:

> [a] prohibition which has greater impact on pharmacies established outside the German territory could impede access to the market for products from other Member States more than it impedes access for domestic products [para 74].

On this basis, the selling arrangement did not apply equally in fact and therefore triggered an analysis under Article 34 TFEU. The wording the CJ uses in this case is broad. Although very similar to the test used in *TK-Heimdienst* and *Gourmet International Products*, it seems not to require an actual impact, but suggests that a potential effect would suffice. This approach suggests that the test for the equal application of selling arrangements is the same as the test used to identify an MEQR in the first place. If this is the case, it renders the *Keck* 'exception' nothing but a detour to come to the same place as an assessment of all rules would have done prior to *Keck*. It is hard to square this approach—or, indeed, that in *TK-Heimdienst* and *Gourmet International Products*—with that in the *infant milk* case (see Box 18.1), handed down shortly after *Keck*. The boundary of Article 34 TFEU seems to have moved, becoming more broadly drawn again.

Karner concerned the Austrian prohibition on misleading advertising in relation to the sale of goods via auction. In this case, the auction catalogue, including the (misleading) statement that the goods in issue were from an insolvent estate, was advertised on the Internet. By contrast to *De Agostini*, the national provision in this case was held not to constitute a total prohibition on all forms of advertising. Consequently, although the Court accepted that the prohibition could affect the total number of sales, it did not affect the marketing of products originating from other Member States more than it affects the marketing of products from the host Member State (para 42) (see also *Dynamic Medien*). Crucially, the CJ pointed to lack of evidence from those seeking to benefit from Article 34 TFEU as to the impact of the national rule. This approach, which implicitly requires an actual impact, does not seem entirely on all fours with the approach in *DocMorris*. It may well be that the different rules did have a differential impact on the facts, justifying a difference in treatment. Nonetheless, any unifying principles on which these judgments are based remain unclear.

18.6.8 Other categories of trading rule: 'Use Rules'

As we noted earlier, *Dassonville* was very broad and covered many areas of law. *Keck* identifies two subcategories: product requirements and selling arrangements and tells us how to treat them. The question is, do all rules fall within these two categories, or are there others? Part of the difficulties with *Alfa Vita* (18.6.6) seems to be the underlying assumption that the measure must fall into one or other of the categories. Presumably, there is scope for viewing rules as satisfying the *Dassonville* test without having to ascribe them either to a category of product requirement or selling arrangement. We might then question whether all rules falling in this third category are equally inimical to trade.

This question could arise in relation to rules relating to the use of a product. If the use of a product is prohibited, we can see that such a rule would deter consumers from buying such products with a potential impact on trade. Equally, a rule limiting the circumstances in which a product can be used (eg, a push bike not being allowed on a motorway) would have little impact on trade. It was suggested, by the Advocate-General in *Åklagaren v Mickelsson and Roos* (case C-142/05), that such rules should be treated as analogous to selling arrangements and that the crucial factor would be whether they applied equally in law and in fact. After that Opinion but before *Mickelsson* had been decided, the issue of a ban on the use of a product, that of tinted film for car windows, came before the CJ (*Commission v Portugal (tinted window film)* (case C-265/06)). In that case, the CJ concluded that the rules were MEQR, and proceeded to determine if they were justified; neither it nor the Advocate-General considered the issue of whether such rules should be treated akin to selling arrangements. This omission is perhaps not surprising: a total ban on a product's use has a direct impact on its marketing and sales. The CJ then followed its ruling in *tinted film* in *Mickelsson* and in another case involving 'use rules', the *motorbike trailers* case, thus establishing the proposition that they should not be treated as a form of selling arrangement. Indeed, in *Mickelsson*, the CJ arguably went further by holding that Article 34 TFEU also catches national rules that merely regulate how, where and when a product may be used.

In *Mickelsson*, the CJ held that the trigger for the application of Article 34 TFEU was the fact that a use restriction rule, 'may, depending on its scope, have a *considerable* influence on the behaviour of consumers, which may, in turn, affect the access of that product to the market of that Member State' (para 26 emphasis added). In *Bonnarde v Agence de Service et de Paiement* (case C-443/10), a case concerning rules relating to ecological subsidies available to demonstration vehicles, the CJ referred to its case law on use restrictions such as those in *Mickelsson*, but in so doing modified its previous approach. The CJ in *Bonnarde* referred to rules that 'may influence the behaviour of consumers' (para 30), omitting the requirement found in *Mickelsson* that a 'considerable influence' be required. While *Bonnarde* did not concern use rules itself, and may therefore be distinguished on that basis, if its approach as to the required level of influence on consumers' behaviour is followed as regards other cases concerning use rules, the scope of Article 34 TFEU would have been broadened.

The lack of consideration given by the CJ to the issue is unfortunate. While a complete ban on use no doubt has an impact, many use rules are not as extreme and variants of use rules are exceedingly common. Examples are the restriction of the sale of certain products (such as alcohol, cigarettes and solvents) to minors, or a ban on the use of a product in certain contexts, such as a ban on the use of mobile phones when driving. In *Countryside Alliance v HM Attorney General* ([2007] UKHL 52), the Supreme Court was faced with the question of whether the ban on hunting with dogs was caught by Article 34 TFEU. It thought the point questionable but opined that even were a restriction to be found such a restriction would be justified. No reference was made on this point. Whether one agrees with the approach of the CJ or prefers that of the Advocate-General in *Mickelsson*, depends on the purpose that is ascribed to Article 34 TFEU, a question which effectively takes us back to the debates before *Keck* (18.6.4).

18.6.9 **Alternative solutions**

Over the years other tests have been suggested. In addition to the approaches already discussed two main proposals arise: (1) a *de minimis* test; and (2) a remoteness test.

18.6.9.1 *De minimis*

A test of 'substantial' hindrance was suggested by Advocate-General Jacobs in *Leclerc-Siplec*, although the Court adopted a different approach in *Keck*. An approach which considers the impact of a measure, nonetheless, seems to have been favoured by the CJ in a number of cases. We have seen that in cases such as *TK-Heimdienst* and *Gourmet International Products*, the CJ has focused on the importers' ease of access to the markets of other Member States, rather than on the issue of whether a rule is a selling arrangement or not. In *DocMorris*, we also find references to ease of access to the market in the context of assessing whether the selling arrangement applies equally in fact. Indeed, in *Gourmet International Products*, the phrasing of the judgment is not in terms of discrimination but of access to the market. On one analysis, these rulings might not be too far from the *Keck* approach, in that *Keck* can be seen as distinguishing between measures which impact directly on the producer/importer and those which have an impact on consumers and thus only an indirect impact on the free movement rights.

18.6.9.2 **Remoteness**

On the other side of the coin, the CJ has also emphasised that the impact of national rules must not be too remote from inter-state trade. Two cases illustrate this point: *BASF AG v Präsident des Deutschen Patentamts* (case C-44/98) and *ED Srl v Fenocchio* (case C-412/97).

> ### BASF
>
> BASF tried to challenge a German law which, as permitted by the European Patent Convention, required patents that were granted by the European Patent Office in respect of Germany to be translated, at the patent proprietor's cost, into German. BASF argued that because of high translation costs, patent proprietors would be forced into choosing the countries in which to have patent protection as they would not be able to afford the translation costs for the entire Union. This, in turn, would affect patent proprietors' decisions about the Member States in which the patented product would be marketed, thus partitioning the internal market, contrary to Article 34 TFEU.

> ### ED Srl
>
> ED argued that Italian rules which precluded the obtaining of summary judgments against debtors who resided outside Italy would dissuade those resident in Italy from contracting with those who resided elsewhere, as debt recovery would be more difficult in respect of non-Italian residents. On this basis, it was argued that the rule should be regarded as incompatible with Article 35 TFEU as it would discourage exports.

In both cases the CJ gave these convoluted arguments short shrift, holding in both instances that the effect on Union law was too uncertain and indirect to constitute a measure having equivalent effect.

The CJ's approach in *BASF* and *ED Srl* was similar to that in the earlier case of *DIP SpA v Commune di Bassano del Grappa* (cases C-140–2/94), although with a different result. *DIP SpA* concerned a challenge to an Italian law permitting the opening of new shops in particular areas only on receipt of a licence, to be issued by municipal authorities on the recommendation of a local committee. The committee, which represented a variety of interest groups, made its recommendations according to specific criteria. Perhaps because the rule did not fall clearly within the category of either 'requirements to be met' or 'selling arrangements' the Court did not apply the *Keck* formulae. Instead it looked at the effect of the measure, and found its restrictive effect 'too uncertain and too indirect' for the obligation which it imposed to be regarded as hindering trade between Member States. It was thus compatible with Article 34 TFEU.

A similar approach has also been used in the context of freedom of establishment (see Chapter 22). These cases are unlikely to constitute a significant shift in the CJ's approach to the scope of Article 34 TFEU in which access to markets is clearly impeded. (Contrast *TK-Heimdienst* in which the Austrian government unsuccessfully tried to argue that the impact of the legislation there would be too uncertain.)

18.7 Prohibition, as between Member States, of quantitative restrictions on exports and of all measures having equivalent effect (Article 35 TFEU)

All the principles relating to imports under Article 34 TFEU will also apply to exports under Article 35 TFEU, including, as seems to have been accepted by the English courts in *International Trader's*

Ferry, the possibility of Member States being under positive obligations by virtue of Article 35 TFEU in conjunction with Article 4(3) TEU, with one important exception.

It seemed that there was a difference in approach between the scope of Articles 34 and 35 TFEU and that measures which are *indistinctly applicable* would not breach Article 35 TFEU merely because they are capable of hindering, directly or indirectly, actually or potentially, intra-Union trade. The *Dassonville* test did not apply, but rather, a test set down in *PB Groenveld (PB) BV v Produktschap voor Vee en Vlees* (case 15/79).

Groenveld

Here, a national law prohibiting the large-scale manufacture of horsemeat sausages and limiting the sale of such sausages by small specialist butchers to consumers only, designed to safeguard exports of such products to countries which prohibit the sale of horseflesh, was found, not to breach Article 35 TFEU, although, as Advocate-General Capotorti pointed out, it presented an almost insuperable obstacle to exports.

The CJ held that to breach Article 35 TFEU such measures must have as their specific object or effect the restriction of patterns of exports and thereby the establishment of a difference in treatment between the domestic trade of a Member State and its export trade in such a way as to provide a particular advantage for national production or for the domestic market of the state in question, at the expense of the production or of the trade of other Member States. Thus there is a double test: not only must there be a 'measure' but it must benefit the domestic market. In other words, they must be overtly or covertly protectionist. The Court's judgment represented a clear departure from the Opinion of the Advocate-General. He had approached the matter along the lines of Article 34 TFEU; he applied the *Dassonville* test, and *Cassis de Dijon*, and found that the measure was not justified since other, less restrictive measures, such as labelling, could have been used to achieve the same ends.

On the other hand measures which are *distinctly applicable* and which discriminate against exports *will* normally breach Article 35 TFEU. In *Procureur de la République v Bouhelier* (case 53/76) the requirement in France of an export licence, following a quality inspection, for watches destined for export was held to breach Article 35 TFEU since the same inspection and licences were not required for watches sold on the domestic market.

The principles of both *PB Groenveld BV* and *Bouhelier* were applied in *Jongeneel Kaas BV*. Here Dutch rules, indistinctly applicable, regulating the quality and content of cheese produced in the Netherlands were found not to breach Article 35 TFEU, even though domestic producers were thereby at a competitive disadvantage vis-à-vis producers from other states not bound by the same standard of quality, since they did not fall within the *PB Groenveld BV* criteria, whereas a distinctly applicable rule requiring inspection documents for exports alone was, following *Bouhelier*, in breach of Article 35 TFEU. This approach was reiterated, for example in *Ravil SARL v Bellon import SARL and Biraghi SpA* (case C-469/00).

The Court's tolerance towards indistinctly applicable, non-protective restrictions on exports introduced in *PB Groenveld BV* is in line with the Court's attitude, noted earlier, towards reverse discrimination. Clearly where there is no danger of protectionism the Court can afford to take a more lenient view. Restrictions on imports, on the other hand, will always raise a suspicion of protectionism. Nonetheless, it seems that there has been a move away from the 'double' test, even if *Groenveld* is the CJ's starting point for cases concerning exports. This approach can be seen in the Grand Chamber decision in *Lodewijk Gysbrechts, Santural Inter BVBA* (case C-205/07).

Gysbrechts

The case concerned a Belgian rule which prohibited vendors from asking for customers' credit card details before the expiry of a cooling off period, even if the vendor undertook not to take payment prior to the end of that period. The CJ accepted that this could constitute a measure having equivalent effect to a quantitative restriction on exports as it deprives traders of an efficient tool with which to guard against the risk of non-payment. The CJ noted a discriminatory effect as such a rule would fall particularly on those who sold direct to consumers in other Member States where transactions were of a small pecuniary value. Thus even if the prohibition on asking for credit card numbers applies to all, it has a greater impact on exports. The CJ then concluded that there was a prohibited MEQR within the scope of Article 35 TFEU, without considering whether there had been an advantage to the domestic market.

It is hard to spot such an advantage in the facts of this case, suggesting that Article 35 TFEU is now being interpreted more broadly. In *Kakavetsos-Fragkopoulos AE Epexergasias kai Emporias Stafidas v Nomarchiaki Aftodioikisi Korinthias* (case C-161/09) this trend was re-emphasised, as the CJ used the *Dassonville* formula rather than the *Groenveld* test: any measure likely to impede, directly or indirectly, actually or potentially, intra-Union trade constitutes a measure having equivalent effect to a quantitative restriction on exports (para 27). This broad approach to Article 35 TFEU based in particular on *Gysbrechts* is continuing, as can be seen in the case of *New Valmar v Global Pharmacies Partner Health* (case C-15/15).

New Valmar

New Valmar, a Belgian company, entered into an agreement for the sale of its products in Italy with Global Pharmacies Partner Health, an Italian company. A dispute arose in relation to the payment of invoices during the course of which a question was referred to the CJ. The question concerned the compatibility of a Belgian law, which required that invoices must be drafted in Dutch, with Article 35 TFEU.

Relying on *Gysbrechts*, the CJ assessed whether there was an impact on trade. It found that there was: disputes about invoices were likely to arise when the parties to a contract were not free to choose the language in which those invoices should be submitted. This legal uncertainty constituted a barrier to trade which would be likely to deter the initiation or continuation of contractual relationships with an undertaking established in the Dutch-speaking region of the Kingdom of Belgium and which was more likely to affect cross-border trade than trade between undertakings established there.

The Court concluded that these effects were not too remote or uncertain to fall within the scope of the prohibition in Article 35 TFEU.

Since only protective or discriminatory measures were thought to breach Article 35 TFEU, it was usually also thought that a rule of reason will not be applied and justification can only be sought under Article 36 TFEU. The beginnings of a change in approach can be seen in *Schmidberger*, where the CJ discussed the justification for a 'measure' within Article 35 TFEU in conjunction with that for a MEQR within Article 34 TFEU. This reasoning suggests that similar principles should be used in assessing derogations from Article 34 and 35 TFEU. The CJ did not, however, address the point directly. In *Lodewijk Gysbrechts*, however, it stated unequivocally that:

[a] national measure contrary to Article [35 TFEU] may be justified on one of the grounds stated in Article [36 TFEU], and by overriding requirements of public interest, provided that the measure is proportionate to the legitimate objective pursued [para 45].

It likewise considered consumer protection, a mandatory requirement, in *Kakavetsos-Fragkopoulos AE Epexergasias kai Emporias Stafidas*, thereby reaffirming the position. Article 35 TFEU now seems to be being interpreted much more in parallel with Article 34 TFEU, though there is still no equivalent of the *Keck* approach here.

18.8 State monopolies (Article 37 TFEU)

18.8.1 Meaning of 'monopoly'

The bodies subject to Article 37 TFEU are those through which 'a Member State, in law or in fact, either directly or indirectly, supervises, determines or appreciably influences imports or exports between Member States' (Article 37(1), para 2).

To qualify as a monopoly it is not necessary to exert total control of the market in particular goods. It is sufficient if the bodies concerned have as their object transactions regarding a commercial product which could be traded between Member States, if they play an *effective* part in such trade (*Costa*).

It seems that state monopolies must be used for the pursuit of a public-interest aim; therefore, the object of Article 37 TFEU is to reconcile the desire of a Member State to do so with the need to maintain the internal market (*Harry Franzén* (case C-189/95)). It is not clear whether monopolies which do not pursue a public-interest aim are compatible with the provisions on the free movement of goods, although it is arguable that state restrictions on granting a monopoly to a body could be characterised as 'selling arrangements' under *Keck* and *Mithouard* (contrast the approach in the *infant milk* case and *DocMorris*).

A state monopoly within the scope of Article 37 TFEU may also exist where an exclusive right to export or import particular goods is given to one body (*Pubblico Ministero v Manghera* (case C-59/75)). However, Article 37 TFEU does not apply where retailers in a Member State need to be authorised to sell a product, such as tobacco (*Banchero*). This is subject to the proviso that the state does not interfere with the *supply* of the goods to be sold and leaves the retailers free to choose the source of the product.

18.8.2 Prohibition on discrimination on grounds of nationality

Article 37 TFEU prohibits discrimination on the grounds of nationality in the operation of the state monopoly. Its aim is not to abolish monopolies per se, but rather to ensure that they do not operate in a discriminatory manner. The overriding objective is to ensure that obstructions to the free movement of goods and distortions of competition within the Union as a result of such a monopoly are kept to a minimum. In *SA des Grandes Distilleries Peureux v Directeur des Services Fiscaux de la Haute-Saône* (case 119/78), rules regarding the French monopoly for the distillation of raw materials were held to be discriminatory and contrary to Article 37(1) TFEU because they prohibited the use of raw materials imported from another Member State. In contrast, in *Franzén*, Swedish provisions on the existence and operation of the monopoly retailer of alcoholic beverages were found to be compatible with Article 37 TFEU. The existence of this monopoly was not of concern, provided that it was set up in such a way that it was not more difficult for suppliers from other Member States to sell alcohol in Sweden.

Subsequently another Swedish monopoly, one concerning the retail sale of medicinal preparations, was successfully challenged (*Krister Hanner* (case C-438/02)). The Court reiterated its position that Article 37 TFEU does not require the abolition of state monopolies; it controls the way they operate. In this instance, the contract establishing the monopoly did not provide for either a purchasing plan or a system of calls for tender which would provide an opportunity for producers of products that are not selected by the monopoly to find out why and, possibly, to challenge the decision. Here, the state monopoly had absolutely free choice as to the products it would stock. The CJ held that the agreement did not therefore ensure that discrimination was ruled out. On this basis the state monopoly's system for selecting the products to stock is liable to place products from other Member States at a disadvantage. It was therefore, in principle, contrary to Union law.

18.9 Relationship with other Treaty provisions

18.9.1 Article 34 TFEU

Article 37 is part of Title I, Chapter 2 of the TFEU on prohibitions of quantitative restrictions between Member States. It is as noted complementary to Articles 34 and 35 TFEU. However, in contrast to these two provisions, it does not benefit from the equivalent of the Article 36 TFEU derogation (see Chapter 19), and it may therefore be important to identify whether a particular provision is subject to the free movement provisions or the state monopoly provision.

It has been held that Article 37 TFEU only applies to activities that are intrinsically connected with the specific business of the monopoly (*SA des Grandes Distilleries Peureux*). However, related activities may be subject to Article 34 TFEU. In *Franzén*, it was argued that the Swedish alcohol monopoly was contrary to both Articles 34 and 37 TFEU. The CJ drew a distinction between those provisions which related to the existence and operation of the monopoly itself, which would be subject to Article 37 TFEU, and provisions which were separable from the operation of the monopoly but which had a bearing on it. The latter would be subject to assessment under Article 34 TFEU. The provisions at issue in *Franzén* concerned both the monopoly itself and the requirement for importers of alcohol to hold a licence. The monopoly itself was not contrary to Article 37 TFEU, but the requirement of an import licence fell foul of Article 34 TFEU and could not be justified under Article 36 TFEU.

18.9.2 Other provisions

Article 37 TFEU only applies to state monopolies in the provision of goods. It does not apply to services. However, if a state monopoly exists in the provision of services, and operates in a discriminatory manner, then it may be caught by the general prohibition against discrimination on grounds of nationality in Article 18 TFEU. It may also be subject to the provisions on the free movement of services (Articles 56–62 and 102 TFEU), which prohibits the abuse of a dominant position. To the extent that there is a comparable provision regarding services, this is Article 106 TFEU, which deals with the provision of services of general economic interest (see also Chapter 28).

18.10 Conclusions

This chapter illustrates the importance of the jurisprudence defining the scope of the prohibition on measures having an equivalent effect to quantitative restriction. The key question is the relationship between free movement and national regulatory competence. This question is affected by the scope of the derogation principles (Chapter 19) and by positive harmonisation measures (Chapter 16). In addition to these provisions, there is also Article 37 TFEU. Although there is very little jurisprudence on Article 37 TFEU, it nevertheless fulfils an important function in ensuring that the free movement of goods in the common market is not restricted any more than is justifiable.

As far as this chapter is concerned, the central problem relates to how to determine the scope of Article 34 TFEU. The CJ's case law has not always been consistent and it seems that during the development of the Union different approaches have been taken ranging from tests based on discrimination, access to the market and the more formalistic approach under *Keck*. Behind all of these runs the underlying questions of how much regulation of trade (and trade-related matters) is desirable and who gets to choose the form of that regulation. With the single market, if not actually completed, being in a more developed phase than when *Dassonville, Cassis de Dijon* and even *Keck*, were handed down, one remaining question is whether the internal market should tolerate more regulation and greater divergence or less.

Further reading

Arnull, A, 'What shall we do on Sunday?' (1991) 16 EL Rev 112.

Ankersmit, L, 'What if Cassis de Dijon were Cassis de Quebec? The assimilation of goods of third country origin in the Internal Market' (2013) 50 CML Rev 1387.

Barents, R, 'New developments in measures having equivalent effect' (1981) 18 CML Rev 271.

Crespo van de Kooij, A, 'The private effect of the free movement of goods: Examining private-law bodies' activities under the scope of Article 34 TFEU' (2013) 40 LIEI 363.

Dawes, A, 'A freedom reborn? The new yet unclear scope of Article 29 EC' (2009) 34 EL Rev 639.

Di Cicco, L, 'The *Visnapuu* case: the narrow interpretation of article 37 TFEU and the consequent failure in the application of the "certain selling arrangements" doctrine' (2016) 43 LIEI 309.

Gormley, L, 'Actually or potentially, directly or indirectly? Obstacles to the free movement of goods' (1989) 9 YEL 197.

Gormley, L, 'Inconsistencies and misconceptions in the free movement of goods' (2015) 40 EL Rev 925.

Horsley, T, 'Unearthing buried treasure: art.34 TFEU and the exclusionary rules' (2012) 37 EL Rev 734.

Jansson, M and Kalimo, H, 'De Minimis meets "Market Access": Transformations in the Substance—and the Syntax—of EU Free Movement Law?' (2014) 51 CML Rev 523.

Mortelmans, K, 'Article 30 of the EEC Treaty and legislation relating to market circumstances: Time to consider a new definition?' (1991) 28 CML Rev 115.

Oliver, P, *Free Movement of Goods in the European Union*, 5th edn (Hart Publishing, 2010).

Quinn, M and McGowan, N, 'Can Article 30 impose obligations on individuals?' (1987) 12 EL Rev 163.

Reich, N, 'The November revolution: Keck, Meng, Audi revisited' (1994) 31 CML Rev 459.

Roth, WH, Casenote on *Keck* and *Hünermund* (1994) 31 CML Rev 845.

Snell, J, 'The notion of market access: A concept or a slogan?' (2010) 47 CML Rev 437.

Spaventa, E, 'Leaving *Keck* behind? The free movement of goods after the rulings in *Commission v Italy* and *Mickelsson and Roos*' (2009) 34 EL Rev 914.

Steiner, J, 'Drawing the line: Uses and abuses of Article 30 EEC' (1992) 29 CML Rev 749.

Szydho, M, 'Export Restrictions within the Structure of Free Movement of Goods: Re-consideration of an old Paradigm' (2010) 47 CML Rev 753.

Weatherill, S, 'After *Keck*: Some thoughts on how to clarify the clarification' (1996) 33 CML Rev 885.

Wennerås, P and Moen, KB, 'Selling arrangements, keeping *Keck*' (2010) 35 EL Rev 387.

White, E, 'In search of limits to Article 30 of the EEC Treaty' (1989) 26 CML Rev 235.

Wils, WPJ, 'The search for the rule in Article 30: Much ado about nothing?' (1993) 18 EL Rev 475.

Woods, L, *Free Movement of Goods and Services in the European Community* (Ashgate, 2004), chs 4–6.

Woods, L, 'Consistency in the Chambers of the European Court of Justice: A case study on the free movement of goods' (2012) 31 CJQ 338.

19 Derogation from the free movement of goods

19.1 Introduction

The previous chapter has explored and emphasised the width of the fundamental principle of the free movement of goods. Article 36 TFEU contains the treaty exception to this principle. Judge-made exceptions have also been developed via the 'rule of reason' in *Cassis de Dijon*. The relationship between principle and exception is about the balance between different policy interests. It determines the scope of Member States' freedom to regulate, whatever the purpose of that regulation. Final review of the scope of Article 36 TFEU or the rule of reason remains at the Union level. Two general points can be made about the CJ's approach. First, as with other freedoms, the CJ has held that any derogation must be interpreted narrowly. Secondly, the CJ has developed the notion of proportionality, found in other areas of EU law to ensure that where a legitimate interest exists, Member States do not try to use it to hide measures that are essentially restrictions on trade.

19.2 Outline of Article 36 TFEU

The principal provision for derogation from Articles 34 and 35 TFEU is Article 36 TFEU, which provides:

> The provisions of Articles 34 and 35 shall not preclude prohibitions or restrictions on imports, exports or goods in transit justified on grounds of public morality, public policy or public security; the protection of health and life of humans, animals or plants; the protection of national treasures possessing artistic, historic or archaeological value; or the protection of industrial and commercial property. Such prohibitions or restrictions shall not, however, constitute a means of arbitrary discrimination or a disguised restriction on trade between Member States.

We saw in Chapter 18 that with *Cassis de Dijon* the CJ introduced the 'rule of reason' allowing national measures additionally to be justified on public interest grounds not mentioned in the Treaty. The substantive scope of the rule of reason is discussed at 19.5.

19.2.1 **Relationship with the 'rule of reason' under *Cassis de Dijon***

The rule of reason as laid down in *Cassis de Dijon* was not set out in terms that confined it to indistinctly applicable measures. Shortly after *Cassis de Dijon*, in *Gilli (Italian cider-vinegar case)* (case 78/79), the Court suggested (para 14) that the principle applied only where national rules apply *without discrimination* to both domestic and imported products, a distinction that it has reiterated (*Aragonesa de Publicidad Exterior and Publivía v Departmento de Sanidad y Seguridad Social de Cataluña* (cases C-1 and 176/90), para 13). Justification of a distinctly applicable measure by reference to *Cassis de Dijon*-style reasoning was tried in *Commission v Ireland (restrictions on importation of souvenirs)* (case 113/80).

Irish Souvenirs

Here the Irish government sought to justify, on *Cassis de Dijon* principles, an order requiring that imported souvenirs be marked 'foreign', or with their country of origin, arguing that the measure was necessary in the interests of consumers and fair trading—to enable consumers to distinguish the 'genuine' (home-produced) souvenirs from the (imported) 'fakes'. The Court held that since the measure applied only to imported souvenirs it could not be judged on *Cassis de Dijon* principles. It could only be justified on the grounds provided by Article 36 TFEU. Since that article created an exception to the principle of free movement of goods, it could not be extended to situations other than those specifically laid down. The measure could not be justified in the interests of consumer protection.

The distinction between indistinctly and distinctly applicable measures therefore assumes significance in terms of the justifications on which Member States may rely when national measures have been found to constitute a MEQR.

Problematically, the CJ has not consistently insisted on this distinction, and has also been inconsistent as to where the boundary between distinctly and indistinctly applicable measures lies (*Commission v Belgium (walloon waste)* (case C-2/90)—prohibition on tipping waste originating from another Member State; *Aher-Waggon v Germany* (case C-389/96)—domestic restrictions on noise emissions from aircraft; *Commission v Austria (prohibition of heavy lorries)* (case C-320/03), all concerning environmental justifications). In many cases concerning indistinctly applicable measures, the CJ has not considered the issue and, perhaps because the line between the two is not always clear, has dealt with the question of justification of indistinctly applicable measures not on *Cassis de Dijon* principles but under Article 36 TFEU (see *Officier van Justitie v Sandoz BV* (case 174/82); more recently, the *hospital pharmacy supply* case). There appear to be two possible reasons for this approach: first, the Court is merely responding to questions submitted by national courts under Article 267 TFEU; secondly, where the 'mandatory requirement' falls under one of the specific heads of derogation provided by Article 36 TFEU, the Court may prefer to rely on the express provisions of that article (see, eg, *Commission v Germany (German sausages)* (case 274/87)—health justification and *Ditlev Bluhme*—protection of biodiversity and the environment/health and life of animals).

The issue is more problematic when a distinctly applicable measure is in issue, as according to cases such as *Aragonesa de Publicidad Exterior and Publivía Cases* and the *Irish souvenirs* case, such measures are limited to the grounds of derogation in Article 36 TFEU. Advocate-General Jacobs in the case of *PreussenElektra AG v Schleswag AG* (case C-379/98) criticised the *walloon waste* case and suggested that the CJ should abandon the distinction between distinctly and indistinctly applicable measures and allow even discriminatory measures to be capable of justification by reference to mandatory requirements, at least where environmental protection is concerned. The ECJ, however, disregarded the suggestions of the Advocate-General, and came to the conclusion that the national rules, which were aimed at encouraging the use of electricity produced from renewable energy sources, did not contravene Article 34 TFEU in the first place. The issue continues to arise, as illustrated by the Grand Chamber ruling in *Ålands Vindkraft v Energimyndigheten* (case C-573/12).

Ålands Vindkraft

Under Swedish law, approved producers are awarded an electricity certificate for each megawatt-hour of green electricity produced; in practice the certificates are awarded only to domestic producers. The certificates are tradable. The demand for electricity certificates stems from the fact that electricity suppliers and certain users are under an obligation to hold, and to surrender to the State on 1 April of each year, a certain number (quota) of certificates corresponding to a proportion of the total quantity of electricity supplied or consumed during the preceding year, with a payment due if insufficient certificates are held. The purchase price for electricity certificates is passed on by the supplier to the consumer.

Ålands Vindkraft sought approval from the competent Swedish authority for the Oskar wind farm—located in the Åland archipelago in Finland—with a view to being awarded electricity certificates. This was refused on the basis that the wind farm was not in Sweden. Ålands Vindkraft claimed this constituted a barrier to trade.

The Court agreed that the measure was an MEQR but did not consider whether it was indistinctly applicable or not. In looking at justification, the Court held:

> The Court has consistently held that national legislation or a national practice that constitutes a measure having equivalent effect to quantitative restrictions may be justified on one of the public interest grounds listed in Article 36 TFEU or by overriding requirements [para 76].

It reiterated the point at para 77:

> According to settled case-law, national measures that are capable of hindering intra-Community trade may inter alia be justified by overriding requirements relating to protection of the environment.

In this, it seems not to recognise that there are state measures (ie distinctly applicable ones) in respect of which mandatory requirements may not be used. Conversely, one might argue that because it accepted Swedish reliance on mandatory requirements, the Court did not view the measure as a distinctly applicable rule. In a subsequent case, *Canadian Oil Company Sweden AB and Anders Rantén v Riksåklagaren* (case C-472/14), which concerned the requirement to register certain chemical products irrespective of whether the products were domestically manufactured or imported, the Advocate General restated the position to be that to benefit from the environmental mandatory requirement, a measure must be indistinctly applicable. The Court, however, quoted para 77 of its judgment in *Ålands Vindkraft* approvingly (para 45) but without clarifying whether the distinction made by the Advocate General remained valid. The Court seems reluctant to address the issue of whether the distinction should stay.

19.3 Proportionality and disguised restriction on trade

Although the grounds listed in Article 36 TFEU appear extensive they have been narrowly construed. The Court has held on many occasions that the purpose of this article is not to reserve certain matters to the exclusive jurisdiction of the Member States; it merely allows national legislation to derogate from the principle of free movement of goods to the extent to which this is, and remains, justified to achieve the objectives set out there (*Commission v Germany (health control on imported meat)* (case 153/78)). A measure is 'justified' if it is necessary, and no more than is necessary, to achieve the desired result (the proportionality principle). There are two elements to satisfy:

- suitability test;
- necessity test.

Both must be satisfied. Thus if a measure is not appropriate to attain the objective or the same objective can be achieved by less restrictive measures, then the national measure will be found to be disproportionate.

The CJ has held that a restrictive measure is suitable for securing the attainment of the objective only if it genuinely reflects a concern to attain that objective in a consistent and systematic manner, which seems to be a question about the consistency of the policy adopted. (See, eg, *Commission v Austria (Austrian lorry case)* (case C-28/09); *Scotch Whisky Association*—measures imposing minimum price on alcohol one of forty measures to tackle alcohol abuse, discussed in Chapter 18.)

Differences between Member States in the level of protection accepted do not automatically mean that a measure is disproportionate. As Member States may choose the level of protection that they wish to award to a public interest objective, legitimate differences can arise from this fact. Thus the assessment of national provisions is assessed solely by reference to the objective pursued and the level of protection which the Member State in question intends to provide.

Moreover, Article 36 TFEU cannot be relied on to justify rules or practices which, though beneficial, are designed primarily to lighten the administrative burden or reduce public expenditure, unless in the absence of such rules or practices the burden of expenditure would exceed the limits of what can reasonably be required (*Officier van Justitie v de Peijper* (case 104/75)).

In the *Scotch Whisky Association* challenge to rules imposing minimum alcohol prices, the Court accepted that a rule, which had the very specific aim of increasing the price of cheap alcoholic drinks, was capable of reducing the consumption of alcohol, in general, and more specifically the hazardous or harmful consumption of alcohol, given that those who drink to excess purchase, to a great extent, cheap alcoholic drinks. Nonetheless, it was not proved that these objectives could not be attained by measures which had less impact on the free movement of goods—for example, by increasing duty on alcoholic beverages. While a Member State does not have to go so far as to prove that there is no other conceivable measure that could enable the legitimate objective pursued to be attained under the same conditions, it still needs to adduce evidence and analysis to support its claims for a derogation.

The enquiry under Article 36 TFEU is very similar to that conducted in applying the rule of reason introduced in *Cassis de Dijon*. In applying the rule of reason to the facts in *Cassis de Dijon*, the Court found that the German law was in breach of Article 34 TFEU. Although the measure aimed at an acceptable goal being enacted in the interests of public health (to prevent increased consumption resulting from lowering the alcoholic content of cassis) and the fairness of commercial transactions (to avoid giving the weak imported cassis an unfair advantage over its stronger, hence more expensive, German rival), the measure was not *necessary* to achieve these ends. Other means, such as labelling, which would have been less of a hindrance to trade, could have been used to achieve the same ends. Thus the word 'necessary' has been interpreted to mean no more than is necessary—that is, subject to the principle of proportionality. An early example can be seen in *Walter Rau Lebensmittelwerke v De Smedt PVBA* (case 261/81).

> ### Walter Rau
>
> Here a Belgian law requiring margarine to be packed in cube-shaped boxes, allegedly introduced in the interests of consumers, to enable them to distinguish margarine from butter, was held to be in breach of Article 34 TFEU. The same objective could have been achieved by other means, such as labelling, which would be less of a hindrance to trade.

Similar arguments have been used successfully to challenge national rules, allegedly in the interest of public health and consumer protection, concerning the permitted ingredients of pasta (*Drei Glöcken GmbH v USL Centro-Sud* (case 407/85)) and sausages (*German sausages*). In *Rocher* a German law prohibiting 'eye-catching' price comparisons in advertisements, designed to prevent consumers from being misled, was held to be disproportionate on the grounds that such advertisements were forbidden *whether they misled the public or not*. It was implied that a ban on *misleading* price comparisons would have been acceptable.

This approach applies even if the public objective aimed at is the protection of fundamental human rights. It is an open question as to whether the CJ uses, or should use, exactly the same test in this regard (*Dynamic Medien*, see also 19.4.2 and Chapter 6), especially given the broad range of rights found in the EU Charter.

> ### Dynamic Medien
>
> In this case, the CJ held that rules which prohibit the mail-order sale of image storage media which have not been examined and classified by the competent national authority for the purposes of protecting young persons and which do not bear a label from that authority indicating the age from which they may be viewed, would be proportionate, unless the procedure for examination, classification and labelling is not readily accessible or cannot be completed within a reasonable period, or that a decision of refusal is not open to challenge before the courts.

As well as being appropriate and necessary, measures must comply with the second sentence of Article 36 TFEU; they must not 'constitute a means of arbitrary discrimination or a disguised restriction on trade between Member States'. Discrimination will be regarded as arbitrary if it is not justified on objective grounds. Even where a legitimate purpose can be identified, should the manner in which the Member State implements its rules benefit domestic producers, the CJ may view this as a disguised restriction on trade. The presumption in favour of goods lawfully marketed in one of the Member States of the Union means that a state seeking to rebut that presumption must itself prove that the conditions for the application of Article 36 TFEU are satisfied. (See cases discussed at 19.4.4.)

19.4 Grounds for derogation under Article 36 TFEU

19.4.1 Public morality

The public morality ground was considered in two English cases, *Henn and Darby* and *Conegate Ltd v Customs and Excise Commissioners* (case 121/85).

Henn and Darby

In *Henn and Darby*, Article 36 was invoked to justify a ban on the import of pornographic materials. To a certain extent the ban was discriminatory, since not all pornographic material of the kind subject to the ban was illegal in the UK. In the UK it was illegal only if likely to 'deprave or corrupt', whereas under UK customs legislation, import was prohibited if the goods were 'indecent or obscene'. On a reference from the British Supreme Court, the CJ found that the ban was in breach of Article 34 TFEU but was justified under Article 36.

Although the measure was discriminatory, the discrimination was not arbitrary. Nor was it a disguised restriction on trade between Member States; there was no lawful trade in such goods in the UK. The measure was genuinely applied for the protection of public morality, not for the protection of national products. It was for each state to determine in accordance with its own scale of values the requirements of public morality in its territory.

The CJ took a stricter view in *Conegate*.

Conegate

Article 36 TFEU was invoked to justify the seizure by HM Customs and Excise of a number of inflatable rubber dolls euphemistically described as 'love dolls', together with other exotic and erotic articles imported from Germany, on the grounds that they were 'indecent and obscene'. The importers claimed the seizure was in breach of Article 34 TFEU, and, since there was no ban on the manufacture and sale of such items in the UK (the sale was merely restricted), it was discriminatory. Their argument succeeded before the CJ.

The Court held that the seizure was not justified under Article 36, since, unlike *Henn and Darby*, there was no general prohibition on the manufacture and marketing of such goods in the UK; nor had the state adopted serious and effective measures to prevent the distribution of such goods in its territory. (Similar reasoning has been applied in the sphere of free movement of persons, see Chapter 25.)

Thus, while Member States retain the freedom to regulate in the area of public morality, in cases such as this, the implication that the national measure is in fact a disguised restriction on trade will preclude the Member State from successfully relying on the derogation in Article 36 TFEU.

19.4.2 **Public policy**

This potentially wide ground has been strictly construed, and has rarely succeeded as a basis for derogation under Article 36 TFEU. However, in *Thompson* a restriction on the import and export of gold collectors' coins was held to be justified on the grounds of public policy, since the need to protect the right to mint coinage was one of the fundamental interests of the state. More recently, it seems that the test developed under the free movement of people in the case of *R v Bouchereau* (case 30/77) is being used across the four freedoms. Thus the CJ will seek to identify if there is a sufficiently serious threat to one of the fundamental interests of society in issue. The CJ has accepted that the need to prevent or detect crime may also fall within public policy. Examples include the need to prevent dealing in stolen cars (SCP *Boscher, Studer et Fromentin v SA British Motors Wright and Others* (case C-239/90)) or to combat fraud in connection with export funds (*Germany v Deutsche Milchkontor* (case C-426/92)). Thus, Member States retain the discretion to determine the issues which as a matter of public policy need tackling, but it is important to note that public order (and public security) cannot be defined solely by reference to the national legal system; it is certainly not enough to state that a matter is a criminal offence in a particular Member State to justify a restrictive national measure. Public policy cannot be invoked solely on the grounds that the activity which the impugned national measure seeks to curb carries criminal sanctions (*Prantl*). Indeed, in many cases, as in *Prantl* itself, Article 34 TFEU has proved a valid defence to a criminal charge.

Unsurprisingly, the Court has repeatedly stated that public policy cannot provide a clause of general safeguard (the *ban on pork imports* case) and can never be invoked to serve purely economic ends (*Commission v Italy (advance payments for imports)* (case 95/81)). In *Evans Medical* it found that a prohibition against the importation into the UK without a licence of the drug diamorphine could not be justified by the need to maintain the economic viability of the sole licensed manufacturer of the drug in the UK, although it might be permitted on public-health grounds to ensure that a country has reliable supplies for essential medical purposes. *Evans Medical* indicates that financial consideration may affect legitimate public-policy concerns, although the precise circumstances in which the CJ would accept this sort of argument are unclear. In *Deutsche Parkinson Vereinigung eV* German rules setting down fixed prices for the sale by pharmacies of prescription-only medicinal products for human use were challenged in the context of an online pharmacy offering discounted prices for members of an association supporting those with Parkinson's disease. While the Court accepted that protecting physical pharmacies, which provided more assistance to consumers especially in emergency situations, from ruinous price competition is important, it was not convinced that the rule did not go beyond this objective; specific evidence must be adduced in support of this argument which had not been provided.

Another question is the extent to which Member States must take action against public protests which affect inter-state trade. In the *angry farmers* case widespread public demonstrations in France prevented foreign produce from reaching local markets. The CJ found that the French authorities, in failing to take any significant action against these demonstrations, despite repeated requests from the Commission, had failed in their obligations under the TFEU. Since they had adduced no evidence justifying this failure, they could not rely on the public-policy derogation under Article 36 TFEU.

In *Schmidberger*, which concerned protests about the environmental impact of excessive road transport, the CJ accepted that the need to protect human rights fell within public policy, an approach which it also implicitly took in *Dynamic Medien*. *Dynamic Medien* concerned a challenge to German rules which precluded the direct sale by mail order of DVDs and similar products to children if the product had not been examined and classified by the competent German authority. The CJ noted that the objective of the measure was the protection of children, an objective recognised by international human rights law in the UN Convention on the Rights of the Child. Whilst the CJ did not expressly state that the rights of the child formed part of public policy (and, indeed, the UK suggested this might be a matter of public morality), it was discussed in that context, and including human rights protection within public policy seems to be common to the other freedoms too (see, eg, *Omega Spielhallen*, discussed in Chapter 6). Whether the standard proportionality text would be applied in such a case, or whether the CJ would adopt a balancing test as it did in the case of *Schmidberger*, seems uncertain. Whilst the proportionality test requires the national measure to be no more than necessary to achieve the objective, it is submitted that a balancing test gives greater emphasis to the value of fundamental rights and is therefore to be preferred.

Even where a public-policy justification appears to be legitimate, as in *Campus Oil Ltd v Minister for Industry and Energy* (case 72/83) (see 19.4.3) in which Advocate-General Slynn was prepared to accept a public-policy justification, the Court has in the past preferred to base its judgment on other grounds. It seems that public policy will be an exception of last resort.

19.4.3 **Public security**

The CJ has held that public policy and public security are independent concepts, but the boundary between them is not completely clear. In the *tinted window film* case, the Advocate-General suggested that the distinction used in some national systems between crime prevention (public security) and punishment (public policy) need not be transferred to the Union level. It would seem that in most cases where there is doubt, argument is made on both grounds and, again, any derogation is interpreted narrowly.

Public security was successfully invoked in *Campus Oil* to justify an Irish order requiring importers of petroleum oils to buy up to 35 per cent of their requirements of petroleum products from the Irish National Petroleum Co (INPC), at prices to be fixed by the minister. The measure was clearly discriminatory and protective. The Irish government argued that it was justified, on public-policy and public-security grounds, to maintain a viable national refinery that would meet essential needs in times of crisis. The Court found it in breach of Article 34 TFEU but, contrary to the view of the Commission, justifiable on public-security grounds, since its purpose was to maintain the continuity of essential oil supplies. Petroleum products, the Court held, are of fundamental importance to a country's existence, since they are needed not only for the economy, but for the country's institutions, its vital services and the survival of its inhabitants. The Court stressed that purely economic objectives would not provide justification under Article 36 TFEU, but provided the measure was justified on other grounds the fact that it might secure economic objectives did not exclude the application of that article. As to whether the measures were necessary, the Court held that a compulsory purchase requirement would be justified only if the output of the INPC refinery could not be freely disposed of at competitive prices, and the compulsory prices only if they were competitive in the market concerned; if not, the financial loss must be borne by the state, subject to the prohibition on state aids.

The reasoning in *Campus Oil* was much criticised and has not been successfully argued since. In *Procureur de la République v Cullet* (case 231/83), which concerned similar rules, the Advocate-General went to some lengths to distinguish the case from *Campus Oil*. In another case involving oil refineries, the CJ found the national rules in issue disproportionate (*Commission v Greece (importation, exportation and marketing of crude oil and petroleum products)* (case 347/88)). (See also position with regard to capital: 20.4.1.) Given the increasing possibility that fuel supplies may run low, it may be that the issue of fuel security will arise more frequently and as a more pressing matter.

19.4.4 **Protection of the health and life of humans, animals and plants**

This is a potentially broad head of derogation containing three separate groups of interests: those of humans, those of animals and those of plants, and covering a range of concerns. In some respects there are links between these issues and environmental considerations (eg, the *Danish bee* case: *Ditlev Bluhme*, see further below). The CJ has repeatedly held that the health and life of humans rank foremost among the assets or interests protected by Article 36 TFEU. The CJ has noted the importance of this ground of derogation beyond the confines of human health—including, for example, some aspects of animal or environmental protection. In *Nationale Raad van Dierenkwekers en Liefhebbers VZW, Andibel VZW v Belgium* (case C-219/07) (prohibition on holding mammals of certain species), the CJ stated 'the protection of the health and life of animals constitutes a fundamental requirement recognised by [Union] law'. The CJ has also recognised that 'more often than not, damage to the environment or to health cannot, by reason of its nature, be eliminated retroactively'. (See, eg, *Commission v Germany* (case C-114/04) concerning pharmaceutical products.) In the *Austrian lorry* case, which concerned national rules seeking to reduce air pollution, the CJ noted the 'transversal and fundamental nature of those objectives' (para 121). The EUCFR notes the need to integrate a high level of health protection into EU policies (Article 35 EUCFR) as well as a high level of environmental protection (Article 37 EUCFR). This latter provision reflects Article 3(3) TEU.

It is for the Member States, within the limits imposed by the Treaty, to decide on the degree of protection which they wish to afford to public health and on the way in which that degree of protection is to be achieved. Although this seems to afford Member States considerable discretion, and variance between the levels of protection chosen by the various Member States is permitted, in practice there are limitations on this discretion. So, while discriminatory measures for which justification may be sought on health grounds may include bans, tests and inspections of imports to ensure that domestic standards are met, and licensing or documentary requirements to provide evidence of this fact, to succeed on this ground it is necessary to prove a real health risk (see also *Duphar BV*) and the burden of proof falls on the Member State (see, eg, *Ahokainen and Leppik v Virallinen syyttäjä* (case C-434/04)—national legislation prohibiting, without prior authorisation, the importation of undenatured ethyl alcohol of an alcoholic strength of more than 80 per cent).

A Member State will not succeed where the exporting state maintains equivalent standards and those standards are adequate to meet that risk. In *Commission v UK (UHT milk)* (case 124/81) the Court found that a requirement that UHT milk should be marketed only by approved dairies or distributors (allegedly to ensure that milk was free from bacterial or viral infections), which necessitated the repacking and retreating of imported milk, was not justified, since there was evidence that milk in all Member States was of similar quality and subject to equivalent controls. Although the measure was prima facie indistinctly applicable, the Court considered it to be discriminatory in effect and examined it for its compatibility with Article 36 TFEU. (See also *Decker* regarding the need to maintain the quality of medical products.)

In contrast, in *Rewe-Zentralfinanz eGmbH v Landwirtschaftskammer* (case 4/75) a plant health inspection applied only to imported apples, designed to control a pest called San José scale, which was clearly in breach of Article 34 TFEU, was found to be justified on health grounds, since the imported apples constituted a real risk which was not present in domestic apples. Although discriminatory, the discrimination was not arbitrary. (Although the inspection was justified, the charge for the inspection was not, since Article 36 TFEU is not available to justify a charge: *Rewe-Zentralfinanz eGmbH* (case 39/73) (discussed in Chapter 17).)

More recently in *Ditlev Bluhme*, a prohibition on the import onto the island of Læsø of Danish domestic bees and reproductive material for them was held to be justified under Article 36 TFEU. The aim of the measure was to protect an indigenous population that was in danger of disappearance as a result of cross-breeding with other bee species. The CJ held that by seeking to protect biodiversity through ensuring the survival of a distinct indigenous species, the measures protect the life of those animals.

The health justification has often failed on proportionality grounds. In *Ahokainen and Leppik* the CJ left it to the national court to assess whether the national rules were such as to combat effectively abuse arising from the consumption of spirits as a drink, or whether less restrictive measures could ensure a similar result. In the view of the CJ, the national court was in a better position to assess the facts that were pertinent to such a decision.

In a number of instances public health measures have been viewed as constituting 'arbitrary discrimination or a disguised restriction on trade between Member States'. In the *UHT milk* case, in addition to the marketing restrictions, UHT milk coming into the UK required a specific import licence. The Court found both requirements disproportionate; it was not necessary to market the products in that way, and the information gleaned from processing the licensing applications could have been obtained by other less restrictive means, for example, by declarations from importers, accompanied if necessary by the appropriate certificates. For similar reasons in

Commission v UK (imports of poultry meat) (case 40/82) a specific import licence requirement for poultry and eggs, allegedly designed to prevent the spread of Newcastle disease, was found not to be justified. Yet in *Commission v Ireland (protection of animal health)* (case 74/82), which also concerned Newcastle disease, a similar import-licence requirement was permitted under Article 36 TFEU on account of the exceptionally high health standards of Irish poultry, a standard which was not matched by British flocks. The Court said it was necessary in each case to weigh the inconvenience caused by the administrative and financial burden against the dangers and risks to animal health. Thus it may be difficult to predict when a specific import-licence requirement will or will not be justified.

In the *British imports of poultry meat* case the same licensing system was found to result in a total ban on imports from six Member States. The Court found that the measure did not form part of a seriously considered health policy and operated as a disguised restriction on trade between Member States. Similar protectionist motives were discovered in *Commission v France (Italian table wines)* (case 42/82). Here the Court found excessive delays in customs clearance of wine imported from Italy into France, pending analysis of the wine to ensure it complied with French quality standards. While it conceded that some analysis in the form of random checks, resulting in minor delays, might be justified, the measures taken by the French, which involved systematic checks greatly in excess of those made on domestically produced wine, were both discriminatory and disproportionate.

Cases concerning pharmaceuticals and other medicinal products have been shown a greater leniency on the part of the Court, especially when there is no evidence of a protectionist motive, perhaps because of the particularly high value accorded to human health. In *Royal Pharmaceutical Society* the Court found that the rules of the Society prohibiting the substitution by pharmacists of other equivalent drugs for proprietary brands prescribed by doctors, although clearly discriminatory in the effect on imports, were justified to maintain patients' confidence and to avoid the 'anxiety factor' associated with product substitution (see also *Lucien Ortscheit GmbH v Eurim-Pharm Arzneimittel GmbH* (case C-320/93)).

Although there have been a number of harmonising directives in the field of pharmaceuticals and similar products, the area is not exhaustively regulated at EU level. There is still then room for the Treaty derogation as we can see in *DocMorris*. The case concerned, inter alia, the sale via mail order of prescription goods. The CJ accepted that Article 36 TFEU could apply to such a restriction given the risks attaching to such products, the need to ensure the patient understands how to use them and the need to ensure that prescriptions reach their intended recipient (para 119). Against this background, it is worth noting that the CJ in the more recent *Ker-Optika* case (see also Chapter 18) held that the Hungarian legislation governing the sale of contact lenses, although appropriate for attaining a public health objective, went beyond what was necessary to achieve it, that is, it was disproportionate. In coming to this conclusion, the CJ focused in particular on the requirement that a customer must be physically present to have his eyes examined, and that follow-up advice be provided in person and deemed them both unnecessary. This determination is not consistent with the approach it took in the much earlier *Laboratoire de Prothèses Oculaires (LPO) v Union Nationale des Syndicats d'Opticiens de France and Others* (case C-271/92), which also concerned conditions of supply of contact lenses. *Ker-Optika* suggests a slight hardening of the CJ's approach to the proportionality of medical justifications, which can be seen again in *Deutsche Parkinson Vereinigung eV* (also discussed at 19.4.2).

Another argument was put forward in *DocMorris*, that the German system to which the Dutch mail-order suppliers were not subject, obliged pharmacies to stock a range of drugs at certain prices. The control of prices was necessary to ensure the functioning of part of the German health system. This is a different kind of public-health argument, one that is linked to the provision of a public service (see also Chapters 24 and 28). Nonetheless the CJ has accepted the argument, at least in principle, here and in other cases. Thus, in *DocMorris*, the CJ held:

> Although aims of a purely economic nature cannot justify restricting the fundamental freedom to provide services, it is not impossible that the risk of seriously undermining the financial balance of the social security system may constitute an overriding general-interest reason capable of justifying a restriction of that kind (see *Kohll*, para 41; *Vanbraekel*, para 47; *Smits and Peerbooms*, para 72; and case C-358/99 *Müller-Fauré and Van Riet* [2003] ECR I-4509, paras 72 and 73). Moreover, a national market for prescription medicines could be characterised by non-commercial factors, with the result that national legislation fixing the prices at which certain medicinal products are sold should, in so far as it forms an integral part of the national health system, be maintained [para 122].

Crucially in *DocMorris*, the German government had not put forward any arguments on this point and so the Court dismissed the point for that reason.

In cases where it is unclear whether a product or additive is safe (and there is no Union legislation on the point), it is possible for individual Member States to restrict the sales of such products, provided that there is a swift and accessible authorisation procedure available. Further, if an authorisation procedure leads to a refusal of authorisation, that decision must be open to challenge before the courts (see, eg, *Greenham v Abel* (case C-95/01); *Commission v France (additives to cheese)* (case C-344/90)). While the CJ has emphasised that Member State discretion in the context of public health is particularly wide, any such measure must be proportionate, and the Court will expect to see evidence in this regard, rather than bare assertions as to the existence of the risk (see, eg, *Monsanto Agricoltura Italia and Others v Presidenza del Consiglio dei Ministri and Others* (case C-236/01)—(safety assessment regarding food from GMOs).

The prohibition in the *Danish bee* case (*Ditlev Bluhme*) was also found to be proportionate. In that case, as well as there being no protectionist motive, the CJ highlighted the fact that the measures formed the basis of a mechanism recognised in international law for the protection of species—the establishment of a conservation area.

19.4.5 Protection of national treasures possessing artistic, historic, or archaeological value

So far these grounds have not been used successfully to provide a basis for derogation under Article 36 TFEU, but it was suggested in the *export tax on art treasures* case that a desire to prevent art treasures leaving the country would have justified a quantitative restriction, even though it could not justify a charge. It is thought that it would normally apply to restrictions on exports. There is also now a directive governing the return of cultural property (Directive 93/7/EC) to complement Regulation 116/2009 ([2009] OJ L39/1), which deals with the export of cultural goods from Member States to third countries.

The CJ has, on a number of occasions, held that cultural diversity does not fall within this heading, but rather must be considered as a mandatory requirement under the rule of reason (*Edouard Leclerc*—concerning minimum book prices, approved by the Advocate-General in *Fachverband der Buch-und Medienwirtschaft v LIBRO Handelsgesellschaft mbH* (case C-531/07)). Since Maastricht, Article 167 TFEU has provided:

> The Union shall take cultural aspects into account in its action under other provisions of this Treaty, in particular in order to respect and to promote the diversity of its cultures.

The inclusion of this provision, and the protection awarded to cultural and linguistic diversity by Article 22 EUCFR does not seem to have extended the scope of the derogation under Article 36 TFEU.

19.4.6 **Protection of industrial and commercial property**

The exception provided by Article 36 TFEU for industrial and commercial property has perhaps been one of the most litigated heads of derogation. It is noteworthy in three main respects.

First, it constitutes the grant of a derogation in respect of actions of private individuals, the intellectual property rights holders; the national law granting the intellectual property rights is protected as a result of Article 345 TFEU. It provides that:

> This Treaty shall in no way prejudice the rules in Member States governing the system of property ownership.

Secondly, the nature of intellectual property rights (which is effectively the groups of rights to which 'industrial property' in Article 36 TFEU refers) is such that they often operate (or can be used) to partition the market; they thus run counter to the basic notion of the internal market.

The third significant point is that the doctrine of proportionality, which is central in the assessment of the acceptability of derogations under other grounds and, indeed, in respect of the rule of reason, rarely arises here (an exception is the case of *Donner* (case C-5/11) concerning *criminal* penalties for copyright infringement), or at least not expressly. It may be that the limitations imposed by the specific subject matter of the right operate to fulfil the same function, or that the exercise of rights beyond those limitations implicitly constitutes a disguised restriction on trade.

Given the possible impact of intellectual property rights on the internal market, the CJ has thus had to reconcile these competing notions. It has done so by developing two main doctrines:

- specific subject matter;
- doctrine of exhaustion

19.4.6.1 **Specific subject matter**

The first doctrine posits that there is a difference between the existence of the right and its exercise. Whilst the former is a matter of national law and protected, the latter is subject to review to ensure that protection claimed by holders of property rights does not exceed the central area protected by the property rights, its 'specific subject matter'. The scope of Article 36 TFEU in this regard was considered in *Deutsche Grammophon Gesellschaft mbH v Metro–SB–Grossmärkte GmbH & Co KG* (case 78/70).

Deutsche Grammophon

Deutsche Grammophon (DG) was seeking to invoke German copyright law to prevent the defendant wholesalers from selling DG's Polydor records, previously exported to France, in Germany. Since a prohibition on reimport would clearly breach Article 34 TFEU, the matter fell to be decided under Article 36. Arguing from the second sentence of that Article, that 'prohibitions or restrictions shall not . . . constitute a means of arbitrary discrimination or a disguised restriction on trade between Member States' the Court concluded that the provision permitted prohibitions or restrictions on the free movement of goods only to the extent that they were justified for the protection of the rights that form the *specific subject matter of the property*.

The Court drew a distinction between the *existence* of industrial property rights, which falls within the specific subject matter of the right and remains unaffected by EU law, and their *exercise*, which may come within the prohibition of the Treaty. The specific subject matter will vary depending on the type of right in issue (eg, trade-marks, see *SA CNL-SUCAL v Hag GF AG (Hag II)* (case C-10/89) (see further 19.4.6.3); on copyright see *Radio Telefis Eireann v Commission (Magill)* (case C-241–2/91P), discussed in Chapter 29). If copyright protection is used to prohibit in one Member State, the marketing of goods brought on to the market by the holder of the rights, or with his consent, in the territory of the other Member State (ie to prevent what are known as 'parallel' imports) *solely* because the marketing has not occurred in the domestic market, such a prohibition, maintaining the isolation of the national markets, conflicts with the essential aim of the Treaty, the integration of the national markets into one uniform market. Thus it would constitute an improper *exercise* of the property right in question and would not be justified under Article 36 TFEU. (See the position with regard to services, Chapter 25.)

19.4.6.2 Exhaustion of rights

The second doctrine which the Court has applied is the doctrine of exhaustion. It was expressed in *Centrafarm BV v Sterling Drug Inc* (case 15/74) and *Centrafarm BV v Winthrop BV* (case 16/74), in the context of a claim for infringement of patents and trade-marks respectively, as a guarantee that the owner of the trade-mark or patent has the exclusive right to use that trade-mark or patent, for the purposes of putting into circulation in the EU products protected by the trade-mark or patent *for the first time*; either directly, or by the grant of licences to third parties. Once the protected product has been put on the market in a particular Member State by or with the consent of the owner, or by a person economically or legally dependent on him, such as a licensee, a subsidiary, a parent company or an exclusive distributor (but not an assignee of trade-mark rights, see further *IHT Internationale Heiztechnik GmbH v Ideal-Standard GmbH* (case C-9/93)), he can no longer rely on national property rights to prevent its import from that state into other Member States. His rights have been exhausted. The CJ has held that it is not permissible to rely on the right to place goods on the market for the first time to prevent the importation of goods lawfully manufactured in one Member State into the territory of another Member State where the goods have not yet been put into circulation but are in transit in order to be placed on the market of a non-Member State (in this instance, Poland prior to its accession) (*Administration des Douanes et Droits Indirects v Rioglass* (case C-115/02) (concerning spare parts for cars)).

This doctrine of 'exhaustion of rights' has been applied by the Court to trade-marks (*Winthrop BV*), patents (*Sterling Drug Inc*), industrial designs (*Keurkoop BV v Nancy Kean Gifts BV* (case 144/81)) and subject to some qualification due to its special nature (see *Warner Brothers Inc v Cristiansen* (case 158/86); *Coditel v Cine Vog Films* (case 62/79)), copyright (*Musik-Vertrieb Membran GmbH v GEMA* (cases 55 and 57/80)).

19.4.6.3 Role of consent

The underlying assumption in the exhaustion doctrine is that the owner has consented to the marketing of the products. Thus, in *Merck & Co Inc v Stephar BV* (case 187/80), the exhaustion principle was applied where the patent owner had sold his product in Italy, where there existed no system of patent protection. The Court held that having allowed the goods to be sold in Italy, he must accept the consequences as regards free circulation in the Union.

In contrast, where a product has been sold under a compulsory licence, without the consent of the owner, the latter is entitled under Article 36 TFEU to rely on his property right to prevent the marketing in a third Member State of that product resulting from the exploitation of the compulsory licence, since, not having consented to its use, he is still entitled to enjoy the substance of his exclusive licence (*Pharmon BV v Hoechst AG* (case 19/84); see also *Thetford Corp v Fiamma SpA* (case 35/87)). Similarly, where the manufacturing or marketing of a product is lawful in a Member State, *not* through the owner's consent but because of the expiry of the protection period provided for industrial property rights under the law of that Member State, a person with exclusive rights in that product in another Member State may prevent the import of the protected product into the Member State in which he holds these rights (*EMI Electrola GmbH v Patricia* (case 341/87), which concerned rights of reproduction and distribution of musical works).

Where a product has been put lawfully on the market in a particular Member State with the owner's consent and the period of protection permitted under national law in that state has *not* expired, its import into another Member State may not be restrained, even though the purpose of an attempt to prevent importation is to prevent parties taking advantage of different price levels in different Member States, whether the reason for the price differences be government policy, legislation or ordinary market forces (*Centrafarm BV v American Home Products Corporation* (case 3/78); *GEMA*).

One gloss on the idea of consent should be noted which arises in the context of company restructuring. In *Hag II*, the Hag company which owned the trade-mark for Hag coffee was split following World War II, resulting in two companies which legitimately owned the trade-mark. In *Hag II*, the Belgian company tried to stop the import into Luxembourg (where it owned the trade-mark) of coffee bearing the Hag mark but manufactured by the German Hag company. The CJ held (contrary to its ruling in the first *Hag* case) that in the absence of consent to a product being marketed or manufactured in another Member State, a trade-mark owner could take action to protect the trade-mark against imported goods.

This situation can be contrasted with *Ideal-Standard* in which the Court had to decide whether a *voluntary* assignment to an independent undertaking of trade-mark rights in Ideal-Standard products in Germany, originating from a French subsidiary of IHT (USA), would exhaust the rights of the owner of the same trade-mark rights in Germany, which was also a subsidiary of IHT (USA). The CJ held that the principle of exhaustion of rights only applied where the owner of the trade-mark in the importing state and the owner of the trade-mark in the exporting state were the same, or where, even if they are separate persons, they are economically linked, for example, as licensee, parent company, subsidiary or exclusive distributor. It did not apply where trade-mark rights have been assigned to an unrelated enterprise such that the assignor and related enterprises no longer have control.

In the absence of consent, the essential concept for the purposes of exhaustion of rights, replacing the concept of common origin, is unitary control. In the absence of consent, or unitary control, guaranteeing uniform standards, there will be no exhaustion of rights.

19.4.6.4 Goods from outside the EU

The principles outlined above will only apply to trade within the Union. Where parties seek to assert their property rights to prevent goods from third countries from entering the Union, the free movement provisions of Articles 34 and 36 TFEU do not apply (*EMI Records Ltd v CBS United Kingdom Ltd* (case 51/75), *Generics UK Ltd v Smith Kline and French* (case C-191/90), *Silhouette International Schmied GmbH & Co KG v Hartlaner Handelsgesellschaft mbH* (case C-355/96)—this last case concerned the Trade Marks Directive).

19.5 Rule of reason

We saw in Chapter 18 and at 19.2 that the CJ introduced the idea of a 'rule of reason' with its decision in *Cassis de Dijon*. For indistinctly applicable national measures, this is an additional basis on which Member States may argue that such measures are justified referring to 'mandatory requirements' or matters of overriding public interest. *Cassis de Dijon* concerned consumer protection, but in that decision the CJ listed other possible public interest grounds of derogation from free movement, such as fairness of commercial transactions and public health. While these can be seen as linked to the facts in *Cassis de Dijon*, the wording of the CJ's ruling there made it clear that the list of mandatory requirements is not closed, and, indeed, this is a key advantage of the *Cassis de Dijon* line of case law. Thus, the CJ has accepted that a wide range of issues could be protected in this way (see Box 19.1).

Box 19.1 Examples of matters of overriding public interest

Oebel—working conditions

Cinéthèque SA—culture

Commission v Denmark (disposable beer cans) (case 302/86)—environment

Torfaen—socio-cultural characteristics

Vereinigte Familiapress—diversity of the press

Dynamic Medien—protection of young people

As noted at 19.3, the rule of reason is also subject to the proportionality test, which takes more or less the same form as under Article 36 TFEU.

19.6 Derogation provisions other than Article 36 TFEU

In addition to the rule of reason and Article 36 TFEU there are further specific provisions of the Treaty allowing for derogation from the principles of Articles 34 and 35 TFEU, mainly in the field of economic and commercial policy; hence the Court's refusal to allow Article 36 TFEU to justify purely economic measures. These comprise:

- measures to meet short-term economic difficulties (Article 121 TFEU);
- measures to meet balance of payment difficulties (Articles 130–2 and 219 TFEU).

Measures taken under the above articles are required to be taken either by the Commission or the Council (on a proposal from the Commission), or, if taken by Member States, subject to authorisation or approval by the Commission. They are subject to strict EU control. As with measures taken under Article 36 TFEU, they must comply with the proportionality principle.

Derogation is also permitted *in the interests of national security* (Articles 346–7 TFEU). Under Article 346(1) (b) TFEU, a state:

> may take such measures as it considers necessary for the protection of the essential interests of its security which are connected with the production of or trade in arms, munitions and war material

provided that such measures do not adversely affect competition within the internal market regarding products which are not intended for military purposes. As the CJ made clear in the context of Greek support for naval shipyards (*Ellinika Nafpigeia AE v Commission* (case C-246/12P)), this provision must be interpreted strictly (para 37); it is not for the Member States to determine its scope. Here, the shipyard was not engaged exclusively in the building of warships, but also engaged in civilian projects. The CJ confirmed that the protection under Article 346 TFEU must not adversely affect competition in relation to products which are not intended for specifically military purposes. Under Article 347 TFEU, Member States may consult with each other and take steps to counteract measures taken by a Member State in the event of war or the threat of war or serious internal disturbances, or to carry out obligations undertaken for the purpose of maintaining peace or international security. Should the Commission or a Member State consider that a Member State is making improper use of its powers under Articles 346–7 TFEU, they may bring that state before the Court under Article 348 TFEU. In *Ellinika Nafpigeia*, the CJ agreed that only aid measures covering military activity should be assessed under the special procedure laid down by Article 348 TFEU. It would seem that for these provisions, as for Article 36 TFEU, where there is an EU measure covering the specific subject, a Member State cannot rely on the derogation provided in the Treaty itself. In *R v HM Treasury, ex parte Centro-Com Srl* (case C-124/95), for example, the UK sought, on the basis of the UN sanctions against Serbia and Montenegro, to prevent the payments of sums held in a London bank account by a Montenegrin to an Italian company. The CJ, however, pointed out that this issue was dealt with by an EU regulation and that the UK could thus not rely on the national security exception in Article 347 TFEU.

19.7 Conclusions

In the area of the derogation from free movement, the CJ has sought to reconcile the tension between the needs of the internal market and those of the individual Member States, a task that is not always easy to accomplish. The approach of the CJ has interpreted the scope of the derogation provisions narrowly. Although the CJ has shown some willingness to accept a Member State's assessment of when a public-interest issue arises, as can be seen in the sphere of public policy, public health and even as regards the existence of intellectual property rights, it has stringently assessed whether any national measures are necessary or whether such measures constitute a disguised restriction on trade. In this context the principle of proportionality has been central even in the context of the protection of human rights. Thus, despite Treaty amendments and grand political statements, it seems that the internal market and trade concerns continue to be high priorities, a state of affairs which means that the protection offered through harmonising legislation (Chapter 16) remains important.

Further reading

Alexander, W, 'IP and the free movement of goods: 1996 caselaw of the ECJ' (1998) 29 IIC 16.

Castillo de la Torre, F, 'Trade marks and free movement of pharmaceuticals in the European Community: To partition or not to partition' (1997) 6 EIPR 304.

Eisenhut, D, 'The special security exemption of Article 296 EC: Time for a new notion of "essential security interests"?' (2008) 33 EL Rev 577.

Ludwig, R and O'Gorman, R, 'A cock and bull story? Problems with the protection of animal welfare in EU law and some proposed solutions' (2008) 20 J Env L 363.

Poncelet, C, 'Free movement of goods and environmental protection in EU law: A troubled relationship?' (2013) 15 International Community Law Review 171.

Weatherill, S, 'Regulating the internal market: Result orientation in the House of Lords' (1992) 17 EL Rev 299.

Weatherill, S, 'Casenote on *Gallaher*' (1994) 19 EL Rev 55.

Woods, L, *Free Movement of Goods and Services in the EC* (Ashgate, 2004), Ch 7.

20 Free movement of payments and capital

20.1 Introduction

The free movement of capital is one of the four freedoms listed in Article 26(2) TFEU. Yet, its treatment had been somewhat different from the liberal approach taken both in the secondary legislation and by the CJ regarding the free movement of persons, services and goods. Indeed, in striking contrast to its approach to these freedoms, the CJ ruled that the original pre-Maastricht capital provisions did not have direct effect (*Casati* (case 203/80)) and could therefore not be relied on before domestic courts (see Chapter 5). The changes introduced by the Treaty of Maastricht changed the position significantly. The relevant provisions are now Articles 63–6 and 75 TFEU.

This chapter will cover the scope of the provisions of the free movement of capital and payments as well as their derogations and the relationship with the other freedoms. For the sake of completeness, given the relationship between movement of capital and monetary union, there will be a brief introduction to the euro and monetary union. A full discussion of this topic, however, lies outside the scope of this book.

20.2 Outline of provisions relating to the free movement of capital

The 'fourth' freedom, capital, can be broken down into two linked elements:

- capital;
- payments.

Article 63 TFEU prohibits all restrictions on the free movement of capital and payments, whether between Member States or between Member States and third countries. Derogations are found in the Treaty and through the development of a rule of reason. In this parallels can be drawn with the other freedoms. There are, however, some aspects which are specific to the free movement of capital, such as the difference in treatment between TCNs and EU nationals, as well as the distinction between Eurozone members and non-members.

20.3 Scope of the free movement of capital

20.3.1 Who can rely on the free movement of capital?

Union nationals, both natural and legal persons, may rely on this freedom. Like the provisions relating to the free movement of goods, and in contrast with the provisions relating to services and people, the capital provisions may be relied on by TCNs. The situation is the same whether the capital movement is intra-Union, or between a third country and the Union.

20.3.2 Direct effect

Article 63 TFEU is directly effective: see *Bordessa* and *Sanz de Lera and Others* (cases C-163, 165 and 250/94). This is the case whether we are considering prohibitions on restrictions on capital movements between Member States or between Member States and third countries and irrespective of the type of capital in issue. Nevertheless, case law suggests that Article 63 TFEU has no horizontal direct effect (*Commission v Germany (Volkswagen)* (case C-112/05); *Federconsumatori v Commune di Milano* (case C-463/04), see also Chapter 5; but note *Commission v Belgium (Eurobonds)* (case C-478/98), discussed in 20.3.3). Issues such as capital restrictions naturally involve the state and so in general give rise to vertical relationships, so the issue of the horizontal effect of that provision will rarely arise. Yet, it is possible to envisage a situation falling within the scope of capital in which private actors are involved. Imagine, for example, a bank or a building society, which offered different mortgage rates depending on whether or not the borrower was resident in the Member State of its operations.

20.3.3 Types of act caught

The CJ has taken a broad approach to the types of act caught by the prohibition in Article 63 TFEU. This was the case even before the Maastricht amendments to the capital provisions. In *Brugnoni and Ruffinengo v Cassa di Risparmio di Genova e Imperia* (case 157/85), the CJ accepted that 'restriction' covered more than just legislative acts, and also covered administrative obstacles to free movement. Equally, it seems not to matter in which capacity a government is acting when a potential restriction under Article 63 TFEU is in issue. This can be seen in the context of the *Eurobonds* case.

> ### *Eurobonds*
>
> Here, the case related to a prohibition on Belgian residents subscribing to securities issued abroad (Eurobonds). The Belgian government argued that it was acting not in its capacity as public authority but on the same terms as a private borrower when it adopted the restriction. The CJ rejected this argument on the facts of the case, although the status of measures not dependent on public powers remains open.

Finally, a regulation which implements economic sanctions as part of the fight against terrorism and prohibits the transfer of economic resources to individuals in third countries, does not fall within the ambit of the provisions on free movement of capital and payments (*Kadi*, para 188, discussed in Chapter 4).

20.3.4 **Meaning of capital**

The prohibition operates on both capital movements and those relating to payments. This could suggest that the two concepts are different, and indeed, early case law, *Luisi and Carbone v Ministero del Tesoro* (case 286/82), distinguished between the two. The need to distinguish between the two has effectively been removed.

Neither term is defined in Article 63 TFEU, although Article 64 TFEU lists some types of capital, such as direct investments and the provision of financial services. This provision has not, however, been referred to by the CJ in determining the scope of 'capital'. In terms of defining capital, the CJ held in *Trummer v Mayer* (case C-222/97) that the prohibition on the creation of a mortgage in a foreign currency under Directive 88/361 ([1988] OJ L178/5), passed before the changes brought in by Maastricht, remained relevant in terms of identifying what constitutes capital. An annex to this Directive contains an indicative 'nomenclature' (a list of categories), listed under 13 headings (eg, property investment, mortgages, administration of real property, sale of real property, inheritances, banknotes and coins, gifts in money, granting credit). As the CJ made clear, this list is not exhaustive. This point is illustrated in the case of *Staatssecretaris Van Financiën v Verkooijen* (case C-35/98).

Verkooijen

Here, the case related to the exemption from direct taxation of the share of dividends. The CJ ruled that the receipt of dividends from investments abroad, a category not listed in the nomenclature, was inextricable from a capital movement and therefore fell within the scope of Article 63 TFEU. Further, it has also held that an inheritance, whether of money, or immovable or movable property, is a movement of capital for the purposes of Article 63 TFEU. Of course, real property cannot move; what is changing is the ownership of that property.

Potentially the scope of Article 63 TFEU *et seq* is wide, especially as the nomenclature in Directive 88/361 includes not only the capital movement itself but also the underlying transaction (see, eg, heading VIII 'Financial Loans and Credits'). This approach opens up the possibility of overlap between the free movement of capital and the freedom to provide services, affecting particularly financial services (see further 20.5).

20.3.5 **Test for application of free movement of capital**

The concept of a 'restriction on the free movement of capital' has been interpreted broadly. It operates to eliminate measures which effectively prevent an individual being able to use a currency of another Member State, such as in *Trummer* and it applies to less stringent measures, such as the requirement for prior authorisation of currency transactions.

The CJ has described the scope of the prohibition in Article 63 in *Festersen* (case C-370/05) as:

> restrictions on the movement of capital, include those which are likely to discourage non-residents from making investments in a Member State or to discourage that Member State's residents to do so in other States [para 24].

Nonetheless, the CJ has not always distinguished clearly between restrictions and discrimination when handing down its judgments. This can be seen in *Commission v Portugal (Portuguese golden shares)* (case C-367/98).

Portuguese Golden Shares

Here, the CJ accepted that the Portuguese national rules precluding investors from other states from acquiring more than a specified number of shares in certain newly privatised companies constituted 'unequal treatment of nationals of other Member States and restricts the free movement of capital' [para 40].

This is a case of direct discrimination. Similarly, in *Konle*, an Austrian rule, which in the interests of planning control exempted Austrian nationals only from having to obtain authorisation before acquiring a plot of land was seen as creating a discriminatory restriction against nationals of other Member States. Even in this case, however, the CJ linked the existence of discrimination to the creation of a restriction. In other cases the CJ has used terms such as 'obstacles' or 'liable to dissuade' (*Trummer*). These phrases seem similar to the approach taken in relation to the freedom to provide services (see Chapter 22). In the British *golden shares* case (regarding the UK government's 'Special Share' in BAA plc), the CJ noted that even rules which apply without distinction to non-nationals and nationals alike can 'deter investors from other Member States from making such investments and, consequently, affect access to the market' (*Commission v United Kingdom* (*golden shares*) (case C-98/01), para 47). In *Commission v Portugal* (*second Portuguese golden shares*) (case C-543/08) (shares in privatised energy company), the CJ elaborated:

national measures must be regarded as 'restrictions' within the meaning of Article [63(1) TFEU] if they are liable to prevent or limit the acquisition of shares in the undertakings concerned or to deter investors of other Member States from investing in their capital [para 47].

This phraseology has been repeated in *Van Hilten-van der Heijden v Inspecteur van de Belastingdienst/ Particulieren/Ondernemingen buitenland te Heerlen* (case C-513/03), para 44.

Van Hilten-van der Heijden

Here, the case related to national rules creating the legal fiction that a national of a Member State who dies within ten years of ceasing to reside in that Member State is deemed to have been resident there at the time of his death. The CJ ruled that this was not contrary to Article 63 TFEU).

In *Festersen*, the CJ ruled that a requirement that someone who acquires agricultural property must take up residence on it was contrary to Article 63 TFEU. Nevertheless, in *Skatteverkert v A* (case C-101/05), the CJ found that the exemption from income tax in respect of dividends conditional on the company making the distribution being established in a state within the EEA or a state with which a taxation convention providing for the exchange of information had been concluded is not contrary to Article 63 TFEU. The CJ noted that it is irrelevant whether the restriction affects the movement of capital between Member States themselves, or between a Member State and a third country. It seems that the Court moved away from a discrimination-based approach and considered the impact on the market of the rule in issue. Certainly, in the *Portuguese golden shares* case, the CJ commented that Article 63 TFEU:

goes beyond the mere elimination of unequal treatment, on grounds of nationality, as between operators on the financial markets [para 44].

The UK government in the British *golden shares* case suggested that the principle in *Keck* (see chapter 18) should apply to Article 63 TFEU. It argued that the rules in issue had an impact on the market which was too indirect to fall within the scope of the prohibition. This approach, indeed, had been suggested by the Advocate-General in the earlier case of *ED Srl* (discussed in Chapter 18), but the CJ did not address the point here. The relevance of *Keck* was raised again in the *second Portuguese golden shares* case. While the CJ held that the restrictions in this case were not analogous to selling arrangements within *Keck*, its reasoning suggests that as a matter of principle, the *Keck* approach could be used in the context of free movement of capital.

The purpose behind a national rule is not determinative, although the CJ will sometimes consider it if a protectionist motive is alleged. It is the effect that is crucial and, as with the other freedoms, there is no *de minimis* exception. The CJ also does not seem to require proof of an actual effect, but accepts the supposition that certain rules could have the claimed dissuasive effect (see, eg, the *second Portuguese golden shares* case).

20.3.6 **Internal situations**

Article 63 TFEU may not be relied on in internal situations. It cannot therefore be used to challenge Member States rules' regarding, for example, the acquisition of property on national territory. However, the CJ has given a restrictive interpretation of what constitutes an internal situation. This can be seen in the case of *Reisch v Burgermeister der Landeshauptstadt Salzburg* (cases C-515, 519–40/99).

Reisch

Under Austrian law, transfer of ownership of land is only confirmed when certain administrative procedures have been completed. These include the making of a declaration to the effect that the purchaser is an Austrian national, or a national of another Member State exercising one of the four freedoms; and that the land will be used as the purchaser's principal residence or to meet a commercial need. Use of the land as a secondary residence would be permitted only if the land was already used for that purpose before 1 March 1993 or if it is located in an area in which secondary residences are permitted. The relevant national authorities may attach conditions and requirements to its authorisation in order to ensure that the acquirer of title uses the land for the stated purpose, in particular by requiring security in an amount not exceeding the purchase price or the value of the land, or by imposing fines for non-compliance with the rules.

The applicants in *Reisch* had variously been refused permission, been required to provide security or had fines imposed and they sought to challenge these decisions arguing that the rules were incompatible with the TFEU. The applicants were Austrian.

The CJ noted:

National legislation such as the SGVG, which applies without distinction to Austrian nationals and to nationals of Member States . . ., may generally fall within the scope of the provisions on the fundamental freedoms established by the Treaty only to the extent that it applies to situations related to intra-[Union] trade.

This suggests that there will be few circumstances in which an interpretation of EU law will not be relevant and that, as a corollary, internal situations will be few.

20.4 Exceptions to the free movement of capital

Article 345 TFEU specifies that '[t]he Treaties shall in no way prejudice the rules in Member States governing the system of property ownership'. The CJ held in *Staat der Nederlanden v Essent NV* (cases C-105–107/12) that the restrictions on the free movement of capital affecting certain undertakings in the electricity and natural gas industries did not violate EU law in the sense that under Article 345 TFEU Member States are entitled to exclude private investors from the ownership of shares in certain industries.

Additionally, Articles 64–6 and 75 TFEU contain the specific exceptions to the general rule set out in Article 63 TFEU These can be divided further into two categories:

- those that relate to capital movement between Member States (Article 65 TFEU; see also Articles 143–4 TFEU);
- those that relate to movement to third countries (Articles 64, 66 and 75 TFEU).

Article 65 TFEU provides that Article 63 TFEU shall be without prejudice to the right of Member States to apply relevant provisions of their tax law which distinguish between taxpayers who are not in the same situation with regard to their place of residence or with regard to the place where their capital is invested. It can be seen as analogous to Articles 36 (goods), 45(3) (workers), and 52 TFEU (establishment/services). Nonetheless, there are also some differences, as Article 65 TFEU contains some exceptions that are unique to capital: Article 65(1)(a) contains provisions specific to Member States' individual tax regimes. Article 65 TFEU also expressly raises the question of the relationship of the free movement of capital with the freedom of establishment (Article 65(2) and (3) TFEU). This issue, as well as the relationship between capital and services, which has significance for the rights of those in third countries, is discussed at 20.5.

20.4.1 Express Treaty derogation

Member States can restrict free movement of capital and payments on the grounds set out in Article 65 TFEU. The express Treaty derogation in Article 65 TFEU can be divided into three broad categories, comprising:

- national taxation systems (Article 65(1)(a) TFEU);
- fiscal supervision and anti-avoidance (Article 65(1)(b) TFEU);
- public policy and public security (Article 65(1)(b) TFEU).

All three of these categories are subject to the limitation in Article 65(3) TFEU that they 'shall not constitute a means of arbitrary discrimination or a disguised restriction on the free movement of capital'. This phraseology reflects that found in Article 36 TFEU in relation to derogation from the free movement of goods, and presumably would be interpreted in a similar manner.

20.4.1.1 National taxation systems

Member States may distinguish between taxpayers who are not in the same situation with regard to their place of residence or with regard to the place where their capital is invested (Article 65(1)(a) TFEU).

As noted earlier, this is a specific exception, unique to the free movement of capital provisions. This is restrictively interpreted: although taxation remains within Member States' competence, this power must be exercised within the scope of Union law. In *Petri Manninen* (case C-319/02), concerning the Finnish tax credit system in relation to dividend payments, the CJ commented that Article 65(1)(a) TFEU:

> cannot be interpreted as meaning that any tax legislation making a distinction between taxpayers by reference to the place where they invest their capital is automatically compatible with the Treaty [para 28].

In particular, it noted that Article 65(1)(a) TFEU is limited by Article 65(3) (see 20.4.2). In *Verkooijen*, the CJ commented that this provision effectively codified the approach that it had taken in *Finanzamt Koln-Alstadt v Schumacker* (case 279/93) and *Bachmann v Belgium* (case C-204/90), which permits Member States to protect the coherence of their internal taxation system. However, an argument based on the need to safeguard the cohesion of a tax system must be examined in the light of the objective pursued by the tax legislation in question (*De Lasteyrie du Saillant v Ministère de L'Economie des Finances et de L'Industrie de Weerd v Bestuur van de Bedrijfsvereniging voor de CGezondheid, Geestelijke en Maatschappelijke Belangen* (case C-9/02), para 67) to see if such rules are actually necessary. In particular, the CJ has held that there must be a direct link between the tax advantage concerned and the offsetting of that advantage by a particular tax levy (see *Deutsche Shell GmbH v Finanzamt für Großunternehmen in Hamburg* (case C-293/06)—taxation of losses incurred through exchange rates on start up capital for subsidiary in another Member State, decided under Article 49 TFEU). Indeed, the CJ has consistently held that reduction in tax revenue cannot be regarded as an overriding reason in the public interest which may be relied on to justify a measure which is in principle contrary to a fundamental freedom (see, eg, *Verkooijen*, para 59; *X and Y v Riksskatteverket* (case C-436/00), para 50). Laws may also be justified where the difference in treatment concerns situations which are not objectively comparable or in the interests of the fight against tax avoidance and the effectiveness of fiscal supervision. These will be similarly strictly reviewed.

Note, however, that Member States still have a certain degree of fiscal autonomy. Thus, where a disadvantage arises from two Member States choosing to exercise their fiscal sovereignty in such a way as to result in double taxation, neither Member State is obliged to amend their taxation system so as to eradicate the double taxation (*Block v Finanzamt Kaufbeuren* (case C-67/08)). The CJ has noted that the Treaty offers no guarantee to a citizen of the Union that transferring his residence to a Member State other than that in which he previously resided will be neutral as regards taxation. Given the disparities in the tax legislation of the Member States, such a transfer may be to the citizen's advantage or not, according to circumstances (*Lindfors v Finland* (case C-365/02), tax levied on car registration consequent on relocation from one Member State to another).

20.4.1.2 Fiscal supervision

Member States may take action to prevent the avoidance of national regulation; to lay down procedures for the declaration of capital movements for the purposes of administrative or statistical information; or in the interests of public policy or public security (Article 65(1)(b) TFEU). This is a three-pronged exception, which is a mixture of concern for fiscal supervision and a standard public-policy consideration. Fiscal supervision has links with the issues relating to national taxation systems and must be interpreted with caution.

In the *Eurobonds* case, the prohibition on the acquisition by Belgian residents of securities of a loan issued abroad was held to be not justified. The CJ commented that 'a general presumption of tax evasion or tax fraud cannot justify a fiscal measure', especially where the national measure constituted 'an outright prohibition of a fundamental freedom' (para 45). Note that the reference to 'national regulation' is not necessarily limited to concerns listed in Article 65(1)(b) TFEU: taxation and the prudential supervision of financial institutions. In *Bordessa*, the CJ held that other types of measure would be permitted where they were aimed at preventing 'illegal activities of comparable seriousness, such as money laundering, drug trafficking or terrorism' (para 21). The CJ recognises, however, that the approach to assessing fiscal supervision is different depending on whether we are looking at movement between Member States or a Member State and a third country. This can be seen in the context of *Skatteverket v A* (case C-101/05) which concerned rules relating to the taxation of dividends.

Case of A

Special rules applied allowing exemption from the tax liability when the dividend comprised the distribution of shares in a subsidiary company. Conditions applied, including rules relating to the location of the company. The exemption also applied where the distribution of shares was carried out by a foreign company which, inter alia, was established in a country with which Sweden had concluded a tax convention containing provision for exchange of information. A owned shares in Company X, which had its registered office in Switzerland and was considering distributing the shares which it held in one of its subsidiaries. There was no information exchange provision in the tax convention between Sweden and Switzerland and so the conditions for the Swedish exemption were not satisfied. The rules were challenged for their compatibility with Article 63 TFEU. The Swedish government argued that the rule was necessary for fiscal supervision.

According to existing jurisprudence, a Member State cannot rely on the fact that it may be impossible to seek cooperation from another Member State in conducting inquiries or collecting information in order to justify a refusal to grant a tax advantage. In this case, however, the CJ noted as regards transactions involving more than one Member State, that 'such movements take place in a different legal context' (para 60) and that:

> it is, in principle, legitimate for that Member State to refuse to grant that advantage if, in particular, because that third country is not under any contractual obligation to provide information, it proves impossible to obtain such information from that country [para 63].

The anti-avoidance element of Article 65(1)(b) TFEU is potentially a broad category, although the CJ will construe all exceptions to Treaty freedoms narrowly. There is also no equivalent provision to this provision in the articles derogating from the other Treaty freedoms. Some of the issues dealt with as a matter of fiscal supervision or anti-avoidance, such as funding for terrorism or money laundering, might in the context of the other freedoms be seen as public policy and public security. Here, their separate identification may mean that jurisprudence developed in relation to the other Treaty freedoms can probably not be used to derive guidance on the likely scope of this derogation, although proportionality will always apply to limit the manner in which Member States may rely on this provision. It seems that some prior *notification* requirements for statistical purposes or to prevent money laundering, for example, may be acceptable, but not prior *authorisation* (see *Sanz de Lera*).

20.4.1.3 Public policy and public security

Looking at the third group of derogations, public policy and public security, the test adopted is that a sufficiently serious threat to fundamental interest exists and is similar to that used in regard to the other freedoms. This can be seen in the context of *Association Eglise de Scientology de Paris and Scientology International Reserves Trust v the Prime Minister* (case C-54/99).

Association Eglise de Scientology de Paris

French law permitted, with a view to ensuring the defence of national interests, the making and realisation of foreign investments in France subject to prior authorisation or control. The applicants sought to have certain legislative provisions laying down a system of prior authorisation for direct foreign investments repealed. The question of the scope of the public-policy and public-security exception was referred to the CJ. After reiterating that derogations must be interpreted strictly, the CJ specified that 'public policy and public security may be relied on only if there is a genuine and sufficiently serious threat to a fundamental interest of society' and they cannot be used to justify ends that are purely economic. In addition to any measures satisfying a proportionality test, the Court held that 'any person affected by a restrictive measure based on such a derogation must have access to legal redress' (para 17). While the Court accepted that there might be circumstances in which a prior notification system would be inadequate (the difficulty in identifying and blocking capital once it has entered a Member State), here this was not the case. The Court reasoned:

> the essence of the system in question is that prior authorisation is required for every direct foreign investment which is such as to represent a threat to public policy [and] public security, without any more detailed definition. Thus, the investors concerned are given no indication whatever as to the specific circumstances in which prior authorisation is required.

Such lack of precision does not enable individuals to be apprised of the extent of their rights and obligations deriving from Article 73b of the Treaty. That being so, the system established is contrary to the principle of legal certainty.

Member States cannot therefore make general statements about public policy and public security, but must tailor their responses to specific issues. In summary:

- Derogations from the fundamental principle of free movement of capital have to be interpreted strictly so that their scope could not be determined unilaterally by each Member State without any EU control.

- Derogations could not be misapplied so as in fact to serve purely economic ends.

- Any person affected by a restrictive measure based on such a derogation needs to have access to legal redress.

- Derogations are subject to the principle of proportionality. For example a prohibition on buying property near military sites would be acceptable only if military interests of the Member State would be exposed to real, specific and serious risks which could not be countered by less restrictive means (*Albore* (case C-423/98)). In the *second Portuguese golden shares* case, the CJ ruled that Portugal had violated the free movement of capital provisions by securing golden shares intended to remain the property of Portugal. Yet, the CJ accepted that the need to secure an energy supply in times of emergency fell within the public security exception, although on the facts the national measures did not survive the proportionality test. In accepting the public security argument, the CJ followed the line taken with regard to free movement of goods (see Chapter 19).

Restrictions may result in restrictions on the right of establishment and must therefore be compatible with those provisions (Article 65(2) TFEU). The relationship between establishment and capital is discussed at 20.5.

20.4.2 **Interpreting the derogations**

As the CJ noted in *Association Eglise de Scientology de Paris* derogations from the fundamental principle of the free movement of capital must be interpreted strictly. Their scope cannot be determined unilaterally by individual Member States without any supervision by Union institutions. Article 65 TFEU gives the Council the power to adopt decisions stating that restrictive tax measures adopted by a Member State concerning one or more third countries are to be considered compatible with the Treaties in so far as they are justified by one of the objectives of the Union and compatible with the proper functioning of the internal market. This is limited in that the Council may only make such a decision in the absence of action on the matter by the Commission, and the Council must act unanimously. In any event, any rule falling within any of the above exceptions cannot constitute a means of arbitrary discrimination or disguised restriction on the free movement of capital or payments (Article 65(3) TFEU). The CJ has reaffirmed that derogations cannot be applied so as to serve purely economic ends (see also the *Portuguese golden shares* case). As with the other exceptions to Treaty freedoms, it would seem that the crucial question will be proportionality of the Member State's measure, whether the Member State is seeking to justify its measure under express Treaty derogations or in relation to a rule of reason-style argument.

More unusually, the CJ in the *Association Eglise de Scientology de Paris* case (see 20.4.1.3) made two more points about the use of derogations. First, any person affected by such a restrictive measure had to have access to legal redress: in this, the CJ is reflecting the general approach to right to a remedy found in Union law (see further Chapters 6 and 8). Secondly, such a person had to be 'apprised of the extent of their rights and obligations deriving from Article [65] of the Treaty' (para 22). Again, this reflects a general principle of Union law. What is interesting is that it is only in respect of the free movement of capital that this point is made express.

20.4.3 **Non-euro Member States**

For Member States which have not joined up to the euro, there are two further provisions which may be relied on where there are balance of payment difficulties—Articles 143–4 TFEU. Although these empower such Member States to take unilateral action (subject only to veto or amendment by the Council acting by qualified majority), the protective measures must cause the least possible disturbance to the common market and must not be wider in scope than is strictly necessary.

20.4.4 **Rule of reason?**

Article 63 TFEU does not just catch those rules which discriminate directly against capital movements, it also catches rules which indirectly restrict capital movements. With a restriction-based test, it seems that Member States may be able to rely on grounds of overriding public interest to justify a national measure. In *Reisch*, the Court, referring to its previous case law in *Konle*, summarised the position as follows:

> It is not in dispute that those measures, by laying down a procedure of prior notification/authorisation for the acquisition of immovable property, restrict, by their very purpose, the free movement of capital.
>
> Such restrictions may nevertheless be permitted if the national rules pursue, in a non-discriminatory way, an objective in the public interest and if they observe the principle of proportionality, that is if the same result could not be achieved by other less restrictive measures [paras 32–3].

This point was re-emphasised in the British *golden shares* cases; see also *Communication of the Commission on Certain Legal Aspect Concerning intra-EU Investment* ([1997] OJ C220/15)). As with the other freedoms, the list of possible public interest justifications, by contrast with the exceptions in Article 65 TFEU, is open-ended. Thus in *Konle*, town-and-country planning was accepted as an appropriate overriding requirement in the general interest; similarly, environmental protection and land management concerns have been recognised (*Reisch*); and the Portuguese and British *golden shares* cases recognised the importance of undertakings which are involved in the provision of services in the public interest. Relying on *Konle*, the CJ accepted in *Woningstichting Sint Servatius v Minister voor Wonen Wijken en Integratie* (case C-567/07) that requirements related to public housing policy in a Member State and to the financing of that policy can also constitute overriding reasons in the public interest. It also held, relying on the case law from the free movement of services (*Watts v Bedford Primary Care Trust* (case C-372/04)), that a restriction could be justified if there was a risk of 'seriously undermining the financial balance of social policies'. While it can be seen from these cases that the Court has accepted that national legislation may constitute a justified restriction when it is dictated by reasons of an economic nature in the pursuit of an objective in the public interest, it cannot be justified when it is purely of an economic nature. In this, there are similarities with the case law on the other freedoms and—as there—the boundary between the two positions (purely economic on the one hand and economic in pursuit of the public interest on the other) might be difficult to draw.

There is some lack of clarity around the consequence of whether a national rule is discriminatory or not. In the *Portuguese golden shares* case, the CJ reiterated the position that overriding requirements of the general interest may be used in relation to rules 'which are applicable to all persons and undertakings pursuing an activity in the territory of the host Member State'; in this it is following the approach already identified in *Reisch*. Nonetheless, in some cases the CJ accepted that an overriding reason in the general interest would apply, although the rule in issue had been characterised as discriminatory. *Gustavvson v Ministre du Logement et de L'Urbanisme* (case C-484/93), provides a number of overriding reasons in the general interest despite the fact that the CJ had held, in para 15 of the same judgment, that there had been discrimination because the rule was based on the place of establishment and that the rule could therefore only be justified by reference to the grounds of derogation set out expressly in the Treaty. In some instances, the Court has equated the grounds in the TFEU with grounds of overriding interest, adding to the conceptual confusion. This is, however, not unique to the free movement of capital but can also be seen in the other freedoms.

Any Member State measure must satisfy the test of proportionality. Proportionality requires that 'the same result could not be achieved by other less restrictive measures' (*Reisch*). In practice it seems that this is a hard test to satisfy: in many cases the requirement of prior authorisation has not been found to be proportionate. It seems that the CJ is more likely to find a requirement to make a declaration acceptable (see, eg, *Bordessa*). The CJ did accept in the *Portuguese golden shares* case that in some instances prior authorisation might be necessary (here the provision of services in the public interest or strategic services), but even then any such system must be proportionate and use non-discriminatory criteria which would be known in advance to the relevant undertakings. Further, all persons affected by a restrictive measure had to have a legal remedy available to them.

20.5 Relationship with other freedoms

The precise scope of these provisions is not clear: some have suggested that the free movement of capital is ancillary to the other freedoms, for example goods or establishment. Certainly, those provisions may be seen as dependent on the freedom of payments—there would be little incentive to export goods, for example, were it not possible to repatriate the value of those costs. The importance of the scope of the free movement of capital and consequently its relationship with the other freedoms is important, as capital is structured differently from the other freedoms. The question has great political significance, especially in these times of financial crisis as Member States seek to use mechanisms (such as golden share rights) to further national goals (eg, the creation of 'national champions'). There is thus a tension between such goals and the economic freedoms in TFEU. This tension has led to an increase in the case law in this field.

It is not entirely clear whether the capital provisions may be applied in tandem with the provisions relating to establishment or those concerning services. The wording of the Treaty with regard to Article 56 TFEU would suggest that it, at least, applies when other freedoms do not. It would seem, however, that in some cases the CJ has not clearly differentiated the different fields of application for the two provisions. The Advocates-General in *Svensson and Gustavsson* and in *Safir v Skattemyndigheten i Dalamas Lan* (case C-118/96) expressed unease with an approach which conflates services and capital. In *Safir*, the Advocate-General suggested that the boundary lay between a direct restriction on capital, which would fall to be considered under Article 63 TFEU, and the situation where the restriction was indirect, which would be considered as affecting services. In its judgment, the CJ merely remarked that it was unnecessary to consider the free movement of capital provisions; it is unclear whether this silence on the reasoning of the Advocate-General connotes agreement with his reasoning or not. In *Fidium Finanz v Bundesanstalt für Finanzdienstleistungsaufsicht* (case C-452/04, Grand Chamber), which involved a Swiss institution granting credit to people in Germany (via an Internet site), the CJ stated that Articles 56 and 63 TFEU 'were designed to regulate different situations and they each have their own field of application' (para 28). The CJ then had to tackle the argument that the free movement of services would only apply when the other freedoms were inapplicable. It rejected that argument, holding:

> Although in the definition of the notion of 'services' laid down in the first paragraph of Article [57 TFEU] it is specified that the services 'are not governed by the provisions relating to freedom of movement for goods, capital and persons', that relates to the definition of that notion and does not establish any order of priority between the freedom to provide services and the other fundamental freedoms. The notion of 'services' covers services which are not governed by other freedoms, in order to ensure that all economic activity falls within the scope of the fundamental freedoms [para 32].

The CJ is here suggesting that there is a distinction between the definition of subject matter (services or establishment) and the decision whether or not to apply a particular rule, though it is unclear from the reasoning in the case how the definitional hierarchy was being applied. If a situation can be assessed by reference to services and capital, the CJ held that in principle, only one provision should apply. It is then necessary to determine which provision, Article 56 or 63 TFEU, is relevant. In determining this question, the CJ relied on its case law regarding the boundaries between other freedoms and suggested that where one freedom is secondary to the other, the CJ would consider the primary freedom. Here, the CJ held that the rules were primarily concerned with the freedom to provide services and that the impact on the free movement of capital was 'merely an inevitable consequence of the restriction imposed on the provision of services' (para 49).

It is implicit in *Fidium Finanz* that, potentially, both freedoms could apply at the same time. Indeed, this question had already arisen in *Commission v Italy (Italian recruitment agencies)* (case C-279/00).

Italian Recruitment Agencies case

Here, the Commission brought an action against Italy in respect of a requirement that undertakings providing temporary workers must lodge a guarantee with a credit establishment having its seat or a branch in Italy. The Commission argued that this rule violated both the freedom to provide services and the free movement of capital.

The CJ analysed this rule both from the perspective of the employment agencies and from that of the banks. The CJ ruled that the provision was a restriction on capital movement as far as the employment agencies were concerned and a violation of the banks' freedom to provide services within Article 56 TFEU.

It has been suggested that given that there are two sets of circumstances arising from the same rule, there is not a concurrent application of the two freedoms—though arguably the real effect is the same as the concurrent application of such rules.

The CJ had cause to consider the relationship between Article 49 and 63 TFEU in *Européenne et Luxembourgeoise d'investissements SA (ELISA) v Directeur général des impôts, Ministère public* (case C-451/05).

ELISA

The case concerned the imposition of a tax on immovable property in France held by a company in Luxembourg, although its effective centre of management was in France. The referring court was unsure whether the provisions on establishment in Article 49 TFEU or those on capital in Article 63 TFEU were relevant. It pointed out the link between Article 49 TFEU in that the right to establish oneself causes capital movements.

The CJ held that the purchase of immovable property constituted a capital movement within the scope of Article 63 TFEU. Whilst Article 49 TFEU implies the existence of a stable and continuous basis in the economic life of the host Member State, in order for Article 49 TFEU to apply:

it is generally necessary to have secured a permanent presence in the host Member State and, where immovable property is purchased and held, that that property should be actively managed [para 64].

Here, there was no evidence that the property was acquired as part of its business, nor that it was actively managed. Article 49 TFEU did not therefore apply.

20.6 Restrictions on free movement of capital between Member States and third countries

Although in principle free movement of capital between Member States and third countries is secured by Article 63 TFEU, the restrictions on free movement of capital set out in Article 65 TFEU apply equally to free movement as regards third countries. This is a less liberalised framework, however, than that relating to intra-Union movements, as we have seen in relation to the interpretation of the derogation found in Article 65 TFEU. Additional restrictions may also apply:

- Article 63 TFEU does not apply to national measures existing on 31 December 1993—although the Council may act to remove such measures (Article 64 TFEU; see 20.7). For recent Member States, a different date applies.

- In limited circumstances where serious difficulties in the operation of EMU arise, the Council may take short-term measures restricting capital movements to third countries (Article 66 TFEU).

- In urgent cases, restrictions which form part of economic sanctions may be introduced (Article 75 TFEU). Note the scope of Union competence under Article 75 TFEU has been discussed in Chapter 3.

20.7 Power to legislate in the field of free movement of capital

Article 64(2) TFEU provides that the Council may, by qualified majority and following a proposal by the Commission, legislate on the free movement of capital to or from third countries. It identifies the categories of measures which can be taken. In *Kadi*, which concerned measures implementing UN economic sanctions aimed at individuals by freezing their assets, the CJ held that the restrictive measures imposed by the contested regulation did not fall within one of the categories of measures listed in that provision and that Article 64(2) TFEU could not therefore be the legal basis for that regulation. This indicates that the categories of measure listed in Article 64(2) TFEU are closed.

There appears to be some tension in this provision. On the one hand, the objective of such action has to be to endeavour to achieve the free movement of capital between Member States and third countries 'to the greatest extent possible'. Nonetheless, the same provision (albeit in the next paragraph, Article 64(3) TFEU) envisages the possibility of a step back in Union law regarding the liberalisation of capital to or from third countries, although this is tempered somewhat by the requirement that any measure constituting a 'step back' must be adopted unanimously. While unanimity is required in Council for a 'step back', this is one of the remaining occasions when the Parliament need only be consulted.

In contrast to the other freedoms, therefore, there is no all-encompassing competence to adopt legislation to facilitate the free movement of capital (and payments) between Member States. Where it is necessary to adopt legislation dealing with the movement of capital between Member States, this has been achieved by relying on Article 114 TFEU. Directive 2007/64 ([2007] OJ L319/1) amended by 2009/111 ([2009] OJ L302/97) and repealing the earlier Directive established a harmonised legal framework for payment services by regulating the conditions of the authorisation process for those providing payment services and by introducing rules by which the competent regulatory authority is identified. The Directive lays down information that service providers must give to customers. It does not apply to payment operations completed in cash or by cheque, and regulates the granting of credit by payment institutions only where it is closely linked to payment services.

The institutions also enacted Regulation 924/2009 ([2009] OJ L266/11), amended by Single Euro Payments Area (SEPA) Regulation 260/2012 ([2012] OJ L 94/22) on charges for cross-border payments in euros. It guarantees that national and cross-border payments made in the Union are subject to the same rules with regard to bank charges (ie, it provides for non-discrimination, not no charges!). For a discussion of the limits of Article 114 TFEU, see Chapter 16.

20.8 Economic and monetary union (EMU)

Linked to the idea of free movement of capital and payments is the idea of a common currency. For those engaged in cross-border trade, it also reduces risks from currency fluctuations, as well as removing currency transaction costs. The introduction of EMU was justified on the basis that it would be an effective way to reduce inflation and maintain price stability, thus helping to achieve the Union's general goals (recognised in Article 127(1) TFEU). It was, and remains, controversial. Critics argued that conditions were not right, particularly as regards the convergence criteria (see Chapter 1). More fundamentally, concerns were expressed about the shift of important areas of policy from Member States to the EU, about the loss of a classic symbol of sovereignty and state-hood, and whether Member States' economies really would operate in tandem.

The relevant provisions, introduced by Maastricht, are now found in Title VIII to the TFEU, at Article 119 TFEU *et seq*. EMU can be divided into two aspects: economic policy (Article 119(1) TFEU), and monetary policy (Article 119(2) TFEU), though the two are closely linked. Much of the discussion in this area lies in the realm of the political and the economic, rather than the legal. What follows is a brief overview of the provisions introduced: a full discussion of the subject lies outside the scope of this book.

Monetary policy aims to maintain price stability (Article 127 TFEU) and falls to the responsibility of the ECB in conjunction with the various national banks (including those of non-Eurozone Member States), known together as the European System of Central Banks (ESCB), but the ECB has the exclusive right to authorise the issue of euro banknotes. Special provisions exist to take account of the positions of Member States that are not part of the Eurozone (Article 139 TFEU *et seq*).

Member States operate against broad economic policy guidelines (BEPG) (Article 121(3) TFEU). Current BEPG are found in Recommendation 2010/410 ([2010] OJ L191). The Treaty laid down only criteria for the adoption of the single currency, without setting out a budgetary policy to be followed after the change to the euro. So, the Member States adopted the stability and growth pact (SGP) (Resolution of the European Council on the Stability and Growth Pact ([1997] OJ C236/1)). Part of the BEPG is that Member States comply with the SGP. The SGP is intended to ensure the sound management of public finances in the Eurozone and seeks to ensure sustained and sustainable convergence among the economies of the Eurozone Member States. Difficulties in the system (including a Commission action against the Council before the CJ: *Commission v Council (stability and growth pact)* (case C-27/04) led to the SGP being revised so as to improve its management (European Council, 22 and 23 March 2005, Presidency Conclusions (7619/1/05 REV 1)). The SGP comprises a European Council resolution and two regulations. These Regulations reflect two aspects of the SGP which aim to ensure Member States avoid excessive deficits as required by Article 126(1) TFEU:

- preventative (Regulation 1466/97 (surveillance) ([1997] OJ L209) amended by 1055/2005 ([2005] OJ L174));
- corrective (Regulation 1467/97 ([1997] OJ L209) amended by 1056/2005 ([2005] OJ L174)).

As regards prevention, Regulation 1466/97 provides for the surveillance of Member States' budgetary positions. Member States must submit annual stability or convergence programmes, showing how they intend to achieve or safeguard sound fiscal positions in the medium term. The Commission has the responsibility of assessing these programmes; the Council will then give an opinion on the programmes. As regards the corrective aspect, where it is decided that the deficit is excessive under Article 126 TFEU, the Council may issue recommendations to the Member States concerned to correct the excessive deficit, giving a time frame for so doing. Non-compliance with any such recommendations may trigger the imposition of sanctions.

The Commission put forward proposals in 2010 to strengthen SGP further, the so-called 'six-pack' of legislative measures, comprising five regulations and one directive, which entered into force in all Member States on 13 December 2011. In particular, the six-pack reinforces both the preventive and the corrective arms of the SGP in relation to the Excessive Deficit Procedure, which applies to Member States that have breached either the deficit or the debt criterion. Key aspects of the six-pack include the possibility of fines and the use of reverse qualified majority voting (RQMV) for most sanctions. As RQMV implies that a recommendation or a proposal of the Commission is considered adopted in the Council unless a qualified majority of Member States votes against it, the use of RQMV means that it is more likely that sanctions will be adopted. Problems remain in the Eurozone resulting in the addition of specific measures to tackle the sovereign debt crisis.

The initial response to the economic crisis of October 2008 consisted of the European Financial Stabilisation Mechanism (EFSM) and the European Financial Stability Facility (EFSF). The EFSM, established by Regulation 407/2010 ([2010] OJ L181), is an emergency funding programme which provides assistance to Member States where there is a severe financial disturbance due to events beyond the control of the Member State concerned. It is reliant upon funds raised on the financial markets and guaranteed by the Commission, using EU budget as collateral for the debt. The EFSF is permitted to issue bonds (or other debt instruments) on the market to provide funds for loans to Eurozone Member States, to buy sovereign debt or to re-capitalise banks, and is backed by guarantees given by the euro area Member States. It is an emergency fall-back mechanism and would not be available if the Member States could borrow on the market at acceptable rates.

The European Stability Mechanism (ESM) is a permanent rescue-funding programme to succeed the temporary EFSF and EFSM, the legal basis of which in the Treaties was not entirely uncontroversial (see generally, Chapter 3). On 16 December 2010 the European Council agreed (Decision 2011/199) an amendment to Article 136 TFEU (a provision which applies only to Eurozone members) which expressly permitted the establishment by Eurozone Member States of a 'stability mechanism to be activated if indispensable to safeguard the stability of the euro area as a whole. The granting of any required financial assistance under the mechanism will be made subject to strict conditionality'. This amendment was done through the simplified revision procedure provided by Article 48(6) TEU, something which, of course, did not go unnoticed. In *Pringle* (discussed in Chapter 2), the Irish Supreme Court asked the CJ whether the procedure that would amend Article 136 TFEU was in compliance with the Treaty framework. The CJ, unsurprisingly, concluded that the stability mechanism is appropriate to safeguard the stability of the euro area as a whole and confirmed its compatibility with the Treaty framework. More recently, in *Gauweiler*, the CJ on a reference from the German Federal Constitutional Court ruled that the OMT programme of the European Central Bank is compatible with the EU law requirements. In both cases, the CJ recognised in effect that specialised EU law bodies are empowered to take certain complex as well as technical decisions. Therefore the Court has exercised limited judicial review powers, confirming that the specialised bodies have not exceeded their discretionary powers in making certain economic assessments.

Additionally, a separate Treaty between the members of the Eurozone, the Treaty Establishing the European Stability Mechanism, was agreed. It relies on the EU institutions for the implementation of the Treaty: post-programme surveillance will be carried out by the European Commission and by the Council within the framework found in Articles 121 and 136 TFEU; and disputes concerning the interpretation and application of the Treaty are to be referred to the CJ, relying on Article 273 TFEU (which gives the CJ jurisdiction in any dispute between Member States which relates to the subject matter of the treaties—if the dispute is submitted to it under a special agreement between the parties).

The majority of the Member States (all except the UK and the Czech Republic) have agreed a further treaty, the Treaty on Stability, Coordination and Governance (TSCG), which includes the 'fiscal compact'. The TSCG came into force on 1 January 2013. It introduces new rules on controlling budget deficits and these budget rules must be implemented in national law through provisions of 'binding force and permanent character, preferably constitutional'. In addition to increased surveillance mechanisms, the TSCG envisages the possibility of fines being imposed for non-compliance. The TSCG also includes provision on economic governance in the euro area, such as the holding of

Euro Summits at least twice a year and reinforced economic cooperation. While there is significant similarity between some provisions in the six-pack and the TSCG, the latter does not replace the former. The two systems will run in parallel. The new treaty will not amend the TEU or TFEU and is in that sense outside the EU framework. Nonetheless, it too envisages relying on the EU institutional framework.

The TSCG is not entirely unproblematic. It reinforced the division between the UK and the Eurozone. It is noticeable that the Eurozone states have chosen not to use the enhanced cooperation mechanism (that has safeguards for non-participating Member States, which can be enforced before the CJ). Other critics have expressed concern about the democratic legitimacy of this system and that it constitutes the start of a drift back towards intergovernmentalism; in particular, the European Parliament would be excluded from discussions relating to the form of an extra-EU treaty. An important issue is that the substance of the Treaty matches EU law requirements. Note that the draft agreement provides that, in the case of conflict between EU law and the new Treaty, EU law should prevail. On this basis, substantive violations of EU law should not arise. One final question relates to the legality of using EU institutions (such as the European Commission and the CJ) to enforce what is essentially an international agreement among sovereign nations. The Council's Legal Service has confirmed that the institutions can be entrusted with this function.

As well as strengthening economic surveillance mechanisms and coordination, the EU has introduced a new framework for the financial sector. This is because of the role this sector was perceived as playing in the economic crisis. One aspect of the reform has been the introduction of harmonised standards for the financial sector, eliminating the possibility of forum shopping (see, eg, minimum capital requirements in CRD IV—comprising Capital Requirements Regulation (CRR) and the Capital Requirements Directive (CRD); Regulation on short selling (Regulation 236/2012) (OJ [2012] L 86/1)).

In addition to specific rules relating to behaviour of companies in this sector, a new supervisory framework has been established to improve cross-border cooperation, consistent enforcement of rules and systemic oversight. There are three European supervisory authorities:

- the European Banking Authority (EBA);
- the European Insurance and Occupational Pensions Authority (EIOPA);
- the European Securities and Markets Authority (ESMA)

together with an overarching body for the sector: the European Systemic Risk Board (ESRB) to monitor and assess potential threats arising from developments within the financial system as a whole (macro-prudential supervision).

A third strand of action was in response to the risk of contagion illustrated by the sovereign debt crisis, and the inter-connected nature of the EU market (especially for those States sharing a currency). The Member States agreed to introduce a Banking Union to replace the fragmented set of systems based on national regulation. A Single Supervisory Mechanism (SSM) carried out by the ECB has been introduced (Regulation 1024/2013 conferring specific tasks on the European Central Bank concerning policies relating to the prudential supervision of credit institution ([2013] OJ L287/63); and Regulation 1022/2013 amending Regulation 1093/2010 establishing a European Supervisory Authority (European Banking Authority) as regards the conferral of specific tasks on the European Central Bank ([2013] OJ L287/5)).

There have been criticisms that this approach has been introduced on inadequate empirical evidence and that the structures and regulation risk damaging the efficiency of the financial sector. The UK in particular seems unhappy with some of the changes: CRD IV was introduced by a 'qualified majority' of EU Member States, with only the UK dissenting. The UK has also sought to challenge the legal basis relating to powers granted to some of the supervisory institutions and their powers (the *ESMA* case). The CJ, however, ruled that Article 114 TFEU constitutes an appropriate legal basis for the adoption of Article 28 of Regulation 236/2012 in relation to the powers of the EU's financial agency. The UK has objected to other regulatory proposals (*United Kingdom v Council (FTT proposal)* (case C-209/13)). It should be noted, however, that this raft of measures is in part driven by the EU's international commitments in respect of financial regulation.

20.9 Conclusions

Since 1992 and the TEU, the number of cases decided under the free movement of capital provisions has increased significantly, and the jurisprudence on this freedom has developed correspondingly. The CJ seems to have been willing to borrow principles from the other freedoms and apply them to the capital case law, resulting in certain parallels between all the freedoms. The result is that the approach to the free movement of capital has been liberalised, with potentially far-reaching effects on Member States' internal policies, particularly their taxation systems, as recent cases show. Problem areas do remain, particularly with regard to the CJ's approach to the relationship between the different freedoms. Despite the increasing parallelism, it must be recognised that certain provisions remain unique to the free movement of capital, and that there may be circumstances in which the difference between the freedoms remains important. Furthermore, the imposed liberalisation via the CJ's interpretation of Article 63 TFEU with regard to the relationship of Member States with third countries seems to have given rise to concern in some Member States and it is, perhaps, as a response to this that we see Lisbon seeking to clarify some aspects of the Council's freedom to 'step back'. In any event, the current financial climate adds to the tension in this area.

Further reading

Andenas, M, and Chin, I H-Y, 'Financial stability and legal integration in financial regulation' (2013) 38 EL Rev 335.

Benyon, FS, *Direct Investment, National Champions and EU Treaty Freedoms: From Maastricht to Lisbon* (Hart Publishing, 2010).

Craig, P, 'The Stability, Coordination and Governance Treaty: Principle, politics and pragmatism' (2012) 37 EL Rev 231.

de Gregorio Merino, A, 'Legal developments in the economic and monetary union during the debt crisis: The mechanisms of financial assistance' (2012) 49 CML Rev 1616.

Hemels, S, et al, 'Freedom of establishment or free movement of capital: Is there an order of priority? Conflicting visions of national courts and the ECJ' (2010) 19 EC Tax Review 19.

Hinarejos, A, *The Euro Area Crisis in Constitutional Perspective* (Oxford University Press, 2015).

Hindelang, S, *The Free Movement of Capital and Foreign Direct Investment* (Oxford University Press, 2009).

Jukka, S, 'Free Movement of Capital: Evolution as a non-linear process' in P Craig and G De Búrca (eds), *The Evolution of EU Law* (Oxford University Press, 2011).

O'Brien, M, 'Company taxation, state aid and fundamental freedoms: Is the next step enhanced cooperation?' (2005) 30 EL Rev 209.

Peers, S, 'Free movement of capital: Learning lessons or slipping on spilt milk' in C Barnard and J Scott (eds), *The Law of the Single Market: Unpacking the premises* (Hart Publishing, 2002).

Ringe, W, 'Company law and free movement of capital' (2010) 69 CLJ 378.

Ruffert, M, 'The European debt crisis and European Union law' (2011) 48 CML Rev 1777.

Van den Bogaert, S and Borger, V, 'Twenty Years After Maastricht: The Coming of Age of the EMU?' in Visser and van der Mei (eds), *The Treaty on European Union 1993–2013: Reflections from Maastricht* (Intersentia, 2013).

Wattel, PJ, 'Red herrings in direct tax cases before the ECJ' (2004) 31 LIEI 81.

21 Citizenship: rights of free movement and residence

21.1 Introduction

The rights relating to free movement of individuals have changed dramatically over the EU's existence. Originally, these rights formed part of the rules creating the single market and had a primarily economic focus. With the jurisprudence of the CJ, we see a broad interpretation being given to these rights. As well as having an economic function, allowing the movement of factors of production, the free movement provisions have also been interpreted in the light of the fact that economic actors are people, not just inanimate objects, allowing them social and ancillary rights. This approach has been given political recognition through the introduction of EU citizenship and reinforced through the CJ's interpretation, not just of the citizenship provision itself, but of the original free movement provisions in the light of citizenship.

This chapter is the first of three dealing with free movement rights and will deal with the right to move to another Member State and live there as well as with the question of who benefits from the free movement rights. The succeeding chapters will deal with economic and social aspects respectively. Limitations will be dealt with thereafter.

21.2 Overview

The free movement right can be seen to comprise three elements. The first is the right to move to another Member State and to live there (including the right to remain). This is a prerequisite to the second right, which is to access the job market in the host Member State (see chapter 22). Finally, but importantly in terms of removing disadvantages to the migrant arising from the exercise of the right of free movement, there are ancillary rights (see chapter 23).

When considering the rights of free movement and residence, it is important to note the layering of different provisions: the citizenship provisions are broad, underpinning the system. The free movement rights (Articles 45, 49 and 56 TFEU) apply to a narrower group but members accord some additional rights. Their rights are all implemented through Union legislation. None of these provisions replaces the other and their relationship gives rise to some quirks in the level of protection awarded in different circumstances. Thus, although citizenship provides a broad framework of rights, diminishing the need for an economic nexus found in the original Treaty freedoms, it is important still to understand the varying scope of categories of beneficiary under Articles 45 TFEU (workers), 49 TFEU (establishment) and 56 TFEU (services) to recognise the different level and scope of protection so awarded.

In this discussion two themes recur. The first concerns the link between migration and the rights claimed; the second, the underlying concern about abuse of Union law rights. It seems that questions about the appropriate scope of rights are now being dealt with by a test focusing on the degree of integration for the immigrant into society in the host Member State. Furthermore, while some rights may be exercised by citizens, others may be exercised by citizens and legal persons, raising the question of the extent to which the same interpretation should be given to the provisions when they are exercised by individuals or inanimate bodies.

21.2.1 Citizenship: Article 21 TFEU

Article 21 TFEU provides:

> (1) Every citizen of the Union shall have the right to move and reside freely within the territory of the Member States, subject to the limitations and conditions laid down in this Treaty and by the measures adopted to give it effect.

Article 21(2) TFEU empowers the European Parliament and the Council to adopt 'provisions with a view to facilitating the exercise of the right' referred to in Article 21(1) TFEU. Article 21(3) TFEU further provides for the adoption of measures concerning social security and social protection where the Treaties do not already provide for the adoption of such measures.

21.2.2 Workers: Article 45 TFEU

The principal Treaty provision governing the free movement of workers is Article 45 TFEU:

> 1. Freedom of movement for workers shall be secured within the Union.
>
> It elaborates the aspects of this freedom and in particular:
>
> . . .
>
> 3. It shall entail the right, subject to limitations justified on grounds of public policy, public security or public health:
>
> . . .
>
> (b) to move freely within the territory of Member States for this purpose; . . .
>
> (c) to stay in a Member State for the purpose of employment in accordance with the provisions governing the employment of nationals of that State laid down by law, regulation or administrative action;
>
> (d) to remain in the territory of a Member State after having been employed in that State, subject to conditions which shall be embodied in implementing regulations to be drawn up by the Commission.

21.2.3 Establishment: Article 49 TFEU

Article 49(1) TFEU:

> Within the framework of the provisions set out below, restrictions on the freedom of establishment of nationals of a Member State in the territory of another Member State shall be prohibited. Such

prohibition shall also apply to restrictions on the setting up of agencies, branches or subsidiaries by nationals of any Member State established in the territory of any Member State.

21.2.4 **Services: Article 56 TFEU**

Article 56(1) TFEU provides:

Within the framework of the provisions set out below, restrictions on freedom to provide services within the Union shall be prohibited in respect of nationals of Member States who are established in a Member State other than that of the person for whom the services are intended.

21.2.5 **Implementing legislation**

As required under Articles 46 and 50 TFEU, secondary legislation was introduced to give further substance to the above principles. The resulting legislation was updated and consolidated by Directive 2004/38, the Citizens' Rights Directive (CRD), which was additionally based on Article 20 TFEU. The CRD repealed Articles 10 and 11 of Regulation 1612/68, leaving the remaining provision extant. All other legislative provisions on free movement were repealed and replaced by the CRD.

21.3 **Enforcement**

As we have seen in Chapter 3, there are different legal consequences from the choice of type of legal measure, regulations being directly applicable and directives being binding on those to whom they are addressed. The fact that the doctrine of direct effect (Chapter 5) cannot be relied on in horizontal situations in respect of directives may have consequences for the enforceability of the rights contained in the CRD, should they need to be relied on against private individuals (eg refusal to give employment to a migrant worker's family member on grounds of nationality—see former Article 11 of Regulation 1612/68). Rights of access to the territory will only be relied on against public bodies and should not therefore cause problems in this regard.

These implementing measures, as the Court held in *Procureur du Roi v Royer* (case 48/75), merely determine the scope and detailed rules for the exercise of rights conferred directly by the Treaty. Article 45 TFEU, being directly applicable, may be relied on by individuals in their national courts. Likewise, Articles 49 (*Reyners v Belgium* (case 2/74)) and 56 TFEU (*van Binsbergen v Bestuur van de Bedrijfsvereniging voor de Metaalnijverheid* (case 33/74)) have direct effect. Clearly, an individual may enforce the rights contained in these articles against public bodies (*Steinhauser v City of Biarritz* (case 197/84) see Chapter 24), but do they have horizontal effect? The implication from early case law was that they should. In *Walrave*, the Association, a legally recognised professional body, was found to be bound by the terms of what is now Article 56. To put an end to any doubt, the CJ, drawing on its previous case law (*Walrave* and *Bosman*, discussed in Chapter 23), stated in its judgment in *Angonese v Cassa di Risparmio di Bolzano SpA* (case C-281/98), in relation to workers, that 'limiting application of the prohibition of discrimination based on nationality to acts of a public authority risks creating inequality in its application' (para 33). In the *Angonese* case, an Italian national applied to take part in competing for a post with a bank in Italy. There was a condition that the certificate of bilingualism was issued only in Italy. The CJ held that the prohibition on discrimination set out in Article 45 TFEU applies to private persons as well as to public bodies (para 36). It seems likely that the *Angonese*-style reasoning will apply to both establishment and the provision of services.

One question which has not been addressed directly is that of whether the horizontal nature of Articles 45, 49 and 56 TFEU will also apply where the acts in question are not directly discriminatory on grounds of nationality, but which nonetheless impede access to the market. It is nonetheless clear that some private bodies—such as sporting bodies—will be bound even in cases of indirect discrimination or access to the market, as *Bosman* illustrates. Two further cases (*Laval un Partneri v Svenska Byggnadsarbetareförbundet* (case C-341/05) and *International Transport Workers' Federation (ITF) and Finnish Seamen's Union (FSU) v Viking Line*, case C-438/05), concerning Articles 56 and 49 TFEU respectively, confirm that industrial action will, in principle, be caught by the TFEU if it impedes the exercise of the right of establishment or the right to give or receive services. The logic of extension to all private bodies would be the same as for *Angonese*, but given the potential breadth of circumstances in which the provision could be applied, it may be very difficult to police.

Originally, it was not clear whether what is now Article 20 TFEU had direct effect. Many Member States, such as the UK, suggested it did not, whereas the Commission took the contrary view. As seen earlier, the mere fact that secondary legislation is envisaged in a policy area, as here, does not preclude the Treaty provision itself from having direct effect. For some time the CJ avoided ruling on whether Article 20 TFEU had direct effect, despite a number of references on this point, dealing instead with the references on other grounds (eg, *Wijsenbeek*). Eventually, however, the CJ confirmed that Article 20 TFEU does have direct effect (see, eg, *D'Hoop v Office National de l'emploi* (case C-224/98)).

21.4 Personal scope: who benefits?

21.4.1 General

'Who benefits' is the first question we need to ask when considering the scope of the free movement provisions. It is possible to identify two common themes running through the jurisprudence relating to Articles 20, 45, 49 and 56 TFEU:

- nationality
- migration v internal situation.

An additional requirement arises in relation to Articles 45, 49 and 56 TFEU—that there is an economic nexus, though this requirement has been phrased in slightly different language in the case of each article. Crucially, the requirement of an economic nexus does not arise in the context of citizenship and Article 20 TFEU, though the extent to which the distinction in treatment, between those who are economically self-sufficient and those who are not, remains questionable (see 21.5.2 and Chapter 23).

21.4.2 Nationality

The rights in Article 20 TFEU *et seq* are granted to all EU citizens. Article 20 TFEU defines European citizens as: 'Every person holding the nationality of a Member State'. Although not expressly required by the wording of Article 45 TFEU itself, a worker must be a national of one of the Member States. The right of establishment and the right to provide services is accorded under the Treaty to EU nationals and to companies formed according to the law of one of the Member States (on companies, see further 21.4.3). To benefit from the freedom to provide services, an EU national (or company) must be established in a Member State. Thus in *Fidium Finanz*, a Swiss company providing credit services could not rely on Article 56 TFEU to challenge German rules requiring authorisation by the relevant German authorities of companies providing such services in Germany. There is here a double requirement of nationality (of one of the Member States of the Union) and residence, and both must be satisfied. This can also be seen in the context of *FKP Scorpio Konzertproduktionen GmbH v Finanzamt Hamburg-Eimsbüttel* (case C-290/04).

FKP Scorpio Konzertproduktionen GmbH

The case concerned a recipient of services, who was contracting with a party in another Member State. Normally this situation would be covered by Article 56 TFEU, but in this case, the contracting party— although established in another Member State—did not have the nationality of one of the Member States. Article 56 did not therefore apply. As the CJ commented, the Treaty 'does not extend the benefit of those provisions to providers of services who are nationals of non-member countries, even if they are established within the [Union] and an intra-[Union] provision of services is concerned' (para 68).

Nationality is determined according to the domestic law of the Member State concerned. As a Declaration to the TEU, first introduced in 1992 makes clear, it is for each Member State to decide for itself who is to be considered a national of that Member State. Questions of nationality of an individual 'shall be settled solely by reference to the national law of the Member State concerned'. Thus, Member States may only require that an individual provide appropriate identity documents and may not criticise the decision of another Member State to recognise an individual as having the nationality of that Member State. The CJ has considered the issue of nationality. In *Mario Vicente Micheletti and Others v Delegación del Gobierno en Cantabria* (case C-369/90), for example, the CJ held that the Spanish could not challenge the claim of Micheletti—who had the nationality of both Italy and Argentina—to be Italian on the grounds that the Spanish did not recognise the concept of dual nationality. According to the CJ, the important point was whether the Italians recognised his claim (see also *Stephen Saldanha and MTS Securities Corporation v Hiross Holding AG* (case C-122/96)). The viewpoint of the Member State is determinative, as can be seen in *R v Secretary of State for the Home Department, ex parte Manjit Kaur* (case C-192/99). The English High Court referred certain questions to the CJ concerning the extent of the freedom of Member States to define citizenship and, in particular, the limitations imposed on this freedom by the need to respect individuals' fundamental rights. The CJ avoided answering the specific questions on the impact of fundamental human rights, but confirmed that the scope of European citizenship, as far as British subjects were concerned, was determined by the relevant British declarations on this subject.

Since this important criterion for access to Union rights is not an EU concept, inequalities as to who may benefit from European citizenship rights may arise across the Union (contrast, eg, the definition of 'worker', which is a Union concept) given the differences in approach of the Member States as to who may or may not be considered a national. The *Chen* case (discussed further at 21.4.4.2) is illustrative. Catherine Chen was born in the UK to Chinese parents and was resident in the UK, but acquired Irish citizenship by virtue of having been born in Belfast. Irish citizenship law at that time provided that anyone born on the island of Ireland had an automatic right to Irish citizenship. As *Chen* also illustrates, following the approach in *Micheletti* and other cases, Member States cannot challenge another Member State's choice about refusing or restricting citizenship/nationality (see *Rottmann v Freistaat Bayern* (case C-135/08)).

This may have particular consequences for recent Member States, many of which have not granted citizenship to a Russian population who are nonetheless legally resident within their territory, and many of whom have been born in territory that now forms part of the EU. As a result of a national policy these people do not acquire European citizenship.

21.4.3 Companies

One final point to note concerns Articles 49 and 56 TFEU. These two rights, unlike citizens' rights and workers' rights, are expressed as capable of being claimed by legal persons. Article 54 TFEU specifies:

> Companies formed in accordance with the law of a Member State and having their registered office, central administration or principal place of business within the Union shall be treated, for the purposes of the chapter, in the same way as natural persons who are nationals of Member States.

A company's 'nationality' is determined by reference to the Member State in which it has its seat. In the same way as a Member State may choose the conditions on which it grants nationality to individuals, it may choose the connecting factors for a company to acquire 'nationality', that is the conditions it must satisfy to be recognised by the law of the Member State as a company established under the laws of that Member State (*Cartesio*). There are two main theories governing the formation of companies: that which posits that a company is established where it has its main administration, or that which determines the question by reference to where the company has its formal head office. The fact that Member States have not taken a common approach to this question has given rise to some problems.

21.4.4 Migration and the internal situation

21.4.4.1 Economic rights

The CJ has long held that the freedoms constituting the internal market do not apply to internal situations; there must be a cross-border element. This was confirmed in *Nino* (cases C-54, 91/88 and 14/89).

> ### *Nino*
>
> Here, Nino, an Italian national, was qualified as a biotherapist and pranotherapist in Italy. These activities fell within the definition of doctor. Italian law made it an offence to practise as a doctor without proper authorisation. Nino provided treatments in Italy without authorisation, and was charged as a result. The CJ held that Article 49 TFEU did not apply to this situation as it was purely internal.

In *D'Hoop*, the claimant of a job-seekers allowance, who had done her school education in another Member State although her parents had not moved from their state of origin, was held not to fall within Article 45 TFEU. The workers in this case were the parents and they had not moved; the person moving had not worked. Nonetheless, the CJ held that she fell within Union law by virtue of Article 20 TFEU. In this, the CJ seemingly rejected the argument of the UK government that to fall within Union law not only must an individual move but also pursue an activity which falls within the scope of the Treaty, such as studying for a vocational course. This is a qualitative shift in approach: the consequence of citizenship is that movement in itself triggers Union law.

Although the rights conferred by Article 20 TFEU arise as a consequence of an individual holding the nationality of a Member State without further requirement (see eg, *Zablocka-Weyhermüller v Land Baden-Württemberg* (case C-221/07), para 26), the CJ has nonetheless repeatedly held that internal situations fall outside the scope of Union law, even where citizenship is in issue. The movement requirement may be easy to satisfy, however, as *de Coster* illustrates. *De Coster* concerned a tax on the installation of satellite dishes. Although the complainant had not exercised his right to free movement, nor were the satellite dishes necessarily imported, the CJ assumed a cross-border element because the dishes could receive satellite television signals which, as they are inherently transnational, might be from another Member State. Here, the CJ accepted the potential for movement as sufficient.

Two subsequent cases on municipal taxes reaffirm this point: *Mobistar SA v Commune de Fléron* (case C-544/03) and *Viacom Outdoor Srl v Giotto Immobilier SARL* (case C-134/03). *Mobistar* concerned a tax on mobile phone masts and *Viacom* concerned a tax on bill posting. Although in both these cases the national rules were found to be acceptable under Article 56 TFEU, the CJ's reasoning still assumed the possibility of a cross-border element, suggesting a desire on its part to have the jurisdiction to scrutinise national rules for compliance with free movement rights.

21.4.4.2 Citizenship

The CJ's approach in cases involving the EU citizen has been very different. If an EU citizen is deprived of the substance of the right of citizenship, the fact that he or she has not moved within the Union is irrelevant. Respect for his rights as an EU citizen is essential. This point is illustrated by the somewhat unusual facts in the case of *Chen*.

Chen

The case concerned a Chinese couple who travelled to the UK when Mrs Chen was six months' pregnant. She gave birth to a daughter, Catherine, in Belfast and both mother and daughter then moved to Cardiff. Catherine did not acquire British citizenship, as birth in the territory of the UK itself no longer confers UK nationality. The operation of Irish nationality laws meant that Catherine did acquire Irish nationality, as any person born on the island of Ireland is an Irish citizen from birth if not entitled to citizenship of any other country. Catherine lost the right to Chinese nationality by virtue of being born in Northern Ireland. None of the parties were entitled to reside in the UK under national law, but Catherine was not entitled to reside in China. The parties were not dependent on the UK welfare services to survive and it was unlikely that they would be so dependent. Nonetheless, the Secretary of State refused Mrs Chen and Catherine long-term residence permits. The UK and Irish governments argued that Catherine could not exercise free movement rights because she had not moved from one Member State to another; she had only ever lived in the UK.

The CJ rejected this argument. Relying on *Garcia Avello*, the CJ held that the situation of a national of one Member State who has only ever lived in the host Member State cannot be assimilated to a purely internal situation (para 19). Further, the ability to exercise free movement rights is not circumscribed by the need to acquire legal capacity; children may exercise free movement rights.

Consequently, Catherine Chen had the right to reside in the United Kingdom by virtue of the EU citizenship. That right would be rendered meaningless if her parent, who is her primary carer, could not reside with her. Catherine's right of residence would be deprived of any useful effect. The CJ had rejected the argument that baby Catherine's mother was dependent upon her but, nevertheless, the CJ has clarified the position of the TCN parent of a baby citizen of the Union.

Another citizenship case, *Zambrano v ONEm* (case C-34/09) disassociated the scope of EU law from the need to show a trans-national element still further.

Zambrano

A Colombian national, Zambrano, moved to Belgium with his wife and young son in 1999. His wife gave birth to two children, both of whom had Belgian nationality. Mr Zambrano, although he did not have a work permit, was employed on a full-time contract of employment. He was thus able to provide for his family. The CJ found that a person in Mr Zambrano's position was entitled to remain and work in Belgium without a work permit. He derived this right from his children who were EU citizens and who, in the absence of the right of their parent to live and work in Belgium, would be deprived 'of the genuine enjoyment of the substance of the rights conferred by virtue of their status as citizens of the Union'.

Had Mr Zambrano not been able to remain in Belgium his dependent children would have had to leave not just Belgium, the country of their birth and residence, but the territory of the Union as a whole and thus be deprived of any opportunity to exercise their citizenship rights. In the words of the CJ:

> It must be assumed that such a refusal would lead to a situation where those children, citizens of the Union, would have to leave the territory of the Union in order to accompany their parents. Similarly, if a work permit were not granted to such a person, he would risk not having sufficient resources to provide for himself and his family, which would also result in the children, citizens of the Union, having to leave the territory of the Union. In those circumstances, those citizens of the Union would, in fact, be unable to exercise the substance of the rights conferred on them by virtue of their status as citizens of the Union [para 44].

The subsequent case of *McCarthy (Shirley) v Secretary of State for the Home Department* (case C-434/09) concerned an adult EU national who could herself exercise citizenship rights.

McCarthy

Shirley McCarthy had dual citizenship: British and Irish. She was born and has always lived in the United Kingdom and has never been economically active. In 2002 she married a Jamaican national who had no right to remain in the United Kingdom. The McCarthys applied to the Secretary of State for a residence permit and residence documents under EU law as, respectively, a Union citizen and the spouse of a Union citizen. Their applications were refused. On a reference from the UK Supreme Court, the CJ held that as a national of a Member State, Mrs McCarthy enjoyed the status of a Union citizen under Article 20(1) TFEU and could rely on rights pertaining to that status and in particular the right conferred by Article 21 TFEU to move and reside freely within the territory of the Member States.

However, in contrast to *Zambrano*, the national measures at issue in this case did not have the effect of obliging Mrs McCarthy to leave the territory of the European Union:

> the failure by the authorities of the United Kingdom to take into account the Irish nationality of Mrs McCarthy for the purposes of granting her a right of residence in the United Kingdom in no way affects her in her right to move and reside freely within the territory of the member States, or any other right conferred on her by virtue of her status as a Union citizen.
> However, no element of the situation of Mrs McCarthy . . . indicates that the national measure at issue . . . has the effect of depriving her of the genuine enjoyment of the substance of the rights associated with her status as a Union citizen, or of impeding the exercise of her right to move and

reside freely within the territory of the Member States, in accordance with Article 21 TFEU. Indeed, the failure by the authorities of the United Kingdom to take into account the Irish nationality of Mrs McCarthy for the purposes of granting her a right of residence in the United Kingdom in no way affects her in her right to move and reside freely within the territory of the Member States, or any other right conferred on her by virtue of her status as a Union citizen [paras 49–50].

This approach was further clarified in *Dereci and Others v Bundesministerium für Inneres J* (case C-256/11) which concerned a series of refusals to grant residence permits to third country national family members of Austrian nationals who had never exercised EU free movement rights. They had entered Austria, in some cases legally, in others illegally, and had never moved to another Member State. The CJ stated what had been implicit in *McCarthy*. Deprivation of the genuine enjoyment of the substance of citizenship rights arises when a Union citizen 'has, in fact, to leave not only the territory of the Member State of which he is a national but also the territory of the Union as a whole'. If such a person does not have to leave the territory of the Union, then the national measures in question cannot be said to deprive him of his citizenship rights because:

the mere fact that it might appear desirable to a national of a Member State, for economic reason or in order to keep his family together in the territory of the Union, for members of his family who do not have the nationality of a Member State to be able to reside with him in the territory of the Union, is not sufficient in itself to support the view that the Union citizen will be forced to leave Union territory if such a right is not granted [para 68].

The Court in these three cases focused upon the person whose citizenship rights were at stake. The Zambrano children, as well as Catherine Zhu (*Chen*), would have been deprived totally of their rights of citizenship under Article 21 TFEU had their parents, upon whom they were totally dependent, not been allowed to remain with them on Union territory. By contrast, Mrs McCarthy and the Austrian nationals in *Dereci* would have preferred for their family members to reside with them in the countries of which they were nationals but they themselves were neither denied the right to move freely within the Union nor obliged to leave the territory of the Union. Their citizenship rights were not prejudiced by the refusal of the national authorities to allow their family members to reside with them.

21.4.4.3 Companies

A similarly broad approach to the existence of the connection with Union law can be seen with regard to companies. Migration occurs not only when a company moves, but when it sets up a branch, agency or subsidiary in another Member State. Establishment rights may be exercised against home and host Member State. This can be seen in *Marks and Spencer v Halsey (Inspector of Taxes)* (case C-446/03).

Marks and Spencer plc

Here, a UK law precluded a parent company from deducting losses made by its subsidiaries in other Member States, though it could deduct losses made by subsidiaries in the UK. The effect of this rule was to deter companies established in the UK from establishing subsidiaries in other Member States. Thus a UK rule was challenged by a UK company; the cross-border element was provided by the impact on its choices about whether to set up subsidiaries in other Member States; actual movement—or relocation—by the company was not required.

21.4.5 Is migration status indefinite?

The question of the longevity of migration status is also important. So, if you have migrated once, are you always a migrant? On the basis of current case law, children whose parents exercised free movement rights, or whose parents hold different EU nationalities, would seem destined to live their lives within the sphere of EU law. Another question then arises: what is the scope of the rights available in such circumstances?

Questions as to scope and longevity of rights are not new, though the impact of citizenship might be significant in terms of the circumstances in which rights can arise. This issue can be seen even before the Maastricht Treaty in the case of *Konstantinidis*.

Konstantinidis

Here, a Greek national was established as a self-employed person in Germany. His claim was based on the fact that his name was wrongly transliterated as 'Konstadinidis' on the marriage register there, instead of the correct 'Konstantinidis', as found on his passport. When he applied for rectification of the register, he was told that German rules required transliteration according to a particular standard, which resulted in the (incorrect) transposition. He challenged the rule as contrary to what is now Article 49 TFEU.

Note that the marriage register did not relate to his business activities; accepting his argument would have meant a broad scope being applied to the right, which was not necessarily tied to the initial exercise of the free movement right or the continuing activity. The Advocate-General took the view that the rules constituted covert discrimination and the fact that this was not directly related to his business was irrelevant. He further considered the question of whether Konstantinidis was entitled to rely on the ECHR (particularly Article 8 with regard to private life) as protected by Union law, and concluded that he was. The CJ, however, took a different approach. It held:

> Rules of this kind must only be considered incompatible with Article 52 EEC [now Article 49 TFEU] in so far as their application creates for the Greek national such a constraint that it actually interferes with the unfettered exercise of the right of establishment conferred upon him by that Article [para 15].

The approach of the CJ is a much narrower conception, making clear the link with the economic function of the provision, rather than the approach suggested by the Advocate-General, which would have had the impact of creating a class of favoured migrants. Whether Article 49 TFEU is still so limited as regards the rights of individuals in the light of the introduction of citizenship rights may, however, be questionable. (contrast *D'Hoop* discussed earlier). We return to the issue of the scope of rights, and particularly Union competence in Chapters 22 and 23.

A right may also be relied on when those who have exercised their rights of free movement seek to return to their state of origin. This approach was confirmed in *Knoors v Secretary of State for Economic Affairs* (case 115/78) in relation to a Dutch national who moved to Belgium where he worked as a plumber. He returned to the Netherlands and relied on his experience in Belgium when he sought to have his qualifications recognised by the Dutch authorities. A similar approach can be seen with relation to workers in the *Singh* case.

Singh

Mr Singh was an Indian who had married a British national in 1982. He and his wife subsequently went to work in Germany, returning in 1985 to open a business in the UK. Their marriage broke down in 1988. Following the issue of a decree nisi but before the decree became absolute, that is before the divorce was finalised, the UK authorities sought to deport Mr Singh. His appeal against the deportation order was successful. Since the divorce was not yet a legal fact, the case still concerned the position of spouses and the rights that spouses could claim under EU law. The question of the effect of the subsequent divorce was not an issue before the Court (although the fact of divorce was known). The CJ held that, as the spouse of an EU national who had exercised her rights to work in Germany, Singh was entitled on their return to claim his rights as a spouse under EU law.

21.4.6 Meaning of 'worker' for Article 45 TFEU

As the CJ held in *Levin v Staatssecretaris van Justitie* (case 53/81), the concept of 'worker' is a Union concept, not dependent for its meaning on the laws of Member States. There are two aspects to the definition of worker:

- a formal aspect;
- an economic aspect.

The formal aspect questions whether an individual is employed, rather than self-employed; while the economic test looks at the nature, duration and quality of the work. These two elements can be seen in *Lawrie-Blum v Land Baden-Württemberg* (case 66/85) which concerned a trainee teacher. The German government contended that, as a trainee, Lawrie-Blum did not fall within the definition of 'worker'. The CJ rejected this argument and in doing so laid down a three-stage test for a worker. It suggested the 'essential characteristics' of a worker is that he:

- performs services for and under the direction of another;
- for a certain period of time;
- in return for remuneration.

Note that remuneration need not be in the form of cash, but could also be benefits in kind (see the discussion of *Steymann v Staatssecretaris van Justitie* (case 196/87)). The essential test is that there should be some consideration for work performed.

As regards the economic element of the test for 'worker', in *Levin* the CJ held that the term 'worker' applied even to those who worked to a limited extent (ie, part-time), provided that the work was 'real' work, and not nominal or minimal. The rights only attach to those who perform or wish to perform an activity of an economic nature. The Court went on to say that this principle applied whether the worker was self-supporting or whether he wished to make do with less than the national minimum income. It was able to side-step the problem of the part-time worker who relies on public funds for his support.

This issue was squarely faced in *Kempf v Staatssecretaris van Justitie* (case 139/85).

Kempf

Kempf was a German, part-time music teacher working in the Netherlands from 1981 to 1982. During this time he was in receipt of Dutch supplementary benefit, both sickness benefit and general assistance. In November 1981 he applied for a Dutch residence permit. He was refused on the grounds that he was not a 'favoured EU citizen', since his income from his work was not sufficient to meet his needs. He challenged that decision before the Dutch courts. The Raad van State referred to the CJ the question whether a part-time worker such as Kempf, whose income was below subsistence level and who did not have sufficient means of support, was a 'worker' entitled to benefit under Union law. The Court replied that he was. Freedom of movement of workers was, it held, one of the fundamental freedoms and must, as such, be defined broadly; a person who pursued a genuine and effective activity as an employed person, even on a part-time basis, could not be excluded from the scope of Union rules merely because he sought to supplement his income, which was lower than the means of subsistence, by other lawful means of subsistence. It was irrelevant whether the income was supplemented out of a private income or from public funds.

The Court has, however, held that the duration of the activity concerned was a factor which might be taken into account in assessing whether the employment was effective and genuine or so limited as to be marginal or ancillary (*Raulin v Netherlands Ministry for Education and Science* (case C-357/89), see further 21.4.7.1 and note similarities with services and establishment case law).

Following *Kempf*, in *Steymann*, the Court held that the claimant's occupation as part of a religious community, entitling him to his 'keep' and pocket money, but not to formal wages, constituted a genuine and effective activity where commercial activity is an inherent part of membership of that community. In contrast, in *Bettray v Staatssecretaris van Justitie* (case 344/87) paid activity provided by the state as part of a drug rehabilitation programme under its social employment law was held by the Court not to represent 'real and genuine economic activity'. To give rise to the status of 'worker', the work performed must fulfil, or derive from, some *economic* purpose. It has been suggested, however, that the principle of *Bettray* does not apply to 'ordinary' sheltered employment. The undertaking in *Bettray* existed solely for the purpose of rehabilitation and re-education of the persons employed therein.

The question of whether an individual who works and receives benefits in kind at a minimal level was raised in *Trojani v Le Centre Public d'Aide Sociale de Bruxelles* (case C-456/02). In this case, the CJ reiterated the points made in its earlier case law: the determination of whether someone is a worker is a question of fact to be assessed by objective criteria.

Trojani

In this case, the applicant was carrying out jobs for approximately 30 hours per week for the Salvation Army as part of a personal reintegration programme. In return, he received benefits in kind. The CJ made two points. The CJ identified that the key question in determining whether Trojani was a worker or not was whether his activities formed part of the 'normal labour market'. Secondly, this was a question of fact over which the national court has exclusive jurisdiction. The CJ consequently did not come to a determination on the facts.

Although the final result in this case is consequently not clear, the principle remains that rehabilitation does not constitute work for the purposes of Article 45 TFEU. It may well be, however, that this issue has lost much of its significance with the introduction of citizenship and the rights flowing from migrant citizen status (see Chapter 23).

21.4.6.1 The position of students

The position of people who migrate and then become students has given rise to difficulties. The status of students as workers was raised in *Brown v Secretary of State for Scotland* (case 197/86) and *Lair v Universität Hannover* (case 39/86). In both these cases the parties, having obtained a place at university, Brown at Cambridge to study engineering, and Lair at the University of Hanover to study languages, claimed maintenance grants from the UK and German authorities, respectively. Although Brown had dual French/English nationality, he and his family had for many years been domiciled in France; Lair was a Frenchwoman. Prior to taking up his place at Cambridge, Brown had obtained university sponsorship from, and worked for, Ferranti in Scotland. The job lasted for eight months. Lair had worked intermittently in Germany for over five years, with spells of involuntary unemployment. Both parties were refused a grant and sought to challenge that refusal on the basis of, inter alia, Regulation 1612/68, Article 7(2)–(3) which have now been codified in Regulation 492/2011 ([2011] OJ L141/1) (these provisions will be discussed in Chapter 23).

The crucial question was whether Brown and Lair were 'workers', and therefore entitled to claim the grants under Article 7 of Regulation 1612/68; the CJ excluded an argument that Brown and Lair could rely on the general principle of non-discrimination in what is now Article 18 TFEU as education was not at that point within the scope of Union competence. Brown had come to the UK primarily to prepare for his engineering studies at Cambridge and his work experience formed part of this preparation; he had obtained his place at Cambridge prior to taking up work in the UK. Lair, on the other hand, had undoubtedly come to Germany many years before, intending to work. The Court, which delivered judgments in both cases on the same day, held that the concept of worker must have a Union meaning. Nevertheless, in Brown's case, although he might be regarded as a worker, he was not entitled to claim the grant as a social advantage because he had acquired the status of worker exclusively as a result of his having been accepted for admission to university. The employment was part of his preparation for his studies and was therefore merely ancillary to the studies to be financed by the grant. With regard to Lair's claim, the Court drew a distinction between a claim by a migrant worker who was *involuntarily* unemployed, who, if legitimately resident, was entitled to the same treatment as regards reinstatement or re-employment as national workers, and one who gave up his work in order to undertake further training in the host Member State. In the latter case, he or she might only claim a grant for such a course if there was some link between the studies to be pursued and his previous work activity.

The Court chose to base its decision in both cases on fine factual distinctions rather than on the 'genuineness' of the claimant's status as a worker, although it did add in *Lair*, in response to the expressed worries of Member States as to the possibility of abuse, that:

> insofar as a worker has entered a Member State for the sole purpose of enjoying, after a very short period of work activity, the benefit of the student assistance system in that State, it should be observed that such abuses are not covered by the [Union] provisions [ie Article 7(2)–(3)] in question [para 43].

This reasoning, which is implicitly based on the possibility of 'abuse', is problematic. It suggests that motive is relevant for the acquisition of worker status. Nonetheless, the tension between acceptable and unacceptable uses of Union law remains, and recurs periodically in the case law.

Further, it is regrettable that in its concern to appease the anxiety of Member States, the CJ chose in *Lair* to limit the scope of Article 7(2) of Regulation 1612/68 by denying a right to 'social advantages' in the form of grants to migrant workers who have not become unemployed but who genuinely want to improve their prospects by retraining in a *new* field of activity. In an era of rapid technological and economic change, flexibility in the workforce is surely to be encouraged; nonetheless, a similar approach is found in the CRD, Article 7(3)(d).

This area continued to give rise to litigation. This can be seen in the context of *Raulin*.

Raulin

Here, in a claim by a French national for a grant to pursue a full-time course in the plastic arts in the Netherlands, following 60 hours' work as a waitress there, the Court followed *Brown* and *Lair*, adding only that in assessing whether the work undertaken was 'effective and genuine' for the purpose of acquiring the status of worker, both the length of time of employment and all the activities undertaken in the host state might be taken into account, but not the activities conducted elsewhere in the Union.

The situation of someone who works for a short period and then becomes a student was considered again in *Ninni-Orasche v Bundesminister für Wissenschaft Verkehr und Kunst* (case C-413/01).

Ninni-Orasche

The applicant was an Italian national who married an Austrian and moved to Austria. After about two years, she took up a fixed-term contract as a waitress and cashier, working for only a couple of months. She also completed a distance-learning diploma in bookkeeping and commerce. She then tried to get a job relying on her diploma but was unsuccessful, so she started studying Romance languages at Klagenfurt University. The case concerned her claim for financial assistance from the Austrian government.

The CJ reiterated its approach in *Lair* and *Raulin*, that is, a worker who ceases to work retains some rights to social assistance provided there is continuity between the previous occupational activity and the studies pursued. Following its previous case law, the CJ also noted that this limitation was not imposed on those who are involuntarily unemployed. In this case, the CJ emphasised that the determination of whether someone is a 'worker' is based on objective criteria and should take into account circumstances as a whole.

The CJ specifically rejected certain factors which the referring court had identified as potentially relevant to the assessment of her status—that is, the fact she did not start work immediately on her entry into Austria, the fact that she became eligible for study by virtue of her diploma, and her attempts to find work. These were not relevant as they preceded or were subsequent to the period of employment.

The expiry of a fixed-term contract does not necessarily mean a person has become voluntarily unemployed. This may vary on facts. Crucially, some of the factors the CJ dismissed as not relevant to the determination of the economic aspect of 'worker' might be relevant in identifying if a worker has become voluntarily unemployed or not. The CJ has repeatedly held that motivation for moving is not a relevant factor in determining whether someone is a worker in the first place, but seems to become relevant where an individual stops work and seeks to rely on continuing rights. This assessment could be based on the implicit concern, already noted, that individuals who migrate and do minimum work for a short period before seeking to claim benefits in the host Member State are manipulating, if not abusing, Union law. The rights granted to workers can be traced to an idea of solidarity, where the migrant has already contributed to the system on which he or she seeks to rely. Nonetheless, the approach here might seem to be taking a more generous line than that adopted in *Raulin*. (See also *Office National de 'l'emploi v Ioannidis* (case C-258/04)–CJ assumed migrant who had completed a paid training course in another Member State was a worker.)

Summarising the position, it would seem as though the position of someone seeking host-state support for studies could be attributed to one of four categories:

(1) The work undertaken was ancillary to another activity (in this case the individual is not a worker and cannot claim rights under Article 45 TFEU or Regulation 492/2011 ([2011] OJ L141/1); but note the impact of citizenship in *Bidar* (discussed also in Chapter 24). A French national, had legal residence in the UK for three years while being in a secondary school. He received financial assistance from the UK authorities for his university tuition fees but his application for maintenance aid was rejected. The CJ has clarified that EU citizens have a legitimate expectation for financial solidarity subject to satisfying the condition of sufficient integration to the host society. Length of time is a particularly important factor when considering the degree of sufficient integration).

(2) The work undertaken is marginal and therefore the individual is not a worker (presumably this would be in cases such as *Raulin*, though it is not possible to state this with certainty, as the CJ has left national courts to assess the facts).

(3) A student was a worker and became voluntarily unemployed, in which case to be entitled to support there must be a link between the previous work and the study (*Bernini*).

(4) A student was a worker and became involuntarily unemployed, in which case the individual retains his or her rights as a worker even if the study is unconnected with the previous work (*Lair; Ninni-Orasche*).

Individuals falling in each of these categories will also be EU citizens and claim rights as such, though the significance of this to such individuals would depend on which category each fell in, and consequently whether they could claim rights as workers and the scope of any such rights. The CJ has not been consistent in this approach, however, as can be seen in a decision of the Grand Chamber, *Förster v Hoofddirectie van de Informatie Beheer Groep* (case C-158/07).

Förster

Here, a German national moved to the Netherlands to be with her partner. She worked for a short while before commencing her studies. During this time she continued to work and received maintenance payments from the Dutch authorities which viewed her as a worker. She then stopped working part-time and the authorities tried to reclaim payments made. The Advocate-General noted that *Förster* fell in the same line of cases as *Lair, Raulin, Ninni-Orasche* etc, and that therefore, as the Dutch authorities had accepted she was a worker, *Förster* was entitled to the payments. The CJ did not consider this possibility, suggesting that, in fact, it viewed *Förster* as falling outside the definition of 'worker'. In the end, the CJ determined that *Förster* was a migrant EU national, but not entitled to payments as she was not sufficiently integrated in the Netherlands, despite her three years' residence there.

Whilst the case law discussed above can be seen as a separate strand of cases relating specifically to students, the cases might also be seen as part of the case law on continuing rights. Continuing rights are rights to which someone is entitled after he stops working, by virtue of having been a worker (see also 21.4.5). The longevity of rights, especially when no longer directly connected with economic activity, is contentious. Whilst the CJ has not come to a coherent theory for all circumstances, since continuing rights remain after a person ceases to be a worker, it could be argued that this justifies a slightly more restrictive view of the scope of the rights available to individuals in such circumstances.

21.4.7 Meaning of establishment for Article 49 TFEU

21.4.7.1 General

A right of establishment is a right to install oneself, to 'set up shop' in another Member State, permanently or semi-permanently, whether as an individual, a partnership or a company, for the purpose of performing a particular economic activity there. The concept of establishment has been held to be 'a broad one, allowing a [Union] national to participate on a stable and continuous basis in the economic life of a Member State other than his own' (*Gebhard*). In *Commission v Germany (insurance services)* (case 205/84) the Court suggested that an enterprise would fall within the concept of 'establishment' even if its presence is not in the form of a branch or agency but consists merely of an office managed by the enterprise's own staff or by a person who is independent but is authorised to act on a permanent basis for the enterprise. Thus in the case of *Gambelli* (case C-243/01), the CJ commented:

> Where a company established in a Member State . . . pursues the activity of collecting bets through the intermediary of an organisation of agencies established in another Member State (such as the defendants in the main proceedings), any restrictions on the activities of those agencies constitute obstacles to the freedom of establishment [para 46].

21.4.7.2 Elements of establishment

Certain elements need to be shown to bring the freedom of establishment into play. We have noted the requirement for migration (21.4.4) and for economic activity (15.3.1). The CJ has borrowed the test for economic activity from both the workers and services spheres to determine that work or service performed is genuine and effective and not such as to be regarded as purely marginal and ancillary (*Jany v Staatssecretaris van Justitie* (case C-268/99), para 33). As regards companies, Article 54(2) TFEU expressly excludes those companies which are non-profit making. This does not mean that the business must make a profit but that it is intended so to do. Charitable work seems to be excluded (cf *Bettray* (case 344/87) discussed at 21.4.6).

The final element is self-employed activity; this is a formal criterion. The cases on workers (at 21.4.6) discuss the definition of employment. We can therefore identify self-employment by a process of elimination. The CJ identified the criteria for self-employed activity in *Jany* starting from this premise. Although the case concerned the Europe Agreements, the principles can nonetheless be applied here, as the same concepts as found in Article 49 TFEU were under consideration. The question before the CJ was whether women working as window prostitutes in Amsterdam could claim the benefit of the freedom of establishment. The question was crucial for the women in *Jany*, as the association agreements did not give the right to take up employment, although it permitted establishment. The CJ held that establishment required:

- the provision of a service;
- outside any relationship of subordination concerning the choice of that activity, working conditions and conditions of remuneration;

- under that person's own responsibility;
- in return for remuneration paid to that person directly and in full (para 71).

The CJ rejected the Dutch government's argument that, given the subordinate relationship of a prostitute to her pimp, she was in an employment relationship; the CJ pointed out the Dutch government had adduced no evidence on the point and furthermore disagreed with the assumption that a relationship of dependency could be equated to an employment relationship. In assessing whether a person is carrying out such activities, it does not matter that he or she is undergoing professional training (*Morgenbesser v Consiglio dell'Ordine degli Avvacati di Genova* (case C-313/01)—recognition of French legal qualifications in Italy, requirement for further training).

21.4.8 Meaning of services for Article 56 TFEU (ex Article 49 EC)

21.4.8.1 General

'Services' are defined as those 'normally provided for remuneration, insofar as they are not governed by the provisions relating to freedom of movement for goods, capital and persons' (Article 57(1)). Services in the field of transport are 'governed by the provisions of the Title [Part Three, Title VI] relating to transport' (Article 58 TFEU). The liberalisation of banking and insurance services connected with movements of capital was to be effected 'in step with the liberalisation of movement of capital'; Article 57 TFEU provides a non-exhaustive list of examples of services. There are a number of key elements in identifying a service for the purposes of Article 56 TFEU.

21.4.8.2 Types of activity caught

Although Article 57 provides a list of services that are definitely caught by Article 56, *Grogan*, discussed later, illustrates that no area of economic activity in principle falls outside the Treaty, no matter what its moral, cultural or ethical status. Article 56 TFEU will, in theory, only apply if none of the other freedoms do—that is, it is a catch-all or fall-back provision—and provided the service does not fall within the Treaty provisions dealing with transport (but cf 20.5).

Because of the special nature of services, lending themselves to promotion and even provision via modern 'distance' methods of communication, a service can be deemed to 'move' within the Union without either the provider or the recipient moving across national borders. Thus, Article 56 TFEU can be used to regulate either the provider, or the service itself. In *Alpine Investments BV v Minister van Financiën* (case C-384/93), a Dutch prohibition on 'cold calling' (the soliciting of business by telephone), by providers of financial advice established in the Netherlands, was held to constitute a barrier to the free provision of services contrary to Article 56 TFEU (although it was found on the facts to be justified). Restrictions on cross-border advertising relating to the distribution of goods will be dealt with under the free movement of goods provisions of Article 34 TFEU (*Leclerc-Siplec*, decided on *Keck* principles, see Chapter 18, but contrast *Karner*). The broad scope of the right means that it can be relied on against both host and home Member State and, as *Alpine Investments* shows, in an 'export' situation as well as when the services are being imported (see also 21.4.4).

Finally, the right to provide services includes the right to receive (*Luisi and Carbonne*). This aspect of the rights is discussed in Chapter 24.

As with establishment and workers, there must be an economic element. The test derived is that the services performed must be genuine and effective and not marginal and ancillary. In *Deliège*, we can see that the CJ has found this requirement to be satisfied quite easily. *Deliège* concerned the case of an amateur athlete. In considering whether or not economic activity was involved, the CJ argued:

> that sporting activities and, in particular, a high-ranking athlete's participation in an international competition are capable of involving the provision of a number of separate, but closely related, services which may fall within the scope of Article [56] of the Treaty even if some of those services are not paid for by those for whom they are performed.

In developing its earlier jurisprudence on television broadcasting (see *Bond van Adverteerders and Others v Netherlands State* (case 352/85), para 16) the CJ suggested that the fact that activities can form the basis of commerce means Article 56 must be engaged. Note it also seems that it does not matter whether remuneration is found in the particular case under consideration, provided the type of service is such that it is usually provided for remuneration (see, eg, *Freskot AE v Elliniko Dimosio* (case C-355/00), para 54).

Although the CJ has repeatedly held that the basic Treaty freedoms must be interpreted widely, there are limits. In *Grogan*, the provision of information about abortion clinics in other Member States by officers of a students' union (abortion at the time being illegal in Ireland) was held not to fall within the scope of Article 56. Although abortion (when legal in the Member State in which the procedure took place) could constitute a service within the Treaty, the link between the provision of an information service about the clinics and the clinics themselves was too tenuous to bring Article 56 into play; specifically it lacked an economic aspect as the students' union was providing this as a free service and did not receive payment from the clinics. Some have suggested that this judgment is an isolated decision and that the CJ's reasoning in this case was motivated by a desire to avoid a sensitive political issue. The Irish position as regards abortion was formalised by a Protocol annexed to the TEU.

21.4.9 **Distinction between the provisions**

The relationship between the freedoms is dealt with in general terms in Chapter 15. Nonetheless, given the similarities in circumstances in which these rights may be exercised, some further consideration is due here. There are two aspects to consider: one may be considered vertical, which permits overlap between the freedoms and citizenship (eg, *Collins v Secretary of State for Work and Pensions* (case C-138/02) and *Grzeczyk v Centre Public D'Aide Sociale D'Ottignies-Louvain-La-Neuve* (case C-184/99)); the second, where the freedoms are mutually exclusive, can be considered horizontal. The relationship may be rendered diagrammatically as seen in Figure 21.1.

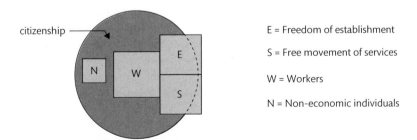

Figure 21.1 Relationship between citizenship, freedom of establishment, free movement of services and free movement of workers

The circle represents citizenship, which incorporates all workers and non-economic individuals (protected by Union legislation), but only those aspects of establishment and services pertaining to individuals. It may be that where economically active citizens cannot rely on the provisions of the Treaty relating to their status as such they may be able to fall back upon the provision relating to EU citizenship. There is no overlap between the freedoms, though the boundary between them may be fine. It has also held that where the more specific provisions apply, for example Article 45 TFEU, there is no need to interpret Article 20 TFEU (see *Stylianakis v Elliniko Dimosio* (case C-92/01), regarding the relationship between Article 20 and Article 56 TFEU; *Skanavi and Chryssanthakopoulos* (case C-193/94), regarding establishment; and *Ministre de l'intérieur v Oteiza Olazabal* (case C-100/01), regarding workers).

Some lack of clarity remains. In some of these cases where free movement provisions could apply, the CJ does not refer to citizenship at all (see, eg, *Stylianakis v Elliniko Dimosio* (case C-92/01)). In others, although the question is determined on the basis of one of the four freedoms, the interpretation of that freedom is affected by the notion of citizenship (see, eg, *Olazabal; Bickel and Franz*), which the CJ has held to be a fundamental status of EU nationals (see, eg, *Grzelczyk*, para 31) (see further Chapter 23). The CJ has, in some cases, referred to one of the economic freedoms and citizenship (see, eg, *Schwarz and Gootjes-Schwarz v Finanzamt Bergisch Gladbach* (case C-76/05) concerning the right to tax deductions against private school fees).

We have noted the difference between workers and establishment at 21.4.7.2. The relationship between establishment and services should, however, be considered further. The difference between the right of establishment and the right to provide services is, in many instances, one of degree rather than of kind, though with the introduction of the Services Directive (see Chapter 22 at 22.8) the distinction may acquire a greater significance. The key distinction seems to be the strength of the connection between the right holder and the host Member State. Whereas establishment suggests some degree of continuity or permanence, the right to provide services connotes the provision of services in one Member State, on a temporary or spasmodic basis, by a person established in another Member State. In the latter case it is not necessary to reside, even temporarily, in the Member State in which the service is provided. The temporary nature of the activities in question should be determined in the light not only of the duration of the service but of its regularity, periodicity and continuity (*Gebhard*). Applying these principles in *Gebhard* the Court found that the setting up of chambers in Italy by a German barrister, a practising member of the Stuttgart Bar, fell within the concept of establishment. A person could be established, within the meaning of the Treaty, in more than one Member State, in particular, in the case of companies, through the setting up of branches or subsidiaries, and, in the case of members of the professions, by establishing a second professional base.

The relationship between the secondary implementing legislation and the underlying Treaty articles deserves further comment. In the context of the free movement of persons, the CJ has relied in some cases on a broad interpretation of underlying Treaty articles, to interpret restrictively the limitations on free movement imposed by the implementing directives, or to limit discretion allowed to Member States by the terms of the directives (see, eg, *Collins* (regarding Articles 45 and 20 TFEU), *Baumbast and R v Secretary of State for the Home Department* (case C-413/99), and *Grzelczyck* (regarding Article 20 TFEU)).

21.4.10 **Families**

It is in the context of determining family rights that the changes introduced by the CRD can be seen. In some respects, the fundamental position has not changed. The rights of family members are derived from the EU national who seeks to exercise free movement rights, if they are not an EU national themselves. As noted in 21.4.4, the citizen must satisfy the migration test before he or she, or any family members, can benefit from the rights granted. In this respect the CRD does not change the position. The changes introduced by the CRD can, however, be seen in the definition of family member, as the CRD not only incorporates judicial developments in this area, but fills in lacunae in protection left by the CJ's jurisprudence.

Much of the jurisprudence relating to families arose in the context of the free movement of workers. Article 2(1)(2) CRD defines family member as:

(a) the spouse;

(b) the partner with whom the Union citizen has contracted a registered partnership, on the basis of the legislation of a Member State, if the legislation of the host Member States treats registered partnerships as equivalent to marriage and in accordance with the conditions laid down in the relevant legislation of the host Member State;

(c) the direct descendants who are under the age of 21 or are dependants and those of the spouse or partner as defined in point (b);

(d) the dependent direct relatives in the ascending line as defined in point (b).

Article 3 identifies the beneficiaries of the rights specified in the CRD. In addition to Union citizens and their family members, Article 3(2) recommends that Member States facilitate the entry of two other groups of people:

(a) any other family members, irrespective of their nationality, not falling under the definition in point 2 of Article 2 who, in the country from which they have come, are dependants or members of the household of the Union citizen having the primary right of residence, or where serious health grounds strictly require the personal care of the family member by the Union citizen;

(b) the partner with whom the citizen has a durable relationship, duly attested.

21.4.10.1 'Spouse' and 'partner'

The definition in Article 2(2) CRD includes both the category of a worker's spouse and that of a worker's partner. In this, the article is broader than the drafting of Regulation 1612/68, Article 10, but in fact reflects the jurisprudence of the CJ, based on the principle of non-discrimination. In *Netherlands v Reed* (case 59/85) the CJ was asked whether the term 'spouse' included a cohabitee.

Reed

The case concerned Ms Reed's right to reside in Holland with her English cohabitee of five years' standing, who was working in Holland. Ms Reed, who was also English, was not herself a worker. The Court held that in the then state of Union law the term spouse referred to marital relationships only. This did not mean that Ms Reed was not entitled to remain in Holland. As her cohabitee was a worker in Holland, and since aliens with stable relationships with *Dutch* nationals were entitled in similar circumstances to reside in Holland, it would be discriminatory, in breach of what is now Article 18 TFEU and Article 45 (also what is now Article 7(2) of Regulation 492/2011 ([2011] OJ L141/1)), not to accord him the same treatment as national workers. Ms Reed was not entitled to remain as a 'spouse', but she was entitled to remain on account of her cohabitee's rights not to be discriminated against under the Treaty.

'Cohabitee' in the *Reed* sense seems to equate to 'partner' in the context of Article 2(1). There are two points to note here. First, non-marital partnerships within the meaning of Article 2 are limited to those which are registered; other partnerships are dealt with under Article 3(2). Secondly, the CRD is based on the principle of non-discrimination with how a registered partnership is treated under the national regime of the host Member State, as was *Reed*. The approach in *Reed* was criticised because it did not introduce equality across the Union; different Member States could treat non-married couples differently. The CRD has not addressed this point. Nonetheless, this line of reasoning may have the benefit of assisting same-sex couples in Member States where they may register their unions.

Since the rights of partners are to some degree limited, the precise extent of the notion of spouse still has meaning; the case law from Regulation 1612/68 is probably still good law in this regard. However, there is uncertainty about how to reconcile the two rules in the event of a conflict. It can be argued that the most favourable rule to the applicants should apply. Another question which arises is whether a divorced spouse is entitled to claim rights as a 'spouse' under EU law. This can be seen as a question about the meaning of the term 'spouse', or as a question of whether someone who was a spouse has residual rights after he or she ceases to be a spouse. In *Diatta v Land Berlin* (case 267/83), the CJ examined whether someone who was a spouse has residual rights after he or she ceases to be a spouse. The Court held that a separated spouse (in this case a Senegalese national), who intended to obtain a divorce and who was living apart from her husband, a worker in Germany, did not lose her rights of residence in Germany merely because she did not live under the same roof. The marital relationship is not dissolved, the Court held, when spouses live separately. As the matter came before the Court on a reference for interpretation it was not necessary for the Court to decide on the effect of divorce on a spouse's rights.

The problem for a divorced spouse is particularly acute where the spouse is not a national of a Member State, as in *Diatta*. A spouse who has EU nationality can always become a worker in her own right, and, after *Kempf*, even for a spouse with family responsibilities this should not prove too daunting a prospect as it does not require self-sufficiency. The position of the divorced spouse where there are children was addressed by the CJ in *Baumbast*, concerning two separate cases referred by the British Immigration Appeal Tribunal. In one of the cases, *R*, a migrant EU national, divorced a US citizen but remained in the host Member State. The non-EU national, the mother, was the principal carer for the children who had the right to remain (discussed later). On this basis the CJ determined that the mother also had the right to remain as a corollary of the children's rights. The fact that she was not an EU national and was divorced from the migrant EU worker made no difference.

It is important to note, however, that this case did not address the position of the divorced spouse in her own right; her position was considered as an adjunct of her children's rights. The position of the divorced spouse without children remained unclear. The matter has now, somewhat inelegantly, been addressed by the CRD. Article 13 provides both EU nationals and TCNs with some protection in the event of divorce, annulment or termination of registered partnerships. The precise phraseology and scope of Article 13 should be noted. There is a drafting point: the right is granted to family members. This approach assumes that for the purposes of EU law, family members remain family members even after divorce or termination of a civil partnership, otherwise the provision has no meaning. The position for family members who are not EU nationals is more limited. To claim the benefit of the continuing rights under Article 13, the TCN must satisfy one of four tests. The four possibilities are:

- prior to initiation of the divorce or annulment proceedings or termination of the registered partnership, the marriage or registered partnership has lasted at least three years, including one in the host Member State;

- by agreement between the spouses or partners or by court order, the person who is not an EU national has custody of the Union citizen's children;

- this is warranted by particularly difficult circumstances, such as having been the victim of domestic violence during the subsistence of the marriage or registered partnership;

- by agreement between the parties or by court order, the spouse or partner who is not an EU national has the right of access to a minor child, provided that the court has ruled that the access must be in the host Member State, for as long is required.

A similar question to *Baumbast* was referred to the CJ from the English courts, asking whether the right to remain for a non-EU national spouse and her EU national children who had accompanied an EU national who came to the UK as a worker, but had subsequently ceased to be a worker and subsequently left the UK, and the non-EU national spouse and children are not self-sufficient and are dependent upon social assistance in the UK exists, and if so whether it is based on the terms of the CRD or on the children's right to education guaranteed by what is now Article 10 of Regulation 492/2011 ([2011] OJ L141/1) (see Chapter 23) (*London Borough of Harrow v Hassan Ibrahim and Secretary of State for the Home Department* (case C-310/08)). In *Teixeira v LBC Lambeth, Secretary of State for the Home Department* (case C-480/08), the Court held that in circumstances such as those of the main proceedings, the children of a national of a Member State who works or has worked in the host Member State and the parent who is their primary carer can claim a right of residence in the latter state on the sole basis of what is now Article 10 of Regulation 492/2011 without such a right being conditional on their having sufficient resources and comprehensive sickness insurance cover in that state (cf *Zambrano* and *Dereci*).

Note that the protection granted by Article 13 does not appear to extend to partnerships which are not registered, nor does it apply to other family members falling within Article 3(2)(a). Presumably a *Reed* style argument could be used to gain equivalence of protection where the host Member State granted rights to remain to those who have not registered their partnership or who were family members within the sense of Article 3(2)(a).

One final area of concern regarding the definition of family members concerns the meaning of 'durable relationship' for the purposes of Article 3(2)(b), which is not defined in the CRD. This question is presumably one for each of the Member States. Although there might be differences in approach between the Member States, the prohibition on discrimination should prevent authorities from discriminating between their nationals and migrants when assessing 'durable relationship'.

21.4.10.2 Dependants and descendants

For the children of the marriage, or the worker's dependent relatives who are EU nationals, problems would not have arisen. Even after divorce they will remain members of the worker's family. They will now benefit from the rights granted by Article 13 (discussed earlier). Problems may have arisen for a spouse's dependent relatives. If they, like the spouse, are not EU nationals, they too risk losing their status as 'favoured Union citizens' on the separation or divorce of their relative.

Families are referred to as 'descendants'. In *Baumbast*, the CJ confirmed that descendants within Regulation 1612/68, Article 10(1) extended:

> both to the descendants of that worker and to those of his spouse. To give a restrictive meaning to that provision to the effect that only the children common to the migrant worker and his spouse have the right to install themselves with them would run counter to the aim of Regulation 1612/68 [para 57].

This ruling now finds its expression in Article 2(2)(c) CRD and the same approach has been taken with respect to relatives in the ascending line. All such persons would be able, in principle, to claim the continuing rights granted under Article 13 CRD.

A family member threatened with loss of EU rights, perhaps because he or she did not satisfy the tests in Article 13(2) could invoke the principle of respect for the right to family life expressed in Article 8 ECHR as well as in Article 7 EUCFR, which in the context of the application of Union law must be respected by the authorities of Member States. The impact of Article 8 can also be seen in *Carpenter*, which concerned the scope of the family rights of a service provider (see 21.5.1.1). Additionally, in *Flora May Reyes v Migrationsverket* (case C-423/12), the CJ clarified the meaning of dependency by a TCN who is a family member of an EU citizen.

Reyes

The case involved a Philippines national who wanted to join her mother, an EU national, in Sweden. Ms Reyes applied for a residence permit in Sweden as a dependent family member of an EU national. Her application was rejected because she could not show that the money she was receiving from her mother was used to satisfy her basic needs. The CJ held that the fact that a family member receives a steady income regularly is enough to secure a situation of dependence and that there is no requirement to show that the dependent family member tried unsuccessfully to find a job in the country of origin.

The CJ has ruled, in *Kreshnik Ymeraga and Others v Ministre du Travail, de l'Emploi et de l'Immigration* (case C-87/12), a case concerning the parents and brothers, all from Kosovo, of an EU law national living in Luxembourg, that the application of Article 20 TFEU does not prevent a Member State from refusing to allow a TCN to reside in its territory if the EU national has never exercised his/her free movement rights. Such a restriction, of course, should not lead to the denial of substance of rights conferred upon the Union citizen.

Note also that TCNs may benefit from the Family Reunification Directive and the directive concerning long-term residents (Directive 2003/109) (see Chapter 26).

21.5 Material scope: rights of access of the host Member State (CRD)

21.5.1 Rights of entry

Rights of movement were seen as ancillary to the economic rights granted under Articles 45, 43 and 56 TFEU. Since they have now a fundamental status, express provision is made in Article 21 TFEU for the right of movement of the European citizen. The rights granted under Articles 45, 49 and 56 TFEU are not unlimited. As we shall see, the rights are not free from formality, as illustrated by the case of *Wijsenbeek* in which the CJ held that the right of free movement is different from the obligation to prove one's identity as an EU national. Equally, the right to free movement is subject to the derogations laid down in the Treaty, which must be interpreted restrictively and in accordance with the principle of proportionality. For example in *R v Secretary of State for the Home Department, ex parte Yiadom* (case C-357/98) the UK authorities were able to refuse a suspected Dutch people smuggler the right to enter the UK on grounds of public policy.

These rights are now regulated by the CRD as part of the citizenship package, replacing Directive 68/360. They comprise, for the EU migrant citizen and his family (as defined earlier: CRD Article 2(2)), the right:

- to leave their home state for another Member State (Article 4);
- of entry to that other Member State.

Note that the right of entry is subject to derogation on grounds of public policy, public security and public health. In *Jipa* (case C-33/07), the CJ confirmed that Member States could derogate from the right of exit on the basis of these interests too, though they would be construed narrowly, as they would in the context of the right of entry (see Chapter 25).

21.5.1.1 TCN family members

The provisions on the right of migrant EU nationals to bring their existing families with them when they exercise their free movement rights also apply on their return. The right in this context is non-contentious: there is a clear link between the right to bring a family member with you and the exercise of the right. An individual would clearly be dissuaded from exercising those rights if he or she could not be accompanied to the host state by family members. What, however, of the position where the family members are not moving from one Member State to another, but are using EU rights to enter the EU (or claim residence there) for the first time? What also of the position where the exercise of free movement rights pre-dates the existence of the family relationship and where there is, therefore, no connection between the decision of whether to exercise the right, and the right of the family member to enter the Member State? These are difficult issues which the CJ has dealt with in a number of much discussed and, in some instances, highly criticised cases.

In *S v Maahanmuuttovirasto* and *Maahanmuuttovirasto v L* (cases C-356/11 and 357/11), the CJ examined the issue of TCNs and their rights under the CRD.

S v M and *M v L*

The *S v M* case related to a Ghanaian national who was living and working in Finland. In 2001, Ms S married a Finnish national and had a child with him. In 2005, she got divorced and she was granted the sole custody of their child. In 2008, S married a TCN with whom she had a child. The child is of a Ghanaian nationality. Ms S's husband applied for a residence permit which was refused on the grounds that he did not have sufficient resources.

The *M v L* case, concerned a TCN; this time, an Algerian woman who possessed permanent residence in Finland as she was married to a Finnish national with whom she had a child of Finnish nationality. Following her divorce, Ms L married an Algerian national, with whom she had a child of Algerian nationality. Ms L applied for a residence permit for her husband, which was refused.

The Finnish Court referred the cases to the CJ asking essentially whether residence permissions need to be given to the TCNs and whether refusal of such a permit will force the spouses as well as the children who are EU nationals to leave Finland in order to accompany their families in their countries of origin.

The CJ interpreted the free movement provisions in a very dynamic way and highlighted a number of issues that are of ultimate importance in relation to the free movement provisions. The CJ emphasised the fact that in both cases the children from the previous marriages are EU nationals and they may rely on Article 20(1) TFEU as Union citizens. According to the CJ, the citizenship provisions preclude the Member States from taking any measure, including refusal to give residency permissions to the family members of the Union citizens, which may restrict the free movement provisions of the Union nationals.

It can safely be derived from the above-mentioned cases that the children who are EU nationals would have to leave the territory of the EU in order to accompany their parents to their countries of origin, unless the carers of the children are given residency rights to reside with them. Consequently, a refusal of residency rights would deprive the EU national's right of residence of any useful effect.

Such a fundamental restriction on the free movement rights of EU nationals cannot be tolerated. This can also be seen in the context of *Carpenter*.

> ## *Carpenter*
>
> Here, the case concerned the right of an individual established in his state of origin, who provided occasional, temporary services in other Member States, to rely on these rights as against the state of origin so as to ensure that his wife, who was a TCN who had outstayed her rights of entry under national law, could nonetheless remain in the EU. She did not seek to move from one EU state to another and, indeed, nor did he.

The approach taken in *Carpenter* was a new departure in the case law. The rationale underlying the right for migrants to have their family members accompany them is the removal of a disincentive to free movement. This argument did not apply in the Carpenters' situation: the exercise of the right to have family members with the service provider did not coincide with the exercise of the right to provide services. On the contrary, the right to provide services actually operated to split the Carpenter family unit, albeit temporarily. Nonetheless, the CJ held that Mr Carpenter could rely on his EU law rights as against his state of origin, and that any derogation from these rights must be assessed in the light of the right to family life contained in Article 8 ECHR.

The question of abuse was not discussed by the CJ; perhaps because the Carpenters had not manipulated their circumstances to fall within Union law. The CJ did not face directly the question of whether EU law should cover the position where a TCN seeks to use EU law to access the territory for the first time: Mrs Carpenter had been legally resident in the UK before her visa expired.

MRAX v Etat Belge (case C-459/99), handed down just two weeks later, suggested the answer to that question. The case concerned the Belgian rules regarding the proof to be supplied to gain access to Belgian territory where the marriage had occurred overseas. The CJ considered the question only from the perspective of an EU migrant worker; as this challenge was abstract (concerning the existence of the rules rather than their application to a particular case), there was no need for the CJ to consider the problem of disassociation of the free movement right from the reunification right. The CJ, basing its reasoning on the requirement on Member States to facilitate entry, and the emphasis given to Article 8 ECHR, concluded:

> it is in any event disproportionate and, therefore, prohibited to send back a TCN married to a national of a Member State where he is able to prove his identity and the conjugal ties and there is no evidence to establish that he represents a risk to the requirements of public policy, public security or public health [para 61].

In the case of a TCN who had entered the host Member State illegally, it would be disproportionate to deport for failure to have a visa; other sanctions may be appropriate. There is no consideration of the question of whether this constitutes the granting of a right of access to EU territory, nor recognition of the fact that the 'administrative formality' is actually the Member State's right to control entry of TCNs to its territory. While *MRAX* may be seen as challenging mere formalities, it was a potentially far-reaching decision.

The next case, *Akrich*, had been referred to the CJ before the judgment in *MRAX* was handed down. *Singh* had illustrated that migrant workers could rely on at least some rights as against their Member State on return but the scope of this right, and its longevity, was somewhat uncertain though potentially far-reaching.

Akrich

The case concerned a Moroccan national who was refused entry into the UK. He subsequently married a UK national. She moved to Ireland to work for a short period and he entered Ireland, relying on EU-law-derived rights. The couple then tried to return to the UK on the basis of *Singh*. It transpired that the motive of the sojourn in Ireland had been for the purpose of bringing the couple within Union law, so seeking to evade British immigration controls.

Whilst the exercise of free movement is clearly tied to the reunification right, this case raises concerns about the abuse of Union law. Were this line of reasoning to be accepted, it would introduce the possibility that no Member State would have any control over immigration into the EU in such cases. Whilst this issue had been elided in the reasoning in *MRAX*, in *Akrich* it was centre stage.

The Advocate-General in *Akrich* noted that the situation in *Singh* was different from that in issue in a number of respects. Crucially, Akrich had not been permitted to enter any Member State under national law. The Advocate-General commented that '*Singh* does not create a right in favour of that national of a non-Member State to enter the territory of the European Union' (para 134). The CJ also found in favour of the UK government, addressing both the issues about the scope of the reunification right. First, it seemed to link the right of family reunification with the right of free movement. It argued that, as Akrich could not lawfully reside with his wife in the UK, there was no disincentive in her not having her husband with her if she moved to another Member State, that is, the prohibition could not 'constitute less favourable treatment than that which they enjoyed before the citizen made use of the opportunities afforded by the Treaty as regards free movement of persons' (para 53).

Nonetheless, the CJ confirmed the point it had made in earlier jurisprudence, that the motives of persons seeking to exercise their rights of free movement are not relevant when assessing whether or not they benefit from those rights (paras 55–6), though the position might be different in the context of marriages of convenience. Secondly, the CJ held that Regulation 1612/68 concerned only movement within the Union and not initial access to the territory of the Union. The CJ then added that to benefit from the rights granted, the spouse of a citizen had to be 'lawfully resident in a Member State when he moves to another Member State to which the citizen of the Union is migrating or has migrated' (para 56).

Although it is submitted that some limits to the reasoning in *Singh* should be found, the reasoning of both the CJ and the Advocate-General in *Akrich* is problematic. The precise scope of the ruling is not clear and does not sit easily with *MRAX*. As noted, *MRAX* did not distinguish between the role of national and Union law in determining the right of access to Union territory, nor did it distinguish between legal and illegal immigrants, a distinction central in *Akrich*. It was suggested that the solution which best reconciles the case law is one which sees *Akrich* as confined to similar factual situations, where a TCN has been illegally resident in a Member State and is using Union law to avoid attempts to deport him and does not affect all TCNs wishing to enter directly into the host Member State.

We have already discussed the case of *Chen* (at 21.4.4). Although the parents of the child had not resided lawfully within the EU prior to the birth of the child and admitted manipulating the national rules to obtain residency as family members of an EU national, the question of abuse was not raised in this case.

Our analysis of *Akrich* would be consistent with that taken in *Jia v Migrationsverket* (case C-01/05).

Jia

Jia concerned an EU worker who had married a non-EU national. The EU worker subsequently moved to another Member State with her husband. Thereafter, she sought to rely on her EU law rights to claim that her mother-in-law, also a non-EU national, had the right to enter and reside in the host Member State, although her mother-in-law had never resided in the EU. Here, the CJ was prepared to allow a TCN access to the EU territory without that person having entered the EU territory on the basis of one of the Member State's immigration systems.

Jia can be distinguished from *Akrich* on the basis that there is no suggestion of manipulation of the system in the same way as in *Akrich*, since in *Jia* the migrant EU national had been resident in the host Member State for approximately eight years before her mother-in-law sought to enter the state. The issue that is not discussed in *Jia* is the link—or rather the lack of one—between the exercise of free movement rights and the family-reunification rights. Despite the CJ's argument in *Mettock* (discussed further later) that the competence of the Member States regarding immigration are respected, as the EU rules relate only to the circumstances of free movement rights, this assessment is contestable. Where an EU national exercises the free movement rights and then subsequently gets married or seeks to have dependent family members join him or her, intra-EU movement rights are not in issue. There is no connection between the decision to move and the circumstances in which the family member's right is subsequently deployed. A different argument in favour of *Jia*, however, is that the migrant had formed a 'real link' with the host Member State. We can see this argument deployed in cases involving rights to social benefits (Chapter 23). There is a difference between the two sets of facts, though. In the social rights cases, immigrants are essentially asking to be treated on a par with nationals of the host Member States; in *Jia* the argument results in preferential treatment for the migrant. The CJ is clearly stepping into a sensitive area here, with the possible consequence of reverse discrimination for nationals who do not seek to exercise their free movement rights.

Following *Jia*, it seemed that *Akrich* was restricted to cases of abuse; whether it is still possible to rely on *Akrich* at all is now highly doubtful. In *Akrich*, the CJ suggested that it was no disincentive to free movement to prohibit the entry of Akrich to another Member State as the couple could not live together anyway in the state of origin. A variant of this argument was raised in *Minister voor Vreemdelingenzaken en Integratie v Eind* (case C-291/05). The case concerned a Dutch migrant worker seeking to return to his state of origin with his daughter, a TCN. His daughter did not have the right of residence in the Netherlands prior to the exercise of the free movement right, but by contrast to the position in *Akrich*, her entry to the EU was not illegal. The CJ held that the fact that she had no right of residence was irrelevant to the determination of whether she had a right to reside with her father (at least until she was 21). The CJ gave two reasons:

- such a requirement is not laid down in Union law, and Union law on free movement should not be interpreted restrictively;
- such a requirement would run counter to the objectives of the Union legislature in protecting family life.

Eind is interesting for a number of reasons. It seems inconsistent with *Akrich*, but there is no specific reference to that case. Did the Court overlook or choose to ignore *Akrich*? Further, although the CJ refers to *MRAX* and *Carpenter*, it does not expressly state that it is following the lines of reasoning in those cases. Significantly, the CJ in its first reason, concerning Union law, is ignoring the limits on

Union competence regarding first access to the EU territory, a division of competence it has elsewhere stated that it respected.

Mettock, a decision of the Grand Chamber on a reference from Ireland, deals directly with the family rights in the CRD for the first time. *Mettock* concerns four cases based on a similar-fact pattern. In each case, a TCN was refused asylum in Ireland and subsequently married a migrant EU national lawfully resident in Ireland. Each couple sought to challenge refusal of residency or deportation on the basis of EU law rights. With the exception of the *Mettock* case, the couples met in Ireland and married within a comparatively short timescale, though the national court accepted that none of the cases concerned a marriage of convenience. In this, the facts are more similar to *Jia*, where the migrant was still residing in the host Member State, than *Akrich*, which concerned the right of return to the home Member State. Nonetheless, our two themes can be seen: (1) the disassociation between free movement and reunification; and (2) the question of access to EU territory. The Irish authorities referred to *Akrich* and sought to rely on the requirement that the spouses must have been lawfully resident within the EU. The CJ dismissed this argument, stating that the conclusion in *Akrich* must be 'reconsidered' (para 58), effectively overruling its decision in that case. It argued that the Union institutions have consistently widened the rights available to individuals, and that those rights are not dependent on preconditions such as the prior lawful residence of such a spouse in another Member State. Perhaps because it was not raised by the Irish authorities, the CJ did not address the issue of the link between the right of free movement and the reunification right. Whilst the decision in *Mettock* may be applauded on humanitarian grounds, it is still problematic. As noted earlier, the issue of duration of the rights consequent on migration have not been addressed by the CJ, but it is submitted that this is an issue that needs addressing as, depending on the scope of the rights awarded by migration, the CJ could create a privileged class of individuals in circumstances which have little to do with integration in a host Member State.

The CJ suggested in *Mettock* that its ruling was not effectively opening the floodgates to uncontrolled immigration from third countries, as Member States were still entitled to exclude family members on the basis of Article 27 CRD (if appropriate—see Chapter 25), and that Article 35 CRD entitles Member States to 'adopt the necessary measures to refuse, terminate or withdraw any right conferred by this Directive in the case of abuse of rights or fraud, such as marriages of convenience'. There have been no cases on the scope of this provision, though any such measures would have to comply with the principle of proportionality, suggesting it will be narrowly construed.

21.5.2 **Right of residence**

With the right of entry comes the right of residence, and many cases concern both the right of entry and the right of residence. It is a necessary precursor for an individual to engage in activities in the host Member State. The original provisions relating to workers were generously interpreted by the CJ. In *Royer* the Court held that the right of entry granted by Article 3 Directive 68/360 included the right to enter *in search of work*. In *R v Immigration Appeal Tribunal, ex parte Antonissen* (case C-292/89), the CJ was asked to rule on the legality of English immigration rules which permit the deportation of migrants after six months if they have failed to find employment. It held that a Member State could, however, deport an EU migrant if he had not found employment after six months unless he provided evidence that he was continuing to seek employment and that he had a genuine chance of being engaged. Significantly the Court chose not to impose a specific time limit. Subsequently, it was held that Belgian legislation, which in effect excluded those seeking work after three months, was in contravention of Union law (*Commission v Belgium* (case C-344/95)). Thus, it seems that at the least those genuinely seeking work were entitled to stay in the host Member State for longer than three months.

Likewise, those providing services or seeking to establish themselves had the right of residence, though that of the service provider would be coterminous with the provision of services. Rights of residence are dealt with under the CRD but apply only to those who have exercised their right of free movement (*McCarthy*). The rights of residence contained within Article 21 TFEU remain, though, as with the rights under Articles 45, 43 and 56 TFEU, they are given greater detail by the implementing legislation. Significantly, the right of residence is available to all, a point the CJ recognised in *Baumbast*, when it held that the right was conferred on every citizen of the Union, irrespective of whether he or she was engaged in an economic activity. In *Baumbast*, the migrant Union citizen did not comply with the formal requirements of the residence directive, (Directive 90/364)—to be insured against medical emergencies—but was not a financial burden on the host Member State. According to the CJ, Article 21 had to be read in accordance with the limitations imposed by the residence directives, but that these limits themselves had to be understood in the light of the principle of proportionality, and the UK's refusal to renew his residence permit on the facts of this case was disproportionate. *Baumbast* can thus also be seen as authority for the proposition, seen in other cases (see, eg, *Kaba v Secretary of State for the Home Department* (case C-356/98) and *Chen*), that Article 20(1) residence rights are not unconditional. In *Trojani*, the CJ held that, contrary to the position in *Baumbast*, a claimant who is carrying out minimal economic activities and is dependent on the host state, does not derive a right to reside in the territory for want of sufficient resources (para 36). As we shall see in Chapter 23, a 'real link' with the host Member State has become key.

The rights are now found in the CRD, but it is important to note that the Directive does not reflect the case law precisely, so it may still be necessary to refer to the underlying Treaty provision. Further, not all citizens have the same rights as is shown in Table 21.1.

Table 21.1 Rights of residence available to citizens

	Right of entry (Art 5)	Right of temporary residence (Art 6)—3 months	Right of settled residence (Art 7)—more than 3 months	Right of permanent residence (Art 17)
Economically active	Yes	Yes	Yes	Provided legally resident for 5 years
Non-economically active	Yes	Yes	If they have sufficient resources and sickness insurance	Provided legally resident for 5 years (ie satisfy conditions in Art 7(b) and (c))
Family members	Yes	Yes	Yes if EU national satisfies conditions; note limitations on family members of students (Art 7(4))	Provided legally resident for 5 years

21.5.2.1 **Temporary residence**

Article 6 provides temporary residence of up to three months to all migrant EU citizens, without any requirement that they be self-sufficient or even looking for work. Note, however, EU citizens will retain this right only as long as they do not become an unreasonable burden on the social assistance system of the host Member State (Article 14(1)). In one sense, this is wider than *Antonissen*, see 21.5.2) because it is not limited to work-seekers; should the Union citizen be a work-seeker then in derogation of Article 14(1), provided he or she can provide evidence that he or she is continuing to seek work and has a reasonable chance of being employed, a Member State may not deport that person (unless there are grounds under Article 27). It is more limited than the existing jurisprudence because the right is expressed to be for three months only. Note that secondary legislation cannot limit Treaty freedoms, so for those seeking work it will remain possible to rely on *Antonissen* and *Commission v Belgium* (case C-344/95), which are ultimately based on Article 45 (for a similar approach in a different context, see *Collins*, discussed in Chapter 23 at 23.2.1.2). Such individuals may be able to rely on Article 7 after the three-month period has expired. Note, family members have matching rights of residence.

21.5.2.2 **Settled residence**

Union citizens have the right to reside for as long as they satisfy the conditions in Article 7, that is if they fall into one of three categories. These are that they:

- are workers or self-employed;
- have sufficient resources for themselves and their family members not to become a burden on the social assistance system of the host Member State;
- are enrolled at a private or public establishment for the principal purpose of following a course of study, including vocational training with sufficient resources.

This may be described as the right to 'settled' or 'lawful' residence. As noted earlier, a worker may retain his or her status in certain circumstances. Article 7(3) reflects this position and clarifies the position for the self-employed. Under Article 7(3) a Union citizen retains their economic status (and consequently does not have to show sufficient resources) in the following situations:

(a) he/she is temporarily unable to work as the result of an illness or accident;

(b) he/she is in duly recorded involuntary unemployment after having been employed for more than one year and has registered as a job-seeker with the relevant employment office;

(c) he/she is in duly recorded involuntary unemployment after completing a fixed-term employment contract of less than a year or after having become involuntarily unemployed during the first twelve months and has registered as a jobseeker with the relevant employment office (in this case, the status of worker shall be retained for no less than six months);

(d) he/she embarks on vocational training. Unless he/she is involuntarily unemployed, the retention of the status of worker shall require the training to be related to the previous employment.

Although the CRD specifically provides that a right of residence does not end if the worker becomes incapable of work through illness or accident or involuntary unemployment, Article 7(3)(b) implies that that right will be lost if he is *voluntarily* unemployed, where the worker has only been working for a period of less than a year. Note that in this case there may also be implications for the individual's right to social rights (Article 24(2)).

21.5.2.3 **Permanent residence**

Unusually, Chapter IV CRD provides for a right of permanent residence. Article 16 specifies that 'Union citizens who have resided legally for a continuous period of five years in the host Member State shall have the right of permanent residence there'. Crucially, this right is not subject to the same conditions as the temporary and settled rights of residence (eg, terms of Article 14). This right is extended to family members, who must each complete their own period of five years' legal residence (Article 16(2)). The Directive defines continuous residence, allowing the migrant to be absent for periods totalling no more than six months in a year, with special exceptions for circumstances such as military service, and pregnancy and childbirth. Once acquired, the right may be lost, but only through a period of absence exceeding two consecutive years. Given that this right is dependent on legal residence, an EU national must either be economically active or self-sufficient for the five-year period. Special provisions apply to protect the position of those who retire or become incapacitated (Article 17).

21.5.3 **Formalities**

Under the CRD migrant EU citizens need only produce a valid identity card or passport (Article 5(1)) to enter a host Member State. Entry visas (or their equivalent) may not be demanded except for members of the family who are not nationals of a Member State. In *Wijsenbeek*, the CJ had to consider whether the introduction of European citizenship rendered border controls illegal. In this case the CJ held that Member States were still entitled to check the identity documents (in this case the passport) of EU nationals travelling between Member States, despite the fact that all EU nationals are now European citizens. The CJ then went on to hold, however, that any penalties for failure to comply with such rules must be proportionate in the light of European citizenship and the right to move from one Member State to another. In this, the CJ made a distinction between the right to move between Member States and the ability to do so without having to prove one's identity or nationality. Thus, this ruling would suggest that citizenship on its own is not enough to create an area without internal frontiers even if it is a lot easier, as an EU national, to cross those borders.

Where a person has a residence card within the meaning of Article 10 CRD, they are exempt from any visa requirement. Member States are required to accord to such persons every facility for obtaining the necessary visas (Article 5(2)). According to *MRAX* (see 21.5.1.1), although Directive 68/360, Article 2(2) made the right of entry conditional on the holding of the visa, the rights of the Member State in respect of this condition are limited indeed. Such a visa should be issued without delay and, as far as possible, at the place of entry into the Member State. These requirements are now found in Article 5(2) CRD.

The CJ further held in *MRAX* that, where a TCN is able to prove his or her identity and provide evidence of a marriage, it would be disproportionate to send a TCN back to his or her state of origin in the absence of evidence that he or she represents a risk to public policy, public security or public health. Article 5(4) CRD incorporates these requirements, additionally specifying that a Member State must give such persons a reasonable opportunity of obtaining the necessary documents or of having them sent or otherwise proving that they are covered by the right of free movement and residence.

An economically active migrant need only register when he or she is resident for more than three months; in such cases the obligation to apply occurs only when the Member State runs a registration scheme. To obtain a registration certificate a worker needs to provide:

- a valid identity card or passport;
- confirmation of engagement from the employer or a certificate of employment (Article 8(3)).

The requirements for members of the family who are Union citizens (Article 9(5)) are:

- their documents of entry;
- a document proving their relationship with the worker, and where relevant documents testifying to their dependent status (Article 3(2)(a)) or proof of a durable relationship (see Article 3(2)(b)).

For family members who are not Union citizens, Article 9 provides for a separate procedure. Member States are required to issue such family members a residence card within six months of the date of application. To obtain a residence card a family member must show:

- a valid passport;
- documentary evidence of their relationship with the worker;
- in the case of relatives identified in Article 2(2)(c) or (d), and Article 3(2)(a) and (b), proof that the conditions specified in the respective provisions are satisfied (see 21.4.9).

The residence permit must be valid throughout the territory of the Member State which issued it; it must be valid for at least five years from the date of issue or for the envisaged term of residence of the Union citizen; and it must be automatically renewable (Article 11). Temporary absences, as detailed in Article 11(2) do not affect the validity of the residence card. A worker's right to reside in the state where he is employed is not dependent on his possession of a certificate of registration. Neither a migrant nor his family can be deported because the identity card or passport on which they entered the host Member State has expired (Article 15(2) CRD). As long as the migrant is economically active, he will be entitled to reside in the host Member State without formalities. And as long as he is entitled to stay, his family will also be entitled to stay. In *MRAX* the CJ confirmed that a Member State is not permitted to refuse a residence permit to a family member who is able to prove his or her identity and the existence of a marriage to a migrant EU worker, purely on the grounds that he or she entered the host Member State illegally (see also *Commission v Spain (Schengen Information System)* (case C-503/03) on the relationship between Union law and the Schengen system with regard to TCNs who are family members, discussed in chapter 26). Nor can that Member State expel such a TCN on the grounds that his or her visa expired before he or she applied for a residence permit. A residence permit may not be refused on these grounds either.

A Member State is, however, entitled to demand that migrant workers and their families comply with its administrative formalities on immigration, as is recognised in Articles 8–9 CRD, and can even impose penalties in the form of fines for non-compliance, provided that the penalties are not disproportionate. In *Messner* (case C-265/88) a time limit of three days from crossing the frontier in which aliens were required to register their presence with the Italian police, sanctioned by criminal penalties, was found to be unreasonable. A failure to comply with such formalities can never be a ground for deportation.

The maintenance of a database of non-nationals so registering has been challenged for constituting discrimination contrary to Articles 18, 20 and 49 TFEU, as well as raising questions about compliance with the Data Protection Directive (Directive 95/46 ([2005] OJ L281/31)) (*Huber v Germany* (case C-524/06)). Although Germany registers the basic details of its citizens in municipal registers, it does not have a centralised system for them. The details of non-nationals are additionally registered on a centralised system, which is more extensive in terms of the information so entered. The German government argued that this difference in treatment is acceptable because of the different residence rights of the two groups. The Advocate-General was not convinced:

this is no more than stating the obvious; it says nothing about how this difference in residence status should relate to the collection and processing of the personal data of German citizens and citizens of other Member States . . . For a finding of non-discrimination, it is not sufficient to point out that German citizens and foreign nationals are not in the same situation. It is also necessary to demonstrate that the difference in their respective situations is capable of justifying the difference in treatment. In other words, the difference in treatment must relate and be proportionate to the difference in their respective situations [para 7].

Whilst the case law of the CJ and the terms of the CRD envisage the collection of some data, it does not mean that the Member States are entirely unfettered in this regard. The Advocate-General emphasised the fundamental status of citizenship, arguing that a system would be discriminatory in so far as it includes data beyond those specified in Article 8(3) CRD and allowed access by authorities other than the immigration service. The CJ, while recognising the need for some data to be held, determined that such data must be limited to that necessary for the purpose and that the storage and processing of personal data containing any individualised (as opposed to anonymised) data cannot under any circumstances be considered necessary. Furthermore, Member States cannot put in place a data processing system which focuses on the personal data of non-nationals for the purposes of fighting crime. Member States' ability to keep data on particular population groups has clearly been limited.

21.6 Conclusions

This chapter has looked first at the scope of the free movement provisions *ratione personae*, that is in terms of who benefits from Union-law rights in this area; and secondly, at the scope of one aspect of the rights (*ratione materiae*), the right of access to the territory of the host Member State. The conditions governing *ratione personae* operate to determine the circumstances in which Union law may be invoked. They thus delimit the scope of Union competence, and the circumstances in which Member State freedom is limited. In general terms, we can say that the CJ has interpreted these matters broadly, as can be seen from its approach, for example, to internal situations. It has also generally adopted a Union approach to key terms. This, of course, is beneficial to the individuals seeking to rely on those rights.

Within this framework, two key strands of case law can be determined: that relating to students as workers; and the case law on TCNs entering the territory of the EU as family members of migrant EU nationals. Here the sensitivity of the issue is not just which EU nationals can claim rights, but the scope of those rights and whether they are necessarily connected with enhancing free movement. It is arguable that we see here the beginnings of a qualitative shift from a focus on facilitating free movement of economic factors, to creating a community of individuals. This, however, is problematic. The case law creates a favoured class of individuals; although the CJ has consistently accepted reverse discrimination, it hardly matches a view of the Union where there is no discrimination. Further, there is a constant concern about abuse of Union law rights, so as to allow social benefit tourism or to evade immigration controls into the EU itself.

Nevertheless, by taking into account the latest jurisprudence of the CJ in cases such as *Reyes, S v M* and *M v L*, it is obvious that the CJ has started to give some guidance to the national courts on how to interpret the concepts found in the CRD and, particularly, the grounds on which a TCN parent can derive the right to move and reside in the EU from the citizenship of a child who is the step-father. It is still true to say that the freedom to move is available to a broad class (individual and legal body alike), a fact which has had, and will continue to have, a huge impact on the freedom of

Member States to regulate, and which has had particular impact on the acceptability of distinguishing between nationals and migrant EU nationals.

Further reading

Adams, S and Van Elsuwege, P, 'Citizenship Rights and the Federal Balance between the European Union and its Member States: Comment on Dereci' (2012) 37 EL Rev 176.

Cygan, A, 'Citizenship of the European Union' (2013) 62 ICLQ 492.

Dougan, M, 'The constitutional dimension to the case law on Union citizenship' (2006) 31 EL Rev 613.

Kochenov, D, 'The right to have *what* rights? EU citizenship in need of clarification' (2013) 19 ELJ 502.

Kochenov, D and Plender, R, 'EU Citizenship: From an incipient form to an incipient substance? The discovery of the treaty text' (2012) 37 EL Rev 369.

Kunoy, B, 'A union of national citizens: The origins of the Court's lack of avant-gardisme in the *Chen* case' (2006) 43 CML Rev 179.

Shaw, J, 'Citizenship: Contrasting dynamics at the interface of integration and constitutionalism' in P Craig and G de Búrca, *The Evolution of EU Law* (Oxford University Press, 2011).

Stalford, H, 'Concepts of family under EU law: Lessons from the ECHR' (2002) 16 International Journal of Law, Policy and the Family 410.

Tryfonidou, A, *The Impact of Union Citizenship on the EU's Market Freedoms* (Hart Publishing, 2016).

Tryfonidou, A, '*Jia* or "*Carpenter II*": The edge of reason' (2007) 32 EL Rev 908.

Watson, P, 'Free movement of workers: A one way ticket?' (1993) 22 ILJ 68.

White, R, 'Conflicting competences: Free movement rules and immigration laws' (2004) 29 EL Rev 385.

White, R, 'Free movement, equal treatment, and citizenship of the Union' (2005) 54 ICLQ 885.

Woods, L, 'Family rights in the EU: Disadvantaging the disadvantaged?' (1999) 11 CFLQ 17.

Woods, L, 'Scope of services I: Definitions' in *Free Movement of Goods and Service within the European Community* (Ashgate, 2004).

22 Economic rights: workers, establishment and services

22.1 Introduction

The four freedoms are fundamental to the creation of the internal market and as such have been interpreted broadly. We have noted that the rights granted by the freedoms relating to people and legal entities have different aspects: a territorial aspect (discussed in Chapter 21); an economic aspect; and a social aspect (discussed in Chapter 23). This chapter will focus on the second aspect: the right to the job market or the right to trade as self-employed.

This chapter begins by reviewing the relevant Treaty provisions and, crucially, the changing approach to the CJEU's interpretation of the Treaty freedoms and the consequent impact on Member States' ability to regulate within their own territory. The case law considered in this chapter raises issues about regulatory competition and the deregulatory impact of the freedom to provide services, as with the other freedoms. This chapter focuses in particular on certain problem areas, such as qualifications (now subject to harmonisation) and the abuse of Union-law rights to evade national regulation, as well as the position regarding companies. We also consider the position of services, where services are provided cross-border without anyone physically moving (eg, broadcasting). Services in this context may be provided in more than one Member State simultaneously, raising questions not only about which Member State should have the right or responsibility to regulate the service provider, but also about the dangers of abuse of Union-law rights to avoid national regulation. These questions have a greater significance with the introduction of the Services Directive (Directive 2006/123 ([2006] OJ L376/36)).

22.2 Overview and Treaty provisions

In their economic aspects, the free movement of workers, the right of establishment and the freedom to provide services, probably show the greatest similarity to the other freedoms (goods and capital). Similar themes can be identified in these freedoms, in particular a broad interpretation of the rights. Furthermore, there has been a move from a discrimination-based test for the application of the article to one based on the notion of an obstacle to the exercise of the right (see also Chapter 17). When we look at economic rights, however, there might be different policy issues in play in different circumstances. To what extent should there be a difference in approach with regard to rules which operate to deter individuals and companies from moving in the first place, those that affect access to the market, and the rules that come into play when running a business? Equally, we might consider whether the same approach is desirable with regard to individuals (who might benefit from citizenship rights) and legal entities which will not have the same social needs.

22.2.1 The free movement of workers

The principal Treaty provision governing the free movement of workers is Article 45 TFEU. As regards the economic aspect of the workers' rights it provides:

> (2) Such freedom of movement shall entail the abolition of any discrimination based on nationality between workers of the Member States as regards employment, remuneration and other conditions of work and employment;
>
> (3) It shall entail the right, subject to limitations justified on grounds of public policy, public security or public health:
>
>   (a) to accept offers of employment actually made; . . .

22.2.2 Freedom of establishment

Article 49 TFEU now provides:

> Within the framework of the provisions set out below, restrictions on the freedom of establishment of nationals of a Member State in the territory of another Member State shall be prohibited. Such prohibition shall also apply to restrictions on the setting up of agencies, branches or subsidiaries by nationals of any Member State established in the territory of any Member State.
>
> Freedom of establishment shall include the right to take up and pursue activities as self-employed persons and to set up and manage undertakings, in particular companies and firms within the meaning of the second paragraph of Article 54, under the conditions laid down for its own nationals by the law of the country where such establishment is effected, subject to the provisions of the Chapter relating to capital.

22.2.3 The freedom to provide services

Articles 56 and 57(3) TFEU provide:

> Within the framework of the provisions set out below, restrictions on freedom to provide services within the Union shall be prohibited in respect of nationals of Member States who are established in a State of the Union other than that of the person for whom the services are intended.

> Without prejudice to the provisions of the Chapter relating to the right of establishment, the person providing a service may, in order to do so, temporarily pursue his activity in the State where the service is provided, under the same conditions as are imposed by that State on its own nationals.

22.2.4 **Public service**

The Treaty limits the right of access to jobs in the public sector. Article 45(4) TFEU specifies that '[t]he provisions of this Article shall not apply to employment in the public service'. Similar provisions apply to establishment and services. Article 51 TFEU provides that '[t]he provisions of this Chapter [establishment] shall not apply, so far as any given Member State is concerned, to activities which in that State are connected, even occasionally, with the exercise of official authority'. Finally, according to Article 62 TFEU, the terms of Article 51 TFEU also apply to services.

22.3 **Right of access to the market**

22.3.1 **Workers**

Regulation 1612/68 was passed to implement Articles 45(2) and 45(3)(a) and (b) TFEU. As it was amended several times over the years, the changes have been brought together in a new, codified version: Regulation 492/2011 ([2011] OJ L141/1). As stated in the preamble of Regulation 492/2011, the attainment of the objective of freedom of movement for workers requires:

> the abolition of any discrimination based on nationality between workers of the Member States as regards employment, remuneration and other conditions of work and employment.

Regulation 492/2011 requires, in order for the right of freedom of movement to be exercised 'in freedom and dignity', equality of treatment in 'all matters relating to the actual pursuit of activities as employed persons'. Regulation 492/2011 contains specific provisions (Articles 1–9) dealing with eligibility for employment as well as the terms of employment. Article 45 TFEU was expressed in terms of a prohibition on discrimination, whether direct or indirect. In *Hartmann v Freistaat Bayern* (case C-212/05) (Grand Chamber), the CJ restated that the prohibition relates not only to discrimination on grounds of nationality but to the 'application of other criteria of differentiation' which would have the same effect. These principles are now reflected in Regulation 492/2011. In particular, Article 1 provides that:

> Any national of a Member State shall, irrespective of his place of residence, have the right to take up an activity as an employed person, and to pursue such activity, within the territory of another Member State in accordance with the provisions laid down by law, regulation or administrative action governing the employment of nationals of that State.

Additionally, a Member State may not discriminate, overtly or covertly, against non-nationals, by prioritising the employment of nationals (Article 1(2)), limiting applications and offers of employment (Article 3(1)), or by prescribing special recruitment procedures or limiting advertising or in any other way impeding recruitment of non-resident workers (Article 3(2)). Member States must not restrict by number or percentage the number of foreign nationals to be employed in any activity or area of activity (Article 4; see the *French merchant seamen* case—ratio of three French to one non-French imposed under Code du Travail Maritime 1926 on crew of French merchant ships held in breach of EU law).

Member States must offer non-national applicants the same assistance in seeking employment as are available to nationals (Article 5). A worker who is a national of a Member State may not, in the territory of another Member State, be treated differently from national workers by reason of his nationality in respect of any conditions of employment and work, in particular as regards remuneration, dismissal and, should he become unemployed, reinstatement or re-employment (Article 7(1)). In *Württembergische Milchverwertung-Südmilch AG v Salvatore Ugliola* (case 15/69) a condition whereby a German employer took into account, for the purposes of calculating seniority, employees' periods of national service *in Germany*, thereby prejudicing an employee such as Ugliola, who was required to perform his national service in Italy, was held unlawful under Article 7(1). Similarly, in *Sotgiu*, the German post office's decision to pay increased separation allowances only to workers living away from home in Germany was held to be *capable* of breaching Article 7(1). In *Schöning-Kougebetopoulou*, the CJ held that a collective wage agreement which provided for promotion on grounds of seniority after eight years' employment in any given group, excluding periods of comparable employment in the public service of another Member State, was contrary to the Treaty. The terms of the agreement manifestly worked to the disadvantage of migrant workers as they are less likely, or it is harder for them, to satisfy the eight-year rule.

Workers are also entitled to social and tax advantages (Article 7(2)); these are discussed in Chapter 23.

Article 7(4) of Regulation 492/2011 deals with collective and individual agreements relating to eligibility for work, as well as terms and conditions of work, remuneration and conditions of dismissal. Any such conditions shall be null and void insofar as they are discriminatory in respect of workers from other Member States. Note that, as can be seen in *Merida v Bundesrepublik Deutschland* (case C-400/02), measures which are indirectly discriminatory may be capable of being justified.

Merida

Here, a collective agreement applicable to civilians employed by foreign armed forces in Germany was in issue. It provided for 'interim assistance' to workers where their contracts were terminated. The payment was subject to the deduction of the German income tax. Merida was a French national. Due to a taxation treaty between France and Germany, Merida's tax should have been calculated on the basis of the country of residence, at that time France, rather than in Germany at the German rate. Merida brought an action arguing that this was contrary to what is now Article 45 TFEU and Article 7(4) of Regulation 492/2011. Although the terms of Article 7(4) do not refer to the possibility of justification, the CJ did note the possibility that indirectly discriminatory measures (such as this one) could be justified in the public interest provided it was proportionate to its aim. The CJ rejected the German government's justifications based on simplified administration and limitation of financial charges.

Under Article 8 of Regulation 492/2011 a migrant worker is entitled to equality of treatment as regards 'membership of trade unions and the exercise of rights attaching thereto, including the right to vote and to be eligible for the administration or management posts of a trade union'.

The precise relationship between trade union and collective-action rights and free movement rights is not clear, especially when the exercise of collective-action rights operates to limit employers' rights under Article 49 or 56 TFEU. In *Laval*, the blockade of a building site to prevent the construction company using foreign labourers who were not covered by a collective agreement and were not therefore entitled to the same level of pay as Swedish workers fell in principle within Article 56 TFEU. (Re Article 49 TFEU, see *Viking*, concerning an attempt to reflag a ship to take the seamen outside the protection of a collective agreement.) *Laval* has been criticised for failing to give adequate protection to social rights.

22.3.2 **Establishment**

Central to the rights in Article 49 TFEU is the right to carry on business in another Member State, whether as a primary business (ie moving and setting up your business entirely within the host Member State), or as a secondary establishment (ie maintaining an establishment in one Member State and having other offices, whatever their legal form, in other Member States). Article 49 TFEU applies not just to the market, but also to the terms under which business may be carried on. For example, the recognition of qualifications (now harmonised, see 22.9) might be seen as affecting the right to enter a profession or business in the first place; codes of conduct control the way businesses are run as an on-going obligation. The central element of these rights is to be subject to the same conditions that apply to nationals of the host Member State.

Article 49 TFEU, together with Article 18 TFEU, may be invoked to challenge a national rule which is discriminatory. For example, in an enforcement case against Italy (the *freedom of estab-lishment* case), the CJ confirmed that rules which required Italian nationality as a precondition for the exercise of certain activities—operation of pharmacies and journalism—were contrary to Article 49 TFEU. As with Article 45 TFEU, this prohibition applies to both direct and indirect discrimination.

The scope of carrying on business for the purposes of Article 49 TFEU is broad, as can be seen in *Steinhauser*.

Steinhauser

Steinhauser, a German national, was a professional artist resident in Biarritz. He applied to the Biarritz authorities to rent a *crampotte*, a fisherman's hut of a type used locally for the exhibition and sale of works of art. He was refused on the grounds of his nationality; under the city's regulations *crampottes* could only be rented by persons of French nationality. He challenged that decision, and the CJ held that freedom of establishment provided under Article 49 TFEU related not only to the taking up of an activity as a self-employed person but also to the pursuit of that activity in the widest sense to include, inter alia, the right to rent premises, to tender and to qualify for licences and concessions.

The breadth of the potential scope of Article 49 TFEU was reiterated in *SEVIC Systems AG v Amtsgericht Neuwied* (case C-411/03).

SEVIC

SEVIC Systems AG was a company registered in Germany. It merged with a company established in Luxembourg. SEVIC applied for registration in the commercial register after the merger, but the local authorities refused on the ground that the relevant German law provided only for mergers between companies established in Germany.

There, the CJ held that:

> the right of establishment covers all measures which permit or even merely facilitate access to another Member State and the pursuit of an economic activity in that State . . . [para 18].

Clearly, this approach will have relevance for social rights, discussed further in Chapter 23. It also suggests that Article 49 TFEU is likely to cover similar issues as are dealt with by Regulation 492/2011 with regard to workers; for example, arrangements for the payment of taxes or the right to join a trade association.

Finally, note that Article 49 TFEU will catch rules which prevent persons from seeking to exercise their rights, whether those rules are imposed by the host or the home Member State (see Box 22.1).

Box 22.1 Examples of rules falling with Article 49 TFEU

Rules relating to treatment of company following cross-border merger:
> *SEVIC.*

Prohibition on more than one place of establishment:
> *Ordre des Avocats v Klopp* (case 107/83).

Tax treatment of losses incurred by a permanent establishment situated in a Member State of the EEA and belonging to a company having its seat in a Member State of the European Union:
> *Finanzamt für Körperschaften III in Berlin v Krankenheim Ruhesitz am Wannsee-Seniorenheimstatt GmbH* (case C-157/07).

Advance on costs for registration of company documents:
> *Innoventif Limited* (case C-453/04).

Rules restricting profession of architect to possession of a diploma or professional qualification:
> *Conseil National de l'Ordre des Architectes v Dreessen* (case C-31/00).

Renewal of 329 horse-race betting licences without inviting competing bids:
> *Commission v Italy* (case C-260/04).

22.3.3 Services

As with Article 49 TFEU, Article 56 TFEU grants the right to carry on business in another Member State. Again, the core element is equal treatment, that is, to be subject to the same conditions as apply to nationals of the host Member State.

Article 56 TFEU, together with Article 18 TFEU, may be invoked to challenge a national rule which is in some way discriminatory, whether directly or indirectly. Article 56 TFEU addresses discrimination arising not only to the taking up of an activity (access to the profession), but to pursuit of that activity (rules relating to the running of a business). Cases concerning the recognition of qualifications (discussed in more detail at 22.9) relate to the taking up of an activity. By contrast, *van Binsbergen* was a case relating to the Dutch rule which required representatives before tribunals to be resident in the Netherlands. *Gouda v Commissariaat voor de Media* (case C-288/89) concerned Dutch rules limiting the carrying of advertising on television channels. Both these cases dealt with regulations on the running of a business. This latter category of restrictions must be viewed in the widest sense. It has caught prohibitions on lotteries, access to museums and rules regulating broadcasting, to name but a few (see Box 22.2) and certainly includes access to public services (see Chapter 24).

Box 22.2 Examples of Article 56 TFEU

Prohibition and limitation of gambling:
> *Läärä, Cotswold Microsystems Ltd, Oy Transatlantic Software Ltd v Kihlakunnansyyttäjä (Jyväskylä)* (case C-124/97); *Schindler.*

Requirement to comply with collective agreement for minimum wage:
> *Rüffert v Land Niedersachsen* (case C-346/06).

Rules relating to broadcasters offering entry to competition via phone:
> *Kommunikationsbehörde Austria v Österreichischer Rundfunk (ORF)* (case C-195/06).

Tax deductibility of school fees:
> *Schwarz, Gootjes-Schwarz.*

As well as including restrictions on those providing services, Article 56 TFEU catches those measures designed to discourage those who want to travel to receive services. See, for example, *Skatteministeriet v Bent Vestergaard* (case C-55/98). In this case, Danish tax rules discriminated between professional training courses held in Denmark and those held abroad. The Danish tax authorities allowed the expenses incurred in respect of Danish courses to be deducted from the tax bill, those incurred in respect of overseas trips were not so deductible.

The case law in both instances now needs to be considered in the light of the Services Directive and, in particular, the country of origin rule in Article 16 of the Services Directive (see 22.8.4).

22.3.4 Linguistic concerns

Under Regulation 492/2011 Member States are entitled to permit the imposition on non-nationals of conditions 'relating to linguistic knowledge required by reason of the nature of the post to be filled' (Article 3(1)). This requirement was considered in *Groener v Minister for Education* (case 379/87).

Groener

The CJ held that a requirement of Irish law that teachers in vocational schools in Ireland should be proficient in the Irish language would be permissible under Article 3(1) in view of the clear policy of national law to maintain and promote the use of the Irish language as a means of expressing national identity and culture. The Irish language was the national language and the first official language of Ireland. Such a requirement must not, however, be disproportionate to the objectives pursued.

A similar approach to the non-discrimination Treaty provision of Article 45(2) TFEU was taken, albeit with a different result, in *Spotti v Freistaat Bayern* (case C-272/92), in the context of a challenge to a German law permitting contracts of limited duration for foreign language teaching assistants. The Court held that such contracts, prima facie in breach of Article 45(2) TFEU, would only be permitted if they were objectively justified. Since the principal justification for the rules was that they ensured up-to-date tuition, it is not surprising that the Court found them not to be justified. Likewise in *Angonese*, a requirement to take a specific language test, rather than proving linguistic capabilities by other means, was held to constitute indirect discrimination contrary to Article 45 TFEU. The burden of proving justification for discriminatory rules will always be heavy: the rules must be designed to achieve legitimate ends, and must be both appropriate and necessary to achieve those ends.

Note that linguistic concerns do not affect just workers; they may be relevant to those seeking to provide services or establish themselves. Thus Directive 2005/36 ([2005] OJ L255/22) on the recognition of qualifications recognises the need for knowledge of the language of the host Member State (Article 53). Again, caution must be exercised about the circumstances in which such provisions may be relied upon as can be seen in *Wilson v Ordre des avocats du barreau de Luxembourg* (case C-506/04).

Wilson

A number of questions were referred to the CJ concerning the circumstances in which Union law allows a host Member State to make the right of a lawyer to practise on a permanent basis in that Member State under his home-country professional title subject to a test of his proficiency in the languages of that Member State. Directive 98/5 ([1998] L77/36) allows a lawyer so to practise, provided he submits a certificate attesting to his registration with the competent authorities in his home Member State. Given that the Directive requires such lawyers to comply with the relevant ethical standards of the bar councils, which include requirements as to linguistic knowledge, a Member State could not make registration under Directive 98/5 subject to a prior examination of his proficiency in the languages of the host Member State.

22.3.5 **Public service**

In the field of employment rights, Member States are entitled under Article 45 TFEU to deny or restrict access to 'employment in the public service' on the basis of a worker's nationality. Given the potential breadth of this provision, it is not surprising that it has been exploited by Member States nor that the CJ has given it the narrowest scope. Freedom of establishment and the freedom to provide services are expressed not to apply to 'activities which in that state are connected, even occasionally, with the exercise of official authority' (Article 51 TFEU and Article 62 TFEU applying Article 51 TFEU to services). Although phrased in slightly different language from Article 45(4), the principles applicable to workers will apply equally to the establishment and services provisions. As in the case of workers, the exception has been given the narrowest scope. The CJ has repeatedly emphasised that the meaning of these provisions is a matter of EU law and cannot be determined by national practice.

The German post office sought to rely on this exclusion in *Sotgiu* to counter Sotgiu's allegations that the post office's rules granting extra allowances to workers living apart from their families in Germany were discriminatory. On a reference from the Bundesarbeitsgericht the CJ held that the exception provided by Article 45(4) TFEU did not apply to all employment in the public service. It applied only to 'certain activities' in the public service, connected with the exercise of official authority. Moreover, it applied only to conditions of *access*; it did not permit discriminatory conditions of employment once access had been granted.

The matter was further clarified in *Commission v Belgium (public employees)* (case 149/79).

Belgian Public Employees

This was an infringement action against Belgium for breach of Article 45 TFEU. Under Belgian law, posts in the 'public service' could be limited to Belgian nationals. This was applied to all kinds of posts: unskilled workers, railwaymen, nurses, plumbers, electricians and architects, employed by both central and local government. The city of Brussels (seat of the European Commission!) was one of the chief offenders. The Belgian government (supported by France and Germany intervening) argued that all these jobs were 'in the public service' within Article 45(4) TFEU. The CJ disagreed. The concept of public service was a Union concept; it applied only to the exercise of official authority, and was intended to apply only to employees *safeguarding the general interests of the state*. The fact that higher levels of a post might involve the exercise of official authority would not justify assimilating the junior levels to that status. Belgium was in breach of EU law.

Similar proceedings were brought, and upheld, against France in *Commission v France (French nurses)* (case 307/84) against a French law limiting the appointment of nurses in public hospitals to French nationals.

When a particular job will involve 'the exercise of official authority' is not altogether clear. It certainly does not apply to civil servants generally. In *Lawrie-Blum* the Court held that access to certain posts could not be limited by reason of the fact that in a given Member State persons appointed to such posts have the status of civil servants. To make the application of Article 45(4) TFEU dependent on the legal nature of the relationship between the employer and the administration would enable Member States to determine at will the posts covered by the exception laid down in that provision. To constitute employment in the public service, employees must be charged with the exercise of powers conferred by public law or must be responsible for *safeguarding the general interests of the state*. In *Bleis v Ministère de l'Education Nationale* (case C-4/91) the Court held that the concept of public service:

> Presume[s] on the part of those occupying such posts the existence of a special relationship of allegiance to the State and reciprocity of rights and duties which form the foundation of the bond of nationality [para 6].

This approach by the CJ might be termed a 'functional' approach to the determination of whether the 'exercise of official authority' is involved, as it considers the responsibilities of each job individually.

On these criteria, it seems that the derogation provided by Article 45(4) TFEU will be of limited use, confined to occupations such as the judiciary and the higher echelons of the civil service, the armed forces and the police. Identical principles will apply to the interpretation of Article 51 TFEU in relation to services and establishment. (See, eg, *Peñarroja Fa* (cases C-372 and 373/09) concerning approved expert translators working in national courts.)

Since most of the posts in the above cases may not be denied to non-nationals, access to these posts by way of examination or training must be open, on equal terms, to workers (or their families) who are non-nationals. Thus in *Lawrie-Blum* a practical training scheme for teachers, organised in Baden-Württemberg within the framework of the civil service, was not within Article 45(4) TFEU and could not be confined to German nationals.

In view of the widespread practice among Member States of excluding non-nationals from a wide range of occupations in the public service on the basis of Article 45(4) TFEU the Commission published a Notice in 1988 ([1988] OJ C72/2) identifying certain sectors of employment which it considered to be for the most part 'sufficiently remote from the specific activities of the public sphere as defined by the Court that they would only in rare cases be covered by the exception of Article 45(4)' (now Article 45(4) TFEU).

These comprise:

- public healthcare services;
- teaching in state educational establishments;

- research for non-military purposes in public establishments;
- public bodies responsible for administering commercial services.

The Commission has brought enforcement actions against certain Member States for failure to take action following the communication (eg, *Commission v Belgium* (case C-173/94); *Commission v Greece* (case C-290/94); *Commission v Luxembourg* (case C-473/93)). In its judgments given on the same day, the CJ confirmed the Commission's approach of identifying types of work which would rarely fall within Article 45(4) TFEU. In these circumstances, it is still open to the national authorities to show, on a functional basis, that specified jobs within such sections do fall within the public service exception.

22.4 Test for the application of Articles 45, 49 and 56 TFEU

22.4.1 Discrimination

The jurisprudence of the early years shows a test based on discrimination. This is not surprising as the terms of Article 45(2) TFEU refer expressly to the abolition of discrimination on the grounds of nationality, whether arising from legislation, regulation or administrative practice. Article 45 TFEU is in this context a specific form of the general prohibition on discrimination on the grounds of nationality found in Article 18 TFEU. Although the wording in Articles 49 and 56 TFEU does not refer expressly to a prohibition on discrimination, the CJ took a similar approach in respect of these two provisions. In *Reyners*, the applicant was a Dutch national residing in Belgium. He had the necessary Belgian qualification in law for admission as an *avocat*, but was refused admission purely because he did not have Belgian nationality. This constituted discrimination contrary to Article 49 TFEU.

Discrimination includes those rules which, although not distinguishing on the face of it, are harder to satisfy for non-nationals (eg, language or residence requirements), disadvantage them (eg, rules about length of service in the host Member State), or put them under a dual burden (ie, non-recognition of qualifications). In *O'Flynn* (see Chapter 15) the CJ made clear that it was not necessary to prove that a national measure in practice affected a higher proportion of foreign workers, but that the measure was intrinsically liable to affect migrants more than nationals of the host Member State.

As in relation to the free movement of goods (and now capital), indirect discrimination is capable of being 'objectively justified'. Direct discrimination as, for example, established in relation to Article 56 TFEU in *Bond van Adverteerders*, could only be justified under Article 52 TFEU, which was strictly construed. (See further 22.6.)

22.4.2 Beyond discrimination

As with the free movement of goods, the CJ has moved to an approach which went beyond a discrimination-based test. It was thought initially that national regulatory rules and professional practices which were not discriminatory, which applied 'without distinction' to all persons working, providing services or established in a particular Member State, and which clearly served a useful purpose, could not be challenged under the Treaty. The rights granted to EU nationals under Articles 49 and 56 TFEU were to provide services in other Member States 'under the same conditions' as applied to the state's own nationals (see also Regulation 492/2011, Article 1(1)). Although national regulatory rules might create barriers to the free movement of services and freedom of establishment, they could only be removed by harmonisation, as provided under Articles 52 and 53 TFEU (on harmonisation generally, see chapter 16).

Since harmonisation proved slow to achieve, some of these measures came to be challenged as 'discriminatory' in that they were harder to satisfy for non-nationals or imposed a dual burden upon migrants. As this category of rule would apply without distinction, it was suggested that they would be permissible provided they could be objectively justified. This can be seen in the context of the *insurance services* case.

Insurance Services

The rules required, inter alia, that a person providing direct insurance must be established and authorised to practise in the state in which the service is provided. The Court held that Articles 56 and 57 TFEU require the removal not only of all discrimination based on nationality, but also all restrictions on his freedom to provide services imposed by reason of the fact that he is established in a Member State other than that in which the services are provided.

So while the analysis of the residence requirement in *van Binsbergen* was based on finding discrimination regarding the provider, in *insurance services* it seemed that the CJ was suggesting a test which focused not so much on the position of the individual but on the impact on the activity (whether work, establishment or services). The case law was, however, slow to develop and the principles were unclear. It was not until 1991 with *Säger* that the Court established a coherent approach to indistinctly applicable rules in the field of services parallel to that pioneered in the sphere of goods in the 1970s in *Dassonville* and *Cassis de Dijon*. In doing so it undoubtedly opened up the possibility for further claims under Article 56 TFEU, and with it, as with any easing of the rules, some abuse.

Säger

Säger v Dennemeyer concerned a specialist in patent renewal services, Dennemeyer, who was based in the UK. He provided these services in Germany, without the licence which German law requires for persons attending to the legal affairs of third parties. Such licences were not normally granted to patent renewal agents. Dennemeyer's right to provide such services in Germany was challenged by Säger, a German patent agent operating in Germany. Dennemeyer argued that the German rules, which limited access to the relevant profession were a hindrance to the freedom of movement of services, contrary to Articles 56 and 57, para 3. A number of questions were referred to the Court. As Advocate-General Jacobs pointed out, while it was clear that Article 56 TFEU applied to discriminatory rules, it was not yet clear whether it applied to rules which were applicable to all providers of services, whether established in the Member State in which the service was provided or not. As noted, the principles laid down in *van Binsbergen* and the insurance cases had proceeded on the basis that the rules in question were discriminatory. While it was not unreasonable to expect compliance with the rules of the Member State by any person established in that state, there was less justification for demanding compliance by those providing services there but who were based elsewhere. In these circumstances he suggested an approach based on the Court's jurisprudence on Article 34 TFEU in relation to indistinctly applicable rules.

The Court endorsed his suggestion. While asserting that:

> Article [56 TFEU] requires not only the abolition of all discrimination against a person providing services on the ground of his nationality but also the abolition of any restriction, even if applied without distinction to national providers of services and to those of other Member States, when it is liable to prohibit or otherwise impede the activities of a provider of services established in another Member State where he lawfully provides similar services [para 12].

it held that:

> Having regard to the particular characteristics of certain specific provisions of services, specific requirements imposed on the provider cannot be regarded as incompatible with the Treaty.

However:

> The freedom to provide services may be limited only by rules which are justified by imperative reasons relating to the public interest and which apply to all persons and undertakings pursuing an activity in the State of destination insofar as that interest is not protected by rules to which the person providing the service is subject in the State in which he is established. In particular, these requirements must be objectively necessary in order to ensure compliance with professional rules and must not exceed what is necessary to attain those objectives.

It may be noted that, to establish a prima facie breach of Article 56 TFEU, the rule challenged must be 'liable to prohibit or otherwise impede' the provision of services. On the face of it, this is a stricter test than the *Dassonville* test applied to goods. On the other hand, the criteria relating to justification, embracing the principles of proportionality and mutual recognition, are substantially the same as the twin principles laid down in *Cassis de Dijon*, albeit lacking examples as to what will constitute 'imperative reasons relating to the public interest'.

The principles laid down in *Säger* have been followed in a succession of cases in which national or professional rules likely to 'prohibit or otherwise impede' the free provision of services have been tested for their compatibility with Article 56 TFEU. Thus in *Commission v France* (case C-154/89) a requirement of French law that tourist guides must obtain a licence by examination, although justifiable in principle in the interest of consumers as contributing to a 'proper appreciation of places and things of interest', was found to be disproportionate. The licence requirement went further than was necessary in order to protect this interest. In *Vander Elst v Office des Migrations Internationales* (case C-43/93) the requirement of a French work permit for TCNs seeking to work in France was held not to be justified by 'overriding reasons in the general interest' (to regulate access to the national labour market), since these workers were already in possession of a work permit obtained in Belgium. On the other hand, in *Ramrath v Ministre de la Justice* (case C-106/91) rules governing the conditions for the provision of auditing services in Luxembourg were found on the facts to be justified and not disproportionate. Similarly in *Alpine Investments* a Dutch prohibition on 'cold calling' by providers of financial advice established in the Netherlands was found to be justified in order to protect consumers and the reputation of the Netherlands' security market and was not disproportionate. In each case the measure in question and its alleged justification were tested on their merits.

22.4.3 **Establishment**

Initially, the principles established in *Säger* appeared to apply only to the provision of services. Paragraph 13 of that judgment, suggested that:

> a Member State may not make the provision of services in its territory subject to the conditions required for establishment . . . and thereby deprive of all practical effectiveness the provisions of the Treaty whose object is, primarily, to provide services.

Clearly, the CJ notes a difference between services and establishment, a difference which also shows when considering justification for restrictive national measures, as services will be regulated by the home Member State. This reasoning also implied that persons who established themselves in a Member State must comply with the conditions laid down in that state for its own nationals. *Gebhard* changed our understanding of Article 49 TFEU.

Gebhard involved a challenge by a German lawyer, a member of the Stuttgart Bar, to a decision by the Milan Bar Council prohibiting him from practising from chambers set up in Italy under the title *avvocato*. He claimed the rules of the Milan Bar breached Articles 56 and 49 TFEU.

The Court held that the possibility for a national of a Member State to exercise his right of establishment, and the conditions for the exercise of that right, had to be determined in the light of the activities which he intended to pursue on the territory of the host Member State. Where an activity was not subject to any rules in the host state, a national of another Member State was entitled to establish himself on the territory of the first state and pursue his activities there. On the other hand:

> Where the taking up and pursuit of a particular activity was subject to certain conditions in the host State a national of another Member State intending to pursue that activity must in principle comply with them.

However, national measures which hinder or make less attractive the exercise of fundamental freedoms guaranteed by the Treaty must fulfil four conditions: First, they must be applied in a non-discriminatory manner; Secondly, they must be justified by imperative requirements in the general interest; Thirdly, they must be suitable for securing the attainment of the objective which they pursue; and Fourthly, they must not go beyond what is necessary in order to attain it.

Member States must take into account the equivalence of diplomas and if necessary proceed to a comparison of the knowledge and qualifications required by their national rules and those of the person concerned. It was left to the national court to decide whether the rules in question were in fact justified. (On qualifications see further 22.9.)

Gebhard can thus be seen as a recognition of an approach to national measures parallel to that taken in respect of services (and goods), which is not to analyse the issues by reference to discrimination but to the existence of a hindrance. As with *Säger* for services, *Gebhard* widened the potential scope of Article 49 TFEU.

22.4.4 **Workers**

Whether the same approach would be taken as regards workers was clarified in *Bosman*. It concerned rules that were not overtly discriminatory but which still had an adverse impact on individuals' ability to exercise their free movement rights.

Bosman

The case centred on Belgian football transfer rules, which accorded with international football rules. These rules provided that a club which sought to engage a player must pay a specified, sometimes considerable, sum to the player's existing club. The rules applied irrespective of the nationality of the player and whether the player was going to be playing for a Belgian team or not. Further, there were limits on how many non-nationals a club could employ. In Bosman's case, he was signed up to play for a Belgian team and the rules effectively stopped him from moving to play for a French team. After a lengthy legal dispute, the matter was referred to the CJ. Bosman argued that the rules were, inter alia, contrary to Article 45 TFEU. The CJ held that, although the rules were not discriminatory, they still 'directly affect[ed] players' access to the employment market in other Member States and are thus capable of impeding freedom of movement of workers'.

In principle, the rules were incompatible with Article 45 TFEU unless they pursued a legitimate aim compatible with the Treaty, were justified by pressing reasons of public interest and were proportionate. In *Bosman*, therefore, the CJ was not concerned with discrimination but with the question of whether cross-border access to the job market of each Member State was safeguarded. In this approach we clearly see parallels to that taken by the CJ in relation to the free movement of goods and 'indistinctly applicable' measures. Indeed in *Bosman*, we see perhaps the strongest statement of the scope of these rights as it is stated clearly to be concerned with 'access to the market' and the level of impact required to trigger Article 45 TFEU is low: 'directly affecting'.

The move away from a discrimination-based test seen in *Bosman* has been adopted subsequently in many cases. *Olympique Lyonnais SASP v Olivier Bernard and Newcastle United FC* (case C-325/08), relates to a provision in a collective agreement regarding training contracts for young footballers, in which a young player at the end of his training period is required, under pain of being sued for damages, to sign a professional contract with the club which trained him, was again dealt with as falling within Article 45 TFEU. The CJ noted the purpose of the free-movement provision was to facilitate free movement and 'preclude[s] measures which might place nationals of the Member States at a disadvantage when they wish to pursue an economic activity in the territory of another Member State.'

Thus, national provisions which 'preclude or deter' free movement are incompatible with the TFEU unless justified by an overriding public interest objective.

22.4.5 Distinctions between different kinds of rule?

A couple of further points should be noted. Some, such as Advocate-General Lenz in *Bosman*, had suggested that there should be a distinction between rules relating to access to a profession and those concerning the operation of a business, as the former would be more damaging to the internal market. This view has not been universally accepted, as can be seen from the comments of Advocate-General Alber in *Lehtonen and Castors Canada Dry Namur-Braine ASBL v Fédération royale belge des sociétés de basket-ball ASBL (FRBSB)* (case C-176/96).

Lehtonen

The International Basketball Federation (FIBA) rules governing international transfers of players do not permit clubs to field players who have already played in another country in the same zone during that season in national championships. Lehtonen was a basketball player of Finnish nationality. He played in a team, which took part in the Finnish championship but was then engaged by Castors Braine, a Belgian club, to take part in the final stage of the Belgian championship. He was transferred after the relevant FIBA deadline. Castors Braine was penalised by the award of matches to its opponents, so it was forced to dispense with Lehtonen's services for the play-off matches. Castors Braine and Lehtonen brought court action to have the penalties imposed against Castors Braine lifted. The national court referred questions on the rules' compatibility with EU law.

The CJ confirmed that while sport is special, the entire sector cannot be removed from the application of EU law. Having confirmed that Lehtonen was a worker, the CJ re-affirmed that the rules could constitute an obstacle and:

> ... that the rules in question concern not the employment of such players, on which there is no restriction, but the extent to which their clubs may field them in official matches is irrelevant. In so far as participation in such matches is the essential purpose of a professional player's activity, a rule which restricts that participation obviously also restricts the chances of employment of the player concerned [para 50].

It seems in general that there is no such distinction made in the CJ's approach and that in some circumstances the CJ has conflated the two issues (eg, *Kraus v Land Baden-Württemberg* (case C-19/92), para 23). It may still be that the latter group of restrictions could be more easily justified.

It had also been thought that a distinction could be discerned between the approach towards personal matters and those relating to professional rules. Rules distinguishing on the basis of nationality, for example, would be dealt with on a discrimination-based analysis, whilst rules which concerned professional matters, would be analysed from an access to the market-style approach. It seems that the CJ has not continued to make this distinction. Whether this means that the distinction between personal and professional rights has been eradicated entirely is not certain. In some instances the CJ seems to use both concepts (eg, *Payroll Data Services (Italy) Srl v ADP Europe and ADP GSI SA* (case C-79/01), concerning rules requiring small enterprises to have their payslips produced by bodies registered with specified bodies). If we look to the case law concerning workers and their social and ancillary rights, the CJ still uses a test based on discrimination (see, eg, *Ioannidis* see Chapter 23) and the Italian rules relating to exchange assistants for languages were likewise held to be indirectly discriminatory (*Delay v Universita degli studi di Firenze* (case C-276/07)). Nonetheless, in the majority of cases concerning the economic rights, a test which focused on the restriction of an activity rather than individual discrimination seems to be more common.

22.4.6 'Exports'

Article 56 TFEU, as with Articles 45 and 49 TFEU, applies to 'export' situations, as we can see from *Alpine Investments*. It is open to debate whether the CJ has (or should) take a more lenient approach to export cases, as it has done in the context of the export of goods. Interestingly, in *Alpine Investments*—concerning a prohibition on cold calling in the financial services sector—the national rules were found to be justified and proportionate.

22.4.7 A common approach, a consistent approach?

A general trend can be identified in all three provisions towards the use of a test based on access to the market irrespective of whether the right is being relied on by an individual or a legal person and irrespective of whether the right is exercised by an employer or employee; recipient or provider of service. Nonetheless, the CJ has not used the same test in respect of the three articles. Thus, the test used in *Gebhard* is, on a strict interpretation of the wording, less demanding than the 'prohibit or otherwise impede' threshold introduced in *Säger*. Whether this test is now to be applied to both establishment and services is not clear. In *Gebhard* the CJ noted that both constitute 'fundamental freedoms provided by the Treaty'. It would thus make sense that the same test is applied to both Articles, and indeed to Article 45 TFEU. The wording used in *Bosman* is again different. In the subsequent *CaixaBank France v Minstere de L'Economie, des Finances et de l'industrie* (case C-442/02) (discussed further later), the CJ adopted yet another test in respect of the freedom of establishment, stating that measures which 'prohibit, impede or render less attractive' the exercise of freedom of establishment are restrictions for the purposes of Article 49 TFEU. This seems to blend the *Säger* and *Gebhard* tests, arguably requiring very little in the way of an impediment to freedom of establishment.

Whilst in subsequent case law on Article 56 TFEU the CJ has, in the main, applied the *Säger* test, there are inconsistencies here too. In *Kohll v Union des Caisses de Maladie* (case C-158/96) (prior authorisation of medical expenses by home state required), the CJ citing *Commission v France* (case C-381/93) applied a slightly different test from that used in *Säger*. It held that what is now Article 56 TFEU 'precludes the application of any national rules which have the effect of making the provision of services between Member States *more difficult* than the provision of services purely within one Member State' (para 33; emphasis added). It is not clear whether the use of this test will become generalised within Article 56 TFEU case law: although this version of the test was found in cases involving transport, it seems to be becoming more widely used (see, eg, *Leichtle v Bundesanstalt für Arbeit* (case C-8/02), reimbursement of expenditure for healthcare). In some cases the CJ seems to be avoiding the issue entirely, using neither of these formulations. For example, in *Gambelli* the CJ merely remarked:

> It is appropriate to inquire whether Article [56 TFEU] precludes legislation such as that in issue in the main proceedings which, although it does not discriminate on grounds of nationality, restricts the freedom to provide services [para 69].

This is a yet more stringent approach than *Säger* or *Kohll*.

The CJ has not adopted a consistent approach to the wording it uses either within the individual freedoms or between them, despite their common objective (noted in, eg, *Olympique Lyonnais* (see 22.4.4)). The CJ's case law on Article 56 TFEU has even been described as 'random'. Despite these uncertainties, it is, in the final analysis, not obvious what difference in practice the use of the different tests would make. In any event, the measure in question must be examined to identify if it is objectively justified: the emphasis in all the cases is on justification for the rules in terms of the *activity undertaken* rather than on the burden imposed on the 'guest' undertaking or worker.

In sum, it seems that these provisions will be easy to trigger, raising the spectre of the problems in the goods case law following the *Sunday trading cases*, and the question of whether the appropriate balance between the competence of the EU and of the Member States has been appropriately drawn. This is illustrated by *CaixaBank*, in which a French rule prohibited a certain type of account from being marketed in France. The CJ argued that the rule hindered subsidiaries of foreign banks by depriving them of the possibility of 'competing more effectively' against established banks because the established banks 'have an extensive network of branches and therefore greater opportunities . . . for raising capital from the public' (para 13).

Implicitly the CJ suggests that the incoming companies need to be allowed to provide a greater range of services to give them a competitive edge. In this, the CJ departed from the opinion of the Advocate-General who noted that the effect of the national measures in question would merely be to 'reduce the economic attractiveness' of carrying on the activity regulated. According to the Advocate-General, such an interpretation would upset the balance of powers between the regulatory powers of the Members States and the Union. He noted that the Union does not have general regulatory powers, such power falling to the Member States subject to the overriding prohibition on discrimination and obstacles to establishment. Further, the impact of such an approach would be de-regulatory as it would enable economic operators to oppose any national measure because that measure could 'in the final analysis narrow profit margins'. As the Advocate-General suggested, this would result in a view of the Treaty freedoms which operated not in order to create an internal market in which conditions are similar to those of a single market and where operators can move freely, but in order to establish a market without rules (*CaixaBank*, Opinion, paras 58–63).

Nonetheless, this is precisely the route the CJ has seemed to take, and which has been recognised in subsequent case law on Article 56 TFEU, as well as Article 49 TFEU (*Corporación Dermoestética SA v To Me Group Advertising Media* (case C-500/06) (rule limiting advertising of services to local television)), and even Article 45 TFEU. As, in the final analysis, any regulatory rule has the effect of making a business less desirable or profitable than if those rules were not in place, the consequence seems to be that any attempt at regulation is capable of being challenged on this approach.

22.5 Limitations on the application of Articles 45, 49 and 56 TFEU

We have noted the breadth of circumstances in which Articles 49 and 56 TFEU can be triggered. Following *Bosman*, it seemed that the CJ was providing limits to these circumstances. The CJ took the opportunity to refine the scope of *Bosman*, and consequently the scope of Article 45 TFEU as regards non-discriminatory rules which nonetheless might affect the functioning of the internal market, in *Volker Graf*.

Volker Graf

The rules challenged in this case concerned Austrian employment legislation which required employers to make certain payments to employees on the termination of an employment contract, when the employee was not leaving the job voluntarily. Graf handed in his notice to go to work in Germany. He claimed the payments, but Filzmoser Maschinenbau refused to make the payments as Graf was leaving voluntarily. He argued that the rules that excluded him from receiving the payments were likely adversely to affect those who sought to move from Austria to another Member State more than those who were leaving employment but staying in Austria. Arguing from the CJ's approach in *Bosman*, Graf claimed that the Austrian rules were incompatible with what is now Article 45 TFEU. The question as to whether this was incompatible with the requirements of the free movement of workers was referred.

The CJ confirmed that Article 45 TFEU not only applies to discriminatory rules but also to rules which, although they are expressed to apply without distinction, impede the exercise of free movement rights. It went on to say, however, that for such rules to constitute an obstacle prohibited under Article 45 TFEU, the provisions 'must affect access of the workers to the labour market'. In this case, the entitlement was only contingent on certain events happening—basically the unfair dismissal of an employee—and therefore any effect on the internal market of this sort of rule was too uncertain and indirect to fall within the prohibition.

Thus, although the CJ's test of measures affecting access to the host market would seem on the face of it to be very broad, the latter part of the judgment clearly focuses on the need for an obstacle to accessing that market to exist. A similar approach can be seen, as regards goods, in *Dip Spa* (discussed in Chapter 18).

The CJ in relation to goods adopted another limitation mechanism, that found in *Keck*, which allows certain types of rule to be treated more leniently (known as 'selling arrangements') (see *De Agostini* and Chapter 18). This has similarities to the approach adopted in *Graf* and in *Dip Spa*, as measures which have an effect which is too uncertain and indirect are not be caught by the prohibition. Indeed, the Advocate-General in *CaixaBank* considered the possibility of limiting Article 49 TFEU in a similar way, suggesting that those measures which have an effect which is too uncertain and indirect should not be caught by Article 49 TFEU. It is striking that the CJ did not even consider this possibility, thus opening a rift between the case law in this regard on establishment not only with that concerning goods but also the workers jurisprudence. Although the *Graf* question does not seem to have been raised before the CJ with regard to services, it seemed to reject the need for a *Keck*-style approach to services in *Alpine*, turning its back on the suggestion of Advocate-General Jacobs that the Court adopt a *de minimis* rule, and that only rules which 'substantially impede' the freedom to provide services should be deemed prima facie in breach of Union law (see also in relation to goods *Leclerc-Siplec*). Although the precise scope of the ruling in *Alpine Investments* in that context has been the subject of some debate, it seems that where the advertising of services is concerned, the CJ does not even consider the question of whether there is a distinction between 'selling arrangements' and 'product requirements'. Thus, in *Corporación Dermoestética SA*, which concerned a limitation on the advertising of advertisements for medical and surgical treatments (the adverts were prohibited on national television but permitted on local television), the CJ merely assessed the national rules as a hindrance to cross-border trade (contrast approach in relation to goods where the CJ has distinguished between total and partial bans on advertising: see Chapter 18).

22.6 A rule of reason?

As we have seen in the field of goods, the CJ seems to have felt the need to balance a broad Union competence to review national legislation with the possibility for Member States to justify their national rules. A similar concern can be seen with the development of the case law on workers, services and establishment to cover indirectly discriminatory measures. Thus we see the CJ ruling, in cases such as the *German insurance cases*, that rules which are indirectly discriminatory may be justified for overriding reasons of public interest and developed in subsequent cases. As is the case for goods, the result of this is the introduction of another group of exceptions to the Treaty freedoms. The possible reasons justifying indirectly discriminatory measures are not limited to those grounds set out in the Treaty; rather they are an open-ended group of justifications, such as consumer protection and cultural diversity (see further Chapter 25). The key distinction is that between discriminatory and indirectly discriminatory restrictions (see Figure 22.1). Unfortunately, as we shall see in Chapter 25, the CJ has not always been clear about where this boundary lies. Finally, as with any exception to a Treaty freedom, the measure must be subject to the test of proportionality. In this there is a distinction between services and establishment as, in the case of services, Member States should take into account any regulation to serve the relevant public interest objective, which occurs in the service provider's home Member State.

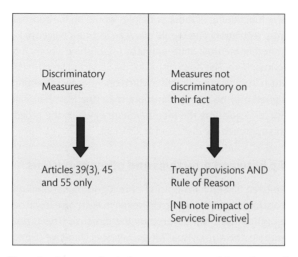

Figure 22.1 Impact of boundary between discriminatory measures and those that apply without distinction

22.7 Harmonisation

Some national rules, particularly those relating to conduct of professions and qualifications, might survive the application of Article 49 TFEU in the interests of protecting the public from unqualified practitioners. The disadvantage is, of course, that the European market could remain segmented. The answer to this particular problem, as we have seen in Chapter 16, is to replace national regulations with European rules, otherwise known as harmonisation.

22.7.1 Mutual recognition and the home-country principle

Because of the problems outlined earlier, and because progress on harmonisation for the purpose of mutual recognition of qualifications had been so slow, the Union decided on a new approach. Instead of attempting to harmonise by profession, known as the sectoral or 'vertical' approach, the Commission adopted a general or 'horizontal' approach, based not on harmonisation but on the mutual recognition of qualifications. This applied not just to individual professions but to all areas of activity for which a higher education diploma was required. Directive 89/48 ([1989] OJ L19/16), based on these principles, was approved in December 1988. The Council then agreed a second directive dealing with secondary education (Council Directive 92/51 ([1992] OJ L209/25)) and also based on the principle of mutual recognition. Both Directives were repeatedly amended and the whole system was replaced by Directive 2005/36 ([2005] OJ L255/22). Directive 2005/36 has now been modernised and amended by the professional Qualifications Directive 2013/55 ([2013] OJ L254/113). The basic systems remain, however, and are discussed at 22.8.2.

Mutual recognition is not limited to the recognition of qualifications, but is an approach used in many directives (and, indeed, underpins much of the CJ's approach to necessity and proportionality of host-state regulations). The approach is based on the following principles:

- the harmonisation of *essential* safeguards and standards applicable to activities as a whole;
- within that framework, acceptance of the standards of other Member States on a basis of mutual trust and recognition, on the principle of home country control and supervision.

Essential to the effective functioning of these principles would be the concept of the single licence known as home-country regulation. This would allow an institution licensed in one Member State to offer its services to another Member State, either by establishing a branch or agency in that state or by supplying its services there. The Audiovisual Media Services Directive (Directive 2010/12), for example, is a minimum-harmonisation directive which operates on the country of origin principle. Although television signals may be received in more than one Member State, only one Member State has responsibility for regulation, the Member State in which the broadcaster is established. (The problems with this approach are discussed at 22.10.3.)

22.7.2 **Relationship between directives and other provisions**

Where directives have been passed harmonising or recognising national rules, the provisions of the directive will be conclusive on the matter. However, in each case it will be necessary to decide whether the rule in question has been covered by the directive. This is not always as simple as it might seem. For example, the Audiovisual Media Services Directive (Directive 2010/13 ([2010] OJ L95/1) (codified version)) covers only television broadcasting and television-like services. In these days of 'web-casting' and on-demand and interactive services, the question does arise, 'what is broadcasting?' The scope of this Directive was considered in *De Agostini*, discussed in Chapter 18, in which the Advocate-General and the CJ came to different conclusions about the scope of the Directive in relation to television advertising. In the *insurance services* case, the insurance Directive was found to be designed to ensure that undertakings were solvent; it did not attempt to harmonise national rules concerning technical reserves. Given the potential impact of the Services Directive (Directive 2006/123), the precise boundaries between directives might become of greater significance.

Harmonisation is discussed in more detail in Chapter 16 and the points made in relation to directives made under Article 114 TFEU can, in general, be transposed to those made under Article 53(2) TFEU.

22.8 **The Services Directive (Directive 2006/123)**

Despite the efforts of the CJ in developing a broad-based test for the application of Article 56 TFEU and the harmonising directives already existing, the Commission concluded that there still existed significant barriers to entry for the cross-border provision of services. To this end, it proposed that a general services directive be enacted, based on the principle of home country regulation, administrative cooperation and administrative simplification. The Directive also contained a number of specific derogation principles to temper the potentially deregulatory impact of the Directive, as well as excluding some sectors of the service industry, such as gambling and gas and water supply, from its scope. The Services Directive proved to be controversial; discontent with its potential impact on the provision of public services has been suggested to have had an influence on the French 'no' vote to Treaty revision. The European Parliament, in expressing concern about the relationship between the Directive and services of general economic interest (ie services that are in the public interest), commented that within the EU legal order trade liberalisation is not an end in itself, nor was it to be benefited at the expense of other tasks of the Union. Others considered the interrelationship between the general services directive and the subject specific directives had been dealt with inadequately. Nonetheless, the Services Directive (Directive 2006/123/EC ([2006] OJ L376/36)) was adopted on 12 December 2006 and was to have been implemented by Member States three years after its publication, by 28 December 2009, at the latest.

22.8.1 **Scope of the Directive**

The Directive applies to all services which are not explicitly excluded from its scope and in principle the definition of services matches that taken under the Treaty. Given that the case law of the CJ has not automatically excluded public services from the scope of the Treaty, in principle some services provided by the state may also be caught by the Directive. The Directive explicitly excludes, however, 'non-economic services of general interest' (Article 2(2)(a)). The Commission has suggested that national primary and secondary education, which is not provided for remuneration, would fall within the excluded category, whereas services in the utilities (such as electricity and gas) would be caught by the Directive. Financial services are excluded (Article 2(2)(b)), as are electronic communication services and networks, and associated facilities and services as defined in Article 2 of the Electronic Communication Framework Directive (Article 2(2)(c)). Transport (Article 2(2)(d)), the service of hiring out workers provided by temporary work agencies (Article 2(2)(e)), healthcare (Article 2(2)(f)), broadcasting (Article 2(2)(g)), gambling (Article 2(2)(h)) and some social services (Article 2(2)(j)) are likewise excluded—though in each case the definition ascribed to the relevant category of service should be checked.

As can be seen in *Ottica New Line di Accardi Vincenzo v Commune di Campobello di Mazara* (case C-539/11), the scope of the healthcare exception was proved to be fairly contentious. In *Ottica New Line di Accardi Vincenzo*, which concerned regional legislation making the establishment of new opticians' shops subject to authorisation based on demographic and geographical limitations, the CJ made the following distinction as regards the scope of 'healthcare' in Article 2(2)(f):

> an optician who is authorised to conduct eye tests, to measure visual acuity, to define and check the ocular correction needed, to detect eye problems and to treat defects of vision using corrective optical devices, to advise customers in that regard and to refer them to an ophthalmic specialist is exercising an activity encompassed by the protection of public health. By contrast, opticians who carry out technical activities, such as assembling frames and repairing spectacles, and who sell products which do not, strictly speaking, form part of the treatment of visual problems, such as non-prescription sunglasses or spectacle care products, exercise a commercial activity which is not associated with the protection of public health [para 20].

In *Fédération des maisons de repos privées de Belgique (Femarbel) ASBL v Commission communautaire commune de Bruxelles-Capitale* (case C-57/12), which concerned care centres for the elderly, the CJ considered the scope of Article 2(2)(f) (healthcare) and Article 2(2)(j) (social services). The CJ noted that the recitals refer to 'healthcare and pharmaceutical services provided by health professionals to patients to assess, maintain or restore their state of health where those activities are reserved to a regulated health profession in the Member State in which the services are provided' (recital 22); this reflects the definition of healthcare in the Patients' Directive (Directive 2011/24). In contrast, the exception does not concern services that are designed to enhance well-being or provide relaxation, such as sports or fitness clubs. Both these cases point to the knowledge base required in the interests of public health being key to the scope of the exclusion. Additionally, the exercise of public authority (Article 2(2)(i)), private security services (Article 2(2)(k)) and bailiffs appointed by an official act of government (Article 2(2)(l)) are excluded. Finally, Article 2(3) states that the Services Directive does not apply to the field of taxation. Although this may seem to constitute a broad range of exclusions, the Services Directive covers many activities, including those in which small and medium-sized enterprises are active, a group which may have found wrestling with 'red tape' particularly challenging.

The Directive covers the activities of those who have the nationality of a Member State or by a legal person under the laws of a Member State and established in a Member State. These reflect the terms of the Treaty provisions. By contrast, services provided by natural persons who are not nationals of a Member State or by entities which are established outside the Union or are not incorporated in accordance with the laws of a Member State are not covered by the Directive.

The Services Directive aims to facilitate the exercise of both the freedom to provide services and the freedom of establishment (Article 1(1)) by requiring Member States to remove restrictions on those freedoms. The Directive concerns 'requirements' relating to the provision of services. According to Article 4(7), the concept of requirement covers any obligation, prohibition, condition or any other limitation imposed on service providers (or recipients of services), such as an obligation to obtain an authorisation or to make a declaration to competent authorities. It does not cover general rules, such as those relating to town planning. The extent to which the Services Directive would cover social and ancillary rights is not clear; it seems principally aimed at restrictions on professional activity. It has also been noted that it is not clear whether the Services Directive will take a discrimination-based or a restriction-based approach to defining 'requirements' and recitals can be found which support either interpretation.

22.8.2 **Administration**

The Directive envisages the simplification of administrative requirements; the provisions attaining this are set out in Chapter II of the Directive. Article 5(1) requires Member States to undertake a process of administrative simplification, to assess whether all procedures and authorisation schemes are necessary and proportionate. Any remaining schemes must be rendered simpler, clearer and more transparent (eg, conditions have to be made public in advance; criteria have to be clear and non-discriminatory). The chapters on establishment (Chapter III) and cross-border provision of services (Chapter IV) deal with permitted regulation in more detail, and Chapter V contains provisions on quality of services.

The Directive also envisages that Member States should introduce 'points of single contact' through which service providers can complete all procedures and formalities needed for access to and exercise of their service activities. Interestingly, the Directive requires the introduction of fully functioning and interoperable electronic procedures to make administrative requirements less burdensome.

22.8.3 **Freedom of establishment**

The Services Directive also contains provisions relating to the freedom of establishment (Articles 9–15). They apply to all cases where a business seeks to establish in a Member State, and cover both the situation where a service provider seeks to establish in another Member State and the situation where a provider seeks to establish in his own Member State: this, then, is wider than merely removing boundaries between Member States. Member States must review authorisation schemes, which—according to the case law of the CJ (eg, *Asociación Profesional de Empresas Navieras de Líneas Regulares (Analir) and Others v Administracion General del Estado (case C-205/99)*) and Article 9 of the Directive—they may only maintain if the schemes are non-discriminatory, justified by an overriding reason relating to the public interest and proportionate—that is, satisfy a rule of reason test. The term, 'overriding reason relating to the public interest' is defined in Article 4(8) of the Directive as reasons recognised by the CJ. Although Article 4(8) gives examples of such reasons, the class is not closed as the definition will continue to reflect any developments in the CJ's case law.

Article 10 contains the criteria against which the process for granting authorisations must be judged. In particular, authorisations must not duplicate controls in the home Member State, a requirement which again follows the jurisprudence of the CJ (eg, *Canal Satélite Digital SL v Administracion General del Estado and Distribuidora de Television Digital SA (DTS)* (case C-390/99)—registration requirement for operators of conditional access television services). All decisions must be fully reasoned and subject to a right of appeal. Article 14 establishes a list of requirements which Member States cannot impose for access to or exercise of a service activity, which reflect the existing case law. An example would be a nationality requirement or a limitation on the number of establishments. By contrast, Article 15 lists the sorts of requirements which usually constitute a restriction but which in some circumstances may be justified, such as territorial or quantitative restrictions (eg, no more than one petrol station per 30 kilometres, but cf *the shopping centres* case, decided under Article 49 TFEU in which the Court found that restrictions on the location and size of large retail establishments constitute a restriction). It does not, however, cover limits imposed on input, output or emissions, for example regarding CO_2 emissions or emissions of other gases.

22.8.4 **The cross-border provision of services**

Articles 16–21 deal with cross-border provision of services, which are subject to a different regime than that applicable to establishment. It is therefore important to distinguish between the two. The Directive follows the distinction made in *Gebhard* (see Chapter 21). According to *Schnitzer* (case C-215/01—entry to skilled trade register in relation to plastering services) establishment requires integration into the economy in the Member State involving the acquisition of customers in that Member State from the basis of a stable professional domicile (para 29).

The cornerstone of the system is Article 16, which applies the country of origin principle. This means that, save in limited circumstances, Member States may not impose host country requirements on cross-border service providers. This is a development of the CJ's case law on the rule of reason which required Member States to take into account country of origin regulation. According to Article 16(b), application of national requirements can only be justified if necessary for the protection of public policy, public security, public health or the environment. This excludes Member States from invoking other public interest objectives. It is the narrow scope of these grounds that has made the scope of the Directive so significant.

Some further derogations are found in Article 17, such as services of general economic interest, matters relating to the posting of workers and matters covered by Directive 77/249 on legal services. Article 17(6) ensures the full application of Title II of the Professional Qualifications Directive (Directive 2005/36 ([2005] OJ L255) discussed at 22.9.2) in the case of cross-border service provision, as by virtue of this provision Article 16 will not apply to matters relating to professional qualifications.

22.8.5 **Provisions to ensure quality of service**

The chapter on quality of services is intended to safeguard the interests of consumers by improving the quality of the services of the regulated professions in the internal market. Thus Article 23 lays down information that Member States must ensure services providers give their customers, including: name; any relevant professional body; price; insurance (Article 22(1); terms defined at Article 23(5)). Service providers whose services present 'a direct and particular risk to the health or safety of the recipient or a third person' may be required to carry professional indemnity insurance or equivalent scheme (Article 23(1)), but host Member States may not require such a provider to take a second insurance/scheme in respect of the host Member State (Article 23(2)). The Commission may establish a list of services covered by Article 23.

Traditionally some activities or professions have been subject to stringent rules which prevent practitioners from advertising or which prevent multidisciplinary activities. According to Article 24(1) all such total prohibitions on 'commercial communications' are to be removed (examples are given in Recital 100), although rules which seek to maintain the independence, integrity or dignity of a profession may be permitted, subject to a proportionality test. It seems the CJ is taking a broad approach to the scope of Article 24(1). In *Société fiduciaire nationale d'expertise comptable v Ministre du Budget, des Comptes publics et de la Fonction publique* (case C-119/09), the CJ held that a prohibition on accountants 'canvassing' for business (an unsolicited personal offer of goods or services to a certain natural or legal person, effectively 'cold-calling') constituted such a total prohibition contrary to Article 24. It argued that because all of *that type* of commercial communication was prohibited, this constituted a total ban; it did not seem to consider the question of whether there were any other forms of commercial communication available (eg, billboard advertising) relevant to the notion of 'total prohibitions'. Interestingly, the CJ referred to *Alpine Investments* to support the conclusion that a ban on cold-calling may affect inter-state trade; it did not follow that decision in finding the prohibition justified.

Rules restricting multidisciplinary activities are permitted in limited circumstances, such as to ensure professional ethics (Article 25(1)(a)). In line with a trend towards self and co-regulation, Article 26 requires Member States to encourage service providers 'to take action on a voluntary basis in order to ensure the quality of service provision', such as through kite mark schemes.

22.8.6 **Administrative cooperation**

The Commission's Report on 'The State of the Internal Market for Services' highlighted lack of trust between the Member States as a reason for multiplicity of regulation and control. It is this issue which the administrative cooperation provisions aim to address. Articles 28–36 legally oblige Member States to give each other mutual assistance, in particular to reply to information requests and to carry out, if necessary, factual checks, inspections and investigations.

To facilitate this process, Member States are required to identify 'liaison points', which have the responsibility for coordinating or supervising cooperation within a given state. The Directive also envisages the establishment of the Internal Market Information System (IMI) to make the exchange of information by electronic means possible. In addition to the provision of information on request, Article 32 lays down a mechanism aiming to ensure that Member States inform all other Member States concerned and the Commission within the shortest possible time if they become aware of acts of a service provider or specific circumstances relating to a service activity that could cause serious damage to the health or safety of persons or to the environment.

22.9 **Professional qualifications**

22.9.1 **Jurisprudence of the CJ**

We have seen that professional qualifications in particular have given rise to barriers to the free movement of self-employed persons and that the legislative process for directives in this area was initially slow. It fell to the CJ to cover the gap in protection offered. A starting point was holding that both Articles 49 and 56 TFEU had direct effect. Further, the CJ has repeatedly held that it is discriminatory, in breach of Article 49, as well as Articles 56 and 57, together with Article 18 TFEU to refuse permission to practise to a person whose qualifications have been recognised as equivalent to those required in the state in which he seeks to practise. This can be seen in the context of *Thieffry v Conseil de l'Ordre des Advocats à la Cour de Paris* (case 71/76).

Thieffry

The Court held that the French Bar Council could not refuse to allow Thieffry, a Belgian national with a Belgian law degree, to undertake practical training for the French bar, as his Belgian degree had been recognised by the University of Paris and he had acquired a qualifying certificate in France for the profession of *avocat*.

(See also *Patrick v Ministre des Affaires Culturelles* (case 11/77), recognition of architecture qualification in the absence of express recognition by French law.)

Where a directive has been issued for the mutual recognition or harmonisation of qualifications in a particular profession, that profession may no longer insist on compliance with its own requirements by persons who have qualified in another Member State according to the terms of the Directive. This approach was confirmed in *C Broekmeulen v Huisarts Registratie Commissie* (case 246/80).

Broekmeulen

Here, the Dutch General Practitioners' Committee was unable to refuse Broekmeulen permission to practise as a GP in Holland even though he had qualified as a GP in Belgium, where it was not necessary to complete the three years' specialised training required for GPs in Holland. The relevant directive (Directive 75/362) did not require GPs to undergo training additional to their original qualification.

Parties may not, however, claim freedom of establishment or freedom to provide services in reliance on a directive until the period provided for its implementation has expired (*Ministère Public v Auer* (case 136/78)), or where they do not fall within the terms of the directive (*Dreessen v Conseil National de l'Ordre des Architectes* (case C-447/93)).

In *Arantis v Land Berlin* (case C-164/94), the CJ held that where a profession was not regulated by an EU directive, Articles 18 and 49 TFEU required the authorities in a host Member State to take into account an individual's qualifications and other relevant experience acquired in the home state. In doing so, the CJ extended its ruling in *Vlassopoulou v Ministerium für Justiz* (case C-340/89), which is discussed later in relation to regulated professions, to unregulated professions. In both *Arantis* and *Vlassopoulou* (and arguably *Thieffry*), we can see the CJ adopting an approach that is based on the idea of mutual recognition—that is, a recognition that, in principle, the training and experience gained throughout all Member States should be acceptable in other Member States and should therefore be taken into account when assessing an individual's qualifications and experience. What is acceptable in one Member State, broadly speaking, is acceptable in all. This will have a significant effect in blocking any remaining gaps in the protection afforded to those with qualifications awarded by a Member State which are not covered by a directive.

22.9.2 **The directives**

The Recognition of Professional Qualifications Directive (Directive 2005/36) (PQD) replaced the previous system, but it broadly adopted the same principles as the previous directives. Directive 2005/36 has now been amended by Directive 2013/55 ([2013] OJ L354/132). The Member States needed to transpose Directive 2013/55 by 18 January 2016. Novelties of the modernised Directive include the introduction of a European Professional Card (Article 4a), the possibility of the development of 'common training frameworks' (Article 49a) and 'common training tests' (Article 49b) to allow for automatic recognition of a qualification. Finally, Article 59 Directive 2013/55 introduces an obligation for Member States to list and describe the professions they regulate and explain why the regulation is necessary to try to eradicate situations where qualifications constitute unnecessary barriers to free movement.

The case law on the previous directives would therefore seem relevant to the understanding of the new Directive. There are nonetheless some key differences. Unlike the previous general directives, the PQD, as amended by Directive 2013/55, deals with both the general system and some of the sectorally regulated professions (eg, medicine). The PQD introduced the idea of 'common platforms' of training. A separate part of the PQD provides for collaboration between the competent administrative authorities of both home and host Member State. The PQD also sought to clarify the criteria for distinguishing between the cross-border provision of services on a temporary and occasional basis on the one hand, and for establishment on the other; different systems apply to the two situations.

Like the previous directives, the PQD applies only to regulated professional activities (Article 2). It will apply to workers as well as the self-employed (Article 2(1)). Although the concept of a regulated activity might seem clear, it has not been unproblematic. The meaning of 'regulated profession' is a question for EU law, not national law. In *Arantis*, the CJ defined the term as meaning that the professional activity in question is governed by laws, regulations or administrative provisions that create a system under which that professional activity is expressly reserved for those who fulfil certain conditions and access is prohibited to those who do not fulfil them. This approach can also be seen in *Peñarroja Fa* (cases C-372 and 373/09).

Peñarroja Fa

Here, the applicant, who was a Spanish–French translator with some 20 years' experience in Spain, applied to be entered on the register of experts used by the French national courts. His application was rejected and he sought to rely on the PQD. The CJ held that the profession was not 'regulated'. According to the CJ, the sole purpose of the provisions establishing the register was 'to facilitate recourse to the services of professionals, whether members of regulated professions or not, and not to lay down rules governing recognition of a particular qualification'. Indeed, the French courts can employ others than those listed on the register as translators. Thus, the rules were insufficient to establish a regulated profession.

This reasoning would seem to exclude voluntary associations and true self-regulatory systems (see by analogy *Christina Ioanni Toki v Ypourgos Ethnikis paideias kai Thriskevmaton* (case C-424/09), concerning Directive 89/48).

It now seems that the profession must be a separate activity from other professions. This point can be seen in *Morgenbesser*.

Morgenbesser

Morgenbesser sought to rely on her French diploma in law to be registered as a *practicante* in Italy. Although the CJ accepted that there was a system which denied precluded persons not fulfilling certain criteria from acting as *practicante*, the CJ also noted that the activities carried out as a *practicante* formed the practical part of the training to become an *avvocato*. The activity of *practicante* could not therefore be considered as a separate regulated activity within Directive 89/48, one of the PQD's predecessor directives.

The starting point for the principle of mutual recognition is that a Member State 'shall recognise professional qualifications obtained in one or more other Member States' so as to allow the beneficiaries 'to gain access in that Member State to the same profession as that for which they are qualified in the home Member State and to pursue it in the host Member State under the same conditions as its nationals' (Article 4). For establishment (or employment), the PQD consolidates the approaches taken with regard to the mutual recognition of higher education diplomas and to diplomas and certificates awarded after a post-secondary education course of at least one year's duration, though the mechanism of recognition established by Directives 89/48 and 92/51 remains unchanged. The PQD recognises that there are different levels of qualification, which are identified in Article 11 (reflecting, eg, the difference between secondary education and higher education). The conditions for recognition are set out in Article 13, which specifies that access to the profession in the host Member State shall be given to 'applicants possessing the attestation of competence or evidence of formal qualifications required by another Member State in order to gain access to and pursue that profession on its territory'.

It was noted with regard to the Diplomas Directive (Directive 89/48) that, although the Directive gave an individual holding a diploma certain rights, the operation of mutual recognition is not automatic (*Morgenbesser*, para 44); Member States may review the qualifications. Although the new system is aimed at facilitating free movement, the system is still based on the idea that the host Member State may set standards for the exercise of a given profession and that it must go through the process of recognising the qualifications and individuals may be required to satisfy compensatory measures. Note, however, that the PQD also covers professions that were subject to sectoral regulation (eg, doctors and vets). Individuals satisfying the coordinated requirements of minimum training shall benefit from automatic recognition of their qualifications (Article 21). The PQD also specifies, in Recital 11, that it is not to be used as a mechanism whereby nationals may evade enforcement of regulation of professions.

22.9.2.1 Rules for lawyers

Directive 98/5 ([1998] OJ L77) gives all qualified lawyers the right to practise in another Member State on a permanent basis, using the professional title gained in the home Member State. They must comply with the professional and ethical rules of both the host Member State and their home state. Article 10 specifies that lawyers who have effectively and regularly pursued, for a period of at least three years, an activity in the host Member State under the home-country professional title are exempted from the aptitude test. For those who have practised for a shorter period, the competent authority of the host Member State must take into account all knowledge and professional experience of the law of the host Member State, as well as any attendance at lectures or seminars on the law of that state. In both instances, the lawyer's experience may be subject to verification. The conditions governing the provision of services on an occasional basis by lawyers established in another Member State, under the home-country professional title, without prior recognition of their qualification, are set out in Directive 77/249 ([1977] OJ L78). Those lawyers who have not completed their professional training are not covered by the Directives, though they may receive some protection through the operation of the jurisprudence of the CJ under Articles 45 and 49 TFEU (*Morgenbesser*).

22.9.2.2 Unregulated activities

Even in areas not covered, or not yet covered, by these Directives, the court has held that professional bodies of a Member State, in deciding whether to allow persons who do not satisfy their own state's professional requirements, must take into account the applicant's qualification and compare them with the 'home' requirements, in order to assess whether they are in fact equivalent. Applicants are entitled to be given reasons for decisions, and must have an opportunity to challenge them in judicial proceedings (*Vlassopoulou*). There is now a consistent line of authority to this effect.

Third country qualifications

A person who has qualified in a non-Member State cannot invoke either the Directives or the Union principle of mutual recognition even though the qualification is recognised in a *particular* Member State and the person has been practising the profession *within that state*: the only entitlement is to practise *in that state*. However, if a Member State chooses to recognise such a qualification, it must take into account practical training or professional experience obtained in other Member States in order to determine whether the requisite national training period has been fulfilled. This approach was confirmed in *Haim v Kassenzahnärtzliche Vereinigung (KLV) Nordrhein* (cases C-319/92 and 424/97).

> ### Haim
>
> *Haim* concerned a dentist whose initial qualification was from Istanbul University but who had practised in Belgium before seeking to be enrolled on the German register of dental practitioners permitted to treat patients who are covered by a social security scheme. This was refused. The CJ held that the competent national authority, in order to verify whether the training period requirement prescribed by the national rules is met, must take into account the professional experience of the plaintiff in the main proceedings, including that which he has acquired during his appointment as a dental practitioner of a social security scheme in another Member State.

Haim can be seen as imposing on Member States the obligation to undertake a *Vlassopoulou* style comparison of experience in such circumstances. *Hocsman v Ministre de l'Emploi et de la Solidarite* (case C-238/98) extended the scope of this obligation.

> ### Hocsman
>
> Hocsman was an EU national who held a doctor of medicine awarded by the University of Buenos Aires in Argentina. The Spanish authorities recognised his degree as equivalent to the Spanish degree so allowing him to practise as a doctor and to train as a specialist. Subsequently he was awarded a diploma of specialist in urology in 1982 by the University of Barcelona. He worked for some years in Spain and then in France, as an assistant. He then sought registration in France to allow him to work in a self-employed capacity, but this was refused by the relevant French authorities, since the Argentine diploma he held did not entitle him to practise medicine in France.

The CJ concluded that the competent authorities of the Member State concerned must take into consideration all the diplomas, certificates and other evidence of formal qualifications of the person concerned and his relevant experience, by comparing the specialised knowledge and abilities certified by those diplomas and that experience with the knowledge and qualifications required by the national rules (para 40).

Crucially in *Hocsman*, the CJ stated that Member States were under an obligation to take into account the qualifications obtained elsewhere, as well as any practical experience. This means that the conditional nature of the obligation found in *Haim*—that the obligation only arose where a Member State had recognised a qualification—has effectively been removed.

22.10 Establishment, services and companies

22.10.1 General

Despite the apparent simplicity of Article 54 TFEU, in practice it has been rather difficult for companies to move around the Union. Companies are entities created by domestic law and only have legal capacity in accordance with these rules. Moving into another jurisdiction might therefore require a company to be wound up in its state of origin, and reformed in the host Member State. Note therefore the potential impact that Article 49 TFEU might have on the rules of the Member States regarding company formation, as well as mergers (*SEVIC Systems*) and takeovers.

The main problem in this area is that the Member States apply different rules for identifying which legal system is applicable to a company (*lex societas*). As we noted in Chapter 21, there are two approaches to this issue. One possibility is to use the 'incorporation' doctrine (sometimes called *siège statutaire*), according to which the location of the company's registered office determines the applicable law. On this theory, the applicable law will be that of the country of incorporation. The second theory is the 'real seat' doctrine (or *siège réel*). Applying the real-seat doctrine, a company is subject to the law of the jurisdiction where its head office or central management is based, and this requires that the company's registered office needs to be located in the same jurisdiction. Quite clearly, the different theories will have an impact on the company law applicable, and therefore will affect the procedures and regulations with which a company will need to comply when running its business. The CJ has been given a number of opportunities to consider the compatibility of these doctrines with EU law, but has not been consistent.

The starting point is *R v HM Treasury and Commissioners of Inland Revenue, ex parte Daily Mail and General Trust PLC* (case 81/87). There, a company incorporated under the laws of England and Wales sought to move its central management to the Netherlands, whilst retaining its status as a British company. The Treasury demanded that certain transactions had to occur before it would permit the move. The company argued that this was a restriction on its right of establishment under Article 49 TFEU. The CJ held that there was no right under Article 49 TFEU for a company to move its head office to another Member State, and the home Member State could impose conditions on a company seeking to leave its jurisdiction.

Daily Mail would seem to suggest that, contrary to the position as regards individuals, some restrictions on the movements of companies would not be affected by Article 49 TFEU. *Daily Mail* has been criticised and it now seems that while Article 49 TFEU does not give a company the unrestricted right to maintain its head office in one Member State whilst remaining incorporated under the laws of another, obstacles to its freedom to move aspects of its business through the establishment of a branch, subsidiary or agency will be prohibited by Article 49 TFEU unless justified. According to the CJ in *Cartesio* there is in fact a distinction to be made between the nationality of the company (determined under Article 54 TFEU) and the right of a company established in one of the Member States to establish itself in another Member State, under Article 49 TFEU.

> ### Cartesio
>
> Cartesio was a limited partnership formed under Hungarian law. Cartesio filed an application with the Hungarian authorities for registration of the transfer of its seat to Italy and, in consequence, for amendment of the entry regarding Cartesio's company seat in the Hungarian commercial register. That application was refused as Hungarian law did not permit the transfer of a company's seat abroad while the company continued to be registered under Hungarian law. Under the Hungarian law, the seat of a company governed by Hungarian law must be the place where its central administration is situated. Cartesio challenged this decision, arguing it was contrary to the freedom of establishment.

When the question was referred to CJ, the Court held that the determination of the nationality of a company was a preliminary matter to be addressed before the issue of freedom of establishment (as it would not be possible to know whether freedom of establishment has been exercised unless the home base of the company is also known). The matter of determining the connecting factor is a matter for national law (see para 109).

So, the CJ in *Cartesio* reaffirmed the approach in *Daily Mail* (and in *Überseering BV v Nordic Construction Company Baumanagement GmBH* (case C-208/00), see further 22.10.2) as to a Member State's right to identify the connecting factor between companies established under its laws and its territories, whether this be by virtue of the doctrine of *siège statutaire* or *siège réel*. This, according to the Court, is the consequence of Article 54 TFEU and has been reiterated since (see, eg, *VALE Építési* KFT (case C-378/10)—when a company removed from Italian companies register with intention to reincorporate under Hungarian law, but the Hungarian registration refused, para 29). The right of the Member State includes the right to remove the status of a company being incorporated under the laws of that Member State if the company ceases to comply with the requirements of national law. This does not mean that the company must be wound up; the company may acquire the status of a company under the laws of another Member State and the original Member State has no right to stop that happening. Equally, the consequences of a change in nationality—such as the loss of a tax exemption—may still trigger Article 49 TFEU.

22.10.2 Regulatory competition

We have seen that there are significant differences in the Member States' individual approaches to company formation and regulation, quite apart from the issue of the rules relating to *siège statutaire* or *siège réel*. It might be easier for someone (whether natural or legal) who wishes to trade in one Member State to establish a company in another Member State and rely on the right to secondary establishment contained in Article 49 TFEU to set up business in the original, target Member State. The question is, is this a legitimate use of freedom of establishment, or does it constitute an abuse of Union law?

Early case law on the question of abuse arose in relation to services. Sometimes the service providers were formally established in one Member State but provided services to another Member State, and relied on Article 56 TFEU so as to avoid compliance with the host Member State's regulation for that sector. At one stage, the CJ sought to avoid difficult questions by re-characterising the provision of services as a question of establishment, for example in *TV10 v Commissariaat voor de Media* (case C-23/93).

TV10

A company established itself in one Member State and broadcast into another Member State, the Netherlands, hoping to avoid the Dutch limitations on broadcast advertising. Here the CJ adopted a broad interpretation of the concept of establishment and decided that the company involved was actually established in the Netherlands. On this basis, the Dutch rules were applicable to the broadcaster.

The CJ here seems to be identifying establishment by reference to a form of the real-seat doctrine. Should the same principles be applied to the establishment of a business as to the regulation of its business activities? This was addressed in *Centros v Erhvervs- og Selskabsstyrelsen* (case C-212/97).

Centros

Here a private limited company registered in the UK but with two Danish shareholders sought to establish a branch in Denmark. At the time, the company had not traded in the UK. In the light of the Danish connection (and the lack of any British business activity), the Danish registrar refused to register the branch because he regarded Centros as a Danish company. Crucially, Centros had failed to comply with a minimum capital rule imposed under Danish law but with no equivalent under the English system. The CJ determined that this was a breach of Article 49 TFEU which could not be justified.

The Court held:

> the fact that a national of a Member State who wishes to set up a company chooses to form it in the Member State whose rules of company law seem to him the least restrictive and to set up branches in other Member States cannot, in itself, constitute an abuse of the right of establishment. The right to form a company in accordance with the law of a Member State and to set up branches in other Member States is inherent in the exercise, in a single market, of the freedom of establishment guaranteed by the Treaty [para 27].

Setting up a company in one Member State and then exercising the right to set up a secondary establishment was not an abuse of the right of establishment, even though it had the effect of circumventing incorporation requirements in the host Member State. The decision was interpreted as holding that in EU law, the jurisdiction where the registered office was based would be the law applicable to the company. Of course, this leaves a potential problem where Member States take a different view about the 'connecting factor' with its territory. If a Member State takes the connecting factor to be the real seat rather than the formal place of establishment, there is the possibility of 'double nationality' if the place of formal incorporation by contrast looks to the *siège statutaire*, as arguably was the case in *Centros*. The analysis of the CJ in *Centros* seems to favour the *siège statutaire* over the *siège réel*.

A similar issue arose in *Überseering*.

Überseering

Here, a Dutch company owned by German shareholders sought to take legal action in the German courts. German law determined a company's legal capacity by reference to its real seat. Since the company had moved its centre of administration to Germany, the German courts found its real seat to be in Germany. Überseering was formally incorporated in the Netherlands, and so complied with that state's rules of incorporation rather than German rules. As the company did not comply with German rules, the German court held that it was not properly incorporated and therefore did not have the capacity to take legal action. The CJ held that because the company had been validly incorporated in the Netherlands, and had not lost this status, the German court's refusal to recognise its legal capacity fell within Article 49 TFEU and was not on the facts justified.

We might suggest that there are similarities here with the *Daily Mail* case. The CJ distinguished the two cases on the facts (implicitly reaffirming *Daily Mail*). Whilst the *Daily Mail* had sought to rely on Article 49 TFEU against its state of incorporation when it sought to emigrate, *Überseering* concerned the rights of an immigrating company against the host Member State. According to the CJ in *Überseering*:

> [t]he requirement of reincorporation of the same company in Germany is therefore tantamount to outright negation of freedom of establishment [paras 80–1].

In its consideration of justification, the CJ also seemed to suggest that, although restrictions on establishment might be open to justification, an absolute prohibition on secondary establishment never could. Articles 49 and 54 TFEU therefore require a host Member State to recognise the legal capacity of a company under the law of its Member State of incorporation. This seems to be yet another blow to the real-seat doctrine.

Slightly different issues arose in *Inspire Art*.

Inspire Art

Dutch law sought to impose a number of restrictions on companies incorporated in a Member State other than the Netherlands, but which were predominantly or exclusively active in the Netherlands. Inspire Art was incorporated under the laws of England and Wales, but had a Dutch sole director. It established a branch in Amsterdam without complying with the Dutch formalities for 'formally foreign' companies and the competent Dutch authorities brought an action against Inspire Art as a consequence. The CJ held that insofar as Dutch law gave effect to certain company-law directives, the rules were compatible with Article 49 TFEU, unless foreign companies were treated differently with regard to penalties for non-compliance. Any rules going beyond the Directives had to be compatible with the TFEU. The additional Dutch rules were caught by Article 49 TFEU and not justifiable on the facts, and therefore infringed EU law.

Once again, the CJ seems to have favoured the incorporation doctrine over the real-seat theory.

It should be noted that in these cases the CJ has refrained from addressing the question directly. It thus remains unclear whether the CJ intends to eradicate the real-seat doctrine in favour of the incorporation theory or not; more recently in *Cartesio*, the CJ has re-emphasised that the question of a company's 'nationality' is one for the Member States. Nonetheless, what remains clear is that Member States will not be able to impose restrictions on companies formed elsewhere, even 'pseudo-foreign' companies without very good (and proportionate) reason. (See also *SEVIC Systems* concerning the impact of a cross-border merger and its relationship with national rules on company formation found to be incompatible with Article 49 TFEU.)

22.10.3 **Taxation: are anti-avoidance measures permissible?**

One area where Member States are concerned about the impact of the use of freedom of establishment is in the area of taxation, as in many Member States different rules apply depending on residency. With freedom of establishment, it is no longer clear that such distinctions are acceptable. With the right legal advice, freedom of establishment can be used to minimise a tax bill, for example by locating profits through a group company to a Member State with a low rate of taxation. The CJ has had to face a series of cases which deal with the boundary between Member State competence and the right of establishment. *Halifax plc and Others v Customs and Excise* (case C-255/02) concerned a corporate structure where payments were made specifically to minimise VAT payments. The CJ distinguished between artificial transactions, which would constitute abuse, and taking advantage of Union law which would be acceptable. The same year another tax case from the UK was decided, this time concerning direct taxation: *Cadbury Schweppes plc v Inland Revenue* (case C-196/04), where Cadbury sought to channel profits through an Irish subsidiary formed to reduce the rate of tax payable. Again the CJ distinguished between artificial transactions, and the right of establishment; the mere setting up of a subsidiary of itself cannot set up a presumption of tax evasion justifying the limitation of a fundamental freedom. So where is the boundary between the two? The CJ noted that the purpose of Article 49 TFEU was to allow an individual or a company 'to set up a secondary establishment in another Member State to carry on his activities there and thus assist economic and social interpenetration within the [Union]'. Abuse, which seems here to be equated to the notion of an artificial transaction, is found where, in addition to there being a subjective element consisting in the intention to obtain a tax advantage, there are objective circumstances showing that, despite formal observance of the conditions laid down by Union law, the objective pursued by freedom of establishment has not been achieved. On the facts of this case, this double element was not sufficiently proven. It has been suggested that the approach here is not consistent with that taken with regard to company law in *Centros*. (See also *Thin Cap Group Litigation v Commissioners of Inland Revenue* (case C-524/04) concerning a rule prohibiting the characterisation of loan interest owed by subsidiary to parent as a dividend, here found disproportionate; and contrast *Columbus Container Services v Finanzamt Bielefeld-Innenstadt* (case C-298/05) where similar rules were found not to constitute a restriction.) A detailed consideration of taxation law lies outside this book.

22.10.4 **Regulatory competition: the position of services—home-country control and abuse**

As we can see from *TV10*, there has been a concern that the exercise of free-movement rights in certain contexts may give rise to a dilution of national standards as businesses establish themselves in the Member State with a lighter regulatory regime and then rely on Article 56 TFEU to trade in Member States with more stringent regulatory regimes. In this there are certain commonalities with the problems arising in the field of establishment, particularly with regard to companies setting up branch offices or subsidiaries (discussed at 22.10.2). The difficulty felt in services, however, is in some ways more acute, as Member States' freedom to regulate incoming services is constrained by the need to take into account home-country regulation; such host Member State regulation is more likely to be assessed as unnecessary or disproportionate (see 22.6). The Services Directive may exacerbate this tendency as it limits the public-interest grounds on which Member States may rely (see 22.8.4).

As with the other freedoms, the CJ made it clear that Union law may not be used (or abused) in order to undermine the legitimate rules and standards of Member States. Thus the CJ has held that establishing oneself in one Member State for the purposes of evading host Member State rules is unacceptable (see, eg, *van Binsbergen*). In *Vereniging Veronica Omroep Organisatie v Commisariaat voor de Media* (case C-148/91), which again concerned a media company broadcasting from one Member State to another to avoid the recipient Member State's regulation on broadcast content, the CJ held that the recipient Member State could rely on its regulations as against the broadcaster. A similar approach can be seen in respect of services regulated by harmonising legislation, for example, in *van de Bijl v Staatssecretaris van Economische Zaken* (case 130/88).

Van de Bijl

The Court was asked to rule on a claim by a Dutch decorator, based on Directive 64/427, which provides, inter alia, for the mutual recognition of qualifications for self-employed persons in small craft industries. Under Directive 64/427 states were required to accept a certification of competence and work experience provided by the appropriate authorities of another Member State in respect of work performed in that state. It was suggested in van de Bijl's case that the certificate issued by the UK authorities, which the Dutch authorities had refused to accept as a basis for registration in Holland, was based on questionable evidence. The Court held that the host (ie Dutch) state was entitled to take steps (eg, verification of evidence) to prevent the relevant Union rules being used for the purpose of circumventing the rules relating to particular occupations applicable to its nationals.

This line of case law does raise difficult questions of what is considered to be abuse. Are we concerned with the intentions of the parties seeking to rely on the right to provide services, or merely with its impact on the host Member State? If we are looking at intention, is it required that the parties sought to rely on the freedom to provide services *always* with the view to exploit the Treaty freedoms, or is it sufficient that the rights holders start *at some point* intending to evade Union law? The case law in this area has not been clear or consistent. Even apart from this difficult question, how is such intention to be proved? Advocate-General Lenz highlighted this problem in the context of broadcasting. If we argue that a broadcaster established in Luxembourg but staffed in the main by Dutch people, broadcasting in Dutch, to the Netherlands is intending to evade national law and thus abuse Union-law rights purely by reference to nationality and language criteria, we are not only undermining the right of those people to exercise rights under Article 45 and 49 TFEU to go to Luxembourg in the first place, but arguably we are indulging in a form of nationality discrimination. The precise scope of this 'exception' to the free movement rights was not clear and subsequent cases interpreted it narrowly (*VT4 Limited v Vlaamse Gemeenschap* (case C-56/96) and see *De Agostini* considered later).

Problems with a perceived downward spiral of standards may also arise when policy areas have been harmonised by directive. Minimum harmonisation (discussed in Chapter 16, and see also 22.8.4 regarding the Services Directive) allows Member States to set different standards, higher than those set out in the directive in question. These rules must of course be compatible with general Treaty objectives. The difficulty in this context arises when there is a market-access clause, which means that a Member State may require those established within its jurisdiction to comply with the higher standards but cannot impose these requirements on those established elsewhere in the Union. Minimum harmonisation therefore introduces the possibility of differing approaches to regulation being taken by the various Member States, which is a situation that is open to abuse. The same general rules apply here as they do to the Treaty articles; companies and individuals are entitled to take advantage of the internal market and the 'abuse' argument will only be accepted in very limited circumstances. Member States must rely on mutual recognition—that is, an acceptance that standards in other Member States are sufficient.

It is clear that in some instances the CJ has difficulty accepting flagrant behaviour by service providers. In addition to the re-characterisation of services as establishment in *TV10*, the CJ has also re-characterised the legal issue in a different way by referring to Article 34 TFEU, again to allow the host Member State some control as can be seen in *De Agostini*.

De Agostini

The question of broadcasting aimed at children in Sweden would seem to fall under the then Television without Frontiers Directive (Directive 89/552, as subsequently amended by 97/36), which contained a market-access clause. The offending broadcaster was established in the UK, which does not prohibit such broadcasts, although Sweden did. On this assessment, given the market-access clause and the rules of the Member State in which the broadcaster was established, the Swedish could do nothing to stop the broadcasts. The CJ, however, took the view that the advertisements should be seen as relating to the sale of the goods they were advertising rather than the service of broadcasting, thereby removing regulation away from the British and allowing the Swedes to maintain their rules (provided such rules operate equally in law and in fact). (See also Chapter 18.)

The difficulty here is that is impossible to predict when the CJ will choose to re-characterise Article 56 TFEU; the certainty is that the CJ will do so only rarely. Interestingly, when the Television without Frontiers Directive was revised by the Audiovisual Media Services Directive (2007/65) ([2007] OJ L332/27) (consolidated 2010/13) an anti-abuse clause was inserted in the Directive.

This area of law is problematic. It highlights the ever-present tension between the need to create and to facilitate the functioning of the internal market and the competence of the Member States and their legitimate concerns. As with the pre-*Keck* case law on the scope of Article 34 TFEU, the Court seems to be encountering some difficulty in distinguishing between legitimate exploitation of rules and their abuse. It is indeed unfortunate that the CJ has not developed a unified principle to deal with cases in this area.

22.11 Conclusions

This chapter has looked at the ways national rules can impede the exercise of free movement as far as access to the job market or the right to trade is concerned. We have considered ways in which the EU institutions have responded, whether through legislation or through the judgments of the CJ. In this, there are three themes.

First, the move from a discrimination-based test, so as to catch measures that are applicable to nationals of the host Member State as to migrants, is clear. In this we see parallels with the free movement of goods, and now the free movement of capital. The precise scope of the test, and consequently the freedoms, is not clear. The CJ has used different language, emphasising different concerns in the various cases before it. The question is, where is the outer boundary of the freedoms, and consequently the boundary of acceptable Member State regulation? As we have seen, in some cases the CJ has adopted a very broad approach indeed. Against this background, we come to the second theme and note the changing political climate and the desire to implement the Lisbon Agenda. Whilst in the early days of the Union harmonising legislation was sectoral, detailed and hard to agree, recent legislative activity shows that the Union (and the Member States) now adopts a horizontal approach, which is based strongly on mutual recognition and limited spheres, particularly as regards services, in which a Member State may legitimately mistrust its fellow Member States.

Secondly, a new emphasis is the focus on administrative cooperation and on the removal of 'red tape'.

The third theme is a familiar one: that of the concern about the legitimate uses of Union-law rights and the problems of abuse. Despite the agreement of the Services Directive, there are still concerns about abuse and a downward pressure on standards, with a desire to retain control over individuals who are, in reality, targeting the host Member State, as are evidenced in the anti-abuse statements in the PQD, the Services Directive and even sectoral directives such as the Audiovisual Media Services Directive. The EU has some way to go before it truly is a single market in services and employment.

Further reading

Biermeyer, T, et al, 'The compatibility of corporate exit taxation with European law' (2012) 9 ECFL Rev 101.

Davies, G, 'The Services Directive: Extending the country of origin principle, and reforming public administration' (2007) 32 EL Rev 232–45.

de la Feria, R, 'Prohibition of abuse of (Community) law: The creation of a new general principle of EC law through tax' (2008) 45 CML Rev 395.

Drury, R, 'The "Delaware syndrome": European fears and reactions' [2005] JBL 709.

Hatzopoulos, V, 'The Court's approach to services (2006–2012): from case law to case load?' (2013) 50 CML Rev 459.

Johnston, A and Syrpis, P, 'Regulatory competition in European company law after *Cartesio*' (2009) 34 EL Rev 378.

Lombardo, S, 'Some reflections on freedom of establishment of non-profit entities in the European Union' (2013) 14 EBL Rev 225.

Meulman, J and de Waele, HCFJA, 'A retreat from *Säger*? Servicing or fine tuning the application of Article 49 EC' (2006) 33 LIEI 207.

O'Brien, M, 'Company taxation, state aid and fundamental freedoms: Is the next step enhanced co-operation?' (2005) 30 EL Rev 209.

Panayi, C, 'National Grid Indus BV: Exit taxes in the European Union revisited' (2012) 1 BT Rev 41.

Paschalidis, P, *Freedom of Establishment and Private International Law for Corporations* (Oxford University Press, 2012).

Ringe, WG, 'Sparking regulatory competition in European company law: The impact of the *Centros* line of case law and its concept of the "Abuse of Law"' in De la Feria and Vogenauer (eds), *Prohibition of Abuse of Law: A New General Principle of EU Law?* (Hart Publishing, 2011).

23 Free movement: social rights

23.1 Introduction

We have noted that the free-movement rights granted by Articles 21 (citizenship), 45 (workers), 49 (establishment) and 56 (services) TFEU comprise three elements: (1) the right to move to another Member State and to live there; (2) the right to access the job market in the host Member State and to take up employment and residence there; and (3) ancillary rights the objective of which is to remove disadvantages to the migrant arising from the exercise of the right of free movement. This third group comprises a broad range of social rights which aim to ensure that the migrant and his or her family integrate into the host Member State. While the preceding two chapters have focused on access to the territory of the host Member State (including family rights, sometimes seen as a form of ancillary right) and access to the labour market, this chapter will focus on the social rights to which a migrant and his family may be entitled in the host Member State.

The granting of social rights has had a long history. As well as having an economic function, allowing the movement of factors of production, the free movement of workers has also been interpreted in the light of the fact that workers are people, who, with their families, should be integrated into the host Member State as opposed to being factors of production. A particularly broad interpretation has been given to the social rights available to economic migrants.

When looking at this area there are a number of recurring themes. As we have noted in earlier chapters, one particular question relates to who obtains the benefit of Union law rights and, as a corollary, what is the extent of that body of rights. There is a difference between the level of entitlement of economic migrants and the non-economically active European citizen, with the former having more rights than the latter. A broad interpretation by the CJ both of the groups entitled to social rights and the nature of the rights themselves, has aroused a certain degree of criticism in the light of concerns about 'social dumping' and 'benefit tourism'. Social justice and schemes for the redistribution of wealth commonly assume either a contribution to the system or some common ground justifying support. Is citizenship at the EU level enough to ground broad-ranging citizenship rights based on individual Member States' social systems? In looking at the scope of the rights, this chapter will take a somewhat historical approach in that it will look at the development of the social rights jurisprudence in the economic context with the main focus being on the cases relating to workers, before looking at the case law on citizenship.

23.2 Economic migrants

23.2.1 Equality of treatment Article 45(2) TFEU and Regulation 492/2011

As we noted earlier, Article 45(2) TFEU prohibits discrimination as regards employment, remuneration and other conditions of work and employment. Regulation 1612/68 was enacted to flesh out the detail of these rights. This Regulation has been amended on numerous occasions and has now been codified by Regulation 492/2011 ([2011] OJ L141/1). Of particular relevance here is Article 7(2) which entitles the migrant worker to 'the same social and tax advantages as national workers'. Such advantages cannot be restricted to migrant workers residing in the host Member State. They must also be made available to cross-border workers who, while employed in the host Member State reside in another Member State (*Elodie Giersch and Others v État du Grandé-Duche de Luxembourg* (case C-20/12)). In assessing the right to social and tax advantages the criterion is where the worker is employed.

The term 'social advantages' has been interpreted in the widest sense and it is here that we begin to understand that while we might initially think these rights were linked to the employment context, in practice they have a much broader ambit. Also relevant are the provisions relating to training and education.

23.2.1.1 Social advantages

No indication is given in Regulation 492/2011 of what constitutes a 'social advantage'. The CJ has adopted a broad approach in defining what it means and who is entitled to such an advantage, ruling that eligibility may not be confined to workers themselves but may extend to their families (*Fiorini (née Christini) v SNCF* (case 32/75) and may encompass advantages not linked to the migrant worker's employment.

Fiorini

The widow of an Italian national who had worked in France, claimed a special fare reduction card issued by the French railways to parents of large families, that is families of three or more children. She had been refused the card on the grounds that she was not of French nationality. She claimed discrimination in breach of Article 18 TFEU and Article 7(2) of Regulation 1612/68. The French tribunal took the view that Article 7(2) was not applicable, since it was concerned only with advantages granted to citizens by virtue of work as employed persons. This would limit the advantages that could be claimed by a worker to those directly linked to his or her employment.

The CJ took a different view. It held that, although certain provisions of Article 7 refer to relationships deriving from the contract of employment, there are others that may extend beyond that relationship. Article 7(2) covers all social and tax advantages, whether or not attached to contracts of employment. Moreover, since the family had a right under Union law (what was then Regulation 1251/70) to remain in France, they were entitled under Article 7(2) to social advantages on the same terms as French nationals.

Subsequently, in *Ministère Public v Even* (case 207/78), the Court held, following *Fiorini*, that the social advantages covered by Article 7(2) were 'those which, whether or not linked to a contract of employment, are generally granted to national workers primarily because of their objective status as workers *or by virtue of the mere fact of their residence on national territory*' (emphasis added). This formula, the '*Even*' formula, has since been applied in a number of cases in the context of claims by both workers and the members of their families to a wide range of social benefits and continues to define the scope of benefits to which migrants may lay claim.

A rule of Dutch law requiring students wishing to study abroad, to have been resident in The Netherlands for three out of the six years preceding the date of their enrolment in a course of studies outside The Netherlands, has been held to be incompatible with Article 45 TFEU and Article 7(2) of Regulation 1612/68 (*Commission v The Netherlands (Dutch student finance (three-in-six rule))* (case C-542/09); *B Martens v Minister van Onderwijs, Cultuur en Wetenschap* (case C-359/13)).

Dutch Student Finance (three-in-six rule)

This case concerned a rule of Dutch law which required students wishing to obtain financing to study outside The Netherlands ('portable funding') to have been lawfully resident within The Netherlands for at least three out of the six years preceding the date of enrolment for higher education outside The Netherlands. The Court found this provision to be contrary to Article 45 TFEU and Article 7(2) of Regulation 1612/68. Although the measure in question was applicable both to nationals and non-nationals 'it primarily operated to the detriment of migrant workers and frontier workers who are nationals of other Member States'.

Social advantages covered not only benefits granted as of right, but also those granted on a discretionary basis (*Reina v Landeskreditbank Baden-Württemberg* (case C-65/81)).

Reina

In this case, an Italian couple living in Germany, where the husband was employed, invoked Article 7(2) to claim a special childbirth loan, state-financed, from the defendant bank. The loan was payable under German law only to German nationals living in Germany. The bank argued that the loan was not a 'social advantage' within Article 7(2), since the loan was granted not as a social right, but rather in the field of political rights, for demographic purposes—that is, to increase the birth rate in Germany. Granting of the loan was, moreover, discretionary. It argued also that the difference in treatment was justified on account of the practical difficulties of recovering loans from workers who return to their own countries. Despite these persuasive arguments the CJ found that, since the loan was granted by reason of the claimant's objective status as a worker or by virtue of the mere fact of residence, it was a 'social advantage' within Article 7(2).

In *Castelli v ONPTS* (case 261/83), on similar reasoning, an Italian mother, who, on being widowed, went to live with her son in Belgium (the son having been a worker and retired there), was held entitled to claim a guaranteed income benefit in the nature of social assistance (not a social security benefit) paid to all old people in Belgium. Since she had a right under Article 10 of Regulation 1612/68 to install herself with her son, she was entitled to the same social and tax advantages as Belgian workers and ex-workers. The Court again applied the *Even* formula; the old-age benefit was one granted to national workers primarily because of their objective status as workers or by virtue of their residence of national territory. The reasoning seems to be that if dependants were not paid benefits, this could constitute an obstacle to the free movement of workers (see, eg, *Deak* (case 94/84)).

The same reasoning was applied in *Hoeckx v Centre Public d'Aide Sociale de Kalmthout* (case 249/83), and *Kenneth Scrivner and Carol Cole v Centre Public d'Aide Sociale de Chastre* (case 122/84), to claims in Belgium for a minimum income allowance, the 'minimex', by a member of the family of a worker and an unemployed worker respectively. (See also *Frascogna v Caisse des Dépôts de Consignation (No 2)* (case 256/86); *Deak* (case 94/84), 'tiding over' allowance paid to young jobseekers a 'social advantage';

Schmid v Belgium (case 310/91), allowance for handicapped child of a retired worker; *Commission v Luxembourg (childbirth allowance)* (case 111/91).) Famously the CJ's judgment in *Lair* opened the door for student grants and loans to be considered as social rights, although, as we have noted at 21.4.6.1, there are limits to this possibility. Similarly in *Matteccci v Communauté Française de Belgique* (case 235/87) a scholarship to study abroad available under a reciprocal arrangement between Belgium and Germany was held to constitute a social advantage to which the child of an Italian, established as a worker in Belgium, was entitled. (See also *Meeusen v Hoofddirectie von de Informatie Beheer Groep* (case C-337/97).) Note, this form of right can also be claimed under the citizenship provisions: *Morgan v Bezirksregierung Köln* and *Bucher v Landrat des Kreises Düren* (cases C-11 and 12/06).

Access to social advantages on the same terms as nationals of the host Member State is conditional upon that individual continuing to satisfy the test of being a worker (*Kaba v Secretary of State for the Home Department* (case C-466/00)). As long as a person retains the status of worker he is entitled to social advantages on the same terms as nationals of the host Member State. The fact that his principal intention on entering the host Member State was to pursue a course of studies there is irrelevant (*L.N.* (case C-46/12)). Thus a person can enter a Member State to pursue studies in the host Member State and, as long as he acquires and retains the status of worker by pursuing an effective and genuine employment activity, he will be entitled to a maintenance granted on the same terms as nationals of that state.

The benefit claimed must be available to the state's own nationals (*Belgium v Taghavi* (case C-243/91)).

Taghavi

The facts of this case were as follows: The Iranian wife of an Italian national residing as a worker in Belgium was held not to be entitled to a benefit for handicapped persons, described as a 'personal' right and not a social security benefit, on the grounds that the benefit was not available to spouses of *Belgian* nationals who were not themselves EU nationals.

Budgetary considerations cannot justify discriminatory treatment in the matter of social advantages. To deny non-nationals social advantages at times when public finances were under pressure would mean that the rights of migrant workers and their families would vary in time and place according to the public finances of a Member State. Budgetary considerations can play a role in formulating social policy in the sense of what social advantages are to be made available, but once such social advantages are put in place they must be granted on equal terms to national and non-national workers and their families.

In this area, as with discrimination in other areas, indirect discrimination may be permitted as 'objectively justified' if the legislation pursues a legitimate end and the measure is no more than is necessary to achieve that end. (For an example of the CJ's reasoning see *O'Flynn*, discussed in Chapter 15.) In this area, as in others, the CJ is moving to a test based on a 'real link' with, or integration into, the host Member State to determine whether restrictions on rights are acceptable (*Wendy Geven v Land Nordrhein-Westfalen* (case C-213/05)).

Geven

This case concerned a claim for the German child-rearing allowance. Geven was a Dutch national living in the Netherlands but working, after the end of the statutory maternity period, in Germany for between 3 and 14 hours per week. The national authorities rejected the claim on the basis that she was neither resident in Germany nor able to satisfy an eligibility test based on the performance of a minimum amount of work. The CJ accepted that Geven was a worker for the purposes of Article 45 TFEU and therefore in principle entitled to the allowance as a 'social advantage'. The German government argued that the allowance was an instrument of family policy aimed at benefiting those with a real link to Germany, whether through residence or by a contribution to the national labour market. This argument the CJ accepted as being appropriate and proportionate to the German government's aim.

In *Giersch* the CJ accepted the fact that the Luxembourg government could impose restrictions on access to financial aid for higher education for the purposes of significantly increasing the proportion of residents holding a higher education degree but found that restricting such aid to residents of Luxembourg went beyond what was necessary to achieve that objective. Less restrictive measures could be used.

Despite the breadth of the *Even* test, not all state support falls within Article 7(2) as can be seen in *Baldinger Pensionsversicherungsanalt der Arbeiter* (case C-386/02).

Baldinger

The payment in issue in this case was a monthly sum granted under Austrian law to former prisoners of war, subject to the condition that the recipient was an Austrian national. The applicant was a former Austrian national, who had been a prisoner of war in the former USSR from 1945 to 1947, but who had become a Swedish national, losing his Austrian nationality, in 1967. He sought to claim equality of treatment. The CJ rejected his argument. The payment, they held, was made to compensate citizens for the hardships they had endured for their country. It was not granted to individuals either because of their status as a worker or because of their lawful residence in a Member State and therefore did not fall within Article 7(2). The payment also had nothing to do with conditions of employment, remuneration or working conditions. It therefore could not fall within Article 45(2) either.

Such rights may be capable of being claimed as a matter of citizenship rights, see 23.4. The right to equal social advantages cannot be claimed by all EU nationals and their families who are lawfully resident in the host state. An important limitation was placed on Article 7(2) by *Centre Public d'Aide Sociale de Courcelles v Lebon* (C-316/85).

Lebon

This case concerned a claim by a French national, Ms Lebon, for the Belgian minimex. She was living in Belgium and her claim was based, inter alia, on the fact that she was looking for work in Belgium. The CJ held that the right to equality of treatment in the field of social and tax advantages granted by Article 7(2) was for the benefit only of workers (ie those in actual employment) and not for nationals of Member States who migrate in search of employment.

In *Lebon*, for the first time, the Court drew a distinction between those who are lawfully entitled to 'settled' residence as a result of obtaining employment, and those who are permitted temporary rights of residence in order to search for work. Only the former will be entitled to equality of treatment in respect of all social advantages. Likewise, EU nationals (and their families) who move within the Union to receive services will not be entitled to full equality of treatment as regards social benefits provided by the host state (see Chapters 24 and 27). *Collins v Secretary of State for Work and Pensions* (case C-138/02) followed the approach of the Court in *Lebon*.

Collins sought to challenge the distinction between those seeking work and those actually work-ing on the basis of the CJ's ruling in *Martinez Sala v Freistaat Bayern* (case C-85/96) (see further 23.5.1) in which the court held that a person seeking work should be considered a worker for the purposes of Regulation 1612/68 (para 32). The CJ reiterated its previous case law to the effect that the notion of 'worker' for the purposes of the Treaty must be interpreted broadly to include those genuinely seeking employment.

Nonetheless the CJ has consistently drawn a distinction between the situation where a person has entered a Member State but not yet worked and a person who is not currently working but has worked (see, eg, *Lair*, paras 32–3). The former group enjoy equality of treatment as regards access to work, whilst the second group, having had the status of worker, may claim the same social and tax advantages by virtue of Article 7(2) as nationals. In confirming that '[t] he concept of "worker" is thus not used in a uniform manner', the CJ reaffirmed its approach in *Lebon* as to workers. Nonetheless, the CJ accepted in *Collins* that discrimination within the scope of the Treaty was not permissible unless justified, which appears to have the effect of undermining the *Lebon* distinction.

As we have seen (at 21.4.6.1), a second important limitation was placed on Article 7(2) in the cases of *Brown* (case 197/86), and *Lair*, also as a result of the claimants' status. In order to benefit from Article 7(2) a person must either be or have been a worker.

23.2.1.2 Continuing rights

In some circumstances, a former migrant worker who ceases to be a worker will continue to retain the benefit of his or her former status, without any condition that he or she should reside in the competent Member State. In a number of cases, the CJ has held that such benefits are those 'the payment of which is dependent on the prior existence of an employment relationship which has come to an end and is intrinsically linked to the recipients' objective status as workers' (*Leclere and Deaconescu v Caisse nationale des prestations familiales* (case C-43/99), para 57; see also *Meints v Minister van Landbouw* (case C-57/96), para 41). This means that a person who is no longer a worker, even if he still receives some benefits, such as invalidity pension, by virtue of his former worker sta-tus, can claim new rights, such as childbirth rights for his family members, which have no links with his former employment (*Leclere and Deaconescu*).

This reasoning was relied upon in *Collins*.

Collins

Collins was born in the United States and, as well as possessing American nationality, had Irish nationality. He spent ten months working in the UK in 1980–1, before returning to the USA. He did not return to the UK until 1998, when he tried to find employment in the social services sector. During his job search, he tried to claim jobseeker's allowance, based on the fact that he had been a worker and migrant workers are entitled to certain rights linked to that status even when no longer employed. Even accepting that the level of work carried out by Collins made him a worker at the time it was performed, he was not entitled to jobseeker's allowance as no link could be established between that work and the search for another job 17 years later (para 28). Given the length of Collins' absence, his position was comparable with that of someone searching for work for the first time, in that the CJ required that there be a link between the original work and the search for another job, though the nature of that link is uncertain.

As with *Geven*, this seems to be a variant of the 'real link' test we find being introduced in citizenship cases. Note, however, that in *Collins*, the CJ also held that migrant EU nationals enjoy equality of treatment in their search for a job (discussed later).

23.2.1.3 **Tax advantages**

The starting point for matters relating to direct taxation is that this area falls within the competence of the Member State, but that competence must be exercised within the framework of the Treaty. Specifically, migrant workers are entitled under Article 7(2) of Regulation 492/2011 to the same tax advantages as nationals of the host state. Moreover, some cases have been considered under the general rules on non-discrimination in Article 18 TFEU (eg, *Turpeinen* (case C-520/04)). Nonetheless, this is an area where a measure such as a residence requirement, which is covertly discriminatory, may be objectively justified, or where the situations of the national worker and the migrant worker will not be regarded as comparable. Such may be the case, as was conceded in *Schumacker* where the worker's residence and principal place of work (and therefore of income) is in another Member State, in which the taxing authorities are better able to take into account his personal and family circumstances (see also *Wielockx v Inspecteur der Directe Belastingen* (case C-80/94), person with main income in a Member State effectively in the same position as a resident there). *Bachmann* and subsequent cases refer to the 'coherence' of national taxation systems as justifying discriminatory treatment of insurance contributions paid outside the taxing Member State.

> ### *Bachmann*
>
> Here the Court found that a Belgian rule, which allowed the deduction from income tax of contributions to health and life insurance policies only if they were paid in Belgium, although indirectly discriminatory, was justified as necessary to ensure the coherence of the tax system. Under this system, tax deductions in respect of insurance contributions could be offset by taxes levied from insurers in Belgium. This would not be possible where insurance was effected in another Member State.

The coherence of the Belgian tax system was also invoked, and accepted by the CJ in infringement proceedings brought against Belgium in respect of a tax concession granted upon the purchase of property in the Flemish region *(Commission v Belgium (Flemish property tax concession)* (case C-269/09)).

> ### *Flemish property tax concession*
>
> This case concerned a tax concession granted by the Flemish region to the purchaser of immoveable property in Flanders, intended as a new principal residence, that was available only if the previous principal residence was in Belgium. It was denied to those whose previous principal residence was in another Member State. The CJ found that this limitation was justified to safeguard the coherence of the tax system.

Bachmann and *Flemish property tax concession* may be contrasted with *Asscher v Staatssecretaris van Financiën* (case C-107/94), a case involving the right of establishment where differential taxation rates were found to be indirectly discriminatory but unjustified and *Petersen v Finanzamt Ludwigshafen* (case C-544/11).

> ### *Petersen*
>
> The Petersens lived in Germany with their daughter. Mr Petersen, a Danish national owned a holiday home in Denmark. Mr Petersen was employed by Hoffmann A/S an undertaking established in Denmark. He was seconded by his employer to Benin as from 2002 for a period of three years to assist

> with a project financed by the Danish International Development Agency. For the fiscal year 2003 Mr Petersen was charged income tax by the German authorities. Had his employer been established in Germany he would not be subject to German income tax. The CJ found this difference in treatment based on the fact that his employer was established in another Member State constituted a restriction on Mr Petersen's right of free movement within the meaning of Article 45 TFEU.

These cases can be seen as examples of the CJ seeking to limit the circumstances in which a Member State may rely on the coherence of the tax system justification found in *Bachmann*. (See also, eg, *Verkooijen*, rebates for income tax limited to residents found to be unjustified.) As in other areas involving indirect discrimination, the Court will in each case scrutinise the justification offered and ensure that the measures adopted are not disproportionate, though it seems to accept arguments based on administrative need more readily than perhaps in other areas (*Pusa v Osuuspankkien Keskinainen Vakuutusyhtio* (case C-224/02); *Turpeinen* (case C-520/04)).

23.2.1.4 Access to training in vocational schools and retraining centres

Article 7(3) entitles workers to access, under the same conditions as national workers, to training in vocational schools and retraining centres.

It seems likely that the CJ will take a broad view of what is meant by access. In *Casagrande v Landeshauptstadt München* (case 9/74) the Court held, in the context of a claim by a child under Article 12 of Regulation 492/2011, that the right to be *admitted* to the host state's educational, apprenticeship and vocational training courses included not only admission but 'general measures to facilitate attendance', which in Casagrande's case, included a grant.

More broadly, differential fees cannot be imposed on migrant EU nationals, as can be seen in the case of *Gravier*.

> ### Gravier
>
> Here, the Belgian authorities sought to charge a special fee levied only on non-nationals, for attendance on a four-year course in the art of strip cartoons in Belgium. The CJ held that access to vocational training was a matter covered by Union law, and to charge fees to non-nationals for attending such courses where no fees were charged to Belgian nationals would constitute discrimination contrary to what is now Article 18 TFEU.

The judgment in *Gravier* was swiftly followed by a number of cases raising the issue of scope of 'vocational training', a concept given a broad interpretation by the CJ to include all forms of teaching which prepares for and leads directly to a particular profession, trade or employment, or which provides the necessary skills for such profession, trade or employment, even if the programme of instruction includes an element of general education. In *Blaizot*, in the context of a claim by university students of veterinary science for reimbursement of the *minerval*, based on *Gravier*, the Court applied the *Gravier* definition of vocational training and held that university education could constitute vocational training:

> not only where the final exam directly provides the required qualification but also insofar as the studies provide specific training (i.e., where the student needs the knowledge so acquired for the pursuit of his trade or profession), even if no legislative or administrative provisions make the acquisition of such knowledge a prerequisite.

In general, university courses would meet these criteria. The only exception would be courses designed for persons seeking to 'improve their general knowledge rather than prepare themselves for an occupation'. Even where, as in veterinary or medical science, the training comprises two stages, the second representing the practical stage, the first, the academic stage must be regarded as vocational. The two stages must be viewed as a single unit.

Similar reasoning informed the Court's decision in *Belgium v Humbel* (case 263/86).

Humbel

This case concerned a claim by the Belgian authorities for the payment of the *minerval* in respect of *secondary* education received in Belgium by the son of a French national living in Luxembourg. Although the course as a whole appeared to be vocational, the fees giving rise to the dispute concerned one year within that course of general education. The Court held that such a course of general education must nonetheless be treated as 'vocational' if it forms an integral part of an overall programme of vocational education. The test therefore is whether the course as a whole (as opposed to its individual elements) is vocational in nature.

Finally, on the same day as the decision in *Humbel*, the Court, in a case brought by the Commission against Belgium (*Commission v Belgium (higher education funding)* (case 42/87)), challenging its rules on access to higher education, revised in the light of *Gravier*, allowing access, inter alia, to only 2 per cent of non-nationals, held that inasmuch as the rules related to vocational training they were in breach of what is now Article 18 TFEU.

On the basis of these cases, where educational courses are concerned, provided they are found *overall* to be vocational, according to the generous interpretation provided by the Court, EU nationals who are neither migrant workers nor the children of migrant workers living in the state in which the education is provided may claim equal access under equal conditions to nationals of the home state, even if the courses are financed or subsidised by the state as a matter of social policy.

23.2.1.5 Housing

A migrant worker is entitled to enjoy 'all the rights and benefits accorded to national workers in matters of housing, including ownership of the housing he needs' (Article 9; see *Commission v Greece* (case 305/87), restrictions on foreigners' right to acquire property held unlawful). The right extends to public and private housing.

More broadly, indirectly discriminatory rules providing for tax rebates for the acquisition of real property were held to be contrary to the principle of non-discrimination in what is now Article 18 TFEU in conjunction with Articles 21 and 45 TFEU (*Commission v Germany (tax rebates)* (case C-152/05)).

23.2.1.6 The rights of workers' families

We have discussed the right of entry to the territory of the host Member State of workers' family members at 21.4.10. Once admitted and installed in a Member State it is submitted that such persons effectively acquire equal-treatment rights within the limits imposed by EU law. In *Lebon* the Court held, in the context of a claim for the Belgian minimex by the adult child of a retired French worker living in Belgium, that the status of dependency resulted from a purely factual situation, that is, support provided by the worker; it did not depend on objective factors indicative of a need for support. The CRD (Directive 2004/38 ([2004] OJ L158/77)), Article 24 extends the principle of equality of treatment to family members who are not nationals of a Member State and who have the right of residence or permanent residence (see 23.5). Family members who are nationals of a Member State are covered by the Directive in their own right.

Article 10(3) of Regulation 1612/68 required that, in order that the family may install themselves with the worker, the worker must have available for his family 'housing considered as normal for national workers in the region where he is employed'. This requirement was dropped in Regulation 492/2011.

Insofar as the rights acquired by family members in their capacity as such should be considered ancillary to the worker's rights on free movement, we should note that family members acquire the right to work in the host Member State. Originally, this right was found in Article 11 of Regulation 1612/68, which has been repealed and replaced by the CRD which provides, in somewhat broader terms: 'Irrespective of nationality, the family members of a Union citizen who have the right of residence or the right of permanent residence in a Member State shall be entitled to take up employment or self-employment there.'

The case law relating to Article 11 of Regulation 1612/68 (*Gül v Regierungspräsident Düsseldorf* (case 131/85)) held that as long as the family member has the qualifications and diplomas necessary for the pursuit of the occupation in question in accordance with the legislation of the host state, and observed the specific rules governing the pursuit of that occupation, he was entitled under Article 11, as the spouse of an EU worker, to practise his profession in that Member State, even though he did not have EU nationality. In the case of a spouse seeking to practise a profession it will be necessary to establish whether the spouse's qualifications are recognised as equivalent, which in Gül's case they were. (For a fuller discussion of this matter see Chapter 22.) It might be of significance in this context to note that the relevant provisions on the rights of a family member to exercise an economic activity in a Member State are now contained in a directive rather than a regulation, which might raise some difficulties should a Member State fail to transpose the provisions correctly. A private employer might discriminate against a TCN either directly on grounds of nationality, or on grounds of qualification. Directives do not have horizontal direct effect and it might be difficult, therefore, to enforce rights in such a case (though note the possibility of indirect effect—see further Chapter 5 and the possibility of directly enforceable rights under Article 45 itself).

23.2.1.7 Children: Access to educational apprenticeship or vocational training courses

The case of *Casagrande* established that Article 12 of Regulation 1612/68 entitled children not merely to admission to such courses, but also to general measures to facilitate attendance, including grants. This right has been held to extend to a grant to study abroad provided it is available to nationals of the host state (*di Leo v Land Berlin* (case C-308/89), and now as a citizenship right). In the *higher education funding* case the Court held that the children of migrant EU workers are entitled to full national treatment as regards *all* forms of state education, even if the working parent has retired or died in that state. The Court went further in *Moritz v Netherlands Minister for Education* (case 390/87).

> ### Moritz
>
> This case involved a claim for an educational allowance from the Dutch authorities by the child of a migrant worker, a German, who had left Holland and returned to his native country. His son sought to return to Holland to complete his studies there since he could not do so in Germany, there being no

coordination of school-leaving certification between the two countries. The Court held that in such a case, having regard to the need to ensure the integration of migrant workers in the host state, and the need for continuity in their children's education, a child was not to be regarded as having lost its status as a 'child of the family' benefiting from the provisions of Regulation 1612/68 merely because his family had moved back to its state of origin. It may be presumed that his rights under Regulation 1612/68 would cease when the course was concluded.

A similarly broad approach was taken in *Landesamt für Ausbildungsförderung Nordrhein-Westfalen v Lubor Gaal* (case C-7/94). Here it held that a child of a (deceased) migrant worker, a Belgian national in Germany, who was over the age of 21 and not dependent on his surviving parent, was entitled to claim equality with nationals under Article 12 in order to obtain finance for studies in Scotland from the German authorities. The Court held that the definition of family in Article 10 could not be invoked to limit financial assistance to students by age or dependency.

The generous interpretation of Article 12 of Regulation 1612/68 has continued. In *Baumbast*, Article 12 was interpreted not just to give the children of a migrant worker the right to stay in the host Member State to study, but also to give the parent with responsibility for their care the right to remain also, irrespective of their nationality or whether the responsible parent was married to a resident migrant worker (*Ibrahim; Teixeira*).

Despite the fact that Article 12 does not give a spouse the right to equal access to educational, apprenticeship or vocational training courses, a spouse was successful in claiming such a right in *Forcheri v Belgium* (case 152/82).

Forcheri

Mrs Forcheri was the wife of an Italian working as a Union official in Brussels. She applied for admission to a social-work training course in Brussels. She was accepted, but required to pay a special fee, the *minerval*, required of all students who were not Belgian nationals. She claimed that the fee was discriminatory, in breach of then Articles 7 and 48 EEC (now Articles 18 and 45 TFEU) and Article 12 of Regulation 1612/68.

The CJ drawing support from the fifth recital in the preamble to Regulation 1612/68, held that to require of a national of another Member State, *lawfully established* in the first Member State, an enrolment fee which is not required of its own nationals constitutes discrimination by reason of nationality which is prohibited by what is now Article 18 TFEU. In Mrs Forcheri's case, the right was deemed to arise not from Article 12 of Regulation 1612/68, now Article 10 of Regulation 492/2011, from which she was clearly excluded, but from the general prohibition on discrimination in the Treaty (now Article 18 TFEU). Had Mrs Forcheri been the spouse of a worker it might have been possible for her to base such a claim for fees levied at the lower Belgian rate, on Article 7(2), as a social advantage.

It should always be borne in mind, as was made clear in *Lebon*, that members of the worker's family are only indirect beneficiaries of the right to equal treatment accorded to the worker under Article 7(2) of Regulation 492/2011; social advantages can only be granted to members of the family under Article 7(2) as advantages to the *worker*. Family members have derived rights only: their rights depend upon and are derived from, the worker. This is a subtle distinction, but an important one. Even though Directive 2004/38, Article 24 also gives family members rights to equal treatment (see 23.5), this right is dependent on the status of being a family member of a migrant EU national.

23.2.1.8 Article 45 and workers' rights

As noted earlier, the rights contained in Regulation 1612/68 are an expression of the rights granted to workers by Article 45 TFEU. It is therefore possible to claim rights on the basis of Article 45, as Collins attempted to do (*Collins*). Despite being unsuccessful in his claims under Article 7(2) of Regulation 1612/68, the CJ accepted that he could argue that there had been discrimination under Article 45(2). The UK government had rejected his application for jobseeker's allowance as he was not habitually resident in the UK. This constituted indirect discrimination in the context of access to employment but was, in the circumstances, justified. The *Collins* reasoning was applied in *Ioannidis*, in which the CJ re-emphasised that nationals of a Member State seeking employment in another Member State fall within the scope of the Treaties and therefore enjoy the right to equal treatment. (Note the position under CRD Article 24(2).)

23.2.2 Establishment

We have noted the huge significance of the CJ's jurisprudence relating to social rights under Regulation 1612/68 both for the worker and the worker's family. Regulation 1612/68 (now amended by Directive 2004/38) had no parallel for the self-employed. Where the self-employed or their families are 'lawfully resident' in a Member State, Article 18 TFEU may, in certain circumstances, be invoked to ensure that they receive equal treatment in the form of 'social' or any other advantages with nationals of the host Member State. For example, in *Commission v Italy (re housing aid)* (case 63/86) the CJ held that a cheap mortgage facility, available under Italian law only to Italian nationals, was in breach of the then Article 7 EEC (now Article 18 TFEU), even where such provision was an aspect of social law, and thus (it was implied) should be available on a basis of equality in Italy to EU nationals providing services *as long as the nature of the services provided was such as to require a permanent dwelling there.* (See similarly the *tax rebates* case, tax rebates for real property.) To a certain extent the significance of the distinction between workers and the self-employed has diminished with the entry into force of the CRD (see 23.5.2).

23.2.3 Services

Whilst the self-employed or their families are 'lawfully resident' in a Member State, Article 18 TFEU may be invoked to ensure equal treatment with nationals of the host Member State; in the case of the provider of services, the matter is less clear. While he or she is undoubtedly able to claim full equality as regards access to, and conditions of, work within the host Member State, it is unlikely that he or she can claim for himself and his family benefits in the form of social assistance, such as may be claimed as social advantages under Article 7(2) of Regulation 492/2011. It could be argued that these should be claimed from the Member State in which the applicant is permanently established. An analogy could perhaps be drawn here with the person migrating in search of employment, who, according to *Lebon* has no entitlement to the social advantages provided by the host Member State. Again, the impact of citizenship rights may be felt here, as well as the impact of fundamental rights, as we can see in the case of *Carpenter*, which concerned the right of a service provider to have his wife, who was a TCN, remain in the EU although she had outstayed her visa. Interestingly, Carpenter's claim was against his country of origin, not the states in which he provided cross-border services.

Note also the impact of the right to receive services on both the rights of the individual who migrates and on the provision on public services by Member States (see Chapter 24).

23.3 **Social security**

In addition to granting the right to 'social advantages' in Article 7(2) of Regulation 492/2011, the Treaty also makes provision for the coordination of social security systems of the Member States. Under the laws of Member States, both eligibility for benefit and the amount of benefit paid may depend on the number and extent of contributions made to the institution responsible for social security in the relevant state. Eligibility may also be conditional on the claimant's residence in the state responsible for payment and benefits.

It was to meet these problems that Article 48 TFEU provided for measures to be adopted in the field of social security to secure for migrant workers and their dependants the implementation of two fundamental principles:

- aggregation, for the purpose of acquiring and retaining the right to benefit and of calculating the amount of benefit, of all periods taken into account under the laws of the several countries;

- payment of benefits to persons resident in the territories of Member States.

To this end, Regulation 1408/71 was passed, replacing the earlier Regulation 3/58. Regulation 1408/71 was implemented and supplemented by Regulation 574/72. Initially applying only to workers and their families, these Regulations were amended to include the self-employed by Regulations 1390/81 and 3795/81. These Regulations were repealed and replaced by Regulation 883/2004 (OJ [2004] L200/1 and Regulation 987/2009 (OJ [2009] L284/1) which came into force on 1 May 2010. Article 48 TFEU allows legislation to be made using the 'ordinary legislative procedure', thus removing the need for unanimity which was hitherto required, but this has been made subject to an 'emergency brake system', whereby a Member State may require a proposal to be discussed by the Council if it feels that any proposal for legislation made under Article 48 would 'affect the financial balance' of its social security system. If such a request is made the ordinary legislative procedure is suspended. After four months the European Council may refer the draft back to the Council or request that the Commission submit a new proposal.

The aim of EU legislation on social security is not to harmonise Member States' social security legislation but to *coordinate* their provisions to attain the objectives of Article 45 TFEU and to ensure that claimants' contributions in different Member States are *aggregated* for the purpose outlined in Article 48(a) of the Treaty and that persons entitled to benefits may receive them wherever they are resident in the EU. The system is designed to abolish, as far as possible, the territorial limitations on the application of the different social security schemes within the Union (*Hessische Knappschaft*). However, in securing these objectives, clearly the territorial scope of the Member States' laws will be modified.

The coordination regulations are detailed and complex, and constitute, in terms of subject matter, the greatest number of cases before the CJ. The vast majority of these cases come to the CJ by way of references for preliminary rulings under Article 267 TFEU. It is beyond the scope of this work to examine this extensive body of law in detail.

23.4 **Citizenship**

Articles 20–5 TFEU govern the rights of the European citizen (see Chapter 21). The European citizen came into being with the Maastricht Treaty, but there was little indication in that Treaty of what rights he could aspire to assuming he was not economically active and therefore in a position to claim rights pertaining to that status. It fell to the CJ to determine what rights attach to the European citizen and his family. This case law is analysed in the following sections. The CRD is also relevant to this discussion.

23.5 Equality of treatment

The central issue is the extent to which the European citizen may claim the same treatment with respect to social rights as citizens of the Member State in which they are resident or present on the basis of Article 18 TFEU. Article 18 TFEU, it will be recalled, prohibits discrimination on the basis of nationality within the scope of the Treaties and 'without prejudice to any special provisions contained therein'. EU citizens have relied on that provision to claim equality of treatment with respect to a variety of rights. *Data Delecta and Forsberg v MSL Dynamics* (case 43/95) held that a foreign plaintiff who was not resident in Sweden could not be required to provide security to guarantee payment of costs of judicial proceedings where Swedish nationals were not subject to such a requirement. *Eckehard Pastoors and Trans-Cap GmbH v Belgian State* (case C-29/95) accepted that, whilst it was justifiable for Belgian law to require a non-national accused of a criminal offence who did not reside permanently in Belgium to be required to pay a deposit to cover the eventual cost of fines and costs orders, the level of the deposit in question the Court found to be disproportionately high. In *Bickel and Franz* the Court held that a national rule which grants residents in a part of its territory the right to use a language other than its official language in criminal proceedings, must be extended to non-nationals. *Garcia Avello* affirmed the right of non-nationals to exceptional treatment under national law in order to respect the rights attaching to their nationality.

> ### Garcia Avello
>
> Under Belgian law children bear the name of their father. By contrast in Spain children carry the name of both parents. Mr Garcia Avello wanted his child to have the name Garcia Weber, Weber being his wife's maiden name. Belgian law did not allow for such a possibility. The CJ held that this rule was discriminatory in the sense that it treated children in dissimilar situations in the same way: that children with dual nationality were treated in the same manner as children of Belgian nationality. Such treatment could have practical consequences in their private and professional lives. (See also *Grunkin and Paul v Standesamt Niebuell* (case C-353/06) and by contrast *Sayn-Wittgenstein v Landeshauptmann von Wien* (case C-208/09).)

The most controversial cases on citizenship social rights have been those concerned with welfare benefits and state student support. To what extent can a European citizen, who is not economically active, claim equality of treatment with respect to such benefits in the host Member State? This is an issue which is sensitive. Whilst the rights of the economically active and their families to welfare benefits in the host Member State on equal terms with nationals of that state is provided by for under EU law and raises little controversy, given the fact that such persons are paying social security contributions and tax in the host Member State and are thus contributing to the state purse (out of which such benefits are paid) in the same way as nationals, the position is otherwise in the case of the non-economically active. Their entitlement to state-financed benefits is often strongly resented by the nationals of the host Member State.

23.5.1 *Martinez Sala*

Any discussion on the rights of the European citizen to social benefits should begin with the seminal case of *Martinez Sala*.

> ### Martinez Sala
>
> Ms Sala was a Spanish national who had lived and work for some years in Germany. She had had successive residence permits and at the relevant time had applied for a renewal of her permit. She applied for a child-raising allowance. This was refused on the ground that she did not have a residence permit. Her file was being processed. She was lawfully resident in Germany in the sense that she could not be deported. The case, according to the German authorities, turned on whether Ms Sala was a worker. The Court took another view—it said that even if Ms Sala was not a worker, she was a European citizen: a national of a Member State lawfully residing in the territory of another Member State. She could therefore rely on what is now Article 18 TFEU, then Article 12 EC.

Martinez Sala marked a huge leap in the thinking of the Court on Article 18 TFEU—it signalled that Article 18 could be used as a source of rights for the European citizen within its scope of application of Treaties.

Martinez Sala appeared to state unconditionally that lawful residence generates entitlement to all socio-economic rights within the scope of the Union legal order. However, it is important to view this case against its factual background: Ms Martinez Sala did have a long-standing connection with Germany, from whose authorities she sought a child-raising allowance, having lived there since the age of 12 and been employed at substantial intervals. Even if the Court in *Martinez Sala* did intend, as its wording would suggest, to give all persons lawfully on the territory of a Member State entitlement to Union socio-economic rights, it has moved away from this stance in subsequent case law. This case law can be divided roughly into two categories according to the subject matter of the proceedings: (1) welfare benefits; and (2) student rights with regard to access to courses and financing of their studies. The reasoning in some of the case law relies on certain provisions in the CRD. It is appropriate therefore to set these out before proceeding any further with a discussion of the case law.

23.5.2 Citizens' Rights Directive (CRD)

The CRD repealed and amended a number of directives governing the right of movement and residence of nationals of Member States within the European Union. Chapter III of the Directive deals with the right of residence. Article 6 provides that Union citizens and their family members (regardless of their nationality) have the right of residence on the territory of another Member State for a period of up to three months. Article 7 provides that Union citizens and their family members have the right of residence on the territory of a Member State for a period of longer than three months if they:

(a) are workers or self-employed persons in the host Member State

(b) have sufficient resources for themselves and their family members not to become a burden on the social assistance system of the host Member State during their period of residence and have comprehensive sickness insurance cover in the host Member State, or

(c)   – are enrolled at a private or public establishment, accredited or financed by the host Member State on the basis of its legislation or administrative practice, for the principal purpose of following a course of study, including vocational training, and

– have comprehensive sickness insurance cover in the host Member State and assure the relevant national authority, by means of a declaration or by such equivalent means as they may choose, that they have sufficient resources for themselves and their family members not to become a burden on the social assistance system of the host Member State.

(d) are family members accompanying or joining a Union citizen who satisfies the conditions referred to in points (a), (b) or (c).

Article 24 is entitled 'Equal Treatment'. It provides in para 1 that Union citizens residing in the territory of the host Member State shall enjoy equal treatment with nationals of the Member State within the scope of the Treaty and subject to any specific provision provided for in the Treaty and secondary law. A Union citizen can claim equality of treatment with the host Member State's nationals only if his residence is in compliance with the CRD (*Elisabeta Dano v Jobcenter Leipzig* (case C-133/13); *Jobcenter Berlin Neukölln v Nazifa Alimanovic and Others* (case C-67/14)). Article 24, para 2 provides, by way of derogation from para 1, that the host Member State is not obliged to confer entitlement to social assistance during the first three months of residence or for a longer period in the case of Union citizens who are jobseekers (and their family members) (*Dano; Vestische Arbeit Jobcenter Kreis Recklinghausen v Jovanna Garcia-Nieto and Others* (case C-299/14)). Nor is a Member State, prior to the acquisition of the right of permanent residence, to grant maintenance aid for studies, including vocational training, consisting of student grants or student loans to persons other than workers, self-employed persons who retain such status and members of their families. As we will see from the case law, some of these provisions appear to have been rendered otiose in the sense that, although they attempt to restrict the rights of citizens to social benefits, reliance can be placed directly on Articles 18 and 20 TFEU to assert those rights (see also 21.4.9). The end result appears to be that whilst the CRD can be used to prevent the entry into the territory of a citizen and deny him the right to reside there if he does not fulfil the conditions set out in the Directive, once he is lawfully resident in the territory of the Member State, there are limits to what benefits he can be denied.

23.5.3 **Welfare benefits**

Welfare benefits can be claimed by citizens of the Union who have a sufficient link with the Member State from which they are claimed. This principle has been developed in a series of cases beginning with *Grzelczyk*. As we have already noted, *Martinez Sala* (see 23.5.1) appeared at first sight to grant citizens lawfully resident on the territory the right to welfare benefits, but although the CJ did not specifically require that a Union citizen should have a link with the Member State from which benefits are claimed, it must not be forgotten that Ms Martinez Sala had a strong link with the country of residence, Germany. The CJ made it plain in subsequent cases that there must be such a link and has indicated what that link might lawfully be required to be.

Grzelczyk

Grzelczyk was a French student studying in Belgium. He supported himself for the first three years of his studies by various small jobs and obtaining loans. In his fourth and final year he found himself in financial difficulties. He therefore applied to the relevant Belgian authorities for a minimum income benefit (the 'minimex'). Initially awarded this benefit, it was subsequently withdrawn on the basis that he was not a Belgian national nor was he a worker. When the case came before the CJ, on a preliminary ruling, the CJ found that a Belgian student in the same circumstances would have received the benefit. There was thus discrimination on the grounds of nationality.

Since *Brown* (see 21.4.6.1) the European citizen had come into being and Directive 93/96 had been adopted, which provided that Member States, subject to certain conditions, must grant right of residence to students who were nationals of other Member States. However, Articles 18 and 19 TFEU precluded entitlement to a benefit such as the minimex from being made conditional in the case of nationals of a Member State other than that of the host state and where they were legally resident from being required to be a 'worker' within the meaning of Regulation 1612/68 where no such similar condition applied to nationals of the host state. As to the requirement of Directive 93/96, repealed and replaced by the CRD, the relevant provisions of which are set out earlier, the CJ had this to say:

> A Member State may withdraw a resident permit or refuse to renew such a permit upon its expiry in the case of a student who has recourse to social assistance. However such measures can in no case be the automatic consequence in the case of a non-national student who has recourse at some point in time of his studies to social assistance. Such a student must not become an unreasonable burden on the public finances of the host state. There is a degree of financial solidarity between nationals and non-nationals in the case of the latter having difficulties which are temporary.

A person who is lawfully resident in a Member State may rely on that fact to establish the necessary link to entitle him to welfare benefits (*Trojani*).

Trojani

The *Trojani* case involved a claim for the Belgian minimex. Trojani was a French national who had been given accommodation in a Salvation Army hostel in Brussels where he did various odd jobs for which he received board and lodging and some pocket money. He claimed the minimex, which he was refused on the ground that he was not a Belgian national, nor was he a worker within the meaning of Regulation 1612/68. At the relevant time he had a valid residence permit, he was therefore lawfully resident in Belgium. This, the CJ held, meant that he could rely upon, what is now, Article 18 TFEU to benefit from the principle of equal treatment with Belgian nationals. A Member State could make the residence of a citizen who is not economically active conditional on his having sufficient resources, but once he was lawfully resident in the country, that citizen could rely upon Article 18 TFEU to claim equality of treatment with respect to the welfare benefits payable to nationals.

Lucy Stewart v Secretary of State for Work and Pensions (case C-503/09) concerned a claim for a benefit in the United Kingdom by a UK national who had moved to Spain. The CJ considered what elements could be taken into account in order to establish a genuine link between the claimant of a welfare benefit and the Member State from which that benefit was claimed.

Lucy Stewart

Ms Stewart had Down's syndrome. She was dependent on her parents with whom she lived in Spain. The CJ considered that the following elements established a 'genuine and sufficient connection' between Ms Stewart and the United Kingdom: (1) she was in receipt of a disability living allowance; (2) national insurance contributions were credited to her national insurance account every week; (3) she had lived for a considerable period of her life in the United Kingdom; (4) her parents upon whom she was dependent received retirement pensions from the United Kingdom where her father had worked before he retired.

By contrast, in the case of *Arthur Gottwald v Bezirkshauptmannschaft Bregenz* (case C-103/08), the CJ found that the necessary link with the Member State (Austria) from which a benefit for disabled persons was not present.

Gottwald

Mr Gottwald was a German national resident in Germany. He was severely disabled. In August 2006 he was driving his car along the Austrian motorway on his way to his holiday destination in Austria. He was fined EUR 200 because he did not have a toll disc affixed to his vehicle as required by Austrian law. Mr Gottwald appealed against this fine arguing that he was entitled to a toll disc free of charge on the same basis as disabled persons resident or ordinarily in Austria. The CJ found that Austria was objectively justified in refusing free toll discs to non-residents such as Mr Gottwald. The availability of the free toll disc to persons unable to use public transport was designed for persons who used the road network relatively frequently with a view to their integration in national society. The requirement relating to residence or ordinary residence therefore appeared to be a criterion suitable to establish a connection between those persons and the Austrian society and, in particular, to distinguish them from other categories of users likely to use the Austrian road network only occasionally or temporarily.

Nevertheless, the approach of the CJ in recent cases shows a different pattern which does not seem to give a significant emphasis on the status of EU citizenship. The latest judicial trend can be seen in the context of *Dano*.

Dano

The case concerned a refusal to grant a special non-contributory benefit to Ms Dano, a Romanian national and her German-born son. It should be noted here that German nationals were entitled to that social benefit. Ms Dano lived with her sister who had been providing them with all the necessary food and accommodation for four and a half years. Ms Dano had never worked and the CJ found no evidence that she had ever looked for a job. On the basis of this, the CJ concluded that a clear distinction should be made with regards to economically active EU citizens and those who are non-economically active. The CJ found that:

> A Member State must therefore have the possibility, . . . of refusing to grant social benefits to economically inactive Union citizens who exercise their right to freedom of movement solely in order to obtain another Member State's social assistance although they do not have sufficient resources to claim a right of residence [para 78].

Dano made it clear that Member States do not violate EU law and are free to deny access to social benefits to EU citizens who are not in a position to reside in the host state without becoming a financial burden on that state.

More recently, the same approach was confirmed in *Alimanovic*.

Alimanovic

Here, a Bosnian mother applied for social welfare benefits from the German government. Ms Alimanovic was living in Germany with her three German-born children of Swiss nationality. The factual background of this case was significantly different to that of the *Dano* case. Ms Alimanovic and her daughter had been working temporarily in Germany for eleven months. They had been receiving social benefits from the German government for the first six months since they became involuntarily unemployed. After that point, the relevant national authority withdrew the welfare benefits. The CJ ruled that:

> To accept that persons who do not have a right of residence under [the CRD] may claim entitlement to social assistance under the same conditions as those applicable to nationals of the host Member State would run counter to an objective of the directive, set out in recital 10 in its preamble, namely preventing Union citizens who are nationals of other Member States from becoming an unreasonable burden on the social assistance system of the host Member State [para 50].

23.5.4 Jobseekers

A number of cases have concerned benefits payable to jobseekers. D'Hoop was a young Belgian who claimed a benefit known in Belgium as a 'tideover allowance', which was paid to young persons who had finished their studies and were looking for their first job (*D'Hoop*). Such persons were required to have completed their secondary schooling in Belgium. D'Hoop had done his secondary schooling in France. He was refused the benefit. The CJ was prepared to accept that the allowance could be refused on the ground that there had to be a sufficient link between the claimant and the host state, but the Belgian requirement that schooling had to have been completed in its territory was disproportionate and did not represent a real and effective link with the Belgian job market (see also *Ioannidis*). Collins was a dual American/Irish citizen (*Collins*). He arrived in the UK to seek work there. He had no connection with the UK apart from the fact that he had a job there as a bartender for some months 17 years previously. He applied for a jobseekers allowance, which was refused to him because he could not satisfy the residency requirement attaching to that benefit. He challenged this decision as being contrary to Union law. The CJ found that ' . . . in view of the establishment of citizenship of the Union . . . it is no longer possible to exclude . . . a benefit of a financial nature intended to facilitate access to employment in the labour market of the Member State', but it was possible to require a jobseeker to have a genuine link with the employment market of that state, for example by requiring that the person has for a reasonable period genuinely sought work in that state, but this residence condition would have to be applied in a proportionate and non-discriminatory manner. *Vatsouras and Koupatantze v Arbeitgemeinschaft (ARGE) Nürnberg 900* (cases C-22 and 23/08) confirmed *Collins*, but also addressed the relevance of Article 24(2) CRD (see 23.5.2) which excluded entitlement to 'social assistance', finding that benefits intended to facilitate access to the labour market could not be classified as 'social assistance'. Therefore, although jobseekers, assuming they had a real link with the labour market which they sought to enter, could claim a jobseekers allowance on the citizenship, they would not be able to claim other benefits which were in the nature of social assistance.

23.5.5 Accessing education and training

We have seen that students must be given access to educational courses of a vocational nature, a concept broadly interpreted to include the vast majority of higher educational courses (see 23.2.1.4). But should a Member State actually be required to provide such courses to non-nationals? If large numbers of non-nationals apply for such courses, is it possible to refuse them entry? These were the issues that arose in *Commission v Austria (recognition of qualifications)* (case C-147/03) and *Bressol and Others v Gouvernement de la Communauté Française* (case C-73/08). In the *recognition of qualifications* case the CJ condemned Austrian rules requiring students who had not completed their secondary education in Austria to have to satisfy a different, more onerous set of entry requirements for certain educational courses. *Bressol* concerned rules relating to the admission to medical and para-medical training designed to ensure that there were sufficient medical professionals to serve the French-speaking Belgian community.

> ### Bressol
>
> At issue in *Bressol* was a rule of Belgian law which required universities and schools of higher education of the French-speaking community to limit the numbers of students not considered to be resident in Belgium at the time of their registration, who may register for their first time in one of the nine medical or paramedical programmes. This rule was designed to ensure that enough Belgian students graduated from these courses in order to be able to provide continuing and quality medical and paramedical care within the French-speaking community in Belgium. The CJ found that the provision was discriminatory, but left it to the referring court to establish whether it was justifiable or not. The CJ accepted that the quality of training and the availability of enough professionals to satisfy the healthcare needs of the national or regional market were relevant considerations in making this assessment, but that the national court should determine whether 'the legislation at issue . . . can be regarded as appropriate for attaining the objective of protecting public health' or whether that objective could be attained by less restrictive measures.

23.5.6 Student finance

We have seen in *Lair* and *Brown* that as Union law stood at the time of those cases, maintenance grants for students could only be claimed either by those who had the status of 'worker' within the meaning of Regulation 1612/68 or were the children of workers (21.4.10.2). As Union law developed in the sphere of education and as the Union citizen came into being, the position with respect to student finance has changed. Union citizens who are not economically active are not in principle entitled to student finance but may be so if they have a sufficient link with the Member State in which they are studying (*Bidar*).

> ### Bidar
>
> Mr Bidar came to London in 1998 and completed his secondary schooling there. In 2001 he began studying economics at University College London. He applied for a student loan. This was refused on the ground that he was not settled in the UK. It was not possible to acquire that status as a student. Mr Bidar argued that this was discriminatory and contrary to what is now Article 18 TFEU. The CJ found that in principle he was entitled to the loan. It fell within the scope of application of the Treaty and therefore he, as a national of a Member State, could rely on Article 18 to claim it but that right was not absolute:
>
> > . . . although the Member States must, in the organization and application of their social assistance systems show a certain degree of financial solidarity with the nationals of other Member States . . . it is permissible for a Member State to ensure that the grant of assistance to cover maintenance costs of students from other Member States does not become an unreasonable burden which could have consequences for the overall assistance which may be granted by that State.

In *Förster* the CJ found that a residence requirement of five years 'does not go beyond what is necessary to attain the objective of ensuring that students from other Member States are to a certain degree integrated into the society of the host Member State'.

Commission v Austria (reduced transport fares for students) (case C-75/11) concerned the discriminatory treatment of students whose parents were not receiving Austrian family allowances.

Reduced Transport Fares for Students

Austrian law granted reduced transport fares to students in respect of whom family allowances were granted under Austrian law. The CJ found this rule was discriminatory:

> ... making the reduced transport fares subject to the grant of Austrian family allowances gives rise to unequal treatment as between Austrian students pursuing their studies in Austria and students from other Member States, pursuing their studies there as well, since such a condition is more easily fulfilled by Austrian students because their parents as a rule receive those allowances [para 50].

23.5.7 **Rights against state of origin**

Much of the case law in this field concerned claims against the host Member State rather than the Member State of origin or by a national returning from another Member State to his Member State of origin. What is the position of a national who wishes to claim from his Member State of origin a benefit to be enjoyed in the host state? Can he claim as a non-economic European citizen to have the right to be in the same position in the host Member State vis-à-vis his Member State of origin?

Tas-Hagen, Tas v Raadskamer WUBO van de Pensioen-en Uitkeringsraad (case C-192/05) concerned an award to civilian war victims by the Netherlands. Both applicants were recognised as civilian war victims, but were refused the payments on the basis that, although they had lived in the Netherlands, they now lived in Spain. The CJ held that national legislation which places at a disadvantage certain of the nationals of the Member State concerned, simply because they have exercised their freedom to move and to reside in another Member State, is a restriction on the freedoms conferred by Article 20 TFEU; this reasoning did not distinguish between restrictions imposed by the host state or the state of origin. Such an approach has been used in a number of other cases concerning war pensions (eg, *Nerkowska v Zaklad Ubezpiezen Społecznych* (case C-499/06); *Zablocka-Weyhermüller*) and has been used in relation to other benefits, such as grants to study abroad (*Morgan v Bezirksregierung Köln* and *Bucher v Landrat des Kreises Düren* (cases C-11 and 12/06)).

It could be argued that this development in the jurisprudence constitutes a qualitative shift in approach. Most importantly, a real link between the claimant and the Member State from which the benefit is claimed must be established, and in ensuring that link Member States enjoy a wide discretion (*Tas-Hagen and Tas*). Moreover, even where such a link has been established, in the case of a social security benefit, it may be justifiable to place restrictions on the receipt of that benefit which may affect the recipient's freedom of movement in the public interest. This would be a case where it was necessary to verify that the recipient continues to satisfy the conditions for the grant of the benefit.

23.6 **Conclusions**

The Union has consistently treated economically active persons be they employed or self-employed as not merely a means of tools in the production process but as persons who, with their families, ought to be integrated fully into the society in which the economic activity is being carried out. Workers and their families are thus entitled to the same social and tax advantages as nationals of the host state. This is entirely reasonable given the fact that workers pay the same level of taxes and social security contributions as nationals of the host state. The CJ has thus adopted a broad approach in interpreting what constitutes social and tax advantages and the circumstances in which they must be granted to workers and their families. Likewise, the CJ has been firm in its approach to discriminatory conduct finding that it can be objectively justified only in limited circumstances. With the advent of the non-economically active migrant—the student and the European citizen—the position became more complex. Such persons did not contribute to the host state's coffers in the same way as the economically active. The question then arose as to what precisely were the rights of such persons to welfare benefits and student finance. The CJ resolved this issue by ruling that the claimant of benefits who was not economically active had to have a 'link' with the Member States from whose welfare system such benefits were claimed in the sense that he must be integrated into the host society to an extent which gives rise to an obligation of 'solidarity' on the part of the citizens of that Member State towards him. The CRD largely reflects this case law.

Further reading

Dougan, M, 'The constitutional dimension to the case law on Union citizenship' (2006) 31 EL Rev 613.

Goudappel, F, *The Effects of EU Citizenship* (TMC Asser Press, 2010).

Guild, E, Peers, S and Tomkin, J, *The EU Citizenship Directive: A Commentary* (Oxford University Press, 2014).

Hailbronner, K, 'Union citizenship and access to social benefits' (2005) 42 CML Rev 1245.

O'Leary, S, 'Equal treatment and EU citizens: A new chapter on cross-border educational mobility and access to student financial assistance' (2009) 34 EL Rev 612.

O'Leary, S, 'The Curious Case of Frontier Workers and Study Finance: Giersch' (2014) 51 CML Rev 601.

Pennings, F, *European Social Security Law*, 5th edn (Antwerp, 2010).

Shaw, J, 'Citizenship: Contrasting dynamics of the interface of integration and constitutionalism' in P Craig and G de Búrca (eds), *Evolution of EU Law*, 2nd edn (Oxford University Press, 2011).

Spaventa, E, 'Seeing the woods despite the trees? On the scope of Union citizenship and its constitutional effects' (2008) 45 CML Rev 40.

White, R, 'Free movement, equal treatment, and citizenship of the Union' (2005) 54 ICLQ 885.

Right to receive services

24.1 Introduction

So far we have discussed the economic rights mainly from the perspective of the provider. While Article 56 TFEU clearly covers the right to supply services, the provision is broader than that. In particular, it raises the possibility of the right to travel and to receive services. The rights of recipients of services were expressly referred to in Article 1(1) Directive 64/221 ([1964] OJ L56/850) which provided for the 'freedom of movement for employed or self-employed persons or the *recipients* of services'. Similarly, Article 1(1)(b) Directive 73/148 ([1973] OJ L172/14)—required Member States to abolish restrictions on the movement and residence of 'nationals of Member States wishing to go to another Member State as *recipients* of services'. But it is the CJ which has developed, in the context of a series of preliminary rulings, the rights of service recipients, particularly in education and healthcare provision. In the case of the latter, this case law has now been codified in legislation (Directive 2011/24 on the applications of patients' rights in cross-border healthcare ([2011] OJ L88/45)) (the 'Patients' Directive).

This chapter will consider, from the point of view of the service recipient, the services to which he may claim the right to receive on the basis of Article 56 TFEU, implementing legislation and the conditions under which such services must be provided.

24.2 General

Articles 56–62 TFEU are expressed in terms of the freedom to *provide* services. The right of recipients of services was raised in *Watson*, where the Commission suggested that the freedom to move within the Union to receive services was the necessary corollary to the freedom to provide services. The point was not decided in that case but it was decided in *Luisi and Carbone*.

Luisi and Carbone

This reference to the CJ was made in the context of criminal proceedings in Italy against Luisi and also Carbone for breach of Italian currency regulations. They were accused of taking foreign currency out of the country in excess of the maximum permitted under Italian law. They had taken the money out for the purposes of tourism and medical treatment. The question referred to the CJ was whether payment for such services represented movement of capital, or payment for the provision of services; if the latter, was it governed by Articles 56–61 TFEU?

Advocate-General Mancini, arguing from *Watson*, suggested that Article 56 was concerned with the receipt of services as well as their provision. The Court, following Advocate-General Mancini, found the money to be payment for services and held that freedom to provide services, as provided by Article 56, includes the freedom for recipients of services to go to another Member State, without restriction, in order to receive a service there. Recipients of services were held to include tourists, persons receiving medical treatment and persons travelling for the purposes of education and business.

The right to enter and remain in another Member State for the purpose of receiving services was further amplified in *Commission v Netherlands (re entry into Dutch territory)* (case C-68/89), where the Court held that nationals of one Member State were entitled to enter another Member State simply on production of a valid identity card or passport. National immigration authorities were not entitled to question EU nationals seeking to enter a Member State except in order to query the validity of the identity card or passport. On the other hand, when applying for a residence permit national authorities may require proof of the applicant's status as a provider or recipient of services. Recipients of services are entitled to reside in a Member State for the period during which the service is provided. Any restrictions on these freedoms will prima facie breach Articles 57–62 TFEU subject to limitation on the grounds of public policy, public security and public health (Articles 52 and 62 TFEU). Articles 56–7 TFEU will apply if neither the provider nor the recipient of services actually travels but the service itself moves cross border towards the recipient, for example if it is provided by internet (online sales), cable, e-mail or by telephone. The question remains whether and to what extent the recipient of services, by reason of his status as such or his right of residence, can invoke these provisions, together with Article 18 TFEU, to claim equality of treatment with nationals of the host state. A number of services, such as education and medicine, are publicly funded and provided not so much as a commercial activity but as a public service. Are these to be available to nationals of the Member States on the same basis as to the states' own citizens?

24.3 Non-discrimination and Union competence

24.3.1 Fees and access to courses

Vocational training was considered in the context of educational services in *Gravier*.

> ### Gravier
>
> The applicant in the main proceedings was a French woman who had applied to and been accepted by the Liège Académie des Beaux-Arts for a four-year course in the art of strip cartoons. As a foreign student she was charged a special fee, known as a *minerval*, for the course. This was not payable by Belgian citizens, whether or not they lived or paid taxes in Belgium, nor by EU nationals working in Belgium, or members of their families. She brought an action before the Belgian courts, claiming the fee was discriminatory.

Her case rested on two arguments. First, she suggested that the *minerval* constituted an obstacle to her freedom of movement to receive services as established in *Luisi and Carbone* in breach of Article 56 TFEU. Her second argument was based on the vocational nature of the course. Vocational education fell within the scope of the Treaty; as a matter covered by EU law it was discriminatory, in breach of Article 18 TFEU, to charge higher fees to EU nationals who were not Belgian citizens or resident in Belgium. The CJ, following the opinion of the Advocate-General, found in Ms Gravier's favour on this second ground. Access to vocational training was a matter covered by Union law; moreover, it was an essential element in promoting freedom of movement for persons throughout the Union. The Court expressly dissociated itself from the wider issues involved, discussed at length by the Advocate-General, concerning the organisation and financing of such courses, and confined its judgment merely to conditions of access to a course affecting foreign students alone, and relating to a particular kind of course, namely vocational education.

The judgment in *Gravier* caused considerable concern amongst Member States. With its wide definition of vocational training, it meant that many courses, including perhaps university courses, often entailing substantial contributions from public funds (the Belgians pointed out that the *minerval* itself only covered 50 per cent of the cost of the education provided), would have to be offered on equal terms to all EU nationals. Underlying this discussion was a more general concern about the right of migrant EU nationals to receive public services on equal terms as nationals of the state in which they were provided.

Gravier was indeed a landmark case, an example of the Court in activist mood. It began to develop the concept of 'vocational training' defining it as:

> . . . any form of education which prepares for a qualification for a particular profession, trade, or employment or which provides the necessary training and skills for such a profession, trade or employment is vocational training, whatever the age and level of training of the pupils or students, and even if the training programme includes an element of general education.

The CJ has applied the principles developed in *Gravier* in the context of equal access to Austrian higher-education institutions (*recognition of qualifications* case). Imposing discriminatory treatment, in this case the requirement on those who did not do their secondary education in Austria to undertake extra tests to prove their academic status, is contrary to Articles 18, 165 and 166 TFEU. In coming to this conclusion, the CJ relied not only on the terms of Article 165(2), which seeks to encourage student mobility, but, significantly, on European citizenship. The CJ reaffirmed the fundamental nature of European citizenship which enables 'those who find themselves in the same situation to enjoy the same treatment irrespective of their nationality' (*recognition of qualifications* case, para 45; see also 23.5).

24.3.2 **Scholarships and grants**

The Court in *Gravier* did not consider whether the right of EU nationals to vocational training carried with it a right to grants and scholarships from the host state to enable them to take up these courses. The matter was resolved in *Brown* and *Lair* (for detailed discussion of these cases see Chapters 21 and 23). Both *Brown* and *Lair* involved claims for maintenance grants for university courses. In both cases their entitlement to the grants as 'workers', or the 'children of migrant workers', was doubtful. So they sought also to rely on *Gravier*, arguing that the course in question constituted vocational training, to which what is now Article 18 TFEU applied. Thus they were entitled to be treated on an equal footing with nationals.

The Court disagreed. Although university courses were capable of constituting vocational training, and EU nationals were therefore entitled to equal treatment with respect to fees, the principle of equality of treatment between nationals set out in Article 18 TFEU did not apply to maintenance grants. Assistance in the form of maintenance grants, the Court held, fell outside the scope of the TFEU. It was a matter of educational policy, and, as such, had not been entrusted to the Union institutions; it was also a matter of social policy, which fell within the competence of Member States insofar as it was not covered by the provisions of the TFEU.

The judgments were greeted with relief by Member States. *Grzelczyck* and other cases in this area suggest that issue may have to be revisited in the light of changes to the Treaty, notably the introduction of European citizenship. As a migrant student, Grzelczyck was not entitled to claim financial support from the state during his studies under Article 7(2) of Regulation 1612/68. As a migrant European citizen, however, he might be so entitled. *Bidar* further held that a non-national could not be subjected to different conditions for eligibility for preferential-rate student loans. EU competence has expanded to include other areas too, such as public health (see 24.5.2).

24.4 Scope of services: corollary to the right to receive

In a number of successful cases, the discrimination principle was used where the recipient was present in the host Member State for business or for tourist purposes: in either situation contributing to the host Member State's economy. We can see such an extension of the equality principle in *Cowan*.

> ### Cowan
>
> The claimant, a British citizen on holiday in Paris, was claiming compensation for personal injuries sustained as a result of a mugging in the Paris Metro. Under French law compensation was provided out of public funds and payable only to French nationals. Cowan claimed that since he was exercising his freedom to receive services, this rule was in breach of Article 18 TFEU. The CJ held that he was entitled to equal protection against, and compensation for, the risks of assault. This right was a corollary of his right to receive services. Since the judgment was expressed in narrow, specific terms, it remains to be seen what rights are to be regarded as a 'corollary' to the right to receive services.

In the *museum admission* case the Court found that in charging discriminatory entrance fees to national museums (lower fees being charged for Spanish citizens and residents and EU nationals under 21 years) Spain was acting in breach of Article 18 TFEU and Article 56 TFEU. The fact that a museum service was a public service financed by the state was not raised by the Spanish government and was not considered by the Court. In subsequent cases concerning discriminatory terms of access to facilities such as museums, the CJ has not addressed the point either, relying instead on its reasoning in *Commission v Spain* (see, eg, *Commission v Italy (museum entry)* (case C-388/01)).

In a rather different context, in *Hubbard v Hamburger* (case C-20/92), a provision of German law requiring a national of another Member State who, in the capacity of executor of a will, had brought proceedings before one of its courts, to lodge security for costs—something which was not required of German nationals—was held to constitute discrimination on grounds of nationality, prohibited by Articles 56 and 57 TFEU. Although in this case both the provider (the executor) and the recipient (the beneficiary) of services were established outside German territory (in the UK), the rule was clearly a barrier to the free provision (or receipt) of services. Discriminatory administrative requirements making cross-border services less attractive than services provided by resident service providers may be incompatible with the Treaty unless they can be objectively justified. This can be seen in *X NV v Staatssecretaris van Financiën* (case C-498/10).

> ### X NV
>
> The Netherlands imposed on recipients of service who had recourse to non-resident service providers in the sports sector an obligation to withhold at source, at the minimum rate of 20 per cent tax on remuneration paid to those non-resident service providers. By contrast, in the case of a resident service provider, the recipient of the services in issue is not under such an obligation. The CJ held that such an

obligation constituted a restriction on the freedom to provide services in that 'it entails an additional administrative burden and related liability risks'. It was also liable to render cross border services 'less attractive for resident recipients than services provided by resident service providers and to deter those recipients from having recourse to non-resident service providers'.

24.5 Remuneration and publicly funded services: where lies the dividing line?

There must be an economic link between the service providers and the recipient of their services. Services provided gratuitously are not covered by Articles 56 and 57 TFEU. Article 57 states clearly:

> Services shall be considered 'services' within the meaning of the Treaties where they are normally provided for remuneration.

There must be an economic link between the service provided and the recipient of that service. Services provided gratuitously are governed by national law and regulation and thus non-nationals are not entitled to receive those services on an equal footing with nationals of the Member State in which they are provided or from which they emanate but if remuneration is received—however minimal—then the activity in question comes within the scope of Article 56 TFEU, as in *Jundt v Finanzamt* (case C-281/06). Jundt, a German national, resident in Germany, taught a 16-hour law course at the University of Strasbourg for which he received a relatively small fee of about £550. The CJ held that his teaching activities were 'services' within the meaning of Article 56 TFEU, even if they were carried out on a 'quasi-honorary basis'. Article 56 simply requires that 'the activity must not be provided for nothing'.

The question of the economic link between the provider and the recipient of services can also be seen in the context of *Grogan*.

Grogan

Irish students' unions distributed information, in Ireland, about the availability of abortion services in the United Kingdom including information as to the identity and location of abortion clinics. SPUC sought an injunction to restrain these activities. It was argued that the distribution of the information in question constituted a service within the meaning of Article 56 TFEU and consequently it was not to be restrained by way of an injunction. The CJ found that the termination of pregnancy, as lawfully practised in several Member States, was a medical activity, which is normally provided for remuneration and thus fell to be classified as a 'service' within the meaning of Article 56. However, in this case there was no economic link between the abortion clinics and the student associations which were receiving the information. Since that information was not distributed on behalf of an economic operator established in another Member State, a prohibition on the distribution of information could not be regarded as a restriction within the meaning of Article 56 of the Treaty.

Article 56 TFEU does not require that services should be paid for by the recipients of those services. The service must normally be provided for remuneration regardless of the source of that payment.

The dividing line between remunerated and non-remunerated services has arisen acutely with respect to publicly provided services, in particular in the fields of education and healthcare: to what extent do such services when they are provided by the state to the population as a whole, and in many cases delivered free of charge at the point of delivery, fall with Article 56 with the result that they can be enjoyed by citizens of another Member State?

24.5.1 **Education**

In *Humbel* the CJ considered the status of state education vis-à-vis Article 56, which is provided free of charge to pupils. It found that state-provided education did not constitute a service because the state was not engaged in gainful activity when providing such services: it was fulfilling its duties towards its population in the educational sphere and such services were paid for out of public funds. In the wording of the judiciary:

> The essential characteristic of remuneration thus lies in the fact that it constitutes consideration for the service in question, and is normally agreed upon between the provider and the recipient of the service.
>
> That characteristic is, however, absent in the case of courses provided under the national education system. First of all, the state, in establishing and maintaining such a system, is not seeking to engage in gainful activity but is fulfilling its duties towards its own population in the social, cultural and educational fields. Secondly, the system in question is, as a general rule, funded from the public purse and not by pupils or their parents.
>
> The nature of the activity is not affected by the fact that pupils or their parents must sometimes pay teaching or enrolment fees in order to make a certain contribution to the operating expenses of the system [paras 17–19].

It is important to note that in addition to looking at how the system of education was funded, the CJ emphasised the purpose of the activity and recognised that the state is acting in its capacity as political unit, with ties to its citizens. This case could be seen as providing an exception to the scope of Article 56 and free-movement logic.

Wirth v Landeshaupt Hannover (case C-109/92) arguably changed the emphasis, by focusing on the nature of the funding mechanism. The case concerned tertiary education rather than second-ary education, but the CJ still recognised that higher education can be provided as a state activity. Crucially, however, it held that, although most higher education institutions would be funded by the state and therefore would fall within the *Humbel* 'exception', those which were funded privately or which sought to make a profit would fall within Article 56. In *Schwarz and Gootjes-Schwarz* the CJ found that a private school which charged fees could be regarded as providing a service for remu-neration and thus fell within the scope of Article 56 TFEU.

Thus the CJ distinguished between education which was provided by private finance, with a view to profit, and education as a public service, financed wholly or partly by the state, as an as-pect of social policy. The position therefore seems to be that—apart from the area of vocational training (access and fees), which is governed by *Gravier*—public services such as health and edu-cation provided by the state for the benefit of its citizens, and not for commercial reasons with a view to profit, cannot be claimed on a basis of equality by EU nationals who are temporarily resident as recipients of services in that Member State but do not enjoy 'lawful residence' on a 'settled' or permanent basis as 'favoured Union citizens'—that is, those who are, or have been, employed and self-employed migrants and their families (see Chapters 21 and 23) in the state providing the services.

24.5.2 **Healthcare services**

As is the case with education, healthcare services can either be provided to the patient in return for payment or free of charge at the point of delivery. There is no problem where the patient pays directly for the services. Such services fall within the scope of Article 56. The situation is more complex where either the patient pays for the services received and is reimbursed either in whole or in part by the state, through, for example, a healthcare insurance scheme, or where the healthcare services are provided free of charge at the point of delivery, the cost being met out of the public purse. This issue was considered by the CJ in *Kohll*.

Kohll

This case concerned the Luxembourgoise requirement that, if an individual wanted to be able to reclaim the cost of medical treatment outside Luxembourg from the state health insurance fund, then prior authorisation granted only in limited circumstances, would be required. Kohll sought to challenge this rule on the basis of Article 56. The Luxembourg government argued that the rule complied with Article 22 of Regulation 1408/71 ([1971] OJ L149/2) concerning social security rights of migrant workers and their families. That provision required that, save in cases of emergency medical treatment, the prior authorisation of the state to whose healthcare system the patient was affiliated was required.

The CJ agreed that, in principle, it is for Member States to organise their own social security systems, including the right or duty to be insured with a social security scheme and the benefits available under any such scheme; it held that in doing so Member States must comply with EU law, including the right to provide and receive services. The CJ held that the orthodontist's treatment in Germany in issue in this case was to be considered 'services' for the purposes of the TFEU, as the treatment was provided for remuneration and constituted a professional activity. Thus the Luxembourg social security rules regarding medical treatment had to be considered in the light of Article 56. They were found to constitute a barrier to the freedom to provide services, in particular the requirement that the treatment to be received in another Member State had to be the subject of a prior authorisation, and was not objectively justified either for the protection of the financial equilibrium of the social security system or for reasons of national health.

This judgment and *Decker*, handed down the same day concerning the provision of spectacles and therefore considered under Article 34 (see Chapter 19) caused some concern among many Member States, as they raised many questions about the scope of the Treaty freedoms in the context of public health.

In this context it should be noted that the *Kohll* situation is different from the cases on education. In those cases, the host Member State bore the cost of providing the educational services for the individuals receiving those services in its territory; here, in the case of healthcare services, the cost is repatriated to the Member State responsible for the healthcare of the recipient. In *Geraets-Smits v Stichting Ziekenfonds* and *HTM Peerbooms v Stichting CZ Groep Zorgverzekeringen* (case C-157/99) the issue was raised of the status of healthcare services, the cost of which was paid for by the recipient at the point of delivery but then reimbursed by the healthcare insurer. The Advocate-General in this case adopted the reasoning in *Humbel* and *Wirth* (discussed at 24.5.1) to suggest that the provision of healthcare in such systems does not fall within Article 56 TFEU, constituting instead part of the Member State's obligation towards its population (para 47). The CJ, however, followed its approach in *Kohll* and held that medical care fell within the scope of Article 56, although certain restrictions could be justified on public policy grounds, such as the need to protect public health by ensuring an appropriate distribution of hospitals, adequately equipped and staffed, so as to meet the needs of the population. The CJ first noted that although the Dutch system (the ZFW) may have provided benefits in kind, the treatment the patients actually did receive was paid for by them. On a separate point the CJ held:

> Furthermore, the fact that hospital medical treatment is financed directly by the sickness insurance funds on the basis of agreements and pre-set scales of fees is not in any event such as to remove such treatment from the sphere of services within the meaning of Article [56] of the Treaty.
>
> First it should be borne in mind that Article [56] of the Treaty does not require that the service should be paid for by those for whom it is performed . . .
>
> Second, Article [56] of the Treaty states that it applies to services normally provided for remuneration and it has been held that, for the purposes of that provision, the essential characteristic of remuneration lies in the fact that it constitutes consideration for the service in question. In the present cases, the payments made by the sickness insurance funds under the contractual arrangements provided for by the ZFW, albeit set at a flat rate, are indeed the consideration for the hospital services and unquestionably represent remuneration for the hospital which receives them and which is engaged in an activity of an economic character [paras 56–8].

In *Müeller-Fauré v Onderlinge Waarborgmaatschappij OZ Zorgverzekeringen UA* (case C-385/99) the Court again focused on the fact that the care provided in that instance had been paid for directly by the patient but the cost to him was subsequently reimbursed. The point of focus therefore seems to be what happens at the point of delivery of the healthcare service. Does the patient pay? If so, the CJ found in *Watts*, the healthcare service received is deemed to be provided for remuneration and so within the scope of Article 56.

Watts

Watts concerned the UK's national health service (NHS), which operates a system whereby healthcare is provided free at point of delivery; furthermore it does not envisage the possibility or reimbursement for treatment provided elsewhere, whether it be private treatment within the UK, or treatment outside the UK, and the trusts operating healthcare in the UK have no funds available for this purpose. Mrs Watts had arthritis and was in pain, but medical authorities put her in a standard category as far as her need for treatment was concerned and she was consequently placed on a waiting list for an operation. She went to France for the operation, which she paid for. Upon her return to the UK she demanded reimbursement for the costs she had incurred, as well as post-operative physiotherapy. On being refused payment by the responsible healthcare trust, Watts brought an action for judicial review, which resulted in a reference to the CJ.

In the arguments before the CJ, much was made of the fact that the NHS was in a parallel situation to the educational system in *Humbel*, in being state funded. The CJ avoided considering whether the provision of healthcare in the UK was a commercial activity, but focused—as it had done in *Smits and Peerboems*—on the fact that Watts paid directly for her treatment received abroad, and the status of the NHS was irrelevant to that assessment (para 89).

Following its approach in *Smits and Peerboems* and *Müeller Fauré* the CJ held that:

> The supply of medical services does not cease to be a supply of services within the meaning of Article [56] on the ground that the patient, after paying the foreign supplier for the treatment received, subsequently seeks reimbursement of that treatment from a national health scheme.

This decision has been much criticised. While the CJ may state that there is scope for Member State choices about the level of healthcare provision and the way that care is provided, in practice the CJ is undermining that freedom where cross-border services are in issue.

In all of the cases discussed above the patient actually paid for the care provided. It is thus unclear as to how the CJ would view healthcare services provided free of charge to the patient at the point of delivery. That said, the service provider will be paid for services delivered even if the payment does not come directly from the service recipient but rather, from the insurer. It will thus be provided for remuneration. But can one classify as 'remuneration' money paid out of state funds to hospitals and other healthcare providers for the provision of care to patients, such funds not being related directly to any particular treatment provided to any given individual? That type of situation would appear to be on all fours with *Humbel* and thus outside Article 56 TFEU.

24.6 **Legislation**

The impact of the Services Directive was discussed in Chapter 22. There we noted that one of the concerns surrounding the enactment of the Directive was its impact on public services. Thus, although the Directive covers the right to receive services, it should be noted that it excludes some sectors from its ambit. Significantly, the recitals to the Services Directive state:

> This Directive covers only services which are performed for an economic consideration. Services of general interest are not covered by the definition in Article [57] of the Treaty and therefore do not fall within the scope of this Directive. Services of general economic interest are services that are performed for an economic consideration and therefore do fall within the scope of this Directive [Recital 17].

This does not clarify the difficulties arising from the case law: presumably state-funded education is a service of 'general interest', as referred to in Recital 17, whilst health is a service of general economic interest. In fact the recitals to the Directive effectively restate the case law from *Humbel*, and whilst cases are to be assessed on their individual facts, Recital 34 specifies that the CJ:

> has recognised that the characteristic of remuneration is absent in the case of activities performed, for no consideration, by the State or on behalf of the State in the context of its duties in the social, cultural, educational and judicial fields, such as courses provided under the national education system, or the management of social security schemes which do not engage in economic activity.

Whilst healthcare is, following the CJ's approach, of necessity not included in this list, the Directive states that the reimbursement of healthcare fees should be dealt with in a separate legal instrument and not under the Services Directive (Recital 23). These exclusions from the scope of the Directive are found in Article 2.

24.6.1 **The Patients' Directive**

Directive 2011/24 on the application of patients' rights in cross-border healthcare ([2011] OJ L88/45) was adopted on 9 March 2011. The objective of the Directive is to set out clearly the rules for facilitating access to cross-border healthcare within the Union, as elaborated in the extensive case law of the CJ, some of which has been considered above in 24.5.2.

Article 2 of the Directive defines 'healthcare' in broad terms: it applies to the provision of healthcare regardless of how it is delivered and financed, or whether it is public or private.

> [H]ealth care means health services provided by health professionals to patients to access, maintain or restore their state of health, including the prescription, dispensation and provision of medicinal products and medical devices.

Certain services are excluded from the scope of the Directive, notably long-term care, the allocation and access to organs for organ transplantation and public vaccination programmes. The Directive requires that the prior authorisation of the Member State to whose healthcare system a patient is affiliated, may be required if the reimbursement for the cost of the healthcare they seek falls within the circumstances set out in Article 8 of the Directive. These include overnight hospital care; treatment which requires the use of highly specialised and costly medical infrastructure or medical equipment; treatment which presents a particular risk to the patient or the population; treatment which is provided by a healthcare provider which 'could give rise to serious and specific concerns relating to the safety or quality of the care'. Article 8(6) lists the circumstances in which the Member States may refuse to grant authorisation, but notably authorisation cannot be refused where the healthcare cannot be provided on their territory within a time limit which is medically justifiable.

24.7 Conclusions

The general theme of the case law is that the CJ has developed a number of mechanisms to extend rights for those who have moved to receive services, particularly public services, whether the purpose of the move was to receive those services or not. This case law has now been codified in the legislative instruments discussed in the previous section. On one level we can commend this, as it supports the rights of individuals, either by making host states provide services without discrimination, as in *Cowan*, or by repatriating the cost of cross-border services, as in *Watts*. On the other hand, essentially, the CJ's approach favours individualistic choices which disturb systems based on scarcity, resource allocation and solidarity. However, to a certain extent, in the sphere of healthcare this concern is addressed in the Patients' Directive.

Further reading

Barnard, C, *The Substantive Law of the EU: The Four Freedoms*, 5th edn (Oxford University Press, 2016), Ch 9.

Barnard, C, 'Unravelling the Services Directive' (2008) 45 CML Rev 323.

Biondi, A, 'Recurring cycles in internal market: Some reflections on free movement of services' in A Arnull (ed), *Continuity and Change in EU Law: Essays in Honour of Sir Francis Jacobs* (Oxford University Press, 2008).

Cygan, A, 'Public healthcare in the European Union: Still a service of general interest?' (2008) 57(3) ICLQ 529.

de la Rosa, S, 'The Directive on cross-border healthcare or the art of codifying complex case-law' (2012) 49 CML Rev 15.

Jørgensen, S, 'The right to cross-border education in the European Union' (2009) 46 CML Rev 1567.

Pennings, F, 'The Cross-border Health Care Directive: More free movement for citizens and more coherent EU Law' (2011) 13 EJSS 424.

Woods, L, 'Scope of services I: Definitions' in *Free Movement of Goods and Services within the European Community* (Ashgate, 2004).

25 Free movement of persons: limitations on grounds of public policy, public security or public health

25.1 Introduction

The last few chapters have shown that the CJ has interpreted the Treaty freedoms applying to persons widely. Nonetheless, as is the case with goods, there are some circumstances where other interests must be balanced against the right to free movement and non-discrimination on the grounds of nationality. We have seen that non-discriminatory measures may be justified on public-interest grounds during the application of the Treaty freedom itself (Chapter 22). There are specific exceptions to the non-discrimination principle in terms of access to jobs and to professions, as regards linguistic capability (see Article 3 of Regulation 492/2011 ([2011] OJ L141/1)), which has codified Regulation 1612/68 ([1968] OJ L257/2) and as regards public services (Article 45(4) TFEU as regards workers and Article 51 TFEU as regards services and establishment). Beyond these specific and limited provisions, the Treaty permits a Member State to derogate from the Treaty freedoms on the grounds of public policy, public security and public health (Articles 45(3) and 52 TFEU). It is these latter provisions on which this chapter focuses. Similarly with other derogation provisions, these articles have been interpreted narrowly.

This chapter will look first at the relationship between the CRD (Directive 2004/38 ([2004] OJ L158/77)) and the Treaty provisions before going on to consider the substantive scope of the derogation provisions and the procedural guarantees in the CRD. We will also briefly consider some of the public interest grounds for limiting the Treaty freedoms.

25.2 Scope of the CRD and its relationship with Treaty provisions

The exception provided by Articles 45(3) and 52 TFEU was originally implemented in Directive 64/221 ([1964] OJ L56/850) to give substance to the rather vague and potentially catch-all provisions of the Treaty. This Directive has now been repealed and replaced by Chapter VI of the CRD. The CRD, although not phrased in exactly the same terms as Directive 64/221, draws on its predecessor Directive and the relevant jurisprudence heavily.

Article 27(1) CRD provides that 'Member States may restrict the freedom of movement and residence of Union citizens and their family members, irrespective of nationality, on grounds of public policy, public security or public health'. There are two aspects to the provisions on derogation found in the CRD. First they lay down the principles on which a state may refuse entry or residence to those who would otherwise be eligible, on the grounds of public policy, public security or public health. Secondly, they lay down procedural safeguards which must be followed by the relevant authorities when they are seeking to exclude non-nationals on one of the permitted grounds.

25.2.1 Scope of provisions

'Measures' taken on the grounds of public policy, public security or public health were defined in *Bouchereau* as any action affecting the rights of persons coming within the field of application of Article 45 TFEU to enter and reside freely in a Member State on the same conditions as apply to nationals of the host state.

25.2.2 Who benefits?

The CRD applies to EU citizens and their family members; their status as employed or self-employed or otherwise satisfying tests of economic sufficiency is *irrelevant*. It applies, however, only to restrictions on the *movement* and *residence* of *natural* persons. The general exceptions on the basis of public policy, public security and public health do not allow for discrimination as regards access to or conditions of employment. Access to employment and social rights will be subject to the derogation provided under Article 3 of Regulation 492/2011 (linguistic knowledge) or Article 45(4) TFEU (public services) or Article 51 TFEU (activities connected with official authority) or non-discriminatory rules in the public interest. Whilst the underlying Treaty provisions may be relied on by legal persons, the CRD, as it covers citizens and their family members, does not apply to legal persons.

The CRD does not apply to TCNs (save those of EEA countries), except to the extent that they formed part of a migrant EU national's family. We will see in Chapter 26 the steps that the institutions have taken to protect the rights of TCNs, especially those that are long-term residents in the EU.

25.2.3 Relationship with Treaty provisions

The grounds of derogation in the CRD are the same as those in Articles 45 and 52 TFEU. To a large extent these provisions may carry the same meaning, and the Court has used decisions under the Treaty provisions to elucidate the meaning of the provisions in the CRD—and vice versa. There are some differences, however. Notably the Treaty provisions apply to a wider group of persons (see 25.2.2) and to the exercise of economic rights (see Chapter 22), as well as access to the territory. This may mean that a straight transfer of jurisprudence may not be appropriate in all circumstances. For example, interpretations of the concept of public policy delivered under Directive 64/221, and now the CRD, which relate to the personal factors justifying discrimination, will not necessarily be appropriate to the public-policy exception applicable to undertakings under Article 52 TFEU. This has not always been recognised by the Court, which has tended to interpret Article 52 TFEU by reference to cases decided under Directive 64/221 (see, eg, Advocate-General Mancini's opinion and the Court's judgment in *Bond van Adverteerders* noted in Chapter 22). Similar problems have arisen in the context of individuals' rights to receive healthcare in other Member States in which the Member State has sought to raise public health—that is, the provision of a public healthcare system—as a justification. This is a different aspect of public health from that envisaged in either Directive 64/221 or the CRD. Nonetheless, it is possible for the underlying Treaty provisions to be relied on where the situation falls outside the scope of the CRD, as cross-border medical-care cases illustrate (*Smits and Peerboom*, discussed in Chapter 24).

25.2.4 Enforcement

Directive 64/221 provided a source of substantive and procedural rights for individuals, since all its main provisions were directly effective. Similarly, the relevant provisions in the CRD are also directly effective.

25.3 Substantive grounds for derogation

25.3.1 Public policy

The meaning and scope of the public-policy derogation was originally not clear but nonetheless potentially broad. In *Van Duyn* the Court held, on a reference from the English High Court, that the concept of public policy must be interpreted strictly; its scope cannot be determined unilaterally by Member States without being subject to control by the institutions of the Union. However, the Court conceded that the concept of public policy must vary from state to state; states must have an area of discretion within the limits defined by the Treaty.

As the European integration project progressed, Member States' individual areas of discretion became narrower, a process which seems to have continued in the terms of the CRD. This narrowing process can be seen even quite early on in the CJ's jurisprudence in the rather stricter view in *Roland Rutili v Ministre de l'Intérieur* (case 36/75). The case related to a legal action by Rutili, an Italian and a noted political agitator, to annul a decision from the minister which restricted his activities to certain regions of France. The Court held that restrictions cannot be imposed on the right of a national of a Member State to enter the territory of another Member State, to stay there and to move within it unless his presence constitutes a *genuine and sufficiently serious threat to public policy*. This principle, the Court added, was an embodiment of the principles contained in the ECHR that no restrictions in the interests of national security or public safety shall be placed on the rights secured by Articles 8–11 ECHR other than such as are *necessary* for the protection of those interests in a democratic society. All restrictions are subject to the proportionality principle.

The concept was narrowed even further in *R v Bouchereau* (case 30/77) where the Court added that the concept of public policy must always presuppose a genuine and sufficiently serious threat to the requirements of public policy *affecting one of the fundamental interests of society*. This case law has now been embodied in the CRD. In particular, Article 27(2) states that the conduct of the individual which forms the basis of a public-policy derogation 'must represent a genuine, present and sufficiently serious threat affecting one of the fundamental interests of society'. This test intro-duces the requirement that there must be a present, or current threat, rather than a threat that has ceased to be (see, eg, *Donatella Calfa* (case C-348/96), discussed at 25.4) or that might arise in the future. This temporal element resurfaces in the case law on spent convictions and in the discussion of 'personal conduct' (see 25.4). The threat must arise in addition to the perturbation of the social order that any infringement of the law involves.

In the early case law, it seemed that behaviour did not have to be illegal to be considered as falling within the public-policy derogation. This can be seen in the context of the well-known *Van Duyn* case.

Van Duyn

Ms Van Duyn, a Dutch national, was refused entry into the UK on the grounds of public policy. She was seeking to enter the UK to take up employment with the Church of Scientology. The practice of scientology was not illegal in the UK but it was regarded as socially undesirable. The refusal was claimed to be on the basis of her personal conduct.

Two questions were referred to the CJ. First, can membership of an organisation count as 'personal conduct' within the meaning of Article 3(1) Directive 64/221? This point is discussed at 25.4. Secondly, if it can, must such conduct be illegal in order to provide grounds for exclusion on public policy grounds? With regard to the second question, the Court held that the conduct does not have to be illegal to justify exclusion of non-nationals, as long as the state has made it clear that it considers the activities in question to be 'socially harmful', and has taken administrative measures to counteract the activities.

Van Duyn must now be read in the light of the more restrictive test advanced in *Bouchereau*; the activities in question must be sufficiently socially harmful to pose a genuine and sufficiently serious threat to the requirements of public policy affecting one of the fundamental interests of society.

The kind of evidence needed to prove that a particular activity is considered by the state to be sufficiently harmful to justify exclusion on the grounds of public policy was considered by the CJ, in the context of many questions referred by the Liège District Court, in the case of *Adoui and Cornuaille v Belgium* (cases 115 and 116/81). The case concerned two prostitutes who were appealing against the Belgian authorities' refusal to grant them a residence permit in Belgium, where they were seeking to practise their arts. The Court held that Member States could not deny residence to non-nationals by reason of conduct that, when attributable to a state's own nationals, did not give rise to repressive measures or other genuine and effective measures to combat such conduct. Evidence of measures of this nature will have to be adduced to prove that the public-policy justification is genuine.

The CRD lays down a number of circumstances in which measures taken on the grounds of public policy or public security will *not* be justified:

(1) They 'shall not be invoked to serve economic ends' (Article 27(1)). Here the Directive makes explicit what was found to be implicit in cases under the derogating Treaty provisions, such as Article 36 TFEU, in the context of goods. To allow an economic justification would clearly run counter to the fundamental aims of the Treaty;

(2) 'Previous criminal convictions shall not *in themselves* constitute grounds for the taking of such measures' (Article 27(2), emphasis added). Thus under certain circumstances past criminal convictions may constitute sufficient grounds, but they will not necessarily do so. (See *Bouchereau* and *Calfa*, discussed at 25.4.) Certainly automatic deportation would seem unacceptable (see opinion of Advocate-General in the *expulsion on criminal conviction case*). Article 27(3) allows a host Member State to check the criminal record of a migrant EU citizen for the purposes of assessing whether an individual might constitute a threat, but the provision specifically states that a Member State cannot make such checks automatically;

(3) The expiry of the identity card or passport used by the person concerned to enter the host country and to obtain a residence permit does not justify expulsion from the host Member State (Article 15(2)). As was noted in *Royer*, the right of residence does not depend on the possession of a residence permit, it merely provides proof of such a right, which derives from the Treaty itself. The same principle applies to identity cards and passports. As was established in *Watson*, a state may impose penalties for failure to comply with administrative formalities, provided the penalties are not disproportionate, but a failure to comply with such formalities can never provide grounds for deportation. (See also *Wijsenbeek*, discussed in Chapter 21.)

It seems that the 'genuine and sufficiently serious threat' test for the use of the public-policy derogation used in respect of cases provided now under the CRD has also been applied in the context of Article 52 TFEU with regard to legal persons. For example, in *Commission v UK (open skies)* (case C-466/98), concerning the refusal to grant an operating licence to an airline on the basis that it constituted a threat to public policy, the CJ applied the *Bouchereau* test. A similar tendency can be seen in relation to the other freedoms.

25.3.2 **Public security**

Although public security has long been identified as a separate head of derogation, there has been little specific discussion of this term; it tends to be considered with public policy. The boundary between public policy and public security came before the Court in *Land Baden-Wurttemberg v Panagiotis Tsakouridis* (case C-145/09). The case concerned a Greek national, Tsakouridis, who was born in Germany but who lost the right to reside there after ten years of residence. He was convicted for a substantial role in narcotics trafficking. The Court noted that matters relating to foreign relations or to military interests may be considered as a matter of public security. In doing so, the Court drew on case law relating to free movement of goods (eg, *Campus Oil*). The Court continued to say that public security was not limited to these interests but could include internal matters such as serious crime. Nevertheless it was for the national court to assess the facts in each case. If the level of severity required to constitute a threat to public security was not shown, the issue could still be considered as a matter of public policy. This distinction becomes important in the light of new procedural guarantees introduced by the CRD (see 25.5.2.3).

The CJ ruled in *PI v Oberburgermeisterin der Stadt Remscheid* (case C-348/09) that the national court enjoys wide discretionary powers under Article 28(3)(a) CRD. Pursuant to this provision, the Member States can consider criminal offences in relation to sexual exploitation of children as something which falls under the derogation of public security. Sexual exploitation of children can constitute a particularly serious threat to one of the fundamental interests of the society as long as the manner in which such offence was committed illustrated particularly serious characteristics. The seriousness of each case is something that can only be examined by the national court, which is the most competent authority to assess whether there is a threat that affects the fundamental interests protected by the society. However, any expulsion measure must respect the principle of proportionality and the host Member State is under an obligation to examine issues such as how long the individual concerned had resided on its territory, his/her state of health, socio-economic situation and issues regarding whether there is sufficient integration into the host society.

Finally, according to Article 27(2), and in the same way as for public policy, measures to protect public security must be based on the individual conduct of the person concerned. Individual conduct is discussed at 25.4. The limitations identified at 25.3.1(1)–(3) in relation to public policy apply also to public security in terms of the procedural guarantees available.

25.3.3 **Public health**

Article 29(1) CRD specifies that the only diseases justifying measures restricting freedom of movement are those 'with epidemic potential as defined by the relevant instruments of the World Health Organisation', as well as other infectious diseases or contagious parasitic diseases provided they are the subject of protection provisions applying to nationals of the host Member State. This is a narrower list than applied under the previous Directive. In its earlier communication (COM(1999) 372), the Commission made the point that all the institutions have clearly stated that the free movement of persons with HIV/AIDS must be safeguarded. Further diseases occurring after a three-month period from the date of arrival cannot constitute grounds for expulsion. There is therefore a distinction between the public-health justification for expulsion and those based on public policy or public security, in that the latter two categories can be relied on at any point during the migrant's stay in the host Member State; whilst reliance on the public-health derogation is limited in time. Again, the host Member State has the right to investigate migrants, this time by requesting an individual to undergo a free medical examination. Such an examination cannot be required as a matter of course.

As suggested at 25.2.3, the scope of public health under the Treaty provisions is somewhat broader than the terms of the CRD, being developed in parallel with the derogation in relation to goods, Article 34 TFEU (see, eg, *Kohll*). In addition to personal health, it includes protection against risks to public health and also arguments based on the need to provide a functioning health service (see Chapter 24).

25.4 **Personal conduct**

Measures taken on the grounds of public policy or public security must be based *exclusively* on the *personal conduct* of the individual concerned (Article 27(2)). This provision reflects the terms of Directive 64/221, Article 3(1), which it replaced; the case law under the old provision would seem to be relevant to our understanding of Article 27(2) CRD.

The CJ has distinguished between past and present association; past association cannot count as personal conduct; present association, being a voluntary act of the person concerned, can. Thus, resignation from a group considered undesirable or illegal would, in the absence of other evidence, suggest that such membership can no longer be taken into account by the relevant authorities. This approach would match the approach taken with regard to criminal convictions. As we have already seen at 25.3.1, Article 27(2) CRD expressly provides that previous criminal convictions shall not in themselves constitute grounds for measures taken on public-policy grounds. The same principle applies to current criminal convictions. This approach was confirmed in *Bonsignore v Oberstadtdirektor of the City of Cologne* (case 67/74).

Bonsignore

Here, Bonsignore, an Italian worker living in Germany, bought a pistol in breach of German firearms law, and accidentally shot his brother. The action against his brother carried no punishment, but he was fined for unlawful possession of a firearm, and his deportation was ordered. The German authorities argued that his deportation was necessary as a general preventive measure to deter other immigrants from committing similar offences. The CJ rejected this argument, holding that the concept of personal conduct expresses the requirement that a deportation order may only be made for breaches of the peace and public security that might be committed by the individual concerned. Thus deportation could not be based on reasons of a general preventive nature.

The above-mentioned principle now finds expression in the CRD. The second paragraph of Article 27(2) provides that justifications which 'are isolated from the particulars of the case or that rely on considerations of general prevention shall not be accepted'.

It should be noted that certain circumstances do permit Member States to take general preventative measures, notably measures connected with gatherings attended by large numbers of people, especially when the people come from different Member States. In its communication, the Commission suggests examples of such events: large sports events, rock concerts and political demonstrations.

The conduct in *Bouchereau* was more serious than in *Bonsignore*.

Bouchereau

The case concerned a French national who took up employment in the UK in 1975. In June 1976 he was found guilty of unlawful possession of drugs. He had already pleaded guilty to a similar offence in January 1976, and had received a 12-month conditional discharge. In June 1976 the court (Marlborough Street Magistrates) wished to make a deportation order against him. He claimed this was contrary to Article 45 TFEU and then Directive 64/221.

One of the questions referred to the CJ concerned Article 3(2) Directive 64/221 (which is replicated in Article 27(2) CRD) and 'previous criminal convictions'. If 'previous criminal convictions' could not 'in themselves' constitute grounds for exclusion, when could they be taken into account? Were they relevant only insofar as they manifested a propensity to act in such a manner, contrary to public policy or public security? The Court held that the existence of previous convictions could only be taken into account as evidence of personal conduct constituting a present threat to the requirements of public policy, as showing a propensity to act in the same way again. Therefore, past conduct alone *could* constitute a threat to the requirements of public policy. Thus, it would depend on the gravity of the conduct, past or present, whether it would in fact constitute a present threat to the requirements of public policy.

This point was re-emphasised in *Calfa*. The case concerned a Greek rule which automatically required the expulsion—for life—of non-nationals who had been convicted of certain offences. Calfa was an Italian tourist who was convicted of offences relating to the possession of drugs. She appealed against her sentence on the basis that it was incompatible with her right to receive services under what is now Article 56 TFEU. The CJ held that her expulsion could only be based on personal conduct *besides* the commission of the offence.

It seems that national authorities must thus look at the individual's conduct in addition to that which gave rise to the criminal offence. In any event, all rules must be proportionate, which an automatic life ban is not. Given the wording of the CRD, it would seem this approach still applies.

Article 3 Directive 64/221 precluded a national practice whereby national courts cannot take into account changes in factual circumstances when reviewing a decision to deport, especially where there has been a lengthy delay. The requirements of personal conduct and 'present threat' are not satisfied (*Oliveri v Land baden-Württemberg* (case C-482/01). Interestingly, this case was brought as a matter of interpretation of Article 3 Directive 64/221, rather than under the procedural provisions (discussed at 25.6.3). Given that the CRD which replaced it also refers to personal conduct and incorporates the test of a present threat, a similar interpretation applies to that provision too.

The requirement of 'personal conduct' has implications for the Schengen implementation system (see further Chapter 26). The Commission brought an action against Spain (the *Schengen Information System* case) for refusing entry to two TCNs, both of whom were married to migrant EU nationals. Spain refused entry automatically on the basis of information in the Schengen Information System entered by the German authorities. The CJ held that, in the case of a migrant EU national's family member, a Member State must check the threat posed by the individual in the light of the *Bouchereau* test.

Since a denial of residence must be based exclusively on personal conduct, it follows that a worker who is entitled to residence cannot be refused entry or deported merely because the worker is involuntarily unemployed or unable to work through incapacity, even if the worker becomes a charge on public funds (see *Lubbersen v Secretary of State for the Home Department* [1984] 3 CMLR 77, Immigration Appeal Tribunal). The same applies to the worker's family. This accords with what was Directive 68/360 (see now Article 7(3) CRD and discussion in Chapter 21).

25.5 Types of measure

The original Directive was silent as to the type of 'measure' that individual Member States would be permitted to take against foreign nationals. There are a range of options, for example registration requirements, though it would seem the most likely would be refusal of entry or expulsion. Case law has developed limitations in respect of both geographical and temporal considerations, driven by the concept of proportionality and, more recently, citizenship.

25.5.1 Partial restrictions

It was originally thought, following the *Rutili* decision that the derogation operated only to justify a total ban on residence in a Member State rather than partial restrictions on the right of residence. Unsurprisingly, this ruling came in for a certain amount of criticism as an unnecessary restriction on Articles 45(3) and 52 TFEU. The derogation exists precisely in order to enable Member States to discriminate against non-nationals on limited and specific grounds. As the CJ pointed out in *Van Duyn*, it is a principle of international law that states cannot deny rights of residence to their own nationals. To require a total ban where a partial ban would suffice is surely to impose on non-nationals greater restrictions than are necessary to protect the particular interest concerned. This issue was revisited in *Olazabal* in which the CJ reviewed its ruling in *Rutili*. In contrast to Olazabal, who had been convicted of offences related to terrorism, Rutili was subject to restrictions because of political and trades-union activities. In *Rutili*, the national referring court had not been sure that national law allowed the adoption of the national measure in question. In *Olazabal*, the national court was clear that Olazabal's activities were of such a serious nature that they justified his deportation. The CJ concluded that a Member State would not be precluded from imposing limitations on the right to residence within the territory of that Member State provided that:

- such action is justified by reasons of public order or public security based on the individual's conduct;
- the only alternative course of action, given the seriousness of that conduct, would consist of a measure prohibiting the individual from residing in the whole of the national territory;
- the conduct which the Member State concerned wishes to prevent gives rise, in the case of its own nationals, to genuine and effective measures designed to combat it (para 45).

This approach is now reflected in Article 22 CRD which provides that limitations may only be imposed on migrants where the same restrictions apply to the Member State's own nationals.

25.5.2 Expulsion

There are two main problems in this area: expulsion in addition to a criminal penalty; and life-long bans. Case law has sought to limit the Member States' power in such circumstances by use of the doctrine of proportionality and by reading the relevant provisions in the light of the requirements of citizenship. This approach in now incorporated into the CRD.

25.5.2.1 Expulsion in addition to a criminal penalty

Bonsignore indicates that deportation cannot be required in addition to a criminal penalty as a matter of course; this would offend against the requirement of personal conduct and, as in the case of *Calfa*, proportionality. Additionally, there are procedural rights concerning the requirement of temporal proximity between the decision to deport and the deportation itself (see 25.4). These concerns now find their expression in Article 33 CRD.

25.5.2.2 Permanent exclusion

If a Member State has grounds for restricting the right of free movement, this does not mean that it can permanently exclude someone. Such an approach could, as we have seen in *Calfa*, be disproportionate. Article 27(2) CRD specifies that any measures shall be proportionate and Article 32 gives the right to apply for the lifting of an exclusion order where there has been a material change in circumstances.

25.5.2.3 Protection against expulsion

An innovation introduced by the CRD is Article 28 which imposes limitations on a Member State's freedom to expel an EU national. Article 28(1) provides that in deciding whether or not to expel an individual, a Member State must take into account factors such as how long the individual has resided on its territory, the age of the person concerned, state of health, family and economic situation, as well as the links with the country of origin. These conditions are the types of consideration that the CJ has highlighted as being required by respect for family life under Article 8 ECHR (see *Orfanopoulos*, citing *Boultif v Switzerland*). Many of these factors reflect a graduated level of protection awarded to migrants, based on their level of integration into the host Member State, which we also see in Chapter 24 regarding citizenship rights.

Article 28 then goes on to identify three specific circumstances: the position of those who have a right of permanent residence (Article 28(2)); those who have resided in the host Member State for the previous ten years (Article 28(3)(a)); and minors (Article 28(3)(b)). For those falling within the scope of Article 28(2), Member States may only take an expulsion decision on serious grounds of public policy or public security. For the other two categories in Article 28(3), an expulsion decision may only be made on 'imperative grounds of public security'; seemingly public policy will not justify such a decision. The use of the words 'imperative grounds' in Article 28(3) mean that a stricter test should be used than in relation to the 'serious grounds' referred to in Article 28(2). Recital 24 CRD indicates that Article 28(3) may be used in only 'exceptional circumstances'. The Court had to determine the meaning of Article 28(3) in *Tsakouridis*. There it held that this test requires not only the existence of a threat to public security (see 25.3.2) but also 'that such a threat is of a particularly high degree of seriousness' (para 44). Any such assessment must be based on the facts of the case and cannot be an automatic consequence of a prison sentence of a specified severity (see 25.4). In *Tsakouridis* it suggested that organised drug trafficking frequently involves transnational elements and 'could reach a level of intensity that might directly threaten the calm and physical security of the population as a whole or a large part of it' (para 47). In *PI*, the Court clarified that it was not just organised crime which can pose a 'direct threat to the calm and physical security of the population', but also severe individual crimes—here repeated sexual abuse of a child by a person in a position of trust.

25.6 Procedural rights

The CRD provides extensive procedural safeguards for parties seeking to assert rights of entry or residence in Member States, based on the provisions in Directive 64/221. Any decision issued in violation of these rights may be challenged as contrary to EU law.

25.6.1 Temporary residence

Directive 64/221 specified that:

> a person awaiting a decision to grant or refuse a first residence permit in a Member State must be allowed to remain temporarily in that state pending that decision. The decision must be taken as soon as possible and not more than six months from the date of application [Article 5(1)].

Given that Union citizens no longer have to apply for a residence permit, there is no equivalent provision in the CRD. Instead, Article 30(3) requires the Member State to specify the time limit within which a person must leave the territory, which save in cases of emergency (duly substantiated) may not be less than one month, and Article 31(2) provides that, where an individual appeals and applies for a suspension of the removal order, such a person will not be required to remove themselves from the territory whilst the matter is pending, save in limited, specified circumstances. By contrast to Directive 64/221 (Article 7), there are no specific time limits contained in the CRD.

25.6.2 Reasons for decisions

The person concerned shall be informed in writing of any decision made under Article 27, in a manner so that he or she is able to understand not only the decision but its implications. Further, the person must be informed, precisely and in full, of the grounds of public policy, public security or public health upon which the decision taken in his or her case is based, unless this is contrary to the interests of the security of the state (Article 30). Any notification must inform the person of where, when and how an appeal may be lodged (Article 30(3)).

The CRD seems to have incorporated the jurisprudence of the CJ in cases such as *Rutili*. The Court held in *Rutili* that the authority making the decision must give the applicant a precise and comprehensive statement of the ground for the decision, to enable the applicant to take effective steps to prepare his or her defence. The Commission in its communication made the point that the duty to give reasons applies also to decisions regarding the applications for visas by family members who are TCNs.

25.6.3 Remedies: rights of defence

The CRD amends the format of the rights of the defence. Directive 64/221 provided for a right of access to remedies by comparison with the position of nationals of the host Member State (Article 8), but then also provided a minimum guarantee that a decision to deport must be reviewed by a competent authority (Article 9). A certain amount of case law arose about the scope and interrelationship of the two provisions, which may be of historic interest only given the changes introduced by the CRD. Article 31 CRD provides:

> The persons concerned shall have access to judicial and, where appropriate, administrative redress procedures in the host Member State to appeal against or seek review of any decision taken against them on the grounds of public policy, public security or public health.

The phraseology represents a change in that individuals under the new system are given a right of access to a judicial remedy and possibly an administrative remedy. The matter is not one of comparison, as under former Article 8, nor of merely showing that a competent authority has reviewed the decision.

Although the terms of the two sets of provisions are different, a number of points from the case law on the old system might well be applicable to the new. Note that neither system specified the precise nature of the remedies to be available; this is consonant with the principle of national procedural autonomy (see Chapter 8). The CJ noted, in relation to Article 9, Directive 64/221, that the provisions incorporated the minimum requirements of natural justice. According to the CJ, they therefore called for a broad interpretation. Whether a review of the case law truly reveals a high level of protection or not, this principle would seem to apply to Article 31 CRD.

In *Royer*, the CJ held that Member States could not execute a deportation order without giving the migrant the chance to avail himself of the right to the remedy granted under Article 8 Directive 64/221. The substance of the CRD reflects this. Not only should a Member State not normally allow less than a month for an individual to leave (Article 30(3)), but Article 31(2) allows for an individual to remain on the territory pending the outcome of the appeal, subject to certain specified exceptions (see also Article 31(4)).

There were two aspects to the case law on Article 9 Directive 64/221: the class of people to whom it applied; and the scope of the rights granted.

The CJ had to consider the question of the beneficiaries of procedural rights in *MRAX*.

MRAX

In this case, the Belgian government argued that Article 9 did not apply to the TCNs who were members of a migrant worker's family, but who had entered the host Member State illegally. Given the importance of Directive 64/221, and particularly these procedural articles, for guaranteeing the rights set out in Article 6 and 13 ECHR, however, the CJ held that the illegality of their original entry to the host Member State could not deprive these individuals of the protection granted by Article 9.

As the CJ pointed out, to require an individual to be in possession of a valid identity document or visa would rob the procedural guarantees of much of their effectiveness. A similar argument could be made in respect of the guarantees in Articles 30–1 CRD.

As regards the scope of the rights, the CJ seems also to have been influenced by the need to ensure a fair trial and the right to an effective remedy contained in the ECHR. The Court pointed out in *Rutili* that the person concerned must at the very least be able to exercise his or her rights of defence before a competent authority, which must not be the same as that which adopted the measure which restricted the person's freedom. Principles of independence must inform an assessment of the appropriateness of bodies providing redress under Article 31 CRD. This can be seen in the context of *R v Secretary of State for the Home Department, ex parte Santillo* (case 131/79).

Santillo

Santillo, an Italian national, had been convicted in the UK in relation to a number of crimes including rape, buggery and indecent assault. He was sentenced to eight years in jail, with a recommendation for deportation at the end of his sentence. Nearly five years later the Home Secretary made a deportation order against him. He applied for judicial review to annul this decision. Two issues were raised in the proceedings. First, whether the trial judge's recommendation was an 'opinion from a competent authority', as required by Article 9(1) Directive 64/221; and secondly, if so, whether a lapse of time between the issuing of this 'opinion' and the making of the order could deprive the judge's recommendation of its status as an 'opinion' under Article 9(1). The CJ, on a reference for interpretation from the English High Court, held that the trial judge's recommendation did amount to an 'opinion' within Article 9(1); but that the safeguard provided by Article 9 could only be a real one if that opinion were sufficiently proximate in time to the decision recommending deportation, to ensure that the factors justifying deportation still existed at the time when the order was made. A change of heart or political climate could mean that the public policy justification had ceased to exist.

The above-mentioned safeguard has been enacted by Article 33(2) CRD, which provides that where an expulsion order is enforced more than two years after it was issued, the Member State is under an obligation to check that the individual concerned is 'currently and genuinely a threat to public policy or public security' and to assess whether there has been any 'material change' in circumstances since the expulsion order was issued.

Like its predecessor, the CRD gives no definition of what appropriate remedies might be. Jurisprudence in respect of Article 9(2) Directive 64/221 was considered in *R v Secretary of State for the Home Department, ex parte Gallagher* (case C-175/94), with particular reference to what could constitute a competent authority and the scope of the information regarding the appeal body that was required to be given to the applicant.

Gallagher

Gallagher had been convicted in Ireland for the possession of rifles for unlawful purposes. He subsequently went to the UK and took up employment there. He was arrested and deported. On arrival in Ireland he challenged the deportation decision as unlawful, and was interviewed in Dublin. His interviewer gave no name and no information concerning the grounds for his expulsion. At his request his case was reconsidered by the Home Secretary, but the deportation decision was not reversed. The CJ found that the matter fell within Article 9(2), but did not specify how the competent authority should be appointed, nor what its composition should be. It was nonetheless essential that it should be independent of the authority empowered to take the measure concerning deportation, and that the person concerned should be able to submit his or her defence. There was no need to notify the claimant of the identity of the authority as long as the national court was in a position to determine whether it was impartial. These questions were left to the national court to decide.

Although one might suggest the level of protection awarded in *Gallagher* was low and perhaps driven by political sensitivities, the underlying principles regarding independence and impartiality as touchstones for determining whether procedural safeguards have been satisfied must remain. Article 31(3) further specifies the scope of the jurisdiction of the appeal bodies. It provides that:

the redress procedures shall allow for an examination of the legality of the decision, as well as of the facts and circumstances on which the proposed measure is based. They shall ensure that the decision is not disproportionate, particularly in view of the requirements laid down in Article 28.

It seems, following *R v Secretary of State for the Home Department, ex parte Shingara* (cases C-65 and 111/95), that where an individual who has been refused admission to a Member State, reapplies for admission to a country after a reasonable length of time (in *Shingara* approximately three years), the procedural safeguards replacing these in Articles 8–9 Directive 64/221 would apply anew to that reapplication. Individuals expressly have the right to apply to have exclusion orders lifted under Article 32. It is submitted that following the *Shingara* reasoning, they too would benefit from procedural rights, although Article 32(2) states that such persons do not have the right of entry to the territory of a Member State while their application is being considered.

25.7 Non-discriminatory measures

As we have seen in 22.6, the court introduced the possibility of justifying non-discriminatory rules in the public interest in relation to workers, establishment and services. These have mainly applied to national rules affecting economic rights, though in principle can be used in relation to the other rights (access to the territory and social rights too). As with the rule of reason for the free movement of goods, the category of justifications is not closed (see Box 25.1), though this must now be understood against the Services Directive (see 22.8) and specifically Article 16 thereof. This provision limits the grounds of derogation to public policy, public security, public health or the environment to services which fall within the scope of the Directive. Case law remains unchanged for services excluded from the Directive, for the establishment and for workers.

Box 25.1 Examples of 'Overriding Reasons Relating to the Public Interest'

- financial equilibrium of the social security system
- combatting fraud
- intellectual property
- cultural policy objectives
- See also: Article 4(8) Services Directive and sport (*Bosman*).

The position regarding the protection of intellectual property rights is interesting, as the derogation provision in Article 52 TFEU does not refer to the protection of industrial property, unlike Article 36 TFEU. The Court has nonetheless held that indistinctly applicable measures can justify intellectual property rights that might otherwise conflict with the operation of Article 56 TFEU (*Coditel; Collins v Imtrat* (case C-92/92)). In *Coditel*, Belgian cable companies were picking up German terrestrial television transmissions of programmes and rebroadcasting them; the doctrine of exhaustion did not apply. The ruling in *Coditel* has been challenged in a reference to the CJ in *Murphy*.

Murphy

The case concerned the right of pub landlords in the UK to subscribe to Greek satellite-television services broadcasting English football matches despite the attempts of Sky (the company in the UK with the right to broadcast the matches) to prevent them. Questions were referred not only on the scope of Article 56 TFEU, but also on the competition provisions. The judgment in *Murphy* was long and dealt with a range of complex issues relating to the directives (partially) harmonising copyright. The Court determined that while national legal orders might protect media rights, it could not place the rights holders in a position to extort the maximum fee possible through partitioning the market. There was a difference between the existence of the right, which could be protected, and its exercise which could be constrained to the specific subject matter of the right protected.

In this there are parallels with the approach adopted in respect of goods. Note also that many questions related to copyright will be dealt with under the Information Society Directive (Directive 2001/29 ([2001] OJ L167/10)).

25.8 A rule of reason?

As in the case of free movement of goods, the CJ seems to have felt the need to balance a broad Union competence to review national legislation with the possibility for Member States to justify their national rules. This is particularly important with regard to the training and educational backgrounds of those seeking employment or to trade in another Member States, as the requirements in the Member States are not uniform. Both Article 49 and Article 56 TFEU recognised the need for Member States to limit the right of individuals and legal persons to trade. The right to equality of opportunity provided by Articles 49(2) can only be exercised 'under the conditions laid down for its own nationals by the law of the country where such establishment is effected'. Article 57, para 3 TFEU, likewise provides in relation to services that it can only be exercised 'under the same conditions as are imposed by that State on its own nationals'. Even within Regulation 492/2011 we can find recognition of this point: an employer may require a non-national to undergo a vocational test provided he expressly requests this when making his offer of employment (Article 6(2)). This provision may not, however, be used as a means of covert discrimination.

These types of rule are likely to be caught by Articles 49 and 56 TFEU, even prior to *Säger*. Equally, striking such measures down would be unlikely to be in the public interest. The CJ seemed aware of the problem even in the relatively early jurisprudence. In *van Binsbergen* it was acknowledged, in the context of a challenge to a residence requirement imposed by the Dutch Bar on those seeking to provide certain legal services in Holland, that specific requirements imposed on a person providing services would not infringe Articles 56 and 57 TFEU where they have as their purpose the application of professional rules justified by the general good—in particular, rules relating to organisation, ethics, qualifications, supervision and liability, which are binding on any person established in the territory of the Member State in which the service is provided. The person providing the service cannot take advantage of his right to provide services to avoid the professional rules of conduct which would be applied to him if he were established in that state.

Professional rules, which inhibit the free provision of services would only be permissible if they were:

- non-discriminatory;
- objectively justified;
- not disproportionate.

These principles were subsequently applied in *Webb* (case 279/80) in the context of the provision of manpower services. The Court added in *Webb* that, in ascertaining whether its own rules are justified, the host Member State must take into account the justifications and safeguards already provided by the applicant in order to pursue the activity in question in his state of establishment (approved in *Commission v Germany (lawyers' services)* (case 427/85)).

The principles expressed in *van Binsbergen* and *Webb* were refined and developed in 1986 in the 'insurance' cases (the *insurance services* case; *Commission v Ireland (co-insurance services)* (case 206/84); *Commission v France* (case 220/83); *Commission v Denmark (insurance services)* (case 252/83)). These actions were based on alleged infringements of Articles 56 and 57 TFEU and Insurance Directive 78/473 by the defendant Member States in their rules regulating the provision of insurance services. The rules and the breaches alleged in each state were similar.

Effectively, the imposition of the rules of the host Member State meant that cross-border service providers were subject to regulation more than once. Because of this, the Court held that not *all* the legislation applicable to nationals or those engaged in permanent activities could be applied to the *temporary* activities of enterprises established in another Member State. It could be applied only if three criteria were satisfied:

- it is justified by imperative reasons relating to the public interest;
- the public interest is not already protected by the rules of the state of establishment;
- the same result cannot be obtained by less restrictive means.

Thus, in the field of services, the Court moved towards a test for professional rules not unlike the *Cassis de Dijon* test applied to goods (see Chapters 18 and 19). As with that test, it is likely that the criteria will be strictly applied to ensure that each rule is necessary and genuinely justified. If not, it will breach Articles 56 and 57 TFEU. In the German *insurance services* case the Court found that the establishment requirement was not justified; indeed, it was the very negation of the freedom to provide services and would only be permissible if indispensable. The authorisation requirement, on the other hand, at least as related to the rules concerning technical reserves, might be justified for the protection of policyholders and insured persons. The Commission's action failed in this respect. Applying the same approach in *Commission v Luxembourg* (case C-351/90) the Court found that a 'single surgery' rule applied in Luxembourg, the effect of which was to prohibit doctors, dentists and veterinary surgeons established outside Luxembourg from opening surgeries in Luxembourg, was not justified, as was argued, in the interest of good professional practice (to ensure proximity to patients). Such a general prohibition (which in any case was applied more strictly to professionals established in other Member States) was found to be 'unduly restrictive', 'too absolute and too general'.

A similar approach can be seen with regard to establishment. As we have seen, *Gebhard* (discussed in Chapter 22), introduced what might be called a 'rule of reason'. Thus, national rules which aim at a legitimate objective will not be struck down under Article 49 TFEU if they satisfy a four-stage test:

- they apply in a non-discriminatory manner;
- they are justified by overriding reasons in the general interest;
- they are suitable for obtaining that objective;
- they do not go beyond what is necessary to attain that objective.

This test, or the last three elements of it, is sometimes referred to as a proportionality test. It is important to emphasise that it is a cumulative test; all elements must be satisfied for a national rule which falls within the *Gebhard* test to be protected. Although the possible categories of justification are not closed (by contrast to those listed in the Treaty), the scope of this rule is, as in other areas, limited in practice by the rigour of the proportionality review.

It should be noted that there seems to be a necessary distinction between the necessity and proportionality assessments under services by comparison with establishment (and possibly workers), as the presumption of home Member State control is greater in the context of the provision of services, which are often seen as temporary; double regulation is less easily justified. Note now, however, the impact of the Article 16 Services Directive, which introduces the principle of country-of-origin regulation, with very limited grounds for derogation. These latter are narrower than the public-interest grounds recognised under the rule of reason by the CJ. Whilst the case law with regard to workers is more often focused on personal rights, there is no reason to suppose that in terms of measures applying without distinction the CJ would not take a similar approach. In this context, there would be a similar distinction between the considerations taken into account in the proportionality assessment between workers and services as with establishment and services.

25.8.1 Boundary between discriminatory measures and those that apply without distinction

The case law so far suggests that we have a model which distinguishes between (directly) discriminatory rules on the one hand and those that apply without distinction (including indirectly discriminatory rules) on the other. The consequence of this distinction is felt in the way the rules may be justified: discriminatory rules may only be justified by grounds specified in the Treaty; the others may be justified on broader grounds of public interest under a 'rule of reason'.

One problem in this area is the distinction between discriminatory measures and those which apply without distinction. There are two elements to this problem. First, it has been suggested that the CJ has not always been clear as to whether measures are discriminatory or not. Secondly, this problem may be exacerbated by the use of an obstacle-based test rather than one that looks at the notion of discrimination, whether direct or indirect, as the CJ no longer has to consider the distinction in its analysis.

We can see this problem with regard to residence requirements. As the CJ has argued, a residence requirement is indirectly discriminatory because it 'is liable to operate mainly to the detriment of nationals of other Member States, since non-residents are in the majority of cases foreigners' (see, eg, the *museum entry* case, para 14). Indirect discrimination can be justified objectively. This approach has been taken in other cases too (eg *Sotgiu*). In the earlier case of *Gouda v Commissariaat voor de Media* (case C-288/89), however, the CJ held that Article 56 TFEU catches 'discrimination against a person providing services on the grounds of his nationality or the fact that he is established in a Member State other than one in which the service is provided' (para 10). The distinction is significant because direct discrimination, as the residence requirement was seen to be in *Gouda*, can be justified only under the terms of the express Treaty derogation (*Gouda*, para 11).

To take an example, should single-surgery rules be viewed as discriminatory? In *Commission v Luxembourg* (case C-351/90), such a rule was treated as applying without distinction though it would make cross-border establishment impossible. In *Marks and Spencer*, the measure in issue could be categorised as discriminatory, as different rules applied depending on the place of establishment. Nonetheless, the CJ went on to consider the possible justifications for the rule and did not limit itself to the grounds set out in the express Treaty provisions derogating from the right of free movement. In this, we can see reflections of the difficulties encountered by the CJ in a number of cases concerning the free movement of goods, specifically in relation to rules designed to protect the environment (eg, the *walloon waste* case (Chapter 19)). In both cases, there have been suggestions from the Advocates-General that the distinction between discriminatory and non-discriminatory rules should be abandoned, but to no avail. Another area which gives rise to difficulties in this context is taxation. The tax cases involving companies can be particularly problematic because of the uncertainties surrounding the determination of the seat of the company (see 22.10). Analyses based on place of residence have become more complex in this context (contrast *Royal Bank of Scotland (RBS) v Elliniko Dimosio (Greek State)* (case C-311/97) and *Lankhorst-Hohorst GmbH v Finanzamt Steinfurt* (case C-324/00); see also *Danner* (case C-136/00)). The problem of residency and whether it should be viewed as indirectly or directly discriminatory arises in relation to social and ancillary rights too.

25.9 **Conclusions**

It can be seen that derogation from the free movement of people has common themes with the derogation from the free movement of goods. Both sets of derogation are interpreted narrowly, with Member States' actions being closely scrutinised. Further, it seems that a 'rule of reason' approach has been developed in relation to workers, services and establishment, so mirroring the approach in relation to goods. This is particularly significant in relation to legal persons, as they do not fall within the scope of the CRD.

As regards the CRD, the interpretation of personal conduct has been of great significance in limiting general actions by Member States against groups of EU migrants on the basis of their nationality. Another important aspect of the case law in this area has been the Court's interpretation of the procedural guarantees contained in the second part of the Directive, which is clearly linked with the guarantees to a fair trial contained in the ECHR (on fundamental rights in the EU, see Chapter 6). Since *Calfa*, it now seems likely that the scope of the derogations will also have to be understood in the light of the impact of European citizenship, again constraining Member States' freedom in this area. In this respect the terms of the Directive do not represent a break with past practice, but rather constitute a codification of that jurisprudence.

Further reading

Ferreira, N, 'The EU free movement of persons from a Spanish perspective: Exploring its evolution and derogations' (2013) 19 EPL 397.

Furse, M and Nash, S, 'Free movement, criminal law and fundamental rights in the European Community' [1997] JR 148.

Morano-Foadi, S and Andreadaksi, S, 'The convergence of the European legal system in the treatment of third country nationals in Europe: the ECJ and ECtHR jurisprudence' (2011) 22 EJIL 1071.

Shuibhne, NN, 'Exceptions to the Free Movement Rules' in C Barnard and S Peers (eds), *European Union Law* (Oxford University Press, 2014), Ch 16.

Van Overbeek, PM, 'Aids/HIV infection and the free movement of persons in the European Economic Community' (1990) 27 CML Rev 791.

Woods, L, *Free Movement of Goods and Services within the European Community* (Ashgate, 2004), Ch 12.

26 The Area of Freedom, Security and Justice: EU justice and home affairs law and policy

26.1 Introduction

The European Union's stated goal for its activities in relation to home affairs is the creation of an 'area of freedom, security and justice' (AFSJ) in Europe. The AFSJ is the continuation and further development of the cooperation in justice and home affairs (JHA) introduced by original TEU (referred to as the Treaty of Maastricht in this chapter). EU activities in this area have developed and changed significantly. Prior to the Treaty of Lisbon, AFSJ was divided between 'pillars', creating a confusing mixture of supranational and intergovernmental measures.

The Treaty of Lisbon marked a turning point both institutionally—with the consequences of 'depillarisation'—and substantively, as fundamental rights and rule of law became centre stage for the Union as a whole (Article 2 TEU) and AFSJ specifically (Article 67(1) TFEU).

This chapter will focus on the following: first, to set out the historical development of home affairs law in the Union; secondly, to give detailed consideration to the EU legislation on immigration; thirdly, to set out the legal framework and principles surrounding the Union's criminal-justice policies. Because a substantial body of law exists, asylum rules lie outside the scope of this chapter. There are also two underlying themes that will be considered. These are: first, the assessment of the degree of protection given to fundamental rights by the Union in its home-affairs policies; and secondly the consideration of the impact of the Treaty of Lisbon on the institutional structure.

26.2 Historical development

26.2.1 From JHA to AFSJ

As we have already seen, the European Union began life as a largely *economic* project. Despite the more ambitious political aims of achieving a unified Europe, the original Treaty of Rome focused upon the creation of the internal market. There were good pragmatic reasons for the narrow focus; achieving agreement on more controversial issues like policing, immigration or the administration of justice would have been difficult. Member States were also reluctant to give up their sovereign powers in such areas. As the single-market project progressed, broader issues that were closely linked to economic development, such as environmental protection and social security for workers, began to be incorporated into the Union's policymaking. In the 1980s and 1990s governments became more concerned about non-economic issues with trans-European dimensions such as organised crime, terrorism, drug-trafficking, asylum and immigration. There had been a growing degree of ad hoc collaboration between Member States in such areas, but it was only with the Treaty of Maastricht that the Union began to acquire formal legal powers in these more politically sensitive fields.

The previous rather disparate home-affairs activities of the Union were eventually grouped together by the ToA under the theme of the need to create an area of 'freedom, security and justice' within Europe. This label was an attempt to provide a grand positive vision (rather like the creation of the internal market) behind various initiatives that had been developed on a piecemeal and pragmatic basis. These ranged from common visa systems for TCNs to police cooperation in combating drug trafficking and organised crime. Post-Lisbon the role of AFSJ is highlighted in Article 3(2) TEU:

> The Union shall offer its citizens an area of freedom, security and justice without internal frontiers, in which the free movement of persons is ensured in conjunction with appropriate measures with respect to external border controls, asylum, immigration and the prevention and combating of crime.

The range of matters covered is not totally logical or complete. It represents the topics over which Member States have felt able to agree to closer cooperation. The one common thread noted by the preamble to the TEU is the need for Member States to 'facilitate the free movement of persons, while ensuring the safety and security of their peoples'. This is a reference to the link between the removal of border controls inherent in the internal market and the need to provide alternative guarantees for Member States against a range of threats. This said, the Member States have given only limited powers to the Union to achieve these goals. There is in no sense a European Union interior ministry or justice ministry with comprehensive powers over policing, criminal procedure, sentencing, prisons, immigration control and so forth.

The emphasis of policy activity within the AFSJ has been set by 'five-year plans' (see Box 26.1), agreed by the European Council (a process now recognised by Article 68 TFEU). It was suggested that each plan reflected a particular characteristic in terms of the overarching focus of policy development. Thus the first phase, in Tampere, was based on expectations and enthusiasm in a 'new' area of EU policy. The Hague plan showed a re-focusing, perhaps as a result of external events (the New York, London and Madrid bombings). In this second phase, this led to the prevalence of the security rationale which was directly reflected in the nature and priorities in The Hague Programme (November 2004), encapsulated by the 'need' to 'balance' individuals' fundamental rights with security concerns. The third phase (Stockholm and also the changes of Lisbon) suggested a further change in emphasis, towards a 'Europe of rights' as the premise upon which any security measures needed to be founded.

Box 26.1 AFSJ Five-year plans

Tampere (1999 to 2004)

The Hague (2004 to 2009)

Stockholm (2010 to 2014)

European Council 'Strategic guidelines' (2015 to 2020)

The programme identified the following as central to create and maintain '[a]n open and secure Europe serving and protecting the citizen':

- citizens' rights;
- law and justice issues;
- internal security (including counter-terrorism, law enforcement and disaster management);
- external border management and visa policy;
- migration and asylum (including integration);
- the external dimensions of freedom, security and justice.

Security and exclusion were key features of the Union agenda on migration. By the same token, there has been ongoing concern that segregation, racism and xenophobia have fuelled extremism within migrant communities in Europe. The legislative programme that has emerged since Tampere has consequently reflected a complex set of sometimes contradictory political objectives: humanitarianism; policing and public-order concerns; economic self-interest; and social or cultural integration.

26.2.2 The acquisition by the European Union of powers over home affairs

There are three stages to the development of the AFSJ, each of which affects the institutional relationship and lawmaking procedures in this field. The three stages are:

- introduction of justice and home affairs as a 'third pillar' by the Treaty of Maastricht;
- split of policy areas between 'third pillar' and former European Community introduced by the ToA;
- 'de-pillarisation' following the Treaty of Lisbon, meaning that AFSJ forms part of TFEU.

Under the Treaty of Maastricht structures, home affairs were not subject to the same degree of integration and loss of sovereignty as matters falling within the internal market. This resulted in methods of decision-making in relation to home affairs which entailed a reduced role for the more supranational institutions of Commission, CJ and European Parliament. Different forms of Union act were also introduced by the Treaty of Maastricht for use here. Power remained concentrated in the Council, the institution which reflects to a greater degree the perceived national interests of the governments of the Member States, and the field was typified by much looser intergovernmental methods than that of mainstream European law.

Following the ToA in 2004, immigration and asylum became incorporated into the 'first pillar' and thereby subject to more usual EU systems. Significantly, roles were assigned to the European Parliament and CJ, so the Commission (through the Director-General (DG) Justice, Freedom and Security) proposed legislation and the ordinary legislative procedure applied, thus giving equal power to the Parliament and Council. There is also now a European border-control agency called Frontex that supports Member State immigration control over the EU borders. By contrast, the other main area of home-affairs policy—policing and criminal justice—remained in the third pillar, and the institutional architecture in relation to policing remained more intergovernmental, so decision-making required, on the whole, unanimity.

We noted in Chapter 1 that the Treaty of Lisbon removed the pillar structure introduced by the Treaty of Maastricht. For AFSJ, this meant that the two sections of policy, dealt with post-Amsterdam within different institutional frameworks, were reunited in the TFEU. This move had consequences: the special regime for AFSJ matters under the old third pillar disappeared. Specifically, the limitations on the preliminary ruling procedure were (with an exception relating to policing decisions and maintenance of law and order—Article 276 TFEU) removed; the prohibition on third pillar measures having direct effect (formerly Article 34 TEU) were repealed (see also Chapter 5); and the legislative procedure now used is the ordinary legislative procedure in most cases. The changes which allow for greater accessibility to the CJ should improve access to justice—or at least enforcement of EU rights. Given the impact of the private individual's claim on the development of the law in other areas, this could be a significant change indeed. The changes also mean that not only is the European Parliament involved in legislation in this area, but it has the right of effective veto (see Chapter 3). Parliament also gains powers with regard to external agreements in these fields, the effect of which can be seen in the following two examples.

SWIFT Agreement

The European Parliament held up the agreement on the SWIFT banking system relating to data transfers on banking transactions to the United States for counter-terrorist purposes by rejecting the first version of the Draft Agreement on bank, as it had concerns about data protection. While this was regarded as an impressive display of power—as well as concern for citizens' rights, the European Parliament backed off: it approved the agreement at a second vote (July 2010), although virtually none of the concerns that were raised at the first vote had been addressed.

PNR Agreement

The European Parliament also delayed the finalisation of the Passenger Name Records (PNR) agreement which the EU entered into with the US which—apparently—permits US authorities to keep credit card details, home addresses and phone numbers of every passenger travelling between America and the EU for up to 15 years, allegedly to prevent terrorism and serious crime. While the European Parliament's Resolution of 5 May 2010 indicated that there were similar concerns here as there were for the SWIFT agreement, it eventually consented to the PNR agreement. Interestingly, a leaked memo (available on Statewatch website) from the European Commission legal service itself indicates that there are serious concerns about the legality of the PNR Agreement in the light of Article 16 TFEU and Article 8 EUCFR. The European Parliament later asked the CJ to rule on these issues as regards a PNR treaty between the EU and Canada (*Opinion 1/15*, pending).

26.2.3 **The need to respect fundamental rights**

One crucial theme that runs throughout the whole field of EU home affairs is that of legal accountability and protection of fundamental rights. Unlike the more economic focus of the internal market hitherto considered, the expulsion of vulnerable refugees or other TCNs, or the arrest and prosecution of suspects puts Union law into more obvious potential conflict with fundamental human rights. There are clear dangers that, in moving away from national towards supranational action, proper checks and balances on police and immigration officials may be neglected. There may be few political incentives to protect the rights of 'outsiders' such as alleged criminals or non-EU citizens. There are thus dangers that standards of human rights protection fall to the level of the 'lowest' Member State. Information may be exchanged and action taken through remote executive agencies that are not open to scrutiny. The move to supra-nationalism may also make it harder to ensure that individuals have ready access to judicial remedies that previously were clearly located in the national legal order. In short, supra-nationalism in home affairs provides much greater dangers for individual rights than almost any other area of Union policy. We have already seen (Chapter 6) that the CJ has previously recognised the risk of a protection gap and developed general principles of EU law to fill it. Thus the Court has drawn upon the ECHR, general international law norms and national constitutional traditions to protect human rights where these are threatened by the Union institutions or the Member States. These principles are of great importance in AFSJ. The change in status—following the Treaty of Lisbon—of the EUCFR, whereby the EUCFR has the same legal status as the Treaties themselves, may be important in re-emphasising the protection of rights, both substantive and procedural, with consequent constraints on state and Union power.

One further concern as regards judicial protection is the delay in obtaining decisions from the CJ where references are made to it. In cases involving individual liberty or deportation, delay may have serious consequences. In 2008 the Rules of Procedure of the CJ were amended to include an expedited urgent procedure to be used in some cases arising in relation to justice and home affairs, where people are in detention or children have been allegedly abducted. As a result such cases are heard within a few weeks. For an example see *Rinau* (case C-195/08 PPU) in which child-custody proceedings were expedited so as to avoid the child being wrongly kept from her parental guardian.

26.3 The migration of TCNs and the need for EU powers

TCNs are relatively new as subjects of mainstream EU law. Apart from the family members of EU citizen migrants who are permitted to move and reside in other Member States under the CRD (Directive 2004/38 ([2004] OJ L158/77)) (see Chapter 21) and certain country-specific agreements, EU law had very little to say about the immigration of such persons. They did not feature in the original EEC Treaty and still do not have Treaty rights as such (all their rights stem from secondary legislation). In fact, for many years, there were no powers to legislate in relation to non-EU citizens. Immigration powers over such persons, a powerful symbol of national sovereignty, were essentially reserved to Member States. However, pressure for completion of a borderless internal market had been growing since the 1980s. This required a common approach to the migration of TCNs in order to allow removal of internal border controls between Member States.

The politically sensitive nature of the issue initially meant the Union did not act, but rather, separate intergovernmental action led to the Schengen Treaty of 1985. That Treaty was followed in 1990 by the Schengen Convention that created a common short-stay visa system and permitted internal movement of TCNs across borders between participating states without border checks. As a quid pro quo, the Convention also better facilitated participating states' policing of the external border through establishing both a common database of persons who should be excluded on security grounds and agreed standards on policing the external borders so as to reduce the numbers of irregular migrants. Security was therefore a key feature of European supranational policy on migration even before the Union itself acquired powers in this field. A very detailed body of rules, institutions and procedures forming the Schengen *acquis* was set up during the 1990s. The area free of internal passport checks is still determined by Schengen, as it includes more Member States and not all Member States are part of the Schengen zone. The UK and Ireland opted out. Most new Member States have joined, save Bulgaria and Romania, whose entry has been blocked by some Schengen signatory states, Croatia and Cyprus.

Any assessment of the Union's lawmaking in this area is complex. We can identify four reasons for this complexity. First, there were already diverging national migration laws governing most of the topics that have now become part of EU law. Thus the extent to which EU law has improved on the previous position depends upon the country of comparison. Secondly, there are important international human rights conventions by which Member States are bound in this area. The most important are the 1951 Refugee Convention and 1950 ECHR. Because these were signed before the EEC Treaty, they override any contrary obligation. This is as a result of Article 351 TFEU which states that:

> rights and obligations arising from agreements concluded between one or more Member States . . . and one or more third countries shall not be affected by this Treaty.

EU migration law has attempted to comply with and implement these Treaties but there are areas of possible conflict. Thirdly, EU migration policy has been to harmonise national laws completely, but in several areas Member States resisted this. Thus, much of the Union's legislation sets minimum standards only. These reflect the lowest standards amongst the Member States' previous laws. Therefore we have three overlapping sets of rules; national, international and European Union. This means it is not always clear which rule applies in any particular case. Finally, Ireland, Denmark and the UK are only bound by measures that they opt into, pursuant to protocols annexed to the Treaty of Amsterdam. In broad terms, these three countries have opted in to some earlier measures on asylum and illegal immigration but not those giving immigration rights.

26.4 Economic migration and integration

26.4.1 Schengen

As noted, the Schengen system has an internal and external aspect. The internal aspect removes the internal borders between Schengen States. It requires a certain amount of cooperation between Member States, so the EU has established a number of information sharing systems. In addition to the system which allows exchange of information on short-stay visa applications (VIS), the main database is the Schengen Information System (SIS, replaced by SIS II), which allows Schengen States to exchange data on suspected criminals, on people who may not have the right to enter into or stay in the EU, on missing persons and on stolen, misappropriated or lost property. A separate system deals with asylum applications (EURODAC).

The Schengen provisions require Member States to remove border controls, and this obligation includes the avoidance of measures that might have an equivalent effect. Thus, Article 23 of the Schengen Borders Code (Codification Regulation 2016/399 ([2016] OJ L77/1)) deals with police checks close to the internal border and Article 24 contains the obligation for Schengen states to remove obstacles to fluid traffic flow, such as speed limitations, at road crossing-points at internal borders. According to the Commission's 2012 review (COM(2013) 326 final), the majority of case law in this field currently concerns these sorts of issues.

Exceptionally, Article 25 Schengen Borders Code permits the temporary reintroduction of borders to deal with a serious threat to public policy or internal security. In its 2012 review, the Commission gave the example of Norway reintroducing controls in respect of the Nobel Peace Prize ceremony in 2012. It is this issue of Member State responses to crises which has been the subject of reform.

The system also provides for evaluation of Member States' compliance with Schengen and its *acquis*.

The external aspect, found in the Schengen Borders Code, governs entry into the EU. It is supported by the common visa policy (the visa list: Regulation 539/2001 ([2001] OJ L81/1), and the visa code: Regulation 810/2009 ([2009] OJ L243/1)).

In its Communication on Strengthening Schengen Governance (COM(2011) 561 final), the Commission suggested the need to reform the system. There are two aspects to the reform: (1) strengthening the management of the Schengen area; (2) defining a European Union decision-making mechanism to protect the 'common interest'. Two regulations were adopted. The first, enacted using the consultation procedure, established a new EU-based Schengen evaluation mechanism to deal with critical situations. It relates to monitoring the implementation of Schengen through announced and unannounced monitoring visits. This is the first time that it will be possible for inspection teams to make unannounced visits to monitor any attempt to introduce illegal border checks at internal borders. The second—using the ordinary legislative procedure—amended the Schengen Borders Code to lay down common rules for the temporary re-imposition of checks at internal borders in exceptional cases (Regulation 610/2013 ([2013] OJ L182/1)).

The second Regulation concerns the exercise by the Member States of their rights under Schengen to allow national authorities exceptionally and temporarily to reintroduce border controls in the case of a serious threat to public policy and internal security. The amended Schengen Borders Code re-emphasises that any reintroduction of border controls at internal borders should remain an exception and should take place only as a measure of last resort, for a strictly limited scope and period of time, based on specific objective criteria and on an assessment of its necessity which should be monitored at Union level. It allows for the possibility of checks being reintroduced for 30 days, and prolonged for up to six months. Where unforeseeable events arise which require immediate action (eg, a terrorist attack), Member States could re-impose border checks unilaterally, for up to ten days. Measures would be subject to review at EU level. In practice, the powers to reintroduce border checks have been used a number of times by some Member States as a response to the perceived 'refugee crisis' starting in 2015.

26.4.2 Integration of long-term residents

One clear message from Tampere was the moral and political need to ensure that established resident migrants were given strong immigration rights to promote their integration into their host communities. Also, in terms of the internal market in labour, the Member States accepted that there should be a more level playing field with each state providing similar levels of immigration status to long-term residents. This would render each Member State equally attractive as a destination for migrant workers. The Union has, however, no power to alter national citizenship laws regarding who can become a citizen of a Member State. Thus there was no possibility of requiring Member States to naturalise long-term residents.

26.4.3 The Long-term Residents Directive

One of the first measures passed to deal with the status of resident TCNs was Directive 2003/109 on the status of long-term residents ([2004] OJ L16/44). It aims to achieve the integration of TCNs who are settled on a long-term basis in the Member States and to ensure the free movement of people within the internal market. It therefore specifies the conditions for residence permits and provides permanent residence for persons who have resided *legally* in a Member State for five years (Article 4). Certain categories of person, whose residence seems by nature temporary, are excluded from protection by Article 3(2)(e): au pairs, seasonal or posted workers and cross-border providers of services. Additionally, those whose rights of residence have been 'formally limited' are likewise excluded. The case of *Singh* concerned a permit that was tied to the occupation as a religious leader but which had been successively renewed for more than five years, but which the Dutch authorities argued had—as a result of the occupational condition—been 'formally limited'. The CJ held that this phrase must be a concept with Union meaning. While Member States have the competence to determine the terms of legal residence, it does not suffice for the purposes of Article 3(2)(e) that the Member States merely declare a residence permit to be 'formally limited'. For the CJ, the key question of whether the permit could be used as the basis of long-term residence or not; this was a question of fact in each case which would be determined by the national court.

The Directive does not provide rights of access in the first place, and the right of permanent residence is made conditional upon proving that long-term residents have stable and regular resources sufficient to maintain themselves and their family members without social assistance from the state as well as sickness insurance to cover all risks normally covered in the Member State concerned (Article 5). Member States may charge administrative fees for the issue of residence permits and they have a certain margin of appreciation in determining the level of those fees in the absence of a specific provision in the Directive regulating the amount of such charges. Nonetheless, recital 10 to the Directive specifies that the charges must be reasonable and fair and they must not discourage TCNs who satisfy the conditions laid down by that Directive from exercising the right of residence conferred on them by that Directive. In *Commission v Netherlands* (case C-508/10) concerning the Dutch system where the fees charged to the TCNs were up to 27 times greater than those imposed on Union citizens for the processing of their applications for residence permits, the CJ held that this level of fee affected the Directive's effectiveness, jeopardising the achievement of the objectives pursued by a directive. It was therefore unacceptable.

There are important differences between EU citizens (and their families) and TCNs. First, it will be recalled that, under the CRD citizens acquire the right of permanent residence after five years without, once they have satisfied this criterion, having to show they will be self-sufficient (Article 16 CRD). Secondly, Member States are entitled to impose 'integration conditions' on TCNs as a condition of acquiring permanent residence status (Article 5(2) Long-term Residents Directive). The nature of these conditions is not spelled out in the Long-term Residents Directive, but would include matters like passing tests in the native language or cultural knowledge. The EU has recognised the significance of language testing and its impact on TCNs. The renewed *European Agenda for the Integration of third-country nationals* (COM(2011) 455) contains specific recommendations to Member States on the provision of language courses which reflect migrants' varying needs at different stages of their integration process, including introductory programmes aimed at newly arrived migrants. These recommendations presumably will also apply to TCNs benefiting from other directives in the 'Legal Migration Package'. Thirdly, TCNs who have been residing as students or under humanitarian/refugee protection cannot gain rights under the Long-term Residents Directive (Article 3(2)). Fourthly, family members of long-term residents are only allowed to acquire permanent residence if the TCN has sufficient resources to support them. This is not the case for the family of EU citizens under the CRD.

The grant of a right of permanent residence in the first instance may also be denied on the grounds of public policy or public security but, importantly, not due to economic considerations such as the level of unemployment (Article 6). In such cases Member States must weigh up the threat posed by the person as against their length of residence and other links with the country of residence but there are no further constraints on their discretion to refuse. Thus before a long-term resident is formally given permanent residence they are more vulnerable to expulsion. By contrast, after a permanent residence permit has been issued, Article 12 gives only a more restricted power to withdraw such a resident permit when the migrant is an 'actual and sufficiently serious threat to public policy or public security'. In this case the proportionality exercise requires weighing up matters such as duration of residence, age, consequences for the person and family members and links with other countries. There must be judicial redress and legal aid must be given on the same terms as for nationals. These provisions reflect standards found in the case law of the CJ in relation to expulsion of EU citizens (see, eg, *Bouchereau*, and Chapter 25). In this sense the Long-term Residents Directive provides a high level of security of immigration status for long-term resident TCNs.

Apart from the right to permanent residence in the host Member State, the Directive confers other important rights. Article 11 requires Member States to grant equal treatment with nationals as regards a broad range of matters: access to employment and self-employment, along with remuneration and conditions; education and training, including study grants; social security, social assistance and social protection; tax benefits; and freedom of association and free access to the entire territory of the host state. This is an important and extensive package of rights, close to that given to EU citizens under Article 24 CRD (see Chapter 23). It does, however, mean that in principle only the entitlements listed are subject to equal treatment. Other benefits may be denied such as those found to fall within the broad concept of 'social advantages' developed by the CJ in relation to Article 7(2) Regulation 492/2011 ([2011] OJ L141/1) (see Chapter 23). Article 24(2) CRD also allows Member States a power to restrict equal treatment in relation to social assistance. It reads as follows:

> By way of derogation from paragraph 1, the host Member State shall not be obliged to confer entitlement to social assistance during the first three months of residence or, where appropriate, the longer period provided for in Article 14(4)(b), nor shall it be obliged, prior to acquisition of the right of permanent residence, to grant maintenance aid for studies, including vocational training, consisting in student grants or student loans to persons other than workers, self-employed persons, persons who retain such status and members of their families.

We should note, however, that the CJ developed the social rights of EU nationals by reference to the principle of non-discrimination on the grounds of nationality. In *Vatsouras* the CJ held that Article 18 TFEU 'is not intended to apply to cases of a possible difference in treatment between nationals of Member States and nationals of non-member countries' (para 52). The CJ, however, confirmed that non-discrimination on the grounds of nationality is part of the general principle of equality and can be relied on within the scope of EU law; the prohibition in the Treaty is an expression of the general principle (*Land Oberösterreich v ČEZ*, case C-115/08)). As in *ČEZ*, it can be invoked even in circumstances in which it is not possible to rely on Article 18 TFEU. It may then be suggested that the principle of equality is not restricted to protecting EU nationals (or their family members). We saw in Chapter 6 that there are many unanswered questions about the CJ's recent approach to general principles as a mechanism to avoid limitations in (written) EU law, and it remains to be seen whether the case law in this area will be developed.

In keeping with the idea of creating an internal market, permanent resident TCNs are given a right to reside in another Member State other than their host for work, studies or any other purpose (Article 14). This is a significant mobility right but again it is not unconditional. The migrant must show they and their family are self-sufficient (Article 15). The Long-term Residents Directive importantly allows the second Member State power to derogate completely from the right by maintaining systems of quotas on TCNs. This could render the right illusory for some Member States if the quota was set at zero or at a very low level. In times of unemployment, this could be a serious issue. Thus again, free-movement rights are less extensive for TCNs than EU citizens, for whom economic factors cannot justify exclusion. Furthermore, preference can be given to EU citizens and other residents over TCNs in access to employment (Article 14(3)). Finally, a more limited range of family members (compared to EU citizens under the CRD) of the permanent resident can accompany them to the second Member State (Article 16).

While the Long-term Residents Directive goes a good way to meeting the Tampere objective of providing nearly equal rights for aliens who are highly integrated, there are significantly less expansive rights in some key areas. Some important rights, like the right to migrate to a second Member

State, are conditional upon the labour market or social policies of Member States. It is not obvious why this should be so for persons who may have lived within the Union for many decades contributing to society, taxation and national income. The shortage of persons of working age within Europe suggests that attracting migration will remain an issue for years to come. The Long-term Residents Directive provides some incentives for migrants to remain in Europe but is not equivalent to the full status of EU citizenship. Nevertheless, for the many millions of long-term migrant workers who have been unable or chosen not to naturalise, the Long-term Residents Directive is a significant step towards their greater security and integration. It removes the ability of the Member States to withdraw residence on economic grounds and effectively ends the possibility of guest-worker systems being reintroduced. It is thus important both as a practical measure for immigrants and as a political expression of a positive European commitment towards resident foreigners.

26.4.4 **The Family Reunification Directive**

Another key immigration instrument is the Family Reunification Directive 2003/86 ([2003] OJ L251/12), which gives rights to non-EU citizens to join their family in the Union. The 'sponsor' must hold a residence permit of at least one year validity (Article 3) but does not need to be a long-term resident.

The range of family members that have the right to be admitted is more limited than for EU citizens under the CRD (which permits adult children, grandparents and certain other dependants to accompany the migrant). For TCNs, by contrast, only the spouse and minor children must be admitted (Article 4(1)). The Directive unsurprisingly confirms that the Member States have powers to refuse entry and residence on public policy, security or health grounds (Article 6). Although Article 4 is limited to the nuclear family, it does seem to include the nuclear family as reconstituted through divorce and re-marriage. Article 4 covers: the sponsor's spouse, the children of the sponsor and the spouse, and the minor children of the sponsor or of the spouse where that person has custody and the children are dependent on him or her.

The Directive, in a similar manner to the Long-term Residents Directive, provides that sponsors must not be dependent on the state as a precondition for reunification, in particular without having recourse to the social assistance system (Article 7). The meaning of this term was considered in *Chakroun v Minister van Buitlandse Zaken* (case C-578/08).

Chakroun

Mr and Mrs Chakroun's application for reunification was rejected on the basis that Mr Chakroun was in receipt of unemployment benefit which left him with an income below the level set in national legislation, which determined these questions by reference to a predetermined figure. The CJ confirmed that the term 'social assistance' had an independent Union meaning. It refers to assistance granted by the public authorities to those who do not have stable and regular resources which are sufficient to maintain himself and the members of his family and who would therefore become a burden to the host state.

In reaching this conclusion, the CJ referred to the case of *End* under the CRD (see generally Chapter 23), suggesting a bridging of interpretation between the Directives. The CJ then determined whether the use of a reference amount was permissible. The Court argued that the approach adopted by a Member State in assessing whether a sponsor under the Directive had enough to live on should not undermine the purposes of the Directive. While a reference amount might be permissible, it could not be used to impose a minimum income level below which all family reunifications will be refused, irrespective of an actual examination of the situation of each applicant, as

Article 17 requires applications to be assessed individually. The Court concluded that a Member State could not exclude an applicant who had enough money to live on normally but who would require state assistance for exceptional costs on the basis of aid available in that state. Moreover, it is the resources of the sponsor, not the member of the family seeking entry, which are in issue.

The Court also held that (with the exception of the position for refugees—see Article 9) the rules apply not just for reunification of existing families but also in the context of 'family formation'. In coming to this conclusion, it referred to both Article 8 ECHR and Article 7 EUCFR, neither of which makes a distinction between the formation of a family unit or its reunification. While *Chakroun* relates to the Family Reunification Directive, the reasoning of the Court in borrowing concepts used under the CRD (albeit in the context of TCN family members) suggests an intention to interpret equivalent provisions in the Directives in parallel. It is unlikely that such an approach will be limited to the Family Reunification Directive, but will be used in the context of the other AFSJ Directives too.

More problematically, the Directive permits derogation in the case of children aged over 12 who have spent some time living apart from the rest of the family. In these cases, some Member States were concerned that such children might be difficult to integrate, being older and thus, allegedly, less adaptable to a new culture. The Directive therefore permits Member States to subject such children to tests, such as language examinations, to see if they meet integration conditions. It also allows Member States to require applications from minor children to be submitted before they reach the age of 15 (Article 4(6)). Finally, Member States were also permitted to require a sponsor to have been resident for two years before allowing family reunion (Article 8).

These provisions restricting family reunion were challenged by the European Parliament on human-rights grounds in the *family reunification* case before the Grand Chamber of the Court. Here, the Parliament was concerned about the concessions made to Member States by the Council. It wished to see EU immigration legislation adopt high standards of protection for the family life of migrants. It argued that the Directive breached Article 8 ECHR, the right to respect for family life. In fact the CJ held that the Directive did not in itself breach Article 8. Rather, the Member States must ensure that each individual decision involving children respected the right to respect for family life. In doing this, Member States were entitled to consider the degree to which older children had close links to their own country and how far they could adapt if admitted to that Member State. It is suggested that the case was correctly decided because Article 8 ECHR does give a wide discretion to states to apply immigration control, particularly when deciding whether to admit a TCN who has not lived there before. The justification for this lower level of rights is said to be the need to ensure that family members of TCNs demonstrate that they can integrate into their host Member State. This concern is not raised in the context of migrant EU nationals, a contrast made stronger by the fact that the families of migrant EU nationals may also include TCNs. It is moreover not clear that immigration policy is the only or even the best way of achieving this objective of integration.

26.4.5 **Students Directive**

Non-EU students have the right to travel to the EU for study purposes, under certain conditions provided initially in Directive 2004/114 ([2004] OJ L375/12), recently replaced by Directive 2016/801 ([2016] OJ L132/21). Subject to these conditions, the Directive (in its 2016 version) provides for the right of entry and the corresponding right of residence for those travelling to a Member State for more than three months for the purposes of studies, pupil exchange, training, research, *au pair* work or voluntary service. The Directive also seeks to facilitate free movement between the Member States of TCN students and researchers, though this is a Directive which does not apply in the United Kingdom, Denmark or in Ireland. The Directive provides for the grant of a residence permit. It lays down provisions regarding transparency of decision-making. It also provides that students shall be entitled to be employed and may be entitled to exercise self-employed economic activity. The situation of the labour market in the host Member State may, however, be taken into account, and Member States may state the maximum amount of time students are permitted to work, which cannot be less than 15 hours a week (Article 24(3)).

As with the Long-term Residents Directive, certain categories of people are excluded: asylum seekers; members of the family of migrant EU nationals; and third-country nationals whose expulsion has been suspended for reasons of fact or of law. Equally those who fall within the Long-term Residents Directive or are workers or self-employed cannot rely on this Directive.

The right is subject to conditions. General conditions (in Article 7) apply to all; specific conditions (such as the obligation to prove a place at a higher education establishment, for students) apply to various categories of people (Articles 8–16).

The general conditions include the requirements to provide documentation, have sickness insurance cover, as well as not being regarded as a threat to public security. This mirrors the equivalent rules for EU citizens. By contrast to the position for the CRD, in which the threat is determined by behaviour not association, the recitals specify:

> [t]he notion of public policy may cover a conviction for committing a serious crime. In this context it has to be noted that the notions of public policy and public security also cover cases in which a third-country national belongs or has belonged to an association which supports terrorism, supports or has supported such an association, or has or has had extremist aspirations [Recital 14].

Note, unlike EU citizens, TCNs can be discriminated against in terms of being charged higher fees for courses. There is no equivalent to Article 24 Directive 2004/38 which forbids this in relation to migrant EU nationals.

26.4.6 **Blue Card Directive**

Directive 2009/50 ([2009] OJ L155/17) provides conditions for entry and residence of TCNs for highly qualified employment. The Directive's primary purpose was not the integration of TCNs or concerns about social justice but to 'provide Member States and EU companies with additional "tools" to recruit, retain and better allocate (and re-allocate) the workers they need' (MEMO/07/423). Thus, the Directive does not create a right of admission (that remains the decision of the relevant Member State); and it permits a 'Union preference', that is the giving of jobs to EU nationals over TCNs. The Directive has three main objectives:

- to facilitate the admission of highly qualified TCNs by harmonising entry and residence conditions throughout the EU;
- to simplify admission procedures;
- to improve the legal status of highly qualified TCNs already in the EU.

The Directive establishes the idea of the 'blue card' granted to TCNs who carry out 'highly qualified employment' which is valid for a period specified by the issuing Member State (between one and four years–Article 7(2)). Essentially 'highly qualified' means a job requiring a higher education qualification or five years' professional experience at a comparable level. Some groups of individuals are excluded, including: asylum seekers; those who fall within the terms of the Long-term Residence Directive; and those who would gain protection as a member of the family of a migrant EU national.

The Blue Card gives the holder the right to enter, re-enter and stay in the territory of the Member State issuing the EU Blue Card; the right of residence in Member States other than that which issued the Blue Card (applicable after 18 months—see Article 18); right of family reunification; rights of access to the labour market (Article 12) and rights of equality in the areas specified in Article 14. This list includes: working conditions, including pay and dismissal, freedom of association, education and vocational training and recognition of qualifications. Equal treatment of EU Blue Card holders does not cover measures in the field of vocational training which are covered under social assistance schemes. The Family Reunification Directive applies to Blue Card holders and their families, but with a number of important differences. For example, while the Family Reunification Directive permits Member States to take into account the likelihood of the TCN having reasonable prospects of obtaining the right of permanent residence and having a minimum period of residence when deciding on family reunification, the rights of a Blue Card holder cannot be so limited (Article 15). As a further benefit to Blue Card holder status, a Blue Card holder who applies for permanent residence (see 26.4.3) may (subject to conditions laid down in Article 16) cumulate periods of residence in different Member States in order to fulfil the requirement concerning the duration of residence. This is more generous than the other directives.

Entry is subject to a number of conditions: a work contract or binding job offer of at least one year in the Member State concerned which guarantees an average gross salary at least 1.5 times the national average, as well as holding the relevant qualifications and other documents. As with the Students Directive, sickness insurance is required, and the same restriction regarding public policy and public security applies. Article 6 permits Member States to continue to restrict the numbers of those coming into its territory on this basis. A Blue Card may be terminated for public-policy reasons or when a holder does not have sufficient resources, or when the holder applies for social assistance. Unemployment in itself will not constitute a reason for withdrawing an EU Blue Card, unless the period of unemployment exceeds three consecutive months (a shorter period than that allowed to workers under the CRD—see Chapter 21).

So while the Blue Card Directive is more generous in its treatment of highly qualified TCNs, the treatment is less generous than that under the CRD. Some of the restrictions show a family similarity to those in the other TCN directives and reflect the familiar concern about benefit tourism and security. Again, the Directive does not apply to the UK, Ireland or Denmark. The Commission proposed a major reform of the Directive in 2016 (COM(2016) 378), which is being discussed by the Council and the European Parliament.

26.4.7 **Other EU immigration measures**

In 2014, two additional EU immigration Directives were adopted. Firstly, Directive 2014/36 ([2014] OJ L94/375) on seasonal workers which covers the direct relationship of seasonal workers and their employers. Secondly, Directive 2014/66 ([2014] OJ L157/1) on the intra-corporate transfer of non-EU skilled workers. This Directive aims to facilitate mobility of intra-corporate transferees in the EU as well as to reduce the administrative work related to their movement in several Member States.

26.5 **The regulation of asylum: harmonisation or exclusion?**

The duty to provide asylum to persons fleeing persecution is one of the oldest human-rights obligations known to international law. It was formally incorporated into a multilateral Treaty in 1951—the Refugee Convention. All Member States of the European Union had signed the Convention and were operating it before their respective accessions to the Treaty of Rome. It may be wondered, therefore, why the European Union began to develop asylum policies given that refugee protection was already a legal obligation upon the individual Member States. The answer lies in the rapid growth in the numbers of asylum seekers entering Europe in the 1980s and 1990s. Many hundreds of thousands of persons sought protection, but the pattern of applications for asylum varied. Some northern states such as Germany and the Netherlands received many of the refugees whilst others, particularly in southern Europe, took very few per capita. There was a perception that 'burden-sharing' was not equitable between different Member States. This was partly ascribed to divergent practices between different states. Although they were all applying the same Refugee Convention, interpretations differed on many questions. Examples included: who qualifies as a refugee; whether social support should be available during the application process; and what appeal rights should be given upon refusal. It was said that some states were thus more attractive as asylum destinations, although the extent to which individuals 'shopped' around for their preferred country of refuge was never really established.

In addition to the harmonisation issue, asylum came to be viewed partly as a border-security issue. Because of European governments' restrictions on the migration of persons from poorer refugee-producing countries, asylum seekers often entered the European Union illegally. In this sense, the Union began to perceive that its external borders should be more secure to prevent illegal entry (including of asylum seekers) and to ensure swift expulsion in such cases. The goal of high levels of refugee protection was therefore not always consistent with the political pressure to better police border controls. Joint action in European border security could in itself more readily lead to genuine refugees being expelled or denied entry.

Thus, we see the beginnings of the attempt to create a Common European Asylum System (CEAS). The first phase of this led, by 2005, to the adoption of the Dublin II Regulation (Regulation 343/2003 ([2003] OJ L50/1)), now replaced by the Dublin III Regulation (Regulation 604/2013 ([2013] OJ L180/31)), the Qualification Directive (Directive 2004/83 ([2004] OJ L304/12)), now replaced by Directive 2011/95 ([2011] OJ L337/9), the Reception Conditions Directive (Directive 2003/9 ([2003] OJ L31/18)), now replaced by Directive 2013/33 ([2013] OJ L180/96) and the Asylum Procedures Directive 2005/85 ([2005] OJ L326/13), now replaced by Directive 2013/32 ([2013] OJ L180/60). There were, however, questions about uniformity of implementation across Member States. The standards adopted had in some cases lowered protection levels below those pre-existing in individual Member States and have even gone below those recommended by the United Nations High Commissioner for Refugees (UNHCR).

Given the lack of consistency between Member States, asylum policy (and particularly the Directive defining who qualified as an asylum seeker—the Qualification Directive) and the sensitivity of many of the issues raised led to many references to the CJ. In key cases, the CJ has interpreted the Qualification Directive broadly. For example, in the important case of *Elgafaji v Staatssecretaris van Justitie* (case C-465/07) the Grand Chamber of the CJ confirmed that subsidiary protection is available to those who can show that indiscriminate violence has reached such a high level that substantial grounds exist for believing that a civilian returned there would face a real risk of death or serious harm to their person. They do not need to show they are individually being targeted. This decision means that the Directive goes beyond existing refugee law and that of the ECHR in affording protection to those fleeing civil war and internal armed conflict.

The amendment of the Qualification Directive (now Directive 2011/95) sought to bring the terms of legislation in line with this case law, and the case law of the ECHR. While the original Directives did achieve some improvements in the system (eg, the Reception Conditions Directive (Directive 2003/9 ([2003] OJ L31/18)) provided a minimum set of rights regarding housing, educational, medical and material support for asylum seekers), deficiencies remained—for example the lack of clarity concerning the circumstances in which it would be permissible to detain refugees, or the extent to which Member States had latitude in determining conditions of access to the labour market.

Against these concerns, in 2007, the Commission issued a Green Paper on the future direction of CEAS, which was followed up by a Policy Plan on Asylum in 2008, which proposed, amongst other things, a need for greater alignment of the Member States' systems, which would require changes to the three Directives, as well as the need to strengthen the Dublin II Convention. This approach was reaffirmed first by the 2008 Pact on Immigration and Asylum and then by the Stockholm Programme.

This resulted in:

- the recast Qualification Directive (Directive 2011/95);
- the revised Asylum Procedures Directive (Directive 2013/32) (provides clearer requirements on Member States for efficient decision-making which recognises the needs of certain groups for special assistance as well as rules on appeals);
- the revised Reception Conditions Directive (Directive 2013/33) (concerns humane material reception conditions (such as housing and access to fresh air) for asylum seekers and that detention is a last resort);
- the revised Dublin Regulation (Regulation 604/2013) (concerns the identification of which state is responsible for the asylum seeker and other matters and now provides, inter alia, for greater guarantees for the applicant in the decision-making process as well as clearer rules regarding process);
- the revised EURODAC system (Regulation 603/2013 ([2013] OJ L180/1)) (allows law enforcement access to the EU database of the fingerprints of asylum seekers under strictly limited circumstances in order to prevent, detect or investigate the most serious crimes, such as murder and terrorism).

A further point is that the EU Charter provides that 'the right to asylum shall be guaranteed with due respect for the rules of the Geneva Convention . . . ' (Article 18 EUCFR). This probably changes nothing of substance, as Article 18 EUCFR continues to specify that the right shall be in accordance with the TEU and TFEU, returning us to the terms of the Treaties and the Directives. Following the perceived refugee crisis beginning in 2016, the Commission proposed new versions of all the EU asylum laws, which are still under discussion. However, given the extensive, technical and specialist nature of the body of law in this field, a full review of the CEAS lies outside the scope of this book.

26.6 Irregular migration and policing the EU border

Another area where the Union has been very active is in attempting to combat illegal migration. Article 3(2) TEU links an internal free movement zone with the need for external border control. There was long-standing concern about people-smuggling routes through southern Europe from Africa. With eastern enlargement, the Union's borders were more exposed to smuggling from Asia through Russia and Turkey. Migrants entering this way could gain access to any of the Member States. Joint policies to secure the external borders of the Union and also action against illegal migrants found within the Union have thus been introduced. These policies are both preventive and remedial. They can also be linked to traditional EU social and employment policies, particularly those aimed at preventing exploitation of irregular migrants by undercutting EU citizens and other lawful residents. Additionally, there is a growing emphasis on security rationales for controlling migration by non-EU citizens.

26.6.1 **People smuggling and people trafficking**

Directive 2002/90 ([2002] OJ L328/17) defines the facilitation of unauthorised entry, transit and residence. The aim of the measure was to combat the aiding of illegal immigration whether in connection with unauthorised crossing of the border in itself or for the purpose of sustaining trafficking networks. The Directive requires the imposition of sanctions for people smuggling (ie for financial gain), save where such actions are for humanitarian purposes, and such sanctions are further specified in Framework Decision (2002/946/JHA) on the strengthening of the penal framework to prevent the facilitation of unauthorised entry, transit and residence. The framework decision thus provides minimum rules for penalties, liability of legal persons and jurisdiction. The UK and Ireland participated in both measures.

One key measure is the Directive on Trafficking in Human Beings (Directive 2011/36 ([2011] OJ L101/1)), replacing Framework Decision 2002/629/JHA. While not initially addressed to Denmark and the United Kingdom, it now binds the latter after the UK government decided to opt in. Not all the Member States which were supposed to implement the Directive have fully done so. This measure is supported by a directive on the residence permit issued to TCNs who are victims of trafficking in human beings or who have been the subject of an action to facilitate illegal immigration, who cooperate with authorities (Directive 2004/81 ([2004] OJ L261/19)), which does not apply to Denmark, Ireland or the UK, and Directive 2009/52 ([2009] OJ L168/24) providing for minimum standards on sanctions and measures against employers. As with much legislation in the AFSJ, mixed motives are in play. One stated aim is to better protect the victims and is to some extent victim orientated. Equally the Member States wish to prevent trafficking, and to prosecute criminals effectively, which also links in to concerns about external security.

The Trafficking Directive establishes minimum rules concerning the definition of criminal offences and sanctions in the area of trafficking in human beings and in doing so adopts a broad definition of trafficking (wider than that in the previous instrument) including trafficking for organ removal purposes, forced adoption or marriage. Article 2(1) specifies that the following is caught by the Directive:

> The recruitment, transportation, transfer, harbouring or reception of persons, including the exchange or transfer of control over those persons, by means of the threat or use of force or other forms of coercion, of abduction, of fraud, of deception, of the abuse of power or of a position of vulnerability or of the giving or receiving of payments or benefits to achieve the consent of a person having control over another person, for the purpose of exploitation.

Exploitation includes:

> the prostitution of others or other forms of sexual exploitation, forced labour or services, including begging, slavery or practices similar to slavery, servitude, or the exploitation of criminal activities, or the removal of organs (Article 2(3)).

It is clear from the terms of the Directive that this is a minimum, so that all Member States must take action in these cases, but that Member States may provide for more extensive protection. Aiding and abetting, as well as attempts, are likewise caught (Article 3). The Directive specifies minimum penalties to be imposed on perpetrators (minimum five years' imprisonment), with greater penalties being imposed on those who exploit in aggravating circumstances, such as in the case of exploiting the vulnerable (minimum 10 years' imprisonment) (Article 4). The Directive contains provisions which seek to facilitate the investigation and prosecution of crimes, including making conditions more 'victim-friendly', in particular in relation to counselling, witness protection and how the trial is carried out. While it is envisaged that victims might apply for compensation, the issue of the right to remain in the EU (which may have been the incentive for some victims becoming trafficked) falls outside this Directive.

Directive 2004/81 does provide the possibility of a residence permit for victims, although this is limited to those who cooperate with the authorities and the residence permit is limited in time. The system envisages that every TCN victim of human trafficking, who is in the EU illegally, should be offered a 'reflection period' during which the victim can make a decision about whether to cooperate with the authorities. During this period the victim is granted access to medical care and treatment. Thereafter, a cooperative victim (as specified in Article 8(1)) can obtain a residence permit, which entitles the victim to receive continued medical care, as well as access to the labour market, vocational training and education as specified in national legislation. This residence permit is not an attempt to integrate the victim (by contrast to economic migrants) and is temporary and may be withdrawn. We might question whether the concern here is for the victim or for the prosecution (and deterrence) of people traffickers. Recital 9 notes that a residence permit offers 'a sufficient incentive to cooperate with the competent authorities while including certain conditions to safeguard against abuse'. In any event, the Directive specifies the criteria for issuing a residence permit, the conditions of stay, as well as the grounds for non-renewal and withdrawal (Articles 13 and 14). In addition to more usual public-policy considerations, one such ground is the termination or discontinuation of the relevant legal proceedings. Of course, victims may apply to stay as asylum seekers. Many points of detail in the implementation of the Directive are left to Member States individually to determine (such as the length of the 'period of reflection'), which has led to a certain variance in practice. The Commission has further questioned (COM(2010) 493 final) whether the Directive is being used effectively, as, of the thousands of identified victims a year, only some 20 receive residence permits.

26.6.2 **The Returns Directive**

The most significant and controversial measure in relation to illegal entry is the Returns Directive (Directive 2008/115 ([2008] OJ L348/98)). The Directive seeks to bolster the policing role of the Union both in relation to external borders and also internally to ensure that migrants not entitled under national or EU law to be present are removed. It creates a harmonised system for the expulsion of non-EU citizens found illegally present in any of the Member States. The clear aim is to require each Member State to contribute towards tackling the issue of illegal immigration rather than to simply allow such migrants to remain when detected. Thus, Article 6 requires Member States to issue a 'return decision' in respect of such persons (subject to exceptions). They must then take 'all necessary measures to enforce' this decision, including coercive methods such as arrest (Article 8). This must not involve more than reasonable and proportionate force (Article 8(4)). Member States are, however, still allowed to grant a residence permit on humanitarian or compassionate grounds (Article 6(4)). Further, note that the effect of an asylum seeker's right to remain while the application is determined means that, during such period, such a person cannot be viewed as 'illegally staying' within the meaning of Directive 2008/115 (*Arslan v Policie Č R, Krajské ředitelství policie Ústeckého kraje, odbor cizinecké policie* (case C-534/11)). In such a case, however, if a return procedure had been started prior to the lodging of the asylum application, the return procedure would not be terminated by such an application, but may be resumed should the claim be rejected. In *Arslan*, it seemed likely that Arslan—who was subject to a return procedure—had made the asylum application with the objective of thwarting the returns process. While the Directive does allow Member

States to be more generous in some respects, the tone and purpose is clearly to remove illegal immigrants. The Directive does require the possibility of an effective remedy to challenge the return decision itself before an impartial body (Article 13), but there is no explicit obligation on the review body to engage with the merits of the case. Where a person raises issues of fundamental human rights then the ECHR requires an independent tribunal to review the merits carefully (see *Conka v Belgium* (Application No 51564/99) 5 February 2001, (2002) 34 EHRR 54). The Directive also suggests an exclusionary bias in EU policy by requiring Member States to impose a ban (subject to exceptions) on re-entry for migrants returned other than voluntarily (Article 11(1)). This operates to prevent the migrant from coming back to *any* Member State. There is a discretion as to the period for which the ban is imposed, but the Directive sets a maximum of five years, possibly longer if the migrant presents a 'serious threat to public policy, public security or national security' (Article 11(2)). The *Filev and Osmani* case (case C-297/12) concerned re-entry bans, imposed by Germany prior to the adoption of the Directive, but which had not been limited in their duration. When the subjects of these orders sought to return to Germany (in one case more than 20 years later), criminal sanctions were imposed. A question was referred to the CJ as to whether such an unlimited ban complied with the terms of Article 11(2). The Court concluded that bans in excess of five years, except where those re-entry bans were made against TCNs who constituted a serious threat to public order, public security or national security (para 44), were unacceptable. Such re-entry bans may lead to breaches of Article 8 of the ECHR if they disproportionately deny such migrants access to family members in the Union (see *Abdulaziz, Cabales and Balkandali v UK* (1985) 7 EHRR 47).

Significantly the Directive authorises detention of persons subject to return decisions pending their expulsion where: (1) there is a risk of absconding, based on objective criteria, or (2) where the detainee 'hampers' or 'avoids' the effort to remove them (Article 15). There is a dangerous lack of clarity in what constitutes 'hampering' and this power suggests that detainees are open to punishment for non-cooperation. The Directive requires that detention should be for shortest possible period but six months is permitted (Article 15(5)). Even then, this can be extended to eighteen months in certain cases (Article 15(6)). If detention was ordered by administrative authorities, it must be subject to initial judicial review (Article 15(2)); there must be further judicial review if this detention is 'prolonged' (a term which is not defined; Article 15(3)). To comply with the ECHR (Article 5(1)(f)), however, the Member State must act with 'due diligence' to effect expulsion (see *Chahal v United Kingdom* [1996] 23 EHRR 413). States must show that they are taking reasonably active steps to expel a detainee. The ECHR also requires that there be mandatory judicial review of detention that extends beyond a few days (see *Shamsa v Poland* (Application Nos 45355/99 and 45357/99) Judgment of 27 November 2003). The very lengthy detention periods may lead to arbitrary imprisonment and abuse of power, and questions have already led to references to the CJ to determine the scope of Member State power in this regard, as can be seen in *El Dridi* (case C-61/11PPU).

El Dridi

El Dridi was a TCN who entered Italy illegally. A deportation decree was issued against him, with which he did not comply. Consequently, he was sentenced to one year's imprisonment. The Italian law in question was enacted as part of a 'security package' ('pacchetto sicurezza') of immigration laws and permits the imposition of custodial sentences of up to four years. Italy had not transposed Articles 15 and 16 Directive 2008/115, on which El Dridi sought to rely. Despite its faults, the Directive provided better protection than the Italian law.

In its judgment, the CJ highlighted that the Returns Directive establishes an order in which the various stages of a returns procedure should take place. This order ranges from the measures which allow the person concerned the most liberty to those which restrict that liberty the most, specifically detention (para 41). While the Returns Directive envisages the possibility of detaining people, it is only justifiable when their actions suggest they risk jeopardising the removal process, and even then only for as short a period as possible and subject to periodic review. A custodial penalty 'risks jeopardizing the attainment of the objective pursued by that directive rather than ensuring a speedy return': effectively, custody could delay a return (para 59). Interestingly, in its reasoning the CJ did not base its conclusion on the individuals' freedom of liberty, merely touching on that point and instead focusing on the objective of the Directive.

The *El Dridi* judgment was affirmed in *Achughbabian v Préfet du Val-de-Marne* (case C-329/11).

Achughbabian

This case concerned an Armenian national whose application for a residence permit had been rejected. An order was served on Achughbabian, requiring him to leave French territory within one month, but an identity check in 2011 revealed Achughbabian had not complied. A deportation order and an administrative detention order were served on him the next day; that is, he no longer had the option to leave voluntarily. On appeal, the national court made a reference to the CJ on the legality under the Returns Directive of the imposition of a sentence of imprisonment on a TCN on the sole ground of his illegal entry or residence in national territory.

The CJ responded in similar terms to those used in *El Dridi*:

> National legislation such as that at issue in the main proceedings is, consequently, likely to thwart the application of the common standards and procedures established by Directive 2008/115 and delay the return, thereby, like the legislation at issue in El Dridi, undermining the effectiveness of the said directive.

It is important to note, however, that the CJ emphasised that the Returns Directive was of limited scope and Member States' freedom as regards criminal sanctions were unrestricted outside it. Thus a Member State could classify an illegal stay as a criminal offence. Further, the CJ confirmed that the Returns Directive does not preclude a TCN being placed in detention with a view to determining whether or not his stay is lawful. It is once a decision to return an individual has been made that the procedures and protections granted by the Returns Directive come into play.

The *El Dridi* and *Achughbabian* decisions, although they did not make big claims for human rights, are important, as they make clear that within the scope of the Directive individuals cannot be imprisoned simply for being illegally present in a country. Contrast the position in *Arslan*, in which the applicant was permitted to be detained, although technically an asylum seeker, because he made the asylum application solely to delay or jeopardise the enforcement of the return decision and because it was objectively necessary and proportionate to maintain detention. Given the current political situation (specifically the influx of migrants from Africa and the Middle East) in which a number of Member States have sought ever broader powers to detain and deport irregular migrants, even re-imposing national border controls within the 'passport free' Schengen zone, the *El Dridi* and *Achughbabian* judgments stand against the current political trend.

26.7 EU criminal justice policy

This chapter does not seek to set out in comprehensive form all the policies relating to criminal law. Indeed, the European Union has not developed a complete set of criminal justice policies. Policy regarding what conduct to make criminal, sentencing, prison policy and court procedures remains largely concentrated at Member State level. The Union only has limited powers to act. This is in contrast to the position in relation to asylum and immigration where EU legislation is now central to the law in all Member States, and despite the link made in Article 3(2) TEU between the fight against crime and strong external borders in the creation of AFSJ. Nevertheless there has been growing cooperation in a number of areas (eg, illegal immigration), despite great reluctance by Member States to accept that the Union has a prominent role in criminal justice. This led to conflict between Member States and European institutions over how far 'normal' principles of law developed under the former EC Treaty, direct effect and supremacy in particular (see Chapters 4 and 5), should apply in relation to criminal law measures taken under the TEU. There has been a renewal of the same dissent, previously shown by national constitutional courts concerned about the lack of fundamental rights protection toward criminal-law measures that arguably infringe their citizens' constitutional rights. Of course, post-Lisbon the EUCFR has legal force and, significantly, there are plans for the EU to accede to the ECHR (see Chapter 6). These developments should strengthen human rights protection within the EU, but whether such strengthening is enough to end dissent is another question. We shall set out here some of the main issues of legal principle that have arisen rather than attempting to summarise the content of the actual legislation passed.

Note that the United Kingdom and Ireland have the benefit of an opt-out in areas covered by the AFSJ, and that this opt-out continues even post-Lisbon. The opt-out does not mean that no AFSJ measures apply, as either state may choose to opt in to individual measures.

26.7.1 Criminal liability arising ancillary to legislation passed under non-AFSJ provisions

The TFEU gives powers to the institutions to pass legislation to regulate the internal market (see Chapter 16). In practice, such legislation sometimes includes criminal sanctions to give effect to its goals or it may require Member States to pass criminal laws to do so.

For example, when the institutions act to pass laws under the internal market provisions, say a directive on financial services regulation, they may wish to impose a penalty upon natural or legal persons for a breach of those regulations. Member States may create criminal offences to ensure compliance by those to whom it is directed. The obligation to impose some form of penalty would ensure that there is a level playing field in terms of economic activity in that market, but that penalty might not take the form of criminal law in every state. In this scenario, criminal sanctions are simply a tool to use to regulate activities falling within the internal market goals. By contrast, the provisions in AFSJ empower the institutions to pass criminal-law measures in relation to cross-border crime such as cybercrime, human trafficking, terrorism, internet pornography and so forth. In these cases, the powers are specifically designed to pass criminal-law measures rather than to regulate markets.

The existence of criminal-lawmaking powers under the former third pillar gave rise to the question of whether the internal market provisions could lawfully be used to make criminal law in relation to the internal market or other Community law issues, or whether in such a case, third pillar powers should be used instead. The significance of the distinction related to the powers of the various institutions. The former third pillar was intergovernmental in its arrangements, meaning that most decisions were made by the Council, acting unanimously; the European Parliament did not have co-legislator status (Chapter 3) and references to the CJ were limited (see Chapter 10). Internal market measures shifted legislative power, so that the European Parliament was effectively a co-regulator and the limitations on references to the CJ did not apply. This was a controversial issue because such a power challenges the reservation of competence to Member States in the field of criminal law.

Prior to Lisbon, the Member States were, however, very reluctant to accept that the then EC Treaty gave a power to enact criminal sanctions. They saw this as reserved to the Member States or falling only under the more limited intergovernmental negotiations outside the EC Treaty frame- work in the old 'third pillar'. Even prior to Maastricht, however, the CJ had held in *Commission v Greece (Greek maize)* (case 68/88), that some EU legislation might impliedly require Member States to impose criminal penalties in order to ensure its effectiveness. These penalties must be 'effective, proportionate and dissuasive'. They must also be set at a level equivalent to those imposed on similar offences in national law. The Commission took this as a sign that criminal sanctions could be included directly in EU legislation.

The CJ again agreed with the Commission in the important *environmental crimes* case.

Environmental Crimes

Here the Commission had proposed a directive on environmental damage liability which included criminal sanctions for serious polluters. The Member States refused to accept that Community law applied to laws imposing criminal sanctions. Instead they had decided in the Council to pass their own framework decision on environmental crime under the third pillar, emphasising that the framework decision was really a measure on criminal law, not the environment. They thereby maintained their monopoly of power over criminal law. The Commission challenged the power of the Council to pass the measure. It reasoned that as an environmental protection law it should have been passed on the basis of provisions found in the then EC Treaty. The European Court agreed, ruling that although criminal law did not generally fall within the competence of the institutions under those provisions, this did not prevent criminal sanctions being imposed where these were necessary to ensure that the environmental protection rules were fully effective.

This approach was confirmed in the *ship source pollution* case.

Lisbon changed the position radically. With the removal of the pillar structure, the institutional limitations on the European Parliament and the CJ, together with the move toward QMV in Council, mean that the question of whether a piece of legislation should have been enacted as a single market measure or under the AFSJ largely loses its force (though the question of whether it should have been enacted as an EU measure at all remains). There is one group of Member States for whom the distinction between single market and AFSJ may remain significant: that is the Member States who have an opt-out of AFSJ. If a measure is deemed to be an internal market measure or a measure within another non-criminal law field, the opt-out will not apply and the Member States will be bound by the measure.

26.7.2 **AFSJ post-Lisbon**

Chapter 4 of Title V TFEU deals with criminal cooperation. Article 83 TFEU is a development of former Article 31 TEU in the old third pillar. Article 83 TFEU allows the enactment of directives, using the ordinary legislative procedure, to establish minimum rules concerning the definition of criminal offences and sanctions relating to such offences in the area of 'particularly serious crime with a cross-border dimension'. While Union action is clearly envisaged, it can be seen that there are sensitivities about Member States' competence here (see also COM(2011) 573 final). As we saw in Chapter 3, a directive is the form of Union legislation which allows Member States to choose a means of implementation that most fits in with the national legal system. Further, minimum standards are to be set: there is no total harmonisation here. Finally, the type of crime selected is of such a nature that joint endeavour is required. The second paragraph of Article 83(1) identifies such areas: terrorism; trafficking in human beings and sexual exploitation of women and children; illicit drug trafficking; illicit arms trafficking; money-laundering; corruption; counterfeiting of means of payment; computer crime; and organised crime. Reflecting the approach of the CJ in the *environmental crimes* case, Article 83(2) TFEU provides that where effective implementation of the Union policy in an area which has been subject to harmonisation requires it, such measures may establish minimum rules with regard to the definition of both criminal offences and sanctions. Sensitivities remained even with the treaty wording selected, so Article 83(3) TFEU provides what has been called an 'emergency brake'. This permits a member of Council to request that a draft directive proposed under either Article 83(1) or (2) be referred to the European Council, in which case the ordinary legislative procedure normally used for these provisions would be suspended. Such a request would not prevent the other Member States from using enhanced cooperation to take matters forward, if discussions on the proposal do not resolve the dispute.

There have also been significant attempts to increase cooperation and information sharing between police forces across the Union (Article 87 TEU). The Hague European Council in 2004 went so far as to say law enforcement officers should in general make available to law enforcement officers in other Member States information needed to perform their duties. These suggestions raise important questions about respect for the right to privacy and the protection of personal data. The Hague Council also gave great prominence to combating terrorism through pooling intelligence and freezing assets. Prior to Lisbon, and perhaps most importantly, there were efforts to secure the 'mutual recognition' of criminal judgments and orders by the courts of each of the Member States. Article 82 TFEU now provides an express Treaty base for judicial cooperation and permits the institutions to legislate so as to lay down rules and procedures for the recognition of judgments, to settle conflicts of jurisdiction and otherwise facilitate cooperation. The aim has been to render borders irrelevant in terms of criminal enforcement. As we shall see below, this has raised serious constitutional issues for the courts of the Member States anxious to maintain national safeguards for criminal suspects.

26.8 Conclusions

Union law has now begun to exert consideration influence on areas falling within AFSJ. This is most clear in relation to immigration and asylum where there are quite comprehensive systems of legislation that provide the main rules governing migration into the Union. Several Member States have not opted in to some of the measures passed, particularly in relation to immigration. The legislation passed so far does not provide a comprehensive set of minimum standards for migrants because there are areas where Member States can opt to provide lower standards. This can be seen in the approach to residence permits for victims of trafficking and also some aspects of asylum rules. Despite the focus on the victim, an underlying concern with control, exclusion and security can still be seen. Turning to immigration the picture is more positive because the Family Reunion and Long-term Residents Directives do provide enhanced standards of respect for migrants within the Union.

These measures provide protection approaching the level offered to EU migrant citizens, although do not fully mirror them. In much of the case law, the impact of fundamental rights is key.

Regarding judicial and policing matters under the AFSJ the picture is rather different. There has not been the same degree of harmonisation of substantive law here, although financial crime and terrorism are exceptions. There has been a great deal of cooperation between police forces. The main legislative emphasis has been upon mutual recognition of criminal court orders and judgments. The European arrest warrant has been the centrepiece of this process. The possible conflict between this measure and national and international fundamental rights protection has not yet been resolved by the CJ and the supreme courts of the Member States. The area of policing and criminal justice does therefore present the potential for serious clashes over the effectiveness and legitimacy of EU law. Whilst the Lisbon changes could lead to an improvement in legitimacy, transparency and human rights protection, the possible increase in Union activity in this sensitive field could give rise to greater conflict.

Further reading

Acosta Arcarazo, D, *The Long Term Residence Status as a Subsidiary Form of EU Citizenship: An Analysis of Directive 2003/109* (Martinus Nijhoff, 2011).

Baker, E and Harding, C, 'From past imperfect to future imperfect? A longitudinal study of the third pillar' (2009) 34 EL Rev 25.

Douglas-Scott, S, 'The rule of law in the European Union: Putting security into "the area of freedom security and justice"' (2004) 29 EL Rev 219.

Errera, R, 'Cessation and assessment of new circumstances: A comment on *Abdulla*' (2011) 23 Int'l J Refugee L 521.

Errera, R, 'The CJEU and subsidiary protection: Reflections on *Elgafaji*—and after' (2011) 23 Int'l J Refugee L 93.

Herlin-Karnell, E, 'From mutual trust to the full effectiveness of EU law: 10 years of the European arrest warrant' (2013) 38 EL Rev 79.

Lenaerts, K, 'The contribution of the European Court of Justice to the area of freedom, security and justice' (2010) 59 ICLQ 255.

Marguery, T, 'European Union fundamental rights and Member States action in EU criminal law' (2013) 20 Maastricht Journal 282.

Mitseligas, V, 'The third wave of third pillar law: Which direction for EU criminal justice?' (2009) 34 EL Rev 523.

Murphy, C, 'The enduring vulnerability of migrant domestic workers in Europe' (2013) 62 ICLQ 599.

O'Neill, M, 'EU cross-border policing provisions, the view from one of the Schengen opt-out states' (2010) 18 Eur J Crime Cr L Cr J 73.

Peers, S, 'Implementing equality? The Directive on Long-term Resident Third Country Nationals' (2004) 29 EL Rev 437.

Peers, S, *EU Justice and Home Affairs Law*, 4th edn (Oxford University Press, 2016).

27 Discrimination

27.1 Introduction

This chapter sets out the development of the law on equality of treatment between persons from the inception of the European Union to the present day. Whilst equality of treatment between men and women has existed for more than three decades now, measures for the prohibition of discrimination on grounds other than sex are relatively recent. This chapter looks at the historical development of the approach of the EU to discrimination generally before looking at the provisions relating to sex discrimination in employment. It then considers discrimination on grounds other than sex.

27.2 Historical development

The law of the EU on discrimination has been developed in three phases, each of which reflects a growing commitment to the principle of equality and respect for human rights.

27.2.1 **Phase 1**

The first phase ran from 1957 to 1987. In its original form, the TFEU contained a number of references to the concept of equal treatment, most of which concerned economic operators. Article 7 EEC, now Article 18 TFEU, prohibited discrimination on the basis of nationality (see Chapters 21–23). Further, there was a provision dealing with sex discrimination. The right to equal treatment between employed persons having the nationality of a Member State with respect to access to employment remuneration and other conditions of work and employment is assured by Article 45 TFEU. Regulation 442/2011 ([2011] OJ L141/1) implements the principle of equal treatment articulated in this provision. Thus, for example, nationals of a Member State who take up employment in another Member State have the right to vocational training under the same conditions as nationals of that state (Article 7). In addition they have the right to the same 'social and tax advantages' as nationals of that state (see 23.2.1.1). The concept of social and tax advantages has been interpreted broadly.

Article 119 EEC in its original form provided for equal pay for men and women doing equal work. It appears to have been drafted originally to address economic concerns by creating a level playing field between operators established in different Member States.

Article 119 EEC did not prohibit discrimination between men and women in the matter of pay, nor did it provide for the adoption of legislative measures to enforce this principle, relying instead on requiring the Member States themselves to bring about equal pay for equal work within their own legal systems by 31 December 1961. This deadline was not respected and the Member States passed a resolution in late December 1961, giving themselves an extension until 31 December 1964 to achieve equality between men and women in pay.

In the meantime, Ms Gabrielle Defrenne, an air stewardess with the now defunct national Belgian airline, SABENA, began a series of actions complaining of discrimination with respect to her pension rights pay and some of her working conditions, all which she claimed were less favourable than those of her male colleagues doing the same work.

In the second of these actions, *Defrenne II*, in support of her claim to parity of pay with her male colleagues engaged in the same employment, Ms Defrenne relied upon what was at that time Article 119. In a preliminary ruling referred to the CJ by the Cour de Travail Brussels, the Court was asked whether Article 119 had direct effect, so that workers could rely on it before national courts, to claim equal pay. The Court held that indeed they could. It began its analysis by stating that the then Article 119 had a double aim: to avoid a situation in which undertakings in Member States where the principle of equal pay for equal work had been implemented suffered a competitive disadvantage as compared to undertakings established in Member States where that principle was not respected, and since Article 119 EEC was part of the chapter in the Treaty devoted to social policy, it had the social aim of improving working conditions and living standards.

The Court went on to find that the then Article 119 EEC was 'directly applicable and may therefore give rise to individual rights which the Courts must protect'. It imposed upon Member States a duty to bring about a specific result within a fixed period. Article 119 was not a vague declaration, nor did it give the Member States any discretion as to the attainment of its objective. The Court pronounced the principle of equal pay to be one of the foundations of the Union which must be attained by raising the lowest salaries rather than lowering the highest. Women's pay was to move up to the level of that of men (reiterated in *Bestuur van het Algemeen Burgerlijk Pensioenfonds v Beune* (case C-7/93) para 28, where the Court held that the meaning and scope of the principle of equal pay could not be determined by a formal criterion which is in itself dependent upon a rule or practice followed in the Member States). This reasoning applies to the article in its current form.

The *Defrenne II* case was, at the time, viewed as being dramatic: far from the Member States meandering gently on their own terms towards equal pay for men and women, this objective was achieved by the CJ declaring this to be a directly effective right, the substance of which could not be limited by national legislation. Given the potentially grave financial consequences of its judgment for many sectors of industry, the Court limited the temporal effect of its judgment: Article 119 EEC could not be relied upon to support claims for pay periods prior to the date of judgment, 8 April 1976, save with respect to those claimants who had instituted proceedings prior to that date.

The Equal Pay Directive (Directive 75/117 ([1975] OJ L45/19)) came into force some eight weeks before the judgment in *Defrenne II* was pronounced. That judgment did not make it in any way redundant and required no amendment to its provisions.

In two further sets of proceedings instituted by Ms Defrenne the Court found that Article 119 related to pay only, it did not require equal treatment with respect to working conditions (*Defrenne III*) or within state social security systems (*Defrenne v Belgium (Defrenne I)* (case 80/70)).

Accordingly, following these judgments two directives were adopted in 1976 and 1979 respectively: the Equal Opportunities Directive (Directive 76/207 ([1976] OJ L39/40)) and the Equal Treatment in Social Security Directive (Directive 79/7 ([1979] OJ L6/24)). In 1986 the Equality of Treatment in Occupational Welfare Schemes were adopted (Directive 86/378 ([1986] OJ L225/40)) in the mistaken belief that the concept of 'pay' did not extend to occupational welfare schemes such as pensions and thus specific legislation was required to ensure the equal treatment of men and women.

27.2.2 **Phase 2**

The second phase in the evolution of equality law ran from 1987 to 1997 with a broadening of the substantive area of legislative activity. This phase saw the adoption of the Pregnancy Directive (Directive 92/85 ([1992] OJ L348/1)); the Burden of Proof Directive (Directive 97/80 (OJ [1998] L14/6)); and the Parental Leave Directive (Directive 96/34 OJ ([1996] OJ L145/4)).

The ToA amended Article 119, renumbering it Article 141 EC and introduced Article 13 into the EC Treaty (now Article 19 TFEU) prohibiting discrimination on the grounds of religion or belief, disability, age and sexual orientation.

27.2.3 **Phase 3**

The third phase in the evolution of EU equality law runs from 1997—the ToA—to the present day. During this period, the Charter of Fundamental Rights was adopted, the Treaty of Lisbon came into being and gender equality was strengthened by the adoption of legislation outlawing discrimination on the basis of gender in the supply of goods and services. The Race Directive and the Framework Employment Directive were adopted. The Recast Directive ([2006] OJ L204/23) was adopted in 2006 (see 27.4).

27.3 **TFEU provisions**

The TFEU deals with discrimination in three provisions relevant to this chapter: Articles 18, 19 and 157 TFEU.

Article 18 TFEU

Within the scope of application of the Treaties, and without prejudice to any special provisions contained therein, any discrimination on grounds of nationality shall be prohibited.

The European Parliament and the Council, acting in accordance with the ordinary legislative procedure, may adopt rules designed to prohibit such discrimination.

Article 18 TFEU has been held to have direct effect with the result that it can be relied upon by individuals seeking to assert their right to equal treatment. Its scope of application has been broadly interpreted by the CJ.

The earliest cases involving claims of equal treatment on the basis of nationality started to come before the CJ in the early 1980s. They concerned the right of equality of treatment between nationals and non-nationals with respect to conditions of access to education.

Subsequently, the CJ extended the principle of equality between nationals broadly into other areas where there was Union competence. In *Cowan* the CJ held that non-national recipients of services had a right to equality of treatment with the citizens of the country in which they were receiving services.

Cowan

Mr Cowan, a UK national, was attacked violently outside a metro station in Paris. The CJ held that, as a recipient of services, he fell within the scope of Article 18 and was thus entitled under French law to compensation for victims of violent crimes on the same terms as French nationals.

Cowan marked the beginning of a period that has lasted until this day, of using what is now Article 18 of the TFEU broadly to achieve equality of treatment among Union citizens. This case law is discussed in Chapters 23 and 24.

Although provision is made in Article 18 TFEU for implementing legislation, none has to date been adopted.

Article 19 TFEU

1. Without prejudice to the other provisions of the Treaties and within the limits of the powers conferred by them upon the Union, the Council, acting unanimously in accordance with a special legislative procedure and after obtaining the consent of the European Parliament, may take appropriate action to combat discrimination based on sex, racial or ethnic origin, religion or belief, disability, age or sexual orientation.

Article 157 TFEU

1. Each Member State shall ensure that the principle of equal pay for male and female workers for equal work or work of equal value is applied.

2. For the purpose of this Article, 'pay' means the ordinary basic or minimum wage or salary and any other consideration, whether in cash or in kind, which the worker receives directly or indirectly, in respect of his employment, from his employer.

Equal pay without discrimination based on sex means:

(a) that pay for the same work at piece rates shall be calculated on the basis of the same unit of measurement;

(b) that pay for work at time rates shall be the same for the same job.

3. The European Parliament and the Council acting in accordance with the ordinary legislative procedure and after consulting the Economic and Social Committee, shall adopt measures to ensure the application of the principle of equal opportunities and equal treatment of men and women in matters of employment and occupation, including the principle of equal pay for equal work or work of equal value.

4. With a view to ensuring full equality in practice between men and women in working life, the principle of equal treatment shall not prevent any Member State from maintaining or adopting measures providing for specific advantages in order to make it easier for the underrepresented sex to pursue a vocational activity or to prevent or compensate for disadvantages in professional careers.

A number of directives have been adopted to implement the principle of equal treatment, as set out in 27.4.

27.4 **Legislation in force**

The current position is as follows. The Equal Pay Directive, the Equal Opportunities Directive, the Equal Treatment in Occupational Social Security Schemes and the Burden of Proof Directive have been repealed and replaced with effect from 15 August 2009 by Directive 2006/54 on the implementation of the principle of equal opportunities and equal treatment of men and women in matters of employment and occupation (recast) (the Recast Directive). Whilst references to specific directives have changed, the substantive rules remain the same. Indeed, Article 34(2) of the Recast Directive (Directive 2006/54) specifies that 'References to the repealed Directives shall be construed as to this Directive' and a table of equivalence is contained in an annex to the Directive.

In addition to the Recast Directive there are five further directives which make up the full complement of legislation dealing with gender discrimination:

- the Equal Treatment in Social Security Directive;
- the Pregnancy Directive;
- the Parental Leave Directive;
- the Equal Treatment for the Self-Employed Directive;
- the Goods and Services Directive.

Two other directives have been adopted pursuant to Article 19 TFEU: (1) Directive 2000/43 implementing the principle of equal treatment between persons irrespective of racial or ethnic origin (the Race Directive ([2002] OJ L180/22)); (2) Directive 2000/78 establishing a general framework for equal treatment in employment and occupation (the Framework Employment Directive (OJ [2000] L303/16)).

There are a number of provisions common to all directives. These are considered in the next section.

27.4.1 **Common provisions**

The eight directives referred to in the preceding paragraph all deal with discrimination. This section will consider their principal features and what have they in common as well as their differences.

At the outset it should be noted that some aspects are common to all the Directives. First and foremost all the Directives prohibit direct and indirect discrimination, and define these concepts in similar terms. And they prescribe enforcement mechanisms to bring about equality of treatment.

In other respects the Directives differ, leading to a fragmentation in the application of the principle of equal treatment regarded by some as regrettable and unnecessary, but by the Commission as inevitable given the differing characteristics of the various grounds of discrimination.

The CJ has, in general, been consistent in its approach to common issues, transposing principles established in one domain of anti-discrimination to others. Yet there is a marked difference in the rigour of its approach to exceptions and derogations, with a generosity of spirit shown in favour of the Member States when determining their social and employment policy with respect to some types of discrimination, notably age, which is denied in others, for example, gender discrimination.

27.4.2 **Minimum standards**

The Directives impose minimum standards only: Member States are free to adopt more favourable provisions if they wish. The Directives, however, should not serve to justify any regression in standards prevailing at the time of its adoption. They are thus measures of upward harmonisation.

27.4.3 **Direct and indirect discrimination**

All the Directives prohibit direct and indirect discrimination, concepts developed by the CJ in its case law and subsequently transposed into legislation. Direct discrimination is defined as the treatment of one person less favourably on one of the prohibited grounds with which the legislation is concerned (sex, racial or ethnic origin, age, religion, disability or sexual orientation) than another person would be treated in comparable circumstances. Indirect discrimination occurs where an apparently neutral provision, criterion or practice would put persons bearing certain characteristics at a particular disadvantage compared with persons who do not possess those characteristics, unless such differential treatment can be objectively justified by a legitimate aim and the means of achieving that aim are proportionate. Discrimination also includes harassment and, where relevant, sexual harassment and instructions to discriminate. Less favourable treatment of women who are pregnant or on maternity leave is also prohibited. Positive action to ensure full equality is permitted both under Article 157(4) TFEU, the Recast Directive, and the Race Directive. The Directives are all expressed to apply both in the public and private sectors and to employment in public bodies—thus they cover all types of remunerated activity. The scope of the Race Directive is broader covering discrimination in a number of non-work related areas.

27.4.4 **Enforcement**

With respect to enforcement, the picture is somewhat mixed. There are some common features in the Directives and at the same time there are differences that result in a higher level of protection against discrimination in some areas but not others.

Laws, regulations or administrative provisions that are contrary to the principle of equal treatment are required to be abolished. Member States are required to make null and void, have declared null and void, or subject to the obligation to amend, any provisions contrary to the principle of equal treatment that are in individual contracts, collective agreements, internal rules of undertakings, rules governing profit-making or non-profit-making organisations, and rules governing the inde-pendent professions and workers' and employers' organisations. Thus, the Directives impose on the Member States the duty to render their provisions effective right across the entire spectrum of those aspects of economic and social life with which it is concerned.

Judicial or administrative remedies must be made available to all persons who consider them-selves to have been the subject of discriminatory acts. These remedies must be available even if the relationship within which the unequal treatment is alleged to have occurred has ended. The right to bring proceedings extends to associations, organisations or other legal entities that have a legiti-mate interest in ensuring compliance with the Directives. Member States may determine which groups have a legitimate interest.

Sanctions for breach of national provisions adopted to implement the Directives must be put in place by the Member States. Such sanctions, which may include the payment of compensation, must be effective, proportionate and dissuasive.

Apart from granting the claimant the right to bring proceedings for the enforcement of the prin-ciple of equal treatment, the Directives institute a number of other enforcement mechanisms, aimed at the prevention of discriminatory conduct. First, they advocate the dissemination of information relating to the provisions of the Directive within the Member States. Secondly, they advocate fos-tering equal treatment in the workplace through social dialogue. Thirdly, they require Member States to encourage dialogue with appropriate non-governmental organisations. Lastly, with the notable exception of the Framework Equality Directive, Member States are required to designate a body responsible for the promotion of equal treatment. Such bodies must be competent to provide independent assistance to victims of discrimination in the pursuit of their complaints, to conduct independent surveys and to make public reports and recommendations on any issue relating to discrimination.

27.4.5 **Burden of proof**

Where a claim for equal treatment requires a claimant to adduce factual evidence, the burden of proving that such evidence does not show unequal treatment shifts to the respondent who must prove that there has not been any discrimination. The plaintiff must simply provide evidence from which it may be presumed that there has been discrimination. Generally this rule does not apply to criminal proceedings or proceedings in which it is for a court or competent body to investigate the case. In *Coleman v Attridge Law* (case C-303/06), where harassment due to associative disability was alleged, the Court held that should Ms Coleman establish facts from which it could be presumed that there has been harassment, the effective application of the principle of equal treatment required that the burden of proof should fall upon the respondents to prove that there had been no harassment in the circumstances of the case. Where an employer is in possession of information from which it might be presumed discrimination had occurred and he refuses to disclose that information, his silence may be a factor to be taken into account in determining whether discrimination has occurred (*Meister*). Whilst national evidentiary rules determine what information is in the possession of an employer such rules must not result in the rights of an aggrieved person being undermined (*Kelly*).

27.5 **Overview of provisions on gender equality**

Article 157 of the TFEU, as we have seen, provides for equal pay for work of equal value. In addition to this provision, which is limited to pay, there are currently six directives dealing with gender dis-crimination (see 27.4).

27.5.1 **Pay**

'Pay' is defined in Article 157 TFEU and the Recast Directive as 'the ordinary basic or minimum wage or salary and any other consideration, whether in cash or in kind, which the worker receives directly or indirectly, in respect of his employment from his employer'. This definition reflects the broad interpretation given to the concept of pay developed by the CJ in the years since *Defrenne II* and the earlier Equal Pay Directive. Neither Article 119 of the EEC Treaty nor the latter Directive defined pay, so it was left to the CJ to elaborate. The CJ did so by relying on the link between monies received by the employee and his employment. It considered whether the employee received the sum in question as a direct result of his contract of employment or employment relationship. If this were the case those sums fell to be classified as 'pay'.

On the basis of this criterion the CJ has held 'pay' to include the following: piece work schemes in which pay depends on the individual output of each worker (*Specialarbejderforbundet i Danmark v Dansk Industri (Royal Copenhagen)* (case C-400/93)); sick leave payments (*Rinner–Kühn v FWW Spezial Gebäudereinigung GmbH & Co KG* (case C-171/88; *Høj Pedersen and Others v Kvickly Skive and Others* (case C-66/96)); pay received during maternity leave either by virtue of the employment contract, a collective agreement or under legislation (*Gillespie v Northern Health and Social Services Board* (case C-342/93); *Boyle and Others v Equal Opportunities Commission* (case C-411/96)); family and marriage allowances (*Commission v Greece* (case C-187/98)); compensation for unfair dismissal following judicial proceedings the amount of which was fixed by legislation (*R v Secretary of State for Employment, ex parte Seymour-Smith* (case C-167/97)); travel concessions paid to employees and to their spouses or long-term partners of the opposite sex or to their dependants (*Garland v British Rail Engineering* (case C-12/81)); an end of year Christmas bonus (*Leven v Denda* (case C-333/97)); supplements paid for specific duties or inconvenient working hours (*Brunnhofer v Bank der österrichischen Postsparkasse AG* (case C-381/99)); paid leave (*Arbeitwohlfahrt der Stadt Berlin v Botel* (case C-360/90)); pay in respect of loss of earnings due to attendance at training courses for staff council members (*Botel*); occupational pensions paid under contractual arrangements with an employer (*Barber*); redundancy payments (*Kowalska v Freie und Hansestadt Hamburg* (case C-33/99)) and severance grants (*Gruber v Silhouette International Schmied GmbH & Co KG* (case C-249/97)).

Pay includes allowances paid to an employee by an employer during maternity leave. This means that a woman whose contract of employment or employment relationship continues to subsist during a period of maternity leave must receive pay rises which are awarded during that period to her fellow employees doing work similar to her usual employment (*Gillespie; Abdoulaye and Others v Régie Nationale des Usines Renault SA* (case C-218/98)).

27.5.2 **Sources of pay**

The source of remuneration is irrelevant: it can derive from a contract of employment, a collective agreement, an ex gratia payment from an employer, under a statutory provision, or by virtue of a judicial decision. It matters not from where pay comes provided it is linked to employment in the sense that it is the employment relationship which gives rise to the right or the opportunity to be paid. For example, compensation for time spent on a training course is pay (*Freers and Speckmann v Deutsche Bundespost* (case C-278/93)).

27.5.2.1 **Collective agreements**

Collective agreements may also be a source of pay, with the result that any discriminatory provisions regarding pay are prohibited.

In *Kowalska*, the Court found a clause in a collective wage agreement applying to the national public service excluding part-time employees, who were largely female, from the benefit of a severance grant on termination of their employment to be contrary to Article 141. In *Krieza* (case C-281/1), an end of year bonus paid under a collective agreement applicable to public sector employees was held to be pay and so the exclusion of large groups of female employees from entitlement to it was found to be contrary to Article 157.

Enderby raised a different issue concerning collective agreements: to what extent can separately negotiated collective agreements be compared for the purpose of determining whether there is gender discrimination in the pay levels fixed by the two collective agreements for two jobs of equal value?

Enderby

Ms Enderby was a speech therapist. She complained that as a member of a healthcare profession which was largely female she was paid less than a pharmacist who she claimed was doing the same work or work of equal value. The rate of pay for both professions was settled by collective bargaining processes. Within each collective agreement there was no difference in the treatment of men and women, but when both were compared there were differences in the pay of both professions. Could the two agreements be compared for the purposes of determining whether the alleged discrimination between the two professions existed or not?

The Court held that they could:

> The fact that the rates of pay at issue are decided by collective bargaining processes conducted separately for each of the two professional groups concerned without any discriminatory effect within each group, does not preclude a finding of prima facie discrimination where the results of these processes show that two groups with the same employer and the same trade union are treated differently. If the employer could rely on the absence of discrimination within each of the collective bargaining processes taken separately as sufficient justification for the difference in pay, he could easily circumvent the principle of equal pay by using separate bargaining processes (para 22).

27.5.2.2 A single source

In the absence of collective agreements or job evaluation schemes affecting undertakings or industries at a national level, it is submitted that comparisons cannot be made *across* undertakings or industries. This principle was established in *Lawrence v Regent Office Care Ltd, Commercial Catering Group and Mitie Secure Services Ltd* (case C-320/00).

Lawrence

The local council, which had employed people directly to carry out cleaning and catering jobs, put these services out to competitive tender. During the tendering period, the women involved in these jobs won a case against the council arguing that their work was equal to work carried out by men for jobs such as gardening, refuse collection and sewage treatment. Thereafter, the women still employed by the council had their wages increased. The contractor who obtained the contract with the council for the cleaning and catering services then re-employed some of the former council workers, but paid them less than they had been paid by the council. The women employed by the contractor then brought a claim on the basis of Article 157, arguing that they were entitled to equal pay with male comparators employed by the council, regardless of whether the appellants had been originally employed by the council or were so employed at present.

The CJ, however, held that where the differences identified in the pay conditions of workers of different sex performing equal work or work of equal value cannot be attributed to a single source, Article 157(1) does not apply.

27.5.2.3 Ex gratia payments

The employer may not necessarily be contractually or otherwise legally bound to furnish the payment or benefit in question. Ex gratia payments paid over voluntarily are pay if linked to employment. *Garland* concerned the right to travel facilities by spouses and children of retired employees. Such facilities were granted to the spouses and children of male employees but not to female employees. The employer, British Rail, was not contractually bound to grant such facilities, but generally did so, with the result that male employees had a legitimate expectation that they would be so granted after their retirement.

The Court found that the facilities in question were pay for the purposes of Article 157 TFEU; provided they were granted in respect of employment, their precise legal nature was not relevant.

Similarly in *Lewen* a Christmas bonus, equal to one month's salary, which was a voluntary benefit revocable at any time payable as an incentive for future work and loyalty, was held to be pay for the purposes of Article 119.

27.5.2.4 Statutory payments

The concept of 'pay' can also cover payments which an employer is obliged to make to an employee under statute irrespective of any agreement between them (*Rinner-Kühn*).

27.5.2.5 Payments resulting from a judicial decision

Seymour-Smith held that a judicial award of compensation for breach of the right not to be unfairly dismissed constitutes pay.

27.5.2.6 Access to pay

The right of access to elements of consideration is also pay (eg, the right to join an occupational pension scheme has been held to be within the scope of now Article 157 TFEU) (*Bilka-Kaufhaus GmbH v Weber von Hartz* (case 170/84)) as has the automatic reclassification to a higher point in the salary scale on the basis of length of service (*Helga Nimz v Freie und Hansestadt Hamburg* (case C-184/89)) and a system for classifying workers converting from job sharing to full-time employment which determines their pay level (*Hill and Stapleton v Revenue Commissioners and Department of Finance* (case C-243/95)).

27.6 Pensions

The precise extent to which employers' contributions to pensions and other social security benefits fall within the scope of Article 157 has been made clear in *Bilka-Kaufhaus* in the context of a claim by a female part-time worker.

> ## Bilka-Kaufhaus
>
> Ms Weber was seeking to challenge her employer's occupational pension scheme. The scheme was non-contributory, financed solely by the employer. Under the scheme part-timers were entitled to benefit only if they had worked with the firm for at least 15 out of a total of 20 years. No such limitation was imposed on full-timers. Ms Weber alleged that the scheme was indirectly discriminatory, in breach of Article 157, since the majority of part-time workers were women.
>
> The Court agreed that it was *capable* of falling within the provision, as the scheme was contractual, not statutory, in origin; it originated from an agreement made between Bilka and the works council representing the employees, and the benefits were financed solely by the employer as a supplement to existing social-security schemes. The benefit constituted consideration paid by the employer to the employee for his employment.

The reasoning in *Bilka-Kaufhaus* seemed to imply that benefits paid by an employer pursuant to or in lieu of a *statutory* scheme might not constitute pay.

In *Barber*, the Court found, in a claim by a group of male employees who were seeking to challenge payments made by their employer under a contracted-out pension scheme, which operated as a substitute for the statutory social-security scheme, and under a statutory redundancy scheme, both of which were payable at different ages for men (65) and women (60), that such payments also constituted 'pay', since the worker received these benefits, albeit indirectly, from his employer for his employment:

> Although it is true that many advantages granted by an employer also reflect considerations of social policy, the fact that a benefit is in the nature of pay cannot be called into question where the worker is entitled to receive the benefit in question from his employer by reason of the existence of the employment relationship [para 18].

This point was re-emphasised in *Beune*, which concerned civil service pensions. The Court held that, even where the pension scheme was affected by considerations of social policy, state organisation, ethics or budgetary concerns (factors usually indicative of a social-security scheme), the pension scheme of a public employer would still constitute pay where: (1) it concerned only a certain category of workers rather than general categories; (2) it was directly related to the period of service; and (3) it was calculated by reference to the employee's last salary (para 45; see also *Schönheit v Stadt Frankfurt am main* (case C-4/02); *Commission v Italy (summary publication)* (case C-46/07)).

Because the ruling in *Barber* was likely to affect seriously the financial balance of contracted-out pension schemes, the contributions and the calculations for which had been based on different retirement ages for men and women; and because, as the Court conceded, both Member States and the parties concerned were reasonably entitled to consider that this provision did not apply to pensions paid under contracted-out pension schemes, the Court held that its ruling as regards such schemes could not be applied retrospectively. Article 157 might not be relied on to claim entitlement to a pension with effect prior to the date of judgment, except in the case of workers, or those claiming under them, who had before that date initiated legal proceedings or raised an equivalent claim under the applicable national law (para 45). Following dispute over the scope of this ruling, as to whether Article 157 applies to all claims for *pensions arising* after the date of judgment or only to claims based on *benefits earned* after this date, the matter was finally resolved by a protocol issued at Maastricht in favour of the latter, more restrictive view (Protocol No 2).

This interpretation of *Barber* has since been applied by the Court in many cases including *Ten Oever v Stichting Bedrijfspensioenenfonds voor het Glazenwassers-en Schoonmaakbedrijf* (case C-109/91), survivors' benefit; *Coloroll Pension Trustees Ltd v Russell* (case C-200/91); *Moroni v Firma Collo GmbH* (case C-110/91), supplementary pension scheme, early retirement; *Neath v Hugh Steeper Ltd* (case C-152/91), supplementary pension scheme, early retirement; and *Defreyn v Sabena SA* (case C-166/99), additional pre-retirement payment. However, in *Vroege v NCIV Institute Voor Volkshuisvesting Bv* (case C-57/93), and *Fisscher* the Court held that the limit on retrospectivity of its ruling in *Barber* did not apply where it should have been clear to the employer that the terms fell within Article 157. In these cases, the provisions related to *access* to pension schemes, which, following *Bilka-Kaufhaus*, should be considered pay. Provided the female employees were prepared to pay the requisite contributions to a pension scheme for any period between *Defrenne* and *Barber*, employers were also obliged to make the relevant employer's contributions to such schemes retrospectively. This principle was affirmed in *Preston and Fletcher*, and the non-retroactivity in *Barber*, as reinforced by the protocol, was affirmed in *Schönheit*.

Further problems arising from the application of Article 157 TFEU to the award of occupational pensions are illustrated in *Neath v Hugh Steeper Ltd* (case C-152/91). The case concerned a contracted-out pension scheme in which men were treated less favourably than women in respect of early retirement and lump-sum payments in lieu of pension payments. Neath claimed that, following *Barber*, this was contrary to Article 157. The Court, however, distinguished between the *accrual of the right* to receive benefits and the *funding* of those benefits. Both the pension payments themselves and the employees' contributions to a pension scheme fell within 'pay' and, therefore, neither should distinguish between the sexes. The funding arrangements established by the employer, however, fall outside the scope of Article 157 because the purpose of those arrangements is to ensure that there are adequate resources to make the pension payments when due. An employer, when calculating its contribution to funding, may therefore rely on actuarial factors which, for example, take into account differing average life expectancies of the sexes and thus may make different payments in respect of men and women (para 22). A corollary to this argument is that capital sum or transfer benefits such as lump-sum payments that are based on the method and amount of funding also do not fall within Article 157 (para 33). *Neath* was a retreat from the position in *Barber*, and has made the boundaries between pay and pensions even less certain than they seemed before.

The Court's judgment in *Neath* does not affect a further principle established in *Barber*, that, in order to comply with Article 157 TFEU, it is not enough that the overall package of remuneration received by men and women be equal. Each element of the consideration paid to both sexes must be equal. The system of pay must be 'transparent', in order that clear comparisons as between men and women may be made in every element.

27.7 Meaning of 'worker'

Article 157 refers to male and female 'workers'. In *Debra Allonby v Accrington & Rossendale College* (case C-256/01), the CJ noted that there was no single definition of this concept in Union law, but that this varied according to the context in which it was used. At the same time, the concept must be given a Union meaning. The Court chose to adopt the *Lawrie-Blum* definition of 'a person who, for a certain period of time, performs services under the direction of another person in return for which he receives remuneration', which included a person who was self-employed where the status as self-employed was notional and disguised an employment relationship. However, independent providers of services who are not in a position of subordination to the person receiving such services are not within the scope of Article 157 (*Allonby*).

A person will also be regarded as a worker where she is a part-time employee working to need, that is, only the hours requested by her employer (*Wippel v Peek & Cloppenburg GmbH & Co KG* (case C-313/02)).

27.8 Equal pay for equal work

Article 157 TFEU provides for 'equal pay for male and female workers for equal work or work of equal value'. Article 4 Recast Directive refers to equal pay for work of equal value.

The Court has consistently adopted a broad approach focusing on the essential objective of the principle of equal pay which is to ensure that men and women who do the same work receive the same remuneration. It has accordingly, for example, laid down principles to ensure that job classification schemes do not contain features that would result in the discriminatory treatment of one sex or the other. It has allowed comparisons to be made between jobs held at different points of time and between jobs having a higher value to the jobs with which a comparison is sought to be made.

27.8.1 Job classification schemes

In the case of different types of work, it may not be easy to determine whether they are comparable in value. In order to facilitate comparisons for the determination of pay rates, employers may choose to set up a job classification scheme in order to evaluate the different components in any given job but that job classification scheme may in itself have discriminatory consequences.

The Recast Directive, in Article 4, provides that where a job classification system is used for determining pay, it must be based on the same criteria for both men and women and so exclude any discrimination on grounds of sex. More precise indications of how this may be achieved are set out in case law (*Rummler v Data-Druck GmbH* (case 237/83); *Brunnhofer*).

27.8.2 Contemporaneity

Macarthys Ltd v Smith (case 129/79) raised the issue of the point in time when job comparisons could be made.

Macarthys

Mrs Smith was employed as a manager of a warehouse at a salary of £50 per week. Her predecessor, who had left that job some four months earlier, had been paid £60 per week. Could Mrs Smith compare herself to him in spite of the fact that they were not both in the employment of Macarthys at the same time? Could her employer offer her a lower rate of pay where there was no change in the work required to be performed but she had been hired some four months after her predecessor had left the post?

The Court held in principle that it could not. The scope of the concept of 'equal work' could not be restricted by the introduction of a requirement of contemporaneity. Where the work was of equal value a female employee had to receive the same pay as her male predecessor even if he had vacated the job some time before she was appointed. If the situation were otherwise, it would be all too easy to avoid the principle of equal pay.

27.8.3 **Equal work**

Macarthys held that the scope of the concept of 'equal work' is entirely qualitative in character in that it is exclusively concerned with the nature of the services in question. The point of focus in determining whether jobs are of equal value is the nature of the work performed not its formal classification within the employer organisation.

Absolute parity is not necessary. Work may be of lesser value than that with which it is sought to be compared (*Murphy and Others v An Bord Telecom Eireann* (case 157/87)). This stands to reason. If work of equal value is required to be remunerated on the same basis, why should work of lesser value not be so required?

Whether work is of equal value or not is a subjective matter to be determined on the basis of the facts of each case. There is no hard and fast rule.

Similarity or differences in professional qualifications are not in themselves decisive. The essential criterion is what the workers actually do or can be required to do, not what qualifications they have. Comparisons based on qualifications alone could be misleading. They must be made in the context of the employment environment.

In *Angestelltenbetriebsrat der Wiener Gebietskrankenkasse v Wiener Gebietskrankenkasse* (case C-309/97) the issue was whether different groups of persons who carried out seemingly identical tasks, but who did not have the same training or professional qualifications performed the same work.

Angestelltenbetriebsrat der Wiener Gebietskrankenkasse

In this case there were three types of psychotherapists employed by the Vienna Health Fund: doctors who had completed their general practitioners' or specialists' training; graduate psychologists qualified to practise in the health sector or on a self-employed basis; and, lastly, those who were neither doctors nor psychologists, but who had a general education and had undergone specialised training in psychotherapy. Were these three categories comparable? The order for reference to the Court stated that although psychologists and doctors employed as psychotherapists by the Health Fund performed identical activities, in treating their patients they drew upon knowledge and skills acquired in very different disciplines, the expertise of psychologists being grounded in the study of psychology, that of doctors in the study of medicine. Even though doctors and psychologists both in fact performed work of psychotherapy the former were also qualified to perform other tasks in a field which is not open to the latter, who could only perform psychotherapy.

The Court held that in those circumstances:

> two groups of persons who have received different professional training and who, because of the different scope of the qualifications resulting from that training, on the basis of which they were recruited, are called upon to perform difference tasks or duties, cannot be regarded as being in a comparable situation [para 21].

The Court was not influenced in its findings by the fact that a single tariff was charged for psychotherapeutic treatment since that may 'be the result of social policy'.

If it is the case that two groups of persons with different professional training do perform different tasks, then they are not in comparable situations. But if in fact those with different professional qualifications are also doing the same tasks, they may be doing the same work or work of equal value. Whether this is the case or not must be ascertained by looking at the tasks assigned to each group and the training requirements for the performance of those tasks. If the tasks are performed by persons having different qualifications but whose training is suitable for the execution of those tasks, it would appear difficult to argue that they are not doing 'equal work'. This may be the case of the 'overqualified' worker whose skills exceed those required for the job in question. Conversely, if persons having the same qualifications are in fact doing different tasks they may not be doing equal work.

27.9 Discrimination

Both direct and indirect discrimination are prohibited.

27.9.1 Direct discrimination

Direct discrimination is easier to discern than indirect discrimination in that it concerns a difference in the rate of pay for male and female employees doing the same work or work of equal value and therefore is, or ought to be, obvious.

Direct discrimination has been found to exist in the following circumstances:

- where a woman receives less pay than a man who previously carried out the same work in the same undertaking (*Macarthys*);
- where a male and female employee performing the same work receive the same basic salary, but the male employee is paid a higher salary supplement than the female employee (*Brunnhofer*);
- where retired male transport employees enjoy travel facilities denied to retired female employees (*Garland*);
- where retirement pensions under an occupational pensions scheme are paid out at different pensionable ages for men and women (*Barber*);
- where the conditions attaching to the receipt of survivors' pensions differ for widows and widowers (*DEI v Evrenopoulos* (case 147/95); *Jean-Marie Podesta v Caisse de Retraite par répartition des Ingénieurs Cadres & Assimilés (CRICA) and Others* (case C-50/98));
- where redundancy payments awarded by virtue of a collective agreement are granted to male workers aged between sixty and sixty-five years, but are denied to female workers within the same age group (*Commission v Belgium* (case C-173/91));
- where pay increases are denied to women during periods of maternity leave (*Alabaster v Woolwich plc* (case C-147/07)).

27.9.2 Indirect discrimination

Indirect discrimination is more difficult to detect (and prove) than direct discrimination, given that pay rates will, in principle, appear to be the same for workers in doing the same work under comparable conditions. The classic case, and one of the first that came before the Court, is that of the part-time worker who tends to be female and may be paid proportionately less or receive less favourable terms of employment than the full-time worker. Equality of treatment for part-time workers has now been ensured in the Part-time Workers Directive (Directive 97/98 ([1998] OJ L14/8)), but the issue of their right to equality arose many years before in the context of equal pay claims in *Jenkins v Kingsgate (Clothing Productions) Ltd* (case 96/80).

Jenkins

Mrs Jenkins worked part-time in the Kingsgate Clothing company. She claimed that she was receiving an hourly rate of pay which was less than that of her male colleagues employed full-time doing the same work. The part-time workforce of Kingsgate Clothing was predominantly female.

The Court held that a difference in pay between full-time and part-time workers does not amount to discrimination prohibited by Article 157 TFEU unless it is in reality merely an indirect way of reducing the level of pay of part-time workers on the ground that that group of workers is composed exclusively or predominantly of women. If the difference in pay between the two groups of workers is attributable to factors which are objectively justified, there is no unlawful discrimination. This might be the case if the employer was endeavouring to encourage full-time work irrespective of the sex of the worker.

Further examples of findings of indirect discrimination in preliminary rulings proceedings before the Court in which part-time workers have been denied benefits or advantages given to full-time employees include:

- the exclusion of part-time workers from membership of occupational pension schemes (*Bilka Kaufhaus*);
- the exclusion of part-time workers from the payment of a severance grant on termination of employment (*Kowalska*);
- non-payment of salary to part-time workers during periods of illness (*Rinner Kühn*);
- the exclusion of workers in minor employment (less than fifteen hours a week) from a special Christmas bonus equivalent to one month's salary (*Kruger v Kreiskrankenhaus Ebersberg* (case C-281/97));
- the placement of job sharers who worked part-time to a pay level less than that for full-time job-sharing staff upon their conversion to full-time employment (*Hill and Stapleton*);
- the non-payment of compensation to part-time workers for attendance at staff training courses outside their normal working hours, where full-time staff receive compensation for loss of earnings due to attendance at such courses during their normal working hours (*Botel* (case C-360/90); *Lewark* (case C-457/93));
- there is a prima facie case of discrimination where the pay level of one group of workers (predominantly women) is less than another group of workers (predominantly men) working for the same employer in jobs which are of equal value (*Enderby*);
- requirement for access to membership of an occupational pension scheme which is more difficult for women to fulfil than men (*Allonby*).

27.9.3 Time rates/piece work

Where work is paid at time rates the employer may take the employee's level of productivity into account (*Brunnhofer*) with the result that different rates may be applicable, but since the pay differentials will not be attributable to sex but to objective differences in the value of the work to the employer, the principle of equal pay will not be violated. Likewise, where the unit of measurement is the same for two groups of workers carrying out the same work at piece rates, the principle of equal pay does not prohibit those workers from receiving different pay if that is due to levels of individual output. Therefore, in a piece work scheme, the mere finding that there is a difference in the average pay of two groups of workers, calculated on the basis of the total individual pay of all workers belonging to one or other group, is not sufficient to establish that there is discrimination with regard to pay (*Royal Copenhagen*).

27.9.4 Computation of pay

The basic methodology by which an employment package is calculated may affect aspects of an employee's remuneration and must therefore be the same for men and women. It is necessary to look at each aspect of the remuneration package and the relationship between those elements. This principle was established in *Worringham and Humphreys*.

Worringham and Humphreys

Lloyds Bank had two retirement schemes, one for men and one for women, established under collective agreements made between Lloyds and the trade union representative of Lloyds' employees. Under the retirement schemes, men under the age of twenty-five years were required to contribute 5 per cent of their salary to these schemes whereas women under thirty-five years were not. In order to cover the compulsory contributions of the young men, Lloyds added the amount of the contribution—5 per cent—to their gross salary. This amount was then deducted and paid directly into the pension scheme. The men in question therefore never actually received the 5 per cent extra pay. But the basis on which other employment-related benefits such as redundancy payments, unemployment benefits, family benefits, mortgage, and credit allowances were calculated included that 5 per cent figure.

The Court found that in the circumstances of the case the pension contributions paid by Lloyds on behalf of the men constituted 'pay' since they directly determined the calculation of other advantages linked to salary with the result that the men received benefits from which women engaged in the same work or work of equal value were excluded, or received on that account greater benefits or social advantages than those to which women were entitled (see also *WGM Liefting and Others v Directie van het Academisch Ziekenhuis bij de Universiteit van Amsterdam and Others* (case 23/83)).

Worringham and Humphreys was concerned with the impact of different methods of calculating gross salary on salary-related benefits. *Newstead v Department of Transport* (case 192/85) differed in the sense that men and women received the same gross salary, but a sum of 1.5 per cent of that was deducted in the case of men as a contribution to a widow's pension fund. The result was that the net pay of men and women was less than that of women doing the same job. The Court in *Newstead*, in contrast to the approach it had adopted in *Worringham and Humphreys*, ignored the patent disparities in net pay finding that there was no discrimination since gross pay for men and women was the same:

> The deduction in question results in a reduction in net pay because a contribution is paid to a social security scheme and in no way affects gross pay, on the basis of which other salary-related benefits…are normally calculated [para 18].

Although the Court referred to the widow's pension scheme as 'social security', this was not in fact the case: the scheme in question was an occupational pension scheme. Had it been a statutory social security scheme, there would have been no issue under Article 157 TFEU as such schemes are not 'pay'.

27.10 Grounds of discrimination: limited to sex

An employer is entitled to restrict employment benefits to married couples thereby excluding couples who are not married. Equally an employer may restrict benefits to spouses (*Newstead*) or persons of the opposite sex who are in a relationship with the employee from whose remuneration the entitlement to those benefits derives. Neither of these situations comes about because of any unlawful discriminatory conduct. Each employee is subject to the same conditions of entitlement. But what if an employee is prevented from getting a benefit related to his employment either for himself or for his partner or family member because under national law he cannot put himself in a position to fulfil the requirements of entitlement? This was the situation in *KB v National Health Service Pensions Agency and the Secretary of State for Health* (case C-117/01).

KB

In *KB*, the Court held that it was in principle contrary to Article 157 TFEU for national legislation to prevent a couple from fulfilling the marriage requirement which must be met for one of them to be able to benefit from the salary benefits of the other. The Court in reaching this conclusion was influenced by the fact that the national provision in issue had been held to be contrary to the ECHR.

Grant v South-West Trains Ltd (case C-249/96) concerned a claim to equal treatment from a woman in a same sex relationship.

Grant

Lisa Grant claimed the right to travel concessions from her employer, South-West Trains, in respect of her female partner. Travel concessions were granted to employees, their spouses and/or partners of the opposite sex with whom the employee has been in a meaningful relationship for two years. Ms Grant's application for these concessions for her partner was rejected on the ground that in the case of unmarried employees travel concessions would only be granted for partners of the opposite sex. Ms Grant claimed that such a restriction constituted discrimination on two counts:

(1) The male worker who had previously occupied her post had obtained travel concessions for his female partner and consequently any refusal to give the same concessions to Ms Grant's partner amounted to direct discrimination based on sex;

(2) The denial of the concessions constituted discrimination on the ground of sexual orientation which was included within the concept of 'discrimination based on sex' in Article 141.

The Court rejected both of these arguments. It held that Ms Grant was refused the concession because she did not live with a spouse or person of the opposite sex, which was a condition for entitlement. That condition applied to all employees regardless of their sex. Travel concessions were not made available to a male worker if he was living with a person of the same sex just as they were unavailable to a female worker if she were living with a person of the same sex. Article 157 did not cover discrimination based on sexual orientation.

27.11 Objective justification

27.11.1 General criteria

As noted earlier, differences in pay (or treatment) which discriminate indirectly against women or men will be permissible if they are objectively justified. Guidelines as to what might constitute objective justification were laid down in *Bilka-Kaufhaus*. There the Court held that in order to prove that a measure is objectively justified the employer must prove that the measures giving rise to the difference in treatment:

- correspond to a 'genuine need of the enterprise';
- are suitable for obtaining the objective pursued by the enterprise;
- are necessary for that purpose.

27.11.2 Justifications based on economic factors, job performance and market forces

Jenkins and *Bilka-Kaufhaus* suggest that economic factors would prove acceptable justification. In *Bilka-Kaufhaus* the defendants argued that part-time workers were less economic; they were less ready to work on Saturdays and in the evening; that it was necessary to pay more to attract full-timers. Justification on these grounds was not disputed in principle. Whether it would in fact be accepted would depend on whether the need for the difference in pay could be proved, and if so whether the proportionality principle was satisfied. In applying this ruling the German court found that it was not.

In *Cadman v Health and Safety Executive* (case C-17/05) the Court examined indirect discrimination against women resulting from the fact that one of the criteria taken into account for the assessment of pay was length of service. It held that rewarding an employee who has acquired experience enabling him to perform better constitutes a legitimate objective of pay policy:

> As a general rule, recourse to the criterion of length of service is appropriate to attain that objective. Length of service goes hand in hand with experience, and experience generally enables the worker to perform his duties better [para 35].

While taking into account length of service in order to determine a worker's remuneration is lawful, the total exclusion of part-time employment from the calculation of length of service will violate the Recast Directive if it affects a much higher percentage of female workers than male workers, unless it can be attributed to objective factors unrelated to sex (*Nikoloudi v OTE AE* (case C-196/02)) (on criteria for the determination of pay, see also *Danfoss*).

Although the Court has been sympathetic to the Member States' concern to control budgetary expenditure (eg, limitations imposed in *Barber; Steenhorst-Neerings*), a *purely* economic justification of discrimination is unlikely to be successful. In *MA de Weerd, née Roks, and Others v Bestuur van de Bedrijfsvereniging voor de Gezondheid, Geestelijke en Maatschappelijke Belangen and Others* (case C-343/92) concerning Directive 79/7 the Court stated that to allow budgetary considerations to justify discrimination between men and women would be tantamount to agreeing that the fundamental principle of equality could vary over time and throughout the Union depending on the state of the Member States' public finances (paras 35–6) (see also *R v Secretary of State for Health, ex parte Richardson* (case C-137/94) and *Schönheit*).

27.11.3 Administrative convenience

In *Kirsammer-Hack v Nurhan Sidal* (case C-189/91), in a claim based on the then Equal Treatment Directive (Directive 76/207), the Court was prepared to concede that an exclusion from employment protection provided under German legislation for employees of firms comprising fewer than five employees, excluding employees working less than 10 hours a week or 45 hours per month, even if indirectly discriminatory against women, would be objectively justified on the grounds of the need to lighten the administrative, financial and legal burdens on small enterprises, acknowledged by the Union in the then Article 154 TFEU and its directives on the health and safety of workers.

27.11.4 Social-policy objectives

In *Rinner-Kühn* the Court suggested that a justification based on a 'genuine objective of social policy' might be acceptable, provided that the means selected were appropriate and necessary to the attainment of that objective.

27.12 Recast Directive: Article 14(2): genuine and determining occupational requirement

The Recast Directive provides:

> Member States may provide, as regards access to employment including the training leading thereto, that a difference of treatment which is based on a characteristic related to sex shall not constitute discrimination where, by reason of the nature of the particular occupational activities concerned or in the context in which they were carried out, such a characteristic constitutes a genuine and determining occupational requirement, provided that its objective is legitimate and the requirement is proportionate.

27.12.1 Positive discrimination

A further exception to the principle of equal treatment is that of positive discrimination, which permits schemes to enable women to compete equally with men. As already noted, the ToA amended Article 119 EC, which became Article 157 TFEU, so as to strengthen the provision for positive discrimination with the addition of a new para (4), which provides that:

> With a view to ensuring full equality in practice between men and women in working life, the principle of equal treatment shall not prevent any Member State from maintaining or adopting measures providing for specific advantages in order to make it easier for the under-represented sex to pursue a vocational activity or to prevent or compensate for disadvantages in professional careers.

Article 3 of the Recast Directive provides for positive discrimination in almost identical terms:

> Member States may maintain or adopt measures within the meaning of Article 157(4) of the Treaty with a view to ensuring full equality in practice between men and women in working life.

This reflects the case law of the CJ developed under Article 119 EEC.

In *Marschall v Land Nordrhein-Westfalen* (case C-409/95), which was decided before the addition of para 4 to Article 157 of the EC Treaty, the Court held that a national provision which gave priority to women applicants was compatible with Union law because it included a qualification that the employer could appoint a male applicant if there were special reasons for such an appointment. Similarly in *Georg Badeck and Others* (case C-158/97), decided after the ToA came into force, the Court ruled in favour of several provisions which gave priority to women in the context of public-service employment because they were not 'absolute and unconditional', but aimed at affording qualified women additional opportunities to enter working life.

Further, positive discrimination measures must respect the principle of proportionality, as can be seen by the judgment in *Lommers v Minister van Landbouw, Natuurbeheer en Visserij* (case C-476/99), where the CJ had to consider whether right of access to subsidised nursery places to female employees was acceptable. The CJ noted that the former Article 2(4) Directive 76/207 (replaced by Article 3 Recast Directive) authorises measures relating to access to employment which give a specific advantage to women to allow them to compete on an equal footing with men. The Court noted that the absence of suitable and affordable nursery facilities leads to parents, mainly women, giving up their jobs. The CJ concluded that such measures would fall within the scope of the former Article 2(4). Nonetheless, any such measure must be proportional. A measure which excludes fathers from all possibility of access to such facilities would be disproportionate. Rules that exceptionally permit fathers who take care of their children would, however, be permissible. The same general approach seems to be taken here as was taken in *Badeck* and *Marschall*.

Interestingly, the CJ noted in *Lommers* that measures such as those in this case, 'might nevertheless also help to perpetuate a traditional division of roles between men and women' (para 41). While there is undoubtedly a risk of stereotyping arising from positive discrimination measures such as this, the alternative may perpetuate a real existing disadvantage. The existence of these conflicting concerns suggests that it is not appropriate to state that all positive discrimination should be viewed as 'good' or 'bad', but that such measures should be assessed individually.

Finally, even now, measures which give automatic priority to certain candidates will be incompatible with the principle of equal treatment. In *Abrahamson and Anderson* the Court examined a rule which provided that candidates of the underrepresented sex would be appointed despite the fact that their qualifications were inferior to those of other candidates if such an appointment could be objectively justified. The Court held that this rule was disproportionate to the aim pursued since it granted automatic preference to the members of the underrepresented group with the result that the selection was ultimately based on the mere fact of belonging to a certain sex.

The effect of the Court's case law on positive discrimination is that rules which grant automatic priority by reference to a candidate's sex will be incompatible with Union law. By contrast, measures which are designed to combat existing inequalities in the marketplace by affording additional employment opportunities to members of the underrepresented sex who are suitably qualified and allow other factors (ie beyond the candidates' sex) to be taken into account are acceptable.

The previously discussed cases involving exemption from the equal treatment principle all concern direct discrimination. Where the discrimination is indirect the same principles apply as apply in the field of pay; a difference in treatment as between one group of workers and another which *affects* one sex disproportionately will require objective justification.

27.13 Scope of the Recast Directive

Article 14 of the Recast Directive prohibits direct and indirect discrimination on grounds of sex in the public and private sectors, including public bodies in relation to:

- conditions for access to employment, to self-employment or occupation, including selection criteria and recruitment conditions, whatever the branch of activity and at all levels of the professional hierarchy, including promotion;

- access to all types and to all levels of vocational guidance and retraining, including practical work experience;
- employment and working conditions, including dismissals, as well as pay;
- membership of and involvement in an organisation of workers and employers, or any organisation whose members carry on a particular profession, including the benefits provided for by such organisations.

27.13.1 Access to employment

'Access to employment' has been given a broad interpretation by the CJ, encompassing not only conditions obtaining before an employment relationship comes into being, but also matters which affect the decision to seek or accept employment. In *Meyers v Adjudication Officer* (case C-116/94) a social security benefit designed to keep low income workers in employment or to encourage them into employment was held to be within the scope of what is now the Recast Directive since it was directly related to access to employment:

> … the prospect of receiving family credit, if he accepts low paid work encourages unemployed workers to accept such work with the result that the benefit is related to considerations governing access to employment [para 22].

27.13.1.1 Vocational training

Article 14(10)(b) Recast Directive provides for the application of the principle of equal treatment with respect to access to all types and levels of vocational training. This provision has direct effect (*Johnston*). In *Schnorbus* (case 79/99) the CJ found that giving preferential treatment in the matter of admission to practical legal training to male applicants who have completed compulsory military or civil service indirectly discriminates against women since they are not required to do military or civil training and therefore not in a position to benefit from the preferential admissions policy. However the CJ went on to find that the differential treatment was objectively justified:

> … it is clear that the provision at issue, which takes account of the delay experienced in the progress of their education by applicants who have been required to do military or civilian service, is objective in nature and prompted solely by the desire to counterbalance to some extent the effects of that delay (para 44).

27.13.1.2 Employment conditions including dismissal

The concept of 'working conditions' has been given a broad interpretation; it concerns all aspects of the conditions in which the worker performs his job. A prohibition on night work by women where there was no equivalent provision applicable to men has been held to be discriminatory and therefore prohibited (*Commission v France* (case C-197/96); *Stoeckel* (case C-345/89)).

In *Burton* it was held that the concept of dismissal must be construed broadly so as to include the termination of an employment relationship between a worker and his employer even as part of a voluntary redundancy scheme.

Roberts v Tate and Lyle Ltd (case 151/84) held that the age limit for compulsory redundancy of workers as part of a mass redundancy falls within the concept of 'dismissal' in the then Equal Opportunities Directive.

Roberts

Joan Roberts worked for Tate and Lyle for twenty-eight years. At the age of fifty-three years she was made redundant along with the other employees at the depot at which she worked in Liverpool, which was closed by Tate and Lyle. Employees were offered either a cash payment or an early pension. All employees both male and female over the age of fifty-five were offered an early pension. The normal retirement age for men was sixty-five and women sixty. Ms Roberts contended that the early pension entitlement under the severance package was discriminatory since men were entitlement to an immediate pension ten years before retirement age whereas women were not so entitled until five years before their normal retirement age.

The Court ruled that there was no discrimination:

…the grant of a pension to persons of the same age who are made redundant amounts merely to a collective measure adopted irrespective of the sex of those persons in order to guarantee them all the same rights. (Judgment, para 36.)

Judgment in *Marshall I* was handed down on the same day as *Roberts*.

Marshall

Miss Marshall was employed as a dietician by an area health authority. She was dismissed at the age of sixty-two years solely because she had reached retirement age. The health authority had a policy which fixed retirement age at the age at which the statutory pension becomes payable, which was sixty years in the case of women and sixty-five years in the case of men. The health authority had exercised its discretion to allow Miss Roberts to continue working until the age of sixty-two years, but she wished to work until the age of sixty-five years.

The Court held:

…a general policy concerning dismissal involving the dismissal of a woman solely because she has attained the qualifying age for a state pension, which age is different under national law for men and women, constitutes discrimination on the grounds of sex (para 38).

27.13.2 **Direct and indirect discrimination**

Both direct and indirect discrimination are prohibited, as is harassment. *Kleist* (case C-356/09) provides an example of direct discrimination.

Kleist

This case concerned a provision of Austrian law which permitted an employer in the public sector to dismiss employees who have acquired the right to withdraw their retirement pension five years earlier than men. Did this difference between men and women in the timing of pension entitlement and the consequences of that constitute discrimination? The Court found that it did. Doctors working in the public health sector could be dismissed when they acquired the right to draw a retirement pension.

> Men acquired that right at the age of sixty-five years. Women at the age of sixty years. The effect of this was that men could be dismissed at the age of sixty-five years but women at sixty years.

Examples of indirect discrimination can be seen in the *Rinke* (case C-25/02), *Kording* (case C-100/95) and *Kirsammer-Hack* cases. In *Rinke*, the Court found that a requirement that general medical training must include periods of full-time training worked to the disadvantage of a much higher percentage of women than men since a '…much higher percentage of women than men wishing to train in general medicine have difficulties working full time during part of their training'. Likewise in *Kording* part-time employees, more than 90 per cent of whom were women, suffered discrimination because they had to work for a number of years longer than full-time employees in order to be exempt from the compulsory qualifying examination for tax advisers. But in *Kirsammer-Hack* the exclusion of the employment force of small businesses from protection against unfair dismissal was held not to be discriminatory since it applied to all employees of such businesses whether they work full-time, part-time, or half-time. However, the Court pointed out that if it were established that small businesses employed a considerably higher percentage of women than men, that would constitute indirect discrimination.

27.13.3 Derogation from the equal treatment principle

Article 14(2) of the Recast Directive permits Member States with regard to access to employment and related training, to provide that 'a difference of treatment which is based on a characteristic relating to sex' is not discriminatory where because of 'the nature of the particular occupational activities concerned or of the context in which they are carried out, such a characteristic constitutes a genuine and determining occupational requirement'. Article 15 provides that the Directive is without prejudice to provisions on the protection of women during pregnancy and maternity leave. In addition, Article 3 of the Recast Directive provides some scope for positive discrimination, by allowing for 'measures within the meaning of Article 157(4) of the Treaty with a view to ensuring full equality in practice between men and women'.

Below the case law that evolved under the Equal Treatment Directive is discussed as it may offer guidance on the interpretation of the derogation provisions in the Recast Directive.

27.13.3.1 Sex as a determining factor

The former Article 2(2) of the original Equal Treatment Directive provided for derogation in respect of 'activities . . . for which . . . the sex of the worker constitutes a determining factor'.

In *Stoeckel* (case C-345/89) a general ban on night work for women, provided for under German law, allegedly to protect women, was held by the Court not permissible under the former Article 2(2). However, in *Ministère Public v Levy* faced with a question of the compatibility of *Stoeckel* with French law imposing restrictions on night work in industry for women, designed to give effect to a provision of the International Labour Organisation (ILO) Convention 1948, the Court suggested that national courts must not apply provisions of national law contrary to Article 5 Directive 76/207 (now deleted) 'unless the application of national law is necessary to ensure compliance with international obligations' resulting from a convention concluded with third countries 'before the entry into force of the EC Treaty'. The point came before the CJ again in the case of *Commission v Italy* (case C-207/96). In this case, Italy prohibited women from working overnight in accordance with the ILO Convention. Italy had, however, following the CJ's previous ruling, denounced the Convention. The CJ thus held that it could not rely on the Convention and that the prohibition was contrary to EU law.

The former Article 2(2) was also raised as a defence in the case of *Johnston* (see Chapter 6).

Johnston

This action was brought by a female member of the Royal Ulster Constabulary (RUC) against a decision by the RUC refusing to renew her contract of employment. The RUC had decided as a matter of policy not to employ women as full-time members of the RUC reserve, since they were not trained in the use of firearms nor permitted to use them.

In proceedings before the CJ concerning the interpretation of Directive 76/207, and in particular the scope for derogation from the equal treatment principle available under EU law (see Chapter 24), the RUC argued, by analogy with what was Article 48(3) EEC (now Article 45 TFEU) that in view of the political situation in Northern Ireland derogation was justified on public safety or public-security grounds; it was also justified under the former Article 2(2) Directive 76/207. To allow women to carry and use firearms, the RUC claimed, increased the risk of their becoming targets for assassination.

The Court held that there was no general public safety exception to the equal treatment principle available under the Treaty. A claim for exemption could *only* be examined in the light of the provisions of Directive 76/207. With regard to the former Article 2(2), the Court held the following:

- the derogation provided under Article 2(2) could be applied only to specific *duties*, not to activities in general. Nonetheless, it was permissible to take into account the *context* in which the activity takes place;
- where derogation is justified in the light of the above, the situation must be reviewed periodically to ensure that the justification still exists;
- derogation must be subject to the principle of proportionality;
- it was for national courts to decide whether these conditions are satisfied.

The scope of the former Article 2(2) also came under consideration in *Sirdar v The Army Board* (case C-273/97). The Army Board refused to transfer a female chef (who would otherwise be made redundant) to the Royal Marines because of her sex. She argued that this was contrary to the approach set down in *Johnston*. The CJ, however, took a different view. It confirmed that Member States have a discretion regarding measures necessary for ensuring public security, although it further noted that any derogation from fundamental Treaty rights (such as equality) must be narrowly construed and be proportionate to its aims. In this case, the CJ focused on the special nature of the Marines, who are, in effect, front-line troops and in respect of whom an absolute rule provides that *all* Marines must be combat ready, irrespective of their normal role. It seems that it was the particularly dangerous nature of the Marines' role that, according to the CJ, justified the UK's decision that the Marines should remain exclusively male. By contrast, in *Kreil v Germany* (case C-285/98) a German rule of more general ambit which precluded women from occupying posts which would involve the use of firearms constituted sex discrimination, even taking into account Member States' discretion regarding the organisation of their armed forces. *Kreil* cannot be interpreted to mean that Member States cannot organise their compulsory national service to apply to men alone (*Dory v Germany* (case C-186/01)). Arguably, then, these rulings continue the approach to the former Article 2(2) which requires a *specific* assessment of the *specific* duties to be performed in individual cases.

In the light of the above case law, the derogation was recast, and the new provision, set out earlier, reflects the very strict interpretation given to the former Article 2(2).

27.13.3.2 **Pregnancy and maternity**

Former Article 2(3) Directive 76/207 permitted 'provisions concerning the protection of women, particularly as regards pregnancy and maternity'. Pregnancy and maternity leave can, potentially, have a detrimental impact on the pay and career progression of women, who will be away from work for a period of time.

Herrero

In *Herrero v Imsalud* (case C-294/04), Ms Herrero, who had already been employed by Imsalud, was successful in applying for a new post whilst she was on maternity leave. She was able to defer taking up that post, but she challenged a rule whereby her seniority would only be calculated from the date she took up her post, rather than the date of appointment. The Court held that this situation was within the scope of Directive 76/207, and that it precluded a rule which excluded maternity leave from calculating the period of seniority of a female employee.

It followed the earlier decision in *Land Brandenburg v Sass* (case C-284/02).

Kiiski

In *Kiiski v Tampereen kaupunki* (case C-116/06) the claimant had been granted 'childcare leave' to enable her to care for her child. On becoming pregnant again, she asked her employer, first, to alter the dates of her childcare leave and, subsequently, to interrupt it, so that she could take maternity leave. Her employer refused because, under the relevant collective agreement and Finnish case law, childcare leave could be interrupted only for an unforeseeable and justified ground, and pregnancy did not constitute such a ground.

The Court held that the refusal was incompatible with the Directive since it was capable of affecting negatively the claimant's right to obtain maternity leave and enjoy its relevant benefits.

Hofmann v Barmer Ersatzkasse (case 184/83) concerned a claim by a father to six months' leave following the birth of his child to look after the child while the mother went back to work. German law, which granted such leave only to the mother, was, he claimed, discriminatory, in breach of Directive 76/207. The Court disagreed. Special provision for maternity leave was, the Court held, permissible under Article 2(3), which was concerned to protect two types of female need. It protected:

- the biological condition of women during and after pregnancy;
- the relationship between mother and child during the period following pregnancy and birth.

Directive 76/207 (and now the Recast Directive) was not intended to cover matters relating to the organisation of the family or to change the division of responsibility between parents.

A second case brought by the Commission against France (*Commission v France* (case 312/86)) related to special privileges in the form of, inter alia, extended maternity leave, lower retirement age, extra time off to allow for children's illness and holidays and extra allowances to meet the cost of nursery schools and child minders, awarded under French law to married women. The French government sought to justify these privileges under Article 2(3)–(4) Equal Treatment Directive (equivalent provision is Article 2(2) Recast Directive). The Court, citing *Hofmann*, found that such measures fell outside the limits of Article 2(3); moreover, there was no indication that the rights claimed corresponded to the situation envisaged under Article 2(4). If such privileges are to be justified, they can only be justified on objective grounds *unrelated to sex*, such as the need to assist persons who carry primary responsibility for the welfare of the family, and particularly of children. As the Court pointed out in *Commission v France*, such responsibility may be undertaken by men. As an example of the application of 'neutral' criteria, see *Teuling* (case 30/85), which is discussed later in this Chapter.

Contrast *Commission v France* (case 312/86) with *Abdoulaye*, albeit a case based on Article 157 TFEU rather than the Recast Directive.

Abdoulaye

In this case a group of men sought to challenge the payment of a lump sum, in addition to their maternity pay, to women going on maternity leave. The men argued that a recent father was not entitled to the same amount and that the measure discriminated against men.

The CJ held the payment of the lump sum to be compatible with Union law as it was intended to compensate woman for the problems inherent in having to take time off work for maternity leave, and which are consequently specific to women.

The precise extent to which, and circumstances in which, a dismissal or refusal to employ a woman for reasons connected with pregnancy and childbirth will breach the Recast Directive remains unclear, although it seems that the CJ has become increasingly unsympathetic to employers. In *Dekker* the defendant employer had withdrawn his offer of employment to the claimant when he discovered she was pregnant. He argued that his action was justified; her absence during maternity leave would not be covered by insurance, and he could not afford to pay for a replacement worker. The CJ held that a refusal to employ a woman on the grounds of pregnancy constituted direct discrimination on the grounds of sex; as such it could not be justified on the basis of financial detriment to the employer.

The effect of this ruling was undermined in the Court's judgment in *Handels-og Kontorfunktion ærernes Forbund i Danmark v Dansk Arbejdsgiverforening (Hertz)* (case C-179/88) delivered on the same day. This case concerned a claim by a female employee against dismissal on the grounds of her extended absence from work as a result of illness which, though connected with pregnancy and childbirth, was suffered some time *after* the end of her maternity leave.

The Court held that in this case there was no need to distinguish between illness resulting from pregnancy and maternity and any other illness such as might be suffered by a man. The dismissal was thus not directly discriminatory and could be justified. The reason for the distinction between *Dekker* and *Hertz*, suggested in *Hertz*, lay in Article 2(3) Directive 76/207 which provided for measures concerning the protection of women, particularly as regards pregnancy and maternity (now Article 2(2) Recast Directive).

The CJ's judgment raises some questions, not the least of which concerns where the boundary lies between being dismissed for pregnancy, which is unacceptable, and being dismissed for being ill, albeit because of pregnancy, which—provided it occurs outside the normal maternity leave—is acceptable (see *Hertz*). In *Handels-og Kontorfunktion ærernes Forbund i Danmark acting on behalf of Larsson v Dansk Handel & Service acting on behalf of Føtex Supermarket A/S* (case C-400/95), the CJ held that a woman could be dismissed for absences other than maternity leave caused by pregnancy-related illnesses occurring both prior to and after the birth of the child, and in *North Western Health Board v McKenna* (case C-191/03), the Court held that where a female worker had been absent due to pregnancy-related illness before her maternity leave, her pay could be reduced if a man who had been absent for the same period would be treated in the same way. The decision in *Larsson* should be contrasted with *Brown v Rentokil* (case C-394/96), where it was held that a woman could not be dismissed at any time during her pregnancy for absences arising from pregnancy-related illnesses. The Pregnancy Directive (Directive 92/85 ([1992] OJ L348/1)) prohibits the dismissal of workers during the period from the beginning of their pregnancy to the end of their maternity leave, save in exceptional circumstances unconnected with their pregnancy. Pregnancy-related illnesses would seem not to justify dismissal during this time. The position after the end of the woman's maternity leave as regards such illnesses is not, however, dealt with expressly and some uncertainty as to the level of protection in this context remains.

A worker's dismissal while she was at an advanced stage of *in vitro* fertilisation treatment came before the Court in *Mayr v Backerei und Konditorei Gerhard Flockner OHG* (case C-506/06). It held that even if the claimant could not rely on Directive 92/85 on pregnant workers, her dismissal would violate what was then Directive 76/207 if it could be established that it was based on the fact that she has undergone such treatment.

Further, if the reason for a worker's dismissal is her pregnancy or childbirth, the dismissal will violate the Pregnancy Directive irrespective of the moment when that decision to dismiss is notified (*Paquay v Societe d'architectes Hoet and Minne SPRL* (case C-460/06)).

A question arising in *Webb* concerned whether availability for work constitutes a fundamental condition of the employment contract. The CJ rejected this contention, but on the basis that the time that the woman would be unavailable for work constitutes only a small proportion of the contract time in an indefinite contract. This did, however, undermine the position of women on short-term contracts. Could they be dismissed on the basis that the period of their pregnancy constitutes too large a proportion of the contract? These issues were clarified in the cases of *Tele Danmark A/S v Handels-og Kontorfunktionærernes Forbund i Danmark* (case C-109/00), *Jiménez Melgar v Ayuntamiento de Los Barrios* (case C-438/99), and *Busch v Klinikum Neustadt GmbH & Co Betriebs-KG* (case C-320/01).

Tele Danmark

In *Tele Danmark*, a woman was employed on a six months' fixed-term contract, two of which were spent on a training course. After commencing employment, she notified her employer that she was pregnant, whereupon she was dismissed. The employer argued that she could not perform a substantial part of her duties and further that, in not mentioning her pregnancy before she was employed, she had violated the principle of good faith.

The CJ rejected these arguments:

Since the dismissal of a worker on account of pregnancy constitutes direct discrimination on grounds of sex, whatever the nature and extent of economic loss incurred by the company as a result of her absence, because of pregnancy, whether the contract was concluded for a fixed term or for an infinite period has no bearing on the discriminatory character of the dismissal. In either case, the employee's inability to perform her contract of employment is due to pregnancy [para 31].

The ruling was applied in *Jiménez Melgar*, which concerned a refusal to renew a fixed-term contract. In *Busch*, the CJ, basing its judgment on *Tele Danmark*, confirmed that a woman was under no duty to tell an employer that she is pregnant prior to accepting a job offer or returning to work.

This case law seems to reflect, if not go further than, the terms of the Pregnancy Directive. The Directive provides core maternity rights including periods of maternity leave and protection from dismissal during such leave, whether the worker is on a short-term or indefinite contract, and will thus protect workers in this position. The Pregnancy Directive does not, though, deal with the position of the woman who is not engaged because she is pregnant. Presumably, this could still fall within the Recast Directive following *Dekker*. Certainly, the CJ held in *Mahlburg v Land Mecklenburg-Vorpommern* (case C-207/98), that a hospital could not refuse to appoint a pregnant woman to a permanent post as a theatre nurse on the basis that she would not be able to carry out her duties while she was pregnant. In this case German legislation prohibited expectant mothers from being exposed to chemicals with which the applicant would have come into contact as part of her job. This demonstrates that where a permanent post is in issue, temporary absence or incapacity (even from the commencement date of the appointment) will not be a legitimate ground for refusal of employment.

The Pregnancy Directive also specifies that women on maternity leave are entitled to an 'adequate allowance'. Maternity pay did not need to be full pay, provided it was an adequate allowance (*Gillespie*). The Court also held, however, that account must be taken of any pay increases during the maternity leave or during the period with reference to which the maternity pay is calculated (see also *Alabaster*). The CJ has also ruled on the impact of maternity leave (in conjunction with sick leave) on a woman's entitlement to be considered for a 'merit increase' (*Caisse Nationale D'Assurance Vieillesse des Travailleurs Salaries (NAVTS) v Thibault* (case C-136/95)). As far as the applicant was concerned, the difficulty arose because she did not satisfy the prerequisite of six months' work because of the time she had had off, and was therefore ineligible for the pay rise. The CJ agreed that this was contrary to the requirements of the then Equal Treatment Directive. It stated that if a woman continued to be bound by her contract of employment, she should not be deprived of benefits which apply to men and other women by virtue of the employment relationship. The CJ, in so holding, emphasised that the Equal Treatment Directive was intended to promote substantive equality, as is the Recast Directive. (See also *Gillespie*.) Whether this desire to safeguard substantive equality is respected in all the CJ's judgments relating to pregnancy issues is, however, another matter. The precise scope of the rights under the Pregnancy Directive will no doubt continue to be the subject of further litigation.

Many of these decisions are now incorporated into the text of the Recast Directive. Thus, Article 15 provides that a woman is entitled to return to her job, or an equivalent post, after the end of her maternity leave, on no less favourable terms and conditions and to benefit from any improvement in working conditions to which she would have been entitled during her absence. The previous case law will continue to be relevant in interpreting this broad rule.

27.13.3.3 Enforcement

The provisions relating to the enforcement of equal treatment are given in Article 23 Recast Directive and have been set out above (27.4.4).

27.14 Directive 2010/41: equal treatment in self-employment

Directive 2010/41 lays down a framework for putting into effect in the Member States the principle of equal treatment between men and women engaged in an activity in a self-employed capacity.

The Directive applies to:

> 'all persons pursuing a gainful activity for their own account under conditions laid down by national law' and to 'their spouses or, when and in so far as recognised by national law, the life partners of self-employed workers, not being employees or business partners, where they habitually . . . participate in the activities of the self-employed worker and perform the same tasks or ancillary tasks' [Article 2].

The principle of equal treatment implies:

> that there shall be no discrimination whatsoever on grounds of sex in the public or private sectors, either directly or indirectly, for instance in the relation to the establishment, equipment or extension of a business or the launching or extension of any form of self-employed activity [Article 4].

Discrimination includes both direct and indirect discrimination, harassment and sexual harassment, and an instruction to discriminate against persons on grounds of sex. Member States are also required: 'Without prejudice to the specific conditions for access to certain activities which apply equally to both sexes' to take the measures necessary to ensure that the conditions for the formation of a company between spouses are not more restrictive than the conditions for the formation of a company between other persons (Article 6).

Where a system for social protection for self-employed workers exists in a Member State, that Member State must take the necessary measures to enable those spouses and life partners to benefit from social protection in accordance with national law. Member States can decide whether this social-protection right is implemented on a mandatory or voluntary basis. Article 8 provides that female self-employed workers and female spouses and life partners should be entitled to a 'sufficient maternity allowance' enabling them to interrupt their occupational activity for a period of at least 14 weeks.

27.15 Directive 2004/113: equal treatment of men and women in access to goods and services

The most recent measure to give effect to the principle of equal treatment between men and women is Directive 2004/113 on equal treatment between men and women in the access to and supply of goods and services ([2004] OJ L373/37). According to Article 3(1), the Directive applies to all persons who provide goods or services to the public and offered outside the area of private and family life. It does not seek to prevent freedom of contract, although it does affect the choice of a contracting partner based on sex (Article 3(2)). The Directive also does not deal with employment matters, for which there is, of course, already existing legislation.

Article 4 then gives effect to the general principle of equal treatment, prohibiting both direct and indirect discrimination in this context. A provision which proved controversial during the legislative process was Article 5, which prohibits 'the use of sex as a factor in the calculation of premiums and benefits for the purposes of insurance and related financial services'. There was concern that this would, for example, outlaw the variations in insurance premiums for male and female drivers. To meet such concerns, Article 5(2) allows Member States to decide before December 2007 to permit 'proportionate differences in individuals' premiums and benefits where the use of sex is a determining factor in the assessment of risk based on relevant and accurate actuarial and statistical data'. In *Test Achats* the CJ found Article 5(2) to be invalid. The possibility of the Member States maintaining for an undefined period of time—possibly indefinitely—an exemption from the requirement in Article 5(1) of unisex premiums and benefits, was contrary to the general principle of equal treatment, and must therefore be regarded as invalid 'upon the expiry of an appropriate transitional period' which the CJ laid down as ending on 21 December 2012. The European Commission has issued a Communication in December 2011, setting out Guidelines aimed at facilitating compliance by the insurance industry with this ruling (COM(2011) 9497 final).

This Directive is regarded as laying down a minimum standard, and Member States may introduce provisions which are more favourable then the equal treatment principle (Article 7; for minimum harmonisation generally, see Chapter 16).

The remainder of the Directive contains provisions on enforcement (Articles 8–11), and on the setting up of a body responsible for promoting and monitoring the equal treatment of all persons (Article 12). The latter provision duplicates provisions found elsewhere, and it seems that entrusting this task to a body generally responsible for equal treatment matters would suffice.

27.16 Directive 2000/43: equal treatment irrespective of racial or ethnic origin

The ToA greatly enlarged the Union's competence in the field of discrimination which hitherto had been confined to the prohibition of discrimination on the grounds of nationality and gender. Following the ToA, Article 13 EC (now Article 19 TFEU) granted the EU powers to adopt measures against discrimination on grounds of race, religion or belief, sexual orientation or disability. On the basis of this provision, Directive 2000/43 ([2000] OJ L180/22) has been adopted to combat discrimination, both direct and indirect, on grounds of racial or ethnic origin, in relation to employment matters, social protection, education and access to public goods and services.

27.16.1 Minimum levels of protection

Directive 2000/43 provides a minimum level of protection. Member States may introduce more stringent standards, but the Directive should not be used to justify any regression in standards prevailing at the time of its adoption (Article 6). In *Firma Feryn* the Advocate-General stated that the Directive should be interpreted in the light of the values of Article 19 TFEU and even though the Directive lays down minimum measures, these should not be construed more narrowly than a reading of those values would warrant.

In *Malgožata Runevič-Vardyn and Łukasz Paweł Wardyn v Vilniaus miesto savivaldybės administracija and Others* (case C-391/09) the Court drew attention to the fact that the Directive is merely an expression of the general principle of equality now enshrined in Article 21 EUCFR with the result that the provisions of the Directive cannot be interpreted restrictively but must reflect that general principle:

> It should be noted... that, in the light of the objective of Directive 2000/43 and the nature of the rights which it seeks to safeguard, and in view of the fact that that directive is merely an expression, within the area under consideration, of the principle of equality, which is one of the general principles of European Union law, as recognized in Article 21 of the Charter of Fundamental Rights of the European Union, the scope of that directive cannot be defined restrictively [para 43].

27.16.2 Scope of application

The Directive applies, within the limits of the powers conferred upon the Union Institutions to all persons and to the public and private sectors, including public bodies, with respect to the following matters:

- conditions for access to employment, to self-employment and to occupation including selection criteria and recruitment conditions, whatever the branch of activity and at all levels of the professional hierarchy, including promotion;

- access to all types and all levels of vocational training, vocational guidance, advanced vocational training and retraining, including practical work experience;

- employment and working conditions, including dismissal and pay;

- membership of, and involvement in, an organisation of workers or employers or any organisation whose members carry on a particular profession, including the benefits provided to such an organisation;

- social protection including social security and healthcare;

- social advantages;

- education;

- access to and supply of goods and services, which are available to the public, including housing.

The Directive thus marks a departure from the approach to gender discrimination which is limited in scope to differences in treatment in employment and social-security matters. Discrimination on grounds of race or ethnic origin is recognised as not being confined to the workplace but extends beyond that into many aspects of life in the Union. The preamble to the Directive explains that the broad scope of the Directive is necessary to achieve its objectives:

> To ensure the development of democratic and tolerant societies which allow the participation of all persons irrespective of racial or ethnic origin, specific action in the field of discrimination based on race or ethnic origin should go beyond access to employed and self-employed activities and cover areas such as education, social protection, including social security and health care, social advantages and access to and supply of services [para 12].

27.16.3 Discrimination

The Directive extends to discrimination in matters such as educational fees, restrictions on the production and sale of foodstuffs such as halal meat or kosher products, the allocation of housing (an area in which discrimination is traditionally rife) and bans on the wearing of clothing with religious significance such as certain types of headwear. The extent of the right to equal treatment with regard to matters unconnected with employment may in reality be limited given that such a right is co-terminous with the extent of the Union's competence. Thus its scope of application with respect to, for example, housing and healthcare may be limited. It is also uncertain to what extent the Directive applies to the provision of services by the private sector in, for example, banks, shops and hotels. The lack of any general provision imposing an obligation to eliminate discrimination in general public services, such as policing, is also a matter of concern.

The Directive applies to all persons regardless of their nationality. Persons who, although not members of an ethnic group receive less favourable treatment or who are otherwise prejudiced by the discriminatory measure also fall within the scope of the Directive (*CHEZ Razpredelenie Bulgaria AD v Komisia za zashtita ot diskriminatsia* (case C-83/14)). Both direct and indirect discrimination on the grounds of race or ethnic origin are prohibited. 'Race and ethnic origin' are Union law concepts. They are not defined in the Directive. Recital 6 of the preamble to the Directive states that the European Union 'rejects theories which attempt to determine the existence of separate human races'.

Direct discrimination is deemed to have occurred where one person is treated less favourably than another or would be treated in a comparable situation on the grounds of racial or ethnic origin

(Article 2(1)). The scope of the concept of direct discrimination was given a broad interpretation in *Feryn*.

Feryn

In this case the Court was asked whether a statement made publicly by the director of a company that he did not wish to employ immigrants was discriminatory for the purposes of the Directive. A body designated to promote equal treatment brought proceedings against the company asking the national court to find that its recruitment policy was discriminatory.

The CJ ruled that the lack of an identifiable complainant did not mean that there was no discrimination. The director's statement was likely to strongly dissuade certain candidates from applying for the job and, thus, hindered their access to the labour market. Therefore, the statement constituted direct discrimination within the meaning of the Directive despite the fact that no one had submitted a complaint claiming to be a victim. Then, the burden fell on the employer to prove before the national court that his actual recruitment practices were non-discriminatory and did not correspond to that statement.

Indirect discrimination occurs when an apparently neutral provision, criterion or practice would put persons of certain racial or ethnic origin at a particular disadvantage as compared to other persons unless that provision, criterion or practice is objectively justified as being in pursuit of a legitimate aim and the means of achieving that aim are appropriate and necessary. The cases of *Belov* and *CHEZ RB* raised issues relating to indirect discrimination.

Belov

This case concerned measures taken by Bulgarian state electricity distribution companies to place meters measuring electricity consumption at a height of seven metres on posts situated outside houses connected to the electricity network in two areas of the City of Montana, mainly inhabited by members of the Roma community.

Electricity meters were usually placed at a height of 1.7 metres in the consumer's home or on the outside wall of buildings or on surrounding fences allowing consumers to easily check their consumption. The question was whether the measure placing meters at an inaccessible level hindering consumers from readily checking their meter readings, in an area heavily populated by the Roma was discrimination on ethnic grounds?

The Court did not address the issue as it found that the referring entity was not a 'court or tribunal' within the meaning of Article 309 TFEU and accordingly it had no jurisdiction over the matter. Advocate-General Kokott had come to a different conclusion. Finding the reference admissible she found that the Bulgarian measure was indirectly discriminatory, but capable of justification to prevent fraud and abuse. Whether it was proportionate was a matter to be decided in the light of several factors including the risk of an ethnic group being stigmatised. In *CHEZ RB* the CJ found that a measure similar to the one in issue in *Belov* could be directly discriminatory if it were established that it was imposed because of the ethnic origin of the inhabitants of the district in question. Even if it were not directly discriminatory it could be regarded as indirectly discriminatory if it affected persons of a particular ethnic origin in considerable numbers. It was for the national court to decide on whether such a measure could be objectively justified as pursuing a legitimate objective and if so whether the measure was proportionate.

Harassment and instructions to discriminate on racial and ethnic grounds are deemed to be discrimination for the purposes of the Directive. Harassment is defined as unwanted conduct relating to racial or ethnic origin, the purpose or effect of which is to violate the dignity of a person and to create an intimidating, hostile, degrading, humiliating or offensive environment.

27.16.4 Exceptions

27.16.4.1 Nationality

Differences of treatment based on nationality are excluded from the scope of the Directive and the Directive provides (Article 3(2)) that it applies without prejudice to the provisions and conditions relating to entry into, and residence of, TCNs and stateless persons on the territory of the Member States and to any treatment which arises from the legal status of such TCNs and stateless persons.

27.16.4.2 Genuine and determining occupational requirement

Member States may provide that a difference in treatment by reason of the nature of a particular job or activity shall not constitute discrimination where it is a genuine and determining occupational requirement. The objective of the discriminatory conduct must be legitimate and the level of discriminatory treatment no more than is necessary to achieve that objective (Article 4).

27.16.4.3 Positive measures

Member States are free to maintain or adopt specific measures to prevent or compensate for disadvantages linked to racial or ethnic origin (Article 5).

27.16.5 Enforcement and remedies

Many aspects of enforcement and remedies for aggrieved persons are common to all the directives considered in this chapter. These have been discussed at 27.4.4. Provisions specific to the Race Directive are considered here.

The right to bring proceedings in respect of discriminatory conduct extends to associations, organisations or other legal entities which have a legitimate interest in ensuring compliance with the Race Directive. Member States may determine which groups have a legitimate interest. But the right to institute proceedings is not autonomous: such entities have no right under the Directive to bring proceedings in their own name. They can only act with respect to a particular complainant on behalf of or with the support of that complainant. However since the Directive only lays down minimum requirements, Member States can give additional redress over and above those measures prescribed by the Directive (*Firma Feryn* (case C-54/07)).

The right to bring proceedings is subject to national time limits (Article 7(1)). Apart from granting an aggrieved person the right to bring proceedings for the enforcement of the principle of equal treatment, the Directive institutes a number of other enforcement mechanisms, aimed at the prevention of discriminatory conduct. First, it advocates the dissemination of information relating to the provision of the Directive within the Member States (Article 10); secondly, it advocates fostering equal treatment in the workplace through the social dialogue (Article 11); thirdly, it requires Member States to encourage dialogue with appropriate non-governmental organisations (Article 12) and fourthly, Member States are required to designate a body responsible for the promotion of equal treatment. Such bodies must be competent to provide independent assistance to victims of discrimination when pursuing their complaints, to conduct independent surveys and to make public reports and recommendations on any issue relating to discrimination.

When a claim for equal treatment requires a claimant to adduce factual evidence, the burden of proof lies on the defendant to show that there has been no discrimination.

27.17 Directive 2000/78: equal treatment in employment and occupation

The Framework Employment Directive (Directive 2000/78 ([2000] OJ L303/16)) has the same legal basis as the Race Directive: Article 19 TFEU. It lays down a general framework for combating discrimination on the grounds of religion or belief, disability, age or sexual orientation with regard to employment and occupation. Its scope is thus narrower than that of the Race Directive, which prohibits discrimination with respect to a number of non-employment related areas in so far as the Union is competent to act in those areas. The Directive prohibits direct and indirect discrimination; harassment and an instruction to discriminate are also deemed to be forms of discrimination (Article 2).

27.17.1 Key concepts

No definition is given of any of the key concepts—religion, disability, age or sexual orientation in either Article 19 TFEU or the Directive but the CJ has urged that they be interpreted restrictively. Advocate-General Geelhoed stated in *Chacón Navas* that the evolution and wording of Article 19 reflected restraint on the part of the authors of the Treaty (see Bell and Waddington in the further reading section at the end of this chapter). The detailed wording of the Directive, in particular Articles 5 and 6 suggested that the Union legislature was aware of the potentially far-reaching economic and financial consequences of the prohibition set out therein. Moreover, the essentially complementary nature of the Union's legislative powers in this area required the 'definitions and delineations' set out therein to be taken seriously.

27.17.1.1 Religion or belief

Religion or belief may be interpreted as going beyond traditional organised religions involving a belief in a divine being or a deity to other philosophical beliefs on major issues. For example, Article 9 ECHR which provides for the right to freedom of religion has been interpreted broadly as extending beyond the major world religions to other groups such as Jehovah's witnesses and the Pentecostal Church both of which have been identified as a form of religion for the purposes of that provision. Article 10(1) EUCFR adopts an equally broad approach. It provides that the right includes freedom to change religion or belief and the freedom in public and in private to manifest religion or belief, in worship, teaching, practice and observance. In *Asma Bougnaoui*, the CJ held that the term 'religion' in Article 1 of the Directive should follow the approach in the ECHR and Article 10(1) of the Charter should be interpreted as covering both the forum internum, that is the fact of having a belief, and the forum exterrnum, that is the manifestation of religious faith in public.

27.17.1.2 Disability

Chacón Navas considered the meaning of disability within the context of the Framework Employment Directive. It held that in the absence of any definition of the term 'disability', or any express reference in the Directive to national law for the purpose of determining its meaning and scope, the term had to be given an autonomous and uniform interpretation throughout the Union. It then looked to the Directive to see what disability might mean and concluded that:

> 'disability' must be understood as referring to a limitation which results in particular from physical, mental or psychological impairments and which hinders the participation of the person concerned in professional life [para 43].

Disability therefore did not include sickness even if the period of sickness was relatively lengthy. In coming to this conclusion, the Court reasoned as follows. The legislature had chosen a term which differed from 'sickness'; the two terms could not therefore simply be treated as being the same. The requirement to provide reasonable accommodation in Article 5 [see 27.17.3] indicates that the Union legislature envisaged situations in which access to, and participation in, professional life is restricted over a lengthy period in time.

Following the accession of the European Union to the UN Convention on the Rights of Persons with Disabilities in December 2010 ([2010] OJ L23/35) the CJ has held that the concept of 'disability' must be understood as referring to

> …a limitation which results in particular from long term physical, mental or psychological impairments which in interaction with various barriers may hinder the full and effective participation of the person concerned in professional life on an equal basis with other workers (cases C-335 and 337/11 *HK Danmark; FOA* (case C-354/13)) [para 41].

The Convention did not define what amounts to a 'long term' impairment. The issue of whether an incapacity for work for a temporary but indeterminate period of time can amount to a disability arose in the recent case of *Mohamed Daouidi v Bootes Plus SL and Others* (case C-395/15).

Daouidi

Mr Daouidi was employed as a kitchen assistant in a restaurant in Barcelona. He slipped on the kitchen floor of the restaurant and dislocated his elbow on 3 October 2014. On 26 November 2014, whilst still unable to work due to his injury, he was dismissed. He brought proceedings alleging that his dismissal was discriminatory on the ground that the real reason for it was his being temporarily unable to work as a result of the accident which had caused his injury.

The CJ found that the concept of a 'long-term' limitation of a person's capacity to work was a matter for EU law and it was up to the national court to make a factual assessment of whether a person's incapacity was long term or not taking into account a number of factors; whether the incapacity of the person in question 'does not display a clearly defined prognosis as regards short-term progress' or whether the incapacity is likely to be 'significantly prolonged before that person has recovered'. Such an assessment must be based on objective evidence, in particular on the documents and certificates relating to that person's condition established on the basis of current medical and scientific knowledge and data.

The concept of disability is to be interpreted as referring to a hindrance in the exercise of professional activity not to the impossibility of exercising such an activity. The fact that a person can only work to a limited extent is not an obstacle to a person's state of health being covered by the concept of 'disability'. The state of health of a person with a disability who is fit to work, albeit only part-time, is thus capable of being covered by the concept of 'disability'. A woman's inability to have a child because she has no uterus has been held not to constitute a disability within the meaning of the Directive as it does not make it impossible for her to carry out her work or constitute a hindrance to the exercise of her professional activity (*Z v A Government Department and The Board of Management of a Community School* (case C-363/12)).

Obesity may constitute a disability if it entails a limitation resulting from long-term physical, mental or psychological impairments, which in interaction with various barriers hinder the full and effective participation of the person concerned in professional life on an equal basis with other workers. Such would be the case, in particular, if the obesity lead to reduced mobility or the onset of medical conditions prevent the carrying out of his/her work or caused discomfort when carrying out his professional activity (*Fag og Arbejde (FOA), acting on behalf of Karsten Kaltoft v Kommunernes Landsforening (KL), acting on behalf of the Municipality of Billund* (case C-354/13)).

The extent to which a person may or may not have contributed to the onset of his/her disability is not relevant (*Kaltoft*). Likewise the origin of the disability is not determinative (*HK Danmark v Dansk almennyttigt Boligselskab* and *HK Danmark v Dansk Arbejdsgiverforening* (cases C-335 and C-337/11); *Kaltoft*). Whether a person has a disability within the meaning of the Directive depends on the effect of that disability upon his ability to participate in working life on equal terms with others.

Whether a person is in a situation of temporary incapacity for work or is subject to a long-term limitation on his ability to participate in profession life is a factual matter to be decided in each case. Evidence which might make it possible to make a finding of a long-term condition includes the fact that, at the time of the alleged discriminatory act, the incapacity of the person concerned does not display a clearly defined prognosis as regards short-term progress or the fact that the incapacity is likely to be significantly prolonged before that person has recovered (*Kaltoft*).

27.17.1.3 Age

Although age is not defined in the Directive, Recitals 6 and 8 of the preamble refer to the 'elderly' and 'older workers' but the wording of a number of provisions, for example Article 6, refers to young people, older persons and persons with caring responsibilities, whilst Article 6(2) permits the fixing of different ages for the administration or entitlement to retirement benefits under occupational social security schemes. The wording of these provisions indicates that more groups than the elderly are envisaged by the Directive, a view confirmed by the CJ (*David Hütter v Technische Universität Graz* (case C-88/08); *Wolf v Stadt Frankfurt am Main* (case C-229/08); *Kücükdeveci*).

27.17.1.4 Sexual orientation

Sexual orientation is not defined in the Directive. In addition to homosexuality, it could be interpreted as extending to heterosexual or bisexual persons. There is no reason why it should be confined to homosexuality, the sole ground of sexual orientation hitherto raised before the Court.

27.17.2 Scope of the Directive

The Directive applies to all persons who exercise an economic activity, either in an employed or self-employed capacity, in the public or private sector including public bodies. Such persons are entitled to equal treatment with respect to:

- conditions of access to employment, to self-employment or occupation including selection criteria and recruitment conditions, whatever the branch of activity and at all levels of the professional hierarchy including promotion;
- access to all types and levels of vocational guidance, vocational training, advanced vocational training and retraining including practical work experience;

- employment and working conditions including dismissal and pay;
- membership and involvement in an organisation of workers or employers or any organisation whose members carry on a particular profession, including the benefits provided by such organisations.

27.17.3 **Reasonable accommodation**

Article 5 requires that disabled persons are given reasonable accommodation, which means that employers must take appropriate measures to enable a person with a disability to have access to or to advance in employment, unless such measures would be disproportionately burdensome for the employer. The Directive gives little guidance on the meaning of reasonable accommodation. Guidance as to what may be appropriate measures can be found in Recital 20 of the Preamble to the Directive which describes them as:

> . . . effective and practical measures to adapt the workplace to the disability, for example, by adapting premises and equipment, patterns of working time, the distribution of tasks or the provision of training and integration resources.

Reasonable accommodation may include alterations in working hours to facilitate a disabled person's participation in the workforce (*HK Danmark*).

In determining whether the burden of providing reasonable accommodation is disproportionate 'account should be taken in particular of the financial and other costs entailed, the scale and financial resources of the organisation or undertaking and the possibility of obtaining public funding or other assistance' (Recital 21).

27.17.4 **Minimum requirements**

The Framework Employment Directive lays down minimum requirements (Article 8(1)). Member States may adopt or maintain more favourable provisions than those envisaged by the Directive, but they cannot rely on it to reduce levels of protection prevailing in the Member States at the time of the adoption of the Directive (Article 8(2), subject to an annual reporting requirement (Article 18)). In *Coleman* (27.17.5), the Advocate-General found that there was nothing in either the Directive or its recitals to indicate that the setting of 'minimum requirements' meant that the intervention of Union law in this area must be at its lowest level. He thus rejected the UK's argument to the effect that it was for the Member States to decide whether to prohibit discrimination by association in the field of employment or occupation.

27.17.5 **Discrimination**

The Directive prohibits direct and indirect discrimination, concepts which have been discussed at 27.4.3.

Coleman established the principle of discrimination by association.

Coleman

The claimant was the mother of a disabled child who argued that, because of her child, she suffered adverse treatment in comparison to employees who did not have disabled children. The Employment Tribunal asked the CJ whether Directive 2000/78 covered direct 'discrimination by association', that is, discrimination suffered by an employee who, while not having himself one of the characteristics listed in the Directive, is associated with a third person who does.

Advocate-General Poiares Maduro noted that the Directive operates 'at the level of grounds of discrimination', its aim being to prohibit completely the use of those characteristics as reasons to treat an employee less well than others.

The Court followed the Advocate-General's opinion and held that the principle of equal treatment which the Directive is designed to safeguard is not limited to people who themselves have a disability within the meaning of the Directive, and that the prohibition of discrimination 'applies not to a particular category of person but by reference to the grounds mentioned in Article 1 [of the Directive]'. Thus, after *Coleman*, it is unlawful for an employer to treat adversely not only employees who themselves have one of the characteristics listed in Article 1 of the Directive, but also employees who are associated with a third person having those characteristics, if the reason for the adverse treatment is that third person's religion, disability, age or sexual orientation.

27.17.5.1 Age discrimination

In *Mangold* (see Chapter 5) it was held that the source of the principle of non-discrimination on the grounds of age is not the Directive itself, but a general principle of law derived from the constitutional traditions common to the Member States and various international instruments; what the Directive does is to lay down the general framework for combating discrimination on the grounds listed therein. Then, the Court went on to hold that the principle of non-discrimination on grounds of age is a general principle of Union law. Accordingly, the fact that the employment contract at issue had been concluded before the period prescribed for the transposition of the Directive into domestic law had expired did not relieve Member States from their non-discrimination obligations. National courts hearing a dispute concerning discrimination in respect of age must ensure that individuals enjoy the protection guaranteed by Union law and that the relevant rules are fully effective, setting aside any conflicting provisions of national law.

This broad ruling in *Mangold* attracted criticism not only from academics but also from some of the Court's Advocates-General. The case of *Lindorfer* concerned an employee of the European Union who argued, among others, that she had suffered age discrimination because the actuarial values used for the calculation of her pension were increasingly less favourable for employees as their age on recruitment increased. Advocate-General Sharpston suggested that what flows from the constitutional traditions common to the Member States and international law is the *general* principle of equality, while the specific prohibition of age discrimination is 'too recent and uneven' to be considered as a general principle of law; rather, it is a particular expression of the general equality principle. The Court held that the claimant had suffered no age discrimination since her situation was not comparable to an employee who had started his career in the Union institutions at an earlier age and, thus, did not discuss the effect of *Mangold*. In *Bartsch*, she reiterated her view, reasoning it at length and with conviction. Subsequently in *Palacios de la Villa* Advocate-General Mazak pointed out that, although reliance had been placed by the CJ in *Mangold* on various international instruments and constitutional traditions common to the Member States, from which it could conclude that there was a general principle of non-discrimination on the grounds of age, those instruments referred for the most part to the general principle of equality rather than the more specific principle of equality on the grounds of age. The Advocate-General therefore did not find the conclusion drawn in *Mangold* to be 'particularly compelling'. He concluded that if the reasoning in *Mangold* were followed to its logical conclusion, not only the prohibition on the grounds of age but all the specific prohibitions of the types of discrimination referred to in Article 1

Framework Employment Directive would have to be regarded as general principles of Union law. The CJ, ignoring this advice, confirmed its view in *Kücükdeveci*, and more recently in *Prigge*, that the prohibition of discrimination on the ground of age is a general principle of Union law. However it adopted a narrow approach in *Bartsch*, in which the Court was asked whether the application of the prohibition under Union law of discrimination on the ground of age was mandatory where the allegedly discriminatory treatment contained no link with Union law.

In *Bartsch*, the claimant was a widow who, after the death of her husband, was refused a survivor's pension because the guidelines of the pension fund stated that no pension would be paid out if the survivor is more than 15 years younger than the deceased person. The Court held that the situation at issue was outside the scope of Union law. First, the pension fund's guidelines did not constitute a measure implementing Directive 2000/78 and when the death of the claimant's husband occurred the period for the transposition of the Directive had not expired. Secondly, Article 19 TFEU could not by itself bring within the scope of EU law situations which were not covered by specific measures adopted under it such as Directive 2000/78.

Examples of direct discrimination on the grounds of age include a provision permitting employers to conclude without restriction fixed-term contracts of employment with workers over the age of 52. Such treatment 'introduces a difference of treatment on the grounds directly of age' (*Mangold*) and a provision in a collective agreement providing that within each salary group basic pay is determined by reference to age (*Sabine Hennigs v Eisenbahn-Bundesamt* and *Land Berlin v Alexander Mai* (cases C-298 and 299/10)). Other examples of direct discrimination include the setting of an age limit or range for recruitment to a particular job (eg, 30 years) which discriminates against those above that age limit (*Mario Vital Pérez v Ayuntamiento de Oviedo* (case C-416/13); *Gorka Salaberria Sorondo v Academia Vasca de Policia y Emergencias* (case C-258/15)) or different retirement ages for professional workers (dentists) according to whether they were employed in the public or private healthcare services (*Domnica Petersen v Berufungsausschuss für Zahnärzte für den Bezirk Westfalen-Lippe* (case C-341/08)). In *Commission v Hungary* (case C-286/12) a Hungarian law lowering the retirement age for judges, prosecutors and notaries from 70 to 62 years was found by the CJ to be directly discriminatory. When persons in those professions reached the age of 62 their employment was automatically terminated. They were therefore treated less favourably than other members of the workforce.

Most of the cases on the Framework Directive have been concerned with age discrimination in dismissal and compulsory retirement. In all of these cases the CJ has made a finding of discriminatory conduct and has then considered whether such conduct falls within one of the exceptions or derogations provided for in the Directive. These cases are considered below at 27.17.7.

27.17.5.2 Sexual orientation

In a number of cases, the CJ has found direct discrimination on the ground of sexual orientation. In *Maruko, Römer v Freie und Hansestadt Hamburg* (case C-147/08) and *Frédéric Hay v Crédit Agricole Mutuel de Charente-Maritime et des Deux-Sèvres* (C-267/12), both Germany and France had created a legal regime to allow persons of the same sex to live in a union of mutual support and assistance which is normally constituted for life. Persons entering into such a union were, the CJ found, to be in a position comparable to marriage between persons of different sexes, and must therefore be treated in the same manner.

> ### *Maruko*
>
> Mr Maruko was refused a widower's pension when his same-sex life partner died in January 2005. He and his partner had entered into a life partnership in November 2001 following the adoption of a law

> in Germany allowing persons of the same sex to live in a union of mutual support and assistance which is normally constituted for life. Mr Maruko's claim for a pension was refused on the ground that the pension scheme did not provide for survivors' pensions for life partners. Entitlement was confined to living spouses.

The CJ held that this refusal amounted to discriminatory conduct prohibited under Articles 1 and 2 Framework Employment Directive. Having chosen not to permit persons of the same sex to enter into marriage, Germany had created for persons of the same sex an equivalent regime, the life partnership, the conditions of which were made equivalent to those applicable to marriage. If therefore a surviving life partner was in a position comparable to a surviving spouse, they must be treated in the same manner with respect to their entitlement to a survivor's pension.

The case of *Römer* concerned similar issues to those raised in *Maruko*.

Römer

> Mr Römer had lived with Mr U continuously since 1969. They entered into a civil partnership in accordance with German law. Mr Römer then applied for a recalculation of the amount of his supplementary retirement pension on the basis of the more favourable tax category applicable to married pensioners. This request was refused on the ground that this favourable tax category applied only to married, not permanently separated, pensioners and pensioners entitled to claim child benefit. There was therefore direct discrimination if spouses and persons in registered life partnerships were in a comparable situation. This was for the national court to assess.

The CJ in *Hay* went further than *Maruko* and *Römer*, finding that the situation of persons who marry and that of persons of the same sex who cannot marry, but who enter into a civil solidarity pact—such as the French Pacte Civil de Solidarité (PACS) arrangement—are in the same position as married persons in the sense they live together and provide material aid and assistance to each other. Thus benefits in terms of pay (a bonus) or working conditions (days of special leave) granted at the time of an employee's marriage must also be given to those who cannot enter into a marriage but who conclude a PACS arrangement.

The recent case of *Parris v Trinity College Dublin and Others* (case C-443/15) found that a legal inability to enter into a civil partnership which made the claiming of a survivor's benefit impossible in circumstance in which such a benefit would have been paid to a spouse did not constitute discrimination contrary to Article 2 of the Directive.

Parris

> Mr Parris was a lecturer in Trinity College Dublin. He was born on 21 April 1946 and has dual Irish and UK citizenship. He had been in a stable relationship with his same-sex partner for over 30 years. Under the pension scheme to which Mr Parris was affiliated a survivor's pension was payable to the spouse or, since 1 January 2011, the civil partner of a member, where the member predeceases the spouse or civil partner. Where a member dies after retirement, the survivor's pension is only payable to the surviving spouse or civil partner if the member married or entered into the civil partnership before reaching the age of 60 years. On 21 December 2005 it became possible to enter into a civil partnership in the United Kingdom under the Civil Partnership Act 2004. On 21 April when he was 63 years old Mr Parris registered a civil partnership in the United Kingdom. On 19 July 2010 (when Mr Parris was 64 years old) the Civil Partnership Act was enacted in Ireland. Mr Parris requested Trinity College Dublin that on

his death his civil partner should receive a survivor's pension. This request was refused on the ground, inter alia, that the rules of the pension scheme excluded the payment of a survivors' pension where the member married or entered into a civil partnership after the age of 60.

The CJ found that the rule in question did not refer directly to a worker's sexual orientation. It was worded neutrally and excludes their partner, without distinction, from receiving a survivor's pension where the marriage or civil relationship is not entered into before the employee reaches 60 years. It followed that civil partners were not treated less favourably than a surviving spouse and there was therefore no direct discrimination on the ground of sexual orientation. The CJ proceeded then to find that there had been no indirect discrimination. Mr Parris had argued that homosexuals who had reached the age of 60 years before the date of entry into force of the Civil Partnership Act in Ireland were the subject of indirect discrimination because it was impossible for them to satisfy the conditions of the pension scheme on survivor's pensions. The CJ, referred to Recital 22 of the preamble to the Directive which states that it is without prejudice to national laws on marital status and the benefits dependent thereon. The Directive did not require Ireland to provide before 1 January 2011 for marriage or a form of civil partnership for same-sex couples nor to give retrospective effect to the Civil Partnership Act. There was thus no indirect discrimination.

27.17.5.3 Disability discrimination

Most of the case law on disability discrimination has been concerned with the definition of disability. This case law has been considered earlier at 27.17.1.2. The case of *Johann Odar v Baxter Deutschland GmbH* (case C-152/11) concerned indirect discrimination on the grounds of disability.

Odar

Dr Odar was disabled. He lived and worked in Germany. From 1979–2008 he had been employed by Baxter. Under the German retirement pension scheme he was entitled to an old age pension as from the age of 65 years old, that is from 1 August 2015, as well as a retirement pension for severely disabled persons as from the age of 60, which in his case was 1 August 2010. In addition he was entitled to compensation under a Contingency Social Plan (CSP) which had been agreed with the company's work council in 2006. This was payable in the case of employees who left their employer company because it was unable to offer them a suitable job. Baxter could not offer Dr Odar a job suited to his physical capabilities. The compensation was calculated by a twofold method: the standard formula and the special formula compensation which took into account, in the case of workers who were more than 54 years old, the date on which their pension entitlement began. In the case of Dr Odar this resulted in an amount considerably less than if the compensation had been calculated on the basis of the standard formula in which no account would have been taken of his pension entitlements—and also less than that which he would have received had the calculation been based on his entitlement to an old age pension scheme. German law permitted differences in benefits under CSPs in the case of workers who were financially secure because they were entitled to a pension. The objective of this rule was to protect younger workers, to facilitate their integration into employment whilst at the same time ensuring a fair distribution of limited financial resources of a CSP.

The CJ found that the calculation method used in the case of Dr Odar gave rise to indirect discrimination on the ground of a disability:

> . . . the first component in the special formula calculation will always be lower for a severely disabled worker than for a non-disabled worker of the same age. In the present case the fact that the calculation is based, in an ostensibly neutral manner, on pensionable age, leads to a situation where severely disabled workers . . . receive less compensation on termination of employment because of a serious disability [para 57].

27.17.5.4 Religious discrimination

The issue of discrimination on the ground of religion has arisen in two cases: *Samira Achbita* and *Asma Bougnaoui*. In both cases women of the Muslim faith complained that they had been dismissed from employment because they wished to wear a veil during working hours.

Samira Achbita

Samira Achbita worked as a receptionist for the Belgian security company G4S Secure Solutions, which provides security and guarding services as well as reception services. After three years of employment she insisted that she should be able to wear an Islamic headscarf at work. She was dismissed. G4S prohibited the wearing of any visible religious, political or philosophical symbols.

The Court found there was no direct discrimination where an employee of the Muslim faith is banned from wearing an Islamic headscarf as a result of an internal rule prohibiting the visible wearing of any political, philosophical and religious sign in the workplace. However, the ban may constitute indirect discrimination based on religion if it is established that the apparently neutral obligation it imposes results, in fact, in persons adhering to a particular religion or belief being put at a disadvantage, unless it is objectively justified by a legitimate aim, such as the pursuit by the employer, in its relations with its customers, of a policy of political, philosophical and religious neutrality, provided the principle of proportionality is respected.

Asma Bougnaoui

Ms Bougnaoui was a Muslin woman who was employed in July 2008 as a design engineer by Micropole SA, an IT consultancy company. Whilst in employment she wore, at times of her choice, an Islamic headscarf which covered her head but left her face exposed. As part of her duties, Ms Bougnaoui was required to meet Micropole's clients on their premises. One of those clients complained that Ms Bougnaoui's headscarf had 'embarrassed' its employees and requested that she should not wear the veil the next time she came to the premises. She refused this request and was dismissed.

In a reference for a preliminary ruling from the Cour de Cassation, the CJ was asked whether Article 4(1) Directive 2000/78 (see para 27.17.6) could be interpretred as meaning that the wish of a customer no longer to have the services of an employee wearing an Islamic headscarf is a 'genuine and determining occupational requirement' by reason of the nature of the particular occupational activities concerned or the context in which they were carried out.

The Court answered this question in the negative. It held that the willingness of an employer to take into account the wishes of a customer no longer to have the services of that employer provided by a worker wearing an Islamic headscarf cannot be considered to be a genuine and determining occupational requirement within the meaning of Article 4(1) Directive 2000/78. In accordance with

Recital 23 of the Directive 'it is only in very limited circumstances that a characteristic related, in particular, to religion may constitute a genuine and determining occupational requirement (para 38)'. Moreover a 'genuinely and determining occupational requirement' is objectively dictated by the nature of the occupational activities concerned or the context in which they are carried out. It cannot cover the subjective considerations such as an employer's desire to accommodate the wishes of his customers.

27.17.6 **Exceptions and derogations**

The principle of equal treatment laid down by the Directive is subject to five exceptions. Additionally, Member States are permitted to make a number of derogations from some of its provisions. Such exceptions or derogations are subject to the principle of proportionality. As a general rule, the Directive applies without prejudice to measures laid down by national law in the interests of public security, public order and the prevention of criminal offences, for the protection of health and the rights and freedoms of others (Article 2(5)). The Directive provides for two other specific exceptions to the principle of equal treatment:

- it has no application to differences in treatment based on nationality or conditions relating to the entry and residence of TCNs and stateless persons (Article 3(2)). Discrimination based on nationality remains subject to Article 18 TFEU and the rights of TCNs to enter and remain in a Member State are within the exclusive competence of that State;

- it does not apply to payments of any kind by state schemes 'or similar', including state social security or social protection schemes (Article 3(3)).

Member States can provide that the Directive does not apply to the following:

- the armed forces in so far as it relates to discrimination on the grounds of disability and age (Article 3(1));

- the fixing, for occupational social security schemes, of differential ages for employees or groups or categories of employees for admission or entitlement to retirement or invalidity benefits including the fixing under those schemes of different ages for employees or groups or categories of employees. The use of age criteria in actuarial calculations does not constitute discrimination on the grounds of age provided it does not result in discrimination on the grounds of sex (Article 6(2));

- differences in treatment based on a characteristic required for a particular occupation. The characteristic in question must be a 'genuine and determining occupational requirement' which has a legitimate objective and the difference in treatment must be a proportionate means of attaining that objective (Article 4 (1));

- occupational activities within churches and other public or private organisations the ethos of which is based upon religion or belief. In such cases a difference in treatment based upon a person's religion or belief does not constitute discrimination where, by reason of the nature of these activities or the context in which they are carried out, a person's religion or belief constitutes a genuine, legitimate and justified occupational requirement having regard to the organisation's ethos. Such organisations can require individuals working for them to act in good faith and with loyalty to the organisation's ethos (Article 4(5));

- differences in treatment on the grounds of age, provided there are objective reasons for the differential treatment and it is reasonably justified, within the context of national law, by a legitimate aim relating to employment policy, labour market and vocational training objectives if the means of achieving those objectives are appropriate and necessary (Article 6(1)).

On a further note, Article 15 recognises the need to achieve a balance of representation of the major religious communities in Northern Ireland both in the police service and in the employment of teachers.

Most of the cases that have come before the CJ under the Framework Employment Directive have been concerned with age discrimination. In all of these cases the CJ found discriminatory conduct but proceeded to consider whether it fell under one of the exceptions or derogations permitted by the Directive. Whilst most of these cases have been concerned with Article 6(1) (justifiable differential treatment necessary for the pursuit of a legitimate aim related to employment policy) a number have relied upon Article 4(1) (differences in treatment based on a characteristic required for a particular occupation). We consider both lines of case law below, beginning with cases concerning Article 4(1).

Wolf is the first case in which Article 4(1) was relied upon to justify age discrimination with respect to access to employment.

Wolf

Wolf applied for a position with the fire services of the city of Frankfurt. His application was turned down on the ground that he was over the age of 30—the limit for recruitment to the particular service he wished to join. The issue was whether this statutory age limit was a 'genuine and determining occupational requirement' within the meaning of Article 4(1) of the Directive.

The CJ held that it was. The task to be performed in that particular service required exceptionally high physical capabilities and could only be performed by young persons.

By contrast, in *Vital Pérez* the CJ found that an age limit of 30 for a post in a local police force was not justified.

Vital Pérez

Mr Vital Pérez challenged a provision in a notice of competition intended to fill 15 local police officer posts which required applicants to be no more than 30 years of age. He argued that the condition had no justification insofar as the physical fitness required by candidates was the subject of a separate specific requirement in the notice of competition which stated that candidates would be required to satisfy certain physical tests.

The CJ found that setting a maximum age of recruitment of local police officers was discriminatory and could not be justified. Distinguishing *Wolf* the Court held that many of the tasks assigned to local police officers did not require physical capacities comparable to the 'exceptionally high' physical capacities regularly required of officers in the fire service. The stringent eliminatory physical tests imposed at the recruitment stage would make it possible to ensure that local police officers possessed the necessary level of physical fitness required for the performance of their professional duties.

More recently in *Salaberria Sorondo* the CJ found that the duties of the police force of the Autonomous Communities in Spain required more physical capacities that those of local police forces such as the one in issue in *Vital Pérez* with the result that a police officer serving in the

Autonomous Communities who is more than 55 years old could not be considered to be in full possession of the capabilities necessary for the proper performance of his duties. This fact justified imposing a maximum age limit of 35 years on new recruits to such forces. A police officer recruited at the age of 34 years old would have to undergo training for two years after which he could be expected to perform policing duties for a maximum of 19 years until he reached the age of 55 years. This being the case, recruitment at a higher age would prejudice the numbers which could be assigned to full policing duties for a sufficiently long period. The objective of ensuring the operational capacity and proper functioning of the police service concerned therefore justified an age limit being imposed on recruits.

Turning now to Article 6(1), we see the CJ affirming the right of Member States to determine their own employment policies and to take measures to execute those policies in an effective manner but at the same time requiring that discriminatory measures in pursuit of legitimate employment policies are no more than is necessary to achieve those policy aims.

Kücükdeveci concerned the disregard of the period of employment of young persons in the calculation of their notice period.

Kücükdeveci

The claimant had been employed from the age of 18 years by Swedex. She was dismissed after ten years of service. Her notice period was calculated as if she had been in employment for three years instead of ten years. This was in accordance with German law under which periods of employment before the age of 25 are not taken into account in calculating the notice period in case of dismissal.

The Court held that such a provision must be regarded as relating to conditions of dismissal. It was discriminatory in that it afforded less favourable treatment between persons with the same length of service. As to whether the difference in treatment could be justified it appeared that the objective of the legislation—adopted in 1926—was to lighten the burden on employers imposed by lengthy notice periods and to introduce some fluidity into the labour market. The legislation reflected the legislature's assessment that younger workers react more rapidly to the loss of their jobs and greater flexibility may be demanded of them. A shorter period of notice for young workers also facilitates their recruitment by increasing the flexibility of personnel management. However the Court was not impressed with this argument, pointing out that the legislation applies to all employees who joined their employing organisation before the age of 25 years old, regardless of when they were dismissed—they could have in fact completed a long period of service and might not therefore be young workers. Accordingly it ruled that the legislation was not appropriate for achieving its purported aim.

Andersen

In *Andersen*, Mr Andersen worked for the Region of Southern Denmark from 1979 until 2006 when he was 63 years old. Danish law grants a severance allowance to workers employed in the same undertaking for at least 12 years. The allowance is not payable to workers who on termination of their employment relationship are entitled to an old-age pension under an occupational pension scheme. Mr Andersen was entitled to such a pension, but he wished to remain on the labour market and registered as a jobseeker with the relevant employment services. He intended to waive his pension rights.

The Court found that the Danish law was discriminatory. It then went on to consider whether such a difference in treatment could be justified under Article 6(1). The objective of the severance allowance was to facilitate employees who had worked for an employer for a long period of time to move jobs by providing them with the means to acquire new skills to get a new job. This the Court found was a legitimate employment policy and labour-market objective within the meaning of Article 6(1). Generally those who were entitled to an old-age pension left the job market. They were not therefore in need of the severance allowance. Although the exclusion of those who left the labour market from entitlement to the severance allowance was not manifestly inappropriate to the attainment of the objective of the legislation, the exclusion of workers who were eligible for a pension was disproportionate. By precluding payment of the allowance to workers who, although eligible for an old-age pension from their employer, nonetheless intended to waive the right to a pension and continue working, the legislation went beyond what is necessary to achieve the objective of governing the severance allowance.

In *Odar* (discussed earlier at 27.17.5.3) the CJ found that the aim of the objective of the German government of ensuring the fair distribution of limited financial resources of CSPs was legitimate but found the measure to have a disproportionate effect on the severely disabled who generally face greater difficulty in finding new employment and whose risks tend to become exacerbated as they approach retirement age.

> ... In ultimately paying a severely disabled worker compensation ... which is lower than the amount paid to a non-disabled worker, the measure ... has an excessive adverse effect on the legitimate interests of severely disabled workers and therefore goes beyond what is necessary to achieve the social-policy objectives pursued by the German government [para 70].

27.17.7 Compulsory retirement

There have been a number of cases on compulsory retirement-age requirements which either require a worker to leave the labour market at a given age or which alter the arrangements under which they continue working—such as moving from tenured posts or indefinite contracts of employment to short-term fixed contracts. *Palacios de la Villa* concerned the dismissal of an employee who had reached the compulsory retirement age. The Court held that the national provision was objectively and reasonably justified by the legitimate aim of facilitating the entry into the labour market of certain categories of workers (Article 6(1) of the Directive); it did not exclude compulsory retirement rules from the scope of its review. In other words, Member States are free to set age limits such as that at issue in the case only if they can establish that there are objective and reasonable social-policy justifications for them, with the CJ having the last word.

Retirement age was again the issue in *Age Concern England*.

Age Concern England

The Employment Equality (Age) Regulations 2006, which transposed Directive 2000/78, provide that an employer may dismiss an employee who has reached retirement age if that measure constitutes 'a proportionate means of achieving a legitimate aim'. The case turned on the interpretation of Article 6(1) of the Directive which empowers Member States to provide that certain differences in treatment on the basis of age shall not constitute discrimination if they are objectively and reasonably justified by a legitimate aim, and then gives examples of what could be considered as an objective and reasonable justification. The 2006 Regulations do not provide for such examples. The claimants argued that the meaning of Article 6 of the Directive is that Member States must set out in their instruments of transposition a specific list of the differences of treatment which may be justified by reference to a

> legitimate aim; thus, if the relevant national law provides only that a difference of treatment on grounds of age, of whatever kind, is lawful if it can be shown that it constitutes a proportionate means of achieving a legitimate aim, it is incompatible with Article 6.

The Court disagreed. It reiterated its earlier case law to the effect that Member States have wide discretion as to the choice of methods for the transposition of a directive, and that their obligation to ensure the effectiveness of a directive does not necessarily mean that its provisions must be incorporated formally in express, specific legislation. Therefore, the lack in the Regulations of a precise list of aims which can justify discrimination does not render them incompatible with the Directive. However, the general content of the national measure should enable courts to identify what the legitimate aim is in each case and assess the proportionality of the means used to achieve it. The spirit of Article 6(1) of the Directive, the Court continued, is that discriminatory measures may be justified by reference to social-policy objectives, such as those related to employment policy, the labour market, or vocational training; it is for the national court to determine whether a particular measure can be justified by such an objective. The effect of the judgment is that Member States enjoy considerable discretion as to the way they design and implement their anti-discrimination legislation which gives effect to relevant rules. The limit of such discretion is the effectiveness of law: national legislation cannot provide for justifications of discriminatory treatment which are not objective and proportionate. This is a test which national courts should perform by applying the principles developed by the CJ, and, if necessary, by making a preliminary reference.

In *Mangold* the Court held that a provision of German law whereby all workers who had reached the age of 52 years old without distinction may, until the age at which they may claim their entitlement to a retirement pension, be offered fixed-term contracts of employment which could be renewed an indefinite number of times, could not be objectively justified. The age of the worker was the only criterion for the application of fixed-term contracts of employment. It had not been shown that the fixing of an age threshold as such, regardless of any other consideration linked to the structure of the labour market or the personal situation of the workers concerned, was objectively necessary to achieve the vocational integration of the unemployed older worker, as had been argued by the German government. The consequence of the law was, the Court found:

> This significant body of workers, determined solely on the basis of age, is thus in danger, during a substantial part of its members' working life, of being excluded from the benefit of stable employment which, however, as the Framework Agreement makes clear, constitutes a major element in the protection of workers [para 64].

In *Petersen*, Ms Petersen was refused authorisation to practise as a panel dentist after the age of 68 years. Panel dentists were obliged to retire at the age of 68 years in order to protect the health of patients insured under the statutory health scheme since it was believed that the performance of those dentists declined from that age. However non-panel dentists were not required to retire at that age. Although the Court accepted patient health to be a legitimate social-policy objective both on the basis of Article 2(5) of the Directive and the general rule that Member States have a broad discretion in organising their social-security and healthcare schemes, it found that the legislation lacked consistency in the sense that non-panel dentists were not required to retire at 68 years old. If dentists over the age of 68 were deemed not to have the requisite skills to provide care of an appropriate standard then all dentists over that age should be prohibited from practising dentistry.

Prigge and *Gerard Fuchs and Peter Köhler v Land Hessen* (cases C-159 and 160/10) may be compared and contrasted with *Petersen*.

> ## Prigge
>
> *Prigge* concerned a collective agreement applicable to the crew of Deutsche Lufthansa which prohibited pilots from working as such after the age of 60. Both national and international law provided that pilots should retire at the age of 65, but that between the ages of 60 and 64 they should work as part of a multi-pilot crew and the other members of that crew should be under 60 years. These rules were designed to ensure air traffic safety in that airline pilots must possess particular physical capabilities which might diminish with age. As such, they could be considered a 'genuine and determining' occupational requirement within the meaning of Article 4(1).

The CJ found the compulsory retirement age of 60 laid down in the collective agreement to be disproportionate given that both national and international law set the age of compulsory retirement at 65. *Fuchs and Köhler* concerned the retirement age of civil servants. This age was set at 65, but exceptionally a civil servant could continue to work until the age of 68 if he so requested and his continued employment was in the interests of the service. In the case of a public prosecutor it might be in the interests of the service if he were allocated a case in which proceedings were not finished by the time he reached 65 years old. Rather than reallocate the case to another prosecutor it might be more efficient for him to continue to deal with it until proceedings had terminated. The Court found in contrast to *Petersen* that the rule in question did not lack coherence when contrasted with the general retirement scheme for civil servants. The compulsory retirement age was 65 and in certain limited cases civil servants could work beyond that age. The position in *Petersen* was otherwise, in that the retirement age of two groups of persons doing work of the same nature in the same profession differed according to their employment status.

In *Rosenbladt v Oellerking GmbH* (case C-45/09), Ms Rosenbladt worked as cleaner in a barracks for 39 years—hardly a comfortable way of life but she was no doubt a sturdy and reliable employee. She was entitled to a very low pension and so wished to remain in employment. Her contract provided that it would terminate at the end of the calendar month in which the employee could claim a retirement pension or at 65 years old at the latest. The German government argued that this rule:

> ... is the reflection of a political and social consensus which has endured for many years in Germany. That consensus is based primarily on the notion of sharing employment between the generations in Germany. The termination of the employment contracts of those employees directly benefits young workers by enabling them to find work [para 43].

The Court accepted this practice of automatic retirement—which it observed had been a feature of employment law in many Member States—could be regarded as objectively and reasonably justified within the meaning of Article 6(1) of the Directive. As to whether it was appropriate and necessary the Court had this to say:

> Legislation such as that in issue in *Rosenbladt* takes account of the fact that persons concerned are entitled to financial compensation by means of a replacement income in the form of a retirement income at the end of their working life [para 48].

Thus it was not unreasonable for a Member State to take the view that a measure such as the authorisation of clauses on automatic termination of employment contracts at a given age was justified. However, was such a measure proportionate given the fact that the termination of employment contracts at a given age could cause financial hardship—precisely the circumstances of Ms

Rosenbladt and indeed others in low paid jobs whose pension entitlement was poor? Given the fact that German employment legislation does not prevent a person who has reached retirement age from continuing to work—there is no obligation to exit the labour market—coupled with the protection from discrimination from age, the Court found that the legislation in question did not go beyond what is necessary to achieve the aims it is designed to pursue. However this reasoning may be queried. Although theoretically a person can re-enter the labour market after retirement, just how easy is it to get employment after retirement age in an employment culture which provides for automatic termination of employment at a given age? What about loss of seniority and other employment rights following the rupture of an employment relationship? What about the consequences for pension entitlement? These are issues which may place a person retired compulsorily in a much less favourable position than before retirement.

27.17.8 **Enforcement**

The mechanism for enforcement of the rights and obligations are similar to those set out in the Race Directive (see 27.16.5) save for one important exception: there is no provision requiring Member States to designate a body responsible for the promotion of equal treatment.

27.18 **Conclusions**

Since the last edition of this work there has been an upsurge in the case law emanating from the CJ. These judgments have all been rendered in cases in which national courts have referred requests for preliminary ruling, pursuant to Article 267 TFEU, to the CJ. Much responsibility has been placed on the CJ which has been called upon to interpret skeletal legal provisions, key concepts in many instruments having been left undefined and with little indication as to what they might mean. The Court's approach in interpreting and applying these provisions has been functional—it has looked upon the objectives of the rules upon which it has been asked to rule and interpreted them in accordance with what they were designed to achieve and wider Union objectives. Exceptions and derogations have been required to be proportionate and appropriate to the objective which they seek to achieve. At the same time, both in legislation and case law, we see differences in the application of the principle of equality. A hierarchy of norms can be detected. Whilst employment-related discrimination is prohibited in all the spheres to which discrimination legislation is addressed, it is only in the case of gender discrimination and racial and ethnic discrimination that non-employment-related discrimination is addressed, and even then it is more widely prohibited on racial and ethnic grounds than on the basis of gender. The Race Directive and the Recast Directive impose a duty on the Member States to designate a body or bodies for the promotion of equal treatment of all persons without discrimination on the grounds of racial or ethnic origin, but there is no comparable obligation in the Framework Employment Directive. Under the Race Directive direct discrimination can be justified on two grounds only (genuine and determining occupational requirements and positive action), whereas the Framework Employment Directive allows many more exceptions and derogations and the Court has adopted a fairly non-restrictive approach to them, being particularly deferential to Member States' social and employment policies where these are invoked to justify age discrimination. Within the gender discrimination directives, disparities can also be noted, particularly in the sphere of indirect discrimination where age-related discrimination in social security can result in the prejudicial treatment of women. The attainment of equal treatment in occupational social welfare schemes is similarly constrained. The end result is a fragmentation of equality rights with variable standards of protection. This in itself leads to inequalities and, moreover, makes it difficult to bring claims of multiple discrimination or intersectional discrimination where disparity of treatment is alleged on more than one ground.

Further reading

Ahtela, K, 'The revised provisions on sex discrimination in European law: A critical assessment' (2005) 11 ELJ 58.

Arnull, A, 'Out with the old . . . ' (Editorial) (2006) 31 EL Rev 1.

Barnard, C, 'The economic objectives of Article 119' in T Hervey and D O'Keeffe, *Sex Equality Law of the European Union* (Wiley, 1996).

Bell, M, 'A patchwork of protectionism: The new anti-discrimination law framework' (2002) 67 MLR 465.

Bell, M, 'Reflecting on inequalities in European equality law' (2003) 28 EL Rev 349.

Bell, M, 'The principle of equal treatment: Widening and deepening' in P Craig and G de Búrca, *The Evolution of EU Law*, 2nd edn (Oxford University Press, 2011).

Bell, M and Waddington, L, 'The 1996 Intergovernmental Conference and the Prospects of a non-discrimination Treaty Article' (1996) 25 ILJ 320.

Besson, S, 'Never shall the twain meet? Gender discrimination under EU and ECHR law' (2008) 8 Human Rights L Rev 647.

Burrows, N and Robison, M, 'Positive action for women in employment: Time to align with Europe?' (2006) 33 J Law & Soc 24.

Ellis, E and Watson, P, *EU Anti-Discrimination Law*, 2nd edn (Oxford University Press, 2012).

Hatzopoulos, V, 'A (more) social group: A political crossroad or a legal one-way? Dialogues between Luxembourg and Lisbon' (2005) 42 CML Rev 1599.

Honeyball, S, 'Pregnancy and sex discrimination' (2000) 29 ILJ 43.

Howard, E, 'Anti-race discrimination measures in Europe: An attack on two fronts' (2005) 11 ELJ 468.

Koldinski, K, 'Case-law of the European Court of Justice on sex discrimination 2006-2011' (2011) 48 CML Rev 1599.

Masselot, A, 'The state of gender equality law in the European Union' (2007) 13 ELJ 152.

Muir, E, 'Enhancing the effects of Community law on national employment policies: the *Mangold* case' (2006) 31 EL Rev 879.

Neuner, J, 'Protection against discrimination in European contract law' (2006) 2 ERCL 35.

O'Brien, C, 'Equality's false summits: New varieties of disability discrimination, "excessive" equal treatment and economically constricted horizons' (2011) 36 EL Rev 26.

Sargeant, M, 'The European Court of Justice and age discrimination' [2011] JBL 144.

Schiek, D and Lawson, A (eds), *European Union Non-Discrimination Law and Intersectionality* (Ashgate Press, 2011).

Watson, P, 'Equality, fundamental rights and the limits of legislative discretion: Comment on *Test Achats*' (2011) 36 EL Rev 896.

28 Introduction to EU competition policy

28.1 Introduction

In previous editions of this book, the chapters on competition law were extensive. Competition law has become increasingly complex, and has now evolved to such an extent that it is a specialist area of study. In a general book on EU law, it is no longer possible to do full justice to this subject, and the discussion both in this chapter and Chapter 29 which follows here has been curtailed to what may be regarded as the fundamental aspects of competition law and the essential structure and principles governing the EU competition regime. Note, however, that with the decentralisation of enforcement, some aspects of enforcement will be affected by the rules on effectiveness (see Chapter 8). When considering the interrelationship between competition rules and intellectual property rights, note the parallels with the approach taken with regard to free movement of goods (Chapter 19).

28.2 Objectives of the competition rules

Article 3(3) TEU sets out as one of the objectives of the Union: achieving a 'highly competitive social market economy'. The role of competition policy is pivotal to the internal market. An effective competition system is essential to the attainment of the internal market. If the restrictions on the free movement of goods and services required to be removed by the Member States could be replaced by restrictive arrangements made between private parties, the internal market would never be achieved. Accordingly, the competition rules, in many senses, are a reflection of the free movement provisions, applicable as between undertakings engaged in economic activity. Both sets of rules have common objectives: the attainment of the single market, the encouragement of economic activity and the maximisation of efficiency by enabling goods and resources to flow freely amongst Member States according to the operation of normal market forces. Any attempt to isolate or divide up markets attracts severe penalties. For example, Nintendo was fined EUR 149 million for preventing the exports of game consoles and related products from the United Kingdom to The Netherlands and Germany ([2003] OJ L255/33).

In addition to market integration, EU competition policy has one fundamental objective in common with all competition systems: consumer welfare. Consumers should have access to goods and services at optimal prices and trading terms. This can be achieved through the efficient allocation of resources and ensuring the competitive structure of the market.

28.3 Structure of the EU competition rules

The EU competition rules are set out in the TFEU, Council and Commission regulations and a range of 'soft law' instruments. Policy initiatives and priorities are set out in a variety of publications such as the European Commission's annual competition reports, and the Competition Policy Brief and specific policy statements made throughout the year by senior officials and the Commissioner.

28.3.1 The competition rules

The competition rules are set out in Chapter 1 of Title VII TFEU. Section 1, containing Articles 101 and 102 sets out the rules applicable to undertakings. Article 101 applies to the conduct of two or more undertakings; Article 102 applies, in general, to the conduct of a single undertaking. Both provisions require that the allegedly prohibited conduct in question be restrictive of competition and have an effect on trade between Member States.

28.3.2 Article 101

Article 101 contains three provisions setting out what acts are prohibited; how an exemption may be available from that prohibition and what consequences flow from engaging in acts restrictive of competition for which no exemption is available.

Article 101

1. The following shall be prohibited as incompatible with the internal market: all agreements between undertakings, decisions by associations of undertakings and concerted practices which may affect trade between Member States and which have as their object or effect the prevention, restriction or distortion of competition within the internal market, and in particular those which:

   (a) directly or indirectly fix purchase or selling prices or any other trading conditions;

   (b) limit or control production, markets, technical development, or investment;

   (c) share markets or sources of supply;

   (d) apply dissimilar conditions to equivalent transactions with other trading parties, thereby placing them at a competitive disadvantage;

   (e) make the conclusion of contracts subject to acceptance by the other parties of supplementary obligations which, by their nature or according to commercial usage, have no connection with the subject of such contracts.

2. Any agreements or decisions prohibited pursuant to this Article shall be automatically void;

3. The provisions of paragraph 1 may, however, be declared inapplicable in the case of:

   – any agreement or category of agreements between undertakings,

   – any decision or category of decisions by associations of undertakings,

   – any concerted practice or category of concerted practices, which contributes to improving the production or distribution of goods or to promoting technical or economic progress, while allowing consumers a fair share of the resulting benefit, and which does not:

(a) impose on the undertakings concerned restrictions which are not indispensable to the attainment of these objectives;

(b) afford such undertakings the possibility of eliminating competition in respect of a substantial part of the products in question.

28.3.3 Article 102

Article 102 is concerned with the behaviour of undertakings in a dominant position. Being 'big' is not an issue in EU law. What offends against the competition rules is certain types of behaviour by dominant undertakings which may prejudice the competitive structure of the market, in particular by foreclosing access by competitors.

Article 102

Any abuse by one or more undertakings of a dominant position within the internal market or in a substantial part of it shall be prohibited as incompatible with the internal market in so far as it may affect trade between Member States.

Such abuse may, in particular, consist in:

(a) directly or indirectly imposing unfair purchase or selling prices or other unfair trading conditions;

(b) limiting production, markets or technical development to the prejudice of consumers;

(c) applying dissimilar conditions to equivalent transactions with other trading parties, thereby placing them at a competitive disadvantage;

(d) making the conclusion of contracts subject to acceptance by the other parties of supplementary obligations which, by their nature or according to commercial usage, have no connection with the subject of such contracts.

Article 103 empowers the Council, on a proposal from the Commission and after consulting the European Parliament, to adopt regulations or directives to give effect to the principles set out in Articles 101 and 102 and in particular to make provision for fines and periodic penalty payments.

Article 106 is concerned with the applicability of the TFEU to the state. It contains specific provisions on the extent to which the competition rules are to be applied to the state.

Section 2, Article 107(1) provides that the grant by Member States of aid which distorts or threatens to distort competition by favouring certain undertakings or the production of certain goods 'in so far as it affects trade between Member States be incompatible with the internal market.' Article 107(2) set out a number of types of aid, which are deemed to be compatible with the internal market, for example aid to make good the damage caused by natural disasters or exceptional occurrences.

On the basis of Article 103 a number of regulations have been adopted to ensure the effective implementation of Article 101 and 102. This legislation has been adopted either by the Council and the Parliament using the ordinary legislative method or by the Commission on the basis of an enabling regulation of the Council. Much of this legislation is concerned with block exemptions. Block exemption regulations provide for exemption from the prohibition set out in Article 101(1). They provide a 'safe harbour' for some of the most common business practices.

Additionally and importantly there are a number of 'soft law' instruments in the form of guide-lines, communications and notices. Drawing on the principles established by its own case law and that of the CJEU the Commission uses these instruments to achieve a number of objectives: to in-dicate how it will apply and interpret the competition rules; its enforcement priorities; and import-antly to distil and clarify the extensive body of law and policy which has emerged over the many years of enforcement of the competition rules. These instruments are not legally binding but the Commission regards itself as being bound by them and will not therefore act in a manner that is incompatible with their provisions. Examples include:

- Notice on the Definition of the Relevant Market ([1997] OJ L372);
- Guidelines on the applicability of Article 101 TFEU to Horizontal Co-operation Agreements ([2011] OJ C11/1);
- Guidelines on Vertical Restraints ([2010] OJ L 130/01).

28.4 Enforcement of EU competition policy: the early years

28.4.1 A strict approach

The basic principles of EU competition policy, as adopted in the original EEC Treaty, were drafted in the broadest terms, leaving the Commission, subject to review by the CJEU, to interpret these provisions and to develop detailed rules. Regulation 17/62 came into force on 1 March 1962. Article 1 confirmed that the prohibition set out in what were then Articles 85 and 86 EEC, now Articles 101 and 102 TFEU, takes effect without any prior decision of the Commission. The remain-ing provisions dealt with the obtaining of exemptions under Article 101(3) TFEU and entrusted the Commission with the exclusive jurisdiction to grant such exemptions. Agreements could be notified to the Commission with a request for either a negative clearance (a declaration that the agreement did not offend against the competition rules) or an exemption. Regulation 17 also dealt with the conduct of complaints alleging violations of the competition rules by aggrieved parties, and invested the Commission with considerable powers of enforcement. Regulation 19/ 65 empowered the Commission to exempt en bloc certain categories of agreements. This in effect meant that agreements which fell within the terms of such a regulation would be automatically deemed to be exempt from the prohibition set out in Article 101(1) TFEU, no notification to or clearance by the Commission being required. The Commission adopted block exemption regula-tions dealing with the most common types of agreement which, although restrictive of compe-tition and thus prohibited under Article 101(1) TFEU would fulfil the criteria set out in what was then Article 101(3) and thus qualify for exemption. The earliest regulations dealt with distribution agreements.

Block exemption regulations generally remain in force for a period of 10 years after which, fol-lowing public consultation, they are revised to reflect changes in business practices and the work-ings of markets. For example, the earliest block exemption tended to be rather formalistic, allowing certain types of clauses and prohibiting others. Latterly the block exemption regulations are based on effects of certain agreements on competition. Thus, for example, the market share of parties to the agreement will be decisive in deciding whether the parties can have the benefit of a block exemption regulation. The benefit of a block exemption can be withdrawn by the Commission or the national competition authorities. In the case of vertical agreements the Commission may, by means of a regulation, disapply the to certain markets.

28.5 The modernisation of the competition rules

Although Articles 101(1) and 102 TFEU were of direct effect and thus enforceable in national courts (*BRT v SABAM* (case 127/73)), the inability of national courts to consider whether an agreement fulfilled the criteria set out in Article 101(3) and hold that an agreement with features restrictive of competition, to be exempt or for national competition authorities to grant exemptions meant that the enforcement of the competition rules was concentrated in the hands of the Commission.

With successive enlargements and the creation of the internal market, the Commission began to struggle to keep pace with the numbers of agreements notified to it. Its resources were stretched leading to long delays in the processing of notifications. More seriously it found itself unable to focus on issues such as the most serious competition infringements and the application of the competition rules to new types of industry and business practices. Accordingly, the Commission began, with the publication of a White Paper in 1999, a long process of reform which resulted in the adoption of Regulation 1/2003 ([2003] OJ L1/1), which entered into force on 1 May 2004. This Regulation repealed and replaced Regulation 17/62 and fundamentally altered the balance of competence in the enforcement of the competition rules between the Commission and the Member States. In essence Regulation 1/2003 decentralised the application of the competition rules, sharing competence with the Member States, by increasing the role of the national competition authorities and courts. The system of prior notification of agreements was abolished; henceforth business itself had to ensure that its practices were in compliance with the competition rules.

The position today is that the responsibility of enforcement of EU competition rules is on two levels: (1) national competition authorities and courts; and (2) the Commission and the CJEU. Enforcement responsibilities are organised within the European Competition Network (ECN) (see Notice on NCA cooperation (OJ [2004] C101/3)).

28.5.1 European competition network

The national competition courts and authorities have more responsibility than hitherto in ensuring that the EU competition rules are complied with. This required a greater than before exchange of information between the various competent institutions. To facilitate the exchange of information among the national competition authorities and the European Commission, and to organise the allocation of cases between them, Regulation 1/2003 provided for the establishment of the ECN which is composed of the national competition authorities and the Commission. Within this network, information (including confidential information) is exchanged. The Commission must transmit a copy of the most important documents in any case it handles and, at the request of the competition authorities, furnish any document necessary to an assessment of the case pursued by it. For their part the national competition authorities are responsible for informing the Commission of any proposed decision relating to the application of Articles 101 and 102 and any decision withdrawing the benefit of a block exemption no later than 30 days before it is adopted.

To avoid any overlap and ensure the uniform and coherent application of the EU competition rules, the Regulation sets out how jurisdiction is to be divided between the various authorities. On any case in which the European Commission initiates proceedings, national competition authorities are relieved of their competence to assume jurisdiction. Before initiating proceedings in any particular case, the Commission must consult the national competition authorities of its intention to do so. Where either the Commission or a national competition authority receives a complaint relating to a matter which is being dealt with by another competition authority, it may suspend proceedings or reject the complaint.

28.5.2 Advisory Committee

Before taking a decision to order an infringement to be brought to an end, to find Article 101(1) or Article 102 not to be applicable, or to impose a fine or a periodic penalty payment on undertakings, the Commission consults the Advisory Committee on Restrictive Practice and Dominant Positions at one of its meetings or in writing. This committee is made up of representatives of the various national competition authorities.

28.5.3 National courts

Regulation 1/2003 provides that national courts may ask the Commission to transmit to them information in its possession or its opinion on questions of the application of the EU competition rules. Furthermore, Member States undertake to transmit to the Commission a copy of any written judgment of national courts relating to the application of Article 101 and 102 TFEU. The Regulation also makes provision for the Commission and national competition authorities to submit written or oral observations to the national courts on issues relating to Articles 101 and 102.

28.6 Powers of the European Commission

The European Commission has extensive powers to investigate and penalise infringements of the competition rules. It can conduct sector inquiries: where the trend of trade between EU countries suggests that competition may be being restricted or distorted within the internal market, the Commission is able to conduct an inquiry into a particular sector of the economy or into a particular type of agreement across various sectors. An example is the inquiry into the workings of the pharmaceuticals sector, the report of which was published in 2009. The Commission may, by simple request or by decision, ask undertakings and associations of undertakings to provide any information it needs to carry out the duties assigned to it by this Regulation; any natural or legal person who might have useful information is required to supply any information asked of them; the Commission may also ask governments and national competition authorities for any information it requires to carry out its duties. The Commission may conduct any necessary inspections of undertakings and associations of undertakings, and the latter are required to submit to such inspections; to this end, its officials are empowered to:

- enter the premises, including the homes of directors, managers or other staff members if a reasonable suspicion exists that books or other records related to the business and to the subject matter of the inspection might be held there. It can also seal any business premises and books or records for the period of the inspection;
- examine and take copies of extracts from the books and other records related to the business;
- ask any representative or member of staff of the undertaking or association of undertakings for information and record their answers.

28.6.1 **Decisions**

Under Regulation 1/2003, if the Commission finds there to be an infringement of Article 101 or 102 TFEU, it may adopt a decision requiring the undertakings and associations of undertakings concerned to bring the infringement to an end or finding that the infringement has been brought to an end. In cases of justified urgency, the Commission, acting on its own initiative, may, on the basis of a prima facie finding of infringement, order interim measures.

28.6.2 **Commitments**

Undertakings which are being investigated for breach of the competition rules may enter into legally binding commitments to rectify their behaviour so as to bring it into line with the competition rules. The file is then closed without any finding as to whether there has been an infringement or not. The Commission may make those commitments binding for a specified period. It may reopen the proceedings if the facts of the case change, the undertakings act contrary to their commitments or the decision is based on incomplete, incorrect or misleading information.

28.6.3 **Settlements**

In 2008 the Commission introduced a settlements procedure whereby during an investigation the parties to a cartel may acknowledge their participation in the cartel and, in return, the Commission will reduce the fine to which they would have been liable had a finding of an infringement been made by 10 per cent (Regulation 662/2008 ([2008] OJ L171/3). By the end of 2016, 22 settlement decisions had been made.

28.6.4 **Procedural rights**

In order to ensure a proper right of defence, the Commission, before taking a decision, will give the undertaking or association of undertakings in question the opportunity of being heard on the aspects to which it objects. The parties concerned also have the right of access to the Commission's file, provided that this does not result in business secrets being divulged. However, in order to safeguard professional secrecy, any information gathered may be used solely for the purpose for which it was acquired. The Commission and the national competition authorities are also under an obligation not to divulge any information they have acquired or exchanged.

28.6.5 **Fines and periodic penalty payments**

The Commission has extensive fining powers. It may impose fines on undertakings and associations of undertakings not exceeding 10 per cent of the total turnover realised in the preceding business year by each of the undertakings which participated in the infringement where they infringe Article 101 or 102 TFEU.

In fixing the amount of the fine, the Commission must take account of the gravity and the duration of the infringement. The methodology used in calculating fines is set out in the Guidelines on the method of setting fines ([2006] OJ C210/2). Fines are regarded by the Commission as being administrative in nature. In recent years the level of fines has gone up quite dramatically. In 2016 fines of EUR 3.7 billion were imposed, up from 1.6 billion in 2013. 2016 saw the highest fine ever imposed—EUR 2.9 billion. This was in respect of a cartel operated by truck manufacturers.

Fines may also be imposed where undertakings intentionally or negligently supply incorrect, incomplete or misleading information in response to a request from the Commission for information.

The Commission may also impose on undertakings and associations of undertakings periodic penalty payments not exceeding 5 per cent of their average daily turnover in the preceding business year per day and calculated from the date appointed by the decision, in order to compel them to: put an end to an infringement, comply with a decision ordering interim measures or submit to an inspection which it has ordered.

28.6.6 Review by the GC and the CJ

Any decisions taken by the Commission may be reviewed by the GC under Article 263 TFEU, and a failure on the part of the Commission to take such a decision may be challenged under Article 265 TFEU (see Chapter 13). Decisions of the GC may be the subject of an appeal to the CJ on a point of law only.

Breach of Articles 101 and 102 may give rise to sanctions imposed by the Commission in the form of heavy fines and penalties. Since companies in breach of competition rules may be subject to substantial fines, the CJEU has been vigilant in ensuring that the companies' procedural rights are not infringed. For example, in *BASF AG v Commission* (cases T-80/89), a decision was impugned because it had not been properly adopted in all relevant official languages. In the *Soda Ash* cases, the GC quashed Commission decisions because the companies' right of access to the file had been denied (*Solvay; ICI* cases (T-57/01 and T-66/01)). (On procedural rights, see Chapter 6; on effectiveness of remedies, see Chapter 8.) Of late the Commission's procedures have been increasingly criticised as failing to respect the rights of defendants. In response to this the Commission has introduced a number of reforms (Notice on Best Practices in the conduct of proceedings concerning Articles 101 and 102 TFEU, [2011] OJ C308/6; Decision 2011/695 on the Functions and Terms of Reference of the Hearing Officer, [2011] OJ L275/29). The CJEU has power to reduce or raise the level of fines imposed by the Commission.

28.7 The state and competition

Although the obligations of Articles 101–2 TFEU are imposed on 'undertakings' and do not prima facie concern the activities of public authorities, Article 106(1) expressly provides that EU competition law applies to 'public undertakings and undertakings to which Member States grant special or exclusive rights', subject to exception for undertakings 'entrusted with the operation of services of general economic interest or having the character of a revenue-producing monopoly' insofar as the application of the rules may 'obstruct the performance of the particular tasks assigned to them' (Article 106(2)). This exception has been strictly construed. Derogation will be permitted only to the extent that it is necessary to the performance of the particular tasks assigned to such undertakings and to ensure the economic equilibrium of the service operated in the general economic interest—for example, by providing a set-off between profitable and unprofitable activities (*Corbeau* (case C-320/91)—re Belgian postal monopoly). The legal framework:

> . . . within which agreements are made or decisions are taken and the classification (ie, public or private) given to that framework are irrelevant as far as the applicability of [Union] rules on competition are concerned [*BNIC v Clair* (case 123/83) para 17].

Even where there is no agreement or behaviour on the part of a public (or semi-public) body such as to give rise to liability under Articles 101–2, a state may not adopt or maintain in force any measures which deprive these articles of their effectiveness. Any public measure that endorses or encourages action in breach of Articles 101 and 102 will be deemed unlawful (*GB-INNO v ATAB* (case 13/77)).

A number of areas, such as transport, were originally excluded from EU competition law. As has been noted, there has been scope under Article 106(2) for exemption for public undertakings. The scope of these exclusions has been considerably reduced in recent years, as the Commission has introduced liberalising measures in the field of communications, postal services, transport, energy, insurance and audiovisual media, with a view to further increasing competition in these spheres.

28.8 Private Enforcement

Directive 2014/104 ([2014] OJ L349/11) which came into force on 27 December 2016 aims to facilitate claims for damages for victims of violations of the competition rules. (See Chapter 29.) Since infringements of Article 101 and 102 may affect a large number of individuals for whom seeking redress on an individual basis may not be practicable, the Commission has issued a Recommendation ([2013] OJ L201/60) inviting Member States to set up collective redress systems and recommends the principles which should govern those systems. At the time the Recommendation was issued, the availability of collective redress differed considerably from Member State to Member State. The Recommendation seeks to establish the right to collective redress and to lay down minimum common conditions under which it will be available.

28.9 Competition and third countries

As with the globalisation of the economy, competition law has become increasingly global. Over 125 countries now have competition regimes and that number is growing. Competition rules are enforced on a national and global level. The growth of international cartels, spanning multiple jurisdictions has led to increased cooperation between enforcement authorities. The EU has signed cooperation agreements with the United States ([1995] OJ L95/47; [1998] OJ L173), Canada ([1999] OJ L175/49), Japan ([2003] OJ L183/12) and Switzerland ([2014] OJ L347). Additionally there is in place a number of Memoranda of Understanding with countries such as China and India. The nature of cooperation varies between countries and can cover the coordination of enforcement actions, sharing of information on cases of mutual interest, dialogue on competition policy issues and, in some cases, capacity building support. The Commission's Annual Report on Competition describes the working of these cooperation agreements. In addition the Commission participates actively in a number of multilateral organisations, such as the International Competition Network (ICN) and the Organisation for Economic Co-operation and Development (OECD), UNCTAD and the World Trade Organisation.

Further reading

Commission's Annual Reports on Competition Policy.

Flynn, L, 'Competition policy and public services in EC law after the Maastricht and Amsterdam Treaties' in D O'Keeffe and P Twomey (eds), *Legal Issues of the Amsterdam Treaties* (Hart Publishing, 1999).

Fox, E, *Global Issues in Antitrust and Competition Law* (West, 2010).

Hofmann, HCH, 'Negotiated and non-negotiated administrative rule making: The example of EC competition policy' (2006) 43 CML Rev 153.

Jones, A and Sufrin, B, *EU Competition Law*, 6th edn (Oxford University Press, 2016).

Maher, I, 'Competition law modernization: An evolutionary tale' in P Craig and G de Búrca (eds), *The Evolution of EU Law*, 2nd edn (Oxford University Press, 2011).

Ross, M, 'Article 16 EC and services of general interest: From derogation to obligation?' (2000) 25 EL Rev 22.

Whish, R and Bailey, D, *Competition Law*, 8th edn (Oxford University Press, 2015).

29 EU competition law

29.1 Introduction

Chapter 28 sketched an overview of the EU competition law system. In this chapter we will consider in more detail those rules, focusing on Articles 101 and 102 TFEU and merger control. Given the breadth of the subject it is not possible to deal with it exhaustively and therefore reference to further specialised competition works is made at the end of this chapter.

29.2 The general scheme

Article 101 TFEU (1) prohibits:

> all agreements between undertakings, decisions by associations of undertakings and concerted practices which may affect trade between Member States and which have as their object or effect the prevention, restriction or distortion of competition within the internal market.

A number of examples of the types of agreements covered by this article are provided in para (1) (a)–(e). Article 101(2) TFEU provides that any agreement or decision in breach of Article 101 'shall be automatically void'. By virtue of Article 101(3) TFEU, the prohibition articulated in Article 101(1) may, however, be declared 'inapplicable' to agreements or decisions fulfilling a number of specified criteria.

29.2.1 Elements of an infringement

Article 101(1) contains three essential elements. There must be:

- an agreement between undertakings, or a decision by an association of undertakings or a concerted practice;
- which may affect trade between Member States;
- which must have as its object or effect the prevention, restriction or distortion of competition within the internal market.

Each of these elements will be considered in turn.

29.2.2 **Agreements between undertakings, decisions by associations of undertakings and concerted practices**

29.2.2.1 **Undertakings**

'Undertaking' is not defined either in the Treaties or secondary legislation. It has been interpreted by the EU Commission and the CJ in the widest possible sense to include any legal or natural person, regardless of the legal status of that entity, engaged in economic activity, whether in the provision of goods or services, including cultural or sporting activities (*Bosman*), banking (*Züchner v Bayerische Vereinsbank AG* (case 172/80)), insurance (*Verband der Sachversicherer eV v Commission* (case 45/85)) and transport (*Commission v Belgium* (case 156/77)). It is not necessary that the activity be pursued with a view to profit (eg, *Fédération Française des Sociétés d'Assurance v Ministère de l'Agriculture et de la Pêche* (case C-244/94)). The activity must simply involve putting goods or services on the market (*Pavel Pavlov and Others v Stichting Pensioenfonds Medische Specialisten* (case C-180/98)). The GC reconsidered the meaning of 'undertaking' in *FENIN v Commission* (case C-205/03P).

FENIN

FENIN was a Spanish association of the majority of undertakings marketing medical goods and equipment in Spain for use in Spanish publicly funded hospitals. Health bodies (hospitals, etc.) in Spain (SNS) purchase their requirements through FENIN. FENIN complained (under Article 102) that the SNS bodies were abusing their dominant position by delaying payment for goods obtained through FENIN. This was rejected because SNS was not an economic actor. FENIN appealed to the GC, which also rejected the claim. A further appeal was made to the CJ which upheld the judgment of the GC to the effect that SNS was not an undertaking.

The GC emphasised that an undertaking must carry on an economic activity, which is characterised by the business of offering goods or services in a particular market, rather than the simple fact of making purchases. Provided that the purpose for which goods purchased are subsequently used is part of an economic activity, then the purchase itself is an economic activity. Consequently, it is necessary to establish some economic activity, however marginal, for an entity to be regarded as an undertaking for the purposes of EU competition law (approach affirmed in *AOK- Bundersverbank and Others* (the *German Sickness Fund* case) (cases C-264, 306, 354, and 355/01)). (Contrast the approach in the case law on the right to receive services; Chapter 24.)

Entities providing health or welfare services which are provided on the basis of 'solidarity' are not considered to be undertakings for the purposes of Articles 101 and 102. By 'solidarity' is meant the 'inherently uncommercial act of involuntary subsidization of one social group by another' (Attorney-General Fennelly, *Sodemare SA and Others v Regione Lombardia* (case C-70/95)). State social security systems are characterised by solidarity—contributions are paid by all members on the basis of the same criteria, benefits are paid to all who are eligible regardless of the level of their contributions and all are accepted as (indeed, required to be) members regardless of the level of exposure to the risks for which they are insured. In *Christian Poucet v Assurances Générales de France and Caisse Mutuelle Régionale du Languedoc-Roussillon* (case C-139/91) the CJ held that French social security offices administering sickness and maternity insurance schemes were not undertakings. By contrast, in *Albany International BV v Stichting Bedrijfspensioenfonds Textielindustrie* (case C-67/96) the CJ found that a pension fund was an undertaking: it made investments on behalf of its members the performance of which determined the amount of benefits the fund would pay to its members.

Article 101(1) applies to undertakings in the public as well as the private sphere (*Italy v Commission (British Telecommunications)* (case 41/83)), but only in so far as they are engaged in economic activity. Note that public undertakings and undertakings charged with special responsibilities, are subject to the competition rules only insofar as the application of these rules 'does not obstruct the performance, in law or in fact, of the particular tasks assigned to them' (Article 106(2) TFEU).

29.2.2.2 Agreements

An agreement within the meaning of Article 101(1) has been interpreted broadly to include both formal and informal agreements. A 'gentleman's agreement' will suffice. There must, however, be a meeting of minds between the parties. In *Bayer AG v Commission* (case T-41/96) the GC held that the concept of an agreement:

> centres around the existence of a concurrence of rules between at least two parties, the form in which manifested being unimportant as long as it constitutes the faithful expression of the parties' intentions [para 67].

Article 101 applies to both horizontal and vertical agreements (*Établissements Consten SA and Grundig-Verkaufs GmbH v Commission* (cases 56 and 58/64)). Horizontal agreements are those made between undertakings operating at the same level in the market, for example agreements between producers or manufacturers. Vertical agreements are those between undertakings operating at different levels in the market, for example agreements between producers and distributors.

29.2.2.3 Decisions by associations of undertakings

The effect of decisions by associations of undertakings may be to coordinate behaviour amongst participant undertakings which has anti-competitive effects, without any need for actual agreement between those undertakings or between them and the association, hence their inclusion in Article 101(1).

It was held in *NV IAZ International Belgium v Commission* (case 96/82) that even a non-binding recommendation from a trade association which was normally followed by its members could constitute a decision within Article 101(1), as could a decision by an association of associations. The position of associations was considered in *Application of the Publishers' Association* ([1989] OJ L22/12).

> ### Re the Application of the Publishers' Association
>
> The Association's Code of Conduct was found by the Commission to have the character of a recommendation to its members and customers, and as such was to be considered as a decision of an association of undertakings, despite its non-binding character. As well as the association itself, its members may be liable for fines if they comply, even unwillingly, with a decision in breach of Article 101(1).

In *Wouters v Algemene Raad van de Nederlandse Orde van Advoccaten* (case C-309/99), a regulation by the Dutch Bar Association (DBA) on multi-disciplinary partnerships was held to be a decision by an association of undertakings because it related to the economic activity of its members (lawyers) rather than to the public law function which the DBA also fulfilled.

29.2.2.4 Concerted practices

A concerted practice is defined in *Imperial Chemical Industries Ltd v Commission (Dyestuffs)* (case 48/69) as a form of cooperation between undertakings which, without having reached the stage where an agreement properly so-called has been concluded, knowingly substitutes practical cooperation between them for the risks of competition.

To constitute a concerted practice, it is not necessary to have a concerted plan. It is enough that each party should have informed the other of the position they intended to take so that each could regulate his business conduct safe in the knowledge that his competitors would act in the same way. Similarly, in a series of cases, the GC has held that meeting to exchange information about pricing structures also constitutes a concerted practice, as the participants cannot fail to take this information into account when devising their own market strategies (eg, *Shell International Chemical Co Ltd v Commission* (case T-11/89)). Clearly, such practices may be just as damaging to competition as agreements or decisions by associations, and are much harder to prove as the *Dyestuffs* case demonstrates.

Dyestuffs

This case concerned three uniform price increases covering the same products introduced by a number of leading producers (including ICI) of aniline dyes, almost simultaneously, in 1964, 1965 and 1967. ICI unsuccessfully challenged a Commission decision that the producers were engaged in a concerted price-fixing practice, arguing that such price increases were common in oligopolies (ie where the market is dominated by a small number of large independent concerns).

The Court held that whilst parallel behaviour does not in itself constitute a concerted practice, it provides strong evidence of such a practice if it leads to conditions of competition which do not correspond to the normal conditions of the market.

In *Ahlström OY v Commission (wood pulp)* (cases C-89, 104, 114, 116–17 and 125–9/85), the CJ took a more cautious approach, finding that the Commission had not established that the undertakings had colluded.

Wood Pulp

In an action for the annulment of a Commission decision fining a number of the world's leading wood-pulp producers, which together held a two-thirds share of the Union market in wood pulp, for announcing quarterly simultaneous and identical price increases, the Court held that these announcements in themselves did not necessarily provide evidence of concerted practices, especially where the system of price announcements represented a 'rational response to the need to limit commercial risk in a long-term market'. It found that the similarity was the result of a high degree of market transparency, and the parallelism of the price increases could be satisfactorily explained by the oligopolistic tendencies of the market.

It was only where there was no 'plausible explanation' for the conduct in issue could it be presumed that it resulted from collusive behaviour.

29.2.2.5 Unilateral conduct

Although Article 101(1) TFEU appears to require some form of agreement or concentration on the part of two or more undertakings, there are circumstances when what appears to be a unilateral act may be found to be prohibited under Article 101(1).

In *AEG-Telefunken v Commission* (case 107/82) the parties had notified their distribution agreements for AEG products and obtained negative clearance from the Commission. AEG was subsequently found in breach of Article 101(1) for having *operated* the agreements in such a way as to restrict competition by systematically refusing to allow dealers into its network who did not comply with the (unofficial) pricing policy apparently observed by existing members. Similarly, in *Ford Werke AG v Commission* (case 25/84) the Court approved the Commission's refusal to grant clearance for what appeared to be a perfectly acceptable standard distribution agreement because Ford was refusing to supply existing distributors in Germany with right-hand-drive cars for export to England, apparently to maintain an artificial partitioning of the market and thereby different price levels in different Member States. Although there was no clear evidence of concerted action, and certainly none of any agreement, the Court held that Ford's decision to cease supplies formed part of the contractual relations between Ford Werke AG and its dealers. Admission to Ford's dealer network implied acceptance by the contracting parties of the policies pursued by Ford. In *Sandoz* ([1987] OJ L222/28) the Commission held that the words 'export prohibited' on all invoices to distributors were part of a continuing relationship between a producer and his distributors and was thus an agreement between them. The *Bayer* case demonstrates a stricter approach by the CJ in assessing whether unilateral conduct on the part of a supplier can constitute an agreement between them thus bringing their conduct within the scope of Article 101.

Bayer

Bayer had reduced the volume of supplies of the drug Adalat to its wholesalers in France and Spain in order to prevent them engaging in parallel exports to the United Kingdom where Adalat was sold at prices considerably higher—around 40 per cent—than in France and Spain. The Commission found that there was a tacit agreement between Bayer and its wholesalers not to export to the United Kingdom.

Whilst the Court acknowledged that there could be an agreement where one person tacitly accepts to engage in conduct or practices imposed by another, it found that the Commission had failed to prove that Bayer had intended to impose an export ban and that the wholesalers had intended to adhere to that policy. It seems therefore that some evidence of an agreement between a supplier and a distributor must be proved.

Subsequently in *General Motors Nederland and Opel Nederland BV v Commission* (case T-368/00) the GC found that the Commission had failed to adduce evidence that a communication from its subsidiary, Opel, to its dealers setting out a policy limiting exports had been agreed to by the dealers.

29.2.2.6 Public authorities

Where public bodies are concerned, a distinction must be drawn between agreements or concerted practices entered into in the course of commercial activities, which are clearly capable of falling within Article 101(1), and executive measures taken in a non-commercial context. In other words where a public body is engaged in commercial activity it will be subject to the competition rules, but not where it is exercising its public law powers which was the case in *Bodson v Pompes Funèbres des Régions Libérées SA* (case 30/87).

Bodson

In this case a licensing arrangement, whereby the local authority granted exclusive rights in respect of certain funeral services to the Société des Pompes Funèbres, was held not to constitute an 'agreement between undertakings' within Article 101(1); but had the municipality imposed a certain level of prices on the licensees the Court suggested it would have been subject to EU competition rules.

In the *COAPI* decision ([1995] 5 CMLR 468), the Commission determined that the Spanish official association of industrial agents (COAPI) fell within the ambit of Article 101, thus rejecting COAPI's argument that it was a public service body since it was established by government regulations, as was its scale of charges. The Commission, however, found that the agents were 'undertakings' and that the regulations constituted an agreement between them. As the scale of charges, which set a minimum charge to be applied to foreign clients, affected trade between Member States, COAPI was in breach of Article 101(1).

29.2.3 Field of application of Article 101(1) TFEU

29.2.3.1 Group companies

For Article 101(1) to apply there must be an agreement between two or more undertakings which are independent of each other. Arrangements between undertakings which form part of the same group of companies may not be subject to the competition rules. An agreement between a parent and its subsidiary will not breach Article 101(1) if the parent controls the subsidiary so that it does not act independently on the market. If that is the case the parent and the subsidiary are regarded as a single economic entity (see Guidelines on the application of Article 101 to horizontal agreements ([2011] OJ C11/1 at para 11)). A subsidiary undertaking which can act independently of its parent, that is, which can adopt its own business decisions, is regarded as an independent undertaking for the purposes of Article 101, and any agreement between such a subsidiary and its parent will fall within the scope of Article 101(1).

In *Viho Europe BV v Commission* (case C-73/95P) the CJ found that Parker Pen and its subsidiaries operated as a single economic entity. There was therefore no agreement between them.

Viho

Parker Pen had an integrated distribution system in Germany, France, Belgium, Spain and the Netherlands. Its products were distributed in those countries by its wholly owned distributor which it controlled. It directed their sales and marketing strategies, and it controlled sales, targets, managed costs, cash flow and stock.

In these circumstances the Court found:

Parker and its subsidiaries thus form a single economic unit within which the subsidiaries did not enjoy real autonomy in determining their course of action on the market but carried out instructions issued to them by the parent company controlling them.

A parent as well as its subsidiary may be liable for acts of the subsidiary vis-à-vis third parties in breach of Article 101(1) where the subsidiary has acted as a result of the parent's promptings.

Similarly members of an 'economic unit' comprising bodies with identical interests and subject to common control may be liable under Article 101 (*Hydrotherm v Compact* (case 170/83)). This means that there may be an 'economic unit' where two companies are controlled by the same shareholder, although that fact is not, in itself, sufficient; there must be additional evidence to show that the companies were operated as an economic unit (*Preinsulated Pipes Cartel* (cases C-189, 202, 205–8 and 213/02P)).

But where a parent company holds all of the share capital in a subsidiary which has contravened Article 101(1), there is a rebuttable presumption that the parent exercises decisive influence on the subsidiary's conduct and that both therefore comprise an economic unit. The onus is on the parent company to rebut that presumption (*Akzo Nobel and Others v Commission* (case T-112/05)).

29.2.3.2 Undertakings situated outside the European Union

An undertaking situated outside the EU may be liable under Article 101(1) if anti-competitive agreements or practices to which it is a party have effects within the internal market. In the *Dyestuffs* case, ICI (UK) was held liable for the acts of its subsidiary in Holland, although the UK was not yet a member of the Union. In the *wood pulp* decision, ([1985] 3 CMLR 474), a number of firms, all from outside the EU, who were not acting through subsidiaries in the EU but who supplied two-thirds of the EU consumption of wood pulp, were fined for concerted practices in breach of Article 101(1) on the grounds that the *effects* of their practices were felt in the Union. Although the Court, on appeal, annulled the decision in part and reduced the fines, since not all the concerted practices were proved, it held that the applicant firms could be liable, even though they were situated outside the EU, as long as their agreement or practices were *implemented* in the Union. Implementation can occur by mere sales within the EU (*Gencor v Commission* (case T-102/96)). More recent cases suggest that Article 101 can become applicable if an agreement or practice affects competition within the EU. Actual effects need not be proved. It suffices that there are foreseeable effects which could threaten the effective functioning of competition within the EU (*Intel v Commission* (case T-286/09)).

29.2.4 'Which may affect trade between Member States'

The agreement or decision by associations of undertakings or concerted practice must be one which may affect trade between Member States to breach Article 101(1). In the absence of an effect on inter-state trade any restriction on competition is a matter for national law alone. However, the question of whether trade between Member States may be affected has been broadly interpreted by the Commission and the Court. In *Société Technique Minière v Maschinenbau Ulm GmbH* (case 56/65), the Court held that an agreement was capable of affecting trade between Member States if, on the basis of objective legal or factual criteria, it allows one to expect that it will exercise a direct or indirect, actual or potential, effect on the flow of trade between Member States. The test is very similar to the *Dassonville* test applied in the context of Article 34 TFEU but broader, since it requires simply an *effect* on, not a *hindrance* to, trade between Member States (see Chapter 18). Clearly, the most obvious effect on trade between Member States occurs when parties attempt to partition the market along national lines by means of restrictions on 'parallel' imports or exports (ie restrictions on the movement of goods or services across internal EU frontiers). (See Guidelines on the effect of trade concept contained in Articles 101 and 102 of the Treaty ([2004] OJ C101/7).)

29.2.5 Agreements within a Member State

An effect on trade between Member States can occur even when an agreement takes place wholly within a Member State and appears to concern only trade within that state. This is so particularly in the case of decisions of associations or national agreements which are intended to operate across the whole national market. As the Court pointed out in *Vereeniging van Cementhandelaren v Commission* (case 8/72)—in the context of a challenge to a Commission decision that a cement dealers' price-fixing scheme, limited to the Dutch market, infringed Article 101(1)—an agreement extending over the whole of the territory of a Member State by its very nature has the effect of reinforcing the compartmentalisation of markets on a national basis, thereby holding up the economic interpenetration which the Treaty is designed to bring about and protecting domestic production.

The Court has on several occasions held that this provision applies to agreements between undertakings in the same state. For example in *Re Vacuum Interrupters Ltd* ([1977] I CMLR D67), a joint venture agreement between three UK manufacturers to design and develop switch-gear apparatus in the UK was held capable of affecting trade between Member States, since in the absence of such agreement they would have attempted to develop the apparatus independently and to market it in other Member States. (See also *Italian Flat Glass* [1982] 3 CMLR 366—agreement between Italian producers and wholesalers of glass representing more than half of the Italian market; *Salonia v Poidomani* (case 126/80)—national selective distribution system for newspapers capable of affecting trade between Member States.)

29.2.6 **The Network Effect: combined effect of similar agreements**

In the case of an agreement between individual traders, it may be necessary to examine the agreement in the context of other similar agreements, to ascertain whether, taken as a whole, they are capable of affecting trade between Member States (*Brasserie de Haecht SA v Wilkin I* (case 23/67)—Belgian tied-house agreement part of a network of similar agreements). The question to be asked is whether the agreements taken as a whole make a significant contribution to the sealing-off of national markets from competition from undertakings situated in other Member States (*Delimitis v Henninger Bräu* (case C-234/89)).

29.2.7 **Actual or potential effect**

Since only a *potential* effect of trade need be proved the enquiry is not limited to existing patterns of trade; possible future patterns of trade are relevant, particularly those which may discourage or foreclose market entry by new competitors. In *Pronuptia de Paris GmbH v Pronuptia de Paris Irmgard Schillgalis* (case 161/84) the Court accepted the Commission's finding that a franchising agreement between Pronuptia in France (the franchisor) and its franchisee in Germany, which restricted the franchisee's power to operate outside a particular territory, was capable of affecting inter-state trade even though there was no evidence, and indeed it seemed highly unlikely, that the franchisee had any intention of extending its activities to other Member States.

The question of effect on trade between Member States is not concerned with the increase or decrease of trade which might result from an agreement; all that is required to be shown is a deviation (actual or potential) from the 'normal' pattern of trade which might exist between Member States (*Consten*). In assessing this question, the agreement as a whole must be assessed to see if it is capable of affecting trade between Member States either by distorting patterns of trade in existing markets or by creating barriers to entry. Essentially the test is quite light: would a trader be prevented or dissuaded from entering the market? (*Windsurfing International Inc v Commission* (case 193/83).)

29.2.8 **'Which have as their object or effect the prevention, restriction or distortion of competition within the common market'**

29.2.8.1 'Object or effect'

If the object of an agreement is to prevent or restrict or distort competition, for example, a naked price-fixing or market-sharing agreement between competing manufacturers, there is no need to prove its effect. Unless the agreement is clearly incapable of affecting competition, an anti-competitive effect will be presumed. Where the agreement is not designed to restrict competition, for example an information sharing agreement, a detailed economic analysis of its effects on the particular market will be necessary before a breach of Article 101(1) can be proved. Cases are thus divided into two categories: 'objects cases' and 'effects cases'. Objects cases are those in which the behaviour in issue will inevitably bring about anti-competitive effects—it is inherently anti-competitive. Cartels fall into this category. Effects cases concern behaviour which may be restrictive of competition but not necessarily so. Their actual impact on the market will have to be assessed.

The scope of the analysis required was considered in *Société Technique Minière*. The case involved an exclusive distribution agreement between a German manufacturer of heavy earth-moving equipment, Maschinenbau Ulm GmbH (MU), and a French distributor, Société Technique Minière (STM), similar to the Consten–Grundig agreement, but without its undesirable features. It contained no restrictions on parallel imports or exports, and no abusive use of trade-marks. STM sought to resile on its agreement, claiming it was in breach of Article 101(1). The CJ held that in order to ascertain whether an agreement is capable of preventing, restricting or distorting competition a number of factors must be examined:

- *the nature and quantity of the products concerned* (ie the product market, and the parties' combined share in that market). The greater the market share held by the parties, the more damaging its impact on competition;

- *the position and size of the parties concerned* (ie their position in the market). The bigger they are, in terms of turnover and *relative* market share, the more likely it is that competition will be restricted;

- *the isolated nature of the agreement or its position in a series* (see also *Brasserie de Haecht*). This is particularly relevant in the case of distribution agreements, which in themselves may appear insignificant, but which often form part of a network of similar agreements;

- *the severity of the clauses.* The more severely restrictive of competition the provisions of an agreement are, the more likely they will be deemed in breach of Article 101(1). However, any clause that is more than is necessary to achieve the desired (beneficial) result will risk infringing Article 101(1) (*L'Oréal NV v De Nieuwe AMCK PVBA* (case 31/80));

- *the possibility of other commercial currents acting on the same products* by means of re-imports and re-exports (ie parallel imports or exports). Thus any agreement which attempts to ban or even limit parallel imports or exports will normally breach Article 101(1): (*LC Nungesser KG v Commission* (case 258/78)).

The agreement between STM and MU was found on the facts not to breach Article 101(1).

The enquiry needed to ascertain whether an agreement has the potential to prevent, restrict or distort competition within the internal market is a wide-ranging one, often involving all the factors outlined above, *always* involving the first two. Such is the importance of the question of market definition that the Commission issued a Notice on the Definition of the Relevant Market for the purposes of Union competition law ([1997] OJ C372/5). In *European Night Services v Commission* (cases T-374 and 375/94), the GC emphasised that where an agreement does not contain obvious restrictions of competition, it is necessary to consider the actual context within which the agreement functions, with a particular focus on the economic context.

The de minimis *principle*

All agreements between business people to some extent curtail each other's freedom of action in the marketplace. Clearly not all such agreements are capable of preventing, restricting or distorting competition to any noticeable extent. It is always a question of size and scale whether in fact they do so. Hence the importance in competition law of the *de minimis* principle. The *de minimis* principle was developed by the court in *Völk v Établissements Vervaecke Sprl* (case 5/69).

> ### *Völk*
>
> This case concerned an exclusive distribution agreement between Völk, a small-scale manufacturer of washing machines in Germany, and Vervaecke, a Dutch distributor of electrical goods. Völk agreed, inter alia, to block all sales of his machines into Vervaecke's territory by third parties (ie parallel imports). They were seeking absolute territorial protection for Vervaecke in relation to Völk's machines in Belgium and Luxembourg.

The Court ruled that in order to come within Article 101(1), competition must be affected to a noticeable extent; there must be a sufficient degree of harmfulness. In this case, the effect of Völk-Vervaecke's agreement on the washing-machine market in Belgium and Luxembourg was insignificant. (In fact Völk's production of washing machines was between 0.2 and 0.5 per cent of the German market, and his share in the Belgian and Luxembourg market was minute.) The size of the parties, and even more important, their share in the relevant product market, will be an essential factor in determining liability.

Since 1986, the Commission has published a number of notices on agreements of minor importance. The current *de minimis* notice was issued in 2014 ([2014] OJ C291/01). The Notice states that agreements between undertakings with a combined market share below a certain threshold will be regarded as *de minimis*. If the aggregate share of the parties to an agreement between competitors does not exceed 10 per cent of the relevant markets, it will not fall within Article 101(1). In the case of an agreement between non-competitors, the parties' market share must not exceed 15 per cent to fall within the *de minimis* principle. If it is not possible to classify the agreement as one involving competitors or non-competitors, the lower threshold will apply. However, if more than 30 per cent of the relevant market is covered by parallel agreements, then the market share of the parties to one such agreement must not exceed 5 per cent.

The 2014 Notice provides that it does not apply to agreements which have as their object the prevention, restriction or distortion of competition within the internal market. This reflects the judgment of the CJ in *Expedia Inc v Autorite de la concurrence and Others* (case C-226/11). The Commission has issued Guidance on restriction of competition by 'object' for the purpose of defining which agreements may benefit from the Notice (SWD(2014) 198 Final).

In *European Night Services*, the GC observed that even where the thresholds in the notice have been exceeded, the agreement in question may still not be sufficiently appreciable as to give rise to a breach of Article 101(1). Where the threshold is exceeded only marginally, the Commission has to produce clear evidence that the agreement is caught by the prohibition in Article 101(1).

29.2.9 **Consequences if agreement is within Article 101(1)**

An agreement which is caught by Article 101(1), and is not within a block exemption (see 29.2.11) or the criteria in Article 101(3) (see 29.2.10), will be 'automatically void' (Article 101(2)). Moreover, parties to such an agreement or concerted practice may be fined for their anti-competitive conduct and may be subject to claims in respect of damage caused by their anti-competitive practices (see 29.5).

However, where undertakings in a particular Member State are subject to binding rules which require them to act in a manner which infringes Article 101(1) without any autonomy as to their ability to act, no sanctions may be imposed on them for such conduct. Instead, the national court must disapply the domestic law, and only if the undertakings do not subsequently change their conduct may they be found liable for infringements of Article 101(1) (*Consorzio Industrie Fiammiferi (CIF)*).

29.2.10 **Article 101(3): exemption**

If an agreement satisfies the criteria in Article 101(3), Article 101(1) becomes inapplicable. The relevant criteria are that the agreement:

> Contributes to improving the production or distribution of goods or to promoting technical or economic progress, while allowing consumers a fair share of the resulting benefit, and which does not:
>
> - impose on the undertakings concerned restrictions which are not indispensable to the attainment of these objectives;
> - afford such undertakings the possibility of eliminating competition in respect of a substantial part of the products in question.

To qualify for an exemption under Article 101(3) the agreement or decision must satisfy four essential criteria discussed below. This paragraph is significant as it is the mechanism that allows the objectives of competition to be balanced against other, sometimes non-trade, concerns.

29.2.10.1 **It must contribute to improving the production or distribution of goods or to promoting technical or economic progress**

The agreement as a whole must show positive benefits. These are expressed in the alternative, although the more benefits that are proved the greater the likelihood of exemption. Different kinds of agreement will produce different benefits.

Production

Benefits in production are most likely to accrue from specialisation agreements. Specialisation enables each party to concentrate its efforts and achieve the benefits of scale; it avoids wasteful duplication.

> ### *Clima Chappée/Buderus*
>
> In *Clima Chappée/Buderus* ([1970] CMLR D7) the Commission granted exemption to a specialisation and reciprocal supply agreement between Clima Chappée in France and Buderus in Germany. Both were engaged in the manufacture of air-conditioning and ventilation systems and central-heating apparatus in their own countries. They agreed each to manufacture a certain range of products exclusively, and to supply the other exclusively with these products in the other's own country. Clearly there was some reduction in competition in the internal market since they were potential competitors. Nonetheless the gains in production and distribution were clear, and the agreement contributed to both technical and economic progress. The other elements of Article 101(3) too were satisfied. The agreement would result in fair shares for consumers because there was sufficient inter-brand competition to ensure that the parties would pass on the benefit of their agreement to the consumers. Nor had they imposed on each other restrictions which were not indispensable; they were not obliged to purchase the other's products unless they were competitive. There was no possibility of eliminating competition in respect of a substantial part of the products in question. Even combined, the parties were subject to strong inter-brand competition for the products in question.

Distribution

Benefits of distribution systems are obvious, but agreements between the distributor and his supplier may be anti-competitive not because the parties necessarily wish to engage in anti-competitive conduct but because of the effect of their arrangements on others in the marketplace. The benefits of such an agreement result from the streamlining of the distribution process and the concentration of activity on the part of the distributor, whether it be in the provision of publicity, technical expertise, after-sales service or simply the maintenance of adequate stocks. These factors were important in the *Transocean Marine Paint Association* decision ([1967] CMLR D9).

Transocean Marine Paint Association

The agreement here was between a number of small and medium-sized manufacturers and distributors of marine paint from inside and outside the EU. The purpose of their collaboration was to produce and market marine paints to identical standards and to organise the sale of these products on a worldwide basis. They hoped thereby to compete with the giants of the paint world. The paints were sold under a single trade-mark, though members were free to add their own name and mark. Markets were to be divided up on national lines, and members were free to sell in each other's territory only on payment of a commission. There was a degree of territorial protection. (Their original plan to prohibit sales on each other's territory was dropped at the request of the Commission.) The advantage claimed for the agreement was the achievement of a worldwide distribution network for the same interchangeable product. Alone, each manufacturer would be too small to offer adequate stocks and expertise.

Exemption was granted. The Commission agreed that the system did improve distribution; it streamlined the service to customers and led to a specialised knowledge of the market. Even the clauses granting limited territorial protection were permitted since they avoided fragmentation of the market, especially important during the launching period. While competition between members was restricted, on an international scale it was greatly increased. The use of the trade-mark too was permitted, as it was used to identify the product, not to partition the market.

Technical progress

Technical progress is most likely to result from specialisation agreements, particularly those concerned with research and development. The *ACEC/Berliet* decision ([1968] CMLR D35) concerned an agreement between ACEC, who were manufacturers, inter alia, of electrical transmission systems for commercial vehicles, and Berliet, who manufactured buses in France. They wished to collaborate to produce a new prototype bus. ACEC was to develop a new transmission system for the bus; Berliet agreed to buy the system only from ACEC; ACEC to supply only Berliet in France and not more than one outlet in any other Member State. ACEC also undertook to give Berliet 'most favoured treatment', and agreed not to reveal to any other manufacturer information acquired from Berliet. Despite these many restrictions the Commission granted them exemption. There were clear gains in production and technical progress.

In *Re Vacuum Interrupters II* ([1981] 2 CMLR 217) an agreement in the form of a joint venture between the three leading British companies engaged in the manufacture of switch gear for research and the development of vacuum interrupters was exempted. It was found to lead to benefits on all four fronts, but particularly technical progress (see also *ICI/BP* [1985] 2 CMLR 330).

Economic progress

Rather surprisingly, economic progress has received scant attention in decisions concerning exemption. It is normally presumed if improvements in production or distribution or technical progress are achieved. However, it did form the basis of a decision granting exemption to an agreement regulating the holding of trade fairs in *Cecimo* ([1969] CMLR D1) on the grounds that it tended to rationalise the operation and avoided wasteful duplication of time and effort.

29.2.10.2 The agreement must allow consumers a fair share in the resulting benefit

Provided there is sufficient (inter-brand) competition from other producers in the relevant market the improvements achieved will inevitably ensure to the benefit of consumers, either in the form of a better product, or a better service, or greater availability of supplies or lower prices. If the parties fail to pass on the benefits to consumers they risk losing out to their competitors. The parties' market share, both in absolute terms and in relation to their competitors, will be crucial. In all the cases considered earlier where exemption was granted the parties faced lively competition.

29.2.10.3 The agreement must not impose on the undertakings concerned restrictions which are not indispensable

This is the familiar proportionality principle, the downfall of many an agreement that would otherwise have been exempted. The Commission will examine each clause in an agreement to see if it is necessary to the agreement as a whole. Fixed prices, even fixed maximum and minimum price limits, as in *Hennessy/Henkell* ([1980] OJ L383/11) will rarely be indispensable, nor will clauses seeking absolute territorial protection (*Consten/Grundig; Hennessy/Henkell; Nungesser*). Even these restrictions may occasionally be justified. In *Transocean Marine Paint Association* some limited territorial protection in the form of a commission payable by the parallel importer to the appointed distributor in the territory in question was deemed to be necessary to avoid fragmentation of the market during the initial launching period. When the agreement was renewed five years later, when the product was launched and the parties had grown in size and strength, that clause was required to be dropped; it was no longer indispensable. In *Pronuptia* there was a suggestion by the Court that some territorial protection for the franchisee might be justified. If the agreement is a desirable one, pro-competitive overall, even quite severe restrictions may be deemed indispensable. In *ACEC/Berliet*, ACEC's undertaking not to divulge to any other customer confidential information received from Berliet, even their agreement to give Berliet 'most favoured' (ie discriminatory) treatment, was considered no more than was necessary to safeguard their investment in the light of the mutual confidence needed and the burden or risk involved in the enterprise.

In the *Carlsberg Beers* agreement ([1985] 1 CMLR 735) a cooperation agreement of 11 years' duration between Carlsberg Brewery Ltd (UK) and Grand Metropolitan plc, whereby Grand Metropolitan agreed to buy 50 per cent of its lager supplies from Carlsberg, was granted exemption. The agreement was necessary to enable Carlsberg to establish itself in the UK market and build up its own independent distribution network.

29.2.10.4 The agreement must not afford such undertakings the possibility of eliminating competition in respect of a substantial part of the products in question

In all the cases in which exemption has been granted, the parties have been subject to substantial inter-brand competition, whether from producers inside the common market or from outside (eg, *Re Vacuum Interrupters*, parties faced competition from the Americans and Japanese). It seems that, in the case of new products the market will not be too narrowly defined.

In *Metropole Television SA (M6) and Others v Commission* (cases T-185, 216, 299, and 300/00), the GC annulled a Commission decision exempting the Eurovision broadcasting agreement because the Commission had been wrong to determine that a sub-licensing scheme to competitors of the European Broadcasting Union (EBU) avoided the elimination of competition in that market when the evidence demonstrated that this was not the case.

29.2.11 **Block exemptions**

29.2.11.1 **Background**

The old-style enforcement system was centralised and concentrated power in the Commission. Because the Commission was unwilling, or felt unable, to apply a rule of reason to many restrictions on competition which were clearly justifiable on the principles outlined earlier, it chose to solve the twin problems of uncertainty (for business people) and workload (for itself) by means of block exemptions. If an agreement for which it might otherwise have been necessary to seek individual exemption fell within a block exemption, it would no longer need to be notified. Indeed, the block exemptions were passed in order to avoid the need for individual appraisal by the Commission, in the hope that parties would tailor their agreements to fit within their confines. In many cases this became standard practice. These block exemptions, being enacted by regulation, may, and where relevant *must*, be applied by national courts.

Most of the original regulations followed a similar pattern. First, they laid down the kinds of restrictions which were permitted, the 'white' list, the restrictions which are deemed 'essential' to the agreement in question; this was followed by the 'black' list—the kind of clauses which will not be permitted. With the Patent Licensing Regulation the Commission introduced a third category, the 'grey' restrictions. These were subject to a special procedure, known as the 'opposition' procedure. Under this procedure the grey restrictions must be notified to the Commission, but if they are not opposed within a specified period, they are deemed to be exempt. The Commission accepted that these 'old-style' block exemptions were too formalistic and generally failed to take into account the real economic impact of particular agreements. It therefore reviewed all of its block exemptions as they expired and adopted new exemptions which are based on a market-share threshold together with a list of prohibited 'hard core' restrictions.

As this is now a highly technical area of law it is not possible in a book of this nature to examine the guidelines and block exemptions in detail. Instead, the general scope of the exemptions, and their limitations, will be considered.

There is now a single block exemption (Regulation 330/2010 ([2010] OJ L102/1)) applying to *vertical restraints* (although special rules continue to apply to some sectors such as petrol distribution). This new block exemption came into force on 1 June 2010. It applies to all agreements containing vertical restraints. It is wider than the previous block exemptions, as it will cover unfinished goods ('intermediate goods') and agreements between multiple parties.

This block exemption, unlike earlier block exemptions in the field, is based on a market-share test; where the parties to the agreement have a combined market share of up to 30 per cent, the agreement will enter a 'safe harbour' where the agreement will automatically be exempt from the Article 101(1) prohibition, unless it contains what are described as 'hard-core restrictions'. Market share will be determined by assessing the relevant geographical and product markets. The definition of these markets is discussed further at 29.3.4.2. Agreements which exceed the safe harbour limit are not necessarily contrary to Article 101 but may need further examination. The vertical agreements block exemption is discussed further at 29.2.12.10.

A number of regulations have now been passed granting block exemption to certain categories of agreement, including:

- specialisation agreements (Regulation 1218/10 ([2010] OJ L335/43));

- research and development agreements (Regulation 1217/2010 ([2010] OJ L335/36));

- technology transfer agreements (Regulation 316/2014 ([2014] OJ L93/17)).

In addition to these general categories, further specific block exemptions have now been agreed (eg, shipping conferences, certain air transport agreements, insurance).

These block exemptions follow the new, economics-based approach first adopted by the Commission in the context of vertical agreements (see 29.2.12.10). In essence, the exemption applies provided that the combined market share of the parties does not exceed a specified threshold.

29.2.12 Horizontal agreements

Article 101 applies to both horizontal and vertical agreements. The most common types of horizontal agreements, that is agreements between two undertakings operating at the same level of the market will be considered first. Vertical agreements will be considered in 29.2.12.6–29.2.12.10.

29.2.12.1 Price fixing

Price is primordial in an effective competition regime; the most effective form of competition is price based.

Price-fixing agreements, because of their obvious anti-competitive effects, are almost always inexcusable. Price fixing, direct or indirect, in any form is prohibited in agreements on recommended prices, maximum and minimum prices, exchanges of information between competitors on pricing policy, the coordination of discounting policies or credit terms are all prohibited. The essential criterion is whether an undertaking acts independently in its pricing policy and any matters which affect that pricing policy. If it is influenced by considerations other than normal market conditions, it may lose the degree of independence required by Article 101(1) in the matter of pricing. *Vimpoltu* ([1983] OJ L200/44) condemned an agreement to observe maximum discounts and to offer the same credit terms to customers. In *Italian Flat Glass*, undertakings agreed to fix prices and to offer identical discounts and to ensure that these applied in the downstream market. In *Belgian Architects* ([2005] OJ L4/10), the Commission fined the Belgian Architects Association for adopting a minimum fee scale for the provision of architectural services in Belgium.

There may be exceptional cases in which they may be exempt from the price-fixing prohibition in Article 101(1).

In *Reims II* ([1999] OJ L275/17) the Commission granted an exemption under Article 101(3) to an agreement between sixteen European postal operators on the fixing of fees for the cost of delivering cross-border mail. More recently an exemption was granted to a banking system which restricted the freedom of banks to decide their own pricing policies (*Visa International* ([2002] OJ L318/17)).

29.2.12.2 Market sharing

Market sharing harms consumer welfare by reducing choice and dampening price competition. It may also affect the attainment of the internal market by dividing up markets along national lines.

Markets can be divided in a number of ways, for example geographically, by product or by customer base. Any attempt to divide up markets will infringe Article 101. Examples of cases in which market sharing has been condemned include *ACF Chemiefarma NV v Commission (Quinine Cartel)* (case 41/69) and *Gas Insulated Switchgear* (case T-117/07).

> ### *Gas Insulated Switchgear*
>
> Here the Commission imposed stiff fines—EUR 750 million—in respect of a number of prohibited practices, including the dividing up of the global market for switch-gear apparatus. Japanese undertakings did not compete for contracts in Europe and European undertakings agreed to stay out of the Japanese market.

29.2.12.3 **Restrictions on output**

Agreements between competitors to restrict output can result in demand led price increases. Producers can agree to keep production at a certain level or to refrain from expanding their capacity, without the approval of their competitors. In *French-West African Shipowners' Committees* ([1992] OJ L134/1), an agreement between ship-owners to a cargo-sharing system in respect of traffic between France and a number of West African countries was condemned as being in violation of Article 101. *Competition Authority v Beef Industry Development Society Ltd (BIDS) and Barry Brothers (Carrigmore) Meals Ltd* (case C-209/07) concerned an agreement between ten of the main beef and veal processors in Ireland which made provision for a reduction of 25 per cent in processing capacity. The agreement was held by the CJ to have as its object the prevention, restriction or distortion of competition.

By contrast, in the earlier case of *Synthetic Fibres* ([1984] OJ L207/17) the Commission authorised an agreement between manufacturers of synthetic fibres to reduce capacity. The industry was at the time suffering severe over-capacity. Market forces alone were unable to achieve the necessary capacity reduction to re-establish and maintain stability to restore the industry to an effective competitive structure.

29.2.12.4 **Collusive tendering**

Collusive tendering arises when a number of firms agree to coordinate their bids for tenders. It is a practice frequently found in the construction industry. Undertakings agree to organise their bid in such a way as to favour one potential bidder for each contract. In *Building and Construction Industry in The Netherlands (SPO)* ([1992] OJ L92/1) 28 associations of firms set up SPO, which established a number of uniform price regulatory rules. Members exchanged information with one another prior to submitting bids and to coordinate their final bid prices. These practices were found to be in violation of Article 101(1) and not capable of exemption under Article 101(3). A further example of collusive tendering is *Saint-Gobain Glass France and Others v Commission (car glass)* (case T-56/09) in which members of a cartel deliberately set bids at a higher level than that of the member of the cartel which it had been agreed would be best positioned to obtain the contract.

29.2.12.5 **Cooperation agreements**

There are many types of agreements or arrangements which may be entered into by competitors which are beneficial to consumer welfare and which therefore either may not restrict competition at all or, if they do, qualify for an exemption under Article 101(3). Examples of such agreements include joint ventures, information agreements, research and development agreements, production agreements, purchasing agreement and standardisation agreements. The assessment of the competitive effects of these agreements, and other horizontal arrangements, has been the subject of an extensive set of guidelines published by the European Commission in 2011 (Guidelines on the applicability of Article 101 of the Treaty on the Functioning of the European Union to Horizontal Co-operation Agreements ([2011] OJ L11/1)). These guidelines reflect Commission practice and case law and the case law of the GC and the CJ.

29.2.12.6 **Vertical agreements**

Goods and services can be distributed to consumers in a variety of ways. They can be distributed by the producer himself through a vertically integrated operation. The producer can set up his own retail outlets, possibly operated by subsidiaries which he owns and controls, or he can use the services of a commercial agent to attract customers. In either of these sets of circumstances

Article 101 will not be applicable since there is no agreement between undertakings. Production and distribution is done by a single economic entity. Alternatively, and possibly more cost-effective, the producer can entrust the distribution of his goods or services to an independent distributor or a network of independent distributors. In this case Article 101 does apply as there will be an agreement between two independent undertakings.

29.2.12.7 Commercial agents

A commercial agency agreement will not attract the application of Article 101. Commercial agents act on behalf of producers or manufacturers. The agent negotiates sales and either passes orders back to the producer who will supply the goods directly to the customer, or he enters into a contract with the customer on behalf of the producer. For those services he will either be paid a salary or commission based on the number of orders he brings in or a combination of both. What distinguishes a commercial agent from an independent distributor is that the agent bears no financial risk himself. No property passes to him. He is a 'go between' linking the customer and the producer. (See Guidelines on Vertical Restraints ([2010] OJ C130/1), paras 12–21.) As such he is acting on behalf of the producer and not as an independent economic entity.

29.2.12.8 Independent distributors

Article 101 applies to agreements between producers and independent producers. Whilst overall distribution arrangement contributes to consumer welfare by ensuring the efficient distribution of goods and services and by encouraging non-price competition and improved quality of customer service, they can have negative effects. Notably they can divide up markets, soften competition between the supplier and his competitors by reducing inter-brand competition and by reducing intra-brand competition between distributors of the same brand. Many common vertical restraints contain provisions which, viewed in isolation, are restrictive of competition but are necessary simply to enable the distributions arrangements to function properly. They therefore qualify for an exemption under Article 101(3) or by virtue of the Vertical Restraints Block Exemption Regulation, which provides a 'safe harbour' for provisions which comply with it. The Regulation is considered later. The Guidelines on Vertical Restraints set out the principles developed by the European Commission, the GC and the CJ over the years. It offers guidance on both the Block Exemption Regulation and the treatment of individual cases which may not fall within the scope of the Block Exemption Regulation and therefore fall to be considered under Article 101(1) and (3).

Types of distribution arrangements

There are two main types of distribution arrangements and each has its own particular characteristics which influence the way they are treated under the competition rules. They are:

- exclusive distribution agreements;
- selective distribution agreements.

An exclusive distribution agreement is one whereby the supplier agrees to sell its products only to one distributor for resale in a particular territory. At the same time the distributor is usually prohibited from actively selling products into other exclusively allocated territories. This may lead to a reduction in intra-brand competition and market partitioning. Where most or all of the suppliers use exclusive distribution this fact may soften competition and facilitate collusion, both at the suppliers' and the distributors' level. Exclusive distribution may also lead to foreclosure of other distributors (Guidelines on Vertical Restraints, paras 151–2).

Selective distribution agreements are like exclusive distribution agreements, in that they restrict the number of authorised distributors on the one hand and the possibilities of resale on the other. The difference from exclusive distribution is that the restriction on the number of dealers does not depend on the number of territories, but on selection criteria linked to the nature of the product. Another important difference from exclusive distribution is that the restriction on resale is not a restriction on active selling to another territory, but a restriction on sales to non-authorised distributors leaving only appointed dealers and final customers as potential buyers. Selective distribution is usually used to distribute final branded products. Such products are generally of the kind sold in a specific type of environment which is suited to their characteristics. Generally they are high end value luxury goods (perfume, cosmetics, luxury clothing) or complex high-tech products.

The competition issues here are a risk of a reduction of intra-brand competition and a softening of competition and facilitation of collusion between suppliers and buyers (Guidelines on Vertical Restraints, paras 174 and 175).

The supplier does not have complete discretion in deciding whether to set up a selective distribution system. The first principle, laid down in *Metro-SB-Grossmärkte GmbH*, is that selective distribution systems will not breach Article 101(1) provided that dealers are chosen on the basis of objective criteria of a *qualitative* nature relating to the technical qualifications of the dealer and his staff and the suitability of his trading premises, and that such conditions are laid down uniformly and not applied in a discriminatory manner.

In *L'Oréal* the CJ followed *Metro-SB-Grossmärkte GmbH*, adding that the qualitative criteria must not go beyond what is necessary. What is regarded as necessary will depend on the nature of the product. In *Re Ideal/Standard Agreement* ([1988] 4 CMLR 627) the Commission found that the characteristics of plumbing fittings were not sufficiently technically advanced to necessitate a selective distribution system in which wholesalers were required to be specialists in the sale of plumbing fittings and sanitary ware and to have a department specialising in the sale of such products. The products were too 'banal' to warrant such a system. With regard to *quantitative* criteria, such as, in *L'Oréal*, requirements that the distributor should guarantee a minimum turnover and hold minimum stocks were held to exceed the requirements of a selective distribution system, and were thus in breach of Article 101(1), although it was suggested that they might be capable of being exempted under Article 101(3).

29.2.12.9 Franchise agreements

Franchise agreements contain licences of intellectual property rights relating in particular to trademarks or signs and know-how for the use and distribution of goods or services. In addition to the licences of intellectual property rights the franchisor usually provides the franchisee during the life of the agreement with commercial or technical assistance. The franchisor is in general paid a franchise fee by the franchisee for the use of the particular business method. Such agreements usually contain a combination of different vertical restraints concerning the products being distributed and/or non-compete and/or exclusive distribution in some form (Guidelines on Vertical Restraints, para 189).

29.2.12.10 The Vertical Agreements Block Exemption Regulations

The Block Exemption on Vertical Agreements Regulation (Regulation 330/2010 ([2010] OJ L102/1)) entered into force in June 2010. It should be read alongside the Guidelines on Vertical Restraints already discussed (29.2.12.8). The Guidelines set out the principles laid down by the European Commission, the GC and the CJ on the treatment of vertical agreements both under the Block Exemption Regulation and Article 101.

Scope

The Regulation grants an exemption to agreements which contain certain vertical restraints. It thus provides a 'safe harbour' for agreements which might otherwise fall foul of Article 101(1). The availability of the exemption is subject to a market share threshold. The market share held by the supplier must not exceed 30 per cent of the relevant market in which it sells contract goods or services and the market share held by the buyer must not exceed 30 per cent of the relevant market in which it purchases goods or services. Previously under Regulation 2790/99, which preceded Regulation 330/2010, the market share of the buyer was not taken into consideration in establishing the applicability of the block exemption. Article 7 sets out how market share is to be calculated.

Key concepts

Article 1 defines certain key concepts. A vertical restraint is a restriction of competition found in vertical agreements. Other concepts such as 'supplier', 'undertaking', 'know how', 'non-compete obligation', 'competing undertaking' and 'selective distribution' are also defined.

The exemption

Article 2(1) declares that Article 101(1) shall not apply to vertical agreements to the extent that they contain vertical restraints. Many, of course, do not and the exemption is not available to every vertical agreement. Aside from the market threshold limit set out earlier, the exemption is not available to vertical agreements entered into by competing undertakings. However, it can apply when competing undertakings enter into certain types of non-reciprocal vertical agreements. Article 2(5) of the Regulation provides that it shall not apply to vertical agreements the subject matter of which falls within the scope of any other block exemption regulation, such as for example, research and development or specialisation agreements. Regulation 330/2010 is thus a residual instrument.

The block exemption is not available to agreements which contain hard-core restrictions. If agreements do contain such restrictions, recourse must be had to Article 101(3) but it is unlikely, save in exceptional circumstances, that they would qualify for an exemption under that provision. Paragraph 47 of the Guidelines on Vertical Restraints states that an agreement containing hard-core restrictions is presumed to fall within the scope of Article 101. Paragraphs 23 and 29 specify that hard-core restrictions are restrictive of competition by object. This appears to eliminate any possibility of an exemption on the basis of Article 101(3).

Hard-core restrictions

As we have pointed out earlier, agreements containing hard-core restrictions cannot benefit from the exemption granted by the Regulation. Recital 10 of the preamble states that vertical agreements:

> containing certain types of severe restrictions on competition should be excluded from the benefits of the block exemption established by the Regulation irrespective of the market share of the undertakings concerned.

Article 4 sets out what is meant by 'hard-core' restrictions. These relate mainly to restrictions on intra-brand competition. The imposition of an obligation to observe fixed or minimum resale prices is prohibited, but maximum pricing limits may be imposed. The reason for this is presumably that it is in the interests of the supplier to ensure that the distributor does not set prices at such a level as to discourage demand.

The use of territorial restrictions is also circumscribed. Whilst exclusive distribution agreements are characterised by a degree of territorial protection, this must not be absolute. Distributors who have territorial protection may be prohibited from making active sales (eg, seeking business through marketing initiatives) in the territory of another exclusive distributor, but passive sales (where the customer comes to the distributor) cannot be banned: distributors have a right to supply on a passive basis outside their allocated territory. Limiting cross supplies between selective distributors is also regarded as a hard-core restriction.

Excluded restrictions

Article 5 sets out a number of restrictions to which the block exemption does not apply: if such restrictions are severable from the agreement as a whole, the block exemption applies to the remaining provisions of the agreement. This position contrasts with that where an agreement contains hard-core restrictions: the presence of a hard-core restriction deprives the agreement in its entirety of the benefit of the block exemption.

Excluded restrictions are mainly concerned with three types of non-compete obligations. Any direct or indirect non-compete obligation which is indefinite or exceeds five years in duration is prohibited. The definition of a non-compete obligation, somewhat obviously is an obligation not to manufacture, purchase, sell or resell goods or services which compete with the goods or services which are the subject of the distribution contract. The concept further encompasses any obligation on the distributor to purchase from the supplier or from an undertaking designated by the supplier more than 80 per cent of the distributor's total purchases of the contract goods or services. This is designed to prevent market access foreclosure. The ceiling of 80 per cent, although apparently high, had been accepted many years ago in *Pronuptia*. In addition to a number of qualitative restrictions relating to layout, shop fittings, advertising and promotion, the Court did allow, as compatible with Article 101(1), a requirement that the franchisee should buy 80 per cent of its wedding dresses from Pronuptia and the remainder only from suppliers approved by Pronuptia. This requirement, like the qualitative requirements, was found essential in a franchising agreement to protect the know-how and reputation of the franchisor.

In addition to this non-compete obligation, which relates to the lifetime of the agreement post-termination non-compete obligations are also prohibited. Article 5(1)(b) excludes from the block exemption 'any direct or indirect obligations causing the buyer after the termination of the agreement, not to manufacture, purchase, sell or resell goods or services'. There is an exception to this rule. A post-term ban on the sale of competing goods or services at the point of sale from which the distributor operated during the lifetime of the agreement, may be imposed for a year after the termination of the agreement in order to protect the know-how of the supplier. Such an obligation must be 'indispensable' to protect the supplier's know-how.

Withdrawal/disapplication of the block exemption

The exemption can be withdrawn from individual agreements by the European Commission or a national competition authority. Article 6 of the Block Exemption provides for the first time for the potential disapplication by the European Commission of the regulation where parallel networks of similar vertical restraints cover more than 50 per cent of the relevant market.

29.2.12.11 Ancillary restrictions

Certain restrictions on competition have been construed as essential to the main agreement, and as such not in breach of the prohibition set out in Article 101(1). They are regarded as being objectively justified in order to facilitate the effective operation of an agreement. Such permissible restrictions and their usage must not be overestimated. In *David Meca-Medina and Igor Majcen v Commission* (case C-519/04P) the CJ found that anti-doping rules operated by the International Olympic Committee which limited the freedom of activities of professional athletes were justified in the interests of the organisation and proper conduct of competitive sport. Their purpose was to ensure healthy rivalry between athletes. Likewise in *Wouters* the Dutch Bar's regulations prohibiting its members from practising in full partnership with accountants was held to be justified as being necessary for the proper practice of the legal profession. Restrictions attached to the sale of a business have also been held to be justifiable (*Reuters/BASF* ([1976] OJ L254/40); *Remia BV v Commission* (Case 42/84)). However, clauses which have as their objective the proper functioning of an agreement in the sense of being essential to the attainment of the objective of the agreement may not be prohibited under Article 101(1). In particular they must be no more restrictive of competition than is necessary to achieve their objectives (*Remia*).

29.2.13 Conclusions on Article 101 TFEU

In recent years, the application of Article 101 has moved from a very rigid, formalistic approach to one that recognises the economic context within which particular agreements operate. The Commission now attempts to base its approach on considerations of market power and market concentration, rather than a simple application of the elements of Article 101(1). Both the new-style block exemptions on vertical agreements and on horizontal cooperation agreements reflect the general view that agreements involving parties who do not have a significant degree of market power will not normally be regarded as anti-competitive and can be exempted. At the same time, the *de minimis* threshold below which agreements are deemed not to fall within Article 101(1) at all has also been increased. The Commission's Guidelines on vertical agreements and horizontal cooperation agreements, which reflect the experiences of four decades of centralised competition law enforcement, provide vital guidance on the types of agreements which are likely to be caught by Article 101 in future. In essence, only agreements in which the parties involved exercise market power and/or agreements which include hard-core restraints will fall foul of Article 101 and will be pursued vigorously both by the Commission and the national competition law authorities.

29.3 Abuse of a dominant position

The previous section examined how Article 101 deals with the dangers to competition which may arise when otherwise independent undertakings come together and coordinate their activities. The unilateral conduct of undertakings enjoying a strong position in a particular market may also give rise to distortions of competition. Indeed, certain actions of such an undertaking may result in the elimination of competition altogether. It would, of course, be wrong to condemn an undertaking for being a strong player in a particular market in the absence of any anti-competitive practice, but where an undertaking in a strong position uses that position in an abusive manner, serious consequences for competition may follow. That is why Article 102 TFEU seeks to deal with undertakings having a strong position in the market by prohibiting activities which could be regarded as an abuse of the undertaking's dominant position in a particular market.

29.3.1 Overview of prohibition

Article 102 TFEU provides that

> Any abuse by one or more undertakings of a dominant position within the common market or in a substantial part of it shall be prohibited as incompatible with the internal market insofar as it may affect trade between Member States.

The prohibition is followed by a list of examples of abuse considered later in this chapter. Article 102 is directly effective, and gives rise to rights and obligations for individuals. Article 102 contains four essential ingredients. There must be:

- an undertaking;
- dominant position;
- an abuse of that position;
- which affects trade between Member States.

29.3.2 **Undertakings**

The term 'undertakings' is subject to the same broad interpretation as is applied to Article 101 TFEU (see 29.2.2.1), and covers the same activities, both public and private.

29.3.3 **Joint dominance**

It was thought originally that Article 102 did not apply to undertakings which were independent of each other, and could not therefore be used to control oligopolies. This has not proved to be the case. In *Italian Flat Glass*, the Commission held that three Italian producers of flat glass, who between them held a 79–95 per cent share of the Italian market in flat glass, had a *collective* dominant position in these markets and had abused that position. While the decision was annulled in part in *SIV v Commission* (cases T-68, 77, and 78/89) for lack of proof of dominance, the application of Article 102 to oligopolies was not disputed by the GC. The potential application of Article 102 to oligopolies has since been affirmed, notably by the CJ in *Municipality of Almelo v Energiededrijf IJsselmij NV* (case C-393/92). In that case, the CJ stated that a collective dominant position would exist when 'the undertakings in question were linked in such a way that they adopt the same conduct on the market'. In *Irish Sugar v Commission* (case T-288/97), the GC accepted the possibility that Irish Sugar, which produced sugar, and its distributor were together dominant, thus raising the possibility of vertical collective dominance as well as horizontal collective dominance. In *Compagnie Maritime Belge and Others v Commission* (case C-395-6/96P), the CJ noted that it was not necessary to find contractual or other links in law. A finding of collective dominance could be based on 'other connecting factors and would depend on an economic assessment and, in particular, on an assessment of the structure of the market in question' (para 45).

In *Airtours Plc v Commission* (case T-342/99), a case under the Merger Regulation (Regulation 139/2004 ([2004] OJ L24/1)), the GC rejected a suggestion that the mere fact that the same institutional investors were found in three out of the four main tour operators was sufficient to give rise to collective dominance because it was not apparent that these shareholders directly influenced management decisions.

Nevertheless, the implications of these decisions for oligopolies are not clear. It remains to be seen whether Article 102 could be invoked to control oligopolistic practices which are not in breach of Article 101(1), but which nevertheless undermine the competitive structure in a particular market. Nonetheless, it seems that Articles 101–2 are not mutually exclusive; where doubt exists as to which article is applicable, both should be pleaded.

29.3.4 **The principle of dominance**

Dominance was defined in *United Brands* at para 65 as:

a position of economic strength enjoyed by an undertaking which enables it to prevent effective competition being maintained on the relevant market by giving it the power to behave to an appreciable extent independently of its competitors, customers, and ultimately of its consumers.

To this the Commission added in *AKZO Chemie BV* ([1986] 3 CMLR 273) at para 67 that:

> The power to exclude effective competition is not . . . in all cases coterminous with independence from competitive factors but may also involve the ability to eliminate or seriously weaken existing competitors or to prevent potential competitors from entering the market.

To assess if an undertaking has sufficient economic strength to behave independently of, or even exclude, competitors, it is necessary first to ascertain the relevant market in which competition is said to exist. As the Court pointed out in *Europemballage Corp and Continental Can Co Inc v Commission* (case 6/72), a position can be dominant within the meaning of Article 102 only if it is dominant in a relevant market. The definition of the relevant market requires consideration of three parameters:

- the relevant product market;
- the relevant geographical market;
- the temporal market.

The determination of whether an undertaking is in a dominant position will depend on how those parameters are set. The following sections consider these aspects in turn, starting with the relevant product market, which is often the most complex aspect of establishing the relevant market.

As a starting point in determining the extent of the relevant market, both in respect of the product market and the geographic market, the Commission, in its Notice on the Definition of the Relevant Market ([1997] OJ C372), suggests a small, but significant and non-transitory increase in prices (SSNIP test) should be postulated and the likely reaction of customers to that change evaluated. The question is, would the consumer switch to readily available substitutes? If such an increase were to result in a loss of profits as consumers switched to alternatives, there would clearly seem to be other suppliers or alternative products in the market. This test would then be reapplied, decreasing the relevant products or areas until there is no such change indicating no competitors.

29.3.4.1 The relevant product market (RPM)

This is defined by the Commission in its Notice on the Definition of the Relevant Market ([1997] OJ C372) and the Court in terms of product substitution. The relevant product market is one in which products are substantially interchangeable (*Istituto Chemioterapico Italiano SpA v Commission* (cases 6 and 7/73)). It includes identical products, or products considered by consumers to be similar by reason of their characteristics, price or use. Two questions are central to this enquiry:

1. To what extent is the customer, or importer, or wholesaler, able to buy goods *similar* to those supplied by the dominant firm, or *acceptable as substitutes?* This is known as cross-elasticity of demand, or 'demand-side' substitutability;

2. To what extent are other firms *able to supply, or capable of producing* acceptable substitutes? This is known as cross-elasticity of supply, or 'supply-side' substitutability.

These questions may be assessed by reference to the characteristics of the product, its price, or the use to which it is to be put. Although the principles are expressed in terms of goods or products they apply equally in the context of services.

End products

Ascertaining the relevant product market is no easy matter. Its difficulties are illustrated in the *Continental Can* case.

Continental Can

This case involved the proposed takeover of a large Dutch packaging firm, Thomassen & Drijver-Vçerblifa NV (TDV) by Europemballage Corporation, a company registered in the USA, held and controlled by another US company, Continental Can Co Inc. Continental Can was a powerful organisation engaged in packaging operations throughout the world. It held an 86 per cent share in a German packaging company, Schmalbach-Lubeca-Werke AG (SLW), prominent in Germany in the manufacture of, inter alia, light metal containers for meat and fish and bottle-sealing machines. Continental Can proposed to transfer its interest in SLW to Europemballage. Thus the whole deal would result in Europemballage and, indirectly, Continental Can, holding significant market power in Europe.

The Commission issued a decision that the takeover of TDV by Continental Can via Europemballage constituted a breach of Article 102.

Continental Can, through its holding in SLW, was alleged to be dominant in Germany in three separate product markets, comprising:

- light metal containers for meat products;
- light metal containers for fish products;
- metal closures for glass containers.

The acquisition of TDV by Europemballage would have further increased its dominance in these markets, since it would have removed an important potential competitor to SLW. Continental Can and Europemballage sought to annul the Commission's decision. Although the Court agreed with the Commission in principle that the takeover could constitute an abuse, it found that the Commission had failed to prove the claimants' dominance in the relevant product market. The Commission had failed to explore the question of product substitution. To be regarded as a distinct market, the Court held, the products in question must be individualised not only by the mere fact that they are used for packing certain products, but by particular characteristics of production which make them *specifically suitable for this purpose*. The Commission had also failed to consider the question of substitution on the supply side—ie whether other potential competitors might not be able to enter the market by simple adaptation.

In *United Brands* the Commission claimed that United Brands, one of the world's largest banana empires, producer of 'Chiquita' bananas, was abusing its dominant position in a number of ways. The question was whether the relevant product market was bananas, branded and unbranded, as the Commission claimed, or fresh fruit, as United Brands claimed. Clearly it was in the Commission's interest to define the market as narrowly as possible, because United Brands would have a larger share of a smaller market. Conversely, it was in the interest of United Brands to define it as widely as possible. The Commission produced research from the Food and Agriculture Organisation which revealed that the existence of other fruit had very little influence on the price and consumption of bananas. Moreover, bananas occupied a special place in the diet of the very young, the sick and the old. For them other fruits were not acceptable as substitutes. This time the Court accepted the Commission's view of the relevant product market.

It has been argued that the relevant product market could have been defined even more narrowly, either as branded bananas, or as bananas bought for the old, the sick or the very young, since there was evidence that customers continued to buy branded bananas even when they were considerably more expensive than unbranded bananas, showing little cross-elasticity of demand, while for the old, the sick and the very young, there was practically no cross-elasticity at all.

On the question of cross-elasticity, both the Commission and the Court will scrutinise the evidence with care, and will not necessarily agree with the experts. In *Eurofix & Bauco v Hilti AG* ([1989] 4 CMLR 677), in the context of a finding of abuse against Hilti, a firm dominant in the market for cartridge strips and nails compatible with Hilti nail guns, the Commission rejected an econometric study produced by Hilti which purported to show significant cross-elasticity between nail guns and power drills, finding that the methodology of the study 'needed further refinement'. Moreover, the findings of the study were inconsistent with the way in which the market operated. The decision in *Eurofix & Hilti* was approved by the Court (*Hilti v Commission* (case 98/88)).

Raw materials

The relevant product market, and the question of substitutability, is not necessarily defined by reference to consumers. In *Istituto Chemioterapico Italiano* the abuse alleged against Commercial Solvents Corporation (CSC) and its subsidiary, Istituto Chemicoterapico Italiano SpA (ICI), was a refusal to supply Zoja with a particular chemical, aminobutanol, which CSC had supplied to Zoja in the past through ICI. The chemical was required for processing into ethambutol, a drug used for the treatment of tuberculosis. CSC had a near monopoly in aminobutanol, which was widely used as the best, and cheapest, for the manufacture of ethambutol. However, ethambutol was not the only drug suitable for treating tuberculosis and ethambutol could be made from other raw materials. In an action before the Court for annulment of the Commission's decision, CSC argued that what mattered was whether consumers had a choice of drugs for tuberculosis, as Article 102 was aimed at abuses which prejudiced the interests of consumers.

The Court disagreed. The article was concerned not only with abuses which prejudiced consumers directly. It was also aimed at abuses which prejudiced consumers indirectly by impairing the competitive structure. The effect of CSC's refusal to supply Zoja was to eliminate one of the principal manufacturers of ethambutol in the common market. Nor was the Court prepared to accept that Zoja could switch to other raw materials for the manufacture of ethambutol. The Court found that it was not feasible for Zoja to adapt its production in this way. Only if other raw materials could be substituted *without difficulty* for aminobutanol could they be regarded as acceptable substitutes. Since they could not, the relevant product market was aminobutanol.

The hard line taken in this case illustrates that the Commission and the Court are not concerned merely with the immediate protection of the consumer; they are concerned to protect competition at the manufacturing level and in particular to prevent the smaller firm from suffering at the hands of its more powerful competitors. Similar thinking lay behind the Commission's and the Court's approach in *Consten*.

Size of relevant product market

In the previously discussed cases the relevant product market was a substantial one and the parties alleged to be dominant in that market wielded considerable power. But the relevant market, whether in goods or services, can be quite small, and provided an undertaking is dominant in that market it does not need to be generally powerful to fall foul of Article 102 TFEU. In *Hugin Kassaregister AB v Commission* (case 22/78) a Swedish firm, Hugin, which manufactured cash registers, supplying them to Liptons Cash Registers and Business Equipment Ltd in the UK through its British subsidiary, Hugin

Cash Registers Ltd, was found to be dominant in the supply of spare parts for Hugin machines to independent repair businesses. (See also *AB Volvo v Erik Veng* (case 238/87).) In *British Brass Band Instruments v Boosey & Hawkes (Interim measures)* ([1988] 4 CMLR 67) the relevant product market, in which Boosey & Hawkes held a 90 per cent share, was held to be instruments for *British-style* brass bands. The fact that the market, or in this case the sub-market, was defined in narrow terms, did not, the Court said, exclude the application of Article 102. 'The essential question is whether the sub-market is sufficiently distinct in commercial reality.' Similarly, certain activities of a firm which seem quite insignificant may constitute a relevant market in which that firm may be dominant. In *General Motors Continental NV* ([1975] 1 CMLR D20) the issuing of test certificates for second-hand imports of Opel cars, carried out exclusively by General Motors in Belgium, constituted the relevant market, even though in one year (1973) only five cars were involved; and in *British Leyland plc* ([1984] 3 CMLR 92), BL was found to be dominant in the provision of national type approval certificates for its vehicles since it alone had the right to issue these certificates. The decision was approved by the Court in *British Leyland plc v Commission* (case 226/84).

29.3.4.2 The relevant geographical market (RGM)

Determining the RGM

To fall within Article 102 an undertaking must be dominant 'within the common or in a substantial part of it'. Thus, the question of dominance must also be assessed in the context of the relevant geographical market. The RGM is the one in which the 'objective conditions of competition are the same for all traders' (*United Brands*). It is the market in which available and acceptable substitutes exist.

Where goods are homogeneous and easily and cheaply transportable, the RGM may be large. The Commission suggested in the *AKZO Chemie BV* decision that in certain circumstances the whole of the Union territory may constitute the RGM. In *Eurofix & Hilti* the whole of the EC was found to constitute the RGM in the nail cartridge market. Where goods are differentiated, or where consumer tastes are inflexible, or where transportation is difficult or costly, a single state or even part of a state may constitute the RGM. Where a service is only needed within one particular state, as in *British Leyland*, clearly that state will represent the RGM. As the Court commented in *United Brands*, in order to ascertain whether a particular territory is large enough to amount to a substantial part of the market, the pattern and volume of the production and consumption of the products as well as the habits and economic opportunities of vendors and purchasers (and the users of services) must be considered. In *B&I/Sealink* ([1992] CMLR 255) the Commission decided that a port or airport, even if not itself a substantial part of the EU, may be considered such insofar as reasonable access to the facility is indispensable for the exploitation of a transport route which is substantial for the purposes of Article 102. Sealink's action as port authority in Holyhead in altering its own ferry times, thereby limiting access to the port by B&I's ships, was found to breach Article 102.

In determining the RGM, the cost of transport is particularly important. When deciding in *Hilti* that the RGM was the whole of the EU, the Commission took into account the fact that nail cartridges could be transported throughout the Union at relatively little cost. Clearly, geographical markets have been growing and will continue to grow as the barriers to the single internal market are removed.

29.3.4.3 The temporal market

In assessing the question of dominance the temporal aspect of the market should also be considered. It has been suggested that the Commission in *United Brands* should have defined the relevant product market by reference to the particular time of the year (eg, the winter months), when there was little opportunity for product substitution. The Commission did take the temporal element into account in *Re ABG Oil* ([1977] 2 CMLR D1) in limiting the market for oil to the period of crisis following the OPEC action in the early 1970s. In particular, the question of the length of time the allegedly dominant firm has held or might continue to hold, its position of dominance needs to be addressed.

29.3.4.4 Dominance in fact

Once the RGM is established, it is necessary to ascertain whether the parties concerned are dominant within that market. An undertaking can be dominant irrespective of whether it is a supplier or a purchaser (*British Airways v Commission* (case T-219/99)—airline dominant in market for purchase of air travel agency services). When will an undertaking be regarded as dominant? The Commission suggested in *United Brands Co* ([1976] 1 CMLR D28) that:

> Undertakings are in a dominant position when they have the power to behave independently without taking into account, to any substantial extent, their competitors, purchasers and suppliers. Such is the case where an undertaking's market share, either in itself or when combined with its know-how, access to raw materials, capital or other major advantage such as trade-mark ownership, enables it to determine the prices or to control the production or distribution of a significant part of the relevant goods. It is not necessary for the undertaking to have total dominance such as would deprive all other market participants of their commercial freedom, as long as it is strong enough in general terms to devise its own strategy as it wishes, even if there are differences in the extent to which it dominates individual submarkets.

In *Michelin v Commission* (case 322/81), the CJ adopted the test for dominance, which is now usually referred to as:

> A position of economic strength enjoyed by an undertaking which enables it to hinder the maintenance of effective competition on the relevant market by allowing it to *behave to an appreciable extent independently of its competitors and customers*, and ultimately of consumers [para 30, emphasis added].

See also *Aéroports de Paris v Commission* (case T-128/98), para 47, which refers to 'the power to behave' rather than 'allowing' (although there seems to be no significant difference in practice between the terms used).

Thus, the question of dominance requires a wide-ranging economic analysis of the undertaking concerned and of the market in which it operates. There are a range of relevant factors for establishing dominance which will now be considered in turn.

Market share

Market share is of prime importance. In *Istituto Chemioterapico Italiano*, CSC (according to the Commission; this was not found proved by the Court) held a virtual monopoly in aminobutanol. In the *Continental Can* case, SLW, owned by Continental Can, held a 70–80 per cent share in the RPM in Germany. In *Tetra Pak International SA v Commission* (case T-83/91) the GC remarked that a market share of 90 per cent would be regarded as dominant save in exceptional circumstances. But such a high figure is not essential. United Brands held only a 40–45 per cent share in the banana market in a substantial part of Europe. Where the share is less than 50 per cent, the structure of the market will be important, particularly the market share held by the next-largest competitor. In *United Brands* the nearest competitors held 16 per cent and 10 per cent shares in the market. Where the market is highly fragmented the Commission has even suggested that a share of 20–40 per cent could constitute dominance (*10th Report on Competition Policy*). The Court has held that the existence of lively competition does not rule out a dominant position (*United Brands*).

A variation on the market share assessment can be seen in *British Airways*. In this case, BA's dominance as a purchaser in the market for air travel agency services was established on the basis of the number of seats which it was able to offer and therefore the number of tickets it might be able to sell through agencies. Its role was that of purchaser because it was 'buying' the service of the travel agencies for each ticket they sold on BA's behalf. It was irrelevant that there were competitors on some of the air routes, because the market for air transport services was different from that of air travel agency services. This, in turn, produced a market share calculation which demonstrated BA's dominance in the relevant market.

The CJEU, reflecting the view of the Commission, emphasised in *Hoffmann-La Roche* that although a high market share is clearly very important, it is not conclusive, and 'its importance varies from market to market according to the structure of the market'. It is therefore necessary to consider other factors, as well.

The Commission in its Guidance on Enforcement Priorities in applying Article 102 ([2009] OJ 45/7) indicates that the assessment of dominance will take into account the competitive structure of the market and in particular the following factors:

- constraints imposed by the existing supplies from, and the position on the market of, actual competitors (the market position of the dominant undertaking and its competitors);
- constraints imposed by the credible threat of future expansion of actual competitors or entry by potential competitors (expansion or entry);
- constraints imposed by the bargaining strength of the undertaking's customers (countervailing buyer power).

Each of these factors will be considered in turn.

1. Market position:
    The Guidance reproduces the principles derived set out earlier in our discussion on market share. The Commission confirms that it will not generally regard an undertaking with a 40 per cent market share or less to be in a dominant position. However, it goes on to say that there may be specific cases below that threshold where competitors are not in a position to constrain effectively the conduct of a dominant undertaking, for example where they face serious capacity limitations.

2. Expansion or entry:
    An assessment of the competitive restraints on an undertaking cannot be based solely on existing market conditions. Future developments also need to be taken into account. The potential impact of expansion by actual competitors or entry by potential competitors, including the threat of such expansion or entry is relevant. An undertaking can be deterred from increasing prices or behaving in other anti-competitive ways, if expansion or entry is likely, timely and sufficient. For the Commission to consider expansion or entry likely it must be sufficiently profitable for the competitor or new entrant, taking into account factors such as barriers to entry (which may be difficult or costly to overcome) and the likely reaction of other undertakings on the market and the risk and costs of failure. For expansion or entry to be considered sufficient, it cannot be simply small-scale entry but must be of such a magnitude as to be able to deter any attempt to increase prices by the allegedly dominant undertaking, Barriers to entry or expansion can take various forms. They may be legal barriers such as tariffs

and quotas or they may take the form of advantages enjoyed by the dominant undertaking such as economies of scale, privileged access to essentially inputs or natural resources or technology (*Hilti*) or an established distribution or sales network (*United Brands*). Barriers to effective entry may also arise out of the dominate undertaking's own behaviour such as the conclusion of long-term contracts with its customers thereby effectively locking them in and eliminating the possibility of access by newcomers.

3. Countervailing market power:
    Competitive constraints may be exercised not only by actual or potential competitors but also by customers. Customers may have sufficient bargaining power to constrain a dominant undertaking's behaviour. This may arise from their sheer size making them an inevitable trading partner for the dominant undertaking or because of the facility with which they could switch to a competing supplier. Such countervailing bargaining power may deter an undertaking from increasing prices or behaving otherwise than in a competitive manner.

The length of time during which a firm has held its position in the RPM

This point was stressed in *Istituto Chemicoterapico Italiano* and *United Brands*. The firm cannot be dominant unless it is dominant *over time*.

Financial and technological resources

A firm with large financial and technological resources will be in a position to adapt its market strategy in order to meet and drive out competitors. It may indulge in predatory pricing, selling below cost if necessary to undercut rivals (see *AKZO Chemie BV*); it can maintain demand for its product by heavy advertising, thereby reducing cross-elasticity of demand, as was clearly the case in *United Brands*. Technological resources will enable a firm to keep ahead of potential competitors.

Access to raw materials and outlets

The greater the degree of vertical integration (ie control over businesses up and downstream in the marketing process), the greater a firm's power to act independently. However powerful Zoja may have been as a manufacturer of ethambutol, it was dependent on CSC for its raw materials. CSC, on the other hand, controlled both raw materials and outlets via ICI. United Brands enjoyed an even greater degree of vertical integration. Its empire extended virtually from the plantation to the table. They owned plantations, fleets of refrigerated vessels and refrigerated warehouses in key ports throughout Europe.

Behaviour

The Commission suggested in *United Brands* that an undertaking's behaviour can in itself provide evidence of dominance. In *United Brands* the firm's discriminatory rebate system was taken, inter alia, as an indicium of independence. In *Eurofix & Hilti* the Commission regarded Hilti's discriminatory treatment of its customers as 'witness to its ability to act independently and without due regard to other competitors or customers'.

Economists have questioned the validity in economic terms of some of these criteria, and even more so their application by the Commission in particular cases. For example, although United Brands had large financial and technological resources and enjoyed a high degree of vertical integration there was evidence that it faced fierce competition from time to time and its share of the market was falling. Moreover, its banana operations were not showing steady profits. These factors would not seem to indicate a power to behave independently of competitors. Such an approach may come close to blurring the line between determination of dominance and the finding of abuse.

Barriers to entry

In assessing dominance, it is not enough to examine the allegedly dominant undertaking's position in the existing state of the market; the question of *potential* competition must be assessed. This requires an examination into the whole range of barriers, geographical, financial, technical and temporal, to entry into that market. The Commission's decision in *Continental Can* was annulled for a failure to explore the possibility of product substitution. Both the Commission and the Court have been criticised for giving undue weight to such barriers, and particularly for failing to take a long-term view as to the prospects of market entry. This may result in a finding of dominance when the market is, in the longer term, contestable (see eg, *Michelin*).

Common barriers to entry are things such as the superior technology and technical resources of the undertaking which could not be matched easily by others. For example, *Hoffmann-La Roche* was a market leader in innovation. Its ability to generate new technology was an important consideration in establishing dominance. Also, trade-marks and brand names owned by the undertaking and its brand identity may make it more difficult for new brands to gain market share.

Associated markets

Proof of dominance in a particular market need not always be required. Where two markets are deemed to be associated, and a company is dominant in one of them, proof of dominance on the other does not need to be illustrated. In *Tetra Pak International SA v Commission* (case T-83/91) the GC held that associative links between two product markets could be shown because the key products were the same in both markets and because many of the manufacturers and consumers in the two markets were also the same. Thus, for a company dominant in one market to be in breach of Article 102 TFEU in respect of an associated market, only abusive behaviour need be shown. The decision of the GC has been confirmed by the CJ (*Tetra Pak International SA v Commission* (case C-333/94P); see also *British Airways*).

29.3.5 **Abuse**

It is not dominance per se but the abuse of a dominant position that brings Article 102 into play and this must be understood bearing in mind the principle that dominant firms are under a special duty not to hinder competition (*Michelin*, at para 10). 'Abuse' is not defined in Article 102 itself. In *Hoffmann-La Roche*, the CJ stated that abuse:

> is an objective concept relating to the *behaviour* of an undertaking in a dominant position which is such as to *influence the structure of a market* where, as a result of the very presence of the undertaking in question, *the degree of competition is weakened* and which, through recourse to *methods different from those which condition normal competition* in products or services on the basis of the transactions of commercial operators, has the effect of *hindering the maintenance of the degree of competition still existing* in the market or the growth of that competition [para 91, emphasis added].

Examples of abuse are provided by Article 102. They comprise:

(a) directly or indirectly imposing unfair purchase or selling prices or unfair trading conditions;

(b) limiting production, markets, or technical development to the prejudice of consumers;

(c) applying dissimilar conditions to equivalent transactions with other trading parties, thereby placing them at a competitive disadvantage; and

(d) making the conclusion of contracts subject to acceptance by the other parties of supplementary obligations which, by their nature or commercial usage, have no connection with the subject of such contracts.

These are merely examples; the list is not exhaustive.

A glance back to Article 101 will reveal that the kinds of abuse prohibited under Article 102 run in close parallel to the examples of concerted behaviour likely to breach Article 101(1). As far as most forms of behaviour are concerned, the difference between Articles 101 and 102 is a difference in degree rather than in kind. The existence of a dominant position merely makes the conduct more dangerous; thus there is no possibility of exemption for a breach of Article 102.

Abuses prohibited under Article 102 have been divided into two categories: exploitative abuses and exclusionary abuses. Exploitative abuses occur when an undertaking seeks to take advantage of its position of dominance by imposing oppressive or unfair conditions on its trading partners. Examples of such abuses are provided under (a), (c), and (d) cited earlier, and some behaviour under (b). Exclusionary abuses are those which, while not in themselves unfair or oppressive, are damaging because they reduce or eliminate competition. Such behaviour would arise under paragraph (b) cited earlier, and certain practices falling under para (d). Many kinds of behaviour fall into both categories (eg, *Istituto Chemioterapico Italiano*). The Commission has issued guidelines setting out its enforcement priorities in applying Article 102 to abusive exclusionary conduct ([2009] OJ L45/7). For the abusive behaviour to fall within Article 102, it is not necessary that the dominant undertaking reaps financial or commercial benefit from the behaviour which is the subject of the complaint. In the *World Cup* case ([2000] OJ L5/55), the non-profit-making organisation with the responsibility for organising the distribution of tickets put forward the argument that it had not benefited from the limitation it had imposed on ticket sales, an argument the Commission dismissed as irrelevant.

29.3.5.1 Exploitative abuses

United Brands provides examples of a number of exploitative abuses.

Unfair prices

According to the Commission, United Brands Co was charging excessively high prices for its branded bananas. Although this point was not found proved by the Court, the Court agreed with the Commission on the matter of principle. An excessive price was defined by the Court as one which bears no reasonable relation to the economic value of the product. In *British Leyland* the fees charged for the type-approval certificates for left-hand drive cars (when issued) were found to be excessive and discriminatory.

Problems arise over the question of 'economic value'. Deciding the economic value of a product or a service is a complex accounting exercise which leaves ample scope for differences of opinion. Economists would disagree as to what constituted the economic value of a product, and indeed, whether it can be accurately ascertained at all. What uniformity, then, can be hoped for from national courts when called upon to apply Article 102?

Unfair trading conditions

United Brands was found to be imposing unfair conditions by refusing to allow importers to resell bananas while they were still green. This meant that only wholesalers with the correct storage and ripening facilities were able to handle the bananas. The fact that the consumer might thereby be assured of obtaining a better, more standardised product did not prevent the Commission and the Court from finding that this requirement constituted an abuse. Again we find EU competition law protecting the 'middleman'.

Discriminatory treatment

United Brands was charging prices with a difference of, in some cases, more than 100 per cent in different common market countries, not, apparently, according to objective criteria, but according to what the market would bear. This constituted discriminatory treatment. Similarly, *British Leyland* charged different prices for type-approval certificates for left-hand drive cars, without objective justification.

In *British Airways*, BA held a dominant position as a purchaser of air travel-agency services. It had offered all UK travel agents a performance reward scheme if sales of BA tickets increased. Following a complaint by Virgin Atlantic, the Commission concluded that BA had abused a dominant position. The GC upheld this finding. One element of the abuse was that it was possible under the scheme that two travel agents with identical sales would receive different rates of commission. BA's scheme therefore had discriminatory effects in the network of travel agents.

29.3.5.2 **Exclusionary abuse**

This kind of abuse is less easy to detect than the exploitative abuse. Here the dominant firm uses its position in such a way as to undermine or even eliminate existing competitors, thereby reinforcing or increasing its dominance. A number of examples may be considered.

Tying and bundling

A good example of tying-in practices is provided by the case of *Hoffmann-La Roche*. La Roche was the largest pharmaceutical company in the world, with a dominant position in seven separate vitamin markets. The alleged abuses lay in a number of tying-in practices. Customers undertook to buy all or most of their requirements from La Roche ('requirements contracts'); as a reward they were entitled to 'fidelity' rebates (discounts). The agreement also contained 'English' clauses. These provided that if customers found other suppliers offering similar products at cheaper prices they should ask La Roche to 'adjust' their prices. If La Roche failed to respond they were free to buy elsewhere. None of these clauses was oppressive as far as La Roche's customers were concerned. But the Commission (approved by the Court) found the practices to be abusive. The tying-in system limited their customers' freedom to buy from competing suppliers; the English clauses were unacceptable because they enabled La Roche to identify competitors and take pre-emptive action—for example, by dropping its prices to its competitors' levels, thereby nipping potential rivals in the bud.

The case law in this area, most recently confirmed in *Microsoft Corp v Commission* (case T-201/04) reveals a four-stage test:

- the tying and tied products are separate products;
- the undertaking is dominant in the tying market;
- consumers do not have the option to obtain the tying product without the tied product;
- competition is foreclosed.

Nonetheless, if objective justification can be shown, there will be no infringement of Article 102 TFEU. (For more on *Microsoft*, see *An 'essential facilities' doctrine* later in this section.)

Predatory pricing

This is a strategy whereby prices are reduced, below cost if necessary, in order to drive competitors out of the market. In *AKZO Chemie BV v Commission* (case 62/96), AKZO, a firm dominant worldwide in the production of organic peroxides, was found to be engaged in such practices. However, as the Commission pointed out, it may be necessary to examine a firm's costs and motives in order to ascertain whether its low prices are predatory or merely the result of efficiency. Where low pricing is susceptible of several explanations, evidence of an anti-competitive intent may be needed. Indeed, the lowering of prices may even be evidence of weakness. In *Hoffmann-La Roche* the Court suggested that the fact that an undertaking is compelled by the pressure of its competitors' price reductions to lower its prices is in general incompatible with that independence which is the hallmark of dominance. The Court, in its first decision on predatory pricing (*AKZO Chemie*), agreed with the Commission. There was a distinction, in competition-law terms, between lowering prices in order to win new customers and trying to eliminate a competitor. In the case of *AKZO* the firm's 'avowed intention' had been to eliminate one of its competitors.

In *Compagnie Maritime Belge Transports SA v Commission* (case T-24–6 and 28/93), the GC emphasised the need to show intent. In this case, it was not clear that the dominant undertakings (this was a case involving collective dominance) had actually traded at a loss; certainly the Commission in its investigation did not carry out an analysis of costs and prices. There was, however, evidence to show that the motive behind the practice complained of was to drive the only existing competition out of the market. In this circumstance, the GC seemed to place the burden on the dominant undertakings to show that their behaviour was not anti-competitive. Although the CJ reduced the fines imposed in this case on appeal, the Court did confirm this aspect of the GC's ruling (*Compagnie Maritime Belge Transports v Dafra Lines* (cases C-395–6/96P)). In *Post Danmark* (case C-209/10) the CJ reiterated the necessity to prove that a pricing policy produces an actual or likely exclusionary effect to the detriment of competition and therefore of consumers' interests (para 44).

In the case of an allegation of abuse, though, how does the dominant undertaking show that its behaviour was normal in the circumstances? The danger is that normal price competition (eg, the reaction of a dominant undertaking to the news that one of its customers has been offered a lower price by a competitor) may be confused with predatory pricing.

Refusal to supply

While Article 102, in principle, respects the right of dominant firms to choose their contractual partners, in exceptional circumstances a refusal to supply may fall foul of Article 102 TFEU. Where supplies (or services) are refused to reduce or eliminate competition, such a refusal will constitute abuse. This appeared to be the case in *Istituto Chemioterapico Italiano SpA* where it was intended that CSC's subsidiary, ICI, would take over production of ethambutol previously undertaken by Zoja (see also *Hugin Kassaregister*). Boosey & Hawkes' cessation of supplies to BBI was designed deliberately to prevent them entering into the market as competitors.

However, a refusal to supply either an existing or a new customer will not necessarily be abusive. Arguing from *Metro-SB-Grossmärkte GmbH*, a refusal may be permissible if it is non-discriminatory and objectively justified. A refusal of supplies, particularly to an existing customer, will require cogent justification, and any signs of an anti-competitive motive will be fatal. In *Radio Telefis Eireann v Commission* (case T-69/89), *British Broadcasting Corporation v Commission* (case T-70/89) and *Independent Television Publications Ltd v Commission* (case T-76/89) the GC upheld a decision of the Commission which condemned, for the first time, a refusal to supply a party with whom it had no pre-existing commercial relationship. Here the applicant television companies were seeking to exploit their copyright in television programme listings to prevent competitors from publishing television programme guides in competition with their own publications, to the detriment of consumers. The CJ upheld this decision on appeal (*Magill*). The CJ focused on the fact that the television companies were the sole source of the information which is needed to produce weekly listings guides for all channels, that there was a market for such a product and the product was not being produced because of the behaviour of the television companies, and that the television companies were therefore *without objective justification* seeking to reserve a secondary market (television guide publishing) to themselves. (See further *An 'essential facilities' doctrine* later in this section.)

More recently, the CJ has held that a refusal to supply, to protect the dominant company from the effects of parallel imports, constitutes abuse where it refuses to supply ordinary orders (*Sot Lélos-kai Sia EE v GSK* (cases C-468–78/06)). The key phrase is 'ordinary orders', as such an undertaking is permitted:

> to counter in a reasonable and proportionate way the threat to its own commercial interests potentially posed by the activities of an undertaking which wishes to be supplied in the first Member State with significant quantities of products that are essentially destined for parallel export [para 71].

An 'essential facilities' doctrine?

The *Magill* case and subsequent developments have been interpreted as the development of an 'essential facilities' doctrine. The doctrine concerns undertakings which own or control a facility that is necessary to carry out a particular type of business, but which could not practically be reproduced by a competing entity or a potential competitor. The Commission Notice on access agreements in the telecommunications sector ([1988] OJ C265/3) described an essential facility as 'a facility or infrastructure which is essential for reaching customers and/or for enabling a competitor to carry on business, and which cannot be replicated by any reasonable means' (para 68).

In the absence of an objective justification, it seems that an essential facility must be made available to a competitor on reasonable terms as can be seen for example, in *Rødby Havn* ([1994] OJ L55/52).

Rødby Havn

Rødby Havn, a Danish port was owned by DSB, a publicly owned port authority, which also operated the only ferry service between there and Germany. Two other companies were interested in running a ferry service on the same route. The Danish government refused permission to use the port or to build another facility close by. This refusal was held to be an abuse within the terms of Article 102 because access to the port, a necessary prerequisite to the provision of the service, was prevented.

Similarly, a ferry company controlling access to a port was not permitted to deny access or schedule departures to the detriment of rival companies providing ferry services out of that port without objective justification (*Sealink*). Where there is no objective justification such behaviour is a prima facie breach of Article 102.

However, in *Oscar Bronner GmbH v Mediaprint* (case C-7/97), the CJ sought to limit the scope of the doctrine.

> ### Oscar Bronner
>
> Bronner published a newspaper which had about 3.6 per cent of the daily market in Austria. Mediaprint's newspapers had a market share of around 44 per cent. Mediaprint had established a nationwide home-delivery scheme for its newspapers. Bronner wanted Mediaprint to include its newspaper within that system. Mediaprint did include another newspaper in its scheme, but refused to allow Bronner's newspaper into its network. Bronner claimed that Mediaprint was abusing its dominant position.

The CJ disagreed with Bronner's claim. It held that four factors were required for a refusal of access to constitute an abuse, comprising:

- refusal likely to eliminate all competition in the downstream market from the person requiring access;
- refusal incapable of objective justification;
- access must be indispensable for the other person for carrying on its business;
- no actual or potential substitute for it.

These criteria had not been fulfilled, as Bronner could have set up his own distribution system, albeit at considerable cost, or developed alternative methods of distribution.

The essential facilities doctrine must therefore be handled with caution. It poses particular challenges in the case of intellectual property rights (such as in *Magill*), where it could prove to operate against innovation and investment in research and development if companies were ultimately compelled to make available the results of their own efforts and expense. However, in *IMS Health v NDC Health* (case C-418/01), the CJ attempted to re-adjust the balance between protecting intellectual property rights and innovation, when it held that a refusal to license the use of a particular system for collecting sales data to another undertaking would be an abuse where the undertaking requesting the licence intends to offer new products or services not offered by the IP owner for which there would be demand.

> ### IMS Health
>
> IMS Health had developed a geographical model of analysis, called a 'brick structure', which is used for making available sales data to IMS Health's customers and which constituted a *de facto* industry standard. The dominance arose because IMS customers had been heavily involved in the development of this 'brick structure' and were therefore dependent on it. The Commission, following a complaint from NDC, had taken the view that IMS Health has a dominant position in the German market for data services on sales and prescriptions of pharmaceuticals. Having concluded that IMS's refusal to license the use of their model of analysis meant that there existed a prima facie case for abuse of IMS's dominant position, the Commission ordered IMS to grant a licence by way of interim measure. This decision was suspended by the GC and an appeal to the CJ against the suspension failed.

The GC (case T-184/01 R) emphasised that:

> the respect for property rights in general and for intellectual property rights in particular is expressly reflected in Articles [36 and 345 TFEU]. The mere fact that the applicant has invoked and sought to enforce its copyright . . . for economic reasons does not lessen its entitlement to rely upon the exclusive right granted by national law for the very purpose of rewarding innovation [para 143].

The evidence suggested that the lack of competition which resulted from the refusal to license was not perceptible, but rather, that the position of particular competitors had become difficult because they could not use similar technology. This, however, was not enough to find a prima facie infringement of Article 102 (note that the Commission subsequently withdrew its decision).

The decision in *IMS Health*, discussed earlier, followed a complaint by NDC to the Commission. This had been prompted by a decision by a German court to grant an injunction in favour of IMS to prevent NDC from using a brick structure derived from IMS's structure. The German court referred a number of questions on the interpretation of Article 102 to the CJ (see *IMS Health*). The Court confirmed that a refusal to license could not, in itself, be an abuse under Article 102, although the manner in which these rights are exercised could. It therefore held that it would be an abuse by a dominant undertaking which owned an intellectual property right in a brick structure indispensable to the presentation of regional sales data to refuse to grant a licence to another undertaking which also intends to provide such data in the same Member State. This was subject to a number of conditions: first, the undertaking requesting the licence intends to offer new products for which there is potential demand and which are not offered by the owner of the intellectual property rights; secondly, there are no objective justifications for refusing to grant the licences; and finally, the refusal is such as to enable the owner of the intellectual property rights to eliminate all competition on the relevant market.

The upshot of this ruling is that there may be circumstances where Article 102 *does* appear to require a degree of compulsory licensing, at least in circumstances where a refusal to do so would eliminate the possibility of innovation, and where there are no objective justifications for this refusal. In *Microsoft*, Microsoft was unsuccessful in challenging the Commission's decision that it had breached Article 102 by refusing to supply interoperability information for its operating system because it had failed to demonstrate that disclosing this information would have a significant negative effect on its incentives to innovate. Some commentators have criticised the reasoning in *Microsoft*, because it takes a broad view of the criteria laid down in *IMS Health* and, arguably, operates to protect Microsoft's competitors rather than competition.

Exclusive reservation of activities

Similar principles to those applicable to a refusal to supply will apply where a dominant undertaking reserves certain activities to itself. This occurred in the *British Telecommunications* case where BT reserved for itself exclusive rights to its telex forwarding services, and in *Centre D'Etudes du Marché-Télémarketing SA v Compagnie Luxembourgeoise de Télédiffusion SA and Information Publicité Benelux (Belgian Telemarketing)* (case 311/84), in which a telephone marketing service was channelled exclusively through RTL's agent. The Court pointed out in *Belgian Telemarketing* that there was no 'objective necessity' for its so doing. This implies that the exclusive reservation of certain activities by a dominant undertaking, whether for itself or for an appointed agent, might be permissible if it were necessary and objectively justified. However the Court was not prepared to accept that the preservation of RTL's image constituted a 'necessity'.

Import and export bans

In view of the hard line of the Commission and the Court over such restrictions under Article 101 it is no surprise that import and export bans have been held to constitute abuse under Article 102 (*Suiker Unie v Commission (European sugar cartel)* (case 40/73)). Apart from when industrial property rights are legitimately exercised to this end it is hard to imagine a situation in which such a ban would not be deemed an abuse.

Margin Squeeze

Margin squeeze is caused when a vertically integrated undertaking which is dominant on an upstream market for an input product or service sets its prices at such a level that competitors on the downstream market cannot compete with it for the supply of downstream products or services. In *Deutsche Telecom* (DT) ([2003] OJ L263/9), the Commission found that DT, by charging its competitors in the retail market in Germany a higher price for access to the 'local loop' than it was charging to its own retail end user customers, was abusing its dominant position. Its pricing policy led to actual exclusionary effects on competitors (see also *Konkurrensverket v TeleSoneria Sverige AB* (case C-52/09)).

29.3.6 Trade between Member States

As with Article 101, there must be some effect on trade between Member States for Article 102 to apply, but such an effect is not hard to establish. The Court held in *British Leyland* that it was not necessary to establish any specific effects, as long as there was evidence that a particular activity *might* affect trade between Member States. A theoretical possibility will be sufficient.

However, in *Hugin Kassaregister* the Court annulled the Commission's decision ([1978] 1 CMLR D19) that Hugin had acted in breach of Article 102. Although it agreed with the Commission on the questions of the relevant product market and abuse, it found that Hugin's refusal to supply Liptons with spare parts did not affect trade between states. Hugin was a Swedish firm and at that time outside the common market, and Liptons was functioning in London on a purely local scale.

An effect on trade between Member States was held in *Istituto Chemioterapico Italiano* to include repercussions on the competitive structure within the common market. This was approved and followed by the Court in *Bodson* and an effect on trade between Member States found despite the Commission's view that a monopoly in funeral services granted to Pompes Funèbres by the municipality of Charleville-Mèziéres did not affect trade between Member States.

29.3.7 Relationship with Article 106(2) TFEU

Some public undertakings (such as utility companies) defending a claim of alleged abuse under Article 102 may seek to rely on Article 106(2). This provides that undertakings entrusted with the operation of services of general economic interest or which have the character of a revenue-producing monopoly are subject to the rules in the Treaty (including competition rules) unless the performance of the tasks assigned to them would be obstructed by the application of those rules. This exception is subject to the proviso that the 'development of trade must not be affected to such an extent as would be contrary to the interests of the Union'.

29.3.7.1 When will Article 102 not apply?

This is a twofold test. To be able to rely on this exception, not only must the entity show, first, that it is the requisite type of undertaking, but, secondly, that it cannot perform the tasks assigned to it without relying on provisions or behaviour which would normally be in breach of competition provisions—in particular, Article 102. In *Corbeau*, Corbeau was prevented from running a postal service because the Belgian postal service had a monopoly. Potentially this could have breached Article 102 unless the Belgian postal service could rely on Article 106(2). The CJ accepted that the Belgian postal service was an undertaking within Article 106(2) and also that a certain amount of restriction of competition was necessary to enable it to remain economically viable. The postal service is required to perform some services which can only be carried out at a loss (eg, delivery to outlying areas) and it funds these activities from profit-making activities. Unrestricted competition would allow other companies to 'cream off' the profitable services without having to carry out the non-profitable activities, leaving the Belgian postal service with the obligation but not the means of paying for it. In *TNT Traco SpA v Poste Italiane SpA* (case C-340/99), therefore, a requirement that economic operators providing an express mail service that fell outside the scope of the universal postal service had to pay the equivalent of the normal postal charges to the universal service provider was compatible with Articles 102 and 106 if the proceeds of such payments were necessary to enable the universal service provider to operate in economically acceptable conditions. Moreover, the universal service provider must be under the same obligation when providing an express mail service which is not part of the universal service.

This does not mean, however, that all competition can be excluded: in deciding if a case falls within Article 106(2), the authorities must identify the extent of restriction necessary to enable the undertaking to perform its tasks, taking into account, 'the economic conditions in which the undertaking operates, the costs which it has to bear and the legislation, particularly concerning the environment, to which it is subject' (*Almelo*, para 49).

29.3.7.2 Interests of the Union

The interests of the Union must also be taken into account. Although it is not clear precisely what this element of Article 106(2) requires, it will clearly curtail the scope of the exception provided under this article. It has been suggested from the terms of the *Almelo* judgment that, broadly speaking, an assessment will be made entailing a balancing of the needs of the undertaking with other EU goals. It is not clear what impact Article 14 TFEU, which obliges Member States to ensure that services of general economic interest 'operate on the basis of principles and conditions, particularly economic and financial conditions, which enable them to fulfil their missions', will have, as on the one hand both the Union and Member States are required to take into account the 'shared values of the Union as well as their role in promoting social and territorial cohesion' and, on the other hand, this provision is expressed to be without prejudice to certain Treaty articles including Article 106. (See also Article 36 EUCFR.)

29.4 Enforcement of Articles 101 and 102

Central to the effectiveness of the competition provisions are the rules on enforcement. Without proper enforcement, the substantive competition rules would lose much of their bite. For four decades, Regulation 17/62 gave the Commission a central role in enforcing the competition provisions within the then EC Treaty, with significant powers of investigation and the right to impose penalties. During this time, two themes emerged in relation to competition enforcement by the Commission. The first concerned the scope of the Commission's powers. Although the decisions of the Commission may have been subject to judicial review, given their extent and their potential impact on undertakings, including individuals, the need to ensure procedural fairness became ever more important. This point remains central today. Secondly, the previously strongly centralised system meant that D-G Competition was subject to a very high workload, resulting in delays in the decision-making process. A thorough process of reform in a number of aspects of competition law in response to this second point was therefore undertaken. The replacement of the original system of enforcement with a new, decentralised system finally came into place when Regulation 1/2003 ([2003] OJ L1/1) entered into force in May 2004. It is supplemented by Regulation 773/2004 relating to the conduct of proceedings by the Commission pursuant to Articles 101–2 TFEU ([2004] OJ L123/18), as well as a 'Modernisation Package' of Commission notices which provide detailed guidance on the operation of the new system and the interpretation of key concepts (see [2004] OJ C101).

These Regulations and Notices replace the earlier Regulation 17/62, and this chapter concentrates on the new system. It should be remembered that the bulk of the *acquis communautaire* in the field of competition law evolved through decisions and cases decided under the previous framework.

Article 1(1) of Regulation 1 states, rather boldly, that 'agreements, decisions and concerted practices caught by Article 101(1) of the Treaty which do not satisfy the conditions of Article 101(3) of the Treaty shall be prohibited, no prior decision to that effect being required' (Article 1(3) contains a similar statement in respect of Article 102 TFEU). The corollary of this basic prohibition is that an agreement caught by Article 101(1) which *does* satisfy the conditions of Article 101(3) is not prohibited, and no prior decision-granting exemption is required (Article 1(2), Regulation 1). Unlike the previous system, it is not necessary to ask the Commission to examine individual agreements to establish whether the criteria for exemption are, in fact, satisfied. Rather, undertakings will have to examine for themselves whether any of their practices conflict with Article 101(1) but are exempt under Article 101(3), thus transferring the workload in making this assessment to the companies involved. This transfer also imposes a certain amount of risk on the companies making the assessment, should their advisers come to the 'wrong' conclusion about the acceptability of their agreements (and this fact comes to competition authorities' attention). Consequently, although the Commission is not involved in this assessment directly, it provides indirect support through its notices and block exemptions, as well as through formal decisions adopted previously and the case law of the courts. In particular, it has issued two documents containing guidelines on the notion of 'effect on trade' ([2004] OJ C101/101) and the application of Article 101(3) ([2004] OJ C101/97).

Although the Commission no longer deals with notifications, it retains the power to investigate specific anti-competitive practices on its own initiative or in response to complaints received from third parties. As the Commission's focus has now shifted towards investigating harmful anti-competitive practices, such as large price-fixing cartels, it seems likely that the Commission's involvement will be restricted (although it has encouraged complaints to be made). Instead, both national competition authorities (Article 3) and national courts (Article 6) now have the power to apply Articles 101–2 TFEU in full. However, this is subject to the requirement in Article 16 of Regulation 1 that national authorities and courts cannot adopt a decision running counter to a decision adopted by the Commission.

National authorities have the power to require that an infringement is brought to an end, to order interim measures, accept commitments and to impose fines, periodic penalty payments, or any other penalty provided by national law.

Where the Commission does investigate, it may similarly order the termination of an infringement and impose structural or behavioural remedies (Article 7). Under Article 9, where the Commission intends to adopt a formal decision that an infringement should be brought to an end, the undertakings concerned may offer commitments to meet the concerns expressed by the Commission. If these are accepted, the Commission may adopt a decision to that effect and thereby make the commitments binding on the parties. However, if there is a material change in the facts on the basis of which the commitments were accepted, or if the undertakings subsequently fail to honour their commitments, the Commission may reopen its investigation (Article 9(2)). Finally, the Commission retains the power to make a finding of inapplicability if it concludes that Article 101(1) TFEU or Article 102 TFEU does not apply at all, or, in the case of Article 101(1) TFEU, that the conditions of Article 101(3) TFEU are satisfied (Article 10). However, this power is only exercisable 'where the [Union] public interest' so requires and where the Commission acts on its own initiative.

The modernised enforcement system is based on the assumption that the relevant principles on the application of the competition rules are now well established, and that the Commission no longer needs to take a central role. However, it has been accepted that 'novel questions' regarding the scope and application of Articles 101–2 may still arise. Where undertakings are unable to assess whether a practice they are involved in constitutes an infringement because neither the various guidance notices, nor the *acquis communautaire*, provide an answer, they may seek informal guidance from the Commission in accordance with the Notice on informal guidance relating to novel questions concerning Articles 101–2 ([2004] OJ C101/78). If appropriate, the Commission will issue an informal guidance letter, which is without prejudice to any subsequent formal investigation.

29.5 Private Enforcement

Infringements of Articles 101 and 102 such as cartels or abusive behaviour on the part of dominant undertakings can cause harm in the shape, such as higher prices or lost profits to concrete victims for example direct and indirect customers of the infringing undertaking as well as their competitors and their customers. The CJ established in *Courage* that victims of unlawful anti-competitive conduct have a right to damages for harm suffered as a result of that conduct. However the rules relating to compensation for damages vary considerably between the Member States and often make it costly and difficult for victims to bring damages actions. With a view to rectifying this situation and to render the enforcement of the competition rules more effective, the Commission in 2013 proposed the adoption of a Directive to remove the main obstacles to effective compensation and to guarantee minimum protection for citizens and businesses throughout the EU. Directive 2014/104 on actions for damages was adopted at the end of 2014 ([2014] OJ L349/1). It was required to be implemented by the Member States by 27 December 2016. A complementary measure to the Directive is the Commission's Recommendation on collective redress which invited the Member States to introduce, by 26 July 2015, collective redress mechanisms, including actions for damages. Collective redress is important for consumers harmed by violations of the competition rules who are generally not in a position to pursue individual claims for damages. The Commission will assess the implementation of the Recommendation by July 2017. A major difficulty encountered by courts and tribunals and parties in damages actions is how to quantify the harm allegedly suffered. The Commission has issued a Communication on quantifying harm in actions for damages to assist national courts and parties in this complex task.

29.6 Mergers and concentrations

29.6.1 Background: from Articles 101 and 102 to the Merger Regulation

Perhaps the most surprising application of Article 102 came in the *Continental Can* case. Here the Commission had applied Article 102 in the context of a proposed merger, namely, the proposed takeover by Continental Can, which owned an 86 per cent share in SLW in Germany, of TDV in Holland, the entire package to be held by Continental Can's subsidiary Europemballage. The Commission issued a decision that the proposed takeover constituted an abuse of their dominant position within the common market (viz Germany). In annulment proceedings Continental Can argued that such action could not be regarded as an abuse. Article 102 was concerned only with behaviour detrimental to consumers. Moreover, it required some causative link between the position of dominance and abuse. Neither Continental Can nor Europemballage had used their power to effect the merger. The Court disagreed. Article 102, the Court said, cannot allow mergers which eliminate competition. Prejudice under that article does not mean affecting consumers directly but also prejudice through interference with the structure of competition itself. Nor was it necessary to prove a causal link between the dominance and the abuse. The mere fact of dominance rendered the proposed takeover an abuse. Although the Court annulled the Commission's decision on the grounds that the relevant product markets had not been fully proved, the principle was established.

Following *Continental Can*, in *Tetra Pak Rausing SA v Commission* (case T-51/89), the takeover by Tetra Pak of a company holding an exclusive licence to new technology for sterilising milk cartons was held to constitute a breach of Article 102. Although the acquisition of an exclusive licence was not per se abusive, Tetra Pak's acquisition of that licence had the practical effect of precluding all competition in the relevant market. The existence of an exemption under the Exclusive Licence Block Exemption Regulation (Regulation 2349/84 ([1984] OJ L 219/15)) did not release a dominant undertaking from its obligation to comply with Article 102.

Continental Can and Article 102 remained the basis on which the Commission exercised control over mergers until the Court decided for the first time, in *BAT & Reynolds*, that mergers could also fall within Article 101(1).

BAT & Reynolds

The case arose from a proposed merger between Philip Morris Inc and Rembrandt Ltd, which would have given Philip Morris a controlling interest in one of its principal competitors, Rothmans Tobacco (Holding) Ltd, in the EU cigarette market. The Commission had been alerted to the proposed merger by the parties' competitors, BAT and Reynolds. Subsequently the agreement was modified by a decision from the Commission reducing Philip Morris's shareholding in Rothmans Ltd, and thereby ensuring that the relationship between them remained competitive. The decision was challenged by BAT and Reynolds.

While the decision was upheld by the Court, the Court affirmed that Article 101(1) could apply in principle to mergers. Although the acquisition of an equity interest in a competitor did not in itself restrict competition, it might serve as an instrument to that end.

This decision paved the way for the acceptance by Member States of a regulation on merger control which had been languishing for many years. The final version of the Regulation, Regulation 4064/89 (corrected version [1990] OJ L257/13), was adopted in December 1989, after much debate among Member States on the appropriate turnover and market-share thresholds required to bring the Regulation into operation. It was replaced with a modernised regulation in 2004 (Regulation 139/2004 ([2004] OJ L24/1)). It requires notification to and approval by the Commission of proposed mergers above certain combined turnover thresholds. Moreover the Merger Regulation applies to 'full-function' joint ventures, which are joint ventures which perform, on a lasting basis, all the functions of an autonomous economic entity (Article 3(4)). Such joint ventures operate in the market in the same way as other undertakings and must have sufficient financial and other resources to be able to operate as a business on a lasting basis (see Commission Notice on Full-Function Joint Ventures ([1997] OJ C66), together with other notices on the notion of undertakings concerned, the notion of concentration and the calculation of turnover). However, a joint venture which does not fall within the definition of full-function joint venture will have to be assessed under Article 101.

29.6.2 **The Merger Regulation**

Regulation 139/2004, which came into effect on 1 May 2004, applies to mergers, acquisitions and certain joint ventures, known as 'concentrations' between firms with a combined worldwide turnover of more than EUR 5,000 million, where at least two of the firms have a combined turnover of more than EUR 250 million in the EU but do not earn more than two-thirds of their turnover in a single Member State (Article 1(2)). Article 1(3) provides that where a concentration does not meet these thresholds, it may still have an EU dimension if:

(a) the combined aggregate worldwide turnover of all the undertakings is more than EUR 2,500 million;

(b) in each of at least three Member States, the combined aggregate turnover of all the undertakings concerned is more than EUR 100 million;

(c) in each of at least three Member States included for the purpose of point (b), the aggregate turnover of each of at least two of the undertakings concerned is more than EUR 25 million; and

(d) the aggregate Community-wide turnover of each of at least two of the undertakings concerned is more than EUR 100 million.

unless each of the undertakings concerned achieves more than two-thirds of its aggregate Community-wide turnover within one Member State.

A 'concentration' is defined in Article 3(1) as:

- the merger of two or more previously independent undertakings; or
- the acquisition, by one or more persons already controlling at least one undertaking, or by one or more undertakings, whether by purchase of securities or assets, by contract or by any other means, of direct or indirect control of the whole or parts of one or more other undertakings.

'Control' confers the possibility of exercising 'decisive influence' on an undertaking. A joint venture will be concentrative if it performs on a lasting basis all the functions of an autonomous economic entity (Article 3(4)). The Commission issued guidance on the concept of a concentration, calculation of turnover and the definition of a full-function joint venture ([1997] OJ C66) under the old Regulation; this had not been replaced at the time of writing.

The principle underlying the Regulation is that of the 'one-stop shop'. Concentrations falling within the Regulation will be subject to the exclusive jurisdiction of the Commission (Article 21(2)) and must be notified to the Commission (Article 4). A failure to notify may result in a fine of up to 10 per cent of the aggregate turnover of the undertaking(s) concerned (Article 14(2)), whereas supplying incorrect or misleading information may result in fines of up to 1 per cent of aggregate turnover (Article 14(1)). Concentrations falling outside the Regulation's thresholds will be subject to control by the relevant national authority. However, a Member State or Member States jointly may ask the Commission to intervene in respect of a concentration falling outside the Regulation which will 'significantly affect' competition within its own territory and have an effect on trade between Member States (Article 22(1)). Similarly, the Commission may refer a matter notified to it to the relevant national authority following receipt of notification by the Member State that a concentration may significantly affect competition in a market within that Member State which has the characteristics of a separate market (Article 9). In this context, the Commission has provided guidance on how to deal with the allocation of cases in a Notice on Case Referral in respect of concentrations ([2005] OJ C56/2).

A concentration will be permitted if it would not 'significantly impede effective competition in the common market or in a substantial part of it, in particular as a result of the creation or strengthening of a dominant position' (Article 2(2)–(3)). It is, however, not clear if the test for 'dominance' would be the same as under Article 102. In the Green Paper (COM(2001) 745 final) leading to the reform, an altogether different test was proposed to avoid the links with Article 102, but this has not survived in the final version of the Regulation.

In making its decision, the Commission must take into account, inter alia, the 'need to preserve and develop effective competition within the common market', as well as 'the market position of the undertakings concerned and their economic and financial power' (Article 2(1)). The Commission has 25 days in which to decide whether to investigate the matter and four months from the date on which proceedings are initiated in which to reach a final decision (Article 10).

Procedures governing notification and detailed provision in respect of hearings and time limit are laid down in Regulation 802/2004 ([2004] OJ L133/1).

29.7 Conclusions

This chapter demonstrates that competition law is a mature area of EU law, and one where there has been a move to decentralised enforcement and a use of more general block exemptions (at least as far as Article 101 is concerned). It is also a very complex one where law and economics interact ever more closely. Difficulties may arise from the degree to which a court can properly be expected to make complex assessments of economics. There is also a tension between the different objectives of the EU—particularly the need to facilitate the internal market. Its contribution to the creation and functioning of the internal market has been immense, ensuring that undertakings do not undermine it by creating artificial barriers along national lines, or act in such a way as to undermine market integration.

Further reading

Bellamy and Child: European Union Law of Competition Law, 7th edn (Oxford University Press, 2013).

Camesasca, P, *European Merger Control: Getting efficiencies right* (Hart Publishing, 2000).

Eilmansberger, T, 'How to distinguish good from bad competition under Article 82' (2005) 42 CML Rev 129.

Ezrachi, A, *EU Competition Law: An Analytical Guide to the Leading Cases* (Hart Publishing, 2016).

Guidance on the Commission's enforcement priorities in applying Article 82 of the EC Treaty to abusive exclusionary conduct by dominant undertakings [2009] OJ C45/7.

Harrison, J and Woods, L, 'Media ownership: Impact on access and content' in *European Broadcasting Law and Policy* (Cambridge University Press, 2007).

Jones, A and Sufrin, B, *EU Competition Law*, 6th edn (Oxford University Press, 2016).

Jones, A, 'The Boundaries of an Undertaking in EU Competition Law' (2012) 8 European Competition Law Journal 301.

Lang, JT, 'Defining legitimate competition: Companies' duties to supply competitors and access to essential facilities' (1994) 18 Fordham Int'l LJ 437.

Mezzanotte, FE, 'Tacit collusion as economic links in article 82 EC revisited' (2009) 30 ECLR 137.

Monti, G, 'The scope of collective dominance under Article 82 EC' (2001) 38 CML Rev 131.

Monti, G, 'Article 81 and public policy' (2002) 35 CML Rev 1057.

Niels, G and Jenkins, H, 'Reform of Article 82: Where the link between dominance and effects breaks down' (2005) 26 ECLR 605.

Odudu, O, *The Boundaries of EC Competition Law: The scope of Article 101* (Oxford University Press, 2006).

Stothers, C, 'Refusal to supply as abuse of a dominant position: The essential facilities doctrine in the European Union' (2001) 22 ECLR 256.

Wesseling, R, 'The rule of reason and competition law: Various rules, various reasons' in Schrauwen (ed), *Rule of Reason: Rethinking another Classic of European Legal Doctrine* (Hogenderp Papers 4) (Europe Law Publishing, 2005).

Whish, R and Bailey, D, *Competition Law*, 8th edn (Oxford University Press, 2015).

Wils, W, 'Ten Years of Regulation 1/2003—A Retrospective' (2013) Journal of European Competition Law and Practice 293.

Wils, W, 'Private Enforcement of EU Antitrust Law and its Relationship with Public Enforcement: Past, Present and Future' (2017) 40 World Competition Law and Economics Review (forthcoming).

Further reading

Principal sources of EU law

Official Journal (L series): Union secondary legislation.

Official Journal (C series): non-binding Union instruments; proposals, notices, -opinions, resolutions, reports of proceedings in Parliament and the Court of Justice.

European Commercial Cases.

European Current Law.

European Court Reports: reports of cases from the Court of Justice.

Common Market Law Reports: reports of cases from the Court of Justice and national courts.

Annual *General Report on the Activities of the European Union.*

Annual *Report on Competition Policy.*

Encyclopedia of European Union Law, (London: Sweet & Maxwell, looseleaf). Constitutional Treaties, together with annexes and protocols. Secondary legislation.

Databases

EUR-LEX—portal to European Union Law (full text)

URL—**http://eur-lex.europa.eu/en/index.htm**

Prelex—database on inter-institutional procedures allowing access to electronic texts available

URL—**http://ec.europa.eu/prelex/apcnet. cfm?CL=en**

LexisNexis—commercial database containing European Court reports, European commercial cases, and Commission competition decisions

General introductory

Szyszczak, E and Cygan, A, *Understanding EU Law*, 2nd edn (London: Sweet & Maxwell, 2008)

Selected textbooks in specialised areas

Mathijsen, P, *A Guide to European Union Law*, 11th edn (London: Sweet & Maxwell, 2010)

O'Neill, A, *EU Law for UK Lawyers*, 2nd edn (Oxford: Hart Publishing, 2012)

(a) General textbooks

Craig, P and de Búrca, G, *EU Law: Text, Cases and Materials*, 6th edn (Oxford: Oxford University Press, 2015)

Weatherill, S, *Cases and Materials on EU Law*, 12th edn (Oxford: Oxford University Press, 2016)

Wyatt, D and Dashwood, A, *European Union Law*, 6th edn (Oxford: Hart Publishing, 2011)

(b) Constitutional, institutional and administrative law

Albi, A, *EU Enlargement and the Constitutions of Central and Eastern Europe* (Cambridge: Cambridge University Press, 2005)

Andenas, M, and Usher, W-H (eds), *The Treaty of Nice and Beyond: Enlargement and Constitutional Reform* (Oxford: Hart Publishing, 2003)

Andersen, S, *The Enforcement of EU Law: The Role of the European Commission* (Oxford: Oxford University Press, 2012)

Avbelj, M and Komárek, J (eds), *Constitutional Pluralism in the European Union and Beyond* (Oxford: Hart Publishing, 2012)

Biondi, A and Eeckhout, P, *EU Law after Lisbon* (Oxford: Oxford University Press, 2012)

Brown, N and Jacobs, F, *The Court of Justice of the European Communities*, 5th edn (London: Sweet & Maxwell, 2000)

Burrows, N and Greaves, R, *The Advocate General and EU Law* (Oxford: Oxford University Press, 2007)

Costa, M, *The Accountability Gap in EU Law* (Oxford: Routledge, 2016)

Craig, P, *EU Administrative Law,* 2nd edn (Oxford: Oxford University Press, 2012)

Craig, P and De Búrca, G (eds), *The Evolution of EU Law*, 2nd edn (Oxford: Oxford University Press, 2011)

Curtin, D (ed), *The EU Constitution: The Best Way Forward?* (The Hague: TMC Asser Press, 2005)

de Búrca, G and Weiler, J, *The Worlds of European Constitutionalism* (Cambridge: Cambridge University Press, 2011) de Vitte, F, *Justice in the EU* (Oxford: Oxford University Press, 2015)

Fahey, E, *The Global Reach of EU law* (Oxford: Routledge, 2016)

Gragl, P, *The Accession of the European Union to the European Convention on Human Rights* (Oxford: Hart Publishing, 2013)

Hartley, TC, *The Foundations of European Union Law*, 8th edn (Oxford: Oxford University Press, 2014)

Hinarejos, A, *Judicial Control in the European Union, Reforming Jurisdiction in the Intergovernmental Pillars* (Oxford: Oxford University Press, 2009)

Hinarejos, A, *The Euro Area Crisis in Constitutional Perspective* (Oxford: Oxford University Press, 2014)

Lenaerts, K, Van Nuffel, P and Bray, R, *European Union Law*, 3rd edn (London: Sweet & Maxwell, 2011)

Linsetti, PL, *Power and Legitimacy* (Oxford: Oxford University Press, 2010)

Mendes, J, *Participation in EU Rule-making: A Rights-Based Approach* (Oxford: Oxford University Press, 2011)

Mendez, M, *The Legal Effect of EU Agreements* (Oxford: Oxford University Press, 2013)

Piris, J-C, *The Lisbon Treaty* (Cambridge: Cambridge University Press, 2010)

Rittberger, B, *Building Europe's Parliament: Democratic Representation Beyond the Nation State* (Oxford: Oxford University Press, 2007)

Tridimas, T, *The General Principles of EU Law* (Oxford: Oxford University Press, 2007)

Tryfonidou, A, *The Impact of Union Citizenship on the EU's Market Freedoms* (Oxford: Hart Publishing, 2016)

Ward, A, *Judicial Review and the Rights of Private Parties in EU Law* (Oxford: Oxford University Press, 2007)

Weiler, JHH, *The Constitution of Europe* (Cambridge: Cambridge University Press, 1999)

(c) Human rights

Gragl, P, *The Accession of the European Union to the European Convention on Human Rights* (Oxford: Hart Publishing, 2013)

Peers, S, Hervey, T, Kenner, J and Ward, A (eds), *The EU Charter of Fundamental Rights: A Commentary* (Oxford: Hart Publishing, 2014)

(d) Substantive law

(i) Agriculture

Churchill, R and Owen, D, *The EC Common Fisheries Policy* (Oxford: Oxford University Press, 2010)

McMahon, J, *EU Agricultural Law* (Oxford: Oxford University Press, 2007)

O'Rourke, R, *European Food Law*, 3rd edn (London: Sweet & Maxwell, 2005)

(ii) Civil jurisdiction and enforcement of judgments

Briggs, A, *Agreements on Jurisdiction and Choice of Law* (Oxford: Oxford University Press, 2008)

Calliess, G-P, *Rome Regulations: Commentary on the European Rules of the Conflict of Law* (The Hague: Kluwer, 2011)

Plender, R and Wilderspin, M, *Private International Law of Obligations: The Rome Convention on the Choice of Law for Contracts*, 3rd edn (London: Sweet & Maxwell, 2009)

(iii) Company law

Bernitz, U and Ringe, W-E (eds), *Company Law and Economic Protectionism: New Challenges to European Integration* (Oxford: Oxford University Press, 2010)

Dine, J, Koutsias, M and Blecher, M, *Company Law in the New Europe: The EU Acquis, Comparative Methodology and Model Law* (Cheltenham: Edward Elgar, 2007)

Gore-Brown on EU Company Law (Chichester: Jordans, looseleaf)

Grundmann, S, *European Company Law* (Oxford: Hart Publishing, 2012)

Usher, J, *Law of Money & Financial Services in the EC*, 2nd edn (Oxford: Oxford University Press, 2000)

Vossestan, G-J, *Modernization of European Company Law and Corporate Governance: Some Considerations of its Legal Limits* (The Hague: Kluwer, 2010)

(iv) Competition law

Akman, P, *The Concept of Abuse in EU Competition Law* (Oxford: Hart Publishing, 2012)

Baquero Cruz, J, *Between Competition and Free Movement* (Oxford: Hart Publishing, 2002)

Bellamy, CW and Child, GD, *The European Community Law of Competition*, 7th edn (Oxford: Oxford University Press, 2013)

Cameron, P, *Competition in Energy Markets*, 2nd edn (Oxford: Oxford University Press, 2007)

Hancher, L, Ottervanger, T and Slot, PJ, *EU State Aids*, 5th edn (London: Sweet & Maxwell, 2016)

Hoeg, D, *European Merger Remedies: Law and Policy* (Oxford: Hart Publishing, 2013)

Khan, N, *EU Antitrust Procedure*, 6th edn (London: Sweet & Maxwell, 2012)

Lindsay, A and Berridge, A, *The EU Merger Regulation*, 4th edn (London: Sweet & Maxwell, 2012)

Lista, A, *EU Competition Law and the Financial Services Sector* (London: Informa Law, 2013)

O'Donoghue, R and Padilla, AJ, *The Law and Economics of Article 102 TFEU*, 2nd edn (Oxford: Hart Publishing, 2013)

Silva Morais, L, *Joint Ventures and EU Competition Law* (Oxford: Hart Publishing, 2013)

Van Gerven, D, *Cross-Border Mergers in Europe* (Cambridge: Cambridge University Press, 2011)

Whish, R and Bailey, D, *Competition Law*, 8th edn (Oxford: Oxford University Press, 2015)

(v) Consumer

Twigg-Flesner, C, *The Cambridge Companion to European Union Private Law* (Cambridge: Cambridge University Press, 2010)

Twigg-Flesner, C, *The Europeanisation of Contract Law: Current Controversies in Law*, 2nd edn (Oxford: Routledge, 2013)

Weatherill, S, *EU Consumer Law and Policy*, 2nd edn (Cheltenham: Edward Elgar, 2005)

(vi) Environment

Krämer, L, *EU Environmental Law*, 8th edn (London: Sweet & Maxwell, 2015)

Lee, M, *EU Environmental Law: Governance and Decision Making* (Oxford: Hart Publishing, 2014)

Scott, J, *Environmental Protection: European Law and Governance* (Oxford: Oxford University Press, 2009)

Wennerås, P, *The Enforcement of EC Environmental Law* (Oxford: Oxford University Press, 2007)

(vii) External law and policy

Dashwood, A and Maresceau, M, *Law and Practice of EU External Relations* (Cambridge: Cambridge University Press, 2011)

Eeckhout, P, *EU External Relations Law* (Oxford: Oxford University Press, 2011)

Koutrakos, P, *EU Law of International Relations Law* (Oxford: Hart Publishing, 2015)

Koutrakos, P, *The EU Common Security and Defence Policy* (Oxford: Oxford University Press, 2013)

(viii) Free movement of goods and services

Andenas, M and Roth, W-H (eds), *Services and Free Movement in EC Law* (Oxford: Oxford University Press, 2003)

Barnard, C and Scott, J (eds), *The Law of the Single European Market* (Oxford: Hart Publishing, 2002)

Gormley, L, *EU Law of Free Movement of Goods and Customs Union* (Oxford: Oxford University Press, 2009)

Janssens, C, *The Principle of Mutual Recognition in EU Law* (Oxford: Oxford University Press, 2013)

Lyons, T, *EC Customs Law*, 2nd edn (Oxford: Oxford University Press, 2008)

Nic Shuibhne, N, *The Coherence of EU Free Movement Law: Constitutionality and the Court of Justice* (Oxford: Oxford University Press, 2013)

Oliver, P, *Oliver on Free Movement of Goods in the European Union*, 5th edn (Oxford: Hart Publishing, 2010)

Sauter, W and Schepel, H, *State and Market in European Union Law* (Cambridge: Cambridge University Press, 2009)

Woods, L, *Free Movement of Goods and Services within the EC* (Aldershot: Ashgate, 2004)

(ix) Health

Eriksen, CC, *The European Constitution, Welfare States and Democracy* (Oxford: Routledge, 2011)

Hervey, T, *Health Law and the European Union* (Cambridge: Cambridge University Press, 2004)

(x) Intellectual property

Hasselblatt, G (ed), *The European Trade Mark Convention and European Design Convention; A Commentary* (Oxford: Hart Publishing, 2013)

Kur, A and Dreier, T, *European Intellectual Property Law: Text, Cases and Materials* (Cheltenham: Edward Elgar, 2013)

Pila, J and Wadlow, C (eds), *The EU Unitary Patent System* (Oxford: Hart Publishing, 2014)

(xi) Remedies

Heukels, T and McDonnell, A, *The Action for Damages in Community Law* (The Hague: Kluwer Law International, 1997)

(xii) Tax

Cerioni, L, *The European Union and Direct Taxation: A Solution for a Difficult Relationship* (London: Routledge, 2014)

Gormley, L, *EU Taxation Law* (Oxford: Oxford University Press, 2005)

Panayi CHJI, *European Union Corporate Tax Law* (Cambridge: Cambridge University Press, 2013)

Van Raad, K, *Materials on International and EU Tax Law 2013/2014: Volumes 1 & 2* (Leiden: International Tax Centre Leiden, 2013)

(xiii) Security and justice

Ball, R, *The Legitimacy of The European Union through Legal Rationality: Free Movement of Third Country Nationals* (London: Routledge, 2014)

Eckes, C and Konstantinides, T (eds), *Crime within the Area of Freedom, Security and Justice: A European Public Order* (Cambridge: Cambridge University Press, 2011)

O'Neill, M, *The Evolving EU Counter-terrorism Legal Framework* (London: Routledge, 2012)

(xiv) The social dimension

Burcusson, B, *European Labour Law*, 2nd edn (Cambridge: Cambridge University Press, 2009)

de Búrca, G, de Witte, B and Ogertschnig, L, *Social Rights in Europe* (Oxford: Oxford University Press, 2005)

Ellis, E and Watson, P, *EU Anti-Discrimination Law*, 2nd edn (Oxford: Oxford University Press, 2012)

Giubboni, S, *Social Rights and Market Freedom in the European Constitution* (Cambridge: Cambridge University Press, 2006)

Guild, E and O'Keeffe, D (eds), *Sex Equality Law in the European Union* (London: J Wiley & Son, 1996)

Harvey, TK and Peers, S, *The EU Citizenship Directive: A Commentary* (Oxford: Oxford University Press, 2014)

Kenner, J, *EU Employment Law: From Rome to Amsterdam* (Oxford: Hart Publishing, 2002)

Nielsen, R and Szyszczak, E, *The Social Dimension of the European Community*, 3rd edn (Copenhagen: Handelshøjskolens Forlag, 1997)

Peers, S, *EU Justice and Home Affairs Law*, 4th edn (Oxford: Oxford University Press, 2016)

Prechal, S and Burrows, N, *Gender Discrimination Law of the European Society* (Dartmouth: Gower, 1990)

van der Mei, P, *Free Movement of Persons within the European Community: Cross-Border Access to Public Benefits* (Oxford: Hart Publishing, 2002)

White, R, *Workers, Establishment and Services in the European Union* (Oxford: Oxford University Press, 2004)

(xv) Transport

Humphreys, M, *Sustainability in European Transport Policy* (Oxford: Routledge, 2010)

Articles, case notes and reviews

American Journal of International Law.

Cahiers de Droit Européen.

Columbia Journal of European Law.

Common Market Law Review.

European Business Law Review.

European Competition Law Review.

European Intellectual Property Review.

European Law Review.

European Public Law.

International and Comparative Law Quarterly.

Journal of Common Market Studies.

Journal of World Trade Law.

Legal Issues of European Integration.

Maastricht Journal.

Yearbook of European Law.

Information

Information Office of the European Commission, Jean Monnet House, 8 Storey's Gate, London SW1P 3AT. Tel: 0207 973 1992.

European Documentation Centres (in most major cities).

European Information Centres (in most major regional centres).

Index